MODERN TRIALS

Second Edition

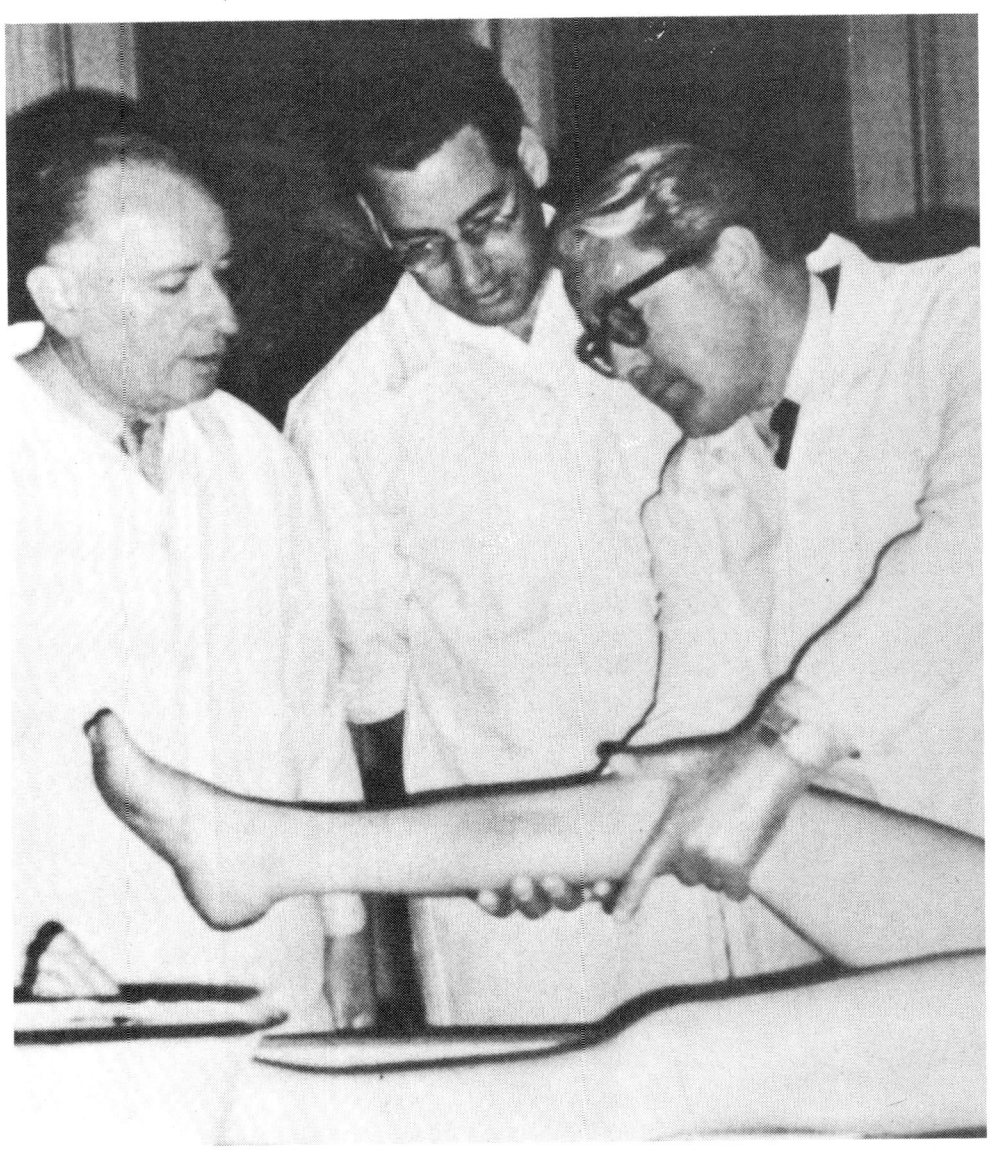

The author, Melvin M. Belli (holding leg), gowned and gloved with the world famous Dr. Kelemen Endre (left) at the Budapest, Hungary morgue, May 1963. Subject: death, self-induced abortion.

MODERN TRIALS

Second Edition

By

MELVIN M. BELLI, SR.

of the
San Francisco and Los Angeles Bars

Volume 1

Sections 1.1 to 30

ST. PAUL, MINN.
WEST PUBLISHING CO.
1982

Other Books by Author

Ready for the Plaintiff
My Life on Trial
Trial and Tort Trends (10 Vols., Yearbooks)
Mel Belli Presents the Wayward Law
The Law Revolt—Civil
The Law Revolt—Criminal
Modern Trials (First Ed., 3 Vols.)
Modern Damages (3 Vols.)
Modern Trials—Student Edition
Over 50 Law Review Articles

COPYRIGHT © 1982 By WEST PUBLISHING CO.
50 West Kellogg Boulevard
P.O. Box 3526
St. Paul, Minnesota 55165

All rights reserved
Printed in the United States of America

Library of Congress Cataloging in Publication Data

Belli, Melvin M., 1907–
  Modern trials.

  Includes index.
  1. Trial practice—United States. 2. Personal injuries—United States. 3. Damages—United States.
I. Title.
KF8915.B42   1982   347.73'7   82-11159
                             347.3077

ISBN 0-314-68804-8

ACKNOWLEDGEMENTS

The author thanks Allen P. Wilkinson, *Esq.*, for his invaluable assistance in the preparation and editing of this new second edition of *Modern Trials* throughout its entire compilation.

We also thank Paul Kleven for his assistance during the latter stages, and Joe Duane for his contribution during the first stage.

Melvin Caesar Belli, Jr. has been of inestimable assistance, though still in his second year of law school at the University of San Francisco.

*

DEDICATION

To old (and by some modern law students unfortunately forgotten) Mr. Winterbottom (of Winterbottom v. Wright) in solace for having suffered a broken wheel too soon, and to gentle Mr. MacPherson (by way of MacPherson v. Buick Motor Co.) with an assist from Justice Cardozo as his recompense for a defective wheel **74** years later!

The dedication of the original edition of *Modern Trials* in **1954** was to my son Melvin Caesar Belli, Jr. (now at the University of San Francisco Law School). I also dedicate this new work to my daughter Melia (now 9), who plans to attend the Yale Law School. I have every reason to believe that between them in years hence they too will take good care of the wagons of both Mr. Winterbottom's and Mr. MacPherson's descendants!

*

WILLIAM O. DOUGLAS REMEMBRANCE

The Introduction to our *Modern Trials, Second Edition*, was to have been done by the Honorable William O. Douglas, Justice, United States Supreme Court.

I had known Bill Douglas and his widow, Cathy, the latter now an excellent lawyer in her own right practicing in Washington, D.C. for a number of years. Like many other trial men, I had marveled and admired the career of Justice Douglas from teacher to administrator, the Securities & Exchange Commission, almost President of the United States, to his long term on the United States Supreme Court. I enjoyed visiting with him in his office in the United States Supreme Court Building when I went to Washington.

The Douglas opinions of the Supreme Court to me were explicit, masterful and prophetic. His books showed his love of the great outdoors and the greater world. I so admired his legal and literary endeavors that I dared take the chance to ask him to do an Introduction to this new edition of *Modern Trials*.

In early 1979 I sent to him Volume I and an outline of the further volumes. I waited weeks. But I knew he was then not well and was still trying to carry a Herculean literary load. Finally came the answer, he not only liked *Modern Trials, Second*, but he would do the Introduction in the manner in which the original one was done by Dean Roscoe Pound.

With an Introduction to the original edition by Dean Pound and to the new work by Justice William O. Douglas, I was greatly encouraged to finish this second work which had become a demanding companion to my trial calendar.

I wrote to Bill from time to time. I only heard back from his wife, but then I was reading in the newspapers that he had had medical setbacks.

Came the day some two months before he died when I received a note from his Clerk that the Justice regretfully would not be able to do my Introduction, that he, the Clerk, was returning my boxes of manuscript.

I suppose for every great man, seeing him at the hour of his greatness, one must have feelings that the very light which one then sees at its brightness must, as with all things living, diminish.

But it was difficult to realize that this oracle soon would write and speak no more of the cause of those for whom our Constitution was writ-

WILLIAM O. DOUGLAS REMEMBRANCE

ten. He could and did write for the least and most of us. But he also could write for those more plentifully endowed with material goods and indeed through his decisions shone the principle that with our national growth more of the former class would join those in the latter.

For the now almost 50 years of trial practice, I've been impressed with the cause of those who have been guaranteed rights not accorded them. So had Bill Douglas.

I've loved the mountains and far away lands all my life and indeed my Shangri-La I just achieved. I was able to go to Tibet. Bill Douglas loved the mountains and far away lands.

There are many, many great lawyers, deans, judges and professors still among us who could have written an Introduction after we lost Bill's to rival that of Dean Pound's.

But I had so wanted Bill Douglas to do it, I haven't had the heart to ask another. I think I shall be satisfied to think and almost know what Bill would have written by way of Introduction, and I hope you will know that too. In the meantime, we do have what Dean Pound thought of the law.

MELVIN BELLI

San Francisco and Los Angeles
May, 1982

INTRODUCTION

by

ROSCOE POUND

Here is an indispensable book for the trial lawyer in personal injury cases. Indeed, it will have much which will give the trial lawyer in general practice food for thought.

If we compare the time of the Civil War, when the formative era of American law seemed to have ended, with the present time, what is perhaps most significant is the radical change from an era of measurable size and relative simplicity to one of unlimited bigness and infinite complexity. Not the least feature of this change is brought out in the practice of law. In 1934 Paul D. Cravath, who came to the bar in 1886, compared the firm of two, which he had headed in 1891, with the firm of seventeen partners and forty-seven associates (in 1948 there were twenty-three partners, seventy-four law-associates, and one hundred and sixty-six members of the office staff) of which he was then the head.

In 1886, when Mr. Cravath came to the bar, in 1890, when I came to the bar, in 1896, when Chief Justice Stone came to the bar, the chief work of the lawyer was advocacy, as it had been in the formative era of our law. But, as Chief Justice Stone put it at the 75th Anniversary of the Bar Association of the City of New York, the era of great advocates was "on the wane." The economic revolution which produced Big Business in the last decades of the nineteenth century largely changed the center of gravity in the legal profession in America from the advocate to the advisor. In an era of increasing specialization, advocacy has become a specialized function—one of many others. The setting up of a multitude of administrative agencies in the development of the service state has made for specialization by individual practitioners as well as for departmentalized specialists associated in large firms. Extreme specialization has been coming to be inevitable for adequate service to big business and even to little business. As Mr. Swaine put it, "The law office with large corporate clients must have partners and associates expert in all the branches of the law which have attained importance; thus arises the further plaint that 'the big firms are as inclusive as department stores.'"

Differentiation and specialization characterize the practice of law today. The large office in the metropolitan city of today, devoted to what Mr. Kales called client-caretaking—to keeping its clients out of court, has to be able to handle at short notice a multiplicity of detail of legislation and administrative regulation and to appear before arbitrators and

INTRODUCTION

administrative agencies, but little before trial courts of first instance and before juries. On the other hand, the trial lawyer whose clients are not to be kept out of courts but must resort to the courts for reparation of injuries they have suffered, has to deal with an enormous mass of detailed causes of injury and of types of injury involved in the highly mechanized activities of our time. His field is provided by the annual total of nine million victims of personal injury in the United States today, to which total of injured, maimed, and slain must be added the widows, orphans and dependents deprived of maintenance to which they are entitled. In a population of about one hundred and sixty million, substantially one in eighteen is injured annually seriously enough to get into the statistics. Tempest, fires, flood, pestilence and famine, which men used to fear, as our prayer books bear witness, still take toll; but no such toll today. Indeed, the two million annually victims of accidents in factories and workshops, and the seven million more injured in automobile, railway, airplane, shipping, store and home accidents make even war take a second place.

Rise of humanitarian ideas as to adequate provision for the injured, not leaving the whole burden of injury in an era of life in mechanized activities to fall upon the luckless victims, makes new and highly specialized work for the trial lawyer beyond anything confronting him in the past. Not only has a body of highly specialized litigation devolved upon him, but he has had to contend with thoroughly organized and specialized legal departments of public utilities, great industries, municipalities, and insurance companies, and under the Federal Tort Claims Act with the Federal Department of Justice.

The ninety years since the close of the Civil War have seen more mechanical achievements, more harnessing of physical nature to man's use than all time before. In that time we have seen the coming of the telephone, electric light, electric power, electric street cars, trolley lines and trackless trolleys, automatic electric elevators, electric refrigerators, and electric heating replacing the steam heat which had replaced the fireplace and the coal stove. We have seen the coming of the phonograph, of X-ray, of the radio, and of television. We have seen the coming of streamlined passenger trains going one hundred miles an hour and freight trains a mile long. We have seen the advent of automobiles, now going at incredible speed, and resulting auto trucks, auto buses, tanks, tractors and bulldozers. We have seen concrete and steel construction emulate the Tower of Babel. We have seen the coming of turbine engines and of the submarine. Above all we have seen the coming of air transportation which has abolished distance. We have even come to see machines perform elaborate mathematical calculations and make arithmetic obsolete. What the dividing of the indivisible atom may yet lead to in the way of destruction of life and limb we have yet to see.

INTRODUCTION

But all this has brought with it an enormous multiplication of types of injury to which the individual of this time is subjected in almost every aspect of his everyday life.

Nor are injuries from the mechanical contrivances with which every one comes in contact in a mechanized world the whole story. In an urban, industrial society a new category of industrial diseases has grown up calling for legislation and judicial decision and disclosing a new type of threat to the general security and ground of imposing liability. To take at random a mere half dozen terms from the current law reports which the nineteenth century had never heard of, asbestosis, beryllium poisoning, caisson disease, granite cutter's disease, silicosis, and tennis elbow (unconnected with tennis) tell of dangers lurking in one's immediate walk of life which may bring him into court.

Moreover, a category of nervous injuries has arisen and has been much developed by advances in neurology, psychology, and psychiatry. When I came to the bar in 1890, except as an additional item of damages in case of physical impact, there was no legal liability for causing fright with serious consequences of even permanent nervous injury. This limitation upon liability was steadily given up in and after the first decade of the present century, and whether or not there has been physical impact a difficult field of traumatic neuroses has come to vex courts and lawyers.

But apart from these new types of injury, the possibilities of injury today have not merely increased enormously, the circumstances of injuries have become vastly complicated. The farm wagon or the family horse and surrey on the highway in the nature of things could not have or give rise to accidents requiring untangling of difficult disputed issues of fact. There were no collisions of farm wagons at cross roads. Even if the farmer was drunk the horses had sense and knew their way home. They ran into or ran over no one. A boy ten years old could drive the old fashioned family horse and surrey and have no accident and endanger no one. When trains ran thirty miles an hour the conventional sign at the railroad crossing served well. There was ample time after stopping, looking and listening to know whether a train was dangerously near. The carpenter worked mostly on the ground. But what he did in entire safety is now done at the mill and he works on scaffolds putting up heavy frames and parts of a building and accidents to employees at the mills and to carpenters from falls or collapsing scaffolds multiply. Indeed, we now have compiled statistics of the cost in life and limb involved in the erection of a building as cold blooded and matter of course as the figures on cost of materials. Agricultural operations are carried on with tractors and complicated machinery so that there is danger lurking about the home farm. We read in the law reports today of huge orchards where hundreds are at work picking fruit and of scores of laborers at work picking tung nuts, and of injuries to these workers which could not have happened fifty years ago. High explosives have come into use also.

INTRODUCTION

We read of them in connection with excavating for foundations, in road building, and in clearing land for cultivation. We read of explosions of trains and ships in transit, and even of supposedly harmless cargoes. Even worse are the injuries inflicted by high tension electric power wires of which we read in so many cases in the current reports. Electricity is brought into the home and raises new dangers there and even more in the streets creates dangers of which we read nothing in the law reports of the last century. Compare, as *loci* of accidents the hand loom and spinning wheel with the textile mill, and livery stable with the garage. The general use of gasoline is another prolific cause of serious injuries.

In other words, the trial lawyer of today must know about and be able to consider the possibilities of a myriad of instrumentalities of injury and the many consequences of contact with each.

Again, in the crowded cities of today, children in search of room for play have raised new questions as to the free liberty of use of land by owners and of duties toward child trespassers. Much of what my generation learned in law school in this connection is obsolete or at most moribund. The lawyer who specializes in personal injury cases has had to do pioneer work in this field of the law. If, as Mr. Swaine thought, the rise of big business in the latter part of the last century pushed the advocate into the background, the increasing volume of injuries to life and limb in the mechanized life of today has given a new importance to advocacy and has called for a new and more effective type of advocate. Trial of injury cases has become a specialized calling and a needed one if the courts are to be able to do justice.

So much for the occasion of Mr. Belli's book. Now as to the method.

It will be worth while to make some comparison with the books which were available to lawyers in the past. In the last century there was an English work, Ram on Facts as Subjects of Inquiry by a Jury (London, 1861) which went through four American editions, the last in 1890. It was taken up with the probative value of testimony, with examination and cross examination of witnesses, with reasoning from facts, and included a chapter on advocacy. The American editions added David Paul Brown's Golden Rules for the Examination of Witnesses, Cox's Practical Advice for Conducting the Examination of Witnesses, and Practical Advice Upon Opening a Case to the Jury (both abridged from Cox, The Advocate, His Training, Practice, Rights and Duties, London, 1852), and a collection of cases of mistaken identity and erroneous conviction. Also there were three books by an English barrister which had much vogue: Harris, Hints on Advocacy, which went through thirteen editions in England, between 1872 and 1906, and an American edition from the second English edition in 1880; Harris, Illustrations in Advocacy (London, 1884, fourth edition, 1904); and Harris, Before Trial; What Should Be Done by Client, Solicitor and Counsel from a Barrister's Point of View (second edition, London, 1887). These books had many American

INTRODUCTION

followers or imitators mostly along the lines of Mr. Harris's. Much valuable forensic experience, especially in criminal cases was set forth in them. Much was set forth also in Memoirs and Reminiscences of American Lawyers. A few recent books, written from forensic experience under the conditions of today are referred to in Mr. Belli's text. But except for these last the available writing upon the problems and methods of the American trial lawyer in the actions for personal injuries that are the staple of litigation in common-law courts in America today speaks directly or indirectly from our formative era. They tell us much about examination and cross examination of witnesses and argument to juries. But under the circumstances of today a great deal has to be done out of court and the office of the lawyer in personal injury practice has to be as organized and departmentalized as that of the client caretaker. Not only must he deal with new and complicated facts of accident and injury and new and complicated disabilities and consequences, but he must struggle with procedural delay and expense and substantive anachronisms holding over from times of fewer and less serious injuries. Mr. Belli's undertaking is to point the way to thorough preparation and convincing presentation based on experience and intelligent appraisal of the cases of one out of eighteen of the population who are likely to be injured in the course of the year.

As the economic order exists it is necessary for the very great majority of the victims of injury to be represented by lawyers compensated by contingent fees. However imbued with the professional spirit of practicing law in the spirit of a public service, the lawyer cannot devote his time, energy, and talent to the cases of the injured who, as is true of most of them, can not afford to meet the expense of investigation and preparation of their cases nor pay an adequate fee to attorney or advocate. There are undoubted serious theoretical objections to contingent fees which to a certain extent make the advocate a party as well. But the gross inequality of positions of the compensation claimant, the injured workingman or sailor, the dependent of an employee killed in an accident in the course of his employment, often without clear knowledge of their rights or of how to preserve them or to assert them effectively against well organized legal departments of utilities, industries, municipalities, and insurance companies calls for something more than leaving the interests of a large and increasing section of the people to self help or charity. The work of investigating and preparing cases and of presenting them to the proper tribunals is necessarily and increasingly expensive. In most cases if it had to be met by the injured person himself the expense would be prohibitive. The alternative would be to do what has been done in England, where contingent fees are not permitted, set up an administrative bureau, supposed to represent both sides, to administer compensatory relief.

INTRODUCTION

When one studies the process of investigation and preparation required to present adequately the case of injured persons today it becomes obvious that routine action of bureau office holders will not suffice to insure equality of treatment and full reparation. A tradition of the duty of the lawyer to the client, to the profession, to the courts, and to the public, authoritatively declared in codes of professional ethics, taught by precept and example, and made effective by the discipline of an organized profession, makes for effective service to the public and to all groups and classes. This professional tradition cannot be replaced with benefit to the public by a political tradition of office holders owing primary allegiance to political parties and depending for advancement on the favor of political leaders. The abuses which may undoubtedly be involved in the practice of contingent fees, as was manifest in the heyday of ambulance chasing, before the advent of the strong bar organizations of today, can be precluded by an organized bar zealous to maintain the highest professional conduct and empowered to make its canons of ethics practically effective. The contingent fee system seems to be the only workable system for the protection of the mass of injured persons in the United States of today.

On the basis of wide experience and with the cooperation of many able and experienced trial lawyers from every part of the land, the author expounds and illustrates the technique of investigation of all cases, particularly complicated or unusual accidents, and complicated or unusual consequences, and the need of thorough medical and at times, neurological or psychological advice, and how to utilize it. He then takes up the technique of determining the appropriate legal remedy and legal procedure, emphasizing the need of thorough critical looking into legislation, municipal ordinances, and administrative regulations covering all items of action and surrounding circumstances which may bear on questions of negligence or contributory negligence or may create or bar liability. The Workmen's Compensation Law, the Federal Employers' Liability Act, the Jones Act, the Federal Tort Claims Act, comparative negligence, the last clear chance doctrine, res ipsa loquitur, the Death Statutes and Survivorship Laws, election of remedies and, indeed, the whole law of torts are reviewed to show what thorough preparation requires and how to go about it.

Next is the technique of preparing for settlement, of appraising the case and determining what would be a reasonable settlement, emphasizing the putting of the parties' cards upon the table and the professional duty of proper settlement when possible and avoidance of litigation. But if fair settlement is not possible, he passes on to the technique of bringing the requisite legal proceedings, the technique of pretrial proceedings and of the procedure by taking depositions which obtains in different jurisdictions.

From this the author turns to the immediate work of the advocate.

INTRODUCTION

The passing for the greater part of the land of the sporting theory of justice; the simplifying and modernizing of procedure which has been going forward everywhere in varying degrees; the strengthening of professional feeling emphasizing methodical exposition of facts and reasoned inferences, in place of the oratory of our formative era, and laying stress on fairness of presentation, make the exposition of advocacy something more wholesome and effective for the administration of justice than what we used to read too much of in the last century. What is set forth most thoroughly and deserves careful study by all lawyers, not merely trial lawyers and practitioners in personal injury cases, is the technique of demonstrative evidence and demonstrative methods of presentation to make clear and intelligible the facts and inferences in case of complicated or confused circumstances and occurrences, complicated machinery or apparatus, and items of loss or damage proper to be considered. The author is a master of this mode of presenting cases, and the fulness of exposition of the technique in application to all manner of cases, and of the legal questions and course of decisions upon the method as a whole and details of its application are a contribution to the administration of justice.

Specifically, the author would make presentation of the just cases of the injured as complete and thorough as possible. He would make the work of the lawyer who undertakes and advocates the cases of the injured as effective for justice as the work of the lawyer who by wise good counsel safeguards the interests of industry and business. Society today needs each type of lawyer. If the latter makes for maintaining the economic order and maintaining the social interest in the security of acquisitions, security of transactions, and security of economic institutions, the former makes for maintaining the social interest in the individual life.

Roscoe Pound

*

OVERVIEW
(WHERE WE'VE BEEN; WHERE WE'RE GOING)

The Seventh Annual Convention of NACCA (National Association Claimant and Compensation Attorneys—now ATLA, American Trial Lawyers Association) was being held in Chicago at the Edgewater Beach Hotel, August 1953. Aboard were many of the early trial lawyers of national NACCA prominence, Jim (later Justice) Dooley, Senator H. Alva Brumfield, Harry Lipsig, Leo Karlin, Perry Nichols, Sam Horowitz, "Spot" Mozingo, Peter Tonkoff, Joe Tonahill, and Lou Ashe, to mention a few.

After the formal convention (as formal as NACCA conventions were in those days) a group of us sat around and spontaneously I led what was to become the first *"Belli Seminar"*. (It was later published as the first in the series of *Trial and Tort Trends*.) Almost every year thereafter there's been a Belli Seminar, if not immediately before ATLA conventions, then in the middle of the trial year. The Belli Seminars were the *first* in legal seminars, later to be copied in form and procedure by the American Bar and bar associations everywhere in America and Canada.

In 1980, for the first time, the Belli Seminars were formally joined with the ATLA convention in July in Montreal, Canada, under the title of "Belli-ATLA Seminar".

Partly from the Belli Seminars grew *Modern Trials* in 1954.

Since writing the original six volumes of *Modern Trials* (three covering *Modern Damages*), there have been many and great changes in the law, civil and criminal. I prognosed some of them in my preface to that work and Dean Roscoe Pound in his Introduction recommending the work, which I preserve in these volumes, wrote of even greater change past and to come.

Comparing the procedures of 1933 law when I came to the bar fresh from Boalt Hall, the University of California Law School at Berkeley, to our 1980's, one almost wonders whether it's the same system. How could we have lived in safety in a society under the law of fifty years ago? How could an innocent defendant in a criminal case have proved his innocence? How could a plaintiff in a meritorious personal injury case ever have achieved an *adequate award*? With the Warren court, criminal law changes were probably more profound and precipitous than those in the civil law, but in recent years, led by the California Supreme Court, civil law changes have caught up.

OVERVIEW

It is hard to conceive today that there was a case in 1936 like my People v. Gosden (6 Cal.2d 14, 56 P.2d 211) and, of all places, in the jurisdiction of California.

California had just amended her constitution allowing trial judges to "comment on the testimony and credibility of any witness as do the federal judges."

Louis Gosden had the misfortune of being charged shortly after this amendment with murdering his wife. Evidence was also introduced that he had killed a former wife by the same method—strychnine.

Earl Warren, later U.S. Chief Justice, District Attorney of Oakland, Alameda County, prosecuted. The late Frank Ogden was trial judge. I, just out of law school that summer, defended. (It was my second homicide case within several months of graduation.)

"Commenting on the evidence" the trial judge referred to the purchase of strychnine by the defendant and stated to the jury in his charge that appellant's explanation did not "appeal to my mind as reasonably consistent with an honest mind!"

As to defendant's witnesses, the court further said that their testimony "may be viewed in the light of the witnesses' interest in the case." As to the state's witnesses, he said, "I see no reason for disbelieving them!"

When it came to punishment the court instructed the jury that they could return a verdict of capital punishment or life imprisonment. But to reduce a verdict from capital punishment to life imprisonment the jury was told "there must be some extenuating circumstances." The court then went on to instruct the jury, "I have been unable to find any!"

The opinion of the California Supreme Court, an appellate body which was later to become, at least for a while, the best state supreme court in the land, in affirming the death penalty must be read to be believed. Said that court on the "I have not been able to find any," "this was purely a comment on the *evidence* in the case and was justified under the authority given the court by the constitutional amendment. . . ."

But what is more, this opinion was affirmed when I later took this case to the United States Supreme Court on certiorari.

Years later, when Earl Warren was sitting as Chief Justice of the United States Supreme Court, I wrote to him about the *Gosden* case and referred him to a then recent California decision, People v. Friend (47 Cal.2d 749, 306 P.2d 463) (1957) where the California Supreme Court now said that even to instruct a jury that they must find "mitigating circumstances" was error. (They can reduce a capital punishment sentence to life imprisonment arbitrarily or on whim or, for example, if they just don't like the color of the hair of the prosecutor.)

OVERVIEW

I never heard back from the Chief Justice, though he remained a good friend of mine until his death. I think he was a great Chief Justice, but he was a district attorney. This did not stop him from being my friend.

Then there was the "accusatory statement": a defendant would be brought into a room with other defendants or suspects and police officers would accuse one or all of a complete set of criminal acts. If the defendant did not reply or try to explain every accusation, later on at trial the accusations would be read to the jury and his *conduct* in the face of them, or his attempt at explanations, would be completely recorded. Of course the jury was told that the accusations were "not evidence. . . . You may consider only the conduct of the defendant in the face of the accusation."

Those of my readers practicing in the forties, fifties and sixties can remember other horrendous examples of legal criminal misconduct. The criminal trial was heavily weighted in favor of the prosecution and police excesses and brutality and horrendous prison conditions were the order of the day. At San Quentin and other prisons throughout the United States there was the "hole" and corporal punishment. Merely to mention that today prisoners have attempted to set up prisoners' unions in the prisons and there is a prisoners' law review counselling about the civil rights of prisoners, suggests the changes.

There was no *Warren* court or great *Miranda* decisions to herald a more evolving than abruptly changing civil law in the last thirty years. But the changes are there and sociologically and philosophically as great and as profound as over on the criminal side. (I suppose it will never be determined whether a changing society demands a changing law or whether changing law is a forerunner of a changing society. Which is the precursor?)

Dean Pound writes of societal changes and law and law practice changes up to 1953. The changes thereafter, and I think they are all to the good as I think the changes in society have been to the good, can be written in the activities of the individual leaders of ATLA, now over 40,000 strong, of the biggest trial bar in the world.

Whereas it was written into our Constitution that the individual man and his life and privacy and pursuits were to be individually protected, the manufacturer, later the corporation, took precedence. Now the rights protected are, as the founding fathers originally intended, both civilly and criminally, individual rights.

It is paramount in personal injury law, which is the great body of civil trial law, that the individual is now more than ever before individually protected. More and diverse plaintiffs now more easily achieve the *"adequate award"*, a phrase which I first used in an article on that sub-

OVERVIEW

ject in 1954 in the California Law Review (39 Cal.Law Rev. 1), than ever before.

I suppose even a law book is somewhat of a biography of its author. I take great pride in being the innovator of many of the procedures now used in modern trials, both on the civil as well as the criminal side. But as with most inventions the bonfire was set from the sparks struck by others. I've had the pleasure of lecturing or doing a seminar before most of the law schools and bar associations in the United States at one time or another. From the questions and comments I learned even more than I gave. It was from these seminars, lectures, letters, communications and friends that the innovations came and went into *Modern Trials*. I am proud of the many changes I have made in trial practices over these almost fifty years.

In my early years at the bar, I tried many more criminal than civil cases. Indeed, I was the lawyer for Father George O'Meara, San Quentin's beloved priest. I remember once I was introduced by Earl Warren as "a recent graduate from Boalt Hall who when the trap was sprung at San Quentin last Friday had half his practice wiped out!" He was in error. I had my entire practice wiped out!

My fee for a major felony representation at San Quentin was a bottle of Vat '69 from Father O'Meara. Even though this was more valuable then than now, it being Prohibition time then, economic necessity drove me over to the civil side. That and the hazardous state of criminal practice in San Francisco at the time. So much illegal practice went on between police and lawyer that a young barrister hazarded his license every time he stepped into the criminal court.

In those days when someone went into the police department he didn't refer to it as going into the "department" but as going into the "business"!

Money would buy anything then in California prisons. For a price, a dinner could be served from one of San Francisco's famed restaurants in a guard's home just adjacent to San Quentin prison with female companionship if desired—and it generally was.

One night, San Francisco Chief of Police O'Brien was dancing at the Bal Tabarin with his wife. Who should go by on the dance floor but a well-heeled murderer after whom the chief personally had led a posse, convicted, and sent to San Quentin with a ten-to-twenty-year sentence. The prisoner was enjoying his well-financed week on the town!

Justice was callow in those days. I remember driving up to the State Capitol in Sacramento one gloomy day with a writ of coram nobis for Chief Justice Waste. I thought it was a justiciable writ for the cause and I argued it over the breakfast table with his honor as time was short and it was the only place I could get him.

OVERVIEW

I had argued quite a while without the justice saying anything when he looked up at the clock and said, "Melvin, have some of this bacon and eggs, it's delicious. Your case is more academic. It's 10:01 and your client was hanged one minute ago." It seemed that capital punishment wasn't as final or as horrendous as it is regarded now.

Since those days almost every state has legislated the "automatic appeal" in a death penalty case, so concerned are we that the unthinkable can happen, the execution of an innocent man. (The reader is referred to the excellent book written by Yale Professor Borchard and his wife "Convicting the Innocent".)

Demonstrative evidence was extensively used in criminal practice: blackboards, diagrams, illustrations, mock-ups, models, microscopic and enlarged pictures of deadly weapons, all sorts of pictures and experiments. Every criminal lawyer used it. But few civil lawyers adopted it. I was the first civil trial lawyer to bring it wholesale over to the civil side!

I remember trying the case of Ernie Smith who was accused of homicide. He was standing over a prone convict in the yard at San Quentin. Ernie suddenly stomped on the prone person and killed him. It seemed like a clear-cut murder one. Indeed, Warden Holahan moved Ernie out of his regular cell over to condemned row even before the trial!

Father O'Meara took me to Ernie Smith and his seemingly hopeless case. I asked Ernie that which the lawyer should have told him, "What shall we plead?"

"Self-defense obviously," readily replied Ernie.

He then went on to tell me that the man lying on the ground had a knife and was about to throw it. Ernie stomped him in self-defense.

I couldn't believe that prisoners were allowed to carry knives in San Quentin. I went to my friend Ralph New, Captain of the Yard and asked him. He took me into his office and showed me a huge drawer of confiscated knives. He told me, "All prisoners can carry knives up to three inches to do their work in the factory. It's only when they've violated rules that we confiscate their knives." In the drawer was the most vicious-looking assortment of store-bought and homemade knives I've ever seen.

We went to trial with our plea of self-defense. I subpoenaed *duces tecum* the whole drawer of knives, learning early that if I had doubt about something, certainly jurors must harbor the same suspicions.

Captain New was on the stand. I was carrying the huge drawerful of knives up to him when (and it's so long ago I don't honestly remember whether deliberately or accidentally) I stumbled and spilled the whole drawer of hundreds of knives at the feet of the horrified jury. It took us (the jury and me) about ten minutes—I was deliberately slow—to pick up

OVERVIEW

the knives and put them into the drawer. But when the drawer and its contents of knives was passed up to the witness there was no doubt in any mind in that courtroom that knives were carried by prisoners in San Quentin yard and the assailant of Ernie had one. Ernie was found not guilty and came off death row. It was one of my first uses of demonstrative evidence.

I've been dropping knives, tire irons, light globes, medicine bottles, scapels, wrenches, pills, exploded appendices in bottles, lanterns, tires, forceps and myriad other offending instruments into the laps of jurors across America ever since—on the civil side!

Demonstrative evidence in the civil trial was a procedure waiting to happen. Today, it has, of course, become something much more sophisticated than dropping a drawerful of knives at the feet of a jury so that they can see and feel rather than be told about the offending instruments.

When I came to the civil law, what seems to be a scant few years ago (though it's almost fifty), most courtrooms, if not all, had no blackboards. It was rarely used in opening statement or cross-examination or in argument. (See § 55.1, infra.) I was to use it extensively and the procedures in this book developed from humble beginnings. Every courtroom now has a blackboard as well as large sheets of "butcher paper" to write on and to preserve as evidence. It's hard now to believe this an innovation. But it was.

The opening statement in the civil case was cursory. The final argument was extended and florid. I began to outline in detail and on the blackboard or on placards my witnesses and my evidence and my damages in the opening statement. (See § 52.1, infra.) I used it as a blueprint for the trial and particularly for the final argument. "I made a bond with you in my opening statement. Now let us see whether I have kept it," I would say in my final argument. Civil trial lawyers everywhere began employing extended opening statements, blackboards, and more detailed, precise, business-like closing arguments.

I began to photostat and enlarge jury instructions, then use them in my final argument. It took some time to educate the trial judges that it was just as fair and honest to show the actual instruction as to read it.

I began to photostat and blow up part of the complaint and answer for cross-examination and argument. I began to photograph and enlarge statements taken by the officer at the scene of the accident and the officer's statement and diagram done by the officer himself. I found these most helpful in cross-examining a witness and I had little difficulty in convincing the court that these could be used.

I began to blow up pages of depositions (admitted into evidence) and use them for cross-examination and I photographed and enlarged pages of the daily transcript making sure to have the actual page number on

OVERVIEW

the exhibit to report actual testimony during the final argument. To my knowledge, I was also the first one to use this procedure.

I photographed whole pages of hospital records and enlarged them and used these in cross-examination and argument and did the same for suspect labels on bottles and in commodity cases.

To my knowledge we were the first to do the obvious in portraying the catastrophe of, for example, quadraplegic injuries. We did a "day in the life of." One of the first of these was a trial in Honolulu in which a young electrician lost both hands. The great scholar, my partner, Lou Ashe, did the direction and produced an hour-long film showing the difficulties the handicapped boy encountered in showering, going to the bathroom, brushing his teeth, eating at the table, driving a car.

I also had evidence that the boy was a saxophone player, not professional, but for his own amusement. I put a saxophone on the witness stand in front of him and then got permission to play a record he had made for his own amusement. The jury could see—demonstratively—that he'd never play a saxophone again. Defendants settled the case after the movie and the demonstration for $265,000, the highest award by far in Honolulu up to that time—an award which would now be over a million dollars.

We also, I believe, were the first to use videotapes in deposition. We did this in the Bonnie Buehler v. Conrad Hilton case, San Bernardino, to show signals to turn the boat being made by the deponee which would not appropriately or dramatically reflect in a written deposition. (Tom Murray of Sandusky, Ohio is the current expert on videotape depositions and has written infra of this in Chapter 59.)

To my knowledge, we were the first to do the obvious with x-rays. We made *positive* x-rays and enlarged them. These are excellent demonstrative evidence though probably not as valuable in diagnoses as the negative.

We took numerous aerial photographs and enlarged them and we took pictures from the top of buildings of intersections to use along with diagrams of the scene of the accident. Once I flew into the Grand Canyon in an aerial commander and almost lost my life in taking pictures of "Smokey Bluff", the scene of the accident.

A TWA and United plane had started out almost liked arrows out of a bow on the same course and at the same time from Los Angeles to Chicago. They had gone off of airways (this was over thirty years ago) and came out of the clouds to meet over the Grand Canyon. The United DC-4 had come up on the Constellation's tail. To prove this I went down into the Grand Canyon and with mules brought pieces of the United propeller and pieces of the empennage of the Constellation out of the canyon.

OVERVIEW

Microscopically I was able to show that there was red, white and blue paint transferred from United's red, white and blue propeller to the Constellation, showing which plane had come on which. Stuart Speiser, later to become one of the outstanding air lawyers in America, sat through this his first airplane case in the Los Angeles court watching me try this one.

I learned from my criminal experience the use of models in the trial. The great Bill Fallon had once disassembled and then assembled a whole New York taxicab in a New York courtroom. He proved that there wasn't room enough to commit rape in the back seat.

In Bonnie Buehler v. Conrad Hilton (see § 53.20, infra), a beautiful starlet and Western Airlines stewardess had lost an arm and a leg in a waterskiing accident. I purloined Mr. Hilton's speedboat and brought it to court but had to be content with bringing the jury down to the courtyard because it was too big for the courtroom.

Modern Trials shows where we have gone from my early use of models in the courtroom from the miniscule—using enlargements of the electronic microscope—to derricks and trucks—and the 650-pound man!

We were the first to "personalize" abstract doctrines. Presumptions became *"Mr.* Presumption" and were argued as a living person. (See Chapter 5, infra.) For example, in the cockpit of an airplane Mr. Presumption put his hand on the throttle to keep it at a reasonably prudent level.

Res ipsa loquitur became *Mr. Res Ipsa Loquitur* in opening statement and argument. In the *Reckenbeil* case we personalized barriers of sound and used aerial photographs and drawings to show how the offending truck seemingly had to go through physical barriers of sound.

I remember when I started to try wrongful death cases the awards of this "utlimate personal injury" were low. My procedure in argument was to detail on the blackboard and on charts life expectancy times earnings. It was simple. In those days defendants never thought of forcing the plaintiff to "reduce to present value" and the judges never instructed on this.

We were the first to use (in the Superior Court in Los Angeles in an FELA case) the appraiser to demonstrate decreased earning capacity. I explained exactly what I needed by way of actuarial, economic, and earning figures but I proved too much. Soon defendants asked for "reduction to present value." Shortly thereafter, specialist appraisers "discovered" our procedures and became instantly available in wrongful death cases all over the United States. Their advertising brochures of their "inventions" describe *my* procedures perfectly. The value in awards and settlements in wrongful death cases trebled in proportion to the amount of those in personal injury cases with the use of these actuaries.

OVERVIEW

In the original volumes of *Modern Trials* there is the first case where a jury in Oklahoma came back with other than a lump sum verdict. They voted a lump sum but ordered it to be paid in *installments* over the life expectancy of the plaintiff. From this I came up with the idea of a *structured settlement* and developed it so that I was able some years ago to convince an insurance company to settle for over a million dollars paid over a term of years with conditions, in a medical malpractice case of a young boy with negligently diagnosed spinal meningitis.

Abe Freedman of Philadelphia and I at about the same time first employed the device of actually taking a cameraman and a reporter into defendant's factory (see Chapter 59, infra) for "sound-movie depositions" by court order.

Some thirty years ago a United aircraft helicopter fell into the waters of San Diego Bay, killing the military pilot when the rear rotor became disassembled. With a court order I went to defendant's factory in Connecticut with an alert cameraman. He photographed everything including a notice on the bulletin board "Safety First—Carelessness in installing lock nut in rear rotor tail assembly has already caused one death."

I learned the lesson early, as will be repeatedly pointed out in this work, that appropriate demonstrative evidence leads to the *adequate award*.

We saw nothing wrong in that which is now commonly done in demonstrative evidence, in displaying to the jury the injured anatomy of the plaintiff. In Gluckstein v. Lipsett (1949, 93 Cal.App.2d 391) we displayed the plaintiff completely naked to the jury in the trial judge's chambers so they could see the errant plastic surgery, malpracticed on the breasts and lower abdomen of plaintiff.

The verdict was $115,000 and that with Sullivan v. San Francisco (1950, 95 Cal.App.2d 745, 214 P.2d 82) for $125,000 were the highest verdicts to reach an appellate court up to that time—so said the California Supreme Court.

In the *Reckenbeil* case (1945), the verdict was $225,000 for head injuries causing plaintiff, a fire captain, to be treated in a mental institution. That award was the highest jury award in a common law jurisdiction up to that time. Nate Richter of Philadelphia was to achieve an award for his client of $265,000 several months later and timorously prophesied that catastrophic verdicts in personal injury cases might even go as high as $500,000. (Just recently a Chicago jury awarded my client $3,125,000.)

It would be some twenty years from that date before I was to achieve my first personal injury award of over a million dollars for a client, this in a wrongful death case in Las Vegas, Nevada (Bank of Nevada v. Sylvester Azbil—$1,220,438.) Verdicts now in personal injury catastrophe cases come in over a million dollars weekly. One is reported

OVERVIEW

infra for 22 million dollars, and another for 120 million dollars with punitive damages.

In 1949 Harvard Law School was on my lecture tour. One of the students was Ralph Nader. I was introduced by the great tort professor Warren Seavey as "A young lawyer from the west who has been doing something interesting with demonstrative evidence—you'd better listen to him and learn what's going on." Ralph tells me he got his inspiration here for going into commodity law and public service. In 1954, because of the demonstrative evidence you'll see in this book, I was profiled and sobriqueted in *Life* magazine as "The King of Torts."

Shortly thereafter, I addressed the Canadian Bar Association at Niagara Falls. In keeping with their effusive hospitality, the chairman introduced me very proudly as "The King of Torts" and then added that "to further honor us, ladies and gentlemen, the King has brought his beautiful wife, the Queen of Tarts!" His embarrassment was profound when I had to explain to the audience, my wife being present, that "tart" was not a nice word to apply to one's wife, and particularly mine wasn't one!

The prognosis for civil and criminal trial practice is healthy because I think the prognosis for society is healthy and societal doings will be reflected in that future law. It will exist for and be more and more useful to the layman. Once was when law, like the priesthood, existed for the lawyers and priests rather than penitents and clients.

But when society changes form, then will law change form? We have been tending towards a more socialistic state since the turn of the century. How will this be reflected in the law if we live under a benevolent socialism rather than a democracy?

The first to go probably would be jury trial. There are those on high who through cries of expediency or economy would do away with jury trial today.

In New Zealand, the personal injury victim goes to a government office, files a piece of paper, and recovers an award like workers' compensation payable by the government. It is the modern concept of the old "bot", "wite" and "wer" of the Middle Ages where regional anatomical areas and appendages had a price tag on them. Justice Burger and others have encouraged lectures in this country by New Zealand lawyers.

I was in China recently and the Dean of the University of Peking Law School told me that never again would there be the institution of "private lawyers" in China. Their new constitution will be activated by layman through arbitration where necessary. Arbitration as an institution has legislatively been encouraged and will continue to be encouraged in the United States.

OVERVIEW

Already there is the six-man jury and voir dire has been largely taken away from the trial lawyer.

In addition, there are now more and more mandatory pre-trial settlements. In Alameda County, California, for example, if one does not get a court on trial day, he goes to another mandatory pre-trial settlement and continues on down the line if that trial court is not forthcoming to another pre-trial mandatory settlement. Personally, I think these pre-trial settlements are useful and now there is the appellate mandatory settlement conference in California before or after appellate argument.

The biggest problem today and in the future in trial law are the crowded calendars. Recently I had a civil case in Sacramento County, California, where I got a court after seven years only to have the trial judge continue the case because he had a criminal case ahead of mine.

The question will sometime have to be answered, "Should criminal cases always usurp the civil docket for precedence and trial?"

Do we have enough judges? Almost. Do we have enough physical facilities for courtrooms? Almost. Do we have enough court attachés, clerks, reporters, bailiffs and such? No.

But I think the solution to crowded calendars is the appointment of pro tempore judges from the rank of lawyers sitting with or without fees. Wherever this has been tried it has been successful. But for some unknown reason, at least to me, it has been abandoned.

A big change in the law was the advent of advertising. Though advertising is now allowed and ethical, few lawyers have made use of it. Those few who have tried it, with the exception of some few multi-office firms, have told me it is not economically rewarding.

Along with advertising, there have been proposals to allow soliciting by lawyers. One such proposal was recently narrowly defeated in the California Bar but these proposals will be renewed. Recently the California Supreme Court allowed the paying of referral fees by lawyers one to another regardless of the amount of the work done by either lawyer in proportion to the fee.

The use of paralegals has been a tremendous step forward in the efficient management of law offices. Most offices now, small and large, use paralegals and the wonder is how we ever got along without them. Any type of law office today not considering a paralegal is overlooking half an efficiency of management.

Since the first Belli Seminars, legal seminars on *all* subjects have become so numerous that a day does not go by that a national or local seminar on some legal or medical or economic subject is not announced in the mail. There are more law journals, even including a journal for prisoners, and the number is increasing as are the specialties. Tapes of arguments and seminars also abound.

OVERVIEW

There is almost the distinction between barrister and solicitor now in the United States, the trial bar being highly specialized. The California Supreme Court recently held that any lawyer taking on a specialized case is held to the care of the proficient specialist in that particular specialty.

As for the actual trial itself, as we shall see later on in these volumes (Chapter 59), video and sound tapes are being more frequently used, particularly in depositions of the expert. I have found that expert testimony of a specialist is just as emphatic and dramatic by sound-movie deposition as it is in person. Again, we were the first to use this procedure as witness *Buehler* (above).

Today's big case, and it will be more so in the future, is a battle of experts with more and specialized experts in the particular area asking higher and higher fees. The other day we flew in an expert medical man from Australia at a cost of $5,000 a day plus expenses.

The "big cases" are becoming more and more expensive to try, with experts and experiments. It is nothing now to have to set aside $50,000–$100,000 for the preparation and trial of a big case, one that will take a long time and one that will go for sizeable damages, compensatory and punitive.

More experiments are being done in the commodity and warranty fields, particularly involving large objects such as motorcycles and automobiles. In fact, whole automobiles are even purchased and destroyed on camera to prepare, preserve and prove a point.

"The day in the life" is commonly used on film in all of the cases that have any great degree of damage.

In the trial itself, blackboards, models, and blow-ups of testimony, depositions, pleadings and instructions are regularly used.

The procedure of going into defendant's factory on discovery with a reporter deposition or moving pictures is widely allowed and used. In drug cases great freedom is allowed on discovery into the manufacturing process as well as into the books and "adverse reaction reports", etc., of the drug manufacturer.

In the *Cutter* case, the quadragen case against Parke-Davis, and the Bendectin case against Merrill Laboratories, a tremendous number of depositions and discoveries were taken of defendant manufacturers and then employees all over America.

Very little can be done by, for example, a president or his advisors to whip inflation. It is a worldwide problem. An oil price increase in one part of the world will reflect itself worldwide. Inflation has progressed regularly since 1776 and it will continue. The quantum of damages is inflated and as we have said above has gone from $225,000 in 1945 to well over $100,000,000 recently.

OVERVIEW

Punitive damages have and will be used much more extensively despite their dislike by some judges, particularly on the federal side. A whole new chapter appears in this work on punitive damages (see Chapter 16, infra).

Realistically, the insurance company has been brought directly into the mainstream of litigation. More states are allowing the insurance company to be sued directly and more states say that if the insurance company doesn't pay a plaintiff's reasonable demand, and promptly, the insurer is held without more for the full amount of an adverse judgment.

As there used to be (and still is) a specialized admiralty bar in personal injury and a railroad bar in F.E.L.A., there is now a specialized airplane accident bar which actively handles cases *worldwide*. The airline cases are, even more than the maritime and railroad cases, generally cases of liability and for large amounts. Discovery and experts range the globe in an airline catastrophe.

Aviation accidents all over the world generally can be sued somewhere in the United States (commonly in Los Angeles County) because most modern aircraft have American manufacturers or principal parts suppliers. Defects causing accidents give America jurisdiction.

Worldwide discovery is commonplace now in the airplane accident litigation, with depositions and interrogatories ranging the globe.

Jorge Ortiz-Brunet of Puerto Rico and I filed (see Chapter 40) a suit against Air France for death and injuries occasioned by assassins in the Tel Aviv airport. The malefactors had boarded a Puerto Rico to Tel Aviv Air France plane at Rome with multiple hand grenades and armaments which we alleged Air France was negligent in allowing on board unscreened.

Jurisdiction was in Puerto Rico where the flight had originated and the tickets were bought. Depositions were taken at the head office of Air France in Paris, Rome and in Tel Aviv in which latter city Golda Meir helped us enlist the testimony of the Ambassador from Israel to France by way of deposition. The case was settled just before trial, U.S. District Judge Gigneaux of Portland, Maine, presiding, for $6,000,000.

But ironically the death of one in another case whose award should have set a record had to be settled for $100,000. Verne Lawyer of Des Moines and I collected the full amount of the insurance policy when Rocky Marciano's rented plane crashed in an Iowa cornfield. There was absolute liability but no financial responsibility above the meagre policy to compensate the family of this high-income earner.

While required statutory limits of insurance in the several states have increased in amount, they still lag much below the level of awards and inflationary values. The insurance carrier is still by far the most used principal in the personal injury case and without a healthy insur-

OVERVIEW

ance industry there would be no collectible adequate awards or no industry for that matter!

One great difference between the lawsuit of the thirties, forties and fifties and its modern counterpart is discovery by way of interrogatories, written or oral (usually both), depositions and other discovery devices. Multitudinous depositions are now taken, and they can become very expensive. I can remember in this regard the *Cutter* case (Gottsdanker v. Cutter Laboratories, 182 Cal.App.2d 602, 6 Cal.Rptr. 320 (1960)) tried in 1957.

We put on our case, lasting three weeks, for the plaintiff. When we were through we had no idea what experts would be called by the defendant.

Some six world-renowned scientists were called. We had not had the opportunity of theretofore examining them by depositions or running biographical material. This would be unheard of now. The trial lawyer, either plaintiff or defendant, who does not know *everything* about his adversary's contentions before opening statement, is almost responsible in malpractice.

The federal courts, and most states by statute or court rules, have granted varied means of discovery by depositions, interrogatories, claims for admissions, etc. Originally these were all thought to be a boon to the plaintiff. And they are—if the plaintiff has the money and manpower to answer the paper deluge rained down upon him by the "big office" representing the "big defendant."

It should not be for me representing the plaintiff to complain about the fees defendant lawyers charge. Of course the laborer in the vineyard is worthy of his hire but I have seen so many cases that could settle or otherwise be disposed of with much less work where the "big firm" modus operandi was to run up a bill for a multitude of lawyers like the meter in a waiting taxicab so as to make it impossible to otherwise dispose of the case. A great share of litigation money that should have gone to the plaintiff went to defense lawyers, or was ultimately paid by taxpayers or consumers in the case of utilities or commodities.

Strict and absolute liability will extend. Chief Justice Traynor's prophetic words in my Escola v. Coca Cola in 1944 (24 Cal.2d 453, 150 P.2d 436) show a striving of the law for practicality and laymen understanding.

I came to the bar when contributory negligence was the order of the day. Some trial judges mumbled through plaintiff's and defendant's instructions until they came upon the one having to do with contributory negligence. Then the judicial eyes would light up and in a voice vibrant and strong the jury would be instructed that *any* amount of contributory negligence would defeat a recovery. Defense counsel would stand in front of the jury and, taking a large piece of paper, tear off the tiniest

OVERVIEW

corner while saying, "Contributory negligence is like this tiniest corner of this paper. If there is *any* of it the whole case is destroyed!"

I "personalized" the defense of contributory negligence (which I learned from my great friend Peter Tonkoff) by drawing what purported to be a bale of hay in the center of a field on the blackboard. Then I put circles around it and argued to the jury that "these circles are fences that the horse has to get over before he can get to the bale of hay. One circle, and it is a high one, is that the burden of proof in showing contributory negligence is on the defendant. The next circle is proximate cause. Contributory negligence, even if there were such, must be the proximate cause of the happening of the accident. And the third fence is the highest of all, that the plaintiff is presumed to have used due care.

Comparative negligence, as in England, is almost universally supplanting contributory negligence in this country.

Then there is the no-fault cases of the future such as in divorce where it has almost come to pass that if a party wants a divorce he has one. Every day that I go to court I hear more and more laymen pleading their own divorce cases. I do not believe that the abandonment of the lawyer in favor of instant divorce or instant probate or instant wills will extend. Too horrendous are the stories known to laymen of tax consequences and otherwise for failing to use a lawyer in tax matters, divorces, income taxes, wills and property transfers.

Last year Ralph Nader and I did a warranty commodity lecture in London to which were invited manufacturers from all over the world. Many attended, particularly from Germany and Japan, because goods from these countries are more frequently being sold in the United States and our courts, particularly federal, have increasingly held that the sale of defective products in an area (see Ch. 43) gives jurisdiction over the manufacturer no matter how far distant geographically he may be. Once a judgment is rendered in this country it's increasingly easier to collect it here than in the foreign country. The Germans and Japanese were aware of the "adequate award" and the "more adequate award" even before my lecture.

If there is an area of the law that has changed since the writing of the original *Modern Trials* it is in commodity and warranty law. What used to be the rat in the Coca Cola bottle or the rock in the can of beans has become the exploding defective tire resulting in quadriplegia or the Datsun or the Ford with the defectively placed gas tank resulting in multiple catastrophic burn injuries. (In my recent $3,125,000 Chicago verdict (supra) the trial judge directed liability leaving only the damage amount to the jury.)

In the last twenty years it has become much easier to sue, much easier to discover and much easier to get an adequate award in commodity litigation. So much is this so that many manufacturers are now com-

OVERVIEW

plaining that awards have gotten so high in consumer cases that they can't afford the accompanying rise in insurance policies.

For example, in 1979 Wilsons Sporting Goods Company, one of the nation's largest manufacturers of athletic equipment, announced it would discontinue making football helmets at the close of that season. A company spokesman cited the "continuing high risk of product liability litigation associated with helmet sales which comprise less than one percent of Wilsons' overall sales" as the major reason for the decision.

In the new chapter, infra, on Punitive Damages (Ch. 16) the applicability of such damages to warranty cases is discussed. In some of the drug cases I have tried I have seen a callous disregard by the manufacturer for humankind about the world. The conduct of Robert Merrill Drug Company for one is particularly reprehensible in the Thalidomide and the MER 29 cases. In the latter, they were punished by exemplary damages in San Francisco and again in Washington, D.C. where an $80,000 fine was levied after a plea of nolo contendere.

Recently, United Press International reported a ten-month investigation done by *Mother Jones*, a consumer-oriented magazine based in San Francisco, wherein banned drugs and dangerous intrauterine devices driven from the market by warranty and consumer suits in the United States were being dumped in Third World countries by the U.S. corporations.

Cited were the instances of several million children's pajamas treated with a carcinogenic fire retardant in the U.S. They were shipped overseas after the U.S. Consumer Product Safety Commission forced them off the U.S. market.

Winstrol, a synthetic male hormone found to stunt growth in children, is now being sold by U.S. manufacturers in Brazil.

The U.S. agency for international development has been encouraging and sponsoring the use in the Third World of the injectible contraceptive Depo-Provera which was banned in the U.S. after it caused cancer in laboratory animals and birth defects in humans.

The psychic injury has come of age. My good friend and great trial lawyer, Marvin Lewis of San Francisco, probably is the leader in this field. Though he is known for his cable car case in which the accident victim was caused to become a nymphomaniac, he has led in other areas of psychic damage.

It has taken us a long while adequately to evaluate that which is probably the most important to man, his mind, and we've just come to realize that a personality or even a mind can be destroyed without any (as yet discovered) corporeal injury.

Recently there was awarded in Los Angeles against the Southern Pacific Railroad a verdict of $1,600,000 (reduced to $1,300,000 because of

OVERVIEW

comparative negligence) for a railroad worker solely because of a severe traumatic neuroses which made it impossible for him to work.

Comment should be made upon the state of military law by those who have not practiced it. I believe military law has developed into the most protective system of law for individual rights now practiced in the world. I've tried military cases in Okinawa, Japan, a number in Vietnam, in the United States, in Naples, Italy, and in Stuttgard and Frankfurt, Germany.

The court or jury composed of army officers is a delight as a hearing body. Almost always I have found them intelligent, considerate of the defendant's rights, understanding of the law and interested in demonstrative evidence.

Sometimes foreign languages do cause a problem. I remember trying a case in Okinawa, Japan, in which all my remarks were translated. I was making a long and laborious opening statement. The prosecutor kept interrupting me in Japanese. I assumed everyone spoke only Japanese.

Finally in exasperation, I turned to my army co-counsel and said, "If this sonofabitch doesn't lay off, I'm going to let him have it!"

Apparently I'd spoken loudly enough so that both court and prosecutor heard me and the prosecutor jumped up and exclaimed in excellent English, "He call me sonofabitch!"

The judge replied resignedly, also in English, "I heard him. Continue!" Embarrassedly and with much more deference, I did.

I tried a Green Beret case in Vietnam. I can attest that some court martials pay well. My defendant's mother brought in a shoe box of $40,000 in $100 bills. Apparently it was left over after a policy raid by my defendant who was also on CIA duty in Cambodia. Since it had nothing to do with the charges, I resolved any ethical considerations and took it.

Recently an allegedly defective Pinto car in which there was a wrongful death gave rise to a criminal suit against Ford Motor Company in a criminal counterpart to a civil suit for breach of warranty. The verdict by the criminal jury went for the Ford defendant. But I prognose more similar criminal-civil cases in the future.

Malpractice has become the order of the day. In some countries, e.g., South America, one would no more think of suing his doctor or his hospital than suing his priest, but I suppose the time may come even there where even the priest may be sued for not securing salvation if the present trend for suing professionals does not abate.

The architect is sued and despite some knotty problems of proximate cause and statutes of repose, recoveries have been allowed. Some lawyers now even specialize in lawyers' malpractice, apparently delighting in

OVERVIEW

suing their seemingly errant brethren. Trial and appellate courts are more reluctant to allow a legal malpractice case to stand than one sounding in medical malpractice. In legal malpractice a case must be tried within a case and then there is the often difficult proof of speculative damages.

But medical malpractice has become big business. Many firms specialize in it and many others specialize in its sibling—drug manufacturer breach of warranty.

When I came to the bar in 1933 it was most difficult to get one doctor to testify against another one. I had one old war horse who now—having long since departed the fields of battle and having done his share in righting malpractice wrongs—I'm sure won't mind my telling this story of him.

He was a delightful, convivial human being, most capable and alert in the medical-legal forensic battle. We always had to get him on the stand in the morning because by noontime a consuming thirst generally overcame him and if he wasn't handcuffed during the lunch hour he'd show up in the afternoon in a manner of glorious abandonment.

Bob Lamb, Oxford graduate and one of the truly great defense trial lawyers of San Francisco, and a good friend of my earlier days, after several bouts with the good doctor wanted no more forensic battles so he would ask but one question of my expert doctor. It was a devastating one: "Doctor, when did you get off probation?"

But Doctor X always did get us by non-suit.

Today, this lone noble medical forensic warrior has many, many counterparts. Not only does the younger breed of medicine man testify in a meritorious medical malpractice case but there are whole organizations who advertise their prowess. These organizations are composed of doctors who will advise as to the worth of one's medical malpractice case and if it is worthy will furnish experts who qualify up to the hilt. But the best use of this organization is in settlement, see infra Chapter 50. They prepare the case so factually, accurately and devastatingly that the insurance company and the doctor or hospital realistically evaluates it.

In quantum of damages the biggest awards have been in medical malpractice and warranty. The anesthesiologist and the neurosurgeon have had to pay the highest awards. Cord damage, paraplegia, quadraplegia and blindness now are being compensated at realistic figures. Birth injuries attend long life expectencies.

There are still jurisdictions where the adequate award has not yet arrived, such as New England. I settled a wrongful death case in Maine for $300,000 during the spring of 1980. I learned to my shock that this was the highest award up to then in Maine. Recently we settled a paraplegic case—worth perhaps 2 to 3 million in Chicago—for $1,250,000 in

OVERVIEW

Portland, Maine. Ironically the jurisdiction which was, in 1953, probably the lowest in awards is now the highest—Alaska. And interest is allowed on the judgment from the date of the filing of the complaint and attorneys' fees are allowed.

Detroit vies with Alaska as a high award area, and Washington, D.C. would also, but the federal judges in that district have effectively and practically frowned on higher awards.

In most of the demonstrative evidence procedures written of in this book, I've had to break new ground with the trial judge. This has been difficult in some cases with blackboards, enlargements of photos and such, simply because lawyers are creatures of stare decisis and "if it hasn't been done before it's just not dignified or safe" and the particular judge doesn't want to "take the chance."

Generally, new procedures are easier to come by in the cities than in the country unless the country judges are particularly learned and well-read. So demonstrative evidence is like most other things, relative to time and place.

I was told about the relativity of European justice one time when I was in Paris representing the late Errol Flynn, a good friend and client of mine. I'm sure the story is not true of French judges but I was worried about a particular French judge we were going before the coming Monday. We were all gathered at the George Cinque hotel in Paris and I expressed my concern to my distinguished French colleague.

He reassured me, "My friend, you have nothing to worry about. We have paid him a substantial sum of money to see it our way."

I was shocked and said, "How can we depend upon the integrity of a judge who 'takes'? He's just as apt to take from the other side."

My friend answered in horror, "Monsieur Le Justice _____ has 'taken' from us. He is a very *honorable* man. He would never, never think of taking from *both* sides!"

The late great tort teacher, Bill Prosser, was critical in reviewing the parent volume of *Modern Trials*. He said it was "unabashedly slanted pro plaintiff." I regard this as a badge of honor because when I came to the bar, a work such as *Modern Trials* was badly needed to elevate the procedures of the plaintiff's civil bar. I think, now looking back these almost fifty years, I did just that.

With my Demonstrative Evidence and my Adequate Award I hope I have helped improve justice generally and I have been pleased to see *Modern Trials* on the shelves of many defendant law office libraries.

In a few months I will be 75 and will have been practicing law almost 50 years. For the next 25 years—God willing—I intend to do more

OVERVIEW

trial work than writing, but I shall do yearly pocket parts to *Modern Trials, Second.*

MELVIN M. BELLI

San Francisco and Los Angeles
May, 1982

SUMMARY OF CONTENTS

Volume 1

PART I. INTRODUCTION

Chapter		Sections
1.	Setting the Stage	1.1–2.0
2.	Investigation and Discovery	2.1–3.0
3.	Have I a Case?	3.1–4.0
4.	Jurisdiction and Venue	4.1–5.0

PART II. BURDEN OF PROOF

5.	Quantum of Proof: Inferences, Presumptions, Possibilities and Probabilities	5.1–6.0

PART III. TORT LIABILITY AND DEFENSES—GENERALLY

6.	Strict Liability	6.1–7.0
7.	Res Ipsa Loquitur	7.1–8.0
8.	Violation of Statute	8.1–9.0
9.	The Rescue Doctrine	9.1–10.0
10.	Comparative Negligence	10.1–11.0
11.	Contributory Negligence	11.1–12.0
12.	Last Clear Chance	12.1–13.0
13.	Assumption of Risk	13.1–14.0
14.	Imminent Peril—"I Can't Let Go!"—The Emergency Rule	14.1–15.0
15.	Wanton or Wilful Misconduct	15.1–16.0
16.	Punitive Damages	16.1–17.0
17.	Contribution Between Joint Tortfeasors	17.1–18.0
18.	Releases	18.1–19.0

PART IV. DEFENSES—SPECIFIC ACTIONS

19.	Federal Tort Claims Act	19.1–20.0
20.	Suing the Insurer	20.1–21.0
21.	Actio Personalis Moritur Cum Persona	21.1–22.0
22.	Wrongful Death	22.1–23.0
23.	Wrongful Birth and Wrongful Life	23.1–24.0
24.	Prenatal Injuries	24.1–25.0
25.	Loss of Consortium	25.1–26.0

SUMMARY OF CONTENTS

Chapter		Sections
26.	Tort Liability and the Familial Relationship	26.1–27.0
27.	Charitable and Sovereign Immunities	27.1–28.0
28.	Uninsured Motorist Coverage	28.1–29.0
29.	The Dramshop Rule	29.1–30.0
30.	Defamation	30.1–31.0

Volume 2

31.	Right of Privacy	31.1–32.0
32.	Nuisance	32.1–33.0
33.	Recovery for Emotional Disturbances	33.1–34.0
34.	Riot Damage	34.1–35.0
35.	Animal Law	35.1–36.0
36.	Persons in Control	36.1–37.0
37.	Landlord's Liability	37.1–38.0
38.	Owners and Possessors of Land	38.1–39.0
39.	Workers' Compensation	39.1–40.0
40.	Aircraft Accident Litigation	40.1–41.0
41.	Railroad Law	41.1–42.0
42.	Maritime Tort Law	42.1–43.0
43.	Products Liability	43.1–44.0
44.	Medical Malpractice	44.1–45.0

Volume 3

45.	Admission of Liability by Words, Acts and Conduct	45.1–46.0
46.	Safety History: Prior Accidents and Subsequent Repairs	46.1–47.0

PART V. TESTS AND MEDICAL EXAMINATIONS

47.	Tests—Lie Detector, Intoxication, Blood	47.1–48.0
48.	The Medical Examination	48.1–49.0

PART VI. PLEADINGS

49.	Pleading the Case	49.1–50.0

PART VII. SETTLEMENT OF THE CASE

50.	The Settlement	50.1–51.0

PART VIII. TRIAL TECHNIQUES

51.	The Jury	51.1–52.0
52.	The Opening Statement	52.1–53.0
53.	Demonstrative Evidence in Civil Cases	53.1–54.0
54.	Demonstrative Evidence in Divorce Cases	54.1–55.0
55.	Trial by Blackboard, Placards and Charts	55.1–56.0

SUMMARY OF CONTENTS

Volume 4

Chapter		Sections
56.	Experiments	56.1–57.0
57.	Models	57.1–58.0
58.	Photographs and Movies	58.1–59.0
59.	Videotape Depositions: A New Frontier of Advocacy	59.1–60.0
60.	Exhibition of Person	60.1–61.0
61.	Medical Demonstrative Evidence	61.1–62.0
62.	Expert Testimony	62.1–63.0
63.	Examining Witnesses	63.1–64.0

Volume 5

64.	General Damages: Pain and Suffering	64.1–65.0
65.	Closing Argument to Jury in Civil Cases	65.1–66.0
66.	Instructing the Jury	66.1–67.0

PART IX. ADEQUACY OF AWARD

67.	The Adequate Award	67.1–68.0

PART X. CRIMINAL TRIALS

68.	The Criminal Trial Framework	68.1–69.0
69.	Criminal Demonstrative Evidence	69.1–70.0
70.	Closing Argument to Jury in Criminal Cases	70.1–71.0

PART XI. APPEAL TECHNIQUES

71.	Demonstrative Evidence on Appeal	71.1–72.0

PART XII. TAX CONSIDERATIONS

72.	Tax Aspects of Litigation Settlements	72.1–72.11

Medical Glossary

Legal Bibliography

Table of Persons

Index

*

TABLE OF CONTENTS

PART I. INTRODUCTION

CHAPTER 1. SETTING THE STAGE

A. INTRODUCTION

Sec.
1.1 Yesterday, Today and Tomorrow.
1.2 NACCA and ATLA.
1.3 New Procedures and the Law.
1.4 The Trial Lawyer of Today.

B. WHO IS THE TORT CLIENT?

1.11 Introduction.
1.12 Accidents and Statistics.
1.13 The Verdict and Social Good.

C. ATTORNEY'S FEES, LIENS AND EXPENSES

1.21 Introduction.
1.22 The Contingent Fee Contract; Advances.
1.23 Amount of Fees; Fee Schedules.
1.24 When Contingent Fee Is Inappropriate.
1.25 Recovery of Fee by Discharged Attorney.

D. POST ACCIDENT REHABILITATION OF PLAINTIFF

1.31 Introduction.
1.32 The Lawyer's Role in Rehabilitation.
1.33 Remarks on Rehabilitation.

E. TRAUMATIC NEUROSES AND HYSTERICAL PARALYSES

1.41 Introduction.
1.42 Traumatic Neurosis Defined.
1.43 Examples of Traumatic Neuroses.
1.44 The "Accident Prone" Person.
1.45 Hysterical Paralysis.

CHAPTER 2. INVESTIGATION AND DISCOVERY

A. PRELIMINARY CONSIDERATIONS

2.1 Introduction.
2.2 Sources of Information.

TABLE OF CONTENTS

B. THE CASE HISTORY

Sec.
- 2.11 Introduction.
- 2.12 Use of the Case History.
- 2.13 Medical Questions and Considerations.
- 2.14 The Lawyer as "Doctor".

C. OFFICE FORMS AND RECORDS

- 2.21 Introduction.
- 2.22 Information to Obtain.
- 2.23 Model Interview Form.
- 2.24 Use of Specialized Forms.
- 2.25 Police Reports.
- 2.26 Medical Records Consent Forms.
- 2.27 Contingent Fee Agreement Forms.
- 2.28 Office Records.
- 2.29 Use of Bound Volumes.
- 2.30 The Disbursal Sheet.

D. PARALEGALS

- 2.41 Role and Duties of Paralegals.

E. THE INVESTIGATOR

- 2.45 Introduction.
- 2.46 Importance of the Investigator.
- 2.47 The Investigator's Tools.

F. "ON-THE-SCENE" INVESTIGATIONS AND PHOTOGRAPHS

- 2.51 Introduction.
- 2.52 Finding "On-the-Scene" Photographs.
- 2.53 "On-the-Scene" Photographs in Head-On Collision.
- 2.54 Railroad Death Case.
- 2.55 Automobile-Truck Accident.
- 2.56 Tank Explosion Case Report.
- 2.57 Personal Injury and Property Damage Caused by Truck.

G. USE OF "ON-THE-SCENE" PHOTOGRAPHS

- 2.61 Introduction.
- 2.62 Use for Impeachment.
- 2.63 To Show Negligence.
- 2.64 To Show Cause of a Fire.

H. "OFFICIAL" PROCEEDINGS AND INQUESTS BEFORE TRIAL

- 2.71 Introduction.
- 2.72 Personal Injury With Criminal Charges.
- 2.73 Utilizing Criminal Investigations.

TABLE OF CONTENTS

I. DISCOVERY

Sec.
- 2.81 In General.
- 2.82 Discovering Demonstrative Evidence.
- 2.83 Privileged Matters.
- 2.84 Lawyer-Client Privilege.
- 2.85 Attorney's Work Product.
- 2.86 Discovery of Experts' Opinions.

J. DISCOVERING LIMITS OF INSURANCE COVERAGE

- 2.91 Discovery of Insurance Generally.
- 2.92 Practical Effects of Refusal to Disclose Insurance Coverage.

K. DEPOSITIONS AND INTERROGATORIES

- 2.101 Introduction.
- 2.102 Sample Written Interrogatories.
- 2.103 Example of Deposition.

L. INVESTIGATION BY DEPOSITIONS AND PICTURES

- 2.111 Use of Pictures to Supplement Deposition.

M. LOCATING WITNESSES

- 2.115 Introduction.
- 2.116 Techniques for Locating Witnesses.

N. FINDING THE ACTUAL INSTRUMENTALITY

- 2.121 Introduction.
- 2.122 Unraveling the "Freak" Accident.
- 2.123 Identification Through Advertisements.
- 2.124 Identification of Manufacturer.
- 2.125 Finding the Offending Product.

O. WHEN THE ACTUAL INSTRUMENTALITY IS NOT AVAILABLE

- 2.131 Introduction.
- 2.132 Illustration—Vehicle Unavailable.

P. DEMONSTRATIVE EVIDENCE OFTEN DEMONSTRATES THE THEORY

- 2.135 In General.

Q. EXEMPLARY INVESTIGATIONS

- 2.141 Introduction.
- 2.142 Hidden Rock Case.
- 2.143 Investigation by Exhumation.
- 2.144 Investigation of Injury on Ship.

TABLE OF CONTENTS

R. INVESTIGATION THROUGH ACCIDENT RECONSTRUCTION

Sec.
2.151 Introduction.
2.152 Train-Bus Collision.
2.153 Automobile-Motorcycle Accident.

S. ENJOINING THE OVERZEALOUS INVESTIGATION

2.161 Introduction.
2.162 Examples of Improper Investigative Techniques.
2.163 Suggested Petition for Order Enjoining Harassment.

T. ETHICAL CONSIDERATIONS AND THE INVESTIGATOR

2.171 In General.
2.172 Communication With Adverse Party.
2.173 Insurance Company's Letter in Chicago Air Crash Disaster.
2.174 Engaging an Investigator.

CHAPTER 3. HAVE I A CASE?

A. INTRODUCTION

3.1 Initial Considerations.

B. DETERMINING THE THEORY

3.5 Introduction.
3.6 Contract v. Tort Actions.
3.7 The Unexplainable Accident.
3.8 Circumstantial Evidence Demonstrates the Theory.

C. *STARE DECISIS* AND THE LAWYER'S DUTY

3.11 Introduction.
3.12 The Doctrine of *Stare Decisis*.
3.13 Combatting *Stare Decisis*.
3.14 English Common Law.
3.15 Statutes.

D. THE CRIPPLED CASE

3.21 Introduction.
3.22 Intoxication.
3.23 Aggravation of Pre-existing Condition.
3.24 Obvious Danger Cases.

E. STATUTES OF LIMITATION

3.31 In General.
3.32 Equitable Arguments.
3.33 Suit in Contract.
3.34 Notice of Claim Statutes.

TABLE OF CONTENTS

Sec.
3.35 Types of Statutes of Limitation.
3.36 Persons Affected.
3.37 Alternative or Collateral Remedies and Defenses.
3.38 Conflict of Laws.
3.39 Computation of Period—Accrual; Estoppel; Tolling.
3.40 Revival of Remedy.
3.41 Notice.
3.42 Claims Against Municipalities.

CHAPTER 4. JURISDICTION AND VENUE

4.1 In General.
4.2 Subject Matter Jurisdiction.
4.3 Jurisdiction Over Persons and Things.
4.4 Notice Requirement.
4.5 Venue.
4.6 Jurisdiction and Venue in Federal Courts.

PART II. BURDEN OF PROOF

CHAPTER 5. QUANTUM OF PROOF: INFERENCES, PRESUMPTIONS, POSSIBILITIES AND PROBABILITIES

5.1 "Possibilities" and "Probabilities"—In General.
5.2 Proximate Cause.
5.3 The "Lost Possibility".
5.4 Prognosis—Generally.
5.5 Prognosis—In Practice.
5.6 Different Standards in Different Proceedings.
5.7 Who May Present Proof.
5.8 Statistics in Criminal Cases.

PART III. TORT LIABILITY AND DEFENSES—GENERALLY

CHAPTER 6. STRICT LIABILITY

6.1 In General.
6.2 History of Strict Liability.
6.3 Worker's Compensation.
6.4 Dangerous Activities.
6.5 Escaping Water.
6.6 Products Liability.
6.7 Restrictions on Strict Liability.
6.8 Absolute Liability in Nuclear Accident—The Karen Silkwood Case.

TABLE OF CONTENTS

CHAPTER 7. RES IPSA LOQUITUR

Sec.
7.1 In General.
7.2 Elements or Conditions.
7.3 Unusual Accident—Expert Testimony and the Balance of Probabilities.
7.4 Control and Multiple Defendants.
7.5 Plaintiff's Conduct.
7.6 Defendant's Superior Knowledge.
7.7 Application—Pleading and Evidence of Specific Negligence.
7.8 Effect—Inference or Presumption.
7.9 Practical Considerations—Defense of Due Care.

CHAPTER 8. VIOLATION OF STATUTE

8.1 In General.
8.2 Legal Effect.
8.3 Criminal Statutes.
8.4 Municipal Ordinances and Administrative Regulations.
8.5 Elements—Causation, Protected Class, and Type of Risk.
8.6 Defenses—Excuses.

CHAPTER 9. THE RESCUE DOCTRINE

9.1 Basis of Liability.
9.2 Attempts to Save Persons from Harm.
9.3 The Rescue as an Intervening Force.
9.4 The Rescue Doctrine as a Defense to Contributory Negligence.
9.5 Right of Rescuer to Recover Hinges Upon Dependent Wrong.
9.6 Attempts to Save Property from Harm.

CHAPTER 10. COMPARATIVE NEGLIGENCE

10.1 In General.
10.2 Forms of Comparative Negligence.
10.3 Proximate Cause—Last Clear Chance—Assumption of Risk.
10.4 Multiple Defendants.
10.5 Cross-Complaints and Set-Offs.
10.6 Non-parties—Joinder.
10.7 Strict Liability Actions.
10.8 Willful Misconduct.

CHAPTER 11. CONTRIBUTORY NEGLIGENCE

11.1 General Considerations.
11.2 Criticism and Defense of the Doctrine.
11.3 Standard of Conduct—Imputed Negligence.
11.4 Avoidable Consequences Rule.
11.5 Non-negligent Torts.

TABLE OF CONTENTS

CHAPTER 12. LAST CLEAR CHANCE

Sec.
12.1 General Considerations.
12.2 Issues—Knowledge, Opportunity, Antecedent Negligence.
12.3 Relation to Other Doctrines.

CHAPTER 13. ASSUMPTION OF RISK

13.1 Origins.
13.2 Relation to Contributory Negligence.
13.3 Express Agreements.
13.4 Implied Acceptance of Risk.
13.5 Demise of the Defense.

CHAPTER 14. IMMINENT PERIL—"I CAN'T LET GO!"—THE EMERGENCY RULE

14.1 General Considerations.
14.2 Availability of Defense.

CHAPTER 15. WANTON OR WILFUL MISCONDUCT

15.1 In General.
15.2 Elements.
15.3 Pleadings.
15.4 Corporate Wilful and Wanton Misconduct.

CHAPTER 16. PUNITIVE DAMAGES

16.1 Introduction.
16.2 History.
16.3 Statements of Purpose.
16.4 Arguments Against Punitive Damages.
16.5 Requirements for Punitive Damages.
16.6 Survival of Claim.
16.7 Measurement of Punitive Damages.
16.8 Pleadings.
16.9 Insurance Coverage of Punitive Awards.
16.10 Contract Actions.
16.11 Punitive Damages in Products Liability Cases.
16.12 Punitive Damages in Drunk Driving Cases.
16.13 Conclusion.

CHAPTER 17. CONTRIBUTION BETWEEN JOINT TORTFEASORS

17.1 Common Law Rule.
17.2 Criticism—Statutory and Judicial Revision.
17.3 Requirement of Common Liability.
17.4 Apportionment—Pro Rata—Comparative Fault.
17.5 Release.

TABLE OF CONTENTS

CHAPTER 18. RELEASES

Sec.
18.1 In General.
18.2 Mutual Mistake.
18.3 Unilateral Mistake of Fact.
18.4 Ignorance of Releasor.
18.5 Mistake of Law.
18.6 Innocent Misrepresentation.
18.7 Fraud.
18.8 Burden of Proof.
18.9 Restoration of Consideration Upon Repudiation of Release.
18.10 What Law Applies.
18.11 Effect of Release—Joint Tortfeasors.
18.12 Distinguished from Covenant Not to Sue.

PART IV. DEFENSES—SPECIFIC ACTIONS

CHAPTER 19. FEDERAL TORT CLAIMS ACT

19.1 In General.
19.2 Construction of F.T.C.A.
19.3 Limitations.
19.4 Subrogation.
19.5 Armed Forces Personnel.
19.6 Impleader.
19.7 Exclusions.
19.8 Strict Liability.
19.9 Compromise.
19.10 Attorney's Fees.
19.11 Damages.
19.12 Discovery.
19.13 Election of Remedy.
19.14 Within Scope of Office or Employment.

CHAPTER 20. SUING THE INSURER

20.1 The Problem.
20.2 Standards for Recovery.
20.3 Duty to Initiate Settlement.
20.4 Duty to Defend.
20.5 Extent of Liability.
20.6 Punitive Damages.
20.7 Who May Sue.
20.8 Duty of Insurance Agent to Insured.

CHAPTER 21. ACTIO PERSONALIS MORITUR CUM PERSONA

21.1 General Consideration.
21.2 Survival Statutes.
21.3 Distinction from Wrongful Death Statutes.
21.4 Punitive Damages.
21.5 Injury to the Person.

TABLE OF CONTENTS

CHAPTER 22. WRONGFUL DEATH

Sec.
22.1 At Common Law.
22.2 Statutes.
22.3 Application—Proximate Cause, Defenses, Conflicts.
22.4 Beneficiaries—Damages.

CHAPTER 23. WRONGFUL BIRTH AND WRONGFUL LIFE

23.1 In General.
23.2 Common Law View—No Damages Suffered.
23.3 Wrongful Birth—Origin of Action—Normal Children.
23.4 —— Defective Children.
23.5 —— What Injuries Are Compensable.
23.6 "Wrongful Life"—In General.
23.7 —— Traditional Damages Incapable of Measurement.
23.8 —— Child's Suit Against Laboratory for Negligent Testing.
23.9 —— Birth Under Adverse Circumstances.
23.10 Injuries Resulting from Pre-conception Negligence.

CHAPTER 24. PRENATAL INJURIES

24.1 Development of the Cause of Action.
24.2 Viability.
24.3 Wrongful Death Resulting from Prenatal Injuries.
24.4 Damages.
24.5 Effect of Statutes of Limitation.

CHAPTER 25. LOSS OF CONSORTIUM

25.1 In General.
25.2 "Consortium" Defined.
25.3 Development of Right.
25.4 Rationales, Given for Extending Right to Wife.
25.5 Procedural Aspects—Derivative v. Non-derivative.
25.6 Requirement of Marriage.
25.7 Parents' Action for Loss of Filial Consortium.
25.8 Child's Action for Loss of Parental Consortium.
25.9 Why Action Is Denied.
25.10 Recovery When Parent "Severely Injured".

CHAPTER 26. TORT LIABILITY AND THE FAMILIAL RELATIONSHIP

26.1 In General.
26.2 Husband—Wife Immunities.
26.3 Parent—Child Immunities.
26.4 Family Law—Vicarious Liability.

TABLE OF CONTENTS

CHAPTER 27. CHARITABLE AND SOVEREIGN IMMUNITIES

Sec.
27.1 Immunity of Charities.
27.2 Immunity of National and State Governments.
27.3 Immunity of Municipalities.
27.4 Immunity of Public Officers.
27.5 Actions under 42 U.S.C.A. § 1983.

CHAPTER 28. UNINSURED MOTORIST COVERAGE

28.1 Introduction.
28.2 "Unsatisfied Judgment" Statutes.
28.3 Financial Responsibility Statutes.
28.4 Uninsured Motorist Statutes.
28.5 Arbitration.
28.6 No-Fault Insurance.

CHAPTER 29. THE DRAMSHOP RULE

29.1 Development of Common Law Liability.
29.2 Proof in a Dramshop Case.
29.3 Dramshop Acts—Construction and Elements.
29.4 Who May Be Liable.
29.5 Extraterritoriality—Exclusiveness of Remedy.

CHAPTER 30. DEFAMATION

30.1 In General.
30.2 Defamation Defined—Who Can Sue.
30.3 Libel and Slander Distinguished.
30.4 Libel and Slander—When Actionable.
30.5 Interpretation of Dafamatory Meaning.
30.6 Requirement of Publication.
30.7 Truth—A Complete Defense.
30.8 Absolute Privilege.
30.9 Qualified Privilege.
30.10 Constitutional Privilege—Public Officials and Public Figures.
30.11 Burden of Proof—Court and Jury.
30.12 Measure of Damages.

MODERN TRIALS

PART I
INTRODUCTION

CHAPTER 1
SETTING THE STAGE

Table of Sections

		Sections
A.	Introduction	1.1 –1.10
B.	Who Is the Tort Client?	1.11–1.20
C.	Attorney's Fees, Liens and Expenses	1.21–1.30
D.	Post Accident Rehabilitation of Plaintiff	1.31–1.40
E.	Traumatic Neuroses and Hysterical Paralyses	1.41–2.0

A. INTRODUCTION

Sec.
1.1 Yesterday, Today and Tomorrow.
1.2 NACCA and ATLA.
1.3 New Procedures and the Law.
1.4 The Trial Lawyer of Today.

B. WHO IS THE TORT CLIENT?

1.11 Introduction.
1.12 Accidents and Statistics.
1.13 The Verdict and Social Good.

C. ATTORNEY'S FEES, LIENS AND EXPENSES

1.21 Introduction.
1.22 The Contingent Fee Contract; Advances.
1.23 Amount of Fees; Fee Schedules.
1.24 When Contingent Fee Is Inappropriate.
1.25 Recovery of Fee by Discharged Attorney.

D. POST ACCIDENT REHABILITATION OF PLAINTIFF

Sec.
1.31 Introduction.
1.32 The Lawyer's Role in Rehabilitation.
1.33 Remarks on Rehabilitation.

E. TRAUMATIC NEUROSES AND HYSTERICAL PARALYSES

1.41 Introduction.
1.42 Traumatic Neurosis Defined.
1.43 Examples of Traumatic Neuroses.
1.44 The "Accident Prone" Person.
1.45 Hysterical Paralysis.

A. INTRODUCTION

§ 1.1 Yesterday, Today and Tomorrow

Alice in Wonderland confirmed the perplexity of many youthful readers when she quizzically announced that she had "often seen a cat without a grin, but a grin without a cat! It's the most curious thing I ever saw in all my life!"[1]

That much respected, and to most laymen feared, legal magician, the trial lawyer, has himself been so long on the "other side of the looking glass" that such wizardry as "grins without cats" have become commonplace. With the numerous "inferences" and "presumptions" the trial lawyer knows the rest of the cat is nonetheless there, even though only the grin is apparent. He is often impatient with the "unpresumptive" who would not understand or follow his seemingly esoteric ways. No doubt he has often said (if not quite aloud, as did Alice's Queen) of those who would not implicitly understand or obey, "Off with their heads!"[2]

1. For the "usual," "customary" and "accepted" book on evidence and related intricate subjects in this perplexing science of law, the author suggests a perusal elsewhere, following Alice, who, leaving both the Hatter and the Cheshire cat behind, said, "The March Hare will be much more interesting, and perhaps as this is May, it won't be raving mad —," Carroll, Lewis, Alice's Adventures in Wonderland, Chapter VI.

2. The author's respect for legal legerdemain came early in his career, when he applied the formula of an early California Supreme Court decision, People v. Hall, 4 Cal. 399 (1854) that "Chinese are Indians." George W. Hall had been convicted of murder on the testimony of one witness, a Chinaman. On appeal, counsel for the defendant pointed out that an Act of 1850 had provided that "No *black* or *mulatto* person, or *Indian*, shall be

But modern substantive and trial law has become quite a practical and empirical body. Common law is being made more and more "common" and understandable to him most frequently in need of it: the common man. How it has evolved to become the cement that holds our civilization together is one of the mysteries that lends it majesty. It may be seen in the opinions of the United States Supreme Court, perhaps more clearly than those of any other tribunal, how modern law has approached consummation with changes in economic, social and political framework.

Yet, this development has taken place within the framework of a constitution promulgated at a time when invention, trade, government and the standard of living were as different from today as is trial by battle from *certiorari*. The student of law must still trace its ancient beginnings, and map the evolution of present day doctrines, forms and remedies from these ancient beginnings, clothed in the disguise of what may now appear to be a formalistic legerdemain.

allowed to give evidence in favor of, or against a white man." Chinamen had not been excluded to testify against a "white" such as was Hall, but the Supreme Court of California had not yet applied its interpretations to the act, so as to decide that "Chinese are Indians." The court reasoned: when Columbus landed upon these shores to discover a western passage to the Indies, he imagined that he had landed on one of the islands of the Chinese Sea, lying near the extremity of India, and therefore called the inhabitants "Indians", meaning thereby an inhabitant of all lands "washed by the Chinese waters"—Chinese, Japanese, Filipinos. In his time, ethnology was not a distinct science, and mankind was considered divided into but three races, the whites, blacks, and Indians. Hence the court held that the Chinese were Indians, excluded the testimony of the Chinaman, reversed the conviction of murder, and released Hall. Had he committed the crime 19 years later, he would have been hanged, for in 1873, the legislature passed a statute making people of all races competent witnesses.

The reasoning of this case came into practical use by me, later for the benefit of a Chinese client. He had moved into an exclusive "White" residential district. (California had previously held segregated districts unconstitutional). He was "waited upon" by officers of the district who showed him the restricted race covenants in the several deeds and asked him to move. When I cited the decision of People v. Hall, which apparently turned my client from a Chinaman into an Indian, and thereby a favored citizen, their complaints were immediately withdrawn. For not only could he not be restricted, but as an Indian he could hunt out of season, and might have claimed certain tax exemptions, which if enjoyed by his fellowmen of like color, might have bankrupted the district.

Seeing the effect of such a magical ethnological pronouncement by a Supreme Court, I have since never been the least confounded with simple confusion as "a grin without a cat"—at least in the law. In fact I was so impressed that I began to do a daily newspaper column, "So That's the Law!" and wrote of the Hall case as my first encounter.

§ 1.1 INTRODUCTION

The lady holding scales and blindfolded (still appropriately portrayed as such) has—certainly her priests, the lawyers and judges have—a number of "grins without cats" remaining. But within the last few decades, the evolution in the trial of a lawsuit has become increasingly manifest. No longer is it a game. It has become a race of disclosures. Both sides now seek a verdict of fact, and not of confusion. To borrow again from Alice's menagerie, the rabbit is not "pulled out of the hat." If he is to appear at all, he is disclosed on the opening statement, and remains in full view during the entire trial! (See chapter 55, Trial by Blackboard, infra.)

No longer are jurors selected because of their lack of intelligence, and to be forgotten during the introduction of evidence and until a verdict is somehow mystically reached. They have become an intelligent entity with a mind of their own. True, they may still desire and expect to be entertained with much more histrionics than the modern lawyer, in good taste, is willing to employ. But primarily they look and listen to be informed, so that when the time for deliberation comes, a verdict will be easy, and some measure of justice may be done.

§ 1.2 NACCA and ATLA

In August of 1946, in Portland, Oregon, there was born an organization of plaintiffs' lawyers called the National Association of Claimants' Compensation Attorneys. This group developed into an institution of thousands of attorneys who specialized in one of the following four branches of law: workman's compensation; personal injury; railroad law; and admiralty law. The official publication of this organization, under the direction of able and dedicated *Samuel B. Horovitz*, was the NACCA Law Journal.[3]

From this group evolved the Association of Trial Lawyers of America [ATLA], which currently has a membership of well over 45,000 trial lawyers, with the number increasing steadily each year. Numerous fields of trial law are covered by ATLA, and it offers many services, such as its monthly magazine *Trial* and the ATLA Law Reporter, to keep the trial lawyer abreast of new developments in tort and trial law. Criminal law, at my urging, is also included.

While not having invented the adequate trial or "the adequate award,"[4] many members of this organization put into daily court-

---

3. See S. Horovitz, NACCA and its Objectives, 10 NACCA L.J. 17 (1952).

4. The "adequate award" is a term I coined some years ago in describing what the objective of the trial lawyer and also the judge and jury should be in relation to an injured plaintiff. See M. Belli, The Adequate Award, 39 Cal.L.Rev. 1 (1951).

room use throughout the United States a method of trial procedure guaranteeing a more efficient administration of justice, a more factual award, and a speedier trial in at least 75% of the cases they try. We still lag woefully in the speedy trial. See § 51.2, infra.

§ 1.3 New Procedures and the Law

The layman has heard how zealously the medical profession probes, experiments, controls and evaluates new procedures before announcing them available for general use. Most laymen have never heard of "stare decisis." Supplementing his natural instinct to hew to the known rather than substitute the uncertain and the untried, there is the training of the trial lawyer and judge, instilling in him respect for precedent and the frequent acceptance of the antique due only to its antiquity. See § 3.11 et seq. infra.

When counsel offers a new procedure at trial, it is recommended that he proceed with caution, and explain to the judge just what it is he is attempting. If ever a new procedure will only add to an already-existing confusion, it is better that the older procedure remain, so as to have at least the soporific distinction of dignity, if nothing else.

Much of this book must be acceptable, not because it has membership in the fraternity of stare decisis, but because it is vouchsafed by the trial judge's "discretion." More than with any other procedure, the abundant measure of discretion reposed in the integrity, common sense and fairness of the trial judge is sufficient to invoke methods of proof, and thereby guarantee the more adequate trial. The lawyer himself is rapidly realizing that the law is not an end in itself, and that his profession, while a license to him, is for the benefit solely of his client, the layman. Where he has not been prompt to appreciate this fundamental, he, like those in other professions, has learned that the law has given to the layman an exclusive province, namely, the power to legislate.

§ 1.4 The Trial Lawyer of Today

For the trial lawyer, today's practitioner is more of a business man than attorney. The "tax expert" relies more and more upon market reports than the law cases. Yet, at least to the author, "law" is trial law. The court is the temple, and other legalistic endeavors,

This determination, of course, varies significantly not only with the type of injury, but also the type of plaintiff, such as his or her sex, age, earning capacity and the like. As we shall constantly see throughout this work, all of these factors must be scrutinized thoroughly in every case in determining what award could be considered "adequate."

less hallowed market places. The imposing Law Courts, the Courts building, Halls of Justice, in the big cities; the "county courthouses" in the center of small towns are still in structure and thought, both the genesis and end of life in America. Therein is birth recorded, marriage licensed, and for the errant, the death penalty imposed. It is both presumptive and permissive to magnify one's own specialty.

Yet such magnification is not out of proportion to the layman's concept of the law. It is for him that law is both kept and made. Delays of trial, technical and often unjust court procedures and inequitable awards excite the layman to more and more displeasure, either in his legislative halls or in his newspapers and magazines. That he, himself, may be the first victim of his determination to do something by way of ill-considered reform is not usually a deterrent to action.

A considerable part of all this trial law is personal injury. We are frank to admit, because we believe the first step toward betterment is recognition of the problem that the personal injury lawyer, like the criminal defense advocate, has not in the past had too savory a reputation. Part of this criticism is due to the courtroom procedure, "tricks of court and lawyers."[5] Part is directed at certain practices

---

5. Mr. Bumble (Oliver Twist) was moved to remark—"The law is a ass." Peter the Great is said to have asked, when being shown through Westminster—"Who are all those people running about in black robes?" Upon being answered that they were lawyers, he remarked in disgust—"Why, I have but four in my entire kingdom and I propose to hang two as soon as I return." Sagacious Benjamin Franklin said, "A countryman between two lawyers is like a fish between two cats." Josh Billings said "Every man should know something of the law. If he knows enough to keep out of it, he is a pretty good lawyer."

It even became necessary for a California court to say, "There is nothing about the practice of the profession of the law which makes the business dangerous to the public. It does not threaten the public health or safety, nor is it demoralizing to the public . . ." City of Sonora v. Curtin, 137 Cal. 583, 70 P. 674 (1902).

Should the layman look too critically at the law, let him be reminded of the dictum in In re Goodell, 39 Wis. 232 (1875): "It is more important that an end should be put to litigation than that justice should be done in every case."

On the character of law and lawyers, the Wisconsin court, in In re Goodell, supra, denied women the right to practice law, stating:

"The peculiar qualities of womanhood, its gentle graces, its quick sensibility, its tender susceptibility, its purity, its delicacy, its emotional impulses, its subordination of hard reason to sympathetic feeling, are surely not qualifications for the lawyer . . . it would be revolting to all female sense of the innocence and sanctity of their sex, shocking to man's reverence for womanhood and faith in women, on which hinge all the better affections and humanity of life, that women should be permitted to mix professionally in all the nastiness

epitomized in the uncomplimentary appellations applied to him by others.[6]

A surprising amount of the invidious criticism is special pleading by business men, such as insurance company executives, who are interested in a favorable balance sheet and consequently distrustful of the successful methods of any lawyer who assists accident claimants to achieve adequate awards. Others, and some judges, lawyers and scholars, base their more disinterested comments as to the "claims racket" and the alarming "big verdict" upon a radical theory of *laissez faire*, and the stoical philosophy of enduring one's own pain and disabilities with a minimum of legal relief as a reasonable price to pay in a mechanistic age. In the true spirit of the common law, it is to be hoped that, with the increasing use of new procedures for trying the bulk of litigated cases, there will be less evasion, concealment, obscurantism and chicanery, and more facing up to the problems that exist.

My friend, the late great Bill Prosser, while lauding the original Modern Trials somewhat retractingly found it "unabashedly pro-plaintiff." It is. But I repeatedly urge throughout this book that every page that can be used by plaintiff should be considered, maybe modified, and used by defendant.

---

[6]. "They have no lawyers among them, for they consider them as a sort of people whose profession is to disguise matters." Sir Thomas More, Utopia.

"[T]hese nice sharp quillets of the law," Henry VI, Act II, Sc. 4.

"Litigous terms, fat contention, and flowing fees," John Milton.

"My business on the jury's done—the quibbling all is through—I've watched the lawyers right and left, and give my verdict true." Will Carleton, "Going Home Today."

Perhaps Shakespeare best summarized public sentiment when he advocated: "The first thing we do, let's kill all the lawyers." King Henry VI, Part II, Act IV. To the contrary, see Samuel Johnson, quoted, Piozzi, Johnsoniana, "The law is the last result of human wisdom acting upon human experience for the benefit of the public."

of the world which finds its way into courts of justice."

§§ 1.5–1.10 are reserved for supplementary material.

B. WHO IS THE TORT CLIENT?

§ 1.11 Introduction

In determining a method of adequate trial, we should first examine him for whom the trial is proposed. As clients of the common law, we find the Lord, the farmer, the soldier, the merchant, the infrequent traveller, the husband and wife and their children, and of course, the testator. These clients have changed with the times, as the men and women themselves have followed different paths and vocations. Today the large majority of the trial lawyer's clients on the civil side are personal injury litigants.

§ 1.12 Accidents and Statistics

To be a prospective plaintiff or defendant in the great mass of litigation, all one must do is live. The potentials of personal injury are as great and as varied as is man's complex modern life. Nothing is more personal to man than the injuries to his person. Also, nothing may be more disastrous than the possible loss of life, limb and livelihood for the plaintiff, and yet at the same time, the financial hazards of probable liability for the defendant, and even his insurance company, may be similarly ruinous. All plaintiff need do is move about to become a statistic.[7]

---

7. "Accidents" take an annual toll in injuries, lives and money far exceeding that of any war in which this country has ever been engaged. During the years 1961–1969, 300,000 American soldiers lost their lives in Vietnam. During that same 8 year period, 400,000 Americans were killed and over 20 million were injured in motor vehicle collisions on United States highways and streets.

J. Finch, M.D. & J. Smith, Jr., J.D., Psychiatric and Legal Aspects of Automobile Fatalities, 3–4 (1970).

The United States Department of Transportation reported on October 13, 1980: "There are approximately 50,000 highway deaths every year—the equivalent of a major airplane disaster every day. Alcohol is involved in half of those deaths and some 8,000 persons are killed each year in pedestrian accidents."

In 1978, there were approximately 104,500 persons killed by accidents in the United States, an increase in about 1,300 deaths from the preceding year. In 1973, 102,500 persons were killed by accidents, while in 1952, the statistics reported in the original edition of Modern Trials, the number was 96,000. An even more telling statistic is that of cost, how much and its increase over the last 25 years. Entirely apart from the intangible cost, ranging from simple inconvenience to the tragedy of broken homes, in 1978 there was a direct computable cost of $68.7 billion. In 1975, the figure was $47.1 billion, while in 1952, it was $8.3 billion. This cost includes loss of wages, medical expenses, overhead, cost of insurance, production delays, damage to equipment (in occupational accidents) and damage to property (resulting from motor vehicle accidents).

Nothing is more dispassionate and final than the reduction of human life to tables of figures. But "sudden death"[8] is just as absolute. The indulgent father, laughter at a late party, a sleek foreign car, the old jalopy, the hotrod, vintage champagne sparkling ebulliently, rare brandy, traffic lights that change unexpectedly, a swinging speedometer needle, the social register, and the unemployment registrant: all achieve their finality in the cold statistics. From a meager part-time job, the law has since unwillingly been forced into an almost full-time position of maid-in-waiting upon negligence cases. Old rules become anachronistic for new situations. The old hearsay rule, formerly in-

Of the 104,500 persons killed accidently in 1978, 51,500 were in street and highway traffic accidents; 23,000 in home accidents; 13,000 in occupational accidents; and 21,500 in other public non-motor vehicle and non-work accidents. The number of persons suffering disabling injuries were 10,200,000. Estimates are that a worker dies every 35 minutes in the United States as the result of an on-the-job accident. Lost wages accounted for $4.2 billion, medical expenses were $2.5 billion, and insurance administrative costs amounted to $3.9 billion. Another $10.6 billion that was lost can be attributed to workers other than those injured and the time required to investigate accidents, write up reports, etc.

The National Safety Council reports that of the 104,500 accidental deaths in 1978, 51,500 could be attributed to motor-vehicle accidents; 13,800 were from falls; 6,900 were due to drowning; 6,300 from fires, burns, or otherwise associated with fire; 3,400 deaths were from poisoning by solids or liquids; 2,900 deaths related to suffocation due to an ingested object; 1,800 from firearms; 1,700 people died from poisoning by gases and vapors; and 16,200 people died from various other accidents, such as air and rail transport, being struck with a falling object, coming into contact with an electric current, and medical complications.

As reported by the National Safety Council, in 1978 51,500 people were killed in traffic accidents. 18,300 of these were in urban areas, while the remaining 33,200 deaths occurred in rural areas; 22,900 persons were killed in collisions between motor vehicles; 13,600 met their death in non-collision accidents; 9,300 pedestrians were killed by motor vehicles; 3,500 people lost their lives when a motor vehicle collided with a fixed object, such as a lamppost or guardrail; 1,100 people died due to automobiles colliding with trains. Collisions with pedalcycles accounted for 1,000 deaths in 1978.

The late Dean Roscoe Pound, eminent scholar and one-time Editor-in-Chief of the NACCA Law Journal, in an address given July 2, 1953 at Philadelphia, and printed in 12 NACCA L. J. 197, entitled "Reparation and Prevention in the Law of Today", stated:

> In a population of about one hundred and sixty millions, one in eighteen is injured annually seriously enough to get into the statistics. Tempest, fires, flood, pestilence, and famine which men used to fear, as our prayer books bear witness, still take toll, but no such toll today. Indeed, the two million annual victims of accidents in factories and work shops and the seven million more injured in automobile, railway, airplane, shipping, store and home accidents make even war take a second place.

8. "Sudden Death" was the title of an article published some years back, intending to shock from complacency the unheeding prospective client.

volved in a breach of warranty claim for the sale of a "milch cow" excludes the testimony of a "speed cop". The majority of litigated cases are made up largely of automobile cases. The appalling statistics of highway death[9] and personal injury[10] daily challenge the remedies provided by the law of negligence.

§ 1.13 The Verdict and Social Good

This is a book primarily about compensation for those to whom the accident has happened. But in reading the pages hereafter, one may not overlook preventive law in impressing that "negligence" can picture a harsh scene. I have often said to a jury:

> "Ladies and gentlemen: It is not necessary in this case that we prove to you that defendant did anything willfully or wantonly.

---

9. In 1978, the total number of accidental disabling injuries, as reported by the National Safety Council Accident Facts, (1979 ed.), was 10,200,000. The total number of accidental deaths was 104,500. These statistics are broken down as follows: occupational non-motor vehicle injuries were 2,000,000; occupational non-motor vehicle deaths were 8,600; occupational motor vehicle injuries were 200,000; occupational motor vehicle deaths were 4,400; public motor vehicle injuries (non-occupational) were 1,800,000; and public motor vehicle deaths (non-occupational) were 46,900.

    In 1978, there were 18,300,000 accidents involving 31,500,000 drivers. 45,400 of the accidents produced fatalities; 1,400,000 resulted in disabling injuries. The remaining 18,300,000 caused property damage and nondisabling injuries.

    The California Highway patrol reports that in 1979, 5,503 persons were killed on California streets and highways, a new "record" despite the fact that drivers had driven 1.4 billion fewer miles than the preceding year. The death toll in California rose by 3.9% over the previous year, while nationwide there was an increase of 0.8%.

    The number of bicyclists killed in California increased from 81 in 1978 to 119 in 1979, and the number of motorcyclists killed rose to 837 from 767. More than half of all the fatalities involved a driver who had been drinking. 309,240 persons were injured in 1979, a 1.1% reduction in the number of injuries from 1978.

10. In 1970, the National Commission on Product Safety presented its final report to the President and Congress. In the report it estimated that each year, over *20 million* Americans were injured in the home as a result of incidents connected with consumer products. Of these persons injured, 30,000 died; 110,000 were permanently disabled; 585,000 hospitalized; and more than 20 million suffered injuries serious enough to require medical treatment, or resulted in their being disabled for a year or more. The annual cost to the nation of product related injuries was estimated in excess of $5 billion.

    Of the products causing injuries with the most frequency, the Commission found that a number of makes, models, or types of the following products constituted "unreasonable hazards": glass; fireworks; floor furnaces; glass bottles; hot-water vaporizers; household chemicals; infant furniture; ladders; power tools; protective headgear; rotary lawnmowers; toys; unvented gas heaters; television sets; and wringer washers.

The gravamen of this complaint is simple negligence and carelessness only. Of all those in the court room within the sound of my voice, there is probably no one more sorry than he, the defendant, that the accident has happened. He would restore the maimed body if he could."

Yet the tragedy of "simple negligence and carelessness" may be just as fatal as the bullet sped from the firing chamber with evil and malicious intent, wanton and wilful purpose, or an abandoned and malignant heart. At the end of the personal injury lawsuit, the accident has been explained. The negligence has been analyzed and dissected.

Unfortunately, too often the verdict of the jury is merely a decision between the parties, and not a social judgment which might stand as a recommendation to change an errant practice.[11] Time and again as the jury found negligence, had the verdict been special, specific blame might have been placed, condemning speeding, intoxication, defective roads, or whatever practice brought about the accident. The social accomplishment of the personal injury lawyer in merely treating his client's economic wounds seems as futile as were the medical practitioner to treat repeatedly for a disease, and knowing its cause, seek only to cure the particular patient without preventing a recurrence to him or others.

Negligence law in recent years has left in its wake a great mass of reported cases. But within the law of these cases, too, there lie facts available for studies in injury prevention.[12]

The surgeon not only may, but *must* become seemingly immune to metal cutting flesh, cauteries searing vessels. He can never become insensitive to his patient's pain. Likewise, the personal injury lawyer has seen so many pictures of "sudden death" that he too may become hardened and bitter about the recklessness of motorists. He

---

11. In criminal law, I was impressed with the English procedure, different from our own, where the jury, after a verdict of guilty, remain in court to hear the pleas and recommendations for probation, and the act of sentencing.

12. The personal injury lawyer should be able to qualify as an expert to sit on traffic, health and safety boards and councils. His community usefulness has not been recognized. From his investigations and preparation of personal injury cases for trial, he has learned the causes for accidents, whether drinking, excessive speed, defective road conditions, or poor mechanical equipment. He should be able to conclude factually the proper age at which one should start and perhaps stop driving, proper penalties for reckless driving and the advisability of leniency in allowing an offender to offend again, and perhaps the last time. And his practical knowledge is not limited to the automobile. He can tell you about elevators, escalators, street cars, buses, electrical appliances, and every instrument which has, or is capable of achieving, momentum. That is his field.

must recall, however, that the arbiter to whom these pictures are presented in court, the twelve jurors (The xii), may have never seen such a picture. He must, of course, carefully observe the members of a jury to make sure that a picture, factual and often brutal, does not offend.

Figures 1 [13] and 2 [14] are "sudden death". The jury will study such pictures. Twelve pairs of eyes will each see something different. In the jury-room there will be a pooling of their observations. They may misinterpret the picture, or see details unnoticed by the lawyer who has introduced it. Before the introduction of such a picture into evidence, it must be minutely scrutinized from all angles, even perhaps with the use of a magnifying glass. The unwary trial lawyer may find after his final argument that an important piece of evidence was in the picture but not pointed out; or that actually the scene is falsified to his detriment by not showing enough, or conversely, too much.

Figure 1. Crash catastrophe means the loss of life and limb. What happened here? Sometimes after the debris and the victims are removed, it is too late to find out.

---

13. See note 13 on page 13.   14. See note 14 on page 13.

Ch. 1 SETTING THE STAGE § 1.13

Figure 2. Sudden death came here, the result of a railroad train and school bus collision. Who was to blame? Who will take care of the loss of life and limb?

13. Photo courtesy of R. T. "Ted" Abrahamson, P. E., Abrahamson & Associates, Consulting Engineers, Suite 536—Petroleum Building, P.O. Box 14025, Amarillo, Texas 79101.

14. Photo courtesy of R. T. "Ted" Abrahamson, P. E., Abrahamson & Associates, Consulting Engineers, Suite 536—Petroleum Building, P.O. Box 14025, Amarillo, Texas 79101. For a complete report of this case, Ortiz v. Atchison, Topeka, & Santa Fe Ry. Co., see "Investigation Through Accident Reconstruction," Section 21.52, infra.

§§ 1.14–1.20 are reserved for supplementary material.

C. ATTORNEY'S FEES, LIENS AND EXPENSES

§ 1.21 Introduction

Accounts and gossip of lawyers' excessive fees and exorbitant court costs are common and notorious. In seeking legal counsel, just as in visiting a doctor or retaining any other services or purchasing goods, the layman is concerned with, and rightly so, "What will it cost me?" Mr. Citizen may be the first to admit that the "laborer in the vineyard is worthy of his hire," and yet there is something to the uninitiated about a lawyer's "fee" that ranks him with the greedy landlord, the spendthrift heir, the profiteers from a government contract, and the unscrupulous corporations.

Generally, the injured plaintiff is a wage earner. (Bank presidents never seem to be personal injury plaintiffs!) When the bankrupting catastrophe of a severe personal injury, or even more so the death of the breadwinner, strikes, the last thing Mr. Wage Earner or his surviving dependents could afford to do is to pay money for a retainer and the lawyer's hourly wages as the claim progresses. How, then, can an injured victim or his surviving dependents avail themselves of the recourse supposedly necessary to afford access to the court? How do they gain access to the hallowed halls of justice?

§ 1.22 The Contingent Fee Contract; Advances

Practically speaking, it is only through the contingent fee contract that such a plaintiff is guaranteed access to the courts. The author believes it is the contingent fee which makes the management of personal injury law workable under a free enterprise system, without the use of administrative tribunals and commissions. Use of the contingent fee, in recognition that without it the injured party may be shut off from any remedy, has now been uniformly accepted in the United States,[15] while in England it remains the butt of vigorous

---

15. Cappel v. Adams, 434 F.2d 1278 (5th Cir. 1970) ("Contingent fee contracts have long been commonly accepted in the United States in civil proceedings to enforce claims. Such arrangements have been traditionally justified on the ground that they provide many litigants with the only practical means by which they can secure legal services to enforce their claims."); Valentino v. Richners Rhederie, G. m. B. H., 417 F.Supp. 176 (E.D.N.Y.1976), aff'd 552 F.2d 466 (2d Cir.) ("In weighing the conflicting interests it is necessary to give substantial weight to the public policy favoring contingent fees because they make it possible for the poor and middle class to vindicate their substantive rights. American law has long recognized contingent fee arrangements as a practical method of permitting workers such as longshoremen to protect their legal rights."); Draper v. Zebec, 219 Ind. 362, 37 N.E.2d 952 (1941), reh. denied

disparagement.[16] However, the costs of the barrister-solicitor system in England has become so expensive it has almost driven these specialists out of business!

219 Ind. 362, 38 N.E.2d 995 ("It may and does happen that persons who have rights, but no means to pursue them, are obliged to resort to this means of procuring legal redress. . . . The fact that the practice of stipulating beforehand for professional fees, contingent on the result of the litigation, is sometimes abused, and exposes the profession to misapprehension and illiberal remark, is not sufficient excuse for refusing to enforce such a contract, when characterized throughout by 'all good fidelity to the client.' "); Couture v. Mammoth Groceries, Inc., 117 N.H. 294, 371 A.2d 1184 (1977) ("In this state contingent fees are not per se unreasonable for the mere fact that an attorney's fees are to be contingent upon his success and are to constitute a share of the proceedings recovered can scarcely be said to offend the public conscience. . . . While contingent fees in criminal cases are against public policy, in civil cases they have long been commonly accepted in the United States in proceedings to enforce claims.").

Ethical Consideration 2–20 of the ABA Code of Professional Responsibility states: "Contingent fee arrangements in civil cases have long been commonly accepted in the United States in proceedings to enforce claims. The historical bases of their acceptance are that (1) they often, and in a variety of circumstances, provide the only practical means by which one having a claim against another can economically afford, finance, and obtain the services of a competent lawyer to prosecute his claim, and (2) a successful prosecution of the claim produces a res out of which the fees can be paid."

See also M. Bloom, The Trouble With Lawyers (1968); F. MacKinnon, Contingent Fees For Legal Services (1964); D. Rosenthal, Lawyer and Client: Who's in Charge (1974); Schwart & Mitchell, Economic Analysis of the Contingent Fee in Personal-Injury Litigation, 22 Stan.L.Rev. 1125 (1970); Note, Contingent Fee: Champerty or Champion, 21 Clev.St. L.Rev. 15 (1972).

John V. Lewis, former Collector of Internal Revenue for San Francisco, and an able lawyer, recounted to the author, that upon one Christmas season he visited the home of Frank Hogan, former President of the American Bar Association, and found the distinguished barrister sitting in front of the fireplace surrounded by munificent gifts from admiring clients. Lewis asked, "What's the matter Frank, you don't seem to like your presents. Just suppose to make you happy, you could have any present you, one of the leading lawyers in the United States, would want. Just what would a lawyer wish for as his finest present on Christmas Day?" Hogan thought for a moment, and then with a gleam in his eye facetiously said, "A very rich man, very solvent, walking up to my door, in a very great deal of trouble."

Forms

See § 2.27, infra, for "Contingent Fee Agreement Forms."

16. The English have traditionally viewed the contingent fee with abhorrence, saying, quite academically, that it breeds champerty and maintenance. See Haseldine v. Hoskin [1933] 1 K.B. 822; Wild v. Simpson [1919] 2 K.B. 544; Swinfen v. Chelnsford, 157 Eng.Rep. 1436 (1860). In 1967, England abolished champerty as a criminal offense. Nonetheless, it retained the ancient rule that a lawyer "who is retained or employed to prosecute any action, suit or proceed-

Another immediate ancillary problem is also presented: Not only does the prospective plaintiff lack the money to hire a lawyer, in many cases he may not be able to afford the usual expenses of litigation, nor will he be able to support himself and his family while pursuing his claim and convalescing. Even with the verdict won, after many months and years, and pending appeal, he may be forced to succumb to the temptation of a severely discounted ready cash offer.

ing, shall not enter into any arrangement to receive a contingency fee . . . ." The American practice of allowing contingent fees is criticized as the lawyer, having obtained a financial interest in the suit, may find himself in a situation where this interest conflicts with his obligations to present the case with the utmost care of his client's interest, and to conduct the case with "scrupulous fairness and integrity." Wallensteiner v. Moir (No. 2), [1975] 1 Q.B. 373.

Another reason the English frown upon the use of contingent fees is because it allegedly reduces the status of the lawyer to that of a merchant motivated by profit: "The English lawyer's hostility 'may reflect historic aversion to the supposed immoralities of commercial life as much as it does a belief that contingent fees will bring harmful effects upon today's lawyers, clients and courts.' By contrast, the American lawyer's approval of this method of financing litigation is partly the product of his acceptance of the profit-motivated commercially oriented society." M. Zander, Lawyers and the Public Interest 115 (1968). The more progressive English scholars concede, however, that the practice of law does indeed have its commercial elements. "Any attempt to deny the commercial aspects of the practice of law in 1978 must be condemned as unreal. No longer can it be pretended that fees are mere honoraria for a service to justice. Lawyers are in business and run their practices in the main as business." Robin C. A. White, Contingent Fees: A Supplement to Legal Aid?, 41 Modern L.Rev. 286 (1978).

What has happened in British society, as confirmed by the publication Post and Insurance Monitor, is that the legal system and judicial recourse are available only to the very wealthy, who can afford it, and the very poor, who are given government assistance. The middle class suffer the most from England's failure to adopt the contingent fee system. Often, the injured party cannot come up with the funds to pay the lawyer and expenses. Even where they can do so, many are inhibited by the fact that the losing party must pay the attorney's fees of the victor. Although intended to dissuade spurious claims, the effect of this practice has seen many with meritorious claims failing to pursue them because of the economic hardships imposed should they not prevail.

To provide the middle class with access to the courts, a number of British lawyers are supporting the institution of the contingent fee contract. Another alternative being studied is a "Contingent Legal Aid Fund" (CLAF). Under this plan, a prospective plaintiff would request monetary assistance from the fund where the suit involved a claim for money damages. The case would then be reviewed by a group of lawyers, and the money would be granted if there were "reasonable grounds" for the suit. See Robert Donin, England Looks at a Hybrid Contingent Fee System, 64 A.B.A.J. 773 (1978).

The traditional strict rule[17] in this situation prohibited an attorney from advancing *any money whatsoever* to his client, regardless of whether the funds were to be used for litigation expenses only, or also for living expenses. This practice was condemned as being champertous and maintenance.[18]

---

17. Gonzalez, Barredo v. Schenck, 287 F.Supp. 505 (S.D.N.Y.1968), rev'd on other grounds 428 F.2d 971 (2d Cir.) (An attorney fee agreement under which an attorney agrees to pay the expenses of litigation held clearly inconsistent with and contrary to the public policy of New York); Kentucky Bar Ass'n v. DeCamillas, 547 S.W.2d 446 (Ky.1977) ("As to the charge relating to the waiving of attorney fees and purchasing furniture, the ethical considerations are also clear that a lawyer shall not advance funds to his client in order to pursue the litigation. The waiving of the fees by itself is perhaps proper, but the fact that he was making this agreement without the consent of his client, without any information to the client about it, was improper."); In re Mason, 203 S.W.2d 750 (Mo.App.1947) (Attorney guilty of unprofessional conduct when he offered to pay court costs which might accrue in a case to be filed by him as plaintiff's attorney, where he would receive a part of the recovery of the suit in compensation for services rendered); In re Gladstone, 16 A.D.2d 512, 229 N.Y.S.2d 663 (1962) (Professional misconduct for attorney to pay various expenses of clients' claims, including process servers' fees, calendar fees, jury fees, and doctors' bills and other medical expenses); Matter of Sandifer, 260 S.C. 633, 198 S.E.2d 120 (1973) (Attorney publicly remanded for extensive and involved loans made to client for latter's expenses, coupled with attorney's rendering of inadequate statement of account to client at time of settlement of action).

See also, Quittner v. Motion Picture Producers & Distributors of America, 70 F.2d 331 (2d Cir. 1934) (Upon petition *forma pauperis* for printing of record on appeal, not necessary for attorney who has contingent contract to also file oath, since he is under no obligation to furnish record for client, —such would be champertous); Sun Life Assur. Co. of Canada v. Casanova, 260 F. 449 (1st Cir. 1919) (Contract to render professional services and to pay all the expenses and costs of litigation held "clearly champertous"); In re Sizer, 306 Mo. 356, 267 S.W. 922 (1924). (Disbarment proceeding, court holding: "A lawyer can loan his client money without violating either ethics or law. Of course, the loan should not be the consideration for the employment."); In re Gilman's Adm'x, 251 N.Y. 265, 167 N.E. 437 (1929) (Agreement by attorney to pay expenses of proceedings held champertous: "The law does not say that an attorney is guilty of misconduct by the voluntary advance of the expenses of a lawsuit to a client too poor to pay the cost of justice. It does say that there is misconduct if he makes or promises the payment to discharge an obligation assumed in return for his retainer."); Stark County v. Mischel, 42 N.D. 332, 173 N.W. 817 (1919) (Contract by which attorney promised to save client harmless from all expenses, if successful, held champertous and void).

18. Schnabel v. Taft Broadcasting Co., Inc., 525 S.W.2d 819 (Mo.App.1975). ("The doctrines of champerty and maintenance were developed at the common law to prevent officious intermeddlers from stirring up strife and contention by vexatious and

Two main rationales were offered in support of this view: First, it was felt that by permitting the lawyer to advance any costs to the client would give the lawyer a personal interest in the outcome of the litigation. This would result in the interests of the client, which should always be paramount, being relegated to a position of lesser importance, thereby resulting in the formation of a conflict of interests.[19] Second, the restriction was designed to discourage lawyers from soliciting and enticing prospective clients[20] by promising them they would pay all costs and advance them money to live on.

Today most courts[21] allow an attorney to advance the expenses of litigation, including court costs, fees for investigative services and

---

speculative litigation which would disturb the peace of society, lead to corrupt practices and prevent the remedial process of the law. . . . Maintenance is defined as 'an officious intermeddling in a suit which in no way belongs to one, by maintaining or assisting either party, with money or otherwise, to prosecute or defend it.' . . . Champerty, a species of maintenance, consists of an agreement under which a person who has no interest in the suit of another undertakes to maintain or support it at his own expense in exchange for part of the litigated matter in the event of a successful conclusion of the cause."); Lo Guidice v. Harris, 98 Ohio App. 230, 128 N.E.2d 842 (1954) ("[C]hamperty is a bargain between one having an interest in a law suit, either as plaintiff or defendant, and another who is a stranger thereto, whereby such stranger, called the champertor, agrees to carry on the prosecution or defense of such suit at his own expense, in consideration of his receiving a part of the proceeds in the event of a favorable determination of the litigation"). See also Boettcher v. Criscione, 180 Kan. 39, 299 P.2d 806 (1956), mod'd 180 Kan. 484, 305 P.2d 1055 (Common barratry and champerty defined as that of frequently exciting and stirring up quarrels at law or otherwise); In re Gilman's Adm'x, 251 N.Y. 265, 167 N.E. 437 (1929) (Contract of retainer whereby attorney agreed to bear "all necessary expenses" held champertous, as inducing plaintiff to place claim in his hands for prosecution).

19. In this respect see ABA Code of Professional Responsibility, Ethical Consideration (ABA–EC) 5–1: "The professional judgment of a lawyer should be exercised within the bounds of the law solely for the benefit of his client and free of compromising influences and loyalties. Neither his personal interests, the interest of other clients nor the desires of third persons should be permitted to dilute his loyalty to his client." See also ABA–EC 5–2: "After accepting employment a lawyer should carefully refrain from acquiring a property right or assuming a position that would tend to make his judgment less protective of the interest of his client."

20. State ex rel. Florida Bar v. Dawson, 111 So.2d 427 (Fla.1959) (Improper for attorney to bear all costs of suit in event there was no recovery; also improper to advance to clients money for funeral services, medical expenses, and automobile repair bills as inducement for clients to employ him as their attorney); Fort Worth & D. C. R. Co. v. Carlock, 33 Tex.Civ.App. 202, 75 S.W. 931 (1903) (Jury question raised as to whether promise to loan money to prospective client for expenses of litigation was inducement to secure employment).

21. See note 21 on page 19.

medical examinations, and expenses incurred in obtaining and presenting evidence and witnesses. The usual requirement, however, is that the client himself must remain ultimately liable for all expenses incurred by the lawyer.[22] Of course, a lawyer may still not promise a prospective client that he will pay all such expenses for the purpose of soliciting his business.

Apart from court costs and related expenses the injured person is often left wondering how he will manage to support his family during the pending litigation. Surely it is unfair and places an undue burden on the injured victim to afford him legal recourse, yet to delay it four or five years during which time he is often pressured into settling for an inadequate amount so he does not have to sit idly by as the car, furniture, and ultimately the family home are repossessed.

Yet most states[3] still prohibit a lawyer from advancing any living expenses, regardless of how meritorious plaintiff's claim may be

---

21. This is in accord with the position taken by the rules of professional responsibility promulgated by the ABA. Disciplinary Rule 5–103(B) reads:

> While representing a client in connection with contemplated or pending litigation, a lawyer shall not advance or guarantee financial assistance to his client, except that the lawyer may advance or guarantee the expenses of litigation, including court costs, expenses of investigation, expenses of medical examination, and costs of obtaining and presenting evidence, provided the client remains ultimately liable for such expenses.

See also Ryan v. Pennsylvania R. Co., 268 Ill.App. 364 (1932) (Holding that making of loan to client for purpose of advancement of costs proper when necessary to prevent inadequate settlement); Johnson v. Great Northern R. Co., 128 Minn. 365, 151 N.W. 125 (1915) (Contingent contract to retain from proceeds moneys advanced for expenses held valid: "An agreement to loan the client funds with which to carry on the suit or to maintain himself during its pendency is not regarded as *per se* opposed to public policy."); Potter v. Ajax Mining Co., 22 Utah 273, 61 P. 999 (1900) (Advances made as loan to client pending litigation held proper).

22. In re Ruffalo, 249 F.Supp. 432 (N.D.Ohio 1965) ("Whether it be the attorney's fee, the expenses of litigation, or unconditional loans, the fact that it might be difficult or unlikely that the client will be able to reimburse the attorney for the same absent a recovery on his claim should not render the attorney's conduct improper"); Sherwin Williams Co. v. J. Mannos & Sons, 287 Mass. 304, 191 N.E. 438 (1934) (Agreement by attorney to prosecute suit for client in consideration of share from amount recovered is void, when there is no right of lawyer to look to defendant for money advanced or for services rendered).

23. Matter of Carroll, 124 Ariz. 80, 602 P.2d 461 (1979) (Improper for attorneys to advance living expenses because, if publicized, such practice would constitute an improper inducement for clients to employ an attorney); Matter of Stewart, 121 Ariz. 243, 589 P.2d 886 (1979) (Improper for attorney to loan client $215.00 to cover living expenses; court held that such practice could lead to lawyer placing his own recovery ahead of that of client, and might, for example, urge a settlement which would be to his best interest, but not to the best interest of his client); Mahoning County Bar Ass'n v. Ruf-

and how debilitating his injuries are. A few courts, however, have held that the attorney was not guilty of misconduct when he advanced his client minimal living expenses, as otherwise plaintiff may have been forced to settle for an inadequate amount out of economic necessity.[24]

The author believes that to make practical the contingent fee, there should be no restrictions except the integrity of the lawyer as an officer of the court in the "financing" of the litigation, and the convalescense as well. It is done in practice to a considerable degree in most states now. If this is an unsound practice, then this very

falo, 176 Ohio St. 263, 199 N.E.2d 396 (1964), cert. denied 379 U.S. 931, 85 S.Ct. 328, 13 L.Ed.2d 342. ("It is obvious that, where the advancement of living expenses is made, as in the instant case, to enable a disabled client and his family to survive, any agreement by the disabled client to repay them would not have the effect of providing the attorney with any reasonable source of repayment other than the proceeds received on trial or settlement of his client's claim. In effect, the attorney has purchased an interest in the subject matter of the litigation that he is conducting."); In re Berlant, 458 Pa. 439, 328 A.2d 471 (1974), cert. denied 421 U.S. 964, 95 S.Ct. 1953, 44 L.Ed.2d 451 (1975) (Holding that although it may be considered as a mitigating factor in determining punishment, fact that money was advanced to indigent client and used for rent, food, and other necessities was irrelevant to the commission of the offense itself).

24. Louisiana State Bar Ass'n v. Edwins, 329 So.2d 437 (La.1976) (Lawyer advanced client $894.00 cash, purchased tires for $30.41, paid three car notes ($67.50 each), paid two other finance notes ($31.04 each), and arranged and paid for plaintiff's hospitalization and operation ($579.25) in connection with a non-accident-related painful condition. Court held that it was unwilling to hold that either the spirit or the intent of the disciplinary rule prohibiting a lawyer from advancing money to his client violated by the advancement of minimal living expenses, of minor sums necessary to prevent foreclosures, or of necessary medical treatment. "If an impoverished person is unable to secure subsistence from some source during disability, he may be deprived of the only effective means by which he can wait out the necessary delays that result from litigation to enforce his cause of action. He may, for reasons of economic necessity and physical need, be forced to settle his claim for an inadequate amount."). See also Dombey, Tyler, Richards & Grieser v. Detroit, T. & I. R. Co., 351 F.2d 121 (6th Cir. 1965) (Suggesting that it may not be improper for attorney to advance money to client where there is a reasonable prospect the latter will be able to repay the loan even if the cause of action proves unsuccessful); Hildebrand v. State Bar of California, 18 Cal.2d 816, 117 P.2d 860 (1941) (Loan to client after being retained not unethical); Mock v. Higgins, 3 Ill.App.2d 281, 121 N.E.2d 865 (1954) (Costs and expenses of suit properly advanced); People ex rel. Chicago Bar Ass'n v. McCallum, 341 Ill. 578, 173 N.E. 827 (1930) (Advancement of money to indigent clients for payment of living expenses or hospital bills approved); Christie v. Sawyer, 44 N.H. 298 (1862) ("It is not uncommon that attorneys commence actions for poor people, and make advances of money necessary to the prosecution of the suit, upon the credit of the cause.").

practical problem should be met in some other manner, but not by ignoring it.

By characterizing the lawyer who engages in these practices as a "merchant," and criticising his action as not within the "ancient dignity of counsel" does not solve the problem. Name calling is not a substitute for the practical necessity for economic support of the injured claimant between accident and trial. Surely the various bar associations should approach the problem in a less academic and more pragmatic manner.

§ 1.23 Amount of Fees; Fee Schedules

The amount of fee when justly determined may be a partial answer to the problem. I have set a fee of 33% if disposition is made by settlement before the filing of a complaint, and 40% should a recovery result either by settlement, trial or otherwise after the complaint is filed. I now tend to 25% if disposition is by settlement.

These percentages are fairly representative of most contingent fee agreements today, although some contingent fee contracts for 50% have been approved.[25] Some states have enacted statutory fee schedules[26] which provide for varying percentages as the amount of the award increases.

---

25. See cases cited in note 33, infra.

26. At one time, many states had *minimum* fee schedules. These were designed to preserve the integrity of the legal profession, and to ensure a prospective litigant that he would be getting competent counsel who would devote a fair amount of time to the case. Such minimum fee schedules once enjoyed strong support from the American Bar Association. "The establishment of suggested or recommended fee schedules by bar associations is a thoroughly laudable activity. The evils of fee cutting ought to be apparent to all members of the Bar." The ABA even went so far as to say that the habitual charging of less than the minimum fees as established by the schedule could be evidence of unethical conduct. ABA Committee on Professional Ethics, Ops. No. 302 (1961). Thirteen years later the ABA reversed its position, recommending that all state and local bar associations who had not yet done so should withdraw or cancel all fee schedules, "whether or not designated as 'minimum' or 'suggested' fee schedules. ABA 1974 Mid-Year Meeting 12–13 (1974). See also Arnould & Corley, Fee Schedules Should Be Abolished, 57 A.B.A.J. 655 (1971); Note, Bar Association Minimum Fee Schedules and the Antitrust Laws, 1974 Duke L.J. 1164. Finally, such minimum fee practices were severely curtailed by the U.S. Supreme Court in the case of Goldfarb v. Virginia State Bar Ass'n, 421 U.S. 773, 95 S.Ct. 2004, 44 L.Ed.2d 572 (1975), reh. denied 423 U.S. 886, 96 S.Ct. 162, 46 L.Ed.2d 118, wherein the Court held that such minimum fee schedules were violative of the Sherman Act.

In *American Trial Lawyers Ass'n v. New Jersey Supreme Court*,[27] the Supreme Court of New Jersey, affirming a decision of the Appellate Court, approved of a fee schedule which read as follows: In any matter where a client's claim for damages is based upon the alleged tortious conduct of another, including products liability claims, and the client is not a subrogee, an attorney shall not contract for, charge, or collect a contingent fee in excess of the following limits: (1) 50% on the first $1,000 recovered; (2) 40% on the next $2,000 recovered; (3) 33½% on the next $47,000 recovered; (4) 20% on the next $50,000 recovered; (5) 10% on any amount recovered over $100,000; and (6) where the amount recovered is for the benefit of an infant or incompetent and the matter is settled without trial the foregoing limits shall apply, except that the fee on any amount recovered up to $50,000 shall not exceed 25%.

The court noted that the New Jersey Constitution made its Supreme Court the exclusive repository of the State's power to regulate the practice of law. The fee schedule was held not to be a violation of the freedom to contract, as guaranteed by that state's constitution, since the fees charged their clients by attorneys had always been subject to judicial review.[28] New York has long had a fee schedule[29]

---

27. 66 N.J. 258, 330 A.2d (1974), aff'g 126 N.J.Super. 577, 316 A.2d 19. The New Jersey Supreme Court adopted *in toto* the decision of the lower court.

28. Concerning judicial review of attorneys' fees, the court stated: "Attorneys have never had the right to enforce contractual provisions for more than a fair and reasonable fee. They are not businessmen entitled to charge what the traffic will bear. Membership in the bar is a privilege burdened with conditions. The court's control over a lawyer's professional life derives from his relation to the responsibilities of a court." 316 A.2d at 27.

29. In Gair v. Peck, 6 N.Y.2d 97, 188 N.Y.S.2d 491, 160 N.E.2d 43 (1959), cert. denied 361 U.S. 374, 80 S.Ct. 401, 4 L.Ed.2d 380, the New York Court of Appeals held that it is the function of the Appellate Divisions to "keep the house of the law in order." Toward this goal, they could promulgate guidelines to be used by attorneys in setting their fees. The schedule in question provided:

"(b) The following is the schedule of reasonable fees referred to above: either,

"(1)(A) Fifty per cent on the first one thousand dollars of the sum recovered,

"(B) Forty per cent on the next two thousand dollars of the sum recovered,

"(C) Thirty-five per cent on the next twenty-two thousand dollars of the sum recovered,

"(D) Twenty-five per cent on any amount over twenty-five thousand dollars of the sum recovered; or

"(2) A percentage not exceeding thirty-three and a third per cent of the sum recovered, if the initial contractual arrangement between the client and the attorneys so provides, in which event the procedure hereinafter provided for making application for additional compensation because of extraordinary circumstances shall not apply."

which, although not given the effect of a rule of substantive law,[30] is utilized as a guide for making an initial determination as to the reasonableness of the fee.

The author has seen the 25% statutory limitation (even reduced by some courts) in Federal Tort Claims work an injustice upon attorneys and, at times, on the client, who could thereby "not afford" adequate counsel. There seems to be no logical reason for the general practice of limiting fees in minor's cases to a lesser amount than an adult.[31] A conscientious lawyer may be more concerned and spend additional time in preparation of a minor's or incompetent's case.

In my experience, a 50% contingent fee is too high in any, except the most unusual case, or maybe where there is an appeal and retrial. Yet this percentage has been approved in a number of cases brought to trial in American courts.[32] On the other hand, an efficient personal injury office cannot operate on less than a 25% fee. Not all cases are won, and all a lawyer has to sell is his time and talents and these become rapidly expendible commodities. Law is a profession, not an occupation.

The penalty for being a professional man is a reward in itself with an accrual of dignity and public recognition. It has become customary for lawyers, when going on the bench, to accept a considerable reduction in income. Yet in considering contingent fees, and with controversial legislation being proposed in many states for control of lawyer compensation, the lawyer can no longer afford to be too "dignified" to analyze the economic facts as to whether his business can be profitable if his income is limited as sometimes proposed. If there is to be a system whereby everyone injured will be automatically

---

30. The fee schedule was instead given the effect of a procedural aid to assist the court in effecting its disciplinary power over lawyers in the case of unlawful contingent fees. The scheduled percentages were given a "merely presumptive effect, like a burden of proof which pertains to procedure and is not substantive law." 160 N.E.2d at 53.

31. The allowance of the ⅓ fee in workman's compensation cases from petitioners already inadequately recompensed, seems unjustifiable, as in some states. However, if workman's compensation schedules of awards cannot be raised to adequacy, without bankrupting our economy, then, how can they be indirectly raised by adding the attorney's fee to the employer's bill, instead of deducting it from the employee's award? The compensation lawyer practicing on a set fee schedule can only exist on "volume." Shall the number of lawyers in this field be then limited?

32. See, e. g., Cappel v. Adams, 434 F.2d 1278 (5th Cir. 1970) (Trial court did not abuse its discretion in restricting attorney's recovery for fees to one-third of award to father and to only one-fifth of award to each of three children, even though contingent fee agreement called for recovery by attorney of one-third to *all* parties).

compensated, there may be no further necessity for judges nor lawyers.[33] The financing of such an arrangement would likely require governmental control, which might very well do away with the business of the nation's private insurance companies. Socialization of all business would then be on the threshold. (New Zealand seems to be moving this way).

Should the percentage of the $200,000 award be the same as that for $2,000? Shall we answer by analogy to our medical brethren,

---

33. Since the purpose of allowing damages is to make a successful litigant whole, it seems logical that only by allowing him to recover his expenses of litigation, which certainly includes his lawyer's fee, can this purpose be accomplished. Yet difficulties immediately present themselves. See Attorneys Fees as an Element of Damages in Alabama, 4 Ala.L.Rev. 93 (1951). This article points out that to provide for including in a judgment reasonable attorney fees would increase litigation of small claims, thereby further crowding the courts, and would also require lengthy evidence to prove reasonableness of such fees.

The suggestion that the jury be permitted to award lawyer's fees in addition to the judgment for the plaintiff, is a dangerous suggestion to be made by counsel for the plaintiff, since it might result in the legislature setting plaintiff's fees in personal injury cases. As in California, bills are presented occasionally in the various legislatures providing that attorney fees in personal injury cases shall be upon the same basis as probate or other similar litigation. Taylor v. Bemiss, 110 U.S. 42, 3 S.Ct. 441, 28 L. Ed. 64 (1881) (Agreement for 50% of claim against United States held valid. "While fifty percent seems to be more than a fair proportion in the division between client and attorney in an ordinary case, we are not prepared to assume that it is extortionate for that reason alone . . ."); Elk Valley Coal Mining Co. v. Willis & Meredith, 149 Ky. 449, 149 S.W. 894 (1912) (Holding

"the 50 per cent damage suit contingent contract fee was customary and reasonable in that community"); In re Kraus, 322 Pa. 362, 185 A. 737 (1936) (Agreement for one-half of a decedent's estate for litigation held unconscionable); Moyers v. City of Memphis, 135 Tenn. 263, 186 S.W. 105 (1916) (50 per cent contract for collecting a Civil War claim from government approved).

Compare: In re Chopak, 43 F.Supp. 106 (D.C.N.Y.1941) ("The majority of the court deems a 50 per cent contingent fee as ipso facto oppressive and unreasonable"); and Buckley v. Surface Transp. Corp. of New York, 277 App.Div. 224, 98 N.Y.S.2d 576 (1950) (Practice of charging 50 per cent of recovery on contingent basis, regardless of trial or settlement, or nature and amount of services, disapproved); with Matter of Friedman, 136 App. Div. 750, 121 N.Y.S. 426, aff'd 199 N. Y. 537, 92 N.E. 1085 (1910) (Contract for 50 per cent of recovery approved). In "The More Adequate Award and The Flying Saucers," the author commented upon criticism by insurance companies that it was the lawyer's fee, intimated as an economic surplusage, that caused the injustice of excessive awards and hardships upon the company, which hardship was in turn passed on to the insured in the form of higher premiums. The author thereupon answered, "Let them pay every one of our clients, before they come to us, 'the more adequate settlement' and there won't be any need for lawyers . . . . But they won't do it."

that the test is the ability to pay? A better answer, and perhaps known only to those few lawyers who have achieved such an award, is that the amount of work that goes into such a case is proportioned to the fee.

I have had my share of "adequate settlements," but I have never had the "one phone call" disposition,[34] or heard of one, except from the layman.[35] To the client, who advises that he is entitled to his award, anyhow, "under the law" and the "constitution," it is my answer that neither the laws nor the constitution are self-executing documents.

But isn't the reward to the personal injury specialist higher than to lawyers practicing other fields? Unfortunately the courses in ethics taught in law schools are more academic than practical. There is truly the lure of the large verdict ever present in personal injury.[36]

---

34. Most states allow the layman to practice before the Industrial Accident Commissions. But apparently the layman still needs "someone" to fight his battles for him. Once there was a bill proposed in the California Legislature to limit lawyers' fees far below the one-third percentage. A lawyer legislator introduced another bill; this proposed enactment would limit the fees of automobile salesmen, insurance salesmen, shoe salesmen, livestock salesmen, and real estate salesmen to the amount proposed for the lawyers. It was obvious that no one, including the lawyers, or any of the others, could make a living at the proposed rates.

35. This is not to say, of course, that the amount of time, effort, and expertise expended by the lawyer in settling the case are not factors to be taken into consideration and weighed when evaluating the reasonableness of his fees. Where the amount of work by the attorney in effecting a settlement is minimal, it may well be unconscionable for him to receive the full agreed-upon fee. See The Florida Bar v. Moriber, 314 So.2d 145 (Fla.1975) (Lawyer's fee of $7,983.14, 33⅓% of gross recovery of estate, clearly excessive where tasks could have "easily been performed by a layman," since most of the money passed to the client by operation of law); and In re DeSautels, 1 Mass. App. 787, 307 N.E.2d 576 (1974) (Subtraction by attorney of almost one-third of funds for Lithuanian heirs invalidated: "The exaction of such a fee for the largely ministerial function of transmitting distributive shares to heirs would be unconscionable . . .").

36. Mr. Royce G. Rowe, General Counsel of the Lumberman's Mutual Casualty Company, before a meeting of the International Association of Insurance Counsel, said in part:

"Trying personal injury cases has become such a nerve wracking experience that I make it a point never to say anything unkind to a trial lawyer. It has been said that trying these cases, like running a delicatessen, has become its own punishment. For many years the elaborate skill employed in making automobiles has gone hand in hand with a similar ingenuity in exploiting the accidents they cause. The enormous sums of money involved compelled car owners to adopt counter measures of comparable worth. The key figures in these counter measures are the local trial counsel and the home office insur-

§ 1.23 INTRODUCTION Pt. 1

There is still the "ambulance chaser" [37] in the field. It is no answer to point out that on the other side of the fence is still the "settlement ance counsel and the local adjusters and branch claims managers. All things considered, this team has done not only a satisfactory, but a superb job. A fifty year record is there to prove that policyholders, injured people, and all other interests, generally have their rights taken care of in a manner that calls for pride and not for an apology."

I have witnessed settlements motivated by the eagerness of the lawyer for his fee, rather than a proper consideration of the client's welfare. But to the steady and conservative personal injury practitioner, the rewards from the "big one" more often than not averages out the time and expense consumed on behalf of the "little ones." The majority of personal injury lawyers I have met are men of distinction, ebullient in personality, generous, intelligent and hardworking. They have been first of all concerned with their client's rehabilitation, and more gratified for adequate monetary restitution for a broken body than all of the glamour, prestige, and publicity for the "big award." Often they waive a fee when the client has suffered an insufficient return, as a sort of apology for the lawyer's shortcomings. They will appeal cases against odds, and expend time and money because they sincerely believe that some inequitable rule of law is ready for a change, and abhor technical perversities that impede justice. In the highest tradition, these lawyers are considerate of their clients, and this means all of them. When a lawyer reaches the elegance to pronounce, "I only take the big ones," he has reduced himself in stature. Often, he has long since spent the fee of the "little ones" before the "big ones" comes into the office.

37. Ohralik v. Ohio State Bar Ass'n, 436 U.S. 447, 98 S.Ct. 1912, 56 L.Ed. 2d 444 (1978), reh. denied 439 U.S. 883, 99 S.Ct. 226, 58 L.Ed.2d 198 (Attorney disciplined for soliciting clients. U.S. Supreme Court held that rules prohibiting solicitation of clients did not constitute an impermissible abridgement of freedom of speech); Younger v. State Bar of California, 12 Cal.3d 274, 113 Cal. Rptr. 829, 522 P.2d 5 (1974) (Attorney suspended six-months for solicitation. Five minutes after "capper" left hospital room of plaintiff, attorney appeared with medical release forms, a form requesting a police report, and an attorney's retainer agreement form.).

See also In re Heirich, 10 Ill.2d 357, 140 N.E.2d 825 (1957) (Employment of investigator not unethical—clear and convincing evidence required to justify disbarment); In re Gavel, 22 N.J. 248, 125 A.2d 696 (1956) ("An attorney in his relations with a client is bound to the highest degree of fidelity and good faith"); In re Gondelman, 225 App.Div. 462, 233 N.Y.S. 343 (1929) (Attorney disbarred for ambulance chasing, even though there was no proof of dishonesty. "The testimony demonstrates very clearly the evils of the system of ambulance chasing. Competition between ambulance chasers, and between ambulance chasers and other attorneys in procuring cases; visits to homes and hospitals to procure retainers at unseemly hours, and when the injured person or the members of his family were in no mental condition to enter into contracts for the engagement of lawyer's services; division of fees with solicitors and procurers; payment of moneys to officials, doctors and others for help in procuring cases; the use of photographs of checks of amounts of recoveries had, and newspaper clippings showing success-

adjuster." [38] It is the author's experience as he has lectured throughout the United States that most liability insurance companies no longer attempt grossly inadequate settlements, if not through altruistic

es in court, for the purpose of procuring clients, all are laid bare.").

38. As appears in the Claim Service Guide, by the publisher of the Insurance Bar, a "statement of principles" was agreed upon between the American Bar Association and five insurance associations, as follows: that the insurance companies and their representatives (1) will not advise the claimant as to his legal rights, (2) will not deal directly with any claimant represented by an attorney without the attorney's consent, (3) will not advise claimants to refrain from seeking legal advice, and the insurance companies will undertake to be responsible for the conduct of their employees in observing the above and other recommended principles of conduct.

In Hildebrand v. State Bar of California, 36 Cal.2d 504, 225 P.2d 508 (1950), a railway union plan to investigate and secure services of attorney for employee-claimants against railroad, with 6% of recovery going to brotherhood for investigation, and 19% to attorneys for legal services held contrary to "solicitation" and "ambulance chasing."

In his dissent, Justice Carter commented: "Merely scratching the surface uncovers the universal provision of liability insurance policies under which the insurer agrees to defend the insured in any legal action arising under such a policy and retains control over that litigation, including the employment of an attorney. The fees of the attorney are paid by the insurer out of the premiums it receives from the insured. The insurer advertises for and solicits business . . . the sale of its policies. It would be folly to suggest that the attorneys employed by such insurers do not know that such is the practice, and that it is common knowledge that some attorneys, while not on a salary-employee basis with the insurer, have an arrangement whereby they are regularly retained to defend the insurer's insured. The situation is not distinguishable from the instant case except possibly it may be said that this is a stronger case from the standpoint of professional ethics. Is this court going to discipline all attorneys who are employed by insurance companies to represent their insured?"

See Dissent of Justices Dell and Thomas Gallagher to adoption of ABA Canon of Ethics 28 (241 Minn. XVII).

"My objection to the adoption of Canon 28 is not in what it contains but in what it fails to contain. It particularizes altogether too much on solicitation of business by attorneys engaged in representing plaintiffs in personal injury litigation without giving due recognition to similar abuses which exist among some attorneys engaged in representing the defense. If we are to adopt a canon so as to particularize, which seems to me wholly unnecessary, then the entire field of all solicitation should be adequately covered so that the bar may thoroughly understand that solicitation of all kinds, organized as well as isolated, by those representing plaintiffs as well as those representing defendants, will not be tolerated. If Canon 28 is to be adopted it should, in my opinion, be amended so as to specifically include and subject to discipline or disbarment attorneys guilty of the following practices in addition to those now particularly contained in the canon, namely:

"1. The practice of attorneys or their representatives at any time, whether organized or in isolated instances, in soliciting directly or indirectly by personal contact, tele-

motives, then, because they are more expensive to the company in the long run.[39]

It is likewise my experience that Mr. Layman is becoming more selective in his choice of legal representation. Still, however, as compared with the care given to choosing a banker or doctor, often, when a family's whole economic future is at stake, a lawyer will be selected with no other criteria than the recommendation of an uninformed friend, or the precipitate and timely appearance of the attorney himself bearing his recommendations.

§ 1.24 When Contingent Fee Is Inappropriate

Contingent fees in a number of situations are generally not possible or permitted.[40] For example, where a lawyer is defending an accused in a criminal case, there is no monetary award from which a per-

phone, or other means, legal business or causes of action of any kind or description.

"2. The practice of attorneys engaged in the defense of personal injury actions for and on behalf of insurance companies in inducing by solicitation, suggestion, or other means, injured parties to retain their services or the services of other attorneys named by them in establishing claims for injuries or property damage, arising out of accidents in which the insurance companies represented by such attorneys carry the liability insurance for the injured party.

"3. The practice of attorneys in expending substantial sums for elaborate entertainment of individuals or corporate representatives at private clubs or otherwise as a means designed for obtaining legal business, or by the bestowal of gifts of substantial value to such parties, for the purpose of inducing such individuals, representatives, or their corporate principals to retain or engage the services of such attorneys in any legal matters of business.

"4. The practice of attorneys in soliciting insurance companies or other corporations by any means to employ or forward legal business to them.

"5. The practice of attorneys for insurance companies, and other corporations or their representatives or claim departments in inducing as a result of an accident for which their principals may ultimately be held liable, to settle their claims before they have had adequate opportunity to confer with and obtain the advice of counsel of their own choice.

"Canon 28, in my opinion, should be sufficiently broadened in its particularities so as to insure the free flow of legal business to lawyers of the client's own choosing, thus protecting the ethical and the independent local lawyer from the abuses and practices referred to in the canon as well as this dissent."

39. See Chapter 18, "Releases," infra.

40. In 1927, as the result of an ambulance chasing scandal in New York City, the Appellate Division of the Supreme Court, First Department, promulgated a rule requiring publication of the facts of a lawyer's retainer, and particularly the manner in which the case was referred. The Second Department adopted a similar rule (§ 691.20) which requires the filing of statements as to retainer with the Court.

centage could be allocated to the lawyer. Contingent fee arrangements [41] are usually invalidated in divorce cases as being repugnant to public policy.[42] One stated reason is that a contingent fee agreement in such a case would give the attorney an interest in avoiding reconciliation.[43] In special circumstances, however, contingent fee agreements have been given effect in actions involving marital disputes.[44]

§ 1.25 Recovery of Fee by Discharged Attorney

If an attorney is discharged by his client, is he entitled to recover a full percentage of the agreed-to contingent fee? Although some courts would give the attorney the full percentage where he has been discharged without cause,[45] the modern trend allows the attor-

---

41. A copy of a contingent fee agreement sometimes used by the author is reproduced at § 2.27, of Chapter 2, infra.

42. McDearmon v. Gordon & Gremillion, 247 Ark. 318, 445 S.W.2d 488 (1969) ("A contract for the payment of a fee to an attorney, contingent upon his procuring a divorce for his client or contingent in amount upon the amount of alimony to be obtained, is void as against public policy"); Valparaiso Bank & Trust Co. v. Sims, 343 So.2d 967 (Fla.App.1977); Sobieski v. Maresco, 143 So.2d 62 (Fla.App.1962); Barrelli v. Levin, 144 Ind.App. 576, 247 N.E.2d 847 (1969); Aucoin v. Williams, 295 So.2d 868 (La.App.1974), writ denied 299 So.2d 798 (Contingent fee agreement invalid in divorce action, regardless of whether the community property consists of realty, personal property, choses in action, or otherwise); Avant v. Whitter, 253 So.2d 394 (Miss.1971); Miller v. Miller, 83 S.D. 227, 157 N.W.2d 537 (1968).

43. Shanks v. Kilgore, 589 S.W.2d 318 (Mo.App.1979) ("Because of the human relationships involved and the unique character of the proceedings, contingent fee arrangements in domestic relation cases are rarely justified"). See also Succession of Butler, 294 So.2d 512 (La.1974), (The court noted that the justification for contingent fee arrangements, i.e., that it provides access to those who would otherwise be unable to afford adequate counsel. "[T]he fee should not be an inducement to either reconcile the parties or dissolve the marital relation. It would in many cases be different if the fee were contingent upon dissolution of the marriage."); Baskerville v. Baskerville, 246 Minn. 496, 75 N.W.2d 762 (1956) ("Since the continuance of the marriage relation is deemed essential to the public welfare, the state is interested in its preservation. Sound public policy demands that, when differences arise between parties to a marriage, no obstacle shall be placed in the way of their reconciliation. Consequently, it is not fitting that it should be for the interest of any attorney that there should be no reconciliation.").

44. Salter v. St. Jean, 170 So.2d 94 (Fla.App.1964) (Holding that contingent fee agreements are enforceable when they relate to the return of a wife's separate property); Burns v. Stewart, 290 Minn. 289, 188 N.W.2d 760 (1971) (Husband deserted wife, taking with him all of their securities and liquid assets, leaving wife destitute. As the desertion had occurred several years earlier and there was little possibility of a reconciliation, and destitute wife could not otherwise afford access to the courts, contingent fee arrangement was upheld.).

45. Zurich Gen. Acc. & Liab. Ins. Co. v. Kinsler, 12 Cal.2d 98, 81 P.2d 913

ney to proceed upon a theory of *quantum meruit*,[46] thereby recovering a reasonable value of his services up to the time of his discharge. Of course, where the lawyer is discharged *after* the contingency has occurred, most courts would probably allow the lawyer full recovery of the contracted fee.[47] Upon any discharge as counsel, one should file a lien and/or write the former client and the carriers of the amount claimed as fees and costs.

(1938) (Holding that "where, with respect to compensation for services thereafter to be performed, an attorney who was employed under a contingent contract . . . was discharged '*without cause*' . . . he [is] entitled to recover a judgment for the full amount that was provided by the terms of such contract"). This case was overruled by Fracasse v. Brent, 6 Cal.3d 784, 100 Cal.Rptr. 385, 494 P.2d 9 (1972). See also Carter v. Dunham, 104 Kan. 59, 177 P. 533 (1919); Harrison v. Johnson, 64 Ohio App. 185, 28 N.E.2d 615 (1940); Dolph v. Speckart, 94 Or. 550, 179 P. 657 (1919); Williams v. Philadelphia, 208 Pa. 282, 57 A. 578 (1904); White v. Burch, 19 S.W.2d 404 (Tex.Civ.App.1929).

46. Fracasse v. Brent, 6 Cal.3d 784, 100 Cal.Rptr. 385, 494 P.2d 9 (1972) (After holding that the client has both the power and the right to discharge an attorney without, as well as with, cause, the California Supreme Court ruled that the correct measure of recovery would be the reasonable value of services rendered to the time of discharge. The court went on to hold that the cause of action to recover compensation for services rendered under the contingent fee agreement would not accrue until the occurrence of the stated contingency.); Sohn v. Brockington, 371 So.2d 1089 (Fla.App.1979) (After noting that in some jurisdictions, an attorney who delayed bringing suit until the contingency occurred ran the risk of being barred by the statute of limitations where the cause of action accrues immediately upon discharge, Florida court held that attorney is entitled to recover *quantum meruit*, the cause of action accruing immediately upon discharge); Johnson v. Long, 15 Ill.App.3d 506, 305 N.E.2d 30 (1973); Finney v. Estate of Carter, 130 Ind.App. 381, 164 N.E.2d 656 (1960); Ambrose v. Detroit Edison Co., 65 Mich.App. 484, 237 N.W.2d 520 (1975); Estate of Poli, 134 N.J. Super. 222, 338 A.2d 888 (1975); Zimmerman v. Kallimopoulou, 56 Misc.2d 828, 290 N.Y.S.2d 270 (1967); Covington v. Rhodes, 38 N.C.App. 61, 247 S.E.2d 305 (1978) (Attorney who was discharged after spending 29½ hours representing clients awarded $2,000); Heinzman v. Fine, Fine, Legum & Fine, 217 Va. 958, 234 S.E.2d 282 (1977) (Noting that a quantum meruit determination looks to "the reasonable value of the services rendered, not in benefit to the client, but, in themselves"). See 92 A.L.R.3d 690.

47. See Milton Kelner, P. A. v. 610 Lincoln Road, Inc., 328 So.2d 193 (Fla.1976) (Attorney who was discharged after recovering full insurance policy limits entitled to recover 40% of $100,000, not 40% of $39,000 actually received by client).

In Fracasse v. Brent, supra, note 46, the court held that where a client executes a settlement "on the courthouse steps" after much work by the attorney, "the factors involved in a determination of reasonableness would certainly justify a finding that the entire fee was the reasonable value of the attorney's services." 6 Cal.3d at 791.

§§ 1.26–1.30 are reserved for supplementary material.

D. POST ACCIDENT REHABILITATION OF PLAINTIFF

§ 1.31   Introduction

Insofar as the injured plaintiff is concerned, the award of damages by the jury does not mark the end of his journey. Beyond the verdict lies rehabilitation.[48] Unless plaintiff is a minor or a guardian has been appointed, the court has no jurisdiction or authority over the deployment of the fund, no matter how large it may be. Unfortunately, plaintiff's attorney likewise has no such power. Frequently the award, this "one lump sum of money,"[49] will be far in excess of the largest single sum this now physically-handicapped person ever had at one time while he was still in a healthy condition.

Further, the award may come to him either in whole or in large part tax free. He has heard counsel argue to the jury that this amount is not a "tremendous" or "outrageous" sum of money; that it is only adequate compensation for the serious injuries received. Yet it at once becomes an "excessive award" unless it is used for those purposes contemplated by the jury, and as actually urged by his lawyer in argument: so much for future hospital care, an amount for future wages, a figure for rehabilitative needs, and so on.

§ 1.32   The Lawyer's Role in Rehabilitation

No authority will be found in the law books as to the lawyer's duty of assisting in this rehabilitation. Indeed, some clients may even regard such attempt as an interference. But it does seem a fraud upon the jury for the lawyer to convince its members that spe-

---

48. "The traditional settlement environment for third party auto bodily injury claims offers nothing to encourage and much to preclude the early introduction of rehabilitation. Not only must fault and degree of disability be agreed to by opposing sides, but a bargain must be struck and dollar value assigned to the damages. Where the claimant has retained legal counsel, the settlement must cover his fees and expenses. The size of the attorney's fee is directly dependent on the size of the settlement, thus heightening the adversary nature of the settlement environment. Thus, considerable time, energy and expense must be devoted to controversy just when rehabilitation measures might most benefit the victim." John Henle, Rehabilitation of Auto Accident Victims, prepared for the Dep't of Transportation, Auto Insurance & Compensation Study (Aug. 1970).

49. The advent of the "Structured Settlement" whereby plaintiff gets an initial sum up front, and the remainder is paid in monthly or yearly instalments, may, to some extent, alleviate the danger of plaintiff dissipating or wasting the "one lump sum" long before he has recovered, or died. For a complete discussion on this topic, see Chapter 50, "Settlement of the Case", infra.

cific sums[50] will be used for special purposes (almost in the nature of an offer to establish a trust), then, in cases where guardianship is unavailable, to make no effort whatsoever to preserve for the client the fruits of the compensation received.[51]

Perhaps such practical considerations as rehabilitation, prudent investment of the monetary award, and supervision of a spendthrift client are without the scope of this book. Yet, in the tragic cases of amputation, paralysis, and other major physical impairments, some thought to the imposition of court guardianship should be given unless the lawyer is willing to assume the moral responsibility.[52] On occasion, I have secured the appointment of a guardian before or during the course of a trial when there was evidence of personality aberration, or excessive drinking on the part of plaintiff. Jurors afterwards have stated that had there not been a guardian, they would have felt that an adequate award would have been worthless, because it would have been squandered, and might, in fact, have been detrimental.

As we shall see later,[53] the trial lawyer must make a preliminary diagnosis of medical and physical conditions in order to determine which medical expert is to be enlisted in the case so that, after the trial is over or a settlement has been reached, the lawyer will have

---

50. It is admittedly incongruous that we talk only of the client's verdict in jury argument, when the judge and every lawyer in the court room, and probably the jurors as well, will know that the attorney will take part as his contingent fee; that to deduct this amount would make completely erroneous his calculations on the blackboard, while to mention it would result in a mistrial.

51. I recall in one case I achieved a settlement of $128,000 for a young wife, partially paralyzed because of alleged malpractice in the administration of caudal anesthesia. After the money was received, I took her to several capable bankers for investment, and she took their advice. Three years after the accident, she not only had her principal intact, but it had increased 10%, and she had paid all of her current obligations.

52. As illustrative of an extreme, yet not all that rare, case was a pitiful story which appeared in a newspaper a few years back:

> A personal injury client had been awarded a $40,000 settlement for his accident. As related by the reporter, he spent $11,000 for lawyer's fees, spent $12,000 more on two cars and clothing, and within two years dissipated the balance of $17,000 for narcotics for his wife. His case was brought to the attention of the press when jailed for passing a bad check, and pleaded with the judge to be released on the ground that, "My beloved wife is now lying dead in the morgue. I need to be out so I can bury her." Apparently the only thing left him, his wife and his money and his reputation being gone, was a long disfiguring scar on his face and a silver plate in his head.

53. See §§ 2.11–2.14, infra, "The Case History", infra.

sufficient information to understand what is necessary and available by way of rehabilitation. Thus, where plastic surgery is advisable, counsel can assist in recommending and arranging for these procedures, and directing the funds to the best ends. Likewise, in an amputation case, for example, counsel should appreciate the possibility of drug addiction for phantom pains, and be able to advise his client of institutions capable of giving proper prosthetic development and training.[54]

§ 1.33 Remarks on Rehabilitation

On the subject of rehabilitation and the lawyer's role, I add some remarks of my late longtime friend and partner, and a legal scholar in his own right, Lou Ashe, J.D., LL.M.:[55]

> "Over a decade ago, there was a growing realization that inter-related social factors outside the physics and chemistry of the body were very much involved in restoring the disabled to a life that is purposeful and satisfying. Rehabilitation reflects the basic American democratic idea that 'each individual is unique, that each person has the right to participate in all aspects of life, that each member of the community should contribute to society to the fullest extent of which he or she is capable.'
>
> "Trial lawyers who have been involved intimately with the victims of trauma and injury from a myriad of causes have,

---

54. There are several programs for rehabilitation open to Insurance Companies and are discussed by John Henle in his work, Rehabilitation of Auto Accident Victims, supra note 48. Several of the alternatives are:

  A. The use of advance payments by the Insurance Company to the injured plaintiff, before any accord has been reached, for the purpose of rehabilitating him. Some of the stated intended social objectives of this program are that it permits securing proper medical care to reduce disability and promote recovery; it provides a humane and much needed service for the innocent casualty victim; it promotes voluntary and speedy settlements; and it stabilizes the cost of liability insurance "by reducing legal and claim investigative expenses";

  B. Use of a State-Federal rehabilitation program involving cooperation between the appropriate agencies and the insurance companies; and

  C. Insurance supported rehabilitation whereby insurance company personnel work closely and cooperatively with the claimant, his family, physician, and lawyer, and everyone else who is concerned with developing and implementing a rehabilitation plan.

55. Lou Ashe, Esquire, Problems Involved in the Failure of Health Care Providers to Provide Proper Rehabilitation Following Injury: A Contribution to the ABA Litigation Section by the Committee on Professional Responsibility at Atlanta, Georgia, August, 1976.

through the years, increased their recognition of the necessity for interdisciplinary understanding of the role of physical medicine and rehabilitation in determining the eventual restoration of the patient, i. e., the client, to his maximal functional capacity. Unless counsel is conversant with the dynamic role of rehabilitation medicine in its modern conception and law, it may affect the life of his client, and there is danger that he may under-evaluate the merits of his case. Without an understanding of the role of rehabilitation, he may fail to understand fully the therapeutic possibilities, i. e., recovery of functional ability, the length of incapacity, and the degree of residual disability. This in turn requires an open and candid and intelligent rapport with the treating physician, psychiatrist, and the rehabilitation team.

"Howard A. Rusk, M.D., one of the 'Fathers' of rehabilitation medicine, divides medicine into three phases: *First phase* being *preventive* medicine; *Second, curative* medicine and surgery; and the *Third,* one in which a dynamic program of *rehabilitation* is carried out. The objectives, too, are three in number: (1) eliminate the physical disability, if possible; (2) reduce or alleviate disability to the greatest extent possible; and (3) return the person with a residual physical disability to live and work within the limits of the disability but to the hilt of his capacities.

"From the lawyer's point of view, the ability of the psychiatrist to 'evaluate and correlate the patient's disability and his ability to become functional as a person, makes the psychiatrist an invaluable witness.'

"We have learned to appreciate the team approach to the patient's problem. These are usually the psychiatrist and his team of paramedical people and we must learn to communicate with the psychologist, the social worker, the vocational counselor, the physical therapist, the occupational therapist, the speech therapist and all others who in any particular case may make the difference in our ability to translate the travail of a severely disabled client.

"From the vantage point of many years' experience in being alert to and observant of the residuals and sequelae of various types of injury and aided by conferences with and writings of rehabilitation specialists, as well as others in the healing arts, it is clear that the injured person has needs over and above his medical restoration. His economic needs and responsibilities do not cease with the correction of the gross pathology. They continue and often are the cause of strain, anxiety and frustration.

Time and again we have observed the emotional complications resulting from medical and psychological stress. A patient's whole personality may change. Repeatedly through the years we have heard the testimony of members of the victim's family of their inability to cope with the short temper, unreasonableness, and even fits of rage, which have been superimposed on a formerly reasonably tranquil personality—by a traumatic event.

"Where liability exists in the event giving rise to the disability, counsel has the great responsibility to produce all available expert testimony in support of the full extent of his client's rehabilitation efforts and the resultant impact upon his life emotionally, psychologically, sexually and economically.

"A few years ago, I was privileged to represent a 58-year-old man with a C-5 spared quadriplegia secondary to a brachial arteriogram which had been performed allegedly for a transient ischemia. He had been appropriately depressed although, as he advised me, he was conscious of his problem and determined to prepare himself for some form of productive accomplishment. He had gone through a long period of rehabilitation procedures which would have tried the strength and soul of any man. Now the consulting psychiatrist, in his report, described him this way:

> "'. . . His physical disabilities are exquisitely disheartening to see and I am surprised that this man is willing to even open up his eyes each morning. He admits to being depressed, admits to feeling quite uncomfortable about the depression, and I merely confronted him with the fact that he's entitled to some unhappiness and that pharmacologically the most we could offer was to give him some medicine to help take the edge off some of the depression. He wept several times during the interview and seemed to have a bit of a speech difficulty as well as some hearing problems, but did not seem to resent or avoid the questions asked. We acknowledged with him the sense of frustration that he must feel in even attempting to do the simplest things, and even when it comes to using specially-devised devices such as a recorded book, he is unable to turn the on-off switch for himself. What else can we do except suggest that he use the resources that he has as effectively as he can?'"

Lou then goes on to describe how, with encouragement and the continued supportive assistance of a number of rehabilitation staff personnel, and by involving his wife and family in the counselling of the injured man, he was able, with a special hand device, to write, to press a contact which activated a telephone, and to communicate

§ 1.33　　　　　　　　INTRODUCTION　　　　　　　　Pt. 1

with others who were disabled. Eventually, he obtained a specially-equipped van into which he could be lifted while he was still in his wheelchair by a power-operated ramp, where he could be placed in a secure position for his transportation from place to place.[56]

56. Lou adds a closing thought paraphrasing that sentiment expressed by the Great Lady in New York Harbor:

> Give us your chronically ill and disabled,
> Your Quads, your paralyzed
> The Frustrated and Depressed.
> The men and women of despair and defeat
> Struck down in one fleeting devastating moment
> At the height of their powers
> (And but too often at the threshold of life)
> By indiscriminate, non-selective trauma
> AND
> We shall, with all that is in us
> Lift up their heads and spirits,
> Strengthen their wasted muscles,
> Inspire a desire to live as whole men and women
> To function each day in a productive way
> Respected by their family and friends, self sufficient
> And all this with consideration, love and a
> Triumphant affirmation of the intrinsic dignity
> And worth of every individual.

§§ 1.34–1.40 are reserved for supplementary material.

E. TRAUMATIC NEUROSES AND HYSTERICAL PARALYSES

§ 1.41 Introduction

In this chapter, as an example of the entire subject, consider the head injury and its sequelae, of which the post traumatic neuroses are frequently the most important part of the syndrome. In this sort of a typical case appear the prolixity of problems confronting a sincere lawyer, mingling law and medicine and economics, and the cherished right to live out one's life free from pain and suffering.[57]

§ 1.42 Traumatic Neurosis Defined

"Traumatic neurosis" is the mental or emotional accompaniment of traumatic injury, triggered by the threat which accompanies the trauma.[58] The victim suffers from such problems as fear or worry about being able to work again, fear of crippling, paralysis or death, or possibly just the fear of a vague unexplainable threat.

Even when the trauma is severe, many people do not suffer this debilitating neurosis. After some period of anxiety, most are able to re-establish mental stability with little psychological damage. Others, however, may be predisposed to these neuroses because their past has caused them to have a major emotional conflict centered around dependency needs. Those brought up by overly protective parents or, conversely, who received no love and attention as children, sometimes develop a strong sense of inadequacy that motivates them toward invalidism. For these people, approximately 10% of the population, the trauma normally accompanying a serious injury may escalate to such a peak that they are effectively immobilized. The injury need not even be serious—a minor accident may trigger an overwhelming neurosis in seriously predisposed individuals, resulting in disabling psychosomatic illness. They respond to stress by getting sick—they have what might be termed an egg-shell psyche.

Like the amputations, loss of sight, disfigurations, and paralyses, traumatic neuroses cases result in very high awards.[59] They are very difficult to evaluate.

---

57. Concussion, epilepsy, and other serious injuries will be discussed in Chapter 48, "Medical Examinations", infra.

58. The following discussion is taken from R. Cohen, Traumatic Neuroses in Personal Injury Cases (1970). The author strongly recommends a perusal of this excellent book by all plaintiffs' lawyers confronted with a plaintiff who may be suffering from such a neurosis.

59. An example of the possible high awards for traumatic neurosis was reported in the Los Angeles Herald Examiner, October 4, 1979, Page A3, Column 2. A 49-year-old railroad worker was awarded *$1.3 million* for

§ 1.42   INTRODUCTION   Pt. 1

Since the majority of plaintiffs with traumatic neuroses have suffered a comparatively trivial physical injury, another factor presents itself, whether the claimed symptoms are fact or fantasy. Smith and Solomon,[60] in analyzing cases of traumatic neuroses on appeal in the British Empire and the United States, divide them into two main classes: (a) those cases following a trivial impact; and (b) cases incident to a serious physical injury. They found that less than 3/8 of all of these cases fell into group (b) despite the great number of serious physical injuries that crowded court dockets.

"Given a person of marginal psychological adjustment, with a potentially serious unconscious conflict under tenuous control, then a relatively minor psychological incident can precipitate a full blown neurotic illness."[61]

To put it more simply, a cracked egg breaks easily.

§ 1.43   Examples of Traumatic Neuroses

Examples are in the files of every personal injury lawyer:[62] a fifty year old man was driving his wife in a Nebraska town. His "severe traumatic neurosis." The verdict was believed to be the largest ever in California for psychological damage. Plaintiff therein was injured in 1974 when he was asked to lift a 100-pound locomotive cylinder head, a task usually performed by a machine. In so doing, plaintiff strained his back and was physically unable to work for about ten years. His attorney argued that plaintiff, a Spanish-American, was very "macho," and because he could not provide for his family, went into a "very, very depressed state that even developed into a psychosis."

60. Smith & Solomon, Traumatic Neurosis in Court, 21 Amer.Int.Med. 367 (1944); Smith, Cobb & Solomon, 30 Va.L.Rev. 87 (1943).

Although a common occurrence, traumatic neurosis is still largely overlooked when plaintiff's lawyer drafts the complaint. See L. Keiser, M.D., Traumatic Neurosis: A Common Problem Relatively Untried in the Courts, 1971 Med.Trial Technique Quarterly 1.

61. Smith, Cross-Examination of Neuropsychiatric Testimony in Personal Injury Cases, 4 Vand.L.Rev. 1 (1950) (comprehensive review of cases and literature. See also S. Schwartz, Medical Testimony in a Case of Soft Tissue Injury with Neurosis, 1969 Med.Trial Technique Quarterly 363, 364.

62. Reed v. McGibbony, 243 Ark. 789, 422 S.W.2d 115 (1967) (Proper to admit medical opinion about the psychological effects scars would have on young girl); Argonaut Ins. Co. v. Allen, 123 Ga.App. 741, 182 S.E.2d 508 (1971) (Plaintiff injured his right hand while working in a carpet mill; since the injury, he had been nervous, jittery, annoyed by loud noises, and unable to work); Thacker v. Ward, 263 N.C. 594, 140 S.E.2d 23 (1965), cert. denied 382 U.S. 865, 86 S.Ct. 134, 15 L.Ed.2d 104, reh. denied 382 U.S. 934, 86 S.Ct. 319, 15 L.Ed.2d 347 (Complaint failed to allege proper cause of action for traumatic neurosis); Ford v. Blythe Bros. Co., 242 N.C. 347, 87 S.E.2d 879 (1955) (Expert testimony admissible to show that before injury, child was not nervous, ate and slept well, but since the accident became excitable, nerv-

car stalled on the railroad tracks and a slowly moving locomotive appeared, and was unable to stop. The automobile was jolted off the track. The ribs of the driver were bruised, and he was frightened, while his wife was relatively unaffected by the impact. However, the slightly injured man gradually developed a sense of weakness, insomnia, sweating, emotional instability, and irrational fears. Eight months after the accident, he was incapacitated by these symptoms. Was the trauma physical or psychological? Regardless of which, it was compensable.

Another example: a workman was hit on the shoulders and neck by a falling sandbag which knocked him to the ground. A bruised shoulder muscle responded in about a week to physical treatment. However, he gradually developed residual symptoms of a twisted neck. When seen approximately seven months later, his neck was twisted grotesquely to one side. This is an example of a common symptom of neurotic hysteria. Was it a physical or psychological trauma? Again the psychological as well as the physical injuries were compensable.

A classic illustration of the problem is contained in the late Paul D. Cantor's, M.D., LL.B., excellent treatise on traumatic injuries.[63] He relates a case in which an 18-year-old girl, her father, and her 17-year-old cousin are injured when another car runs into their own. The driver of the other car is killed; the father is severely injured, and his 18-year-old daughter sustains a concussion and multiple fractures. The 17-year-old cousin is uninjured, and as a newspaper recounted, "miraculously escaped without a scratch."

Eight weeks later, the father and daughter have substantially recovered. The unscathed cousin, however, is constantly nervous and apprehensive, suffers from nightmares, is unable to resume her schoolwork, and is generally listless and unhappy. Six months after the accident, she is very anxious about traveling or even leaving home, and has suffered several acute attacks of anxiety or anxiety-panic. One year after the collision, she continues to be nervous, pale and underweight. Caused by the accident, the 17-year-old girl has developed chronic symptoms of an anxiety neurosis. And this despite the fact she had been physically unharmed by the accident.

ous, afraid of noises and neither ate nor slept well).

63. Paul D. Cantor, M.D., LL.B., Traumatic Medicine & Surgery for the Attorney 77–78 (1962).

Another interesting study on this subject was done by A. Sims, A. White & T. Murphy, Aftermath Neurosis: Psychological Sequelae of the Birmingham Bombings in Victims not Seriously Injured, 19 Med.Sci. & Law 78 (1979). The study, conducted two years after the bombings, showed that there was considerable and severe psychological sequelae in persons who had not been seriously hurt in the bombings some years earlier.

In these cases neighbors and friends readily bear witness to the health of the victim prior to the accident, and the calamitous changes they notice after what may have been only a trivial impact.[64] Of course these lay observers do not see the underlying neurosis, the roots of psychopathic disturbance, and only see the outward manifestations. Their testimony is true and accurate. On the other side, a psychoanalyst's determination is likewise true and accurate that the disease began long before. On the legal side, compensation should be forthcoming because there is the picture of a person able to cope with the world prior to the minor incident which was the precipitating force.[65]

Every man has his "breaking point." For some it may be the ten-ton truck, for others the five-ton truck, for others perhaps the twenty-pound scooter. Witness the military man under stress. The majority do not break at all, but some become neurotic before arriving at the induction station; another group breaks down during basic training and lands in the Psychiatric Ward of a military hospital; others collapse in advance training when subjected for the first time to live ammunition; still others hold up until hit by "gang plank fever" while boarding a transport; and an additional group acquires symptoms overseas from the strain of waiting to be sent into combat; still others disintegrate only after being subjected to the horrors of intensive fighting; finally an interesting group becomes neurotic after V day while awaiting discharge. Some doctors will testify quite sincerely that psychotics admitted to Veterans Administration Hospitals as late as five years after separation from service can trace a mental illness to a tour of duty.

Then there is the compensation neurosis, an insidious, yet completely involuntary and honest disease. Most accident victims after an injury receive kindlier attention than they ever had in their lives. Often, tragically, this plaintiff has "become somebody," with his picture in the paper, his personality an object for comment. Then he will be told that he is entitled to be adequately compensated. Of course the best therapy for this type of person may be to get back to his normal life as soon as possible, and certainly back to work, and his mind off his case.[66] Compensation must be secondary. If the trial is

---

64. Smith, Cross-Examination of Neuropsychiatric Testimony in Personal Injury Cases, 4 Vand.L.Rev. 1 (1950); Smith, Cobb & Solomon, 30 Va.L.Rev. 87 (1943).

65. Would it be fair to allow defendant to argue that since a strong man can lie down and have a ten-ton truck drive over him as a display of strength, none of us should be allowed to complain if we turn up with a permanent and totally incapacitating disability if a mere five-ton truck ran over us?

66. Conversely, I have seen some lawyers deliberately return a client to

long delayed, there should be no thought of keeping the client on the "sick list." Damage so done is difficult to repair. To do his job with a sincere regard for the welfare of his plaintiff, the lawyer must be a psychiatrist himself in his treatment.[67]

§ 1.44 The "Accident Prone" Person

Is there such a thing as "accident proneness"?[68] Do some persons have an unconscious drive toward self-destruction which promotes within them an urge to seek out an accident?

It is a frightening thing to hear the modern psychologists contend that most accidents are not accidents at all but are caused largely by the victim's own disposition. Strictly speaking, an accident is an occurrence, the cause of which is outside a person's control. A brick falling on a pedestrian's head is a completely accidental event, particularly if the pedestrian is not warned by a sign that such an event is likely to occur at a particular place.

However, some industrial, traffic and home accidents, if we would believe the psychiatrists, are of a different nature. The prospective plaintiff has had some active part in its causation. The layman says the victim was tired or absent-minded or inattentive, otherwise he could have avoided the accident. The psychiatrists say most accidents are not due to such simple human qualities. Some people are prone to have more accidents than others, not because they are clumsy or absent-minded, but because of the total structure of their personality and the influence of their unconscious neurotic processes.

Marbe, a German psychiatrist, more than forty-five years ago showed the higher incidence of subsequent accidents in one who had already had an accident, and statistical studies tend to support the psychiatrists' theory.[69]

work too soon, and have him laid off because of his obvious incapacity, then remain idle longer than necessary. This sort of fraudulent effort is sometimes successful in convincing a jury that plaintiff cannot work.

67. I have actually had people call me with broken backs and legs, expressing a sense of accomplishment. Recently a husband called me, early in the morning, and said with elation, "Well, I've done it." When I inquired sleepily what he had done, he went on, "My wife has broken her leg in an accident, and the other driver was drunk." I knew that he and his wife were entirely devoted, and that he was the most sympathetic of men.

68. See L. Shaw & H. Sichel, Accident Proneness (1971).

69. One large company employing a great number of truck drivers, and being concerned about the high cost of its automobile accidents, tried to analyze the cause in order to reduce the frequency. By shifting those with the highest accident records of frequency, they were able to reduce the subsequent rate to one-fifth of its original level. The most interesting

§ 1.44 INTRODUCTION Pt. 1

Is the accident prone individual the plaintiff or the defendant? He may become the plaintiff, but in one sense it is the defendant, frequently, who is really the victim, involved in an accident by the irrational will of the plaintiff, who received the actual injuries.

Traumatic neurosis is aptly named because the two factors involved in its production are (1) precipitating trauma; (2) neurotic pre-disposition. These two factors usually operate in inverse proportion; the more trivial the trauma, the more severe the pre-disposition.

It might be well for both plaintiff and defendant's counsel to appreciate the function of dynamic psychiatry. It is concerned with understanding the unconscious conflict and forces which disturb the functioning personality into a state of psychological illness called neurosis. By many techniques of treatment, the psychiatrist is frequently successful in unearthing these unconscious conflicts sufficiently to alleviate the neurotic incapacity and aid the person's attainment of a satisfactory adjustment.

Among the concepts of dynamic psychiatry of particular relevancy to medical jurisprudence are those of secondary gains or compensation neurosis, and accident proneness. Some patients cannot resist unconsciously exploiting a psychological illness, particularly the need for security and economic stability or revenge against a wealthy defendant guilty of gross negligence.[70] The psychiatrist might also

factor in the study was that the drivers who had the highest accident rate and were shifted, retained this "accident proneness" in their new occupation! See Alexander, Psychosomatic Medicine. W. W. Norton Co., New York, 1950.

The National Safety Council has discovered the same propensity for accidents among automobile drivers. People with four accidents were approximately fourteen times as numerous as they should have been on the basis of the theory that bad luck might be only pure chance, while people with seven accidents each during the time of the study were nine thousand times commoner than the law of chance would require. Furthermore, those persons who had numerous accidents showed a pronounced tendency to repeat the same kind of accidents. (See Menninger,

Man Against Himself, Harcourt Brace & Co., New York, 1938).

Is complete social disregard only the symptom of "accident proneness"?

70. This is not a modern trend: The Gold Hill (Nevada) Daily News of May 10, 1876 carried the story of a man in Decorah, Iowa, who "got some whiskey at a drug store," and, while under its benign influence had his hands and feet so badly frozen that they had to be amputated. Then his wife sued the druggist for damages, and recovered $9,000.00, which was probably twice as much as she expected to get. Ever since then, whenever a man starts down town, his wife follows him to the drug store and tenderly says: "It looks like its gwin to be monsus cold on towards the shank o' the evenin' and you na-t'rally be tol'ble tired agin that time,

42

SETTING THE STAGE § 1.45

analyze the motive of the insurance adjuster who, though he cannot personally profit, settles a case for an utterly fraudulent amount, even against the policy of his company. Is it jealousy, egoism, or what "drive" causes this?

§ 1.45 Hysterical Paralysis

Like traumatic neurosis, hysterical paralysis [71] can have a much more devastating effect upon the injured party than those purely physical injuries sustained. Attorney *Daniel G. Lilley* [72] reports a case he tried in which the jury awarded plaintiff $70,000.00 for "psychological neurosis, conversion type."

In that case, plaintiff, a 39-year-old airplane parts inspector, was injured when the truck he was driving was rear-ended while he was stopped at a stop sign. The other vehicle was a company-owned panel truck being driven by the son of the corporation president. Plain-

---

if I was you I'd come by the drugstore and hist in a nice, warm drink of good spirits, and fetch a drap or two home with you, which you had better drink it all, as you come along, yourself."

See Herbert C. Modlin, M.D., "Psychiatric View of Traumatic Neurosis," a paper presented at the Central States Conference of NACCA, Wichita, Kansas, March 15, 1952 10 NACCA L.J. 213. (Senior psychiatrist to Menninger Foundation, Topeka, Kansas).

71. An hysterical paralysis is a recognized pathological and compensable condition. Let us suppose: A prominent doctor married his office nurse, one who had been with him for a number of years. In that time she had acquired considerable medical training and helped build his practice. Their marital life became beset with turbulence. On one particular evening, the doctor, displaying a rather gross "medical procedure," hit the wife over the head with a chair. The next morning she did not get up. She explained to her husband that her left leg was paralyzed for he had hit her on the left parietal area. The medical husband, stricken with remorse at the result of his "malprac-

tice", hired a nurse for his wife and put her under the care of another competent doctor. From that time on she became an invalid. Some three years later her physician told her that she had an hysterical paralysis. She denied this and challenged him to straighten her leg under sodium pentathol (anesthesia). The doctor explained that permanent major contractures (shortening or distortion of the muscles) had set in, and that the minor contracture that she had the morning after she was struck should have been flaccid (soft and pliable) and have disappeared in about two weeks.

The nurse asked, "Are you going to tell my husband?" The doctor answered, "No, I think you are far better off paralyzed, so from now on, you stay that way because you will have to and it will be to your advantage."

We may inquire at what dates the hysteria becomes malingering (feigning illness) and malingering a real physiological disability? Should such an injury be compensable?

72. Daniel G. Lilley, Esquire, 805 Maine Savings Plaza, Portland, Maine 04101.

tiff sustained no apparent injuries, and appeared to be unharmed on the day of the accident. Several months later, however, plaintiff developed an inability to move various limbs of his body, and was ultimately confined to a wheelchair.

Plaintiff sought the attention of various physicians, neurologists, orthopedic surgeons and the like, but none could find any basis for the condition. The local Veterans Administration Hospital diagnosed plaintiff as having a mental problem which they later specifically diagnosed as hysterical neurosis, conversion type. The prescribed treatment for his condition consisted of extensive counseling with a psychologist. Through this, plaintiff was able to regain movement in and control of his limbs, and returned to full employment.

At the time of trial, plaintiff was fully employed, but his treating psychologist testified that because of his diminished abilities, especially the difficulty he had in moving, it was more probable than not that he would eventually lose his job. The psychologist further stated that plaintiff might even become unemployable. Plaintiff's condition was analogized with that of a time-bomb waiting to explode, with the rear-end collision being the precipitating event which set-off the condition.

Counsel was offered $4,500.00 by an insurance adjuster prior to trial as the top price for the case. Later, Attorney Lilley was offered $35,000.00 by defense counsel immediately prior to and during the trial. The jury awarded plaintiff $70,000.00, and apportioned liability among the corporation and driver in the amounts of 65% and 35% respectively. The corporation was held liable under the theory that it had negligently entrusted the vehicle to the boy, who had had previous convictions for speeding, and once had his license suspended.

§§ 1.46–2.0 are reserved for supplementary material.

CHAPTER 2

INVESTIGATION AND DISCOVERY

Table of Sections

		Sections
A.	Preliminary Considerations	2.1 –2.10
B.	The Case History	2.11 –2.20
C.	Office Forms and Records	2.21 –2.40
D.	Paralegals	2.41 –2.44
E.	The Investigator	2.45 –2.50
F.	"On-the-Scene" Investigations and Photographs	2.51 –2.60
G.	Use of "On-the-Scene" Photographs	2.61 –2.70
H.	"Official" Proceedings and Inquests Before Trial	2.71 –2.80
I.	Discovery	2.81 –2.90
J.	Discovering Limits of Insurance Coverage	2.91 –2.100
K.	Depositions and Interrogatories	2.101–2.110
L.	Investigation by Depositions and Pictures	2.111–2.114
M.	Locating Witnesses	2.115–2.120
N.	Finding the Actual Instrumentality	2.121–2.130
O.	When the Actual Instrumentality Is Not Available	2.131–2.134
P.	Demonstrative Evidence Often Demonstrates the Theory	2.135–2.140
Q.	Exemplary Investigations	2.141–2.150
R.	Investigation Through Accident Reconstruction	2.151–2.160
S.	Enjoining the Overzealous Investigation	2.161–2.170
T.	Ethical Considerations and the Investigator	2.171–2.180

A. PRELIMINARY CONSIDERATIONS

Sec.
2.1 Introduction.
2.2 Sources of Information.

B. THE CASE HISTORY

2.11 Introduction.
2.12 Use of the Case History.
2.13 Medical Questions and Considerations.
2.14 The Lawyer as "Doctor".

INTRODUCTION

C. OFFICE FORMS AND RECORDS

Sec.
2.21 Introduction.
2.22 Information to Obtain.
2.23 Model Interview Form.
2.24 Use of Specialized Forms.
2.25 Police Reports.
2.26 Medical Records Consent Forms.
2.27 Contingent Fee Agreement Forms.
2.28 Office Records.
2.29 Use of Bound Volumes.
2.30 The Disbursal Sheet.

D. PARALEGALS

2.41 Role and Duties of Paralegals.

E. THE INVESTIGATOR

2.45 Introduction.
2.46 Importance of the Investigator.
2.47 The Investigator's Tools.

F. "ON-THE-SCENE" INVESTIGATIONS AND PHOTOGRAPHS

2.51 Introduction.
2.52 Finding "On-the-Scene" Photographs.
2.53 "On-the-Scene" Photographs in Head-On Collision.
2.54 Railroad Death Case.
2.55 Automobile-Truck Accident.
2.56 Tank Explosion Case Report.
2.57 Personal Injury and Property Damage Caused by Truck.

G. USE OF "ON-THE-SCENE" PHOTOGRAPHS

2.61 Introduction.
2.62 Use for Impeachment.
2.63 To Show Negligence.
2.64 To Show Cause of a Fire.

H. "OFFICIAL" PROCEEDINGS AND INQUESTS BEFORE TRIAL

2.71 Introduction.
2.72 Personal Injury With Criminal Charges.
2.73 Utilizing Criminal Investigations.

I. DISCOVERY

2.81 In General.
2.82 Discovering Demonstrative Evidence.

Ch. 2   INVESTIGATION AND DISCOVERY

Sec.
2.83   Privileged Matters.
2.84   Lawyer-Client Privilege.
2.85   Attorney's Work Product.
2.86   Discovery of Experts' Opinions.

J. DISCOVERING LIMITS OF INSURANCE COVERAGE

2.91   Discovery of Insurance Generally.
2.92   Practical Effects of Refusal to Disclose Insurance Coverage.

K. DEPOSITIONS AND INTERROGATORIES

2.101   Introduction.
2.102   Sample Written Interrogatories.
2.103   Example of Deposition.

L. INVESTIGATION BY DEPOSITIONS AND PICTURES

2.111   Use of Pictures to Supplement Deposition.

M. LOCATING WITNESSES

2.115   Introduction.
2.116   Techniques for Locating Witnesses.

N. FINDING THE ACTUAL INSTRUMENTALITY

2.121   Introduction.
2.122   Unraveling the "Freak" Accident.
2.123   Identification Through Advertisements.
2.124   Identification of Manufacturer.
2.125   Finding the Offending Product.

O. WHEN THE ACTUAL INSTRUMENTALITY IS NOT AVAILABLE

2.131   Introduction.
2.132   Illustration. Vehicle Unavailable.

P. DEMONSTRATIVE EVIDENCE OFTEN DEMONSTRATES THE THEORY

2.135   In General.

Q. EXEMPLARY INVESTIGATIONS

2.141   Introduction.
2.142   Hidden Rock Case.
2.143   Investigation by Exhumation.
2.144   Investigation of Injury on Ship.

R. INVESTIGATION THROUGH ACCIDENT RECONSTRUCTION

2.151 Introduction.
2.152 Train-Bus Collision.
2.153 Automobile-Motorcycle Accident.

S. ENJOINING THE OVERZEALOUS INVESTIGATION

2.161 Introduction.
2.162 Examples of Improper Investigative Techniques.
2.163 Suggested Petition for Order Enjoining Harassment.

T. ETHICAL CONSIDERATIONS AND THE INVESTIGATOR

2.171 In General.
2.172 Communication With Adverse Party.
2.173 Insurance Company's Letter in Chicago Air Crash Disaster.
2.174 Engaging an Investigator.

A. PRELIMINARY CONSIDERATIONS

§ 2.1 Introduction

In this chapter we are concerned with finding the true and complete facts of the case. Unless the trial lawyer has ascertained all the facts relative to the case, he is not in a position properly to evaluate either the basis for liability or the extent of property damage and injury to the plaintiff. Thorough investigation and effective use of the numerous discovery tools available to the modern trial lawyer and his investigator are the means by which the trial lawyer finds all pertinent information about the case. (I serve papers for depositions and discovery with the complaint—if state law allows—or as soon thereafter as possible.)

§ 2.2 Sources of Information

I am frequently asked, "Where do you get all of your information on investigation; and doesn't it cost a considerable amount to prepare a case so thoroughly with demonstrative evidence?"

The answer to the first question comes when one considers that countless specialists are contributing their efforts; that city, county, state and federal officers, as well as private and semi-private citizens devote themselves to determining facts which will start, and perhaps even *complete*, the investigation of almost every case.

Ch. 2   INVESTIGATION AND DISCOVERY   § 2.2

The young lawyer should learn just what studies and findings are at his disposal: What type of investigations are made by and information released by the medical examiner's office;[1] what reports are available from the highway patrol, and city and county police departments; what his city attorney does. He could well reflect: What does the newsboy, the taxi-cab driver, the gas-meter reader, and the trash collector see and hear? What would a house-to-house canvass on different days and at different hours produce? What information can be found in trade journals, medical libraries, and governmental press releases and studies? What boards have jurisdiction over the accident, and have they issued a report or held a hearing? What do fellow employees of plaintiff say about his conduct, and what do defendant motorman's (for instance) friends and co-workers say about him, particularly his driving, health, police encounters, eyesight, domestic life, school achievements, and financial and credit records.

The title of a very practical and intriguing course, as yet offered in no law school curriculum, might well be: "Discovering those who investigate the world about us."[2]

1. Most attorneys are aware only of the autopsy report. The work of the medical examiner goes far beyond that, however. Counsel should visit the nearest medical examiner's office to learn everything they do.

2. Two cases illustrate the finding of the "fortuitous witness." The "accident" was there for everyone to see. The witness was available for anyone to find.

"If the night has a thousand eyes, the law has a million. Where is the happening that has not witnesses? He is there . . . riding on the streetcar, stepping out of the elevator, coming home from a late party, as ever-present as man's occupation is varied.

"Find him. It is upon him and his story that our mode of trial is based.

"There was a case tried in Oregon over a disputed claim for fire insurance. To prevail, it was essential for the lawyer to prove that the fire had originated on certain premises. A ship's captain testified against the lawyer . . . said he saw the whole fire from the bridge of his ship. His story was convincing. The lawyer heard of a Japanese photographer who, like many of his race, took pictures of everything. Maybe he had a picture of the fire. After months of tedious day and night search, the lawyer found his man. Yes, he had pictures of the fire!

"The lawyer eagerly looked at the pictures. In none of them was the captain's boat present, because the captain actually hadn't been a witness. As the lawyer suspected, the captain had perjured himself. That witness won the case for the lawyer.

"In Kingston, Jamaica, in 1808, an earthquake and fire destroyed practically the whole town. The damage ran into thousands of dollars. Most of the people carried insurance.

"Yet this region was so subject to earthquakes that premiums for earthquake insurance were prohibitive. Only fire insurance was carried. If the fire came first, the defendant insurance carriers had to pay; if the earthquake came first, there was no recovery.

"When the case first came to court, plaintiffs produced first two officers of the Port Kingston, a boat in the harbor at the time of the catastrophe. Both testified that they had noticed a pillar of smoke at 3:30; at 3:35, the earthquake struck. The captain of

§ 2.2 INTRODUCTION Pt. 1

"Where do I get all of this scientific proof?" the trial lawyer asks. "Where can I find answers to chemical and physical problems, have my models built, my photographs taken, and my case prepared?" We refer him to the hundreds of private investigators throughout the country. My office frequently receives letters and advertising from a variety of services advising that experienced consultants can be employed concerning such happenings as transportation accidents, fires, explosions, chemical damage, airborne collisions and the like.

If the trial lawyer does not have a trained investigator and a photographer attached directly to his office, he may avail himself of an investigating organization of which there are various types throughout the United States.[3]

---

another ship corroborated this testimony.

"But what won the case was the curiosity of a third witness who lived on a hill in back of the town. He had noticed the pillar of smoke, had taken angles of it and swore it was 255 feet high before the earthquake struck. The case went through the highest courts of England, but the insurance companies eventually paid for the strange coincidence of an earthquake preceded by a fire, memorialized by the curiosity of a not too unique witness." (From Melvin M. Belli, So That's the Law).

3. These investigators appreciate the necessity for finding the facts, so that demonstration may be made before a jury. I once received an advertisement stating:

"Lethal quantities of carbon monoxide are often formed in the ordinary woodburning home fireplace. Accidentally closing the damper, or a downdraft, may push the odorless, colorless death dealing fumes into the room. Cause of explosions of soft drink or beer bottles, can often be determined if sufficient glass is obtained for analysis. Failure may be due to imperfect molds, defective glass, excess pressure or mishandling. Icy pavement may be the cause of an accident though the temperature at a nearby weather station was 50 degrees Fahrenheit or more at the time. Early morning temperatures can vary 20 degrees F. or 30 degrees F. in a short distance, particularly in irregular terrain. Gasoline burns at the rate of about five feet per second. This may be an important factor in determining the origin of a fire. Worn tires are often more effective than new tires at stopping cars on wet surfaces at speeds of less than twenty miles an hour. Paint on homes may turn black if exposed to certain sulphur gases released by industry or natural sources. (The lead in the paint reacts with the sulphur to form a dark compound—lead sulphite.) Popular belief that metal crystallizes, thus causing it to break, is not true. Metals normally have a crystallizing structure. Failure occurs when repeated loads cause metal fatigue. Wind direction is given as the direction from which the wind is coming—not going. A north wind is from the north and is moving toward the south."

The original problem, when formulating the case, should be discussed with this type of investigator or photographer as well, as should damages, of course, be discussed with the doctor, since there are two aspects to the case.

§§ 2.3–2.10 are reserved for supplementary material.

B. THE CASE HISTORY

§ 2.11 Introduction

One of the most important steps in preparing any case is the taking of a detailed, factual case history, starting as soon as the client walks in or calls the lawyer to discuss a possible lawsuit. Most of the facts which subsequently lead to investigation by deposition, police reports, collateral witnesses, friends, doctors, the newsboy on the corner, to every testimonial possibility are first elicited from a carefully taken case history.

The interviews with the client may be taken upon a mechanical recording machine, or the lawyer may make notes. Ultimately, however, the whole factual case history should be reduced to typewriting, and made a part of the file for reference by anyone who may subsequently be investigating or processing the case. The trial lawyer in his office is like the contractor determining whether there is enough material to build a house, but more than that, he is also architect, plumber, painter, landscaper, and finally realtor. He must envision the whole structure from the case history and the investigation it suggests.

§ 2.12 Use of the Case History

Suppose the client has given a factual statement of the accident. Then assume that on cross-examination, his adversary contends that these facts are a "recent fabrication." It then becomes important to have at hand, in the history, the people to whom the party told the same account, when and where in the past. This testimony, although seemingly self-serving, may be admissible to answer the contention of the other party.[4]

An accurately taken and minutely described recital of facts prevents the embarrassment to the lawyer after a surprise on cross-examination when he is informed by his client, "You didn't ask me that." The prudent lawyer will appreciate the natural reluctance of a client to confess something damaging to the case, and the necessity to pry out all possible facts whether favorable or not. Conversely,

---

4. Warrick v. Brode, 428 F.2d 699 (3d Cir. 1970); United States v. Stamey, 423 F.2d 1223 (4th Cir. 1970); United States v. Zito, 467 F.2d 1401 (2d Cir. 1972); Applebaum v. American Export Isbrandtsen Lines, 472 F.2d 56 (2d Cir. 1972); People v. Armstrong, 275 Cal.App.2d 30, 79 Cal.Rptr. 668 (1969); Kellam v. Thomas, 287 So.2d 733 (Fla.App.1974); State v. Galloway, 247 A.2d 104 (Me.1968); Brown v. Pointer, 41 Mich.App. 539, 200 N.W.2d 756 (1972) rev'd 390 Mich. 346, 212 N.W.2d 201; Sas v. Strelecki, 110 N.J.Super. 14, 264 A.2d 247 (1970); State v. Jones, 215 Tenn. 206, 385 S.W.2d 80 (1964); State v. Epton, 10 Wash.App. 373, 518 P.2d 229 (1974).

too, the client should be asked the sources of damaging information. "Who else knows about this?" "Who else saw you do this?" "Who else will be able to testify against you?" Armed with this information, the lawyer can go to these witnesses and determine, quite properly and ethically, just how damaging such testimony is going to be. Some of these witnesses might best be called by him to remove some of the sting.

Any case history should be factual, but the patient herself does not write it, and often could not accurately evaluate her complaints. Often the records of a nurse or doctor, made under pressure for time, give a conclusion that does not correctly portray the facts. Thus the nurse may write, "Patient complains of being dizzy." Then when this case comes on for trial, there may be a differential diagnosis desired between the "dizziness" occasioned by a diabetic condition antedating the accident, and that due to a subdural hematoma (effusion of blood under lining of brain). But all that may appear in the hospital record is "dizziness." The cross-examiner will ask the patient on the stand, "Did you not tell the nurse that you were dizzy before the accident?" The patient, now witness, may honestly attempt to distinguish, but the record is there—"dizzy," and before the accident.

The incomplete case history, or one without reference to antecedents is also factually vulnerable. Thus, a failure properly to read an x-ray indicating spurs or arthritic changes may confuse, in differential diagnosis, subsequent x-ray photographs after an injury when there is a true traumatic arthritis claimed.[5]

§ 2.13 Medical Questions and Considerations

Upon taking the case history of a potential plaintiff, the personal injury lawyer, like his legal brethren representing the defendant, has the immediate question as to liability, and the possibilities of convincing proof. He must also promptly concern himself, with the "injuries," and how best to ascertain the actual physical condition of his client, and to determine the probable recoverable damages. Medicolegal questions are his added responsibility. He must become a referring "doctor," and a specialist in the medical information relevant to the prosecution of such cases, as well as being a legal general practitioner. Indeed, he must be able to make a preliminary diagnosis and

---

5. The story is told of a perverse and terse entry in a ship's log that, because of its complete silence as to prior activity, was a devastating notation. During a certain voyage, a seaman had been roughly treated by the captain, or at least he thought he had received inconsiderate treatment from the master. When the ship finally reached port, this sailor logged a quite accurate and proper entry, as far as it went: "June 15, 19—. Captain sober today."

prognosis of his client's ailment, and be able to recommend doctors, who will be able to advise properly as to any disability, as well as to any remedial treatment. Of course he cannot evaluate the case before him in dollars and cents for demand and settlement, or for the preparation of a complaint and prayer for damages without expert medical assistance and advice. But after this consultation with the chosen doctors, it is he, not the doctor, who will have to put the dollar sign on the medical report. This is the end result of the case history towards which the lawyer must work. He must determine what sum, for all time, would be an adequate award for his client.

Generally, the lawyer sees the client after the family physician or the emergency surgeon has done the first repair. Very often this individual will give a good working diagnosis, but the whole course of this patient-client's economic future may be dependent upon the lawyer's knowledge of medical specialties and to whom to send the client for a proper evaluation of the particular malady. Is the pain in the chest symptomatic of traumatic endocarditis (inflammation of the lining of the heart), so that the sufferer should be sent to a physician familiar with these disorders, or should he be sent to a chest man for x-rays of the rib cage, or to an orthopedist (bone specialist)? In some communities the patient cannot be sent directly to a radiologist, but must first consult a regular physician for reference to the specialist. If the complaint is a pain in the lower back, shall the lawyer send his client to a neurologist or an orthopedist? If surgery is indicated for a laminectomy and fusion, both the orthopedist and the neuro-surgeon will work as a team. Suppose there are fainting spells, and a negative neurological report is returned. The lawyer then must be able to diagnose sufficiently to direct his client to a gastrointestinal, a cardiac, or a lung man, perhaps even to a psychiatrist. He must be able to appreciate psychosomatic problems. Very often the internist, or the family physician, may be able to answer a number of these questions satisfactorily, with the exception of placing the dollar sign on the probable verdict for the trial lawyer.

The lawyer is not practicing medicine by conducting simple medical and neurological tests in his own office, like the Romberg (swaying of the body when standing with the feet close together and eyes closed, a sign of nervous disorders). A good book explaining such tests is invaluable. Suppose the client complains of persistent headaches. The family doctor, who is a general practitioner, returns a negative report. Is it not incumbent upon the trial lawyer to exhaust the services of an ear, nose and throat man, an ophthalmologist, and, when indicated, a psychiatrist, and to have appropriate studies done, when advisable?

§ 2.14 The Lawyer as "Doctor"

Is this too heroic a procedure? Let me recount the case of a woman who came to me complaining of injuries received in a bus accident. The lawyer who referred her to me advised of her stable family history, and reported no remarkable accident background. I took her case history, but was entirely unalerted to any neurological signs or symptoms of psychopathic disorder. Here was a case, however, of absolute liability, a res ipsa loquitur (common carrier utmost care situation). Since she complained of headaches, I sent her to a neurologist who reported:

"It was felt that at the time of the accident, she suffered a crushing injury to the left chest which resulted in five fractured ribs with contusion of the left thoracic viscera including the lung and the heart. The slight changes in the electrocardiogram are consistent with a mild traumatic miocarditis which, however, will in all probability not cause any permanent disability. The patient also suffered an injury to her head which resulted in lacerations of the scalp and moderate cerebral concussion. The electroencephalogram study indicated that no serious inter-cranial pathology resulted. However, the patient has had a difficult post-concussional state which will take several weeks completely to resolve." [6]

Confronted with this report, and observing a complete healing of the fractured rib cage, and no apparent permanency whatever, I negotiated a settlement at $4500. When I told my client that she would be "crazy" not to accept the offer, she replied that she would not accept it, and said, "I may be crazy." Subsequently she went to several other lawyers, but returned to me several months later. This time she advised me that she had seen snakes in the water of the bath tub, was being poisoned, and feared murder in her bed. The storm signals were now fully flying, and even an amateur mariner would have hesitated to fly a settlement flag in the face of them. Immediately I dispatched her to a psychiatrist, another neurologist, and a neurosurgeon.[7] In retrospect, had I been more detailed in taking the case

---

6. Electrocardiogram—graphic tracing of electric current produced by contraction of heart muscle.

Electroencephalogram—graphic recording of electrical currents developed in cortex of brain.

7. I am neither a neurologist nor a psychiatrist. But I take issue with the learned gentlemen in these two specialities who report that traumatic psychoses are rare, that slight injuries do not precipate the predisposed into a mental disorder. I cannot speak from the knowledge of medical learning. I only report of the number of cases I have actually seen in which it is too much of a coincidence to have a case history of complete self-dependence, and no other contributing factor except an accident followed by an actual state of psychosis, without feeling that the trauma was responsible.

history, more of a "doctor," I might not have been so close to committing the error which could have proven so colossal.

One of the reports from my now experts read,

"It is my opinion that the patient is suffering from a hysterical psychosis following the automobile accident. Her contact with reality is not in keeping with the diagnosis of chronic schizophrenia. The paresthesia and other discomforts are in my opinion conversion phenomena. It is my feeling that her present symptoms are directly attributable to the accident in an individual who was predisposed to such reaction."[8]

Another report read,

"In conclusion I may say that both the concussion symptoms, the phobic symptoms, and the psychotic symptoms are, in my opinion, directly attributable to the head injury which patient received—and that the psychotic symptoms may be considered either as a traumatic psychosis with schizophrenic symptoms or as a true schizophrenia precipitated by the injury."

The third report, in part, stated,

"Apparently there is no history of previous mental illness— Her symptoms so far as she described them dated specifically from the time of her accident and developed immediately thereafter. The experiences of auditory and visual hallucinations, the defective thinking and concentration, are all consistent with the diagnosis of schizophrenia. The psychological picture is not that of a patient with deterioration following a head injury, but is consistent with the psychological picture of a patient suffering from an intense emotional disturbance. It is impossible to state accurately on this one cross-section impression whether it is a severe hysterical reaction, or whether it is a schizophrenic psychosis. In either case, the patient appears now to be totally incapacitated and unable to make an adequate working and social adjustment, and it would appear that this is directly related to the accident, and that the accident was the precipitating factor in the development of the mental illness."

This case which I had advised my client to settle for $4500 was now compromised at $72,500! But it was my client's judgment, not mine, that brought it about.

For an in-depth look at these subjects, see § 1.41 et seq. in Chapter 1, supra.

8. Schizophrenia—psychosis of split personality; paresthesia—abnormal sensation.

§§ 2.15–2.20 are reserved for supplementary material.

C. OFFICE FORMS AND RECORDS

§ 2.21 Introduction

Many forms have been published for use in the investigation of the several types of tort cases. Experienced lawyers have some of their own, either written or carried in the mind. A prudent attorney should prepare a detailed list of his own, adapted to the particular state where used, setting out the information he needs to look for in a typical case, with blank pages for the crucial facts peculiar to that accident alone. Office word processing equipment can now greatly facilitate this task.

§ 2.22 Information to Obtain

Information which should be considered in every case include: Plaintiff's full name (along with any aliases), address and telephone number for both his residence and his work, marital status, number and ages of children, and any information concerning others who may be living with and dependent upon him. Also included should be a complete narration of the facts and events leading up to the accident, including the place, date and time thereof. Names and addresses of witnesses and possible defendants should also be noted.

The prospective plaintiff should be asked whether he may have made any statements or admissions concerning the accident and its cause, or if a defendant made such statements; and if so, to whom they were said. The inquiry should include questions as to the nature and severity of the injuries plaintiff sustained, the names and addresses of treating physicians and their prognoses, medical costs already incurred and wages lost to date. An in depth probe of plaintiff's medical, employment, familial and educational history should also be made. Our office utilizes a comprehensive form encompassing all this material, and more.

§ 2.23 Model Interview Form

The following is a reproduction of the form usually employed by my office when interviewing the client:

Client Information Sheet
(Confidential)

Date: _____
Ref. by: _____

Please fill out what you know.

I. PLAINTIFF
Name: _____ Age: _____ Birthdate: _____
Address: _____
Telephone: (Home) _____ (Business) _____
Present employer: _____
Employer's address: _____
Married: ____ Single: ____ Divorce: ____ Spouse's name: ____
Dependents: _____ (Name) _____ (Age) _____
(Relationship) _____

II. OCCURRENCE
Date of accident: _____ Admin. claim: _____
Place of accident: _____
Defendants: (Give full names and addresses) _____
_____

Witnesses: (Give full names and addresses) _____
_____

Facts: (Give a brief description of what happened) _____
_____

Injuries received as a result of this accident: _____
_____

Present physical condition and future prognosis: _____
_____

Names and addresses of treating physicians/hospitals: _____
_____

Defendant's insurance: _____
_____

Your insurance: _____
_____

§ 2.23   INTRODUCTION   Pt. 1

Other than defendants and yourself (and your family) were any other persons involved? If so, give name, address and a brief statement as to their involvement, damages and/or injuries: _____

_____

Was occurrence Reported to Police or others: _____
Did you give a statement, and if so, to whom (attach copy): _____
Was the statement oral or written: _____
Give the name and address of person having copy of the statement:

_____

Was statement signed: _____ Date of statement: _____
Was anyone present when you gave statement: _____
Do you know of any other statements given? If so, describe: _____

_____

III. DAMAGES

Medical: It is important that you collect and attach copies of all medical bills incurred to date as a result of this occurrence. Please be sure to forward copies of all future medical bills, drug bills, etc. as they are incurred. This should include *all* bills paid by insurance.
Total medical costs to date: _____
Total pharmacy costs to date: _____

Wages: Monthly income: _____ Income lost to date: _____
Time lost from work: _____ Date returned to work:

Property: Describe all property lost or damaged and its repair or replacement cost _____

IV. HISTORY

Medical: List any prior injuries, hospitalizations and explain:

_____

_____

Give a general history of physical condition prior to the accident in question: _____

_____

List any injuries or illnesses since the accident in question: _____

Employment: Social security number: _____
List all previous employers, their addresses and the dates you worked for them: _____

_____

Ch. 2   INVESTIGATION AND DISCOVERY   § **2.24**

List your annual income for the past five years: _____
_____

Family: Children: (If not living with you, give their address and telephone number) _____
_____

Parents: _____
Brothers and sisters: _____
Previous marriages: (Give dates and how dissolved)
_____

Education: Highest grade completed: _____
Vocational training: _____

Military: Branch: _____
Discharge date: _____

Legal: Prior claims or lawsuits: (Please describe) _____
Prior accidents: (Please describe) _____
Arrests and/or convictions: _____

V. DIAGRAM

§ **2.24**   Use of Specialized Forms

The lawyer practicing in a particular specialty will eventually prepare his own office forms to be used in interviewing the client and gathering a complete case history. Reproduced below is an interview or case history report for seaman cases. Such a form will necessarily differ as to the type of information required, whether, e.g., railroad (FELA), aviation, or automobile cases.

SEAMAN'S ACCIDENT REPORT FORM

Union _____   Date _____
Book No. _____   Taken by _____
                                  Referred by _____

Seaman's Accident Report

Name _____ Age _____ Wt. _____ Height _____ Cert. No. _____
Place of Birth _____ Date of Birth _____ Soc. Sec. No. _____
Single
Married _____ Children _____ Dependents _____ Address _____
Present Address _____ Home Address _____
Mailing Address _____
Occupation and Experience _____

§ 2.24 INTRODUCTION Pt. 1

Certificates
Licenses _____

Name of ship _____ Owner
Operator _____
Rating _____ What watch _____

Rate of pay _____ Average overtime _____ Unpaid wages _____
Prior service with company _____

Where signed on _____ Date signed on _____
Where he left vessel _____ Date he left vessel _____
Date discharged _____
Reason for leaving vessel _____

Period of articles or employment contract _____
Nature and description of voyage _____
Port of beginning of voyage _____
Port where vessel paid off _____
Nature and destination of cargo _____
Date of accident _____ Exact time _____
Location of ship at time of accident _____
Nature of work at time of accident _____
Locate exact point on ship where accident occurred _____
Conditions at point of accident (weather, light, slipperiness, etc.) _____

Who was in charge of work and watch _____
Who was present at time of accident _____
To whom was accident reported (date and time) _____

Was medical attention given and by whom _____

Was hospital slip given and by whom, where and when _____

Did he miss any watches—If so specify _____

Nature of injuries _____

Hospitals—Doctors—Dates of attendance _____

Period of disability—Giving date of return to work _____

Is there any permanent or additional disability or after effect _____

Was there any prior medical history _____

Names and addresses of witnesses (stating also what witness probably knows) _____

Causes of Accident _____

Were any reports made (If so, by whom and to whom) _____

What log books are pertinent—In whose possession are they _____

Sources of information for statements—Pertinent government records ___

Did client sign any statements—Specify _____
Client referred to Dr. _____
Suggestions and matters requiring development _____

§ 2.24 INTRODUCTION Pt. 1

Legal questions involved _____

Law Memo on questions involved (give brief statement and list authorities)

Exact and Full Details of Accident (giving exact dates—places and all relevant circumstances) _____

§ 2.25 Police Reports

Where the injuries and damage arise out of an automobile accident, plaintiff's lawyer should obtain a copy of the Vehicle Accident Report made by the investigating police officer. Therein contained will usually be names and statements of the parties involved and any witnesses, road, weather, traffic conditions, and frequently, a diagram of the scene. Also appearing may be the officer's notation of whether any provision of the vehicle code was violated by either or both drivers.

While information supplied by the police reports are helpful to an investigation, one must not come to rely too heavily thereupon. Often the information contained in the report may be erroneous or misleading, and while useful in supplying leads, should be carefully rechecked point by point.

Nonetheless, the information contained in the report should not be overlooked for its value as an impeachment tool. The interrogatories and depositions of the defendant and eyewitnesses should be checked against those statements contained in the report. If a discrepancy is found, then the investigating officer should be deposed. The written report may be used to refresh his memory, or in the event of a total lack of recall, the writing may be read into evidence if the proper foundation has been laid (past recollection recorded). If the investigating officer can qualify as an expert in accident investigation, or took measurements at the scene of skid marks, position of the car, and the like, his testimony should be fully explored for use at trial.

It should be noted here that a number of states have laws which render the accident reports confidential. However, upon submission of a formal consent of a person involved, information contained in the official police report is made available to his attorney. Several copies of such consent should be obtained from the client. An example of a consent form follows:

> The undersigned, _____, authorizes _____ to inspect any and all records regarding injuries sustained by me in an auto accident at _____ _____ on _____.
>
> Signed: _____
>
> Subscribed and sworn to before me, a Notary Public, this _____ day of _____ _____, 19__.
>
> My commission expires _____.

§ 2.26 Medical Records Consent Forms

At the initial interview between the lawyer and his client, the client should be required to sign at least four consent forms authorizing the hospital, treating physician or others to disclose all medical records and such to the attorney or his authorized representative. Some states have enacted laws which must be complied with to the letter, or the information will not be released. For instance, California, in 1979, enacted its "Confidentiality of Medical Information Act."[9] Among other provisions, the Act requires that to be valid, an authorization for the release of medical information must in writing, clearly set apart from any other claim or language on the same page, must be signed by the patient, and must state the names of the persons authorized to see the material, what material is to be disclosed, and the length of time the authorization is to remain in force. An example of an authorization form follows:

GENERAL AUTHORIZATION

To:

You are hereby authorized to disclose and deliver to my attorney, **MELVIN M. BELLI, Sr.** or his authorized representative, any and

---

9. Calif.Civil Code § 56 et seq.

all records or documents of any kind they desire, and pursuant to the Confidentiality of Medical Information Act, to release any and all medical reports and records, hospitalization records, including but not limited to, inpatient, outpatient or otherwise, doctors' notes, nurses' notes, correspondence, x-rays, charts and diagrams, laboratory and pathological reports and tests, examinations and analyses, surgical and non-surgical procedures, diagnosis and prognosis, history, statements, bills or charges for any or all of such services; all personnel, employment and earnings records, including but not limited to insurance coverage and claims, accidents and sick leave; and police, accident or investigative reports.

MELVIN M. BELLI, Sr. or his representatives are further authorized to photocopy, microfilm or otherwise reproduce said records for use in my behalf. I have been informed that such information about me will not be released to any person or agency other than as stated above. This authorization shall remain valid until _____ or upon further notice or condition. I understand and have been informed that I have a right to receive a copy of this authorization.

My lawyers are investigating and/or proceeding on a claim in my behalf, and pursuant to California Evidence Code § 1158, your cooperation in supplying the information requested and allowing release or copying of the documents will be appreciated.

Dated: _____.

If Applicable Complete the Following:

I hereby also consent to the release of any and all alcohol and/or drug abuse or psychiatric treatment records under the same conditions as stated above. I understand that such information cannot be released without my specific consent.

Dated: _____.

§ 2.27 Contingent Fee Agreement Forms

It is imperative at this first meeting that the lawyer and client enter into a frank discussion of the lawyer's fees and costs of suit. The client should sign the contingent fee agreement (or retainer) after the lawyer has fully explained all of its contents, and given the client a chance to read it over carefully, and thoroughly digest its contents. In California, because of laws specifically addressing the amount of fees in medical malpractice cases, and setting limitations thereon, it is necessary either to have an entirely separate contract or, as we sometimes do, make an addendum to the standard contingent fee contract.[10] An example of a "Contingent Fee Agreement" follows:

CONTINGENT FEE AGREEMENT

Re: _____ vs. _____

I hereby retain the Law Offices of MELVIN M. BELLI, Sr. (hereinafter referred to as "BELLI") as my lawyers in all cases of property damage or personal injury or any claim otherwise arising directly or indirectly therefrom.

Should a recovery result by settlement before the filing of a complaint, BELLI is to receive one-third ($1/3$) of this recovery and I am to receive two-thirds ($2/3$), less any expenses or costs if these have been advanced by BELLI.

Should a recovery result either by settlement, trial or otherwise, after the filing of a complaint, BELLI is to receive forty (40%) per cent of the recovery and I am to receive sixty (60%) per cent, less any expenses or costs if these have been advanced by BELLI.

Should a recovery, either by settlement, trial or otherwise, not result, I am to owe BELLI nothing for their time and services.

---

10. § 6146 of the California Business and Professions Code imposes the following limits on the amount of fees an attorney may recover in a medical malpractice case:

(1) Forty percent of the first fifty thousand ($50,000) recovered;

(2) Thirty-three and one-third percent of the next fifty thousand dollars ($50,000) recovered;

(3) Twenty-five percent of the next one hundred thousand ($100,000) recovered;

(4) Ten percent of any amount on which the recovery exceeds two hundred thousand dollars ($200,000).

Because of these limitations, it is necessary for our office to have the client sign, in addition to the standard contingent fee agreement, the following addendum thereto:

ADDENDUM TO RETAINER AGREEMENT
(MEDICAL MALPRACTICE CASE ONLY)

The Medical Injury Compensation Reform Act of 1975 (Assembly Bill 1 and Senate Bill 24) purports to regulate contingency fee agreements by statute. To the extent that said purported legislation is binding upon the attached RETAINER AGREEMENT and upon the facts giving rise to the action contemplated by attorney and client in entering into this AGREEMENT, the contingency fee percentages set forth in said legislation shall be utilized in determining attorney's fees in lieu of the percentages stated above in the body of the attached AGREEMENT. In no event, however, shall the attorney's fees percentages exceed those set forth in the attached AGREEMENT.

Dated: _____.

_____
Client

Law Offices of MELVIN M. BELLI, Sr.
By _____

§ 2.27   INTRODUCTION

It is agreed that if a settlement offer is tendered in the case by the defendants and BELLI believes in good faith that settlement should be accepted and communicates this to client and client does not agree to the settlement offer, BELLI may require client to advance the reasonable costs of trial in the case. In the event that client refuses to accept a reasonable settlement offer and refuses to advance costs, client thereby agrees to permit BELLI to withdraw from the case.

I hereby give BELLI my power of attorney to execute all complaints, claims, contracts, settlements, checks, drafts, compromises, releases, dismissals and orders as I could myself. I grant BELLI, as my attorneys, an assignment to the extent of their fees and expenses and costs advanced and a lien on my cause of action.

BELLI is authorized to see and make copies of all my hospital and medical records of any kind.

Dated: _____.   Client: _____

                                                    _____

We accept: (Address)

MELVIN M. BELLI, Sr.   _____

                                                      (Telephone)

_____

The Belli Building
722 Montgomery Street   _____
San Francisco, California   94111   (Business Address)
415–YUkon 1–1849

                                                       (Telephone)

§ 2.28   Office Records

Proficiency is experience. In argument, cross-examination, deposition, direct examination, instructions, and investigations, eventually the one proficient in the art will overlook neither the minute nor the obvious. Nevertheless, even the careful practitioner will have a "mental check list" or a written outline in all of the above legal procedures. So that all required information is not overlooked, many offices have prepared their own forms for investigation. An example of such an office record follows:

PERSONAL INJURY OFFICE RECORD

Statute of Limitations

Date Done

Preliminary Case

_____Initial Conference   _____Periodic Appointments

_____Report (Motor Vehicle Dept.) filed

_____Medical Authorization permits signed

Forwarded to M.D.

    1. _____ on _____. Rec'd. _____

    2. _____ on _____. Rec'd. _____

    3. _____ on _____. Rec'd. _____

_____Retainer signed

_____Police Report secured

Officer conference _____

Witnesses Screened:

	Name	Address	Date
1.	_____	_____	_____
2.	_____	_____	_____
3.	_____	_____	_____
4.	_____	_____	_____

_____Pictures of

    _____Scene

    _____Injuries

    _____Cars

_____Measurements

Conference with M.D.'s

    1. _____ Date _____

    2. _____ Date _____

    3. _____ Date _____

_____Special Damages outlined.

Reserve Estimate

Pre-trial Pleadings

_____Complaint filed

_____Answer filed

_____Memo to Set filed, accompanied by Jury Fee.

Set for Trial on _____ At _____

_____Notice of Time and Place of Trial Served

§ 2.28   INTRODUCTION   Pt. 1

Pre-trial Preparation

Deposition of Adverse Party Set for _____ Taken on _____
Other depositions desired? _____
Client need specialized Medical Attention? _____
_____Specialist consulted   Date of Report _____
_____Photographs of X-rays
Demonstrative Aids secured or securable at _____
Upon _____ days notice.
Demonstrative evidence aids required:

    1. _____
    2. _____
    3. _____
    4. _____

Medical Texts secured or securable at _____
Upon _____ days notice.
_____Brochure forwarded to defense
Demand _____ Jury Value _____ Settle Value _____
_____Subpoenas issued
Subpoenas served upon:

    1. _____ Date _____
    2. _____ Date _____
    3. _____ Date _____
    4. _____ Date _____
    5. _____ Date _____
    6. _____ Date _____

Trial Preparation

_____Jury list received
_____Jury list investigated
_____Fact Brief prepared
_____Jury questions prepared
_____Opening Statement
    Blackboard? _____
    Map? _____
_____Instructions prepared

    The use of a form office record serves the double purpose of providing the trial lawyer with complete information on the case

showing what work has been done, and serves as a checklist for that which remains to be completed. Most personal injury attorney offices, on defense as well as plaintiff's side, use some such procedure. While a secretary may keep the record, the trial lawyer should review it regularly to determine the progress of the case and to prepare it thoroughly, not at the last minute, that being the purpose of the chart.

In every such file, the author uses a blue sheet of paper upon which *law* citations are noted, and a pink sheet upon which all *settlement* notations are recorded. The distinctive color of these sheets easily enables location of this data.

A case history sheet makes up the first covering sheet. Many offices number their files, rather than give them a name. Regardless of the description of the particular file, there should be a central catalog or "docket" containing dockets of filing, deposit of jury fees, statutes of limitations and other "procedural vital statistics," so that upon current inquiry or office conference all the office cases may be shown in summary. Some offices use a large rubber stamp or printing on the file itself to afford a place for this information. In smaller offices financial data may be kept in this record.

§ 2.29 Use of Bound Volumes

The magnitude of pretrial preparation and investigation may be appreciated when one outlines each step to be completed before the first juror is sworn. It has been the author's practice to employ bound volumes for preparation and trial notes. Each case is indexed in the front of each volume (which may contain many cases—some tried, some settled), and the volume, when filled, is filed.

The bound volume is also used during selection of the jury. One page is divided into twelve parts (or whatever the number of jurors in the state happens to be), and notations made as to who is selected and who is challenged. Thus, a permanent record is made of the jury selection.

§ 2.30 The Disbursal Sheet

Closed files should be kept accessible and a "disbursal sheet," generally the last entry, attached. In addition to having the client acknowledge receipt of the money on the disbursal sheet, some lawyers also have him acknowledge termination of the attorney-client relation.

Reproduced at the end of this section is a disbursal sheet we employed showing the disbursal of the proceeds of a settlement we made on behalf of a widow and her 7 children. The disbursal sheet indicates the amount of money paid to all the interested parties, the trial lawyer, the witnesses, and the client. It shows the expense of modern litigation. It is a record for both client and lawyer, and four copies are made: one to be retained in the file which is closed upon disbursal, one copy goes to the disbursal sheet file, a copy goes to the client, and a copy to any associate counsel. (The client is, of course, advised of the tax consequences, if any.)

Some lawyers absorb the costs of investigation and notarial services, considering it a part of general office overhead. It is the practice of the author to charge the client for these costs.

Some lawyers have had the sad experience of disbursing proceeds of defendant's check in settlement of the judgment before this instrument has cleared the bank. The author is familiar with several instances in which the check did not clear, and with one instance in which defendant became insolvent between the time of the draft and the time it reached the paying bank. The lawyer had advanced the proceeds to the client from his account, hence the notation, "Defendant's check cleared _____."

The author deems it good practice to have the senior partner of the office approve, with his initials and date, each disbursal sheet, and have any associated lawyers do likewise. The client must execute the sheet before payment. It is likewise prudent practice to have the client note by his signature that the case is "closed" to his satisfaction, and the date thereof. This formally terminates the relationship of client and attorney in the particular case.

If the above procedure of disbursal is followed in each case and a copy of the disbursal sheet sent to a disbursal file, at the end of the taxable year the lawyer not only has an invaluable aid to check his gross income for tax purposes, but can refer a tax audit to the particular case under question, if necessary.

The client should know what "advances" are, and he should likewise know not only that they are taken "off the top" of the award, but that should there be no recovery, he is obligated to return these expenses to the lawyer under modern rules.[11]

11. Brown & Huseby, Inc. v. Chrietzberg, 242 Ga. 232, 248 S.E.2d 631 (1978) ("[A]n attorney may obligate himself to advance the cost of obtaining depositions, provided the client remains ultimately liable for such expenses"). See § 1.21 et seq., "Attorney's Fees, Liens and Expenses," supra.

DISBURSAL SHEET

Re: G. v. S. D. HOME CO.

SETTLEMENT:		$ 250,000.00
LESS COSTS:		
See Exhibit "A" attached hereto		2,745.12
		$ 247,254.88

DISTRIBUTIVE SHARE OF SETTLEMENT:

M. L. C. de G.,
    Widow–⅔ share $ 164,836.59

G. G., a minor
O. G., a minor
I. G., a minor
R. G., a minor   ⅓ share $ 82,418.29
S. G., a minor
J. F. G., a minor
L. G.

LESS FEES:

40% of Mrs. C's distributive share	$ 65,934.64	
25% of minor children's share	$ 20,604.57	
		$ 86,539.21

NET DISTRIBUTIVE SHARE TO CLIENTS:

M. L. C. de G.	$ 98,901.95
G. G., a minor	$ 8,830.53
O. G., a minor	$ 8,830.53
I. G., a minor	$ 8,830.53
R. G., a minor	$ 8,830.53
S. G., a minor	$ 8,830.53
J. F. G., a minor	$ 8,830.53
L. G.	$ 8,830.54

RECAPITULATION:

Total fees	$ 86,539.21
Total costs	2,745.12
M. L. C. de G.	98,901.95
M. L. C. de G., Trustee for G., O., I., R., S., J. and L. G., minors	61,813.72
	$ 250,000.00

§ 2.30 INTRODUCTION Pt. 1

COSTS ADVANCED
SETTLEMENT: $ 250,000.00

LESS COSTS:

Copying charges	$ 51.00
Police Report	2.00
County Clerk–filing fee	25.00
Telephone calls	20.74
Lipset Service–Investigation	147.80
ABC Legal Service–service of summons	23.00
" " " " "	17.00
Investigation	281.82
ABC Legal Service–service of summons	13.00
" " " " "	13.50
City of F.–Engineering specif.	10.00
Office of Procurement–Safety Orders	2.10
County Clerk–Probate information	6.00
ABC Legal Service–service of summons	13.50
H. M. V. & Son–bond premium	10.00
P. V.–witness fee	30.00
D. E. W.–witness fee	30.00
S. E. F., Esq.–reimburse costs	87.50
Sacramento Deposition Reporters	327.44
Attorneys Filing Service–serve subpoenas	75.00
J. L., CSR–Deposition of Shilts	100.67
Sacramento Deposition Reporters	280.86
Mail–a–Way Service–photographs	82.01
G. W.–witness fee	16.00
F. B.–witness fee	13.00
P. V.–witness fee	19.00
J. H. R–witness fee	115.00
Solano County Reporters–transcript	7.50
S. A. F., Esq.–retainer fee	200.00
P. V.–witness fee	26.00
Attorneys Filing Service–serve subpoena	7.00
J. P. C.–Interpreter fee	60.20
Solano County Court Reporters–transcript	7.50
Sacramento Deposition Reporters	538.98
Attorneys Filing Service–Serve Subpoenas	30.50
" " " " "	12.50
" " " " "	35.00
County Clerk–certified copy of Order (7)	7.00

                                                      2,745.12
                                                     $ 247,254.88

PRO-RATA SHARE OF COSTS:

M. L. C. de G.	2/3	$1,830.08
Minor children (7)	1/3	915.04
		$2,745.12

§§ 2.31–2.40 are reserved for supplementary material.

D. PARALEGALS

§ 2.41 Role and Duties of Paralegals

One of the great changes in recent years in the practice of law is the advent of the paralegal. These persons may be either formerly trained in paralegal schools, or trained "on-the-job" in the law office setting—often advancing from the position of legal secretary.

Certainly, along with specialization and advertising, the work of the paralegal has changed the actual practice of law to a great extent. If the practicing lawyer, even in a small office, has not tried paralegals, he is missing the opportunity to more efficiently utilize his or her time.

Paralegals are so new that the limits of their role is not yet clearly defined or delineated. Apparently, they can do anything in the practice of law but try a case and give legal advice, *if* they are *supervised by a full fledged lawyer*. Although they can't try cases, they certainly may sit at the counsel table (although some courts will not allow this yet), and assist the trial lawyer in the trial of the case as the detective sits with the District Attorney to help try the criminal case.

Can they interview clients on the first call? This has not yet been fully determined, and particularly if the paralegal is the one who is going to tell the client if there is or isn't a case or otherwise give legal advice. However, if the activity is restricted (e.g. information gathering) and is supervised by a lawyer, perhaps they can interview clients.

I believe my office is the first to carry paralegals, designating them as such, on my legal letterhead. I do this because I think they should be recognized and it is of assistance to the client to know who are the lawyers and who are the paralegals.

The registered nurse is the right hand of the doctor in the doctor's office. Taking histories and such, she frees the doctor for specific medical work. The paralegal taking histories, doing interrogatories, managing the office, etc., can free the trial lawyer for that which he does best and should want to do away from the details and turmoil of the office—try cases.

I cannot recommend too highly the use of paralegals in one's law office *regardless* of his specialty or general practice. In some of the fields, such as probate, the lawyer may find, if he is so inclined, that he can increase his workload two or three times and raise his billings accordingly.

I've asked one of our paralegals, *Valerie Lambertson*, to outline some of the litigation work which our paralegals perform. I see them doing even more "law" work as time goes on, provided, of course, that they are under the constant and close supervision of a lawyer.

Herewith are the comments of Valerie Lambertson[12] on the role and duties of the paralegal:

A litigation paralegal may perform as wide a variety of tasks as the *supervising* attorney cares to assign. She[13] may work on just one assignment for any given case, or may be involved totally in one specific case throughout the entire litigation process. In the latter situation, the attorney may find that introducing his paralegal to the client as a team member who is able to assist in his case will facilitate matters later on when the paralegal needs to contact the client on behalf of the attorney.

This rapport is particularly helpful when a paralegal is asked to assist a client in such matters as answering interrogatories. It should be noted that a paralegal may not only assist in the drafting of the answers, but may well draft the interrogatories themselves.

Document production is another area in which a paralegal can perform many valuable services. She may review client documents for privileged materials, designate those documents that are subject to a protective order, and ascertain which documents fall within the scope of requests for documents.

The client's documents should be organized and an index prepared, as well as a control system established for client documents to be copied by the opposition. The paralegal may either produce or supervise the production of client documents to the opposition, and serve as the liaison to the opposition with respect to the mechanical aspects of document production and reproduction.

In regard to document inspection, a paralegal can work with attorneys, clients and experts to determine the type of documents to be requested and then arrange for the copying of the designated materials. The copied documents should be organized and a detailed inventory prepared so that the paralegal can identify any deficiencies in the document production and deal with the opposition in respect to those deficiencies.

---

12. The author of the following article, Valerie Lambertson, would like to acknowledge her appreciation to the San Francisco Association of Legal Assistants for notes from its utilization seminar.

13. The term "she" is used because presently, most paralegals are women. There are, however, a growing number of men in the field.

A paralegal can provide much assistance in the area of depositions. She can review all documents to identify possible deponents and compile information regarding designated witnesses. She can schedule the depositions and should then attend them for the purpose of managing documents, and may also provide notetaking assistance. After the depositions are completed, the paralegal should summarize the transcript and develop an index to the testimony that will enable the attorney to make the best possible use of the information. She herself cannot take depositions.

Drafting Requests for Admissions, responses to admission requests and serving as liaison to clients with respect to those responses can well be a part of a paralegal's job.

A paralegal's skills can be extremely helpful when it comes to analyzing and utilizing the factual information in a case. She may identify information from depositions, documents, pleadings or clients in order to support oral or written argument; review drafts of correspondence, pleadings or briefs for the accuracy of factual information; identify all testimony supporting or conflicting with allegations; identify weak or unsupported client claims and conflicts between client testimony and documentation. She may also assist an expert in compiling damages and in preparing pretrial and trial briefs.

During the pretrial period, a paralegal is able to prepare graphs, charts, visual aids, trial exhibits and witness files. At the actual trial, she may assist in controlling and logging the documents and exhibits, and be the liaison with the witnesses. When the trial is concluded, the paralegal can digest or summarize the trial transcript and prepare findings of fact.

These tasks are all aimed at freeing the attorney to do the work that only he can do. All indications are that as attorneys discover this fact, the use of paralegals will continue to grow.

§§ 2.42–2.44 are reserved for supplementary material.

E. THE INVESTIGATOR

§ 2.45 Introduction

Several years ago in Chicago, *Edward Williams* and I addressed the National Bar Association, the Bar composed of distinguished and able black lawyers. Williams and I gave what we thought were learned addresses on the trial of cases in both criminal and personal injury fields. We asked for questions. One spectator raised his hand, and I acknowledged him. He said, "Brothers Williams and Belli, you've told us how to try these cases. Now would you mind giving us a lecture on how to get them!"

If I could have conclusively answered that question, or could do so in this book, I probably could shed the greatest enlightment since the original Blackstonian lectures to lawyers.

§ 2.46 Importance of the Investigator

The investigator is one source of the lawyer's business. The lawyer cannot solicit cases.[14] The investigator cannot solicit them for him.[15] In California, there is a movement to abandon the crime and ethical admonition against solicitation. (Other states apparently are considering similar rules.) With advertising now allowed to professional men by United States Supreme Court fiat, doctors and den-

---

14. ABA Code of Professional Responsibility, DR 2–103(A); Kentucky State Bar Ass'n v. Stivers, 475 S.W.2d 900 (Ky.1971), cert. denied 406 U.S. 968, 92 S.Ct. 2412, 32 L.Ed.2d 666 (Attorney suspended from practice for one year for sending the following letter:
    "Dear Mrs. V———:
    "According to the May 29, 1969 issue of the local Jeffersonville Indiana newspaper, you were involved in an automobile accident recently, in Clark County, Indiana. The newspaper account indicates that you were not at fault and therefore entitled to recover any damages you suffered, as a result of the accident, from the party at fault.
    "In my practice of law, I handle cases of this nature and am admitted to practice in all courts, both in Kentucky and Indiana. I am in a position to represent you and prosecute the case all the way through suit, if necessary.
    "If I can be of service to you in this matter, please call me at the above number and I will arrange an appointment for you to come into my office for a conference.
    "Sincerely,
    "s/———.").
    See also Ohralik v. Ohio State Bar Ass'n, 436 U.S. 447, 98 S.Ct. 1912, 56 L.Ed.2d 444 (1978), reh. denied 439 U.S. 883, 99 S.Ct. 226, 58 L.Ed.2d 198.

15. Younger v. State Bar of California, 12 Cal.3d 274, 113 Cal.Rptr. 829, 522 P.2d 5 (1974) (Attorney arrived in hospital room of injured person five minutes after his "capper" had left her side).

tists as well as lawyers,[16] it is pretty hard to say where advertising ends and solicitation begins. I suppose it's a practical thing and each case has to be judged on its own merits. Some courts have used "good taste" as a common denominator, but in my humble opinion, I feel good taste is the father of *ethical* confusion.

I think that defendants—all sorts of defendants, big firms, and little firms—chase their cases more vigorously and vehemently than do plaintiff's lawyers. Maybe the chasing is more subtle, i. e., on the 18th tee or after the fourth olive in the bottom of the martini glass, but nevertheless chasing it is. And while this doesn't particularly concern me since my specialty is more on the plaintiff's side, I deeply resent the hypocrisy of the leaders of the various bar associations representing defendants whom they have considerably chased, criticizing the at-one-time less organized plaintiff or the plaintiff's Bar.

On the plaintiff's side, the FELA case was generally chased by the business agent to a friendly lawyer who more frequently than not repaid the not inconsiderable efforts of the chaser in monetary reward. This was similarly true with the admiralty and Jones Act cases.

Various unions have various business agents who rightly or wrongly send the cases of that union to the particular business agent: rightly, without kickback; wrongly, with kickback.[17]

In the small but rapidly growing fraternity of aviation lawyers, "chasing" worldwide is at its maximum and is generally done directly, i.e., by the heads of the firm. Though the chances of organized bar reproval are minimal, the opportunities of emolument are tremendous.

---

16. Bates v. State Bar of Arizona, 433 U.S. 350, 97 S.Ct. 2691, 53 L.Ed.2d 810 (1977), reh. denied 434 U.S. 881, 98 S.Ct. 242, 54 L.Ed.2d 164; Virginia Pharmacy Bd. v. Virginia Citizens Consumer Council, 425 U.S. 748, 96 S.Ct. 1817, 48 L.Ed.2d 346 (1976).

17. Matter of Jaques, 407 Mich. 26, 281 N.W.2d 469 (1979). Therein an attorney had "solicited" potential clients—union members—through the union business agent. Such conduct was held *not* prohibited. "I am unconvinced that the particular conduct attributed to Jaques . . . rises to the level of 'fraud, undue influence, intimidation, overreaching, and other forms of "vexatious conduct" ' which the disciplinary rules may properly seek to prevent.

. . . Jaques did not directly contact any prospective client. His solicitation was directed to a union business agent who ostensibly represented the interests of union members with potential claims. The union agent possessed the expertise to make a detached and informed evaluation of Jaques' qualifications before passing any recommendation along to his members. There is no claim that the union official was in fact nothing more than a 'runner' or agent for Jaques. Under these circumstances, the union agent served as a buffer between the attorney and prospective clients thus alleviating the potential for overreaching and undue influence."

What has the investigator got to do with this? In most active personal injury offices, it is the investigator who first sees the client and can ethically "sign him up" provided the client or a friend or relative has first asked for this. I've heard it said by many personal injury lawyers on the plaintiff's side that their investigator held their ticket to practice in his hand!

I've been fortunate in my investigators these past 40 years. There was *Bob Callahan*, a member of the San Francisco Fire Department, who helped me out for years. He had no particular experience, except on-the-job training. In the early days there were few schools for "investigators", and no schools for paralegals. A paralegal was unheard of and would have been uncontinenced.

I then had an ex-actor *Vince Silk*, who, like all of my other investigators, was loyal unto the calls of his master. Came then an ex-county clerk, a thorough Irishman, now deceased, who knew the whereabouts of every piece of paper that had been filed at City Hall since the first spade of earth was turned for its building, *Harold McGlennon*. Then came my chief investigator, the only really one I've ever had who had any formal investigative experience. He was in charge of narcotics in the Caribbean area and investigated for Bobby Kennedy and a number of committees in Washington, *Eugene Marshall*.

To say that the investigator must be loyal is unnecessary. But he must be as imaginative as he is intelligent and loyal. He must be willing to canvass a neighborhood at different times and at different hours to see if a witness absent on one occasion is present on the other. The investigator should know how to read medical reports as well as expert witness reports, but he cannot substitute for the expert, except it may be his judgment when first reviewing the case on a particular technical piece of evidence as to whether there is a case. But I would say principally it is the expert's job to see that more than one lawyer in the office gives his judgment as to whether "I have a case".

My present investigator has two assistants. See Figure 3. All are on the "house" payroll. Some lawyers prefer to hire outside investigators, to have them completely separated from the office. I prefer to have a man whom I deeply know and completely trust available 24 hours. He can never afford to be away or on vacation or asleep. The investigator for Old Holy Grail Insurance Company pops out of his defendant's exhaust pipe within seconds after the accident. The first investigator to cover the accident, get the pictures and interview the witnesses has a distinct advantage.

Ch. 2   INVESTIGATION AND DISCOVERY   § **2.46**

Figure 3. Creative and intelligent investigators are a most valuable asset to the trial lawyer. They must find witnesses, elicit statements, and find the facts which make (and sometimes destroy) the case. Standing with some of the equipment they use, from left to right, are investigators *Craig Zurkey, Eugene J. Marshall* and *Dale Roberts.*

[Photo by Chuck DeCuir.]

The investigator should be able to take pictures and it is no great difficulty to instruct him as to how to do this. He must have sense enough to go to expert photography for the detailed analysis that he should know is necessary, and early in the case to preserve the evidence.

I make it a rule never to give one of my investigators an oral instruction, or if I do, say the night before in emergency, I put it in writing for the file the next morning. (I follow the same rule in our research department, which I think is one of the finest in San Francisco. A researcher is not required to do *any* work unless the request is put specifically in writing. The benefit of this is to allocate praise or blame: Was it an errant question or an errant answer that gave the wrong research?)

§ 2.47 The Investigator's Tools

Investigation of the lawsuit, either criminal or civil, often requires the employment of a trained investigator, a man or agency specializing in finding facts. His modern equipment is much more extensive than that portrayed as the trademark of the detective of fiction: the meerschaum pipe, magnifying glass, and two-visored hat. It is also much more expensive.[18]

Almost everyone today is familiar with the scientific aids of the great criminal laboratories such as the FBI lab in Washington, D.C. While the lawyer who does his own investigating need not, of course, set up such an extensive laboratory or even have available all of the equipment shown here, nevertheless he should be familiar with the uses of some of these fact-finding devices. Certainly he should know what these instruments may do for or against his client in order that he may be prepared, either on direct or cross-examination, for the introduction of their results.

Figure 4 shows noted San Francisco investigator *Hal Lipset* [19] standing with some of the equipment regularly utilized in his profession. The same photograph is reproduced in Figure 5, with each item individually numbered for identification.

18. See Figure 4. The cost of the investigation equipment shown in this picture is in excess of $27,000.

19. Hal Lipset, Lipset Service, Investigations, 2509 Pacific Avenue, San Francisco, California 94115.

Ch. 2   INVESTIGATION AND DISCOVERY   § **2.47**

Figure 4. Investigator Hal Lipset is shown standing beside some of the investigation tools he frequently employs in his trade. (Photo by James Campbell, Lipset Service, San Francisco.)

Figure 5. Picture reproduced and marked for identification purposes.[20]

Item #1 is the most important, most often employed tool of the investigator: his automobile. The car shown is a high-performance, medium-sized sedan, and is equipped with a mobile radio. Its cost is in the neighborhood of $10,000.

20. Item # 1 – investigator's automobile; Item # 2 – mobile radio; Item # 3 – cassette recorder; Item # 4 – frequency scanner; Items # 5 & 6 – video tape recorder and camera; Item # 7 – cassette recorder; Item # 8 – Nagra recorder; Item # 9 – Pearlcorder; Item # 10 – portable radios; Item # 11 – movie camera with telephone lens; Item # 12 – binoculars; Item # 13 – magnifying glass; Item # 14 – tape measure; Item # 15 – 35mm Nikon camera with 680mm precision mirrored lens attached; Item # 16 – camera film; Item # 17 – Polaroid camera; Item # 18 – wide-angle lens; Item # 19 – standard 50mm lens; Item # 20 – 35mm Konica camera with zoom lens attached.

Most investigators' cars have in them a recording device which allows them to pick-up and record conversations in the car without the knowledge of the passenger. Thus, the witness who is willing to talk freely but who will not "give a statement," while he sits in the investigator's car, may find his words perpetuated and may be confronted with them when he comes to trial.

Item #2, which is barely visible in the hand of investigator Lipset, is a microphone attached to the mobile radio in the vehicle. The mobile radio is a multi-channel UHF, operating through multiple mountain-top repeater sites. Such radios have the capability of base to radio communication and radio to radio communication, as well as a discreet surveillance channel. These radios currently sell for around $1200 each.

Item #3 is an Akai cassette recorder, used to copy previously recorded interviews, and has a value of $300. Depicted in Item #4 is a scanner, which can monitor 50 channels on UHF and VHF frequencies. The scanner sells for about $200.

Items #5 and 6 are a video tape recorder and camera. These are used for surveillance, and also for taking statements of witnesses. They are also utilized wherever instant review is desired, such as accident reconstruction. The camera and recorder are valued at $4,000.

Item #7 is a Sony cassette recorder, which is used to tape individual interviews for transcription purposes. This recorder is worth approximately $225. Item #8 is a Nagra recorder. This is a Swiss-made, precision recording device which is capable of recording three hours on reel-to-reel tape, and sells for $3,000. Item #9 in the photograph is a Pearlcorder, a recorder capable of voice/noise activation, and comes equipped with an electrically amplified condensor microphone. Both the microphone and the recorder sell for $450.

The items shown in #10 are hand-held portable radios. Due to their circuitry, these radios are very expensive, costing $1800 each. They are multi-channel UHF frequency, and operate through multiple mountain-top repeater sites. These radios may be operated from a base station to the portable radio, or from one portable radio to another.

Item #11 is a Bolex 16mm movie camera with a telephoto lens. This combination is worth $1,500, and is used chiefly for surveillance photography. Item #12 is a pair of binoculars, which are also used mainly for surveillance. They are valued at $300. Item #13 is a magnifying glass which costs about $20. Item #14, although a relatively inexpensive item, costing approximately $12, nonetheless is frequently employed by the investigator. This is a tape measure, and can be used for measuring distances of automobile tire skid marks, and other distances.

The camera in Item #15 is a 35mm Nikon, and in the photograph it is shown with a 680mm precision mirrored lens attached. This combination is used for photo surveillance, scene photography, and precision photographs. The camera sells for around $300, while the lens costs $1,000. The items in #16 are 35mm color and black and white film which are used for scene and surveillance photography. Kodak has recently made available a faster color film having a 400 ASA, which greatly expands the use of color film.

Item #17 is a Polaroid camera which is used for ID photos and close-ups of evidence items. The pictures taken by this type of camera are ready for viewing within minutes after the scene has been captured on film, and do not require the services of a photo lab.

Items #18, 19, and 20 are some of the lenses more frequently used by the investigator. Item #18 is a wide-angle lens which is used for scene photography where it is desired to include as much of the scene as possible from a closer distance. Such a lens costs about $150. Item #19 is a 50mm lens, which is generally classified the "standard" lens in the photography world. This lens sells for $100.

Item #20 is a Konica 35mm camera with a telephoto zoom lens, which is used for routine and surveillance photography. The advantage of a zoom lens is that it permits the photographer to take pictures using different milimeter settings, without the necessity of changing lenses. The camera and lens shown sell for $600. Like telephoto lenses, zoom lenses make it possible for a picture to be taken of a subject from long distances. Thus, pictures may be taken from an automobile, the top of a building, or a position far enough away that the operator may remain unnoticed and at a discreet distance, yet accurately photograph the subject matter.

While the above items do not purport to be an exhaustive list of all of the tools available to the investigator, they are fairly representative of those which are most important and most commonly utilized. It may be assumed that the investigator has at his disposal means with which to "bug" a room and for wire-tapping. Also, a complete photography lab is a valid asset to the investigator.

§§ 2.48–2.50 are reserved for supplementary material.

F. "ON-THE-SCENE" INVESTIGATIONS AND PHOTOGRAPHS

§ 2.51 Introduction

Nothing gives the jury a description of an accident's occurrence and resulting damages as do pictures of the accident scene taken immediately after the incident has occurred, or better still, while it is actually happening. Where there is an intersection, highway, crosswalk or double line involved—things that can be photographed at leisure—a study may be made for possible camera angles, aerial photos and even color pictures to determine the best way vividly, yet factually, to portray the scene to the jury. Upon proper request, of course, the jury may even be permitted to visit the scene of the event.

§ 2.52 Finding "On-the-Scene" Photographs

How does one capture the actual occurrence in pictures? A great deal may depend upon sheer luck. Few trial lawyers, however, fully realize the source and availability of such photographs in their preparation.

A defendant, through his immediately notified insurance company,[21] or an employee through his superintendent, generally has the first opportunity to investigate and preserve the facts. As we shall see,[22] liberal discovery procedures under state as well as federal rules pertaining to discovery, make these first-discovered facts available to the other side. With the growth of unions, representatives of the plaintiff-employee also have an early opportunity for an on-the-spot investigation.[23]

---

21. It frequently happens that an injured plaintiff has insurance of his own to cover damage not encompassed in a prospective claim. While he is called upon to furnish data to his own insurance carrier (failing which he may be cancelled for non-cooperation) nevertheless, he should appreciate that, despite protestations to the contrary, this information might find itself into a "clearing house" and into the files of an adversary in his subsequent personal injury case. His only recourse is to be as factual as possible, remembering that actually he may be "deposing" to his future law suit.

Thus defendant lawyers may ascertain the facts of any prior suits brought, hospital and medical treatments, a full past history of plaintiff, and indeed a rating of the particular lawyer involved, and his expert witnesses. Informal investigations of this nature, in the large cities, are "traded" among the members of a cooperative plaintiff's bar, but they do not approach the detail of defendant's information.

22. See § 2.81 et seq., "Discovery", infra.

23. Wallace E. Sedgwick, defense counsel of San Francisco, in a talk before Casualty & Surety Claims As-

Another source which should always be checked into are the local newspapers printed at about the date of the accident, which may always be examined at the public library. The search should not stop here, though, because a newspaper photographer generally takes many more pictures than those which are eventually printed in the newspaper. Often, no pictures may be printed; that does not necessarily mean that none were taken. A visit to the newspaper morgue might uncover some striking photographs. See Figure 6.

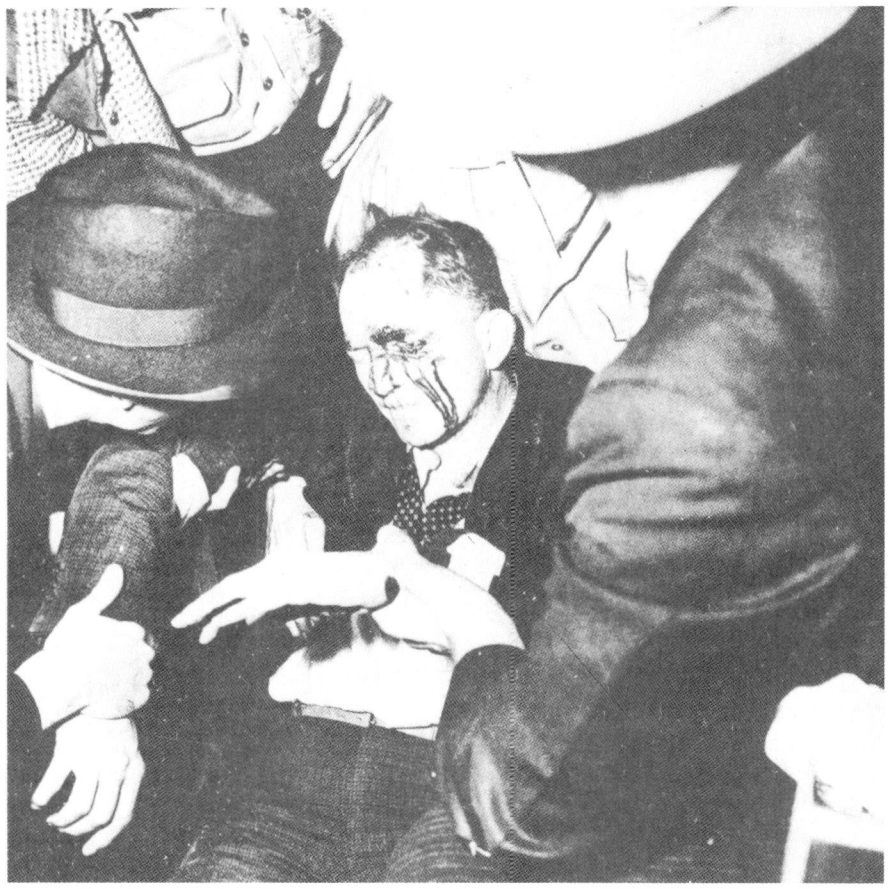

Figure 6. Pain and suffering vividly depicted at a moment the injured man may believe to be his last. Witnesses are at hand and Last Rites are being given. Notice the outstretched hands indicating extreme anguish.

sociation of San Francisco, is reported to have said,

"I have personally several times had the experience of being associated for one reason or another with several of our leading plaintiff's attorneys in the handling of a case. In each instance the plain-

Whether used or not, such pictures often give important clues for other pictures, or investigation leads. Pictures of the physical yard, road, engine, boat, cars, tracks, etc. involved should be in one's files as soon as possible after the accident. A court order will enable one to go onto a party's premises to take such pictures when necessary.

§ 2.53 "On-the-Scene" Photographs in Head-On Collision

On-the-scene photographs played a major role in the successful handling of an automobile accident case handled by attorney *Gerald A. Facchini*.[24] Plaintiffs in the case where injured when the car being driven by defendant's decedent, traveling eastbound, crossed over and into the westbound lanes, resulting in a head-on collision.

The accident occurred on Interstate 90, also known as the Northwest Tollway, a limited access highway leading to and from Chicago. The highway is designed as, and generally used as, a six-lane road, and is divided by a median strip. On the date of the accident, however, the southernmost two travel lanes were being repaved and were therefore closed. To accommodate the flow of traffic going east, the traffic lanes immediately on either side of the median strip were used.

Rubber cones were placed atop double yellow lines to separate the eastbound from the westbound traffic. See Figure 7. The cones were about two feet high, painted yellow, and had a square base. Tires were placed on the bases of the cones to provide more ballast to prevent them from being blown over by the wind generated from the passing traffic.

tiff's investigation was better and more complete than ours. The truth of this situation is generally recognized and is most surprising in view of the far greater resources and experience of the insurance companies in this field. The answer is that the investigators for plaintiff's lawyers handle far fewer cases than do the company claims men doing similar work. The plaintiff's investigator can and does spend far more time on a particular case than is the usual practice by insurance company representatives simply because the claims men do not have sufficient time to completely investigate all aspects of a given case. How often have we all heard a competent claims man say in effect, that he simply did not have sufficient time or personnel to do a particular job the way it should be done at the time it should be done."

24. Gerald A. Facchini, Esquire, Facchini & Minton, 1211 West 22nd Street, Suite 830, Oak Brook, Illinois.

Figure 7. Picture taken shortly after accident had occurred shows skid marks made by plaintiffs' car. The routing of traffic due to construction is clearly demarcated by yellow cones.

The repaving process involved laying asphalt over the old road and paved shoulder surface. This resulted in the raising of the level of the new road and shoulder above that of the median strip. The median was then to be filled to even its height with that of the newly-paved road. The fill work had not yet been completed, and at the time of the accident, a four-to-six inch difference was allowed to exist at the berm point. No barricades or other signs were used to mark the berm differences, even though the contract required barricades to be placed where there was a difference of three or more inches between the "existing shoulder" and the road.

Defendant's decedent was traveling eastbound at less than forty miles per hour. To avoid cones which had fallen over, either from contact with passing cars or because of wind, decedent veered to the right, onto the shoulder. One of her wheels went off the shoulder onto the unpaved, earthen median strip, resulting in the wheel becoming caught in the area of the berm difference. This caused the decedent to lose control of her car, resulting in its crossing over the westbound lanes, where it collided with plaintiff's vehicle.

Figure 8 shows the decedent's car resting upside-down after the impact. Skid marks caused by the vehicle's tires having come into contact with the berm can be seen on the inside of the right front tire. The damage caused to plaintiff's car is shown in Figure 9, which picture was taken shortly before the car was removed.

Figure 8. On-the-scene photograph of decedent's car shows not only extent of damage, but also marks caused by berm can be seen on the inside of the right front tire.

Figure 9. Damage to plaintiff's car is dramatically portrayed as car is pulled away from the accident by tow truck. The effect of such picture can not be duplicated by a picture taken at a later date.

Defendants at trial were the Illinois Tollway, the general contractor in charge of the repaving, and various consulting engineers. Plaintiffs' expert testified that the "reverse flow" concept was unsafe, especially when one considered the condition of the berm and the fallen cones.

The jury awarded Mr. Facchini's clients, husband and wife, $700,000. Decedent's estate also filed suit against these same defendants,[25] and was awarded $400,000. Had it not been for the availability and use of the photos showing the marks caused by the berm, such results very well might not have been achieved.

§ 2.54 Railroad Death Case

In a wrongful death case handled by the author and *William H. DeParcq* in the Hennepin County Court of Minnesota, on-the-scene

---

[25]. William J. Harte, Esquire, 111 West Washington Street, Suite 2025, Chicago, Illinois, was the attorney for decedent's estate in its capacity as plaintiff.

photographs were obtained and utilized to obtain satisfactory results. The accident occurred on the main line track near Bismarck, North Dakota. The deceased was an engineer for defendant's railway at the time of the accident, and was 58 years of age and in excellent health. The accident was caused by a washout of the main tracks.

The investigation, while including a complete history of the deceased and of plaintiff, their earnings, habits, service record and witnesses' statements, a long list of maps and technical drainage information and meteorologists' and Interstate Commerce Commissions reports, hospital records, and physicians' and nurses' statements, contained that which is even more important: the actual pictures taken of the accident while it was occurring and immediately thereafter. See Figures 10 and 11.

Figure 10. The body of a deceased need not be seen to depict the sudden death. Here we see the futility of rescue.

§ 2.55   INTRODUCTION   Pt. 1

Figure 11. Workers digging desperately to attempt the rescue of a victim of an overturned railroad car. Such pictures often can be obtained from newspaper reporters. The jury is entitled to the facts, too.

§ 2.55   Automobile-Truck Accident

Sometimes newspapers will have on-the-scene photographs. Often the investigating police and an occasional onlooker will have captured the unfolding event on film. But whatever the source, these pictures provide the most dramatic, visually effective (yet entirely factual) presentation possible.

This was demonstrated in *State of Indiana v. Thompson*,[26] a case handled by *C. Richard Marshall*, Esquire,[27] his partner *Robert L. Stevenson*, and attorney *Tom G. Jones*.[28] Skillful and effective use of on-the-scene photos played an integral role in a jury award of $1.24 million, the largest personal injury verdict ever obtained to that date in the state of Indiana.

---

26. State of Indiana v. Thompson, —— Ind.App. ——, 385 N.E.2d 198 (1979).

27. C. Richard Marshall, Esquire and Robert L. Stevenson, Esquire, Stevenson & Marshall, Franklin Square, 522 Franklin Street, P.O. Box 427, Columbus, Indiana.

28. Tom G. Jones, Esquire, Jones, Loveall & Coachys, P.O. Box 365, Franklin, Indiana.

Plaintiff therein was driving home one night at about 10:15 p. m., with his girlfriend riding beside him. They were proceeding at about 60–65 miles per hour, and were traveling southbound on a divided four-lane highway. Plaintiff was injured when his car collided with a flat-bed trailer which was being pulled by a tractor, and was blocking an unlighted intersection. The danger was multiplied in this particular case by the fact that a flat-bed trailer of this type has very little side surface to reflect the headlights of an approaching automobile. Plaintiff, because of the lack of proper lighting, was unable to see the slow-moving truck until it was too late.

Due to the force of the impact, plaintiff was trapped inside his car for a time. During this period, photographs were taken of the event as it was happening. Figure 12 shows the car and truck in the position they were in immediately after the accident. Plaintiff's left shoulder is barely visible through the twisted metal. Figure 13 is a photograph taken after the car had been pulled back a few feet. This picture was shown to the jury who with it were able to see for themselves, and thereby experience, the severity of plaintiff's injuries and damages, and his pain and suffering. The award of $1.24 million was upheld on appeal.

Figure 12. Photograph taken of accident before plaintiff had been extricated from car. Plaintiff's left shoulder is barely visible (arrow).

Figure 13. In this picture, the car has been pulled back a few feet. The pain and suffering of plaintiff, still wedged in the car, is dramatically portrayed.

§ 2.56 Tank Explosion Case Report

As was true in the preceding case, use of on-the-scene pictures were instrumental in obtaining the highest verdict ever in the state of Alabama. Attorney *Neal C. Newell* and his partner *Alex W. Newton*, from Birmingham, Alabama,[29] were successful in obtaining a $5 million jury verdict for the death of two men who were killed when a tank exploded. The two victims were welders for a construction company and were putting on the final touches when the tank exploded.

Plaintiffs contended that the explosion occurred when a tanker truck loaded 3,500 gallons of Zylene, a highly-explosive substance, into a nearby tank. As the liquid went in, plaintiffs alleged that vapors therefrom escaped through a vent, settling over the adjoining tank where the two men were working. The explosion was set-off

---

29. Neal C. Newell, Esquire, and Alex W. Newton, Esquire, Hare, Wynn, Newell & Newton, Seventh Floor City Federal Building, Birmingham, Alabama.

when sparks from the welding operation came into contact with the vapors.

Figure 14 is an aerial photograph which was taken while the fire was raging out of control. The fury of the inferno, so clearly seen in the picture, could not be equalled by oral testimony alone. Figure 15 is a shot of the fire showing the closest horizontal tank on which the two decedents were welding the walkways at the time of the initial explosion. The two vertical white tanks to the left are those from which the explosive vapors allegedly escaped.

Figure 14. Aerial photograph taken while fire, caused by storage tank explosion, was raging. This type of picture lets each juror know in no uncertain terms just how devastating the event was.

Figure 15. Photograph taken from the ground identifies tank which had exploded. By the time this picture was taken, the fire and heat had subsided sufficiently to allow a closer inspection of the inferno.

The final photograph, Figure 16, which was taken after the fire was extinguished, shows the tanks and walkway upon which the decedents had been working.

One of the men, a 22-year-old worker, died almost instantly. His 43-year-old colleague ran from the fire with his clothing aflame, and died several hours later. The jury awarded $2.5 million in punitive damages to the mother of the youth, and an equal award was given to the widow of the older worker. This was in accord with the wrongful death statute of Alabama which does not permit compensatory damages in wrongful death actions. The total sum of $5 million represented the highest award to that date—June, 1978—in Alabama.

Figure 16. Ladder upon which two welders had been working can be seen connecting the two tanks after the fire had been put out.

§ 2.57 Personal Injury and Property Damage Caused by Truck

Another example showing the value of on-the-scene photographs is presented by *Leonard M. Ring*, Esquire, a past president of ATLA.[30] In *Kunde v. South Bend Freight Lines, Inc.*,[31] plaintiffs were injured when defendant's southbound semi-truck/trailer rig went off the road at 3:00 a.m., running into and through plaintiff's farmhouse. See Figure 17.

30. Leonard M. Ring, Esquire, 111 West Washington Street, Suite 1333, Chicago, Illinois.

31. Herbert F. and Norma Kunde v. South Bend Freight Lines, Inc., filed May 1, 1979, in the Circuit Court, Cook County, Illinois (# 74L–6761).

Figure 17. Photograph taken shortly after accident occurred shows sharp curve truck, traveling at too high of speed, failed to negotiate. Truck was proceeding from the background to the foreground in picture. Plaintiffs' house may partially be seen to the left.

At the time, plaintiffs were asleep in a second floor bedroom. The truck/trailer combination caromed through the house. The top of the trailer hooked on the first floor ceiling, which was the floor of the plaintiff's bedroom. As the vehicle continued its destructive path, it ripped the first floor ceiling/second floor wall out of its place.

Plaintiffs were thrown from their bed onto the top of the trailer, which they rode out of the house. Somewhere enroute plaintiff-wife fell off the trailer and landed in some debris in the backyard. The fall allegedly caused a spinal cord injury which rendered her a paraplegic.

The incident occurred near a sharp curve in the road. It was foggy on the morning in question, and plaintiffs' contention was that the driver of the rig had been traveling too fast, and due to the heavy fog, did not see the curve in time to navigate it successfully. Defendant originally contended that its vehicle had been cut-off by an oncoming car which was coming around the curve in the wrong lane. After the jury was selected, however, the defendant admitted liability.

On-the-scene photographs were used to show the extent of the destruction caused by the truck and trailer. Figures 18 and 19 show some of the resulting havoc. The photograph appearing in Figure 20 shows the back of the trailer, and clearly and dramatically portrays the extensive damage caused to the house. The floor of plaintiffs' bedroom can be seen in this picture. Mr. Ring had a big blow-up made of this picture, and used it on opening statement, throughout the testimony of certain witnesses, and during closing argument.

Figure 18. On-the-scene photograph shows destruction of house, and efforts being undertaken by local rescue squad.

Figure 19. Pictures such as these give the jury as good a view as had they been among the gatherers who congregated shortly after the accident occurred. Through scenes like this which show the accident in progress, a jury is able almost to "feel" the vibrations and hear the sounds of wood being ripped from its place as the truck barreled through the house.

Figure 20. This picture was blown-up and used to show jurors extent of devastation caused to house by truck. View is from front yard of plaintiffs, looking through house to back of truck (arrow).

Plaintiff-wife, a 54-year-old housewife, was awarded $1,133,000 for her injuries, which included a traumatic paralysis at T-12. Plaintiff-husband was awarded $116,000 for his injuries, which consisted primarily of a fracture of the left scapula and five broken ribs.

§§ 2.58–2.60 are reserved for supplementary material.

G. USE OF "ON-THE-SCENE" PHOTOGRAPHS

§ 2.61 Introduction

On-the-scene pictures can be invaluable in preserving evidence, proving liability and showing how the mishap might have occurred. A good lawyer makes every effort to get pictures of the scene taken as soon as possible. In this section, we shall consider the use of on-the-scene pictures and pictures taken shortly after the accident as a means of proving liability or impeaching a defendant's testimony.

§ 2.62 Use for Impeachment

Unscrupulous defendants can make swift investigative work not simply helpful but actually vital to a successful plaintiff's suit. In *Murphy v. L & J Press Corporation*, defendants falsely claimed that a safety guard had been installed on the offending machine *prior* to the accident. Luckily, plaintiff's attorney, *Vincent Igoe* of St. Louis, Missouri,[32] had visited the accident site on the day after the incident with a photographer. He was therefore able to preserve the evidence as it was at the time of the accident, and his pictures dramatically exposed defendant's false testimony at trial.

The case involved an industrial accident which occurred in 1972. The plaintiff had placed his hand into the point of operation of a punch press and had lost four fingers. The press, when manufactured, did not provide point-of-operation protection. Plaintiff's experts testified that it was both desirable and feasible for the manufacturer to have provided such protection. The case was tried on the theory of strict liability.

Mr. Igoe and a photographer went to the accident site the day following the incident. Photographs of the machine were "pirated by unlawful trespass." At trial, the manufacturer and employer insisted that a guard installed after the accident (Figure 21) had been on the machine when plaintiff was injured.

Figure 22, however, shows the machine as it appeared the day after the accident. The circle indicates where the guard was later installed; clearly, there is neither a guard nor any holes drilled to mount the guard. To duplicate the conditions existing on the day of the ac-

---

32. Vincent M. Igoe, Esquire, Igoe & Igoe, 800 International Building, 722 Chestnut Street, St. Louis, Missouri.

Figure 21. Defendants insisted that a guard had been present on the punch press at the time of the injury. Investigation by plaintiff's lawyer Vincent Igoe demonstrated the falsity of this claim.

cident, then, it was necessary to remove the guard completely, as shown in Figure 23.

Mr. Igoe blew up the photographs of the punch press to a size of 3 by 5 feet so that the jury could see the pictures from anywhere in the courtroom. Evidence was given as to the dates the pictures were

Figure 22. This picture, taken the day after the accident by plaintiff's lawyer and his investigator, clearly shows that there was no guard at the time of the accident (circle).

taken. The photographs made plaintiff's case, as the pictures were graphic illustrations of defendant's incorrect testimony. The jury responded with a large compensatory and, not surprisingly, a huge punitive judgment.

Figure 23. To duplicate the dangerous condition existing at the time plaintiff was injured, the guard was removed for inspection by the jury. Had plaintiff's lawyer and his investigator not acted as quickly in taking photographs of the machine, it is not improbable that plaintiff would have received an adverse verdict.

§ 2.63 To Show Negligence

Attorney *Jerry L. Sumpter* [33] of Cheboygan, Michigan, took advantage of his early involvement in a personal injury case to win

---

33. Jerry L. Sumpter, Esquire, Sumpter & Loznak, 11118 Straits Highway, P.O. Box 286, Cheboygan, Michigan.

§ 2.63   INTRODUCTION   Pt. 1

a large verdict in *Neil v. DMH, et al.* His on-the-scene photographs so persuasively demonstrated defendant's ineptitude that the jury awarded his client $304,250 against a defendent whose negligence only aggravated a relatively minor injury.

The case involved a journeyman carpenter who was first injured at an automobile manufacturing company when he fell against a car bumper, traumatizing his sterno clavicular joint. He went on full worker's compensation and began a course of weight exercise programs to strengthen the muscles in the offended joint area.

A year later plaintiff purchased a 14' x 65' mobile home from defendant. The home was to be equipped with a gas furnace and LP gas appliances. Defendant's subsidiary hooked up the gas tanks one day when no one was present. The gas lines were connected to the mobile home without turning on the gas or checking for leaks in the system.

When plaintiff brought some friends over to see the mobile home, he turned on the gas tanks and stepped inside. One of the friends lit a cigarette near the furnace area, causing a low-grade explosion. Plaintiff suffered only first-degree burns at the time, but noticed that he began to lose ground in his exercise program. He had surgery to remove the meniscus from the joint in an effort to stop a clicking sensation there and later had an inch of his clavical removed. His condition caused him discomfort when lifting heavy weights or working overhead, but otherwise plaintiff functioned normally. He claimed at trial that the explosion had aggravated and accelerated his condition.

Mr. Sumpter had been contacted several hours after the accident, and within 18 hours he had an expert on the scene examining the mobile home with a photographer. The cause of the explosion was obvious: somewhere along the assembly line at the factory, an oil furnace had been substituted for the gas furnance called for by the plans. Although the system was changed, no one had bothered to cap the gas line pipe leading into the mobile home. The gas had flowed out of the pipe through the fresh-air intake of the oil furnace and into the home, where it was ignited by the cigarette.

With the expert already on the scene, he could direct the photographer to take precisely the pictures he needed to present a persuasive argument. Figure 24 convincingly depicts the ludicrous but tragic situation at the motor home. The pipe leading to the half-inch elbow was the offending gas line. There was no plug or pipe compound at the elbow opening, though pipe compound was clearly used on all other joints. There was no doubt that gas could easily escape into the air vent.

Figure 24. This picture, taken shortly after the explosion in a mobile home depicts the dangerous condition which led to the tragedy. Plaintiff's expert was on the scene 18 hours after the explosion occurred.

The furnace/stove area is depicted in Figure 25. This photograph demonstrates that the home was equipped with an oil furnace, rather than the gas type that would be used with the pipe in Figure 24. It also shows the high concentration area of the fire, which helped plaintiff to establish that the fire had its origin in the furnace

Figure 25. This photograph shows that the mobile home was equipped with an oil furnace, not a gas type which would be used with the pipe in the preceding figure.

area where the alleged defect was located. Finally, the expert used a transparency to further cement his case. Although it was supposedly a print-out of the home's gas piping, *none* of the lines going to the furnace was present in plaintiff's unit.

These exhibits had a dramatic and gratifying effect on the jury, which could not quite conceive of such gross incompetence as that exhibited in Figure 24. Their astonishment and disbelief were quite evident from their actions: some even stood up to look over the jury rail at the exhibits. Attorney Sumpter credits this extraordinary documentary evidence, attributable to his swift action in the first hours after the accident, with the award of $304,250.

§ 2.64 To Show Cause of a Fire

Attorney *Robert B. Wallis* [34] reports the case of *Buning v. Reynolds Metals Co. et al.*, filed in Harris County, Texas, which he tried with Attorney *Buddy Hanby*. This case exemplifies the value of an immediate investigation and the use of immediate pictures to prove the cause of a fire.

The body of decedent, a doctor, was discovered in the bedroom of his apartment by a friend. The apartment was on fire at the time the body was found. The autopsy report revealed no significant burning and reported the cause of death as an unusually high saturation of carbon monoxide poisoning.

The fire was superbly investigated by the Houston Fire Department—Arson Division. Through the diligent work of these expert investigators, the fire was traced to an electrical outlet on the south wall of the bedroom. See Figure 26.

Figure 26. Attorneys Robert B. Wallis and Buddy Hanby, Houston, Texas, utilized the reports and findings of the Houston Fire Department's investigation. The fire was traced to an electrical outlet on the south wall of the bedroom.

34. Robert B. Wallis, Esquire; Buddy Hanby, Esquire, Haynes & Fullenweider, 2701 Fannin, Houston, Texas.

After conducting its investigation, the Arson Division theorized that the fire had been caused by the aluminum-wired outlet in the bedroom. Pictures of the debris were taken to support this conclusion. Among them was Figure 27, a photograph of the exposed outlet.

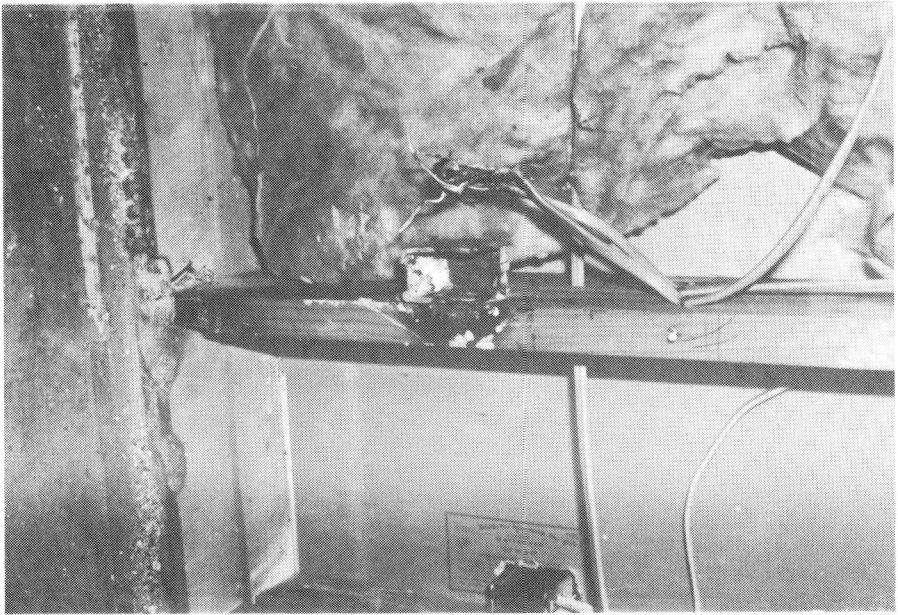

Figure 27. The aluminum-wired outlet, after the sheetrock had been removed. Plaintiff's lawyers took advantage of an early investigation by the local fire department, and its conclusion that the fire had been caused by the outlet.

From this picture, it can be clearly seen that the fire started *inside* the outlet and burned out, and not conversely. This picture was one of the strongest pieces of demonstrative evidence presented to the jury during the trial.

Approximately one year after suit was filed, the apartment owners made a settlement with plaintiffs for $85,000.00 and delivering their expert. The apartment owner's expert, a consulting engineer, had performed an extensive fire investigation beginning twenty-four hours after the fire and continued for several days. This expert independently reached the same conclusion as the Arson Division: The fire started from the aluminum-wired outlet, not from other sources. The apartment owner's expert ultimately became plaintiff's chief witness at trial.

On the first day of trial, plaintiffs cleared the deck by settling with most defendants, leaving only the manufacturer and installer. Although the suit prayed for $2,000,000.00 in damages, plaintiffs offered to settle for $230,000.00. The lower demand was justified in view of the fact that the widow had remarried seven months after the incident and divorced shortly before trial, and under Texas law, these facts could be shown at trial. Furthermore, the children were 17 and 19 years old at the time of the trial. Defendants rejected the demand, giving a counter-offer of $150,000.00.

During the three-week trial, numerous experiments, both in and out of court, were performed to illustrate such diverse points as comparing characteristics of different brands of aluminum wire among themselves and against copper wire on the one hand, and to show the degradation time of a plastic face-plate on the other. See Section 56.18, infra.

The jury found for plaintiffs, and awarded a total of $1.5 million. As is true of most complex products liability cases, the instant case resolved into a battle of experts. Here, the deciding factor proved to be the photographs taken by the Arson Division in making its investigation.

Aluminum wire cases are controversial and will likely continue to present themselves for at least another quarter of a century. They are extremely expensive to prosecute from the plaintiff's standpoint, but as the author has stressed countless times, it does cost a large sum on most large modern trials, but usually they are well worth the cost.

In these aluminum wire cases, and there will be many before aluminum wire is universally approved or discarded, plaintiff's lawyer should call or write directly to one of the lawyers who handled an aluminum wire case reported in this book.

§§ 2.65–2.70 are reserved for supplementary material.

H. "OFFICIAL" PROCEEDINGS AND INQUESTS BEFORE TRIAL

§ 2.71 Introduction

The jury trial may actually be the second, third, or even fourth "trial" in the lawsuit. Criminal preliminary hearings, coroners' inquests, official investigations, administrative proceedings, and the several depositions may of themselves comprise a "trial." A single extensive deposition, of itself, may be almost an entire trial.

In the preliminary hearing of the criminal case, there may be an actual court trial prior to the jury trial, with some evidence being produced thereat. The transcript at such preliminary hearing may be of inestimable value in the subsequent civil case. Likewise, coroners' inquests, proceedings for violation before administrative boards, workmen's compensation hearings, and all proceedings in which testimony is preliminarily taken may be the basis for the subsequent trial the "main event."

While such proceedings are referred to as "preliminary" hearings, they are that in name only.[35] They deserve, and should be given, just as much attention, preparation, and care as the actual trial. In fact, failure to prepare fully and properly at the preliminary stage may cause severe damage to the case that no amount of later preparation could expunge. With the witnesses being sworn and under oath, testimony adduced in these "preliminary hearings" is generally irrevocable, and may establish for all times the liability or lack of liability in the subsequent "main case."

Some civil defense lawyers, as a rule of thumb, instruct the potential civil defendant, the actual defendant in the criminal case, to refuse to testify at the coroner's inquest or similar proceeding. The author believes this to be a mistake since the refusal to testify, under an asserted "constitutional" privilege, may be shown in the subsequent civil case and is damaging evidence. In *Nelson v. Southern Pacific Co.*,[36] the California Supreme Court ruled that the trial court erroneously refused to permit plaintiff's counsel to question the engineer of a train as to whether he had refused to testify at the coroner's inquest on the basis of invoking the privilege against self-incrimination. The court therein stated: "Such a question was proper for

---

35. Slotnick v. Hilleboe, 38 Misc.2d 1039, 237 N.Y.S.2d 406 (1963) ("The determination of the Coroner and the entries on the death certificate as to his findings may not be disturbed unless it is established that the Coroner's decision or determination was arbitrary and an abuse of discretion").

36. Nelson v. Southern Pacific Co., 8 Cal.2d 648, 67 P.2d 682 (1937).

impeachment purposes since the claim of privilege gives rise to an inference bearing upon the credibility of his statement of lack of negligence upon his part.[37]

This evidence will be produced. Defendant's counsel, following the above procedure of non-testimony, only temporizes and is penalized in most states by the subsequent permissible reference to and comment upon his failure to testify.

The author has followed the procedure of subpoenaing for deposition, in the civil suit, a defendant who is at that time under information or indictment in a criminal charge growing out of the civil suit or, stated conversely, the civil suit which has grown out of the criminal case. Generally, defendant's counsel instructs the client to refuse to testify in the deposition because he then is presently a potential defendant in a criminal case and anything that he says "may be used against him." This refusal again so to testify in the deposition may be shown on the subsequent civil case and is most damaging to defendant therein. The author believes this is a serious mistake for defendant's counsel to urge upon his client.

Unless it fairly appears that a defendant charged in a criminal case on preliminary hearing will not be held to answer, the author deems it good criminal law procedure to expand the preliminary hearing into a searching deposition. Thus, when counsel for a defendant who is charged with having committed a crime believes his client will be held to answer regardless of the testimony addressed, the committing magistrate not being held to the same quantum of proof that the triers of fact in the subsequent "main trial" must adhere to,[38] he should force the prosecution to call all the witnesses, or call them himself. In this situation immediately above, when representing a criminal defendant, I use the complete process of the criminal court to call every witness upon whom the prosecution may likely depend, for their case in chief in the higher court. Thus, even though the prosecution puts on only one witness to make out a *prima facie* case for a holding to the higher court, in the lower court, I subpoena all the police officers, all of the defendant's witnesses with all of their

---

37. 8 Cal.2d at 654–55. This decision was recently reaffirmed by the California Supreme Court. Shepherd v. Superior Court, 17 Cal.3d 107, 130 Cal.Rptr. 257, 550 P.2d 161 (1976) (Wherein the court stated that "when a witness' invocation of the privilege in a prior proceeding gives rise to an inference bearing upon his credibility on an issue in a later proceeding, no infringement of the privilege results from a disclosure of that fact").

38. Gerstein v. Pugh, 420 U.S. 103, 95 S.Ct. 854, 43 L.Ed.2d 54 (1975), on remand 511 F.2d 528 (5th Cir.), on remand 422 F.Supp. 498 (S.D.Fla.) ("Probable cause" is the governing standard at preliminary hearing).

§ 2.71　　　　　　　　INTRODUCTION　　　　　　　　Pt. 1

statements, and fully depose every witness, "milking" the prosecution's case in a manner I might not be privileged to do by deposition.[39]

This is a most important procedure available to learn the entire facts and strength of the prosecution's case. Physical exhibits, statements, and even hearsay may be adduced. I make no objection to relevancy of evidence, hearsay or any testimony a witness wants to tell the Judge in a case that is predestined to subsequent trial on its merits.

§ 2.72　Personal Injury With Criminal Charges

On the Continent today, civil and criminal cases can be tried together. Of course, this makes for speedier trials and saves a lot of time. Much could be said for adopting this procedure in this country, once we could get over certain constitutional hurdles, such as the privilege against self-incrimination, evidence obtained through illegal searches and seizures, etc.

But what of a defendant whose tortious act is also a crime? If defendant *pleads* guilty, this "admission" can be used in the subsequent civil trial.[40] If he is *found* guilty by criminal trial, generally the result cannot be used in the later civil trial.[41]

---

39. Jennings v. Superior Court, 66 Cal.2d 867, 59 Cal.Rptr. 440, 428 P.2d 304 (1967) (Trial court limited cross-examination of arresting officers at preliminary hearing for illegal possession of narcotics. California Supreme Court reversed, stating that such cross-examination should be given "wide latitude, particularly in cases involving a 'witness against a defendant in a criminal prosecution.'"); Johnson v. Strickland, 300 So.2d 50 (Fla.App.1974) ("We should make it plain that the county judge has ample authority to prevent the preliminary hearing from becoming a discovery proceeding, but that authority should not be exercised by the curtailment of legitimate inquiry into the ground for belief that the defendant should be held answerable to the charge. Let us assume a clear-cut but improbable hypothetical case: Given the testimony we have quoted above, suppose that the defendant then offered to produce Detective Smith to show that at the time of the alleged offense the defendant was in fact in custody. There is no reason why the defendant should await ultimate trial to prove that she is the victim of mistaken identity. We are aware that the courts are busy and that preliminary hearings should not be prolonged unnecessarily. So long, however, as the inquiry is directed in good faith to the issue of probable cause, Rule 3.131(f) does afford the defendant the right to cross-examine the state's witnesses and offer his own.").

But see State v. Hudson, 295 N.C. 427, 245 S.E.2d 686 (1978) ("A probable cause hearing may afford the opportunity for a defendant to discover the strengths and weaknesses of the State's case. However, discovery is not the purpose for such a hearing.").

40. State Farm Mut. Auto. Ins. Co. v. Worthington, 405 F.2d 683 (8th Cir. 1968) (Plea of guilty is admissible as an admission against interest, but is

41. See note 41 on page 115.

What if the civil plaintiff seeks to elicit information from the defendant before the criminal trial? Is this, too, privileged? Further, suppose defendant invokes the fifth amendment. Can this be shown in the subsequent civil trial? We have seen that it can be brought in at the civil trial.

Generally, a defendant may not shield himself from a pretrial examination as a whole by asserting the fifth amendment. Instead, the privilege against self-incrimination is available only when a specific objectionable question is asked.[42]

This very question arose recently in *Starr v. Bailey*, handled and reported by attorney *James L. Lowry* of Danville, Indiana.[43]

The decedent, Ralph W. Starr, was proceeding westbound on U. S. Highway 40 in Hendricks County, Indiana. Defendant was traveling east on the same highway when he turned abruptly in front of Starr's car. Starr was killed as a result of the accident. See Figure 28.

not conclusive and defendant may offer his explanation of plea and his version of occurrence that occasioned criminal charge); Teitelbaum Furs, Inc. v. Dominion Ins. Co., 58 Cal.2d 601, 25 Cal.Rptr. 559, 375 P.2d 439 (1962), cert. denied 372 U.S. 966, 83 S.Ct. 1091, 10 L.Ed.2d 130; Arenstein v. California State Bd. of Pharmacy, 265 Cal.App.2d 179, 71 Cal.Rptr. 357 (1968); Gregorie v. Hartford Acc. & Indem. Co., 348 So.2d 186 (La.App. 1977), writ denied 350 So.2d 1210, 1213 (La.).

41. See, e. g., Tidwell v. Booker, 290 N.C. 98, 225 S.E.2d 816 (1976), quoting from Durham Bank & Trust Co. v. Pollard, 256 N.C. 77, 123 S.E.2d 104 (1961) (" 'The general and traditional rule supported by a great majority of the jurisdictions is that, in the absence of a statutory provision to the contrary, evidence of a conviction and of a judgment therein, or of an acquittal, rendered in a criminal prosecution, is not admissible in evidence in a purely civil action to establish the truth of the facts on which the verdict of guilty or of acquittal was rendered, or when there is a verdict of acquittal to constitute a bar to a subsequent civil action based on the same facts. While the same facts may be involved in two cases, one civil and the other criminal, the parties are necessarily different, for, whereas one action is prosecuted by an individual, the other is maintained by the state.' ").

42. United States v. Lustig, 16 F.R.D. 138 (S.D.N.Y.1954) (Court held that defendant's assertion of privilege against self-incrimination was premature and furnished no ground to vacate the proposed examination. "The time to assert the plea is when specific questions are put to the defendant during the course of the examination.")

43. James L. Lowry, Esquire, Kendall, Stevenson, Lowry & Wood, 1 S. Washington Street, Danville, Indiana.

Figure 28. Attorney James L. Lowry, Danville, Indiana, exhibits photographic display of accident prepared for use in settlement negotiations and for possible trial. Expert use of the discovery procedure by Mr. Lowry while defendant stood accused of criminal charges arising from same accident resulted in a settlement for over $2 million.

It was contended that Bailey was driving without headlights and was having difficulty in seeing through his windshield due to the fact that the windshield was accumulating ice. A witness testified to these occurrences and conditions, and that there was no excessive speed.

Defendant Bailey was arrested at the scene of the accident for operating a vehicle while under the influence of intoxicating beverages and on a breathalizer test tested out at .15% blood alcohol. A blood-alcohol test was taken of the decedent at the scene of the accident, and the decedent tested out at .2% blood alcohol.

Starr was 34 years of age at the time of his death, and left surviving him his wife and one minor child. He had been employed earning $34,000 a year, and was also raising Arabian horses.

Plaintiff's lawyers immediately filed suit and sent interrogatories, oral and written, for defendant, who contended through his lawyer that he did not have to reply until after the criminal trial. All questions were resolved before trial and the case was settled for a structured settlement worth $2,049,472. The case is noteworthy as it exemplifies the diligent efforts of plaintiff's lawyer in seeking "official" information; i. e., interrogatories while defendant is still a criminal defendant. Such procedure is useful in pushing settlement even if all the information is not obtained, and certainly worries the defendant.

§ 2.73 Utilizing Criminal Investigations

In many automobile accidents, the Highway Patrol or local police department will often conduct an investigation to determine whether either or both parties were at fault, and if so, whether a citation should issue. Not as often, a federal agency will intervene and conduct its own investigation.

Attorney *C. Robert Beltz* of Flint, Michigan [44] reports a rather unusual motor vehicle accident case [45] he handled in which he skillfully and successfully utilized numerous pictures and other material obtained through an investigation performed by the Department of Transportation. His creativity and ingenuity were rewarded with a settlement of $1.6 million.

The accident occurred when a tractor pulling a 1963 Fruehof tank trailer carrying 39,000 pounds of flammable liquid petroleum gas fell from an interstate overpass. The vehicle landed immediately behind a car being driven by the 18 year old plaintiff. Her mother, a passenger in the car, also sustained severe burn injuries.

The Department of Transportation conducted an investigation, and Mr. Beltz was able to obtain many of the photographs the Department had taken. Figure 29.

[44] C. Robert Beltz, Esquire, Hick, Beltz, Behm & Nickola, 6th Floor, Genesee Bank Building, Flint, Michigan.

[45] Gearing v. Aero Liquid Transit, Inc., filed in the Circuit Court for the County of Genesee, Michigan (# 78–47085NI).

§ 2.73 INTRODUCTION Pt. 1

Photograph # 17

View of Bridge Parapet from right side of bridge

Photograph # 18

View of Exit Ramp from Northbound I 75 to Miller Road from bridge

Photograph # 19

View of Bridge Deck – Final portion of driver cab and body of Aero driver

Photograph # 20

View of Exit Ramp showing merge to Northbound I 75 to left, merge to Miller Road Exit Ramp to right (Note fire damage to overhead signing)

Figure 29. Official criminal investigations by governmental bodies can produce extensive, well-documented pictures which plaintiff's attorney can use in the civil case. Here, attorney C. Robert Beltz obtained photos from the Department of Transportation, which had conducted its own investigation.

Due to the spectacular nature of the crash, the local newspapers sent reporters to the scene. Attorney Beltz managed to obtain many of these pictures which he utilized during settlement negotiations. Figure 30. The local sheriff's department also conducted an on-the-scene investigation of the accident, and photos taken by that department were also obtained and utilized by Mr. Beltz.

Figure 30. Newspapers and local police and sheriff's departments are also major sources of pictures and information. Plaintiff's lawyer may avoid the expense of conducting his own investigation if he obtains the results of "official" investigations.

§ 2.73   INTRODUCTION

Many cases are investigated by local police or fire departments, and sometimes state and federal agencies.[46] Plaintiff's lawyer may be able to take advantage of these investigations and reports, as did Mr. Beltz, which may be so complete as to make an independent investigation unnecessary.

46. The trial lawyer should make every effort to learn what agencies may be involved in a particular case, and whether they have made or intend to make an investigation in his case. It is quite possible that a governmental body will perform so complete of an investigation that plaintiff's lawyer will not have to perform one himself.

§§ 2.74–2.80 are reserved for supplementary material.

I. DISCOVERY

Library References:
C.J.S. Federal Civil Procedure § 526.
West's Key No. Digests, Federal Civil Procedure ⚞1261 et seq.
Wright & Miller, Federal Practice and Procedure: Civil, § 2001 et seq.

§ 2.81 In General

Perhaps the most significant "revolution" in legal practice during the last quarter-century has been the widespread adoption among the states (following the lead of the federal courts) of liberal rules and techniques of discovery.[47] Today, the availability of procedures such as depositions, interrogatories, requests for admissions, and motions for inspection guarantee in actual practice the philosophy of this book: a full disclosure by all parties of the facts before trial, so that a justiciable settlement may be achieved by counsel without recourse to the court or, failing this, that the verdict will be one based on fact, and not on confusion or surprise.

A means is now available to assure that litigation can be conducted "with all of the cards on the table." "The sporting theory of justice," which unfortunately in the past has so often horrified the layman and, perhaps unconsciously, delighted the lawyer in his own esoteric game, is abolished, at least to counsel vigilant in adopting the new procedure.[48] As expressed by Justice Douglas in *United States v. Proctor & Gamble Co.*:[49] "Modern instruments of discovery serve a useful purpose . . . . They together with pretrial procedures make a trial less a game of blind man's bluff and more a fair contest with the basic issues and facts disclosed to the fullest practicable extent."

It is no longer a valid objection that counsel's discovery proceedings may constitute a "fishing expedition," if there appears any reasonable possibility that there be fish in the pond. The modern scope of "relevance" in discovery proceedings is considerably broader than the admissibility requirements of evidence at trial. "Relevancy of

---

47. See Wright & Miller, Federal Practice & Procedure: Civil § 2002.

48. See Greyhound Corp. v. Superior Court, 56 Cal.2d 355, 15 Cal.Rptr. 90, 364 P.2d 266 (1961) (Peters, J.: "Certainly, it can be said, that the legislature intended to take the 'game' element out of trial preparation while yet retaining the adversary nature of the trial itself. One of the principal purposes of discovery was to do away 'with the sporting theory of litigation—namely, surprise at the trial.' ").

49. 356 U.S. 677, 78 S.Ct. 983, 2 L.Ed. 2d 1077, 1082 (1958); Hickman v. Taylor, 329 U.S. 495, 507, 67 S.Ct. 385, 91 L.Ed. 451 (1947); Greyhound Corp. v. Superior Court, supra, n. 48.

the subject matter" encompasses all matters which "will aid in a party's preparation for trial." [50] It is generally recognized that "no precise or universal test of relevancy is furnished by the law," [51] and that "the question must be determined in each case according to the teachings of reason and judicial experience." [52] The courts have squarely held, however, that substantial leeway is to be granted in discovery proceedings. The California Supreme Court put litigants on notice with the following language: "[I]n accordance with the liberal policies underlying the discovery procedures, doubts as to relevance should generally be resolved in favor of permitting discovery . . . . Given this very liberal and flexible standard of relevancy, a party attempting to show that a court abused its discretion in finding material relevant for purposes of discovery bears an extremely heavy burden. An appellate court cannot reverse a trial court's grant of discovery under a "relevancy" attack unless it concludes that the answers sought by a given line of questioning cannot as a reasonable possibility lead to the discovery of admissible evidence or be helpful in preparation for trial." [53]

The First Circuit Court of Appeals remarked of the federal rule that it "apparently envisions generally unrestrictive access to sources of information, and the courts have so interpreted it." [54]

Reversal of a verdict is rarely granted on grounds of improper discovery. While extraordinary writs are theoretically available to review discovery orders before proceeding to trial,[55] they are uniformly discouraged. In fact, the California Supreme Court has urged that the writ be withheld even in cases where the trial court's ruling appears to be erroneous: "The prerogative writs have been used frequently to review interim orders in discovery cases [citations]. But this does not mean that these discretionary writs will or should issue

50. Pacific Tel. & Tel. Co. v. Superior Court, 2 Cal.3d 161, 84 Cal.Rptr. 718, 465 P.2d 854 (1970); Cox v. Du Pont de Nemours & Co., 38 F.R.D. 396 (D.C.S.C.1965) ("Fortunately, in the search for the ultimate truth, the Federal Courts, blessed with the rules of discovery, are not shackled with strict interpretations of relevancy").

51. Regents of Univ. of California v. Superior Court, 200 Cal.App.2d 787, 794, 19 Cal.Rptr. 568 (1962), quoting Moody v. Peirano, 4 Cal.App. 411, 88 P. 380 (1906).

52. Patton v. Southern Bell Tel. & Tel. Co., 38 F.R.D. 428 (N.D.Ga.1965); Broadway & Ninety-Sixth St. Realty Co. v. Loew's Inc., 21 F.R.D. 347 (S.D.N.Y.1958).

53. Pacific Tel. & Tel. Co. v. Superior Court, 2 Cal.3d 161, 84 Cal.Rptr. 718, 465 P.2d 854 (1970).

54. Horizons Titanium Corp. v. Norton Co., 290 F.2d 421, 425 (1st Cir. 1961).

55. Greyhound Corp. v. Superior Court, 56 Cal.2d 355, 15 Cal.Rptr. 90, 364 P.2d 266 (1961); Singer v. Superior Court, 54 Cal.2d 318, 5 Cal.Rptr. 697, 353 P.2d 305 (1960); Dowell v. Superior Court, 47 Cal.2d 483, 304 P.2d 1009 (1956).

as of course in all cases where this court may be of the opinion that the interim order of the trial court was erroneous. In most such cases, as is true of most other interim orders, the parties must be relegated to a review of the order on appeal from the final judgment. As inadequate as such review may be in some cases, the prerogative writs should only be used in discovery matters to review questions of first impression that are of general importance to the trial courts and to the profession, and where general guidelines can be laid down for future cases." [56]

Although the liberal application of discovery techniques can be said to have removed the "sporting element" from the litigation process, it should not be assumed that the *adversary* nature of trial practice has been in any measure diminished.[57] Rather, the effect of liberal discovery has been to broaden the arena for exercise of adversarial expertise. As noted by one commentator: "The rules simply develop discovery, which has its antecedents in English chancery practice, into an efficient technique for fact ascertainment, to take its place in the common law's arsenal along with the advocate's other efficient weapons such as testimony in open court, cross-examination, impeachment, forensic skill, and mastery of legal principles." [58] Besides affording counsel greater latitude in probing for facts, the discovery process allows counsel, through deposition proceedings, to fully prepare for examination and cross-examination in the court room. The memorialized record of testimony deposed under oath, in the hands of a skillful practitioner, can be a devastating instrument of cross-examination of a witness whose testimony is more creative than genuine. By introduction of a prior deposition into the record, the testimony of a witness who is unavailable at time of trial, through death or otherwise, may be presented to the trier of fact. Under the Federal rules, the deposition of a witness who is greater than 100 miles distant from the place of trial may be introduced into evidence.[59]

---

56. Oceanside Union Sch. Dist. v. Superior Court, 58 Cal.2d 180, 186, n. 4, 23 Cal.Rptr. 375, 373 P.2d 439 (1962). Followed in: Associated Brewers Distributing Co. v. Superior Court, 65 Cal.2d 583, 55 Cal.Rptr. 772, 422 P.2d 332 (1967). But note: Roberts v. Superior Court, 9 Cal.3d 330, 107 Cal. Rptr. 309, 508 P.2d 309 (1973) (Writ available when party asserts that compelling discovery would violate a privilege).

57. See Hickman v. Taylor, 329 U.S. 495, 67 S.Ct. 385, 91 L.Ed. 451 (1958) ("[A] common law trial is and always should be an adversary proceeding. Discovery was hardly intended to enable a learned professional to perform his functions either without wits or on wits borrowed from the adversary.").

58. Louisell, Discovery and Pretrial, 36 Minn.L.Rev. 633, 639 (1952).

59. FRCP Rule 32(a)(3)(B). See Wright & Miller, Federal Practice and Procedure: Civil § 2141 et seq.

§ 2.81   INTRODUCTION   Pt. 1

This rule affords counsel the opportunity to utilize the testimony of an expert who would be inconvenienced if required first to reserve an extended schedule of availability for an uncertain trial date, then to travel to a distant forum to give evidence. The expert may be deposed at his convenience in his own office and his testimony subsequently read to the jury.

Although the many benefits of modern discovery practice to the litigation process are undisputed, it may be admitted that, like any legal procedure, discovery devices are open to abuse by practitioners unencumbered by ethical restraints in strategy and tactics.[60] The principal form of abuse is to employ lengthy and unnecessary discovery as a means to harass and preoccupy the adversary, while inflicting significant expense of time and money. A lawyer whose case has passed the pleading stage may find his desk literally swamped with interminable stock interrogatory forms, designed and propounded to impede rather than facilitate the fact finding process. Protective devices do, of course, exist, primarily in the form of protective court orders.[61] The California statute allows the court to make any order "which justice requires to protect the party or witness from annoyance, embarrassment, or oppression."[62] In addition, the Federal rule wisely provides for protection from discovery which imposes undue burden and expense.[63]

§ 2.82 Discovering Demonstrative Evidence

Through discovery, it is often possible to obtain crucial demonstrative evidence which clearly shows that a component was defective, and that defendant had reason to know, or did in fact know, of its defectiveness. Attorney *W. W. Watkins* of Houston, Texas[64] reports the case of *Hopkins v. General Motors Corp.* which clearly illustrates this occurrence. The facts of the case are:

Plaintiff, a seventeen-year-old, purchased new a Chevrolet pick-up truck. The truck came equipped with a four barrel quadrajet carburetor. After he had driven the vehicle about 25,000 miles, plaintiff replaced said carburetor with a new Holly carburetor.

---

60. Court rules commonly provide protections for discovery abuses; see e.g. FRCP § 26(c) (protective orders), and 30(d) (motion to terminate or limit examination).

61. FRCP § 26(c). See Wright & Miller, Federal Practice and Procedure: Civil § 2035 et seq.

62. CCP § 2019(b).

63. FRCP § 26(c). See Wright & Miller, Federal Practice and Procedure: Civil § 2035 et seq.

64. W. W. Watkins, Esquire, Kronzer, Abraham & Watkins, 800 Commerce Street, Houston, Texas. The appeal of the instant case was handled by Mr. Watkins' partner, W. James Kronzer, Esquire.

Shortly thereafter plaintiff learned that the engine would not accommodate a Holly, thus he reinstalled the original one.

Admittedly, plaintiff had taken some shortcuts when he reinstalled the original carburetor. Within three or four days after having put the original piece of equipment back into the engine, plaintiff was approaching a sharp curve on a narrow dirt road. As he reached the turn, plaintiff depressed the accelerator pedal, it being his intention to let up on the gas pedal as he was about to round the curve. However, when he removed his foot from the pedal, rather than slowing, the truck continued to proceed at a faster rate of speed. This resulted in his losing control of the truck, which then overturned, breaking his neck.

An examination of the carburetor later revealed that the lockout pin and lockout lever were jammed, thus causing the rear barrels to be partially open to the extent that the engine would be programmed to reach a speed of 80 miles per hour or greater. See figure 31.

Figure 31. Arrow points to jammed lockout pin and lever. Defendant denied that its tests proved this could happen. Exemplary discovery by plaintiff's attorney W. W. Watkins demonstrated otherwise.

Defendant General Motors contended that the quadrajet carburetor was constructed and designed in such a manner that a jamming of the lockout pin and the lockout lever would be a physical impossibility. Defendant's engineers took the position that the cause of the malfunction was due to plaintiff's not having reinstalled the carburetor properly, in that he had done 12 things incorrectly. Among the procedures plaintiff had not done correctly were: He had placed the thermostatic coil cover on backwards, and in a raised position; the lockout pin had been sawed and hammered, and had a burr on the end; there was a nail instead of a cotter pin in the main accelerator rod linkage; and the accelerator return spring was misreplaced and had been stretched.

While taking the deposition of one of General Motors' chief engineers, it developed that he had a photograph of a quadrajet carburetor made on General Motors' proving ground showing that the lockout pin and lever did jam. This photograph, along with numerous written communications circulated because of this event, were discovered in the files of defendant General Motors. See Figure 32. The photograph is a reproduction of a rather poor polaroid picture made by an engineer at the proving grounds. This picture was taken approximately two years before the carburetor in plaintiff's truck had been manufactured. This photograph was invaluable in refuting defendant's contention that it was "impossible" for the lockout pin and lever to jam, and further, to establish that defendant knew of this occurrence.

After plaintiff was hurt, General Motors re-designed the lockout pin and lever. See Figure 33. The pin was flattened and the lever, instead of having a straight radius, has since been shaped in such a manner that it now contacts the pin at a 45 degree angle. Needless to say, the picture made at the proving grounds proved to be the single most important piece of demonstrative evidence to plaintiff's cause. Skillful use of the discovery process had uncovered this "crucial" photograph.

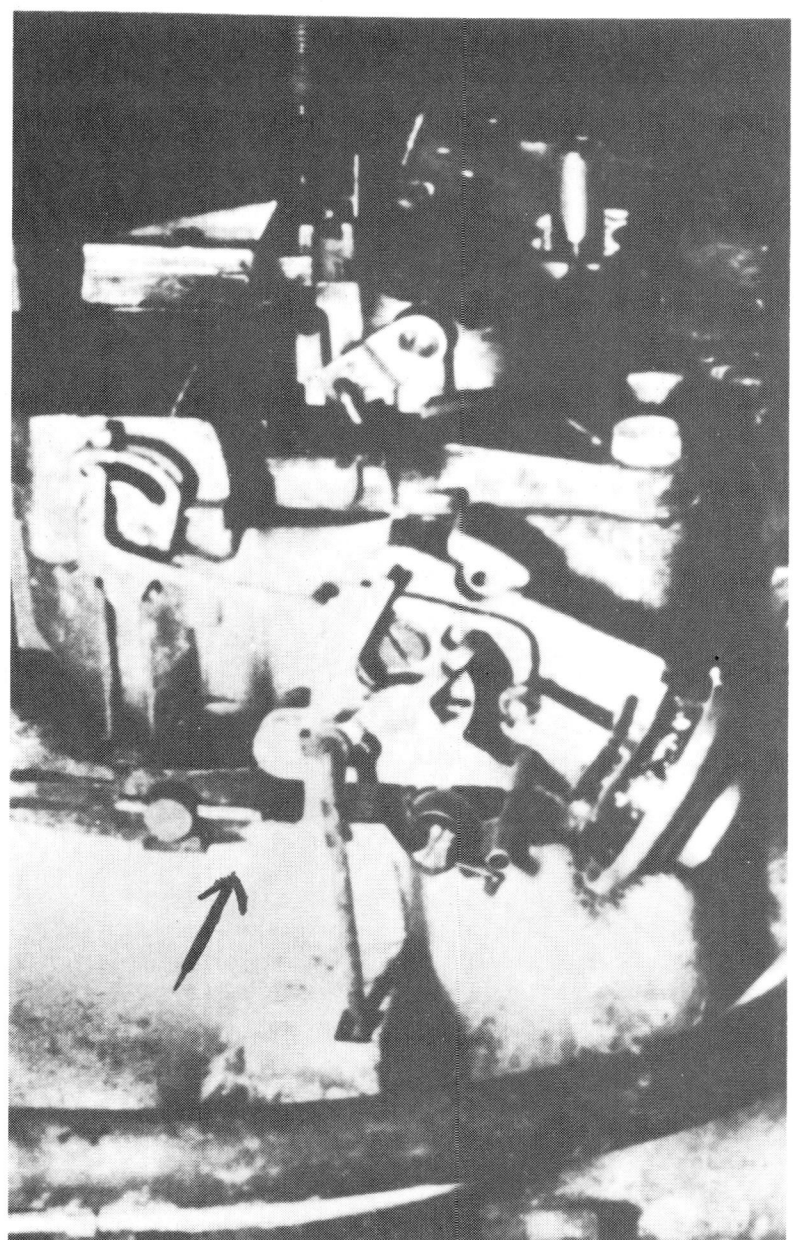

Figure 32. This photograph showing jammed lockout pin and lever was discovered in the files of defendant General Motors. Attorney Watkins was able to prove that the photograph was made by defendant while performing tests on the car.

Figure 33. As a result of this case, General Motors redesigned the system to prevent future occurrences of the same problem.

§ 2.82 INTRODUCTION Pt. 1

Another interesting case in which demonstrative evidence obtained through discovery is an escalator injury case handled by Attorney *Betty C. Love*.[65] This was a case against the Montgomery Elevator Company, Inc., and involved an eleven-year-old girl who lost part of her little toe to an escalator.

Through interrogatories and requests for production, defendant Montgomery Elevator Company, Inc., furnished Attorney Love with a *computer printout* showing the number of children's toes, feet, and other parts of the body which had been caught and severed by its escalators over a given period of time. The printouts further showed the amount the company had been paying for each lost toe or foot.

Armed with these printouts and other demonstrative evidence, Attorney Love was able to reach a settlement of $25,000 for the young girl. Upon hearing of this settlement, and the existence of the printouts, other trial lawyers contacted Attorney Love to obtain copies thereof. Among them was Attorney *Norman J. Landau*[66] who presented these and other demonstrative evidence to a jury (including a box similar in size to one in which sneakers which had been caught by the escalator were placed) in a trial wherein a young boy had lost most of the toes on one foot to an escalator. Attorney Landau's client was awarded $400,000 by the jury in compensation for his tragic injuries.[67]

§ 2.83 Privileged Matters

Although the philosophy of modern discovery supports a broad concept of relevancy, the scope of discoverable material is not unlimited. Irrelevance may be raised to bar discovery when the information sought is clearly so remote that disclosure would avail no practical benefit to the moving party.[68] And since relevancy in discovery is a fluid concept, with great latitude for its determination vested in the trial judge, borderline relevancy combined with significant burden in complying will often act to bar discovery.[69]

---

65. Betty C. Love, Esquire, Love, Love, Lawrence & Burton, P.O. Drawer 297, 130 East Street, North, Talladega, Alabama.

66. Norman J. Landau, Esquire, 233 Broadway, New York, New York.

67. For a complete report of this case, see § 53.14, infra.

68. Biliske v. American Live Stock Ins. Co., 73 F.R.D. 124 (D.C.Okl.1977)

(Request for all correspondence over 6 month period, whether or not related to subject matter, held overbroad).

Los Angeles v. Superior Court, 13 Cal. 3d 721, 119 Cal.Rptr. 631, 532 P.2d 495 (1975) (Motives of legislators in enacting legislation are irrelevant to validity of act and therefore.

69. Kolta v. Tuck Indus., Inc., 20 F.R. Serv.2d 1049 (S.D.N.Y.1975) (Answers to 250 interrogatories would require

Most successful objections to discovery, however, are based on privilege[70] rather than relevancy. The major categories of privileged information are discussed below. In federal practice, state privilege law will be relied on in diversity cases.[71] In cases arising under federal law, the traditional rule was that state privileges need not be honored.[72] The new Federal Rules of Evidence, however, defer to state law when an issue is presented on which state law supplies the rule of decision.[73] A conflicts of law question may arise when the law of the state where the deposition is being taken differs from the law of the forum of the underlying action. Federal courts in general will apply the choice-of-law rule of the forum state.[74] If there is no state law resolving the question, federal courts have applied the law of the state where the deposition is being taken.[75]

§ 2.84 Lawyer-Client Privilege

The absolute privilege afforded to confidential communications made by a client to a lawyer, in his professional capacity, has been

---

considerable time searching corporate records and could produce only marginally relevant information); Burroughs v. Warner Bros. Pictures, Inc., 14 F.R.D. 165 (D.C.Mass.1953) (Burdensome interrogatories, requested information seemed to have little relevance).

70. FRCP Rule 26(b)(1): "Parties may obtain discovery regarding any matter, *not privileged*, which is relevant to the subject matter involved in the pending action . . . ." [emphasis supplied]. See Wright & Miller, Federal Practice and Procedure: Civil (1970), Vol. 8, Ch. 6, §§ 2016–2028.

71. Blackledge v. Eby Constr. Co., Inc., 542 F.2d 474 (8th Cir. 1976); Scott v. McDonald, 70 F.R.D. 568 (D.C.Ga.1976); Reeves v. Pennsylvania R. R. Co., 8 F.R.D. 616, 12 F.R.Serv. 34, 411, case 2 (D.C.Del.1949); Palmer v. Fisher, 228 F.2d 603 (7th Cir. 1955), cert. denied 351 U.S. 965, 76 S.Ct. 1030, 100 L.Ed. 1485 (Accountant's privilege); Merlin v. Aetna Life Ins. Co., 180 F.Supp. 90 (D.C.N.Y. 1960) (Husband-wife privilege). See Kaminsky, State Evidentiary Privileges in Federal Civil Litigation (1975) 43 Fordham L.Rev. 923.

72. Colton v. United States, 306 F.2d 633 (2d Cir. 1962), cert. denied 371 U.S. 951, 83 S.Ct. 505, 9 L.Ed.2d 499; Fraser v. United States, 145 F.2d 139 (6th Cir. 1944), cert. denied 324 U.S. 849, 65 S.Ct. 684, 89 L.Ed. 1409; See Louisell, Confidentiality, Conformity and Confusion. Privileges in Federal Courts Today (1956) 31 Tul.L.Rev. 101; Stafford, Evidential Privileges in Federal Courts (1964) 52 Cal.L.Rev. 640.

73. Federal Rules of Evidence, Rule 501. See Swartz, Privileges Under the Federal Rules of Evidence—A Slip Forward? (1976) 38 Pitts.L.Rev. 79. See also Wright and Graham, Federal Practice and Procedure: Evidence (Vol. 23), Rule 501; M. Graham, Handbook of Federal Evidence, Rule 501.

74. Cepeda v. Cohane, 233 F.Supp. 465 (D.C.N.Y.1964). See Note, Privileged Communications under Rule 26(b): Conflict of Laws in Diversity Cases (1956) 23 U.Chi.L.Rev. 704.

75. Palmer v. Fisher, 228 F.2d 603 (7th Cir. 1955), cert. denied 351 U.S. 965, 76 S.Ct. 1030, 100 L.Ed. 1485; Hill v. Huddleston, 263 F.Supp. 108 (D.C. Md.1967).

characterized as a basic principle not only of Anglo-American society, but of the entire Western World.[76] In safeguarding the integrity of the lawyer-client relationship, the rule safeguards society under law. The privilege is a necessity to full disclosure of the facts from client to lawyer, promoting thereby "the interest and administration of justice."[77] As expressed in the Model Code of Evidence: "Unless he makes known to the lawyer all the facts, the advice which follows will be useless, if not misleading; the lawsuit will be conducted along improper lines, the trial will be full of surprises, much useless litigation may result. Thirdly, unless the client knows that his lawyer cannot be compelled to reveal what is told him, the client will suppress what he thinks to be unfavorable facts."[78]

While many courts are zealous in recognition and defense of this "sacred" privilege,[79] others are apt to urge a strict construction of the privilege on the grounds that it tends to *suppress* facts from

---

76. Louisell, supra note 52, at 110. See also Wright & Miller, Federal Practice & Procedure (1970) Vol. 8, § 2017. McCormick, Evidence (1972, 2d Ed), § 87–97.

77. Hunt v. Blackburn, 128 U.S. 464, 470, 9 S.Ct. 125, 32 L.Ed. 488 (1888); United States v. United Shoe Machinery Corp., 89 F.Supp. 357 (D.C.Mass. 1950) ("As stated in the Comment to Rule 210 of the A.L.I. Model Code of Evidence: In a society as complicated in structure as ours and governed by laws as complex and detailed as those imposed upon us, expert legal advice is essential. To the furnishing of such advice the fullest freedom and honesty of communication of pertinent facts is a prerequisite. To induce clients to make such communications, the privilege to prevent their later disclosure is said by courts and commentators to be a necessity. The social good derived from the proper performance of the functions of lawyers acting for their clients is believed to outweigh the harm that may come from the suppression of the evidence in specific cases.") (emphasis added); Jacobi v. Podevels, 23 Wis.2d 152, 127 N.W.2d 73 (1964).

78. San Francisco v. Superior Court, 37 Cal.2d 227, 234, 231 P.2d 26, 29 (1951).

79. People v. Kor, 129 Cal.App.2d 436, 277 P.2d 94 (1954) ("The privilege of confidential communication between client and attorney should be regarded as sacred. It is not to be whittled away by means of specious argument that it has been waived. Least of all should the courts seize upon slight and equivocal circumstances as a technical reason for destroying the privilege . . . . Defendant's attorney should have chosen to go to jail and take his chances of release by a higher court. This is not intended as a criticism of the action of the attorney. It is, however, a suggestion to any and all attorneys who may have the misfortune to be confronted by the same or a similar problem."); Grand Lake Drive In, Inc. v. Superior Court, 179 Cal.App. 2d 122, 3 Cal.Rptr. 621 (1960) ("Also, we point out that the requirement of showing of good cause can have no application when the matter sought to be discovered is within the attorney-client privilege. No possible showing of good cause can dissipate or destroy that privilege where it truly applies.").

disclosure.[80] Thus, the privilege and its elements have been delineated with great particularity: ". . . The privilege applies only if (1) the asserted holder of the privilege is or sought to become a client; (2) the person to whom the communication was made (a) is a member of the bar of a court, or his subordinate and (b) in connection with this communication is acting as a lawyer; (3) the communication relates to a fact of which the attorney was informed (a) by his client (b) without the presence of strangers (c) for the purpose of securing primarily either (i) an opinion on law of (ii) legal services or (iii) assistance in some legal proceeding, and not (d) for the purpose of committing a crime or tort; and (4) the privilege has been (a) claimed and (b) not waived by the client."[81] Other courts have approached the privilege in more general terms: ". . . where legal advice of any kind is sought from a professional legal advisor in his capacity as such, the communications relevant to that purpose, made in confidence by the client, are at his instance permanently protected from disclosure by himself or by the legal advisor except the protection be waived."[82]

There is general agreement to the principle that unprivileged matters cannot be made privileged merely by the client's communicating them to his lawyer.[83] "[A] document, report, or photograph that would otherwise be admissible in evidence does not become privileged merely because the client delivers it to his attorney. Unless a report or photograph is created for the purpose of communicating information to the attorney, it cannot have the character of a privileged communication when it comes into existence and accordingly cannot become privileged if it is later delivered to the attorney."[84] However,

80. Radiant Burners, Inc. v. American Gas Ass'n, 320 F.2d 314 (7th Cir. 1963), cert. denied 375 U.S. 929, 84 S.Ct. 330, 11 L.Ed.2d 262; Underwater Storage, Inc. v. United States Rubber Co., 314 F.Supp. 546 (D.C.D. C.1970).

81. United States v. United Shoe Machinery Corp., 89 F.Supp. 357, 358–59 (D.C.Mass.1950) (Wyzanski, J.).

82. Wonneman v. Stratford Securities Co., 23 F.R.D. 281, 285 (S.D.N.Y. 1959).

83. San Francisco Unified Sch. Dist. v. Superior Court, 55 Cal.2d 451, 11 Cal.Rptr. 373, 359 P.2d 925, 82 A.L. R.2d 1156 (1961). See In re Natta, 264 F.Supp. 734, 741 (D.Del.1967), aff'd on other issues 388 F.2d 215 (3rd Cir.); Georgia-Pacific Plywood Co. v. United States Plywood Corp., 18 F.R.D. 463, 464 (S.D.N.Y.1956); Zenith Radio Corp. v. Radio Corp. of America, 121 F.Supp. 792, 794 (D. Del.1954).

84. Holm v. Superior Court, 42 Cal.2d 500, 511, 267 P.2d 1025 (1954), reh. denied 42 Cal.2d 500, 268 P.2d 722 (concurring and dissenting opinion) (Where city claims investigator obtained statement from plaintiff regarding circumstances of accident, later transmitted statement to city attorney did not make it privileged). See Fish v. United States, 425 U.S. 391, 96 S.Ct. 1569, 48 L.Ed.2d 39 (1976)

where it can be shown that the dominant purpose in creating the material was to prepare for anticipated litigation, it should be deemed privileged and not discoverable.[85]

The privilege attaches only to communications made to the lawyer in his professional capacity. Where the lawyer's services are in a lay capacity, the privilege may be denied.[86] A salutary approach is that of Dean Wigmore,[87] adopted by the Eighth Circuit Court of Appeals in *Diversified Industries, Inc. v. Meredith*,[88] that a matter committed to a professional legal adviser is prima facie committed for the sake of legal advice, so that the privilege attaches absent a clear showing to the contrary. When one consults with a lawyer with a view to obtaining legal services, communications made in confidence are privileged, even though a lawyer-client relationship does not ensue.[89] Communications made without such purpose are not protected.[90] Communications made in the course of a lawyer-client relationship remain privileged despite termination of employment.[91]

85. Jessup v. Superior Court, 151 Cal. App.2d 102, 311 P.2d 177 (1957) (Report of drowning incident in municipal pool held privileged, since prepared for litigation); Heffron v. Los Angeles Transit Lines, 170 Cal.App.2d 709, 339 P.2d 567 (1959) (Bus driver's accident report transmitted to insurance company, then to attorney, held privileged as prepared in anticipation of litigation).

86. Georgia-Pacific Plywood Co. v. United States Plywood Corp., 18 F.R. D. 463, 464 (S.D.N.Y.1956). ("Communications dealing exclusively with the solicitation or giving of business advice, or with the technical engineering aspects of patent procurement or with any other matters which may as easily be handled by laymen are not privileged"); In re Natta (D.C.Del.1967) 264 F.Supp. 734, aff'd 388 F.2d 215 (3d Cir. 1968).

87. 8 Wigmore, Evidence, § 2296 (McNaughton rev. 1961) ("It is not easy to frame a definite test for distinguishing legal from nonlegal advice. . . . [T]he most that can be said by way of generalization is that a matter committed to a professional legal adviser is *prima facie* so committed for the sake of the legal advice which may be more or less desirable for some aspect of the matter, and is therefore within the privilege unless it clearly appears to be lacking in aspects requiring legal advice. Obviously, much depends upon the circumstances of individual transactions." [emphasis added]).

(Accountant's tax workpapers prepared for client not privileged by later transmission to attorney).

88. 572 F.2d 596 (8th Cir. 1978). See also McLaughlin, The Treatment of Attorney-Client Privileges in the Proposed Rules of Evidence for the U.S. District Courts, 26 The Record 31 (1971).

89. Harkobusic v. General American Transp. Corp., 31 F.R.D. 264 (D.C.Pa. 1962); People v. Canfield, 12 Cal.3d 699, 117 Cal.Rptr. 81, 527 P.2d 633 (1974).

90. Air-Shield, Inc. v. Air Reduction Co., 46 F.R.D. 96 (D.C.Ill.1968).

91. People v. Singh, 123 Cal.App. 365, 11 P.2d 73 (1932).

Information or statements obtained by a lawyer from a witness are not privileged because no lawyer-client relationship exists.[92] However, an expert, such as an examining physician or specialist, may be deemed to be the client's *agent* who functions to transmit confidential information from the client which the client is incapable of discovering, understanding, or expressing technically. In such cases the communications are privileged,[93] but the privilege is waived if the expert will be called as a witness, since the intent to disclose the information destroys its confidential character.[94] A communication made by the client to the lawyer through the lawyer's agent,[95] including a medical expert retained by the lawyer,[96] is privileged.

Only those communications made to a lawyer with intentions of *confidentiality* are privileged.[97] Thus the presence of a third party at the time of the communication can destroy the privilege.[98] Where the third party is present in furtherance of the client's interest, the privilege is not waived.[99]

A corporation enjoys the same privilege as an individual in regard to communications to its legal representative.[1] An uncertainty persists, however, as to exactly who represents the corporate interests for this purpose, and thus whose communications enjoy the privilege. The Seventh Circuit, in *Harper & Row Publishers, Inc v.*

92. Greyhound Corp. v. Superior Court, 56 Cal.2d 355, 15 Cal.Rptr. 90, 364 P.2d 266 (1961).

93. Cold Metal Process Co. v. Aluminum Co. of America, 7 F.R.D. 684 (D.C.Mass.1947); Suezaki v. Superior Court, 58 Cal.2d 166, 23 Cal.Rptr. 368, 373 P.2d 432, 95 A.L.R.2d 1073 (1962); San Diego Professional Ass'n v. Superior Court, 58 Cal.2d 194, 23 Cal.Rptr. 384, 373 P.2d 448, 97 A.L.R.2d 761 (1962).

94. Sanders v. Superior Court, 34 Cal. App.3d 270, 109 Cal.Rptr. 770 (1973).

95. United States v. Kovel, 296 F.2d 918 (2d Cir. 1961); See Annotation 96 A.L.R.2d 125, 150.

96. San Francisco v. Superior Court, 37 Cal.2d 227, 231 P.2d 26 (1951); Lindsay v. Lipson, 367 Mich. 1, 116 N.W.2d 60 (1962); State v. Kociolek, 23 N.J. 400, 129 A.2d 417 (1957) (Psychiatrist).

97. Mission Film Corp. v. Chadwick Pictures Corp., 207 Cal. 386, 278 P. 855 (1929); Solon v. Lichtenstein, 39 Cal.2d 75, 244 P.2d 907 (1952) (Communication intended to be transmitted to third party not privileged).

98. Bolyea v. First Presbyterian Church, 196 N.W.2d 149, 55 A.L.R.3d 1304 (N.D.1972); McCaw v. Hartman, 100 Okl. 264, 122 P.2d 999 (1942); People v. Cox, 263 Cal.App.2d 176, 69 Cal.Rptr. 410 (1968) (Where information was communicated by telephone to lawyer of defendant in police custody, presence of police matron who overheard destroyed privilege).

99. Cal. Evidence Code § 952.

1. Radiant Burners, Inc. v. American Gas Ass'n, 320 F.2d 314 (7th Cir. 1963), cert. denied 375 U.S. 929, 84 S.Ct. 330, 11 L.Ed.2d 262; See Comment, 10 Stan.L.Rev. 297, 76 Harv.L. Rev. 655.

§ 2.84   INTRODUCTION   Pt. 1

Decker[2] rejected the prevalent "control group" test which limited the privilege to corporate employees who wield decision-making power.[3] The broader *Harper & Row* approach grants the privilege to communications to the corporations' counsel from corporate employees "where the employee makes the communication at the direction of his superiors in the corporation, and where the subject matter upon which the attorney's advice is sought by the corporation and dealt with in the communication is the performance by the employee of the duties of his employment."[4] That the lawyer is "house counsel" does not affect the privilege,[5] but internal communications among corporate officers advising that legal advice be sought are not privileged.[6]

There are various circumstances under which the lawyer-client privilege will be deemed to have been waived. Since the client is the "holder of the privilege," he alone may waive it.[7] The lawyer is under a duty to claim the privilege on behalf of the client. Unless otherwise instructed, he *must* claim it.[8] If he fails to do so at trial, the court may exclude the privileged communication on its own motion,[9] but a lawyer's failure to raise timely objections may be held against the client and the privilege waived.[10] Disclosure of the communication to third parties waives the privilege.[11] Where the client divulges part of the communication, the privilege is waived as to the whole,[12]

2. (7th Cir. 1970) 423 F.2d 487, aff'd 400 U.S. 348, 91 S.Ct. 479, 27 L.Ed.2d 433, reh. denied 401 U.S. 950, 91 S.Ct. 917, 28 L.Ed.2d 234.

3. See City of Philadelphia v. Westinghouse Electric Corp., 210 F.Supp. 483 (E.D.Pa.1962), mandamus and prohibition denied; General Electric Co. v. Kirkpatrick, 312 F.2d 742 (3d Cir. 1962), cert. denied 372 U.S. 943, 83 S.Ct. 937, 9 L.Ed.2d 969.

4. Harper & Row Publishers, Inc. v. Decker supra, n. 54, at 491–492.

See also Note, Attorney-Client Privilege for Corporate Clients: The Control Group Test, 84 Harv.L.Rev. 424 (1970); Kobak, The Uneven Application of the Attorney-Client Privilege to Corporations in the Federal Courts, 6 Ga.L.Rev. 339 (1972).

5. New York Underwriters Ins. Co. v. Union Constr. Co., 285 F.Supp. 868 (D.C.Kan.1968).

6. United States v. IBM Corp., 415 F.Supp. 668 (D.C.N.Y.1976).

7. Republic Gear Co. v. Borg-Warner Corp. (2d Cir. 1967) 381 F.2d 551; Tillotson v. Boughner, 350 F.2d 663 (7th Cir. 1965).

8. Cal.Evid.Code § 955.

9. Stearns v. Los Angeles City Sch. Dist., 244 Cal.App.2d 696, 53 Cal. Rptr. 482 (1966).

10. Curry v. Wilson, 405 F.2d 110 (9th Cir. 1968), cert. denied 397 U.S. 973, 90 S.Ct. 1090, 25 L.Ed.2d 268.

11. Velsicol Chem. Corp. v. Parsons, (7th Cir. 1977) 561 F.2d 671.

12. Handgards Inc. v. Johnson & Johnson, 413 F.Supp. 926 (D.C.Cal.1976). ("[A] party may not insist on the protection of the attorney-client privilege for damaging communications while disclosing other selected communications because they are self-serving.").

limited, however, to the specific subject of the conversation divulged in part.[13] A document used by a witness to refresh his recollection for deposition or trial testimony loses its privileged status.[14] A lawyer's duty to protect the confidentiality of privileged communications terminates when he is accused by the client of wrongful doing and disclosure of the communications is necessary to defense of his own professional conduct.[15]

Where the client's consultation with his lawyer is in furtherance of a crime or fraud, the privilege will not protect against its disclosure,[16] even in a proceeding other than a trial for the crime or fraud disclosed.[17] A prima facie showing of crime or fraud will operate to trigger the exception,[18] and the intention of the client, not the lawyer, is relevant.[19]

§ 2.85 Attorney's Work Product

In the celebrated decision of *Hickman v. Taylor*,[20] the United States Supreme Court announced the "work product of the lawyer"

13. Goldman, Sachs & Co. v. Blondis, 412 F.Supp. 286 (D.C.Ill.1976); Perrignon v. Bergen Brunswig Corp., 77 F.R.D. 455 (D.C.Cal.1978).

14. Kerns Constr. Co. v. Superior Court, 266 Cal.App.2d 405, 72 Cal. Rptr. 74 (1968).

15. Sullivan v. Chase Inv. Services of Boston, Inc., 434 F.Supp. 171 (N.D. Cal.1977); People v. Morris, 20 Cal. App.3d 659, 97 Cal.Rptr. 817 (1971); People v. Vargas, 53 Cal.App.3d 516, 126 Cal.Rptr. 88 (1975).

16. Clark v. United States, 289 U.S. 1, 53 S.Ct. 465, 77 L.Ed. 993 (1933) ("The privilege takes flight if the relation is abused."); Alexander v. United States, 138 U.S. 353, 11 S.Ct. 350, 34 L.Ed. 954 (1890); United States v. Goldstein, 456 F.2d 1006 (8th Cir. 1972), cert. denied 416 U.S. 943, 94 S.Ct. 1951, 40 L.Ed.2d 295; United States v. Bartlett, 449 F.2d 700 (8th Cir. 1971), cert. denied 405 U.S. 932, 92 S.Ct. 990, 30 L.Ed.2d 808; United States v. Billingsley, 440 F.2d 823 (7th Cir. 1971), cert. denied 403 U.S. 909, 91 S.Ct. 2219, 29 L.Ed. 2d 687; 8 Wizurne, Evidence (McNaughton Rev. 1961) § 2298.

17. A. B. Dick Co. v. Marr, 95 F.Supp. 83 (D.C.D.C.1950), appeal dism'd 197 F.2d 498 (D.C.Cir.), cert. denied 344 U.S. 878, 73 S.Ct. 169, 97 L.Ed. 680, reh. denied 344 U.S. 905, 73 S.Ct. 282, 97 L.Ed. 699 ("Nevertheless, it is quite clear that the privilege disappears if it is provoked merely to cloak a fraudulent scheme, and that when a client consults an attorney as to how to concoct or perpetrate a fraud the privilege is unavailing"). Securities & Exchange Comm'n v. Harrison, 80 F.Supp. 226 (D.C.D.C. 1948), appeal dism'd 184 F.2d 691 (D. C.Cir.), vacated as moot 340 U.S. 908, 71 S.Ct. 290, 95 L.Ed. 656.

18. United States v. Aldridge, 484 F.2d 655 (7th Cir. 1973), cert. denied 415 U.S. 921, 94 S.Ct. 1423, 39 L.Ed.2d 477.

19. United States v. Hodge & Zweig, 548 F.2d 1347 (9th Cir. 1977).

20. 329 U.S. 495, 67 S.Ct. 385, 91 L.Ed. 451 (1947). For additional discussion of the "Work Product Rule", see Wright & Miller, Federal Practice and Procedure: Civil § 2021 et seq.

rule of qualified immunity from discovery. The *Hickman* case involved the death of five crewmen when a tugboat sank in the Delaware River. After a public hearing on the case, lawyers representing the defendant tug company and their insurers took statements from the surviving crewmembers who had testified. They subsequently interviewed additional witnesses, and committed the information obtained to memoranda. Plaintiffs' lawyers, by interrogatories, requested discovery of all statements, records, reports, or memoranda made concerning any matter relative to operation of the tug or the accident in question. Defendants' refusal to comply was overruled by the District Court, who cited them in contempt. The Court of Appeals reversed. The Supreme Court affirmed the Court of Appeals, not, however, on grounds that the materials requested were "privileged." Rather, the Court enunciated the theory that a lawyer's "work product"—materials gathered in preparation for litigation—could not be discovered without a showing that they were necessary to the moving party's case, or that non-production would result in prejudice or hardship. The Court observed:

"Historically, a lawyer is an officer of the court and is bound to work for the advancement of justice while faithfully protecting the rightful interests of his clients. In performing his various duties, however, it is essential that a lawyer work with a certain degree of privacy, free from unnecessary intrusion by opposing parties and their counsel. Proper preparation of a client's case demands that he assemble information, sift what he considers to be the relevant from the irrelevant facts, prepare his legal theories and plan his strategy without undue and needless interference. That is the historical and the necessary way in which lawyers act within the framework of our system of jurisprudence to promote justice and to protect their clients' interests. This work is reflected, of course, in interviews, statements, memoranda, correspondence, briefs, mental impressions, personal beliefs, and countless other tangible and intangible ways aptly though roughly termed by the Circuit Court of Appeals in this case as the 'work product of the lawyer.' Were such materials open to opposing counsel on mere demand, much of what is now put down in writing would remain unwritten. An attorney's thoughts, heretofore inviolate, would not be his own. Inefficiency, unfairness and sharp practices would inevitably develop in the giving of legal advice and in the preparation of cases for trial. The effect on the legal profession would be demoralizing. And the interests of the clients and the cause of justice would be poorly served.

"We do not mean to say that all written materials obtained or prepared by an adversary's counsel with an eye toward litigation are necessarily free from discovery in all cases. Where relevant and non-privileged facts remain hidden in an attorney's file and where production of those facts is essential to the preparation of one's case, discovery may properly be had. Such written statements and documents might, under certain circumstances, be admissible in evidence or give clues as to the existence or location of relevant facts. Or they might be useful for purposes of impeachment or corroboration. And production might be justified where the witnesses are no longer available or can be reached only with difficulty. Were production of written statements and documents to be precluded under such circumstances, the liberal ideals of the deposition-discovery portions of the Federal Rules of Civil Procedure would be stripped of much of their meaning. But the general policy against invading the privacy of an attorney's course of preparation is so well recognized and so essential to an orderly working of our system of legal procedure that a burden rests on the one who would invade that privacy to establish adequate reasons to justify production through a subpoena or court order. That burden, we believe, is necessarily implicit in the rules as now constituted." [21]

The *Hickman* decision did not establish a rule of absolute immunity, but established the moving party's burden of showing "special circumstances" [22]—a sort of "extreme good cause"—in order to obtain disclosure of materials deemed "work product." The *Hickman* rationale was essentially a balancing test—weighing a demonstrated "necessity or justification" for disclosure against the presumption in favor of protecting "the privacy of a man's work." *Hickman* provided no detailed rules, but committed the doctrine to the discretion of the trial courts, to be applied on a case by case basis.[23] The resulting body of adjudication was described by one court as a "huge jungle of conflicting decisions." [24]

Federal Rule 26(b)(3) was intended to refine and codify the *Hickman* rule. It excludes from disclosure "documents and tangible things" which have been "prepared in anticipation of litigation or for trial by or for another party or by or for that other party's representative," unless the moving party can show "substantial need of the materials" *and* that he is "unable without undue hardship to obtain the substantial equivalent of the materials by other means."

21. 329 U.S. at 510–12; 91 L.Ed. at 462–63.

22. See Gardner, Agency Problems in the Law of Attorney-Client Privilege: Privilege and "Work Product" under Open Discovery, 42 U.Det.L.J. 105 (1964); Wright & Miller, Federal Practice and Procedure: Civil § 2022.

23. Wright & Miller, Federal Practice and Procedure: Civil, § 2022, p. 190.

24. Monier v. Chamberlain, 35 Ill.2d 351, 221 N.E.2d 410, 18 A.L.R.3d 471 (1966). See also comment, Attorney's Work Product—An Area of Confrontation, 31 Ind.L.Rev. 530 (1963).

§ 2.85   INTRODUCTION   Pt. 1

The California code section codifying the work product immunity rule[25] was enacted in response to the State Supreme Court's ruling that there was no work product immunity in California.[26] The statute provides that the protected materials will not be disclosed unless their denial will "unfairly prejudice" the other party, or "result in injustice." This broad language is conditioned by the appended policy statement, providing: "It is the policy of this state (i) to preserve the rights of attorneys to prepare cases for trial with that degree of privacy necessary to encourage them to prepare their cases thoroughly and to investigate not only the favorable but the unfavorable aspects of such cases and (ii) to prevent an attorney from taking undue advantage of his adversary's industry or efforts."[27]

Application of the work product immunity rule, under such guidelines, is thus primarily a discretionary function of the trial court. Determination of what materials constitute "work product," and what work product materials are immune from discovery, can vary widely on a case by case basis.[28] Generally, courts are prone to grant protection in direct proportion to the extent that the materials represent the mental processes of the lawyer.[29] As expressed by the Wisconsin Supreme Court: "For example, if a matter or writing is classified work product because it reflects the mental impressions of the investigating attorney, only a showing of nonavailability after diligent search and of great prejudice to preparation could justify an

---

25. CCP § 2016(b).

26. Greyhound Corp. v. Superior Court, 56 Cal.2d 355, 15 Cal.Rptr. 90, 364 P.2d 266 (1961).

27. CCP § 2016(g). See also McCoy, California Civil Discovery: Work Product of Attorney, 18 Stan.L.Rev. 783, (1966). Comment, Work product doctrine in California, 6 Southwestern U.L.Rev. 677 (1974).

28. State ex rel. Dudek v. Circuit Court, 34 Wis.2d 559, 150 N.W.2d 387 (1967) ("This approach to the problem requires the exercise of sound judicial discretion by the trial judge confronted with the problem. It is a question of fairness tempered by the basic concepts of our adversary system and the desirable aspects of pretrial discovery. We recognize that this is a rather nebulous test that will cast upon counsel and primarily the trial judge the duty to articulate the reason for enforcing the privilege or recognizing an exception and ordering that discovery be permitted. The trial judge will also be required to determine the scope of the permitted discovery and the terms, if any, to be imposed. While we are reluctant not to fashion more exact rules, the subject is one that does not lend itself to exactness. We believe the ends of justice will be better served by relying on the judicious discretion of our trial courts to fairly meet a multitude of variable situations than to announce stereotyped rules that do not always accommodate a particular problem."); City of Long Beach v. Superior Court, 64 Cal.App.3d 65, 134 Cal.Rptr. 468 (1976).

29. In re Murphy, 560 F.2d 326 (8th Cir. 1977); Handgards, Inc. v. Johnson & Johnson, 413 F.Supp. 926 (D.C. Cal.1976).

order for production. On the other hand, a report classified work product though not reflective of an attorney's mental impressions, such as an expert's report so classified in order to encourage diligent investigation by both parties, may be discoverable upon a showing of the uniqueness or unavailability of the experiment giving rise to the report and a possible offer to share costs of the experiment." [30] Federal Rule 26(b)(3) provides that in ordering discovery, "the court shall protect against disclosure of the mental impressions, conclusions, opinions, or legal theories of an attorney or other representative of a party concerning the litigation." The California statute goes further and provides that "any writing that reflects an attorney's impressions, conclusions, opinions, or legal research or theories shall not be disclosed under any circumstances." [31]

Any question of "work product" immunity from discovery involves three factors: (1) Do the materials constitute "work product?", (2) If so, has the moving party shown justification for their disclosures? and (3) Has the work product immunity of the materials been waived?

The *Hickman* ruling has been construed to hold that "a lawyer's work product consists of the information he has assembled and the mental impressions, legal theories and strategies that he has pursued or adopted as derived from interviews, statements, memoranda, correspondence, briefs, legal and factual research, mental impressions, personal beliefs, and other tangible or intangible means." [32]

As in the case of lawyer-client privilege, pre-existing materials do not qualify for protection under work product immunity by their subsequent "adoption" by a lawyer.[33] Only those materials which are

---

30. State ex rel. Dudek v. Circuit Court, 34 Wis.2d 559, 150 N.W.2d 387 (1967).

31. CCP § 2016(b). American Mut. Liab. Ins. Co. v. Superior Court, 38 Cal.App.3d 579, 113 Cal.Rptr. 561 (1974).

32. McCoy, California Civil Discovery: Work Product of Attorneys, 18 Stan. L.Rev. 783, 797 (1966) ("[T]he work product of an attorney is the product of his effort, research, and thought in the preparation of his client's case. It includes the results of his own work, and the work of those employed by him or for him by his client, in investigating both the favorable and unfavorable aspects of the case, the information thus assembled, and the legal theories and plan of strategy developed by the attorney— all as reflecting in interviews, statements, memoranda, correspondence, briefs, and any other writings reflecting the attorney's 'impressions, conclusions, opinions, or legal research or theories,' and in countless other tangible and intangible ways.").

33. Natta v. Hogan, 392 F.2d 686 (10th Cir. 1968); Colton v. United States, 306 F.2d 633 (2d Cir. 1962), cert. denied 371 U.S. 951, 83 S.Ct. 505, 9 L. Ed.2d 499; Bank of the Orient v. Superior Court, 67 Cal.App.3d 588, 136 Cal.Rptr. 741 (1977); Brunswick

§ 2.85 INTRODUCTION Pt. 1

actually prepared for litigation[34] and are presently a part of the lawyer's work files[35] are immune. The test is not whether litigation has begun, but whether the materials have been prepared or obtained in anticipation of litigation.[36] Materials that are prepared in the ordinary course of business are not protected, however, even though litigation may be in prospect.[37]

It is not necessary that the materials be the handiwork of the lawyer himself. They are protected if prepared by lawyer's agent[38] or by the party at the discretion of the agent.[39] The Federal rule refers to materials prepared by or for a party or his "representative," thus including work done in anticipation of litigation by the party's "attorney, consultant, surety, indemnitor, insurer, or agent."[40] The California rule, however, is specifically restricted to the work of the attorney and his agents. Thus, in California, materials prepared by an insurance investigator before counsel is retained are not immune from discovery.[41]

A lawyer's work product is produced only in the course of his preparation for trial, in his professional capacity representing a client.[42] A lawyer's independent work, which is not performed on behalf of a client, is not included.[43] For instance, a district attorney's investigative notes concerning a party may be discoverable in a subsequent civil court action where the district attorney has completed

Corp. v. Aetna Cas. & Sur. Co., 27 A. D.2d 182, 278 N.Y.S.2d 459 (1967).

34. Virginia Elec. & Power Co. v. Sun Shipbuilding & Dry Dock Co., 68 F.R.D. 397 (D.C.Va.1975); Scourtes v. Fred W. Albrecht Grocery Co., 15 F.R.D. 55 (D.C.Ohio 1953).

35. Virginia Elec. & Power Co. v. Sun Shipbuilding & Dry Dock Co., 68 F.R.D. 397 (D.C.Va.1975); United States v. Kelsey-Hayes Wheel Co., 15 F.R.D. 461 (D.C.Mich.1954).

36. Arney v. Geo. A. Hormel & Co., 53 F.R.D. 179 (D.C.Minn.1971).

37. Goosman v. A. Duie Pyle, Inc., 320 F.2d 45 (4th Cir. 1963), appeal after remand 336 F.2d 151; Galambus v. Consolidated Freightways Corp., 64 F.R.D. 468 (D.C.Ind.1974); Burns v. New York Central R. Co., 33 F.R.D. 309 (D.C.Ohio 1963); Nordeide v. Pennsylvania R. Co., 73 N.J.Super. 74, 179 A.2d 71 (1962).

38. Alltmont v. United States, 177 F.2d 971 (3d Cir. 1949), cert. denied 339 U.S. 967, 70 S.Ct. 999, 94 L.Ed. 1375; United States v. Maryland Shipbuilding & Drydock Co., 51 F.R.D. 159 (D.C.Md.1970); J. A. Utley Co. v. Borchard, 372 Mich. 367, 126 N.W.2d 696 (1964); Rakes v. Fulcher, 210 Va. 542, 172 S.E.2d 751 (1970).

39. Berger v. Central Vermont Ry., 8 F.R.D. 419 (D.C.Mass.1948).

40. FRCP Rule 26(b)(3). See Wright & Miller, Federal Practice and Procedure, § 2007 et seq.

41. Wilson v. Superior Court, 226 Cal. App.2d 715, 38 Cal.Rptr. 255 (1964).

42. Weisgold v. Kiamesha Concord, Inc., 51 Misc.2d 456, 273 N.Y.S.2d 279 (1966).

43. State ex rel. Missouri Public Serv. Co. v. Elliott, 434 S.W.2d 532 (Mo. 1968).

his investigation and announces, after failing to obtain an indictment, that no further action will be taken by him.[44] A lawyer's memorandum in a prior case involving different parties may not qualify for "work product" protection in another suit providing the same transaction, since it was not "prepared in direct relation to the case at bar."[45] Some courts have held to the contrary, where the cases were "closely related."[46]

The work product doctrine protects "documents and tangible things,"[47] but does not protect *facts* learned from or contained in protection documents.[48] Thus, in Federal cases and in many states, an investigator for an adverse party may be deposed as to all substantive facts which he knows.[49] Facts developed through the work

---

44. Shepherd v. Superior Court, 17 Cal.3d 107, 130 Cal.Rptr. 257, 550 P.2d 161 (1976).

45. Honeywell, Inc. v. Piper Aircraft Corp., 50 F.R.D. 117, 119 (D.C.Pa. 1970); Hanover Shoe, Inc. v. United Shoe Machinery Corp., 207 F.Supp. 407 (D.C.Pa.1962); Tobacco and Allied Stocks, Inc. v. Transamerica Corp., 16 F.R.D. 534 (D.C.Del.1954).

46. Republic Gear Co. v. Borg-Warner Corp., 381 F.2d 551 (2d Cir. 1967); United States v. O. K. Tire & Rubber Co., 71 F.R.D. 465 (D.C.Idaho 1976); Hercules, Inc. v. Exxon Corp., 434 F.Supp. 136 (D.C.Del.1977); LaRocca v. State Farm Mut. Auto. Ins. Co., 47 F.R.D. 278 (D.C.Pa.1969). See Wright & Miller, Federal Practice and Procedure, § 2024.

47. FRCP Rule 26(b)(3). See Wright & Miller, Federal Practice and Procedure: Civil § 2007 et seq.

48. Lance, Inc. v. Ginsburg, 32 F.R.D. 51 (D.C.Pa.1962). See Advisory Committee Note to FRCP 26(b)(3): "No change is made in the existing doctrine, noted in the *Hickman* case, that one party may discover relevant facts known or available to the other party, even though such facts are contained in a document which is not itself discoverable." Wright & Miller, Federal Practice and Procedure (1970) § 2023: "The courts have consistently held that the work product concept furnishes no shield against discovery, by interrogatories or depositions, if the facts that the adverse party's lawyer has learned, or the persons from whom he has learned such facts, or the existence or nonexistence of documents, even though the documents themselves may not be subject to discovery."

49. Floe v. Plowden, 10 F.R.D. 504 (D.C.S.C.1950) ("Neither the Defendant nor the investigator will be allowed to withhold the knowledge of substantive facts in his possession. . . . [T]his investigator may be called as a witness and may be interrogated as to just what he did, what he saw at the place of collision, the condition of the colliding vehicles, the condition of the roadway, character of pavement, location of ditches, sideroads, curves, elevations or any and all other physical facts that came to his attention. I think that he may be called upon to produce any photographs or delineations of any of the foregoing matters or other similar or pertinent things. He may be required to state whom he interviewed and give their names and addresses."); Baltimore Transit Co. v. Mezzanotti, 227 Md. 8, 174 A.2d 768 (1961); Newton v. Yates, 170 Ind. App. 486, 353 N.E.2d 485 (1976); Southern Pacific Co. v. Superior Court, 3 Cal.App.3d 195, 83 Cal.Rptr. 231 (1969).

of experts, may be disclosed although the experts' reports are immune as work product.[50] The expert's "conclusions," however, will be protected.[51] *Information* possessed by a party generally is discoverable even when the source of that information may qualify as a lawyer's work product.[52] Even facts which have been developed through legal reasoning and theories may be ordered disclosed.[53] Thus, although a party's legal theories are not discoverable,[54] the facts upon which a relevant legal contention is based may be discovered.[55]

Information regarding the existence, and names and addresses, of witnesses or persons having knowledge of relevant facts is not protected by the work product doctrine.[56] Generally, a party will not be required to disclose which (non-expert) witnesses it intends to call at trial,[57] since this decision is a derivative product of the "judgment, discretion, and mental processes" of the lawyer.[58] In regard to expert witnesses, however, the rule is reversed, and a party will usually be compelled to declare which experts will be called.[59]

50. United States v. IBM Corp., 72 F.R.D. 78 (S.D.N.Y.1976); Meese v. Eaton Mfg. Co., 35 F.R.D. 162 (N.D.Ohio 1964).

51. Walsh v. Reynolds Metals Co., 15 F.R.D. 376 (D.C.N.J.1954); United States v. 284,392 Square Feet of Floor Space, 203 F.Supp. 75 (D.C.N.Y.1962).

52. Kenford Co., Inc. v. County of Erie, 55 A.D.2d 466, 390 N.Y.S.2d 715 (1977).

53. Burke v. Superior Court, 71 Cal.2d 276, 78 Cal.Rptr. 481, 455 P.2d 409 (1969).

54. Sav-on Drugs, Inc. v. Superior Court, 15 Cal.3d 1, 123 Cal.Rptr. 283, 538 P.2d 739 (1975).

55. Burke v. Superior Court, 71 Cal.2d 276, 78 Cal.Rptr. 481, 455 P.2d 409 (1969).

56. McCall v. Overseas Tankship Corp., 16 F.R.D. 467 (D.C.N.Y.1954) (Identification of documents and witnesses); Roberson v. Ryder Truck Lines, Inc., 41 F.R.D. 166 (D.C.Miss. 1966); Cedolia v. C. S. Hill Saw Mills, Inc., 41 F.R.D. 524 (D.C.N.C. 1967); Borse v. Superior Court, 7 Cal.App.3d 286, 86 Cal.Rptr. 559 (1970); Clarkson Indus., Inc. v. Price, 135 Ga.App. 787, 218 S.E.2d 921 (1975); City of Long Beach v. Superior Court, 64 Cal.App.3d 65, 134 Cal. Rptr. 468 (1976).

57. Wirtz v. Continental Fin. & Loan Co., 326 F.2d 561 (5th Cir. 1964); United States v. Procter & Gamble Co., 25 F.R.D. 252 (D.C.N.J.1960); *contra:* United States v. 216 Bottles, 36 F.R.D. 695 (D.C.N.Y.1965); Lewis v. J. P. Stevens & Co., 20 F.R.Serv.2d 1091 (D.C.S.C.1975).

58. McNamara v. Erschen, 8 F.R.D. 427 (D.C.Del.1948); Griffin v. Memphis Sales & Mfg. Co., 38 F.R.D. 54 (D.C.Miss.1965); Employers Mut. Liab. Ins. Co. of Wisconsin v. Butler, 511 S.W.2d 323 (Tex.Civ.App.1974), refused n. r. e.; Frankel v. Sussex Poultry Co., 45 Del. 264, 71 A.2d 754 (1950); Atlantic Northern Airlines v. Schwimmer, 12 N.J. 293, 96 A.2d 652 (1953); City of Long Beach v. Superior Court, 64 Cal.App.3d 65, 134 Cal. Rptr. 468 (1976).

59. FRCP Rule 26(b)(4)(A) allows discovery of the identity of each person

Discovery of statements taken in preparation for litigation is the subject of conflicting rulings. Most jurisdictions agree that a party has a right to disclosure of any statement of his own in the possession of his adversary.[60] The Federal rule also allows any non-party witness to obtain a copy of his own statement, without any special showing.[61]

§ 2.86 Discovery of Experts' Opinions

Rule 26(b)(4) of the Federal Rules of Civil Procedure [62] allows a party to discover, through interrogatories, the identity [63] of any and expected to be called as an expert witness at trial, the subject matter on which he is expected to testify, and the substance of his testimony. See Wright & Miller, Federal Practice and Procedure: Civil § 2029 et seq.

60. F.R.C.P. Rule 26(b)(3): "A party may obtain without the required showing a statement concerning the action or its subject matter previously made by that party."

Nedimyer v. Pennsylvania R. R. Co., 6 F.R.D. 21 (D.C.Pa.1946) ("Here is a situation where it is plain that the defendant can gain nothing except the advantage of surprise by withholding the statement asked for. It is, of course, easy to say that the plaintiff knows what the facts of the accident were and what he said in his statement, but the accident occurred some three years ago and the statement requested was taken shortly thereafter. Whatever recollection of it the plaintiff may have, it is certain that he cannot carry in his mind, word for word, exactly what the statement shows he said. Words are susceptible of many shades of meaning and when the defendant, at the trial, produces the statement for cross-examination or offers it as containing an admission, the plaintiff may unexpectedly find that, as written down, it admits of a construction which he never intended. The precise words used, the phraseology, and the descriptive and technical terms applied to machinery, structures, places, etc., may well turn out to be critical.

"The statement was in all probability phrased by the defendant's agent who wrote it down and it will be carefully studied by the defendant's attorney when he prepares his case. To the plaintiff it is, to all practical intents and purposes, unknown—at best, only vaguely remembered. He may be perfectly honest and yet his statement, unless fairly and adequately explained, may be damaging.")

61. FRCP Rule 26(b)(3): "Upon request a person not a party may obtain without the required showing a statement concerning the action or its subject matter previously made by that person."

62. Concerning rule 26(b)(4), the Advisory Committee on the 1970 amendment to the Federal Rules of Civil Procedure stated: "Past judicial restrictions on discovery of an adversary's expert, particularly as to his opinions, reflect the fear that one side will benefit unduly from the other's better preparation. The procedure established in subsection (b)(4)(A) holds the risk to a minimum. Discovery is limited to trial witnesses, and may be obtained only at a time when the parties know who their expert witnesses will be. A party must as a practical matter prepare his own case in advance of that time, for he

63. See note 63 on page 146.

all expert witnesses opposing counsel intends to call at trial. Additionally, he may require the other party to state the subject matter on which the expert will testify, the substance of the facts and opinions to which he will testify, and a summary of the grounds for each opinion.[64]

If counsel determines that more information is required, and the court agrees, the court may, upon proper motion, order further discovery by other means, such as deposition or the production of written reports.[65] It has been stated that Rule 26(b)(4) is a two-step procedure, first requiring the use of interrogatories before other means of discovery may be pursued.[66]

Where an expert has been retained or specially employed by defense counsel in anticipation of litigation or preparation for trial, but

can hardly hope to build his case out of his opponent's experts.
"Subdivision (b)(4)(A) provides for discovery of an expert who is to testify at the trial. A party can require one who intends to use the expert to state the substance of the testimony that the expert is expected to give. The court may order further discovery, and it has ample power to regulate its timing and scope and to prevent abuse. Ordinarily, the order for further discovery shall compensate the expert for his time, and may compensate the party who intends to use the expert for past expenses reasonably incurred in obtaining facts or opinions from the expert. Those provisions are likely to discourage abusive practices." See also Weiss v. Chrysler Motors Corp., 515 F.2d 449 (2d Cir. 1975) (Policy behind Rule 26(b)(4) was not merely for the convenience of the parties and the court, but was designed to make the task of the trier of fact more manageable by means of an orderly presentation of complex issues of fact); Grinnell Corp. v. Hackett, 70 F.R.D. 326 (D.C.R.I.1976) (Purpose of rule is to provide a way, consistent with recognized privileges, for the parties to obtain the fullest possible knowledge of the issues and facts before trial).

63. Discovery of an expert witness' identity does not mean that defendant must release only his name. Defendant must also furnish plaintiff with the expert's present address, his current occupation or profession, and his particular specialty. Olmert v. Nelson, 60 F.R.D. 369 (D.D.C.1975); Rupp v. Vock & Weiderhold, Inc., 52 F.R.D. 111 (N.D.Ohio 1971).

One court has held that "identity" includes the qualifications of the witness. Clark v. General Motors Corp., 20 F.R.Serv.2d 679 (Mass.1975).

64. Breedlove v. Beech Aircraft Corp., 57 F.R.D. 202 (N.D.Miss.1972); Wilson v. Resnick, 51 F.R.D. 510 (D.C.Pa. 1970).

65. In order for the court to grant the motion for further discovery, the moving party must show additional circumstances which warrant the discovery. Quadrini v. Sikorsky Aircraft Div., United Aircraft Corp., 74 F.R.D. 594 (D.C.Conn.1977); United States v. 145.31 Acres of Land, 54 F.R.D. 359 (M.D.Pa.1972) aff'd without opinion 485 F.2d 682 (3d Cir.).

66. United States v. International Business Machines Corp., 72 F.R.D. 78 (S.D.N.Y.1976); Herbst v. International Tel. & Tel. Corp., 65 F.R.D. 528 (D.C.Conn.1975).

who is not expected to be called as a witness, Rule 26(b)(4)(B) provides that a party may discover facts known or opinions held by that expert only upon a showing of "exceptional circumstances."[67] Section (b)(4)(C) of Rule 26 states that the court shall require the party seeking discovery pay the expert a reasonable fee for his time spent in responding to discovery, unless manifest injustice would result.

67. Pearl Brewing Co. v. Joseph Schlitz Brewing Co., 415 F.Supp. 1122 (S.D. Tex.1976) (Exceptional circumstances met where only plaintiff's non-trial experts knew what was represented by coded symbols and lines of computer program print-out); Seiffer v. Topsy's Int'l, Inc., 69 F.R.D. 69 (D.C. Kan.1975) (Holding "exceptional circumstances" are met when it is impracticable to obtain facts or opinions on the same subject by other means); Sea Colony, Inc. v. Continental Ins. Co., 63 F.R.D. 113 (D.C. Del.1974) (Exceptional circumstances not required where party seeks only to discover *identity* of expert who is not expected to be called to trial, not his opinions).

§§ 2.87–2.90 are reserved for supplementary material.

J. DISCOVERING LIMITS OF INSURANCE COVERAGE

§ 2.91 Discovery of Insurance Generally

The first major case dealing with discovery of insurance policy limits was *Superior Insurance Co. v. Superior Ct.*,[68] a California Supreme Court case in which our office intervened as *amicus curius*. That case gave to plaintiff that which many insurance companies theretofore refused to divulge, to wit, policy limits. Prior to the *Superior Insurance Co. v. Superior Ct.* case, our office pursued the practical procedure of demanding policy limits, and when they were not forthcoming, moving "to perpetuate testimony" of defendant.

On our perpetuation proceedings we asked the defendant if he had insurance and his insurance limits. This was allowed under the theory that this was an asset legitimately within the subject of inquiry on a perpetion proceeding. Finally, the Superior Insurance Company in Los Angeles objected to this proceeding, and *Superior Insurance Co. v. Superior Ct.* resulted.

Although some courts are still hesitant and refuse for the most part to allow plaintiff to discover insurance policy limits in the absence of a sufficient independent reason,[69] many courts now routinely allow policy limits to be discovered.[70] Most states [71] so providing have

---

68. 37 Cal.2d 749, 235 P.2d 833 (1951).

For comprehensive discussion of discovery of existence and limits of insurance, see Wright & Miller, Federal Practice and Procedure, § 2010. See also West's Key No. Digests, Federal Civil Procedure ⚖1595.

69. Muck v. Claflin, 197 Kan. 594, 419 P.2d 1017 (1966) (Policy limits not discoverable); but see Cropp v. Woleslagel, 207 Kan. 627, 485 P.2d 1271 (1971) (Limits of insurance policy held subject to disclosure as essential adjunct to the encouragement of settlement); Fort v. Neal, 79 N.M. 479, 444 P.2d 990 (1968) (Court held that under rule of civil proceeding providing for examination of deponent regarding any matter relevant to the subject matter of the suit, insurance policy limits were *not* discoverable. "Plaintiff's counsel, having accepted employment, must proceed with equal diligence whether he can collect a large judgment, in full, in part, or not at all. Knowing that insurance is available, he should not agree to a settlement for less than he reasonably appraises the injuries justify as an award by a fair and unbiased jury of the locale of the action."); Hall v. Paul, 549 P.2d 343 (Okl.1976) (Policy limits not relevant, and hence not discoverable even where punitive damages are sought); Great American Ins. Co. v. Murray, 437 S.W.2d 264 (Tex.1969) (Policy limits not subject to discovery on grounds they materially reflected on witnesses' credibility).

70. State Nat'l Bank v. Gregorio, 68 Misc.2d 926, 328 N.Y.S.2d 799 (1971) (Disclosure of policy limits proper to aid in settling cases); Evans v. Grange Mut. Cas. Co., 12 Ohio Misc. 108, 230 N.E.2d 751 (1964).

71. Miffitt v. Statler Hilton, Inc., 28 Conn.Sup. 32, 248 A.2d 581 (1968)

§ 2.92 Practical Effects of Refusal to Disclose Insurance Coverage

even gone so far as to statutorily enact this rule, and in 1970, it was incorporated into the Federal Rules of Civil Procedure.[72]

It seems to the author that companies refusing to give policy limits place themselves at a disadvantage. For instance, when the policy limits is refused us, we immediately assume that it is a large policy and make a settlement demand solely upon the liability and the injuries not tempered with the expediency of a low policy limit.

If the policy is a small one, both sides are prejudiced by the short-sightedness of the insurance company. Plaintiff may go to court and obtain a large verdict that exceeds the policy limits. If the insured be insolvent, the plaintiff has not triumphed because he might have settled for the policy limits had he known them. Plaintiff's attorney has wasted his own time and hazarded his client to the caprice of trial, and the insurance company has had to pay the full policy limit, plus the cost of defense. Defense counsel who advise me that, "We can't even find out the limits of our own client's policy," have thereby abruptly terminated any negotiations for settlement.

("Pretrial procedures designed to facilitate the disposition of cases are recognized in the rules of practice adopted by the Superior Court. The disclosure of policy limits frequently aids in the disposition of cases in pretrial proceedings. There has been no unconstitutional interference with the judicial department by the General Assembly in enacting [rule permitting discovery of insurance policy limits]."); Montano v. Wigfield, 239 So.2d 609 (Fla.App.1970); Scott v. Kreuger, 151 Ind.App. 479, 280 N.E.2d 336 (1972); Walls v. Horbach, 189 Neb. 479, 203 N.W.2d 490 (1973); Marks v. Thompson, 282 N.C. 174, 192 S.E.2d 311 (1972) ("Sole purpose of the 1971 Act was to permit discovery of the existence and contents of insurance agreements"); Szarmack v. Welch, 456 Pa. 293, 318 A.2d 707 (1974) (Plaintiff entitled to discovery of automobile policy limits); Williams v. Carr, 84 S.D. 102, 167 N.W.2d 774 (1969); Young v. Barney, 20 Utah 2d 108, 433 P.2d 846 (1967); Ellis v. Gilbert, 19 Utah 2d 189, 429 P.2d 39 (1967) (Holding that while copy of automobile liability policy should be made available to plaintiff upon proper demand, such information should not be disclosed to the jury).

72. Fed.R.Civ.P. 26(b)(2), effective July 1, 1970, provides as follows:

"(2) Insurance Agreements. A party may obtain discovery of the existence and contents of any insurance agreement under which any person carrying on an insurance business may be liable to satisfy part or all of a judgment which may be entered in the action or to indemnify or reimburse for payments made to satisfy judgment. Information concerning the insurance agreement is not by reason of disclosure admissible in evidence at trial. For purposes of this paragraph, an application for insurance shall not be treated as part of an insurance agreement."

I have sometimes ascertained that an offer of settlement at policy limits has not been communicated to the insured by the lawyer for the insurance company. It would perhaps be unethical for me to communicate the offer directly to the personal defendant when he is represented by the insurance company lawyer. However, if I suspect that the insured has not been advised that settlement is possible within the policy limits,[73] when their case is called for trial I invite defendant's counsel and defendant personally into the Judge's chambers, asking the reporter to be present. I then state that since it would be unethical for me to advise the defendant personally that we are willing to settle the case for his policy limits, I now advise his counsel and the court, in his presence, of such settlement offer, and ask the reporter to make the record.

On numerous occasions I have seen heated conferences being carried on in the hallway by the insurance company lawyer and his client, following such an offer of settlement made by me in the Judge's chambers. Furthermore, such a statement obviates any questions of plaintiff's counsel himself being called by either the insurance company or the personal defendant if a verdict goes over policy limits and defendant has to pay personally, then sues the insurance company on the ground of bad faith.[74]

---

73. Conversely, must plaintiff's attorney report to his client an offer of settlement, even though it is far below the demand? Years past, on several occasions the author has not done so. Fortunately, the verdict in one instance was three times the offer, and in another instance was seven times the offer. However, upon reflection, I believe this to be a very dangerous and unrecommended practice. If the verdict were for defendant, in such instance, failure to report an offer might be adjudged malpractice if the client were to claim, in hindsight, that he would have accepted the offer even though it were below the demand.

Almost without exception in the author's experience, upon an offer being reported to the client, he has asked the author's advice. The lawyer cannot say, "I'm going to leave it up to you," for the technical knowledge of the lawyer is so far superior in his appraisal of the case that he should influence his client. He should state, as nearly as possible, in "percentages" or "chances," the probabilities of verdict. Being in better position to counsel and answer the layman than is the layman himself the lawyer can take into account his client's economic condition, his age, his family, or other personal consideration, and adopt the role of the conservative business counselor in giving advice, rather than that of an attorney who would be willing to hazard a trial for the possibility of a much higher award.

74. Parsons v. Continental Nat'l American Group, 113 Ariz. 223, 550 P.2d 94 (1976) (Insurance carrier held liable for $50,000.00, although policy limits were only $25,000.00, for refusal to deal in good faith. Attorney retained to defend claim advised insurer that injury was "worth the full amount of the policy," yet insurance company refused to settle within policy limits on the ground settlement figure was completely unrealistic.); Johansen v. California State Auto Ass'n Inter-Insurance Bureau, 15 Cal. 3d 9, 123 Cal.Rptr. 288, 538 P.2d 744 (1975) (Insurer breached its duty to insured when it failed to accept settlement offer at policy limits on belief that policy did not provide appropriate coverage); Cain v. State Farm Mut. Auto. Ins. Co., 47 Cal.App.3d 783, 121 Cal.Rptr. 200 (1975) (Insurer tortiously breached duty of good faith and fair dealing in refusing to settle within policy limits where investigation produced facts which showed that its insured was driving at time of accident); Rector v. Husted, 214 Kan. 230, 519 P.2d 634 (1974) (Insurer liable for damages awarded in excess of policy limits occasioned by its refusal to accept $6,000.00 settlement offer); Lange v. Fidelity & Cas. Co. of New York, 290 Minn. 61, 185 N.W.2d 881 (1971) (Insurer liable for its wrongful refusal to settle a verdict of $29,000.00 in a personal injury verdict against its insured for the $25,000.00 limits of policy); Poland v. Transamerica Ins. Co., 53 A. D.2d 140, 385 N.Y.S.2d 987 (1976) (Evidence raised factual issue as to whether insurer's refusal to accept offer to settle within limits of $100,000.00 was wrongful, where it knew that trial could result in judgment of over $500,000.00, and later, pursuant to a settlement agreement of $193,750.00, paid full policy limits); Hernandez v. Great Ins. Co. of New York, 464 S.W.2d 91 (Tex. 1971) (Insured entitled to sue insurer for failing to accept reasonable offers within policy limits); Hamilton v. State Farm Ins. Co., 83 Wash.2d 787, 523 P.2d 193 (1974) (Flat refusal of insurance company's lawyer to negotiate, under circumstances of substantial exposure to liability, a demonstrated receptive climate for settlement, and limited insurance coverage may show lack of good faith). Some plaintiffs' counsel have the mistaken idea that once judgment goes over policy limits, plaintiff can sue the insurance company directly for the excess if it has refused to settle within the policy limits, and an offer within policy limits has been made. This is obviously incorrect. It is only when a personal defendant has been made to pay the excess that he, himself, can sue the insurance company under the several theories of liability (whether negligence or bad faith in the particular jurisdiction). Of course, the defendant may assign this right to the plaintiff, a common practice. See Chapter 20, "Suing the Insurer," infra.

§§ 2.93–2.100 are reserved for supplementary material.

K. DEPOSITIONS AND INTERROGATORIES

Library References:

C.J.S. Federal Civil Procedure § 548.
West's Key No. Digests, Federal Civil Procedure ⚷1311 et seq., 1471 et seq.
Wright & Miller, Federal Practice and Procedure: Civil § 2071 et seq.

§ 2.101 Introduction

Written interrogatories [75] and oral depositions [76] are the means by which most of the information concerning the cause of an injury, extent of the damage, and the identity of those responsible are gathered.

Since depositions comprise a complete trial in and of themselves, and settle a theory of the case which, except in rare instances, must be followed during the trial, the preparation for a deposition must be as thorough as that for actual trial. As we have seen,[77] depositions may to some extent be used as a "fishing expedition." Their only limitation is that there is a reasonable possibility that admissible evidence may be discovered. Deposition by video tape is now an accepted practice in most state courts,[78] and is likewise permitted by the Federal Rules of Civil Procedure.[79]

---

75. FRCP Rule 33(a) provides that written interrogatories may be served upon defendant with or after service of the summons and complaint. For additional discussion, see Wright & Miller, Federal Practice and Procedure, § 2161 et seq.

See Universal Underwriters Ins. Co. v. Superior Court, 250 Cal.App.2d 722, 58 Cal.Rptr. 870 (1967) ("A sworn statement as to the contention of the party in answer to a relevant interrogatory is binding."); Seiden v. Allen, 135 N.J.Super. 253, 343 A.2d 125 (1975) (Held improper for party to answer interrogatory with but general references to transcript of deposition. "Neither the letter nor the spirit of the rule allows a party to supply answers which cast upon his adversary the impossible burden of ferreting out of a deposition transcript that which the answeror intends as his answer. If the called-for information is contained in the transcripts of the deposition, it is the answeror's obligation to collect it and supply it in the form required by the rule.").

76. Under FRCP Rule 30(a), deposition of any person upon oral examination may be taken after the action is commenced without leave of court, except leave of court is required where plaintiff seeks to take a deposition prior to the expiration of 30 days after service of process. For additional discussion, see Wright & Miller, Federal Practice and Procedure, § 2101 et seq.

77. See section 2.81 supra.

78. Mayor and Alderman of Savannah v. Palmerio, 135 Ga.App. 147, 217 S. E.2d 430 (1975) ("[A] deposition is at best a poor substitute for the live testimony of a witness, but the use

79. See note 79 on page 153.

While a deposition may be used somewhat as a "fishing expedition," nevertheless, counsel asking the questions may be bound by a theory set forth in his questions. Both the question and answer may be introduced subsequently at the trial and be more damaging to the party asking the question than to the adversary. In the rare case, it is conceivable that counsel, having a complete investigation and needing no information from the adverse party, should waive deposition rather than unnecessarily expose his theory by the questions, if the theory be unknown.

To prevent his overlooking any permissible subjects of inquiry, even the most adept counsel who has taken hundreds of depositions should, at least mentally, have a chart of all the subjects to be covered.

In the automobile case, ages, addresses, license numbers, familial history, military records, health histories, employments, wages, education, marital history, contributions of support should all be consid-

---

of video tape is far superior to the reading of a stenographic transcript of a deposition, when it is considered that the appearance and the demeanor of the witness is apparent through the use of the video taping process. The objective of all legal investigations is the discovery of truth, and it is our sincere belief that the use of video taping for depositions will provide a more accurate record of the witness' testimony than the mere reading of a stenographic transcript by persons other than those who actually gave the deposition."); State ex rel. Lucas v. Moss, 498 S.W.2d 289 (Mo.1973); Mills v. Dortch, 142 N.J. Super. 410, 361 A.2d 606 (1976) ("Unless waived by the parties, the deposition shall be recorded by the usual stenographic method as well as by videotape, in order to protect the parties against mechanical defects"); Rubino v. G. D. Searle Co., 73 Misc. 2d 447, 340 N.Y.S.2d 574 (1973) ("Because a videotape is 'nothing more than a motion picture synchronized with a sound recording.' . . ., the rationale permitting the use of electronic recording devices would allow the use of videotapes."); State ex rel. Johnson v. Circuit Court of Milwaukee County, 61 Wis.2d 1, 212 N.W.2d 1 (1972) (trial court has discretion to allow videotape recordings of depositions of witnesses to be made).

79. FRCP Rule 30(b)(4) provides: "[A] court may upon motion order that the testimony at a deposition be recorded by other than stenographic means, in which event the order shall designate the manner of recording, preserving, and filing the deposition, and may include such other provisions to assure that the recorded testimony will be accurate and trustworthy."

Concerning the use of videotaped depositions, the court in Carson v. Burlington Northern, Inc., 52 F.R.D. 492, 493 (D.C.Neb.1971) stated:

"[T]he finder of fact at trial often will gain greater insight from the manner in which an answer is delivered and recorded by audio-visual devices. Moreover, a recording, a video tape, or a motion picture of a deposition will avoid the tedium that is produced when counsel reads, lengthy depositions into evidence at trial."

ered that further investigation may be made. This applies both to defendant and plaintiff questioner.

A subpoena duces tecum should also be liberally used to bring to the lawyer's office photographs from the newspaper morgue, health records, hospital records, doctor's charts and the like and these should be given to the officer authorized under the particular state procedure to administer the oath that he may photostat or photograph these to incorporate in the deposition. Such a deposition may then be referred to an expert for further evaluation.

Counsel for plaintiff should keep in mind that all depositions taken go to the home office of the interested insurance company, and that these documents are material in deciding questions as to amount of settlement. Therefore it is ordinarily prudent to supplement depositions, whenever counsel for the defense omits questions as to such matters as loss of wages, hospital bills, pain and suffering and the like, by asking the questions. In any event, care should be exercised so that the answers given by the plaintiff, or that of any other witness under the guidance of plaintiff's counsel, appear clear and correct in the deposition taken. Otherwise, at the trial, the issue of changed testimony may arise. By additional questions, the witness should be given the chance to clear up any uncertainties, or apparent misstatements.

Under most rules of practice, a witness has the right to correct his deposition after it has been typed and presented to him for examination and approval.[80] However, many changes, if at all material, at once reflect upon the credibility of the witness, and are subject to comment by opposing counsel at the trial.

As a preamble to depositions, counsel often stipulate that the "usual stipulations" shall prevail, but unless these are well known, it

---

80. FRCP Rule 30(e) requires the fully-transcribed deposition to be submitted to the witness for his examination. The witness may then make any changes he desires as to its form or substance, but he must state his reasons for doing so. These changes are to be entered by the officer conducting the examination. Rogers v. Roth, 477 F.2d 1154 (10th Cir. 1973) (When witness gives deposition and signature is not waived, deponent may later make changes and give reasons therefor); Architectural League of New York v. Bartos, 404 F.Supp. 304 (S.D.N.Y.1975) (Changes made by witness in his own hand and without statement of his reasons were inoperative). See also De Seversky v. Republic Aviation Corp., 2 F.R.D. 113 (E.D.N.Y.1941) (Where plaintiff made substantial changes in his answers, he was ordered to appear and submit himself to additional examination. "Such examination should not be considered finished if a witness seeks to recant his testimony or feels that to be 'truthful' he must directly contradict the answers already given by him on most material points.").

is better to write them out, and avoid subsequent misunderstandings. If a witness is to be unavailable at trial it is devastating to have his testimony stricken because of the "leading question" on the deposition or because his most important answer may be "hearsay." If counsel taking a deposition has such "evidence," he should be sure to ask the question in a different manner so that this evidence will be legally admissible.

Under the practice in some states, plaintiff's deposition may be introduced and read completely, and does not have to be used solely for "impeachment."[81] Likewise, a deposition may be read even if the reporter is dead or the deposition unsigned.[82]

Unlike the lawsuit in chief, the deposition is not limited by State or even national boundaries.[83] However, the author disfavors written interrogatories in foreign depositions. The oral interrogatories are preferable, provided the representing counsel is given a full resume of the case and the desired testimony.

In seamen's cases, the defendant ship owner often has first opportunity at interrogation because the witness may be at sea, on the boat, immediately after the accident. However, libellant's proctor

---

81. See, e. g., Calif.Code of Civil Procedure, § 2016(c)(2):

"The deposition of a party to the record of any civil action or proceeding or of a person for whose immediate benefit said action or proceeding is prosecuted or defended, or of anyone who at the time of taking the deposition was an officer, director, superintendent, member, agent, employee, or managing agent of any such party or person may be used by an adverse party for any purpose."

Most state statutes allow depositions to be admitted where the witness is absent or lives at a specified distance from the place of trial. FRCP Rule 32(a)3(B) allows a deposition to be so used where the witness lives more than 100 miles from the place of trial, or is outside of the United States. For additional discussion see Wright & Miller, Federal Practice and Procedure, Rule 32.

82. Rochland Chem. Co. v. F & F Mfg., Inc., 184 Neb. 235, 166 N.W.2d 735 (1969); Hill v. Rich, 522 S.W.2d 597 (Tex.Civ.App.1975), refused n. r. e. (holding that mere lack of signature would not justify suppression of a deposition, unless the reasons for not signing it impugn the verity or reliability of the deposition).

FRCP Rule 30(e) permits the officer to sign the deposition if the witness has not signed it within 30 days after its submission to him, and to state on the record the fact of the waiver, the illness, or absence of the witness, or the refusal of the witness along with any reason given therefor. For additional discussion, see Wright & Miller, Federal Practice and Procedure Civil § 2142 et seq.

83. State ex rel. Von Pein v. Clark, 526 S.W.2d 383 (Mo.App.1975) (Lower court abused its discretion when it ordered defendants in dog-bite case to travel from their residence in Belgium to be deposed in Missouri.).

§ 2.102 Sample Written Interrogatories

Herewith is presented an example of written interrogatories and the answers appended. It will be seen how much information may be realized from the adverse party by this method. The case was against a negligent driver who had injured our client, a motorcyclist. The questions and answers are as follows:

Interrogatory No. 1. State your full name, present resident address, telephone number, date and place of birth.

Answer. NORMAN HARPER and BRENDA HARPER (CHRONISTER): 5243 South Clovis, Fresno, California; September 23, 1919 and January 19, 1951.

Interrogatory No. 2. State your age.

Answer. NORMAN HARPER: 52; BRENDA HARPER CHRONISTER: 20.

Interrogatory No. 3. State your former residence addresses for a period of five years prior to the date of these Interrogatories, giving the dates during which you lived at each of said addresses.

Answer. Both defendants have lived at the same address for the past 15 years.

Interrogatory No. 4. State your marital status at the present time and at the time of the within accident and, if married, the name and address of your spouse.

Answer. NORMAN HARPER: married; BRENDA HARPER CHRONISTER: single at the time of the accident but now married.

Interrogatory No. 5. State whether you have been issued a driver's license authorizing you to operate a motor vehicle.

Answer. Yes.

Ch. 2 INVESTIGATION AND DISCOVERY § 2.102

Interrogatory No. 6. If so, state as to each said license:
    a. The full name and address shown on such license;
    b. The date of original issuance;
    c. The state of issuance;
    d. The number of the license;
    e. The date of expiration, and
    f. The name and address of all persons who signed the application for such license.

Answer.
    a. See answer to Interrogatories 1 and 3 above.
    b. Unknown.
    c. California.
    d. Brenda Harper Chronister: E621607.
    e. NORMAN HARPER: Birthdate, 1974; BRENDA HARPER CHRONISTER: Birthdate, 1973.
    f. Both parents signed for Brenda Harper Chronister's drivers license.

Interrogatory No. 7. State whether you ever had a driver's license which had put on it any restrictions of any sort.

Answer. No.

Interrogatory No. 8. If so, with respect to each restriction to each license, state:
    a. The name of the issuing state;
    b. The date of issuance;
    c. All restrictions recorded on the license;
    d. The nature of such restriction; and,
    e. Whether such restriction was recorded on the license.

Answer. Not applicable.

Interrogatory No. 9. State whether you ever had a driver's license suspended, cancelled or revoked.

Answer. No.

Interrogatory No. 10. If so, with respect to each such suspension, cancellation or revocation, state:
    a. The name of the state suspending, cancelling or revoking such license;
    b. The date of such suspension, cancellation or revocation;
    c. The reasons therefor;

§ 2.102　　　　　　　　INTRODUCTION　　　　　　　　Pt. 1

Interrogatory No. 10.
—Continued

         d. The action taken by the state; and,
         e. The reasons therefor.

Answer.   Not applicable.

Interrogatory No. 11. State whether you have ever been denied the issuance of a driver's license.

Answer.   No.

Interrogatory No. 12. If so, for each occasion, state:
         a. The date of denial;
         b. Whether the denial was made; and,
         c. The reasons for such denial.

Answer.   Not applicable.

Interrogatory No. 13. State and set forth the number of months or years, and the extent of your driving experience prior to the accident referred to in plaintiff's Complaint herein (hereinafter called "said accident"),

Answer.   NORMAN HARPER: 34 years; BRENDA HARPER CHRONISTER: 4 years.

Interrogatory No. 14. List all offenses or violations recorded on your driver's license.

Answer.   None.

Interrogatory No. 15. In the five (5) years preceding said accident, state whether you have been involved in any collisions involving motor vehicles.

Answer.   No.

Interrogatory No. 16. If so, as to each state:
         a. The date, time and location of accident;
         b. All of the names and addresses of people involved;
         c. Whether legal proceedings were commenced; and
         d. The names of parties and status they occupied in any action.

Answer.   Not applicable.

Interrogatory No. 17. What was the condition of your health during the six (6) months prior to and including the date of said accident?

Answer.   Good.

Ch. 2 INVESTIGATION AND DISCOVERY   § 2.102

Interrogatory No. 18. Had you been under the care of any physician, doctor or practitioner of the healing arts during the six (6) months prior to and including the date of said accident?

Answer. No.

Interrogatory No. 19. If so, state:
    a. Name and address of such practitioner;
    b. Dates under care of such practitioner; and
    c. The nature of the condition for which you were under such care.

Interrogatory No. 20. Have you ever had epilepsy or been subject to fainting, dizzy spells or blackouts?

Answer. No.

Interrogatory No. 21. If so, describe and set forth:
    a. Nature of any such problem;
    b. Frequency of same;
    c. Name and address of any attending physician for any such conditions;
    d. Name and address of any person or persons you have told about any such conditions, who knows about it, or who has witnessed the same;
    e. If so, state the time of day and location when this occurred; and
    f. Describe such occurrence in detail.

Answer. Not applicable.

Interrogatory No. 22. State whether you consumed any intoxicating or alcoholic beverages within twenty-four (24) hours preceding the said accident or occurrence in question.

Answer. No.

Interrogatory No. 23. If so, state:
    a. The time and place of each such item consumed;
    b. The kind and amount of each such item consumed;
    c. The name and address of all persons present at the consumption of each such item or drink;
    d. Have you ever been advised not to consume intoxicating or alcoholic beverages;

§ 2.102

    e. If so, state the name and address of the person or persons who so advised you, and state whether you were advised not to consume intoxicating or alcoholic beverages in all situations or whether such advice pertained only to certain circumstances;

    f. Did you consume any food while partaking, or after having partaken, of any such intoxicating or alcoholic beverages; and

    g. If so, state when and where you consumed same and the amount.

Answer. Not applicable.

Interrogatory No. 24. State whether you took any drugs or narcotics, whether by prescription or otherwise, in any manner whatsoever in the twenty-four (24) hour period immediately preceding the said accident or occurrence in question.

Answer. No.

Interrogatory No. 25. If so, state:

    a. The time and place of consumption of each such drug or narcotic;

    b. The kind and amount of each such drug or narcotic consumed;

    c. The name and address of all persons present at the consumption of each such drug or narcotic;

    d. Whether you had been advised to take a drug or narcotic;

    e. If so, the present name and address of the physician who advised you to take the same, and whether or not a prescription for the same had been issued to you by said physician; and

    f. Had you consumed any such drug or narcotic which you had been advised to take at regular intervals of time in accordance with the advice of said physician within the twenty-four (24) hours period preceding the said accident or occurrence in question, or had you omitted any time at which you were advised to partake of same, or had you partaken of same at irregular intervals of time?

Ch. 2 INVESTIGATION AND DISCOVERY § 2.102

Answer. Not applicable.

Interrogatory No. 26. At the time of this accident:
- a. Did you have any impairment of vision in either eye?
- b. If your answer to part (a) of this Interrogatory is affirmative, state:
  1. Which eye; and
  2. Describe the impairment.
- c. Were you wearing corrective lenses or any glasses at the time of said accident?
- d. If so,
  1. Were the lenses tinted or colored?
  2. Were the lenses bifocal?
  3. State the name and address of the doctor or optometrist who prescribed them and the date thereof.
  4. For what conditions were said glasses prescribed?
  5. Where are the glasses at the present time?
- e. State the name, address and telephone number of the last doctor or optometrist who gave you an eye examination, and the dates thereof; and,
- f. If you were not wearing corrective lenses or glasses,
  1. Have corrective lenses or glasses ever been prescribed for or recommended to you?
  2. State the name, address and telephone number of the last doctor or optometrist who did so, and the date thereof.

Answer.
- a. NORMAN HARPER: no; BRENDA HARPER CHRONISTER: yes.
- b. BRENDA HARPER CHRONISTER: required to wear glasses because she was nearsighted.
- c. Yes.
- d. 1. No.
  2. No.
  3. Dr. Hugh Awtrey, opthalmologist, 1045 "S" Street, Fresno.
  4. Nearsighted.
  5. Defendant has them on her person.

§ 2.102   INTRODUCTION   Pt. 1

         e. Dr. Hugh Awtrey, approximately two years ago.
         f. Not applicable.

Interrogatory No. 27. State all names, addresses and telephone numbers known to you, your attorney or your insurance carrier, of any and all persons who claim to have been at the scene of said accident or who claim to have heard any of the events or happenings that occurred at the scene of said accident.

Answer. The only persons that these defendants have knowledge of that were witnesses to the accident involved the occupants of both vehicles which includes the parties and Margaret Summers who is the daughter of the defendant NORMAN HARPER.

Interrogatory No. 28. State whether you or any of your representatives have obtained a written statement, recording, or a transcription of any oral statement concerning the accident of any injuries claimed to have resulted from said accident, from any party herein, any agent or employee of a party herein, any witness or witnesses.

Answer. No.

Interrogatory No. 29. If so, state:
     a. The name of such person or persons;
     b. The address of such person or persons;
     c. The date and place wherein such statement was taken;
     d. The name, address and telephone number of the person who has custody of such statement(s); and,
     e. The name, address and telephone number of the person taking such statement(s).

Answer. Not applicable.

Interrogatory No. 30. Have any photographs or motion pictures been taken concerning the accident or occurrence or injuries claimed to have resulted from said accident?

Answer. No.

Interrogatory No. 31.	If so, state:
	a. What photographs or motion pictures have been taken concerning the facts of the accident or occurrence, and further state:
	  1. When were these taken?
	  2. Who took them?
	  3. How many were taken?
	  4. Size or footage involved?
	  5. Who has possession of them?
	b. What photographs or motion pictures have been taken showing injuries to person or damage to property or lack of same, and further state:
	  1. When were these taken?
	  2. Who took them?
	  3. How many were taken?
	  4. Size or footage involved?
	  5. Who has possession of them?

Answer.	Not applicable.
Interrogatory No. 32.	Have you ever heard anything said by any plaintiff in this action concerning any facts of this accident, how this accident occurred, who was at fault or the nature or extent of injuries involved?
Answer.	No.
Interrogatory No. 33.	If your answer to the above Interrogatory is affirmative, state in chronological order: a. The date, time and place of each statement; b. The name, business address and telephone number and residence address and telephone number of each person present; and c. What each person said, and the name of the person making each statement.
Answer.	Not applicable.
Interrogatory No. 34.	Have you ever said anything to any plaintiff in this action, or in said plaintiff's presence, concerning any facts of this accident, how this accident occurred, who was at fault or the nature and extent of injuries involved?
Answer.	No.

§ 2.102 INTRODUCTION Pt. 1

Interrogatory No. 35. If your answer to the above Interrogatory is affirmative, state in chronological order:
    a. The date, time and place of each statement;
    b. The name, business address and telephone number, and residence address and telephone number of each person present;
    c. What you said; and
    d. What each other person, including any plaintiff, said at that time and name of person making each statement.

Answer. Not applicable.

Interrogatory No. 36. Have you ever said anything to anyone (excluding plaintiff and your attorney, insurance company and their representatives) concerning the facts of this accident, how this accident occurred, who was at fault or the nature or extent of injuries involved?

Answer. No.

Interrogatory No. 37. If your answer to the above Interrogatory is affirmative, state in chronological order:
    a. The date, time and place of each statement;
    b. The name, business address and telephone number and residence address and telephone number of each person present;
    c. What you said; and,
    d. What each other person said at that time and name the person making such statement.

Answer. Not applicable.

Interrogatory No. 38. With respect to the vehicle you were operating at the time of the accident, state:
    a. The name, address and last known whereabouts of the registered owner; and,
    b. The name, address and last known whereabouts of the legal owner.

Answer.
    a. NORMAN HARPER.
    b. NORMAN HARPER.

Interrogatory No. 39. If you were not the registered owner of said automobile at the time of said accident, state if you were driving the automobile:
a. With the permission and consent of the registered owner; and,
b. Under any other claimed authority.

Answer. BRENDA HARPER CHRONISTER was driving her father's automobile with his permission.

Interrogatory No. 40. Did you have the permission of the owner to drive such vehicle:
a. Generally; and,
b. At the specific time of the accident.

Answer. Yes.

Interrogatory No. 41. Were you engaged in the pursuit of any business activity, performing acts on behalf of any other person, or acting as the agent of any person or firm at the time of said accident?

Answer. No.

Interrogatory No. 42. If your answer to the preceding Interrogatory is affirmative, state the name and address of the person or firm and nature of business or activity you were pursuing at the time of the accident.

Answer. Not applicable.

Interrogatory No. 43. Was your vehicle damaged as a result of said accident?

Answer. Yes.

Interrogatory No. 44. If your answer to the preceding Interrogatory is affirmative, state:
a. What parts of your vehicle were damaged by said accident;
b. Describe the full extent of this damage;
c. Whether all of said damage has been repaired;
d. If all of said damage has not been repaired,
   1. What portions were not repaired?
   2. Was the vehicle sold for salvage?
e. If the vehicle was sold for salvage, state the name, address and telephone number of the buyer;

§ 2.102　　　　　　　　　INTRODUCTION　　　　　　　　　Pt. 1

    f. The name, address and telephone number of each person or organization that made repairs, and the amounts of their respective repair bills; and,

    g. The name, address and telephone number of each person who now has possession, custody or control of each of said estimates, repair bills or bill of salvage sale.

Answer.   The right front fender was damaged and it has not been repaired.

Interrogatory No. 45.   State the number and names of all insurance companies whose policies afford you any bodily injury or public liability coverage, whether primary or excess, concerning said accident, and further state:

    a. The policy numbers of each;

    b. The extent of the bodily injury or public liability monetary limits for which you are covered by each or any of these insurance policies; and,

    c. The complete wording of all named insureds on each policy.

Answer.   Travelers Insurance Company.

    a. 007468372

    b. $100,000 single limit coverage

    c. NORMAN Q. and BRENDA R. HARPER

Interrogatory No. 46.   Was there in effect at the time of the accident referred to in plaintiff's complaint herein any insurance policies where a question or controversy exists as to whether such policies afford you any bodily injury or public liability coverage, whether primary or excess, in connection with said accident?

Answer.   No.

Interrogatory No. 47.   If the answer to the preceding Interrogatory is affirmative, state the names of all said insurance companies, their policy numbers and the bodily injury or public liability limits of each policy.

Answer.   Not applicable.

Interrogatory No. 48.	State the name, business address and telephone number and the residence address and telephone number, of each person not named elsewhere in your answers to these Interrogatories known to you or anyone acting in your behalf, who has any knowledge or relevant information regarding any facts or circumstances in this case.
Answer.	Margaret Summers.
Interrogatory No. 49.	State whether you know, or are acquainted with any of the persons whose names have been given in answer to any of the Interrogatories herein.
Answer.	Yes.
Interrogatory No. 50.	If your answer to the preceding Interrogatory is affirmative, state: a. The name of each such person; b. The nature of said acquaintanceship; c. For how long you have been acquainted with each; and, d. Which of said persons are your present or past agents, servants or employees, and state the dates of their employment.
Answer.	a. Margaret Summers. b. Daughter of NORMAN HARPER and sister of BRENDA HARPER CHRONISTER.

Signature [84]

Interrogatories furnish information which is the missing key in a case. Illusive facts appear because it is the first opportunity that counsel has to question the opposing party.

---

84. In California, the interrogatories must be verified by the person answering them. A sample of such a verification is set out below:

VERIFICATION

I, _____, declare:
I am one of the defendants in the above-entitled action; I have read the foregoing Answer to Interrogatories and know the contents thereof; I certify that the same is true of my own knowledge, except as to the matters which are therein stated upon my information or belief, and as to those matters I believe them to be true.
I certify under penalty of perjury that the foregoing is true and correct.
Executed on _____, 19___, at _____, California.

Signature

Interrogatories may furnish gold, too, in the sense of materials to be used in trial. (Written first, then oral interrogatories, i. e., depositions, should both be employed.)

Walter Gerash, Esquire,[85] was plaintiff's attorney in a wrongful death case. In written interrogatories, plaintiff was asked, *"How were you dependent on your son?"*

Herewith the answer, which has the complete factual and emotional thrust of a survivor in a wrongful death case. Such answer should be read to the jury in toto on closing plaintiff's argument:

"We were dependent upon Stephen to return our investment in him (estimated at in excess of $100,000 in after-tax money) in the form of an annuity to take care of his mother and father in their old age and to shelter us against the onslaught of inflation.

We were dependent upon him to the extent that it allowed us a dependency tax deduction each year of his all-too-short life.

We were dependent upon him to absorb some of our estate development through the transferral to him of a non-taxable gift of $6,000 a year estimated to have cost us, predicated on our life expectancy, approximately $189,000 of estate value and the resultant tax that this will add to our estate.

We were dependent on him to carry as much of his own weight financially as he could to permit us to successfully cross to the other side of the tracks.

We were dependent upon him to perpetuate the family name, to continue the contributions to America and human society that started with the arrival of his grandparents from Italy.

We were dependent upon him for continuation of our right to life, liberty, and the pursuit of happiness. You denied him the right to life, thereby eroding the very foundation of our rights and destroyed our pursuit of happiness on this earth.

I was dependent upon him to follow in my footsteps in terms of his engineering training and the application of his honest labor, his native intelligence and his business acumen to successfully run the wholly-owned business which I acquired after consultation with and consideration of Stephen's desires and aspirations.

I was dependent upon him to perpetuate my philosophy in my company to help and aid the working peoples, the true creators of wealth in our society, against the inroad and onslaught of the leeches.

---

85. Walter Gerash, Esquire, Gerash & Springer, P.C., Suite 2317, 1700 Broadway, Denver, Colorado 80290.

I was dependent upon him to see that all my financial obligations, normal and philosophic, implied or stated, incurred by virtue of my purchase of this business (the purchase started in 1973 and was completed in 1976), were met and fulfilled in the event of my demise.

I was dependent upon him to acquire the technical and business knowledge required with the continuing success of this business.

We were dependent upon Stephen for the peace of mind to keep us both constructive, compassionate human beings.

We were dependent upon Stephen for our mental and physical health, both of which you have denied us through his wrongful death.

I was dependent upon Stephen to economically hold the family group together in the event of my demise.

I was dependent upon Stephen to look out for the welfare of Mrs. Meoli, who is not a financial nor a business sophisticate.

We were dependent upon Stephen for the love, warmth, humor and disposition that he brought into our lives.

We were dependent upon Stephen for his company and the warm relationship of those many friends that he was responsible for developing.

I depended upon Stephen as the only member of my immediate family with the ability to read and to be shown my company's audited report for the fiscal year 1975. We spent two days discussing this report, its ramifications, his obligations and his future responsibilities. Up to that point (January, 1976), he was the only son to be shown this report and to whom I layed out the entire business aspects of my company.

I was dependent upon Stephen for, in his words, my "ticket to early retirement." I have worked long and hard to come from the bowels of Brooklyn and poverty to have earned an early retirement. It is my just due and right which you have denied me of . . .

I consider this question oppressive and ridiculous. I can tell you that on August 6, 1975, on the occasion of our 25th anniversary, Stephen in conjunction with his two brothers, gave Mrs. Meoli and myself a set of sterling silver goblets, provided the champagne, photographed the event, took us to dinner, along with his grandmother and grandfather. I will also tell you that Stephen on his return in December, 1975, during the Christmas vacation from Colorado State broke into tears and said, "Jesus, I never thought I would miss you guys as much as I have. I love the two of you so much!" These gifts and others are of incalculable value to us. *You place a value on it.*"

§ 2.103 Example of Deposition

The following is a condensed and excerpted transcript of a deposition taken by *John E. Kalin,* Esquire, one of the author's associates, in a case involving a collision between an automobile and a motorcycle. The person being deposed is the defendant in the case, who was driving the car.

The deponent should be instructed verbally to answer every question, not to shake his or her head or make other gestures in response to the inquiry. Initially, the lawyer should inform the deponent as to the effect of the deposition, that is, that it is taken under oath and may be used in the subsequent trial to impeach his testimony and the like. The witness should also be made aware that he is not to answer a question he has not heard clearly, or does not understand.

In our Los Angeles office we have a videotape showing prospective witnesses a sample deposition.

The deposition:

EXAMINATION BY MR. KALIN

MR. KALIN: Q. Mrs. Newhall, would you please state your name and address for the records.

A. Jane Newhall, 2950 P_____ Avenue, San Francisco, California.

Q. And do you spell your name N-e-w-h-a-l-l?

A. Yes.

MR. HOTHEM: May we have the standard stipulations?
MR. KALIN: Yes.

Q. Have you had an opportunity to prepare for this deposition with your lawyer, Mr. Hothem?

A. Yes.

Q. And he's explained to you what a deposition is?

A. Yes.

Q. So you understand that I'm going to be asking you questions, and you will answer them under oath, and it's as though you were giving testimony in court.

My questions and your answers will be taken down by the court reporter and later transcribed and put in booklet form for your review.

A. Yes.

Q. I want you also to understand that if, after reviewing the transcript of the deposition, if you make any changes, that I can comment upon them and anyone can comment upon them in court at the trial of this matter. You understand that?

A. Yes.
Q. Are you taking any medication at this time?
A. Thyroid pills. And Dyazide.
Q. Would either of those pills affect your ability to think and answer questions at the deposition?
A. I think not.
Q. Have you reviewed any documents pertaining to this lawsuit before coming to the deposition?
A. No.
Q. Have you looked at the police report regarding this accident?
A. Shortly after the accident happened.
Q. Have you looked at it since that time?
A. No.
Q. Have you gone over or looked at any witness statements?
A. No.
Q. I note that there are no restrictions on your driving on that license; is that correct?
A. That's right.
Q. Do you wear glasses?
A. Not to drive.
Q. For reading purposes?
A. Yes.
Q. Any other reason?
A. No.
Q. I'm going to be asking you some questions about the accident which occurred at the intersection of Irving and 11th Streets on May 26th, 1978.

Do you recall that accident?
A. Yes.
Q. Now, was there anyone present with you in the car that you were driving?
A. No.
Q. Where were you going at the time of the accident?
A. I was going to the corner of 11th and Irving.
Q. Which corner of 11th and Irving?
A. Northwest.

Q. When you turned onto Irving, did you make a left or a right-hand turn?
A. A left turn onto Irving.
Q. This would be a left-hand turn onto Irving from 12th?
A. Yes.
Q. Then, you proceeded approximately one block, a little more than a block, before the accident occurred.
A. Yes.
Q. And immediately prior to the accident, which direction were you headed on Irving?
A. East.
Q. Are either of those intersections at 12th and Irving or 11th and Irving controlled by a stop sign?
A. I think both 12th and 11th are. But Irving is not.
Q. And there are no stop lights at either intersection?
A. No.
Q. Now, at the time of the accident when you were traveling east on Irving, do you recall what the flow of traffic was like? Was it light, heavy, medium?
A. I'd say light right at that time.
Q. Now, is Irving street a two-lane or a four-lane road?
A. Two lane.
Q. Immediately before the accident, what lane were you traveling in?
A. I was driving in the easterly lane.
Q. I take it that the thrift shop is on the northwest corner of 11th?
A. Yes.
Q. Were you going to pick someone up there or drop something off or—
A. Pick up the lady who had been working with me.
Q. I see.
And do you remember approximately—the approximate time of day that that would have been?
A. 4:40.
Q. Now, when did you first notice Mr. Baron on his motorcycle?
A. When he was on the ground.
Q. Did you see the impact between your two vehicles; that is, between your car and his motorcycle?

Ch. 2   INVESTIGATION AND DISCOVERY   § 2.103

A. I felt it.
Q. But you didn't see it?
A. No.
Q. How far into the intersection were you at the time of the impact?
A. About the center.
Q. And approximately how far into making your turn were you at the time of the impact?
A. I had just started.
Q. Do you recall how fast you were traveling at the time of the impact?
A. No.
Q. Can you give an approximation of your speed?
A. (Witness shakes head negatively.) I would say slowly.
Q. Was your car moving?
A. As I was making the turn (indicating).
Q. And by "slowly," what do you mean? Do you mean 10 to 15 miles per hour?
A. I would say under 10.
Q. Can you tell me how far into your turn were you? You had begun your turn—
A. Yes.
Q. —was your car at the time of impact headed in a northern direction?
A. Not yet.
Q. Would it be fair to say it was headed in a northerly direction?
A. Yes.
Q. Were you about halfway—were you about in the middle of your turn? In other words, you had not completed your turn, but you were about in the middle of the turn.
A. I'd say closer to the beginning of it.
Q. So, it was somewhere in between the beginning and the middle of the turn.
A. Yes.
Q. Were you into the westerly lane on Irving?
A. Just barely.
Q. By "barely," can you put that in terms of feet for us?
A. No, I couldn't.

§ 2.103 INTRODUCTION Pt. 1

Q. Well, would you say it would be more than ten feet?
A. I would have no idea about the measurement.
Q. Was there a car traveling in front of you as you traveled from the intersection of 12th and Irving to the intersection of 11th and Irving?
A. Not that I remember.
Q. Do you remember cars passing you going the opposite direction?
A. No. There was a car coming toward me as I approached 11th.
Q. And did that car pass through the intersection of 11th and Irving before you reached the intersection?
A. It indicated that it was to turn south on 11th.
Q. And that would be a left-hand turn in front of you?
A. Yes.
Q. And did it turn in front of you?
A. Yes. It began its turn in front of me.
Q. And where was your vehicle located when it began its turn?
A. Well, I was—when it began to make its turn, I realized I could make my turn.
Q. So, are you saying that you were stopped at the intersection of 11th and Irving and saw this other car making its turn, and then started to make your turn?
A. Stopped or going very slowly.
Q. You were stopped or going very slowly.
A. Uh-huh.
Q. After he started to make his left-hand turn, then you saw that you could make your left-hand turn, and you started to make it; is that correct?
A. Yes.
Q. Now, where was that vehicle located? By "that vehicle," I mean the vehicle that was making the left-hand turn in front of you when you started to make your left-hand turn. In other words, had he come over into the eastern lane or was he still in the western lane?
A. He was still in the western lane.
Q. Were there any cars in back of him?
A. Not that I know of. I didn't see any.
Q. Did you see him complete his left-hand turn?
A. No.

Q. Did you see him pass by to your right?

A. Um, if we go back a minute, can I explain?

Q. You don't have to go back; you can just explain.

A. He started to make his turn, and I started to make my turn, and then there was the impact. And after the impact, Mr. Baron was sliding along the street. And when he had come to a stop, I glanced to see where that—the car making the turn was, and he was going down—he was going along—in other words, I don't know whether it's down or not—going along 11th.

Q. When you got to the intersection of 11th and Irving, were there any vehicles on 11th at the stop signs?

A. No. (Witness shakes head negatively.) Not that I know of.

Q. And you don't remember any car in front of you making a left- or right-hand turn?

A. No.

Q. Did your car move after the impact?

A. No. Stopped.

Q. Anytime prior to the impact, did you use your brakes?

A. No.

Q. Do you remember whether or not there was a crosswalk anywhere at that intersection?

A. Gee, I don't remember whether they're marked or not. I think they are.

Q. Did you see the impact between the two vehicles, between the motorcycle and your car?

A. No.

§§ 2.104–2.110 are reserved for supplementary material.

L. INVESTIGATION BY DEPOSITIONS AND PICTURES

§ 2.111 Use of Pictures to Supplement Deposition

The late *Abraham Freedman*[86] often utilized a most effective method of pictures to supplement factual investigations.

In *Trowbridge v. Abrasive Co. of Philadelphia*,[87] plaintiff was seriously injured by the explosion of an abrasive wheel while he was grinding a fin off a coupler. Plaintiff alleged that the fracture of the wheel was due to a defect; however, the explosion had destroyed the wheel completely and, thereby, all evidence of any defect, and a formal check for demonstrative evidence appeared to indicate that none was available because of the destruction of the subject matter.

Under such circumstances it should be remembered that analogous or comparable demonstrative evidence may be just as effective, that it is generally factually and always legally available.

Mr. Freedman first filed a series of interrogatories identifying and outlining the various practices of defendant, specifying the manufacture of a comparable wheel. He then called the general manager of defendant company for oral examination under the discovery rules, and filed petitions for leave to take photographs of the plant of defendant and of the various relative matters complimentary to the oral examination.

On the day scheduled for examination, Mr. Freedman appeared at defendant's plant with a court reporter and professional photographer, and, after developing preliminary foundations in oral interrogatories and examination, he then proceeded to interrogate the witnesses regarding each and every step in the manufacture of the product, starting from the very beginning.

As the witnesses testified, the photographer was directed to preserve the process by pictures, and each picture was identified and explained by the witness as the deposition proceeded. Upon conclusion of the deposition, plaintiff had a complete set of pictures of the entire manufacturing process of the abrasive wheels with a comprehensive explanation relating to each picture and each step in the manufac-

---

86. The late Abe Freedman was one of the leading admiralty lawyers of America, and appeared in leading maritime cases through the Supreme Court of the United States, in a manner reminiscent of the famous Silas Axtel of New York, father of the Jones Act, and personal counsel for Andrew Furuseth.

87. 190 F.2d 825 (3d Cir. 1951).

ture. These were identified with the particularity required to offer them into evidence in any court.[88] See Figure 34.

Figure 34. Series of pictures of the manufacture of an abrasive wheel used by Attorney Abraham Freedman, Philadelphia, to supplement depositions, in case where abrasive wheel exploded.

Upon transcription of the deposition and printing of the pictures, Mr. Freedman called his own expert to investigate the practices of defendant, contemplating a placing of responsibility for the explosion. This gave plaintiff's expert a complete education regarding the method of manufacture employed by defendant. The pictures were shown as the depositions were read. It then became strikingly apparent, that although the wheels were customarily tested at the end of the production line, there was no proof that the particular wheel had been tested according to the prescribed standards, and further

---

88. The pictures shown were taken under court order to supplement deposition as to the processes in the manufacture of an abrasive wheel. The verdict was $150,000. Mr. Freedman shown in the picture.

that the tests generally performed were inadequate to determine the usability for the purposes for which the product was offered for use. The pictures, together with the explanations given, demonstrated a test only for particular operations.

A picture of the coupling, with the fin on it, placed alongside the testing machine, disclosed that in actual practice, the abrasive wheel, when used to grind a fin off a coupling, was subjected to stresses and strain entirely different than those which the testing apparatus encompassed. Thus the jury understood the explicit cause of the accident.[89]

In *Bowser v. Publicker Industries, Inc.*,[90] the facts presented a worker on a crane electrocuted when the boom of the crane either came into contact with, or close proximity to, high tension lines. Defendant contended that the property owner had no responsibility since the high tension lines were identified by signs conspicuously posted on the property and further alleged that the accident was due to the negligence of the crane operator.

Again, under court order, Mr. Freedman was able to obtain a series of pictures of every part of the building and of the adjoining lines serving the building. After the pictures had been taken, a model was made from the pictures. Subsequent visits to the scene of the accident showed the cramped area within which the crane had to work. The location of the sign showed that the crane operator could not have seen it, and further that the operations of the crane were in full view of the property owner's managing representatives who knew, or should have known, of the dangers inherent in the work going on. The model of the crane was placed in the exact position in which the offending crane was at the time of the accident. In the course of trial, it became manifest from the model that the work in which the crane was engaged was so dangerous, and which danger could not have been known to the crane operator, as to make it virtually criminal negligence on the part of defendant owner in failing to give adequate warning or to take appropriate measures to insure the safety of plaintiff.

The model posed the inevitable conclusion that one or more people might be electrocuted if it was operated as it was presented to the

---

89. There is no law of trial procedure against making a case interesting to a jury, particularly when it is something entirely foreign to their ordinary or past experience, and which will, at the end, give a logical, factual and honest answer to the "who done it."

90. 101 F.Supp. 386 (E.D.Pa.1951), aff'd 192 F.2d 933 (3d Cir.).

jury, and it was presented to the jury in the same factual manner as it was operated at the time of the accident. It was impossible to swing the boom with any degree of freedom escaping contact with the high tension lines.[91]

91. On appeal, the defendant attorneys again insisted on the signs and other precautions that had been taken. Milton Borowsky, who tried the case for the Freedman firm, was able to dispute each of these contentions by pointing to the "invisible" signs both on the enlarged pictures and the model. This factual presentation destroyed any oral argument that proper precautions had been taken.

Mr. Freedman advises that the judges came off the bench, and tried their hands at operating the model crane. One remarked in substance, "Why, he couldn't help but hit that high tension line."

§§ 2.112–2.114 are reserved for supplementary material.

M. LOCATING WITNESSES

§ 2.115 Introduction

Locating those persons who stood watching as an accident unfolded before them is one of the prime concerns of the trial lawyer. Without witnesses, it amounts to plaintiff's word against that of the defendant. While plaintiff's theory may often be substantiated by circumstantial evidence and demonstrations, nonetheless, it is to plaintiff's advantage to find independent observers who will testify to the same sequence of facts.

Rarely will a plaintiff walk into a lawyer's office bringing with him an exhaustive list of witnesses' names, addresses, and statements. He may only know that there were people in the general vicinity of the accident, some of whom surely must have seen it.

§ 2.116 Techniques for Locating Witnesses

The search for the prospective witness is best begun with a perusal of the police report, if one has been made. Therein may be included the names, addresses, and statements of the principals involved, as well as any onlookers. Often, representatives of the local news media will be on the scene shortly afterwards. In the newspaper the following day may be the names of witnesses and clues as to their residence. Once the name of a witness has been discovered, a search through local telephone books often provides one with his home address and telephone number.

The newspaper may include a photo of the accident scene from which witnesses may be identified, if the story omits their names. Where the license plate of a witness' vehicle has been taken down or made known to plaintiff's lawyer, a check with the Department of Motor Vehicles, through established procedures, will yield the owner's name and address.

The author remembers once filing a complaint for a soldier in uniform who had been badly injured. He was unconscious for a number of days after the accident from a severe cerebral injury, and suffered complete retrograde amnesia to a point in time and distance entirely behind the events in the picture. A picture of the accident appeared in the daily newspaper, and we advertised for anyone therein shown to communicate with a post office box number. Unfortunately, the only answer we received was from some person who wrote in, and made claim to the "prize." (None of course had been offered.) He said that he recognized the third man from the end as being George Raft, although we had made the contest very difficult by disguising him! Regardless of the results in this specific case, the procedure is recommended.

Another procedure which has been known to produce rewarding results is a house-to-house canvass with picture in hand. Even if the first attempt proves fruitless, it is recommended that the trial lawyer or his investigator return on another day, at another hour. Once one witness has been discovered, this usually leads to a chain reaction whereby many others will be found.

It is worth noting here that in a civil case especially, the prospective witness does not normally make any attempt to conceal his identity. Thus, he may usually be discovered through these standard procedures. The earlier in the case identities of witnesses are sought, the easier the task will be, as the chances they have died, moved, or forgotten the incident will be substantially reduced.

§§ 2.117–2.120 are reserved for supplementary material.

N. FINDING THE ACTUAL INSTRUMENTALITY

§ 2.121 Introduction

If discovery will not produce the actual instrumentality, or if a party claims it is no longer in his possession, then minute search should be made, quietly and independently. Certain registrations may be of assistance. Available are pawn shop records, police department records, auto and gun registrations, city permits, etc. Where the object is bulky, the chances are that at least part of it will still be available, if intensive investigation is followed.

§ 2.122 Unraveling the "Freak" Accident

Often the careful investigation will prove cases that look to be hopeless: A number of years ago, a California woman suffered a severe skull fracture in what was termed by the newspapers "a freak accident."

A number of months after the accident the plaintiff's husband came to the author and almost apologetically asked if he had "a case." He explained that his wife was a passenger in a pick-up truck being driven by him, when suddenly and without any warning, an object flew through the windshield striking her in the forehead. A truck was passing by at the time. It did not stop.

The husband was fortunately still able to produce the object that came through the windshield and the author, by making inquiries, found that it was a "corner iron". See Figure 35. Upon making further inquiry we ascertained that this corner iron was used solely in the lumber industry to secure lumber on trucks. We then determined the manufacturer of the iron. He advised us of the names and addresses of every person to whom he had supplied the irons.

From that point it was easy to interview each of the lumber carriers and ascertain from their records if any of their trucks were at the scene of the accident at the time of accident. Finally we came to the only trucking concern that had a truck at the time and place of the accident. We immediately filed suit making this concern a defendant and alleged that the corner iron flew off the bed of the truck as it was coming around the corner. We had ascertained that the truck was empty from defendant's own records.

Defendants first contended that "perhaps" they ran over an iron dropped by someone else causing it to fly through the windshield. Finally they admitted it was their truck and iron! The case was settled before trial for a figure approaching policy limits.

Figure 35. Truck corner iron that went through plaintiff's windshield, later used to find the offending vehicle—a lesson in investigation.

§ 2.123 Identification Through Advertisements

·The case of *Batsford v. Doe Store* [92] is another case which illustrates the value of a thorough, though necessarily delayed, investigation involving the identity of the injury-causing instrumentality. Plaintiff was a five-year-old boy whose shirt ignited when he attempted to warm his hands over an electric stove. The instantaneous combustion of the cotton material inflicted severe third-degree burns over the upper torso of the child.

Plaintiff's counsel, Attorney *Daniel J. Monaco*,[93] was not consulted by plaintiff's parents until *four years* after the incident. At that time, the remnants of the burned shirt had long been discarded. Plaintiff had an excellent case of liability, only he had no identifiable defendant to sue.

Careful and thorough questioning of plaintiff's mother elicited the memory that she had purchased the flammable shirt at the store of defendant J.C. Penney Co., at the special sale price of only $1.00 per shirt. Based on the mother's recall of the general time period in

---

92. Batsford et al. v. Doe Store et al., San Mateo, California, Superior Court (1974).

93. Daniel J. Monaco, Esquire, Monaco, Anderlini & Finkelstein, 400 So. El Camino Real, Suite 200, San Mateo, California.

which the purchase had been made, plaintiff's counsel instituted a search through the archives of the local newspapers for an advertisement of the sale. The described merchandise fit the price and description remembered by the mother.

This particular make of shirt was no longer on the market at the time of plaintiff's suit. Plaintiff's counsel then directed his investigation efforts to local used-clothing retail stores. Two shirts were found which could be identified as similar to the one which plaintiff had been wearing. These shirts were given to experts in flammability, and tests were subsequently conducted. These tests verified the fact that the shirt had had a dangerous and unreasonably low ignition point, and that it would emit intense heat once ignited.

This testimony dovetailed with that of plaintiff's expert medical witness. An analysis of the severity of the burn injuries indicated that the fabric involved must have been extremely flammable. The case was settled prior to trial for $200,000.00. Had it not been for the investigative efforts of Attorney Monaco, four years after the accident, plaintiff's cause would have been worthless.

§ 2.124 Identification of Manufacturer

Roman T. Plaszczak, Esquire,[94] also handled a case in which identification of the maker of the injury-causing instrumentality was crucial to his case. The suit involved the death of a four-year-old child. The youngster was killed when a one-cubic-yard, slant-sided trash container upon which he was playing, fell on him, covering his whole body with the exception of his head. The trash container had been sitting in soft dirt on an unlevel surface.

The child lingered for several days, then died. No one had actually seen the trash container fall over. Suit was filed against the owner of the property where the trash container had been located (Dispos-O-Waste Company, Inc.), and the manufacturer of the container. The latter was Bynal Products, Inc., of Franklin Park, Illinois, who had sold out to Waste Management, Inc., a national corporation heavily involved in the trash and disposal industry.

One of the principal problems in the case was the *identification* of the trash container as one made by Bynal. Bynal denied that the trash container was theirs, and identification was further stymied by the fact there were no serial numbers, name plates, or any other identifying marks on it. Dispos-O-Waste Company, Inc., which owned the container, had no invoices or other records to show that it

---

94. Roman T. Plaszczak, Esquire, Plaszczak & Bauhof, P.C., 137 North Park Street, Suite 203, Kalamazoo, Michigan.

had been made by Bynal, but merely felt that it was a Bynal from their experience with trash containers. From Attorney Plaszczak's point of view, he very badly wanted to establish liability against Bynal as the latter had been sued many times before for the same type of accidents.

In order to prove the trash container was in fact made by Bynal, Attorney Plaszczak travelled about and finally found a Bynal trash container with a Bynal label on it in a junk yard. That container was purchased, and plaintiff's expert compared it with the one the child had been playing on. A point-by-point examination of the two containers showed there were similarities in all of the construction methods in both of them.

The expert also examined all other trash containers made by other manufacturers which could be found. The expert found dissimilarities in all those containers, and in the known Bynal and alleged Bynal containers. In order to illustrate the testimony, a video tape was made wherein plaintiff's expert compared the known Bynal container with the alleged one on a point-by-point basis. In addition, close-up photographs were exhibited to the jury.

After the court ruled that the video tape of the comparison of the trash containers was admissible, defendants raised their settlement offers, which had been very low at the outset, to a more substantial amount. The owner of the property had been sued on a negligence theory regarding the improper placement of the trash container on soft, uneven ground. The refuse company which had actually placed the container there was also sued for negligence.

Bynal Products, Inc. was sued on the basis that it was negligent and had breached an implied warranty because the container was of an unstable design. About one week into trial, the case was settled for $83,500.00.

§ 2.125 Finding the Offending Product

The case of *Dorsey v. Honda Motor Company, Ltd.*,[95] tried by *Larry S. Stewart*, Esquire,[96] of Miami, Florida, illustrates that there is just no substitute for *thorough* and methodical investigation in the preparation of a personal injury lawsuit. Investigative work itself may not be particularly inspiring—it involves long hours of telephon-

---

[95]. Dorsey v. Honda Motor Co. Ltd., et al., United States District Court, Southern District of Florida, Miami Division, Case No. 76-592-CIV-PF, June 1979.

[96]. Larry S. Stewart, Esquire, Frates, Floyd, Pearson, Stewart, Richman & Greer, P.A., One Biscayne Tower, 25th Floor, Miami, Florida.

ing, tracing leads, sifting records, and pounding pavements. But the rewards of conscientious investigative work may indeed be inspiring, as when witnesses or exhibits crucial to plaintiff's case are brought to light.

The fruits of Larry Stewart's investigation of the Dorsey case was a verdict of nearly *$6,000,000*!

Stewart's firm was retained to represent Glen Dorsey about three and a half years after he had suffered severe injuries in an automobile accident. In 1972 Glen Dorsey was employed by McDonnell Douglas Astronautics as a computer engineer at a salary of $17,000 a year. He worked on the computer testing aspect of the Apollo and Skylab programs at Cape Kennedy, Florida.

In early 1972, Dorsey purchased a 1971 Honda AN600 automobile. This tiny compact, which utilized an air cooled engine, had made a brief splash at the time as the second smallest car on the market. It was also the least expensive car on the market at the time of its introduction by U.S. Honda dealers, selling for $1395.00. The AN600 model was sold in 1971 and 1972 only, and was subsequently taken off the market.

On the morning of March 9, 1972, Dorsey was driving his Honda to work, traveling north on US Highway 1 in Cocoa Beach, Florida. He was traveling at a speed of 30–35 miles per hour when a Ford automobile, making a left turn, turned into his path. At the moment of the collision, the Ford was moving at a few miles an hour or had just come to a stop.

The left front of plaintiff's Honda collided with the Ford. The left front of the Honda passenger compartment collapsed approximately 10 inches. Although the 6' 1" tall plaintiff was wearing his seat belt and shoulder harness, the set track failed, and he was thrown forward. His feet jammed under the pedals, his knees were forced under the dashboard. His head struck the A-pillar post between the front and the side of the car.

Plaintiff suffered a severe concussion, broken shoulder and collarbones, two broken legs, one of them with the bone protruding through his pants. Most serious, however, were plaintiff's brain injuries, which included damage to the frontal lobes. As a result of the accident plaintiff suffers permanent double vision, speech impairment, and left side hemi-paresis. The accident abruptly ended what Dorsey's employers testified were prospects for a bright career, and saddled him with medical bills in excess of $50,000.

Attorney Stewart's law firm was not retained in the case until about three and a half years after the accident. Their investigation began by combing the files of local newspapers. They found a newspaper reporter who had been traveling by at the time of the accident, and had taken a few photographs on the scene. The photographs included the one reproduced in Figure 37, a clear portrayal of the damage to the Honda.

Attorney Stewart's investigators then began attempting to locate the vehicle itself, which proved obviously to be an immense task. They began with the police accident report, which identified the company that had removed the vehicle from the scene. By examining the records at each of the several locations where the car had been, they were able to trace the route of the wreck as it had been forwarded from junk yard to junk yard across the state of Florida. Finally, the Honda's body was located in a junk yard in Tampa, Florida.

Although the wreck had been "cannibalized" and had suffered a great deal of deterioration due to exposure to the elements, it had not been totally destroyed nor turned into scrap metal. **See Figures 38 & 39.** Attorney Stewart secured the vehicle, and ultimately introduced it into evidence as an exhibit at trial.

Figure 37. On-the-spot photo of plaintiff's car taken by passing newspaper photographer immediately after accident. Plaintiff's counsel found this photo by combing files of local newspapers.

§ 2.125 INTRODUCTION Pt. 1

Figure 38. The wreck of plaintiff's car, found in a junk yard three and a half years after the accident. The car itself was introduced into evidence at trial.

Figure 39. Although the vehicle had been "cannibalized" and had deteriorated through exposure, it was still probative of the damage sustained in the collision.

The owner of the Ford had been insured by State Farm Insurance, and an adjuster had taken one photograph of plaintiff's car immediately following the accident, though after it had been removed from the scene. Figure 40. A copy of that photograph was obtained by subpoena.

Figure 40. Photo of plaintiff's car taken by insurance adjuster of other driver, shortly after the accident. This photo was obtained by subpoena, and admitted into evidence to show the damage sustained at the time of the collision.

A comparison between the remains of the actual vehicle and the photographs taken immediately following the accident enabled Attorney Stewart fairly well to document the precise amount of damage that occurred in the accident. Attorney Stewart then supplemented his exhibits by the purchase of an undamaged Honda of the same year and model. This was to prove a profitable investment.

The complaint was founded on a general crashworthiness theory —that the combination of the size of the vehicle, together with the construction of the occupant compartment and the restraint system, was inadequate. In addition to negligence and failure to warn, a count alleging that Honda had acted with "wantonness, willfulness or reckless indifference to the rights of others" was added to the complaint.

§ 2.125   INTRODUCTION   Pt. 1

The named defendants in the case were Honda Motor Company Ltd., the Japanese manufacturer, and American Honda Motor Company, Inc., their wholly owned American subsidiary. The Japanese corporation contended that the United States Federal District Court had no jurisdiction over them.

Counsel for plaintiff founded their argument for jurisdiction over Honda on Rule 4 of the Federal Rules of Civil Procedure, which authorizes service of process upon a non-resident where any statute of the state in which the District Court is located so provides. Florida had two pertinent long-arm statutes. Florida Statute Section 48.-181 provided for jurisdiction over non-resident persons and corporations who carry on business activities in the state, when the cause of action arises out of any transaction or operation connected with the business. Section (3) of the Statute provides that any person or corporation who sells property "through brokers, jobbers, wholesalers or distributors" in the state shall be conclusively presumed to be conducting business within the state.

Florida Statute Section 48.182 provided for jurisdiction over any non-resident person or corporation who commits a wrongful act outside the state which causes injury, loss or damage to persons or property within the state. *Youngblood v. Citrus Association of New York Cotton Exchange, Inc.*,[97] had established the conditions under which F.S. § 48.182 could be used:

> ". . . (1) The non-resident committed a wrongful act (2) outside the state (3) which caused injury or damage to (4) persons or property within this state, (5) if the non-resident expected or should reasonably have expected the act to have consequences (6) in this state or any other state or nation and (7) derives substantial revenue from inter-state or international commerce. . . ."

The District Court held that Honda's activities in manufacturing cars in Japan which were sold in Florida met the requirements of F. S. § 48.182, and subjected the Japanese corporation to the jurisdiction of the Federal District Court in Florida. Plaintiffs thus did not need to "pierce the corporate veil" of the wholly owned American subsidiary.

The discovery process was utilized by Attorney Stewart as a further stage of investigation. Honda was asked to produce the results of any crash testing of the AN600 model. In response, Honda pro-

---

97. Youngblood v. Citrus Ass'n of New York Cotton Exchange, Inc., 276 So.2d 505 (Fla.App.1973).

duced a single crash test report, which plaintiff's counsel interpreted as indicating serious problems with the vehicle.

Counsel then went to Japan to carry out further discovery. Plaintiff's theory at that time was that, since only one crash test report had been produced, there had been inadequate testing of the vehicle before production and distribution. However, when counsel arrived in Tokyo, Honda took the position that there had been a great deal more testing of the vehicle than previously divulged. Additionally, the Honda engineers testified that they had fortified the vehicle by the inclusion of "bones" in all of the surfaces surrounding the passenger compartment. They testified that these structural components rendered the vehicle as strong as American cars built during the same time.

When counsel returned from Tokyo, they filed a series of motions addressing the fact that Honda had not produced all of the testing which they claimed had occurred. In response, Honda produced six test reports written in Japanese. The Court required Honda to translate these test reports into English, and to supply a witness in Florida to testify with respect to that testing.

The translations, which had been done on a rush basis, showed even more problems in the design of the vehicle. In fact, in one report the Honda engineering personnel had specifically recommended making the cabin space larger because test dummies were striking the forward portion of the cabin in the tests. This was precisely the injury which plaintiff Dorsey had sustained when his head struck the A-pillar support post located at the side of the front windshield.

Several months later, plaintiff's counsel received from Honda a second translation of the Japanese test reports. Honda claimed errors in the first translation—but even the second translation continued to show serious problems. About a month before trial, a third translation of the test reports was offered. Although the incriminating portions were by now somewhat watered down, the reports still contained very damaging evidence relating to Honda's lack of regard for human safety in the design of this automobile.

Also, on return from Tokyo, Attorney Stewart investigated Honda's claims that the passenger compartment had been fortified by the addition of structural "bones". He had the right front quarter of the undamaged Honda AN600 purchased earlier cut out to determine exactly and conclusively what fortifications, if any, had been added to strengthen the passenger compartment. See Figure 41. There were no "bones" present. See Figure 42.

Figure 41. Plaintiff's counsel purchased an undamaged vehicle of the same make, model, and year as plaintiff's. The vehicle was sectioned and introduced into evidence at trial to demonstrate clearly and conclusively its inadequate construction and design.

Ch. 2 INVESTIGATION AND DISCOVERY § 2.125

Figure 42. A close-up of the sectioned vehicle introduced into evidence to refute defendant's claims that the passenger compartment had been fortified by the addition of structural "bones".

Further investigation by deposition in Florida revealed that Honda had run tests on designs for the floor channel located in the front part of the passenger compartment. The tests showed that a design, designated Design No. 5, *failed*. A later design, identified as Design No. 6, barely passed the tests, but the Honda engineers recommended that the channel be made even stronger for production models. Plaintiff's counsel photographed the drawings contained in the test reports, and consolidated them into one photograph so that Design No. 5 and Design No. 6 could be easily compared. See Figure 43. In deposition in Miami, Honda claimed that the version of the AN600 marketed in America contained the beefed-up Design No. 6. Plaintiff's counsel then proceeded to cut a section from the channel in both the undamaged car, as well as from plaintiff Dorsey's car. They found that both those floor channels used Design No. 5—the one that had failed the tests!

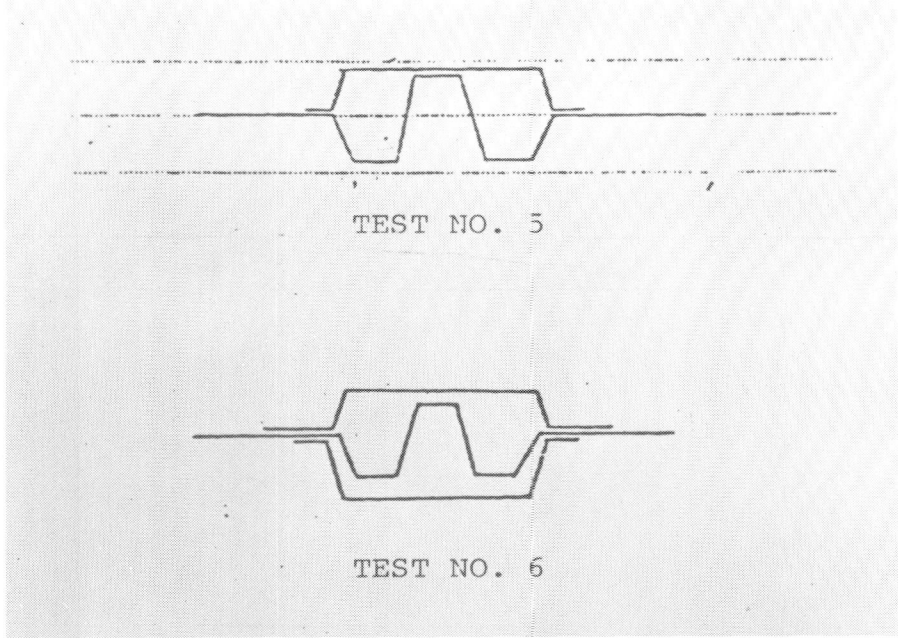

Figure 43. Plaintiff's composite photograph of exhibits taken from defendant's test reports, showing alternative designs of floor channels. This presentation to the jury made a comparison of the crucial elements easy and obvious.

Another aspect of Attorney Stewart's investigation related to other lawsuits in which Honda had been involved. Through Attorney *Herbert Resner* of the *Belli office* in San Francisco, plaintiff's counsel discovered an Experimental Safety Vehicle report prepared by Honda. This ESV report showed how the car could be substantially improved to provide significantly more occupant protection. It proved to be a very valuable piece of evidence at trial.

Investigation into other litigation involving Honda revealed that Honda used the same team of defense experts in most of their cases. Stewart obtained copies of their testimony and reports in previous cases. These also turned out to be extremely helpful. This cooperation of other plaintiffs' counsel was freely given and proved to be an extremely effective factor at trial, particularly so since the defense did not know that plaintiff had the material until it was used.

At trial, plaintiff's counsel introduced into evidence both the remnants of the Dorsey vehicle and the undamaged Honda that had been sectioned. Both exhibits were so large, however, that they could not physically be brought into the courtroom. The trial took place on the sixth floor of the building and the elevators were not large enough to accommodate either vehicle. Therefore, arrangements were made to have the vehicles placed in a storage area on the first floor. The Court was then removed from the sixth floor to the storage area for the experts' testimony. The judge, witnesses, counsel, and six-man federal jury all rode down in an elevator to the storage area. There, plaintiff's expert went over the two vehicles, illustrating his testimony by direct reference to the actual instrumentality. Plaintiff's counsel learned later that this had a major impact on the jury.

As part of their original investigation, plaintiff's counsel had contacted *all* of the witnesses whose names had been included in the original police investigation report. A nurse who had participated in extricating plaintiff from the vehicle at the time of the accident was unavailable, since she had both moved and married. Through persistent investigative efforts her present location was determined by information obtained from her family. Plaintiff's counsel contacted her and obtained her statement, in which she was asked to describe everything that she did in rescuing plaintiff. In her statement she mentioned that she had cut Mr. Dorsey out of the seatbelts. The remains of the vehicle, exhibited at trial, still had the cut belt in it. This proved beyond a shadow of a doubt that plaintiff was wearing his seatbelt at the time of the accident.

At trial, Honda undertook every effort to try to escape the devastating impact of their own testing. They brought witnesses from Japan to testify that the reported testing had been performed on a 360 Model Honda. The 360 Model was a car made solely for the Japanese domestic market. It was much smaller and less substantial than the 600 Model. Defendants flew in from Japan a 360 Model to show to the jury.

Plaintiff's counsel, however, had earlier secured a motion picture that had been made by defendant Honda in conjunction with one of their tests. This was a test in which a Honda was crashed into an American car. The film showed a devastating result for the Honda.

After the Honda experts had testified that the test had been performed on a 360 Model, plaintiff's counsel introduced a blow-up of one frame of the movie film which had been made in conjunction with the test. See Figure 44. The picture of the front end of the Honda taken immediately after the crash with the American car clearly shows the number 600 on the grill ornament. This photograph was introduced as the very last piece of rebuttal evidence for the jury to see at the end of the trial.

Figure 44. Blow-up of frame from defendant's movie of test crash, showing "600" emblem affixed to grill. This exhibit refuted defendant's testimony at trial that the test had been performed on a "360" model.

In final argument, counsel was able to argue these facts in relation to the question of exemplary damages. Counsel argued that Honda had gone to great lengths to escape the test results because these tests clearly showed Honda's knowledge of the car's inadequate design. The conclusion that Honda was reckless in marketing the car notwithstanding that knowledge was inescapable.

After a nine day trial, the jury deliberated for only three hours. They ruled that the product was defective and the company had been both negligent and reckless. Plaintiff Dorsey was awarded *compensatory* damages in the amount of $750,000.00. Plaintiff's wife was awarded $75,000 for loss of consortium. These compensatory payments were ordered collected from both the parent company in Japan, Honda Motor Company, Ltd., and its American subsidiary, American Honda Motor Company, Inc. The jury further awarded *punitive* damages in the amount of $5,000,000 against the parent company in Japan.

That this salutary result could be achieved is attributable to the exhaustive and unrelenting investigative efforts of Attorney

Larry Stewart in his approach to preparation of the case. Undaunted by the disadvantages of entering the case three and one half years after the incident, Attorney Stewart pursued every avenue of investigation—newspapers, police reports, witness statements, repeated discovery, intensive examination of the product itself and of the defense exhibits—to the fullest. There is no other way—a superlative result can be achieved only through a superlative effort.

§§ 2.126–2.130 are reserved for supplementary material.

O. WHEN THE ACTUAL INSTRUMENTALITY IS NOT AVAILABLE

§ 2.131 Introduction

Having the actual instrumentality available to inspect and run tests on is generally of critical importance to a case, as we have just seen in *Dorsey v. Honda Motor Company, Ltd.* and the several other cases in the preceding section. Every effort should be made by plaintiff, the investigating officers, plaintiff's lawyer, and even the representatives of the insurance company to preserve intact the evidence exactly as it was immediately after the accident. Sometimes, however, obtaining the actual instrumentality is entirely beyond one's control. It may have been wholly obliterated in the accident; or the thought of preserving it may have come much too late, long after the instrumentality, or records concerning its ultimate disposition and whereabouts, have been lost or destroyed. In such an instance it is only through a herculean effort on the part of plaintiff's counsel, his investigator, and experts that the burden may be lessened.

§ 2.132 Illustration—Vehicle Unavailable

Illustrative of the difficulty inherent in this situation is *Hakim v. Downtown Datsun*,[98] a single-car accident handled by our office.

Plaintiff therein was injured while driving his brother's Datsun 510, which had been purchased new some nine months earlier. In attempting to negotiate a rather sharp curve, the vehicle went out of control, and struck a lamppost. See Figure 45. Plaintiff was severely injured in the wreck. He suffered brain damage, retrograde amnesia, and paralysis of the left side. For two months after the accident, he had lain in a coma, during which time he developed pneumonia and other complications. Additionally, plaintiff had suffered a fractured femur, multiple fractures and deformation of facial bones and his nose, serious internal injuries, and psychological damage and disabilities.

---

98. Hakim v. Downtown Datsun, filed in Superior Court, State of California, City and County of San Francisco, April 1, 1974 (# 673199).

Figure 45. From this angle, the degree of the curve plaintiff was trying to navigate is clearly seen. Defendant contended that one of the possible causes of the accident was the sand apparent in the left foreground.

[Photo by Rodman Bingham, Menlo Park, California.]

Our allegation was that a defect in the car, to-wit a serious misalignment problem, had caused the car to go out of control. Defendant Downtown Datsun contended that the accident was due to any or a combination of the following: plaintiff had been driving too fast; he was an inexperienced driver; he had run the car into the curb; or the wheels had come into contact with some sand on the edge of the road while rounding the curve.

For us to prove that there was a defect in the car which had precipitated the accident, a careful study of the vehicle by experts was vital to our case. The experts could dismantle the car piece-by-piece, and find the cause of the tragic event. To our chagrin and despair, the vehicle had been repossessed by the insurance company, who then sold it to an automobile wrecker. This despite repeated requests by plaintiff's brother (who owned the car) that the car was to be preserved!

§ 2.132   INTRODUCTION   Pt. 1

An inquiry to the claims representative of the insurance company regarding the car's disposal and its current location proved frustrating. The car, came the reply, had been rendered a total loss by the collision. Title thereto had reverted to the insurance company after plaintiff's brother had refused to make any further payments thereon. The Datsun was then sold to an automobile wrecker who had already destroyed it. In response to our question as to why he had scrapped the car in view of the fact plaintiff's brother had informed him that a defect in the steering or alignment of the car may have caused the accident, and thus the vehicle was to be preserved, the agent stated: "There is a distinct possibility that steering failure was mentioned at the time, however, even if it was, I would have dismissed the possibility after a cursory inspection of the vehicle, as I hear basically the same excuse i. e. Mechanical failure in the majority of accidents involving loss of control." Thus, the callous snap judgment of an insurance claims representative had led to the loss of the car.

Without the car, the "actual instrumentality", it was going to be extremely difficult, if not impossible, for us to prove liability. To ascertain the cause of the accident, we began by questioning the plaintiff. Unfortunately, due to retrograde amnesia, he could remember nothing.

In cases involving retrograde amnesia, sometimes it is possible to break through the subconscious mental block by use of hypnosis with good results. Such was done in this case, and the end result was productive. Under hypnosis, plaintiff remembered that he had placed his foot on the brake pedal and pushed, but the car wouldn't stop. [Plaintiff's car fell within those which had been recalled due to a defect in the brake housing system which could result in the brakes becoming ineffective.] He was able to remember further that the car was not steady, that it was "shimmying" as he went into the turn, and that something was causing it to go faster than 45 miles per hour.

We then deposed plaintiff's brother, who was able to relate the numerous problems he had had with the car since the date of its purchase, especially the problem with its misalignment and handling. Less than one month after he had purchased the car, he noticed that it idled rough, would shake while in neutral, and that bad vibrations were emanating from its front end while traveling at 40–45 mph.

Over the following months, there were numerous other problems with the car. The vehicle was taken to defendant Downtown Datsun was not steady, that it was "shimmying" as he went into the turn, several times, and on each occasion they informed plaintiff's brother the various problems had been corrected. According to his brother, not only had the problems not been rectified, but new ones could also be found. Plaintiff's brother's frustration grew to the extent that he sought the advice of counsel on several occasions on how he could get out of the contract of purchase.

Statements and depositions were taken of the two eye-witnesses to the accident, whose names and addresses had been supplied by the police report. One of the investigating officers had even managed to capture one of the witnesses on film. See Figure 46.

Figure 46. On-the-scene photograph taken of the car shortly after the accident. Potential witnesses often may be discovered by inspecting this type of picture. For example, the young man standing behind the bicycle was one of the few eyewitnesses to the accident.

Both witnesses stated that the car had been going fast, anywhere from 45 to 55 mph, but not nearly so fast as to be unable to successfully negotiate the curve. One of the witnesses stated that he saw the two right-side wheels in the air as the car was rounding the turn. The other witness testified that it looked like the car had hit some sand, causing it to slide around the corner. However, this was refuted as neither he nor the other witness could remember noticing any sand in the immediate vicinity. Significantly, neither eye-witness had seen the car hit the curb.

Although we were unable to obtain the actual car, we were able to acquire some on-the-scene photographs taken by the investigating officers which proved invaluable to our case. In Figure 47, the scuff marks made by the tires skidding on the road surface may be seen. This picture evidences the point that the brakes were not functioning, as the marks were made by the car sliding sideways. We were able to obtain a picture of the car taken shortly after the accident, while the car was still in police custody. See Figure 48. From this photograph, we had an expert photographer make an enlargement of the right front tire area. In this picture, reproduced in Figure 49, the horizontal scuff marks further attesting to the cause of the skid marks on the road, can be clearly seen.

Figure 47. Skid marks on the road show the automobile's path as it headed toward the light fixture. Unfortunately, the car was towed away and destroyed before experts could test and inspect for possible defects.

Figure 48. Through herculean efforts, we were able to uncover this picture which had been taken while the car was still in police custody. It is the only picture taken after the accident in which the right front tire is visible. Although the quality of the print was poor, we were able to have an enlargement made which supported our contentions.

Figure 49. An enlargement made from the preceding photograph substantiated our claim that the cause of the accident was a defect in the vehicle's steering mechanism. Without this picture, it would have been much more difficult for us to prevail. Note the horizontal marks on the tire caused by its skidding.

We next employed the services of several experts in accident reconstruction, among them Gene McCall of the California Highway Patrol. After pouring over the facts, police report, depositions, and pictures, Mr. McCall came to the following conclusions:

1. The speed of the car had been less than 50 mph while rounding the corner. This was determined by, among other things, the amount of damage to the car when it hit the pole.

2. Although the recommended speed for traversing this curve was 30 mph, our expert had easily negotiated it at 50 mph in a car

which did not have as good suspension as the Datsun. This had been done with little difficulty, and no tire marks had been left at this speed.

3. The scuff marks had been made by a car trying to turn too tight of a radius for the speed it was traveling. The expert further concluded that the car's brakes had not been used, or if applied, did not work.

4. The fact that the car had been balanced on two wheels was not due to its having hit the curb. McCall's evidence and opinion showed that the car, traveling at 40–50 mph, would surely have left a rubber mark on the curb, which there was not. Further, the path of the skid marks were such that it would have been impossible for the car to hit the curb and maintain that trajectory. Finally, McCall was of the opinion that had the car hit the curb, it would have rolled over at that point, and would not have continued on as it did.

As to why the accident happened, it was McCall's opinion that "an erratic, touchy steering car, such as described by this owner, could have been a major factor in causing the accident."

We were fortunate to reach a settlement of just over $200,000 for the injuries suffered by plaintiff. So many factors had been against us when the case first came to us: the car could not be examined minutely by our experts; plaintiff's speed in rounding the turn, while making it not impossible to successfully traverse the sharp curve, was nonetheless a factor leading to the crash; and there were strong possibilities that the car had come into contact with the curb or some sand. To combat these problems, a creative, innovative investigation had to be launched.

Fortunately, we succeeded in our Herculean task, and obtained for the plaintiff, in light of all of the surrounding circumstances, an adequate settlement. Had the car been properly preserved, our task would have been much simpler, and perhaps plaintiff's award would have been larger.

§§ 2.133–2.134 are reserved for supplementary material.

Ch. 2 INVESTIGATION AND DISCOVERY § 2.135

P. DEMONSTRATIVE EVIDENCE OFTEN DEMONSTRATES THE THEORY

§ 2.135 In General

Occasionally, after listening to a client's detailed history and in interviewing witnesses, I have had an intuition of liability, but could not bring it within accepted legal terms. In 1951, I tried a case in Yolo County, California.[99] The several plaintiffs were riding in two passenger cars, traveling a short distance apart, on the right-hand side of the highway, proceeding south on U.S. Highway 101, above Willits, California. Defendant's sixty-foot truck (60 feet was the maximum legal length) came down the highway from the south, traveling north on the right hand side of the highway.

On a narrow curve over a bridge, the lead passenger car came into contact with the after-part of the defendant's truck. The second passenger car was forced into the ditch. When stillness settled over the highway after the crash of the impacts, a baby in the lead car had been decapitated, and two other plaintiffs severely injured. See Figure 50.

Figure 50. Yolo county curve where defendant truck crossed center line. Picture doesn't show the crucial fact that curve was too sharp for truck, which had to be demonstrated by models.

99. Hanks and Taylor v. Minatta Trucking Co., Yolo County Superior Court, Calif.

§ 2.135　　　　　　INTRODUCTION　　　　　　Pt. 1

The Highway Patrol, coming upon the scene of the accident shortly thereafter, felt that defendant's truck was over the center of the highway, but there were no tire marks to corroborate this theory, as the rain had washed the highway clean. No capable witnesses were available. The Highway Patrol, though they felt to the contrary, had no facts to sustain their intuition, and had to note in their report "no violation." [1]

An amateur photographer, happening upon the scene of the accident, along with the Highway Patrol, took some seventy pictures which we subpoenaed at the time of the trial.[2] See Figure 51.

Figure 51. Yolo county curve where the truck went around the curve and crossed the center line, but the picture doesn't show whether it did or not. A model was needed for that.

1. The exact opinion and conclusion of the officer, taken from his official report made after the accident, shows what the author had to contend with: "Opinions and conclusions: Believe truck was overdriving but impossible to prove due to the driver stating he speeded up to straighten tractor after it started to jackknife. No citation at this time. Pending further investigation." (No further investigation was ever done.)

2. Sections 488 and 488.5 of the Vehicle Code provided that motor vehicle officer's files were to be made available after the termination of any possible criminal prosecution.

Ch. 2 INVESTIGATION AND DISCOVERY § 2.135

Upon examining these pictures in detail, I was disappointed. Not only did they fail to prove liability on the part of defendant's truck, but there appeared to be a gouge mark on the truck tire and reconstruction of the position of the passenger cars seemed to indicate that the passenger car, not the truck, was over the double yellow line. Yet both the Highway Patrol and I still had the "feeling" that the fault was completely with the truck.

I visited the scene of the accident two times, and sat alongside the highway as cars went around the curve. Still I could not determine the cause of the accident. I next had a surveyor go to the scene and draw a diagram of it. Then I hired an airplane and had a number of aerial photos made showing the road behind the curve, and the curve, itself but still there was no actual demonstrative evidence of liability.

I then sent a model maker to the scene to make a model, demanding that it be made precisely to scale, as he would have to testify to every inch of the highway on his model before it would be received in evidence. When the model was brought to my office, the model maker also had a model truck and trailer, and the two automobiles, exactly to scale. I put the truck on the curve, and pushed it around. The back seemed to protrude over the double line. I told the model maker that the truck could not go around the curve without going over the double line, and that he must have made a mistake. The truck was of the legal length, and if drawn to scale, then the highway must have been made disproportionate on the model. My expert model maker said that he would testify in court, under oath, that the model was to scale. Not being satisfied, I sent him again to the scene of the accident to re-check his entire drawings and his model, and had him take a State surveyor with him. He came back and would not change an inch of the model.

The County in which this case was to be tried was one of the lowest verdict centers in California, the highest verdict theretofore (that is, prior to 1951) having been awarded in the sum of $35,000. Furthermore, no "demonstrative evidence", blackboards, or the like had been used in that county.

When I drove from San Francisco to court, some fifty miles away, the morning of the trial, it was necessary for me to rent a trailer to bring the demonstrative evidence. There was a blackboard in court. I brought along a skeleton, the model, the aerial photos, the diagrams, and the small pictures.

Before employing the blackboard in opening statement, or using any of the demonstrative evidence, I advised the trial Judge of my purpose and told him that it would be impossible to explain fully to the jury what had happened without the use of this evidence, and that every bit of it was factual and to scale. (Incidentally, the skeleton had a drape over it in the courtroom and appeared as merely an object under a white sheet.)

I made an opening statement of over an hour, using the blackboard completely. See Figure 52. Illustrated were the positions of the various cars, and the monetary claims of several plaintiffs. On the left of the board is a square with an arrow indicating that the defendant truck was going north ("N") while there were two cars going south ("S"), in which the various plaintiffs were riding. In this manner, the separate claims for wrongful death and injuries are set out, as well as the theory of liability presented.

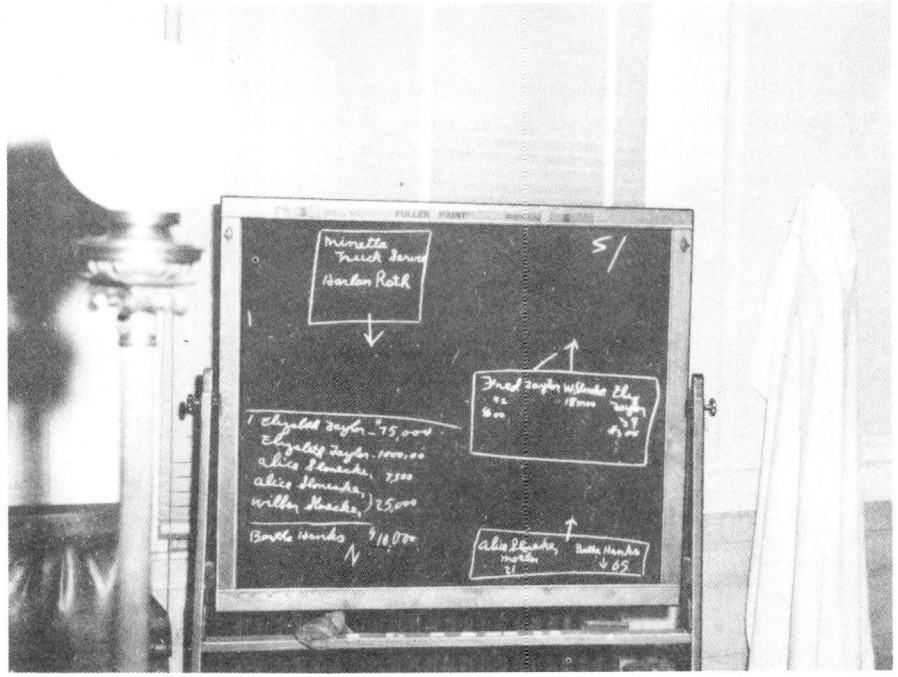

Figure 52. Blackboard used in opening statement, Yolo county accident, illustrating the positions of the vehicles, monetary claims, and names of witnesses. The skeleton to be used in demonstrating injuries stands draped until used.

The photograph reproduced in Figure 53 shows the courtroom during a recess. The blackboard with the opening statement on it is in view, the skeleton from which the doctor demonstrated the bony injury hangs from its mounting before the jury, two aerial photos are in view, the stack of the seventy pictures is on counsel's table, and the model is directly in front of the jury.

Ch. 2   INVESTIGATION AND DISCOVERY   § **2.135**

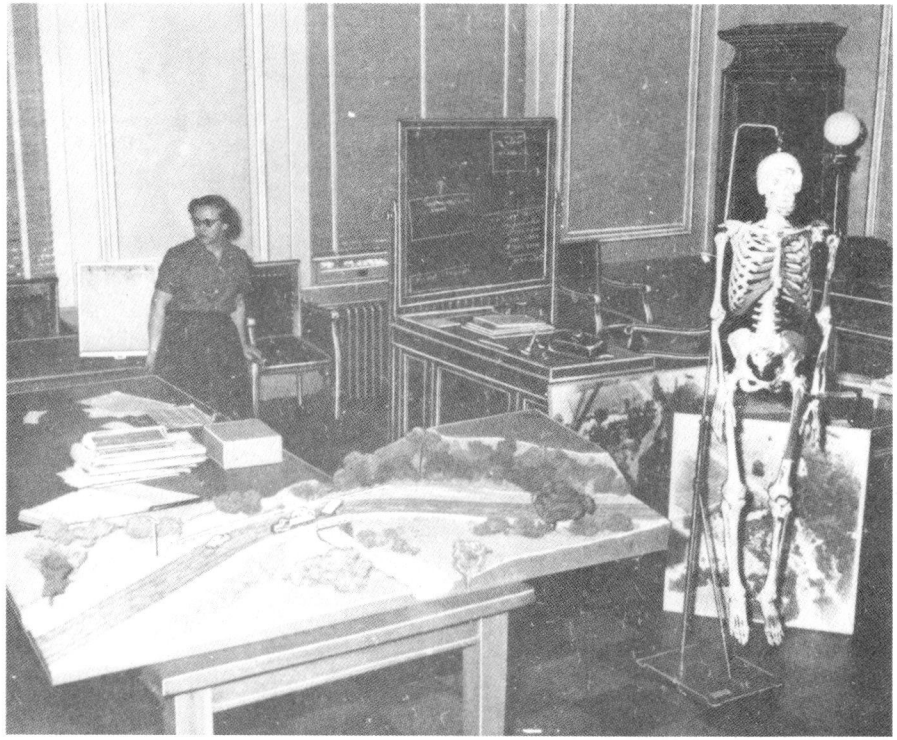

Figure 53. Yolo county curve accident, courtroom scene showing exhibits, skeleton and model in foreground, drawn to scale, which by use of toy vehicles also to scale it was conclusively demonstrated that the defendant truck must have crossed the center line.

When the Highway Patrolman testified from the model, His Honor came from the Bench to watch the demonstration. I could see the jury becoming firmly convinced that the accident was the fault of the truck being across the highway, that a vehicle of its size and length physically could not traverse that curve at any speed without going over the double line. It was so apparent that some of the observers in the courtroom subsequently asked me why I had not joined the State because of a defective highway. The case was settled during the course of trial because of policy limitations.[3] This amount was warranted by the injuries, but it was only made possible by the employment of the several phases of demonstrative evidence.

3. The Woodland Democrat, November 8, 1951: "Yolo Superior Court was turned into a virtual art gallery yesterday as props, which are to be used in evidence, started making an appearance in the trial of a $218,000 lawsuit in which a Woodland man is one of the defendants. In a county where $15,000 previously was a high verdict, the defendant here paid $70,000 to settle during this trial."

§ 2.135

The most frequently traversed intersection, the most customarily used highway and curve, is often deceptive in measurement, and in appearance. I recall in Moncton, in Eastern Canada, there is a hill, which, because of an optical illusion, causes it to appear that cars allowed to coast on this hill, run up hill. The driver of an automobile coasting on this hill would swear that he was "coasting up hill," yet it is a slight down hill grade.

Very often a curve, a cross-walk, a path, or a stairway, does not reveal the dangers existing until viewed in a number of perspectives. Just because other people have traversed it safely, does not mean that danger may not exist. If there is recognition of the unsafe conditions before complaint is filed, the blame may be placed where it justly belongs, perhaps on the driver of defendant's vehicle, or some sovereign body, or a lessor or owner. Such preparation aids settlement as well as success on trial.

In the Yolo County case, the photographs taken showed the most painstaking effort to discover clues to liability, but the true cause was obvious, although difficult to see, because hid by the respectability that had come from long and notorious use. A thorough and varied investigation again showed the existence of a case.

§§ 2.136–2.140 are reserved for supplementary material.

Q. EXEMPLARY INVESTIGATIONS

§ 2.141 Introduction

The following case reports are examples of superbly investigated cases which resulted in most favorable outcomes, attesting to the value of a thorough expert investigation.

§ 2.142 Hidden Rock Case

One of the most unusual investigations resulted in my former partner, *Vasilios B. ("Bill") Choulos* donning wet suit and skin-diving gear to conduct a search for a rock upon which our client had struck his head while diving into a man-made lake, rendering him a quadriplegic.

Folsom Lake is a large, man-made lake in Northern California, near Sacramento. Like many other artificial lakes, the water fills an area previously covered by trees, and strewn with croppings of rock. When the trees are cut down, many of the remaining stumps are left intact, and their removal may be years off. Dangerous croppings of rock may also be left untouched.

At Folsom Lake, the tree stumps and rock croppings had been removed only from a few of the areas which were designated "improved" beaches. The lake was used for irrigation purposes, resulting in the water level rising and falling in accordance with the needs of the farmers. Because of this, the tree stumps were sometimes exposed, while at other times, they were hidden by the shallow, murky waters of the lake.

One section of the large lake was designated "Granite Bay." This bay harbored several beaches, only one of which, Granite Beach, was improved (that is, the tree stumps and rock croppings had been removed to make the area safe for swimming and boating). Not far removed from Granite Beach was an unimproved beach, commonly known as Five Percent Beach. Although unimproved, Five Percent Beach was a popular area, especially among teenagers and young adults. See Figure 54. Often the crowd here would surpass the number at the improved beach.

Figure 54. This picture demonstrates the amount of use of Five Percent Beach. Note the number of bathers in the water. Shouldn't there have been signs prohibiting swimming, or at least warning of the tree stumps, rock croppings, and other submerged hazards?

To reach Five Percent Beach, it was necessary to traverse about two hundred feet on a trail. Swimming at this beach was a popular activity, notwithstanding the fact that there existed the tree stumps and hidden boulders.

On the day of the accident, plaintiff had arrived at approximately 3:15 p.m. Upon arriving, plaintiff encountered an acquaintance who gave him one-half a can of beer, which plaintiff drank. About thirty minutes later, plaintiff suggested the two youths go for a swim. Plaintiff ran to the water, continued running a few steps when he had reached the water line, then dove in. See Figures 55 and 56.

Lauren Deposition August 13, 1969
Plaintiff's ex 4 For id

Figure 55. Park employees assume positions where plaintiff was when he dove into the water, and where he landed.

Figure 56. Same view as preceding picture, taken from different angle. Could the offending rock be found?

Due to his dislike of cold water, plaintiff's friend stopped at the water's edge at the last moment. From there, he watched as plaintiff dove into the water, his hands outstretched. As quickly as plaintiff entered the water, he shot back up, feet first. Observers on the beach thought he had pushed off of the bottom with his outstretched hands, and was lying face down on the surface as a "joke."

When plaintiff's friend realized he had been lying face-down in the water for an inordinate length of time, the friend pulled him to the shoreline. When he had initially grabbed plaintiff to move him to a position of safety, the youth observed a "shadow" in the water, which could very well have been a rock. After he had dragged plaintiff to the shore, he picked up a rock and placed it under plaintiff's head. The rock was later removed, and a towel put in its stead. This rock could not be found afterwards.

No signs in or around the area had stated that swimming was prohibited on this unimproved beach. One sign contained the following caution: "WARNING—Lake contains many navigation hazards. Use caution while boating." Another declared: "DANGER—Unusual low water. Unmarked hazards." The only sign which gave even the slightest intimation that one should not swim in this area read: "Hazardous water area. No lifeguards available." See Figure 57. Clearly, then, there were no signs adequately advising against swimming, and informing of the true nature of any unseen dangers.

Ch. 2 INVESTIGATION AND DISCOVERY § **2.142**

Figure 57. Sign on approach to Five Percent Beach does not serve adequately to discourage swimming, or sufficiently to inform bathers of numerous sunken hazards. It says: "Hazardous Water Area—No Lifeguards Available."

Lifeguards were regularly stationed at the three so-called "improved" beaches around the lake. Another lifeguard would make rounds in the state-owned pickup truck. This roving lifeguard would occasionally patrol the Five Percent Beach area, but despite the fact that many youths were seen swimming at various times by these lifeguards, no attempt was made to inform the youths that swimming in this area was either prohibited or dangerous.

We contended that the tree stumps and rock croppings abundant in this unimproved beach made them too dangerous for swimming. The State of California, acting through its Parks and Recreation Department, was at fault in failing to prohibit swimming in these areas, especially in light of the frequent use by the teenagers.

To prove our theory of liability, it would be necessary to show that a rock hidden on the bottom of the lake was the direct cause of plaintiff's injuries. Plaintiff's friend had informed us that he had seen a "shadow" in the water which looked like a rock, and further, that he had placed a rock beneath plaintiff's head. A cursory search by two of the Park employees immediately after the incident, however, had failed to turn up the rock in question.

§ 2.142 INTRODUCTION Pt. 1

An extensive hunt for the offending boulder was undertaken by our office at a later date. Bill Choulos had donned a wetsuit and appropriate skin-diving gear to enable him to make a thorough search for the actual rock, or a similar one. See Figure 58.

Figure 58. Attorney Vasilios ("Bill") Choulos donned a wetsuit to conduct own exclusive search for rock.

The search proved rewarding. Bill was able to find a watermelon-sized boulder, measuring nearly 24 inches in length. See Figure 59. This was discovered in the general area where plaintiff had dived into the lake.

Figure 59. The fruit of a thorough investigation—a watermelon-sized boulder which may have caused plaintiff's injuries. At least we showed that rocks similar to the one which we claimed caused plaintiff's injury were in fact present at the site.

Pictures of the rock were shown to the lifeguard supervisor who had been on duty the day in question. On deposition, he stated that while it was only infrequently, nonetheless he had seen users of the beach throwing similar large boulders to and fro in the water. He further testified that swimming and diving were not prohibited in the Five Percent Beach area, notwithstanding the hazards in the water, and that he had often seen bathers running and diving into the water.

The rock uncovered by Bill Choulos was then placed in the spot where plaintiff had landed, and this was done under similar conditions to those which existed at the time of the tragic incident. This reenactment demonstrated that the rock would have been hidden from plaintiff's view at the time he dived into the water. We were also able to show from the frequent use of the unimproved beach that it was foreseeable that plaintiff and others like him would dive into the water and be injured in this manner.

Through the investigative efforts of Mr. Choulos, we were able to reach a favorable settlement with the State of California, it being fairly represented by the present Secretary of Defense, Casper Weinberger, who was adequately impressed with our own investigation.

§ 2.143 Investigation by Exhumation

Another unique case involving an imaginative investigation was *Estate of Diamond:* Barney Diamond was a bridge builder in Georgia and other Southern states. He had gone the "rags-to-riches" route, and at the time of his death was worth more than $20,000,000. By the terms of his will, his wife Delores, who was to become our client, was to receive an income of only $400 per month.

Several years before his death, Barney and Delores, his second wife, had broken up. But before the will had been executed, they had reconciled. Part of the reconciliation was based on Barney's promises that he would stop drinking, and that he would bequeath to Delores one-third of his estate. Barney, however, did not follow through on this latter promise. It was to be our task to discover the reasons underlying his failure to do so.

Some of the men who had been closest to Barney firmly maintained that he exhibited no signs of being mentally ill or deficient. Four of these were officers of several companies owned by Diamond, and were also trustees of the will's prime beneficiary—the Diamond Foundation. Barney's personal physician attributed the cause of death to old age: Barney was 68 when he died.

Delores, on the other hand, vehemently insisted that there was something wrong with Barney, something radically wrong. I had a hunch that we might be able to break the will if we could show that Barney had suffered some brain damage that would have affected his memory and dispositive capacity. To do this, we would have to exhume the body.

Others expressed their doubts that anything wrong could still be proved. After all, they continued, Barney had been dead two months. Being familiar with the work pathologists were now doing, I persevered. If there was anything organically wrong with his brain, we would be able to find it.

To exhume the body, the permission of Delores and the local health authorities had to be obtained. This was difficult in Georgia. I employed two of the best pathologists in the world to conduct the autopsy: Dr. Milton Helpern and Dr. Andrew Cyrus. Dr. Cyrus is a neuropathologist from the Wisconsin School of Medicine (formerly Marquette) and Dr. Helpern is from Bellevue in New York.

Each expressed doubts about my hunch, but went along with it.

The body was exhumed from the red Georgia clay. At the trial, Drs. Cyrus and Helpern told the jury why this will could not have been Barney Diamond's: Barney could not have been of sound mind for the past several years. Dr. Cyrus testified that he found ten cysts in

Barney's brain, and added that he probably walked with a gimpy left leg, couldn't read, and would have had some speech impediments. All of these observations were then confirmed by witness friends of the deceased. Dr. Halpern testified that Barney's brain was deteriorated from the ingestion of too much alcohol.

The testimony of the pathologists resulted in the jury finding in our favor. The case was eventually appealed to the Supreme Court of Georgia,[4] which upheld the award of one-third of the estate to our client.

Defendants then attempted to have the tainted will probated, but the jury was unable to reach a decision on this. The trustees for the estate finally consented to give Delores one-third of the figure they had computed as the full value of the estate, which was considerably less than the estimated $20 million, but still a great deal more than the original $400 per month. Were it not for my hunch and the examination of the exhumed body by two of the country's top pathologist's, none of this would have been possible.

§ 2.144 Investigation of Injury on Ship

Another example of a thorough investigation is *Crisp v. Matson Navigation Company*, a case we filed in United States District Court for the Northern District of California. Therein we utilized a combination of extensive demonstrative evidence and depositions of both experts who reenacted the procedures and on-the-scene witnesses who had seen the accident happen. *Vasilios B. Choulos* Esq. and investigator *Eugene J. Marshall*, conducted and exhaustive investigation which led to a settlement of $2.3 million.

Plaintiff, a 54-year-old able-bodied seaman, sustained severe brain damage by reason of a near drowning. The accident occurred on November 21, 1977, as the gangway of the S.S. Hawaiian was being stowed during unloading procedures in the Port of Seattle, Washington. The gangway collapsed and fell some 15 feet while plaintiff was engaged in stripping procedures. Figure 60.

When the end of the gangway gave way, plaintiff was thrown into the cold water of the ocean. During the fall, it was believed that plaintiff struck his body against several portions of the gangway. By the time he was in the water, his condition was such that he could not extricate himself, or even tread water until rescuers reached him. The rescue was delayed due to a malfunction in the same gangway

---

4. Liberty Nat'l Bank & Trust Co. v. Diamond, 231 Ga. 321, 201 S.E.2d 400 (1973).

Figure 60. The gangplank is shown here in its down position.

which prevented it from being lowered to the water's edge. When the rescuers finally did reach him, plaintiff exhibited no vital life signs. In effect, he was dead from drowning.

Resuscitation efforts ultimately revived plaintiff; however, he did not regain consciousness immediately, and in fact remained in a coma for 40 days following the tragic event. The incident left plaintiff a spastic quadriplegic.

We contended that the case was one of liability, as the facts clearly showed defendant's vessel was unseaworthy and that defendants were negligent as follows:

1. The condition of the starboard gangway (the one involved in the unfortunate occurrence) was unseaworthy in that it fell;

2. The designated method of stowing the gangway was unseaworthy in that plaintiff was required to do his work by going onto the gangway, which was hanging outside of the hull of the ship over the water, without a safety line or safety net, after the vessel had undocked and was in the process of navigating in the harbor under substandard lighting. Rather than performing the stowing procedures while they were still docked at the pier, it was the usual practice of this ship to get underway first. In our case, the procedure was commenced only after the ship had traversed ½ mile out to sea.

3. The ship owners and officers were at fault in having failed to provide a Mate, Bosun, or other designated supervisory personnel to supervise the procedure.

4. Due to the further malfunction of the gangway which prevented its immediate lowering to water's edge, plaintiff was left unconscious in the cold water for an unduly long period of 15 minutes.

Defendant Matson Navigation Company alleged that the gangway had collapsed by reason of plaintiff's own weight in going on the gangway before it was safe to do so. This, defendant contended, was the result of plaintiff's impaired judgment occasioned by the latter's drunkenness.

Plaintiff's blood alcohol reading taken at the emergency room was 0.150%.) Defendant offered proof that plaintiff had ingested apis 0.150%.) Defendant offered proof that plaintiff had ingested approximately 17 "screwdrivers" within several hours of the vessel's sailing time. We countered this argument by claiming that defendant, under the rules of the Union and the Sea, should not have allowed plaintiff on duty to begin with in his drunken condition. We further maintained that he had been an alcoholic some 20 years, and as such, his judgment was not impaired by reason of said alcohol ingestion, as he had developed a tolerance thereto.[5]

For us to prevail at trial, it would be necessary to gather facts showing that plaintiff's weight had nothing to do with the gangway's dropping, and further that the entire procedure of stowing the gangway, especially at sea, was unreasonably dangerous. Through the exhaustive efforts of our staff, we managed to do so.

We deposed a number of experts whose backgrounds ranged from retired captains to bosuns and seamen, all experienced in and familiar with various methods of stowing the gangway. These experts would testify as to the ship's seaworthiness under conditions similar

---

5. The subject of handling a case wherein plaintiff was drunk is discussed in § 3.22, "The Crippled Case", infra.

to those existing when plaintiff was injured, and would express their opinions as to the safety of the entire procedure.

Hundreds of pictures of the operation were taken, some of which are reproduced in Figures 60 through 63. We also managed to take some motion pictures of the actual techniques used to stow the gangway, which supported our theories.

Through discovery, we were able to obtain documents which greatly assisted us in proving the procedure was unsafe.

In the Report of Personal Injury or Loss of Life dated November 24, 1977, it was therein recommended that sailors be closely supervised while performing stowing procedures. A report of the Master of the S.S. Hawaiian to the Vessel Manager of the same ship advised that from that date on, there would be better lighting, closer supervision, and better instruction with respect to the stowing operation.

In an earlier, more significant inter-office memo from the Master to the Vessel Manager, the Master reported: "There was a *very unsafe practice* being used in the procedure. . . . In the future, this practice will not be used and also the Bosun will be at the scene of the work prior to the work being done." These inter-office memos showed that defendant recognized and admitted the procedure as being unsafe, and recommended the same preventive measures which we were alleging should have originally been taken!

Together with the testimony of those seamen familiar with the stowing procedures employed on the S.S. Hawaiian, and the pictures and movies taken by us and accompanied by a number of experts, we conducted a *reenactment* of the entire procedure aboard the ship. Figures 61 to 63. This reenactment further substantiated our contention that the entire procedure was unsafe.

Figure 61. A proper investigation often requires careful scrutiny by qualified experts, especially in unusual or technical cases.

Figure 62. An expert recreates the stowing procedure leading to plaintiff's injuries.

Ch. 2 INVESTIGATION AND DISCOVERY § **2.144**

Figure 63. Attorney Vasilios B. Choulos personally investigates the procedure used to stow the gang way. Counsel should actively participate in investigation whenever possible.

Through this investigation, we were able to achieve a favorable settlement of $2.3 million, structured.

§ 2.151 INTRODUCTION Pt. 1

R. INVESTIGATION THROUGH ACCIDENT RECONSTRUCTION

§ 2.151 Introduction

One of the best methods to investigate the causes of an accident is to obtain the services of an expert trained in the reconstruction of accidents. The following two cases, contributed by *R. T. "Ted" Abrahamson*, P.E., of *Abrahamson & Associates*, Consulting Engineers, Amarillo, Texas,[6] were investigated in this manner, and the results achieved attest to the value in utilizing this method.

§ 2.152 Train-Bus Collision

Ortiz v. Atchison, Topeka, & Santa Fe Railway Co. involved a train and school bus collision in which seven schoolchildren were killed, and fifteen others injured. Figures 64 and 65. The investiga-

Figure 64. The aftermath of a bus-train collision in which 7 children were killed and fifteen injured. Expert reconstructionist Ted Abrahamson, Amarillo, Texas was called in to determine the cause of the accident.

6. R. T. "Ted" Abrahamson, P.E., Abrahamson & Associates, Consulting Engineers, Suite 536—Petroleum Building, P.O. Box 14025, Amarillo, Texas.

228

Figure 65. A close-up of the bus shows the extent of damage caused by the collision. An expert reconstruction was necessary to prove that the cause of the collision was due to the excessive speed of the train.

tion by the Railroad Safety Board placed blame for the accident on the school bus driver's failure to remain stationary after stopping short of the crossing.

The bus driver had gone through the standard procedures of stopping the school bus prior to crossing a spur track which led up to the dock next to the train depot. The driver then proceeded forward, looking both ways at service poles, switching operations, other vehicles, and what he could see of the main line track toward the approaching train. Although there were flashing lights and bells allegedly in operation at the time, the sun was in such a position behind and above the driver that the illumination of the flashing red lights could not be detected. As to the noise being made by the bells, it would have been very difficult for the bus driver to detect any train whistles or bells through the sounds made by a bus full of children who had just been let out of their classrooms.

Reconstruction of the accident scene by Ted Abrahamson involved taking measurements of the site, and of the positions of the school bus and the train after the collision. Photographs from various angles were taken of the scene. From this information Abrahamson was able to make a model of the site which demonstrated the problems and sight restrictions the bus driver encountered as he proceeded from his initial stopped position to the point where he was able to see the approaching train.

A diagram of the location was made by Mr. Abrahamson, Figure 66, which along with some pictures of the site, illustrated the difficulty the bus driver met while approaching the main line of the track. Abrahamson enlisted the aid of another expert to substantiate the claim that the sun had been in such a position that it would have obscured the flashing red lights. The expert reported, "This letter is to confirm . . . the position of the Sun at 4 PM CST on February 6, 1972, as seen from latitude 33°39′ and longitude 101°49′. The results of the calculation gave a solar position of Azimuth of 198°38′, elevation of 23°17′."

Through the measurements and observations he had made of the crossing and the final resting place of the train, Abrahamson was able to determine the train's speed as 58 MPH. Motion pictures and still photographs were then made from the train cab, the bus driver's position, and on the site using the actual speeds of the units as they approached each other immediately before the actual collision.

Through this accident reconstruction, Abrahamson was able to show that had the train been traveling less than 58 MPH, the bus driver would have had one-half of a second more from the time he saw the train and "floorboarded" the gas pedal, to the time the rear-end of the bus would have cleared the path of the train. This instant of time would have avoided the accident completely, rather than the train striking the bus 4.7 feet from its end as did actually occur.

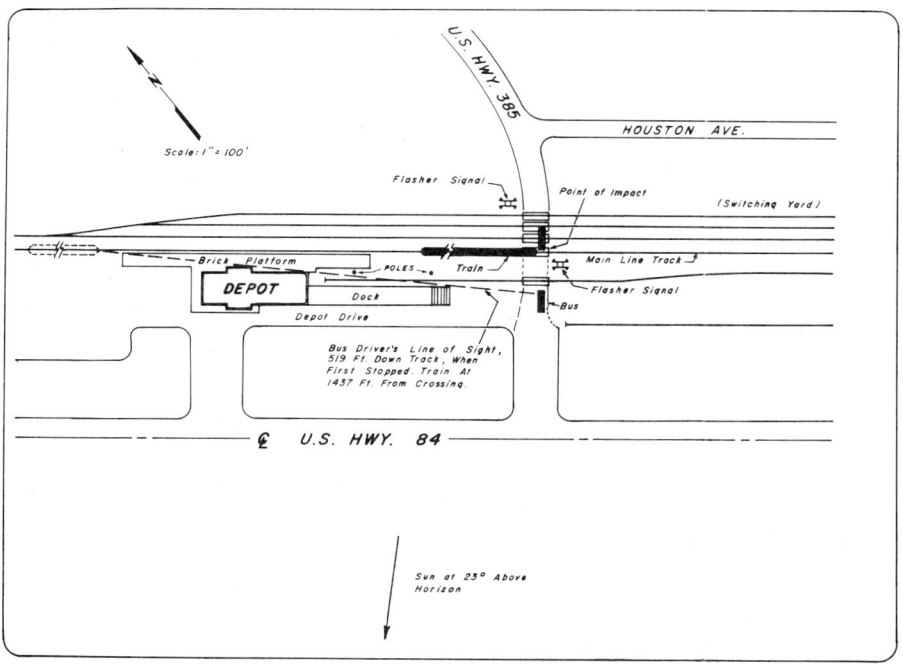

Figure 66. Part of the reconstruction included the preparation of a detailed scale map showing the relative positions of the train, the school bus, the flashing lights and other important objects.

§ 2.153 Automobile-Motorcycle Accident

Another case in which *Ted Abrahamson* participated as expert reconstructionist was *Price v. Producer's Grain Corp.* The action arose out of a head-on collision between a 64-year-old man driving a standard-sized car which was attempting to make a left turn at an intersection when it collided with a 22-year-old motorcyclist. Despite the fact he was wearing a helmet, the young motorcycle driver suffered fatal injuries.

The collision initially appeared to be the entire fault of the automobile driver. On-the-spot pictures taken before either of the vehicles had been moved showed their positions immediately after the incident. Figures 67 and 68.

Figure 67. Expert Ted Abrahamson was also employed to determine the cause of a fatal motorcycle-automobile collision. Reconstruction of the accident often proves, or disproves, a theory.

Figure 68. Another angle shows the final positions of the two vehicles. Studies of on-the-scene photographs are of crucial importance to the expert reconstructionist's determination of fault.

Further investigation by Mr. Abrahamson, however, demonstrated that the car driver was not solely to blame for the mishap. Measurements of the skid marks made by the motorcycle and other information obtained by Abrahamson were used to adduce that the motorcycle had been exceeding the speed limit. Figure 69.

A reconstruction of the accident by Abrahamson proved that had the motorcyclist been traveling at the speed limit, he would have been able to swerve around the car, without crossing the double yellow line which divided the road. Even if the motorcyclist had hit the car, at this reduced speed, his injuries would have been much less severe. The following is a copy of the report made by Abrahamson, replete with the information he relied upon, difficulties he encountered, and the conclusions he reached. The report:

"In reference to our meeting and your request on July 26, 1979, an investigation and accident reconstruction has been made of the subject collision whereby a northbound motorcycle collided with a

Figure 69. In accidents involving automobiles, motorcycles, and trucks, skid marks are used to assist the expert reconstructionist in his decision as to liability. The marks can be measured and the relative speed of the vehicle computed therefrom.

southbound automobile making a left turn from South Washington Street onto South 48th Avenue in Amarillo, Texas on May 19, 1979.

"A greater than normal amount of investigation and reconstruction was necessary to gather and evaluate the most accurate, pertinent data and available information.

"Some of these factors were:

"1. No definite information was available from the drivers.

"2. Severe damages occurred to the motorcycle.

"3. Insufficient measurements and photographs were taken prior to the removal of the units and drivers.

"4. Damages to the motorcycle could not be readily determined from the pictures taken at the scene nor where the motorcycle had been stored which would reveal the actual direction and force of the impact.

"5. The automobile was repaired before its damages could be evaluated.

Ch. 2   INVESTIGATION AND DISCOVERY   § 2.153

"6. Several witnesses saw different phases of the collision before, during and after the actual impact.

"In order to gain as much information as possible concerning this collision between the motorcycle and the car, the following data and information were obtained by personal inspection of the accident site, personal inspection of the motorcycle, and the inspection and study of photographs, measurements and various data gained by myself and/or supplied by others:

"1. A copy of the Texas Peace Officer's Accident Report by the Amarillo Police Department was received.

"2. The data, specifications and weights of the two units were obtained.

"3. An inspection, various measurements and photographs of the accident site, each of the units, (and/or their same year and model, and their component parts) the motorcyclist's helmet and clothes, and related items were made by me.

"4. A copy of the roadway plans and an aerial photograph where this collision occurred were obtained from the City of Amarillo.

"5. A survey of the roadway, adjacent fences, pavement markings, curbs, signs, and other relevant data was made.

"6. Photographs made by the Amarillo Police Department were received.

"7. Statements of witnesses along with other pertinent data relative to this collision were received.

"A basic drawing of the accident site was made to a scale whereby one inch represented twenty feet. The conclusions established by the investigation of the foregoing data were calculated and plotted on the drawing. This drawing along with other engineering-based information and engineering expertise were used to perform certain calculations from which additional information was gained and used to reconstruct this accident. Both vehicles involved in this collision are assumed to have been in good operating condition with no malfunctioning equipment relative to the physical reconstruction of this accident.

"This accident was reconstructed by starting from the final or 'rest' positions of both of the vehicles and the location where the motorcycle driver was picked up by the ambulance attendants, and working backwards to the positions of both vehicles immediately prior to the time either driver began taking evasive action. This accident was then reconstructed as the various events occurred during the normal time sequence.

§ 2.153 INTRODUCTION Pt. 1

"The primary purpose of this report is to reconstruct this accident to determine:

"1. The location of each of the vehicles and the motorcycle driver in their final positions.

"2. The speed and location of each of the vehicles and the motorcycle driver at the Point of Impact.

"3. The speed and location of each of the vehicles at the instant their respective drivers performed any evasive action.

"4. The probable events which caused this accident to occur, and what actions each of the drivers may have taken to avoid the collision.

"Since there were several sources of information stated at the beginning of this report, only those data which are logical and consistent with relative information have been utilized during the accident reconstruction process. The primary purpose of this report was then followed as numbered in the preceding paragraph.

"1. The final positions of the vehicles were determined from the pictures and the measurements made by the Amarillo Police Department. The location of the final position of the motorcycle driver was determined from the statements of the witnesses and subsequent conversations with them. From this information, the locations of the final positions of the vehicles and the motorcycle driver were drawn on the drawing.

"2. Knowing the location where the motorcycle rider landed, and the location and direction of the movement of the vehicles at their point of impact, the intensity of the impact of the collision could be calculated. The motorcycle driver had vaulted 62 Feet through the air after his impact with the upper left-hand corner of the automobile windshield. The car had skidded to a stop 1.0 Feet beyond the point of impact. The motorcycle had rotated 180 Degrees clockwise after the initial point of impact. The speed of the motorcycle driver as he left the top of the automobile windshield was 31.36 MPH, and as he left the motorcycle on impact was 32.76 MPH. The speed of the car was 6.38 MPH at the Point of Impact.

"3. From the skidmarks of the motorcycle and the car, their initial speeds at the time their wheels began leaving skidmarks can be calculated. The motorcycle was travelling 50.5 MPH and the car was travelling at 9.37 MPH. Allowing for brake-force build up, brake lag, brake reaction, and driver reaction time through their relative distances and retarding forces, the motorcycle was travelling 52.5 MPH and the car was travelling at 7.69 MPH when their respective drivers reacted to the impending collision.

236

"4. Subconsciously, the driver of the car may have seen the oncoming motorcycle, but because the motorcycle appeared to be far enough away—along with the difficulty of a person being able to judge the speed of an oncoming motorcycle—the driver of the car felt no threat of a collision until the point in time he realized the motorcycle was coming faster than he had subconsciously thought at which time he began evasive maneuvers by applying his brakes.

"If the driver of the car had proceeded to complete his left turn, the motorcycle would have hit the right side of the car 0.37 Feet behind the center of the right-front wheel.

"If the motorcycle was travelling 45 MPH instead of 52.5 MPH when its driver began his evasive actions while the driver of the car stopped as he did, the motorcycle would have hit the right side of the car 0.90 Feet in front of the center of the right-front wheel at a speed of 12.06 MPH.

"If the motorcycle was travelling 45 MPH when its driver began his evasive actions while the driver of the car proceeded to complete his left turn, the motorcycle would have cleared the rear of the car by 1.90 Feet.

"If the motorcyclist had proceeded at 45 MPH and the driver of the car proceeded to complete his left turn, the motorcycle would have hit the car on the right side 0.39 Feet behind the right-front corner of the car if the motorcycle had followed the same path as it did in the actual collision.

"If the motorcyclist had travelled at 45 MPH and steered toward the centerline of Washington Street (but not cross the centerline) and tried to go around the back of the car as the car was proceeding to turn left, the motorcycle would have cleared the car by 2.0 Feet.

"In conclusion, if the motorcyclist was travelling at 45 MPH while the driver of the car was completing his left turn, the motorcyclist could have:

"1. Continued on its path and try to stop whereby he would have hit the right-front fender of the car at a speed of about 12 MPH which would have created must less injurious effects to the motorcycle and its driver;

"2. Steered toward the centerline of South Washington Street and cleared the rear end of the car by about 2.0 Feet without going over the centerline of South Washington Street.

"A motorcycle, like any other vehicle, is easier to control at 45 MPH than at 52.5 MPH."

§§ 2.154–2.160 are reserved for supplementary material.

S. ENJOINING THE OVERZEALOUS INVESTIGATION

§ 2.161 Introduction

The defendant is, of course, entitled to investigate all phases of plaintiff's claim. He may take moving pictures, interrogate neighbors, employers and friends, check government and educational records, and so forth. However, if the defendant becomes so enthusiastic as to violate the plaintiff's privacy, or actually annoys or harasses him, then the plaintiff's counsel should have no hesitancy in protecting his clients' rights by injunction or some other appropriate court order against the defendant.[7]

§ 2.162 Examples of Improper Investigative Techniques

On one occasion, I represented a plaintiff who had received a severe head injury in an intersection accident.[8] In this case there were gross personality disturbances in the plaintiff which we felt were easily demonstrable. However, the damage was in the frontal lobes, and no neurological signs manifested.

We obtained our own neurological and physical examinations of the plaintiff, and then prepared a brochure and submitted it to the

---

7. Rule 26(c) of the Federal Rules of Discovery permits a court to issue a protective order as follows:

    "Upon motion by a party or by the person from whom discovery is sought, and for good cause shown, the court in which the action is pending or alternatively, on matters relating to a deposition, the court in the district where the deposition is to be taken may make any order which justice requires to protect a party or person from annoyance, embarrassment, oppression, or undue burden or expense, including one or more of the following: (1) that the discovery not be had; (2) that the discovery may be had only on specified terms and conditions, including a designation of the time or place; (3) that the discovery may be had only by a method of discovery other than that selected by the party seeking discovery; (4) that certain matters not be inquired into, or that the scope of the discovery be limited to certain matters; (5) that discovery be conducted with no one present except persons designated by the court; (6) that a deposition after being sealed be opened only by order of the court; (7) that a trade secret or other confidential research, development, or commercial information not be disclosed or be disclosed only in a designated way; (8) that the parties simultaneously file specified documents or information enclosed in sealed envelopes to be opened as directed by the court."

    For additional discussion, see Wright & Miller, Federal Practice & Procedure §§ 2035 et seq.

8. An intersection case always presents the problem of liability, and remains potentially dangerous until verdict, because of the ever-present issue of plaintiff's own negligence.

defendant's insurance company. This brochure included all of the law, all of the pictures, examinations, hospital records, and results of the several tests. Additionally, defendants were allowed not only independent medical examinations by doctors of their own choosing, but defendants' doctors were permitted to speak with plaintiff's doctors without our presence.

On the eve of trial, I first learned that someone representing the defendants, despite all this cooperation and candor in the above proceedings, had hired private detectives to take the plaintiff for a ride in an automobile (at the time he was under court guardianship), and had grilled him to a point that he eventually become utterly confused. They had him do multiplication tests, introduced him to various people, asked about his future plans, and generally harassed him to the point that when they returned him home he was hysterical, requiring that medical aid be summoned.

Associate counsel and I immediately went into court where the cause was pending, had an order issued for the liability carrier and other interested persons to appear, and after a hearing, the defendants' insurance company, lawyers, detectives, investigators, agents and servants were enjoined from visiting, seeing, talking to, harassing or annoying plaintiff.[9]

In a recent case, a defense investigator fraudulently tampered with evidence and obtained a statement from the plaintiff by falsely representing that he was from plaintiff's own insurance company. The jury awarded plaintiff $8 million in punitive damages for this wrongful conduct.[10]

In another case,[11] defendant's investigator gained admittance to the hospital room wherein plaintiff was confined, and by deception secured from plaintiff the address of a man who had accompanied her on her shopping trip, during which she was injured. Plaintiff brought suit alleging invasion of privacy, to which defendant objected on the ground it was investigating the claim. Said the court: "[W]e hold that an unreasonably intrusive investigation may violate a plaintiff's right to privacy."[12]

9. Several days later this case was settled before trial for $50,000, which settlement, while it did not approach adequacy for the injuries, nevertheless, measured in terms of liability weighed with possible contributory negligence, was satisfactory.

10. Blackwell v. Reliance Ins. Co., Indio Superior Court, California, # 15354 (July 25, 1975).

11. Noble v. Sears, Roebuck & Co., 33 Cal.App.3d 654, 109 Cal.Rptr. 269 (1973).

12. 33 Cal.App.3d at 660, 109 Cal.Rptr. at 272. See also Redner v. Workmen's Comp. Appeals Bd., 5 Cal.3d 83, 94 n. 13, 95 Cal.Rptr. 447, 455, 485 P.2d 799, 807 (1971) ("In such cases, the private investigators may well make an intrusion into the in-

Overzealous plaintiffs' counsel have been known, on occasion, to aid or abet their injured or bereaved clients by calling on the defendant for a "friendly" visit and a discussion of the "facts," and attempt to melt him with sympathy; and then testify either that the cold-hearted and indifferent fellow refused to talk, or that he did talk and admitted liability. Such conduct is likewise to be condemned.

§ 2.163 Suggested Petition for Order Enjoining Harassment

Set out below is a suggested form which can be used in order to prevent a litigant from being harassed:

PETITION RE ORDER TO SHOW CAUSE

Comes now _____, Guardian (or Guardian ad Litem) of _____, plaintiff above named, and as such Guardian of the person and estate of said _____, an incompetent, represents to the court as follows:

I.

That the _____ Company is the insurance company and has issued to the defendants named herein its policy of insurance insuring said defendants against damages for public liability and property damage.

II.

That petitioner herein is the duly acting, appointed and qualified Guardian of the person and estate of plaintiff _____.

III.

That said incompetent is seriously ill and in poor health, and is now and ever since the happening of the accident described in plaintiffs' complaint on file herein on the _____ day of _____, _____, has been under medical care and supervision; that his condition is such at this time that the slightest disturbance of the routine care and treatment he receives from petitioner upsets him emotionally and

dividual's right of privacy which would be objectionable or offensive to the reasonable man. . . . Courts have permitted such an individual to maintain an action for damages against the intruders."); Tucker v. American Employers' Ins. Co., 171 So.2d 437 (Fla.App.1965) (Florida Supreme Court recognizes that an investigation done by trailing or shadowing a claimant could amount to an actionable invasion of privacy if it is unreasonably intrusive); Pinkerton Nat'l Detective Agency, Inc. v. Stevens, 108 Ga.App. 159, 132 S.E.2d 119 (1965) (Investigation done in frightening manner may provide cause of action against detective agency); Souder v. Pendleton Detectives, Inc., 88 So.2d 716 (La.App. 1956).

causes him to cry for long periods of time, renders him physically and mentally ill and makes it quite difficult for petitioner to properly care for him and administer to his needs.

IV.

That the within personal injury action has been set for jury trial _____, _____, and the outcome of said action is of great concern to said incompetent whose thoughts are constantly on said trial and the part he is to take in said trial.

V.

That it is vital and material to the interests of said incompetent in said action that strangers be kept away from said incompetent and not permitted to engage him in conversation in that such action by strangers upset and disturb said incompetent mentally and thereby cause him to be physically and mentally sick; that any interference with said incompetent at this time shortly before the trial of the within action would seriously hamper, endanger and prejudice the successful prosecution of said action.

VI.

That on _____, _____, while petitioner was away from the home of petitioner, and said incompetent, leaving said incompetent home alone, a stranger representing himself as a "Mr. Doe" and driving a Ford automobile prevailed upon said incompetent to accompany him in said automobile to view some property which he asserted he was interested in buying for the purpose of raising chickens; that on _____, _____, again while petitioner was working in the fields and while incompetent was home alone, said stranger returned accompanied by a woman he introduced as his wife, leaving the woman alone with said incompetent for a long period of time; that upon petitioner's return to the house, said woman was still there alone with said incompetent; that said stranger and said woman attempted to take petitioner and said incompetent out to dinner and invited them to go to a festival then being held, stating that they did so because the incompetent _____ had been so nice to help; that the petitioner refused both invitations stating that it was the doctor's orders that _____ could do neither of these two things; that on _____, when said stranger returned with said incompetent, petitioner told him that said incompetent was not to be taken away from the house for a drive in an automobile; that despite this warning and request, when said stranger and said woman returned, they took him for a drive contrary to their instructions not to do so.

VII.

That on _____, _____, the day following said stranger's first arrival at the _____ home, and as a result of his experience with said stranger and the drive in said automobile, said incompetent suffered a relapse in his mental and physical state, was emotionally upset to the point that his coordination became badly affected and he cried throughout the entire day.

VIII.

That while said couple represented themselves to be chicken ranchers, petitioner noted that their hands were too white to be those of chicken ranchers.

IX.

That said stranger further represented that he, himself, had been in an accident and had, like _____, suffered a head injury.

X.

That said stranger was a man about 35 or 40 years of age, of a fair complexion, brown hair, wore glasses, was about six feet in height, was well and neatly dressed, and nice looking; that he was slow and deliberate in his speech.

XI.

That petitioner is further informed and believes and upon such information and belief alleges that said stranger and his alleged wife were investigators, detectives, employees or agents of the _____ Company, and that their acts, hereinbefore alleged, were performed and done at the express direction and request of said _____ Company and for the express purpose of upsetting, disturbing and exciting the said incompetent and rendering him emotionally unfit and unable to withstand the excitement and strain of the approaching trial.

XII.

That petitioner is further informed and believes and upon such information and belief alleges that unless restrained by order of this court said _____ Company, its officers, agents or employees will send other investigators, detectives, agents or employees to petitioner's home for the purpose of talking to said incompetent and injuring, disturbing, exciting and upsetting his mental and physical health.

Wherefore, petitioner prays for an order of this court directed to the _____ Company, its duly constituted officers, agents and employees requiring said company, its officers, agents and employees to appear at a time and place to be fixed in said order, then and there to show cause, if any they may have, why the court should not issue its order enjoining and restraining said _____ Company, its duly constituted officers, agents and employees from directly or indirectly interviewing and meeting said incompetent, from harassing, annoying or molesting said incompetent in any manner, from visiting or entering upon the premises of petitioner and said incompetent for any purpose or purposes whatever, and from employing or authorizing any investigators, detectives or individuals to do any of the things herein complained of.

Dated this _____.

_____
Petitioner

_____
Attorney for Petitioner

ORDER TO SHOW CAUSE AND TEMPORARY RESTRAINING ORDER

TO _____ COMPANY, ITS DULY CONSTITUTED OFFICERS, AGENTS AND EMPLOYEES:

You and each of you, are hereby ordered to appear before the above-entitled Court on the _____ day of _____, 19__, in Department _____ thereof, located in the Court House in the City of _____, County of _____, State of _____, then and there to show cause, if any you have, why:

Pending the trial of this action you, _____ Company, your duly constituted officers, agents, employees, investigators and detectives, should not be, and pending the hearing on this order you are hereby, enjoined and restrained from directly or indirectly interviewing and meeting _____, plaintiff herein; from harassing, annoying or molesting said plaintiff in any manner; from visiting or entering upon the premises of said plaintiff for any purpose or purposes whatever.

Dated this _____.

_____
Judge of the Superior Court

§§ 2.164–2.170 are reserved for supplementary material.

T. ETHICAL CONSIDERATIONS AND THE INVESTIGATOR

§ 2.171 In General

Every busy lawyer knows the importance of a capable secretary. She is no ordinary office girl. In many states, she is given the same "privilege" as the lawyer, the churchman, the doctor and the newspaper man, that is, the privilege not to testify as to the conversation with a client.[13] Those who seek the lawyer are just as troubled in mind as the sick person who seeks a physician is troubled in body. Fortunate indeed is the lawyer whose secretary is familiar with his files, and his clients—their demands, difficulties and idiosyncracies. This girl can actually give her boss half a day extra for his legal work, and save him the "clerking" so many men must routinely do, as a part of the burden of practicing law.

Likewise for the personal injury lawyer, the investigator is of the utmost importance. He, too, may make or win the case for the trial lawyer. Most trial specialists must, necessarily, depend to a large degree upon someone trained to find out the facts. If he has had legal training, his reports will be all the more valuable, since he can first of all evaluate the evidence he is gathering, and appreciate its importance at the trial.

§ 2.172 Communication With Adverse Party

Neither counsel should interview the opposing party once the latter has retained counsel.[14] (However, in criminal cases, the courts

---

13. Section 952 of the California Evidence Code governing "confidential communication between client and lawyer," states that a communication made by a client to his lawyer is privileged notwithstanding that third persons were in a position to hear the communication, if the third person was present to further the interest of the client, or whose presence is reasonably necessary for the transmission of the information, or for the accomplishment of the purpose for which the lawyer has been consulted.

This section replaced prior Code of Civil Procedure section 1881 which provided:

". . . 2. Attorney and client. An attorney cannot, without the consent of his client, be examined as to any communication made by the client to him, or his advice given thereon in the course of professional employment; nor can an attorney's *secretary, stenographer,* or *clerk* be examined, without the consent of his employer, concerning any fact the knowledge of which has been acquired in such capacity."

14. Disciplinary Rule 7–104(A)(1) of the ABA Code of Professional Responsibility provides:

"(A) During the course of his representation of a client a lawyer shall not:

(1) Communicate or cause another to communicate on the subject of the representation

have held it not improper for defendant's counsel to interview the complaining witness even after indictment.)[15] A prospective plaintiff may, of course, be interviewed and his statement taken, as is frequently the case by an insurance adjuster, prior to his engaging counsel. Plaintiff also may secure a statement from defendant before he has counsel engaged, and indeed, it is good practice for such a statement to be taken at the earliest possible moment. In states where process is actually served by someone from counsel's office, an interview and a statement may well be secured when the service is accomplished.

An anomaly exists between plaintiff's or defendant's office, and the insurance company: Every now and then bar associations will complain of banks and trust companies "practicing law" by drawing deeds and wills and other documents through their legal departments or by unlicensed employees. However, the author has yet to hear criticism directed at an insurance company for practicing law when, daily, the insurance adjuster actually practices the highest type of law with his negotiating and settling cases. Paradoxically, it is considered "unethical" for plaintiff's lawyer to allow his secretary or his investigator or any unlicensed person in his office to negotiate a settlement, yet daily, throughout the United States, the great proportion of settlements are negotiated by plaintiff's lawyer with an unlicensed adjuster, investigator or clerk at the insurance company. No such privilege is accorded the employee of the plaintiff's attorney.[16]

§ 2.173 Insurance Company's Letter in Chicago Air Crash Disaster

Illustrative of the fact that insurance companies regularly deal in the practice of settling cases, thereby affecting the legal rights of a prospective plaintiff, and the extent to which they sometimes go, I include relevant excerpts from a letter to the survivors of passengers who

with a party he knows to be represented by a lawyer in that matter unless he has the prior consent of the lawyer representing such other party or is authorized by law to do so."

15. People v. Cordero (1925) 72 Cal. App. 526, 237 P.2d 786 ("The right of counsel to interview witnesses prior to a trial of a case is just as sacred, and just as full and complete, as is the right of district attorneys to ascertain all the facts concerning the cause to be tried"). See also In re Malone, 44 Cal.2d 700, 284 P.2d 805 (1955).

16. The author once employed a lawyer licensed to practice in a foreign state and awaiting his bar examination in California. Against specific instructions, this lawyer sat in on a deposition, representing the plaintiff, while defendant's counsel, for the insurance company, took plaintiff's deposition. The author was actually publicly reproved by the California State Bar for this.

had been killed in the air crash at O'Hare International Airport in Chicago on May 25, 1979. The letter is dated June 1, 1979, one week after the incident. As may be gleaned from the letter, representatives of the insurance company had already contacted the bereaved.

Dear Mr. and Mrs. _____:

By the time you receive this letter, one of our representatives will have contacted you in connection with the death of _____ who was a passenger aboard the American Airlines' aircraft which was involved in the accident at O'Hare International Airport, Chicago, Illinois, on May 25, 1979. We represent the insurers of American Airlines, Inc., in connection with this accident and it is our intention on behalf of American, and its insurers, to see that everything possible is done to ease the burden of this difficult time.

We wish to again express our sincere condolences which were originally communicated to you when our personnel first made contact with you. It certainly is not our intention to invade your family's personal privacy at this time of grief; however, it has been our experience that next-of-kin have questions at a time like this, only some of which are ordinarily answered expeditiously and completely. It is for this reason that we undertake to communicate with you and attempt to place ourselves at your disposal with respect to these areas of inquiry.

. . .

We have arranged to pay for all costs associated with the preparation and shipment of the deceased to the airport destination (or city) directly to the parties who performed the services. It would be our request that you have your own funeral director invoice you for those services which he completes for you locally. We will then, upon receipt of this invoice from you, expeditiously pay to that funeral director (or reimburse you for) all reasonable expenses incurred in the interment.

During this period of time, you may be in need of funds because unexpected expenses have been incurred, or as a result of losing the one to whom you normally look for financial support. In order to attempt to minimize any such current hardship, we are prepared to advance funds to you periodically as you need them if you will call or write to one of the above persons.

Money damages can never compensate for the loss of a loved one but this is the medium recognized by the law for compensating victims and the families of victims in air disasters. We will be writing to you again within the next two weeks to obtain certain information to assist us in evaluating the loss which you have incurred. Upon receipt of this information, we will extend an offer to settle your claim.

It is our intention to see that you receive fair compensation for the loss which you have sustained. It is also our hope that you ultimately retain as much of the compensation as is properly due you without unnecessary diversion of large amounts to legal expenses.

You may find yourselves under pressure to sign a contingent fee retainer with an attorney whereby his fee is a percentage of the final award. The rationale for such a percentage fee is that the lawyer risks getting no fee if there is no recovery. There is no such contingency in this case. There is also nothing to be gained by a precipitous lawsuit. We do suggest that it would be in your best interest to evaluate the offers which will be made to you and obtain the help of your attorney based upon a fee for the work involved rather than a percentage of the settlement or award.

Immediate legal action is unnecessary to avoid permitting applicable time periods (i. e., statutes of limitations, etc.) to expire. Should settlement discussions not ultimately result in a termination of any claims that might exist, we provide a reasonable extension of any applicable time limitation based upon the facts and circumstances of the individual case in order that you will have ample time to take any path you choose as to counsel you retain, the basis upon which he is paid or whether you wish to institute a lawsuit. Please do not be rushed into limiting your alternatives or committing yourselves needlessly to an inordinate legal expense.

Very truly yours,

———————————.

§ 2.174 Engaging an Investigator

Some lawyers employ an outside investigator, paying him either by the hour or by the case. Other firms have an investigator in their employ solely upon salary. The California Supreme Court, in *Hildebrand v. State Bar* [17] held it to be proper to engage an investigator on a contingent fee basis. However, in *Hildebrand v. State Bar* it was held improper for a representative of the Railroad Brotherhood to contribute part of his fee in each case to a "legal aid fund." [18]

---

17. 18 Cal.2d 816, 117 P.2d 860 (1941). However in a later decision by an appellate court, Cain v. Burns, 131 Cal.App.2d 439, 280 P.2d 888 (1955), the court held that contingent payment to an investigator constituted impermissible fee-splitting between a lawyer and a layperson. The court found that the investigator was "working on a percentage basis without regard to the work done, the time consumed or the difficulties encountered." 131 Cal.App.2d at 441, 280 P.2d at 889. This is in accord with the present view of most, if not all, jurisdictions.

18. Hildebrand v. State Bar, 36 Cal.2d 504, 225 P.2d 508 (1950).

§ 2.174 INTRODUCTION Pt. 1

It is no secret that the great majority of union employees injured, and particularly in the seamen and railroad cases, either seek the business agent of the particular union for advice on selection of a lawyer or the business agent himself initially recommends the "union lawyer". Because of this selection, admiralty and railroad cases, on the plaintiff side, are generally presented by a select number of lawyers in each city of the United States. These lawyers obviously are specialists in the law and problems of the particular union.

On the defendant's side, rarely does the insured defendant select his own lawyer. His lawyer is selected for him by a corporation, the insurance company. The author recalls no case wherein this practice has been criticized as a "corporation practicing law." This method of selection, on the defendant's side, has become so universal that the layman even speaks of the lawyer as the "insurance company lawyer" rather than "his" lawyer.[19]

The "private eye" is a well recognized figure. One need but look at the classified section in the telephone book of any modest-sized city in the United States to see not only his well-advertised address and telephone (the latter with "24 hour service") but, generally, his alleged prowess characterized as well. Some of these gentlemen are used in personal injury cases for investigation but generally they belong to other fields of fact finding, particularly the domestic.[20] Indeed many of the "great investigators" were so proficient in their investigations that their exploits and solutions would have made the services of an attorney surplusage.[21]

There are many nationally known investigators available to trial counsel. Some lawyers prefer to send an investigator from their own locality (one whom they know personally) to a distant location. Others employ the services of a younger lawyer in the firm to accomplish this work. Others, sometimes pressed by time, employ an investigator located at the actual place, feeling he is more familiar with the customs and procedures there and more acquainted with the local law enforcement officials from whom information may be needed.

19. Universal knowledge by the layman that the majority of the cases are "fought" by "insurance company lawyers," that obviously the insurance company is the actual defendant, and further that most people carry insurance today, should minimize the characterization of "mistrial and misconduct" when the forbidden subject of insurance is mentioned during the trial. It takes credulity to assume that jurors, seeing the same defense counsel, representing defendant after defendant, would not correctly infer the true facts of the situation.

20. Their fees in these cases often exceed those of the lawyer.

21. See James B. Horan and Howard Swiggett, The Pinkerton Story; Alva Johnston, A Profile of Ray Schindler, New Yorker; also not to be omitted, is the legendary Sherlock Holmes.

The author has experienced, almost universally, a distrust by jurors and judges of an investigator's testimony, unless it is circumstantially corroborated. A juror reflects in his verdict his dislike to be found out, to be spied upon. No less a person than Justice McReynolds [22] once said, "The most exemplary resent having their footsteps dogged by private detectives. All know that men who accept such employment commonly lack fine scruples, often wilfully misrepresent innocent conduct and manufacture charges!"

Knowing, therefore, the disposition of the average juror to accept with reluctance the testimony of an investigator, it is good practice, when a statement is taken, and there may be a possibility of subsequent denial, that a court reporter be present, and reduce what is said to writing. If the lawyer, himself, does the talking, he may find himself unable to testify in a good many jurisdictions as to the circumstances, without withdrawing from further participation in the cause.[23]

---

22. Sinclair v. United States, 279 U.S. 749, 49 S.Ct. 471, 73 L.Ed. 938 (1928).

In the Sinclair case the Burns Detective Agency was held in contempt when 14 of its operators shadowed jurors even though it was admitted that no juror was contacted, and no juror knew that he was being shadowed. Evidence of the practice of the Department of Justice of the United States to shadow jurors was rejected as irrelevant.

23. Most, if not all, states now have rules requiring an attorney to withdraw from a cause when he or his firm may be called as a witness on behalf of a client, with few exceptions. See e. g., Comden v. Superior Court, 20 Cal.3d 906, 145 Cal.Rptr. 9, 576 P.2d 971 (1978), cert. denied 439 U.S. 981, 99 S.Ct. 568, 58 L.Ed.2d 652. This rule is partly based upon the fact that the attorney would have to argue to the jury his own credibility, and also upon the idea that a lawyer, as an officer of the court, is disinterested, even though a hired partisan.

§§ 2.175–2.180 are reserved for supplementary material.

CHAPTER 3

HAVE I A CASE?

Table of Sections

		Sections
A.	Introduction	3.1 –3.4
B.	Determining The Theory	3.5 –3.10
C.	Stare Decisis and The Lawyer's Duty	3.11–3.20
D.	The Crippled Case	3.21–3.30
E.	Statutes of Limitation	3.31–4.0

A. INTRODUCTION

Sec.
3.1 Initial Considerations.

B. DETERMINING THE THEORY

3.5 Introduction.
3.6 Contract v. Tort Actions.
3.7 The Unexplainable Accident.
3.8 Circumstantial Evidence Demonstrates the Theory.

C. *STARE DECISIS* AND THE LAWYER'S DUTY

3.11 Introduction.
3.12 The Doctrine of *Stare Decisis*.
3.13 Combatting *Stare Decisis*.
3.14 English Common Law.
3.15 Statutes.

D. THE CRIPPLED CASE

3.21 Introduction.
3.22 Intoxication.
3.23 Aggravation of Pre-existing Condition.
3.24 Obvious Danger Cases.

E. STATUTES OF LIMITATION

3.31 In General.
3.32 Equitable Arguments.
3.33 Suit in Contract.
3.34 Notice of Claim Statutes.

Sec.
3.35 Types of Statutes of Limitation.
3.36 Persons Affected.
3.37 Alternative or Collateral Remedies and Defenses.
3.38 Conflict of Laws.
3.39 Computation of Period—Accrual; Estoppel; Tolling.
3.40 Revival of Remedy.
3.41 Notice.
3.42 Claims Against Municipalities.

A. INTRODUCTION

§ 3.1 Initial Considerations

This chapter is the next step after one's client says with awesome brutality, "I'm going to see my lawyer!"

We are concerned herein with tort trends, practical as well as legal answers. Before the lawyer advises his client against the pursuit of a fancied claim, or how serious may be the defense of a suit against him, he must know that the answer he would have given in 1979 is still the law in 1982. He must realize as never before the growing guarantee to the ancient and heretofore academic *"ubi jus ubi remedium."* The currency of modern law is becoming readily exchangeable and strikingly fashionable in the market place.

Before taking the dramatic step of "going to law," the layman has generally given his own common sense interpretation to his grievances. Rather than discount the reasons he thinks he has a case, the lawyer should ask why he thinks he is right and the other fellow wrong. Then should the lawyer attempt to fit the fancied rights and wrongs into the various "duties" hereinafter set forth. This is not a return to "forms of action" but a suggestion for more searching and specific investigation, both of fact and law.[1] A case seemingly hopeless, whether for prosecution or defense, at the first interview, requires the more reason to examine into a possible remedy or defense. Were the case not so desperate, my client would not have accorded me the compliment of bringing the cause to one he credits with knowing more than he. But notwithstanding the enthusiasm, often entirely emotional, of the client, counsel must be just as determined in advising *against* suit or determined defense, if the cause does not warrant.[2]

In most other fields of law, the attorney has at least a mental "check list" before him when analyzing and preparing for a particu-

1. See § 2.11 et seq., "The Case History," supra.

2. See § 3.21 et seq., "The Crippled Case," infra.

lar transaction. When drawing a contract, generally the attorney has a form which contains the essential clauses, ordinarily included in similar documents, and as he goes through his preparation he (or more often his secretary) checks off those included, and then rechecks to see that nothing important is left out. In preparing Articles of Incorporation, by-laws, tax documents, or wills, the same is done.

This method of avoiding oversight of a possible theory should be also available to the personal injury lawyer, as well. The modern commercial airliner is checked and double checked by the mechanics before it is even taken onto the runway. Yet when one watches the pilots before take-off, he will see them again checking off, on a "double check," the various operating parts of the plane. Thus, radio, wheels, pressure, lights, gas, flight plan, etc. are all called out by one pilot and checked by the other.

Herein is our "check list," which trial counsel may well consider before advising a client that he "has no case." [3] Somewhere in the activity and complexity of human living someone has failed in his "check list." He has been careless. Our paragon, the "ordinarily prudent person," has failed to check. He has been negligent. Someone has suffered an injury or death. Unfortunately, we cannot restore sight, limbs, eyes, life, or smiles for sadness. Yet in a vicarious sense, the personal injury lawyer, too, is entrusted with life, liberty, and the pursuit of happiness. Prosaically put, he cannot afford to be careless in this, his trust, by neglecting his check list for an available theory; a last clear chance, perhaps, that some seemingly remote statutory violation, a newly announced familial doctrine, or some other remedy, subtle perhaps, but often potent, may offer hope for his client.[4]

3. It may well be that the lawyer reader in going over the section headings hereinafter indicated, may reconsider some of the cases in which he has advised his client, "You have no case."

4. Ours is a noble profession. Those among us who specialize in the personal injury field are particularly privileged. A doctor may bind up the physical wounds after personal injury but it is only the plaintiff's lawyer in the personal injury case who rehabilitates economically the client, his widow, his children. Were it not for the personal injury lawyer, the state, the federal government, and the county hospitals would have to accept the burden of rehabilitation.

There is a fascination about the "personal injury lawyer." We make no apologies for calling ourselves "damage suit lawyers," "trial lawyers," "personal injury lawyers," or "plaintiffs' lawyers." For a great lawyer once said, "Anyone who can successfully obtain verdicts in damage suits and have those verdicts sustained on appeal, is capable of entering any type of litigation." In our field, one encounters not only the human element, present in every law suit, but also

No client ever walked into a lawyer's office with a placard on his back heralding, "I am the *Dartmouth College Case*,"[5] or, *"MacPherson v. Buick Motor Co.,"*[6] *"Marbury v. Madison,"*[7] *"Pennoyer v. Neff,"*[8] or *"Dred Scott Case."*[9] These landmarks of law walked into offices, indistinguishable from hundreds of others, only as humble human beings, perhaps in working garments, some stumbling, often incoherent and incapable of adequate expression. But these became the great cases of law. The lawyer will interpret rights, and perhaps discover a new and neglected cause of action, as Samuel D. Warren and Louis D. Brandeis did in calling attention to the rights of privacy.[10] In any event, he will see to it that justice is not always as blind as sometimes depicted.

employs all of the mechanics necessary to obtain a judgment, and to perfect that judgment to its ultimate conclusion.

Let us speak frankly. There are those among us who malign the "personal injury lawyer." On *voir dire* of a jury, I often have the defendant sarcastically comment to the jury, "Do you know the plaintiff in this case is asking for a money judgment—dollars?" My reply, as I shall try to show you later on when we speak of the use of the blackboard, is that under our system of jurisprudence compensation can only be allowed in terms of dollars—money. I bring this home to the jury adequately and in direct reply on voir dire. As I shall show you later on, tears and laughter and pain can only be translated into the compensation of dollars—money.

5. 17 U.S. (4 Wheat.) 518, 4 L.Ed. 629 (1819).

6. 217 N.Y. 382, 111 N.E. 1050 (1916).

7. 5 U.S. (1 Cranch) 137, 2 L.Ed. 60 (1803).

8. 95 U.S. 714, 24 L.Ed. 565 (1877).

9. 60 U.S. (19 How.) 393, 15 L.Ed. 691 (1859).

10. 4 Harv.L.Rev. 193 (1890).

§§ 3.2–3.4 are reserved for supplementary material.

B. DETERMINING THE THEORY

§ 3.5 Introduction

Now that the case history has been taken in long or shorthand, or by dictaphone, etc., typed and placed in the file for reference (but always open for expansion as further investigation requires), the vital question recurs: *Is there a case?* The author recalls a 1947 California case, wherein the appellate court had reversed a judgment against my client, and said:

> "The trial of a lawsuit is not a game where the spoils of victory go to the clever and technical regardless of the merits, but a method devised by a civilized society to settle peaceably and justly disputes between litigants. The rules of the contest are not an end in themselves. Unless the rules tend to accomplish justice, strict compliance is not always required." [11]

Despite such disarming promises of "fireside equity" and "armchair justice," notwithstanding announcements in code states that the code "makes no distinction in matters of form between actions of contract and those of tort, and relief is administered without reference to the technical and artificial rules of the common law—," [12] this burst of exuberant confidence repeated in many phrases by courts everywhere, should not dissuade counsel from formalizing his legal theory [13] whether in the complaint or an answer.

---

11. Simon v. City and County of San Francisco, 79 Cal.App.2d 590, 600, 180 P.2d 393, 399 (1947).

12. Jones v. The Cortes, 17 Cal. 487, 497, 79 Am.Dec. 142, 144 (1861).

Most states have pleading rules patterned on Federal Rule of Civil Procedure 8(e)(2) which provides: "(2) A party may set forth two or more statements of a claim or defense alternately or hypothetically, either in one count or defense or in separate counts or defenses. When two or more statements are made in the alternative and one of them if made independently would be sufficient, the pleading is not made insufficient by the insufficiency of one or more of the alternative statements. A party may also state as many separate claims or defenses as he has regardless of consistency and whether based on legal, equitable, or maritime grounds. All statements shall be made subject to the obligations set forth in Rule 11."

13. Fleming v. Lockwood, 36 Mont. 384, 92 P. 962 (1907) ("While it is true that by adopting a Code we have abolished common-law forms of pleading, this abolition does not in any sense change the fundamental rules of substantive law, and we must still resolve questions presented in our litigation with reference to those ancient rules of law which had reason, experience, and the necessities of society for their foundation").

See B. Witkin, "Forms of Action: Return of the Zombies," NACCA, 1951 San Francisco Convention Proceedings, at 585: "Black's Law Dictionary says, 'Zombi legalis' or legal zombi:

In legally theorizing the case, however, counsel should be aware of various alternative possibilities: Is the case in contract or tort? Should there be a count in *both* contract and tort? What measure of damages and limitations apply depending on the form of action? If the cause lends itself to pleading as "wanton," or "gross negligence," the rule of exemplary damages may prevail, even when the civil offense is no more than drunken driving.[14] Is it necessary to plead Last Clear Chance? Will specific facts avoid *res ipsa loquitor*? How should attractive nuisance be alleged? Should the defense of "unavoidable accident" be pleaded?

§ 3.6 Contract v. Tort Actions

A 1976 decision by a California appellate court attests to the continued importance between actions *ex contractu*—those based on a contract—and actions *ex delicto*—founded in tort. In *Voth v. Wasco Public Util. Dist.*,[15] this difference was crucial to the case: under one action, plaintiff would have been precluded from bringing suit under a 100 day time limit, while under the other action, plaintiff could still pursue his claim.

In the *Voth* case, plaintiff was the assignee of an agricultural lease on land owned by defendant. Because the wells on the property did not produce a sufficient quantity of water for irrigation, the water from a sewage plant had to be used to irrigate the crops. When the land failed to produce a normal crop, plaintiff sued on a breach of an implied promise of fitness of water for use on growing crops.

Defendant asserted that the claim was barred by Section 911.2 of the California Government Code, which provided: "A claim relating to a cause of action for death or for injury to person or to personal property or growing crops shall be presented . . . not later than the 100th day after the accrual of the cause of action. A claim relating to any other cause of action shall be presented . . . not later than one year after the accrual of the cause of action."

nonentity, normally invisible, located in the interstices of every complaint. During pleading stages usually quite dead. When necessary conditions for resurrection occur—such as questions of jurisdiction, venue, or remedy—it is brought to a semblance of life by the peculiar necromancy of courts and lawyers known as construction of the pleadings. When thus made to appear in soulless, living form, it is known as a 'gravamen' or 'gist.' It discloses its presence by characteristic sonic manifestations in the upper ranges, and the complaint is then said, e. g., to 'sound' in tort or in contract."

14. See Chapter 16, "Punitive Damages," infra.

15. 56 Cal.App.3d 353, 128 Cal.Rptr. 608 (1976).

The court noted that whether an action is contractual or tortious depends upon the nature of the right sued upon, not the form of the pleading or demanded relief. One based on a breach of a promise is contractual; if noncontractual, it is in tort. But where, as in the case at bar, the breach is both contractual *and* tortious, then the court must ascertain which duty is the quintessence of the action. After considering prior decisions and the facts of the instant case, the court came to the conclusion that here, the action was based solely on a promise implied in the lease. Thus, it was contractual in nature, making the 100 day limit inapplicable.[16]

Consider two cases: *Bee v. Cooper*[17] and *Dougherty v. California Kettleman Oil Royalties*.[18] In the former, a number of directors of the defendant corporation fraudulently disposed of corporate assets to the injury of plaintiff shareholders. In the latter, a number of defendants, in violation of the contract, fraudulently concealed and failed to pay oil royalties to plaintiffs. Thus, in each case, the plaintiffs were injured by the activities of several defendants who fraudulently acquired property in which plaintiffs had an interest. In each case, plaintiffs, for consideration, released some of the guilty parties. In each, the remaining defendants were guilty of a wrong.

However, in the *Bee* case, the remaining defendants were held to be released, while in the *Dougherty* case, the remaining defendants were held liable. The reason? In the former, the action was said to be brought on the theory of fraud and sounded in tort, hence the release of one or more joint tortfeasors released all. But in the latter case, the action was to declare defendant a constructive trustee, and in contract, and here there was merely a release of a joint contract debtor, while the rights against the others were reserved.[19]

16. 56 Cal.App.3d at 359–60. "In summary, appellant's claim for damages, resulting from the poor 1971–1972 alfalfa crop allegedly caused by respondent's failure to provide water that was fit for irrigation purposes is based solely on a promise inferred from the provisions of the lease; therefore, the action is contractual in nature and the one-year claims-filing period applies."

See also the dissenting opinion of Judge Talbot in Baatz v. Smith, 361 Mich. 68, 76, 104 N.W.2d 787, 791 (1960): "The pleader insists he is relying on the contractual cause of action, and so, in truth, the declaration reads, but it is hopeless to rely upon verbiage alone, unless the wheel has come full circle and lawsuits will once more, as in medieval times, stand or fall upon the words employed in the writ.

"We should in determining the cause of action pleaded, examine the essential allegations of the complaint as a whole, stressing neither particular words nor particular allegations taken out of context . . . . If the substantive cause of action, the tort limitation would follow. If contract, the longer period."

17. 217 Cal. 96, 17 P.2d 740 (1932).

18. 13 Cal.2d 174, 88 P.2d 690 (1939).

19. See also Nicholson v. Han, 12 Mich.App. 35, 162 N.W.2d 313 (1968)

Even a court having both equitable and legal jurisdiction, as in most states, sometimes overlooks the former. Thus in a California case [20] a complaint alleged that R, plaintiff's intimate friend and family advisor negligently killed the son of the plaintiff, and afterwards conspired with the defendant insurance company fraudulently to represent to the Industrial Accident Commission that the son was R's employee, and that, as a result, the Commission took jurisdiction and awarded only burial expenses.

In an action against R and the insurance company, plaintiff sought damages. However, the court held that the award of the Commission was conclusive on the issue of employment, and a bar to any action at law for damages. Obviously there was a good cause of action in equity to set aside the Commissioner's award for the alleged extrinsic fraud, since R, the real adverse party defendant, who was primarily liable for the wrong, acted on behalf of plaintiff to prevent them from bringing the right kind of suit.[21]

Perhaps plaintiff desires an attachment. In California, as in numerous other states, unless the statutory procedure otherwise provides, the action must sound *ex contractu,* not *ex delicto.* In an older California case [22] plaintiff sued as trustee for corporate stockholders alleging that defendant fraudulently obtained stock of a corporation. An attachment was sought on the theory that the action was quasi-contractual for the recovery of money, the value of the stock obtained by fraud. The court held that the action, as pleaded, was for damages, and that no attachment would lie.

Sometimes, as in surgery, it is necessary to make a "working diagnosis." The surgeon may have to explore (laparotomy); so may

(While undergoing marriage counselling with defendant doctor plaintiff's wife and defendant doctor became intimate, leading to the total disintegration of the marriage. Although plaintiff attempted to establish claim was for breach of contract, court held action was in tort for alienation of affections and criminal conversation. Since statute had been enacted abolishing actions for such torts, plaintiff was denied recovery.); Meeker v. Shafranek, 112 Ohio App. 320, 176 N.E.2d 293 (1960) (Purchasers of land and buildings brought suit against vendors, claiming that garage purchased encroached upon adjoining landowner's property. Court held that action was one in contract, and suit was thus not barred by four year statute of limitations pertaining to action in tort.).

20. Gerini v. Pacific Employers Inc., 27 Cal.App.2d 52, 80 P.2d 499 (1938).

21. Perhaps the court was as remiss in theory as the plaintiff. Could not the pleadings have been held sufficient for equitable relief against the judgment, the award of the Commission, the statute of limitations, and then consideration of the cause for wrongful death—all in one action?

22. Hallidie v. Enginger, 175 Cal. 505, 166 P. 1 (1917).

§ 3.6   INTRODUCTION   Pt. 1

the lawyer for both facts and law before he irretrievably commits himself, (1) as to a theory that will promote recovery if he decides to take the case, to (2) justify his action in saying, "There is no case." With pleading requirements more tolerant, and with the distinct trend toward socialized compensation, but still fortunately without the conception of "generalized absolute liability," the modern trial lawyer representing a plaintiff must be aware of the "check points" that may entitle his client to recover.

However, sometimes adept trial men overlook pleading possibilities, obvious in sister states, and perhaps available although untried in their own jurisdiction. The rules of Last Clear Chance, the Rescue Doctrine, Attractive Nuisance, are only a number of legal doctrines which should be explored in every case. Perhaps wanton or wilful misconduct may be alleged, and contributory or comparative negligence avoided.[23] If the defendant is insured under a liability policy, it may be important to know whether judgments for wilful or intentional fault are excluded.

Since some states allow a plea of wantonness as sufficient to invoke exemplary damages, the allegation of this offense instead of wilfulness may bring the action within the insurance. In the jurisdictions that still hold to the rule that contributory negligence of a spouse will defeat a cause of action by the other, because of the identity of interest, a waiver or release of a husband's interest may avoid the claim of imputed negligence on part of wife. These are only a few of the many check points that must be reviewed in the trial lawyer's mind before he decides whether he has a case, or a defense.

§ 3.7   The Unexplainable Accident

Regardless of the utmost investigation and preparation, every now and then a case presents itself as completely unexplainable, and with no workable theory. (Even then sometimes trial and cross-examination will supplement the missing facts.) Such a case was recently tried by Attorney *Richard Hobbs* of Arkansas.[24]

Plaintiff's decedent was a 74-year-old retired professor in chemistry and physics who, with his wife, was vacationing in Hot Springs National Park, taking advantage of the bathing in the hot springs thermal baths. The water supplied by the hot springs flowed at a temperature of 147 degrees Fahrenheit. Before the water was piped

---

23. See Chapter 11, "Contributory Negligence," infra.

24. Richard W. Hobbs, Esquire, Hobbs, Longinotti & Bosson, 500 Ouachita Avenue, Hot Springs National Park, Arkansas.

to local bath houses, the temperature was lowered by running the water through cooling tanks.

The attendant who gave decedent his bath on the day of the accident was the same attendant who had attended him the day before. After the attendant placed the professor in a tub and filled it with hot water, he left the area to talk with a professional athlete from Kansas City. When the attendant returned to check on his charge, the professor was unconscious and probably dead at that time.

The professional athlete attempted to resuscitate the professor by pressing on the chest area and giving artificial respiration, but was unsuccessful in getting any sign of life. Where the athlete pressed on the chest of the decedent with the heel of his hand, the skin had peeled off. Figure 70.

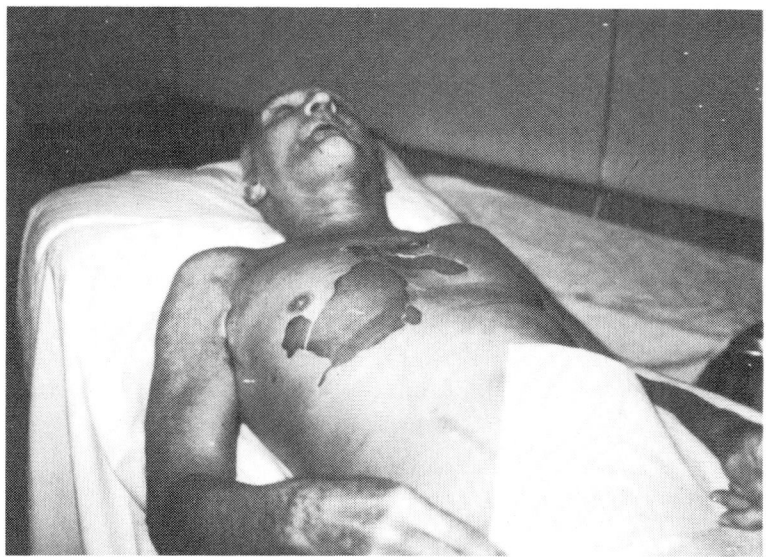

Figure 70. Even reliance on *res ipsa loquitur* could not provide an answer to this "unexplainable accident." Skin on chest peeled away during rescue efforts, due to hot mineral springs water.

An ambulance was called. Care had to be used handling the body because of the tendency of the skin to peel. The man was pronounced dead on arrival at the local hospital by the physician on duty. An autopsy was performed by a local pathologist who testified at the trial that the cause of death was the second and third degree burns suffered by the doctor. The pathologist testified that he had eliminated any other cause of death by examining the body and its organs.

The evidence presented on behalf of the plaintiff consisted of a deposition from the athlete from Kansas City who testified that he was taking a bath at the same time as the decedent and that "Speedy", the bath attendant, spent a great deal of the time discussing past athletic activities of the witness. The witness had not seen "Speedy" paying any attention to the decedent who was at the end of the row of tubs.

Another witness was a Vice President of a Texas bank who testified that he was taking a bath at the same time as the decedent. Although the witness had had one of the baths the day before, the water "Speedy" put into the tub this particular day was very hot. The witness commented to "Speedy" about the water temperature. The banker pointed out to the attendant that he, the banker, belonged to an athletic club in Houston, was used to taking Sauna baths, could stand great heat, but that the water in the tub was too hot for anyone and that he could not finish his bath.

"Speedy" maintained that the decedent himself kept turning the hot water valve on and that the attendant told the decedent not to increase the temperature in the tub. The decedent's wife testified that her husband did not like to take hot baths, but liked only lukewarm water, such as was normally put into the tubs in the bath houses in Hot Springs.

There was testimony from witnesses for the defense that no person could suffer burns from the water placed in the tubs in bathing houses in Hot Springs. According to the defendant, this was due to the fact that all hot waters and bathing facilities were under the supervision of the Hot Springs National Park officials and the water temperature was always cooled before going to the houses.

The plaintiff's argument to the jury was to the effect that the decedent was a normal healthy individual who had taken the baths the day previous with absolutely no ill effects, and that on the day in question he had entered the bath house for the same purpose as the day before. He had placed himself under the supervision of the bath attendant, and ended up with third degree burns which resulted in his death. The jury was out for approximately two hours and returned with a verdict for the defendant.

The foreman of the jury told the court reporter the next day that the jury decided the decedent did not die from the burns received. When reminded by the reporter than the undisputed testimony of the pathologist was to the effect that death was caused by the burns, the foreman stated that the jury did not agree with the medical findings!

A motion for new trial was duly filed but refused by the trial judge. An appeal was taken to the Arkansas Supreme Court on the ground that there was no substantial evidence to contradict the facts alleged in the complaint. The Supreme Court affirmed the lower Court.

Plaintiff relied heavily on the use of *res ipsa loquitur,* but even this legal crutch could not counter the belief of an "unexplained accident," and the plaintiff failed on the burden of proof. In the absence of facts, the cause of death was not explained.[25]

§ 3.8 Circumstantial Evidence Demonstrates the Theory

Another recent case, *Rafferty v. Weimer,*[26] reported by *Alan J. Bloom*[27] and *Henry Holzman,*[28] both practicing Maryland lawyers, illustrates a more positive result in a case crippled by lack of facts. Plaintiff Rafferty had left his home in Baltimore City on the evening of December 4, 1973, to visit his father, who had been hospitalized that morning for a heart attack. At approximately 9:00 PM a tractor-trailer, owned by defendant B. and P. Motor Express, Inc. and driven by defendant Weimer, collided with the Rafferty vehicle. At the time of the collision, plaintiff's vehicle was stopped without lights on the shoulder of the highway, extending about two feet into the right westbound lane.

The collision was a side-swipe, resulting in extensive damages to the entire left side of plaintiff's vehicle, Figure 71, and damages to the front end of the tractor-trailer, Figure 72, and the tires on its

---

25. The author recalls trying a case involving an "unexplainable accident" in San Francisco in 1949. In Murray v. Southern Pac. Co., 91 Cal.App.2d 107, 204 P.2d 636 (1949), the plaintiff was a San Francisco fireman who was injured while walking from his firehouse through the Southern Pacific railroad depot. He recalled walking up to the tracks upon which he was found, but nothing more. The only available witness was a flagman of the railroad, who died shortly after the accident, without making any statement or giving a deposition as to what he knew. The tracks and the engine under which the plaintiff was lying as well as the injured man himself was discovered were demonstrated to the jury by photographs. The remarkable fact was that no one, including the plaintiff, had any knowledge of how he got under the engine. More astonishing, the engine had to be jacked up and off him before he could be gotten out.

    The trial was a valiant but futile effort because of want of facts. The plaintiff escaped a nonsuit, but the jury, after five hours deliberation, returned a verdict for the defendant.

26. 36 Md.App. 98, 373 A.2d 64 (1977).

27. Alan J. Bloom, Esquire, 401 Washington Avenue, Suite 406, Towson, Maryland.

28. Henry Holzman, Esquire, 218 E. Lexington Street, Baltimore, Maryland.

right side, Figure 73. Plaintiff's vehicle was lodged against the guardrail on the shoulder of the road. The key was in the ignition in the on position, but the engine was not running. The only skid marks found were those directly beside the left front tire, indicating the vehicle had moved six inches from left to right. Grease marks were found on the hood of the car, and on plaintiff's right hand.

Figure 71. Demolished left side of plaintiff's car after mysterious accident in *Rafferty v. Weimer*.

Figure 72. Damage to right front corner of defendant's truck.

Figure 73. Plaintiff's car inexplicably wedged against guardrail.

Plaintiff was found unconscious approximately twenty feet from his car across the guardrail in the median strip adjacent to the shoulder of the road. His trousers had been torn off; there were severe injuries to his left hand and several brush burns on his body. The back of his head was injured, apparently when it struck a steel-grated drain located in the underbrush. In addition, a red substance, which appeared to be blood, was found on the guardrail.

A subsequent examination of plaintiff disclosed that he had sustained contusions of the right leg and both thighs, a compound fracture of the left forearm and hand, and a closed fracture of the right hand. He also had suffered a permanent, irreversible brain stem injury, which expert testimony indicated was caused by a vehicular accident. Plaintiff has been hospitalized or in a nursing facility since the accident. He is a cerebral cripple, unable to tell anything about the accident.

Prior to the collision, defendant driver was driving in the right lane and within the speed limit. There was no traffic in front or on the side of him and he had a clear and unobstructed view of the highway for at least one-quarter mile. The area in which the accident occurred was well-lighted and the roadway was dry. Defendant indicated that before the accident he never saw plaintiff or plaintiff's vehicle.[29]

29. 373 A.2d at 66.

On this set of facts, lawyers for plaintiff proceeded to trial. The jury found against defendants on the issues of both negligence and causation. Plaintiff Rafferty was awarded $300,000.00 for his injuries, and his wife was awarded $40,000.00 for loss of consortium. After rendition of the jury verdict, the court entered judgment N.O.V. in favor of defendants owner and driver of the tractor-trailer, on the grounds that plaintiff was guilty of contributory negligence as a matter of law. Plaintiffs appealed.

The Maryland Court of Special Appeals reversed the judgment N.O.V. and entered judgment on the jury verdict. The Appeals Court found that although the defendants-appellees had not conceded, they apparently had not contested the fact that defendant driver was negligent in side-swiping plaintiff's vehicle. The court noted that defendant driver had a clear and unobstructed view of the highway, and reasoned that if he had looked, as alleged, he would have seen plaintiff's vehicle.[30]

The Appeals Court also found that plaintiff had produced evidence sufficient to support a finding of proximate cause. The circumstantial evidence noted above was sufficient to support plaintiff was standing in front of his vehicle with his hands on the hood; that when the tractor-trailer collided with the vehicle, the resulting impact hurled plaintiff into and over the guardrail adjacent to the shoulder of the road.

Defendants-appellees argued that the same circumstantial evidence rendered plaintiff's theory untenable and totally contrary to scientific principles. They argued that the skid marks indicated that plaintiff's vehicle had moved only six inches sideways without any forward movement. On this basis, they claimed an indisputable inference that plaintiff could not possibly have been thrown forward a distance of twenty feet by reason of the collision.

The Appeals Court found that this inference was not indisputable, holding that skid marks, without more, are not conclusive as to movement.[31] The court stated that the absence of forward skid marks merely suggested that the tires had been pointed straight ahead without application of the brakes. The weight of the circumstantial evidence—the severity of the impact, grease on both the hood and plaintiff's hands, blood on the guardrail, and medical testimony that the injuries resulted from a vehicular accident—was held to con-

---

30. Bush v. Mohrlein, 191 Md. 418, 423, 62 A.2d 301, 303 (1948) ("We accept the rule that where a witness testified that he looked and listened, but did not see or hear a certain object, which if he had actually looked and listened, he must necessarily have seen and heard, his testimony is not worthy of consideration.").

31. York Motor Exp. Co. v. State for Use of Hawk, 195 Md. 525, 535, 74 A.2d 12, 16 (1950).

stitute legally sufficient circumstantial evidence to support an inference of causation.

The court cited Prosser:[32] "Plaintiff is not, however, required to . . . negative entirely the possibility that the defendants' conduct was not a cause, and it is enough that he introduces evidence from which reasonable men may conclude that it is more probable that the event was caused by the defendant than it was not. The fact of causation is incapable of mathematical proof, since no man can say with absolute certainty what would have occurred if the defendant had acted otherwise."

Defendants-appellees' alternative contention, by contrast, was held to constitute the sort of theory that fails to rise above the level of speculation and conjecture as to what actually occurred.[33] Defendants' theory, that plaintiff was struck by some other motor vehicle at some time while he was walking or standing in one of the traveled westbound lanes of the highway, was unsupported by any evidence adduced at trial.

The court cited *Fowler v. Smith*:[34] ". . . Maryland has gone almost as far as any jurisdiction that we know in holding that meager evidence of negligence is sufficient to carry the case to the jury. The rule has been stated as requiring submission if there be any evidence, however slight, *legally sufficient* as tending to prove negligence, and the weight and value of such evidence will be left to the jury."[35]

32. Prosser, The Law of Torts, § 44 (4th ed.).

33. 373 A.2d at 68.

34. 240 Md. 240, 213 A.2d 549 (1965) (emphasis in original).

35. See chapter 5, "Quantum of Proof," infra.

§§ 3.9–3.10 are reserved for supplementary material.

C. *STARE DECISIS* AND THE LAWYER'S DUTY

Library References:
C.J.S. Judgments §§ 592, 593, 686, 687.
West's Key No. Digests, Judgments ⚖︎634 et seq.

§ 3.11 Introduction

A client walks through the front door of an attorney's office one morning, sits down and proceeds to relate an astounding array of facts concerning how he comes to the lawyer in his injured state. Obviously, a wrong has been done to this man. The lawyer remembers the old maxim: where there's a wrong, the law provides a remedy. Although he is somewhat unfamiliar with the particular legal question being posed, counsel feels confident that the law must afford some reparation. He tells the client it sounds as though he has a good case, but to cover himself, counsel further states that in order to be sure, he'll have to do some research.

In dusting off the books on his shelves, counsel (or his junior partner or law clerk to whom the task has been delegated) happens upon a holding of an authoritative court of last-resort dealing with the precise set of facts the client just told him. So much so counsel thinks the client might have memorized this case word for word. As he reads the case, everything seems to be in his favor . . . Everything, that is, except the court's decision.

Believe it or not (and the lawyer can't) the court has ruled that recovery in such a situation must be denied. Counsel tries to come up with alternatives. Should he call the client, tell him of the discovery, that he has no hope for recovery and that counsel wants to be released from the case? Or does counsel inform the client of the decision, telling him that in good faith counsel believes the decision to be erroneous, especially in light of any changed circumstances, and that he honestly feels there is a good chance the court will reverse itself?

§ 3.12 The Doctrine of *Stare Decisis*

Such is a fairly common quandary encountered through use of the doctrine known as *stare decisis* (again the danger of a slogan, with its abrupt literal translation "to follow decisions"). The decision one makes, of course, will be based upon the date of the holding, the unanimity thereof, and the level of the court's authority (such as a 9–0 decision handed down a week earlier by the U.S. Supreme Court), and whether there are facts in your case which could sufficiently distinguish it from the precedent.

Stare decisis has evolved into a rule at once more abbreviated and awesome than ever intended. It may be well to examine its full impact. It is a deliberate decision of a judge or court made after argument on a question of law properly arising and necessary to the determination of a case, which thereby becomes a precedent in the same court, or to other courts of lesser standing in the same jurisdiction. But, like all statements of law applied to the changing panorama of human affairs, its correctness is relative to the *exigencies* of new cases to be decided by different judges with variant judicial views.[36]

One of the main policies underlying *stare decisis* is the need for a stable set of rules [37] so there may be some type of order to people's

---

36. Bracton's Note Book (decisions covering 1217–1240) gave impetus to the doctrine by directing the attention to preceding decisions in an attempt to "bring back the law to its ancient principles."

In the Yearbooks (1454) Chief Justice Prisot stated that the overruling of old decisions would be a "bad example to your apprentices in shaking their confidence in the books."

Blackstone states, ". . . it is an established rule to abide by former precedents, where the points come up again in litigation." Commentaries 3d Ed. p. 69.

37. Moragne v. States Marine Lines, 398 U.S. 375, 90 S.Ct. 1772, 26 L.Ed. 2d 339 (1970) on remand 446 F.2d 906:

"Very weighty considerations underlie the principle that courts should not lightly overrule past decisions. Among these are the desirability that the law furnish a clear guide for the conduct of individuals, to enable them to plan their affairs with assurance against untoward surprise; the importance of furthering fair and expeditious adjudication by eliminating the need to relitigate every relevant proposition in every case; and the necessity of maintaining public faith in the judiciary as a source of impersonal and reasoned judgments. The reasons for rejecting any established rule must always be weighed against these factors.

"The first factor, often considered the mainstay of stare decisis is singularly absent in this case. The confidence of people in their ability to predict the legal consequences of their actions is vitally necessary to facilitate the planning of primary activity and to encourage the settlement of disputes without resort to the courts. However, that confidence is threatened least by the announcement of a new remedial rule to effectuate well-established primary rules of behavior."

Cobb v. Georgia, 187 Ga. 448, 200 S.E. 796 (1939), conformed to 59 Ga.App. 695, 2 S.E.2d 116:

"Where a ruling made by an able bench, after full argument by able counsel, has been followed and applied in divers case, and has been left unmolested by the General Assembly, it should not, unless for impelling reasons, thereafter be changed by the court. The application of the doctrine of stare decisis is essential to the performance of a well-ordered system of jurisprudence. In most instances it is of more practical utility to have the law settled and to let it remain so, than to open it up to new construction, as the personnel of the court may change even though

§ 3.12 INTRODUCTION Pt. 1

lives, and the workings of society. Law makes our democracy work and holds it together. With this we do not take issue. But blindly to apply *stare decisis* would be to enshrine the laws of the Pharisees in a world bearing little resemblance to that of so long ago.[38] Common law is custom of the *particular time*. The duty of every court is to do justice,[39] not to perpetuate error or antiquity for old times sake alone.

grave doubt may arise as to the correctness of the interpretation originally given to it."

Ellison v. Georgia R. R. & Banking Co., 87 Ga. 691, 13 S.E. 809 (1891):

"With these exalted tribunals, who live only to judge the judges, the rule of stare decisis is not only a canon of the public good, but a law of self-preservation. At the peril of their lives they must discover error abroad, and be discreetly blind to its commission at home. Were they as ready to correct themselves as others, they could no longer speak as absolute oracles of legal truth; the reason for their existence would disappear, and their destruction would speedily supervene. Nevertheless, without serious detriment to the public or peril to themselves, they can and do admit now and then, with cautious reserve, that they have made a mistake. Their rigid dogma of infallibility allows of this much relaxation in favor of truth unwittingly forsaken. Indeed, reversion to truth, in some rare instances, is highly necessary to their permanent well-being."

38. O. W. Holmes, Collected Legal Papers 187 (1921):

"It is revolting to have no better reason for a rule of law than it is as laid down in the time of Henry IV. It is still more revolting if the grounds upon which it was laid down have vanished long since, and the rule simply persists from blind imitation of the past."

Brooks v. Robinson, 259 Ind. 16, 284 N. E.2d 794 (1972):

"Judicial devotion to the doctrine of *stare decisis* is indeed a justifiable concept to be followed by our courts. However, it cannot and must not be so strictly pursued to the point where our view is opaqued and reality disregarded. To do so is to envision the common law to be as immutable as the laws of the Medes and Persians, and thus render our system of jurisprudence forever impotent. The strength and genius of the common law lies in its ability to adapt to the changing needs of the society it governs."

Woods v. Lancet, 303 N.Y. 349, 102 N. E.2d 691 (1951):

"[I]f that were a valid objection, the common law would now be what it was in the Plantagenet period".

39. Swift & Co. v. Wickham, 382 U.S. 111, 86 S.Ct. 258, 15 L.Ed.2d 194 (1965):

"We believe that considerations for stare decisis should not deter us from this course. Unless inexorably commanded by statute, a procedural principle of this importance should not be kept on the books in the name of stare decisis once it is proved to be unworkable in practice; the mischievous consequences to litigants and courts alike from the perpetuation of an unworkable rule are too great."

County of Los Angeles v. Faus, 48 Cal. 2d 672, 312 P.2d 680 (1957):

"The rule of stare decisis is not so imperative or inflexible as to preclude a departure therefrom in any case, but its application must be determined in each instance by the discretion of the court. Previous decisions should not be followed to the extent that error may

The changes inherent in a progressive civilization demand that when there exists no longer the reasons for the rule, *a fortiori*, the rule should likewise cease.[40]

be perpetuated and that wrong may result."

Humthlett v. Reeves, 211 Ga. 210, 85 S.E.2d 25 (1954):
"The doctrine of stare decisis should not be followed to the extent that error may be perpetuated."

The court continued later:
"Minor errors, even if quite obvious, or important errors, if their existence be fairly doubtful, may be adhered to, and repeated indefinitely; but the only treatment for a great and glaring error affecting the current administration of justice in all courts of original jurisdiction is to correct it. When an error of this magnitude, and which moves in so wide an orbit, competes with truth in the struggle for existence, the maxim for a supreme court—supreme in the majesty of duty as well as in the majesty of power,—is not stare decisis, but fiat justitia ruate coelum [let justice be done, though the heavens should fall]."

Hall v. Hopper, 234 Ga. 625, 216 S.E.2d 839 (1975):
"Stability and certainty in law are desirable: stare decisis is a valid and compelling basis of argument . . . When a majority of this court determines that stability must give way to justice to the prisoner, then justice prevails."

40. Moragne v. States Marine Lines, 398 U.S. 375, 90 S.Ct. 1772, 26 L.Ed. 2d 339 (1970), on remand 446 F.2d 906 (5th Cir.):
"Finally, a judicious reconsideration of precedent cannot be as threatening to public faith in the judiciary as continued adherence to a rule unjustified in reason, which produces different results for breaches of duty in situations that cannot be differentiated in policy. Respect for the process of adjudication should be enhanced, not diminished by our ruling today."

Funk v. United States, 290 U.S. 371, 54 S.Ct. 212, 78 L.Ed. 369 (1933):
"Its rules [the rules of the common law] are modified upon its own principles and not in violation of them. Those rules being founded in reason, one of its oldest maxims is, that where the reason of the rule ceases the rule also ceases."

People v. Pierce, 61 Cal.2d 879, 40 Cal. Rptr. 845, 395 P.2d 893 (1964):
"Defendants finally contend that the long-established rule formulated by this court that would afford them immunity, should not now be overruled except by the Legislature. In effect the contention is a request that courts abdicate their responsibility for the upkeep of the common law. That upkeep it needs continuously, as this case demonstrates. In view of the fact that the fiction underlying the rule in question has long been dead, we overrule People v. Miller [which had held that a husband and wife would not be charged with conspiracy]."

Bickford v. Nolen, 142 Ga.App. 256, 235 S.E.2d 743 (1977), aff'd 240 Ga. 255, 240 S.E.2d 24:
"There are no longer any valid reasons for adhering to our judicially created guest rule. Continued adherence to the guest rule's common law distinctions can only lead to injustice or, if injustice is to be avoided, further fictions resulting in complexity and confusion. Accordingly, we would de-

The continued stability of the law juxtaposed with the requirement that justice in all cases be done is exemplified in a 1960 decision [41] of the Michigan Supreme Court in which it extended to the wife a cause of action for loss of consortium when her husband was negligently injured by another:

> These precedents are venerable. Their chains may be moss-encrusted and rusty but only a few courts have held that they no longer control or confine. Thus again we reach the conflict that divides us, for the law, as Dean Pound put it, must be stable, and yet it cannot stand still. Were we to rule upon precedent alone, were stability the only reason for our being, we would have no trouble with this case. We would simply tell the woman to be-gone, and to take her shattered husband with her, that we need no longer be affronted by a sight so repulsive. In so doing we would have vast support from the dusty books. But dust of the decision would remain in our mouths through the years ahead, a reproach to law and conscience alike. Our oath is to do justice, not to perpetuate error.

The common law was never meant to be a stagnant, rigid doctrine standing in the way of change and justice.[42] As society evolves,

---

cline to follow and perpetuate the guest rule's classifications."

Haney v. City of Lexington, 386 S.W. 2d 738 (Ky.1964):

> "The acceptance or use of a theory does not prove the truth or validity of the rule of law it supports. If its worth has been proven by extended experience, we can be content with that theory. But when a theory supporting a rule of law is not grounded upon sound logic, is not just, and has been discredited by actual experience, it should be discarded, and with it, the rule it supports."

41. Montgomery v. Stephan, 359 Mich. 33, 101 N.W.2d 227 (1960).

42. Larsen v. General Motors Corp., 391 F.2d 495 (8th Cir. 1968):

> "The common law is not sterile or rigid and serves the best interests of society by adapting standards of conduct and responsibility that fairly meet the emerging and developing needs of our time."

O'Dell v. School Dist. of Independence, 521 S.W.2d 403 (Mo.1975), cert. denied 423 U.S. 865, 96 S.Ct. 125, 46 L. Ed.2d 94:

> "[T]he common law is not a static but a dynamic and growing thing. Its rules arise from the application of reason to the changing conditions of society. It inheres in the life of society, not in the decisions interpreting that life . . . ."

Digby v. Digby, —— R.I. ——, 388 A.2d 1 (1978):

> "In the light of these precedents, we are free to abandon our self-imposed stay of judicial action and to examine the rationales that gave meaning and coherence to the judicially created rule for the purpose of determining whether those rationales retain their vitality. If that examination discloses that the rule has become inconsonant with the needs of our contemporary society and that its further application will work injustice, a court

so, naturally, should the law.⁴³ Indeed, one of the most significant and beneficial aspects of the common law is its "flexibility and capac-

43. Green v. Superior Court of City and County of San Francisco, 10 Cal. 3d 616, 111 Cal.Rptr. 704, 517 P.2d 1168 (1974):

"To remain viable, the common law must reflect the realities of present day society; an implied warranty of habitability in residential leases must therefore be recognized.

"The recent decisions recognize initially that the geographic and economic conditions that characterized the agrarian lessor-lessee transaction have been entirely transformed in the modern urban landlord-tenant relationship. We have suggested that in the Middle Ages, and, indeed, until the urbanization of the industrial revolution, the land itself was by far the most important element of a lease transaction; this predominance explained the law's treatment of such leases as conveyances of interests in land. In today's urban residential leases, however, land as such plays no comparable role. The typical city dweller, who frequently leases an apartment several stories above the actual plot of land on which an apartment building rests, cannot realistically be viewed as acquiring an interest in land; rather, he has contracted for a place to live. As the Court of Appeal for the District of Columbia observed in Javins v. First Nat'l Realty Corp., 138 D.C.App. 369, 428 F.2d 1071, 1074 (1970), cert. denied 400 U.S. 925, 91 S.Ct. 186, 27 L.Ed.2d 185: When American city dwellers, both rich and poor, seek 'shelter' today, they seek a well known, package of goods and services—a package which includes not merely walls and ceilings, but also adequate heat, light and ventilation, serviceable plumbing facilities, secure windows and doors, proper sanitation, and proper maintenance." (Fn. omitted.)

not only has the authority but also the duty to reexamine its precedents rather than to apply by rote an antiquated formula."

Crowder v. Department of State Parks, 228 Ga. 436, 185 S.E.2d 908 (1971), appeal dism'd cert. denied 406 U.S. 914, 92 S.Ct. 1768, 32 L.Ed.2d 113, Felton, J., dissenting:

"[C]ourt-made common law rules not altered by statute or constitution, may be adjusted to different government and different social needs, different from those existing at common law."

Renslow v. Mennonite Hosp., 67 Ill.2d 348, 10 Ill.Dec. 484, 367 N.E.2d 1250 (1977):

"Professor Corbin, whose thinking was reflected by Cardozo, expressed his concept of the judicial function thus: 'It is the function of our courts to keep the doctrines up to date with the mores by continual restatement and by giving them a continually new content. This is judicial legislation, and the judge legislates at his peril. Nevertheless, it is the necessity and duty of such legislation that gives to judicial office its highest honor; and no brave and honest judge shirks the duty or fears the peril.'"

Hungerford v. Portland Sanitarium & Benev. Ass'n, 235 Or. 412, 384 P.2d 1009 (1963):

"We must likewise reject the defendant's contention that stare decisis binds us absolutely to the past. The pull of stare decisis is strong, but it is not inexorable. . . . When litigants come into court, they expect the court to apply to their case the best rule of law available to the court. The

§ 3.12 INTRODUCTION Pt. 1

ity for growth and adaptation." [44] As Lord Atkin stated [45] in discussing long-ago precedents and modernity: "When these ghosts of the past stand in the path of justice clanking their medieval chains the proper course for the judge is to pass through them undeterred."

§ 3.13 Combatting *Stare Decisis*

Historical, social, economic and certainly legal debate may fill volumes upon volumes of learned treatises as to the policy and propriety of changing decisions once made. We shall partake no further, save to state our premise and to give our suggestion. Our premise: if an appellate decision denying recovery is not consonant with obviously changed economic, social, or political changes, it is our suggestion that it is the lawyer's *duty* to vigorously urge a change in that appellate rule. Our further suggestion: most likely this type of

---

44. Funk v. United States, 290 U.S. 371, 54 S.Ct. 212, 78 L.Ed. 369 (1953):
"To concede this capacity for growth and change in the common law by drawing its inspiration from every fountain of justice and at the same time to say that the courts of this country are forever bound to perpetuate such of its rules as, by every reasonable test, are found to be neither wise nor just, because we have once adopted them as suited to our situation and institutions at a particular time, is to deny to the common law in the place of its adoption a flexibility and capacity for growth and adaptation which was the peculiar boast and excellence of the system in the place of its origin."

Hurtado v. California, 110 U.S. 516, 48 S.Ct. 111, 28 L.Ed. 232 (1884):
"But if stare decisis must always be paramount the law would be deprived of its capacity for growth and adaptation which has been considered to be the peculiar boast and excellence of the common law."

fact that a rule has been followed for fifty years is not a convincing reason why it must be followed for another fifty years if the reasons for the rule have ceased to exist."

Smith v. Arbaugh's Restaurant, Inc., 469 F.2d 97 (D.C.Cir. 1972):
"It is the genius of the common law that it recognizes changes in our social, economic, and moral life. Legal classifications such as trespasser and licensee are judicial creations which should be cast aside when they are no longer useful as controlling tools for the jury. The principle of stare decisis was not meant to keep a stranglehold on developments which are responsive to new values, experience, and circumstances."

Rodriguez v. Bethlehem Steel Corp., 12 Cal.3d 382, 115 Cal.Rptr. 765, 525 P.2d 669 (1974):
"The inherent capacity of the common law for growth and change is its most significant feature. Its development has been determined by the social needs of the community which it serves. It is constantly expanding and developing in keeping with advancing civilization and the new conditions and progress of society, and adapting itself to the gradual change of trade, commerce, arts, inventions, and the needs of the country."

45. United Australia, Ltd. v. Barclay's Bank, Ltd. [1941] A.C. 1, 29.

case may require two trials; one with the law as it now stands, followed by an appeal, and then the second trial under the new law. This conceivably could be obviated where counsel could persuade a trial judge to exercise the courage and wisdom to rule against *stare decisis* the first time.

Counsel's procedure and strategy should be determined thusly: he may choose to go up on the pleadings, without more; take a nonsuit on opening statement; at the close of his case; or appeal from the various orders made after final judgment. He must consider how much of his case should come before the appellate court for decision, for the law of the case and, practically, so that he may convince the opposing party to settle without a further trial once the higher court has made its determination to no longer follow *stare decisis* on this point of law.

Counsel is often faced with a mixed question of "ideas and practice," "costs and justice." Certainly there is ample authority, even urging, by appellate justices that their own decision be continually critically examined.[46] A California court once declared one of its

---

46. Helvering v. Hallock, 309 U.S. 106, 60 S.Ct. 444, 84 L.Ed. 604 (1940), conformed to 111 F.2d 143:
 "We recognize that stare decisis embodies an important social policy. It represents an element of continuity in law, and is rooted in the psychologic need to satisfy reasonable expectations. But stare decisis is a principle of policy and not a mechanical formula of adherence to the latest decision, however recent and questionable, when such adherence involves collision with a prior doctrine more embracing in its scope, intrinsically sounder, and verified by experience."

 Hurtado v. California, 110 U.S. 516, 48 S.Ct. 111, 28 L.Ed. 232 (1884):
 "But if stare decisis must always be paramount the law would be deprived of its capacity for growth and adaptation which has been considered to be the peculiar boast and excellence of the common law."

 McKenna v. Austin, 134 F.2d 659 (1943):
 "The majority are not unmindful of the force of stare decisis. But it is not a doctrine of mortmain. It does not exclude room for growth in the law, nor does it require adherence to a highly technical rule which, at its inception, was substantive liability to which it was applied; which has been maintained by lip service, while being chipped away in its substantive effect through multiplying though equally artificial distinctions; and which has found hold in our own law by only a single and a highly ambiguous decision."

 Norton v. Randolph, 176 Ala. 381, 58 So. 283 (1912):
 "The authority of precedents, however, must often yield to the force of reason, and to the paramount demands of justice as well as the decencies of civilized society, and the law ought to speak with a voice responsive to these demands."

 Ficke v. Prudential Ins. Co. of America, 305 Ky. 171, 202 S.W.2d 429 (1947):
 "We have due regard for the stare decisis doctrine, but feel that when our former decisions are predicated on misconceptions of well settled principles of law, and out of line with the majority of

precedents so bad that a lawyer would confess his own incompetence by relying on it.⁴⁷ Consider the decisions of the highest court in the land in recent years, when it is a rarity for the learned gentlemen unanimously to agree even among themselves what the law is, or should be.⁴⁸ The opinions of the State courts, and the Federal Courts of Appeals, more often than not reveal a wide divergence of ideas, and each dissent may be the harbinger of a variant of some sacred

other courts, there is no reason for blindly following them when no rule of property has been established which would be overturned with resulting hardship on persons who have relied upon such erroneous decisions."

Immer v. Risko, 56 N.J. 482, 267 A.2d 481 (1970):
"The nature of the common law requires that each time a rule of law is applied it be carefully scrutinized to make sure that the conditions and needs of the times have not so changed as to make further application of it the instrument of injustice."

Baker v. Lorriland, 4 N.Y. 257 (1850):
"It is 'the duty of every judge and every court to examine its own decisions—without fear, and to revise them without reluctance.'"

McDowell v. Oyer, 21 Pa. 417 (1953):
"Of course I am not saying that we must consecrate the mere blunders of those who went before us, and stumble every time we come to the place they have stumbled."

Whitaker v. Lane, 128 Va. 317, 104 S.E. 252 (1920):
"If the rule established by precedent is highly technical, and finds its origin in reasons which no longer exist, and the courts have from time to time found it necessary to make exceptions thereto to meet the needs and methods of doing business in modern times, it would seem that the courts should adapt their procedure to the age in which we live, and cease to follow a precedent for which they have always to apologize, and declare that it is highly technical and not justified either by reason or policy."

See also Douglas, *Stare Decisis,* 49 Columbia L.Rev. 735 (1949).

47. Alferitz v. Borgwardt, 126 Cal. 201, 58 P. 460 (1899).

48. See e. g., Morland v. Sprecher, 443 U.S. 709, 99 S.Ct. 3086, 61 L.Ed.2d 860 (1979) (Brennan and White, JJ., dissenting); Washington v. Washington State Fishing Vessel Ass'n, 443 U.S. 658, 99 S.Ct. 3055, 61 L.Ed.2d 823 (1979) (Powell, Stewart, and Rehnquist, JJ., dissenting), on remand 605 F.2d 492 (9th Cir.), on remand 92 Wash.2d 939, 603 P.2d 819; Bellotti v. Baird, 443 U.S. 622, 99 S. Ct. 3035, 61 L.Ed.2d 797 (1979) (Rehnquist, Stevens, Brennan, Marshall and Blackmun, JJ., concurring; White, J., dissenting), reh. denied 444 U.S. 887, 100 S.Ct. 185, 62 L.Ed.2d 121; Jones v. Wolf, 443 U.S. 595, 99 S.Ct. 3020, 61 L.Ed.2d 775 (1979) (Powell, Stewart, White, JJ., and Burger, Ch. J., dissenting); Rose v. Mitchell, 443 U.S. 545, 99 S.Ct. 2993, 61 L.Ed.2d 739 (1979) (Rehnquist, Stewart, and Powell, JJ., concurring; White and Stevens, JJ. dissenting); Columbus Bd. of Educ. v. Penick, 443 U.S. 449, 99 S.Ct. 2941, 61 L.Ed.2d 666 (1979), reh. denied 444 U.S. 887, 100 S.Ct. 186, 62 L.Ed.2d 121, (Stewart, J., and Burger, Ch. J., concurring; Powell and Rehnquist, JJ., dissenting); Gannett Co., Inc. v. DePasquale, 443 U.S. 368, 99 S.Ct. 2898, 61 L.Ed. 2d 608 (1979) (Burger, Ch. J., Powell and Rehnquist, JJ., concurring; Blackmun, Brennan, White, and Marshall, JJ., dissenting).

stare decisis. And what of those cases where the appeals court splits 5–4 on what a reasonably prudent man would have done!

The trial lawyer confronted with a case of "bad law" need not necessarily despair. A dark view of this prospect is that of Justice Owen J. Roberts, who in a dissent [49] stated:

> The evil results from overruling earlier considered decisions must be evident. In the present case, the court below naturally felt bound to follow and apply the law as clearly announced by this court. If litigants and lower federal courts are not to do so, the law becomes not a chart to govern conduct but a game of chance; instead of settling rights and liabilities it unsettles them. Counsel and parties will bring and prosecute actions in the teeth of the decisions that such actions are not maintainable on the not improbable chance that the asserted rule will be thrown overboard. Defendants will not know whether to litigate or to settle for they will have no assurance that a declared rule will be followed. But the more deplorable consequence will inevitably be that the administration of justice will fall into disrepute. Respect for tribunals must fall when the bar and the public come to understand that nothing that has been said in prior adjudication has force in a current controversy.

But it all boils down to plaintiffs' lawyer thinking enough about his law—and his client to go up—and sometimes, unfortunately, not having the funds to do it.

§ 3.14 English Common Law

It is not to be implied from the above decision that neither *stare decisis* nor the common law of England has a place in modern American jurisprudence. Many states, in enacting their statutory law, codified English common law into their jurisdiction. An example of this is the Virginia reception statute:

> "The common law of England, insofar as it is not repugnant to the principles of the Bill of Rights and Constitution of this State, shall continue in full force within the same, and be the rule of decision, except as altered by the General Assembly." [50]

---

49. Mahnich v. Southern Steamship Co., 321 U.S. 96, 104, 64 S.Ct. 455, 459, 88 L.Ed. 561, 568 (1944).

50. Va.Code Ann. § 1–10 (1950).

§ 3.14 INTRODUCTION

Using this statute, Attorney *James Eichner*[51] successfully utilized an 1843[52] and a 1927[53] English case as precedents in a 1971 Virginia case. Attorney Eichner's case[54] involved an incident wherein a woman sitting in an aluminum frame chair beside a motel swimming pool suffered severe injuries when the chair collapsed. Eichner argued that the defendant motel was liable for breach of an implied warranty. The court of appeals concurred, quoted the above-statute, and then continued:

> "Apt then is *Silverman v. Imperial London Hotels*.[55] A guest, after taking a Turkish bath at the defendant's hotel, spent the night there. Bitten by bugs in the bed, he sued the hotel keeper. Passing beyond the question of negligent innkeeping, the Court concluded primarily: '. . . that by the contract made between the plaintiff and the defendants the latter impliedly warranted that their premises were reasonably fit for use as Turkish baths in the way that such baths are ordinarily used, and, amongst other things, that the beds or couches . . . were reasonably fit for reclining or sleeping on after the bath had been taken.'"

The importance of the Virginia case cannot be overstated in that many jurisdictions have adopted reception statutes similar to Virginia's. In these jurisdictions, if counsel cannot find a local case or point to a particular fact situation, counsel should look to English case law and ascertain if a case in point can be found. As attorney Eichner states: "It is probably useless to try to get a court to ignore one of its own prior decisions in favor of an English case, but absent such a prior decision, a well-reasoned English case can be urged as strongly persuasive and possibly technically binding."

§ 3.15 Statutes

Sometimes an enterprising lawyer faces not merely an opposing case on point, but an actual statute which on its face disposes of his suit. Although such a statute may make the ultimate conclusion almost inevitable, some cases involve secondary interests which make them worthy of trial despite a high likelihood of failure. Kansas Attorney *Scott Harrison Kreamer*[56] recently confronted this dilemma

---

51. James Eichner, Allen, Allen, Allen & Allen, 1809 Staples Null Road, Post Office Box 6855, Richmond, Virginia.

52. Smith v. Marrable, 11 M. & W. 5 (Exch.1843).

53. Silverman v. Imperial London Hotels, 137 L.T. 59 (King's Bench 1927).

54. Schnitzer v. Nixon, 439 F.2d 940 (4th Cir. 1971).

55. 137 L.T. 59 (King's Bench 1927).

56. Scott Harrison Kreamer, Esquire, Breyfogle, Gardner, Davis & Kreamer, Court Square Building, 110 South Cherry, Olathe, Kansas.

when he brought a suit based on the unauthorized autopsy of a sixteen year old girl.

Although a statute made a victory unlikely and a summary judgment quite possible, Attorney Kreamer believed that the facts of the case warranted some action, and he achieved his objective of reform: the local coroner's office drastically changed their procedures, and the various national groups of coroners and pathologists who followed the case will undoubtedly alter their sometimes callous attitude toward decedents' families.

Plaintiff woke up in the middle of the night with a severe headache and stomach pains. She screamed; when her parents rushed to her aid, she said that something had "burst" in her head. She became comatose, and an ambulance was called to transport her to the hospital.

Doctors at the hospital diagnosed her problem as a subarachnoid hemorrhage and saw little chance of saving her life. She died without regaining consciousness. All doctors agreed on the cause of death. Plaintiff's family doctor assured the family that there was no need for an autopsy and directed the nurse to note on the death report that no autopsy was to be performed.

A deputy county coroner, however, became interested in the decedent when he learned that a drug screen indicated morphine was in her system. Without notifying the family, he seized the body and performed a full-scale autopsy at a local funeral home.

The funeral director notified the father, who became deeply upset and refused to tell his wife for fear of upsetting her. Just before the funeral, the mother reached down into the casket to embrace her daughter. The father, not knowing the after-effects of an autopsy, then told his wife that she should not lift her daughter because an autopsy had been performed. His wife became violently sick, dropped her daughter and refused to touch her again. The autopsy has since become a recurring nightmare for the entire family.

Although a Kansas statute essentially left the decision to perform an autopsy entirely in the discretion of the coroner, Attorney Kreamer felt that he had to file some type of protest. Defendant claimed that he wanted to check for a possible drug overdose, but admitted that no morphine would have been present by the time he performed the autopsy. Incredibly, he further admitted that he already knew the cause of death when he began the autopsy. Finally, he had made this totally unnecessary and unwarranted invasion of decedent's body without making any attempt to secure the family's permission or even to notify them.

While he feared the suit might not survive summary judgment, Attorney Kreamer brought the case in the hopes that it would make an example to the local coroners which might in some way advance the social welfare.

The case did survive summary judgment, but at trial the jury regrettably concluded that, under Kansas law, they had no alternative but to accept the coroner's discretionary decision.

Despite the adverse outcome, Attorney Kreamer decided that an appeal was unnecessary—shortly after the trial, a front-page article in the Kansas City Star reported that local coroners were so concerned about performing indiscriminate autopsies that in the future they would not proceed without the district attorney's approval. This gratifying effect was not merely local, because groups of pathologists and coroners from around the country had been closely following the case and its aftermath. These groups are now much more likely to explain their position to the decedents' families before violating bodies on a whim.

Attorney Kreamer was therefore able to accomplish all that he had hoped even though the case he brought seemed to be doomed from the outset. This is a perfect example of a case in which the lawyer must be able to take a sufficiently broad perspective to realize that the outcome in the courtroom is sometimes a poor indication of success or failure in a case.

§§ 3.16–3.20 are reserved for supplementary material.

D. THE CRIPPLED CASE

§ 3.21 Introduction

We have suggested throughout this book that candor and frankness are the points of entry to settle one's cause; likewise, honesty and sincerity are the basis upon which to try it before a jury. Whether the reader believes in the author's theory of this method of trial, he must agree as to its efficacy in the "crippled case."

The case may, at first scrutiny, be "crippled" because of too many obvious defects. In any accident case, there may be intoxication on the part of the claimant, the presence of an obvious and known danger, a pre-existing condition or injury, or many other factors that may make the winning of the case difficult. However, many of these cases have been lost for the plaintiff—indeed in many of them, the client has been dissuaded from going to trial at all—when there might have been success. Frequently, on trial, these cases have been lost because counsel has tried to hide facts from the jury, which sometimes might even become the strongest offense.

The "crippled case" remains so only until counsel equips it with legitimate and available strong, legal crutches. The weakness then may become a strength. For example, more care must be accorded an intoxicated person in some instances than one who is sober. Greater damages should be awarded for an injury to an already disabled limb than one that is normal. In an obvious danger case, defendant's negligence may be patently proved. As may be seen hereafter, the "crippled cases" may be actually stronger than the "healthy" ones, but it must be remembered that only by a procedure of candor is this brought about. Thus, plaintiff should disclose his seeming weakness in the opening statements, and fully acquaint the jury with the evidence to be produced and the applicable law. If the defendant were to present this evidence leaving the plaintiff to deny, the jury might feel that the case for the plaintiff was indeed crippled, if not totally disabled.

The author recognizes the practical problem of distinguishing between the *"crippled case"* and the *"completely disabled case."* Obviously, there are cases which present themselves to the lawyer's office which should never be taken to court. Unfortunately, some of them are won, just as some deserving causes are lost. This still makes the law something of a game, so that when one lawyer hears that an associate has won one that was desperate or "completely disabled," he is tempted to try his "luck" again. Nonetheless, often a case which at first blush seems "completely disabled," upon closer inspection does not appear unduly handicapped. Recently, our office took on a supposedly completely disabled case, and through thorough investigation and accident reconstruction, we were able to prove that defendant could have easily avoided the collision, yet took no steps in that direction, and thus his actions were a proximate cause of the injuries to our plaintiff who was admittedly negligent.

The case, *Papazekos v. Jones,* filed in Superior Court, Alameda County, California, involved a young girl who, at the age of six months, had been tragically and severely injured in an automobile accident. Figure 74. There was no question that the injuries she had sustained were substantial. The last medical report was done shortly before trial was scheduled to commence. At the time of this report, the child was five years old.

The child had suffered major injuries, including subdural and intracerebral hemorrhaging. She was comatose for two weeks following the accident, and was hospitalized for a month. The medical report related that the girl was markedly retarded, suffered from cortical blindness, and had a permanent mental age of two months or less, despite her chronological age. Due to the massive brain injuries suffered, the child was having five or more seizures a day, and had no control over her bowels or bladder.

The effect of the injuries upon the girl are best contained in the following excerpt of the doctor's report:

> I cannot place this child in any particular category as far as mental development and physical development. At best I can tell she has a motor and social development of a child two months of age or less. She does not fit into any of the developmental screening tests that are available.
>
> In my opinion this child has an extremely poor prognosis for return of function. With reasonable medical care, however, she would do quite well from a physical standpoint and would probably succumb only to intercurrent infections.
>
> Her "lot in life" is relegated to that of a severely mentally retarded child who is at the mercy of her environment for life support. At the present time this is being provided by the parents. If the parents are not available and no family was available she certainly would have to be institutionalized for the rest of her life.

Such was the extreme condition of our client. But who, then, was to be held responsible for her injuries, and the costs involved?

At the time of the accident, the then six-month-old infant was being held in her mother's lap while the two were riding as passengers in a car being driven by another woman. The car, a small Volkswagen, began drifting across the solid double yellow line which divided the road in half, and subsequently collided head-on with defendant's car. The position of the two cars immediately after the accident can be seen in Figures 74 and 75. In Figure 74, only the damage to the Volkswagen is apparent, but not the fact it had indeed crossed over the double line. This fact is clear in Figure 75. The rear right side tire of the Volkswagen is resting directly on top of the double line. The remainder of the car is entirely in the fast lane of on-coming traffic.

Figure 74. Photo showing damage to plaintiff's Volkswagen in Papazekos.

Figure 75. From this angle, the position of both cars is evident. The case seemed to be crippled because, as the picture shows, both cars were in defendant's lane.

To complicate matters further, the investigating peace officer was of the opinion that the driver of the Volkswagen had violated section 21460a of the California Vehicle Code, which prohibits driving to the left of a double yellow line. From the second photograph and the opinion of the police officer, a jury would find it unlikely that the driver of the second car, a Chevrolet, had in any way caused the injuries. Our task then, was to do the impossible: we had to show that somehow, the driver of the Chevrolet had been remiss in his obligation to drive prudently, which led to the collision, despite the fact that at all times he had been driving in an otherwise proper lane of traffic.

Investigation of the case began with an inspection of the accident report and pictures taken by the police, and pictures taken by the local news media. The police accident report noted that the weather had been clear, the surface of the road dry, and the lighting good (the accident occurred on a clear day). The police officer had included in the report a statement made to him by the driver of the Chevrolet which read: "He first observed the other involved vehicle when it was approximately *300 feet* away, WB [westbound] in the inside lane of [the street], approaching from the opposite direction. When he first observed the other vehicle, he noticed that it seemed to [be] drifting into his lane. He felt the other vehicle would take corrective action but when the other vehicle continued to drift into his lane, he sounded his horn. The other vehicle did not respond, he sounded his horn again and applied his brakes at which time the other vehicle struck the left front of his vehicle."

We took this statement from the report, then looked once again at the photograph reproduced in Figure 75. From this, we noticed that while it was true that the car in which our plaintiff was riding was almost completely in the other lane, it was likewise obvious that the driver of the Chevrolet had made no attempt to change lanes.

A visit was then made to the scene of the accident. (The attorney who will actually try the case should always make at least one visit to the scene, preferably as soon as possible after he is contacted.) The road was found to be a wide, four-lane street, divided by the solid yellow double line. Two lanes on either side of the double line were clearly demarcated by a single, broken yellow line. Information obtained from the police report and from further inquiry showed that there had been no other traffic on the time and date of the accident, nor had there been any vehicles parked adjacent to the curb within the immediate vicinity of the accident.

It was next determined that we should engage the services of some accident reconstructionists to see whether the driver of the Chevrolet could have easily avoided the accident under the conditions of our case. The experts, for both plaintiff and defendant, agreed that the Volkswagen was traveling at 20 to 22 miles per hour, and that defendant had been proceeding at 25 to 27 mph in his Chevrolet. Given these speeds and the fact defendant first spotted the Volkswagen drifting into his lane from a distance of 300 feet, the experts determined that defendant would have had four to five seconds in which to take some evasive action.

According to his statements to the police officer, defendant's entire evasive action consisted of hitting his horn (from a distance where it would be barely audible at best), waiting to see what the driver of the Volkswagen would do, again sounding his horn, and finally applying his brakes immediately before impact. Our human factors expert was prepared to testify that even if defendant had done all these things, he still would have had ample time in which to take further, appropriate evasive action. That action, we contended, was simply to turn the steering wheel to the right, thereby changing lanes.

§ 3.21 INTRODUCTION Pt. 1

To test the theory of the experts, we set out to re-create the events of the collision. To fulfill the requirements of the law of demonstrative evidence, we had to make the demonstration under similar circumstances which existed at the time of the accident. Thus, we had to schedule the event for the same hour of the day, and under similar road and weather conditions. To do our demonstration, it was necessary for us to obtain permission from the city and the local police department. Permission to block off the street as necessary was granted, upon the conditions that we obtained an insurance policy in the amount of $1,000,000, agreed to indemnify and hold the city harmless against any property damage or personal injury claim, and that we hired city policemen on a contractual basis to coordinate traffic activity. It cost us $6,500 to stage this demonstration, and while expensive, the results justified its need.

The entire scene was marked off by rubber pylons. We had been able to locate cars identical to those in the accident, which made the demonstration all the more realistic. A camera was mounted on the Chevrolet, which represented defendant's vehicle. A second camera was mounted on a helicopter we had hired, and aerial pictures of the reconstruction were taken from it.

Basing the speeds of the Volkswagen and Chevrolet on the experts' opinions of 22 mph and 25 mph respectively, the accident was re-created from distances of 300 feet and 180 feet. The reconstruction proved that even at the lesser distance, defendant could have easily avoided the collision with the on-coming, drifting Volkswagen by simply changing lanes, with no danger to himself or others at the low speeds.

To effectuate a settlement, copies of the videotapes from both the car and the helicopter were sent to defendant and his attorney for their inspection. Additionally, we had prepared a "day-in-the-life" film which was also given to them for viewing the daily life of this tragically-handicapped girl. Along with this videotape, we also sent a copy of the last medical report.

A week before trial was set to begin, a fair structured settlement was reached. The case was not one of good liability, and did require a grand effort on the part of our attorneys and investigators. Nonetheless, it was not a *completely* disabled case, and through our efforts, we were able to provide the injured child with a lifetime of financial security. The settlement of $2,300,000 was structured.

§ 3.22 Intoxication

Cases may initially appear "crippled" because of intoxication. Even so, plaintiff's intoxication may entitle him to a higher degree of care than that accorded a sober person.[57] It may even entitle him to the last clear chance whereas his sober friend would not be so entitled.[58] Again, the defendant's conduct toward the "drunk" may be such as to invoke wanton or wilful fault, and thus remove contributory negligence entirely. (I have yet to hear a defendant exculpate himself by lowering the standards of care applying to him—that he

---

57. Marshall v. Van Meter, 438 S.W.2d 504 (Ky.1969) (Carrier must exercise due care to provide for the safety of a passenger who is known to be completely or partially disabled due to intoxication, and must bestow on him such special care and attention beyond that given to an ordinary passenger as may be reasonably required); Johnson v. New Orleans Public Serv., Inc., 139 So.2d 7 (La. App.1962) (Plaintiff's decedent was killed when he fell into a canal after alighting from bus. The complaint alleged that defendant was negligent in discharging the obviously intoxicated passenger 112 feet from regular bus stop. The court held: "The care which is required of the common carrier is higher when the passenger is intoxicated and the duty of special care applies not only when such intoxication is known to the carrier but also when that intoxication, by proper diligence, could have been known to the carrier's employees.).

See also McMahon v. New York, New Haven & Hartford R. Co., 136 Conn. 372, 71 A.2d 557 (1950); Brown v. Wilmington, 4 Boyce (Del.) 492, 90 A. 44 (1914); Fox v. Michigan Central R. R. Co., 138 Mich. 433, 101 N.W. 624 (1944).

See in addition Brown v. Stevens, 136 Mich. 311, 99 N.W. 12 (1904) (Where plaintiff was business invitee, and his appearance was like that of one intoxicated, although as a fact he merely suffered from partial blindness and deafness, the defendant owed him the care due an incompetent person, known to be such).

The author is informed of a Nevada trial court decision where a business visitor to defendant's establishment (equipped with 5 bars and an escalator) was warned by the employees not to use the moving stairway, but she persisted to her sorrow. As it seemed to the plaintiff, "the handrail went faster than the stairs, pulling her forward." She fell and suffered injuries. It was held that "the duty owed to intoxicated business visitors who intend to use the escalator is not only to warn them, but is coupled further with the high degree of care owed to users of the escalator, and qualified by the additional requirement that special caution is necessary even to the extent of preventing them from using the moving stairs."

58. Pence v. Ketchum, 326 So.2d 831 (La.1976) (Patron of bar brought suit against owners of bar and another to recover damages for injuries sustained when she was struck by an automobile after being ejected from the bar in an intoxicated condition. "If a person is in an advanced state of intoxication so as to render him helpless, or incapable of self-protection, the law accords him the benefit of the doctrine Last Clear Chance.").

See also Simmer v. City and County of San Francisco, 116 Cal.App.2d 724, 254 P.2d 185 (1953) (Plaintiff alleged to have been intoxicated fell to street when bus against which he was leaning unexpectedly pulled away); Morlan v. Hutchinson-Hyatt, 116 Kan. 86, 225 P. 739 (1924); Shipp v. St. Louis Southwestern R. Co., 188 So. 526 (La.App.1939); Aydlett v. Keim, 232 N.C. 367, 61 S.E.2d 109 (1950).

was too drunk.) In any event, the drinking must have been a proximate cause.[59]

The practical danger in drinking cases is the "one or two beers only" testimony, or recalling the "highball and a half", even though true. The jury generally concludes more, and plaintiff arguing complete sobriety loses the advantage of "drunk" law. Thus the seemingly crippled case of confessed intoxication may actually bring an unearned premium. In criminal law, drinking gives a "diminished capacity" to defendant and a lessened sentence accountability.

In a 1975 Ohio Supreme Court decision,[60] an intoxicated passenger who had alighted from defendant's taxi cab was killed when she was unable to cross the road without difficulty. The trial judge apparently ruled that the deceased was contributorily negligent as a matter of law because of her intoxicated condition, and granted defendant's motion for a directed verdict. The Court of Appeals reversed, which reversal was upheld by the Ohio Supreme Court.

The court ruled that the decedent had been negligent in becoming intoxicated, but once she was inebriated, the defendant was bound to exercise reasonable care for her as she was. Quoting Judge Cardozo, the court ruled, "[Her] intoxication previous to and at the time the defendant unlawfully placed [her], as its passenger, in the hazardous situation is not a direct and proximate cause of the injury, and therefore, not contributory negligence." [61]

In a California case,[62] the decedent fell to the street in a drunken stupor, voluntarily induced. The defendant, while negligently operating his automobile, ran over and killed the drunkard. The trial court granted a nonsuit on the ground that decedent's intoxication constituted contributory negligence as a matter of law. The cause was reversed on the ground that, although intoxication may be contributory negligence, whether it is a bar depends on whether it is a proximate cause, and also on last clear chance, and hence should have been submitted to the jury.

---

59. Allen v. Pearson, 89 Conn. 401, 94 A. 277 (1915); Powell v. Berry, 145 Ga. 696, 89 S.E. 753 (1916) ("If ordinary care under certain circumstances would require that a certain thing should be done, the requirement is binding on a man whether sober or drunk; and getting drunk will not relieve the person from that duty. To hold otherwise would be to put a premium upon drunkenness.).

60. Brinkmoeller v. Wilson, 41 Ohio St.2d 223, 325 N.E.2d 233 (1975).

61. 325 N.E.2d at 235, quoting Judge Cardozo's concurring opinion in Fagan v. Atlantic Coast Line R. Co., 220 N.Y. 301, 312, 115 N.E. 704, 709 (1917).

62. Coakley v. Ajuria, 209 Cal. 745, 290 P. 33 (1930).

In one case tried by the author,[63] in association with *William Reed* of San Diego and *John Moran* of San Francisco, it was actually legally necessary to prove that plaintiff was "dead drunk" in order to win the case, and a jury verdict of $75,000. Plaintiff was a young sailor attached to the San Diego Naval Base. He recalled leaving church on the Sunday morning of the accident, and having several drinks at a bar after visiting a girl's house, and then nothing further until he woke up standing on his feet in the Santa Fe Railroad yards where, according to his testimony, he was jostled by a train washing crew, and fell down on the tracks. The next thing he knew, a box car was shunted at him, and it ran over, and amputated his leg. His intoxication was not denied, and it was likewise admitted that the accident took place not in the Santa Fe yards, adjacent to the station, but on private property.[64] It was contended that this railroad station is one of the most dangerous in the United States, and that there were no fences to warn or keep people from the private yards which adjoin the main station, and that in fact, people frequently did walk across these yards and into the public station. As proof, and to corroborate the oral testimony, an aerial photo was taken, Figure 76, to show the proximity of the San Diego ball park to the station and the anchorage for the fleet. The actual evidence was that when the fleet was in, sailors swarmed across these private railroad yards. It was argued that this was notice to defendant railroad. Another aerial showed the ball park areas to, and from which, permissive use was claimed along the "path." Another photograph, Figure 77, looks into the passenger station. The "freight shed," scene of the accident, is to the left.[65]

---

63. Ellis v. Santa Fe Railway, Superior Court for San Diego, California.

64. On the first trial, the jury was "hung" 6–6. Preparing for the second try, plaintiff called every employee having anything to do with the maintenance of the railroad on the particular evening. Every witness that was available to the defendant was called by the plaintiff, and every fact relevant was put before the jury by the plaintiff. (Under California Rules of Civil Procedure, either party may call and cross-examine as an adverse witness any defendant, or corporate officer or employee of a defendant, without being bound by their testimony.).

65. A motion was made to take the jury to the scene, and was granted by the trial judge. On the day of the visit, fresh white paint had been used to warn people out of the area into which plaintiff had wandered.

Figure 76. Aerial of San Diego naval base and freight station to show the proximity of the fleet anchorage where sailors congregate to the dangerous yards; significant points are labeled on the photo for jury inspection.

Figure 77. A view of the passenger station, San Diego, with freight shed scene of accident to the left, demonstrating the proximity of danger to the public ways.

I also argued in this case that defendant was guilty of wanton misconduct, since under the circumstances, what would have been ordinary negligence to an ordinarily prudent plaintiff, became wantonness to a drunken person. Of course, if wantonness was proven, then contributory negligence would be no defense. The verdict was $75,000.[66] While this was hardly adequate for an amputated leg and crushed hand, it was the second highest ever to be awarded in San Diego county, one of the low verdict centers of California. This verdict again was a reflection of candor on trial.[67] The law of Torts is becoming more humanitarian with each appellate court decision.[68]

66. The author follows a practice definitely not to be recommended—allowing an associate to take the verdict. I left San Diego while the jury was out, and went to Los Angeles. As soon as I had entered my hotel room, the phone rang. The first words of the plaintiff were, "We've struck it." When I asked the amount of the verdict, he said, "Verdict, hell. We've hit oil on our property in Texas." He then went on to say that while the jury was out he had received a telegram from his family that oil had come in on his Texas land. Finally he said, "Oh, yes, the jury brought in $75,000 for us." I had left him in San Diego utterly impoverished except for plane fare back to Texas.

67. It was reported that before the verdict was reached, two of the jurors wanted to give the full amount of the prayer, $225,000, five were for $50,000, and only one was against liability.

68. Rowland v. Christian, 69 Cal.2d 108, 119, 70 Cal.Rptr. 97, 104, 443 P.

§ 3.22   INTRODUCTION   Pt. 1

In our case *Crisp v. Matson Navigation Co.*, discussed earlier,[69] the reader will recall that therein defendant was contending that plaintiff's self-induced drunkenness was the proximate cause of his injury. To recapitulate briefly, the case involved a 52-year-old able-bodied seaman who was injured when the gangway he was in the process of stripping for stowage collapsed, throwing him into the cold water, where he remained for about 15 minutes in an unconscious state.

Defendant alleged that plaintiff's extreme state of intoxication resulted in his being where he should not have been, that is, on the gangway. Plaintiff's blood alcohol level was 0.257%. The legal rate of presumed intoxication in California is 0.15%. Because plaintiff had been an alcoholic some 20 years, he had acquired a resistance to the effects of alcohol, and, even though the amount of alcohol in his body normally would have resulted in a drunken stupor for a non-alcoholic, for him, the effects were less.

Among the authority we were able to gather for our proposition that plaintiff had developed such a resistance was a study done by the American Medical Association entitled *Alcohol & The Impaired Driver*. In it were published the results of studies of the correlation between the concentration of alcohol in the blood and intoxication.

2d 561, 568 (1968) ("The proper test to be applied to the liability of the possessor of land . . . is whether in the management of his property he has acted as a reasonable man in view of the probability of injury to others, and although the plaintiff's status as a trespasser, licensee, or invitee may in the light of the facts giving rise to such status have some bearing on the question of liability, the status is not determinitive").

The classic example is given of the person struck by a train at a crossing, and carried some distance on the pilot of the engine. The engine crew removed what they erroneously supposed was a dead, or dying man, and deposited him in a warehouse for the night. In the morning, he was found some paces from where he had been placed, and dead from bleeding, a leg having been crushed in the accident. The court held the railroad liable, because once having taken charge of a helpless person, it was bound to have completed the task. Northern Central Ry. Co. v. State, To Use of Price, 29 Md. 420, 96 Am.Dec. 545 (1808).

"In different jurisdictions defendants are liable for discoverable as well as actually discovered peril under the last clear chance rule. Our humanitarian doctrine is reasoned upon precepts of humanity—that tender regard every man must have for the life and limb of other men in times of peace—and is not sought to be justified on theories involving proximate cause, comparative negligence, wilfulness, recklessness or wantonness. It is not to be distinguished, on the issue under discussion, from holdings in jurisdictions imposing liability for a discoverable peril." Krause v. Pitcairn, 350 Mo. 339, 167 S.W.2d 74 (1942).

69. See § 2.141 et seq., "Exemplary Investigations", supra.

The studies indicated that at levels of 0.15%, more than 50% of those studied were grossly intoxicated. Only a few were drunk when the level of alcohol present in the bloodstream was 0.05%, while almost all were drunk when the level reached 0.35%. The study then noted: "Persons with histories of long use of alcohol are less likely to show signs of gross intoxication at lower levels, since they have learned to control their behavior. They deliberately attempt to conceal their intoxication and *have a greater degree of tolerance than persons with less experience in repeated alcohol consumption.*"

For a tee-totaller, then, a minimal amount of alcohol could produce a state of intoxication, yet for one accustomed to its effects, a small amount would be of absolutely no consequence. We were able to show the latter in the *Crisp* case, and ultimately reached a settlement of $2,300,000.

I recall trying a passenger-common carrier case many years ago which is illustrative of how drunkenness does not necessarily preclude plaintiff from recovering. A Spanish-American war veteran, some 70 years of age, was enroute home from a meeting of his comrades, and was boarding a street railway car. It was charged that he had sampled freely of the liquids present as well as reminiscences of the nostalgic past. The car immediately started, and plaintiff was thrown to the ground, fracturing his femur. An open reduction and a pin through the "surgical neck" was required. I contended that my client, having boarded the car, as a passenger, was not accorded the "highest degree of care" required of a common carrier in California.[70] After plaintiff's res ipsa loquitur showing of accident, plus testimony as to the specific negligence of abrupt starting, defendants attempted to prove that plaintiff was intoxicated. With a fair degree of initial success, counsel for defendant began to insist that the injured man was much drunker than was actually the fact.[71] I oblig-

---

70. The relationship of passenger and carrier begins even before plaintiff boards the car, and does not end immediately after disembarkation. The passenger is entitled to a safe place to board and to alight. This should, of course, be agreed and explained to the jury in instructions. Lee v. Dade County, 342 So.2d 846 (Fla.App.1977) (Bus driver parked bus so that exit door was positioned directly over a recessed sewage drain; 80-year-old woman passenger was injured when she alighted); Atlantic Transit System, Inc. v. Smith, 141 Ga.App. 87, 232 S.E.2d 580 (1977) (Passenger injured while attempting to board bus); Miskunas v. Chicago Transit Auth., 42 Ill.App.3d 202, 355 N.E.2d 738 (1976); Johnson v. New Orleans, 284 So.2d 794 (La.App.1973); Alexander v. New Orleans Public Serv., Inc., 262 So.2d 538 (La.App.1972).

71. This recalls the truly imaginative (it is hoped) story of a plaintiff's counsel whose client claimed to have been injured on a street car, upon which she had not actually been a passenger. The story goes that during the course of the trial, her attorney became conscience stricken, even

ingly allowed them to proceed with the theory that my client was drunk and went along with defendant so far that he finally had my old soldier so drunk that he was unable to take any care of himself. Consequently on instructions to the jury, it was necessary for the court to instruct in accordance with the law that a common carrier takes a passenger as it finds him, the lame, halt and blind—and intoxicated—and once having so accepted him, although not initially bound to do so, it must leave him in no worse condition than it found him. Therefore the street railway, having accepted a passenger, as they themselves tried to prove, who was unable to care for himself, practically admitted their own liability by proof of the accident.

In argument to the jury, I emphasized that the utmost, the highest degree of, care must be accorded a passenger for hire. Then in accord with my general practice, I read the dictionary definition of the word "utmost," "the highest," so that the jury would have a full appreciation of the term. I have found that a word in common usage may not be understood with its full connotation unless the meaning is pointed out. Synonyms and repetitions impress. This is done solely for the purpose of having the trier of facts understand the exact standard the word provides. Then, after giving the definition of "utmost," I argued that this was the standard of care to be accorded an ordinary passenger, but that when a helpless person was involved, the operator of the streetcar had to employ even higher care than "utmost" and become practically a guarantor of his safety.[72] The verdict was $15,000, which, in the author's opinion, even in 1944 was not adequate for the injury. Yet this amount was reduced to $10,000 because of the man's age.

though his case was going very well. He asked to approach the bench, and began, "Your Honor, I want to make a very serious charge and statement with reference to liability in this case. I—," when he was interrupted by defendant's counsel, who said, "Just a minute, Your Honor, before the plaintiff goes any further, You will recall I haven't had the opportunity of making an opening statement, but I want Your Honor here and now to know that we have five unimpeachable witnesses who are prepared to testify that the plaintiff was completely intoxicated when she was riding on our streetcar."

One may humorously, as the sequel to this story, pose the question of morals: under this state of the record should plaintiff's counsel have continued the case?

72. Very often the Court in instructing on common carriers will give the instruction that the "utmost care" must be accorded a passenger, and then emasculate it by the argumentative instruction that this does not mean that the carrier is an insurer of the safety of its passengers. This is unwarranted because there has been no such contention by the plaintiff.

The unavoidable accident instruction is similarly argumentative, wherein the court instructs on this subject over and above full instructions on contributory negligence.

In arguing the case of an aged plaintiff, particular care should be exercised in pointing out that the years left, although few, are the dearest to a human being, because so limited. In these twilight years, towards which men work and look forward to a life of freedom and comfort, are the years in which pain and suffering should be compensated at a higher rate than those for the younger person. The youth may have the intervention of surgical procedures, and look for help from new advances in medicine to alleviate his handicaps and pain. The shorter the life of the oldster, the more magnified is his suffering.

Several years later I tried another case for a drinking plaintiff.[73] Again in this case the defense emphasized the intoxication of the plaintiff, and thereby imposed such a high degree of care that the appellate court was moved to comment:

> "In the present case it is probably true that the evidence of plaintiff and the evidence of Mahoney would not be sufficient to raise the last clear chance doctrine. That is so because plaintiff testified that he was sober, and Mahoney testified that until just before the moment of impact, and too late to prevent it, plaintiff was in an apparent place of safety and was not in an apparent position of peril. Such facts would probably have precluded the doctrine from applying. . . . But that is not the only evidence in the case. Through the witness Kolish the defendants make plaintiff out very drunk indeed. They have him staggering and stumbling over the street, mumbling to himself, hardly able to maintain his balance. Through other witnesses they have him possessing a 'heavy,' a 'very' and a 'strong' alcoholic breath. The defendants perhaps proved too much, at least as far as the last clear chance doctrine is concerned. If just before the accident plaintiff was so drunk that he was staggering and stumbling and hardly able to maintain his balance, it is a reasonable and permissible inference that he was staggering and stumbling during the period after he was observed by Mahoney, and that was at least one hundred feet before the accident. If Mahoney saw plaintiff staggering and stumbling five feet from the tracks on which the streetcar was approaching, then plaintiff was in a place of peril from which, because of his condition, he could not extricate himself." [74]

An older decision of the California Supreme Court [75] is informative and enlightening on the subject of the standard of care owed an

---

73. Not all of the author's clients drink, although I have the honor of a life membership, and one of the very few gold cards, in the bartenders' union of San Francisco.

74. Simon v. City and County of San Francisco, 79 Cal.App.2d 590, 601, 180 P.2d 393 (1947).

75. Robinson v. Picche, Bayerque & Co., 5 Cal. 460, 461 (1855).

intoxicated person: "If the defendants were at fault in leaving an uncovered hole in the sidewalk of a public street, the intoxication of the plaintiff cannot excuse such gross negligence. A drunken man is as much entitled to a safe street, as a sober one, and much more in need of it."

§ 3.23 Aggravation of Pre-existing Condition

The trial procedure in a California case, in the approach to the aggravation of prior existing condition, exemplifies the necessary candor. It also shows how like Bacon's "Myth of the Market Place," we are slaves to common expressions, words and ideas. When this case was brought to me, there was an ultimate offer of $2,500 in settlement, and the plaintiff was described as "a crazy person with a sprained ankle."

The facts: the plaintiff, a woman 53 years of age, had boarded a Municipal street car. Shortly after paying her fare, and while she was standing near the conductor's stand, the car lurched, and she was thrown abruptly to the floor. Her stocking was torn, and her ankle sprained. Helped to her seat, she continued the ride, and refused medical attention. The testimony was that at this time she began to perspire profusely, felt sick at her stomach, did not vomit, but became so confused that she rode beyond her station, and had to take another car back. Upon arriving home, she was unable to cook dinner, and immediately went to bed. There was further evidence that medical care was sought within several days for the ankle, and that within several weeks she began to develop psychotic tendencies, and within two months was admitted to a State Institution as being psychotic. The evidence was that her past history had shown no grossly abnormal conduct, but that she was regarded by her neighbors as "mildly unusual." She had suffered no prior broken bones or serious illnesses; at 43 surgical menopause had been performed.[76] In preparing the case medically, one of the examining doctors advised the theory of a possible petechial (minute) brain hemorrhage as a result of her fall, but no evidence supported this type of cranial damage, so this was discarded.

Plaintiff was undoubtedly a candidate for a mental disorder. Rather than play down a pre-existing condition, I stressed it. Open-

---

76. A "female operation" can be hysterectomy (surgical removal of the uterus); oophorectomy (removal of one or both ovaries); salpingectomy (removal of one or both oviducts or tubes). Generally all three sets of organs are removed in neoplastic (tumorous) disorders, and particularly when the growth is malignant, or when the woman is beyond child-bearing.

ing statement was based on complete candor, fact, and law. The plaintiff had lived 53 years without any disorder; she had enjoyed life, married, had children, cooked for her family, did her shopping, had her pleasures, religious and social activities. She took her place as a member of the community, and voted for president. The law was stated; the street car company takes passengers as it finds them, the lame, halt, blind, and even persons that may be predisposed to mental disorders.

The Superintendent of the State Asylum testified that, in his opinion, a formula was necessary to show causation in the case: (1) a prior existing condition; (2) a "trigger mechanism" to set this condition off into psychosis. There was the prior existing condition of border line stability, and there was the minor injury on the street car. (Minor to a normal person, but tragically severe to this passenger.) I recall one of the doctors being asked, while a witness, "Would your testimony be the same if plaintiff merely fell down her own stairs?" He answered, "I doubt it—because such trauma to the mind of this person would not be the same as a fall in unfamiliar circumstances with all of the embarrassment attendance thereupon."

Plaintiff was brought into the courtroom by a subpoena from the hospital, with nurses in attendance, and the State Medical Superintendent gave objective testimony concerning her condition. The original prayer was for $25,000, and during the course of the trial the case was settled for $52,000, the prayer being amended accordingly. This settlement was proof that candor pays.[77] (These were the days before the Adequate Award.)

A classical example of aggravation of a pre-existing condition is found in a 1978 decision of the Texas Court of Civil Appeals.[78] Plaintiff was dining at a cafeteria when she came upon a roach in her dessert. Upon seeing the creature, she became nauseated, notified defendant's employee, and left with her dinner partner, a psychologist.

Plaintiff's testimony revealed that when she discovered the roach, she immediately became sick and vomited into her napkin. The nausea continued for two days. As a result of the incident,

---

77. One time I had occasion to take a jury for a "view" of a plaintiff-patient in an asylum, the superintendent being reluctant to transport the person to court. When the jury visited the institution, I had arranged with several of the attendants to take them in the back way, through the more violent wards, instead of through the front and more genteel doors. The opportunity was thus given of revealing a complete asylum to my horrified jury, with the assistance, of course, of my uncooperative superintendant.

78. Cavitt v. Jetton's Greenway Plaza Cafeteria, 563 S.W.2d 319 (Tex.Civ. App.1978).

plaintiff's eating habits changed, resulting in a substantial weight loss. She was unable for a time thereafter to eat when she was out in company, which proved very embarrassing to her.

Defendant brought in proof showing that approximately one year prior to this episode, plaintiff had been treated for a stomach ailment, the symptoms of which were identical to those resulting from the roach incident. The jury found that defendant was guilty of serving unwholesome food, but failed to award any money damages to plaintiff.

The Court of Civil Appeals reversed on the issue of damages, holding that a person is injured if he receives damage or harm to the physical structure of his body. "Such damage or harm includes aggravation of any previously existing disease or condition by reason of such damage or harm to the physical structure of the body." [79]

In a Tennessee case,[80] an employee of a security company, assigned to patrol and guard defendant hospital's premises, fell down an unlighted elevator shaft. Two weeks later, plaintiff, still confined in defendant hospital, was injured when a piece of equipment used to pull himself up broke.

Liability for the initial injury was denied by the jury on the basis that it was proximately caused by plaintiff's own negligence, not the hospital's. Plaintiff was awarded $8,000 for the second incident, from which he appealed. The appellate court ruled that when a wrongful act aggravates or increases a permanent partial disability already existing in the injured party, then it does not matter to what extent the wrongful act aggravates or increases the disability; any increase of the pre-existing condition renders the tort feasor liable for all.[81]

The court then went on to hold, "If the jury finds the wrongful act increased the pre-existing permanent disability of the right leg to any degree, the jury fixes damages for the whole. In so doing the jury is not speculating nor basing its verdict on conjecture or surmise, because the *extent of the increase* in the permanent injury is of no significance." [82] Other examples of this may be found in the footnote below.[83]

---

[79] 563 S.W.2d 319 at 322.

[80] Foster v. Baptist Memorial Hosp., 506 S.W.2d 775 (Tenn.App.1973).

[81] 506 S.W.2d 775 at 778.

[82] 506 S.W.2d 775 at 779.

[83] Sweet Milk Co. v. Stanfield, 353 F.2d 811 (9th Cir. 1965) (Plaintiff injured in a separate accident one day before); City of Scottsdale v. Kokaska, 17 Ariz.App. 120, 495 P.2d 1327 (1972) (Plaintiff incurred more severe back injuries than ordinary person would have sustained due to "an ana-

One of the most pathetic "crippled cases" I have seen involved a psychotic plaintiff and a taxicab. This case remained "crippled" until there was an appreciation that the relation of passenger and carrier begins before plaintiff seats himself within the cab, and the relationship is one of utmost care: Plaintiff in my case, a young father, was brought home from overseas by the military services with the message that his wife was "dying." Death of his wife so upset plaintiff that eventually he became psychotic. His family and children on several occasions had him committed to the psychopathic ward of the Emergency Hospital. But on the several occasions of his incarceration he was kept only overnight and was returned to his home and job.

Upon the last occasion before the accident, plaintiff had voluntarily gone to the psychopathic ward because he felt a "spell coming on." While he was sitting on a bench waiting to be admitted, he received a "telepathic message" that his wife was waiting at home and was urging him to "come home." The boy got up, went out of the psychopathic ward and, seeing a cab in front, hailed it, saying "Take me home." The cabbie said "Where's your home?" The boy answered, "Don't you know?" He then got in the cab.

After several more questions, the cab driver was told to drive to a certain neighborhood, that plaintiff would show him his home although he could not tell him where it was. During the course of the

tomically different spine than that of a 'normal' person"); Ng v. Hudson, 75 Cal.App.3d 250, 142 Cal.Rptr. 69 (1977) (Accident aggravated an existent yet dormant vertebral disc condition); Hastie v. Handeland, 274 Cal. App.2d 599, 79 Cal.Rptr. 268 (1969) (Decedent suffered from degenerative disc diseases and disc protrusion prior to accident); Fischer v. Moore, 183 Colo. 392, 517 P.2d 458 (1973) ("Under the common-law principles of tort law, it is axiomatic that the tort feasor must accept the plaintiff as he finds him and may not seek to reduce the amount of damages by spotlighting the physical frailties of **the injured party at the time the tortious force was applied to him**"); Johnson v. Bender, 369 N.E.2d 936 (Ind.App.1977); Taylor v. Rome, 303 So.2d 844 (La.App.1974) (Preexisting arthritis in wrists and knees); Seitz v. Department of Fire, City of Syracuse, 55 A.D.2d 829, 390 N.Y.S.2d 308 (1976); Silcox v. Smith County, 487 S.W.2d 652 (Tenn.App.1972) (Defendant liable for damages resulting to foundation of home, in which cracks already existed. A workman suffered a severe heat stroke and immediately had a recurrence of an old schizophrenia (psychosis), which left him unemployable. Plaintiff's jury award affirmed, holding aggravation of a preexisting disease is compensible. The attending doctor testified that he believed the heat stroke was "one factor or precipitating element of his becoming ill again." Another expert testified that he believed it "shocked his nervous system so that it brought on a recurrence." This was sufficient to sustain the award even though the cause of this type of insanity is unknown.); Jacobson v. Department of Labor and Industries, 37 Wash.2d 444, 224 P.2d 338 (1950).

short ride the boy made several comments to the cab driver which should have indicated an abnormal state of mind, perhaps not to one using "ordinary care," but certainly to one held to the standard of "the utmost care."

After the cab had driven five blocks, the passenger suddenly screamed "That flash—there it is—the atomic bomb—duck down!" Simultaneously he hit the cab driver over the head. (On the cab driver's deposition I asked, "Weren't you at least by this time surprised—didn't you think something was wrong"? The answer was, "Mister, when you've been driving a cab as long as I have, you're not surprised at anything—furthermore, how did I know they weren't dropping one of those eggs"?)

The plaintiff passenger, the cab being abruptly stopped, jumped out of the conveyance, ran across the highway and, struck by a passing automobile, received serious permanent injuries.

Considering this case, that the common carrier first had the duty of utmost care, that he picked up plaintiff in front of the psychopathic ward, that the plaintiff asked several strange questions before getting into the cab, that he continued with strange questions and conversation after he was seated, should not the cab driver legally have been warned of the eventuality of the subsequent conduct? Rather than a case of apparent non-liability, this is a "crippled case" that warrants recovery under the applicable standard of utmost care.

§ 3.24   Obvious Danger Cases

Counsel may discourage a deserving plaintiff because the facts of his case present an apparency of obvious danger, leading counsel to believe that a jury would deny liability on the grounds of contributory negligence: "Why, he certainly should have seen that." However, it should be remembered that even forgetfulness of a known danger will not operate to prevent a recovery, for to forget is not negligence, unless it shows a want of ordinary care. Generally, this determination is one for the jury.[84]

84. Chase v. Shasta Lake Union Sch. Dist., 259 Cal.App.2d 612, 66 Cal. Rptr. 517 (1968) (Adult plaintiff, playing in an evening softball league on defendant school district's field, ran into cement incinerator in left field while chasing down a fly ball); Iden v. Zeeman Clothing Co., 50 Cal.App. 2d 111, 122 P.2d 626 (1942) ("Forgetfulness of a known danger may or may not show want of ordinary care, and whether it does or not is a question for the jury"); Calerich v. Cudahy Packing Co., 170 Colo. 222, 460 P. 2d 801 (1969) ("Justifiable distraction or forgetfulness may excuse a party injured thereby"); Stueber v. Maintenance, Inc., 205 So.2d 305 (Fla.App. 1967) (Plaintiff's mind on ordinary business *not* sufficient distraction);

A plaintiff is injured. True, this fact alone cannot predict liability, and *res ipsa* is not available. But if the injured person is otherwise a prudent person, and if the act was not wilfull, nor purely accidental (i. e., defendant not at fault), may not the mere fact of accident raise, at least in counsel's mind, an inference of the lack of contributory negligence, and thereby a good case of negligence against the defendant?

Many times, patrons of stores are injured by "obvious" obstructions, their minds and attention distracted by the barrage of advertising, the charm of display and decoration, and the sheer numbers of the crowd. It is held that store owners owe their patrons a higher duty of due care, and that complete safety of stairs, floors, rails and other obstructions are accepted as part of the invitation.[85] Similarly, in automobile accidents, the prudent motorist or pedestrian may assume that the other fellow will not be negligent.[86] In many cases in-

Ousley v. Allstate Ins. Co., 234 So.2d 478 (La.App.1970) (Court stating that hurry, confusion, undivided attention to other matters, or sudden diversion may be consistent with due care); Pigg v. Bloom, 22 Mich.App. 325, 177 N.W.2d 441 (1970) (Question for jury whether plaintiff tenant was justifiably distracted when she tripped over worn carpeting, which she knew existed for at least six months).

85. Pensacol Restaurant Supply Co. v. Davison, 266 So.2d 682 (Fla.App.1972) (Customer struck her toe on edge of wooden platform, causing her to fall); Chauvin v. United States Fidelity & Guar. Co., 223 So.2d 441 (La.App. 1969), application denied 254 La. 790, 226 So.2d 921 (Plaintiff tripped over "barn door" which had fallen across walkway leading to and from defendant's establishment, a Dairy Queen; not unreasonable for plaintiff not to discover obstruction, in light of distraction by crowds and advertising on front of building); Borsa v. Great Atlantic & Pac. Tea Co., 207 Pa.Super. 63, 215 A.2d 289 (1965) (Decedent tripped over bench near flower display table).

See also Neel v. Mannings, Inc., 19 Cal.2d 647, 122 P.2d 576 (1942) (Customer bumped her head on obvious ceiling board as she was descending into defendant's store); Sears, Roebuck & Co. v. Geiger, 123 Fla. 446, 167 So. 658 (1936) (Bicycle rack extending into aisle of store); La Sell v. Tri-States Theatre Corp., 233 Iowa 929, 11 N.W.2d 36 (1943) (Theatre seat above level of aisle); Nelson v. F. W. Woolworth & Co., 211 Iowa 592, 231 N.W. 665 (1943) (Customer fell down open stairway behind counter).

86. See, e. g., Logan v. McPhail, 208 Kan. 770, 494 P.2d 1191 (1972) ("Our rule long has been that the operator of an automobile may assume that other motorists using the streets will comply with the law of the road and he is not chargeable with negligence in acting upon that assumption until he has knowledge to the contrary").

See also Pfisterer v. Key, 218 Ind. 521, 33 N.E.2d 330 (1941) (Where pedestrian walking on left side of paved highway approached motor vehicle, and neither apparently observed each other, and collision occurred, verdict of jury upheld for walker. "When the facts are such as to bring the issues within this twilight zone (where reasonable minds may differ upon the question of negligence) the question of negligence or contributory negli-

§ 3.24 INTRODUCTION Pt. 1

volving so-called obvious dangers, there remains a question of fact for the determination by a jury whether the danger was really as "obvious" as may at first seem.[87]

One of the more interesting "crippled" cases in recent years is *Beeson v. Kerlan Constructors, Inc.*,[88] decided in 1980 by the Colorado Court of Appeals. Plaintiff brought suit for the wrongful death of her husband who was killed while "mooning" one of his fellow employees.

Decedent was a member of a crew employed to install a pipeline in Colorado. He commuted to and from the work-site with two of his fellow employees, one of whom was the crew supervisor. The crew supervisor took the other two to and from the site in a company-owned truck. Another one of the workers drove his own truck for commuting, and paid for his own gasoline and other car expenses. The company paid for such expenses on the other vehicle.

After completing their usual 8:00 a. m. to 4:30 p. m. shift, a nearby property owner, for whom the men had done a favor, gave them a case of beer, which they consumed. Afterwards, they went to a nearby tavern where among them, they drank three or four pitchers of beer. About 8:15 p. m., the four men started home, leaving as they had come: three of the men, including decedent, left in the company-owned truck, and the fourth left in his own truck.

The men riding in the company-owned truck arrived at the top of Loveland Pass before the other employee. As they were approach-

gence, is a mixed question of law and fact, and is a proper question to present to a jury").

87. Paluch v. Erie Lackawana R. R. Co., 387 F.2d 996 (3d Cir. 1968) (FELA case—railroad employee injured when telegraph pole he was climbing gave way due to rot, after he was informed by experienced worker it was safe; court ruled that it is not contributory negligence to fail to discover a danger when there is no reason to apprehend one); Huxol v. Nickell, 205 Kan. 718, 473 P.2d 90 (1970) (Night watchman on college campus injured when he fell into eight-foot-deep hole; no contributory negligence, as no dirt was piled on side of hole from which he approached, and there were no warning signals around hole); White v. Burkeybile, 386 S.W.2d 418 (Mo.1965) ("A person is not required to look for danger where he has no cause to anticipate it . . ."). Welsh v. City of South Omaha, 98 Neb. 148, 152 N.W. 302 (1915) (Pedestrian who knew of sidewalk excavation: "Want of ordinary care, and not knowledge of the danger is the test of contributory negligence"); Stevens v. United Gas & Elec. Co., 73 N.H. 159, 60 A. 848 (1905) (Workman coming in contact with live wire: "The fact of actual or constructive knowledge on the part of the plaintiff must appear, either directly or by necessary inference from the evidence and the uniform experience of man, before the court can order a nonsuit or direct a verdict upon this ground: and this result must follow after the evidence has received a construction most favorable to the plaintiff").

88. Beeson v. Kelran Constructors, Inc., 608 P.2d 369 (Colo.App.1980).

ing the summit, the three men decided to "moon" the other, who was a named defendant in the suit. The crew supervisor parked the pickup on the side of the road. The three men got out of the truck, ran into the highway at the top of the pass, and pulled down their pants and bent over, exposing their buttocks. Decedent was killed when the pickup truck being driven by his co-worker struck him.

The lower court dismissed the claim against the construction company on the ground that all of the employees were on a personal frolic at the time of the incident, and thus *respondeat superior* was inapplicable. With this conclusion, the appellate court was in accord.

As to the individual defendant, however, the Court of Appeals felt it was for the jury to decide whose negligence was the proximate cause of injury. Although it was dusk when the accident occurred, the police officer who investigated the accident testified that a reasonably prudent driver could have seen the three men 300 feet from the point of impact. Defendant had told the officer that his attention had been diverted by looking at the company truck parked on the roadside, and he therefore did not see the men until he was about 50 feet from them. The case did not involve the question of defendant's intoxication, as the officer testified that he did not think defendant was drunk nor did his driving abilities seem to be impaired.

Concerning the obvious danger and the conduct of decedent in relation thereto, the Court of Appeals held, "[N]otwithstanding the conduct of decedent, one who voluntarily exposes himself to a known danger does not necessarily consent to the negligence of another." The court then reversed the trial court's decision as to the culpability of the defendant, and held it was for the jury to decide whose negligence had caused the accident.

§§ 3.25–3.30 are reserved for supplementary material.

E. STATUTES OF LIMITATION

Library References:
>C.J.S. Limitation of Actions § 1 et seq.
>West's Key No. Digests, Limitation of Actions ⚖1 et seq.
>Blashfield, Automobile Law & Practice, § 454.1 et seq.

§ 3.31 In General

A client may have a case, except for one disability: the time within which to prosecute his action appears to have lapsed. If otherwise there seems to be no defect to the anticipated suit, before warning the prospective client against precipitous litigation, his lawyer should examine carefully all possibilities of presenting or reviving the suit.

Statutes of limitation were intended as shields, not swords.[89] Claims and notice requirements, usually with much shorter periods than statutes of limitation, have often become traps for conscientious plaintiffs rather than safeguards against harassment of defendants. Consequently, neither moral nor legal criticism should be directed at a lawyer who seeks to protect an otherwise valid claim through a "loophole" in the limitation statutes. If it is one of the rules of play, seemingly without criticism, in other fields of law—taxation, for example—to determine the "loophole," certainly statutes of limitation, notices and claims should be given a thorough analysis in order to extricate the plaintiff.

There may be many possibilities of suit in the case that, at cursory consideration, seems barred. Does a one-year statute of limitation mean 365 days? The political as well as other codes, and the case law of the individual state, may indicate that, mathematically, 365 days is not a year.[90] Holidays may be excluded in computing the year, and the particular state must determine its "legal" holiday.[91] Most statutes provide that a holiday will be excluded only if it coincides with the first or last day of the limitation period.[92]

---

89. See Witkin, California Procedure (2d ed. 1970) Vol. 2, Actions § 228.

90. I recall once, when a member of my family was refused admission to an elementary school because she lacked one day of requisite age that I was able to have her admitted, picking up the extra day by proving that one's birthday is the day before one is born: see Wells v. Wells, 6 Ind. 447 (1855); Erwin v. Benton, 120 Ky. 536, 548, 87 S.W. 291, 295 (1905); 27 Ky.L.J. 909; Ross v. Morrow, 85 Tex. 172, 19 S.W. 1090, 16 L.R.A. 542 (1892).

91. Once, I was granted a new trial after a non-suit to one defendant. A new trial in California must be granted within 60 days to be effective

92. See note 92 on page 303.

I recall the hurried trip to the City Hall on more than one occasion to file a complaint when the client appeared upon the afternoon of the last day for filing. I recall, also, that the naming of "Does" may not toll the statute against ascertainable persons.[93]

Another recollection is the seemingly desperate situation in which plaintiff was not several days without the statute, but a whole two weeks. We were still able to save his cause of action: Generally, the codes of the several states provide that statutes of limitation are tolled while a potential defendant is without the jurisdiction of the state.[94] In this particular case, I filed a complaint and alleged on information and belief that defendant had been without the state for two weeks during the running of the one-year period. Fortunately, defendant had; he had been vacationing out of California for one month.

Statutes are generally tolled by incompetence,[95] infancy,[96] and other such disabilities. But, where a guardian ad litem is appointed,

---

(Code Civ.Proc. § 660). Seemingly through the court's inadvertence, the new trial was granted on 63rd day. One day was picked up by a legal holiday within the 60 day period, but two days were lacking. I ascertained that a newly enacted law provided that the County Clerk's office in the Superior Court of San Francisco was to be closed henceforth on Saturdays. The last, day, or 60th, fell on Saturday. It appeared to the author that one further day would be tolled by this Saturday holiday, and the next day being Sunday, the order being filed on the following Monday, would be timely. However, the California Code (Code of Civ.Proc. 12a) specifically provides that a holiday intervening, Memorial Day, had to be the first or the last date to be effective.

92. If the last date to file suit is a Sunday or legal holiday, the statutory period is extended until the end of the next day which is neither a legal holiday nor a Sunday. Moorey v. Eytchison & Hoppes, Inc., 338 So.2d 558 (Fla.App.1976); Bowling v. Webb Gas Co., 505 S.W.2d 39 (Mo.1974).

93. Scherer v. Mark, 64 Cal.App.3d 834, 135 Cal.Rptr. 90 (1976) (Plaintiff could not substitute true name of known defendant after statute of limitations had run). Statute tolled where defendant's identity unknown; see California State Auto Ass'n v. Cohen, 44 Cal.App.3d 387, 118 Cal. Rptr. 890 (1975).

See also Lawrence v. Bauer Pub. & Printing, Ltd., 143 N.J.Super. 387, 363 A.2d 357 (1976), reversed 154 N.J.Super. 271, 381 A.2d 358; Wall Funeral Home, Inc. v. Stafford, 3 N.C.App. 578, 165 S.E.2d 532 (1969).

94. Garcia v. Flores, 64 Cal.App.3d 705, 134 Cal.Rptr. 712 (1976) (Plaintiff's claim timely filed one year and two days after accident, since statute did not begin to run until defendant returned to California from Mexico, eight days after accident).

But see Dovie v. Hibler, 254 Cal.App.2d 673, 62 Cal.Rptr. 228 (1967) (Statute not tolled by defendant's absence from state which amounted to only a few hours, less than one day in aggregate).

95. There may be a factual question presented as to whether plaintiff actually is incompetent from head inju-

96. See note 96 on page 304.

§ 3.31 INTRODUCTION Pt. 1

the statute begins to run against the one under disability, by acting upon the guardian. Yet, even here, if the guardian ad litem neglects his opportunity, it may be possible to discharge him and appoint another guardian, the one under disability thereby being saved.[97] The California statute provides that an action for injuries sustained prior to or during birth must be brought within six years of the child's birth [98] where injuries are sustained immediately subsequent to birth, the statute does not begin to run until majority.[99]

Statutes of limitation may become inoperative by estoppel.[1] Thus, where plaintiff is advised "not to sue, we'll take care of you," defendant may be estopped from asserting a statute.[2] Some statutes require that the promise be in writing.[3] Defendant may be estopped where he has promised to fulfill his obligations,[4] promised to settle without litigation,[5] or promises to be governed by the determination of other pending litigation.[6]

Most lawyers are familiar with the Soldiers and Sailors Relief Act and moratorium. Many were the subterfuges to abate a suit during the military service of the defendant.[7] Legislators take similar refuge.

ries or otherwise. The litigation of this question may necessarily precede the determination of his ability to sue when the statute of limitations is in question.

See also State ex rel. Hi-Ball Contractors, Inc. v. District Court, 154 Mont. 99, 460 P.2d 751 (1969); Gottesman v. Simon, 169 Cal.App.2d 494, 337 P.2d 906 (1959).

96. West's Ann.Cal.C.C.P. § 352(a)(1).

See also Scott v. School, 568 P.2d 746 (Utah 1977); Williams v. Los Angeles Metropolitan Transit Auth., 68 Cal.2d 599, 68 Cal.Rptr. 297, 440 P.2d 497 (1968).

97. C.J.S. Limitations of Actions §§ 19, 240.

98. West's Ann.Cal.Civ.Code § 29.

99. Fay v. Mundy, 246 Cal.App.2d 231, 54 Cal.Rptr. 591 (1966).

1. See C.J.S. Limitations of Actions § 25.

2. Dupuis v. Van Natten, 61 A.D.2d 293, 402 N.Y.S.2d 242 (1978); Benner v. Industrial Acc. Comm'n, 26 Cal.2d 346, 159 P.2d 24 (1945); Farrell v. Placer County, 23 Cal.2d 624, 145 P.2d 570, 153 A.L.R. 325 (1944).

3. West's Ann.Cal.Code Civ.Proc. § 360.5.

4. Langdon v. Langdon, 47 Cal.App.2d 28, 117 P.2d 371 (1941).

5. Benner v. Industrial Acc. Comm'n, 26 Cal.2d 346, 159 P.2d 24 (1945); Carruth v. Fritch, 36 Cal.2d 426, 224 P.2d 702 (1950).

6. Adams v. California Mut. Bldg. & Loan Ass'n, 18 Cal.2d 487, 116 P.2d 75 (1941). See also Atlas Finance Corp. v. Kenny, 68 Cal.App.2d 504, 157 P.2d 401 (1945).

7. Once, on the eve of trial, the author had presented to him a motion to abate a suit against defendant doctor going into military service. The court abated the proceedings.

HAVE I A CASE? § 3.32

The malpractice suits may present different considerations than the ordinary negligence claim. A plaintiff who is unaware of his cause of action does not have the statutes of limitation run against him, generally, until his awareness—knowledge—of his condition is equal to that of the doctor.[8]

§ 3.32 Equitable Arguments

In a federal case [9] reported by *James A. Eichner*,[10] the Court of Appeals reversed the trial court's dismissal of plaintiff's personal injury action based on *equitable principles*. Plaintiff had been injured on June 22, 1961, in Virginia, when he became entangled in a machine manufactured and sold by the defendant. The defendant's only place of business was in Louisville, Kentucky. Virginia had no "long-arm statute" until 1964.

Thus, plaintiff, at the time he initially sought to institute suit, reasonably concluded that the defendant could not be sued in Virginia. Suit was brought in the United States District Court for the

In actions for relief under the Act, U. S.C.A. Title 50, Appx. 522, when the defendant is involved in personal injury litigation, certain factors are important: (1) The grant of relief is discretionary, (2) Relief should be denied, if the facts by deposition or otherwise are available even though the defendant may be absent, (3) If defendant has adequate liability insurance (This is one instance where courts frankly consider the facts as to liability insurance, and the rights of the parties, including the unnamed insurer.). See Boone v. Lightner, 319 U.S. 561, 63 S.Ct. 1223, 87 L.Ed. 1587 (1943), reh. denied 320 U.S. 809, 64 S.Ct. 26, 88 L.Ed. 489; Gross v. Williams, 149 F.2d 84 (8th Cir. 1945) (Refusal of stay not abuse of discretion where Army sergeant had testified fully on deposition, other witnesses were available, and demand was reduced to maximum liability under insurance policy); Johnson v. Johnson, 59 Cal.App.2d 375, 139 P.2d 33 (1943) (Where deposition had been taken of defendant and he was protected by insurance, discretion of court properly exercised in denying relief); Koons v. Nelson, 113 Colo. 574, 160 P.2d 367 (1945) (Where trial court had deposition of defendant, and properly considered the fact that he carried insurance, denial of stay was not error).

8. West's Ann.Cal.Code Civ.Proc. § 340.5 provides period of one year after discovery (or constructive discovery), or four years from injury, whichever comes first.

See Layton v. Allen, 246 A.2d 794 (Del. Super.1968); Mathis v. Hejna, 109 Ill. App.2d 356, 248 N.E.2d 767 (1969); Fernandi v. Strully, 35 N.J. 434, 173 A.2d 277 (1961); Flanagan v. Mount Eden Gen. Hosp., 24 N.Y.2d 427, 301 N.Y.S.2d 23, 248 N.E.2d 871 (1969); Berry v. Branner, 245 Or. 307, 421 P.2d 996 (1966).

9. Atkins v. Schmutz Mfg. Co., 401 F. 2d 731 (4th Cir. 1968), reh. denied 435 F.2d 527, cert. denied 402 U.S. 932, 91 S.Ct. 1526, 28 L.Ed.2d 867.

10. James A. Eichner (George E. Allen, Jr. on brief), Allen, Allen, Allen, & Allen, 1809 Staples Mill Road, P.O. Box 6855, Richmond, Virginia.

Western District of Kentucky on June 19, 1963. The suit in Kentucky was brought more than one year, but three days less than two years, after the date of injury. The Virginia statute applicable to the plaintiff's alleged cause of action prescribes two years as the period of limitations;[11] the comparable period under Kentucky law is one year.[12]

At the time plaintiff brought suit in Kentucky, Kentucky decisions were understood in the federal courts to hold that in a suit filed in Kentucky, based upon a cause of action arising in another state, the statute of limitations of another state, if longer, was applicable. However, while plaintiff's suit was pending in the Kentucky district court, the Kentucky Court of Appeals held that in such cases the Kentucky one-year statute of limitations would prevail over a longer period of another state. The decision was applied retroactively. Thus plaintiff's case was dismissed in Kentucky. On March 13, 1967, almost six years after the injury occurred, plaintiff filed suit in Virginia. On resubmission, the Fourth Circuit Court of Appeals stated:

"Dismissal of [plaintiff's] suit shocks the conscience, as the trial judge recognized but saw no escape. We think rejection of the plea is demanded by the attending equitable considerations. The amputee is denied trial of his claim despite his strenuous vigilance to get a hearing. His defeat is accomplished by resort to a statute of limitations. Laws of this kind have always been merely to give assurance against stale or ancient claims, lest the defense be impeded by disappearance of proof through lapse of time. Here the statute defies plaintiff's alacrity. True, he waited two years, but never to the defendant's prejudice. At all times it was aware of Atkins' hurt . . . . Utterly unforeseeable to the plaintiff was the about-face of the Kentucky State Court."[13]

Therefore, if a statute of limitation has been missed, but due diligence had been maintained, counsel should consider the feasibility of an equitable argument to preclude dismissal of a cause of action based upon the running of the statute.

§ 3.33 Suit in Contract

There is always the possibility of suing in contract, where the statute usually is longer, when the period has been tolled against the tort.

---

11. 2 Code of Virginia (1957 Repl.Vol.) § 8–24.

12. K.R.S. § 413.140.

13. Atkins v. Schmutz Mfg. Co., 401 F.2d 731 (4th Cir. 1968), reh. denied 435 F.2d 527, cert. denied 402 U.S. 932, 91 S.Ct. 1526, 28 L.Ed.2d 867.

Construction of a complaint as to whether based on contract or tort may become crucial where a limitation period is involved.[14] If the tortfeasor admitted his negligence and promised to pay a just amount, may not the plaintiff sue on the "contract" even though the period has run against the tort? Generally, bill collectors for professional men will not bring suit for services until after the period has run within which the prospective plaintiff could have sued in malpractice. (The period for the bill, being in contract, is generally longer than that for the tort). Most states have extended periods in execution statutes. Thus, for example, long after the debtor has ceased to worry about a claim and has begun to amass a further fortune, he may find that he is still subject to execution.[15]

§ 3.34 Notice of Claim Statutes

Even more vicious to plaintiff's case than the statutes of limitation are the notice of claim statutes, allowing a shorter period for action. Examples of this are the Federal Acts, and requirements by the sovereign (states, municipalities) of action within 30 to 60 days prerequisite to the filing of a complaint.[16] While the justiciableness of these statutes may now be open to doubt, nevertheless, their efficacy, unfortunately, is still felt. The layman may inquire of the time within which to bring his suit and may be advised by another layman of the general tort action period without a consideration of the prior necessary notice or claim acts.

Most claim statutes require that the amount the prospective plaintiff demands be stated.[17] Nevertheless, generally this does not necessarily limit subsequent suits for a higher amount. Likewise, the doctrine of "substantial compliance" has been affectionately received by the courts in notice and claim cases. Thus, while in the past a failure strictly to name a street address, a proper name, a

---

14. See C.J.S. Limitations of Actions §§ 44–51, 125 et seq., 73–81, 168 et seq.

15. At the other extreme, most states provide that the transfer of assets after accident, and even after suit is filed, does not effect their inviolability. Indeed, such transfer may present an evidentiary problem as to whether this action may be shown as an admission of guilt.

16. See e.g. Chapter 27, "Charitable and Sovereign Immunities," infra. See also § 3.41, infra.

17. The author recalls one case, Sullivan v. San Francisco, 95 Cal.App.2d 745, 214 P.2d 82 (1950), wherein he offered to settle for $15,000 and filed a claim for $50,000: then he subsequently amended his claim to conform with the subsequent prayer of the complaint for $150,000, and a verdict was returned and sustained at $125,000.

§ 3.34   INTRODUCTION   Pt. 1

cause of action and other requirements was reason to bar a subsequent complaint, most courts now are more lenient.[18]

§ 3.35   Types of Statutes of Limitation

There are three types of limitations of actions.[19] First, there are "statutes of limitation." Statutes of limitation were enacted in England as early as 1236 A.D., and in Rome as early as 424 A.D.[20] In the United States today, general statutes of limitation are found in every state.[21] These statutes take many forms and govern most types of actions.

Second, it is usually possible for the parties to a contract to set a period of limitation either shorter or longer than that of the pertinent statute of limitation, absent express legislation to the contrary.[22] Such contract provisions may be held void as against public policy if the period of limitation is unreasonably short, however.[23] There is a

---

18. Ala.—Tolbert v. City of Birmingham, 262 Ala. 674, 81 So.2d 336 (1955) (Notice of claim filed against city for injuries sustained as result of alleged defect in sidewalk not fatally defective even though two different locations were given as place where accident occurred).

Cal.—Johnson v. City of Los Angeles, 134 Cal.App.2d 600, 285 P.2d 713 (1955) (Where the hole in the sidewalk which was the cause of plaintiff's injury was erroneously described as being the southeast rather than the southwest corner of the intersection but the dimensions were accurately described variance immaterial); Holm v. San Diego, 35 Cal.2d 399, 217 P.2d 972 (1950) (Home address); Parodi v. San Francisco, 160 Cal.App.2d 577, 325 P.2d 224 (1958) (Location of accident); Knight v. Los Angeles, 26 Cal.2d 764, 160 P.2d 779 (1945) (Date of occurrence).

19. One of the best treatments of statute of limitations since 1916 is a note in 63 Harv.L.Rev. 1177 (1950). There are several reasons for periods of limitation of actions: to prevent suits upon fraudulent or stale claims, where much of the evidence and many of the witnesses are no longer available; valid claims are not usually allowed to remain neglected over a period of years with no attempt to enforce them; a desire to relieve the courts of the burden of adjudicating stale or tenuous claims; a bad effect on commerce of unsettled claims; protection of property rights of "bona fide purchasers."

20. Pollock and Maitland, The History of English Law 81 (2d ed. 1898); Sohm, The Institutes of Roman Law 318–22 (Leslie's transl. (3d ed. 1907)).

21. (1945) 21 Ind.L.J. 23; (1931) 3 Rocky Mt.L.Rev. 106.

22. W. J. Kroeger Co. v. Travelers Indem. Co., 112 Ariz. 285, 541 P.2d 385 (1975); Rumsey Elec. Co. v. University of Delaware, 358 A.2d 712 (Del. 1976); Wiseman v. Arrow Freightways, Inc., 89 N.M. 392, 552 P.2d 1240 (1976). See 6 A.L.R.3d 1197.

23. City of Hot Springs v. National Surety Co., 258 Ark. 1009, 531 S.W.2d 8 (1975) ("A period of time so short as to amount to an abrogation of the right of action would be unreasonable. . . . But it is implicit in the decisions on the subject that the stipulated period is not unreasonable if the time allowed affords a plaintiff sufficient opportunity to investigate his claim and prepare for the controversy." 531 S.W.2d at 10.

split of authority as to the validity of contract provisions extending the period of limitation beyond that of the applicable statute.[24]

The third type of limitation of action is judicial limitation in equity suits, the doctrine of laches. Today, where law and equity courts have concurrent remedies for the same cause of action, the equity court usually finds that the statute of limitations applicable to the action at law is presumptive evidence of laches.[25] However, the equity court sometimes grants relief in exceptional or unusual cases even after the analogous statute of limitation has run.[26]

The typical statute of limitation begins with the words, "No action shall be brought. . . ."[27] In general it is held that the effect of such a statute is to bar the remedy only, and not to impair the right or underlying obligation.[28]

Gary, City of v. Russell, 123 Ind.App. 609, 112 N.E.2d 872 (1953) (Typing of name of claimant to notice by attorney sufficient signing).

24. Holding such a provision invalid is: National Bond & Inv. Co. v. Flaiger, 322 Mass. 431, 77 N.E.2d 772 (1948); Pine v. Okoniewski, 256 App. Div. 519, 11 N.Y.S.2d 13 (1939); E. L. Burns Co. v. Cashio, 302 So.2d 297 (La.1972).

However, some states hold such provisions valid on principles of waiver: see Brownrigg v. DeFrees, 196 Cal. 534, 238 P. 714 (1925); Dexter v. Pierson, 214 Cal. 247, 4 P.2d 932 (1931); Thomas v. Hudson, 190 Ga. 622, 10 S.E.2d 396 (1940).

25. Mitchell v. Mitchell, 575 S.W.2d 311 (Tex.Civ.App.1978); Baker v. Cummings, 169 U.S. 189, 18 S.Ct. 367, 42 L.Ed. 711 (1898); Gillons v. Shell Co. of California, 86 F.2d 600 (9th Cir. 1936); Bovay v. H. M. Byllesby & Co., 27 Del.Ch. 381, 38 A.2d 808, 174 A.L.R. 1201 (1944); Hughes v. Brown, 88 Tenn. 578, 13 S.W. 286 (1890); see (1950) 63 Harv.L.Rev. 1177; (1945) 43 Mich.L.Rev. 978; (1931) 79 U. of Pa. L.Rev. 341; (1941) 2 Pomeroy, Equity Jurisprudence, § 418 (5th ed.); Minion v. Warner, 238 N.Y. 413, 144 N.E. 665 (1924); Gilbert v. David, 235 U.S. 561, 35 S.Ct. 164, 59 L.Ed. 360 (1914).

26. Kelley v. Boettcher, 85 F. 55, 29 C.C.A. 14 (8th Cir. 1898).

27. The official Federal Form for pleading the statute of limitations is: "The right of action set forth in the complaint did not accrue within six years next before the commencement of this action." (Form 20, Fourth Defense).

28. Campbell v. Haverhill, 155 U.S. 610, 15 S.Ct. 217, 39 L.Ed. 280 (1895); Western Coal & Mining Co. v. Jones, 27 Cal.2d 819, 167 P.2d 719 (1946).

However, the contrary result is reached with time limitations for adverse possession of real property, and with statutory causes of action in derogation of common law which include their own limitations: see First Nat'l Bank of Madison v. Kolbeck, 247 Wis. 462, 19 N.W.2d 908 (1945).

§ 3.36 Persons Affected

The general rule is that statutes of limitation are effective to give a defense to the obligor, and cannot be asserted by a third party.[29] However, a transferee of an interest in property may assert the bar of a statute of limitation even though the statute began to run against the transferor prior to the transfer.[30] Similarly, a personal representative or trustee may be held to be under a duty to plead the statute for the benefit of the distributees or beneficiaries.[31]

If there be no statutory authority to the contrary,[32] the ancient doctrine of sovereign immunity extends to prevent the bar of a statute of limitation from being asserted against a state or the federal government in courts within its own territorial jurisdiction.[33] However, municipal corporations and state political subdivisions are generally held subject to statutes of limitation when acting in a proprietary capacity as distinguished from a governmental capacity.[34] On the other hand, the statute of limitations always runs in favor of the sovereign in suits against it.[35]

A successor in interest of a claim dependent upon and derivative from the predecessor in interest is barred at the same time his predecessor would be barred.[36] Thus, assignees, heirs, and subrogees make

---

29. Goldberg, Bowen & Co. v. Demick, 77 Cal.App. 535, 247 P. 261 (1926); Gurske v. Strate, 166 Neb. 882, 87 N.W.2d 703 (1958).

30. Gurske v. Strate, 166 Neb. 882, 87 N.W.2d 703 (1958).

31. However, the result might differ where the trustee incurs the debt himself, or in the case of corporate debts incurred by the directors, where the stockholders cannot force the directors to assert the bar.

32. Compare statutes with respect to taxes and criminal law.

33. Utah Power & Light Co. v. United States, 243 U.S. 389, 37 S.Ct. 387, 61 L.Ed. 791 (1916); United States v. Whited, 246 U.S. 552, 38 S.Ct. 367, 62 L.Ed. 879 (1917); People v. Hammill, 259 Ill. 506, 102 N.E. 1052 (1913); United States v. John Hancock M. L. Ins. Co., 364 U.S. 301, 5 L.Ed.2d 1, 81 S.Ct. 1 (1960). However, the state or federal government must be acting in its sovereign capacity: United States v. Beebe, 127 U.S. 338, 8 S.Ct. 1083, 32 L.Ed. 121 (1888); Denver & R. G. R. R. Co. v. United States, 241 F. 614, 154 C.C.A. 372 (8th Cir. 1917).

34. City of Fullerton v. Orange Co., 140 Cal.App. 464, 35 P.2d 397 (1934); People v. Hale, 320 Ill.App. 645, 52 N.E.2d 308 (1943); compare City of Pendleton v. Holman, 177 Or. 532, 164 P.2d 434 (1945); (1944) 38 Ill.L. Rev. 418.

35. United States v. Verdier, 164 U.S. 213, 17 S.Ct. 42, 41 L.Ed. 407 (1896). For further discussion, see Chapter 27, infra.

36. See C.J.S. Limitations of Actions, § 18, Successor in Right or Title.

Ch. 3   HAVE I A CASE?   § 3.37

derivative claims. However, persons claiming independently and distinct from a claim already barred are not barred.[37]

Once an action has been begun, a substitution of parties or amendment that does not materially change the cause may be made beyond the limitation period.[38]

§ 3.37 Alternative or Collateral Remedies and Defenses

Sometimes alternative or collateral remedies or defenses present a problem as to which of two different periods of limitation is applicable. For example, when plaintiff suffers personal injuries as a result of defendant's breach of a contractual duty, such as the contractual duty of a doctor or a common carrier, and there is a different statutory period for contract and personal injury actions, this problem is presented. Thus, plaintiff should best avoid a bar under the shorter personal injury statute, and sue in contract. The same situation arises in actions for personal injury arising from breach of an implied warranty of quality or fitness of a product, as well as between the period for liability by statute and the personal injury period, when an employee sues his employer for personal injury caused by failure of the employer to meet certain statutory requirements for working conditions. Likewise, the right to "waive the tort and sue in assumpsit" may give rise to the problem when a plaintiff can choose between quasi-contract and conversion for his recovery. There appears to be a wide split of authority in solving these problems.[39]

---

37. For example, a statute of limitation for adverse possession should not run against a reversioner or remainderman until he has a cause of action against the possessor. Likewise, a beneficiary under a wrongful death statute of the Lord Campbell's Act type should have an independent claim with the statute of limitation running as of the time of death of the decedent. See 167 A.L.R. 894 for a discussion of the many cases arising under different statutes as to limitations in death actions.

38. Denver & Rio Grande Western R. Co. v. Clint, 235 F.2d 445 (10th Cir. 1956) (amendment); Cabot v. Clearwater Constr. Co., 89 So.2d 662 (Fla. 1956) (parties changed); Nelms v. Bright, 299 S.W.2d 483 (adding party plaintiff) (Mo.1957); Leyen v. Dunn, 62 Tenn.App. 239, 461 S.W.2d 41 (1970).

39. For cases holding that the action "sounds in tort" and therefore the contract statute is not applicable, see Basler v. Sacramento Elec., Gas & Ry. Co., 166 Cal. 33, 134 P. 993 (1913); Cretcher v. Winona R. Co., 209 Ind. 414, 199 N.E. 241 (1936); Coulter v. Sharp, 145 Kan. 28, 64 P.2d 564 (1937); Loehr v. Eastside Omnibus Corp., 259 App.Div. 200, 18 N.Y.S.2d 529 (1940), aff'd 287 N.Y. 670, 39 N.E.2d 290; Gulf, C. & S. F. Ry. v. Gordon, 218 S.W. 74 (Tex.Civ.App.1919); Birmingham v. Chesapeake & Ohio Ry., 98 Va. 548, 37 S.E. 17 (1900).

However, the presence of fraud or an express contract may alter the result: see Conklin v. Draper, 229 App.Div. 227, 241 N.Y.S. 529 (1930), aff'd 254 N.Y. 620, 173 N.E. 892; Krestich v. Stefanez, 243 Wis. 1, 9 N.W.2d 130 (1943).

There is often room for argument as to which statute of limitation should apply where there is a shorter period for liabilities created by statute, but the liability in question also existed at common law prior to the particular statute.[40] Sometimes the courts allow the longer limitation even though plaintiff is obviously trying to avoid the shorter period by suing on an alternative remedy where the proof is the same under either theory.[41]

"Since the statute of limitation is considered as barring only the direct remedial right of action, and not the underlying claim, the claim may still be of considerable use to its possessor in a variety of situations. It may be asserted defensively, in an action by the debtor, and even offensively where certain possessory interests are endangered. Other rights collateral to the barred claim may still be asserted, and it may be that the remedy of self-help is not affected. But if the time limit is considered 'substantive,' it bars the underlying claim as well, and all remedial rights are extinguished." [42]

If the barred claim is not sufficient to defeat plaintiff's action entirely, it may nevertheless be asserted to reduce it by way of recoupment.[43] Personal representatives of a deceased creditor who has allowed the statute to run are allowed to offset a barred debt against a distributee's share.[44]

Also, due to the fact that most courts say that the statute of limitations bars only the remedy and not the underlying obligation, a creditor's mortgage, security, pledge, or vendor's lien may survive the limitation on collection of debt.[45] Similarly, even though the collateral remedy of foreclosure or sale is barred, the underlying claim

---

40. Southern Counties Thrift Co. v. Rairdon, 47 Cal.App.2d 770, 118 P.2d 828 (1941) (Corporate director liable on common law agency principles, though conduct unlawful by statutory standards. Liability by statutory period of limitations not applied).

41. Chouteau v. Hornbeck, 125 Okl. 254, 257 P. 372 (1927); but compare Deaton v. Rush, 113 Tex. 176, 252 S.W. 1025 (1923).

42. (1950) 63 Harv.L.Rev. 1177, 1244.

43. Jones v. Mortimer, 28 Cal.2d 627, 170 P.2d 893 (1946); Grand Rapids v. McCurdy, 136 F.2d 615 (6th Cir. 1943).

Recoupment requires that defendant's claim arise out of the same transaction as plaintiff's, and that it be used only to decrease or extinguish plaintiff's recovery. As to even broader possibilities for recoupment of taxes, see (1947) 47 Col.L.Rev. 1338; (1949) 63 Harv.L.Rev. 369.

44. (1931) 15 Minn.L.Rev. 590.

45. (1950) 63 Harv.L.Rev. 1177, 1247; see Osborne, Mortgages, 2d (1970) § 296.

Contrary results arise under certain express statutes, and in a few jurisdictions which hold that foreclosure is incidental to the underlying obligation.

survives.⁴⁶ Furthermore, the mortgage when foreclosure suit is barred, may prevent the mortgagor from clearing his title to the property.

§ 3.38 Conflict of Laws

The traditional majority rule is that the law of the forum determines the period of limitation.⁴⁷ Thus, a cause of action may be brought in the forum although it would be barred if sued upon in the jurisdiction where the cause of action arose, and vice versa. However, the forum may adopt the period of the jurisdiction in which the cause of action arose where the period is substantive rather than procedural.⁴⁸ Therefore, the running of an adverse possession statute in the lex loci, or the running of a statutory period of limitation, which is a part of a statute creating a new cause of action in itself, would usually be considered a substantive time limit by the forum, and thus extinguish the right itself. Limitation provisions of wrongful death statutes are usually considered a part of the substantive right, and applied by the forum.⁴⁹ Limitation periods, a part of a Federal Act, are usually binding on a state forum.⁵⁰

---

46. Osborne, Mortgages, 2d (1970) § 296.

47. Restatement, Conflict of Laws 2d § 142(1).

See also Nelson v. Browning, 391 S.W. 2d 873 (Mo.1965); Central Vermont R. Co. v. White, 238 U.S. 507, 35 S. Ct. 865, 59 L.Ed. 1433 (1915); Pearson v. Northeast Airlines, Inc., 309 F.2d 553, 92 A.L.R.2d 1162 (2d Cir. 1962), cert. denied 372 U.S. 912, 83 S.Ct. 726, 9 L.Ed.2d 720. (State does not violate full faith and credit by barring cause of action still available in locus delicti.)

48. See Richardson v. Watkins Bros. Memorial Chapels, 527 S.W.2d 19 (Mo.App.1975).

See also Central Vermont R. Co. v. White, supra, n. 61; Davis v. Mills, 194 U.S. 451, 24 S.Ct. 692, 48 L.Ed. 1067 (1904); Pritchard v. Norton, 106 U.S. 124, 1 S.Ct. 102, 27 L.Ed. 104 (1882); California v. Copus, 158 Tex. 196, 309 S.W.2d 227, 67 A.L.R.2d 758 (1958), cert. denied 356 U.S. 967, 78 S.Ct. 1006, 2 L.Ed.2d 1074; Maki v. George R. Cooke Co., 124 F.2d 663, 146 A.L.R. 1352 (6th Cir. 1942), cert. denied 316 U.S. 686, 62 S.Ct. 1274, 86 L.Ed. 1758.

49. Wells v. Simonds Abrasive Co., 345 U.S. 514, 97 L.Ed. 1211, 73 S.Ct. 856 (1953). (Forum may apply own shorter limitations under full faith and credit clause notwithstanding longer statutory period in state of wrong and decisional law making limitation period substantive right); Martinez v. Missouri Pacific R. Co., 296 S.W.2d 90 (Mo.1956). (Action in Missouri—timely bringing of prior action in Louisiana interrupts running of statute pursuant to Louisiana law); Drinan v. A. J. Lindemann & Hoverson Co., 238 F.2d 72 (7th Cir. 1956).

50. Cox v. Roth, 348 U.S. 207, 75 S.Ct. 242, 99 L.Ed. 260 (1955). (Jones Act— noncompliance with state statute requiring that claim against decedent's estate be filed within specified time does not defeat action since Federal law prevails); Davis v. Foreman, 239 F.2d 579 (7th Cir. 1956)(FTCA).

§ 3.38

Under the majority rule, a certain amount of "forum shopping" for a jurisdiction with a longer period of limitation should be considered for plaintiff whose cause of action might be barred at home. The case of *Union National Bank v. Lamb* [51] requires that if a barred cause of action is revived by a new valid judgment in another jurisdiction, the forum must then grant full faith and credit to the new judgment. Of course, defendants will be able to argue that the foreign revival is not in fact a valid judgment. Many states, however, have enacted borrowing statutes barring causes of action not yet barred by the forum if they would be barred by the lex loci.[52]

Federal courts have always applied the appropriate state period of limitation in enforcing state created causes of action.[53] This rule is even more mechanically applied since *Erie R. Co. v. Tompkins*.[54] The holding in *Ragan v. Merchants Transfer & Warehouse Co.*,[55] to the effect that state law prevails even over Rule 3 of the Federal Rules of Civil Procedure may have been overruled by the ruling in *Hanna v. Plumer* [56] that Rule 4(d)(1) of the FRCP prevails over conflicting state law. The courts are now split on whether *Ragan* remains valid law,[57] and the Supreme Court has yet to resolve the controversy.[58]

---

51. 337 U.S. 38, 69 S.Ct. 911, 93 L.Ed. 1190 (1949), reh. denied 337 U.S. 928, 69 S.Ct. 1492, 93 L.Ed. 1736.

52. Arneil v. Ramsey, 550 F.2d 774 (2d Cir. 1977); Cope v. Anderson, 331 U.S. 461, 67 S.Ct. 1340, 91 L.Ed. 1602 (1946); Richardson v. Watkins Bros. Memorial Chapels, 527 S.W.2d 19 (Mo.App.1975). (Adoption of "most significant relationship" choice of law rule does not alter operation of borrowing statute); Long v. Pettinato, 394 Mich. 343, 230 N.W.2d 550 (1975). (Borrowing statute applies to claims accruing in foreign country.)

53. Arneil v. Ramsey, 550 F.2d 774 (2d Cir. 1977); Bauserman v. Blunt, 147 U.S. 647, 13 S.Ct. 466, 37 L.Ed. 316 (1893).

54. 304 U.S. 64, 58 S.Ct. 817, 82 L.Ed. 1188, 114 A.L.R. 1487 (1938).

55. 337 U.S. 530, 69 S.Ct. 1233, 93 L.Ed. 1520 (1949), reh. denied 338 U.S. 839, 70 S.Ct. 33, 94 L.Ed. 513; (1949) 62 Harv.L.Rev. 1030.

As to rights created by federal statutes, and equitable rights in relation to conflict of laws, see (1950) 63 Harv. L.Rev. 1177; (1946) 19 So.Cal.L.Rev. 432; (1944) 44 Col.L.Rev. 915. The period of limitation in the Federal Tort Claims Act applies in preference to shorter local statutes of limitation: see (1951) 64 Harv.L.Rev. 1205.

56. 380 U.S. 460, 85 S.Ct. 1136, 14 L.Ed.2d 8 (1965).

57. Cases holding *Ragan* overruled in Smith v. Peters, 482 F.2d 799, 17 F.R.Serv.2d 929 (6th Cir. 1973), cert. denied 415 U.S. 989, 94 S.Ct. 1587, 39 L.Ed.2d 886; Grabowski v. United States, 294 F.Supp. 421 (D.C.Wyo. 1968); Wheeler v. Standard Tool & Mfg. Co., 311 F.Supp. 1177 (S.D.N.Y. 1970); Alford v. Whitsel, 52 F.R.D. 327 (N.D.Miss.1971); Manatee Cablevision Corp. v. Pierson, 433 F.Supp. 571 (D.C.D.C.1977).

---

58. See note 58 on page 315.

§ 3.39 Computation of Period—Accrual; Estoppel; Tolling

Most statutes of limitation compute the period from the time the cause of action accrues. However, courts have modified this rule in certain instances. If substantive harm to the plaintiff is really the gravamen of the action, as distinguished from a mere invasion of plaintiff's rights, then, generally, the statute of limitations begins to run only as of the time of such harm. Thus, breach of contract and intentional torts should start the statute running immediately,[59] whereas the statute will begin to run when harm occurs to plaintiff in a negligence case.[60] There is a split of authority, however, as to when the statute begins to run in the case of negligent breaches of contract.[61]

The commencement of the period of limitation should be postponed in cases of "inherently unknowable harm," such as gradually developing occupational disabilities,[62] or even in breach of contract or intentional tort cases, such as an underground trespass.[63] However, it is usually held in personal injury actions that the statute of limitations runs from the time of the commission of the wrongful act rath-

---

Cases holding *Ragan* not overruled in Groninger v. Davison, 364 F.2d 638 (8th Cir. 1966); Witherow v. Firestone Tire & Rubber Co., 530 F.2d 160 (3d Cir. 1976); Tanner v. Presidents-First Lady Spa, Inc., 345 F.Supp. 950 (E.D.Mo.1972).

For discussion, with comprehensive citations, see Wright & Miller, Federal Practice and Procedure: Civil §§ 1057, 1164.

58. Two cases involving the *Ragan* issue were denied certiorari subsequent to *Hanna*: Smith v. Peters, supra, n. 57, and Prashar v. Volkswagen of America, 480 F.2d 947 (8th Cir. 1973), cert. denied 415 U.S. 994, 94 S.Ct. 1596, 39 L.Ed.2d 891.

59. Roberts v. Richard & Sons, Inc., 113 N.H. 154, 304 A.2d 364 (1973); City of Beach v. Goepfert, 147 F.2d 480 (8th Cir. 1945); Niles v. Louis H. Rapoport & Sons, 53 Cal.App.2d 644, 128 P.2d 50 (1942) (Breach of contract); Sonbergh v. MacQuarrie, 112 Cal.App. 771, 247 P.2d 133 (1952). (Assault and battery); Caudill v. Arnett, 481 S.W.2d 668 (Ky.1972).

60. Walker v. Pacific Ind. Co., 183 Cal.App.2d 513, 6 Cal.Rptr. 924 (1960). (Inadequate insurance policy.)

61. White v. Schnoebelen, 91 N.H. 273, 18 A.2d 185 (1941). (Holding that the statute runs as of the time the damage is caused and not as of when a lightning rod was negligently installed); contra, Powers v. Planters Nat'l Bank & Trust Co., 219 N.C. 254, 13 S.E.2d 431 (1941); 19 N.C.L.Rev. 599.

62. Urie v. Thompson, 337 U.S. 163, 69 S.Ct. 1018, 93 L.Ed. 1282. (Occupational disease gradually developing and culminating in disability); Coots v. Southern Pac. Co., 49 Cal.2d 805, 322 P.2d 460 (1958). (Occupational exposure to silver cyanide resulted in dermatitis); Krug v. Sterling Drug, Inc., 416 S.W.2d 143 (Mo.1967).

63. Bell Corp. v. Bell View Oil Syndicate, 24 Cal.App. 748, 76 P.2d 166 (1938).

er than from the time of the resulting injurious consequences or from the plaintiff's knowledge of such consequences.[64]

Also, commencement of the running of the statute is sometimes delayed in cases of continuing or repeated wrongs where there is a possibility that no injury will result, or that defendant may abate or remove the harmful condition.[65] On the other hand, the statute begins running immediately in cases of anticipatory breach of contract.[66]

Some statutes provide that an action once begun, although dismissed, tolls the running of limitations.[67]

Generally speaking, a plaintiff may not postpone the running of the statute by delaying certain acts entirely within plaintiff's control. Thus, where a notice or claim is a condition precedent to a suit for personal injury against an insurance company or a municipal corpo-

---

64. Eistrat v. Cekada, 50 Cal.2d 289, 324 P.2d 881 (1958); Priola v. Paulino, 72 Cal.App.3d 380, 140 Cal.Rptr. 186 (1977).

65. United States v. Dickinson, 331 U.S. 745, 67 S.Ct. 1382, 91 L.Ed. 1789 (1947). (Government dam flooded plaintiff's land.)

See also Handler v. Remington Arms Co., Inc., 144 Conn. 316, 130 A.2d 793 (1957). (Action for permitting defective cartridge to be sold for future use—action accrues at time of accident and not purchase where failure); Vilcinskas v. Sears, Roebuck & Co., 144 Conn. 170, 127 A.2d 814 (1956). (Action for sale of air rifle to child—action accrues at time of wrongful sale).

Fla.—Seaboard Air Line R. Co. v. Ford, 92 So.2d 160 (Fla.1957). (FELA—action for occupational disease accrues at time employee should have known disease was occupational).

Md.—Gracie v. Koppers Co., Inc., 213 Md. 109, 130 A.2d 754 (1957). (W.C.—action for occupational disease accrues when it becomes reasonably apparent).

N.Y.—Wright v. Carter Products, Inc., 244 F.2d 53 (2nd Cir. 1957). (Injury from using deodorant—time runs from last exposure).

Pa.—Ciabattoni v. Birdsboro Steel Foundry & Mach. Co., 386 Pa. 179, 125 A.2d 365 (1956). (Occupational disease—accrual when medical diagnosis completed to knowledge of claimant).

Atlas Chemical Ind., Inc. v. Anderson, 524 S.W.2d 681 (Tex.1975).

Wis.—Delta Oil Co. v. Industrial Comm'n, 273 Wis. 285, 77 N.W.2d 749 (1956). (W.C.—occupational disease claim accrues with knowledge of disability resulting and not knowledge of disease).

66. See, however, Winegar v. Earle, 108 R.I. 464, 276 A.2d 468 (1971).

67. See Hughes v. Hebert, 106 N.H. 176, 207 A.2d 432 (1965).

Okl.—Morris v. Wise, 293 P.2d 547 (1955).

Tenn.—Turner v. Nashville, C. & St. L. Ry. Co., 199 Tenn. 137, 285 S.W.2d 122, 54 A.L.R. 1225 (1955). (Statute permitting bringing of new action after dismissal strictly construed to one).

See 54 A.L.R.2d 1229. (Construction of statutory provision permitting successive actions after nonsuit of judgment not on merits).

ration or political subdivision of the state, the plaintiff cannot postpone the running of the statute merely by failing to give notice or make the claim.[68]

In causes of action for fraud, mistake, breach of trust, undue influence and duress, the commencement of the statutory period is delayed until the plaintiff knows, or ought to have known, of the wrong.[69] For the same reasons, when defendant fraudulently conceals from plaintiff the cause of action, the statute does not begin to run.[70]

Closely related to fraudulent concealment is estoppel of defendant as preventing him from raising the bar of the statute of limitations, if plaintiff has relied on representations or conduct of defendant in forebearing to bring suit.[71] If defendant's representations are more in the nature of a promise or a contract with plaintiff not to sue, the doctrine of waiver is applied by the courts to remove the bar of the statute of limitations.[72]

State legislatures have almost uniformly suspended the running of the statute while defendant is outside the jurisdiction of the

---

68. Provident Life & Acc. Ins. Co. v. Heidelberg, 228 Ala. 682, 154 S. 809 (1934); Fuller v. St. Highway Comm'n, 140 Kan. 558, 38 P.2d 99 (1934).

See Beury Coal & Coke Co. v. Fayette County Court, 76 W.Va. 610, 87 S.E. 258 (1915). (Where the contract or statute provides that plaintiff's suit must be delayed after presentment of the claim until investigated, the courts usually allow plaintiff a reasonable time to make the claim before the statute begins to run).

69. Costello v. Atlas Corp., 297 F.Supp. 19 (D.C.Cal.1967); Akin v. Warner, 318 Mass. 669, 63 N.E.2d 566 (1945).

(1936) 20 Minn.L.Rev. 481; (1933) 31 Mich.L.Rev. 591.

70. Kimball v. Pacific Gas & Elec. Co., 220 Cal. 203, 30 P.2d 39 (1934); St. Clair v. Bardstown Transfer Line, Inc., 310 Ky. 776, 221 S.W.2d 679, 10 A.L.R.2d 560 (1949). (Where defendant motorist, after collision, failed to stop and give information and report to State Police, as required by statute, limitations tolled until plaintiff acquired knowledge as to identity of offender, but statute excuses plaintiff from making any effort to ascertain the necessary facts); Dotson v. Alamo Funeral Home, 577 S.W.2d 308 (Tex.Civ.App.1979).

Courts have applied the doctrine of constructive fraud or fraudulent concealment to malpractice cases, sometimes even where the doctor is not aware of his misconduct: see Morrison v. Acton, 68 Ariz. 27, 198 P.2d 590 (1948); Krestich v. Stefanez, 243 Wis. 1, 9 N.W.2d 130 (1943).

71. Exploration Co. v. United States, 247 U.S. 435, 38 S.Ct. 571, 62 L.Ed. 1200 (1918).

72. Kyle v. Green Acres at Verona, Inc., 44 N.J. 100, 207 A.2d 513 (1965); Noel v. Baskin, 131 F.2d 231 (D.C. 1942); Oliver v. Basle, 55 A.D.2d 975, 390 N.Y.S.2d 466 (1977).

forum.[73] Similarly, it has been held that the Soldier's and Sailor's Civil Relief Act of 1940 enables a civilian plaintiff to toll the statute of limitations while defendant is engaged in active military duty.[74] Successive absences of defendant may be aggregated,[75] and a secret return may be deemed insufficient to set the statute in motion.[76] But plaintiff's ignorance of an open, unconcealed return will not toll the running of the statute.[77] There is some difference of opinion as to whether mere absence for very brief periods will operate to suspend the statute, or whether a change of domicile or residence is required.[78] There is a split of authority whether the absence exception applies to defendants who reside outside the forum, and also where, in addition, the cause of action arose outside the forum.[79]

The absence exception is complicated, especially as to non-resident defendants, by legislation in many jurisdictions providing for substituted service, and attachment of property within the jurisdiction. Some jurisdictions rule that where substituted service is possible, defendant's absence will not suspend the limitation period.[80]

---

73. Absence from within territorial boundaries of the state is what is contemplated by statutory provision that if a person against whom there is a cause of action shall be without the limits of the state at the time of the accruing of the action, or at any time during which the action might have been sustained, the time of such person's absence shall not be taken as a part of the time limited by the provisions of the statute: see McNutt v. Cox, 133 Tex. 409, 129 S.W.2d 626, 122 A.L.R. 941 (1939). (However, the Texas statute tolling the limitation period where the defendant is "without the limits of this state" at the time of the accruing of the cause has been held inapplicable where the defendant is a nonresident at the time of such accrual; but the courts have held that if defendant is physically present in the state at the time of such accrual, or at the time an obligation arises, and thereafter departs from the state, the suspensory provision becomes effective so as to prevent the running of the statute during any subsequent absence, despite his status as a nonresident.)

74. Blazejowski v. Stadnicki, 317 Mass. 352, 58 N.E.2d 164 (1944).

Similarly the time spent by a plaintiff in military service is not to be included in a period during which the statute of limitations runs: see Perkins v. Manning, 59 Ariz. 60, 122 P.2d 857 (1942).

75. Wetzel v. Weyant, 41 Ohio St.2d 135, 323 N.E.2d 711 (1975); Schneider v. Schneider, 82 Cal.App.2d 860, 187 P.2d 459 (1947). (Honeymoon and business trips aggregated to 40 days.)

76. Stewart v. Stewart, 152 Cal. 162, 92 P. 87 (1907).

77. Id.
See Westhoven v. Snyder, 40 Ohio App.2d 91, 318 N.E.2d 167 (1973).

78. Connor v. Timothy, 43 Ariz. 517, 33 P.2d 293 (1934). (Where the absence of 5 days was deducted); cf. Nelson v. Sandkamp, 227 Minn. 177, 34 N.W.2d 640 (1948).

79. (1947) 25 Chi.Kent.L.Rev. 349.

80. Gulf Nat'l Bank v. King, 362 So.2d 1253 (Miss.1978).
See also Bolduc v. Richards, 101 N.H. 303, 142 A.2d 156 (1958); Jarchow v. Eder, 433 P.2d 942 (Okl.1967); Byrne

Ch. 3 HAVE I A CASE? § 3.39

Even though a plaintiff might be able to obtain a judgment against an absent defendant by virtue of these statutes, enforcement of the judgment may be difficult for the plaintiff. Thus other courts suspend the running of the statute for plaintiff even where full relief is available in quasi in rem proceedings, or by an in personam judgment by means of substituted service.

If there is no present controlling statute, the courts have generally refused to suspend the running of the statute after the death of a plaintiff or defendant and before the appointment of a personal representative as to causes of action which arose prior to plaintiff's or defendant's death.[81] Defendant's distributees might deliberately delay the appointment of a personal representative until time to sue has elapsed. However, where the cause of action arises after a defendant or a plaintiff has died, courts usually postpone the running of the statute for either until a personal representative is appointed.[82]

Where the plaintiff is insane,[83] an infant,[84] or imprisoned[85] as of the time his cause of action arises, the statute is suspended usually

v. Ogle, 488 P.2d 716, 55 A.L.R.3d 1151 (Alaska 1971); Friday v. Newman, 183 So.2d 25 (Fla.App.1966); Whittington v. Davis, 221 Or. 209, 350 P.2d 913 (1960); Cal-Farm Ins. Co. v. Oliver, 78 Nev. 479, 375 P.2d 857 (1962).

81. Wrinkle v. Trabert, 174 Ohio St. 233, 188 N.E.2d 587 (1963).

See also Chesnut v. McGinnis, 467 P.2d 500, 47 A.L.R.3d 175 (Okl.1970).

82. Gaudette v. Webb, 362 Mass. 60, 284 N.E.2d 222 (1972). See also Matthews v. Matthews, 177 So.2d 497, 28 A.L.R.3d 1128 (Fla.App.1965), cert. dismissed 189 So.2d 629.

Contra: Graybiel v. Burke, 124 Cal. App.2d 255, 268 P.2d 551 (1954); Valente v. Boggiano, 107 N.J.L. 456, 154 A. 817, 74 A.L.R. 834 (1931).

83. There is a split of authority as to what constitutes insanity for this purpose: see Bowman v. Lemon, 115 Ohio St. 326, 154 N.E. 317 (1926); Woodruff v. Shores, 354 Mo. 742, 190 S.W.2d 994 (1945); Weinstein v. Eissler, 224 Cal.App.2d 212, 36 Cal.Rptr. 537 (1964).

See also Kyle v. Green Acres at Verona, Inc., 44 N.J. 100, 207 A.2d 513 (1965). ("Insane" means mental condition preventing understanding of legal rights or institution of legal action); Browne v. Smith, 119 Colo. 469, 205 P.2d 239 (1949) (Mentally incompetent to handle own business affairs).

84. Vance v. Vance, 108 U.S. 514, 2 S. Ct. 854, 27 L.Ed. 808 (1883) (Tolling of statute on account of infancy based on statutory provisions, not common law). See also Gasparro v. Horner, 245 So.2d 901 (Fla.App.1971) (In absence of statutory provision, limitations statute not tolled by infancy of plaintiff, orphaned and without guardian or legal representation).

85. Black v. City Nat'l Bank & Trust Co., 321 S.W.2d 477 (Mo.1959), cert. denied 360 U.S. 920, 79 S.Ct. 1439, 3 L.Ed.2d 1536, reh. denied 361 U.S. 857, 80 S.Ct. 49, 4 L.Ed.2d 97 (Plaintiff's imprisonment does not toll statute of limitations, absent specific statutory provision).

Hileman v. Knable, 266 F.Supp. 317 (D. C.Pa.1967) (Plaintiff's imprisonment

for the duration of the infirmity by legislative provision, and not by common law. However, courts refuse to suspend the statute for such infirmities when the cause of action arises prior to the infirmity and after the statute has begun to run.[86] The existence of a guardian for an infant or an insane person may deprive the plaintiff of this exception.[87]

Absent a statutory definition of what constitutes initiation of suit by plaintiff, courts require at least a diligent attempt by plaintiff to serve the defendant in order to comply with the statute, and the filing of a complaint and issuance of summons.[88]

§ 3.40 Revival of Remedy

A cause of action is revived for a full new statutory period by an acknowledgment of the debt or action by defendant debtor or a new promise or part payment by him, made either before or after the statute has run.[89] This doctrine of revival does not apply to causes of action in tort, or ones created by statute, nor a contract obligation calling for performance other than payment of money.[90] The general test for revivability is whether the cause of action would have constituted an action in general assumpsit at common law. Many states require such new promises to be in writing if unsupported by legal consideration.[91]

did not toll statute of limitations in absence of Pennsylvania statutory provision).

86. Vann v. Rogers, 225 Ala. 186, 142 So. 539 (1932) (Imprisonment); Larsson v. Cedars of Lebanon Hosp., 97 Cal.App.2d 704, 218 P.2d 604 (1950) (Incompetence).

87. Johnson v. Pilot Life Ins. Co., 217 N.C. 139, 7 S.E.2d 475, 128 A.L.R. 1375 (1940); Spann v. First Nat'l Bank, 240 Ala. 539, 200 So. 554 (1941); In re Sheehan's Estate, 290 Ill.App. 551, 9 N.E.2d 63 (1937).

Contra: Callaway v. Perdue, 238 Ark. 652, 385 S.W.2d 4, 13 A.L.R.3d 1300 (1964) (Guardianship of minor does not bar tolling of statute); Aronson v. Bank of America, 42 Cal.App.2d 710, 109 P.2d 1001 (1941) (Statute does not run against minor when guardian appointed since cause of action held by minor, not guardian).

88. Mayo Clinic v. Kaiser, 383 F.2d 653 (8th Cir. 1967).

89. Shepherd v. Thompson, 122 U.S. 231, 7 S.Ct. 1229, 30 L.Ed. 1156 (1886); Buescher v. Lastar, 61 Cal. App.3d 73, 132 Cal.Rptr. 124 (1976); United States v. Calumet Steel Co., 74 F.2d 429 (7th Cir. 1934); Sterling v. Title Ins. & Trust Co., 53 Cal.App. 2d 736, 128 P.2d 31 (1942). (Acknowledgement or promise in writing takes cases out of statute of limitations).

90. Mutual Trust & Deposit Co. v. Boone, 267 S.W.2d 751 (Ky.1954); Yudin v. Carroll, 57 F.Supp. 793 (D.C.Ark.1944); Maier v. Independent Taxi Owner's Ass'n, 96 F.2d 579, 68 App.D.C. 307 (D.C.1938). But see language in Broussard v. Missouri Pac. R. R., 47 F.Supp. 750, 761 (D.C.La.1942).

91. There is a split of authority as to the revivability of specialties and money judgments: see (1950) 53 Harv.L.Rev. 1177, 1255; (1910) 19 Yale L.J. 221.

§ 3.41 Notice

In addition to the necessity of jurisdiction over defendant [92] and commencing the action within the time prescribed by the statute of limitations, it must always be kept in mind that the filing of notice of the accident or of a claim may be a pre-requisite to the right to bring suit.[93]

This is especially true if the defendant is a governmental body. As the governmental body most frequently sued is a municipal corporation, the following discussion will describe problems of notice and claims in actions against such bodies.[94] Similar statutes and problems will arise in actions against a state or a subdivision of the state.

Notice of an accident is not required in the absence of statute.[95] Usually, however, such a requirement is spelled out by a statute or by a provision in the municipal charter.[96] Such a statute or charter provision generally requires that the notice be given by the claimant, be written, be given to a specified officer of the municipality, and be given within a certain time after the cause of action accrues.[97] The notice must state with reasonable certainty the time, the place, the nature and general circumstances of the injury and contain a statement that the injured party will seek damages from the municipality. In addition to the above, some statutes require that the notice contain the amount of the claim, the residence of the claimant, and the names and addresses of the claimant's witnesses. The statute may also require that the notice be verified. Although there is a diversity of opinion on the matter, most courts hold that substantial compliance with the requirements specified is sufficient.[98]

---

92. See, Chapter 4, "Jurisdiction," infra.

93. Ghiozzi v. South San Francisco, 72 Cal.App.2d 472, 164 P.2d 902 (1946); Lamberti v. Stamford, 131 Conn. 396, 40 A.2d 190 (1944); Bernardine v. New York, 294 N.Y. 361, 62 N.E.2d 604 (1945).

94. See McQuillin, Municipal Corporations (3d ed. rev'd 1968) §§ 48.01 et seq., §§ 53.150 et seq.

95. Green v. Spencer, 67 Iowa 410, 25 N.W. 681 (1885).

96. Welch v. Chicago, 323 Ill. 498, 154 N.E. 226 (1926); Ajamian v. Watertown, 317 Mass. 242, 57 N.E.2d 642 (1944); Munroe v. Booth, 305 N.Y. 426, 113 N.E.2d 546 (1953) (Action against school district—notice must be served on designated officials).

97. McQuillin, Municipal Corporations (3d ed. rev'd 1968).

98. Stewart v. Rio Vista, 72 Cal.App. 2d 279, 164 P.2d 274 (1945); Medeiros v. Somerset, 306 Mass. 557, 29 N.E.2d 21 (1940); Schwartz v. New York, 250 N.Y. 332, 165 N.E. 517 (1929).

But note: Miami Springs, Town of v. Lasseter, 60 So.2d 774 (Fla.1952) (Requirement of written notice to town attorney not satisfied by claimant's relating account of accident to town's liability adjuster who wrote it down); Peters v. City and County of San

§ 3.41 INTRODUCTION Pt. 1

The purpose of these statutes, which are uniformly upheld,[99] is to avoid unnecessary litigation [1] by giving the municipality a chance to investigate the claim, determine its merits and possibly settle it. Such being the purpose of these statutes it has been held that if the injured party or his agent removes the alleged defective condition before notice has been given, any notice subsequently given is ineffectual, as no opportunity to investigate was provided.[2] Variance between the contents of the notice filed and subsequent allegations and proof may become significant.[3]

When notice is required by statute the requirement is regarded as mandatory [4] and a condition precedent to any suit. Once proper notice has been given, the injured party's complaint may be filed anytime before the running out of the applicable statute of limitation.[5]

Notice may not be required for every tort action against a municipal body. It may only be required for personal injury actions and not for actions for damage to property.[6] It may only be required where the injury has been caused by some specific type of negligence

Francisco, 41 Cal.2d 419, 260 P.2d 55 (1953) (Action not defeated by failure to file with municipal board of supervisors where claim was filed with city comptroller and carbon copy with clerk of board of supervisors and city attorney received both copies within the statutory time); George v. School Dist. No. 24, 157 Neb. 791, 61 N.W.2d 401 (1953) (Although statute did not specify with whom the claim was to be filed, allowance for school pupils' transportation denied where written claim was not filed with proper school district board); Ringgold v. New York City Transit Auth., 286 App.Div. 806, 141 N.Y.S.2d 365 (1955) (Mailing notice of injury on bus to city comptroller instead of Transit Authority as required by statute fatal).

99. Jackson v. Santa Monica, 13 Cal. App. 376, 57 P.2d 226 (1936); Hampton v. Duluth, 140 Minn. 303, 168 N.W. 20 (1918); O'Neil v. Richmond, 141 Va. 168, 126 S.E. 56 (1925).

1. Marino v. East Haven, 120 Conn. 577, 182 A. 225, 103 A.L.R. 295 (1935); Lutsch v. Chicago, 318 Ill. App. 156, 47 N.E.2d 545 (1943); Weisman v. New York, 219 N.Y. 178, 114 N.E. 70 (1916).

2. Wornecka v. St. Paul, 118 Minn. 207, 136 N.W. 561 (1912).

3. Cloutier v. City of Owosso, 343 Mich. 238, 72 N.W.2d 46 (1955). (Notice sufficient where no substantial variance from more detailed complaint); Rottschafer v. City of East Grand Rapids, 342 Mich. 43, 69 N.W.2d 193 (1955). (Variance fatal where notice read "I stubbed my toe on a very bad break in the sidewalk" and complaint alleged a gap between slabs, one raised above the other, while at trial plaintiff claimed heel trapped.)

4. Shea v. San Bernardino, 7 Cal.2d 688, 62 P.2d 365 (1936); Wood v. Oxford, 290 Mass. 388, 195 N.E. 321 (1935); Sykes v. Battle Creek, 288 Mich. 660, 286 N.W. 117 (1939).

5. Galloway v. Winchester, 299 Ky. 87, 184 S.W.2d 890 (1944).

6. San Antonio v. Pfeiffer, 216 S.W. 207 (Tex.Civ.App.1919).

on the part of the municipality, as where the injury was caused by a defective sidewalk.[7] Some courts say the requirement of notice only applies where the municipality was acting in its governmental capacity at the time of the injury.[8] The fact that the injured party is a servant of the municipality [9] or is now dead [10] may dispense with the notice requirement. Mere ignorance of the requirement [11] of notice by the municipality from another source will not operate as an excuse.[12]

There is a strong difference of opinion as to whether or not notice may be waived by the municipality or one of its officers.[13] Whether or not there was in fact a waiver depends, of course, on the circumstances of the individual case.[14] All that is really clear is that any attempt by the city to waive notice will be ineffectual after the time for filing notice has elapsed.[15]

The fact that the claimant was disabled from giving notice may operate to toll the notice requirement until the disability ceases.[16] Most, but not all, courts hold that in the absence of express statutory provision, the fact that claimant is an infant will not excuse him.[17]

7. Campbell v. Helena, 92 Mont. 366, 16 P.2d 1 (1932).

8. Borski v. Wakefield, 239 Mich. 656, 215 N.W. 19 (1927).

9. Quackenbush v. Slayton, 120 Minn. 373, 139 N.W. 716 (1913).

10. Prouty v. Chicago, 250 Ill. 222, 95 N.E. 147 (1911); McKeigue v. Janesville, 68 Wis. 50, 31 N.W. 298 (1889).

11. Derlicka v. Leo, 259 App.Div. 607, 19 N.Y.S.2d 949 (1940), rearg. denied 259 A.D. 1001, 20 N.Y.S.2d 985, aff'd 284 N.Y. 711, 31 N.E.2d 47.

12. Nicholaus v. Bridgeport, 117 Conn. 398, 167 A. 826 (1933); Ballinger v. Harlan, 294 Ky. 72, 170 S.W.2d 912 (1943).

But see Viles v. California, 66 Cal.2d 24, 56 Cal.Rptr. 666, 423 P.2d 818 (1967). (Plaintiff relied on insurance adjuster's advice that he had one year to file suit. Held, "honest mistake", where public entity not prejudiced, merits relief.)

13. The following cases state that waiver will be allowed by the municipality: Mount Dora v. Green, 117 Fla. 385, 158 So. 131 (1934); Waco v. Thralls, 128 S.W.2d 462 (Tex.Civ.App.1939), error dism'd (Held agent of limited authority cannot waive); contra, Huntington v. Calais, 105 Me. 144, 73 A. 829 (1909); Blumrich v. Highland Park, 131 Mich. 209, 91 N.W. 129 (1902).

14. Winter v. Niagara Falls, 190 N.Y. 198, 82 N.E. 1101 (1907).

15. Brownsville v. Galvan, 139 Tex. 128, 162 S.W.2d 98 (1942).

16. Randolph v. Springfield, 302 Mo. 33, 257 S.W. 449 (1923); Murphy v. Fort Edward, 213 N.Y. 397, 107 N.E. 716 (1915); contra, Sherfey v. Brazil, 213 Ind. 493, 13 N.E.2d 568 (1938); Hall v. Spokane, 79 Wash. 303, 140 P. 348 (1914).

17. Davidson v. Muskegon, 111 Mich. 454, 69 N.W. 670 (1897); Szroka v. Northwestern Bell Tel. Co., 171 Minn. 57, 213 N.W. 557 (1927); contra,

§ 3.41 INTRODUCTION Pt. 1

Claimant may usually amend the notice he has given,[18] unless the time for giving notice has lapsed.[19]

Claimant must plead and prove notice.[20] In addition, he has the burden of showing any excuse for his failure to give proper notice.[21]

In a suit against the United States under the Federal Tort Claims Act, 28 CFR, § 14.2 provides for the written notification of an incident, "accompanied by a claim for money damages in a sum certain for injury to or loss of property, personal injury, or death alleged to have occurred by reason of the incident." Failure to present a timely and complete claim will result in the barring of plaintiff's action.

Notice may occasionally be required in suits other than those against governmental bodies. Suits against airline companies furnish an excellent example of this.[22] Most air carrier cargo contracts provide that the shipment is subject to tariff provisions that have been filed with the Civil Aeronautics Board in Washington. These provisions usually provide that the airline company will not be liable for any property injury or loss claim unless notice of claim is sent to the main office of the airline within 30, 60, or 90 days after the loss. These provisions have been upheld by the courts.[23]

Notice may also be required to recover insurance for injury.[24] Likewise, notice is a condition precedent to recovery under many Worker's Compensation acts.[25]

McDonald v. Spring Val., 285 Ill. 52, 120 N.E. 476, 2 A.L.R. 1359 (1818); Murphy v. Fort Edward, 213 N.Y. 397, 107 N.E. 716 (1915).

18. Brown v. Winthrop, 275 Mass. 43, 175 N.E. 50 (1931).

19. Berry v. Helena, 56 Mont. 122, 182 P. 117 (1919).

20. Indianapolis v. Evans, 216 Ind. 555, 24 N.E.2d 776 (1940); Winter v. Niagara Falls, 190 N.Y. 198, 82 N.E. 1101 (1907).

21. Townsend v. Boston, 232 Mass. 451, 122 N.E. 395 (1919).

22. See, infra, Chapter 40, Aircraft Accident Litigation.

23. Life Sciences, Inc. v. Emery Air Freight Corp., 341 So.2d 272 (Fla. App.1977). See also Butler's Shoe Corp. v. Pan Am. World Airways, Inc., 514 F.2d 1283 (5th Cir. 1975). (120-day limitation period for filing claim for lost goods not in conflict with provisions of Warsaw Convention nullifying provisions relieving carriers of liability.)

24. Generally such notification is not regarded as a condition precedent to liability in the absence of express stipulation; see Home Indem. Co. v. Banfield Bros. Packing Co., 188 Ark. 683, 67 S.W.2d 203 (1934).

25. See Arkansas Workmen's Compensation Act, § 17. (Arkansas Stats. 81–1317), Voris v. Eikel, 346 U.S. 328, 74 S.Ct. 88, 98 L.Ed. 5 (1953). (Where stevedore was burnt by flash-fire, known to foreman in charge, provisions of 33 U.S.C.A. § 901 et seq., satisfied as to notice to employer, even though no actual knowledge shown.)

§ 3.42 Claims Against Municipalities

The first requirement of any claim against a municipality is that the claim be valid. If the claim is based on a contract, the contract must be one which the municipality had power to make.[26] If there is another basis for the claim, e.g., a statute, such must be shown.[27]

Although presentation of a claim within a certain time was not required at common law,[28] most municipalities today demand such presentment by statute or charter. Such statutes and charter provisions are universally upheld,[29] and generally regarded as mandatory [30] and as a condition precedent to any suit.[31] The purpose of these claims statutes is the same as the purpose of the notice statutes described above.[32] Note that there may be a general state statute applicable to a particular claim. If there is, it is the statute that has to be met, even if it is in conflict with a municipal ordinance or charter.

What is a claim or demand within the usual statute? Speaking generally, any cause of action against a municipality other than one for unliquidated damages, as a tort action, may so qualify.[33] A more precise definition is impractical here; reference must be made to local applicable law.

The requirements of the usual claims statute are very similar to the requirements of the usual notice statute. The claim must be filed in writing by the one to whom the cause of action has accrued, must be presented to a certain officer, within a certain time after the accrual of the cause of action and in the manner prescribed by law.[34] In addition, claims for certain things, as for labor and services, must

---

26. See McQuillin, Municipal Corporations, ch. 29 (3d ed. rev'd 1968) as to the power of municipal corporation to contract.

27. Statutes may authorize the payment of claims that do not constitute legal obligations: see Evans v. Berry, 262 N.Y. 61, 186 N.E. 203 (1933). (Accidental shooting by policeman).

28. Crumly v. Birmingham, 244 Ala. 634, 15 So.2d 273, 275 (1943).

29. Geimann v. Board of Police Comm'r, 158 Cal. 748, 112 P. 553 (1910); Winter v. Niagara Falls, 190 N.Y. 198, 82 N.E. 1101 (1907).

30. Solastic Products Co. v. Seattle, 144 Wash. 691, 258 P. 830 (1927) (Water from sluicing damaged plaintiff's property).

31. First Trust & Sav. Bank v. Pasadena, 21 Cal.2d 220, 130 P.2d 702 (1942) (Action for over-assessment); Bernardine v. New York, 294 N.Y. 361, 62 N.E.2d 604 (1945) (Run down by police horse).

32. Eastlick v. Los Angeles, 29 Cal.2d 661, 177 P.2d 558 (1947) (Defective sidewalk).

33. Harrigan v. Brooklyn, 119 N.Y. 156, 23 N.E. 741 (1890).

34. McQuillin, Municipal Corporations, §§ 48.02–48.08 (3d ed. rev'd 1968).

be itemized, show the municipality is the debtor and show to whom the debt is due.[35]

Claims must generally be verified [36] and may be amended.[37] Substantial compliance with the requirements above is usually deemed adequate.[38] In the absence of a specific statute or an express agreement municipalities are not chargeable with interests on claims made against them.[39]

Claims can only be allowed by the person designated by law and in the manner and for the amount and purposes prescribed by law.[40] Usually the action of the proper legal authorities in auditing accounts and demands are regarded as conclusive in the absence of a showing of fraud.[41] However, the rejection of a claim does not automatically cut off the claimant's cause of action; claimant may still appeal to the proper body or court.[42]

Usually the municipality has power to compromise and arbitrate claims.[43]

For additional discussion of claims and actions against municipalities, see Chapter 27, infra.

35. See McQuillin, Municipal Corporations, § 48.07 (3d ed. rev'd 1968).

36. Oda v. El Grove Union Grammar Sch. Dist., 61 Cal.App.2d 551, 143 P. 2d 490 (1943) (Negligent bus driver); Ponsrok v. Yonkers, 254 N.Y. 91, 171 N.E. 917 (1930) (Sewer case).

37. Carroll v. New York, 189 Misc. 50, 69 N.Y.S.2d 610 (1947).

38. Stewart v. Rio Vista, 72 Cal.App. 2d 279, 164 P.2d 274 (1945) (Open ditch case—complaint verified by plaintiff's attorney); Missano v. New York, 160 N.Y. 123, 54 N.E. 744 (1899) (Child run over and killed by street cleaner's horse).

39. McNutt v. Los Angeles, 187 Cal. 245, 201 P. 592 (1921) (City lowered grade without sufficient notice); Morgan v. Rockford, 375 Ill. 326, 31 N.E.2d 596 (1940) (Minimum wages for police, but no interest).

40. People ex rel. Spence v. Louisville & N. R. Co., 350 Ill. 274, 183 N.E. 233 (1932) (Tax sale judgment reversed); Kelley v. Flint, 251 Mich. 691, 232 N. W. 407 (1930) (Suit on assigned claims).

41. Weston v. Syracuse, 158 N.Y. 274, 53 N.E. 12, 43 L.R.A. 678 (1899) (City council resolution to modify contract held voidable).

42. Maki v. Lommen, 188 Minn. 78, 246 N.W. 531 (1933) (One notice for three claims held sufficient).

43. McQuillin, Municipal Corporations, §§ 48.17–48.22 (3d ed. rev'd 1968).

§§ 3.43–4.0 are reserved for supplementary material.

CHAPTER 4

JURISDICTION AND VENUE

Table of Sections

Sec.
4.1 In General.
4.2 Subject Matter Jurisdiction.
4.3 Jurisdiction Over Persons and Things.
4.4 Notice Requirement.
4.5 Venue.
4.6 Jurisdiction and Venue in Federal Courts.

Library References:

C.J.S. Courts §§ 1, 15, 28; Venue §§ 1–4; 75.
West's Key No. Digests, Courts ⇨1 et seq.; Venue ⇨1 et seq.
Blashfield, Automobile Law & Practice, § 450.1 et seq., § 451.1 et seq.

§ 4.1 In General

Prior to filing suit in a particular court, the lawyer must determine whether that court has jurisdiction over both this *type* of case and the *parties* involved. Jurisdiction is the power of a court to hear and determine a pending action,[1] and to issue a judgment which will be binding both in the forum state and in all sister states, as well.[2]

In order for a court to render such decree, it must have: (1) the power to hear this particular type of case (i. e., subject matter jurisdiction); (2) the defendant or his property must be amenable to the power of the court (i. e., in personam, in rem, or quasi in rem jurisdiction); and (3) the requirement of due process must be fulfilled (i. e., adequate notice and opportunity to be heard).

§ 4.2 Subject Matter Jurisdiction

Subject matter jurisdiction deals with the nature of the cases any court can hear. It is peculiar to every state. Legislatures statutorily create or restrict jurisdiction. Jurisdiction is of two types, limited or general.[3]

---

1. Harrington v. Superior Court, 194 Cal. 185, 188, 228 P. 15, 16 (1924).

2. Berry v. Chitwood, 362 S.W.2d 515, 517 (Mo.1962).

3. Austin v. Director, Patuxent Inst., 245 Md. 206, 225 A.2d 466 (1967); Daniels v. Jordan, 161 Miss. 78, 134 So. 903 (1931). Examples of limited jurisdiction are federal courts, probate courts, and family courts.

§ 4.2 INTRODUCTION

Subject matter jurisdiction is so fundamental to the court's power to hear a case that it may *not* be conferred by the consent of the parties.[4] Neither may it be waived, nor may a party be estopped to object to the court's lack of subject matter jurisdiction.[5] Because of its importance, lack of subject matter may be raised *at any stage of any proceeding*.[6]

The diversity of court systems among the several states is too great to be adequately covered in this study. Suffice it to say that the attorney should be aware of which court has the power to hear a case of this nature and amount. Without proper subject matter jurisdiction, the court is precluded from rendering an effective judgment.[7]

§ 4.3 Jurisdiction Over Persons and Things

Once the court having proper subject matter jurisdiction has been found, the next inquiry delves into the court's jurisdictional power over the defendant or some property. Jurisdiction here may be one of three kinds: (1) in personam, (2) in rem, and (3) quasi in rem. Which kind depends on what relief is sought.

For the court to issue a decree binding the defendant *personally*, it must have in personam jurisdiction. If title to property is to be adjudicated, then the action will be either in rem or quasi in rem.

A. In Personam Jurisdiction

In personam jurisdiction gives the court the power to issue a decree personally binding a person to pay a monetary obligation, to do some act, or to refrain from doing an act.[8] A person is not bound by such a decree unless the rendering court had jurisdiction over his person.

---

4. Rauch v. Day & Night Mfg. Corp., 576 F.2d 697, 699–700 (6th Cir. 1978). See also City of Kenosha v. Bruno, 412 U.S. 507, 511, 93 S.Ct. 2222, 2225, 2226, 37 L.Ed.2d 109, 115 (1973); Silver Star Citizens' Committee v. City Council of Orlando, 194 So.2d 681, 682 (Fla.App.1967). Berry v. Chitwood, 362 S.W.2d 515, 517 (Mo.1962) ("It *is* a sound and uniform rule that the parties cannot create jurisdiction of a court over the subject matter by agreement where it otherwise does not exist").

5. Nelson v. Iowa-Illinois Gas & Elec. Co., 259 Iowa 101, 143 N.W.2d 289 (1969).

6. Consolidated Theatres, Inc. v. Theatrical Stage Employees Union, Local 16, 69 Cal.2d 713, 721, 73 Cal.Rptr. 213, 219, 447 P.2d 325, 331 (1968); Piper v. Olinde Hardware & Supply Co., Inc., 288 So.2d 626 (La.App. 1974).

7. Ex parte Cavitt, 47 Cal.App.2d 698, 118 P.2d 846 (1941).

8. Hanson v. Denckla, 357 U.S. 235, 78 S.Ct. 1228, 2 L.Ed.2d 1283 (1958), reh. denied 358 U.S. 858, 79 S.Ct. 10, 3 L. Ed.2d 92; International Shoe Co. v. Washington, 326 U.S. 310, 66 S.Ct. 154, 90 L.Ed. 95 (1945); Milliken v. Meyer, 311 U.S. 457, 61 S.Ct. 339, 85 L.Ed.

(i) Traditional Bases

At common law, three bases existed for exercising jurisdiction over a person: presence, domicile, and consent.[9] Personal service while present within the territorial boundaries of a state is the classic method of acquiring in personam jurisdiction.[10] This has been true historically irrespective of the *temporary* nature of the presence of the party served,[11] and has been upheld even under the most tenuous and extreme circumstances.[12]

Domicile was also considered to be a sufficient basis at common law for exercising jurisdiction.[13] This was due to the nature of the relationship domicile created between the domiciliary and the state. Since the state accorded its domiciliaries the privileges and protections of its laws, it also had the right to exact reciprocal duties from them. This authority of a state over one of its domiciliaries did not terminate by the fact the citizen was temporarily absent therefrom.[14]

The third basis recognized at common law for conferring jurisdiction was consent. Unlike subject matter jurisdiction, personal jurisdiction may be conferred on the court by consent or may be waived by the parties.[15] The two most common means of manifesting consent to the jurisdiction of a court are through a voluntary personal appearance or by contract.

A party consents to a court's jurisdiction when he makes a voluntary appearance in the action, without first having raised the issue

---

278 (1940), reh. denied 312 U.S. 712, 61 S.Ct. 548, 85 L.Ed. 1143, conformed to 107 Colo. 295, 111 P.2d 232.

9. Jonnet v. Dollar Sav. Bank of City of New York, 530 F.2d 1123, 1132 (3d Cir. 1976) (Gibbons, J., concurring).

10. Harris v. Balk, 198 U.S. 215, 25 S. Ct. 625, 49 L.Ed. 1023 (1905).

11. James H. Rhodes & Co. v. Chausovsky, 137 N.J.L. 459, 60 A.2d 623, 625 (1948).

12. In Grace v. MacArthur, 170 F. Supp. 442 (E.D.Ark.1959), the defendant was served in Arkansas while en route in an airplane on a non-stop flight from Tennessee to Texas. In personam jurisdiction based on this personal service while physically present within Arkansas was upheld. However, the recent decision of Shaffer v. Heitner, 433 U.S. 186, 97 S.Ct. 2569, 53 L.Ed.2d 683 (1977), may now require something more than mere fortuitous presence in order to subject a nonresident defendant who is temporarily in the forum state to that State's jurisdiction, at least insofar as his presence is unrelated to the cause of action.

13. Milliken v. Meyer, 311 U.S. 457, 463, 61 S.Ct. 339, 342, 343, 85 L.Ed. 278, 283 (1940), reh. denied 312 U.S. 712, 61 S.Ct. 548, 85 L.Ed. 1143, conformed to 107 Colo. 295, 111 P.2d 232.

14. Id.

15. Bania v. Royal Lahaina Hotel, 37 Ill.App.3d 661, 347 N.E.2d 106 (1976); Gland-O-Lac Co. v. Franklin County Circuit Court, 230 Ark. 919, 327 S. W.2d 558, 561 (1959).

of the court's lack of personal jurisdiction.[16] Thus, by filing an answer or a demurrer without making any reference to the lack of the court's jurisdiction over him, the defendant is deemed to have consented to the court's jurisdiction over him.

The other method by which a party may consent to the jurisdiction of a court is by contract.[17] Historically, forum selection clauses have not been favored by the courts, and courts often refused to enforce them on the grounds they were contrary to public policy, or that their effect was to oust the jurisdiction of the court.[18]

Modernly, in light of the greatly increased commerce among states and between nations, the courts generally uphold these clauses which operate to confer on a court jurisdiction it otherwise would not have had. In order for this type of provision to be valid, it must be freely negotiated, and unaffected by fraud, undue influence, or unequal bargaining power.[19]

The one universal limitation on clauses governing jurisdiction is that such agreements must not purport to exclude *completely* adjudication by the courts. In the case of such a clause, courts will refuse to enforce it on the basis it is violative of public policy.[20]

(ii) Development of Minimum Contacts

At earlier common law, it was uniformly held that the power of a state to exercise its jurisdiction was limited by its territorial boundaries. Any attempt to exercise extraterritorial jurisdiction was decried as a mere abuse of power.[21] This explains why in personam jurisdiction was initially predicated on presence and domicile.

The development of corporations posed serious jurisdictional problems for the common law courts. Unlike persons, it was hard to hold a corporation was "physically present" anywhere. Still, courts

---

16. Rauch v. Day & Night Mfg. Corp., 576 F.2d 697, 700 (6th Cir. 1978).

17. National Equipment Rental, Ltd. v. Szukhent, 375 U.S. 311, 84 S.Ct. 411, 11 L.Ed.2d 354 (1964); Comprehensive Merchandising Catalogs, Inc. v. Madison Sales Corp., 521 F.2d 1210, 1212 (7th Cir. 1975). See also D. H. Overmyer Co., Inc., of Ohio v. Frick Co., 405 U.S. 174, 185, 92 S.Ct. 775, 782, 31 L.Ed. 124, 134 (1972).

18. M/S Bremen v. Zapata Off-Shore Co., 407 U.S. 1, 9, 92 S.Ct. 1907, 1912–1913, 32 L.Ed.2d 513, 520 (1972).

19. Id. at 12, 92 S.Ct. at 1914, 32 L.Ed.2d at 522.

20. Carbon Black Export, Inc. v. The S. S. Monrosa, 254 F.2d 297, 300–01 (5th Cir. 1958), cert. dismissed 359 U.S. 180, 79 S.Ct. 710, 3 L.Ed.2d 723, reh. denied 359 U.S. 999, 79 S.Ct. 1115, 3 L.Ed.2d 986.

21. Pennoyer v. Neff, 95 U.S. 714, 720, 24 L.Ed. 565, 568 (1878).

would do so, rationalizing that where the quantum of business it was doing was substantial, the corporation would be deemed to be present within the forum state.[22]

Another theory propounded by the courts to denude corporations of the protective cloak which shielded them was the theory of implied consent. Under this "legal fiction", a corporation doing business within a state was presumed to have impliedly consented to the jurisdiction of that state for any suits arising from its activities therein.[23] The same approach was later applied to out-of-state motorists who caused an accident while using the forum state's highways.[24]

Such legal fictions were perpetuated by the courts until *International Shoe v. Washington* [25] was decided in 1945. International Shoe was incorporated in Delaware and had its principal place of business in Missouri. International Shoe argued that there was not sufficient business activity on their part to make them "present" in Washington. After all, they argued, they had no office or warehouses in Washington, nor did they enter into any contracts for the sales or purchase of merchandise there.

The court answered these contentions by stating that if a person is not present within the forum, due process requires only that "he have certain minimum contacts with it such that the maintenance of the suit does not offend 'traditional notions of fair play and substantial justice'." [26] The court moved away from the *quantity* of the contacts, focusing its attention instead upon the *quality* and *nature* of the activities in relation to the state and the cause of action,[27] which were substantial.[28]

During its *systematic and continuous* activities in Washington, International Shoe had enjoyed the benefits and protection of that state's laws. As such, it was obligated to respond to a suit arising out of its activities in Washington. Making International Shoe ame-

22. Philadelphia & Reading R. Co. v. McKibbin, 243 U.S. 264, 37 S.Ct. 280, 61 L.Ed. 710 (1917); International Harvester Co. v. Kentucky, 234 U.S. 579, 34 S.Ct. 944, 58 L.Ed. 1479 (1914).

23. St. Clair v. Cox, 106 U.S. 350, 356, 1 S.Ct. 354, 27 L.Ed. 222, 225 (1882).

24. Hess v. Pawloski, 274 U.S. 352, 356–57, 47 S.Ct. 632, 633–634, 71 L.Ed. 1091, 1095 (1927).

25. 326 U.S. 310, 66 S.Ct. 154, 90 L.Ed. 95 (1945).

26. Id. at 316, 66 S.Ct. at 158, 90 L.Ed. at 102; see also Milliken v. Meyer, 311 U.S. 457, 463, 61 S.Ct. 339, 342–343, 85 L.Ed. 278, 283 (1940), reh. denied 312 U.S. 712, 61 S.Ct. 548, 85 L.Ed. 1143 (1941), conformed to 107 Colo. 295, 111 P.2d 232.

27. 326 U.S. at 319, 66 S.Ct. at 159, 160, 90 L.Ed. at 104.

28. Id. at 313–14, 66 S.Ct. at 156, 157, 90 L.Ed. at 100.

nable to suit under such circumstances could hardly be considered a violation of due process.[29]

The application of the "minimum contacts" doctrine with differing results is demonstrated in a comparison of two of the leading cases in this area which were decided within six months of each other. These two cases are *McGee v. International Life Ins. Co.*,[30] and *Hanson v. Denckla.*[31] Both of these cases deserve much more attention than can fairly be devoted to them herein. The determinative factor in the opposing results was that in the *McGee* case, the court found that defendant had *actively solicited* in California, purposefully availing itself of the privilege of conducting business there. In *Hanson*, it was the conduct of the testator, *not the defendant*, which resulted in Florida having any connection with the transaction, which, it was held, was insufficient for conferring jurisdiction on the Florida court.[32]

Before a state may constitutionally exercise jurisdiction over a nonresident based upon the minimum contacts doctrine, it is a prerequuisite that the state have enacted an appropriate "long-arm" statute. Two basic types of the long-arm statute exist; one is restrictive, the other permissive.

The first type allows a state to exercise jurisdiction over a nonresident person or a corporation only in *specific instances* which are enumerated in the statute. The most typical of these instances are: the transaction of any business within the state;[33] the making of a

29. Id. at 319, 66 S.Ct. at 159, 160, 90 L.Ed. at 104.

30. 355 U.S. 220, 78 S.Ct. 199, 2 L.Ed. 2d 223 (1957). Accord: Ross v. American Income Life Ins. Co., 232 S.C. 433, 102 S.E.2d 743 (1958).

31. 357 U.S. 235, 78 S.Ct. 1228, 2 L. Ed.2d 1283 (1958), reh. denied 358 U. S. 858, 79 S.Ct. 10, 3 L.Ed.2d 92, conformed to 106 So.2d 549 (Fla.).

32. See also Carey v. National Oil Corp., 592 F.2d 673, 676 (2d Cir. 1979) (Court finding no purposeful availment by defendant, hence no jurisdiction); English v. 21st Phoenix Corp., 590 F.2d 723, 728 n. 6 (8th Cir. 1979), cert. denied 444 U.S. 832, 100 S.Ct. 61, 62 L.Ed.2d 41; Telco Leasing, Inc. v. Marshall County Hosp., 586 F.2d 49, 50 (7th Cir. 1978); Charia v. Cigarette Racing Team, Inc., 583 F.2d 184, 186 (5th Cir. 1978) (Requiring some interconnection between the defendant and the state); Swafford v. Avakian, 581 F.2d 1224, 1228 (5th Cir. 1978), cert. denied 440 U.S. 959, 99 S.Ct. 1500, 59 L.Ed.2d 772. ("The act of sending love letters and making phone calls cannot be said to connote an interest to obtain nor expectancy of receiving a corresponding benefit from Georgia that would make fair the assertion of that state's jurisdiction over appellee"); American & Foreign Ins. Ass'n v. Commercial Ins. Co., 575 F.2d 980, 982 (1st Cir. 1978).

33. Merrill Lynch, Pierce, Fenner & Smith, Inc. v. Alexio, 397 F.Supp. 1292 (S.D.N.Y.1975); Shaw v. Aurora Mobile Homes & Real Estate, Inc., 36 Colo.App. 321, 539 P.2d 1366 (1975).

contract to be performed within the state;[34] the commission of a tortious act within the state;[35] and the ownership, use or possession of any real property situated within the state.[36]

This type of long-arm statute is to be construed literally and strictly.[37] If the defendant's actions do not come within the enumerated terms, the state may not exercise jurisdiction over him.[38] Also, it is important to note that these statutes are generally *not* given retroactive application.[39] Thus, unless the statute covered defendant's act *at the time such act occurred,* subsequent amendment thereof will not serve to give the court power over the nonresident defendant.

The second type of long-arm statute is all-inclusive. It permits a court to exercise judicial jurisdiction over nonresident defendants to the fullest extent possible under both the Federal Constitution and its State Constitution.[40] The minimum contact necessary to establish

34. First Nat'l Bank of Kansas City v. Ward, 380 F.Supp. 782 (N.D.Mo.1974); Drilling Engineering, Inc. v. Independent Indonesian American Petroleum Co., 283 So.2d 687 (La.1973). *Compare with* Bank of Wessington v. Winters Government Securities Corp., 361 So.2d 757 (Fla.App.1978). The Florida court held it had *no* jurisdiction where the only contact with that state was a phone call and an alleged oral contract as a result thereof. No performance was required by the nonresident defendant to be done in the forum state.

35. Memorial Lawn Cemeteries Ass'n, Inc. v. Carr, 540 P.2d 1156 (Okl.1975); Stepnowski v. Avery, 235 Pa.Super. 492, 340 A.2d 465, 467 n. 2 (1975). See also Bradley v. Cheleuitte, 65 F.R.D. 57 (D.C.Mass.1974) (Negligent release of plaintiff from hospital in Puerto Rico was not considered an act or omission within Massachusetts, state of plaintiff's residence, and wherein suit was filed); Glover v. Wagner, 462 F.Supp. 308 (D.C.Neb. 1978) (Decedent, Nebraska resident, was negligently administered to in Iowa hospital. Held, Nebraska did not have jurisdiction over Iowa hospital and employees.).

36. First Nat'l Bank of Kansas City v. Ward, 380 F.Supp. 782 (W.D.Mo. 1974); Dwyer v. District Court, 188 Colo. 41, 532 P.2d 725 (1975). However, since Shaffer v. Heitner, 433 U.S. 186, 97 S.Ct. 2569, 53 L.Ed.2d 683 (1977), this basis has been severely restricted.

37. Bank of Wessington v. Winters Gov't Securities Corp., 361 So.2d 757 (Fla.App.1978).

38. Spencer Boat Co., Inc. v. Lieutermoza, 498 F.2d 332 333, (5th Cir. 1974), reh. denied 503 F.2d 568; McDaniel v. Joseph, 409 F.Supp. 1003 (W.D.Pa.1976) (No jurisdiction over nonresident defendant who had been engaging in meretricious relationship with Pennsylvania resident's husband in state other than Pennsylvania.

Compare with: Flying Saucers, Inc. v. Moody, 421 F.2d 884, 887 (5th Cir. 1970), cert. denied 398 U.S. 904, 90 S.Ct. 1692, 26 L.Ed.2d 62 (Earlier case construing same statute broadly).

39. International Graphics, Inc. v. MTA–Travel Ways, Inc., 71 F.R.D. 598, 601 (S.D.Fla.1976).

40. Great Western United Corp. v. Kidwell, 577 F.2d 1256, 1266 (5th Cir. 1978), probable juris noted 439 U.S. 1065, 99 S.Ct. 829, 59 L.Ed.2d 30, rev'd 443 U.S. 173, 99 S.Ct. 2710, 61

jurisdiction may consist of a single act within the state, considered in light of all the surrounding circumstances.[41] So long as it is not repugnant to the due process clause, a state following this approach may exercise its jurisdictional power in any instance.[42]

The determination of reasonableness and the test of minimum contacts do not lend themselves to mechanical application. The United States Supreme Court itself has avowed this. "We recognize that this determination is one in which few answers will be written 'in black and white. The greys are dominant and even among them the shades are innumerable'."[43]

The following factors should be taken into consideration when applying the minimum contacts rule: (1) the *nature* and *quality* of the contacts with the forum state; (2) the *quantity* of the contacts; (3) the *relation* of the cause of action to the *contacts*; (4) the *interest of the forum* in providing a forum for its residents; and (5) the *convenience* of the parties.[44]

The best advice is to argue *all* of the facts. Every contact between the nonresident defendant and the forum state should be clearly pointed out to the court. Wherever possible, interrelate such contacts with the pending cause of action, and show the court why it would be reasonable and just to make the defendant defend in this particular forum.

(ii)(a)   "Minimum" v. "Minimal" Contacts

In the past decade, many courts seem to have confused the requirement of "minimum" contacts with the existence of "minimal"

L.Ed.2d 464, on remand 602 F.2d 1246; Messerschmidt Development Co., Inc. v. Crutcher Resources Corp., 84 Cal.App.3d 819, 824, 149 Cal.Rptr. 35, 38 (1978).

41. Dublin Co. v. Peninsular Supply Co., 309 So.2d 207, 209 (Fla.App. 1975): See also McGee v. International Life Ins. Co., 355 U.S. 220, 78 S.Ct. 199, 2 L.Ed.2d 223 (1957).

42. Telco Leasing, Inc. v. Marshall County Hosp., 586 F.2d 49, 50 (7th Cir. 1978); Mathes v. P. T. National Utility Helicopters Ltd., 68 Cal.App. 3d 182, 189, 137 Cal.Rptr. 104, 108 (1977). The contacts must have some scintilla of substantial connection with the form. Contacts consisting merely of long distance telephone calls have been held *not* to satisfy the minimal constitutional contacts requirement of due process. McBreen v. Beech Aircraft Corp., 543 F.2d 26 (7th Cir. 1976); American Steel, Inc. v. Cascade Steel Rolling Mills, Inc., 425 F.Supp. 301 (S.D.Tex. 1975), aff'd 548 F.2d 620 (5th Cir.), reh. denied 551 F.2d 863; Friberg v. Schlenske, 396 F.Supp. 124 (D.C. Mont.1975).

43. Kulko v. California Superior Court, 436 U.S. 84, 92, 98 S.Ct. 1690, 1696–97, 56 L.Ed.2d 132, 141 (1978), reh. denied 438 U.S. 908, 98 S.Ct. 3217, 57 L.Ed.2d 1150:

44. Aaron Ferer & Sons Co. v. American Compressed Steel Co., 564 F.2d 1206, 1209 (8th Cir. 1977).

contacts. However, the U.S. Supreme Court, in *World-Wide Volkswagen Corp. v. Woodson*,[45] made it clear that "minimum" does not necessarily include "minimal" contacts.

In that case, respondents had purchased a new Audi automobile from petitioner Seaway Volkswagen in New York. One year later, while driving the car from their New York residence to their new residence in Arizona, respondents were involved in an automobile accident in Oklahoma. They brought a products liability action in Oklahoma state court against petitioners Seaway, the retailer, and World-Wide Volkswagen Corp., the wholesale distributor.

Both defendants were incorporated and had their business offices in New York. There was no evidence that either defendant did any business whatsoever in Oklahoma. They appeared specially to challenge the jurisdiction of the court on the basis that they had no "minimum contacts" with the State of Oklahoma.

The U.S. Supreme Court reaffirmed the proposition that there must be some meaningful activity on the part of defendant by which it purposefully avails itself of the privileges of conducting business within a forum state. Said the court: "[E]ven if the defendant would suffer minimal or no inconvenience from being forced to litigate before the tribunals of another State; even if the forum State has a strong interest in applying its law to the controversy; even if the forum State is the most convenient location for litigation, the Due Process clause, acting as an instrument of federalism, may sometimes act to divest the State of its power to render a valid judgment." [46]

The court noted that the only contact between the defendants and Oklahoma was the fortuitous circumstance that the car happened to be involved in an accident in Oklahoma. The court went on to say that whatever marginal revenue petitioners might have received by virtue of the fact that their product was capable of use in Oklahoma was far too attenuated a contact to justify that state's jurisdiction over them.

Attorney *John Wm. Ringer* of Dexter, Missouri [47] reports a similar problem he faced in trying to obtain jurisdiction over a non-resident defendant, but his results were more successful. The case involved damage to plaintiff's cabbage crop caused by Xanthomonas Campsestris, or black rot. Figures 78 and 79.

---

45. 444 U.S. 286, 100 S.Ct. 559, 62 L.Ed.2d 490 (1980).

46. 444 U.S. 286, 294–296, 100 S.Ct. at 565, 566, 62 L.Ed.2d at 499–500.

47. John Wm. Ringer, Esquire, Powell, Ringer & Ringer, 21 Vine Street, Dexter, Missouri.

§ **4.3** INTRODUCTION Pt. 1

Figure 78. Damage caused to cabbage field by black rot. In this case, like so many others, obtaining personal jurisdiction over the defendant proved a major obstacle.

Figure 79. Close-up of cabbage shows damage caused by black rot.

Plaintiff was a cabbage farmer in southeast Missouri. Through a Memphis broker he purchased 155,000 cabbage plants from defendant's farms in Valdosta, Georgia. The plants were shipped to the broker's premises in Memphis, where plaintiff's trucks met them. Plaintiff planted the cabbage in a field alongside plants purchased from other suppliers. Defendant's plants thereafter developed black rot, a disease which normally causes only minor damage but which, under the conditions present that year, could and did cause plaintiff to suffer a considerable loss.

While liability seemed clear, plaintiff had to establish personal jurisdiction before he could proceed to trial. Defendant claimed that it sold primarily to local farmers, that it made no solicitations or deliveries, and that it was not really in the general plant-growing business at all. Defendant further contended that it had not purposefully availed itself of Missouri's benefits and therefore could not be subjected to personal jurisdiction there.

Missouri had a typical long-arm statute granting jurisdiction over anyone who made a contract or committed a tort within that state. Plaintiff claimed that the statute required only a "single act" to confer jurisdiction and filed a products liability claim based on the defective cabbage. Plaintiff argued that there was no distinction between a manufactured product and one which is the fruit of the producer's labor in the soil. Liability should be imposed, he claimed, not only for producing a defective product, but also for placing that product in the purchaser's hands.

Despite the lack of any prior Missouri case closely on point, plaintiff successfully established both personal jurisdiction and a products liability claim and proceeded to trial. The case resulted in a settlement favorable to the plaintiff.

(ii)(b) Shopping for a Forum

Every trial lawyer has read a decision wherein the court stated that forum shopping, if not forbidden outright, is a practice which should not be engaged in. However, sometimes it is beneficial to "forum shop," and sometimes absolutely necessary, as was the situation in a case my firm just settled for $265,000.

Plaintiff in *Roorda v. Volkswagenwerk, A. G.*[48] was rendered quadriplegic in an accident in California some seven years prior to this writing. One of my lawyers filed suit in Federal court in California against Volkswagenwerk of America. This was a case of "will the true Volkswagenwerk step forward" because, as is customary, the

---

48. Roorda v. Volkswagenwerk, A. G., 481 F.Supp. 868 (D.C.S.C.1979).

German Volkswagenwerk Corporation did not step forward until after the one-year-period statute of limitations for torts had run in California. They then came in and moved to dismiss the case forevermore on the ground that plaintiff had not sued the right Volkswagenwerk.

While the lawyer who so filed this case is no longer with me, he can probably be excused for not picking the right Volkswagen since this is probably the first Volkswagen case out of 10,000 in which the true German company should have been sued. The automobile was originally purchased in Germany by a service man stationed there, and the car was subsequently sold to our plaintiff in the United States.

The usual Volkswagen distributor in the United States had had nothing to do with the sale, importation or distribution of this particular car.

We were completely and forevermore thrown out on the one-year statute in California, it being too late by several days to sue the proper defendant, that is, the German Volkswagenwerk.

In many instances law is a game and the spoils go to the acute. But if Volkswagen in Germany was cute, we were cuter because we found that the true Volkswagen in Germany was doing business in South Carolina, and that state has a *six-years* statute of limitations —which we were well within.

Jim Toms of South Carolina and I filed suit there. Volkswagen, with precise German morality, now said: "Law is not a game—you cannot forum shop!" Our plaintiff had, of course, moved to South Carolina and set up his domicile there. Said U.S. District Judge Blatt: "Defendant has asserted, as a bar to jurisdiction here, that plaintiff moved to South Carolina because South Carolina has a six-year statute of limitations for this type of action, and that South Carolina is one of the few states where plaintiff could bring suit because of the time lapse between his injuries—(1970) and the institution of suit here—(1976). Plaintiff admits this to be a fact; however, a change of domicile for such reason is no bar to jurisdiction if the defendant is factually 'present' in this jurisdiction under the principles of *International Shoe* . . . . Citizenship may be changed for the purpose of obtaining federal jurisdiction; however, for there to be a legal change of residence, there must be true intent to reside indefinitely in the new domicile. It is immaterial if a bona fide change to acquire jurisdiction, as is clearly the case here, is made for the purpose of bringing suit in the United States District Court in this state; such bona fide transfer of residence for that purpose is not a new notion." [49]

---

49. Id. at 880.

§ 4.3 JURISDICTION AND VENUE

This case was settled shortly before trial for $265,000.

(iii) Limited v. General Jurisdiction over Defendant

If a nonresident defendant has *some* contact with the forum state, the court may nevertheless *not* have jurisdiction if the cause of action is *unrelated* to the contact with the forum. This raises the difference between general and limited jurisdiction.[50]

General jurisdiction over a party allows a court to subject a defendant to *any* cause of action, even one unrelated to his contact with the forum state.[51] Limited jurisdiction restricts the defendant's amenability to suit within the forum state to actions *arising out* of its activities therein.[52]

If the defendant's forum-related activities are *substantial, systematic,* and *continuous,* the relationship between the defendant and the state is sufficient to support jurisdiction even if the cause of action is unrelated to the defendant's forum activities.[53] Where the activities are less substantial, a defendant may not be subject to the court's jurisdiction where the cause of action does not arise out of the forum-related activities.[54]

Jurisdiction may still lie, however, if the *nature and quality* of the acts make it fair and reasonable to assert jurisdiction over the particular cause of action.[55] *International Shoe Co. v. Washington*[56]

---

50. General as opposed to limited jurisdiction over a defendant is wholly separate and independent from general or limited subject matter jurisdictional of a court, discussed supra at § 4.2. See Stutsman v. Patterson, 457 F.Supp. 189, 191 (C.D.Cal.1978). This basically is the same concept of the common law theory of a corporation's being present. Perkins v. Benguet Consol. Mining Co., 342 U.S. 437, 72 S.Ct. 413, 96 L.Ed. 485 (1952), reh. denied 343 U.S. 917, 72 S.Ct. 645, 96 L.Ed. 1332.

51. Data Disc, Inc. v. Systems Technology Associates, Inc., 557 F.2d 1280, 1287 (9th Cir. 1977).

52. International Shoe Co. v. Washington, 326 U.S. 310, 317–19, 66 S.Ct. 154, 158–160, 90 L.Ed. 95, 102–04 (1945).

53. H. Ray Baker, Inc. v. Associated Banking Corp., 592 F.2d 550, 552 (9th Cir. 1979), cert. denied 444 U.S. 832, 100 S.Ct. 63, 62 L.Ed.2d 42; Data Disc, Inc. v. Systems Technology Associates, Inc., 557 F.2d 1280, 1287 (9th Cir. 1977).

54. Forsythe v. Overmyer, 576 F.2d 779, 782 (9th Cir. 1978), cert. denied 439 U.S. 864, 99 S.Ct. 188, 58 L.Ed.2d 174; Foster v. Mooney Aircraft Corp., 68 Cal.App.3d 887, 893, 137 Cal.Rptr. 694, 698 (1977); Tucker v. Vista Financial Corp., 192 Colo. 440, 560 P.2d 453 (1977).

55. H. Ray Baker, Inc. v. Associated Banking Corp., 592 F.2d 550, 552 (9th Cir. 1979), cert. denied 444 U.S. 832, 100 S.Ct. 63, 62 L.Ed.2d 42.

56. 326 U.S. 310, 90 L.Ed. 95, 66 S.Ct. 154 (1945).

and *McGee v. International Life Ins. Co.*[57] are two well known and classic examples of limited jurisdiction.

(iv) Limitations on the Exercise of Jurisdiction

Some of the more important limitations on the exercise of jurisdiction should be noted. Just because a defendant is personally served while present in the forum state does not absolutely confer jurisdiction on the court in all instances.

If personal service has been procured by fraud, trickery or artifice, then the court may not exercise jurisdiction over the person so served.[58] Another important limitation is the immunity from process enjoyed by witnesses or defendants in either a criminal[59] or civil[60] case.

Unlike the fraud limitation, immunity is a privilege of the court, not the individual. It allows the court to expedite its business, and insures that justice is duly administered by granting immunity to persons whose presence is necessary to the trial, and who would not otherwise attend.[61]

Forum non conveniens is another major limitation on the exercise of jurisdiction. It is a determination made *after* the court has found sufficient contacts to justify the exercise of jurisdiction over a defendant.[62] Broadly speaking, it stands for the proposition that a court should not accept jurisdiction if it is inconvenient to try the case in that court.[63] It is based on the inherent power of the courts

---

57. 355 U.S. 220, 78 S.Ct. 199, 2 L.Ed. 2d 223 (1957).

58. Buchanan v. Wilson, 254 F.2d 849 (6th Cir. 1958); Cushing v. Cushing, 263 N.C. 181, 139 S.E.2d 217, 222 (1964); Forbess v. George Morgan Pontiac Co., 135 So.2d 594, 596 (La. App.1961); Zenker v. Zenker, 161 Neb. 200, 72 N.W.2d 809, 816 (1955).

59. Crusco v. Strunk Steel Co., 365 Pa. 326, 74 A.2d 142, 143 (1950); Gekoski v. Starer, 223 Pa.Super. 560, 302 A.2d 398, 399–400 (1973).

60. Stewart v. Ramsay, 242 U.S. 128, 129, 37 S.Ct. 44, 45, 61 L.Ed. 192 (1916) (Granting immunity to nonresident parties and witnesses in a civil case while attending trial and traveling to and from forum state).

61. Crusco v. Strunk Steel Co., 365 Pa. 326, 74 A.2d 142, 143 (1950); Gekoski v. Starer, 223 Pa.Super. 560, 302 A.2d 398, 399–400 (1973).

62. Buckeye Boiler Co. v. Superior Court, 71 Cal.2d 893, 899, 80 Cal. Rptr. 113, 118, 458 P.2d 57, 62 (1969).

63. The ultimate question to be decided in determining whether the doctrine of *forum non conveniens* is applicable is whether "the forum chosen by the plaintiff is so completely inappropriate and inconvenient that it is better to stop the litigation in the place where brought and let it start all over again somewhere else". Paper Operations Consultants Int'l, Ltd. v. S. S. Hong Kong Amber, 513 F.2d 667, 670 (9th Cir. 1975).

to decline jurisdiction in exceptional cases, and is left to the sound discretion of the court.[64]

In order for a court to dismiss a case under *forum non conveniens*, it must be shown that plaintiff can bring suit elsewhere.[65] If for any reason plaintiff cannot, such as the statute of limitations having expired in other jurisdiction,[66] the court will not dismiss the case and will instead proceed to hear the case on its merits.

Plaintiff's choice of forum is to be given great weight [67] and will be disturbed only where the balance is *strongly* in favor of the defendant.[68] The factors scrutinized by the court in reaching its decision include the ease of access to proof; the availability of compulsory process to obtain the presence of unwilling witnesses; the costs of obtaining witnesses; the possibility of viewing the scene in question; the residences of the parties and witnesses; and the place where the cause of action arose.[69] The court may also inquire into plaintiff's motive in choosing a court to see whether it was to vex, harass, or oppress the defendant.[70]

(B) In Rem Jurisdiction

In rem jurisdiction is founded upon the court's power to adjudicate title and affect interests in property situated within its territorial boundaries.[71] A *true* in rem action seeks to affect the interests of all persons (i. e., the whole world) in certain property.[72]

---

64. Paper Operations Consultants Int'l, Ltd. v. S. S. Hong Kong Amber, 513 F.2d 667, 670 (9th Cir. 1975).

65. Tivoli Realty v. Interstate Circuit, 167 F.2d 155, 156-7 (5th Cir. 1948), cert. denied 334 U.S. 837, 68 S.Ct. 1494, 92 L.Ed. 1762; Del Rio v. Ballenger Corp., 391 F.Supp. 1002, 1006 (D.C.S.C.1975). But see Schertenleib v. Traum, 589 F.2d 1156, 1159-60 (2d Cir. 1978). That court held that lower court had the power to apply doctrine of *forum non conveniens* even if there was no alternative forum in which plaintiff could have originally filed suit without defendant's consent.

66. Paper Operations Consultants Int'l, Ltd. v. S. S. Hong Kong Amber, 513 F.2d 667, 672-73 (9th Cir. 1975).

67. Gulf Oil Corp. v. Gilbert, 330 U.S. 501, 508, 67 S.Ct. 839, 843, 91 L.Ed. 1055, 1062 (1947).

68. Id. See also Fitzgerald v. Texaco, Inc., 521 F.2d 448, 451 (2d Cir. 1975), cert. denied 423 U.S. 1052, 96 S.Ct. 781, 46 L.Ed.2d 641; Harry David Zutz Ins., Inc. v. H. M. S. Associates, Ltd., 360 A.2d 160 (Del.Super.1976).

69. Gulf Oil Corp. v. Gilbert, 330 U.S. 501, 508, 67 S.Ct. 839, 843, 91 L.Ed. 1055, 1062 (1947).

70. Detrick v. Baltimore & Ohio R. R. Co., 330 F.Supp. 257, 259 (E.D.Pa. 1971).

71. Hanson v. Denkla, 357 U.S. 235, 246, 78 S.Ct. 1228, 1235-36, 2 L.Ed.2d 1283, 1293 (1958), reh. denied 358 U.S. 858, 79 S.Ct. 10, 3 L.Ed.2d 92, conformed to 106 So.2d 549 (Fla.); Steele v. G. D. Searle & Co., 483 F.2d 339, 347 (5th Cir. 1973), reh. denied 485 F.2d 688, cert. denied 415 U.S.

72. See note 72 on page 342.

True in rem actions are few. The more common are proceedings in probate,[73] condemnation proceedings,[74] actions to forfeit property used in violation of the law,[75] libel actions in admiralty,[76] and actions to determine status,[77] such as sanity or divorce.

In order for a court to obtain jurisdiction in a true in rem action, two requirements must be fulfilled. First, the property, or *res*, must be situated within the state at the time the action is commenced.[78] Secondly, notice which is reasonably calculated to apprise interested persons of the proceedings must be given.[79]

(C) Quasi In Rem Jurisdiction

Unlike true in rem actions, which bind the interests of the whole world in some particular property, quasi in rem proceedings determine the interests of the property only as between the parties brought before the court.[80] There are two types of quasi in rem ac-

---

958, 94 S.Ct. 1486, 39 L.Ed.2d 572, on remand 422 F.Supp. 560 (S.D.Miss.), motion denied 428 F.Supp. 646; Curtis Pub. Co. v. Golino, 383 F.2d 586, 589 n. 2 (5th Cir. 1967); Podolsky v. Devinney, 281 F.Supp. 488, 493–94 (S.D.N.Y.1968); Wilcox v. Richmond, Fredericksburg & Potomac R. R. Co., 270 F.Supp. 454, 458 (S.D.N.Y.1967).

72. McAndrews v. Krause, 245 Minn. 85, 71 N.W.2d 153, 159 (1955); Linn County v. Roselle, 177 Or. 245, 162 P.2d 150 (1945); In re Bergman's Survivorship, 60 Wyo. 355, 151 P.2d 360 (1944); Combs v. Combs, 249 Ky. 155, 60 S.W.2d 368 (1933).

73. In re Estate of Radovich, 48 Cal.2d 116, 308 P.2d 14 (1957); In re Estate of Nilson, 126 Neb. 541, 253 N.W. 675 (1934).

74. City of Winooski v. State Highway Bd., 124 Vt. 496, 207 A.2d 255 (1965); San Bernardino Val. Municipal Water Dist. v. Gage Canal Co., 226 Cal. App.2d 206, 37 Cal.Rptr. 856 (1964); Mitchell v. State Highway Dept. of Georgia, 216 Ga. 517, 118 S.E.2d 88 (1961).

75. Moore v. Purse Seine Net, 18 Cal. 2d 835, 118 P.2d 1 (1941), aff'd 318 U.S. 133, 63 S.Ct. 499, 87 L.Ed. 663, reh. denied 318 U.S. 801, 63 S.Ct. 848, 87 L.Ed. 1165.

76. Poseidon Schiffahrt, G. M. B. H. v. M/S Netuno, 474 F.2d 203 (5th Cir. 1973), on remand 361 F.Supp. 412 (S.D.Ga.); Riverview State Bank v. Dreyer, 188 Kan. 270, 362 P.2d 55 (1961).

77. Gibson v. Westoby, 115 Cal.App.2d 273, 251 P.2d 1003 (1953); Hamm v. Hamm, 30 Tenn.App. 122, 204 S.W.2d 113 (1947).

78. Martin v. Better Taste Popcorn Co., 89 F.Supp. 754 (S.D.Iowa 1950).

79. Milliken v. Meyer, 311 U.S. 457, 463, 61 S.Ct. 339, 342–343, 85 L.Ed. 278, 283 (1940), reh. denied 312 U.S. 712, 61 S.Ct. 548, 85 L.Ed. 1143, conformed to 107 Colo. 295, 111 P.2d 232.

80. Hanson v. Denckla, 357 U.S. 235, 246 n. 12, 78 S.Ct. 1228, 1235 n. 12, 2 L.Ed.2d 1283, 1293 n. 12 (1958), reh. denied 348 U.S. 858, 79 S.Ct. 10, 3 L. Ed.2d 92, conformed to 106 So.2d 549; Freeman v. Alderson, 119 U.S. 185, 7 S.Ct. 165, 30 L.Ed. 372 (1886).

tions. In the first type, the plaintiff is seeking to secure a pre-existing claim in the property and to extinguish or establish the nonexistence of similar interests of specified persons. This is found on actions to foreclose liens,[81] ejectments, actions to quiet title, and the like.[82]

In the second variety, the plaintiff, unable to acquire personal jurisdiction over him, attaches the property of a nonresident defendant in order to satisfy a claim against him, such claim generally being unrelated to the property.[83] The classic example of this occurs when a plaintiff has been injured out of state due to the tortious conduct of a defendant, who is a nonresident of the forum state. Upon learning that the nonresident defendant owns a substantial amount of land in the forum, the plaintiff attaches it and brings it before the court. The traditional rule allowed the court to then exercise quasi in rem jurisdiction, and the court could award the plaintiff the lesser between the value of the property and the extent of his damages.[84]

One of the noted cases involving quasi in rem actions is *Harris v. Balk*.[85] In this seminal case, Harris was indebted to Balk for $180. Both were residents of North Carolina, which also was the location where the debt was entered into. While Harris was temporarily in Maryland, Epstein, a resident of that state whom Balk owed $300, garnished the $180 that Harris owed Balk.

The court held that the debt, i. e., the obligation to repay, was a sufficient property interest capable of attachment. Being an intangible, its situs was that of the debtor; it clung to and followed him wherever he went. Therefore, the attachment procedure, the court held, was constitutionally valid. The decision was grounded in those lines of cases holding that a state has absolute and exclusive jurisdiction over property within its limits, irrespective of the domicile and contact of the owner thereof.[86]

---

81. Epperson v. Halliburton Co., 434 P.2d 877, 880 (Okl.1967).

82. See generally Comment, The Reasonableness Standard in State Court Jurisdiction: Shaffer v. Heitner and the Uniform Minimum Contacts Theory, 14 Wake Forest L.Rev. 51, 72–73 (1978).

83. Harris v. Balk, 198 U.S. 215, 25 S. Ct. 625, 49 L.Ed. 1023 (1905); Pennoyer v. Neff, 95 U.S. 714, 24 L.Ed. 565 (1878).

84. M. Green, Jurisdictional Reform in California, 21 Hast.L.J. 1219, 1222 (1970).

85. 198 U.S. 215, 25 S.Ct. 625, 49 L.Ed. 1023 (1905).

86. Pennoyer v. Neff, 95 U.S. 714, 722, 24 L.Ed. 565, 568 (1878); Arndt v. Griggs, 134 U.S. 316, 10 S.Ct. 557, 33 L.Ed. 918 (1890).

§ 4.3 INTRODUCTION

This reasoning remained in force until 1977 when the United States Supreme Court handed down its decision in *Shaffer v. Heitner*.[87] The Court, speaking through Justice Marshall, held that in order to attach the property of a nonresident defendant pursuant to the traditional procedure, there must now exist *certain minimum contacts* between the forum, the defendant, the cause of action, *and the property*, so that maintenance of the suit does not offend traditional notions of fair play and substantial justice.[88]

Shaffer was not the result of some sudden celestial inspiration. Rather, it was a logical extension of the minimum contacts doctrine which had for some time been advocated by many courts and authors.[89] For example, in *United States Indus. v. Gregg*,[90] the Third Circuit held that the doctrine of minimum contacts must be applied to a quasi in rem action to ensure traditional notions of fair play and substantial justice.

The Supreme Court of New Hampshire held that the court must apply the in personam test (i. e., minimum contacts) to quasi in rem proceedings.[91] One writer neatly summed it up when he succinctly stated, "The time has come to abolish jurisdictional attachment and to approach all jurisdictional problems on terms of 'minimum contacts'." [92]

---

87. 433 U.S. 186, 97 S.Ct. 2569, 53 L.Ed.2d 683 (1977).

88. International Shoe v. Washington, 326 U.S. 310, 66 S.Ct. 154, 90 L.Ed. 95 (1945). What the court did was extend the *International Shoe* doctrine to quasi in rem proceedings.

89. See, e. g., Jonnet v. Dollar Sav. Bank, 530 F.2d 1123, 1130–43 (3d Cir. 1976) (Gibbons, J. concurring); Atkinson v. Superior Court, 49 Cal.2d 338, 316 P.2d 960 (1957), appeal dismissed sub nom. 357 U.S. 569, 78 S.Ct. 1381, 2 L.Ed.2d 1546 (1958); Bekins v. Huish, 1 Ariz.App. 258, 401 P.2d 743 (1965).

Von Mehren & Trautman, Jurisdiction to Adjudicate: A Suggested Analysis, 79 Harv.L.Rev. 1121 (1966).

90. 540 F.2d 142, 154 (3d Cir. 1976), cert. denied 433 U.S. 908, 97 S.Ct. 2972, 53 L.Ed.2d 1091, on remand 457 F.Supp. 1293.

91. Camire v. Scieszka, 116 N.H. 281, 358 A.2d 397, 399 (1976).

See also Atkinson v. Superior Court, 49 Cal.2d 338, 316 P.2d 960 (1957), appeal dism'd sub nom. 357 U.S. 569, 78 S.Ct. 1381, 2 L.Ed.2d 1546.

92. J. Zammit, Quasi-In-Rem Jurisdiction: Outmoded and Unconstitutional, 49 St. John's L.Rev. 668, 683 (1975). The U.S. Supreme Court itself had grown increasingly uncomfortable with prejudgment attachment procedures.

See Sniadach v. Family Fin. Corp. of Bay View, 395 U.S. 337, 89 S.Ct. 1820, 23 L.Ed.2d 349 (1969); and Fuentes v. Shevin, 407 U.S. 67, 92 S.Ct. 1983, 32 L.Ed.2d 556 (1972), reh. denied 409 U.S. 902, 93 S.Ct. 177, 34 L.Ed.2d 165. See also North Georgia Finishing, Inc. v. Di-Chem, Inc., 419 U.S. 601, 95 S.Ct. 719, 42 L.Ed.2d 751 (1975); In re Law Research Servs., Inc., 386 F.Supp. 749 (S.D.N.Y.1974).

The extension in *Shaffer* was the result of the Court's rejection of a theory set forth in *Pennoyer v. Neff* [93] years earlier. That theory was that a proceeding in rem, or quasi in rem, was against property, not a person. The owner's rights were only *indirectly* affected by the outcome. In *Shaffer*, it was stated that, "The phrase, judicial jurisdiction over a thing, is a customary elliptical way of referring to jurisdiction over the *interest of a person in a thing.*" [94] Actually, this idea had been formulated many years earlier when Oliver Wendell Holmes, then Chief Justice of the Supreme Judicial Court of Massachusetts, said "All proceedings, like all rights, are really against persons." [95]

The impact of *Shaffer* has been to toll the death knell for those actions designed solely to secure jurisdiction over a controversy which the state could not have obtained otherwise.[96] No longer will the fortuitous presence of property within a State, without more, be an adequate ground for exercising jurisdiction.[97]

With the extension of minimum contacts, no longer is the court's attention singularly focused upon whether the property brought before it is tangible or intangible, capable or incapable of attachment. It is clear that the courts will look to the totality of the circumstances to determine whether it would be fair and just, in this particular instance, to exercise jurisdiction.

One question remains unanswered by the courts. Will fortuitous, temporary physical presence within a state continue to be an adequate basis for jurisdiction over any cause of action? I believe minimum contacts will be extended here, too, in keeping with the courts' recent policy of fair play and justice.

(D) The Seider v. Roth Anomaly

In *Seider v. Roth*,[98] a New York Court of Appeals case, an insurance policy was issued by a foreign corporation to a nonresident pursuant to a contract entered into in a foreign state. The plaintiff, a resident of New York, was injured in Vermont due to the insured's negligent operation of an automobile.

---

93. 95 U.S. 714, 24 L.Ed. 565 (1878).

94. Restatement, Second, Conflict of Laws § 56 (Introductory note, 1971), quoted in Shaffer v. Heitner, 433 U.S. 186, 207, 97 S.Ct. 2569, 2581, 53 L.Ed.2d 683, 699 (1977) (emphasis added).

95. Tyler v. Judges of Court of Registration, 175 Mass. 71, 55 N.E. 812, 814 (1900).

96. Comment, The Reasonableness Standard in State Court Jurisdiction: Shaffer v. Heitner and The Uniform Minimum Contact Theory, 14 Wake Forest L.Rev. 51, 72–73 (1978).

97. J. Zammit, Reflections on Shaffer v. Heitner, 5 Hastings Con.L.Q. 15, 20 (1978).

98. 17 N.Y.2d 111, 269 N.Y.S.2d 99, 216 N.E.2d 312 (1966).

The Court of Appeals, basing its decision in large part on *Harris v. Balk* [99] and its progeny, held that the obligation of the insurance company to defend the insured anywhere an accident occurred constitutes a debt for jurisdictional purposes. Thus, the obligation could be attached for jurisdictional purposes by a New York plaintiff so long as the insurance company did business in New York.[1]

Recognizing the precariousness in the constitutionality of its application, the court subsequently restricted the *Seider* ruling. This type of attachment procedure was then made available only to a New York resident plaintiff,[2] or a nonresident who is injured in New York.[3] One court held that where a nonresident plaintiff attempted to institute this type of proceeding against a nonresident defendant, a court could refuse to exercise jurisdiction based on *forum non conveniens*.[4]

Seider drew immediate criticism, both from within its own ranks [5] and from most other states, which refused to allow this type of jurisdictional attachment.[6] In California, an appellate court [7]

---

99. 198 U.S. 215, 25 S.Ct. 625, 49 L.Ed. 1023 (1905).

1. The court reconsidered its decision in *Seider* one year later in Simpson v. Lochman, 21 N.Y.2d 305, 287 N.Y.S.2d 633, 234 N.E.2d 669 (1967). An infant resident of New York was injured when the propeller of a boat owned by a nonresident defendant cut him in waters off of Connecticut. The defendant was insured by a Pennsylvania corporation which was doing business in New York. The court allowed attachment of the foreign insurance company's obligation to defend, holding such obligation constituted a "debt". The one limitation was that recovery could not exceed the face value of the policy.

2. Donawitz v. Danek, 42 N.Y.2d 138, 397 N.Y.S.2d 592, 366 N.E.2d 253 (1977); Farrell v. Piedmont Aviation, Inc., 411 F.2d 812 (2d Cir. 1969), cert. denied 396 U.S. 840, 90 S.Ct. 103, 24 L.Ed.2d 91. Farrell involved a wrongful death action by New York administrators of estates of nonresident decedents who had been killed in an airplane accident in North Carolina. The court held that the liability policies of defendants who were not subject to in personam jurisdiction in New York could not be attached, even though the insurers did business in New York.

3. Jonnet v. Dollar Sav. Bank of the City of New York, 530 F.2d 1123, 1132 (3d Cir. 1976) (Gibbons, J., concurring).

4. Minichiello v. Rosenberg, 410 F.2d 106, 110 n. 6 (2d Cir. 1968), cert. denied 396 U.S. 844, 90 S.Ct. 69, 24 L.Ed.2d 94, reh. denied 396 U.S. 949, 90 S.Ct. 370, 24 L.Ed.2d 254.

5. Seider v. Roth, 17 N.Y.2d 111, 115–18, 269 N.Y.S.2d 99, 102–05, 216 N.E.2d 312, 315–17 (1966) (Burke, J., dissenting); Simpson v. Lochmann, 21 N.Y.2d 305, 316, 287 N.Y.S.2d 633, 641, 234 N.E.2d 669, 674 (1967) (Breitel, J., concurring); Donawitz v. Danek, 42 N.Y.2d 138, 143–51, 397 N.Y.S.2d 592, 595–601, 366 N.E.2d 253, 256–61 (1977) (Jason, J., concurring).

6. Belcher v. Government Employees Ins. Co., 282 Md. 718, 387 A.2d 770 (1978); Rocca v. Kenney, 117 N.H. 381, 381 A.2d 330 (1977); Hart v.

7. See note 7 on page 347.

adopted *Seider*, but this was unanimously overruled by the California Supreme Court in *Javorek v. Superior Court*.[8] That court held that the obligation of the insurer to defend and indemnify was too contigent for attachment since the obligation would not arise in law *until a judgment had been entered against the insured.*

After *Shaffer v. Heitner* was decided, the New York courts had considerable difficulty in determining the continued viability of *Seider* in light thereof. Some of the courts opined that jurisdiction predicated on the *Seider* procedure must now necessarily fail.[9] The rest were of the view that *Seider* was still permissible, as all along it had taken minimum contacts into consideration.[10]

The New York Court of Appeals then heard the issue,[11] ultimately holding in a brief *per curiam* decision that *Seider* still withstands any constitutional challenge, including attacks premised on *Shaffer v. Heitner*. The court bifurcated its opinion, re-examining and then affirming the basic premise for allowing this type of procedure.

Minnesota also permitted an attachment procedure similar to that in question in *Seider v. Roth*, and, like the New York court, held that even in light of the *Shaffer* case, the procedure was still constitutionally permissible.[12]

In 1980, the U.S. Supreme Court, for the first time, ruled on the validity of this procedure and held that it violated guarantees of due process.[13] The Court found that the mere fact that defendant's in-

Cote, 145 N.J.Super. 420, 367 A.2d 1219 (1976); Werner v. Werner, 84 Wash.2d 360, 526 P.2d 370, 376 (1974); Howard v. Allen, 254 S.C. 455, 176 S.E.2d 127 (1968); Housley v. Anaconda Co., 19 Utah 2d 124, 427 P.2d 390 (1967).

7. Turner v. Evers, 31 Cal.App.3d Supp. 11, 107 Cal.Rptr. 390 (1973).

8. 17 Cal.3d 629, 131 Cal.Rptr. 768, 552 P.2d 728 (1976).

9. Torres v. Towmotor Div. of Caterpillar, Inc., 457 F.Supp. 460 (E.D.N.Y.1977); Wallace v. Target Store, Inc., 92 Misc.2d 454, 400 N.Y.S.2d 478 (1977); Katz v. Umansky, 92 Misc.2d 285, 399 N.Y.S.2d 412 (1977); Kennedy v. Deroker, 91 Misc.2d 648, 398 N.Y.S.2d 628 (1977).

10. O'Connor v. Lee-Hy Paving Corp., 579 F.2d 194 (2d Cir. 1978), cert. denied 439 U.S. 1034, 99 S.Ct. 638, 58 L.Ed.2d 696, reh. denied 441 U.S. 918, 99 S.Ct. 2023, 60 L.Ed.2d 392; Alford v. McGaw, 61 A.D.2d 504, 402 N.Y.S.2d 499 (1978); Rodriquez v. Wolfe, 93 Misc.2d 364, 401 N.Y.S.2d 442 (1978).

11. Baden v. Staples, 45 N.Y.2d 889, 410 N.Y.S.2d 808, 383 N.E.2d 110 (1978); Erneta v. Princeton Hosp., 66 A.D.2d 669, 411 N.Y.S.2d 13 (1978); D'Agostino v. Watt, 67 A.D.2d 762, 412 N.Y.S.2d 793 (1979).

12. Savchuk v. Rush, 272 N.W.2d 888 (Minn.1978), overruled 444 U.S. 320, 100 S.Ct. 571, 62 L.Ed.2d 516.

13. Rush v. Savchuk, 444 U.S. 320, 100 S.Ct. 571, 62 L.Ed.2d 516 (1980).

surance company did business in the forum was not a sufficient contact for imposing jurisdiction, including quasi-in-rem jurisdiction, on defendant.

The Court stated: "Here, the fact that the defendant's insurer does business in the forum State suggests no further contacts between the defendant and the forum . . . . State Farm's decision to do business in Minnesota was completely adventitious as far as [defendant] was concerned. He had no control over that decision, and it is unlikely that he would have expected that by buying insurance in Indiana he had subjected himself to suit in any State to which a potential future plaintiff might decide to move. In short, it cannot be said that the defendant engaged in any purposeful activity related to the forum that would make the exercise of jurisdiction fair, just, or reasonable . . . merely because his insurer does business there." [14]

The Court also considered an alternative argument in support of the *Seider* doctrine: The attachment proceeding against the insured is the functional equivalent of a direct action against insurer. The Court found that *Seider* actions were not equivalent to direct actions. "The State's ability to exert its power over the 'nominal defendant' is analytically prerequisite to the insurer's entry into the case as a garnishee. If the Constitution forbids the assertion of jurisdiction over the insured based on the policy, then there is no conceptual basis for bringing the 'garnishee' into the action." [15]

The Court concluded its discussion by holding that since the defendant had no ties or contact with the State of Minnesota, that state could not impose jurisdiction over him.

(E) Contesting Jurisdiction

Assume for the moment that plaintiff, a resident of State A, has filed suit in that state's court against defendant, a resident of State B. Defendant does not think that the court in State A has any basis for exercising jurisdiction over him.

Can the defendant go to State B to litigate the sole question of jurisdiction without submitting himself to the jurisdiction of the court? Or must he abstain altogether, waiting until plaintiff brings suit against him in State B upon the judgment before he raises the issue of jurisdiction?

If it is *patent* that the court does *not* have jurisdiction over the defendant, the defendant is better off not making an appearance. This way he saves time and money, and may raise the issue of juris-

---

[14] 444 U.S. at 328, 100 S.Ct. at 577, 62 L.Ed.2d at 525.

[15] 444 U.S. at 331, 100 S.Ct. at 578, 62 L.Ed.2d at 526.

diction when plaintiff seeks to enforce the default judgment in defendant's home state.[16]

Where, however, serious question exists as to a court's jurisdiction, or lack thereof, the defense should put in a *special appearance*,[17] which is provided for in almost all states. The tactical advantage of a special appearance is this: if defendant loses the question of jurisdiction he nonetheless may proceed to trial on the merits of the case. If the defendant had not made a special appearance, and it turns out the court did in fact have jurisdiction, he will not have the opportunity to have the case heard on the merits when plaintiff brings suit upon the judgment.

A special appearance has but one function—to litigate the question of jurisdiction. When a defendant makes it known to the court that he wishes to contest jurisdiction, usually in the form of a motion to quash service, he submits himself to the jurisdiction of the court for this issue alone.[18] Where the defendant has properly made such a motion, the burden then shifts to the plaintiff to establish the facts of jurisdiction by a preponderance of the evidence.[19]

Perhaps the most important thing to be remembered here is *when* to raise the issue of lack of jurisdiction. Generally speaking, the defense of lack of jurisdiction must be made when the defendant makes his first defensive move.[20] If he fails to object at the proper time, he is deemed to have consented to the court's jurisdiction and will be bound by the outcome.

When the defendant makes a special appearance, and the court concludes it does *not* have jurisdiction over him, the defendant is free to go. On the other hand, where the court finds it *does* have jurisdiction, the defendant has two options: (1) to proceed and defend the case on its merits, or (2) to appeal the adverse ruling to the next highest court, and up to the United States Supreme Court, if need be.[21]

What the defendant *cannot* do is lose the special appearance, drop out of the suit allowing default judgment to be entered against him,

---

16. Sprague & Rhodes Commodity Corp. v. Instituto Mexicano Del Cafe, 566 F.2d 861, 863 (2d Cir. 1977).

17. Harkness v. Hyde, 98 U.S. 476, 25 L.Ed. 237 (1878).

18. Buehne v. Buehne, 190 Kan. 666, 378 P.2d 159, 165 (1963); Johnson v. Haley, 357 Mich. 411, 98 N.W.2d 555, 558 (1959).

19. Messerschmidt Development Co., Inc. v. Crutcher Resources Corp., 84 Cal.App.3d 819, 825, 149 Cal.Rptr. 35 (1978).

20. The "first defensive move" would be the filing of a special appearance. Otherwise, the defense may be lost.

21. Baldwin v. Iowa State Traveling Men's Ass'n, 283 U.S. 522, 525, 51 S.Ct. 517, 518, 75 L.Ed. 1244, 1247 (1931).

§ 4.3   INTRODUCTION   Pt. 1

and then relitigate the issue of jurisdiction when plaintiff brings suit upon the judgment in defendant's home state.[22] This is true even though the court may have made an error as to law or fact when it determined it had jurisdiction over defendant.[23]

Res judicata will be applied to preclude relitigation of the personal jurisdiction question.[24] The heart of the res judicata doctrine is the public policy that all litigation must at some time end and once tried, issues which were or should have been tried are settled forever, as between the parties.[25] The reason for this is that public policy dictates an end to litigation.[26] While it is true that a defendant is entitled to his day in court, it has been interpreted as meaning just that —one day, not a series of days.[27]

§ 4.4   Notice Requirement

Before a party may be deprived of life, liberty or property, due process requires at a minimum that such adjudication be preceded by notice and the opportunity for a hearing appropriate to the case.[28] It has been said that the fundamental requisite of due process is the opportunity to be heard.[29] *A fortiorari*, unless a party is given notice, he will never have that opportunity, thereby failing to satisfy the demands of due process.

The classic form of notice which is always adequate in any type of proceeding is personal service of written notice while present within the forum state.[30] Substituted service is also valid so long as there

---

22. In re Universal Display & Sign Co., 541 F.2d 142, 144 (3d Cir. 1976).

23. Johnson v. Haley, 357 Mich. 411, 98 N.W.2d 555, 558 (1959).

24. Zoriano Sanchez v. Carribean Carriers, Ltd., 552 F.2d 70, 72 (2d Cir. 1977), cert. denied 434 U.S. 853, 98 S.Ct. 168, 54 L.Ed.2d 123.

25. Ligon v. Maryland, 448 F.Supp. 935, 942 (D.C.Md.1977).

26. Baldwin v. Iowa State Traveling Men's Ass'n, 283 U.S. 522, 51 S.Ct. 517, 75 L.Ed. 1244 (1931); S. E. C. v. United Financial Group, Inc., 576 F.2d 217, 221 (9th Cir. 1978).

27. Johnson v. Haley, 357 Mich. 411, 98 N.W.2d 555, 558 (1959).

28. Mullane v. Central Hanover Bank & Trust Co., 339 U.S. 306, 313, 70 S.Ct. 652, 656, 657, 94 L.Ed. 865, 873 (1950); Connell v. Shoemaker, 555 F.2d 483, 487 (5th Cir. 1977); Drollinger v. Milligan, 552 F.2d 1220, 1227 (7th Cir. 1977); In re Nissan Motor Corp. Antitrust Litigation, 552 F.2d 1088, 1103 (5th Cir. 1977).

29. Grannis v. Ordean, 234 U.S. 385, 394, 34 S.Ct. 779, 783, 58 L.Ed. 1363, 1368 (1914).

30. See, e. g., Harris v. Balk, 198 U.S. 215, 25 S.Ct. 625, 49 L.Ed. 1023 (1905); Grace v. MacArthur, 170 F.Supp. 442 (E.D.Ark.1959).

is a reasonable assurance that the defendant will actually be notified.[31]

Modernly, in determining whether the notice given has fulfilled the requirements of due process, the test applied by the courts is whether the method of service employed is *reasonably calculated* to give the defendant actual notice and opportunity to be heard.[32] The notice must be of such nature as reasonably to convey the required information, and it must afford a reasonable time for interested persons to make their appearance.[33]

Whereas traditionally the types of notice required depended upon the nature of the proceeding (i. e., in personam, in rem, quasi in rem), it is clear that now it depends entirely upon the surrounding circumstances.[34] Where the address and present whereabouts of a defendant are known, merely posting notice on the property is insufficient. No longer does the law blindly assume that insofar as notification is concerned, property is always in the possession of its owners or his agent,[35] and that its seizure would automatically inform him thereof.

Publication in a newspaper of general circulation may still be sufficient, but only in the case of missing or unknown persons. The court has allowed this while nonetheless recognizing that publication is an indirect and most likely futile means of publication.[36]

---

31. International Shoe Co. v. Washington, 326 U.S. 310, 320, 66 S.Ct. 154, 160, 90 L.Ed. 95, 104 (1945).

32. Milliken v. Meyer, 311 U.S. 457, 463, 61 S.Ct. 339, 342, 85 L.Ed. 278, 283 (1940), reh. denied 312 U.S. 712, 61 S.Ct. 548, 85 L.Ed. 1143, conformed to 107 Colo. 295, 111 P.2d 232; Top Form Mills, Inc. v. Sociedad Nationale Industria Applicazioni Viscosa, 428 F.Supp. 1237, 1251 (S.D.N.Y.1977).

33. Memphis Light, Gas & Water Div. v. Craft, 436 U.S. 1, 13, 98 S.Ct. 1554, 1562, 56 L.Ed.2d 30, 41 (1978); Mullane v. Central Hanover Bank & Trust Co., 339 U.S. 306, 313, 70 S.Ct. 652, 656, 94 L.Ed. 865, 873 (1950); International Controls Corp. v. Vesco, 593 F.2d 166, 176 (2d Cir. 1979), cert. denied 442 U.S. 941, 99 S.Ct. 2884, 61 L.Ed.2d 311; Stateside Machinery Co., Ltd. v. Alperin, 591 F.2d 234, 241 (3d Cir. 1979); North Alabama Exp., Inc. v. United States, 585 F.2d 783, 787 (5th Cir. 1978).

34. Cooper v. Reynolds, 77 U.S. (10 Wall.) 308, 19 L.Ed. 931 (1870).

35. This was the basis for notification used during the days of Pennoyer v. Neff, 95 U.S. 714, 24 L.Ed. 565 (1878). It was felt that since property was always in the possession of its owner, seizure of the property would inform him of the action brought. This rule acted to deprive persons of their property without ever having received actual notice, even though their current whereabouts were easily ascertainable.

36. Mullane v. Central Hanover Bank & Trust Co., 339 U.S. 306, 317, 70 S.Ct. 652, 658, 94 L.Ed. 865, 875 (1950).

Plaintiffs are now required to take notification of the defendant seriously. Due diligence must be made to discover the whereabouts of the defendant. No longer may a plaintiff make a feeble effort through publication or posting notice on the courthouse door. The courts are emphatic on holding that, when notice is a person's due, process which is a mere gesture is not due process.[37]

These guarantees, however, are not absolute and may be waived by the parties. They may agree to a particular manner and method of notice, and so long as the bargain is not tainted with unequal bargaining power, unconscious ability and so forth, it will be enforced.[38] As acknowledged by the United States Supreme Court in *Boddie v. Connecticut*, "the hearing required by due process is subject to waiver." [39]

§ 4.5 Venue

The final consideration in determining which court to sue in is the question of venue. In which judicial district should suit be filed? The term "venue" comes from the French language and literally means "to have come". Use of the word is derived from early English common law. During that period the jury was composed of townfolk who knew the parties and were familiar with the facts involved.[40] Originally, because of this, all actions had to be tried in the county where the cause of action arose.[41] The jurors were said "to have come" from X county, hence use of the word "venue".[42]

---

37. Id. at 315, 70 S.Ct. at 657, 94 L.Ed. at 874.

38. Comprehensive Merchandising Catalogs, Inc. v. Madison Sales Corp., 521 F.2d 1210, 1212 (7th Cir. 1975). See also M/S Bremen v. Zapata Off-Shore Co., 407 U.S. 1, 11, 92 S.Ct. 1907, 1913, 32 L.Ed.2d 513, 521 (1972), conformed to 464 F.2d 1395 (5th Cir.).

39. 401 U.S. 371, 378–79, 91 S.Ct. 780, 786–787, 28 L.Ed.2d 113, 119 (1971), conformed to 329 F.Supp. 844 (D. Conn.). See also D. H. Overmyer Co., Inc. v. Frick Co., 405 U.S. 174, 185, 92 S.Ct. 775, 782, 31 L.Ed.2d 124, 134 (1972).

40. Crawford v. Carson, 138 W.Va. 852, 78 S.E.2d 268 (1953).

41. McCoubrey v. Pure Oil Co., 179 Okl. 344, 66 P.2d 57 (1937). See also Little v. Chicago, St. P., M. & O. Ry. Co., 65 Minn. 48, 67 N.W. 846 (1896); Coleman v. Lucksinger, 224 Mo. 1, 123 S.W. 441 (1909).

42. Brown v. State, 219 Ind. 251, 37 N.E.2d 73 (1941); State ex rel. McAllister v. Slate, 278 Mo. 570, 214 S.W. 85 (1919); Hardenburgh v. Hardenburgh, 115 Mont. 469, 146 P.2d 151 (1944).

As it is employed today, venue means the place, that is, the county or district where a cause of action is to be tried.[43] It refers to the geographical area in which a *defendant* has a *right to be sued*.[44]

At common law, subsequent to the change in the make-up of the jury to impartial persons having no knowledge of the parties or facts involved, venue was dependent upon whether the action was local or transitory. An action was transitory if it could have arisen anywhere,[45] and suit could be tried wherever one could obtain personal service on the defendant.[46] If, by its nature, the cause of action could have arisen in only one place, then the action is local and must be tried in that one place.[47] The distinction between local and transitory action, once determinative, had largely disappeared.[48] In most, if not all, jurisdictions today, venue is governed entirely by statute.[49]

The usual statute provides for the bringing of transitory actions at the place of the defendant's residence. Some statutes allow such

---

43. Minnesota Val. Canning Co. v. Rehnblom, 242 Iowa 1112, 49 N.W.2d 553, 554 (1951); Stanton Trust & Sav. Bank v. Johnson, 104 Mont. 235, 65 P.2d 1188, 1189 (1937); Public Utility Dist. No. 1 of Kitsap County v. Puget Sound Power and Light Co., 43 Wash. 2d 1, 260 P.2d 315, 317 (1953).

44. Stewart v. Carr, 218 So.2d 525, 527 (Fla.App.1969); Bledsoe v. State, 223 Ind. 675, 64 N.E.2d 160, 161 (1945); Fireproof Constr., Inc. v. Brenner-Bell, Inc., 152 Ohio St. 347, 89 N.E.2d 472, 474 (1949).

45. Texas & P. R. Co. v. Cox, 145 U.S. 593, 12 S.Ct. 905, 36 L.Ed. 829 (1891); Taylor v. Sommers Bros. Match Co., 35 Idaho 30, 204 P. 472 (1922); Roberts v. Cooter, 184 Kan. 805, 339 P.2d 362 (1959). Examples of transitory actions are those on contracts or for personal injuries.

46. Little v. Chicago, St. P. M. & O. Ry. Co., 65 Minn. 48, 67 N.W. 846 (1896); Bagdon v. Philadelphia & Reading Coal & Iron Co., 217 N.Y. 432, 111 N.E. 1075 (1916).

47. Reasor-Hill Corp. v. Harrison, 220 Ark. 521, 249 S.W.2d 994, 997 (1952) (McFadden, J., dissenting); Western Union Tel. Co. v. Bush, 191 Ark. 1085, 89 S.W.2d 723 (1936); Phillips v. Baltimore, 110 Md. 431, 72 A. 902 (1909); Calder v. Third Judicial Dist. Court, 2 Utah 2d 309, 273 P.2d 168 (1954).

48. The distinction may still be important where the local statute does not cover all of the problems that arise, as where such statute must be interpreted, or when suit is brought on a cause of action arising in another jurisdiction. Ohio River Contract Co. v. Gordon, 244 U.S. 68, 37 S.Ct. 599, 61 L.Ed. 997 (1917); Kansas City Western R. Co. v. McAdow, 240 U.S. 51, 36 S.Ct. 252, 60 L.Ed. 520 (1916).

49. In the absence of any express constitutional provision the legislature can determine venue as it sees fit, so long as it does not arbitrarily discriminate against particular persons or groups. State v. First State Bank, 52 N.D. 231, 202 N.W. 391 (1925), followed 52 N.D. 83, 202 N.W. 404; Allen v. Smith, 84 Ohio St. 283, 95 N.E. 829 (1911); Deese v. Williams, 236 S.C. 292, 113 S.E.2d 823 (1960); Perfecto Gas Co. v. State, 228 S.W.2d 918 (Tex.Civ.App.1950).

actions where the plaintiff resides, where the cause of action arose, or the place of the transaction out of which the cause of action arose.[50] Local actions generally may still only be brought where the cause of action arose.[51]

By statute, actions may often be brought against a corporation at any place where it is doing business.[52] The legislature may also provide for suits against corporations in the county where the cause of action arose [53] or where the corporation is domiciled.[54] In the absence of an applicable statute, no unincorporated association can be sued as an entity; the law of venue as it relates to individuals applies.[55] However, statutes often allow action to be brought in the association name.[56]

Venue, even though fixed by statute, may be conferred upon a court by the consent of the parties,[57] or may be waived either contractually [58] or by the failure to make a timely, proper objection.[59]

50. Minnesota Val. Canning Co. v. Rehnblom, 242 Iowa 1112, 49 N.W.2d 553 (1951) ("The legislature may fix the venue of place of trial of civil actions as long as constitutional provisions are not violated").

51. Turlock Theatre Co. v. Laws, 12 Cal.2d 573, 86 P.2d 345 (1939); United Biscuit Co. of America v. Voss Truck Lines, 407 Ill. 488, 95 N.E.2d 439 (1950); Smith v. Wells, 271 Ky. 373, 112 S.W.2d 49 (1937); First Nat'l Bank of Seminole v. Henshaw, 169 Okl. 49, 35 P.2d 898 (1934).

52. Allen v. Smith, 84 Ohio St. 283, 95 N.E. 829 (1911).

53. Bain Peanut Co. v. Pinson, 282 U.S. 499, 51 S.Ct. 228, 75 L.Ed. 482 (1931); Forman v. Mississippi Publishers Corp., 195 Miss. 90, 14 So.2d 344 (1943).

54. Forman v. Mississippi Publishers Corp., 195 Miss. 90, 14 So.2d 344 (1943).

55. Ivanhoe Grand Lodge A. F. & A. M. v. Most Worshipful Grand Lodge of Ancient Free & Accepted Masons of Colorado, 126 Colo. 515, 251 P.2d 1085 (1952); Karges Furniture Co. v. Amalgamated Woodworkers Local Union No. 131, 165 Ind. 421, 75 N.E. 877 (1905); Lafayette Chapter of Property Owners Ass'n v. Lafayette, 129 Ind.App. 425, 157 N.E.2d 287 (1959).

56. McNulty v. Higginbotham, 252 Ala. 218, 40 So.2d 414 (1949); Hall v. Walters, 226 S.C. 430, 85 S.E.2d 729 (1955), cert. denied 349 U.S. 953, 75 S.Ct. 881, 99 L.Ed. 1277.

57. Industrial Addition Ass'n v. Commissioner of Internal Revenue, 323 U.S. 310, 65 S.Ct. 289, 89 L.Ed. 260 (1945); Neirbo Co. v. Bethlehem Shipbuilding Co., 308 U.S. 165, 60 S.Ct. 153, 84 L.Ed. 167 (1939). This is so because venue statutes are not interpreted as limiting jurisdiction that otherwise attaches. United States v. Hvoslef, 237 U.S. 1, 35 S.Ct. 459, 59 L.Ed. 813 (1915).

58. Mittenthal v. Mascagni, 183 Mass. 19, 66 N.E. 425 (1903).

59. Generally, failure to make objection to improper venue before demurring or pleading constitutes a waiver of that objection. Thames & Mersey Marine Ins. Co. v. United States, 237 U.S. 19, 35 S.Ct. 496, 59 L.Ed. 821 (1915); Iselen v. LaCoste, 147 F.2d 791 (5th Cir. 1945); Kentucky Utilities Co. v. Steenman, 283 Ky. 317, 141 S.W.2d 265 (1940).

Usually only parties to the case can apply for a change of venue.[60] If there are several parties on the same side, generally they must all unite in an application for a change of venue before it will be granted.[61] A statutory right to a change in venue is ordinarily available to either side.[62]

Local statutes generally prescribe the grounds for a change of venue. In the majority of jurisdictions, the grounds specified by the statute are the only ones available.[63] Local prejudice, bias, or inability to obtain a fair and impartial trial at the place venue is laid is a ground for a change of venue.[64] Likewise, bias or prejudice of the trial judge is also a ground.[65] Frequently, a motion to transfer venue of a case on the ground such will serve the convenience of witnesses and will promote justice is addressed to the discretion of the trial court.[66] The judge's decision will be upheld unless it is arbitrary.[67]

60. State ex rel. Young v. Niblack, 229 Ind. 596, 99 N.E.2d 839 (1951).

61. Klein v. German Nat'l Bank, 69 Ark. 140, 61 S.W. 572 (1901); In re Greybull Val. Irrigation Dist., 52 Wyo. 479, 76 P.2d 339 (1938), followed 52 Wyo. 513, 76 P.2d 351, reh. denied 52 Wyo. 479, 77 P.2d 617.

62. Olsom v. Sioux Falls, 63 S.D. 563, 262 N.W. 85 (1935). Plaintiff, however, cannot be granted a change of venue on the ground that the action was laid in the wrong county.

63. State ex rel. Young v. Niblack, 229 Ind. 596, 99 N.E.2d 839 (1951); Elliot v. Wallowa County, 57 Or. 236, 109 P. 130 (1910).

64. Rice v. Schubert, 101 Cal.App.2d 638, 226 P.2d 50 (1951); Reynolds v. Coburn, 285 Ky. 544, 148 S.W.2d 705 (1941); State ex rel. Stephens v. District Court, 43 Mont. 571, 118 P. 268 (1911) (Lists grounds for change of venue by judge; cannot have impartial trial; convenience of witnesses; judge is disqualified); Shelton v. Southern Kraft Corp., 195 S.C. 81, 10 S.E.2d 341 (1940).

65. Bentley v. Lucky Friday Extension Mining Co., 70 Idaho 511, 223 P.2d 947 (1947); Rugenstein v. Ottenheimer, 78 Or. 371, 152 P. 215 (1915).

66. Roof v. Tiller, 195 S.C. 132, 10 S.E.2d 333 (1940). In Indiana in a civil suit, either party may have one change of venue from the judge and one from the county by filing a proper affidavit setting up the statutory grounds, and within the time specified by statute and Supreme Court Rules. The granting of the change does not present any issue of fact, except as the form of the affidavit and the granting thereof is mandatory. See also State ex rel. Lindsey v. Beavers, 225 Ind. 398, 75 N.E.2d 660 (1947); State ex rel. Bradshaw v. Probate Court, 225 Ind. 268, 73 N.E.2d 769 (1947); State ex rel. Smith v. Chambers, 211 Ind. 640, 6 N.E.2d 950 (1937).

67. Smith v. Mathers' Adm'r, 281 Ky. 213, 135 S.W.2d 889 (1940); Wilson v. Southern Furniture Co., 224 S.C. 281, 78 S.E.2d 890 (1953).

§ 4.6 Jurisdiction and Venue in Federal Courts

Because the federal courts have only limited jurisdiction, one should know exactly what is required to get a case heard in a federal court. Unless a *federal question* is involved, or Congress has *statutorily* created the right to bring suit in federal courts in a particular situation, jurisdiction must come within the parameters of 28 U.S.C. § 1331—jurisdiction based on *diversity of citizenship*.

For a comprehensive discussion of jurisdiction and venue in federal courts, reference is made to Wright and Miller, Federal Practice and Procedure, § 3501 et seq.

A. Diversity Defined.

Diversity jurisdiction does not exist unless *each* defendant is a citizen of a different state from *each* plaintiff.[68] Diversity is determined at the time suit is filed,[69] and jurisdiction is unaffected by subsequent changes in the citizenship of the parties.[70] In order for a person to be deemed a citizen of a particular state, he/she must be domiciled in that state and must be a citizen of the United States.[71]

---

68. Owen Equipment & Erection Co. v. Kroger, 437 U.S. 365, 98 S.Ct. 2396, 57 L.Ed.2d 274 (1978); Iowa Public Serv. Co. v. Medicine Bow Coal Co., 556 F.2d 400 (8th Cir. 1977); Simon & Flynn, Inc. v. Time, Inc., 513 F.2d 832 (2d Cir. 1975); Harrison v. Prather, 404 F.2d 267 (5th Cir. 1968); Pilkinton v. Pilkinton, 389 F.2d 32 (8th Cir. 1968), cert. denied 392 U.S. 906, 88 S.Ct. 2057, 20 L.Ed.2d 1364; Sacks v. Reynolds Securities, Inc., 434 F.Supp. 37 (D.D.C.1977); Alexander v. Allister Constr. Co., 424 F.Supp. 277 (N.D.Ill.1976); Trivett v. Bank of Delaware, 421 F.Supp. 827 (D.C.Del.1976); Barrett v. Covert, 354 F.Supp. 446 (E.D.Pa.1973); Schetter v. Heim, 300 F.Supp. 1070 (E.D.Wis.1969).

69. Hoefferle Truck Sales, Inc. v. Divco-Wayne Corp., 523 F.2d 543 (7th Cir. 1975); Ray v. Bird & Son & Asset Realization Co., Inc., 519 F.2d 1081 (5th Cir. 1975); Mullins v. Beatrice Pocahontas Co., 489 F.2d 260 (4th Cir. 1974), on remand 374 F.Supp. 282 (W.D.Va.); Krasnov v. Dinan, 465 F.2d 1298 (3d Cir. 1972); American Foundation, Inc. v. Mountain Lake Corp., 454 F.2d 200 (5th Cir. 1972); Spears v. Ohio River Co., 406 F.2d 344 (3d Cir. 1969); Alexander v. Allister Constr. Co., 424 F.Supp. 277 (N.D.Ill.1976); Wright v. Redding, 408 F.Supp. 1180 (E.D.Pa.1975); Anderson v. Cecil, 407 F.Supp. 1354 (E.D.Tenn.1975).

70. Mas v. Perry, 489 F.2d 1396 (5th Cir. 1974), reh. denied 492 F.2d 1242, cert. denied 419 U.S. 842, 95 S.Ct. 74, 42 L.Ed.2d 70; Television Reception Corp. v. Dunbar, 426 F.2d 174 (6th Cir. 1970); Johnston v. Cordell Nat'l Bank, 421 F.2d 1310 (10th Cir. 1970); Lefkowitz v. Lider, 443 F.Supp. 352 (D.C.Mass.1978).

71. Mas v. Perry, 489 F.2d 1396 (5th Cir. 1974), reh. denied 492 F.2d 1242, cert. denied 419 U.S. 842, 95 S.Ct. 74, 42 L.Ed.2d 70; Kaufman & Broad, Inc. v. Gootrad, 397 F.Supp. 1054 (S.D.N.Y.1975); McGlynn v. Employers Commercial Union Ins. Co. of America, 386 F.Supp. 774 (D.C.P.R.1974); Codagnone v. Perrin, 351 F.Supp. 1126 (D.C.R.I.1972).

Domicile is in turn based on residence and an intent to remain for an indefinite period of time.[72]

It is conceivable to have a case in which a party is a citizen of the United States but not a citizen of any state for purposes of diversity jurisdiction. This might be possible in the case of a person who is consistently mobile [73] and does in fact occur when a citizen of the United States is domiciled outside the country.[74]

B. Class Actions.

Special rules apply to class actions. Diversity in such cases is determined by the citizenship of the *named representatives* only, not the citizenship of the class members.[75] However, in a class action based on diversity, *each* member must have a claim in excess of $10,000, unless a common and undivided interest among the members of the class can be shown.[76]

Class actions in federal courts are subject to many other procedural restrictions. It is suggested that the attorney fully acquaint himself with Rule 23 of the Federal Rules of Civil Procedure before filing a class action in federal courts.

C. Corporations.

Corporations, for diversity of jurisdiction purposes, are citizens of the state wherein they are incorporated, and the state where they

---

72. Stifel v. Hopkins, 477 F.2d 1116 (6th Cir. 1973); Johnston v. Cordell Nat'l Bank, 421 F.2d 1310 (10th Cir. 1970).

73. Wasson v. Northrup Worldwide Aircraft Serv., Inc., 443 F.Supp. 400, 405 n. 13 (W.D.Tex.1978). ("It may be possible to have a case in which a party is a citizen of the United States and yet is not a citizen of any state for diversity purposes. One of the aspects of diversity jurisdiction that 'is inherently not founded in reason' is that a party who is consistently mobile or who travels from one job to another could find the door to a federal forum entirely closed should he seek to invoke diversity jurisdiction.")

74. Kaufman & Broad, Inc. v. Gootrad, 397 F.Supp. 1054 (S.D.N.Y.1975); Fakrner v. Gentzach, 355 F.Supp. 349 (E.D.Pa.1972); McGlynn v. Employers Commercial Union Ins. Co. of America, 386 F.Supp. 774 (D.C.P.R.1974); Hernandez v. Lucas, 254 F.Supp. 901 (S.D.Tex.1966); Clapp v. Stearns & Co., 229 F.Supp. 305 (S.D.N.Y.1964); Berhalter v. Irmisch, 75 F.R.D. 539 (W.D.N.Y.1977).

75. United States ex rel. Sero v. Preiser, 506 F.2d 1115 (2d Cir. 1974), cert. denied 421 U.S. 921, 95 S.Ct. 1587, 43 L.Ed.2d 789; Rocket Oil & Gas Co. v. Arkla Exploration Co., 435 F.Supp. 1303 (W.D.Okl.1977).

76. Zahn v. International Paper Co., 414 U.S. 291, 94 S.Ct. 505, 38 L.Ed.2d 511 (1973); Holloway v. Bristol-Myers Corp., 158 U.S.App.D.C. 207, 485 F.2d 986 (1973); Dierks v. Thompson, 414 F.2d 453 (1st Cir. 1969); Brown v. Tahoe Regional Planning Agency, 385 F.Supp. 1128 (D.C.Nev.1973); LeBlanc v. Spector, 378 F.Supp. 301 (D.C.Conn.1973); Weiss v. Sunasco Inc., 316 F.Supp. 1197 (E.D.Pa.1970).

have their principal place of business.[77] A corporation's principal place of business is its "nerve center," that location from which it "radiates out to its constituent parts and from which its officers direct, control and coordinate all activities without regard to locale, in furtherance of the corporate objective."[78]

D. Amount in Controversy.

Section 1332 of 28 U.S.C.A. requires the amount in controversy to be in excess of $10,000 for "diversity" jurisdiction.[79] This amount is exclusive of interest and costs.[80] The test used to determine the existence of this amount is not the sum actually awarded plaintiff, but the sum demanded in good faith.[81] If the plaintiff claims damages in excess of $10,000, the court will not dismiss the case for want of jurisdiction unless it appears to a *legal certainty* that he will not recover that amount.[82]

In order to discourage plaintiffs from filing inflated claims for the purpose of creating federal jurisdiction, the court may deny costs to the plaintiff, or even *impose* costs against him, if the returned verdict is less than $10,000.[83]

---

77. 28 U.S.C.A. § 1332(c); Mississippi Pub. Corp. v. Murphree, 326 U.S. 438, 66 S.Ct. 242, 90 L.Ed. 185 (1945); Ellis v. J–R–M Corp., 324 F.Supp. 768 (D.C.Hawaii 1971); General Foods Corp. v. Struthers Scientific & Int'l Corp., 297 F.Supp. 271 (D.C.Del.1969); Harris Diamond Co. v. Army Times Pub. Co., 280 F.Supp. 273 (S.D.N.Y. 1968); Vogel v. Tenneco Oil Co., 276 F.Supp. 1008 (D.D.C.1967).

78. Uniroyal, Inc. v. Heller, 65 F.R.D. 83, 86 (S.D.N.Y.1974). See also Horwat v. Paulsen-Webber Cordage Corp., 336 F.Supp. 1020 (W.D.Pa. 1971); Inland Rubber Corp. v. Triple A Tire Serv., Inc., 220 F.Supp. 490 (S.D.N.Y.1963); Wear-Ever Aluminum, Inc. v. Sipos, 184 F.Supp. 364 (S.D.N.Y.1960).

79. Note that § 1331 of 28 U.S.C.A. was amended in 1980 to no longer require a jurisdictional amount for "federal question" jurisdiction.

80. Fehling v. Cantonwine, 522 F.2d 604 (10th Cir. 1975); Lonquist v. J. C. Penney Co., 421 F.2d 597 (10th Cir. 1970); White v. North American Acc. Ins. Co., 316 F.2d 5 (10th Cir. 1963).

81. Etheridge v. Piper Aircraft Corp., 559 F.2d 1027 (5th Cir. 1977); Fehling v. Cantonwine, 522 F.2d 604 (10th Cir. 1975); Gibson v. Jeffers, 478 F.2d 216 (10th Cir. 1973); Johns-Manville Sales Corp. v. Mitchell Enterprises, Inc., 417 F.2d 129 (5th Cir. 1969); Jones v. Landry, 387 F.2d 102 (5th Cir. 1967).

82. Wood v. Stark Tri-County Bldg. Trades Council, 473 F.2d 272 (6th Cir. 1973); Jeffries v. Silvercup Bakers, Inc., 434 F.2d 310 (7th Cir. 1970); Bridgess v. Youree, 436 F.Supp. 458 (W.D.Okl.1977); Griffith v. Southwestern Bell Tel. Co., 428 F.Supp. 284 (W.D.Okl.1976); Jeter v. Jim Walter Homes, Inc., 414 F.Supp. 791 (W.D. Okl.1976); Cunningham v. Ford Motor Co., 413 F.Supp. 1101 (D.C.S.C. 1976).

83. 28 U.S.C.A. § 1332(b).

E. Removal of Cases from State Courts.

If the plaintiff files suit in state court, the defense has the right to remove the case to the federal court in that judicial district.[84] This right to removal is dependent upon the following three factors:

1. The federal court must have original jurisdiction (i. e., complete diversity and more than $10,000 in controversy).[85]

2. The state court must have had proper jurisdiction. If not, the federal court must dismiss the case without prejudice.[86] This is true even though the federal courts have exclusive jurisdiction, and jurisdiction would have been proper had suit originally been filed in the federal district court.[87]

3. The petition for removal must be filed within 30 days after the defendant has been served.[88]

Once a case has been properly removed to the federal court, that court has jurisdiction to hear all of the claims involved, even if some may otherwise be non-removable.[89] The retention or remand of any claims not within the district court's original jurisdiction is subject only to the discretion of the district court.[90]

---

84. 28 U.S.C.A. § 1441(a).

85. Snow v. Ford Motor Co., 561 F.2d 787 (9th Cir. 1977); DiAntonio v. Pennsylvania State Univ., 455 F.Supp. 510 (M.D.Pa.1978); City of Princeton v. Francisco, 454 F.Supp. 33 (S.D. Iowa 1978); Shelly v. Pennsylvania, 451 F.Supp. 899 (M.D.Pa.1978); Housing Auth. of Dauphin County v. Danner, 448 F.Supp. 152 (M.D.Pa.1978); City of New York v. New York Jets Football Club, Inc., 429 F.Supp. 987 (S.D.N.Y.1977); Kerbow v. Kerbow, 421 F.Supp. 1253 (N.D.Tex.1976); Selected Risks Ins. Co. v. Kobelinski, 421 F.Supp. 431 (E.D.Pa.1976); Genie Machine Products, Inc. v. Midwestern Machinery Co., 367 F.Supp. 897 (W. D.Mo.1974).

86. Bancohio Corp. v. Fox, 516 F.2d 29 (6th Cir. 1977); Wamp v. Chattanooga Housing Auth., 384 F.Supp. 251 (E.D.Tenn.1974), aff'd 527 F.2d 595 (6th Cir.), cert. denied 425 U.S. 992, 96 S.Ct. 2203, 48 L.Ed.2d 816.

87. Guthrie v. Dow Chem. Co., 445 F. Supp. 311 (S.D.Tex.1978); McNeil v. Suffolk County Painters Ins., 431 F. Supp. 387 (E.D.N.Y.1977); McMahon Chevrolet, Inc. v. Davis, 392 F.Supp. 322 (S.D.Tex.1975); J. J. Ryan & Sons, Inc., v. Continental Ins. Co., 369 F.Supp. 692 (D.C.S.C.1974); Joyce v. Federal Crop Ins. Corp., 356 F.Supp. 928 (E.D.Mo.1973).

88. 28 U.S.C.A. § 1446(b).

89. 28 U.S.C.A. § 1441(c); Johnson v. Alexandria Scrap Corp., 445 F.Supp. 1171 (D.C.Md.1971); Bond v. Doig, 433 F.Supp. 243 (D.C.N.J.1977); Raleigh-Durham Airport Auth. v. Delta Air Lines, Inc., 429 F.Supp. 1069 (D. C.N.C.1976).

90. People of State of Illinois ex rel. Bowman v. Home Fed. Sav. & Loan Ass'n, 521 F.2d 704 (7th Cir. 1975); Griffin v. Hooper-Holmes Bureau, Inc., 413 F.Supp. 107 (M.D.Fla.1976); Leinberger v. Webster, 66 F.R.D. 28 (E.D.N.Y.1975).

§ 4.6 INTRODUCTION Pt. 1

If the court drops the claim which gave the federal court jurisdiction, the federal court may nonetheless still hear the remaining non-removable claims.[91] Its only other alternative is to remand the case to the state court.[92] In such an event, it is improper for the federal court to dismiss the action.

F. Venue and Change of Venue.

(i) Persons, Corporations, and Partnerships.

In a diversity action, venue is proper in the district where *all* plaintiffs or *all* defendants reside, or in which the cause of action arose.[93] A corporation, for venue purposes, may be sued in any judicial district in which it is incorporated, licensed to do business, or is doing business.[94]

The residence of a partnership is determined by applying state law. If the state does not recognize a partnership as a separate legal entity, then venue is determined by the residence of each partner.[95]

(ii) Section 1404(a)—Change of Venue.

If jurisdiction and venue were proper when suit was filed, the federal court, for the convenience of the parties and in the interests of justice, may transfer the case to any district where it might have been brought.[96] Although the basis of this rule is the doctrine of *forum non conveniens*,[97] it allows a court to grant transfers upon a lesser showing of inconvenience than was required at common law.[98]

Before a court will abstain from hearing a case under Section 1404, the availability of a more convenient forum must be

---

91. Watkinns v. Grover, 508 F.2d 920 (9th Cir. 1974); Brough v. United Steelworkers of America, AFL–CIO, 437 F.2d 748 (1st Cir. 1971); Murphy v. Kodz, 351 F.2d 163 (9th Cir. 1965).

92. Ondis v. Barrows, 538 F.2d 904 (1st Cir. 1976).

93. 28 U.S.C.A. § 1391(a). See also Peebles v. Murray, 411 F.Supp. 1174 (D.C.Kan.1976).

94. 28 U.S.C.A. § 1391(b). See also Richards v. Upjohn Co., 406 F.Supp. 405 (E.D.Mich.1976); Radiation Researchers, Inc. v. Fischer Indus., Inc., 70 F.R.D. 561 (W.D.Okl.1976).

95. Thee v. Marvin Glass & Associates 412 F.Supp. 116 (E.D.N.Y.1976). ("[U]nder the law of the State of New York which is applicable in the instant case, it is well established that a partnership is not a separate jural entity from that of its individual partners, and that its residence is that of the individual partners").

96. 28 U.S.C.A. § 1404(a). See also Watson v. DeFelice, 428 F.Supp. 1276 (D.D.C.1977).

97. Farmanfarmaian v. Gulf Oil Corp., 437 F.Supp. 910 (S.D.N.Y.1977); Coffill v. Atlantic Coast Line R. R. Co., 180 F.Supp. 105 (E.D.N.Y.1960).

98. DeLay & Daniels, Inc. v. Allen M. Campbell Co., Gen. Contractors, Inc., 71 F.R.D. 368 (D.C.S.C.1976); Hughes v. Scaffide, 53 Ohio St.2d 85, 372 N. E.2d 598 (1978).

demonstrated.[99] The plaintiff's choice of forum will be disturbed only where the evidence and circumstances are *strongly* in favor of the transfer.[1] Some of the factors the court considers include access to sources of proof, availability of compulsory process, residences of witnesses, plaintiff, and defendant, and so forth.[2]

A limitation on change of venue is that the case may be transferred only to a district *"where it might have been brought."* This means that plaintiff originally could have filed suit in the transferee court.[3] This requires that a court could have obtained in personam jurisdiction over the parties [4] and venue would have been proper.[5]

If the case is transferred, the transferee court must apply the state law which the transferor court would have applied had there been no change of venue.[6] With respect to state law, any change of venue under Section 1404 operates merely to change the courtroom.

99. Weiner v. Shearson, Hammill & Co., Inc., 521 F.2d 817 (9th Cir. 1975); Mohr v. Allen, 407 F.Supp. 483 (S.D. N.Y.1976); Watwood v. Barber, 70 F.R.D. 1 (N.D.Ga.1976).

1. Pope v. Missouri Pac. R. R. Co., 446 F.Supp. 447 (W.D.Okl.1978); Bussey v. Safeway Stores, Inc., 437 F.Supp. 41 (E.D.Okl.1977); American Can Co. v. Crown Cork & Seal Co., Inc., 433 F.Supp. 333 (E.D.Wis.1977); National Ass'n for Advancement of Colored People v. Levi, 418 F.Supp. 1109 (D. D.C.1976); Magnavox Co. v. Bally Mfg. Corp., 414 F.Supp. 891 (N.D.Ill. 1976); Poncy v. Johnson & Johnson, 414 F.Supp. 551 (S.D.Fla.1976); St. Hilaire v. Shapiro, 407 F.Supp. 1029 (E.D.N.Y.1976).

2. Alcoa S. S. Co., Inc. v. M/V Nordic Regent, 453 F.Supp. 10 (S.D.N.Y. 1978); Scott & Fetzer Co. v. McCarty, 450 F.Supp. 274 (N.D.Ohio 1977); Dale Metals Corp. v. Kiwa Chem. Industry Co., Ltd., 442 F.Supp. 78 (S.D. N.Y.1977); Texaco Trinidad, Inc. v. Astro Exito Navegacion S. A., Panama, 437 F.Supp. 331 (S.D.N.Y.1977).

3. Schreiber v. Allis-Chalmers Corp., 448 F.Supp. 1079 (D.C.Kan.1978), rev'd 611 F.2d 790; Northwest Animal Hosp., Inc. v. Earnhardt, 452 F. Supp. 191 (W.D.Okl.1977); McLouth Steel Corp. v. Jewell Coal & Coke Co., Inc., 432 F.Supp. 10 (E.D.Tenn. 1976); ITT Thorp Corp. v. Firemen's Ins. Co. of Newark, 428 F.Supp. 62 (E.D.Wis.1977).

4. McCoy v. United States Bd. of Parole, 537 F.2d 962 (8th Cir. 1976); Schreiber v. Allis-Chalmers Corp., 448 F.Supp. 1079 (D.C.Kan.1978), rev'd 611 F.2d 790; Weltmann v. Fletcher, 431 F.Supp. 448 (N.D.Ohio 1976); American Tel. & Tel. Co. v. Milgo Electronic Corp., 428 F.Supp. 50 (S.D.N.Y.1977); Garner v. Enright, 71 F.R.D. 656 (E.D.N.Y.1976).

5. In re Pope, 580 F.2d 620 (D.C.Cir. 1978); Caleshu v. Wangelin, 549 F.2d 93 (8th Cir. 1977); United States v. Casey, 420 F.Supp. 273 (S.D.Ga.1976); Peebles v. Murray, 411 F.Supp. 1174 (D.C.Kan.1976).

6. Van Dusen v. Barrack, 376 U.S. 612, 84 S.Ct. 805, 11 L.Ed.2d 945 (1964), on remand 236 F.Supp. 645 (E.D.Pa.); Cohen v. Ayers, 449 F.Supp. 298 (N. D.Ill.1978), aff'd 596 F.2d 733 (7th Cir.); Brick v. Dominion Mort. & Realty Trust, 442 F.Supp. 283 (W.D. N.Y.1977); Placek v. Winnebago Indus., Inc., 427 F.Supp. 359 (W.D. Pa.1977); Raymond-Dravo-Langen-

§ 4.6 INTRODUCTION Pt. 1

(iii) Section 1406—Cure or Waiver of Defects.

If venue is *improper* in the federal district court where the suit was originally filed, then Section 1406 is applicable. This section provides for the dismissal of the action, *or transfer* to any district in which it could have been brought.[7] The district court may transfer the case if the transferee court has subject matter jurisdiction over the case, the defendant is amenable to its personal jurisdiction, and proper venue exists in the transferee court.[8]

felder v. Microdot, Inc., 425 F.Supp. 614 (D.C.Del.1976); Harriman v. E. I. Du Pont de Nemours & Co., 411 F. Supp. 133 (D.C.Del.1975) (Transferee court must apply conflicts of law rules of transferor court).

7. 28 U.S.C.A. § 1406(a); Corke v. Sameiet M. S. Song of Norway, 572 F. 2d 77 (2d Cir. 1978); O'Neal v. Hicks Brokerage Co., 537 F.2d 1266 (4th Cir. 1976); De La Fuente v. I. C. C., 451 F.Supp. 867 (N.D.Ill.1978); Papercraft Corp. v. Procter & Gamble Co., 439 F.Supp. 1060 (W.D.Pa.1977); Nanz Trustee Inc. v. American Nat'l Bank & Trust Co. of Chicago, 423 F. Supp. 930 (E.D.Wis.1977).

8. Lowery v. Estelle, 533 F.2d 265 (5th Cir. 1976); Rixner v. White, 417 F. Supp. 995 (D.C.N.D.1976); Thee v. Marvin Glass & Associates, 412 F. Supp. 1116 (E.D.N.Y.1976).

§§ 4.7–5.0 are reserved for supplementary material.

PART II

BURDEN OF PROOF

CHAPTER 5

QUANTUM OF PROOF: INFERENCES, PRESUMPTIONS, POSSIBILITIES AND PROBABILITIES

Table of Sections

Sec.
5.1 "Possibilities" and "Probabilities"—In General.
5.2 Proximate Cause.
5.3 The "Lost Possibility".
5.4 Prognosis—Generally.
5.5 Prognosis—In Practice.
5.6 Different Standards in Different Proceedings.
5.7 Who May Present Proof.
5.8 Statistics in Criminal Cases.

§ 5.1 "Possibilities" and "Probabilities"—In General

The other chapters of this work ultimately concern themselves with what the jury can and cannot consider; i. e., evidence, and how presented. This chapter, still attempting to answer the client's query, "Have I a Case?" more closely approaches the finality of the lawsuit than any other chapter. The question, "How much will I have to prove?" is discussed. ("Won't the jury believe me? I don't need any witnesses. I'm telling the truth.")

How "much" must be proved before a sufficient amount of certainty [1] is presented to establish "truth"? [2] What is the quantum

---

1. "Certainty" defined as a fixed or real state; truth; fact; full assurance of mind; exemption from doubt; exemption from failure; regularity; settled state.

2. "Truth" defined as the quality or state of being true; conformity to facts or reality, as of statements to facts, words to facts, motives or actions to profession; exact accordance with what is, has been, or shall be; the quality or state of being made or constructed, true or exact; the proper and correct representation of any object in nature, or of whatever subject may be under treatment.

of proof [3] necessary in a civil suit? It is to a "preponderance" of the evidence.[4] But as distinguished from the criminal standard, "beyond a reasonable doubt and to a moral certainty," can a civil verdict be sustained on "possibilities" [5] or must it be based upon "probabilities" only? [6] If probabilities only can sustain an award, then is a trial judge justified in admitting "possibilities"?

§ 5.2 Proximate Cause

There is universal recognition that some uncertainty must attach to all human affairs. So the general quantum of civil proof required is recognizably not perfection ("absolute") but "reasonable certainty" [7] or "reasonable probability" [8] which may be established by the "preponderance of the evidence".[9]

"Preponderance of the evidence" is generally recognized as the "greater weight" of evidence [10] which tips the scales of justice in favor of the prevailing party. It need not "satisfy the minds" of the

3. "Proof" defined as any effort, process or operation that ascertains truth or fact; what serves as evidence; what proves or establishes; a convincing token or argument; means of conviction; that amount of evidence which convinces the mind of the certainty of truth or fact and produces belief.

4. "Preponderance" defined as superiority or excess of weight.

"Evidence" defined as clearness, an outward sign; indication; also that which furnishes any mode of proof.

5. "Possible" defined as that which may or can happen, be, or exist; that may be done; not contrary to the nature of things; liable to happen or come to pass; capable of being, existing, or coming to pass, but highly improbable.

6. "Probable" defined as likely; having more evidence than the contrary, or evidence which inclines the mind to believe, but leaves some room for doubt; rendering something probable; probable evidence; probable presumption, that may be proved.

Lord Mansfield said, "As mathematical and absolute certainty is seldom to be attained in human affairs, reason and public utility require that judges and all mankind, in forming their opinion of the truth of facts, should be regulated by the superior number of probabilities on the one side over the other."

7. Hetzel v. Baltimore & Ohio R. R. Co., 169 U.S. 26, 18 S.Ct. 255, 42 L. Ed. 648 (1898); Texas, & P. Ry. Co. v. Marshall, 136 U.S. 393, 10 S.Ct. 846, 34 L.Ed. 385 (1890) (The "assurance" is not exact but only approximately perfect).

8. Wirz v. Wirz, 96 Cal.App.2d 171, 214 P.2d 839, 15 A.L.R.2d 1129 (1929).

9. Coleman v. Baker, 382 S.W.2d 843 (Ky.1964).

10. Cincinnati Butchers Supply Co. v. Conoly, 204 N.C. 677, 169 S.E. 415 (1933).

Figure 80. Melvin M. Belli, Sr. illustrating quantum of proof. [Photo by Larry Nimmer]

§ 5.2 BURDEN OF PROOF Pt. 2

jury to the establishment of the facts,[11] but need only allow reasonable men to conclude that the greater probability lies with the plaintiff.[12]

A plaintiff need not conclusively negate the *possibility* that defendant's actions were not the proximate cause of the injury sustained.[13] But a recovery affirmatively based only on a "possibility" of proximate cause will be deemed based on conjecture and not be sustained.[14] And where the evidence or the inferences drawn from it is equally supportive of contrary possibilities, the trier of fact will not be allowed to select its theory on pure speculation, and proximate cause will be held not to be established.[15]

The problem is frequently encountered in medical testimony, since, as a rule, a reliable physician will be loathe to couch his testimony in "certainties", but be willing to relate the range of "possibilities" of pathological development of a given condition, based upon his experience, observation, and learning. Counsel for defendant will therefore claim that no "proof" has been adduced, but only "possibilities", and that any verdict based thereon can be founded only on speculation and conjecture.

The rule generally adhered to is that it is the jury's function to determine proximate cause to a "reasonable certainty", not the expert witness'.[16] The failure of a medical witness to testify to causation as

11. American Products Co. v. Villwock, 7 Wash.2d 246, 109 P.2d 570, 132 A.L.R. 1010 (1941); Murphy v. Waterhouse, 113 Cal. 467, 45 P. 866 (1896).

12. Consolidated Edison Co. v. N. L. R. B., 305 U.S. 197, 59 S.Ct. 206, 83 L.Ed. 126 (1938). (Evidence sufficient to support a finding must be "more than a mere scintilla. It means such relevant evidence as a reasonable mind might accept as adequate to support a conclusion.").

See also Hill v. Polar Pantries, 219 S.C. 263, 64 S.E.2d 885 (1951); Harmon v. Richardson, 88 N.H. 312, 188 A. 468 (1936); Burch v. Reading Co., 240 F.2d 574 (3d Cir. 1957), cert. denied 353 U.S. 965, 77 S.Ct. 1049, 1 L.Ed.2d 914; State of Maryland for Use of Pumphrey v. Manor Real Estate & Trust Co., 176 F.2d 414 (4th Cir. 1949).

13. Blackhawk Hotels Co. v. Bonfoey, 227 F.2d 232 (8th Cir. 1955); Ogilvie v. Aetna Life Ins. Co., 189 Cal. 406, 209 P. 26 (1922).

14. Francis v. Sauve, 222 Cal.2d 102, 34 Cal.Rptr. 754 (1963).

See also Travelers Ins. Co. v. Industrial Acc. Comm'n, 33 Cal.2d 685, 203 P.2d 747 (1949); Pacific Employers Ins. Co. v. Industrial Acc. Comm'n, 182 Cal.App.2d 162, 5 Cal.Rptr. 738 (1960).

15. Mehra v. Bentz, 529 F.2d 1137 (2d Cir. 1976), cert. denied 426 U.S. 922, 96 S.Ct. 2628, 49 L.Ed.2d 375; Cole v. Swagler, 308 N.Y. 325, 125 N.E.2d 592 (1955); McAfee v. Overberg, 51 Ohio Misc. 86, 367 N.E.2d 942 (1977); Lane v. White, 167 So.2d 14 (Fla. App.1964) (Hernia); LePrince v. McLeod, 171 So.2d 189 (Fla.App.1965), cert. denied 179 So.2d 856 (Fla.).

16. Sentilles v. Inter-Caribbean Shipping Corp., 361 U.S. 107, 80 S.Ct. 173, 4 L.Ed.2d 142 (1959).

a factual certainty does not impair the jury's power to draw reasonable inferences,[17] and many courts will indeed protect this function as the exclusive domain of the jury, and exclude the attempts of an expert witness to advance a "legal" conclusion of causation.[18]

In the U.S. Supreme Court case of *Sentilles v. Inter-Caribbean Shipping Co.*,[19] the majority, in a rare review of a lower case's facts and specific evidence, reinstated plaintiff's District Court verdict. The Court held that the failure of medical experts to testify that plaintiff's tubercular condition had *in fact* been caused by a work-related accident did not preclude the jury from drawing a legal conclusion of liability.[20]

Even where the witness has described his opinion as based on "conjecture", the legal meaning of the term has been held not to attach where the testimony is properly supported by experience and observation.[21] Expert testimony as to causation, whether expressed as "possibility", "likelihood", or "probability" is generally admissible [22] for consideration by the trier of fact, where the factual

17. Id.

18. DeGroot v. Winter, 261 Mich. 660, 247 N.W. 69 (1933) "[W]hen a result *could* have been occasioned by one of two or more causes, the ultimate fact of which cause occasioned the result is for determination by the jury, and a medical expert may not, in case of conflicting evidence, invade the province of the jury and testify that the result was in fact occasioned by one cause only").

See also Dean v. Carolina Coach Co., Inc., 287 N.C. 515, 215 S.E.2d 89 (1975).

19. 361 U.S. 107, 80 S.Ct. 173, 4 L.Ed. 2d 142 (1959).

20. "The jury's power to draw the inference that the aggravation of petitioner's tubercular condition, evident so shortly after the accident, was in fact caused by that accident, was not impaired by the failure of any medical witness to testify that it was in fact the cause. Neither can it be impaired by the lack of medical unanimity as to the respective likelihood of the potential causes of the aggravation, or by the fact that other potential causes existed and were not conclusively negated by the proofs. . . . The members of the jury, not the medical witnesses, were sworn to make a legal determination of the question of causation. They were entitled to take all the circumstances, including the medical testimony, into consideration." (361 U.S. at 109–110).

21. Cullum v. Seifer, 1 Cal.App.3d 20, 81 Cal.Rptr. 381 (1969).

See also Bauman v. San Francisco, 42 Cal.App.2d 144, 108 P.2d 989 (1940) ("[N]or should the technical definition of words constitute a controlling factor in determining the question of admissibility. But, as stated in Ballard v. Kansas City, 110 Mo.App. 391 [86 S.W. 479 (1905)], 'the main object is not to draw fine distinctions based upon accurate definitions or words, but to ascertain the real idea expressed.' ").

22. Generally, see Colson, Memorandum of Law on Reasonable Medical Possibility, Journal of the Academy of Florida Trial Lawyers, Vol. 22

basis for the expert's opinion and expertise is established.[23] And such testimony is generally, though not uniformly, sufficient to support a jury's finding of proximate cause.[24]

Library References:

C.J.S. Negligence § 103 et seq.; Torts §§ 27–30.
West's Key No. Digests, Negligence ⌐56 et seq.; Torts ⌐15.
Prosser, Law of Torts (4th ed. 1971).
Blashfield, Automobile Law & Practice, § 53.1 et seq.

§ 5.3 The "Lost Possibility"

An interesting question is presented where plaintiff (or plaintiff's decedent) suffered from a preexisting condition, and defendant's negligence consisted in the omission of proper treatment. Plaintiff wishes to show that absent defendant's failure to act, the injuries would not have occurred. Defendant wishes to establish that plaintiff (or decedent) never had a chance anyway, and thus the omission was not the proximate cause of the ultimate injury.

Plaintiff's recovery, therefore, is based on the value of the "lost possibility." A leading case is *Hicks v. United States*,[25] where a decedent's intestinal obstruction was diagnosed by Navy doctors as gastroenteritis, and decedent died shortly thereafter of a massive hemorrhagic infarction of the intestine. The government, in defense, asserted that even if negligence were established, there was no proof that the erroneous diagnosis and treatment were the cause of death, since decedent would have required immediate surgery and it would be mere speculation to assert that it would have been successful.

The Court opined for the contrary, noting that both of plaintiff's experts had testified without contradiction that, with prompt surgery, decedent would have survived. The Court analogized to the liability of a ship's captain who took no steps to reverse course and

(1963); Trial Technique: Medical Testimony in a Fracture of the Sternum and Lung Cancer Case, Med.Tr. TQ (March 1972); Expert Evidence—Exclusion of Opinion Testimony, Defense L.J., Vol. 22, No. 3 (1973); Jackson, Presenting Expert Testimony, Law Notes, Vol. 11, No. 1 (1975); Gibbons, Rules 701–706: Opinions and Expert Testimony, The Tr.Law Guide, Vol. 20, No. 4 (1977).

23. Bachran v. Morishige, 52 Hawaii 61, 469 P.2d 808 (1970) (Expert witnesses' testimony need not be restricted to "reasonable medical certainty" or otherwise).

Lockwood v. McCaskill, 262 N.C. 663, 138 S.E.2d 541 (1964); Pygman v. Helton, 148 W.Va. 281, 134 S.E.2d 717 (1964).

24. Sentilles v. Inter-Caribbean Shipping Co., 361 U.S. 107, 80 S.Ct. 173, 4 L.Ed.2d 142 (1959); Robison v. Leigh, 153 Cal.App.2d 730, 315 P.2d 42 (1957).

25. 368 F.2d 626 (4th Cir. 1966).

search for a missing seaman,[26] and held: "When a defendant's negligent action or inaction has effectively terminated a person's chance of survival, it does not lie in the defendant's mouth to raise conjectures as to the measure of the chances that he has put beyond the possibility of realization.

"If there was any substantial possibility of survival and the defendant has already destroyed it, he is answerable. Rarely is it possible to demonstrate to an absolute certainty what would have happened in circumstances that the wrongdoer did not allow to come to pass. The law does not in the existing circumstances require the plaintiff to show to a *certainty* that the patient would have lived had she been hospitalized and operated on promptly." [27]

The *Hicks* rationale was followed in *Kallenberg v. Beth Israel Hospital* [28] where medication to reduce decedent's blood pressure had been directed, but never administered, and decedent died of a cerebral aneurysm hemorrhage. Plaintiff's expert testified that had the medication been administered, and had surgery been undertaken, decedent would have had a 20%–40% chance of survival. The Court upheld the jury's finding that proximate cause had been established and plaintiff was entitled to wrongful death damages.[29]

---

26. Gardner v. National Bulk Carriers, Inc., 310 F.2d 284, 91 A.L.R.2d 1023 (4th Cir. 1962), cert. denied 372 U.S. 913, 83 S.Ct. 728, 9 L.Ed.2d 721, reh. denied 372 U.S. 961, 83 S.Ct. 1012, 10 L.Ed.2d 13. "Once the evidence sustains the reasonable possibility of rescue, ample or narrow, according to the circumstances, a total disregard of the duty, refusal to make even a try, as was the case here, imposes liability."

27. 368 F.2d at 632.

28. 45 A.D.2d 177, 357 N.Y.S.2d 508 (1974), motion denied 35 N.Y.2d 849, 363 N.Y.S.2d 87, 321 N.E.2d 878, aff'd 37 N.Y.2d 719, 374 N.Y.S.2d 615, 337 N.E.2d 128.

See also Thomas v. Corso, 265 Md. 84, 288 A.2d 379 (1972) (On-call physician failed to come to hospital to examine emergency room patient recently struck by car. Proximate cause established for decedent's subsequent death from shock, where evidence sufficient to justify a jury finding of a substantial possibility of survival destroyed by defendant's failure to examine, diagnose, and treat.).

29. See also Cullum v. Seifer, 1 Cal. App.3d 20, 81 Cal.Rptr. 381 (1969) (Malpractice action for delay in diagnosis and treatment of lymphosarcoma. Grant of new trial over defendant's verdict sustained, with finding that trial testimony supported inference that it was a reasonable medical probability that plaintiff would have benefited from earlier diagnosis, by possible lengthening of life and/or personal comfort: "The fact is that in this case, evidence of delay in treatment is a failure to conform to the standard of care in the community. The delay itself prevented more certain proof by plaintiff that had treatment been instituted sooner, her disease *would* have been arrested or cured.").

Hernandez v. Clinica Pasteur, Inc., 293 So.2d 747 (Fla.App.1974) (Decedent's

§ 5.4 Prognosis—Generally

A problem is also presented explicitly in expert medical testimony where the doctor is asked to prognosticate (advise the outcome) "permanency of disability." The question will occur, "Will plaintiff have pain in his hips as long as he lives, Doctor?" "How long will it be before the headaches subside, doctor?" [30]

If the doctor should be asked for a medical opinion, he might state, "prognosis guarded," or "failure disability uncertain." If he were a "defendant's doctor" he might testify that plaintiff might "return to work in six months;" if a "plaintiff's doctor," he might state "disability a total impairment."

But if the medical man were pressed for an answer by the patient, he would give a different sort of opinion, an answer perhaps partially intended as therapeutic good wishes. Yet none of these replies will suffice for the courtroom. There the medical witness, to his discomfiture, and sometimes plaintiff's legal concern, must state almost categorically, "to a reasonable medical certainty." This is apparently an easy standard, but it is theoretic and not so readily achieved in practice.

Let us assume a compound comminuted fracture of both tibia and fibula in the middle third of both shafts, the area of notorious non-union; arrested osteomyelitis and non-union after surgical orthopedic intervention; one unsuccessful plating, two unsuccessful bone grafts: what is this patient's disability? A totally permanent disabled lower extremity? Amputation?

Most medical men would recommend further conservative treatment and possibly a further graft before amputation. What are the *probabilities* of amputation, and, assuming an amputation, intractible "phantom pains" as a result? They are incurable by successive resections of the stump. Is cordotomy, even lobotomy, "probable," medically recommended, so that the testimony of a neurosurgeon should be admitted?

This man's disability is both "possibly" and "probably" a partial-permanent disabled lower limb. He "faces" the complete loss of

---

cardiac condition diagnosed as gastric distress. J.N.O.V. granted for defendants, on grounds that plaintiff had not proved that deceased could have been saved, reversed: "The issue of proximate cause was as to whether appellees' malpractice contributed to the cause of death. In this connection, the testimony that appellant's decedent would have had a better chance to survive if he had received prompt medical attention was sufficient to form a basis for the submission of the issue to the jury.").

30. For a philosophical discussion of probabilities and possibilities in judicial proof, see Michael and Adler (1934) 34 Cl.L.Rev. 1224, 1462.

this limb (although this result cannot be stated as a "certainty") not only in function but as a member.

Phantom pains to the amputee are very factual, yet most medical testimony would contend that the "probability" of these heroic surgical procedures (lobotomy, cordotomy) is extremely rare. Unless plaintiff can lay a sufficient foundation, it may be error to admit evidence of the surgical procedures which plaintiff himself hopes to avoid, but to which he may have to submit.

To the layman, for whom the law must, through its stewards, the lawyers, ultimately present its reasonableness of custom and procedure, it is presently an almost insurmountable problem that a jury put one dollar sign and one lump sum on such a permanently injured person, with such a disputed prognosis. Yet they, the jury, cannot come back in 5 months, 5 years, 15 years further to evaluate the case. This is plaintiff's and defendant's one and only day in court.

Often, the jurors are called upon to give a prognosis more certain than the medical men on either side of the case may be able to offer. They are aided by the instructions of the court, but these statements of rules and formulae do not help much. Indeed, the demonstrative evidence presented by counsel for both sides may be too divergent (although entirely sincere) to warrant the "conviction" of certainty on each side.[31]

§ 5.5 Prognosis—In Practice

Most courts require that an award for the future consequences of an injury be supported by evidence establishing "reasonable certainty" that the future consequences will occur. The standard is identical for future damages of pain and suffering,[32] loss of future earnings,[33] or permanent injuries,[34] in that they must rest on some-

---

31. "Convince" is defined as to persuade or satisfy by evidence; to subdue the opposition of (the minds) to truth, or to what is alleged and compel (it) to yield assent; or, to convince a man of his errors; or to convince him of the truth; to persuade.

32. Rouse v. Chicago, R. I. & P. R. Co., 474 F.2d 1180 (8th Cir. 1973); Weeks v. Latter-Day Saints Hosp., 418 F.2d 1035 (10th Cir. 1969); Adams v. Atchison, T. & S. F. Ry. Co., 280 S.W.2d 84 (Mo.1955); Knotts v. Valocchi, 2 Ohio App.2d 188, 207 N.E.2d 379 (1963); Burnett v. Caho, 7 Ill.App.3d 266, 285 N.E.2d 619 (1972); Jindra v. S. M. S. Trucking Co., 187 Neb. 502, 192 N.W.2d 139 (1971).

33. Fifer v. Nelson, 295 Minn. 313, 204 N.W.2d 422 (1973); Pueblo v. Ratliff, 131 Colo. 381, 281 P.2d 1021 (1955).

34. St. John's Hosp. & Sch. of Nursing, Inc. v. Chapman, 434 P.2d 160 (Okl. 1967); Lobred v. Mann, 395 S.W.2d 778 (Ky.1965).

thing more than mere speculation.[35] In some jurisdictions, "reasonable probability" will suffice,[36] and in one instance, the insistence on proof to a "reasonable medical certainty" was struck down as too strict,[37] since existence of permanent injuries could be inferred from other evidence.

The standard for *admissibility* of testimony is generally lower than that necessary to prove the consequences,[38] on the grounds that the testimony is to be weighed by the jury together with other evidence introduced.[39] A minority of courts, however, impose the standard of "reasonable certainty"[40] or "reasonable probability"[41] on admissibility. Some courts require a higher standard of testimony relating to future disabilities non-existent at time of trial than of testimony relating to future developments of an existing condition.[42]

Where the injuries imparted have created a "susceptibility" to a future condition, the majority of courts admit relevant testimony regardless of the probabilities involved. Testimony that plaintiff, who had suffered a head injury, had a 3% to 25% chance of developing epilepsy as a result, was held sufficient to support an award for future damages in a Federal District Court case in Virginia.[43]

35. Driver v. Anheuser, 397 S.W.2d 11 (Mo.App.1965); Seymour v. House, 305 S.W.2d 1 (Mo.1957).

36. See discussion in McElroy v. Luster, 254 S.W.2d 893 (Tex.Civ.App. 1953), error refused.

37. Carpenter v. Nelson, 257 Minn. 424, 101 N.W.2d 918 (1960).

38. See Annotation, 75 A.L.R.3d 9, Admissibility of Expert Medical Testimony as to Future Consequences of Injury as Affected by Expression in Terms of Probability or Possibility; 2 Wigmore on Evidence § 663; 7 Wigmore on Evidence § 1976.

39. Cordiner v. Los Angeles Traction Co., 5 Cal.App. 400, 91 P. 436 (1907) (Competency of evidence not to be confused with sufficiency.)

40. Redmon v. Sooter, 1 Ill.App.3d 406, 274 N.E.2d 200 (1971); Williams v. Daniels, 48 Tenn.App. 112, 344 S. W.2d 555 (1960).

41. Standard Oil Co. v. Sewell, 37 F.2d 230 (4th Cir. 1930); Howell v. Cussons, 29 Colo.App. 572, 489 P.2d 1056 (1971); Riegel v. Aastad, 272 A.2d 715 (Del.App.1970); Nunez v. Wilson, 211 Kan. 443, 507 P.2d 329 (1973); Rogers v. Sullivan, 410 S.W.2d 624 (Ky.1966); Davidson v. Miller, 276 Md. 54, 344 A.2d 422 (1975).

42. Peligri v. Cat Serv. Corp., 36 Misc.2d 257, 232 N.Y.S.2d 177 (1961).

43. McCall v. United States, 206 F. Supp. 421 (D.C.Va.1962) ("However taking into consideration Fred's pain and suffering, his permanent handicaps, the possibility of a character change for the worse, his physical handicaps and the possibility of still more serious trouble that may ultimately ensue, I believe that $40,000.00 is a reasonable figure at which to assess his damages, feeling that that figure is somewhat excessive for the damages sustained to date, the excess being allowed because of the possibility of future difficulties").

A Pennsylvania court held that testimony that plaintiff had a 1 in 20 chance of developing epileptic seizures was properly admitted to be weighed by the jury in their assessment of damages.[44] Where a medical expert testified that epileptic seizures "might occur," but refused to state that they were "reasonably certain" to develop, the testimony was held improperly stricken and plaintiff granted a new trial on damages.[45]

Testimony as to the possibility of "post-traumatic personality disorder",[46] of "character change for the worse",[47] and of suicide as the result of depressive neurosis,[48] have been admitted for consideration by the jury. Recovery has been allowed for future damages of "fear of amputation"[49] and "fear of cancer"[50] as damages apart from the possibility of the condition actually developing.

Statements by the expert witness such as "only God knows" or "only time will tell" have been held sufficient to justify an award for future damages, where the permanence of the injury has been established with "reasonable certainty."[51] Language such as "conjecture" or "speculation" will be viewed in context when used by expert witnesses and will not automatically disqualify the testimony.[52]

It is one thing to debate the "probabilities" and the "possibilities," the "beyond a reasonable doubt" and the "to a preponderance" standards. It is another thing to see them in actual practice.

Human speech is slave to contradictions in certainty and quantum of proof even in everyday affairs. Examine the expression, "I'm certain!" But just how "certain" is he who so remarks? "I'm positive!" Just how "positive" is he? These are the expressions used by the layman, unfamiliar with quantums of proof and legal ni-

---

44. Schwegel v. Goldberg, 209 Pa.Super. 280, 228 A.2d 405 (1967).

See also Feist v. Sears, Roebuck & Co., 267 Or. 402, 517 P.2d 675 (1973) (Possibility, but not probability, of meningitis).

45. Bauman v. San Francisco, 42 Cal.App.2d 144, 108 P.2d 989 (1940).

46. De Santis v. Parker Feeders, Inc., 547 F.2d 357 (7th Cir. 1976).

47. McCall v. United States, 206 F.Supp. 421 (D.C.Va.1962).

48. Metropolitan Dade County v. Dillon, 305 So.2d 36 (Fla.App.1974)

($900,000.00 verdict for wrongful death of 6-year-old daughter).

49. Hayes v. New York Central R. R. Co., 311 F.2d 198 (1962) (Frostbitten feet).

50. Dempsey v. Hartley, 94 F.Supp. 918 (E.D.Pa.1951).

51. Jordon v. Bero, 210 S.E.2d 618 (W.Va.1974); Riggs v. Gasser Motors, 22 Cal.App.2d 636, 72 P.2d 172 (1937).

52. Cullum v. Seifer, 1 Cal.App.3d 20, 81 Cal.Rptr. 381 (1969) ("Conjecture").

ceties. But these same laymen are the witnesses who will use these expressions in court.

§ 5.6 Different Standards in Different Proceedings

There are different quantums of required proof to justify decision for a litigant, depending upon the subject matter and the forum of the law suit. The quantum, it seems, varies with the subject matter to be determined. Thus if it be man's life or liberty, i. e., the criminal case, proof must be "beyond a reasonable doubt, to a moral certainty," and the state, or plaintiff, has the "burden of proof," while the defendant is clothed with a "presumption of innocence."[53]

In the ordinary civil case, property generally being the subject of inquiry, a mere "preponderance of evidence" will suffice. If the "scales of proof hang evenly," then decision goes against him having the burden of proof, the plaintiff.

While the amount of proof does not vary in ordinary civil cases, certain presumptions[54] are often set up that, though they do not change the primary burden (or quantum) of proof, give the "presumption side" at least a head start; e. g., res ipsa loquitur, the presumption of due care by the deceased. The burden of exercising "the highest," or "the utmost" degree of care sometimes imposed upon a common carrier, practically lessens the amount of proof of negligence necessary to be advanced by a plaintiff passenger.

---

53. See People v. Lamson, a celebrated California criminal case, 1 Cal.2d 648, 36 P.2d 361 (1934). (Defendant's wife was found dead in their bathroom. Did she slip and fall) fracturing her skull on the edge of the bathtub, or did defendant bludgeon his wife to death with the iron pipe produced by the state as an exhibit? The jury found Lamson guilty of murder in the first degree. He was therefore sentenced to death, but the California Supreme Court reversed the conviction saying it was based entirely upon circumstantial evidence. The court held that the quantum of proof in a "circumstantial evidence trial" must be not only consistent with the hypothesis of guilt but must be inconsistent with any other rational hypothesis. Lamson was re-tried, the jury was unable to agree, and the district attorney elected not to prosecute him again. He went free.).

54. "Presumption" is defined as supposition of the truth or real existence of something without direct or positive proof of the facts, but grounded on circumstantial or probable evidence which entitles it to belief; strong probability; something taken for granted or assumed to be true until proved otherwise.

"Inference" is defined as to infer; to bring on; to induce; to draw or derive, as a fact or consequence; as, from the past we infer that certain conditions have existed; an inference, a truth or proposition drawn from another which was admitted or supposed to be true; a conclusion.

See Waters v. New Amsterdam Cas. Co., 393 Pa. 247, 144 A.2d 354 (1958).

Many other presumptions sufficient to shift the burden of going forward with the evidence are often vitally important, such as the presumption of motor vehicle ownership and agency,[55] motor vehicle operation by owner occupant,[56] mental capacity,[57] continued life,[58] self-preservation,[59] receipt of a properly addressed stamped letter,[60]

55. Barber Pure Milk Co. v. Holmes, 264 Ala. 45, 84 So.2d 345 (1956) (Name on truck); Sears, Roebuck & Co. v. Hamm, 38 Ala.App. 258, 81 So.2d 915 (1955) (Name of corporate owner on truck); Robinson v. Workman, 9 Ill.2d 420, 137 N.E.2d 804 (1956); Grier v. Rosenberg, 213 Md. 248, 131 A.2d 737 (1957); Ross v. Burgan, 163 Ohio St. 211, 126 N.E.2d 592, 50 A.L.R. 1275 (1955); Ross v. Griggs, 41 Tenn.App. 491, 296 S.W.2d 641 (1955) (Statutory—rebuttable); Callen v. Coca-Cola Bottling, Inc., 50 Wash.2d 180, 310 P.2d 236 (1957) (Rebuttable); Irvine v. Wilson, 137 Cal.App.2d 843, 289 P.2d 895 (1955) (Under statute imputing negligence of permittee to owner, person registering vehicle conclusively presumed to be owner); Eggerding v. Bicknell, 20 N.J. 106, 118 A.2d 820 (1955) (Automobile dealer who violates statute by permitting purchaser to operate vehicle with dealer's plates estopped to deny ownership).

56. Gaul v. Noiva, 155 Conn. 218, 230 A.2d 591 (1967).

See also Drahmann's Adm'r v. Brink's Adm'r, 290 S.W.2d 449 (Ky.1956) (Applying Georgia law—airplane crash where owner experienced pilot and passenger inexperienced); Hayden's Estate, In re, 174 Kan. 140, 254 P.2d 813, 36 A.L.R.2d 1278 (1953) (Airplane crash—presumption denied as conjectural); Rodney v. Staman, 371 Pa. 1, 89 A.2d 313, 32 A.L.R.2d 988 (1952) (Automobile operation—rebuttable presumption).

57. Presumption of mental competency; see Church v. Capital Freight Lines, 141 Cal.App.2d 246, 296 P. 563 (1956) (Mental competence of juror); Brown v. Panhandle & Santa Fe Ry. Co., 294 S.W.2d 223 (Tex.Civ.App. 1956) (Where 15 year old boy crawled under railroad train and was injured—normal mentality presumed); Binder v. Binder, 50 Wash.2d 142, 309 P.2d 1050 (1957) (Execution of instrument).

58. Basman v. Frank, 250 S.W.2d 989 (Mo.1952).

See also Justin v. Ketcham, 297 Mich. 592, 298 N.W. 294 (1941) (Instantaneous death under survival act ordinarily considered as meaning resulting from accident and not prior thereto); Fretz v. Anderson, 5 Utah 2d 290, 300 P.2d 645 (1956) (Under survival of action against wrongdoer statute, plaintiff does not have burden of proving that deceased was alive immediately before collision).

59. Robinson v. Workman, 9 Ill.2d 420, 137 N.E.2d 804 (1956); Holloway v. Bankers Life Co., 81 N.W.2d 453 (Iowa 1957); National Postal Transport Ass'n v. Hudson, 216 F.2d 193 (8th Cir. 1954); Graham v. Nassau & Suffolk Lighting Co., 308 N.Y. 140, 123 N.E.2d 813 (1954); Vaughn v. Payne, 75 S.D. 292, 63 N.W.2d 798 (1954).

60. New York New Jersey Producer Dealers Coop., Inc., v. Mocker, 59 A. D.2d 970, 399 N.Y.S.2d 280 (1977).

See also American Fidelity Fire Ins. Co. v. Winfield, 225 Ark. 139, 279 S.W.2d 836 (1955); Jensen v. Traders & Gen. Ins. Co., 141 Cal.App.2d 162, 296 P.2d 434 (1956) (Proof that letter not received justifies inference of no mailing); Employers' Liability Assur. Corp., Ltd. v. Maes, 235 F.2d 918 (10th Cir. 1956) (Failure to receive

presumptions imposed by statute,[61] and the like. In the absence of direct evidence, or the applicability of a recognized presumption, valid findings of fact may be based upon a recital of circumstances and reasonable inferences therefrom.[62] In determining the speed of a motor vehicle at the time of collision, evidence of driving speed prior thereto may be admissible as the basis for a reasonable inference.[63] Conflict of laws issues as to evidentiary matters will be decided by the rules of lex fori.[64]

raises presumption of no mailing); Start v. Shell Oil Co., Inc., 202 Or. 99, 273 P.2d 225 (1954); Crow v. City of San Antonio, 294 S.W.2d 899 (Tex.Civ.App.1956) (Notice to city of personal injury).

61. Azvedo v. Benevolent Soc'y of California, 125 Cal.App.2d 894, 270 P.2d 948 (1954) (Simultaneous Death Act conclusive presumption not applicable where evidence on non-simultaneous death); Davis v. Loftin, 75 So. 2d 813 (Fla.1954) (Against railroad operations—changes burden of proof); Litchford v. Iowa-Illinois Gas & Elec. Co., 247 Iowa 947, 75 N.W.2d 346 (1956) (Statute providing that negligence will be presumed on part of person or corporation operating an electric transmission line construed as applicable to lines over private property).

62. Sigety v. Leventhal, 42 N.Y.2d 953, 398 N.Y.S.2d 137, 367 N.E.2d 644 (1977); Savarese v. State Farm Mut. Auto. Ins. Co., 150 Cal.App.2d 518, 310 P.2d 142 (1957) (Inference may be based on inference if first inference is reasonably probable); Pierce v. Albanese, 144 Conn. 241, 129 A.2d 606 (1957) (Dramshop Act violation); Smith v. General Motors Corp., 227 F.2d 210 (5th Cir. 1955) (Automobile manufacturer's liability—circumstantial evidence insufficient where no clear preponderance of inferences); Voelker v. Combined Ins. Co., 73 So. 2d 403 (Fla.1954) (Uncontradicted reasonable inference amounts to established fact); Soreide v. Vilas & Co., 247 Iowa 1139, 78 N.W.2d 41 (1956) ("An inference may not be based upon evidence which is too uncertain or speculative or raises only a conjecture or possibility"); Fegles Constr. Co., Ltd. v. McLaughlin Constr. Co., 205 F.2d 637 (9th Cir. 1953) ("Once the facts are established from which an inference logically flows or legally arises, whether such basic facts are established by circumstantial evidence or by direct testimony, it is the province of the trier of fact to deduce the inference"); First Nat'l Bank v. Simko, 384 Pa. 603, 122 A.2d 47 (1956); Burkett v. Johnston, 39 Tenn.App. 276, 282 S. W.2d 647 (1955) (Where owner of wrecked automobile found dead under wheel and plaintiff also dead in seat beside him and no eye witnesses, jury could infer that owner was driver, plaintiff an invited guest); Ice Serv. Co. v. Scruggs, 284 S.W.2d 185 (Tex.Civ.App.1955).

63. Dawson v. Olson, 97 Idaho 274, 543 P.2d 499 (1975); Fleming v. Lawson, 240 F.2d 119 (10th Cir. 1956) (Discretionary); Comins v. Scrivener, 214 F.2d 810, 46 A.L.R.2d 1 (10th Cir. 1954) (Terrific speed some 5 to 10 miles from scene of accident); Lovejoy v. Tidwell, 212 Ga. 750, 95 S.E.2d 784 (1956) (Speed 10 to 15 minutes before accident); Siegrist v. Wheeler, 178 Kan. 286, 286 P.2d 169 (1955) (Quarter mile from accident); Shields v. Buffalo County, 161 Neb. 34, 71 N.W.2d 701 (1955) (1½ miles from scene).

64. Rodney v. Staman, 371 Pa. 1, 89 A.2d 313, 32 A.L.R.2d 976 (1952).

See also Restatement of Conflict of Laws, Second § 133 et seq.

Between the criminal and the civil case is the quasi criminal action, sometimes the administrative board, sometimes the professional association empowered by law to judge and govern; i. e., a state bar association hearing to discipline a professional member. Various courts have held that proof of "guilt" must be all the way from "substantial" to "beyond a reasonable doubt" in these proceedings.[65]

At the lower end of the scale of certainty (the highest being "beyond a reasonable doubt" plus corroborative evidence required in some criminal prosecutions such as treason) are the hearings before boards and commissions. Proof here, while generally to the standard of "a preponderance," nevertheless in practice suffices to the least degree of "certainty" because of the relaxation of the rules of evidence. This is not a confusion of the quantum of proof with other rules of evidence, but practically means that the requisite amount of proof is more easily satisfied when the evidentiary rules are relaxed. For instance, letters and hearsay, not admissible elsewhere, may qualify to establish the required proof in those administrative and commission cases.[66]

§ 5.7 Who May Present Proof

Who presents proof if not the lawyer? Every trial attorney is familiar with the judge who, in practice, "takes over the case." But does the judge have the right to call witnesses on his own motion? Although the statutes of most states provide for the examination, civil and criminal, by experts appointed by the court (such as medical ex-

---

65. Bar Ass'n v. Sullivan, 185 Cal. 621, 198 P. 7 (1921) ("Clear and satisfying proof"); People ex rel. Cline v. Kerker, 315 Ill. 572, 146 N.E. 439 (1925) (Beyond reasonable doubt where charges were of crimes); In re Mayberry, 295 Mass. 155, 3 N.E.2d 248 (1936) (Cause for disbarment may be established by fair preponderance of evidence); Copren v. State Bar, 64 Nev. 364, 183 P.2d 833, 173 A.L.R. 284 (1947) (Clear and convincing evidence); In re Otterness, 181 Minn. 254, 232 N.W. 318, 73 A.L.R. 1319 (1930) (Clear and convincing proof).

66. See: Davis, An Approach to Rules of Evidence for Non Jury Cases, 50 A.B.A.J. 723 (1964) ("We have rules of evidence for the 3 percent of trials that use juries but we have no rules of evidence for the 97 percent that are without juries"); Richardson v. Perales, 402 U.S. 389, 91 S.Ct. 1420, 28 L.Ed.2d 842 (1971) (Medical reports admissible in Social Security disability hearing despite hearsay character and lack of opportunity to cross examine author, and may constitute sufficient evidence to support adverse finding, despite plaintiff's presentation of opposing medical testimony).

Peters v. United States, 187 Ct.Cl. 63, 408 F.2d 719 (1969) (Air Force placement officer removed on uncorroborated hearsay evidence. Held, permissible, since "corroborated" by declarant. Dissent: "corroboration" of declarant without personal knowledge adds nothing: "Adding hearsay to hearsay is like adding zero to zero which still equals zero.").

§ 5.7   BURDEN OF PROOF   Pt. 2

aminers, alienists, etc.), the rule is not so well known that the judge, being dissatisfied with the evidence adduced, may proceed to call witnesses himself and undertake examinations. Justice Frankfurter, dissenting in *Johnson v. United States*,[67] emphasized:

> "While a courtroom is not a laboratory for the scientific pursuit of truth, a trial judge is surely not confined to an account obviously fragmentary, of the circumstances of a happening, here the meagre testimony of Johnson, when he has at his command the means of exploring and fully, or at least more fully, before passing legal judgment. A trial is not a game of Blind Man's Bluff; and the trial judge—particularly in a case where he himself is the trier of the facts upon which he is to pronounce the law—need not blindfold himself by failing to call an available vital witness simply because the parties, for reasons of trial tactics, choose to withhold the testimony. Federal judges are not referees at prize fights but functionaries of justice. See *Herron v. Southern Pac. Co.*, 283 U.S. 91, 95, 51 S.Ct. 383, 384, 75 L.Ed. 857; *Quercia v. United States*, 289 U.S. 466, 469, 53 S.Ct. 698, 699, 77 L.Ed. 1321. As such they have a duty of initiative to see that the issues are determined within the scope of the pleadings, not left to counsel's chosen argument. See *New York Cent. R. Co. v. Johnson*, 279 U.S. 310, 318, 49 S.Ct. 300, 73 L.Ed. 706."

§ 5.8   Statistics in Criminal Cases

Let us assume a robbery suspect is apprehended. He denies guilt and stands trial. The evidence is uncontroverted that upon apprehension the suspect had (1) a small smear of red paint on the side of one shoe; (2) that a piece of cloth was found on a nail at the place of robbery, and, when examined, appeared to be within the classification of ten to twelve threads to an inch; defendant wore a suit with the same thread pattern; (3) a No. 6 Cuban heel mark was left at the scene of the crime; a plaster cast was made of this and defendant's heel print fitted precisely into the mold; (4) there was loose, cream-colored plaster about the side of the building burglarized, and minute particles of cream colored plaster were found in the cloth of defendant's pants; (5) there was charred lath at the building burglarized from a recent fire; pieces of charred lath were found in defendant's pants cuff when he was taken into custody; (6) $1250 was stolen in the burglary; defendant had on his person when apprehended $992; upon questioning he admitted having spent some

---

67. 333 U.S. 47, 68 S.Ct. 391, 92 L.Ed. 470 (1948), motion denied 333 U.S. 865, 68 S.Ct. 788, 92 L.Ed. 1143.

money on an automobile the day of the burglary; upon investigation it was determined that $270 was expended.

When this actual case came on for argument defense counsel took up each piece of this evidence separately and asked of the jury, "Does this prove guilt beyond a reasonable doubt?" He wrote a large question mark on the blackboard and argued that the series of "coincidences" might even rise to the dignity of a "possibility" but not proof beyond a reasonable doubt.

In arguing the case, the District Attorney used the blackboard in Figure 81, and, following a modus operandi available in any case having several factors of evidence (and nearly every case tried does, civil as well as criminal) to show proof beyond a reasonable doubt, asked the jury, "just to what numerical figure or percentage would you have me reduce the chances of a 'reasonable doubt' to satisfy you? Would you be satisfied if it were '1 in 1,000,' '1 in 10,000,' '1 in 100,000'? Certainly you would be satisfied if I were to show you that it was 'one chance in a million.' Well, I am going to satisfy you beyond 'one chance in a trillion' that defendant was the burglar!"

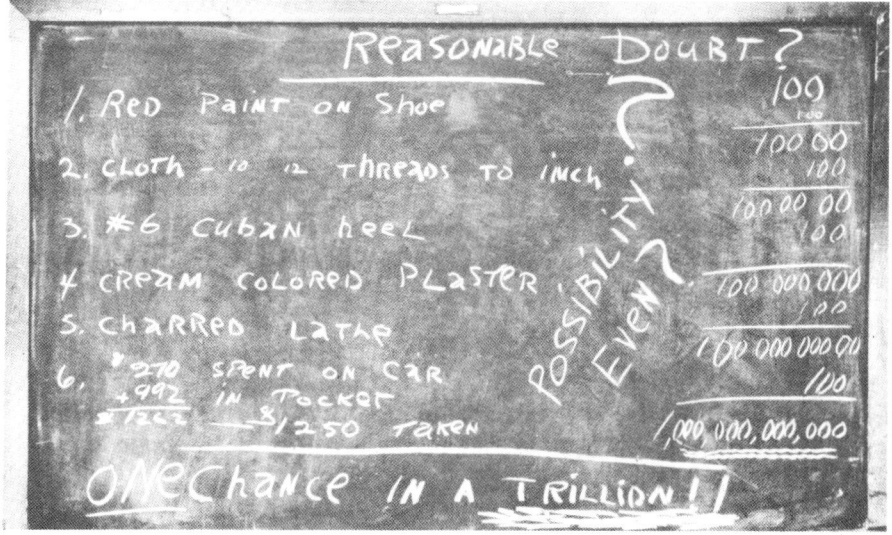

Figure 81. Blackboard was used in this criminal case to show jury the meaning of reasonable doubt, and in this instance to argue that evidence for conviction was sufficient. A factual issue as to identification was in question, and the jury had been instructed that there must be a finding as to the identification of the defendant beyond a reasonable doubt. On the left of the blackboard counsel has written the evidence produced to positively identify the defendant as the one under trial, and to the right a mathematical calculation as to the chance that this strong evidence could be wrong. The conclusion is "one chance in a trillion," and that is certainly beyond any reasonable doubt.

The District Attorney then asked the jury to consider, of all the people in Los Angeles, how many had a smear of red paint on one shoe. Would it be a fair statement to say that none in the courtroom qualified? Would it not be a fair statement, too, to say that but one out of a hundred people from all walks of life in a city the size of Los Angeles would so qualify, taking painters, bankers, doctors, lawyers, actors, collecting one from a hundred in this group?

The District Attorney said, "But if this were the only proof, then there might be the reasonable doubt with this sole clue, 99 chances out of 100 it would be that a man would not have red paint on his shoes but you may say reasonable doubt can be 1 out of 100."

The District Attorney then asked the same question with reference to those wearing cloth clothes with ten to twelve threads to the inch, and requested the obviously fair admission that one out of a hundred would be so clothed. He proceeded likewise to the Cuban heels, the cream colored plaster, the charred lathe, the $1250, securing the obviously fair assumption that it would be difficult even to find one out of 100 persons possessing each of the individual items or descriptions.

But, when a man with red paint on his shoes also has a suit of cloth with 10 to 12 threads to the inch (admitting one out of 100 in each of these classifications); when he also has the precise same Cuban heel, the plaster, the lathe, the money, when these six "clues" are all combined on the blackboard the certainty must be that there is "only one chance in a trillion" that defendant was not the burglar! Proof beyond a reasonable doubt?

The argument and blackboard demonstration, reducing proof to a "mathematical certainty" is, of course, available to a defendant in criminal cases. Indeed it may be used to advantage in a number of combinations both by plaintiff and defendant in the civil as well as the criminal case.

But, is the argument accurate?[68] To ask this question challenges not so much this demonstration as it does a whole system of

---

68. See Evidence: Admission of Mathematical Probability Statistics held Erroneous for Want of Demonstration of Validity. (1967) Duke L.J. 665; The Use of Statistics in Criminalistics. 55 J.Crim.L.C. & P.C. (1964).

See also Tribe, Trial by Mathematics: Precision and Ritual in the Legal Process, 84 Harv.L.Rev. 1329 (1971).

People v. Collins, 68 Cal.2d 319, 66 Cal.Rptr. 497, 438 P.2d 33, 36 A.L.R. 3d 1176 (1968) (Defendant and wife convicted on mathematical probability evidence. Reversed for prejudicial error since testimony unfounded in evidence or statistical theory, and used to distract jury from proper function of weighing evidence on issue of guilt).

State v. Sneed, 76 N.M. 349, 414 P.2d 858 (1966), appeal after remand 78 N.M. 615, 435 P.2d 768: (Defendant convicted on evidence of Mathematical Probability granted new trial on grounds that valid foundation of figures used not established).

trial and method of proof. Illustrative cases actually have shown "convicting proof" in the six categories above combined and yet, after conviction, defendant was proved innocent.[69] Professor Borchard, a Professor of Law at Yale University, concluded that the major source of convicting errors was identification of the accused by a victim of a crime by violence.[70]

In the summer and fall of 1913, there was a flood of forged and bad checks in Boston, Massachusetts. Some time in October, 1913, a police inspector received from a Boston merchant a check for $30,000 which had been given in purchase by one Herbert T. Andrews. It was a bad check. Herbert T. Andrews was located and arrested. He was a cashier for a large Boston store, a family man, thought well of by his friends. Arrested and brought to trial, Andrews was found innocent of issuing a check without funds since there was actually money in the bank.

But by the time of his dismissing, at the urging of the Police Department to "check identification", many victims of the bad check racket had positively identified Andrews as the man who had cashed the other checks. One police inspector, when Andrews' father was endeavoring to plead for his son, stated that he was "absolutely sure of his man" and that he "had never made a mistake in forty years." The Grand Jury, considering the evidence of identification against Andrews, returned an indictment covering 43 counts of forging and uttering, bad checks.

A handwriting expert engaged by the defense advised he could be of no help since the handwriting on the forged checks and Andrews' handwriting was essentially the same. The Burns Detective Agency was hired by the defense to help, but without success.

Seventeen witnesses, men and women, took the stand and identified Andrews as the man who had passed the checks upon them. Many of them were so positive in their identification that there was little defendant could do but deny all knowledge of or connection with the checks and deny that he had ever seen any of the witnesses who testified against him.

Andrews was found guilty February 26, 1914, on 17 counts.

But after Andrews' conviction, bad checks in the same handwriting continued to appear. With considerable police investigation, an

---

69. Such cases are collected by Professor Borchard, Convicting the Innocent, Errors of Criminal Justice (Yale Univ. Press, 1932).

70. Professor Borchard has collected 65 cases from a larger number in refutation of the common expression that innocent men are never convicted. He points out that juries seem disposed to credit the veracity of the victims of an outrage rather than the evidence brought forward by an accused defendant. In six of the cases cited, the person alleged to have been murdered, later turned up hale and hearty, and sometimes after the supposed murderer had entered upon his sentence in the penitentiary. Professor Borchard calls for the employment of impartial experts to find facts in criminal cases and avoid such miscarriages of justice.

Earle Barnes was arrested and confessed that he had written the checks charged against Andrews. By comparing the handwriting with the checks the authorship was obvious.

Andrews was discharged.

Writing about this case some ten years later, Prosecutor Lavelle observed, concerning the appearance of the two men in Judge Chase's court on June 12, 1914:

"As the two men stood at the Bar I wondered how so many persons could have sworn that the innocent man was the one who had cashed the bad checks. There were several inches difference in height and there wasn't a similarity about them. To this day I can't understand the positiveness of those witnesses. I know that the police felt that the man was guilty. So this was a case where 'seeing was not believing,' as the reverse of the old adage goes." [71]

Andrews' "quantum of proof" could have appeared upon the blackboard. The same argument of "one out of a hundred" could have been made as to each of the four items, and the chance that Andrews was not the man could have been argued as one out of 100,000,000.

Yet how mathematics can dissipate verity. The "bad check" wasn't bad. The inspector who "hadn't been fooled in 40 years" was for the first (?) time fooled. The "same handwriting" was the same handwriting of the man who confessed and actually was the check passer. Seventeen witnesses were wrong. Counsel might even have written the name of each witness, given them a mathematical value, and gotten a figure higher than the "one out of 100,000,000 chance."

Both of the above procedures show a method of proof in demonstrative evidence by use of the blackboard, to appraise the jury in summary of the facts tending toward conviction. Both, as the above examples will show, have their limitations, but so, too, have most arguments and proofs concerning the certainty of human beings and their human capacity not only to err but to make it "possible," "probable," or even "certain" for other persons mistakenly to believe that they had erred.[72]

---

71. Borchard, supra n. 69, at 5.

72. Newsweek of May 11, 1953, reported a "conviction of a 43-year old bass fiddler for robbery." At his trial, he was identified by four woman clerks who refused to admit the slightest doubt. However, the greatest ignominy was added when a juror, so certain of guilt, during cross-examination asked in open court, "Do we have to listen to all this?" The result was a mistrial, leaving defendant with no chance to present his alibi—that he was on a farm near Cornwall, New York, at the time of the robbery. When he came up for another trial, the police had happily apprehended another man who confessed the holdup.

§§ 5.9–6.0 are reserved for supplementary material.

PART III

TORT LIABILITY AND DEFENSES—GENERALLY

CHAPTER 6

STRICT LIABILITY

Table of Sections

Sec.
6.1 In General.
6.2 History of Strict Liability.
6.3 Worker's Compensation.
6.4 Dangerous Activities.
6.5 Escaping Water.
6.6 Products Liability.
6.7 Restrictions on Strict Liability.
6.8 Absolute Liability in Nuclear Accident—The Karen Silkwood Case.

Library References:
  C.J.S. Products Liability §§ 7, 8.
  West's Key No. Digests, Products Liability ⟐5.
  Prosser, Law of Torts (4th ed. 1971), pp. 492–540.
  Kimble, Products Liability (West's Handbook Series).

§ 6.1 In General

One of the most significant legal developments of the past 30 years has been the extension of liability without fault, or strict liability.[1] Worker's compensation,[2] no-fault car insurance [3] and products liability [4] cases are just a few examples of this recent expansion, which has allowed many injured people to recover who would otherwise have been remediless.

Ironically, this modern trend is premised, not on a startlingly new theory of liability, but on the ancient common law concept that one who injures another is responsible for that injury. Perhaps the most striking example of this contemporary use of old doctrines is *Silkwood v. Kerr-McGee*,[5] in which plaintiff relied on the hoary maxim that people keep wild animals at their own peril to recover for a death due to plutonium poisoning.

§ 6.2 History of Strict Liability

The common law originally imposed liability regardless of the nature of the defendant's conduct.[6] Jurists of that time hoped that by applying the maxim that "he who breaks must pay" they might provide a substitute for private vengeance.[7] The dominant theme of Anglo-Saxon law was that man acts at his own peril.[8] From this

1. See Comment, Return to Anonymous: The Dying Concept of Fault, 25 Emery Law Journal 163 (1976); Foster, Some Comments in Favor of the Abolition of Fault Law, 8 Akron L.Rev. 57 (1974); O'Connell, Expanding No Fault Beyond Auto Insurance: Some Proposals, 59 Va.L.Rev. 749 (1973).

2. See Chapter 39, infra.

3. See Chapter 28, infra.

4. See Chapter 43, infra.

5. See § 6.8 infra.

6. See Wigmore, Responsibility for Tortious Acts: Its History, 7 Harv.L. Rev. 315, 383, 441 (1894).

7. O. W. Holmes, The Common Law 2, 3 (1881); Peck, Negligence and Liability Without Fault in Tort Law, 46 Wash.L.Rev. 225 (1971); Harper and James, The Law of Torts, § 14.1 ("There are good grounds to believe that the very early concept of justice in the common law was . . . that the law required anyone who caused harm to his neighbor to make good the loss irrespective of any fault or intent to harm on the part of the actor"); Weaver v. Ward, Hobart 134, 80 Eng.Rep. 284, K.B. 1616 (Defendant injured plaintiff with his musket in a military company engaged in field exercises. The court held that unless he could prove that the incident was pure accident—involving no act of his at all—which he could not do, there was liability.).

8. Holdsworth, 2 History of English Law 42.

strict beginning, the law gradually evolved toward a system which predicated responsibility on negligence or fault, leaving plaintiff without a remedy unless the defendant had somehow erred.[9]

Although the general rule was that liability was denied in the absence of fault, public policy dictated certain exceptions to this principle. Insane people, though incapable of comprehending their actions, were held liable for their torts,[10] as were infants.[11] Keepers of wild animals were said to be insurers of the public's safety and held accountable for damages despite using due care.[12] Where damage to land was involved, courts often imposed liability under the doctrines of nuisance or trespass.[13]

9. Stanley v. Powell, 1 Q.B. 86, 63 L.T. 809 (1891) (No liability without fault); Brown v. Kendall, 60 Mass. (6 Cush.) 292 (1850) (History of fault requirement).

See Ehrenzweig, Negligence Without Fault (1951), p. 1; Wigmore, Responsibility for Tortious Acts (1894), 7 Harv.L.Rev. 315, 383, 441; Smith, Tort and Absolute Liability (1916), 30 Harv.L.Rev. 241, 319, 409; Harris, Liability Without Fault (1932) Tulane L.Rev. 337; Isaacs, Fault and Liability (1918) 31 Harv.L.Rev. 954 (Alternating periods of strict liability with periods of fault).

10. Van Vooren v. Cook, 273 App.Div. 88, 75 N.Y.S.2d 362 (1947) rearg. denied 273 App.Div. 941, 78 N.Y.S.2d 558 ("If the tort is committed by an insane person, there is no reason why the person who is offended against by the tort should stand a loss instead of the offending actor." Public policy to make insane people liable.); McGuire v. Almy, 297 Mass. 323, 8 N.E.2d 760 (1937) (Insanity *no* defense to assault; "Fault is by no means at the present day a universal prerequisite to liability"); Seals v. Snow, 123 Kan. 88, 254 P. 348 (1927) (Insane person is liable for compensatory damages).

11. Ellis v. D'Angelo, 116 Cal.App.2d 310, 253 P.2d 675 (1953). (4 year old liable for assault); Peterson v. Haffner, 59 Ind. 130, 26 Am.Rep. 81 (1877) ("An infant is liable for his torts"); Huchting v. Engel, 17 Wis. 230, 84 Am.Dec. 741 (1863) (Infant under 7 liable for trespass).

12. May v. Burdett, 9 Q.B. 101, 115 Eng.Rep. 1213, 3 Eng.Rul.Cas. 108 (1846) (Leading case for doctrine of absolute liability for keeping wild animals); See also Baugh v. Beatty, 91 Cal.App.2d 786, 205 P.2d 671 (1949) (Owner of wild animal "is an insurer against the acts of the animal to anyone who is injured").

13. Snow v. Marian Realty Co., 212 Cal. 622, 299 P. 720 (1931) (Injury to property is nuisance "irrespecting of care or lack of care"); Cunningham v. Miller, 178 Wis. 220, 189 N.W. 531 (1922) (Embalming business in residential section was nuisance); Perry v. Jeffries, 61 S.C. 292, 39 S.E. 515 (1901) (Honest mistake *no* defense in trespass); Coker v. Birge, 9 Ga. 425, 54 Am.Dec. 347 (1851) (Nuisance to do any act that "must necessarily tend to the prejudice of one's neighbor").

§ 6.2

The rationale for these exceptions was aptly stated in *Rylands v. Fletcher*,[14] an 1868 House of Lords opinion: "We think the true rule of law is, that the person who, for his purposes, brings on his lands and collects and keeps there anything likely to do mischief if it escapes, must keep it at his peril, and, if he does not do so, is prima facie answerable for all the damage which is the natural consequence of its escape."[15] The doctrine was almost immediately rejected in the United States, primarily because it was felt that its literal acceptance would thwart industrial growth.[16] Using the doctrine of nuisance,[17] however, courts were able to impose strict liability in selected cases while rejecting *Rylands v. Fletcher* by name.[18]

14. [1868] L.R. 3 H.L. 330.

15. Id. at 279. Of course, many problems were immediately presented. For example, what is a natural use or consequence? See A. L. Goodhart, Liability for Things Naturally on the Land (1930), 4 Cambridge L.J. 13; Stallybrass, Dangerous Things and the Non-Natural User of Land, 3 Cam.L.Rev. 376 (1929); Restatement, Torts, §§ 519–520. Liability for damages caused by atomic accidents is governed by the Price-Anderson Act, 42 U.S.C.A. § 2210 (1970).

16. Luthringer v. Moore, 31 Cal.2d 489, 190 P.2d 1 (1948); Reynolds v. W. H. Hinman Co., 145 Me. 343, 75 A.2d 802 (1950); Brown v. Collins, 53 N.H. 442, 16 Am.Rep. 372 (1873); Marshall v. Welwood, 38 N.J.L. 339 (1876); Losee v. Buchanan, 51 N.Y. 476, 10 Am.Rep. 623 (1873); Turner v. Big Lake Oil Co., 128 Tex. 155, 96 S.W.2d 221 (1936); Bohlen, the Rule in Rylands v. Fletcher, 59 U. of Pa. L.Rev. 298, 373, 423 (1911).

17. See n. 13 supra.

18. Berger v. Minneapolis Gaslight Co., 60 Minn. 296, 62 N.W. 336 (1895) (Escape of petroleum onto adjoining premises; "The essential condition of liability, without proof of negligence on the part of the owner, for injury to others by the escape of things kept by him on his own premises, is that the natural tendency of the things kept is to become a nuisance or to do mischief, if they escape"); Kall v. Carruthers, 59 Cal.App. 555, 211 P. 43 (1922) (Percolating water); Weaver Mercantile Co. v. Thurmond, 68 W.Va. 530, 70 S.E. 126 (1911) (Escape of impounded water); Prosser, Nuisance Without Fault, 20 Tex.L. Rev. 399 (1942).

§ 6.3 Worker's Compensation

As the industrial revolution continued, the risks created by man's mechanization forced the courts to realize that it was the people, not the corporations, who needed protection. Worker's compensation was an early acknowledgment that different theories of liability were required in a civilized society. As Justice Frankfurter explained in a Federal Employers' Liability Act case, *Wilkerson v. McCarthy*,[19] "The difficulties in these cases derive largely from the outmoded concept of 'negligence' as a working principle for the adjustments of injuries inevitable under the technological circumstances of modern industry. This cruel and wasteful mode of dealing with industrial injuries has long been displaced in industry generally by the insurance principle that underlies workmen's compensation laws."[20]

§ 6.4 Dangerous Activities

The *Rylands v. Fletcher* doctrine also became more acceptable after it was included, with some variations, in the first Restatement of Torts. The Restatement limited recovery to "ultrahazardous activities,"[21] thereby recognizing an established group of nuisance cases involving blasting and explosions.[22] Ultrahazardous activities were defined as those which necessarily included a risk of serious harm to the person, land or chattels or others, which could not be eliminated by the exercise of the utmost care, and were not a matter of common usage.[23]

The restatement rule was criticized from both directions, both for going beyond the English rule by ignoring the location of the activity, and for falling short of the *Rylands* rule by requiring the activity to involve extreme danger.[24]

---

19. 336 U.S. 53, 64, 69 S.Ct. 413, 93 L. Ed. 497 (1949), reh. denied 336 U.S. 940, 69 S.Ct. 744, 93 L.Ed. 1098 (Frankfurter, J., concurring). See also Larson, The Nature and Origins of Workmen's Compensation, 37 Corn.L.Q. 206 (1952).

20. Id. at 65. For additional treatment of workers' compensation, see Chapter 39, infra.

21. Restatement of Torts § 519 (1938).

22. Longtin v. Persell, 30 Mont. 306, 76 P. 699 (1904) (Blasting); Sullivan v. Dunham, 161 N.Y. 290, 55 N.E. 923 (1900) (Blast caused tree to strike plaintiff); Heeg v. Licht, 80 N.Y. 579, 36 Am.Rep. 654 (1880) (Explosion of gunpowder); McAndrews v. Collerd, 42 N.J.L. 189, 36 Am.Rep. 508 (1880) (Explosives).

23. Restatement of Torts § 520 (1938).

24. Prosser, The Principle of Rylands v. Fletcher, Selected Topics on the Law of Torts § 147 (1953).

§ 6.4 TORT LIABILITY AND DEFENSES Pt. 3

The Restatement 2d of Torts substituted the "abnormally dangerous activity" test for the "ultrahazardous activity" test of the original Restatement. The Restatement 2d test is treated by the courts as more of a balancing test than is the First Restatement test, and the Second Restatement test enlarges the circumstances under which the rule of strict liability will apply.[25] Thus, in *Yommer v. McKenzie*,[26] the court held that owners of a gasoline station were strictly liable for damages caused by a gas seepage from storage tanks into a neighbor's water well.[27] In another case, downstream property owners were allowed to recover on a strict liability basis for damages caused when water allegedly stored behind a dam on defendant's upstream property was released.[28]

In determining whether any particular activity is to be deemed "abnormally dangerous," the Restatement 2d sets out the following factors: "(a) Whether the activity involves a high degree of risk of some harm to the person, land or chattels of others; (b) Whether the gravity of the harm which may result from it is likely to be great; (c) Whether the risk cannot be eliminated by the exercise of reasonable care; (d) Whether the activity is not a matter of common usage; (e) Whether the activity is inappropriate to the place where it is carried on; and (f) The value of the activity to the community." [29]

The number of states adopting the Restatement Second remains small. To date, states adopting the test are Massachusetts, New York, Oregon, and Washington. Intermediate appellate courts have done the same in Florida, Maryland, and New Mexico.[30]

Strict liability is applied, however, in a wide variety of dangerous situations, including gases,[31] oil wells,[32] piledriving,[33] blasting

---

25. Yommer v. McKenzie, 255 Md. 220, 257 A.2d 138, 140 (1969).

26. Id.

27. Compare with: Greene v. Spinning, 48 S.W.2d 51 (Mo.App.1932) (Contra result).

28. Clark-Aiken Co. v. Cromwell-Wright Co., Inc., 367 Mass. 70, 323 N.E.2d 876 (1975).

29. Restatement, Second, Torts § 520.

30. See Note, The Rylands v. Fletcher Doctrine in America: Abnormally Dangerous, Ultrahazardous, or Absolute Nuisance, 1978 Arizona State Law Journal 99, 101–102.

31. Luthringer v. Moore, 31 Cal.2d 489, 190 P.2d 1 (1948) (Strictly liable for asphyxiation caused by escaping hydrocyanic acid gas used to fumigate adjoining premises); McLane v. Northwest Natural Gas Co., 255 Or. 324, 467 P.2d 635 (1970).

32. Green v. General Petroleum Corp., 205 Cal. 328, 270 P. 952 (1928).

33. Vern J. Oja & Associates v. Washington Park Towers, Inc., 89 Wash.2d 72, 569 P.2d 1141 (1977); Sachs v. Chiat, 281 Minn. 540, 162 N.W.2d 243 (1968).

operations,[34] chemical sprays and cropdusting.[35] The old rule requiring strict liability for wild animals has also been used in some interesting recent cases.[36]

The law of air carrier liability has not followed the general trend. After a start toward the direction of strict liability,[37] there has been a return to the position of holding air carriers only to the same standard of care and liability as ground carriers.[38] However, through the use of the doctrine of res ipsa loquitur, we may see the imposition of stricter liability.[39] The Warsaw Convention is really an absolute liability to a certain level or amount, somewhat akin to worker's compensation.[40]

§ 6.5 Escaping Water

Although *Fletcher v. Rylands* dealt with the escape of water, only a few American courts impose strict liability in such a case.[41] In the case of water escaping from a dam, strict or absolute liability is generally denied, usually on the basis that the construction of a dam is not an unusual practice, or that its value to the community outweighs its attendant risk.[42]

---

34. Coalite v. Aldridge, 285 Ala. 137, 229 So.2d 539 (1969), on remand 45 Ala.App. 721, 229 So.2d 541; Galbreath v. Engineering Constr. Co., 149 Ind.App. 347, 273 N.E.2d 121 (1971); Spano v. Perini Corp., 25 N.Y.2d 11, 302 N.Y.S.2d 527, 250 N.E.2d 31 (1969); Halpert v. Ingram & Greene, Inc., 70 Misc.2d 872, 333 N.Y.S.2d 913 (1972).

35. Bella v. Aurora Air, Inc., 279 Or. 13, 566 P.2d 489 (1977) (Strict liability for damages caused by spraying 2,4–D); Langan v. Valicopters, Inc., 88 Wash.2d 855, 567 P.2d 218 (1977).

36. See Chapter 35, "Animal Law" infra. See also Keyser v. Phillips Petroleum Co., 287 So.2d 364 (Fla.App. 1973) (Rattlesnake); Isaacs v. Powell, 267 So.2d 864 (Fla.App.1972) (Chimpanzee); Wenndt v. Latare, 200 N.W.2d 862 (Iowa 1972) (Bull); Granger v. U. S. Fidelity & Guar. Co., 266 So.2d 526 (La.App.1972) (Bull); Clark v. Brings, 284 Minn. 73, 169 N.W.2d 407 (1969) (Siamese cat); Whitefield v. Stewart, 577 P.2d 1295 (Okl.1978) (Monkey).

37. Conn.Laws 1911, c. 86, Sec. 11, repealed by Laws 1925, c. 249. Kingsley and Bates, Liability to Persons and Property on Ground (1933), 4 J. of Air Law 515.

38. Rhyne, Aviation Accident Law (1947). See also Chapter 40, "Aircraft Accident Litigation," infra.

39. Goldin, the Doctrine of Res Ipsa Loquitur in Aviation Law, 18 So.Cal. L.Rev. 15, 124 (1944). O'Connor, Res Ipsa in the Air, 22 Ind.L.J. 221 (1947); McLarty, Res Ipsa Loquitur in Airline Passenger Litigation, 37 Va.L.Rev. 55 (1951).

40. See Chapter 40, "Aircraft Accident Litigation," infra.

41. See, e. g., Clark-Aiken Co. v. Cromwell-Wright Co., Inc., 367 Mass. 70, 323 N.E.2d 876 (1975).

42. Chicago & Northwestern Ry. Co. v. Tyler, 482 F.2d 1007 (8th Cir. 1973)

§ 6.5   TORT LIABILITY AND DEFENSES   Pt. 3

My law firm has handled extensive flood litigation and bases a cause of action on strict liability when appropriate. The most recent example occurred when we filed a case for multiple plaintiffs who suffered damages in the floods of February and March, 1978, in Maricopa County, Arizona.[43] Though negligence was alleged, strict liability was also alleged in that:

"The flooding, as aforesaid, was caused by the excessive discharge of water from the Bartlett Dam, Stewart Mountain Dam, and other dams and waterways which are owned, maintained and operated by the Defendants in that said Defendants diverted and changed the natural drainage channels of the Verde River, Salt River and Agua Fria Rivers. The changing and diversion of said river channels was done in such a manner so as to inhibit the natural flow of said rivers, and to cause the water released at an excessive rate by Defendants to flow onto the Plaintiffs' properties where these waters did substantial damage to the Plaintiffs' homes, yards and environs in March, 1978, and December, 1978."

Whether we shall be successful on the strict liability count in this case remains to be seen. Defendants in the case have entered a motion to dismiss this particular count of a four count complaint.[44] The fact remains, however, I believe we will be successful in arguing that maintenance of the dams is an abnormally dangerous activity for which defendants should be strictly liable. Even if we are not successful in this particular case, I foresee that most courts will eventually adopt the more practical Restatement, Second Torts test.

§ 6.6 Products Liability

Strict liability is most frequently involved in the area of products liability. Such use is discussed extensively elsewhere in this work,[45] but the vast expansion of the doctrine can be illustrated here

---

("The land owner did no more than construct a dam, normally empty, across a dry watercourse for erosion purposes. The record discloses that the construction of dams in this area for similar purposes is, if not a common practice, certainly not unusual"); Dye v. Burdick, 262 Ark. 124, 553 S.W.2d 833 (1977) ("We recognize that there are jurisdictions in which the doctrine of absolute or strict liability would be applied to a case such as this, upon the theory espoused in Rylands v. Fletcher. . . . There are numerous jurisdictions (a majority that might be called overwhelming) that reject it."); Bowling v. City of Oxford, 267 N.C. 552, 148 S.E.2d 624 (1966) (Holding that while absolute liability is not available, plaintiff may invoke *res ipsa loquitur*).

43. Pearson v. Salt River Valley Water Users Ass'n, Superior Court of Maricopa County, Arizona, No. C-385454.

44. Strict liability negligence, inverse eminent domain, and res ipsa loquitur.

45. See Chapter 43, infra. See also Kimble & Lesher, Products Liability (West Handbook Series).

by reference to an old case of mine, *Gottsdanker v. Cutter Laboratories.*[46] My co-counsel (*Lou Ashe*, and *Dick Gerry*) and I agonized over the complaint in this "drug case." We decided to sue in various counts and causes of action: negligence (and res ipsa liquitur), statutory violation, breach of contract, express and implied warranty, and strict liability. Although we finally went to the jury on breach of implied warranty (our best argument in those days), *Gottsdanker* is now cited as a strict liability decision, and today most lawyers would probably rely almost exclusively on the strict liability count.

§ 6.7 Restrictions on Strict Liability

Although the doctrine of strict liability relieves the plaintiff of the burden of proving negligence or fault, liability is not so "absolute" that plaintiff can recover simply because he was injured. Even where a statute imposes "absolute liability," for example, there can be no recovery unless it is possible to show a causal nexus between defendant's behavior and the injury.[47] Similarly, the defendant is not an insurer of all injuries, but only those which lie within the extraordinary risk that makes strict liability applicable. If a totally unforeseen injury occurs there is no liability, even though the harm was proximately caused by defendant's activity.[48] An intervening "act of God" can also absolve defendant of liability, as it would in a typical negligence case.[49]

Finally, contributory negligence and assumption of the risk may be valid defenses in an appropriate case.[50]

§ 6.8 Absolute Liability in Nuclear Accident—The Karen Silkwood Case

The Lion is getting closer and closer to our back door. He's chained, but the chains aren't adequate. No one really knows His strength or what damage He's going to do when He does get loose.

The nuclear bomb and energy controversy has inevitably found its way into court. Unfortunately, and I think, catastrophically, our society will meet head-on with the Lion again before we have a resolution.

46. 182 Cal.App.2d 602, 6 Cal.Rptr. 320 (1958).

47. Morales v. Houston Fire & Cas. Co., 342 So.2d 1248 (La.App.1977), cert. denied 345 So.2d 49.

48. Foster v. Preston Mill Co., 44 Wash.2d 440, 268 P.2d 645 (1954) (Risks of blasting did not include frightening mother mink into killing her kittens).

49. Lee v. Mobil Oil Corp., 203 Kan. 72, 452 P.2d 857 (1969).

50. See Products Liability Chapter 43, infra.

There have been nuclear "misadventures" or downright accidents, and always in plants where "it couldn't happen" [51]. Drastically do we need atomic energy, but just as drastically do we need it harnassed and docile except for its turbulent and majestic purpose. Many plaintiff lawyers have been and will be presented with nuclear cases. Because of their subtle causality and complex medicine, they can't be recognized off hand. Then, too, the cost factor in fighting these "big cases" is sometimes frightening.

Gerry L. Spence, Casper, Wyoming, tried a plutonium case, *Silkwood v. Kerr-McGee Corp.*,[52] before a learned Federal judge in Oklahoma. He heartily enjoyed the trial and the result echoed his pleasure: Karen Silkwood, a young unmarried girl, was working in the Kerr-McGee Corporation's plant. It dealt with and manufactured plutonium. She had been a protester for safer conditions in the plant. Somehow she was radiation contaminated and later radiation materials were found in her refrigerator at home.

Defendant contended she self-induced the radiation. She denied this, but the fact that she received the radiation at home, not in the plant, took the case out of worker's compensation (a plausible argument could have been made that the injuries were work connected).

Before the trial, young Karen was killed in a car accident under sinister and suspicious circumstances. The case arose around the time of "The China Syndrome" and other anti-nuclear movies and these certainly lent an air of ominous portent to Karen's mysterious accident.

Gerry Spence used "all sorts of demonstrative evidence" and particularly did he "use the blackboard like I breathed". He used it in cross-examination, in the opening during voir dire, and then he put key words on the blackboard so that "we could look at them and talk about them and define them and cuddle up and play with them. It is the only decent device a trial lawyer has. I drew pictures and cartoons, and all kinds of things that brought me joy and the jury and me closer together."

Gerry enlarged a letter from Mr. McGee, of defendant Kerr-McGee, telling the workers that the nuclear industry is the safest industry in the world. It was about the size of an ordinary door by "the time I got finished with the blowup and of course I used it in final argument".

"One of the things that delighted me was to have the Kerr-McGee representative demonstrate the use of a respirator that these

---

51. Gerry Spence, Esq., Spence, Moriarty & Schuster, Casper, Wyoming.

52. 485 F.Supp. 566 (W.D.Okl.1979).

poor workers had to use when working in a contaminated room. I had him put on the respirator and then proceeded to ask him a series of questions—and the answers came through in the silliest, distorted rumbles with rolling of eyes and waving of hands you can imagine. The whole courtroom broke up and the jury thought that the whole scene was hilarious."

Gerry added a new note to the seriousness of the "big case": "What we attorneys most often fail to recognize is that part of our duty in the courtroom is to entertain not only the jury but the judge. And the $10,000,000 in the verdict suggested to me that the jury enjoyed and appreciated it."

The key in the *Silkwood* case was "strict liability" and Gerry told the jury the story of the lion in the old common law who was captured and put in a cage by a man who brought the lion home to his property to display to the people. He was very careful. He put the lion behind a double cage, with a double bar and double padlock and all sorts of things, but one night somehow the lion got out—no one knows for sure how—and went roaring into the streets mauling people.

When suit was brought against the owner, the court ruled that "if the lion gets away, you have to pay because he is so dangerous and you brought him on to your land. You have liability even though you used great care". Gerry told the jury that if the lion got away from Kerr-McGee they had to pay. The lion was, of course, the plutonium.

Rylands v. Fletcher,[53] which held that the escape of underground waters from one's land to another posed strict liability under the English common law, is not followed in all American jurisdictions, but its principle is followed with reference to explosions and dangerous animals.

Spence was particular in clearing up scientific jargon used by defendants and simplifying plutonium and its processes: "It is obvious that a jury cannot understand all of the esoteric and sophisticated ideas that go into a trial dealing with complex issues such as radiation and medical issues of radiation. It isn't that juries can't understand the basic concepts because they can. It's simply defendants like to talk in very intimidating jargon and extremely complicated thought processes which don't clear up the propositions at all but simply muddy the waters."

Judge *Theis* (a U.S. District trial judge) during the trial once made the very colorful remark that "If you are going to clear up the water, you will have to get the hogs out of the spring".

53. [1868] L.R. 3 H.L. 330.

§ 6.8   TORT LIABILITY AND DEFENSES   Pt. 3

"I used the quotation in final argument admonishing the jury not to get stuck in muddy springs over the barrage of technical testimony that was given to them. I pointed out that it was the duty of defendant to make their proposition clear and understandable instead of complicated and muddy and that the defendant ought not to be permitted to use a muddy spring to avoid liability."

Ten million dollars of the $10,505,000 award was for punitive damages and was sustained as against post-trial motions.

Of prime importance in the case were Judge Theis' instructions to the jury that:

(1) While Federal safety standards for and regulation of the nuclear industry were "entitled to a high degree of respect and belief" compliance with such regulation would not foreclose or preclude the finding of Kerr-McGee's liability.

(2) Because of the inherent hazard and abnormally dangerous nature of plutonium, defendants could be held strictly liable or liable without fault to those in the vicinity injured by the escape from the defendant's plant of radioactive substances.

(3) If the jury found that Silkwood's contamination was caused by defendant's gross negligence or recklessness in permitting the escape of plutonium from it, the jury in its discretion could award punitive damages in addition to actual or compensatory damages.

The jury in answering special interrogatories found defendant liable both in strict liability and aggravated negligence.

In many cases, from the drug cases on up to nuclear cases, the Federal government has enacted regulation setting certain standards of compliance. A defendant will often assert non-liability because he has complied fully with these regulations. However, mere compliance with them does *not* preclude a finding by the jury that ordinary care was not exercised,[54] and defendant is therefore responsible.

These regulations generally are at the lowest rather than highest level of consumer safety. Moreover, these "government" regulations frequently are suggested and compiled by the "regulated" industry, and are most favorable to the industry.[55]

54. See generally Stevens v. Parke, Davis & Co., 9 Cal.3d 51, 107 Cal. Rptr. 45, 507 P.2d 653 (1973); Stromsodt v. Parke-Davis & Co., 257 F. Supp. 991, 997 (1966), aff'd 411 F.2d 1390 (8th Cir.).

55. Unfortunately, I have found that many government employees in a particular field are looking for a job in private industry in that field and, most unfortunately for the government and the consumer, attempt to curry favor from their prospective employee by favorable actions. Thus, the general in the Pentagon sees himself in a few years off the government warhorse and at the seat

Worth particular mention here is defendant's argument that, since it was engaging in this unusually dangerous activity pursuant to government authorization, it should not be held liable for injuries resulting from any non-negligent conduct. In answering this contention, Judge Theis relied on a factually related case [56] wherein the defendant, pursuant to state authorization, stored large amounts of natural gas in a populated area. That court held that it did not believe that the fact the state had authorized defendant to engage in the abnormally dangerous activity demonstrated any intention to predetermine where responsibility should lie in the case of a non-negligent miscarriage of the activity.[57]

---

behind a desk working for Lockheed or General Dynamics. Unfortunately, he sometimes begins his work for the latter before he leaves government employ.

56. McLane v. Northwest Natural Gas Co., 255 Or. 324, 467 P.2d 635 (1970).

57. 467 P.2d at 641. See also Comment, The Irradiated Plaintiff: Tort Recovery Outside Price-Anderson, 6 Env.L.Rev. 859, 886–87 (1976).

§§ 6.9–7.0 are reserved for supplementary material.

CHAPTER 7

RES IPSA LOQUITUR

Table of Sections

Sec.
7.1 In General.
7.2 Elements or Conditions.
7.3 Unusual Accident—Expert Testimony and the Balance of Probabilities.
7.4 Control and Multiple Defendants.
7.5 Plaintiff's Conduct.
7.6 Defendant's Superior Knowledge.
7.7 Application—Pleading and Evidence of Specific Negligence.
7.8 Effect—Inference or Presumption.
7.9 Practical Considerations—Defense of Due Care.

Library References:
C.J.S. Negligence §§ 220.1 et seq., 220.24, 220.26.
West's Key No. Digests, Negligence ⚖121.2, 121.3.
Prosser, Law of Torts (4th ed. 1971), pp. 228–235.
Blashfield, Automobile Law & Practice, § 418.1 et seq.

§ 7.1 In General

Res Ipsa Loquitur is a crutch. So when trying an otherwise "crippled case," which badly needs its support, I use the crutch constantly during the entire trial. From the voir dire to and including argument, the expression "res ipsa loquitur" is mentioned as frequently as possible.[1] I try to explain to the jurors as simply as possible this doctrine of law—they having read no law books and being perhaps, not confused at all—realizing that lawyers as well as courts of last resort are often confused as to the true purport of the rule.

Thus, I have often told jurors the story, which surpasseth none, and is surpassed by many in literary counterpart, but is nevertheless very legal: that once I tried a case that seemed to me to be as clear a case of liability as any I ever tried. I relate that while addressing

---

1. The author feels that as a method of trial procedure, plaintiff should discuss res ipsa and its implications in his opening statement and advise the jury that the law upon it will be left to His Honor. The jury should appreciate that this is a departure from ordinary rules of negligence, and that the term res ipsa loquitur should be called out and recognized as a legal entity. Later, the judge in using the same words will emphasize and corroborate the correctness of the statement made by counsel from voir dire through final argument.

the former jury, I advised that I would prove my case by "res ipsa loquitur." I thought that I had tried the perfect case, and made out a complete proof of liability. But when the jury returned the verdict, so I tell, it was definitely for the defendant. After the entry of judgment, when the case was over and the jury discharged, I spoke to the body of them in the hall, so I relate to the present jury, and I asked them, "What conceivably caused you to return a verdict for the defendant in this cause? Why, I thought the proof was abundantly clear, and the law certainly warranted a recovery." But then, that jury, as one voice, and in indignation, answered me, "Why, Mr. Belli, how can you say that? You told us at the very outset of the case, and you reminded us all the way through, that you were going to prove your case by Res Ipsa Loquitur, and you never even called that Mexican as a witness!"

I then go on to relate to the present jury, and before whom I am trying another res ipsa case, "Ladies and Gentlemen of this jury, I don't want you to make that mistake. Res Ipsa Loquitur is not a witness. It is a rule of law that means I don't have to call any witness because the law calls one for me when it says, 'Res ipsa loquitur,' the thing speaks for itself, and, therefore it is not necessary to bring anyone to speak or testify or prove it. Now you can understand why I don't call 'Mr. Res Ipsa Loquitur.' He was here from the beginning of the case, and 'he' being a rule of law, and not a person, is in this court room all of the time, telling you that I had already proved my case to you!" [2]

Herein, we do not intend to exhaust authorities pertaining to the doctrine, but to defend it as a practical and just legal rule, and to show its trends and extensions.[3] In observing the recent trends, it is

---

2. In a dissenting opinion Johnson v. United States, 333 U.S. 46, 50, 68 S. Ct. 391, 92 L.Ed. 468, 473 (1948) Mr. Justice Frankfurter criticized the majority opinion for applying res ipsa loquitur in a Jones Act case, arguing that the doctrine was inapplicable since there was an available witness who might have testified as to the instrument which caused the accident, in the exclusive control of this witness, a servant of the defendant. Since the parties failed to call the witness, or use his deposition already taken, the court might have done so. The history of accident law reveals an increased use of the evidentiary rule of res ipsa loquitur in the judicially sanctioned trend to facilitate compensation to accident victims. (See, James, Accident Liability: Some Wartime Developments, 55 Yale L.J. 365, 388 (1946); Prosser, The Procedural Effect of Res Ipsa Loquitur, (1936) 20 Minn.L.Rev. 241.

3. A sycophant's ease of criticism often passes both for learning and social attainment. We do not, of course, class the myriad reviewers who have criticized res ipsa in this group, but there is hardly a rule of law that has come in for such unfavorable discussion as this doctrine. The author frankly admits his inability to appreciate and understand some of the criticism. He has had consid-

§ 7.1 TORT LIABILITY AND DEFENSES

helpful to consider the origin and progress of the doctrine as it has developed in the last 120 years. Chief Baron Pollock presided at its accouchement in *Byrne v. Boadle*.[4] Some 54 years before this holding, under a different rule, the same burden was placed upon a common carrier in *Christie v. Griggs*.[5] From the rules enunciated in these two cases, one a common carrier case, wherein the carrier had the obligation of using the utmost care, and the other, where the plaintiff could not prove directly the negligence which caused the accident, there has developed the doctrine of res ipsa loquitur.

§ 7.2 Elements or Conditions

Traditionally, three conditions have been recognized as necessary to invoke the doctrine: (1) an accident which ordinarily does not occur in the absence of negligence; (2) caused by an instrumentality under the exclusive control of defendant; (3) not due to any voluntary act or contribution on the part of plaintiff.[6] Some jurisdictions

erable success in achieving the adequate award and settlement through its application. Jurors understand it when homely examples are given in explanation. By such use a particular type of tortious conduct is labeled within their understanding. The "lawyer talk" is explained.

4. 159 Eng.Rep. 299 (1863):
 "There are certain cases of which it may be said res ipsa loquitur, and this seems to be one of them—. The present case upon the evidence comes to this, a man is passing in front of the premises of a dealer in flour and there falls upon him a barrel of flour. I think it apparent that the barrel of flour was in the custody of the defendant who occupied the premises, and who is responsible for the acts of his servants and who had the control of it; and in my opinion the fact of its falling is prima facie evidence of negligence, and the plaintiff who was injured by it is not bound to show that it could not fall without negligence, but if there are any facts inconsistent with negligence, it is for the defendant to prove them."

5. 170 Eng.Rep. 1088 (1809), Justice Mansfield declared:
 "In a case where the axle of a stage coach broke and a passenger was injured, that the burden lay upon the carrier to show that the coach was as good as a coach could be, and that the driver was as careful a driver as could anywhere be found. What other evidence can the plaintiff give? The passengers were probably sailors like himself; and how do they know whether the coach was well built, or whether the coachman drove skilfully? In many other cases of this sort, it must be equally impossible for the plaintiff to give the evidence required. But when the breaking down or turning over of a coach is proved, negligence on the part of the owner is implied."

6. Wigmore, Evidence, (1st ed. 1905) § 2509. Southern Arizona York Refrigeration Co. v. Bush Mfg. Co., 331 F. 2d 1 (9th Cir. 1964); Nuclear Corp. of America v. Land, 480 F.2d 990 (8th Cir. 1973); Ryerson & Son, Inc. v. H. A. Crane & Brother, Inc., 417 F.2d 1263 (3d Cir. 1969); Federal Ins. Co.

impose the condition that defendant possess superior knowledge or means of information regarding the cause of the mishap as a variant on either the second or third element.[7] Although these "elements" of res ipsa loquitur have commanded attention from courts, litigants, and commentators alike,[8] they often tend to obscure, rather than clarify, the essential import of the doctrine:[9] That a trier of fact may find a defendant liable upon circumstantial evidence alone where there may be drawn a reasonable inference that: (1) The injuries were caused by negligence, and that (2) The negligence was that of defendant.[10]

§ 7.3 Unusual Accident—Expert Testimony and the Balance of Probabilities

The requirement of "unusual accident" is a term of art, sometimes misleading, which actually refers to the requirement of a factual basis for a reasonable inference of negligence. The requirement is more appropriately expressed as an "event which ordinarily does not occur in the absence of negligence."[11]

The "unusual accident" element is generally not difficult to establish. However, more is required than a showing of the happening of the event itself.[12] Plaintiff must establish a basis for a reasonable

v. United States, 538 F.2d 300 (10th Cir. 1976); United States v. Chesapeake & Delaware Shipyard, Inc., 369 F.Supp. 714 (D.C.Md.1974); Traub v. Holland-America Line, 278 F.Supp. 814 (D.C.N.Y.1967).

7. Bianchini v. Humble Pipe Line Co., 480 F.2d 251 (5th Cir. 1973), reh. denied 478 F.2d 1402; Oresman v. G. D. Searle & Co., 321 F.Supp. 449 (D.C.R.I.1971).

See infra, § 7.6.

8. See, infra, §§ 7.3–7.5.

9. Seeley v. Combs, 65 Cal.2d 127, 52 Cal.Rptr. 578, 416 P.2d 810; ("The inferences resulting from the application of the doctrine of res ipsa loquitur are but a form of circumstantial evidence. The use of that battered and somewhat ambiguous phrase does not change the fact that what we are talking about is a special appliction of the rules surrounding the use and weight of circumstantial evidence . . ..").

10. Restatement, Second, Torts § 328 D.

11. Zentz v. Coca Cola Bottling Co., 39 Cal.2d 436, 247 P.2d 344 (1952); Di Mare v. Cresci, 58 Cal.2d 292, 23 Cal.Rptr. 772, 373 P.2d 860 (1962); Brannon v. Wood, 251 Or. 349, 444 P.2d 558 (1968).

12. United States v. Johnson, 160 F.2d 789 (9th Cir. 1947), aff'd in part and rev'd in part 333 U.S. 46, 68 S.Ct. 391, 92 L.Ed. 468, motion denied 333 U.S. 865, 68 S.Ct. 788, 92 L.Ed. 1143. (Seaman operating block and tackle injured by falling block.)

See also Calvert v. Katy Taxi, Inc., 413 F.2d 841 (2d Cir. 1969). (Taxicab-pedestrian collision); Ridgway Nat'l Bank v. North American Van Lines, Inc., 326 F.2d 934 (3d Cir. 1964). (Two car automobile collision); Whit-

inference of negligence.[13] The mere occurrence of a fire, for instance, does not in itself permit an inference of negligence, since fires may commonly occur without negligence on anyone's part.[14]

In drawing the conclusion that the event in question is one which would not ordinarily happen in the absence of negligence, the jury may rely upon common experience and knowledge.[15] Where the event in question is outside the sphere of the layman's general knowledge and experience, plaintiff may introduce expert testimony to show that the occurrence was, indeed, "unusual".[16] Plaintiff, in some cases

ney v. Brann, 394 F.Supp. 1 (D.C. Del.1975), aff'd 530 F.2d 966, cert. denied 426 U.S. 922, 96 S.Ct. 2628, 49 L.Ed.2d 375, reh. denied 429 U.S. 874, 97 S.Ct. 194, 50 L.Ed.2d 156. (Horse riding accident); Washington v. Pierce, 307 F.Supp. 1157 (D.C.N.C. 1969). (Collision of car and two mules, preceding collision of two cars.)

13. Restatement, Second, Torts § 328 D, comment e.

14. A. Shapiro Realty Corp. v. Burgess Bros., Inc., 491 F.2d 327 (1st Cir. 1974); Dodge v. McFall, 242 Iowa 12, 45 N.W.2d 501 (1951); Weaver v. Shell Co. of California, 13 Cal.App.2d 643, 57 P.2d 571 (1936). (Fire on premises to which defendant delivered gasoline.)

See also Prosser, The Law of Torts, (4th ed. 1971) p. 216; Note, Torts—res ipsa loquitur—application to fires of unknown origin (1973) 27 Ark.L. Rev. 138.

15. Restatement, Second, Torts § 328 D, comment d. See also Prosser, The Law of Torts (4th ed. 1971) p. 217.

16. See Note, Use of Expert Testimony in Res Ipsa Loquitur Cases, (1958) 106 U.Ap.L.Rev. 731, reprinted (1959) Trial & Tort Trends—Belli Seminar 190.

Siverson v. Weber, 57 Cal.2d 834, 22 Cal.Rptr. 337, 372 P.2d 97 (1962) (Jury may rely on both common knowledge and expert testimony);

Felch v. D'Amico, 326 Mass. 196, 93 N.E.2d 406 (1950) (Where defendant's sewer pipe broke and sewage backed into plaintiff's basement, held that expert evidence necessary as to probable cause of breaks); Williams v. Penn. R. R. Co., 90 F.Supp. 69 (D.C. Del.1950) (Plaintiff, a railroad employee, was run over by a crane while working under a railroad car, and sought recovery by application of res ipsa. Held not justified as an unusual accident.); Logan v. Montgomery Ward & Co., Inc., 216 Va. 425, 219 S.E.2d 685 (1975) (Mere fact of explosion did not establish negligence of either manufacturer or seller of gas stove, since it could be attributed to many causes including use of owner); Gordon v. Aztec Brewing Co., 33 Cal.2d 514, 203 P.2d 522 (1949) (Exploding beer bottle, where expert testified as to the types of bottles ordinarily used by manufacturers in testing bottles); Escola v. Coca-Cola Bottling Co. of Fresno, 24 Cal.2d 453, 150 P.2d 436 (1944) (The real importance in using the testimony of an expert is demonstrated in comparing the case of Honea v. City Dairy, Inc., 22 Cal.2d 614, 140 P.2d 369 (1943), with the *Escola* case, supra, where the court said at page 460:

"In the Honea case, we refused to take judicial notice of the technical practices and information available to the bottling industry for finding defects which cannot be seen. In the present case, however, we are supplied with evidence of the standard method used in

may be *required* to introduce such testimony.[17] Yet plaintiff's counsel should note that, even in a medical case, the jury may be justified in relying on common knowledge in inferring negligence.[18] For instance, when a towel marked "Medical Department, U.S. Army" was found in the abdomen of plaintiff, who months earlier had been operted on in an Army hospital, the jury was entitled to rely on res ipsa loquitur, rejecting the possibility that the towel had been swallowed.[19]

Plaintiff's counsel should also note that expert testimony may be introduced by defendant to bar the application of res ipsa, by showing alternative possible causes of the accident.[20] Where such testimony is uncontradicted by plaintiff, res ipsa may be ruled inapplicable.[21]

testing bottles."). Morse v. Riverside Hosp., 44 Ohio App.2d 422, 339 N.E.2d 846 (1974) (Mere fact that patient contracted hepatitis following blood transfusion does not establish negligence of hospital or blood bank).

17. Folk v. Kilk, 53 Cal.App.3d 176, 126 Cal.Rptr. 172 (1975) ("[T]he etiology of brain abscesses and the standards of care prevailing in the medical community as concern tonsillectomies are not matters of common knowledge and therefore we are bound by the expert testimony").

18. Bardessono v. Michels, 3 Cal.3d 780, 91 Cal.Rptr. 760, 478 P.2d 480 (1970) (Injections of cortisone and xylocaine resulting in paralysis of shoulder: ("[C]ourts have followed the test that if the routine medical procedure is relatively commonplace and simple, rather than special, unusual and complex, the jury may properly rely upon its common knowledge in determining whether the accident is of a kind that would ordinarily not have occurred in the absence of someone's negligence . . ."); Kerr v. Bock, 5 Cal.3d 321, 95 Cal.Rptr. 788, 486 P.2d 684 (1971). (Failure to give post-operative instruction not to lift leg: "Neither such a warning nor the breaking of the leg is so uncommon or so complicated that expert testimony would be required in order to render a res ipsa loquitur instruction appropriate"); Meier v. Ross Gen. Hosp., 69 Cal.2d 420, 71 Cal.Rptr. 903, 445 P.2d 519 (1968). (Patient in psychiatric hospital committed suicide. Negligence of "ordinary type", not involving medical matters.).

19. Jefferson v. United States, 77 F. Supp. 706 (D.C.Md.1948), aff'd 340 U.S. 135, 71 S.Ct. 153, 95 L.Ed. 152.

20. Eversmeyer v. Chrysler Corp., 192 So.2d 845 (La.App.1966) (Defense experts offered numerous possible causes of unexplained fire in car other than manufacturer's negligence).

See also McMorris v. Insurance Co. of North America, 289 So.2d 208 (La. App.1974) (Exploding propane tank); Kentucky Power Co. v. Dillon, 345 S. W.2d 486 (Ky.1961) (Electrical fire).

21. Kramer v. R. M. Hollingshead Corp., 5 N.J. 386, 75 A.2d 861 (1950) (Explosion occurred when plaintiff poured solvent into car motor. Uncontradicted defense testimony that nothing in solvent could have caused explosion led court to bar res ipsa instruction, on theory that it was equally possible that defect in car caused explosion.).

§ 7.3   TORT LIABILITY AND DEFENSES   Pt. 3

Since the plaintiff has the burden of proving his case by a preponderance of the evidence, he has the burden of showing by the circumstances of his case alone, or by the aid of expert testimony in connection therewith, that the probabilities of the defendant's negligence are in his favor. This has acquired the name of "balance of probabilities test".[22] Plaintiff need not exclude with certainty every *possible* cause other than defendant's negligence.[23] But he must present evidence from which reasonable men may infer that "on the whole it is more likely that there was negligence associated with the cause of the event than that there was not." [24] Where the probabilities are equally balanced between negligence of the defendant and its absence, plaintiff will have failed in his burden of proof.[25]

---

22. Raber v. Tumin, 36 Cal.2d 654, 226 P.2d 574 (1951). (Business visitor struck by falling ladder leaned against wall and standing on waxed floor. "Under the circumstances related, it appears that the 'balance of probabilities test' has been met."); Dierman v. Providence Hosp., 31 Cal. 2d 290, 188 P.2d 12 (1948) ("Not only is there a prima facie showing that the accident is one which in the ordinary course of events would not have happened if the defendant had used due care, but the defendants themselves have established the 'possibility' or 'probability' that they used an impure and under the circumstances dangerous anesthetizing agent"); Washington Loan and Trust Co., Inc. v. Hickey, 137 F.2d 677 (D.C.Cir. 1943) (Window ventilator fell upon pedestrian, held landlord liable. The court quoted from Thayer, Liability Without Fault, 29 Harv.L.Rev. 801, "The phrase is nothing but a picturesque way of describing a balance of probabilities on a question of fact on which little evidence either way has been presented.").

23. Federal Ins. Co. v. United States, 538 F.2d 300 (10th Cir. 1976). (Fire in electroplating lab); Higginbotham v. Mobil Oil Corp., 545 F.2d 422 (5th Cir. 1977), cert. denied 434 U.S. 830, 98 S.Ct. 110, 54 L.Ed.2d 89, reh. denied 434 U.S. 960, 98 S.Ct. 494, 54 L. Ed.2d 321. (Helicopter crash); Domany v. Otis Elevator Co., 369 F.2d 604 (6th Cir. 1966), cert. denied 387 U.S. 942, 87 S.Ct. 2073, 18 L.Ed.2d 1327. (Escalator.)

24. Prosser, The Law of Torts (4th ed., 1971) p. 218; See also Graham v. Oak Park Mobile Homes, Inc., 546 S. W.2d 394 (Tex.Civ.App.1977); Haldeman v. Bell Tel. Co. of Pennsylvania, 387 F.2d 557 (3d Cir. 1967).

25. La Porte v. Houston, 33 Cal.2d 167, 199 P.2d 665 (1948). (Stationary car slipped into gear and struck plaintiff—held doctrine inapplicable: "It was at least equally probable that the accident was caused by some fault in the mechanism of the car for which defendants were not liable as that it resulted from any negligent act or omission of the mechanic."); Carrick v. Pound, 276 Cal.App.2d 689, 81 Cal.Rptr. 234 (1969). (Boating accident where balance of probabilities did not favor negligence.); Du Bois v. De Bauche, 262 Wis. 32, 53 N.W.2d 628 (1952). (While seated in locker room plaintiff was struck on head by bowling ball from some unexplained cause. Held that res ipsa did not support verdict because the circumstances were not clear to show that the accident could not have happened without negligence by the defendant); Bone v. General Motors Corp., 322 S.W.2d 916, 71 A.L.R.2d 361 (Mo. 1959); Plains Transport of Kansas,

§ 7.4 Control and Multiple Defendants

The requirement of showing control by defendant may prove a more difficult task. Although the rule is generally stated that the accident must have been caused by an agency or instrumentality within the exclusive control of the defendant,[26] such a statement is not literally true. In some cases where the defendant has actually not had the exclusive control of the instrumentality or agency, the courts have inferred or implied such to the defendant, based on his right to control.[27] Generally speaking, however, plaintiff's failure to establish defendant's actual or implied control will bar application of the doctrine [28] on the theory that although plaintiff may have established the probability of operative negligence, he has not provided a basis

Inc. v. Baldwin, 217 Kan. 2, 535 P.2d 865 (1975) ("One of the chief elements required for the doctrine to apply is that the instrumentality or thing causing the injury must have been within the exclusive control of the defendant").

26. Scott v. London and St. K. Docks Co., 159 Eng.Reprint 665 (1865) ("The rule is predicated, amongst other things, upon the condition that the agency which has produced an injury is within the exclusive possession, control and oversight of the person sought to be charged with negligence"); Menth v. Breeze Corp., 4 N.J. 428, 73 A.2d 183 (1950) ("It is also essential to the application of the res ipsa loquitur doctrine that those seeking to obtain the benefit of its presumptive effect must show that in all probability the direct cause of the injury and so much of the surrounding circumstances essential to its occurrence were in the exclusive control of the defendant, or, his agents or servants.")

27. Birmingham v. Gulf Oil Corp., 516 S.W.2d 914 (Tex.1974) (Defendant not absolved of responsibility for crane which plaintiff controlled; distinction between control of movement and responsibility); Jesionowski v. Boston and Maine R. Co., 329 U.S. 452, 67 S.Ct. 401, 91 L.Ed. 416, 169 A.L.R. 947 (1947); Black v. Partridge, 115 Cal.App.2d 639, 252 P.2d 760 (1953) (Where tenant was poisoned by carbon monoxide fumes from unvented gas heater installed by landlord: jury question as to control—"all that is required is that defendant exercise some control over the article involved in the accident or exercise a right to control. Once it is shown that defendant had some degree of control over such agency, then it is for the jury to say whether it is more probable that defendant's negligence caused the accident or not.").

28. Trouser Corp. of America v. Goodman and Theise, 153 F.2d 284 (3d Cir. 1946) (Where water escaped from purifier on upper floor, and leaked into premises of defendant below, the "exclusive control" rule applied); Morner v. Union Pac. R. Co., 31 Wash.2d 282, 196 P.2d 744 (1948) (Passengers in one automobile collided with a truck, both being enveloped with steam from a locomotive of the railroad defendant. Held that control of circumstances in several agencies, and therefore rule did not apply.); Olson v. Whittborne and Swan, 203 Cal. 206, 263 P. 518 (1928) (Injury from a swinging door does not evoke the doctrine because of lack of exclusive control); Roberts v. Bank of America Nat'l Trust & Sav. Ass'n, 97 Cal.App.2d 133, 217 P.2d 129 (1950) (Ladder in control of plaintiff's employer).

§ 7.4   TORT LIABILITY AND DEFENSES   Pt. 3

for the inference that the negligence was defendant's.[29] In the well-known case of *Larson v. St. Francis Hotel*,[30] plaintiff, a pedestrian on the sidewalk in San Francisco on V-J Day, was struck and knocked unconscious by an armchair thrown from a hotel window. Plaintiff relied on res ipsa loquitur and was non-suited, the court holding that: "A hotel does not have exclusive control, either actual or potential, of its furniture. Guests have, at least, partial control." [31]

The control requirement has been utilized successfully to bar application of the doctrine in products liability cases, such as those involving exploding bottles,[32] where the injury is inflicted after the instrumentality has left the exclusive control of the defendant.[33] The better rule, widely accepted today, is that announced in my *Escola v. Coca Cola Bottling Co.*,[34] which requires a showing of defendant's

29. Morse v. Riverside Hosp., 44 Ohio App.2d 422, 339 N.E.2d 846 (1974); Zentz v. Coca Cola Bottling Co., 39 Cal.2d 436, 247 P.2d 344 (1952) (Exploding bottle).

30. 83 Cal.App.2d 210, 188 P.2d 513 (1948).

31. 83 Cal.App.2d at 212, 188 P.2d at 515.

32. Cunningham v. Parkersburg Coca Cola Bottling Co., 137 W.Va. 827, 74 S.E.2d 409 (1953) (Rule has no application where cardboard cartons holding bottles were delivered to retail store some days before plaintiff was injured, so that control had passed from defendant); Slack v. Premier-Pabst Corp., 40 Del. (1 Terry.) 97, 5 A.2d 516 (1939) (Rule not applicable to exploding bottle case unless control solely in hands of defendant); Smith v. Coca Cola Bottling Co., 97 N.H. 522, 92 A.2d 658 (1952) (Plaintiff, not an employee of defendant, while unloading cases of drinks, one bottle exploded. Held nonsuit properly granted. "—the plaintiff's activity could have caused or contributed to cause the injury and there cannot, therefore, be an inference of causal negligence—We are of the opinion that when the instrumentality is no longer in the exclusive control of the defendant and where someone else's negligence may cause or contribute to cause the accident the reason for the doctrine of res ipsa loquitur is no longer present."); Maybach v. Falstaff Brewing Corp., 359 Mo. 446, 222 S.W.2d 87 (1949) (Res ipsa alone cannot support finding of negligence of party entirely out of control of instrumentality at time of injury).

33. Smith v. Kelly, 246 Md. 640, 229 A.2d 79 (1967) (Coin-operated washing machine not in exclusive control of defendant); Bryan v. Otis Elevator Co., 2 N.C.App. 593, 163 S.E.2d 534 (1968) (Elevator not in exclusive control of defendant maintenance contractor); Seay v. General Elevator Co., 522 P.2d 1022 (Okl.1974) (Defendant not in exclusive control of elevator at time of injury); McBride v. Proctor & Gamble Mfg. Co., 300 F.Supp. 1150 (D.C.Tenn.1969) (Plaintiff suffered eye injury while unloading boxcar of detergent. Held, not under defendant manufacturer's control.); Owen v. Brown, 447 S.W.2d 883 (Tex.1969) (Defective air conditioner which flooded building not under defendant maintenance contractor's exclusive control).

34. 24 Cal.2d 453, 150 P.2d 436 (1944). See also Gadde v. Michigan Consol. Gas Co., 377 Mich. 117, 139 N.W.2d 722 (1966); Lorenc v. Chemirad Corp., 37 N.J. 56, 179 A.2d 401 (1962).

control at the time of the negligent act, rather than at the time of the accident. Under this rule it is plaintiff's burden to show that the product's condition was not changed after leaving defendant's possession.[35] The burden may be satisfied by producing general evidence of careful handling and absence of unusual incidents.[36] But where the product has been altered,[37] or the time lapse is substantial,[38] res ipsa loquitur may be held inapplicable. Where the

35. Zentz v. Coca Cola Bottling Co., 39 Cal.2d 436, 247 P.2d 344 (1952) (Plaintiff injured by exploding bottle in restaurant:—"It is settled that the fact that the accident occurred some time after the defendant relinquished control of the instrumentality which causes the accident does not preclude application of the doctrine provided there is evidence that the instrumentality has not been improperly handled by the plaintiff or some third persons, or its condition otherwise changed, after control was relinquished by the defendant."); Gordon v. Aztec Brewing Co., 33 Cal.2d 514, 203 P.2d 522 (1949) (Bottle of beer exploded); Palleson v. Jewell Co-op Elevator, 219 N.W.2d 8 (Iowa 1974) (Exploding gas furnace); Jankelle v. Bishop Indus., Inc., 354 Mass. 491, 238 N.E.2d 374 (1968) (Broken bottle of hair lotion cut plaintiff's hand. Directed verdict for defendant improper where evidence of proper handling by distributors supported inference of defendant's negligence).

36. Gordon v. Aztec Brewing Co., 33 Cal.2d 514, 203 P.2d 522 (1949) (Evidence presented of absence of accidents throughout course of distribution, and excellent condition of case when delivered); Jankelle v. Bishop Indus. Inc., 354 Mass. 491, 238 N.E.2d 374 (1968); Mahoney v. Hercules Powder Co., 221 Cal.App.2d 353, 34 Cal.Rptr. 468 (1963) (Blasting caps not mishandled or changed); Ewer v. Goodyear Tire & Rubber Co., 4 Wash.App. 152, 480 P.2d 260 (1971) (Exploding tire, condition unchanged since leaving defendant's control).

37. Erickson v. Sears, Roebuck & Co., 240 Cal.App.2d 793, 50 Cal.Rptr. 143 (1966) (Wooden stepladder altered by plaintiff); Lutheran Church v. Canfield, 233 So.2d 331 (La.App.1970), writ refused 256 La. 360, 236 So.2d 497 (Heating unit causing fire had been modified by installer). But note: Reynolds v. Natural Gas Equipment, 184 Cal.App.2d 724, 7 Cal.Rptr. 879 (1960) (Where adjustment in gas burner expected and required by manufacturer, issue of control was question of fact).

38. Andrews v. Barker Bros. Corp., 267 Cal.App.2d 530, 73 Cal.Rptr. 284 (1968) (Doctrine inapplicable against manufacturer where chair had been in store 60 to 90 days); Haas v. Carrier Corp., 339 S.W.2d 727 (Tex.Civ.App.1960) (Summary judgment for defendant in heater case despite evidence negativing intervening negligence, where product used for 14 months before accident); Kansas City Fire & Marine Ins. Co. v. Bituminous Cas. Corp., 209 So.2d 785 (La.App. 1968) (Gas furnace used by plaintiff for seven months before fire); Polly Chin Sugai v. General Motors Corp., 137 F.Supp. 696 (D.C.Idaho 1956) (Car driven for 2,000 miles over 3 months); Vandercook & Son, Inc. v. Thorpe, 322 F.2d 638 (5th Cir. 1963), appeal after remand 395 F.2d 104. (Printing press used for four months). But note: Thompson v. Burke Engineering Sales Co., 252 Iowa 146, 106 N.W.2d 351, 84 A.L.R.2d 689 (1960) (Ceiling fell 15 months after installation. Res ipsa held applicable); Wojciuk v. U. S. Rubber Co., 19 Wis.2d 224, 120 N.W.2d 47 (1963),

§ 7.4 TORT LIABILITY AND DEFENSES Pt. 3

time lapse is short,[39] or the instrumentality is factory-sealed,[40] the absence of intervening negligence may be inferred. All possible alternative causes need not be totally excluded, but only sufficiently reduced so that defendant's fault may reasonably be inferred from a preponderance of the evidence.[41] In nearly all jurisdictions it is well settled that the mouse,[42] roach,[43] worm,[44] or piece of glass [45] in the Coca Cola bottle,[46] the wire baked into the cake,[47] and the human toe in the chewing tobacco [48] speak convincingly for themselves.[49]

modif. on reh. 19 Wis.2d 224, 122 N.W.2d 737 (Tire blow out after 3,100 miles driven in 2 weeks. Doctrine refused); Koktavy v. United Fireworks Mfg. Co., 160 Ohio St. 461, 117 N.E.2d 16 (1954) (Prematurely exploding fireworks had been in warehouse for 2 months after leaving manufacturer).

39. Plunkett v. United Elec. Serv., 214 La. 145, 38 So.2d 704, 3 A.L.R.2d 1437 (1948) (Gas heater installed in plaintiff's house, and a fire was started nearly some 39 hours later. Held that rule applied); Lewis v. U. S. Rubber Co., 414 Pa. 626, 202 A.2d 20 (1964) (New tire exploded while being inflated). But see: Kimmey v. General Motors Corp., 262 S.W.2d 530 (Tex.Civ.App.1953), refused n. r. e. (Although car burned up one day after purchase, plaintiff failed to account for periods when car was unattended).

40. Deveny v. Rheem Mfg. Co., 319 F.2d 124 (2d Cir. 1963) (Water heater control unit was factory sealed); Ryan v. Zweck-Wollenberg Co., 266 Wis. 630, 64 N.W.2d 226 (1954) (Plaintiff suffered electric shock from refrigerator 3 years after manufacture. Doctrine applicable because motor was a sealed unit).

41. Higginbotham v. Mobil Oil Corp., 545 F.2d 422 (5th Cir. 1977), cert. denied 434 U.S. 830, 98 S.Ct. 110, 54 L.Ed.2d 89, reh. denied 434 U.S. 960, 98 S.Ct. 494, 54 L.Ed.2d 321. (Helicopter crash); Traylor v. The Fair, 101 Ill.App.2d 268, 243 N.E.2d 300 (1968).

(Permanent wave solution); Weggeman v. Seven-Up Bottling Co., 5 Wis.2d 503, 93 N.W.2d 467 (1958), amended 94 N.W.2d 645. (Exploding bottle); Evangelio v. Metropolitan Bottling Co., 339 Mass. 177, 158 N.E.2d 342 (1959). (Exploding bottle); American Elevator Co. v. Briscoe, 93 Nev. 665, 572 P.2d 534 (1977). (Elevator malfunction.)

42. Coca-Cola Bottling Co. of Jonesboro v. Misenheimer, 222 Ark. 581, 261 S.W.2d 775 (1953); Zarling v. La Salle Coca-Cola Bottling Co., 2 Wis.2d 596, 87 N.W.2d 263 (1958).

43. Oklahoma Coca-Cola Bottling Co. v. Dillard, 208 Okl. 126, 253 P.2d 847 (1953); Rogers v. Coca-Cola Bottling Co., 156 S.W.2d 325 (Tex.Civ.App. 1941).

44. Coca-Cola Bottling Co. v. Bennett, 184 Ark. 329, 42 S.W.2d 213 (1931); Norfolk Coca-Cola Bottling Works v. Land, 189 Va. 35, 52 S.E.2d 85 (1949).

45. Atlanta Coca-Cola Bottling Co. v. Ergle, 128 Ga.App. 381, 196 S.E.2d 670 (1973); Rutherford v. Huntington Coca-Cola Bottling Co., 142 W.Va. 681, 97 S.E.2d 803 (1957).

46. Wallace v. Coca-Cola Bottling Plants, Inc., 269 A.2d 117 (Me.1970) (Prophylactic); Coca-Cola Bottling

---

47. See note 47 on page 407.

48. See note 48 on page 407.

49. See note 49 on page 407.

Where the case involves multiple defendants, the exclusive control requirement does not necessarily prevent plaintiff's use of res ipsa loquitur.[50] In the case of *Ybarra v. Spangard*,[51] plaintiff emerged from a routine appendectomy with a traumatic injury to his shoulder. Faced with the notorious "conspiracy of silence"[52] on the part of the medical personnel involved, plaintiff's only evidence was res ipsa loquitur. Defendants contended that the doctrine was inapplicable where plaintiff could not isolate the instrumentality or indicate which particular defendant exercised control of it. This theory was rejected by the California Supreme Court, which held "that where a plaintiff receives unusual injuries while unconscious and in the course of medical treatment, all those who had any control over his body or the instrumentalities which might have caused the inju-

Works of Evansville v. Williams, 111 Ind.App. 502, 37 N.E.2d 702 (1941) (Bits of concrete); Claxton Coca-Cola Bottling Co. v. Coleman, 68 Ga.App. 302, 22 S.E.2d 768 (1942) (Kerosene).

47. Holley v. Purity Baking Co., 128 W.Va. 531, 37 S.E.2d 729 (1946).

48. Pillars v. R. J. Reynolds Tobacco Co., 117 Miss. 490, 78 So. 365 (1918).

49. Possibility of tampering by third-party unlikely in absence of evidence: Coca-Cola Bottling Co. of Tucson v. Fitzgerald, 3 Ariz.App. 303, 413 P.2d 869 (1966); Coast Coca-Cola Bottling Co. v. Bryant, 236 Miss. 880, 112 So. 2d 538 (1959).

But see: Macon Coca-Cola Bottling Co. v. Chancey, 216 Ga. 61, 114 S.E.2d 517, 522 (1960); Dr. Pepper Bottling Co. v. Harris, 112 Ga.App. 360, 145 S.E.2d 288 (1965).

50. Schroeder v. City & County Sav. Bank of Albany, 293 N.Y. 370, 57 N. E.2d 57 (1944), motion denied 293 N. Y. 764, 57 N.E.2d 842 (Plaintiff injured by collapsing barricade at bank. Res ipsa applicable to bank, construction company, and contractors.).

See also Du Val v. Boos Bros. Cafeteria Co., 45 Cal.App. 377, 187 P. 767 (1919). (Sidewalk elevator, where the elevator and its doors were under the joint management of the owner of the building and the company making the delivery of purchases to the cwner); Woods v. Kansas City etc. R. Co., 134 Kan. 755, 8 P.2d 404 (1932) (Passenger on railway car operated by two defendants, rule applicable against both); Biondini v. Amship Corp., 81 Cal.App.2d 751, 185 P. 2d 94 (1947) (Scaffold collapsed resulting in fall and injuries to plaintiff. The court held that there was joint control between two or more of the defendants and that it was not necessary that the scaffold be within the "exclusive management" of any particular defendant.).

51. 25 Cal.2d 486, 154 P.2d 687 (1944).

52. See Kelner, The Silent Doctors—The Conspiracy of Silence (1970) 5 V. Richmond L.Rev. 119.

Note: Overcoming the "Conspiracy of Silence": Statutory and Common Law Innovations (1961) 45 Minn.L. Rev. 1019. Markus, Conspiracy of Silence (1965) 14 Cleveland-Marshall L.Rev. 520.

Seidelson, Medical Malpractice Cases and the Reluctant Expert (1966) 16 Cath.U.L.Rev. 187.

Maki v. Murray Hosp., 91 Mont. 251, 7 P.2d 228 (1932).

ries may properly be called upon to meet the inference of negligence by giving an explanation of their conduct." [53]

The *Ybarra* reasoning has been applied in non-medical cases, where multiple defendants have exercised control. The modern trend is to allow res ipsa against the manufacturer, distributor, and retailer in products liability cases,[54] or against the owner, contractor, and sub-contractor in appropriate cases,[55] against co-tortfeasors who concurrently inflict damage,[56] or who may jointly be charged with control.[57]

---

53. 25 Cal.2d at 494, 154 P.2d at 691.

Accord: Cavero v. Franklin, etc. Benevolent Soc'y, 36 Cal.2d 301, 223 P.2d 471 (1950) (Death of child during tonsillectomy); Seneris v. Haas, 45 Cal. 2d 811, 291 P.2d 915 (1955) (Woman paralyzed after delivery of child); Beaudoin v. Watertown Memorial Hosp., 32 Wis.2d 132, 145 N.W.2d 166 (1966).

Rule rejected: Rhodes v. De Haan, 184 Kan. 473, 337 P.2d 1043 (1959); Talbot v. Dr. W. H. Groves Latter-Day Saints Hosp., Inc., 21 Utah 2d 73, 440 P.2d 872 (1968).

See Thode, The Unconscious Patient: Who Should Bear the Risk of Unexplained Injuries to a Healthy Part of his Body. (1969) Utah L.Rev. 1; Frost v. Des Moines Still College, 248 Iowa 294, 79 N.W.2d 306 (1956) (Burns sustained while under anesthesia); Voss v. Bridwell, 188 Kan. 643, 364 P.2d 955 (1961) (Total incapacitation following administration of anesthesia).

54. Blackshere v. Kemper Ins. Co., 352 So.2d 275 (La.App.1977) (Explosion of valve on oxygen tank. Res ipsa applicable against manufacturer and distributor.); Reynolds v. Natural Gas Equipment, 184 Cal.App.2d 724, 7 Cal.Rptr. 879 (1960) (Explosion of gas burner. Res ipsa applicable against manufacturer and seller-installer.).

But see Huggins v. John Morrell & Co., 176 Ohio St. 171, 198 N.E.2d 448 (1964) (Doctrine, inapplicable against packer & retailer together).

55. Knell v. Morris, 39 Cal.2d 450, 247 P.2d 352 (1952) (Water leaking from a cast-iron water heater in a beauty shop which had been repaired improperly by the defendant-plumber, the court held that both the owner of the property and the plumber exercised sufficient control to come within the rule of res ipsa. "The accident occurred either while the heater was in the control of the independent contractor, or in the control of MacMar, or in the control of both of them. It was for the trier of fact to say whether either or both had control.").

See also Schroeder v. City & County Sav. Bank of Albany, 293 N.Y. 370, 57 N.E.2d 57 (1944), motion denied 293 N.Y. 764, 57 N.E.2d 842; Poulsen v. Charlton, 224 Cal.App.2d 262, 36 Cal.Rptr. 347 (1964) (Landlord, general contractor, roofing contractor); Gilbert v. Korvette's, Inc., 457 Pa. 602, 327 A.2d 94 (1974) (Res ipsa applicable to store and escalator company).

56. Gauthreaux v. Hogan, 185 So.2d 44 (La.App.1966) (Plaintiff's building damaged by collision of two drivers).

57. Bond v. Otis Elevator Co., 388 S. W.2d 681 (Tex.1965), on remand 391 S.W.2d 519 (Elevator in joint control of building owner and elevator company); Coca-Cola Bottling Co. v. Lowe, 275 S.W.2d 47 (Ky.1955) (Bottling company and store owner in joint control of sign which fell); Enslein v. Hudson & M. R. Co., 8 Misc.

§ 7.5 Plaintiff's Conduct

Res ipsa loquitur is often denied to plaintiff when he fails to exclude himself as a proximate contributor to the injury.[58] For instance, the doctrine has been ruled inapplicable to the unexplained crash of an airplane outfitted with dual controls, on the theory that plaintiff's decedent could have been the responsible party.[59] Similarly, where the instrumentality was in the sole control of plaintiff, the doctrine may be denied.[60] The better view rejects this rigid formal-

2d 87, 165 N.Y.S.2d 630 (1957), aff'd in part, rev'd in part 6 A.D.2d 833, 176 N.Y.S.2d 70, aff'd 6 N.Y.2d 723, 185 N.Y.S.2d 810, 158 N.E.2d 504 (Escalator owner and service company); Ozark v. Wichita Manor, Inc., 252 F.2d 671 (5th Cir. 1958), reh. denied 258 F.2d 805.

58. Charlton v. Lovelace, 351 Mo. 364, 173 S.W.2d 13 (1943) ("In order to make a prima facie case under the res ipsa loquitur doctrine the evidence must be such as to reasonably exclude the negligence of the injured as a contributing cause of the injury —"); Hollander v. Smith and Smith, 10 N.J.Super. 82, 76 A.2d 697, 21 A.L.R.2d 902 (1950) (Where patient was under care of defendant ambulance attendants, he fell from stretcher, held rule not applicable since movement of plaintiff herself may have caused fall); Ayers v. Amatucci, 206 Okl. 366, 243 P.2d 716 (1952) (After used automobile had been driven by purchaser for 36 days and some 1940 miles, fire as a result of a leak from gas tank, was not imputable to seller on theory of res ipsa loquitur. The rule "—does not apply where the facts shown are equally consistent with the hypothesis that the injury sued for was caused by the negligence of either party or of both combined—".); Hook v. Lakeside Park Co., 142 Colo. 277, 351 P.2d 261 (1960) (Injury sustained in amusement park ride: "Furthermore the possibility that plaintiff's sudden forward movement was attributable to her failure to hold the bar or rod in the car is as persuasive an explanation of her injury as the possibility that it resulted from the looseness of the strap").

59. Towle v. Phillips, 180 Tenn. 121, 172 S.W.2d 806 (1943) (Where airplane which crashed had dual controls, passenger-plaintiff had joint control, so that rule was not invoked); Budgett v. Skoo Sky Ways, 64 S.D. 243, 266 N.W. 253 (1936) (Dual control plane fell—fall may have been caused by defendant's pilot or by plaintiff's decedent); Lejeune v. Collard, 44 So.2d 504 (La.App. 1950) (Where airplane was being flown by plaintiff's decedent, held rule does not apply because under control and knowledge of decedent at time of accident).

60. Kilgore v. Shepard, 52 R.I. 151, 158 A. 720 (1932) (Where customer in store sat on chair and it collapsed. "—we find that plaintiff is not entitled to the benefit of the doctrine, because it appears that the chair was under her exclusive control and use from the time she moved it from the table."); Landers v. Safeway Stores, 172 Or. 116, 139 P.2d 788 (1943) (Hands of plaintiff injured by use of bleaching solution, rule not used because instrumentality which is claimed to have produced the injury was at the time in the exclusive possession and control of the plaintiff); Doherty v. Arcade Hotel Co., 170 Or. 374, 134 P.2d 118 (1943) (Hotel guest attempted to turn off hot water faucet, handle broke and cut his hand); Fisher v. Minneapolis etc. R. Co., 199 F.2d 308 (8th Cir. 1952) (Not applica-

ism in favor of a rational inquiry into the probable relation of defendant's negligence to the injuries sustained.[61] In the leading case of *Jesionowski v. Boston & Maine R. Co.*,[62] the U.S. Supreme Court reversed a Circuit Court of Appeals ruling which had denied a res ipsa loquitur instruction where defendant's evidence pointed to plaintiff's decedent's conduct as responsible for a train derailment. The Supreme Court stated:

> "We cannot agree. Res ipsa loquitur, thus applied, would bar juries from drawing an inference of negligence on account of unusual accidents in all operations where the injured person had himself participated in the operations, even though it was proved that his operations of the things under his control did not cause the accident. This viewpoint unduly restricts the power of juries to decide questions of fact, and in this case the jury's right to draw inferences from evidence and the sufficiency of that evidence to support a verdict are federal questions. A conceptualistic interpretation of res ipsa loquitur has never been used by this Court to reduce the jury's power to draw inferences from facts. Such an interpretation unduly narrows the doctrine as this Court has applied it."

Res ipsa thus may be applied in situations where plaintiff participates in the events leading to the accident, such as driving a car with faulty brakes,[63] mounting a tire which explodes,[64] turning on a defective oven,[65] or unpackaging a caustic chemical which burns his hands,[66] where the evidence excludes plaintiff's conduct as the responsible cause. Wisconsin, apparently alone, has held that plaintiff need

---

ble when carload of logs, one of which rolled off, was under the immediate control of the plaintiff).

61. Rose v. Melody Lane, 39 Cal.2d 481, 247 P.2d 335 (1952) (Plaintiff injured by fall from defective bar stool. Although "in one sense plaintiff was in control of the stool while using it," still "so far as construction, inspection, or maintenance of the stool were concerned, defendant had exclusive control"); Albers v. Greyhound Corp., 4 Cal.App.3d 463, 84 Cal.Rptr. 846 (1970) ("The mere fact that the box was in the custody and control of the plaintiff at the time the accident occurred does not prevent the application of the doctrine"); Gow v. Multnomah Hotel, 191 Or. 45, 224 P.2d 552 (1950), motion granted 191 Or. 45, 228 P.2d 791 (Broken counter stool—plaintiff's mere possession does not bar res ipsa where no abnormal use).

62. 329 U.S. 452, 67 S.Ct. 401, 91 L.Ed. 416, 169 A.L.R. 947 (1947).

63. Dunn v. Vogel Chevrolet Co., 168 Cal.App.2d 117, 335 P.2d 492 (1959).

64. Baker v. B. F. Goodrich Co., 115 Cal.App.2d 221, 252 P.2d 24 (1953).

65. Peterson v. Minnesota Power & Light Co., 207 Minn. 387, 29 N.W. 705 (1940).

66. Lorenc v. Chemirad Corp., 37 N.J. 56, 179 A.2d 401 (1962).

not eliminate himself as a possible cause in order to apply res ipsa, since under comparative negligence his own contribution would not be a bar to recovery.[67]

§ 7.6 Defendant's Superior Knowledge

Some jurisdictions require, as a condition of applying res ipsa loquitur, that the nature of the accident be such that defendant have superior knowledge to plaintiff regarding its causation.[68] The majority of jurisdictions reject this factor as an essential condition for application of the doctrine,[69] yet consideration of plaintiff's ignorance and defendant's superior access to information regarding the accident is frequently involved in determining whether res ipsa is appropriate.

---

67. Turk v. H. C. Prange Co., 18 Wis. 2d 547, 119 N.W.2d 365 (1963).

68. Bianchini v. Humble Pipe Line Co., 480 F.2d 251 (5th Cir. 1973), reh. denied 478 F.2d 1402 (Res ipsa not available to plaintiff oyster farmers in suit against pipeline company for damages caused by oil spill. Louisiana law requires that defendant have superior knowledge regarding cause of mishap. Here, defendant proved third-party cause and lack of own negligence.); McCall v. United States, 206 F.Supp. 421 (D.C.Va.1962) (Tail gate of trailer struck plaintiff on head: "The first element [for application of res ipsa] is that the defendant must have superior knowledge of the cause of the accident. But in the case at bar both parties know that the accident was caused by leaving the tail gate upright with the retaining bolt or pin removed."); Furlong v. Stokes, 427 S.W.2d 513, 34 A.L.R. 3d 1059 (Mo.1968) (Plaintiff suffered burn during operation. Defendant's knowledge required to apply res ipsa. Verdict for defendant affirmed, on lack of control and failure to show causation.); Szafranski v. Radetzky, 31 Wis.2d 119, 141 N.W.2d 902, 23 A.L.R.3d 1071 (1966) (Injuries from explosion of gunpowder in defendant's home: "[T]he doctrine of res ipsa is available only under those circumstances when the conduct is peculiarly within the knowledge of the defendant . . .").

   See also Sample v. Schwenck, 243 Iowa 1189, 54 N.W.2d 527 (1952) (Where granary fell off lifting jacks, and injured employee, res ipsa not involved: "The first condition has been held to mean the management must be so much under the exclusive control of defendant as to charge him with superior knowledge or means of information as to cause of accident"); Seffert v. Los Angeles Transit Lines, 56 Cal.2d 498, 15 Cal.Rptr. 161, 364 P.2d 337 (1961).

69. Zentz v. Coca Cola Bottling Co., 39 Cal.2d 436, 247 P.2d 344 (1952) ("[T]he doctrine may be applied even though the defendant is not in a better position than plaintiff to explain what occurred if it appears more probably than not that the injury resulted from negligence on the part of defendant"); Faust v. Benton County Public Util. Dist. No. 1., 13 Wash. App. 473, 535 P.2d 854 (1975) ("Equal accessibility to the cause of the accident is not a controlling factor and is at best a make-weight argument").

   Prosser, The Law of Torts (4th ed., 1971) p. 226: Plaintiff's comparative ignorance "cannot be regarded as an indispensable requirement, and there are few cases in which it can be said to have had any real importance."

Defendant's lack of superior knowledge in combination with lack of control has been cited in support of refusing a res ipsa instruction.[70] Defendant's lack of superior knowledge is sometimes referred to in connection with the availability of direct evidence to plaintiff.[71] More frequently, however, it is defendant's superior access to information regarding the mishap which is cited by the court in justification of applying the doctrine.[72] An example is *Fowler v. Seaton*,[73] where plaintiff, a three-year-old child, suffered a bump on the forehead while attending defendant's nursery school. The injury resulted in crossed eyes, requiring surgery. Defendant, at separate times gave two unsatisfactory explanations for the child's accident. The California Supreme Court reversed the non-suit, noting: "Where, under the evidence, an explanation is called for, if the defendant refuses to explain or gives a false explanation, it is reasonably inferable that the defendant is hiding something which, more probably than not is his negligence. . . . Under the circumstances it is inferable that defendant had a consciousness or guilt, knew the cause of the injury, was under a duty to explain, and was trying to conceal it. Thus it may be reasonably inferred that the duty was violated. Certainly it is more probable than not that the injury was the result of defendant's faulty supervision. Thus the jury could find that the doctrine of res ipsa loquitur is applicable, and for that reason it was error to grant the nonsuit." [74]

---

70. Lyons v. Jahncke Serv., Inc., 125 So.2d 619 (La.App.1960) (Res ipsa inapplicable against bailor of elevator as distinguished from manufacturer who could be presumed to have superior knowledge); Wallace v. Knapp-Monarch Co., 234 F.2d 853 (8th Cir. 1952) (Vaporizer erupted and scalded infant. Res ipsa denied: "Plaintiff was in a better position to show the circumstances causing the injury and defendant is not possessive of any superior knowledge.").

71. See § 7.8, infra.

72. E. g., 9 Wigmore, Evidence (3d ed.) § 2509: ("The particular force and justice of the rule, regarded as a presumption throwing upon the party charged the duty of producing evidence, consists in the circumstance that the chief evidence of the true cause, whether culpable or innocent, is particularly accessible to him but inaccessible to the injured person"). Quoted in Ybarra v. Spangard, 25 Cal.2d 486, 154 P.2d 687 (1944).

73. 61 Cal.2d 681, 39 Cal.Rptr. 881, 394 P.2d 697 (1964).

74. Id. at 689, 690.

§ 7.7 Application—Pleading and Evidence of Specific Negligence

Many courts hold that res ipsa loquitur is a doctrine of necessity, to be applied only where the demands of justice make it essential, and then with extreme caution.[75] Thus the doctrine has been refused when it appears that evidence of specific negligence is available to plaintiff.[76] A verdict for plaintiff was reversed in *Ford Motor Co. v. Fish*,[77] for example, on grounds that res ipsa loquitur had been erroneously applied. Plaintiff, who had been injured when his truck suddenly veered off the road, claimed that a defective brake mechanism had caused the accident, and prevailed at trial on res ipsa loquitur.

The Arkansas Supreme Court, however, took the view that since the brake mechanism had been retrieved and inspected, and expert testimony relative to its condition presented at trial, that submission of the issue to the jury on res ipsa was improper. The general practice, however, is to admit evidence of specific acts of negligence along with res ipsa loquitur, where the specific evidence does not itself amount to a complete explanation which leaves no room for inference.[78]

---

75. Starr v. Starr, 35 Del. (5 W. W. Harr.) 556, 170 A. 924 (1934) (Not applicable when motor vehicle slid off road. "[T]he doctrine is of limited and restricted scope, ordinarily to be applied sparingly and with caution, in peculiar and exceptional cases, and only where the facts and demands of justice make the application essential."); Miller v. Gerber Products Co., 207 Ga. 385, 62 S.E.2d 174 (1950) ("The doctrine of res ipsa loquitur, when applicable, should be applied with caution, and should be drawn by the jury only in extreme cases"); Venditti v. St. Louis Public Service Co., 360 Mo. 42, 226 S.W.2d 599 (1950) ("[T]he rule is of restricted scope, to be applied in peculiar and exceptional cases where the demands of justice make its application essential"); Morner v. Union Pacific R. Co., 31 Wash.2d 153, 196 P.2d 744 (1948) ("[T]he maxim, when properly applied, is of value in the administration of justice, its scope is nevertheless limited, and ordinarily it is to be sparingly applied, in peculiar and exceptional cases, and only where the facts and the demands of justice make its application essential").

76. Johnson v. Latimer, 180 Kan. 720, 308 P.2d 65 (1957) (Injury claimed from defective furnace leaking carbon monoxide; res ipsa denied: "There was no destruction of the instrumentality alleged to be defective. It remained intact for plaintiff's inspection . . . it was in his possession at all times, and accessible to him . . . there is nothing on the petition to indicate that direct proof of negligence is lacking nor that direct evidence of negligence is unavailable to plaintiff."); Linam v. Murphy, 360 Mo. 1140, 232 S.W.2d 937 (1950) (Dual control airplane, actually operated by defendant's employee, held rule not applicable. "Both occupants of the plane are still alive and the facts are not in dispute.").

77. 232 Ark. 270, 335 S.W.2d 712 (1960).

78. Citrola v. Eastern Air Lines, Inc., 264 F.2d 815 (2d Cir. 1959) (Res ipsa charge proper, despite introduction of specific evidence: "Should this court hold that such a charge is erroneous, plaintiffs in the future would hesitate to introduce whatever evidence they

§ 7.7   TORT LIABILITY AND DEFENSES   Pt. 3

The rule in most jurisdictions allows pleading in alternative counts, so that charges of specific negligence may be coupled with a general charge of negligence under res ipsa.[79] A minority, however, holds that pleading of specific negligence precludes any reliance on res ipsa loquitur.[80] A majority of jurisdictions further will allow plaintiff to rely on res ipsa at trial even where his pleadings include only charges of specific negligence,[81] although some require a charge of general negligence to put defendant on notice.[82] A middle ground

might have available as to the cause of injury for fear that thereby they would be deprived of an otherwise appropriate *res ipsa* charge"); Throop v. F. E. Young & Co., 94 Ariz. 146, 382 P.2d 560 (1963) (Head-on auto collision—permissible to argue res ipsa after introducing evidence of defendant's decedent's heart condition); Hugo v. Manning, 201 Kan. 391, 441 P.2d 145 (1968) (Injuries sustained in stampede from a fire in a crowded building: "We think that in cases in which a plaintiff is entitled to rely on the doctrine of res ipsa loquitur, he should not be penalized by the loss of the presumption because he has been willing to go forward and do the best he can to prove specific acts of negligence"); DiMare v. Cresci, 58 Cal.2d 292, 23 Cal.Rptr. 772, 373 P.2d 860 (1962) (Fall from stairway. Res ipsa not precluded by evidence of specific acts of negligence.); Abbot v. Page Airways, Inc., 23 N.Y.2d 502, 297 N.Y.S.2d 713, 245 N.E.2d 388 (1969) (Helicopter crash, evidence of specific acts only enhanced probability that accident was caused by negligence); Mobil Chem. Co. v. Bell, 517 S.W.2d 245 (Tex. 1974) (Proof of specific acts not inconsistent with doctrine in case where valve spurted out acid on plaintiff).

79. Voss v. Bridwell, 188 Kan. 643, 364 P.2d 955 (1961) (Medical malpractice); Fink v. New York Central R. Co., 144 Ohio St. 1, 56 N.E.2d 456 (1944) (Train derailed); Metz v. Central Illinois Elec. & Gas Co., 32 Ill.2d 446, 207 N.E.2d 305 (1965); Southeastern Aviation, Inc. v. Hurd, 209 Tenn. 639, 355 S.W.2d 436 (1962), appeal dism'd 371 U.S. 21, 83 S.Ct. 120, 9 L.Ed.2d 96; Honea v. Coca Cola Bottling Co., 143 Tex. 272, 183 S.W.2d 968 (1944).

See e.g. Fed.R. Civil Proced. 8(e)(2) (permitting alternative pleading); which rule is followed by most states.

80. Crawford v. Rogers, 406 P.2d 189 (Alaska 1965) (Aircraft accident); Tucson v. Sanderson, 104 Ariz. 151, 449 P.2d 616 (1969); Roos v. Consumers Public Power Dist., 171 Neb. 563, 106 N.W.2d 871 (1961) (Falling power line); McAlester Coca-Cola Bottling Co. v. Lynch, 280 P.2d 466 (Okl.1955) (Exploding bottle).

81. Fassbinder v. Pennsylvania R. Co., 322 F.2d 859 (3d Cir. 1963) (FELA case—res ipsa is rule of evidence, need not be pleaded); Rigney v. Cincinnati St. Ry. Co., 99 Ohio App. 105, 131 N.E.2d 413 (1954); Johnson v. Greenfield, 210 Ark. 985, 198 S.W.2d 403 (1946); Loos v. Mountain Fuel Supply Co., 99 Utah 496, 108 P.2d 254 (1940); Wenzel v. St. Louis Public Serv. Co., 361 Mo. 448, 235 S.W. 2d 312 (1950) (Passenger thrown from bus).

82. Whitby v. One-O-One Trailer Rental Co., 191 Kan. 653, 383 P.2d 560 (1963); Erckman v. Northern Illinois Gas Co., 61 Ill.App.2d 137, 210 N.E.2d 42 (1965).

is to allow res ipsa in this situation only where the inference to be drawn supports the specific allegations framed in the pleadings.[83]

Although res ipsa loquitur has been held inapplicable to actions in strict liability,[84] since negligence is not at issue, nevertheless the essence of the doctrine, as inferential proof by circumstantial evidence, may be applied to products liability cases in warranty and strict liability.[85] Plaintiff is required to present a factual basis for a reasonable inference that the cause of the injury was a defect in the product,[86] that the defect existed while the product was in defend-

83. Wallace v. Norris, 310 Ky. 424, 220 S.W.2d 967 (1940); Short v. D. R. B. Logging Co., 192 Or. 383, 235 P.2d 340 (1951); Zumwalt v. Gardner, 160 F.2d 298 (8th Cir. 1947) (FELA case).

84. Lewis v. American Hoist & Derrick Co., 20 Cal.App.3d 570, 97 Cal.Rptr. 798 (1971); Haas v. Buick Motor Div. of General Motors Corp., 20 Ill.App. 2d 448, 156 N.E.2d 263 (1959) (Res ipsa not available to show defect in warranty action where new car caught fire); Berry v. American Cyanamid Co., 341 F.2d 14 (6th Cir. 1965) (Oral polio vaccine).

85. Wade, Strict Tort Liability of Manufacturers, 19 S.W.L.J. 5, 20: ("It is necessary, of course, that the plaintiff show not only that the product was unsafe but also that defendant was responsible for its condition . . . [T]he plaintiff will often have to resort to circumstantial evidence to supply his proof.")

Prosser, The Law of Torts (4th ed., 1971) p. 673: ("[T]he inferences which are the core of the doctrine remain, and are no less applicable"); Lindsay v. McDonnell Douglas Aircraft Corp., 460 F.2d 631 (8th Cir. 1972), on remand 352 F.Supp. 633 (D.C.Mo.), aff'd 485 F.2d 1288 (Air crash over Gulf of Mexico—circumstantial evidence competent to establish defect and causation: "There would be little gain to the consuming public if the court would establish a form of recovery with one hand and take it away with the other by estab- lishing impossible standards of proof"); State Farm Mut. Auto Ins. Co. v. Anderson-Weber, Inc., 252 Iowa 1289, 110 N.W.2d 449 (1961) (Circumstantial evidence may be resorted to to establish breach of warranty); Kroger Co. v. Bowman, 411 S.W.2d 339 (Ky.1967) (Bottle fell from carton and injured plaintiff. Although res ipsa inapplicable to strict liability action, "We think it is proper in the case before us to apply the same principle", to determine "whether the nature and circumstances of the occurrence presented substantial evidence that the carton was in a dangerously defective condition when delivered to Kroger by Dr. Pepper.").

See Barker, Circumstantial Evidence in Strict Liability Cases (1973) 38 Albany L.R. 11.

See also Chapter 43, Products Liability.

86. Lindsay v. McDonnell Douglas Aircraft Corp., 460 F.2d 631 (8th Cir. 1972), on remand 352 F.Supp. 633 (D.C. Mo.), aff'd 485 F.2d 1288 (Defect inferred by circumstantial fact that aircraft was on fire before crashing); Thomas v. American Cystoscope Makers, Inc., 414 F.Supp. 255 (D.C.Pa. 1976); Bailey v. Montgomery Ward & Co., 6 Ariz.App. 213, 431 P.2d 108 (1967) (Defect inferred where pogo stick broke shortly after purchase); Powers v. Hunt-Wesson Foods, Inc., 64 Wis.2d 532, 219 N.W.2d 393 (1974) (Defect inferred where ketchup bottle broke when plaintiff lightly tapped bottom).

ant's control,[87] and that plaintiff's own conduct was not an equally probable proximate cause of the injuries.[88] A res ipsa loquitur instruction substituting "defect" for "negligence", however, may be refused.[89] But plaintiff in a products case generally may present both a res ipsa loquitur theory in negligence and a strict liability theory to the jury.[90]

§ 7.8 Effect—Inference or Presumption

The majority of jurisdictions treat res ipsa loquitur as a rule of evidence which *permits* an inference of negligence, but does not *compel* such an inference.[91] By its application, plaintiff may avoid a non-

---

87. Paoletto v. Beech Aircraft Corp., 464 F.2d 976 (3d Cir. 1972) (Defect in aircraft which crashed 21 years after manufacture not shown to exist at time of manufacture); Moerer v. Ford Motor Co., 57 Cal.App.3d 114, 129 Cal.Rptr. 112 (1976) (No inference that broken tie rod was defective at time of manufacture of car); Kerr v. Corning Glass Works, 284 Minn. 115, 169 N.W.2d 587 (1969) (No proof that baking dish which exploded was defective at time of manufacture); Clarke v. Brockway Motor Trucks, 372 F.Supp. 1342 (D.C.Pa. 1974) (Truck brake failure 18 days after purchase sufficient to infer defect at time vehicle left manufacturer); Bombardi v. Pochel's Appliance & TV Co., 9 Wash.App. 797, 515 P.2d 540 (1973), modified 10 Wash.2d 243, 518 P.2d 202 (Evidence that TV set which caught fire had been serviced by authorized repairman who used only manufacturer's replacement parts sufficient to prove defect at time TV left manufacturer).

88. Martinez v. Nichols Conveyor & Engineering Co., 243 Cal.App.2d 795, 52 Cal.Rptr. 842 (1966) (Plaintiff's abnormal use of paper baler could have been cause of accident—liability denied); Winnett v. Winnett, 57 Ill.2d 7, 310 N.E.2d 1 (1974) (Plaintiff 4 year-old put fingers in forager mechanism—liability denied); Swain v. Boeing Airplane Co., 337 F.2d 940 (2d Cir. 1964), cert. denied 380 U.S. 951, 85 S.Ct. 1083, 13 L.Ed.2d 969 (Verdict for defendant sustained since jury could have found misuse rather than defect as cause of accident).

89. Tresham v. Ford Motor Co., 275 Cal.App.2d 403, 79 Cal.Rptr. 883 (1969) ("There is no reason in law or logic why the doctrine embedded in the instructions requested by appellants should be extended to include the type of case before this court").

90. Jiminez v. Sears, Roebuck & Co., 4 Cal.3d 379, 93 Cal.Rptr. 769, 482 P.2d 681 (1971) ("No valid reason appears to require a plaintiff to elect whether to proceed on the theory of strict liability in tort or on the theory of negligence").

91. Sweeney v. Erving, 228 U.S. 233, 33 S.Ct. 416, 57 L.Ed. 815 (1913) ("Res ipsa loquitur means that the facts of the occurrence warrant the inference of negligence, not that they compel such an inference; that they furnish circumstantial evidence of negligence where direct evidence of it may be lacking, but it is evidence to be weighed, not necessarily to be accepted as sufficient; that they call for explanation or rebuttal, not necessarily that they require it; that they make a case to be decided by the jury, not that they forestall the verdict. Res ipsa loquitur, where it applies, does not convert the defendant's general issue into an affirmative

suit, but a verdict in his behalf will not be directed.[92] Under this view, the doctrine does not raise a presumption in favor of plaintiff, or shift the burden of proof to defendant.[93] The plaintiff who has presented a res ipsa loquitur case has met his burden of establishing a prima facie case of negligence, and, in this sense only, the burden then shifts to defendant to produce evidence to rebut or run the risk of non-persuasion.[94] The burden of proof by a preponderance of the evidence still rests with plaintiff,[95] and where defendant introduces evidence sufficient to balance the inference he is entitled to a verdict for plaintiff's failure to sustain his burden.[96]

defense. When all the evidence is in, the question for the jury is, whether the preponderance is with the plaintiff.") Id. at 240; Kroger Co. v. Bowman, 411 S.W.2d 339 (Ky.1967); Easterling v. Walton, 208 Va. 214, 156 S.E.2d 787 (1967) (Medical malpractice—failure to remove pad from abdominal cavity after surgery); Hornbeck v. Homeopathic Hosp. Ass'n of Delaware, 57 Del. (7 Storey) 120, 197 A.2d 461 (1964) (Contraction of infection after injection of drug); Kahalili v. Rosecliff Realty, Inc., 26 N.J. 595, 141 A.2d 301, 66 A.L.R.2d 680 (1958).

92. Nuclear Corp. of America v. Lang, 480 F.2d 990 (8th Cir. 1973) (Plaintiff by res ipsa meets his burden); Domany v. Otis Elevator Co., 369 F.2d 604 (6th Cir. 1966), cert. denied 387 U.S. 942, 87 S.Ct. 2073, 18 L.Ed.2d 1327 (Plaintiff not entitled to directed verdict if defendant presents no rebuttal evidence); Trihey v. Transocean Air Lines, 255 F.2d 824 (9th Cir. 1958), cert. denied 358 U.S. 838, 79 S.Ct. 62, 3 L.Ed.2d 74 (Air crash verdict for defendant: "The facts of an unexplained crash into the ocean may warrant an inference of negligence, but do not compel that inference").

93. Brown v. Potomac Elec. Power Co., 236 F.Supp. 815 (D.C.D.C.1964). (Doctrine does not shift burden of proof, question is whether preponderance is with plaintiff.); A. Shapiro Realty Corp. v. Burgess Bros. Inc., 491 F.2d 327 (1st Cir. 1974). (Doctrine does not shift burden of proof).

See also Lowman v. Housing Auth. of Stamford, 150 Conn. 665, 192 A.2d 883 (1963); Johnson v. Coca Cola Bottling Co., 235 Minn. 471, 51 N.W. 2d 573 (1952); Thurman v. Johnson, 330 S.W.2d 179 (Mo.App.1959).

94. United States v. Chesapeake & Delaware Shipyard, Inc., 369 F.Supp. 714 (D.C.Md.1974); Colditz v. Eastern Airlines, Inc., 329 F.Supp. 691 (D.C. N.Y.1971). (Doctrine shifts burden of explanation to defendant, not burden of proof.)

95. Commercial Molasses Corp. v. New York Tank Barge Corp., 314 U. S. 104, 62 S.Ct. 156, 86 L.Ed. 89 (1941); Chaisson v. Williams, 130 Me. 341, 156 A. 154 (1931).

96. Kahalili v. Rosecliff Realty, Inc., 26 N.J. 595, 141 A.2d 301, 66 A.L.R.2d 680 (1958). (Equipoise in evidence entitles defendant to verdict.); Hamilton v. Southern Ry. Co., 162 F.2d 884 (4th Cir. 1947). (Bridge collapse. "The jury should have been instructed that if they believed the testimony of the plaintiff as to the manner in which the truck entered the bridge, an inference of negligence on the part of the defendant arose, but that the burden of proof remained with the plaintiff, and if in the minds of the jury the question of the defendant's negligence was in equal balance, their decision on this point should be for the defendant.")

§ 7.8   TORT LIABILITY AND DEFENSES   Pt. 3

The alternate view, that res ipsa loquitur creates a presumption in favor of plaintiff, is exemplified by the California res ipsa statute.[97] Under this view, a plaintiff who has established the elements of a res ipsa loquitur case is entitled to a directed verdict, unless defendant introduces evidence to support a finding that the accident resulted from some other cause than his negligence.[98] Defendant's burden is not satisfied merely by a showing of other *possible* causes.[99] And where the defendant introduces substantial evidence to rebut the presumption, the determination of liability by a preponderance of the evidence is still for the trier of fact.[1] In a *presumption* vs. *inference* the presumption prevails.

---

97. West's Ann.Cal.Evid. Code § 646(b) ("The judicial doctrine of res ipsa loquitur is a presumption affecting the burden of producing evidence").

98. West's Ann.Cal.Evid. Code § 646, Law Revision Commission Comment (1970) ("Therefore, when the plaintiff has established the three conditions that give rise to the doctrine, the jury is required to find that the accident resulted from the defendant's negligence unless the defendant comes forward with evidence that would support a contrary finding"); Newing v. Cheatham, 15 Cal.3d 351, 124 Cal. Rptr. 193, 540 P.2d 33 (1975) (Air crash: "Since the facts giving rise to the doctrine were undisputed, the inference of negligence arose as a matter of law; . . . to put it another way, the conclusion is compelled that there is a balance of probabilities pointing to the [defendant's] negligence"); Weiss v. Axler, 137 Colo. 544, 328 P.2d 88 (1958) ("The doctrine of res ipsa loquitur creates a compulsive presumption of negligence which continues to exist until the defendant has satisfied the court or jury, whichever is to find the fact, by a preponderance of the evidence that he was not negligent"); Coca-Cola Bottling Co. of Helena v. Mattice, 219 Ark. 428, 243 S.W.2d 15 (1951).

99. Newing v. Cheatham, 15 Cal.3d 351, 124 Cal.Rptr. 193, 540 P.2d 33 (1925) (Defendant "has at most argued that the crash *could* have resulted from causes other than the negligence of his decedent. Mere speculation of this sort is insufficient to discharge defendant's burden of explanation"); Dierman v. Providence Hosp., 31 Cal.2d 290, 188 P.2d 12 (1947) (Defendant in res ipsa case will not be held blameless except on a showing either:

"(1) of a satisfactory explanation of the accident, that is, an affirmative showing of a definite cause for the accident, in which cause no element of negligence on the part of the defendant inheres, or (2) of such care in all possible respects as necessarily to lead to the conclusion that the accident could not have happened from want of care, but must have been due to some unpreventable cause, although the exact cause is unknown."

Roberts v. Trans World Airlines, 225 Cal.App.2d 344, 37 Cal.Rptr. 291 (1964) (Pilot landed airliner in mud to avoid accident. Defense verdict sustained, since showing of compliance with FAA standards constituted substantial evidence of due care.).

1. Ybarra v. Spangard, 25 Cal.2d 486, 154 P.2d 687 (1944).

See also Ybarra v. Spangard, 93 Cal. App.2d 43, 208 P.2d 445 (1949) (Verdict for plaintiff sustained despite rebuttal evidence by defendants. "There is nothing inherent in direct testimony which compels a trial court to accept it over the contrary references which may reasonably be drawn from circumstantial evidence." Id. at 46).

§ 7.9 Practical Considerations—Defense of Due Care

The author believes that plaintiff, having the burden of proof, should rely on res ipsa loquitur if the rules of procedure allow him to do so, taking full advantage of the Court's instructions. However, he should not wait for the defendant to prove his case for him. The advantages of detailed opening statement and full disclosure to the jury as early as possible should be utilized. But once this is done, plaintiff falls flat if merely the facts of the accident and injuries are adduced before resting. Defendant would then be given the opportunity to show the details for the first time, and when rebuttal comes (if the rules of court so permit) plaintiff's experts, now called, may cause the jury to believe that the cause is really desperate.

There are, however, situations when the plaintiff must rely on res ipsa alone. He has no other evidence. But if he has none, lay or expert, the defendant probably has none either. In the exploding bottle case, and similar accidents (including foreign objects found in bottles), I have found that use of this rule of evidence, solely, is the safest procedure. Plaintiff shows that the bottle exploded, or that the foreign object was found therein, proves his damages and rests. What can defendant say? He can, and generally does bring in a score of experts to prove that the glass was of the proper tensile strength, that the beverage was not overcharged, that the cap was properly secured, that there were no defects in the bottle, that he even had watchers on the capping line, observing each bottle as it passed by. (These watchers "were relieved every fifteen minutes so that they would not suffer from eye strain, and be alert to catch any defect.") But what has he actually proved? He has proved two things in aid of plaintiff's case: one, that the thing he emphatically denies can happen, has happened; and, secondly, he has demonstrated scienter by showing the great preparations taken to prevent a recurrence of foreign objects in bottles, or explosions.[2]

---

2. Samuel A. Rosenthal, of Los Angeles advised the author of his argument in Gordon v. Aztec Brewing Co., 33 Cal.2d 514, 203 P.2d 522 (1949), a part of which is as follows: "I wish this little bottle could talk, and do you know what it would have said? It would have said, 'Ladies and Gentlemen of the Jury, when I was born I had some defect. They didn't give me a strong body, and I slipped by the manufacturer with several others because I looked well, you couldn't tell by looking at me what my body was like, but I had some defect there. I had some pain along the side. One side wasn't quite as strong as the other side, but you couldn't tell by just looking at me unless—sure, I have seen some of my brothers placed in a machine. I don't know what to call it, and they were looking at some of my brothers and sisters in the same batch, but they passed me by. And I also heard and saw them taking hammers and rapping some of my brothers and sisters, and they rapped me a little but some-

Accordingly, the courts have generally ruled that a manufacturer's evidence of routine precautions, however elaborate, will not suffice to take a res ipsa case from the jury.[3] In *Baker v. B. F. Goodrich Co.*,[4] an exploding tire case, both sides presented expert testimony regarding the condition of the tire in question. Defendant introduced further evidence of its general manufacturing processes, and escorted the jury to its plant to tour operations there. The trial court's subsequent refusal to grant a res ipsa loquitur instruction was reversed by the Appellate Court, which stated:

> "Neither may we undertake to determine, as respondent invites us to do, whether the evidence adduced by respondent upon

---

3. Webb v. Brown & Williamson Tobacco Co., 121 W.Va. 115, 2 S.E.2d 898 (1939) ("In this case, testimony of the superintendent of the manufacturing plant tends to establish the fact that precautions were taken to prevent the presence of foreign substances in the manufactured product . . . . But the fact remains that, notwithstanding the care exercised by the manufacturer, and the possibility that the injury complained of might have resulted from some development not traceable to its acts, a worm or a moth did get into the tobacco plug, and from this fact resulting injury was sustained by the consumers. . . . The jury had the right to believe that the system used by the manufacturer was not sufficient to prevent the presence of a foreign substance in the manufactured product involved in the case."); Bustamante v. Carborundum Co., 375 F.2d 688 (7th Cir. 1967) (Disintegrating grinding wheel: "[I]t is for the jury to further determine where the permissive inference of negligence . . . is to prevail over a defendant's countervailing proof of due care"); Reynolds Metals Co. v. Yturbide, 258 F.2d 321 (9th Cir. 1958), cert. denied 358 U.S. 840, 79 S.Ct. 66, 3 L.Ed.2d 76 (Res ipsa instruction granted in fluoride poisoning case despite defendant's evidence that it "was utilizing and had installed the latest and best known means of protecting against the escape of fluorides"); Ryan v. Zweck-Wollenberg Co., 266 Wis. 630, 64 N.W.2d 226 (1954) (Plaintiff suffered electric shock from refrigerator door handle. Res ipsa not barred by defendant's showing use of best known testing for short circuits.).

See Kimble and Lesher, Products Liability, §§ 83, 222 (West's Handbook Series).

4. 115 Cal.App.2d 221, 252 P.2d 24 (1953).

[Quoted testimony in left column of footnotes:] "how it didn't seem to indicate to them that I had a weak body. I got by that, too. Then they let me go on down to the brewery. They filled me up with beer. I was sent out and I came back, but I had pain constantly and I wasn't very happy. Then came a day that I deeply regret, because after several times, maybe fifty or a hundred times, maybe more, I would take these trips to and from, and then one day I came into the establishment of Mr. Gordon, a very nice fellow. He didn't mishandle me at all, he didn't drop me. He did nothing at all to me. He just took me out, but by that time I couldn't stand it any longer. I gave way. I made a lot of noise and I went to pieces, and a part of me entered Mr. Gordon's eye and it blinded him. It wasn't my fault, and it certainly wasn't his fault. They just didn't take good care of me. I wish they could take me back and give me a new life and give him a new eye. But they can't.' I wish this little bottle could talk.").

the trial was sufficient to rebut the inference of negligence arising from the application of the doctrine of res ipsa loquitur for this is purely a factual question for the determination of the jury." [5]

5. Id. at 232.

§§ 7.10–8.0 are reserved for supplementary material.

CHAPTER 8

VIOLATION OF STATUTE

Table of Sections

Sec.
8.1 In General.
8.2 Legal Effect.
8.3 Criminal Statutes.
8.4 Municipal Ordinances and Administrative Regulations.
8.5 Elements—Causation, Protected Class, and Type of Risk.
8.6 Defenses—Excuses.

Library References:
C.J.S. Negligence § 203 et seq.
West's Key No. Digests, Negligence ⚖121.1(9).
Prosser, Law of Torts (4th ed. 1971), pp. 190–204.
Blashfield, Automobile Law and Practice § 101.37 et seq.

§ 8.1 In General

Legal research should begin with possible legislative enactments that might affect the case: federal and state statutes, ordinances of cities, and regulations of every legislative or administrative board that might be relevant. Sometimes administrative and regulatory bodies may decree upon a subject, apparently not within their field, and such pronouncements may have the effect of law. With inadequate guides and indices to this type of ordinances and regulations, and possible amendatory and supplemental provisions, the researcher may find the search difficult. However, the importance of finding one of these "laws" in any way pertaining to the case and proscribing defendant's conduct may be of vital importance. When the author tries a lawsuit, the statute, ordinance, or regulation, and its violation may be the backbone of plaintiff's case. He relies upon it to explain why he is suing in making opening statement.[1] Often this proved vi-

---

1. The author prefers to read all ordinances, regulations, and statutes to the jury, even if they are judicially noticed. Many trial judges are confused on this procedure because "the lawyer (not the judge) is reading law to the jury." It would seem if the statute, or other legislative action, is applicable, the jury should know what it is first off, why plaintiff is suing (because he claims defendant violated this, reading it, law). It should be read, therefore, on opening statement, offered into evidence by reading during the trial, read again during argument, instructed upon by the judge, and a written copy given to the jury if asked during delibera-

olation may be sufficient in itself to take him safely past non-suit and directed verdict. Then, during the trial, effective use may be made of the rule that everyone is assumed to know the "law" by asking the defendant if he knew about the ordinance or regulation, and, if so, why he acted as he did.[2] At closing argument, the ordinance or regulation is argued by counsel[3] and given to the jury by the court as a

tions. I feel that it is a mistake, as some judges do, to start the trial without a definite prior ruling whether statutes invoked by counsel are pertinent, and whether they will be allowed in evidence and read to the jury. This information and ruling can and should be made available before opening statement. The jurisdictions are divided on whether the practice is impermissible, is within the court's discretion, or is a recognized right. See cases listed: 9, Cincinnati St. Ry. Co. v. Adams; 33 Ohio App. 311, 169 N.E. 480 (1929) ("In our opinion neither the Constitution, nor the statutes or decisions of the courts of this state, authorize a debate of legal questions before a jury in the opening statements. There is nothing to indicate that such is the function of an opening statement. We can see where such practice would result in confusion in the minds of the jury, who are, under the law, to take the law of the case from the court at the proper time.").

2. United States v. International Minerals & Chem. Corp., 402 U.S. 558, 91 S.Ct. 1697, 29 L.Ed.2d 178 (1971) ("The principle that ignorance of the law is no defense applies whether the law be a statute or a duly promulgated and published regulation").

See State ex rel. Rice v. Hasson Grocery Co., 177 Miss. 204, 170 So. 234, 238, 107 A.L.R. 663 (1936) ("A person is charged at his peril, with knowledge of the law."); City of Plattsmouth v. Murphy, 74 Neb. 749, 105 N.W. 293 (1905) (" 'Ignorantia juris neminem excusat' is a maxim sanctioned by centuries of experience. That it works a hardship in individual instances is a matter of common knowledge; but is of little importance, when compared with the evils which would result from measuring the rights of a litigant, not by the law as it is, but by the law as he understands it to be.").

Knowledge of statute required

Henderson v. St. Louis etc. R. Co., 248 S.W. 987 (Mo.App.1923) ("[K]nowledge of the ordinance, or the want of such knowledge, is to be considered in determining the question of contributory negligence").

3. Mahan v. Hafen, 76 Nev. 220, 351 P.2d 617 (1960).

Permitted

Wiles v. Mullinax, 270 N.C. 661, 155 S.E.2d 246 (1967) (Special statute); City of Anniston v. Oliver, 28 Ala. App. 390, 185 So. 187 (1938) ("It is permissible for counsel in argument to read to the jury the law as it is written either in the Code or in published decisions of the Appellate Court of the state pertinent to the questions involved in the case on trial, and containing correct exposition of the law applicable therein"); Jones v. Detroit Taxicab and Transfer Co., 218 Mich. 673, 188 N.W. 394 (1922) (When acting in good faith, "counsel may, both in stating his case in the first instance, and in his argument of the case to the jury, state what he believes the law applicable to the case to be").

Discretionary

Saunders v. State, 208 Tenn. 347, 345 S.W.2d 899 (1961); Dendy v. Eagle Motor Lines, Inc., 292 Ala. 99, 289

§ 8.1 TORT LIABILITY AND DEFENSES Pt. 3

guide for their deliberations. The ordinance or regulation is photographically blown up and *shown* to the jury. It is the law. Finally, if this is not enough, plaintiff [4] may have assurance that there will be at least several of the jurors who, during their own argument, will say, "Defendant violated the law. The Judge told us what it was. That's enough for me."

§ 8.2 Legal Effect

There are various views as to the effect of a violation of statute. At the extreme is the position that violation of statute imposes absolute liability for injuries resulting therefrom, so that contributory negligence and assumption of risk may not be raised in defense.[5]

So.2d 603 (1974); Baron Tube Co. v. Transport Ins. Co., 365 F.2d 858 (5th Cir. 1966).

Discouraged

Hoffman v. All Star Ins. Corp., 288 So. 2d 388 (La.App.1974), writ refused 290 So.2d 909 (La.).

Not Permitted

Tenenbaum v. Chicago, 60 Ill.2d 363, 325 N.E.2d 607 (1975); Halford v. Yandell, 558 S.W.2d 400 (Mo.App. 1977); Butler v. McDougal, 120 So.2d 832 (Fla.App.1960); Owen v. People, 118 Colo. 415, 195 P.2d 953 (1948).

4. The effect of statutory or other regulatory violation may be similarly effective when applicable to the plaintiff as comparative or contributory negligence so that procedures herein set forth can be likewise beneficial to defendants. Beauchamp v. New York City Housing Auth., 12 N.Y.2d 400, 240 N.Y.S.2d 15, 190 N.E.2d 412 (1963); Sloan v. Coit Int'l, Inc., 292 So.2d 15 (Fla.1974) (Violation establishes negligence per se, which is treated as imposing liability without causal relationship).

5. Osborne v. Salvation Army, 107 F. 2d 929, 931 (1939) (Violation of NY Labor Law requiring owners of public buildings to provide safety devices for window washers. "If the plaintiff's injuries arose from the violation, defendant's liability was absolute irrespective of any proof of negligence."); Mayes v. Byers, 214 Minn. 54, 7 N.W.2d 403, 144 A.L.R. 821 (1943) (Patron fell down defective basement stairs in an "on sale" liquor dealer's establishment, held that contributory negligence no defense to charge of violation of ordinance of city and state statute, and suit on penal bond); Little v. Nashville, Chattanooga & St. Louis Ry. Co., 39 Tenn. App. 130, 281 S.W.2d 284 (1955) (Statutory Precautions Act to prevent accidents at designated crossings is imperative). Does plaintiff's lawyer, in advocating more absolute liability in statutory violations, unthinkingly encourage the abandonment of jury trial in favor of findings by commissions? It is conceivable that as legislatures enact more and more comprehensive systems of legislation covering more and more of man's conduct —building regulations, health and safety codes, motor vehicle statutes, live stock codes, etc.—there could be comprehensive systems of regulations covering every conceivable phase of personal injury law. When and if this situation arises, the problem of trial of a particular case will be changed considerably. There will be no longer any question of proof of negligence, the only question being whether or not there is a statute or regulation that has been violated, and

Many safety[6] and employment[7] statutes are held to impose such liability, and the excuse that defendant was in reasonable ignorance of the statute,[8] or acted with reasonable care,[9] will not constitute a defense.

In *Pitzer v. M. D. Tomkies and Sons*,[10] a young boy of 13 years, while delivering groceries for his employer on a bicycle, was injured by an automobile. On reaching his majority the boy sued his employer, setting up the statutory prohibition of child employment under 16 and another statute permitting recovery of damages. On the trial the boy admitted that the accident was his fault, but there was a verdict for plaintiff. Verdict was affirmed on appeal against the contention of contributory negligence and intervening cause. The court said, "We are of the opinion that contributory negligence of a child whether the plaintiff was within the group intended to be protected, whether the injury was proximately caused by the violation, and whether contributory negligence was a factor may entirely disappear. When this situation arises, legislatures may determine that there is no longer any need for the age old methods of trial, and they may then decide that these comprehensive systems of regulation could be administered by a tribunal similar to a Workman's Compensation Board, or Industrial Accident Commission. The next step would be an established scale of damages and a mechanical determination for a particular injury as related to forbidden conduct.

6. Trout v. Pennsylvania R. Co., 300 F.2d 826 (3d Cir. 1961) (Federal Safety Appliance Act); Continental Can Co. v. Horton, 250 F.2d 637 (8th Cir. 1957) (Scaffolding); Fonseca v. Orange County, 28 Cal.App.3d 361, 104 Cal.Rptr. 566 (1972) (Scaffolding).

See Remington, Liability Without Fault Criminal Statutes, 1956 Wis.L.Rev. 625.

7. Beauchamp v. Sturges & Burns Mfg. Co., 250 Ill. 303, 95 N.E. 204 (1911), aff'd 231 U.S. 320, 34 S.Ct. 60, 58 L.Ed. 245 (Child labor laws); Louisville, H. and St. L. R. Co. v. Lyons, 155 Ky. 396, 159 S.W. 971, 48 L.R.A. (N.S.) 667 (1913), reh. denied 156 Ky. 222, 160 S.W. 942. (Employment of child in dangerous occupation contrary to statute renders employer liable, and contributory negligence and assumption of risk is no defense. "The lives and limbs of children are too valuable to be sacrificed in dangerous employments, and if an employer, in violation of the statute, engages the services of a child in such an employment, he must see to it that no harm comes to him, in so far as money can do, for the injury inflicted".); Pitzer v. M. D. Tomkies and Sons, 136 W. Va. 268, 67 S.E.2d 437 (1951). ("The assumption of risk and the fellow servant rules are not available as defenses where the gist of the tort is the violation of the child labor statute." 13 year old minor hired in violation of labor laws and struck by automobile while at work, and subsequent suit against employer).

8. York v. Pennsylvania R. Co., 73 Ohio App. 323, 56 N.E.2d 341 (1943), appeal dism'd 142 Ohio St. 636, 53 N.E.2d 646.

9. Inland & Sea-Board Coasting Co. v. Tolson, 139 U.S. 551, 11 S.Ct. 653, 35 L.Ed. 270 (1891); Northern Indiana Transit v. Burk, 228 Ind. 162, 89 N.E.2d 905 (1950).

10. 136 W.Va. 268, 67 S.E.2d 437, 442 (1951).

employed in violation of Code, 21–6, as amended and reenacted, is not available as a defense in an action based on such violation.—It is a reasonable assumption that the statute was designed and intended to protect him against the dangers he would encounter in making such deliveries, and therefore there was no break in causal relation between the injury and original negligence of defendant."

Violation of statute is more often held to establish "negligence per se," that is, conclusive evidence of negligence not defensible by a showing of due care [11] but open to the defenses of comparative or contributory negligence and assumption of risk.[12] Plaintiff bears the burden of establishing proximate cause and statutory protection of the injured party.[13] Some courts employ the term "negligence per se," yet apply it so as to impose absolute liability ("liability per se") in effect.[14]

A third view is that violation of statute creates a presumption of negligence, which may be rebutted by defendant's showing that in fact he acted with due care.[15] This position is codified in the California Evidence Code.[16] Other jurisdictions hold that violation of stat-

11. See Restatement, Second, Torts, § 488(b).

See also Basso v. Miller, 40 N.Y.2d 233, 386 N.Y.S.2d 564, 352 N.E.2d 868 (1976); Anderson v. Morgan, 73 Ariz. 344, 241 P.2d 786 (1952) (Driving while intoxicated); Brotemarkle v. Snyder, 99 Cal.App.2d 388, 221 P.2d 992 (1950) (Dog unleashed on street); Ferner v. Casalegno, 141 Cal.App.2d 467, 297 P.2d 91 (1956) (Pedestrian failure to yield right-of-way); Northern Indiana Transit v. Burk, 228 Ind. 162, 89 N.E.2d 905, 17 A.L.R.2d 572 (1950) (Auto safety standards); Rosenblatt v. United States, 112 F.Supp. 114, 12 N.A.C.C.A.L.J. 227 (D.C.N.C. 1953) (Motor vehicle lights).

12. See Prosser, The Law of Torts (4th ed. 1971) p. 201.

But also see Sloan v. Coit Int'l Inc., 292 So.2d 15 (Fla.1974).

13. Sloan v. Coit Int'l Inc., 292 So.2d 15 (Fla.1974).

14. Johnson v. Boston & M. R. Co., 83 N.H. 350, 143 A. 516, 61 A.L.R. 1178 (1928); Vassillion v. Sullivan, 94 N.H. 97, 47 A.2d 115 (1946) (Only issues for jury were whether defendant committed the act, and damages); Beauchamp v. New York City Housing Auth., 12 N.Y.2d 400, 240 N.Y.S.2d 15, 190 N.E. 2d 412, 99 A.L.R.2d 454 (1963).

15. Lister v. Campbell, 371 So.2d 133 (Fla.App.1979); Alarid v. Vanier, 50 Cal.2d 617, 327 P.2d 897 (1958).

16. West's Ann.California Evidence Code § 669 provides:

(a) The failure of a person to exercise due care is presumed if:

(1) He violated a statute, ordinance, or regulation of a public entity;

(2) The violation proximately caused death or injury to person or property;

(3) The death or injury resulted from an occurrence of the nature which the statute, ordinance, or regulation was designed to prevent; and

(4) The person suffering the death or the injury to his person or

ute establishes prima facie negligence,[17] which is nearly identical in effect to the presumption of negligence. Some courts hold that violation of statute only supports an inference of negligence.[18]

The extreme view is that it constitutes merely evidence of negligence,[19] and the common law standard of care must be established by plaintiff. Even in a negligence per se jurisdiction, the statute in question may expressly limit its applicability to "evidence of negligence".[20] If the violation of statute is completely unrelated to the cause of injury, then, of course, it is not even evidence of negligence and has no bearing on liability.[21] Some types of ordinances, agency regulations, or statutes may be judicially noticed;[22] some

property was one of the class of persons for whose protection the statute, ordinance, or regulation was adopted.

(b) This presumption may be rebutted by proof that:

(1) The person violating the statute, ordinance, or regulation did what might reasonably be expected of a person of ordinary prudence, acting under similar circumstances, who desired to comply with the law; or

(2) The person violating the statute, ordinance, or regulation was a child and exercised the degree of care ordinarily exercised by persons of his maturity, intelligence, and capacity under similar circumstances, but the presumption may not be rebutted by such proof if the violation occurred in the course of an activity normally engaged in only by adults and requiring adult qualifications.

17. Ney v. Yellow Cab Co., 2 Ill.2d 74, 117 N.E.2d 74, 51 A.L.R.2d 624 (1954). (Statute prohibiting leaving an unattended automobile without removing ignition key.); Lynghaug v. Payte, 247 Minn. 186, 76 N.W.2d 660 (1956). (Statute requiring owner to maintain muffler on automobile sufficient to prevent carbon monoxide gas from entering vehicle where passenger killed by the gas); Kolatz v. Kelly, 244 Minn. 163, 69 N.W.2d 649 (1955). (Intersectional automobile collision—rules of road.); Lemons v. Holland, 205 Or. 163, 284 P.2d 1041, 286 P.2d 656 (1955). (Exceeding posted automobile speed limits.)

18. Phillips v. Scrimente, 66 N.J.Super. 157, 168 A.2d 809 (1961).

19. Krieger v. Bausch, 377 F.2d 398 (10th Cir. 1967); Fireman's Fund Ins. Co. v. Aalco Wrecking Co., Inc., 466 F.2d 179 (8th Cir. 1972), cert. denied 410 U.S. 930, 93 S.Ct. 1371, 35 L.Ed. 2d 592; Frank's Plastering Co. v. Koenig, 341 F.2d 257 (8th Cir. 1965); New Amsterdam Cas. Co. v. Novick Transfer Co., 274 F.2d 916 (4th Cir. 1960).

20. Carr v. Murrows Transfer, Inc., 262 N.C. 550, 138 S.E.2d 228 (1964); Hysell v. Iowa Public Serv. Co., 534 F.2d 775 (8th Cir. 1976), appeal after remand 559 F.2d 468.

21. Exner v. Sherman Power Constr. Co., 54 F.2d 510 (2d Cir. 1931); Robertson v. Yazoo & M. V. R. Co., 154 Miss. 182, 122 So. 371 (1929).

22. Lilly v. Grand Trunk Western R. R. Co., 317 U.S. 481, 63 S.Ct. 347, 87 L.Ed. 411 (1943) (Rule adopted by Interstate Commerce Commission acquires force of law, and is judicially noticed); Stanislaus Lumber Co. v. Pike, 51 Cal.App.2d 54, 124 P.2d 190 (1942) (Judicial notice taken of proclamations of Governor of state);

must actually be offered into evidence and read to the jury.[23] Judicial construction of a relevant statute by the trial court is often an essential part of an adequate instruction.[24] Just as important in instructing and arguing upon a particular statute or ordinance is the knowledge of the limitations, exclusions, and qualifications in its use. The appellate courts are particularly prone to reverse for error in instructions not so qualified.[25]

Kraetsch v. Stull, 238 Iowa 944, 29 N.W.2d 341 (1947) (Courts take judicial notice of orders and directives of Federal Agencies, including Home Owners' Loan Corporation); Strout v. Burgess, 144 Me. 263, 68 A.2d 241, 12 A.L.R.2d 939 (1949) (Under Uniform Judicial Notice of Foreign Law, courts may inform themselves and invoke authority of law of any state); Powell v. Anderson, 147 Neb. 872, 25 N.W.2d 401 (1946) (State courts will take judicial notice of rules and regulations of Federal Agencies).

23. United Mercantile Agencies v. Bissonnette, 155 Fla. 22, 198 So.2d 466 (1944); Allen v. Allen, 201 Okl. 442, 209 P.2d 172, 14 A.L.R.2d 216 (1948) (Judicial notice not taken of laws and statutes of sister state, but must be pleaded and proven); Evans v. Sheriden, 28 Tenn.App. 90, 186 S.W.2d 911 (1944) (Judicial notice will not be taken of rules and regulations of Federal Agencies when relied upon to defeat an otherwise valid instrument); Brannon v. Perkey, 127 W.Va. 103, 31 S.E.2d 898, 158 A.L.R. 631 (1944) (Judicial notice not taken of ordinances); Wergin v. Voss, 179 Wis. 603, 192 N.W. 51, 26 A.L.R. 933 (1923) (Although municipal court takes notice of ordinances, the Supreme Court will not take such notice).

24. Jesse v. Wemer & Wemer Co., 248 Iowa 1002, 82 N.W.2d 82 (1957) (Statute prohibiting vehicles from stopping, standing or parking not applicable to motorist who stopped momentarily to permit an approaching vehicle to go through a narrow underpass and was struck from behind); Mc-

Beth v. Merchants Motor Freight, Inc., 248 Iowa 320, 79 N.W.2d 303 (1957) (Statute permitting stopping of disabled automobile on highway when "impossible" to avoid means "not reasonably practicable"); Jack Cole Co. v. Hoff, 274 S.W.2d 658, 51 A.L.R.2d 1 (1955) (Where defendant's truck parked on highway to assist another motorist such vehicle not excepted from prohibitions of statute as emergency vehicle); Hinson v. Dawson, 241 N.C. 714, 86 S.E.2d 585, 50 A.L.R.2d 333 (1955). (Speed limits of motor vehicles in business district—meaning of "business district"); Jones v. Santel, 164 Ohio St. 93, 128 N.E.2d 36 (1955) (Boy pushing bicycle up highway on left side a pedestrian and not required to operate vehicle on right side); Fleischman v. City of Reading, 388 Pa. 183, 130 A.2d 429 (1957) (Having motor vehicle under such control as to be able to stop within the "assured clear distance ahead" means a clear distance that can reasonably be depended on, and does contemplate unexpected contingencies).

25. Schumer v. Caplin, 241 N.Y. 346, 150 N.E. 139 (1925) ("The violation of the rule of the commission which the learned judge read to the jury, since it did not have the force of a statute, did not constitute negligence as a matter of law. A correct charge in this respect would have been that the violation of this rule did not establish negligence per se, but was simply some evidence of negligence which the jury could take into consideration with all the other evidence bearing on that subject").

§ 8.3 Criminal Statutes

One problem that has troubled the courts is whether criminal legislation should result in civil liability. Pointing up this problem is the California case of *Hudson v. Craft*,[26] in which plaintiff, a minor, was severely injured in a fight with a "promoter's beast" at a carnival. The complaint alleged that the defendant promoter was conducting prize fights in violation of section 412 of the Penal Code and Chapter 2, div. 8, of the Business and Professional Code (no license to conduct fights from the State Athletic Commission). A general demurrer to plaintiff's complaint was sustained without leave to amend, and judgment entered thereon. There was appellate reversal. The court said that a violation of a criminal statute can be the basis of civil liability when the plaintiff is a member of a class of persons the statute was enacted to protect: "[T]he controlling factor is whether or not the expressed public policy is sufficiently urgent, . . . and explicit." The court further stated, "It is not necessary in the instant case to state a general rule inasmuch as each situation must have individual consideration. The nature and scope of the legislation herein involved and above shown, requires liability, especially when we consider that it calls for continuous and single 'on-the-spot' supervision of boxing matches. That factor alone is sufficient to distinguish it from such cases as a person operating a car without an operator's license and the like." [27]

Criminal statutes designed to protect against injury or loss of life are generally held to establish a standard of care greater than that required by common law, and their violation will usually be treated as constituting negligence per se.[28] Some jurisdictions which so hold, nevertheless, treat traffic laws as merely evidence of negligence.[29] Other jurisdictions refuse to recognize any standard as

---

26. 33 Cal.2d 654, 204 P.2d 1 (1949).

27. Id. at 660.

28. Martin v. Herzog, 228 N.Y. 164, 126 N.E. 814 (1920) (Cardozo, J.: "By the very terms of the hypothesis, to omit, willfully or heedlessly, the safeguards prescribed by law for the benefit of another that he may be preserved in life or limb, is to fall short of the standard of diligence to which those who live in organized society are under a duty to conform").

See Lowndes, Civil Liability Created by Criminal Legislation, 16 Minn.L.Rev. 361 (1932); Morris, The Relation of Criminal Statutes to Tort Liability, 46 Harv.L.Rev. 453 (1933).

See also Rudes v. Gottschalk, 159 Tex. 552, 324 S.W.2d 201 (1959) (Legislature's standard considered a more accurate test of negligence than judicial test); Brownstone Park, Ltd. v. Southern Union Gas Co., 537 S.W.2d 270 (Tex.Civ.App.1976), refused n. r. e.

29. Hansen v. Kemmish, 201 Iowa 1008, 208 N.W. 277, 45 A.L.R. 498 (1926).

§ 8.3   TORT LIABILITY AND DEFENSES   Pt. 3

having been established by a penal statute unless expressly provided for.[30]

If the statute is explicit in the imposition of civil liability, there is no problem. However, in the usual case the prohibited conduct is made a crime without reference to civil liability. Various rationalizations are given to impose this liability,[31] but the best explanation is probably that the judiciary is attempting to further the legislative policy for the protection of individuals intended to be shielded by the statute.

§ 8.4 Municipal Ordinances and Administrative Regulations

A "municipal" ordinance is generally considered to have the same force and effect as a statute in relation to the civil liability of the violator.[32] A minority of jurisdictions, however, limit the application of municipal ordinances to providing evidence of negligence only, on the theory that the creation of liability through negligence per se is a power limited to state government.[33]

Administrative regulations, rules, or orders, when legislatively empowered by enabling statutes are generally held to have the force and effect of statutes in regard to liability of violators.[34] Safety reg-

---

30.   Richmond v. Warren Inst. for Sav., 307 Mass. 483, 30 N.E.2d 407, 132 A.L.R. 859 (1940).

31.   "Presumed intent" to impose civil liability is one rationalization. Loundes, Civil Liability Created by Criminal Legislation, (1932) 16 Minn.L.Rev. 361.

Another rationalization is that a reasonable man would obey the criminal law, and if he does not, he is unreasonable, and negligent. Clinkscales v. Carver, 22 Cal.2d 72, 136 P.2d 777 (1943); Mathers v. Riverside, 22 Cal.2d 781, 141 P.2d 419 (1943). (Standards fixed by criminal statute not always applicable in civil suit).

Thayer, Public Wrong and Private Actions (1914) 27 Harv.L.Rev. 317.

32.   Hayes v. Michigan Cent. R. Co., 111 U.S. 228, 4 S.Ct. 369, 28 L.Ed. 410 (1884); McCleod v. Tri-State Milling Co., 71 S.D. 362, 24 N.W.2d 485 (1946); Marusa v. District of Columbia, 484 F.2d 828 (D.C.Cir. 1973).

33.   Philadelphia & R. R. Co. v. Ervin, 89 Pa. 71, 33 Am.Rep. 726 (1879); Schumer v. Caplin, 241 N.Y. 346, 150 N.E. 139 (1925); Rockford City R. Co. v. Blake, 173 Ill. 354, 50 N.E. 1070 (1898); Major v. Waverly & Ogden, Inc., 7 N.Y.2d 332, 197 N.Y.S.2d 165, 165 N.E.2d 181 (1960).

34.   Anderson v. Blackfoot Livestock Comm'n Co., 85 Idaho 64, 375 P.2d 704 (1962); Presser v. Siesel Constr. Co., 19 Wis.2d 54, 119 N.W.2d 405 (1963); Bowman v. Redding & Co., 449 F.2d 956 (D.C.Cir. 1971); Ruddy v. U. S. Fidelity & Guar. Co., 288 F.Supp. 315 (D.C.Pa.1968); Porter v. Montgomery Ward & Co., 48 Cal.2d 846, 313 P.2d 854 (1957); Halliday v. Greene, 244 Cal.App.2d 482, 53 Cal.Rptr. 267 (1966); Toole v. United States, 443 F.Supp. 1204 (D.C.Pa. 1977).

ulations in particular are often held to establish a standard of negligence per se,[35] but where they have not been given force of law by legislative sanction, they are of lesser import,[36] and even may be held inadmissable as evidence.[37] While some Federal regulations, such as the FAA regulations,[38] are deemed to have force of law,[39] the O.S.H.A. regulations,[40] a potentially fertile ground of liability, have not yet achieved consistent application in Federal or state court actions.[41] The recommendations of an *information manual* published by a regulatory agency have been distinguished from regulations and held inapplicable to the issue of negligence, other than as evidence of custom.[42]

---

35. Daniel v. Oklahoma Gas & Elec. Co., 329 P.2d 1060 (Okl.1958); Lutz Indus., Inc. v. Dixie Home Stores, 242 N.C. 332, 88 S.E.2d 333 (1955); Bowman v. Redding & Co., 449 F.2d 956 (D.C.Cir. 1971).

36. Jorgensen v. Horten, 206 N.W.2d 100 (Iowa 1973).

37. Swaney v. Peden Steel Co., 259 N.C. 531, 131 S.E.2d 601 (1963); Burly v. Louisiana Power & Light Co., 319 So.2d 334 (La.1975), on remand 327 So.2d 585, cert. denied 331 So.2d 455, writ denied 332 So.2d 278.

38. Federal Aviation Agency, established by Pub.L. 85–726, 72 Stat. 737, 49 U.S.C.A. § 1301 et seq. (1958).

39. Hochrein v. United States, 238 F.Supp. 317 (D.C.Pa.1965); United States v. Schultetus, 277 F.2d 322, 86 A.L.R.2d 375 (5th Cir. 1960), cert. denied 364 U.S. 828, 81 S.Ct. 67, 5 L.Ed.2d 56; Gatenby v. Altoona Aviation Corp., 268 F.Supp. 599 (W.D.Pa. 1967), aff'd 407 F.2d 443 (3d Cir.).

40. Occupational Safety and Health Act of 1970 (29 U.S.C.A. §§ 651 et seq.)

See Hogan & Hogan, Occupational Safety and Health Act (1977); Hogan, "OSHA Regulations as Evidence of Negligence" 5 Alabama T.L.J. (1977); Marow, "The Use of OSHA in Products Liability Suits Against the Manufacturers of Industrial Machinery" 21 Trial Lawyers Guide 297 (No. 3, 1977).

41. Violation of OSHA Regulations Held Negligence Per Se:
See Arthur v. Flota Mercante Gran Centro Americana S.A., 487 F.2d 561 (5th Cir. 1973), reh. denied 488 F.2d 552 (Maritime); Koll v. Manatt's Transp. Co., 253 N.W.2d 265 (Iowa 1977) (". . . [W]e hold violation by an employer of an OSHA or IOSHA standard is *negligence per se* to his employee. Such a violation is *evidence of negligence* as to all persons who are likely to be exposed to injury as a result of the violation.").

Violation Held Evidence of Negligence
Buhler v. Marriott Hotels, Inc., 390 F.Supp. 999 (D.C.La.1974); Knight v. Burns, Kirkley & Williams Constr. Co., Inc., 331 So.2d 651 (Ala.1976); Dunn v. Brimer, 259 Ark. 855, 537 S.W.2d 164, 79 A.L.R.3d 958 (1976); Disabatino Bros. Inc. v. Baio, 366 A.2d 508 (Del.1976).

Violation Inadmissable as Evidence
Otto v. Specialties, Inc., 386 F.Supp. 1240 (D.C.Miss.1974).

For additional discussion of O.S.H.A. decisions, see Rothstein, Occupational Safety and Health Law (West's Handbook Series).

42. Diamond v. Grow, 243 Cal.App.2d 396, 52 Cal.Rptr. 265 (1966) (Flight Information Manual published by FAA, including "Good Operating Practices").

§ 8.5 Elements—Causation, Protected Class, and Type of Risk

Where violation of the statute is deemed to impose absolute liability or negligence per se, some courts hold that plaintiff must show only a reasonable causal connection between the violation and the injury, rather than meet the full common law requirements of proximate cause.[43] Intervening acts, in particular, are often inapplicable as a defense where defendant's original act was in violation of a statute.[44] Ordinarily, plaintiff has the burden of establishing that defendant's violation was the proximate cause of the injury,[45] and the determination of proximate cause is a jury function.[46]

Where plaintiff's claim is based on defendant's violation, plaintiff must show that he is in the class of persons intended to be protected by the statute.[47] Where a statute is designed to protect the interests of the state, or the public, an injured plaintiff cannot necessarily base his action upon defendant's violation.[48] A wartime statute fixing speed at 35 miles per hour, for instance, was held to be intended to conserve fuel and, thus, afford no basis for liability of a violater to an injured party.[49] That defendant drove without a driv-

---

43. Daggett v. Keshner, 284 App.Div. 733, 134 N.Y.S.2d 524 (1954), aff'd 7 N.Y.2d 891, 199 N.Y.S.2d 41, 166 N. E.2d 324.
Ross v. Hartman, 139 F.2d 14, 158 A.L. R. 1370 (D.C.Cir. 1943), cert. denied 321 U.S. 790, 64 S.Ct. 790, 88 L.Ed. 1080.

44. Ayers v. Atlantic Greyhound Corp., 208 S.C. 267, 37 S.E.2d 737 (1946); Butts v. Ward, 227 Wis. 387, 279 N.W. 6, 116 A.L.R. 1441 (1938).

45. Earl W. Baker & Co. v. Lagaly, 144 F.2d 344, 154 A.L.R. 1098 (10th Cir. 1944); Gatenby v. Altoona Aviation Corp., 268 F.Supp. 599 (W.D.Pa.1967), aff'd 407 F.2d 443 (3d Cir.); Johnson v. St. Paul Mercury Ins. Co., 219 So. 2d 524, 36 A.L.R.3d 1349 (La.1969); Shafer v. Mountain States Tel. & Tel. Co., 335 F.2d 932 (9th Cir. 1964).

46. Kendrick v. Atchison, T. & S. F. R. Co., 182 Kan. 249, 320 P.2d 1061 (1958); Rucker v. Wabash R. Co., 418 F.2d 146 (7th Cir.); Almond v. Pollon, 198 F.Supp. 301 (D.C.Pa.1961), aff'd 300 F.2d 763 (3d Cir.).

47. Union Pac. R. Co. v. McDonald, 152 U.S. 262, 14 S.Ct. 619, 38 L.Ed. 434 (1894); Beauchamp v. New York City Leasing Auth., 12 N.Y.2d 400, 240 N.Y.S.2d 15, 190 N.E.2d 412 (1963); Lynghaug v. Payte, 247 Minn. 186, 76 N.W.2d 660, 56 A.L.R.2d 1090 (1956).

48. Restatement, Second, Torts § 288(a), (b).
Boruski v. Stewart, 381 F.Supp. 529 (D. C.N.Y.1974) (Criminal statutes pertaining to judicial system for protection of government interests, and violation is not evidence of duty of care to individual).
Ordinances requiring abutting property owners to remove ice and snow from sidewalks cannot be used as basis for civil liability since such enactments create only a public duty. W. T. Grant Co. v. Casady, 117 Colo. 405, 188 P.2d 881 (1948); Calhoun v. Corning, 328 Ill.App. 493, 66 N.E.2d 303 (1946); Grooms v. Union Guardian Trust Co., 309 Mich. 437, 15 N.W. 2d 698 (1944).

49. Cooper v. Hoeglund, 221 Minn. 446, 22 N.W.2d 450 (1946).

er's license is similarly irrelevant, because the statute does not set a standard of care.[50] Courts by and large will be liberal in their construction of the protected class and often will consider a statute's intent to be the protection of anyone likely to be injured by its violation.[51] Even if plaintiff is not in the protected class, the violation may be admissable as evidence of the failure to exercise due care.[52]

To impose liability, the injury must be of the type the statute was designed to prevent.[53] Thus, in a California case, where a plaintiff in a hotel roof sat on a mattress resting in a parapet and fell through to the bottom of an open shaft, liability was claimed on the basis that the parapet surrounding the shaft was only 27 inches high instead of the statutory 30. The trial judge's instruction on negligence per se based on the statutory violation was held in error, since

---

50. Hertz Driv-Ur-Self System v. Hendrickson, 109 Colo. 1, 121 P.2d 483 (1942).

51. Aldridge v. Hasty, 240 N.C. 353, 82 S.E.2d 331 (1954) (Traffic laws intended to protect persons in and about highways).

Ill.—Ney v. Yellow Cab Co., 2 Ill.2d 74, 117 N.E.2d 74, 51 A.L.R.2d 624 (1954) (Statute prohibiting leaving vehicle unattended without removing ignition key for benefit of persons injured when vehicle stolen and involved in collision).

See also Dini v. Naiditch, 20 Ill.2d 406, 170 N.E.2d 881 (1960).

Minn.—Mottinger v. Halfman, 247 Minn. 115, 76 N.W.2d 689 (1956) (Statute requiring drivers on servient road to yield right-of-way for benefit of both vehicles and pedestrian injured by collision between vehicles); Lynghaug v. Payte, 247 Minn. 186, 76 N.W.2d 660 (1956) (Statute requiring maintenance of muffler on automobile so as to prevent carbon monoxide gas from entering vehicle was for benefit of gratuitous guest killed by gas).

Nev.—Scott v. Smith, 73 Nev. 158, 311 P.2d 731 (1957) (Ordinance regulating speed in town for benefit of guest passenger in automobile).

N.H.—Sullivan v. Le Blanc, 100 N.H. 311, 125 A.2d 652 (1956) (Statute requiring motorists to give signals of intention to turn, stop or slow down for benefit of any person who might be endangered including automobile passenger).

N.C.—Duvall v. United States, 312 F. Supp. 625 (D.C.N.C.1970) (Violation of statute enacted for safety and protection of public is negligence per se).

52. Daggett v. Keshner, 284 App.Div. 733, 134 N.Y.S.2d 524 (1954), aff'd 7 N.Y.2d 891, 199 N.Y.S.2d 41, 166 N.E.2d 324.

53. The leading English case is Gorris v. Scott, [1874] L.R. 9 Ex. 125 in which defendant violated a sanitation measure which required sea carriers to provide separate pens for animals. This violation resulted in sheep being washed overboard. Recovery was denied because the damage wasn't of the nature contemplated by the statute; Muhammad v. United States, 366 F.2d 298 (9th Cir. 1966), cert. denied 386 U.S. 959, 87 S.Ct. 1029, 18 L.Ed.2d 108; Freeman v. United States, 509 F.2d 626 (6th Cir. 1975).

§ 8.5   TORT LIABILITY AND DEFENSES   Pt. 3

the intent of the statute was to protect against someone walking into the shaft, and compliance would not have protected against the injury which actually occurred.[54] In another California case, plaintiff, a party guest at an apartment house complex, dived into the shallow end of the swimming pool and sustained injuries resulting in quadriplegia. In her complaint, she relied upon defendants' failure to equip the pool with ropes and buoys as required by safety regulations in the California Code. The trial court's refusal to instruct on a presumption of negligence by violation of statute on the reasoning that the regulation was designed to prevent drowning accidents and not to protect against diving accidents was upheld on appeal of verdict for defendants.[55]

Although courts occasionally impose a narrow construction on the "type of risk" requirement,[56] the more general practice is to include all risks reasonably to be foreseen from violation of the statute.[57] Occasionally, a court will go further and include all risks incurred following the violation.[58]

§ 8.6   Defenses—Excuses

That the statute or ordinance was technically invalid is immaterial, for the statute's standard may still be applied.[59] That the statute itself imposes a civil penalty is no bar to defendant's liability to

---

54. Nunneley v. Edgar Hotel, 36 Cal.2d 493, 225 P.2d 497 (1950).

55. Atkins v. Bisigier, 16 Cal.App.3d 414, 94 Cal.Rptr. 49 (1971).

56. Beauchamp v. New York City Housing Auth., 12 N.Y.2d 400, 240 N.Y.S.2d 15, 190 N.E.2d 412 (1963) (Statute requiring demolition of dilapidated housing held intended to prevent injury from collapse only and inapplicable to child's fall from open window); Kalkopf v. Donald Sales & Mfg. Co., 33 Wis.2d 247, 147 N.W.2d 277 (1967) (Statute prohibiting placing dangerous substances on highways held applicable only to injuries to vehicles and irrelevant to injuries of child pedestrian who fell into spilled sulfuric acid).

57. Bowman v. Redding & Co., 449 F.2d 956 (D.C.Cir. 1971).

See Note, 19 Minn.L.Rev. 666, 674 (1935).

58. Ney v. Yellow Cab Co., 2 Ill.2d 74, 117 N.E.2d 74 (1954) (Cab company held liable where cab left running with keys in ignition in violation of statute was stolen and crashed into plaintiff's car).

See also Ross v. Hartman, 139 F.2d 14, (D.C.Cir. 1943), cert. denied 321 U.S. 790, 64 S.Ct. 70, 88 L.Ed. 1080.

59. Clinkscales v. Carver, 22 Cal.2d 72, 136 P.2d 777 (1943). (Ordinance authorizing particular stop sign not enacted.); Phoenix Refining Co. v. Powell, 251 S.W.2d 892 (Tex.Civ.App. 1952), refused n. r. e.; Kern v. Autman, 54 Del. 402, 177 A.2d 525 (1961); Curtis v. District of Columbia, 363 F.2d 973 (D.C.Cir. 1966).

an injured plaintiff.[60] Ignorance of the law, as noted earlier, is no excuse.[61]

A minor who causes injury while in violation of a statute is not necessarily held to the same standard as an adult violator.[62] In *Alabama Power Co. v. Bowers*,[63] plaintiff's 12 year old son, while riding his bicycle, failed to give the signal required by statute as he crossed the highway. He was struck and killed by an automobile driven by defendant's servant. The court refused to instruct the jury that the boy's violation of the statute was contributory negligence per se, barring recovery. The judgment was affirmed on appeal, the court stating that a minor from seven to fourteen who violates a statute is not contributorily negligent unless he possesses "the discretion, intelligence and sensitiveness to danger which the ordinary child possesses when he is fourteen years of age."

But where the minor may be appropriately held to an adult standard, his minority is no defense to negligence per se for the violation.[64] And even where a minor is by law incapable of negligence, the violation may be admissable in evidence on the issue of due care exercised by defendant.[65]

Authority or approval of defendant's conduct from a state supervisory department will not excuse liability where the conduct is in violation of statute.[66] Due care, of course, is no defense or excuse where violation is held to establish negligence per se.[67] But, where

60. Restatement, Second, Torts § 287.

Zajkowski v. American Steel & Wire Co., 258 F. 9 (6th Cir. 1918).

But see Lavalle v. Kaupp, 240 Minn. 360, 61 N.W.2d 228, 40 A.L.R.2d 539 (1953).

61. See note 2 supra.

62. Morris v. Stone, 33 Ohio App.2d 101, 292 N.E.2d 891 (1972); Simmons v. Holm, 299 Or. 373, 367 P.2d 368 (1961); Daun v. Traux, 56 Cal.2d 647, 16 Cal.Rptr. 351, 365 P.2d 407 (1961).

63. 252 Ala. 49, 39 So.2d 402 (1949); See Pitzer v. M. D. Tomkies and Sons, 136 W.Va. 268, 67 S.E.2d 437 (1951). (Contributory negligence of child employed in violation of child labor laws not a defense.)

Also see Smith v. Arnold, 60 So.2d 281, 11 NACCA L.J. 185 (Fla.1952) (Child killed while employed in violation of child labor laws, wrongful death action may be maintained notwithstanding Workmen's Compensation Act.)

64. Hopkins v. Droppers, 184 Wis. 400, 198 N.W. 738, 36 A.L.R. 1156 (1924); Dellwo v. Pearson, 259 Minn. 452, 107 N.W.2d 859 (1961).

65. Russell v. Corley, 212 Ga. 121, 91 S.E.2d 24 (1956), conformed to 93 Ga.App. 267, 91 S.E.2d 320.

66. Pitcher v. Lennon, 12 App.Div. 356, 42 N.Y.S. 156 (1896) (Approval of construction plans by building department).

67. *Ind.*—Northern Indiana Transit v. Burk, 288 Ind. 162, 89 N.E.2d 905, 17 A.L.R.2d 572 (1950).

Cal.—Gallichotte v. California Mut. Bldg. & Loan Ass'n, 4 Cal.App.2d 503, 41 P.2d 349 (1935).

Ohio—Bush v. Harvey Transfer Co., 146 Ohio St. 657, 67 N.E.2d 851 (1946).

less than absolute liability is imposed, the excuses of emergency,[68] lack of control,[69] impossibility,[70] or circumstances making compliance more dangerous than violation [71] may be advanced to excuse the violation and defeat negligence per se on the presumption of negligence. "Customary noncompliance" is no excuse.[72]

Compliance with statutory requirements is no defense to a general charge of negligence [73] as the statute may be construed as creating merely a minimum standard and the common law duty of care held to requiring more. Thus, in an Arizona case where a truck was hauling a 70-foot pole through city highways, the fact that a red flag was tied to the end of the poles did not establish defendant's due care when the pole, flag included, broke through an automobile's windshield and struck plaintiff in the face.[74]

Where *plaintiff* is in violation of statute, the ancient rule that he is an outlaw without right to redress in the courts [75] is generally

68. Grantham v. Bulik, 137 Conn. 640, 80 A.2d 515 (1951); Burlie v. Stephens, 113 Wash. 182, 193 P. 684 (1920) (Child dashed into street).

See generally Prosser, The Law of Torts (4th ed. 1971) p. 199.

69. Martin v. Nelson, 82 Cal.App.2d 733, 187 P.2d 78 (1947); Giancarlo v. Karabanowski, 124 Conn. 223, 198 A. 752 (1938) (Auto out of control due to prior collision); Adarid v. Vanier, 50 Cal.2d 617, 327 P.2d 897 (1958) (Brakes failed); Stogdon v. Charleston Transit Co., 127 W.Va. 286, 32 S.E.2d 276 (1944).

70. Gigliotti v. New York, C. & St. L. R. Co., 107 Ohio App. 174, 157 N.E.2d 447 (1958); McConnell v. Herron, 240 Or. 486, 402 P.2d 726 (1965).

Contra: Andrew v. White Bus Line Corp., 115 Conn. 464, 161 A. 792 (1932).

71. Tedla v. Ellman, 280 N.Y. 124, 19 N.E.2d 987 (1939) (Walking on wrong side of street where heavy traffic on other side); Cameron v. Stewart, 153 Me. 47, 134 A.2d 474 (1957) (Walking on wrong side of street where sidewalk defective).

72. Stogdon v. Charleston Transit Co., 127 W.Va. 286, 32 S.E.2d 276 (1944); McDonald v. Foster Memorial Hosp., 170 Cal.App.2d 85, 338 P.2d 607 (1959).

73. Pangborn v. Central R. Co., 18 N.J. 84, 112 A.2d 705 (1955).

See Prosser, The Law of Torts (4th ed. 1971) p. 203 ("Thus the requirement of a hand signal on a left turn does not mean that the legislature has conferred immunity upon a driver who is otherwise negligent in making the turn, and that he is absolved from all obligation to slow down, keep a proper lookout, and proceed with reasonable care").

74. Peterson v. Salt River Project Agric. Improvement & Power Dist., 96 Ariz. 1, 391 P.2d 567 (1964).

75. See Davis, The Plaintiff's Illegal Act as a Defense in Actions of Tort, 18 Harv.L.Rev. 505 (1905); Thayer, Public Wrong & Private Action, 27 Harv.L.Rev. 317 (1914); Altshuler, Use and Operation of Automobiles in Violation of Statute, 10 Boston U.L. Rev. 211 (1930); Note, 46 Harv.L.Rev. 319 (1933).

See also Prosser, The Law of Torts (4th ed. 1971) p. 202; Bosworth v. Inhabitants of Swansey, 53 Mass. (10 Metc.) 363 (1845).

abandoned,[76] and his violation will be treated just as violation by defendant—as negligence per se, or evidence of negligence, etc.[77]

76. Comeau v. Harrington, 333 Mass. 768, 130 N.E.2d 554 (1955).

See also Prosser, The Law of Torts (4th ed. 1971) pp. 202–203.

77. Restatement, Second, Torts §§ 469 (1), (2), 475(a), (b).

See Shelby v. Southern Pac. Co., 68 Cal.App.2d 594, 157 P.2d 442 (1945).

§§ 8.7–9.0 are reserved for supplementary material.

CHAPTER 9

THE RESCUE DOCTRINE

Table of Sections

Sec.
9.1 Basis of Liability.
9.2 Attempts to Save Persons from Harm.
9.3 The Rescue as an Intervening Force.
9.4 The Rescue Doctrine as a Defense to Contributory Negligence.
9.5 Right of Rescuer to Recover Hinges Upon Dependent Wrong.
9.6 Attempts to Save Property from Harm.

Library References:
C.J.S. Negligence §§ 63(143), 124.
West's Key No. Digests, Negligence ⚙️74.
Blashfield, Automobile Law & Practice.

§ 9.1 Basis of Liability

"It is interesting to observe—how the icy barriers of 'lack of foreseeability,' 'supervening acts of third persons,' and 'remote causation' melt before the warm sunshine of judicial admiration of the self-sacrificing heroism of a plaintiff whose rescue of another has been 'invited' by defendant's negligent creation of danger." [1]

---

1. Annual Survey American Law, (1949).

Compare these two paradoxical cases, Regina v. Dudley and Stephens (1884) L.R. 14 Q.B.Div. 273, 15 Cox C.C. 624, and United States v. Holmes, Fed.Cas.No.15,383 [1 Wall.Jr. 1] (1842). In the former, three men and a boy had been cast adrift, after shipwreck, in a lifeboat. To prevent starvation, two of the men killed and ate the boy. Indicted for murder on the high seas, a special verdict reported that the two otherwise saved would have probably not survived, and that the deceased boy would likely have died before rescue because of his weakened condition. Sentences of death by the court were remitted to six months, without hard labor. The Judge in passing sentence said, "We are often compelled to set up standards we cannot reach ourselves, and lay down rules we could not ourselves satisfy. But a man has no right to declare temptation to be an excuse, though he might himself have yielded to it, nor allow compassion for the criminal to change or weaken in any manner the legal definition of crime."

In the *Holmes* case, a mate with a lifeboat full of passengers, also after shipwreck, threw overboard some of them to keep the longboat from swamping. The Federal court in sentencing to 6 months and fining $20, said, "Promulgate as law that the prisoner is guiltless, and our marine will be disgraced in the eyes of all civilized nations." (President Taylor remitted the fine of $20, but would not grant a pardon.)

§ 9.1 THE RESCUE DOCTRINE

Such is the rescue doctrine (and quite often another strong crutch for the "crippled case"). Phlegmatic indeed must be plaintiff's personal injury lawyer, who could not rise from counsel table with saddened (and literally golden) words, yet purposeful mien, to vie for the crown of victory in a verdict for his heroic client (disdaining the prosaic and "ordinarily prudent man"), who had accomplished such feats of bravery as to evoke such majestic language as "Contributory negligence, Sir, of my valiant client? I challenge you, Sir. You insult us. We were *grossly* negligent!"

The Rescue Doctrine is separated into cases of attempts to save persons, and attempts to save property. The doctrine's utility to plaintiff is two-fold: first, to establish defendant's liability to plaintiff rescuer; and second, to overcome the defenses of contributory negligence and assumption of risk.

Though traditionally a negligence doctrine, the Rescue Doctrine has been extended to tortious conduct other than negligence. In a New York case in 1969, a sewer worker had succumbed to gas fumes due to a defect in his gas mask. Defendant manufacturer's liability to the victim, based on breach of warranty, was held sufficient to support recovery by those injured in a rescue attempt.[2]

Where plaintiff is professionally engaged in rescue activity, the issue is treated as assumption of the risk and in general, the rescue doctrine will not apply to injuries sustained as a result of the foreseeable hazards of the trade.[3] Thus, the general rule is that a property owner is not liable to an injured fireman for negligence in creating the fire.[4] But where the injury resulted from a tortiously created

---

2. Guarino v. Mine Safety Appliance Co., 25 N.Y.2d 460, 306 N.Y.S.2d 942, 255 N.E.2d 173 (1969).

3. Maltman v. Sauer, 84 Wash.2d 975, 530 P.2d 254 (1975) (Volunteer Army helicopter rescue team crashed enroute to scene of car accident. Deaths held incident to normal risks of professional rescue activity, and rescue doctrine therefore unavailable to establish liability: "Those dangers which are inherent in professional rescue activity, and therefore foreseeable, are willingly submitted to by the professional rescuer when he accepts the position and the remuneration inextricably connected therewith.").

4. Krauth v. Geller, 31 N.J. 270, 157 A.2d 129 (1960) (Fireman has assumed risk of hazards of his profession, and has received compensation for that acceptance).

See 19 Van.L.Rev. 407 (1966).

Giorgi v. Pacific Gas & Elec. Co., 266 Cal.App.2d 355, 72 Cal.Rptr. 119 (1968) (Fire fighters, whose occupation by its very nature exposes them to particular risks, "cannot complain of negligence in the creation of the very occasion for [their] engagement"); Nastasio v. Cinnamon, 295 S.W.2d 117 (Mo.1956) (Decedent, regular fireman then off duty, responded as a volunteer to a fire alarm, and was injured by the collapse of a porch which had deteriorated and of which the defendant owner negligently failed to warn him; rescue doctrine does not apply since plaintiff

"undue risk", which constitutes an "unusual, serious *hidden* danger of a totally unexpected kind," the fireman is not always held to have assumed the risk, and the property owner's liability may be established.[5] In a Louisiana case, where a medical doctor regularly engaged in rendering emergency service under hazardous diving conditions, and reflected his acceptance of the hazards in his fees, the actor whose negligence created the emergency was not liable for death resulting from the strain of the rescue activity.[6] However, in a California case, a doctor who agreed to provide medical care at a construction site was held not to have assumed the risk of falling on the slopes of a caved-in trench while attempting to reach and treat injured workers.[7]

Whether the rescuer is an invitee, a licensee, or even a trespasser, should be irrelevant.[8] A real and imminent danger, not a mere

was only licensee; cogent dissent argues firemen shouldn't be treated as licensees, but that even licensees are owed the duty to be warned of an unusual hazard).

See Comment, Negligence Actions by Police Officers and Firefighters: A Need for a Professional Rescuers Rule, 66 Cal.L.Rev. 585 (1978).

5. Spenser v. B. P. John Furniture Corp., 255 Or. 359, 467 P.2d 429 (1970) (Whether accumulated dust constituted "unusual, serious hidden danger" for fireman a question for jury); Jackson v. Velveray Corp., 82 N.J.Super. 469, 198 A.2d 115 (1964) (Whether storage of chemicals and removal of part of sprinkler system constituted creation of undue risk for fireman a question for jury); Langlois v. Allied Chem. Corp., 258 La. 1067, 249 So.2d 133 (1971) (Fireman injured by inhalation of gas did not voluntarily and knowingly assume risk of being injured by poisonous gas while driving fire truck to premises of fire).

6. Carter v. Taylor Diving & Salvage Co., 341 F.Supp. 628 (E.D.La.1972), aff'd 470 F.2d 995 (5th Cir.) ("In this case, there was no duty to Dr. Carter, as a professional surgeon, engaged at a special rate, to avoid creating a risk of hard work under great emotion. Nor can it be said that the negligence was, as to him, a proximate cause of his injury in any usual sense. Indeed, as has been indicated, he was well paid to undertake the exact sort of risk that caused his injury.").

7. Solgaard v. Guy F. Atkinson Co., 6 Cal.3d 361, 99 Cal.Rptr. 29, 491 P.2d 821 (1971) ("It is not, however, a doctor's business to cope with steep, slippery embankments. Plaintiff agreed only to furnish medical aid to injured employees; he did not further agree to expose himself to risks and hazards not necessarily inherent in the performance of his services."); Landby v. New York N. H. & H. R. Co., 199 Misc. 73, 105 N.Y.S.2d 836 (1950), aff'd 278 App.Div. 965, 105 N.Y.S.2d 839, appeal denied 278 App.Div. 1026, 106 N.Y.S.2d 1008 (Where decedent entered on property of railroad to remove a bare wire hanging from high tension line, and was electrocuted, held that his negligence prevented recovery, there not being any emergency of any kind, and rescue doctrine did not apply); Wolff v. Light, 169 N.W.2d 93 (N.D.1969) (Policeman injured removing broken glass from window; rescue doctrine unavailable where no one in imminent peril).

8. George A. Fuller Constr. Co. v. Elliott, 92 Ga.App. 309, 88 S.E.2d 413

suspicion or possibility of harm, is required to invoke the doctrine.[9] In some instances where peril to a person is involved without negligence, the duty of one who undertakes a rescue to exercise reasonable care in doing so may be imposed.[10]

(1955) (Death of volunteer, technically a trespasser, who attempted to flag train to prevent collision with boxcars—action maintainable); Neal v. Home Builders, Inc., 232 Ind. 160, 111 N.E.2d 280 (1953), reh. denied 111 N. E.2d 713 (Recovery denied where child climbing ladder in partially completed house and mother who went to rescue both considered trespassers); Swift & Co. v. Baldwin, 299 S.W.2d 157 (Tex.Civ.App.1957) (Plaintiff, an employee of the store in front of which defendant's sign had been negligently erected, was on a ladder attempting to prevent it from falling onto children below during the course of violent wind when the sign suddenly came loose knocking plaintiff to the sidewalk—rescue doctrine was properly submitted to the jury—whether plaintiff was an invitee or licensee irrelevant).

9. Eversole v. Wabash R. Co., 249 Mo. 523, 155 S.W. 419 (1913) (Volunteer tried to assist engineer to recouple cars. Court found that life was not endangered. "It requires more than mere suspicion that accident might follow to justify the invocation of the doctrine of 'imminent peril.' "); Walsh v. West Coast Coal Mines, 31 Wash.2d 396, 197 P.2d 233 (1948) (Mine inspector assisted in timbering a mine following a cave-in, but no one in immediate danger, when a second slide occurred, killing him. Held that doctrine did not apply since he acted deliberately and no one was "in imminent and serious peril").

But note: Provenzo v. Sam, 23 N.Y.2d 256, 296 N.Y.S.2d 322, 244 N.E.2d 26 (1968) (Plaintiff injured while going to aid of accident victim whom plaintiff assumed had suffered heart attack. "It is also to be noted that the wisdom of hindsight is not determinative on the issue of the doctrine's applicability. So long as the rescue attempted can be said to have been a reasonable course of conduct at the time, it is of no import that the danger was not as real as it appeared.").

10. See Montega Corp. v. Grooms, 128 Ga.App. 333, 196 S.E.2d 459 (1973) (Doctrine inapplicable where defendant not negligent); Robinson v. Northeastern S. S. Corp., 228 F.2d 679 (2d Cir. 1955), cert. denied 351 U.S. 937, 76 S.Ct. 834, 100 L.Ed. 1465, reh. denied 352 U.S. 860, 77 S.Ct. 24, 1 L. Ed.2d 70. (Jones Act—act of seaman negligently undertaking to assist intoxicated fellow-seaman held not within scope of employment); Buckeye S. S. Co. v. McDonough, 200 F.2d 558 (6th Cir. 1952) (Jones Act—shipowner liable for negligence of fellow-seaman in assisting intoxicated shipmate back to ship); Abresch v. Northwestern Bell Tel. Co., 246 Minn. 408, 75 N.W.2d 206 (1956) (Failure of telephone company to deliver message to fire department); Depue v. Flateau, 100 Minn. 299, 111 N.W. 1, 8 L.R.A.(N.S.) 485 (1907) (Cattle buyer-invitee became ill on premises of defendant but refused shelter resulting in injury from freezing); Clark v. State, 195 Misc. 581, 89 N.Y.S.2d 132 (1949), rearg. denied 276 App.Div. 940, 94 N.Y.S.2d 202, aff'd 302 N.Y. 795, 99 N.E.2d 300 (Plaintiff injured on bobsled run where delays in securing hospitalization, held emergency care sufficient).

§ 9.2 Attempts to Save Persons from Harm

Where one person is exposed to peril of life or limb by the torticus conduct of another, the latter will be liable in damages for injuries received by a third person in a reasonable effort to perform a rescue.[11] Recognition of the social forces, and respect for human life, has led the courts to allow the plaintiff to recover. *Lynch v. Fisher*[12] is one of the broadest extensions of the doctrine, and a suggested delight for a bar examination question: Defendant's car, negligently parked on the highway was hit by another automobile carrying one Gunter and wife, who were exercising due care. Plaintiff, who dragged the Gunters to safety from their burning car, was shot by Mr. Gunter with a gun the plaintiff had removed from the vehicle and handed to Gunter. The court decided that Gunter had no intent to shoot the plaintiff, and attributed his action to something like tem-

---

11. Prosser, The Law of Torts (4th Ed., 1971) p. 277; Guarino v. Mine Safety Appliance Co., 25 N.Y.2d 460, 306 N.Y.S.2d 942, 255 N.E.2d 173 (1969); Betz v. Glazer, 325 S.W.2d 611 (Mo.App.1969) "([T]he basic theory of the rescue doctrine is that the negligence or wrong that imperiled life is not only a wrong to the imperiled victim, but also a wrong to his rescue"); Seaboard Air Line Ry. Co. v. Johnson, 217 Ala. 251, 115 So. 168 (1928), cert. dism'd 278 U.S. 576, 49 S.Ct. 95, 73 L.Ed. 515 (Under FELA, brakeman injured when he attempted to stop a "kicked" car, and save men in caboose some distance down the track. "Neither contributory negligence nor assumption of risk is charged to him who comes to the rescue of others in peril without their fault, unless the act of the rescuer is manifestly rash and reckless to a man of ordinary prudence acting in emergency. One cannot be said to act rashly or recklessly in such case, if the element of danger to himself is less imminent than that of his fellow servants he is charged with the duty of protecting."); Brugh v. Bigelow, 310 Mich. 74, 16 N.W.2d 668, 158 A.L.R. 184 (1944) (Rescuer went to relief of automobile driver in response to his call for help, and in attempting to extricate occupants of disabled car, was injured. "Defendant's claim that he owed himself and his rescuer no duty is without merit. His cries for help belied his claimed freedom from duty."); Neal v. Home Builders, 232 Ind. 160, 111 N.E.2d 280 (1953), reh. denied 111 N.E.2d 713 (Mother attempted to rescue child from a building being constructed, fell and died from injuries. Court held that defendant owed duty to protect child from known dangers, and therefore was negligent as to the rescuer. "The mother responded to wholesome human instincts."); Blanchard v. Reliable Transfer Co., 71 Ga.App. 843, 32 S.E.2d 420 (1944) (Defendant negligently caused a collision between an ambulance and a gasoline truck at an intersection. Owner of ambulance, while in bed nearby heard the noise, and came to the scene, and engaged in caring for the dead and seriously injured, thereby becoming ill himself from exposure and shock. Held that persons were in need of rescue and defendant was "charged with the knowledge that if it injured a person by its negligence, someone might reasonably be expected to attempt a rescue, and it does not matter by what circumstances the rescuer appears on the scene.").

12. 41 So.2d 692 (La.App.1949).

porary insanity. The plaintiff succeeded in the court below against the initial defendant and his verdict was affirmed on appeal. The court also decided that the plaintiff, as a rescuer, could not be considered to have been guilty of contributory negligence.

§ 9.3 The Rescue as an Intervening Force

"An intervening force is one which actively operates in producing harm to another after the actor's negligent act or omission has been committed." [13]

The attempted rescue thus is an intervening force, but generally it has been held not to supersede the defendant's liability because it is either considered to be foreseeable or a normal and expected consequence of the defendant's acts.[14] But when the act of rescue is so

---

13. Restatement, Second, Torts §§ 441, 443, 444. Scott v. Shepherd, 2 W.Bl. 892, 96 Eng.Rep. 525 (1772), 1 Smith, Leading Cases 797.

14. See Henneman v. McCalla, 260 Iowa 60, 148 N.W.2d 447 (1967); Rovinski v. Rowe, 131 F.2d 687 (6th Cir. 1942) (Plaintiff injured while trying to remove disabled truck from highway caused by defendant motorist's negligence); New York Central Ry. Co. v. Brown, 63 F.2d 657 (6th Cir. 1933), cert. denied 290 U.S. 634, 54 S.Ct. 52, 78 L.Ed. 551 (Railroad yardman while attempting to stop runaway car, touched charged third rail, and fell to his injury. "[I]t has long been settled that the chain of causation is not broken by an intervening act which is a normal reaction to the stimulus of the situation created by negligence, and such normal reaction has been held to include the instinct toward self-preservation, Scott v. Shepherd, 2 W.Bl. 892, 96 Eng. Rep. 525 (1772), 1 Smith, Leading Cases 797 (the lighted squib case) and the equally natural impulse to rush to others' assistance in emergency—".); Chicago Great Western Ry. Co. v. Scovel, 232 F.2d 952 (8th Cir. 1956), cert. denied 352 U.S. 835, 77 S.Ct. 53, 1 L.Ed. 2d 54 (F.E.L.A.—plaintiff and another, both employees of defendant railroad, rode on pushcar in course of employment. The other employee fell from the pushcar and plaintiff was injured in an attempt to rescue him. Held for plaintiff: "'The law has so great a regard for human life that it will not impute negligence to an effort to preserve it, unless made under such circumstances as to constitute rashness in the judgment of prudent persons.'"); George A. Fuller Constr. Co. v. Elliott, 92 Ga.App. 309, 88 S.E.2d 413 (1955) (Attempt to flag main track train and prevent collision with boxcars—only rash wanton conduct would constitute contributory negligence); Superior Oil Co. v. Richmond, 172 Miss. 407, 159 So. 850 (1935) (Oil company defendant negligently permitted oil tank to overflow resulting in explosion and fire. The deceased tried to extinguish fire and was killed. The court held that the negligence of its servants was not superseded. "The conduct of the intervener does not supersede the original negligence, although it is beyond that which is usual and customary in such situations and involved 'an unreasonable risk of harm to' himself or to others. In order to supersede the original negligence, the intervener's conduct must be so extraordinary and dangerous to himself or to others that the person guilty of the original negligence could not 'have realized that a third person might so act.'").

§ 9.3 TORT LIABILITY AND DEFENSES Pt. 3

foolhardy or unusual as no longer to be regarded a part of the risk, it will then be considered a superseding cause, relieving the defendant of liability because of a "lack of legal or proximate cause." [15] However, if the act is merely unreasonable, it may not amount to a superseding cause. Such unreasonable responses to defendant's negligence are considered to be foreseeable and normal.[16] These unforeseeable, unreasonable acts of rescue may amount to contributory neg-

15. Atchison, Topeka & Santa Fe Ry. Co. v. Calhoun, 213 U.S. 1, 29 S.Ct. 321, 53 L.Ed. 671 (1909). (Injury sustained by child in hopeless effort to catch departing train.); Bacon v. Payne, 220 Mich. 672, 190 N.W. 716 (1922), cert. denied 261 U.S. 623, 43 S.Ct. 519, 67 L.Ed. 832. (Action under FELA, employee of railroad ran to close a switch, and was struck. Held, that his recklessness was the proximate cause of his injuries, and an intervening force reasonably to have been foreseen by him.); See Sulpher Springs Val. Elect. Coop. Inc. v. Verdugo, 14 Ariz.App. 141, 481 P.2d 511 (1971). (Doctrine inapplicable where plaintiff reckless or contributed to dangerous condition.)

16. Wagner v. International Ry. Co., 232 N.Y. 176, 133 N.E. 437 (1921). ("Danger invites rescue. The cry of distress is the summons to relief. The law does not ignore these reactions of the mind in tracing conduct to its consequences. It recognizes them as normal. It places their effects within the range of the natural and probable."); Marks v. Wagner, 52 Ohio App.2d 320, 370 N.E.2d 480 (1977). (Look to mental state of rescuer, not actual circumstances as long as belief justified.); Coulton v. Caruso, 195 So. 804 (La.App.1940). (Where plaintiff rushed to rescue his infant niece who was swinging around a porch post, and forgot about hole in porch floor, and fell, he was held not contributorily negligent. 'It may be said that he did not act wisely but persons acting under stress or fear cannot be expected to exercise the judgment which would be required of them under different conditions."); Dixon v. New York, N. H. & H. R. Co., 207 Mass. 126, 92 N.E. 1030 (1910). (Plaintiff attempted to restrain horses frightened by train. "[S]uch a voluntary exposure is not to be regarded as rash or reckless if there appears to be a fair chance of success, and even though the person attempting the rescue, knows that it involves great hazard to himself, without a certainty of accomplishing the intended rescue."); Maryland Steel Co. v. Marney, 88 Md. 482, 42 A. 60, 42 L.R.A. 842 (1898) (Plaintiff, an employee in a steel mill, heroically saved many men by undertaking to stop a leaking tap-hole, and was seriously injured. He could have saved himself by stepping back. Held that his acts were not intervening contributory negligence. "[N]o wrongdoer ought to be allowed to apportion or qualify his own wrong, and that, as a loss has actually happened whilst his own wrongful act was in force and operation, he ought not to be permitted to set up as a defense that there was a more immediate cause of the loss, if that cause was put into operation by his own wrongful act."); Sarratt v. Holston Quarry Co., 174 S.C. 262, 177 S.E. 135 (1934) (Death of rescuer caused while attempting to save quarry worker from electric shock from uninsulated wires, held compensable notwithstanding his peril. "He should simply be required to act as any normal person would likely act under similar situations and circumstances, trying to rescue a fellow man from apparent immediate danger.").

ligence barring recovery of the rescuer, although not necessarily preventing defendant's liability to a third person.[17]

Where too much time elapses between the breach of defendant's duty and the impulsive act of rescue, the application of the doctrine on behalf of the injured rescuer has been denied as a nonforeseeable intervention, although ordinarily so long as defendant's negligence is still producing direct results, the rescuer will be protected.[18]

§ 9.4 The Rescue Doctrine as a Defense to Contributory Negligence

"The law has so high a regard for human life that it will not impute negligence to an effort to preserve it, unless made under such circumstances as to constitute rashness in the judgment of prudent persons." [19]

"The law does not discriminate between the rescuer oblivious of peril and the one who counts the cost. It is enough that the act, whether impulsive or deliberate, is the child of the occasion." [20]

This is one of the earliest statements of the theory that prevents the attempted rescuer of life from becoming a victim of his own heroism. The rule is well settled that an attempted rescuer cannot be charged with contributory negligence as a matter of law.[21] Whether

---

17. Calliari v. Fisher, 190 Mich. 56, 155 N.W. 689 (1916) (Owner injured while trying to stop his runaway horses frightened by defendant's negligence); Roach v. Los Angeles and S. L. R. Co., 74 Utah 545, 280 P. 1053 (1929), cert. denied 280 U.S. 613, 50 S.Ct. 162, 74 L.Ed. 655.

18. Parks v. Starks, 342 Mich. 443, 70 N.W.2d 805 (1955) (Attempt of rescuer to protect children from canopy nine hours after negligence).

19. Eckert v. Long Island Ry. Co., 43 N.Y. 502, 3 Am.Rep. 721 (1871).

20. Wagner v. International Ry. Co., 232 N.Y. 176, 133 N.E. 437 (1921).

21. Restatement, Second, Torts § 472. Provenzo v. Sam, 23 N.Y.2d 256, 296 N.Y.S.2d 322, 244 N.E.2d 26 (1968); Woodruff Elec. Co-op. Corp. v. Weis Butane Gas Co., 225 Ark. 114, 279 S. W.2d 564 (1955) (Truck stopped at side of highway to render aid to persons injured in another accident—rescue instructions appropriate); Hymes v. Pollock, 108 Cal.App.2d 536, 238 P.2d 1056 (1952) (Plaintiff noticed car at night parked at right angles to four-lane highway, and after stopping his automobile, walked back on highway to investigate, and was injured when another automobile struck parked car. Held that the contributory negligence of the would-be rescuer was for jury); Petersen v. Lang Transp. Co., 32 Cal.App.2d 462, 90 P. 2d 94 (1939) (Deceased was struck by automobile while attempting to stop other cars approaching scene of collision. "In the ordinary case any negligence, no matter how slight, will defeat recovery, but in this exceptional case such negligence must amount to rashness or recklessness."); Peoples Drug Stores v. Windham, 178 Md.

the act was so reckless or rash as to constitute contributory negligence becomes a fact for the jury. Again, mere "unreasonableness" will not suffice—errors of judgment will be weighed against the excitement and confusion of the moment, and the rescuer will not be required to have chosen what hindsight judges to have been the wisest alternative course of conduct.[22]

Involuntary and instinctive acts in attempting rescue will not bar liability in many situations, for instance, in cases involving parents and children.[23] It has been held that the act of a mother at-

172, 12 A.2d 532 (1940) (Plaintiff suffered injuries when he parked his automobile on highway beyond a smoke cloud in order to assist a disabled motorist inside the smoke. "The mere fact that he left a position of safety in an honest and generous effort to perform that duty (moral) cannot be characterized as negligence in law."); Hammonds v. Haven, 280 S.W.2d 814 (Mo.1955) (Attempt to warn motorists on dark and stormy night of highway obstruction); Doran v. Kansas City, 237 S.W.2d 907 (Mo.App.1951) (Where older brother aged 9 attempted to rescue his younger brother, from a city excavation, and both were drowned, held not contributory negligence as a matter of law, in that the brother was justified in taking risks); Oklahoma Power and Water Co. v. Jamison, 188 Okl. 118, 106 P.2d 1097 (1940) (Rescuer not excused from his contributory negligence as a matter of law by reason of a rescue since Oklahoma constitution requires that this defense be left to the jury); Corbin v. Philadelphia, 195 Pa. 461, 45 A. 1070, 49 L.R.A. 715 (1900) (Deceased descended into a trench to rescue another overcome by gas and died in the attempt. "A rescuer—one who, from the most unselfish motives, prompted by the noblest impulses that can impel men to deeds of heroism, faces deadly peril—ought not to hear from the law word of condemnation of his bravery, because he rushed into danger, to snatch from it the life of a fellow creature imperiled by the negligence of another, but he should rather listen to words of approval, unless regretfully withheld on account of the unmistakable evidence of his rashness and imprudence.").

22. Alford v. Washington, 244 N.C. 132, 92 S.E.2d 788 (1956) (Decedent was electrocuted when he attempted to rescue motorists trapped under electric wires negligently knocked down by defendant—jury could properly find defendant not guilty of contributory negligence; "When one sees his fellow man in such peril, he is not required to pause and calculate as to court decisions, nor recall the last statute as to the burden of proof, but he is allowed to follow the promptings of a generous nature and extend the help which the occasion requires, and his efforts will not be imputed to him for wrong, according to some of the decisions, unless his conduct is rash to the degree of recklessness; and all of them say that full allowance must be made for the emergency presented."); Bond v. Baltimore & O. R. Co., 82 W.Va. 557, 96 S.E. 932, 5 A.L.R. 201 (1918) ("In almost every instance of rescue, there is an emergency calling for quick determination of the course of action and leaving practically no time for deliberation. When this happens in the exercise of other rights, the law makes due allowance for it and does not hold the injured party responsible for his error of judgment as to his course of conduct.").

23. Cote v. Palmer, 127 Conn. 321, 16 A.2d 595 (1940) (Where mother ran across railroad track to rescue infant daughter, and was killed by the train,

tempting to save her child, no matter how desperate, can never constitute negligence on her part.[24] Where the trial court has non-suited a rescuer-plaintiff for contributory fault, there is often reversal.[25]

There are two other related rules within this doctrine. First, it is generally held that the rescuer is not immune from the defense of contributory negligence when he is responsible for the peril that invites him to the act of the rescue.[26] Second, the weight of authority holds that the antecedent negligence of the rescued is not imputed to the rescuer,[27] although some jurisdictions rule to the contrary.[28]

but the daughter was not injured, held proper for jury to decide as to her conduct. "[H]er conduct is to be judged, not in the light of cold reason but in view of the aroused emotions which would animate a mother situated as was the decedent, and of the lack of opportunity for deliberation and the exercise of a cool judgment." "[A]n outstanding factor is the instinctive reaction of human nature to the need of one in danger, and where he stands in a close relationship of blood or affection to the rescuer, as in a case like this, a young child to a mother, the reactions naturally incident in such a case."); Wilford v. Salvucci, 117 Vt. 495, 95 A.2d 37 (1953), followed 117 Vt. 501, 95 A.2d 41. (Mother ran in front of truck to protect children from being struck).

24. Walters v. Denver Consol. Elec. Light Co., 12 Colo.App. 145, 54 P. 960 (1898) (Mother attempted to rescue child from live electric wire. "The law is not the creature of cold-blooded, merciless logic, and its inherent justice and humanity will never for a moment permit the act of a mother in saving her offspring, no matter how desperate it may have been, to be imputed to her as negligence, or at any time, or in any manner, used to her detriment").

25. De Gregorio v. Malloy, 356 Pa. 511, 52 A.2d 195 (1947).

26. Restatement, Second, Torts § 472, comment (a).

Rose v. Peters, 82 So.2d 585 (Fla.1955) (Plaintiff's failure to warn his subordinates of the danger caused them to expose themselves to the peril from which he attempted to rescue them); Sulpher Springs Val. Elect. Coop., Inc. v. Verdugo, 14 Ariz.App. 141, 481 P.2d 511 (1971) (Plaintiff's negligence in erecting antenna).

27. Pierce v. United Gas and Elec. Co., 161 Cal. 176, 118 P. 700 (1911) (Where one boy attempted to rescue brother from charged electric wire, held that any negligence of the imperiled boy was not imputed to the rescuer); Robertson v. Atchison T. & S. F. Ry. Co., 105 S.W.2d 996, 151 A. L.R. 131 (Mo.App.1937) (Pedestrian attempted to flag approaching train when truck stalled on track. Held that the antecedent negligence of the truck driver was not imputable to the rescuer.); Highland v. Wilsonian Inv. Co., 171 Wash. 34, 17 P.2d 631 (1932) (Employee of tenant went to rescue of another employee overcome by ammonia fumes due to negligence of landlord, held that any negligence of endangered person not imputable to rescuer).

28. Scates v. Rapid Transit Ry. Co., 171 S.W. 503 (Tex.Civ.App.1914), error refused (Plaintiff attempted to remove intoxicated companion from defendant's railroad tracks. Defendant, having no liability to intoxicated person, was not liable to plaintiff).

The California case of *Scott v. Texaco, Inc.*[29] demonstrates the trend to extend the rescue doctrine defense to the charge of contributory negligence to causes of action against defendants other than the creator of the original danger. In *Scott*, plaintiff stopped on the highway behind an overturned car to set flares and warn other motorists. In doing so, she and her car were struck by an approaching gasoline truck, allegedly negligently driven. Verdict for defendants was reversed on the grounds that plaintiff was entitled to a rescue instruction despite the fact that the truck driver had not created the situation inducing the rescue attempt. The court stated: "We think the force of the rule should properly be centered on the rescuer, for it is the quality of his conduct which is being weighed. Whether he was induced to enter a position of danger as a result of the act of a particular defendant or as a result of some outside force is inconsequential to the process of evaluating his behavior." [30]

When plaintiff has established the elements of the doctrine, the question of contributory negligence in fact remains, and it is a jury question whether his conduct was that of a reasonable man under the circumstances. Where a truck driver stopped to assist at a highway accident, without setting flares as required by statute, the doctrine was held to be no defense to the action of a third party who collided with the truck.[31]

§ 9.5 Right of Rescuer to Recover Hinges Upon Dependent Wrong

The right of the rescuer is not derivative from the right of the rescued, but is dependent.[32] Whether the right of the rescuer is a dependent right is important in at least one other situation in addi-

---

29. 239 Cal.App.2d 431, 48 Cal.Rptr. 785 (1966).

30. 239 Cal.App.2d at 436, 48 Cal.Rptr. at 789.

31. Jobst v. Butler Well Servicing, Inc., 190 Kan. 86, 372 P.2d 55 (1962).

32. See supra, n. 27.

Neal v. Home Builders, Inc., 232 Ind. 160, 111 N.E.2d 280 (1953), reh. denied 111 N.E.2d 713 (Where mother injured while rescuing child from stepladder in partially completed house—held no recovery allowed under rescue doctrine since no duty to prevent entrance of trespassing children—dissenting opinions argue for liability); Hawkins v. Palmer, 29 Wash.2d 570, 188 P.2d 121 (1947) (Where defendant was not negligent "for causing the perilous situation of the person sought to be rescued, to invoke the doctrine the defendant must be guilty of some negligence toward the rescuer after the rescuer has begun to attempt the rescue"); Brady v. Chicago & N. W. R. Co., 265 Wis. 618, 62 N.W.2d 415 (1954) (Where 9 year old boy fell into river from overhead bridge and 13 year old boy jumped to save him and both died—held no liability since both found to be gratuitous licensees).

tion to the above mentioned contributory negligence. In *Carney v. Buyea*,³³ defendant was also the object of the rescue, and was held liable to plaintiff rescuer on the reasoning that a lack of self-protective care can constitute negligence towards one in the immediate vicinity who is thereby induced to attempt rescue. In *Talbert v. Talbert*,³⁴ a son's claim for damages for injuries sustained in rescuing the father from an attempted suicide, was held to constitute a cause of action. In *Longacre v. Reddick*,³⁵ plaintiff suffered burns from an explosion of a butane gas truck owned by the defendant, and driven by his employee. The servant was negligent. Plaintiff's rescue might have been reasonably foreseen by a "negligent defendant" and the negligence of defendant's servant was imputed to his master.

§ 9.6 Attempts to Save Property from Harm

The uniform acceptance of the rescue doctrine applied to attempts to save human life is not paralleled in cases relating to the protection of property.³⁶ However, there seems little doubt that the extension of the doctrine to the rescue of property is generally conceded.³⁷ The cases are divided into three categories: (1) Rescue of one's own property; (2) rescue of property belonging to one to whom some duty is owed or relationship exists; (3) rescue of property belonging to a stranger.

Most courts, dealing with this problem, conclude that one who negligently endangers the property of another, is liable for the per-

---

33. 271 App.Div. 338, 65 N.Y.S.2d 902 (1946), appeal denied 271 App.Div. 949, 68 N.Y.S.2d 446.

34. 22 Misc.2d 782, 199 N.Y.S.2d 212 (1960).

35. 215 S.W.2d 404 (Tex.Civ.App.1948), 228 S.W.2d 264 (Tex.Civ.App.1950).

36. Cook v. Johnston, 58 Mich. 437, 25 N.W. 388, 5 Am.Rep. 703 (1885) (Attempt of plaintiff to rescue horse from burning building; held that voluntary assuming risk prevented recovery as a matter of law); Holle v. Lake, 194 Kan. 200, 398 P.2d 300 (1965) (Plaintiff injured in saving truck; "a person is not excused of contributory negligence merely in an effort to save property").

37. Wardrop v. Santi Moving and Exp. Co., 233 N.Y. 227, 135 N.E. 272 (1922) (Where owner of automobile attempted to stop truck by seizing bumper, and was injured, held that his contributory negligence was for the jury. "Undoubtedly more risks may be taken to protect life than to protect property without involving the imputation of negligence, but the rule is that a reasonable effort may be made even in the latter case.").

Heber v. Puget Sound Power and Light Co., 34 Wash.2d 231, 208 P.2d 886 (1949) (Where owner attempted to move a broken electric wire to save chicken house from burning by use of a board, and was electrocuted, the question of his contributory negligence was properly given to jury as to whether "the decedent acted as a reasonably prudent person in his desire to save his property from damage and destruction").

See Restatement, Second, Torts § 472.

sonal injuries incurred by the person who attempts to save it, if such effort is reasonably necessary and prudent under the circumstances.[38] A child of 13 years was held not to be contributorily negligent as a matter of law when she ran into an oil sump in an attempt to rescue her dog.[39] It would seem that in the contrary cases, there is an unreasonable attempted rescue considered contributory negligence by the jury.[40] The question is generally a balancing of the degree of risk taken to the value of the endangered property.

Plaintiff's case is bolstered in those jurisdictions which impose a duty upon plaintiff to mitigate damages to property threatened by defendant's harm.[41] One jurisdiction has held, however, that plain-

38. Breslin v. State, 189 Misc. 547, 72 N.Y S.2d 62 (1947) (Inmate of State Boys School, while attempting to assist instructor in moving burning trash barrel—negligent accumulation of waste—from storage room was not contributorily negligent. "The blazing barrel presented potential danger to both life and property. Immediate action was necessary."); Rague v. Staten Island Coach Co., 288 N.Y. 206, 42 N.E.2d 488 (1942), motion denied 262 App.Div. 1029, 30 N.Y.S.2d 1012 (Where truck driver opened door to warn bus driver of impending collision, held jury question of reasonableness of action. "The plaintiff had the right after he felt the first contact between the bus and his truck to take prudent measures to protect his property from further damage, provided he exercised reasonable care for his own safety in doing so."); Woodcock's Adm'r v. Hallock, 98 Vt. 284, 127 A. 380 (1925) (Effort to protect fence and horse from stallion negligently allowed loose, was not contributory negligence as matter of law).

39. Blaycock v. Coates, 44 Cal.App.2d 850, 113 P.2d 256 (1941).

See also Kirk v. Los Angeles Ry. Corp., 26 Cal.2d 833, 161 P.2d 673 (1945) (Where a woman who stopped to pick up the contents of her spilled purse while crossing an intersection was injured by a motorist, held not to have been contributorily negligent as a matter of law).

40. Hedgecock v. Orlosky, 220 Ind. 390, 44 N.E.2d 93 (1942) (Motorist went between cars to unhook bumpers, and was injured by another car. Held that owner entitled to exercise prudent means to save his property, but that his going between the cars without care as to other vehicles was contributory negligence as a matter of law.); Taylor v. Home Tel. Co., 163 Mich. 458, 128 N.W. 728 (1910) (Plaintiff soaked by water when she attempted to close window and shut out stream caused by negligence of defendant in removing valve from water main); Chattanooga Light and Power Co. v. Hodges, 109 Tenn. 331, 70 S.W. 616, 60 A.L.R. 459 (1902) (Employee rushed into burning building to give alarm over telephone); Foster v. New York Central Ry. Co., 115 W.Va. 682, 177 S.E. 871 (1935) (Deceased killed in attempted rescue of his cow from track. "No one should be permitted to recover for injuries sustained in attempting to rescue mere property in the face of obvious danger such as no reasonably prudent man would, under the circumstances, incur."); Jones v. Virginian Ry. Co., 116 W.Va. 201, 179 S.E. 71 (1935) (Attempt to flag train with blazing newspaper when automobile stalled on track).

41. Mississippi Tank Co. v. Roan, 254 Miss. 671, 182 So.2d 582 (1966).

tiff cannot subject defendant to liability greater than that originally incurred in relation to the property threatened,[42] a holding which seems to lose sight of the fundamental reasoning of foreseeability.

Where plaintiff is employed by the owner of the endangered property, the weight of authority holds that he is protected in his reasonable attempts at rescue,[43] particularly where he can show a duty to prevent the threatened harm.[44]

There is some authority that the rescuer need be under no obligation at all with respect to the property he attempts to rescue.[45] In a Georgia case,[46] defendant's servant, while parking his master's automobile, negligently failed to secure the brakes. At defendant's request, plaintiff police officer attempted to enter the car after it had started to roll, hoping to avert a possible collision. In so doing, he slipped on a stone and was injured. Defendant demurred to the complaint on the ground that plaintiff was contributorily negligent as a matter of law, and that the rescue doctrine should not apply, but the court held with the plaintiff, even though the property rescued was not that of the rescuer. It was a question for the jury to pass upon the facts.

To support a similar holding, the Iowa court [47] advanced the theory that there was a social duty on the plaintiff to prevent unneces-

---

42. Tayer v. York Ice Machinery Corp., 342 Mo. 912, 119 S.W.2d 240, 117 A.L.R. 1414 (1937).

43. Atlantic Coast Line Ry. Co. v. Russell, 215 Ala. 600, 111 So. 753 (1927) (Switchman attempted to prevent cars from sideswiping by switching and kicking); Henshaw v. Belyea, 220 Cal. 458, 31 P.2d 348 (1934) (Efforts of servant to stop truck hauling excavating shovel; jury question as to negligence); Illinois Central Ry. Co. v. Stith's Adm'x, 120 Ky. 237, 85 S.W. 1173 (1905) (Train employee moved train to main track by water tank to save overheated engine, struck by oncoming train despite safety precautions); Rollins v. Boston and Maine Ry. Co., 321 Mass. 586, 74 N.E.2d 664 (1947) (Deceased was protecting property of railroad from fire. "[A] reasonable attempt by an employee to save his employer's property, which the latter's negligence has endangered, is not, as matter of law, such a remote conse-quence of the employer's negligence as to relieve him from liability to the employee for injuries sustained during the attempt.").

44. Boyd v. Terminal R. Ass'n of St. Louis, 289 S.W.2d 33, 59 A.L.R.2d 1222 (Mo.1956) (Recovery allowed under FELA, where employee foreman had duty to prevent train collision in railyard).

45. Schmartz v. Hanger, 22 Conn.Sup. 308, 171 A.2d 89 (1961) (Neighbor may recover after voluntarily attempting to save defendant's home); Pike v. Grand Trunk Ry. Co., 39 F. 255 (1st Cir. 1889) (Plaintiff voluntarily attempted to assist in extinguishing fire on railroad, and was burned to death).

46. Rushton v. Howle, 79 Ga.App. 360, 53 S.E.2d 768 (1949).

47. Liming v. Illinois Central R. Co., 81 Iowa 246, 47 N.W. 66 (1890) (Vol-

sary destruction to property, and that he would have been subject to public censure if he had failed to come to the aid of his neighbor. In any comparison between rescue of person or property, and the application of the "ordinarily reasonable hero," it is well to keep in mind that a jury will tolerate much more risk taking when the effort is to rescue persons.

unteer attempted to save horses from barn endangered by prairie fire. "It is the duty of everyone, according to the requirements of an enlightened and just public sentiment, to use reasonable efforts to preserve the property of others from threatened destruction".).

§§ 9.7–10.0 are reserved for supplementary material.

CHAPTER 10

COMPARATIVE NEGLIGENCE

Table of Sections

Sec.
10.1 In General.
10.2 Forms of Comparative Negligence.
10.3 Proximate Cause—Last Clear Chance—Assumption of Risk.
10.4 Multiple Defendants.
10.5 Cross-Complaints and Set-Offs.
10.6 Non-parties—Joinder.
10.7 Strict Liability Actions.
10.8 Willful Misconduct.

Library References:

C.J.S. Negligence §§ 131, 169–172.
West's Key No. Digests, Negligence ⚖︎97–101.
Prosser, Law of Torts (4th ed. 1971) pp. 433–439.
Blashfield, Automobile Law & Practice, § 63.1 et seq.

§ 10.1 In General

Dissatisfaction with the harshness of the contributory negligence doctrine [1] has led to the application of the more refined rule of *comparative negligence* in most civil law jurisdictions.[2] Under this doctrine, the negligence of both parties is compared and in accordance with the degree of negligence displayed by each, the damage is apportioned.[3] Adoption of the comparative negligence rule in Ameri-

---

1. See Chapter 11, "Contributory Negligence", infra.

2. Comparative negligence was included in the Napoleonic Code (1804), the Austrian Civil Code (1811) and the German Civil Code (1812). See Dooley, Modern Tort Law (1977) § 5.01 Preceding the general acceptance of the doctrine of comparative negligence in the civil law jurisdictions is the early statement of the theory in Mosaic law. In Exodus, XXI, 35–6 it is written that if an ox killed the ox of another, the live ox was sold and the proceeds of it and of the dead ox were divided between the owners.

   And following the civil law the nation where the doctrine of contributory negligence was born rejected Butterfield v. Forrester 146 years after its inception by the passage of the English Reform Act of 1945, which provides that in case of mutual fault a claim for damages shall not be defeated by the presence of fault on the part of the victim, but that the damages shall be apportioned as the court shall think just.

   See Prosser, The Law of Torts (4th ed. 1971) p. 435. Turk, Comparative Negligence on the March (1950) 28 Chicago-Kent L.Rev. 189, 238–244.

3. *Example:* if plaintiff's damage is $100 and 20% of the fault is his, the remaining 80% due to defendant, then plaintiff would get $80.

§ 10.1   TORT LIABILITY AND DEFENSES   Pt. 3

can jurisdictions has ordinarily been by legislation,[4] although Florida,[5] Alaska,[6] and California[7] were converted by decisions of their Supreme Courts—the California holding despite the existence of a contributory negligence statute.[8] Comparative negligence today is applied in thirty-three jurisdictions—Alaska,[9] Arkansas,[10] California,[11] Colorado,[12] Connecticut,[13] Florida,[14] Georgia,[15] Hawaii,[16] Idaho,[17] Kansas,[18] Maine,[19] Massachusetts,[20] Minnesota,[21] Mississippi,[22] Montana,[23] Nebraska,[24] Nevada,[25] New Hampshire,[26] New Jersey,[27] New York,[28] North Dakota,[29] Oklahoma,[30] Oregon,[31] Puerto Rico,[32] Rhode Island,[33] South Carolina,[34] South Dakota,[35] Texas,[36] Utah,[37] Vermont,[38] Washington,[39] Wisconsin,[40] and Wyoming.[41]

4. See Maki v. Frelk, 40 Ill.2d 193, 239 N.E.2d 445, 32 A.L.R.3d 452 (1968), wherein the Supreme Court of Illinois reversed an Appellate decision which had adopted comparative negligence, on grounds that such change was properly a legislative matter. For discussion of this case, see 21 Vand. L.Rev. 889 (1968).

5. Hoffman v. Jones, 280 So.2d 431 (Fla.1973).

6. Kaatz v. Alaska, 540 P.2d 1037 (Alaska 1975), app. after rem'd 572 P.2d 775.

7. Li v. Yellow Cab Co., 13 Cal.3d 804, 119 Cal.Rptr. 858, 532 P.2d 1226 (1975).

8. West's Ann.Cal.Civil Code § 1714.

9. See, n. 6, supra.

10. Ark.Stat.Ann. § 27.1763.

11. See, n. 7, supra.

12. Colo.Rev.Stat. § 41-2-14.

13. Conn.G.Stat.Ann. § 52-572h.

14. See, n. 5, supra.

15. Ga.Code Ann. § 105-603.

16. Hawaii Rev.Stat. § 663-31.

17. Idaho Code § 6-801.

18. Kan.Stat.Ann. § 60-258a.

19. Me.Rev.Stat.Ann. tit. 14 § 156.

20. Mass.Ann.Laws, ch. 231, § 85.

21. Minn.Stat.Ann. § 604.01.

22. Miss.Code Ann. § 11-7-15.

23. Mont.Rev.Codes § 58-607.1.

24. Neb.Rev.Stat. § 25-1151.

25. Nev.Rev.Stat. § 41.141.

26. N.H.Rev.Stat.Ann. § 507.7a.

27. N.J.Stat.Ann. § 2A 15-5.1.

28. N.Y.CPLR §§ 1411-13.

29. N.D.Cent.Code § 9-10-07.

30. Okla.Stat.Ann., tit. 23 § 11.

31. Ore.Rev.Stat. § 18.470.

32. Puerto Rico Laws Ann., tit. 31, § 5141.

33. R.I.Gen.Laws Ann. § 9-20-4.

34. S.C.Code § 46-802.1.

35. S.D.Comp.Laws Ann., § 20-9-2.

36. Vernon's Ann.Tex.Civ.Stat. art. 2212a.

37. Utah Code Ann. § 78-27-37.

38. Vt.Stat.Ann., tit. 12, § 1036.

39. Wash., West's RCWA 4.22.010-190.

40. Wis.Stat.Ann. § 895.045.

41. Wyo.Stat.Ann. § 1-7.2.

§ 10.2 Forms of Comparative Negligence

The forms of the comparative negligence doctrine fall generally into two categories: the "pure" form and the "modified" form. The "pure" form of comparative negligence is the rule in seven American jurisdictions,[42] as well as under the FELA,[43] Jones Act,[44] and English and Canadian statutes.[45] Under this doctrine, plaintiff's recovery is reduced in proportion to the amount of his own negligence. Or, conversely put, defendant may be held liable only for the percentage of fault attributed to him.[46]

The "modified" form, of which there are three main variants, applies apportionment based on fault up to the point where plaintiff's negligence is either equal to or greater than that of defendant, whereupon the contributory negligence rule reappears to bar any recovery by plaintiff.[47] Eight jurisdictions[48] apply the "50%" rule whereby plaintiff may recover if his negligence is less or equal to, but not greater than that of defendant. Thirteen jurisdictions[49] apply the "49%" rule, whereby plaintiff may recover only if his negligence is less than that of defendant. The difference between the two rules can be critical in a close case, given the propensity of a jury to use even numbers and find plaintiff and defendant each 50% at fault, rather than 49%–51% at fault. Thus the latter rule may bar plaintiff from any recovery in a case where the "50% rule" will grant him 50% of his damages. In Georgia, the 49% rule is modified by the provision that plaintiff cannot recover if by ordinary care he could have avoided the consequences to himself caused by defendant's negligence[50]—a sort of plaintiff's last clear chance rule.

---

42. Alaska, Cal., Fla., Miss., N.Y., R.I., Wash.

43. 45 U.S.C.A. § 53.

44. 46 U.S.C.A. § 688.

45. Dooley, § 5.03.
For Canadian statutes, see Prosser, The Law of Torts (4th ed.1971) p. 436.

46. See Hoffman v. Jones, supra, n. 5 ("If plaintiff and defendant are both at fault, the former may recover, but the amount of his recovery may be only such proportion of the entire damages plaintiff sustained as the defendant's negligence bears to the combined negligence of both the plaintiff and the defendant").

47. See Li v. Yellow Cab, supra, n. 7 (The modified form "simply shifts the lottery aspect of the contributory negligence rule to a different ground." 13 Cal.3d at 827, 119 Cal. Rptr. 858 at 874, 532 P.2d 1226 at 1242).

48. Conn., Mont., Nev., N.H., N.J., Tex., Vt., Wis.

49. Ark., Colo., Ga., Hawaii, Idaho, Me., Mass., Minn., N.D., Okl., Or., Utah, Wyo.

50. Southern Ry. Co. v. Daniell, 102 Ga.App. 414, 116 S.E.2d 529 (1960).

§ 10.2 TORT LIABILITY AND DEFENSES Pt. 3

Two jurisdictions—Nebraska and South Dakota—employ the "slight-negligence" rule, which provides that a negligent plaintiff may recover only when his negligence was "slight" in comparison with that of the defendant.[51] Nebraska further requires that defendant's negligence be found to be "gross".[52]

The devastating effect of the 49% and 50% comparative negligence rules, completely barring plaintiff's recovery if the "magic number" is reached, is a particular hazard in jurisdictions where the jury may not be informed of the consequences of their findings.[53] The more enlightened rule allows counsel for both sides to educate the jury as to the operation of the comparative negligence rules and the legal consequences of their findings,[54] in recognition that justice cannot be reached by a jury deliberating in the dark.

§ 10.3 Proximate Cause—Last Clear Chance—Assumption of Risk

Generally speaking, comparative negligence may be invoked by defendant under the same conditions which would have made the common law doctrine of contributory negligence available.[55] Plaintiff must establish a prima facie case that defendant's negligence was a proximate cause of the injuries,[56] and defendant, invoking the doctrine, must establish that plaintiff's negligence constituted a concurrent proximate cause.[57] Negligence on the part of any party intended to be included for purposes of determining proportional comparison must be shown to constitute proximate cause.[58]

---

51. *Neb.*—Johnson v. Roueche, 188 Neb. 716, 199 N.W.2d 1 (1972).

    S.D.—S.D.Comp.Laws 1967, § 20–9–2.

52. Pearson v. Schuler, 172 Neb. 353, 109 N.W.2d 537 (1961).

53. De Groot v. Van Akkeren, 225 Wis. 105, 273 N.W. 725 (1937).

    See also Haw.Rev.Stat. 1968 § 663–31(b); Mass.Gen.Laws Ann., Ch. 231, § 85; N.J.Stat.Ann. § 2A:15–5.2.

54. Cobb v. Atkins, 239 Ark. 151, 388 S.W.2d 8 (1965). Smith v. Gizzi, 564 P.2d 1009 (Okl.1977).

    See also Colo.Rev.Stat. 1973 § 13–21–111(4); Idaho Code Ann. § 6–801; Minn.Stat.Ann. § 604.01(1).

55. See Chapter 11, Contributory Negligence.

56. Romo v. Southern Pac. Transp. Co., 71 Cal.App.3d 909, 139 Cal.Rptr. 787, (1977).

57. Stephens v. Massey, 118 Ga.App. 376, 163 S.E.2d 849 (1968); Howard v. Bachman, 524 S.W.2d 414 (Tex. Civ.App.1975).

58. Walker v. Kroger Grocery & Baking Co., 214 Wis. 519, 252 N.W. 721, 92 A.L.R. 680 (1934); Lovsee v. Allied Development Corp., 45 Wis.2d 340, 173 N.W.2d 196 (1970).

Where plaintiff's negligence is held to constitute the "sole" proximate cause of his injuries, plaintiff may be completely barred from recovery,[59] under the theory of "intervening cause." [60] In practice, however, courts and juries are more likely to avoid the harsh consequences of "sole proximate cause" in favor of apportioning liability via comparative negligence.[61]

Adoption by a jurisdiction of the comparative negligence doctrine usually entails the demise of the rule of "last clear chance",[62] since the primary purpose of this rule is to ameliorate the harshness of the contributory negligence doctrine.[63] Some states, however, viewing the last clear chance rule as a question of proximate cause, see no inconsistency and thus allow a plaintiff to avoid a comparative negligence reduction of recovery by showing that defendant had the last clear chance to avoid the injury.[64] Legal writers tend to stress the inapplicability of last clear chance in a comparative negligence jurisdiction.[65] Although the argument may be valid in respect to a "pure" comparative negligence system, it loses sight of the contributory negligence aspect of the modified systems,[66] wherein "last clear chance" may be crucial to plaintiff's recovery of even partial damages.

Several jurisdictions retain the doctrine of assumption of risk [67] under comparative negligence as a defense barring plaintiff's recovery.[68] Other jurisdictions hold that the assumption of risk de-

---

59. Illinois Central R. R. Co. v. Smith, 243 Miss. 766, 140 So.2d 856 (1962).

60. Menden v. Wisconsin Elec. Power Co., 240 Wis. 87, 2 N.W.2d 856 (1942).

61. See, e. g., Presser v. Siesel Constr. Co., 19 Wis.2d 54, 119 N.W.2d 405 (1963).

See also Schwartz, The Impact of Comparative Negligence, (1974) Defense Law J., Vol. 23.

62. See Kaatz v. State, supra, n. 6; Cushman v. Perkins, 245 A.2d 846 (Me.1968); Li v. Yellow Cab, supra, n. 7; Burns v. Ottati, 513 P.2d 469 (Colo.App.1973).

63. See, Chapter 12 Last Clear Chance, infra.

64. Vlach v. Wyman, 78 S.D. 504, 104 N.W.2d 817 (1960); Underwood v. Illinois Central R. Co., 205 F.2d 61 (5th Cir. 1953); Tiedeman v. Chicago, M. S. P. & P. R. Co., 513 F.2d 1267 (8th Cir. 1975) (Applying Minnesota law); Bezdek v. Patrick, 170 Neb. 522, 103 N.W.2d 318 (1960).

65. See, e. g., Prosser, Law of Torts, (4th ed. 1971) p. 439. See also MacIntyre, The Rationale of Last Clear Chance, 53 Harv.L.Rev. 1225.

66. See text accompanying n. 46, supra.

67. See infra Chapter 13, Assumption of Risk.

68. *Ark.*—Arkansas Kraft Corp. v. Johnson, 257 Ark. 629, 519 S.W.2d 74 (1975).

Ga.—Roberts v. King, 102 Ga.App. 518, 116 S.E.2d 885 (1960).

Miss.—Saxon v. Rose, 201 Miss. 814, 29 So.2d 646 (1947).

§ 10.4 Multiple Defendants

Under the "pure" form of comparative negligence, the contributory fault of each party is compared, and plaintiff is entitled to recovery of his damages reduced by the proportion of fault attributed to him. For example, if plaintiff is found 20% negligent, while defendant A is found 70% and defendant B 10% negligent under the "pure" system, plaintiff is entitled to recover 80% of his damages.

Under the modified forms of comparative negligence, however, plaintiff may be barred from recovery against a joint defendant whose apportioned negligence is less than plaintiff's. In the above hypothetical, under the rules of jurisdictions such as Colorado,[70] plaintiff would be barred from recovery against B because plaintiff's negligence is greater than B's. Other jurisdictions applying the modified systems, however, bar plaintiff from recovery only when his negligence is greater than the *aggregate* of the negligence of all the defendants combined.[71] Thus under the systems of jurisdictions such as Arkansas,[72] plaintiff in the above hypothetical would be entitled to recovery of 80% of his damages, which he may enforce against any defendant, including B.

The rule of joint and several liability, whereby all defendants liable to plaintiff are liable for the entire amount of damages recoverable by him, is not altered by application of comparative negligence.[73]

Neb.—Brackman v. Brackman, 169 Neb. 650, 100 N.W.2d 774 (1960).

S.D.—Snodgrass v. Nelson, 369 F.Supp. 1206 (D.C.D.C.1974), aff'd 503 F.2d 94 (8th Cir.).

Tenn.—O'Brien v. Smith Bros. Engine Rebuilders, Inc., 494 S.W.2d 787 (Tenn.App.1973).

69. Cal.—Li v. Yellow Cab Co., supra, n. 7.

Me.—Wilson v. Gordon, 354 A.2d 398 (Me.1976).

Minn.—Springrose v. Willmore, 292 Minn. 23, 192 N.W.2d 826 (1971).

Miss.—Braswell v. Economy Supply Co., 281 So.2d 669 (Miss.1973).

N.H.—Hagenbuch v. Snap-On-Tools Corp., 339 F.Supp. 676 (D.C.N.H.1972).

N.D.—Wentz v. Deseth, 221 N.W.2d 101 (N.D.1974).

Wash.—Lyons v. Redding Constr. Co., 83 Wash.2d 86, 515 P.2d 821 (1973).

Wis.—Decker v. Fox River Tractor Co., 324 F.Supp. 1089 (D.C.Wis.1971).

70. Colorado, Hawaii, Idaho, Minnesota, Montana, Nevada, New Hampshire, New Jersey, North Dakota, South Carolina, Utah, Wisconsin, Wyoming.

71. Arkansas, Connecticut, Kansas, Maine, Massachusetts, Oregon, Pennsylvania, Texas, Vermont.

72. Riddell v. Little, 253 Ark. 686, 488 S.W.2d 34 (1972).

73. Lincenberg v. Issen, 318 So.2d 386 (Fla.1975); Walton v. Tull, 234 Ark. 882, 356 S.W.2d 20 (1962); Chille v. Howell, 34 Wis.2d 491, 149 N.W.2d 600 (1967); American Motorcycle

Thus, again referring to our hypothetical, plaintiff under a "pure" comparative negligence system may recover his full 80% judgment from defendant B who was only 10% "at fault."[74] And, under the modified "aggregate" system, plaintiff may recover his full 80% from B.[75] Only under a modified system where plaintiff's negligence is compared individually to that of each defendant, may defendant B find himself exempt from liability,[76] although plaintiff may still recover his full 80% from A.[77] The Texas variation is to limit the liability of a defendant whose proportional negligence is less than that of plaintiff to liability only for a proportional share of the damages.[78] In Texas, defendant B would be liable only for 10% of plaintiff's damages, but defendant A could be held liable for 80%. A minority of states have abandoned joint and several liability in comparative negligence cases not involving a joint enterprise among defendants, and apply a system of separable liability among defendants in proportion to their attributed negligence.[79] In the majority of jurisdictions, however, plaintiff is free to recover his judgment from any defendant, and a joint defendant's only recourse is for contribution or indemnity from his co-tortfeasors. A few jurisdictions have instituted systems of apportioned contribution[80] or equitable indemnity[81] in order to apply the principles of comparative negligence to defendants.

Ass'n v. Superior Court, 20 Cal.3d 578, 146 Cal.Rptr. 182, 578 P.2d 899 (1978); Packard v. Whitten, 274 A.2d 169 (Me.1971).

See also Schwartz, Comparative Negligence § 16.4, p. 253.

74. See, e. g., Baxter v. Scottish Rite Temple Ass'n, 86 Cal.App.3d 492 150 Cal.Rptr. 511 (1978) (Deleted on direction of California Supreme Court by order dated January 24, 1979) (Jury apportioned negligence 60% to employer, 25% to plaintiff, and 15% to defendant, whose liability for 75% of the $330,000 damages was affirmed).

75. Walton v. Tull, supra, n. 70.

76. Schwenn v. Loraine Hotel, 14 Wis.2d 601, 111 N.W.2d 495 (1961); Walker v. Kroger Grocery, supra, n. 55.

77. Chille v. Howell, 34 Wis.2d 491, 149 N.W.2d 600 (1967).

78. Vernon's Ann.Tex.Civ.St. art. 2212a, § 2(c): "Each defendant is jointly and severally liable for the entire amount of the judgment awarded the claimant, except that a defendant whose negligence is less than that of the claimant is liable to the claimant only for that portion of the judgment which represents the percentage of negligence attributable to him."

79. *Ga.*—Higginbotham v. Ford Motor Co., 540 F.2d 762 (5th Cir. 1976) (Where defendants are not "joint tort-feasors").

Kan.—Kan.Stat.Ann. § 60–258a(a).

Minn.—Kowalske v. Armour & Co., 300 Minn. 301, 220 N.W.2d 268 (1974).

Nev.—Nev.Laws 1973, § 41.141(3).

N.H.—N.H.Rev.Stat. § 507.7.

Vt.—Vt.Stat.Ann.1959, Title 12, § 1036.

80. See Chapter 17, Contribution Between Joint Tortfeasors, infra.

81. Id.

§ 10.5 Cross-Complaints and Set-Offs

Comparative negligence systems do not preclude a defendant from bringing a cross-complaint against plaintiff for damages arising out of the same incident.[82] California virtually requires defendant to assert his claim in cross-complaint by restricting his recovery to a consolidated action.[83] The trier of fact in such cases will assess damages and allocate negligence with regard to injuries suffered by both parties.

An important question, particularly where the parties are insured, is whether damages in this situation are to be set-off, so that only the difference is to be paid. For example, assume a case where plaintiff's damages are $10,000 and his comparative negligence is 25%, and defendant/cross-complaint's damages are $28,000 and his comparative negligence is 75%. Plaintiff is entitled to recover $7,500 and defendant is entitled to recover $7,000. Compulsory set-off will limit effective liability to a $500 recovery by plaintiff. This may have no impact if neither plaintiff nor defendant are insured. But if both carry insurance, the set-off results in a windfall to the insurers, while denying recovery to the injured parties. A similar injustice results where only one party carries insurance. If our plaintiff were insured, his $7,000 payment to defendant could be retained by equitable lien and applied to his own damages, but mandatory set-off could leave him with nothing but an unenforceable judgment for $500. To remedy this situation, one jurisdiction has provided by statute that there shall be no set-off of damages between parties.[84] The Florida court in *Hoffman v. Jones* [85] originally suggested that set-off would be a proper disposition of damages in a comparative negligence case. When directly faced with the issue in *Stuyvesant Ins. Co. v. Bournazian*,[86] however, the court reconsidered, and held that set-off could apply *only* to uninsured liabilities, and that the obligations of an insurer could not be diminished by application of comparative negligence in a suit involving insured parties. Most jurisdictions, however, have not yet expressly dealt with the problem.

---

82. Hoffman v. Jones, supra, n. 5.

Levy, Pure Comparative Negligence—Set-Offs, Multiple Defendants and Loss Distribution.

83. West's Ann.Cal. CCP § 426.30.

84. Rhode Island Gen.Laws 1956 § 9–20–4.1; Pierringer v. Hoger, 21 Wis. 2d 182, 124 N.W.2d 106 (1963); American Motorcycle Ass'n v. Superior Court, supra, n. 73.

85. 280 So.2d 431 (Fla.1973).

86. 342 So.2d 471 (Fla.1976).

§ 10.6 Non-parties—Joinder

Most comparative negligence jurisdictions provide that plaintiff's negligence is to be compared with that of all parties whose negligence proximately caused or contributed to plaintiff's injuries, whether named as defendants or not.[87] The rule is particularly important where plaintiff's employer is immune by virtue of workers' compensation exclusion. For example, in one case in a "pure" comparative negligence jurisdiction,[88] plaintiff was found 25% negligent, his employer 60%, and defendant 15%. Plaintiff's damages were set at $333,000. Total workers' compensation benefits received were $14,435.38, leaving a balance of $318,564.62. Of this latter figure, defendant was held liable for 75%—diminished only by plaintiff's comparative 25%—despite defendant's arguments that plaintiff's negligence should be compared only with that of defendant.

Adoption of the comparative negligence doctrine does not alter plaintiff's right to join as many or as few defendants as he wishes.[89] Some jurisdictions provide that only the negligence of those absent tortfeasors against whom the plaintiff could recover at law may be added to the aggregate of negligence for purposes of comparison.[90] Others, as in the workers' compensation example above, hold that the negligence of a tortfeasor against whom plaintiff's claim would be barred may nevertheless be added to the aggregate.[91] Florida and Oregon allow causal comparison only with those tortfeasors who are actually joined as defendants.[92]

Under the majority view, even those tortfeasors who have settled with plaintiff may be included in the comparative aggregate.[93] The questions of good faith or collusion which commonly arise in this situation primarily involve the right of contribution among the tortfeasors, and its measurement. The legal implications and responses to these problems are discussed infra in Chapter 17, Contribution Among Joint Tortfeasors.

---

87. See e. g., California Jury Instruction BAJI No. 14.90.
American Motorcycle Ass'n v. Superior Court, supra, n. 73.

88. Baxter v. Scottish Rite Temple, supra, n. 74.

89. Kapchuck v. Orlan, 332 So.2d 671 (Fla.App.1976).

90. Greenwood v. McDonough Power Equipment Inc., 437 F.Supp. 707 (D.C.Kan.1977) (Interpreting Kan.Stat. Ann.1963 § 60–258(a)).

91. Walker v. Kroger Grocery & Baking Co., 214 Wis. 519, 252 N.W. 721 (1934) (Plaintiff passenger's action against host driver barred, but negligence of both drivers was combined for comparison with plaintiff's negligence).

92. Kapchuck v. Orlan, supra, n. 89; Conner v. Mertz, 274 Or. 657, 548 P.2d 975 (1976).

93. Pierringer v. Hoger, 21 Wis.2d 182, 124 N.W.2d 106 (1963); Johnson v. Heintz, 73 Wis.2d 286, 243 N.W.2d 815 (1976).

§ 10.7 Strict Liability Actions

Many jurisdictions deny the application of comparative negligence principles to actions based on strict liability, since negligence or conduct of the tort-feasor is not in issue.[94] Plaintiff's actions, however, may constitute an unforeseeable abnormal use of the product,[95] or be found to constitute the sole proximate cause of the injury,[96] and thus completely bar his recovery.

Other jurisdictions reject the notion that comparing plaintiff's negligence to a producer's strict liability for a dangerously defective product is as irrational a process as comparing apples to oranges. The California Supreme Court, which had taken the lead in establishing the doctrine of strict products liability in *Greenman v. Yuba Power Products, Inc.*,[97] and had further held that in such cases plaintiff's contributory negligence was no bar to recovery,[98] nevertheless by a 4-3 decision in *Daly v. General Motors Corp.*,[99] ruled that in strict products liability actions, plaintiff's recovery would be reduced to the extent that his own lack of reasonable care contributed to his injury. Plaintiff's decedent in *Daly* was killed when he was thrown from his car which had collided with a freeway divider fence. Plaintiff asserted that a defective door latch had allowed decedent to be ejected and suffer fatal injuries, whereas he would have sustained only minor injuries had the door not opened. The trial judge allowed testimony relating to decedent's intoxication and failure to use either the shoulder-seat belt or the door lock. A verdict for defendants en-

---

94. Kinard v. Coats Co., 37 Colo.App. 555, 553 P.2d 835 (1976) (In products liability cases under Restatement § 402A, "the focus is upon the nature of the product, and the consumer's reasonable expectations with regard to that product, rather than on the conduct either of the manufacturer or of the person injured because of the product"); Melia v. Ford Motor Co., 534 F.2d 795 (8th Cir. 1976) (Decedent killed when thrown from car in accident due to faulty door. Held that application of Nebraska's slight/gross comparative negligence statute—would be "extremely confusing and inappropriate in a strict liability case."); Parzini v. Center Chem. Co., 134 Ga.App. 414, 214 S.E. 2d 700 (1975) (Plaintiffs injured while trying to open bottle of drain cleaner. Held, plaintiff's negligence should not be injected into instructions relating to strict tort liability.); Kirkland v. General Motors Corp., 521 P.2d 1353 (Okl.1974) (Held that comparative negligence statute has no application to manufacturer's products liability). Connecticut Pub.L. No. 77–335.

95. See, Chapter 43, Products Liability, infra.

96. Kirkland v. General Motors, supra, n. 94 (Cause of accident found to be plaintiff's intoxication rather than automobile's defect).

97. 59 Cal.2d 57, 27 Cal.Rptr. 697, 377 P.2d 897, 13 A.L.R.3d 1049 (1963).

98. Luque v. McLean, 8 Cal.3d 136, 104 Cal.Rptr. 443, 501 P.2d 1163 (1972).

99. 20 Cal.3d 725, 144 Cal.Rptr. 380, 575 P.2d 1162 (1978).

sued. The California Supreme Court reversed the verdict holding that decedent's negligence should not *completely* bar plaintiffs' recovery, but held further that the principles of comparative negligence should apply to reduce their recovery.

Similar holdings have been rendered by the Supreme Courts of Alaska [1] and Florida,[2] which like California had judicially adopted comparative negligence.[3] The Texas Supreme Court held that the "pure" comparative negligence rule applied to products liability actions, although the state's statute provides a "modified" rule for negligence cases.[4] Other courts have declared existing comparative negligence statutes applicable to strict products liability actions.[5] The Ninth Circuit Court of Appeals in a ruling applying strict liability to admiralty cases, at the same time held that comparative negligence would apply in such actions.[6]

Where comparative negligence is applied to strict liability cases, the defense of assumption of the risk is generally subsumed into comparative negligence and is not available as a defense to totally bar plaintiff's recovery.[7] There also seems to be a trend to subsume the

1. Butaud v. Surburban Marine & Sporting Goods, Inc., 555 P.2d 42 (Alaska 1976) (Snowmobile accident).

2. West v. Caterpillar Tractor Co., Inc., 336 So.2d 80 (Fla.1976) conformed to 547 F.2d 885 (5th Cir.) (Decedent crushed by defectively designed roadgrader).

3. See, § 10.1 supra.

4. General Motors Corp. v. Hopkins, 548 S.W.2d 344 (Tex.1977) ("Runaway carburetor" in pickup truck. $1.8 million verdict not reduced because defendant failed to raise comparative negligence or argue plaintiff's misuse).

5. Busch v. General Motors Corp., 312 Minn. 566, 262 N.W.2d 377 (1977) (Plaintiff suffered quadriplegic injuries in automobile accident); Hagenbuch v. Snap-On-Tools Corp., 339 F. Supp. 676 (D.C.N.H.1972) (Plaintiff lost eye when defective hammer chipped); Sun Val. Airlines v. Avco-Lycoming, 411 F.Supp. 598 (D.C.Idaho 1976) (Air crash, plaintiff airline found 90% negligent, manufacturer 10%); Dippel v. Sciano, 37 Wis.2d 443, 155 N.W.2d 55 (1967) (Pool Table collapsed and crushed plaintiff's foot); Edwards v. Sears, Roebuck & Co., 512 F.2d 276 (5th Cir. 1975) (Plaintiff's decedent killed in auto accident involving defective tires. "The court further instructed the jury that if it found that the decedent was contributorily negligent, but that the defendants also proximately caused or contributed to [decedent's] death, damages could be recovered but must be reduced in proportion to the extent to which decedent's negligence contributed to the accident. We believe the trial court took the correct path through the thicket of strict liability and contributory negligence").

6. Pan-Alaska Fisheries, Inc. v. Marine Constr. & Design Co., 565 F.2d 1129 (3d Cir. 1977) (Fishing vessel caught fire and sank, due to defective oil filter, but owner-operator found 66% responsible for negligence in fire prevention and fire fighting).

7. Daly v. General Motors Corp., supra, n. 97; Hagenbuch v. Snap-On-Tools Corp., supra, n. 5.

"misuse" defense under comparative negligence.[8] Plaintiff's negligence in the form of failure to inspect or discover the defect is generally held *not* to constitute negligence for comparative purposes.[9]

The trend to adoption of comparative negligence principles in strict liability cases is not without vigorous criticism.[10] The dissents in the *Daly* decision [11] point out the regressive nature of the holding from the perspective of the development of strict products liability:

> "This decision seriously erodes the pattern of the law which up to now reflected a healthy concern for consumers victimized by defective products placed on the market in this mechanized age through the dynamics of mass production, national and international distribution, and psychologically subtle marketing." [12]

The proponents, on the other hand, view the extension of comparative principles into strict liability as consistent with the modern trend to "equitable allocation of loss among all parties legally responsible in proportion to their fault," [13] and dismiss objections as primarily problems of "formalism" and "semantics".[14] Divergence of opinion

---

8. General Motors Corp. v. Hopkins, supra, n. 5; Sun Val. Airlines v. Avco-Lycoming, supra, n. 5.

   See Noel, Defective Products: Abnormal Use, Contributory Negligence, and Assumption of Risk (1972) 25 Vanderbilt L.Rev. 93.

9. Busch v. G. M., supra, n. 5: ("To insure protection of this interest, we hold that a consumer's negligent failure to inspect a product or to guard against defects is not a defense and thus may not be compared with a distributor's strict liability. All other types of consumer negligence, misuse, or assumption of the risk must be compared with the distributor's strict liability under the statute.")

   Cf. Restatement, Second, Torts § 402A, comment n.

   Contra: Pan Alaska Fisheries v. Marine Constr. & Design Co., supra, n. 6.

10. See, e. g., Levine, Strict Products Liability and Comparative Negligence: The Collision of Fault and No-Fault (1977) 14 San Diego L.Rev. 337.

11. Daly v. G. M., supra, n. 93, 20 Cal.3d at 757, 144 Cal.Rptr. at 399, 575 P.2d at 1181 ("This will be remembered as the dark day when this court, which heroically took the lead in originating the doctrine of products liability . . . and steadfastly resisted efforts to inject concepts of negligence into the newly designed tort . . ., inexplicably turned 180 degrees and beat a hasty retreat almost back to square one. The pure concept of products liability so pridefully fashioned and nurtured by this court for the past decade and a half is reduced to a shambles." Mosk, J., dissenting.).

12. Id., 20 Cal.3d at 764, 144 Cal.Rptr. at 404, 575 P.2d at 1186.

13. Id., 20 Cal.3d at 737, 144 Cal.Rptr. at 387, 575 P.2d at 1169.

14. Id., 20 Cal.3d at 735–736, 144 Cal. Rptr. at 385–386, 575 P.2d at 1167.

    Pan Alaska, supra, n. 6 (Quoting Butaud, supra, n. 1: "The problem is more apparent than real").

§ 10.8 Willful Misconduct

Attorney *Lowell Sucherman* [16] writes of an interesting case, *Lovy v. Kondrack* [17], where defendant's attorney asserted a unique comparative negligence ground: Plaintiff, a 24-year-old computer repairman trainee, was temporarily attending his company's training school. The Company had a policy of allowing its trainees, who were generally out of state residents brought to the company headquarters in Sunnyvale, California for an eight week training program, to rent cars over long weekends in order to see California. The Company suggested that small groups share in the car rental and assisted by paying mileage for the first 200 miles.

Plaintiff and defendant, who was observing his 23rd birthday, and another student, 22 year old Thibeault, all went together to Larry Hopkins Pontiac to rent a car for use on the three-day weekend. Plaintiff signed for the car with the consent of the other two. The car was a Honda Civic. The three intended to drive to Reno, Tahoe and Yosemite over the long weekend.

Evidence was presented that the three people prepared for the long weekend by purchasing a styrofoam cooler and liberally supplying themselves with food items and alcoholic beverages. Both the driving and the beer were shared equally.

A couple of hours before the accident the plaintiff took the wheel and attempted to "race car drive" the car on the mountain roads between Tahoe and Yosemite. After he nearly drove into a lake, Kondrack and Thibeault suggested it might be preferable if one of them drove.

After a short stop, defendant Kondrack took the wheel and proceeded to "race car drive" the car. On at least one occasion the plaintiff assisted him by shifting gears while the defendant depressed the clutch. Although Thibeault requested that Kondrack slow down

---

15. See Brewster, Comparative Negligence in Strict Liability Cases (1976) 42 J.Air Law & Commerce 107; Schwartz, Strict Liability & Comparative Negligence (1974) 42 Tenn.L.Rev. 171; Jensvold, A Modern Approach to Loss Allocation Among Tortfeasors in Products Liability Cases (1974) 58 Minn.L.Rev. 723; Wade, Strict Tort Liability (1973) 44 Miss.L.J. 825, 850.

16. Lowell H. Sucherman, Cartwright, Sucherman, Slobodin & Fowler, Inc., 160 Sansome Street, Suite 900, San Francisco, CA.

17. Santa Clara Superior Court Case No. 307491, March, 1979.

and suggested to him that Thibeault should drive, Kondrack paid no heed. Kondrack lost control of the car and in trying to drive back onto the pavement, defendant turned the car over.

A blood alcohol test taken four (4) hours after the accident showed that the defendant had a .10 BA. (This converts .14 to .18 BA at the time of the accident.) All three in the car admitted to having the same amount to drink.

Defendant contended that the trip was a joint venture and that the plaintiff should be responsible for at least 50% of the negligence. Defendant also contended that since the plaintiff signed for the car a bailor or bailee relationship existed between plaintiff and defendant and that plaintiff was responsible in entrusting the car to an obviously intoxicated driver. (The Court gave both a joint venture and bailor/bailee instruction).

Defendant further contended that the plaintiff himself was as much a driver at the time of the accident in that he was assisting in shifting gears, that the plaintiff was admittedly just as drunk as the defendant, and that the seatbelts were available which, if used, would have probably prevented the type of injury which was sustained.

As a result of the accident the plaintiff is a quadraplegic.

The trial lasted for approximately 18 days with the jury returning a special verdict finding defendant responsible in willful and wanton misconduct, awarding damages of 1.7 Million Dollars, and finding the plaintiff 20% contributorily negligent.

Based upon these special findings, plaintiff contended that his contributory negligence was not a partial defense to the defendant's *willful* or *wanton* misconduct and that judgment in the amount of $1,700,000.00 should be entered. Defendants contended that the plaintiff's contributory negligence was a partial defense to willful or wanton misconduct and that judgment in the amount of $1,360,000.00 should be entered. The court entered judgment in the sum of $1,360,000.00.

Appeal on the limited question of whether or not contributory negligence is a partial defense to willful or wanton misconduct is currently in process. Theoretically and legally I believe plaintiff should prevail because generally contributory negligence is no defense to a willful or wanton act. (Note: in some jurisdictions "wantonness" has been pleaded instead of "wilfulness" on the theory that an insurance policy is not thereby voided.)

§§ 10.9–11.0 are reserved for supplementary material.

CHAPTER 11

CONTRIBUTORY NEGLIGENCE

Table of Sections

Sec.
11.1 General Considerations.
11.2 Criticism and Defense of the Doctrine.
11.3 Standard of Conduct—Imputed Negligence.
11.4 Avoidable Consequences Rule.
11.5 Non-negligent Torts.

Library References:
C.J.S. Negligence §§ 116 et seq., 150, 151.
West's Key No. Digests, Negligence ⚖=65 et seq.
Prosser, Law of Torts (4th ed. 1971), pp. 416–427.
Blashfield, Automobile Law & Practice, § 61.1 et seq.

§ 11.1 General Considerations

In *Butterfield v. Forrester*,[1] 1809, Lord Ellenborough announced the doctrine of contributory negligence: "One person being in fault will not dispense with another's using ordinary care for himself."

The doctrine is more fully enunciated as follows:

"Contributory negligence is conduct on the part of the plaintiff which falls below the standard to which he should conform for his own protection, and which is a legally contributing cause co-operating with the negligence of the defendant in bringing about the plaintiff's harm."[2]

The legal effect of contributory negligence is to completely bar plaintiff's recovery.

The doctrine, now for the most part abandoned, was favorably accepted in England. One reason may lie in the fact that, for several decades following the pronouncement, the country experienced an expansion of its economy, and there might have been economic hazards in the imposition of liability freely for tort claims.[3] Similar economic

---

1. 11 East 60, 103 Eng.Rep. 926.

2. Restatement, Second, Torts § 463.

3. For a historical analysis of the sources of the doctrine of contributory negligence, see Turk, (1950) "Comparative Negligence on the March," 28 Chicago-Kent L.Rev. 190. See James, Contributory Negligence, (1953) 62 Yale L.J. 691; Malone

conditions favored the reception of the *Butterfield* doctrine in the United States about the year 1824.[4]

It has also been suggested that the desire of the court to control the jury is another explanation for the willing acceptance of this doctrine into American law.[5] It is argued that the average juror's tendency to be plaintiff-minded in the wake of much litigation against large and remote railroads and other corporations required some restriction. Through the application of the rules of contributory negligence, a court could non-suit the plaintiff, or grant New Trials, and thus control the litigation without a jury.[6]

§ 11.2 Criticism and Defense of the Doctrine

Authorities on the law of negligence have pointed out that the application of the doctrine is often unfair, since the entire loss is placed on the injured plaintiff, when both he and the defendant may have been at fault.[7] The doctrine may have had its merits in the early days of the 19th century, when infant industry stood in need of judicial help against oversympathetic injuries.[8] But, today the doctrine has become overwhelming in its harshness. In the complex interrelationships of our mechanized society the fact is obvious that all conduct becomes even more imperfect than normally is the case. It is compellingly argued that the rule permitting the injured plaintiff to go unrewarded, because he was negligent in some small degree, while the defendant leaves the court free from responsibility, even though his fault was greater, should be mitigated.

There is considerable dissatisfaction with the defense of contributory negligence, as evidenced by the criticism of legal scholars.[9]

(1946), "The Formative Era of Contributory Negligence," 41 Ill.L.R. 151.

See also Tiller v. Atlantic Coast Line R. Co., 318 U.S. 54, 63 S.Ct. 444, 87 L. Ed. 610, 143 A.L.R. 967 (1943).

4. Smith v. Smith, 19 Mass. (2 Pick), 621, 13 Am.Dec. 464 (1824); Bush v. Brainard, 1 Cow. (N.Y.) 78, 13 Am. Dec. 513 (1823); Noyes v. Town of Morristown, 1 Vt. 353 (1828); Washburn v. Tracy, 2 D Chip (Vt.) 128, 15 Am.Dec. 661 (1824).

5. Malone, supra n. 3, pp. 155 et seq.

6. See Atlantic Coast Line R. Co. v. Glenn, 198 F.2d 232 (4th Cir. 1952), 11 NACCA L.J. 199. (Gross contributory negligence of decedent at railroad crossing precludes recovery as matter of law).

Also see, Malone, supra n. 3 p. 164; James, Contributory Negligence (1953) 62 Yale L.J. 691.

7. See Prosser, The Law of Torts (4th ed., 1971) p. 433; Green, Illinois Negligence Law (1944) 39 Ill.L.Rev. 36, 116; Lowndes, Contributory Negligence (1934) 22 Geo.L.J. 674; James, Last Clear Chance: A Transitional Doctrine, (1938) 47 Yale L.J. 704; James, Contributory Negligence (1953) 62 Yale L.J. 691.

8. See Turk, supra n. 3 p. 201.

9. Prosser, The Law of Torts (4th ed. 1971) p. 418: "Criticism of the denial

Dean Prosser has pointed out,[10] with his customary clarity, that in the civil law countries, and also in most parts of the British Commonwealth of Nations which follow the common law, the defense has been abolished, and damages have been divided between the parties.[11] Such sentiment has led to attempts to mitigate the severe effects of the doctrine: Last Clear Chance,[12] Wanton or Willful Misconduct,[13] and, most importantly, Comparative Negligence.[14]

In defense of contributory negligence, it is often said that the rule promotes caution by making the plaintiff responsible for his own safety. It has been well argued, however, that negligence is encouraged by allowing careless defendants to go free to err again.[15] Also, the large number of negligence cases in the face of the universality of the contributory theory as a defense, is evidence contradicting the "deterrent" theory.[16] It has also been said that the plaintiff is being punished for his own negligence, but the many cases decided under the last clear chance theory giving complete recovery to plaintiff, regardless of his contributory negligence, seems to neutralize this argument. That the plaintiff is in pari delicto is a poor argument, as the negligence of the plaintiff is only carelessness towards himself while the delict of the defendant is a breach of duty to another.[17]

One legal authority has commented that the best defense he can present for the doctrine is that of simplicity of administration.[18] In this connection, see the defense of one judge that comparative negligence is a doctrine fostered by the lawyers.[19]

of all recovery was not slow in coming, and it has been with us for more than a century. The history of the doctrine has been that of a chronic invalid who will not die. With the gradual change in social viewpoint, stressing the humanitarian desire to see injuries compensated, the defense of contributory negligence has gradually come to be looked upon with increasing disfavor by the courts . . ."

See also 2 Harper & James, The Law of Torts (1956) § 22.3; Keeton, Comments on Maki v. Frelk, 21 Vand.L. Rev. 889, 916 (1968).

10. Prosser, The Law of Torts (4th ed. 1971) p. 435.

11. Turk, supra n. 3 p. 206 (thorough historical treatment).

12. See Chapter 12, infra.

13. See Chapter 15, infra.

14. See Chapter 10, supra.

15. Prosser, The Law of Torts (4th ed. 1971) p. 433.

16. See Turk, supra n. 3, p. 202.

See also, Mole and Wilson, A Study of Comparative Negligence (1932) 17 Cornell L.Q. 333, 604.

17. See Turk, supra n. 3, p. 203.

18. Id.

19. William J. Palmer, Judge, Let Us Be Frank About Comparative Negligence, 28 Los Angeles Bar Bulletin, p. 37 (1952).

§ 11.3 Standard of Conduct—Imputed Negligence

The very label, contributory "negligence" has been criticized as inapplicable,[20] since negligence requires a duty—an obligation of conduct to another person—whereas, contributory negligence involves no duty.[21] Nevertheless, the standard of conduct applied is that of ordinary negligence—the conduct of a reasonable man under the same or similar circumstances.[22] Contributory negligence may consist of an act or an omission which fails to observe that standard.[23]

The question of what particular conduct constitutes reasonable prudence under the circumstances is properly a jury question.[24] A finding of contributory negligence as a matter of law is justified only "when the facts are such that all reasonable men must draw the same conclusion from them." [25]

Identical conduct, however, is not necessarily required between plaintiff and defendant.[26] The argument may be made that plaintiff's standard of reasonable care for his own safety is less than defendant's required standard of care for the safety of others.[27] Fur-

20. Prosser, The Law of Torts (4th ed. 1971) p. 418.

21. "[U]nless we are to be so ingenious as to say that the plaintiff is under an obligation to protect the defendant against liability for the consequences of his own negligence." Prosser, p. 418.

22. Stephenson v. Grand Trunk Western R. Co., 110 F.2d 401, 132 A.L.R. 455 (7th Cir. 1940), cert. denied 311 U.S. 720, 60 S.Ct. 1107, 85 L.Ed. 469, overruled on other grounds; Trust Co. of Chicago v. Pennsylvania R. Co., 183 F.2d 640, 21 A.L.R.2d 238 (7th Cir.); Morris v. Uhl & Lopez Engineers, Inc., 468 F.2d 58 (10th Cir. 1972) (Standard that reasonably prudent person would observe in order to avoid injury to himself); Mroz v. Dravo Corp., 429 F.2d 1156 (3d Cir. 1970) (Standard of reasonably prudent person under the circumstances); Cincotta v. United States, 362 F.Supp. 386 (D.C.Md.1973) (Reasonable care under the circumstances to insure own safety).

23. Sandifer v. Sale, 196 F.Supp. 721 (D.C.S.C.1961) (Contributory negligence is an act or omission of plaintiff amounting to want of ordinary care); Little v. Hackett, 116 U.S. 366, 6 S.Ct. 391, 29 L.Ed. 652 (1886).

24. Rogers v. Missouri Pac. R. Co., 352 U.S. 500, 77 S.Ct. 443, 1 L.Ed.2d 493 (1957), reh. denied 353 U.S. 943, 77 S.Ct. 808, 1 L.Ed.2d 764; Brant v. Robinson Inv. Co. v. Ives, 435 F.2d 1345 (1971); Lazar v. Cleveland Elec. Illuminating Co., 43 Ohio St.2d 131, 331 N.E.2d 424 (1975); Eder v. Lansberry, 459 Pa. 621, 331 A.2d 165 (1975); Boeing Co. v. Shipman, 411 F.2d 365 (5th Cir. 1969).

25. Grand Trunk Ry. Co. v. Ives, 144 U.S. 408, 12 S.Ct. 679, 36 L.Ed. 485 (1892); Nuckoles v. F. W. Woolworth Co., 372 F.2d 286 (4th Cir. 1967); Logullo v. Joannides, 301 F.Supp. 722 (D.C.Del.1969).

26. Glaum v. Cummings, 317 Ill.App. 655, 47 N.E.2d 359 (1943); Cushman Motor Delivery Co. v. McCabe, 219 Ind. 156, 36 N.E.2d 769 (1941).

27. James, Contributory Negligence (1953) 62 Yale L.J. 691; James and Dickinson, Accident Proneness and

ther, in a given situation, defendant may have more knowledge than plaintiff of the danger,[28] or plaintiff may be justified in his reliance on defendant's observance of due care.[29]

To bar plaintiff's recovery, his contributory negligence must be found to have been a proximate cause of his damage.[30] His negligence thus must be shown to have been a "substantial factor" in bringing about his harm.[31] Yet once proximate causation is established, plaintiff's cause will be barred regardless of the degree in which his fault was operative.[32] An instruction which makes reference to degrees or percentages in determining contributory negligence will generally be reversible error whether it favors plaintiff or defendant.[33]

Violation of a statute by plaintiff is relevant to the question of his contributory negligence in the measure as it applies to a determination of ordinary negligence.[34] Plaintiff's action will be barred if the statute fixes a standard of care,[35] the violation is a proximate cause of the injury,[36] and the harm incurred is of the type the statute was designed to prevent.[37] According to the rules of the jurisdiction,[38] the violation will be considered either as evidence of

Accident Law (1950) 63 Harv.L.Rev. 769.

Stubbs v. Pancake Corner of Salem, Inc., 254 Or. 220, 458 P.2d 676 (1969); Sollinger v. Himchak, 402 Pa. 232, 166 A.2d 531 (1961).

28. Haverly v. State Line & S. R. Co., 135 Pa. 50, 19 A. 1013 (1890).

29. Warner v. Baltimore & O. R. Co., 168 U.S. 339, 18 S.Ct. 68, 42 L.Ed. 491 (1897); Humbyrd v. Spurlock, 345 S.W. 499 (Mo.App.1961).

30. Leichner v. Basile, 144 Mont. 141, 394 P.2d 742 (1964); Bahm v. Pittsburgh & Lake Erie R. Co., 6 Ohio St. 2d 192, 217 N.E.2d 217 (1966); Gillson v. Osborne, 220 Minn. 122, 19 N. W.2d 1 (1945).

31. Restatement, Second, Torts § 465. Mack v. Precast Indus., Inc., 369 Mich. 439, 120 N.W.2d 225 (1963); Busch v. Lilly, 257 Minn. 343, 101 N.W.2d 199 (1960).

32. Moore v. United States, 217 F. Supp. 289 (D.C.Pa.1963), aff'd 332 F. 2d 372 (3d Cir.); Snyder v. Bicking, 115 N.J.L. 549, 181 A. 161, 102 A.L.R. 409 (1935).

33. Mack v. Precast Indus., Inc., supra, n. 31; Krackomberger v. Vornado, Inc., 119 N.J.Super. 380, 291 A.2d 842 (1972); Coleman v. Lurey, 199 S.C. 442, 20 S.E.2d 65 (1942).

34. See Chapter 8, Violation of Statute, supra.

See also Mechler v. McMahon, 184 Minn. 476, 239 N.W. 605 (1931).

35. Restatement, Second, Torts § 475(a)(b).

36. Restatement, Second, Torts § 286.

37. Restatement, Second, Torts § 256.

38. See Chapter 8, Violation of Statute, supra.

negligence [39] or as negligence per se.[40] Compliance with a statute does not establish due care.[41]

Under some circumstances, misconduct of a third party can be imputed to plaintiff to constitute contributory negligence. A spouse is not necessarily charged with the negligence of the other,[42] although some states provide for imputation where the recovery will be treated as community property.[43] A parent's negligence generally will not bar a child's action,[44] although there is authority to the contrary.[45] A driver's negligence will not ordinarily be imputed to a passenger,[46] though it may if the passenger is the owner of the

39. East Hampton DeWitt Corp. v. State Farm Mut. Auto. Ins. Co., 490 F.2d 1234 (2d Cir. 1973); Bixenmann v. Hall, 251 Ind. 527, 242 N.E.2d 837 (1968); McConnell v. Pic-Walsh Freight Co., 432 S.W.2d 292 (Mo. 1968).

40. Logullo v. Joannides, 301 F.Supp. 722 (D.C.Del.1969); Parrot v. Garcia, 436 S.W.2d 897 (Tex.1969); Leap v. Royce, 203 Or. 566, 279 P.2d 887 (1955); Thomas v. Bruton, 270 F. Supp. 33 (D.C.S.C.1967), aff'd 390 F. 2d 658 (4th Cir.); Rice v. Merritt-Chapman & Scott, Inc., 326 F.2d 122 (4th Cir. 1963).

41. See Chapter 8, Violation of Statute, supra.

42. Winter v. Eon Production, Ltd., 433 F.Supp. 742 (D.C.La.1976); Wright v. Standard Oil Co., Inc., 470 F.2d 1280 (5th Cir. 1972), cert. denied 412 U.S. 938, 93 S.Ct. 2772, 37 L.Ed.2d 398, reh. denied 471 F.2d 650 (5th Cir.); Thompson v. Kane, 58 Misc.2d 364, 295 N.Y.2d 515 (1968).

See also Restatement, Second, Torts § 487.

43. Muhammad v. United States, 366 F.2d 298 (9th Cir. 1966), cert. denied 386 U.S. 959, 87 S.Ct. 1029, 18 L.Ed. 2d 108; Choate v. Ransom, 74 Nev. 100, 323 P.2d 700 (1958). (Applying Idaho law); Tinker v. Hobbs, 80 Ariz. 166, 294 P.2d 659 (1956).

44. Porter v. United Steel & Wire Co., 436 F.Supp. 1376 (D.C.Iowa 1977); Eshback v. W. T. Grant's & Co., 481 F.2d 940 (3d Cir. 1973); Mann v. Anderson, 477 F.2d 533 (7th Cir. 1971); McCormack v. Hankscraft Co., 278 Minn. 322, 154 N.W.2d 488 (1967); Orefice v. Albert, 237 So.2d 142 (Fla. 1970), conformed to 239 So.2d 46.

See also Restatement, Second, Torts § 488(1).

45. Bessey v. Salemne, 302 Mass. 188, 19 N.E.2d 75, 123 A.L.R. 1156 (1939) (Where child too young to exercise care for own safety, negligence of custodian will be imputed to him).

See also Day v. Cunningham, 125 Me. 328, 133 A. 855, 47 A.L.R. 1229 (1925).

46. Runge v. Welch, 307 F.2d 829 (5th Cir. 1962), cert. denied 371 U.S. 954, 83 S.Ct. 50, 9 L.Ed.2d 501; Duckworth v. Greyhound Lines, Inc., 469 F.2d 424 (6th Cir. 1972); Evans v. Pennsylvania R. Co., 255 F.2d 205 (3d Cir. 1958) (Delaware law); Bailey v. Branin, 279 F.2d 344 (3d Cir. 1960); Ernst v. Baltimore & O. R. Co., 316 F.2d 856 (6th Cir. 1963); Dreyer v. United States, 349 F.Supp. 296 (D.C. Ohio 1972), aff'd Freeman v. United States, 509 F.2d 626 (6th Cir.) (Negligence of aircraft pilot not imputed to passengers).

vehicle.⁴⁷ Negligence of an employee will generally be imputed to the employer as against a third party if the employee was acting within the scope of his duties.⁴⁸ An employer's negligence, however, generally will not be imputed to an employee.⁴⁹ Where negligence is established on the part of a beneficiary to the action,⁵⁰ or to a member in a joint enterprise,⁵¹ it may be imputed to plaintiff.

§ 11.4 Avoidable Consequences Rule

Contributory negligence is to be distinguished from the "avoidable consequences rule". Contributory negligence takes place prior to the injury, and totally bars plaintiff's recovery. Avoidable consequences are those which plaintiff, by the exercise of due care, should have averted *subsequent* to the infliction of the legal wrong.⁵² He is barred from recovery only for that portion of his damages which is attributed to his own lack of care.⁵³ Thus, where plaintiff fails to take reasonable steps to obtain proper medical treatment for his injuries, an apportionment will be made to determine what part of his damages were aggravated by his own negligence.⁵⁴

In some instances the avoidable consequences rule has been applied to plaintiff's antecedent conduct,⁵⁵ particularly in connection

---

47. Miller v. United States, 196 F. Supp. 613 (D.C.Mass.1961) (Negligence of driver chargeable to owner-occupant if owner had right to control operation of vehicle).

Knudson v. Boren, 261 F.2d 15 (10th Cir. 1958).

48. Miller v. United States, supra, n. 47 (Mass. law); Drewery v. Shell Oil Co., 317 F.2d 425 (5th Cir. 1963); Sellner v. McKee, 167 Colo. 213, 446 P.2d 909 (1968); Naegele-Kelly Mfg. Co. v. Hannak, 13 Mich.App. 427, 164 N.W.2d 540, 53 A.L.R.3d 658 (1968).

Contra: Weber v. Stokeley-Van Camp, Inc., 274 Minn. 482, 144 N.W.2d 540 (1966).

See also Restatement, Second, Torts § 486.

49. New England Tel. & Tel. Co. v. Reed, 336 F.2d 90 (1st Cir. 1964); Sullivan v. Shell Oil Co., 234 F.2d 733 (9th Cir. 1956), cert. denied 352 U.S. 925, 77 S.Ct. 221, 1 L.Ed.2d 160.

50. Bolen v. Rio Rancho Estates, Inc., 81 N.M. 307, 466 P.2d 873 (1970) (Wrongful death); City of Louisville v. Stuckenborg, 438 S.W.2d 94 (Ky. 1968) (Wrongful death).

51. Restatement, Second, Torts § 491(1).

52. Prosser, The Law of Torts (4th ed. 1971) p. 423.

53. Prosser, The Law of Torts (4th ed. 1971) p. 423.

See also Dippold v. Cathlamet Timber Co., 111 Or. 199, 225 P. 202 (1924).

54. Wingrove v. Home Land Co., 120 W.Va. 100, 196 S.E. 563 (1938); Dohmann v. Richard, 282 So.2d 789 (La. App.1973) (Refusal of plaintiff to undergo electroshock treatment for psychotic state of depression precipitated by accident not unreasonable and did not require reduction of recovery).

55. O'Keefe v. Kansas City Western R. Co., 87 Kan. 322, 124 P. 416 (1912) (Intoxication).

with the failure to use seatbelts.[56] Failure to fasten seatbelts generally will not be deemed to constitute contributory negligence, since it does not contribute to the happening of the accident.[57] Yet, such failure is relevant to aggravation of injuries, and may be considered as grounds for reduction of damages.[58]

§ 11.5 Non-negligent Torts

In theory, contributory negligence presumes primary negligence on the part of the defendant as a proximate cause of plaintiff's damage.[59] Plaintiff's contributory negligence may not be raised as a defense to defendant's liability for an intentional tort,[60] or for "willful and wanton" misconduct.[61] Plaintiff's own reckless conduct may con-

---

56. See Walker and Beck, Seat Belts and the Second Accident (1967) 34 Ins.Couns.J. 352.

Note, Seat Belts and Contributory Negligence (1967) 12 S.D.L.R. 130.

Comment—A Basic Analysis of the Seat Belt Defense. 34 Albany L.Rev. 593 (1970).

57. Pritts v. Walter Lowery Trucking Co., 400 F.Supp. 867 (D.C.Pa.1975); Melesko v. Riley, 32 Conn.Sup. 89, 339 A.2d 479 (1975); Myles v. Lee, (La.App.1968) 209 So.2d 533; Glover v. Daniels, 310 F.Supp. 750 (D.C. Miss.1970); Sonnier v. Ramsey, 424 S.W. 684 (Tex.Civ.App.1968), refused n. r. e. (Judgment that plaintiff take nothing for failure to use seatbelts reversed since it did not contribute to cause of accident).

58. Spier v. Barker, 35 N.Y.2d 444, 363 N.Y.S.2d 916, 323 N.E.2d 164 (1974); Henderson v. United States, 429 F.2d 588 (10th Cir. 1970); Josel v. Rossi, 7 Ill.App.3d 1091, 288 N.E.2d 677 (1972); Truman v. Vargas, 275 Cal. App.2d 976, 80 Cal.Rptr. 373 (1969).

Contra: Moore v. Fischer, 31 Colo.App. 425, 505 P.2d 383 (1973), aff'd 183 Colo. 392, 517 P.2d 458; Stallcup v. Taylor, 62 Tenn.App. 407, 463 S.W.2d 416 (1970); Robinson v. Bone, 285 F. Supp. 423 (D.C.Or.1968). (Oregon law).

See Annotations, 15 A.L.R.3d 1428 (Nonuse of seatbelts as contributory negligence); 80 A.L.R.3d 1033 (Nonuse of seatbelts as failure to mitigate damages).

Note: An expert should be called by a defendant in the seat belt case to make its non-use relevant.

59. Baltimore & Potomac R. Co. v. Cumberland, 176 U.S. 232, 20 S.Ct. 380, 44 L.Ed. 447 (1900); Brown v. General Motors Corp., 355 F.2d 814 (4th Cir. 1966), cert. denied 386 U.S. 1036, 87 S.Ct. 1474, 18 L.Ed.2d 600; Rentfrow v. Grand Trunk Western R. Co., 9 Mich.App. 655, 158 N.W.2d 69 (1968).

60. Restatement, Second, Torts § 481.

See also Ridgeway v. North Star Terminal & Stevedoring Co., 378 P.2d 647 (Alaska 1963); Jenkins v. North Carolina Dept. of Motor Vehicles, 244 N. C. 560, 94 S.E.2d 577 (1956).

61. Restatement, Second, Torts § 482(1).

See also Kellerman v. J. S. Drug Co., 176 Ohio St. 320, 199 N.E.2d 562 (1964); Billingsley v. Westrac Co., 365 F.2d 619 (8th Cir. 1966); Boyce v. Pi Kappa Alpha Holding Corp., 476 F.2d 447 (5th Cir. 1973); Galvin v. Jennings, 289 F.2d 15 (3d Cir. 1961); Wilson v. American Chain & Cable Co., 364 F.2d 558 (3d Cir. 1966).

stitute the defense in the latter case, however.[62] In jurisdictions where "gross negligence" is distinguished from "willful and wanton" misconduct, plaintiff's contributory negligence is generally recognized as a proper defense to gross negligence.[63] Where defendant's conduct is in violation of statute, and thereby regarded as "negligence per se," [64] some jurisdictions will disallow the defense of plaintiff's contributory negligence.[65] Contributory negligence is no defense to an action based on nuisance [66] unless the nuisance rests upon, or is "intertwined with" negligence.[67]

Products liability actions brought in warranty or strict liability in tort are not founded in negligence.[68] (Historically they may be.) Nevertheless, several jurisdictions have allowed the defense of plaintiff's contributory negligence, particularly when plaintiff's use of the commodity was other than that intended or reasonably anticipated by the manufacturer.[69] The "misuse" defense is not actually an aspect of contributory negligence, but more properly goes to the question of

See Prosser, The Law of Torts (4th ed. 1971) p. 426.

See also Chapter 15, Wanton or Wilful Misconduct, infra.

62. Restatement, Second, Torts § 482(2).

See Ardis v. Griffin, 239 S.C. 529, 123 S.E.2d 876 (1962); Tabor v. O'Grady, 61 N.J.Super. 446, 161 A.2d 267 (1960); Graham v. Seaboard Air Line R. R. Co., 250 F.Supp. 556 (D.C.S.C. 1966).

See also Prosser, The Law of Torts (4th ed. 1971) p. 426.

63. Poole v. James, 231 Ark. 810, 332 S.W.2d 833 (1960); Banks v. Braman, 188 Mass. 367, 74 N.E. 594 (1905); Nass v. Mossner, 363 Mich. 128, 108 N.W.2d 881 (1961).

64. See Chapter 8, Violation of Statute, supra.

65. Bowman v. Redding & Co., 449 F.2d 956 (1st Cir. 1971) (Defense available only if plaintiff chargeable with recklessness).

See also Mayes v. Byers, 214 Minn. 54, 7 N.W.2d 403, 144 A.L.R. 821 (1943);

McCallie v. New York Central R. R. Co., 23 Ohio App.2d 152, 261 N.E.2d 179 (1969).

66. See Prosser, The Law of Torts (4th ed. 1971) pp. 608–610; Seavy, Nuisance: Contributory Negligence and Other Mysteries (1952) 65 Harv.L. Rev. 984; Prosser, Private Action for Public Nuisance (1966) 52 Va.L.Rev. 997.

Flaherty v. Great Northern R. Co., 218 Minn. 488, 16 N.W.2d 553 (1944).

67. Schiro v. Oriental Realty Co., 272 Wis. 537, 76 N.W.2d 355 (1956); McFarlane v. City of Niagara Falls, 247 N.Y. 340, 160 N.E. 391 (1928); Merrick v. Miller, 27 Conn.Sup. 330, 237 A.2d 381 (1967); Jones v. Rumford, 64 Wash.2d 559, 392 P.2d 808 (1962).

68. See, Chapter 43, Products Liability, infra.

69. Codling v. Paglia, 32 N.Y.2d 330, 345 N.Y.S.2d 461, 298 N.E.2d 622 (1973); Brandenburg v. Weaver Mfg. Co., 77 Ill.App.2d 374, 222 N.E.2d 348 (1966).

foreseeability.[70] Since the entire thrust of modern products liability establishes that defendant's negligence or lack of it has no relevance to his liability,[71] plaintiff's contributory negligence is equally irrelevant in defense and should not be admissible.[72] The Restatement view, adopted by most courts, is that plaintiff's assumption of the risk [73]— "voluntarily and unreasonably proceeding to encounter a known danger"—constitutes a defense to strict liability.[74] A minority of courts

70. Thompson v. Package Machinery Co., 22 Cal.App.3d 188, 99 Cal.Rptr. 281 (1972) (Manufacturer liable if misuse foreseeable); Helene Curtis Indus., Inc. v. Pruitt, 385 F.2d 841 (5th Cir. 1967), cert. den. 391 U.S. 913, 88 S.Ct. 1806, 20 L.Ed.2d 652 (No liability where plaintiff's mixture of defendant's product with another cosmetic was not reasonably foreseeable); Ford Motor Co. v. Eads, 224 Tenn. 473, 457 S.W.2d 28 (1970) (Hotwiring of tractor, thereby bypassing safety system and causing injury, was not foreseeable use).

See Noel, Defective Products: Abnormal Use, Contributory Negligence and Assumption of Risk (1972) 25 Vand.L.Rev. 93.

71. Chapter 43, Products Liability, infra.

Prosser, The Fall of the Citadel (Strict Liability to the Consumer) 50 Minn. L.Rev. 791 (1966).

72. *Ariz.*—O. S. Stapley Co. v. Mather, 103 Ariz. 556, 447 P.2d 248 (1968) (Contributory negligence in failing to discover defect no defense to strict liability.)

Conn.—DeFelice v. Ford Motor Co., 28 Conn.Sup. 164, 255 A.2d 636 (1969).

Idaho—Shields v. Morton Chem. Co., 95 Idaho 674, 518 P.2d 857 (1974).

Ill.—Williams v. Brown Mfg. Co., 45 Ill.2d 418, 261 N.E.2d 305 (1970).

La.—Khoder v. A.M.F., Inc., 539 F.2d 1078 (5th Cir. 1976). (Under Louisiana law, plaintiff's failure to exercise ordinary care for his own safety not a defense to strict liability.)

Mich.—Baker v. Rosemurgy, 4 Mich. App. 195, 144 N.W.2d 660 (1966).

Mo.—Keener v. Dayton Elec. Mfg. Co., 445 S.W.2d 362 (Mo.1970).

N.M.—Bendorf v. Volkswagenwerk Aktiengesellschaft, 88 N.M. 355, 540 P. 2d 835 (1975), cert. denied 88 N.M. 319, 540 P.2d 249, appeal after remand 90 N.M. 414, 564 P.2d 619, cert. denied 90 N.M. 636, 567 P.2d 485.

Okl.—Kirkland v. General Motors Corp., 521 P.2d 1353 (Okl.1974).

Pa.—McCown v. International Harvester Co., 463 Pa. 13, 342 A.2d 381 (1975).

Tex.—Henderson v. Ford Motor Co., 519 S.W.2d 87 (Tex.1975).

73. Restatement, Second, Torts § 402A.

74. *Conn.*—DeFelice v. Ford Motor Co., supra, n. 71.

Idaho—Rindlisbaker v. Wilson, 95 Idaho 752, 519 P.2d 421 (1974).

Ill.—Martinet v. International Harvester Co., 53 Ill.App.3d 213, 10 Ill.Dec. 901, 368 N.E.2d 496 (1977).

La.—Hastings v. Dis Tran Products, Inc., 389 F.Supp. 1352 (D.C.La.1975).

Mich.—Baker v. Rosemurgy, supra, n. 71.

Minn.—Magnuson v. Rupp Mfg., Inc., 285 Minn. 32, 171 N.W.2d 201 (1970).

Mo.—Collins v. B. F. Goodrich Co., 558 F.2d 908 (8th Cir. 1977).

Neb.—Waegli v. Caterpillar Tractor Co., 197 Neb. 824, 251 N.W.2d 370 (1977).

N.H.—Buttrick v. Arthur Lessard & Sons, Inc., 110 N.H. 36, 260 A.2d 111 (1969).

hold that all forms of contributory negligence are relevant in defense,[75] and some courts apply comparative negligence to strict liability cases.[76]

N.M.—Jasper v. Skyhook Corp., 89 N. M. 98, 547 P.2d 1140 (1976), rev'd on other grounds 90 N.M. 143, 560 P.2d 934.

Okl.—Kirkland v. General Motors Corp., supra, n. 71.

Pa.—Ferraro v. Ford Motor Co., 423 Pa. 324, 223 A.2d 746 (1966).

S.D.—Poches v. J. J. Newberry Co., 549 F.2d 1166 (8th Cir. 1977).

Tex.—Borel v. Fiberboard Paper Products Corp., 493 F.2d 1076 (5th Cir. 1974), cert. denied 419 U.S. 869, 95 S.Ct. 127, 42 L.Ed.2d 107.

See Note, Plaintiff Misconduct As A Defense in Products Liability (1975) 25 Drake L.Rev. 189; Twerski, Old Wine in a New Flask—Restructuring Assumption of Risk in Products Liability Area, (1974) 60 Iowa L.Rev. 1; Note, Awareness of Condition Without Appreciation of Its Hazard Precludes Recovery Under Theory of Strict Products Liability (1972) 55 Minn.L.Rev. 1051; Wade, on the Nature of Strict Tort Liability For Products (1973) 44 Miss.L.J.; On the distinction between Contributory Negligence and Assumption of Risk, see infra, § 35.2, Assumption of Risk.

75. *Mont.*—Oltz v. Toyota Motor Sales, U. S. A., Inc., 166 Mont. 217, 531 P.2d 1341 (1975).

N.H.—Stevens v. Kanematsu-Gosho Co., 494 F.2d 367 (1st Cir. 1974).

N.Y.—Bass v. Firestone Tire & Rubber Co., 497 F.2d 1223 (2d Cir. 1974).

76. See, Chapter 10, Comparative Negligence, supra.

Alaska—Butaud v. Suburban Marine & Sporting Goods, 555 P.2d 42 (Alaska 1976).

Cal.—Daly v. General Motors Corp., 20 Cal.3d 725, 144 Cal.Rptr. 380, 575 P. 2d 1162 (1978).

Fla.—West v. Caterpiller Tractor Co., 336 So.2d 80 (Fla.1976), conformed to 547 F.2d 885 (5th Cir.).

Miss.—Edwards v. Sears, Roebuck & Co., 512 F.2d 276 (5th Cir. 1975).

Wis.—Dippel v. Sciano, 37 Wis.2d 443, 155 N.W.2d 55 (1967).

See Schwartz, Strict Liability and Comparative Negligence (1974) 42 Tenn. L.Rev. 171.

See also Brewster, Comparative Negligence in Strict Liability Cases (1976) 42 Journal of Air Law and Commerce 107.

§§ 11.6–12.0 are reserved for supplementary material.

CHAPTER 12

LAST CLEAR CHANCE

Table of Sections

Sec.
12.1 General Considerations.
12.2 Issues—Knowledge, Opportunity, Antecedent Negligence.
12.3 Relation to Other Doctrines.

Library References:
C.J.S. Negligence § 136(2).
West's Key No. Digests, Negligence ⊙83.1.
Prosser, Law of Torts (4th ed. 1971), pp. 427–433.
Blashfield, Automobile Law & Practice, § 65.1 et seq., 66.3.

§ 12.1 General Considerations

Prior to the now general acceptance of comparative negligence, an increasing dissatisfaction with the doctrine of contributory negligence was prevalent. In the legislature this manifested itself through the adoption of comparative negligence statutes. In the courts it became apparent with an increasing and broader acceptance of the doctrine of the last clear chance.[1] This broader use of this humanitarian doctrine allowed the attorney for a plaintiff to predicate liability in cases in which he formerly might have felt that his client was barred by contributory negligence.

Thus "the last clear chance" while in the first analysis may seem more desperation than "chance" and more confused than "clear," is another strong crutch for the "crippled case," and an everpresent hazard for the defendant, and should always be thoroughly considered. Its extensions are more inclusive in the several jurisdictions than most trial counsel realize, and it has, at its outset, a factual basis of frankness. Tactically, plaintiff admits his dereliction and can

---

1. The cases are multitudinous. See: Annotations, 81 A.L.R.2d 460, 3 A.L.R.3d 180, 20 A.L.R.3d 124, 287, 34 A.L.R.3d 570.

   See also Comment, 27 La.L.Rev. 269 (1967); Comment, 28 Albany L.Rev. 69 (1964); Note, 9 St. Louis U.L.J. 285 (1964); Comment, 48 Iowa L.Rev. 743 (1963); Gozansky, Last Clear Chance Doctrine in Florida, 17 U.Miami L.Rev. 582 (1963); Mortensen, Arizona's Last Clear Chance Doctrine, 4 Ariz.L.Rev. 72 (1962); Hale, Last Clear Chance—Trend in California, 13 Hastings L.J. 141 (1961); Note, 29 U.Kan.City L.Rev. 104 (1961); Note, 6 S.D.L.Rev. 96 (1961); Note, 10 Western Res.L.Rev. 286 (1959); Note, 56 Mich.L.Rev. 1358; Note, 36 N.C.L.Rev. 545 (1958).

begin immediately to concentrate upon the defendant's fault, since a consideration of plaintiff's contributory negligence at once disappears. It is a humanitarian doctrine lending itself to strong impelling argument.[2]

After the turn of the nineteenth century, defendant's liability for his negligent conduct was subjected to the qualification that plaintiff's contributory negligence acted as a bar to his recovery.[3] In order to avoid this harsh result of no recovery, especially when plaintiff was but slightly negligent compared to a high degree of negligence of defendant, the doctrine of the Last Clear Chance was developed.[4] The first rationalization of the rule,[5] and the one most often reiterated to this day,[6] is that the plaintiff's negligence was not the proxi-

---

2. Esrey v. Southern Pac. Co., 103 Cal. 541, 37 P. 500 (1894) ("The party who last has a clear opportunity of avoiding the accident, notwithstanding the negligence of his opponent, is considered solely responsible").

Plaintiff in trial tactics may allow an aggressive defendant to prove plaintiff's case by showing such complete and aggressive contributory negligence that defendant conversely must have violated the Last Clear Chance in not exercising ordinary care by failing to recognize plaintiff's so obvious danger-negligence. This procedure may be followed even on deposition before trial.

See Girdner v. Union Oil Co., 216 Cal. 197, 13 P.2d 915 (1932) ("The real issue in the cases of the character here involved is not whose negligence came first or last, but whose negligence, however it came, was the proximate cause of the injury").

In any event, the question as to Last Clear Chance is ordinarily for the jury: see McCormick v. Gilbertsen, 41 Wash.2d 495, 250 P.2d 546 (1952).

3. Butterfield v. Forrester, 11 East 60 (1809).

4. The doctrine is generally said to have originated in the English case of Davies v. Mann, 10 Mees & W. 546 (1842) (Defendant negligently drove into plaintiff's ass fettered on the highway. In allowing recovery the court stated: "As the defendant might, by proper care, have avoided injuring the animal, and did not, he is liable for the consequences of his negligence, though the animal may have been improperly there.").

For a sampling of some of the discussion stirred up by the doctrine see Schoefield, Davis v. Mann, (1809) 3 Harv.L.Rev. 263; Bohlen, Contributory Negligence (1908) 21 Harv.L.Rev. 233; Smith, Last Clear Chance (1916) 82 Cent.L.J. 425; Lowndes, Contributory Negligence (1934) 22 Georgetown L.J. 674; James, Last Clear Chance—A Transitional Doctrine (1938) 47 Yale L.J. 704; MacIntyre, Rationale of Last Clear Chance (1940) 53 Harv.L.Rev. 1225; "Last Clear Chance was developed and is used by the courts to avoid the rule of contributory negligence, the harshest doctrine known to the common law of the nineteenth century." Green, Illinois Negligence Law (1944) 39 Ill. L.Rev. 36.

See, Chapter 11, Contributory Negligence, supra.

5. Dowell v. General Steam Co., 5 El. & Bl. 195 (1855); Tuff v. Warman, 2 C.B.N.S. 740, 5 C.B.N.S. 573, 27 L.J. CP 263 (1857).

6. "It follows that the decisive question, in each case where a plaintiff

mate cause of the harm. Other courts conclude that the doctrine is in reality a rule of comparative negligence imposing liability on the defendant because of his higher degree of fault.[7] It has also been stated that the doctrine merely bridges the transition from contributory

injured is found to have been at fault in the premises from his failure to exercise the required degree of care, resolves itself into one as to whether that fault was or was not a proximate cause of the injury, and that the answer to that question will infallibly determine whether or not it will bar a recovery." Nehring v. Connecticut Co., 86 Conn. 109, 84 A. 301, 304 (1912).

"A remote fault in one party does not of course dispense with care in the other. It may even make it more necessary and important, if thereby a calamitous injury can be avoided, or an unavoidable calamity essentially mitigated. Common justice and common humanity, to say nothing of law, demand this; and it is no answer for the neglect of it to say that the complainant was first in the wrong, since inattention and accidents are, to a greater or less extent, incident to human affairs." Isbell v. New York & N. H. R. Co., 27 Conn. 393, 71 Am. Dec. 78 (1858).

"The doctrine of 'Last Clear Chance' is a special application of the doctrine of proximate cause. It can make no difference, except from the standpoint of precise historical appropriation of legal terminology, whether it is applied in favor of a plaintiff to allow a recovery, or in favor of a defendant, to defeat recovery." Island Exp. v. Frederick, 35 Del. 569, 171 A. 181 (1934)."

"The doctrine of Last Clear Chance is but the doctrine of proximate cause under another name." Louisville and N. R. Co. v. Patterson, 77 Ga.App. 406, 49 S.E.2d 218 (1948).

Garibaldi v. Borchers Bros., 48 Cal.2d 283, 309 P.2d 23 (1957) ("When all the essential elements for the application of the Last Clear Chance are present, then the negligence of the defendant, who failed to exercise the Last Clear Chance to avoid the accident, is deemed in law to be the sole proximate cause of the accident"): Doran v. City and County of San Francisco, 44 Cal.2d 477, 283 P.2d 1 (1955) (Plaintiff struck by defendant's trolley when he walked across its path—held as matter of law that Last Clear Chance not applicable since plaintiff not "totally unaware" of danger so that it could not be said that plaintiff's negligence was "remote in causation," there being no "appreciable interval after the time that plaintiff has reached a state of helplessness as to enable defendant to gain an actual knowledge of plaintiff's state of helplessness, and to have a Last Clear Chance to avoid the accident,"—see dissent of Justice Carter disapproving). Sparks v. Redinger, 44 Cal.2d 121, 279 P.2d 971 (1955).

For criticism of the proximate cause rationale, see Prosser, The Law of Torts (4th ed. 1971) p. 427.

Goldsmith v. Martin Marietta Corp., 211 F.Supp. 91 (D.C.Md.1962) (The principle of Last Clear Chance is simply a rule governing establishment of proximate cause).

7. Moreno v. Los Angeles Transfer Co., 44 Cal.App. 551, 186 P. 800 (1920); Wilson v. Southern Traction Co., 111 Tex. 361, 234 S.W. 663 (1921).

See also St. Louis Southwestern R. R. Co. v. Simpson, 184 Ark. 633, 43 S.W.2d 251 (1931), rev'd 286 U.S. 346, 52 S.Ct. 520, 76 L.Ed. 1152; Stanley v. Chicago R. I. & Pac. R. Co., 113 Neb. 280, 202 N.W. 864 (1925); Seiffert v. Hines, 108 Nev. 62, 187 N.W. 108 (1922).

negligence to a rule of apportioning damages.[8] These latter views lose sight of the essential fact that the operative effect of the doctrine is "all-or-nothing" and not apportionment of damages between plaintiff and defendant.[9] In the last analysis, last clear chance operates simply to protect plaintiff in certain situations from the harsh results of the contributory negligence rule.[10]

In its ordinary application, the doctrine presupposes negligence on the part of the plaintiff which would constitute contributory negligence barring a recovery were it not for the application of the doctrine.[11] There has been a variety of judicial formulation of the doctrine with the result that there is much confusion in its application.[12] From the plethora of factual situations involved, the following categories have emerged: (1) *Discovered peril or conscious Last Clear Chance.* In this category are those cases where the defendant has actually discovered the peril and the plaintiff, because of his prior negligence, is unable to escape. Illustrative of this is the case of *Chadwick v. City of New York.*[13] Plaintiff's intestate, a ten year old boy, and his twelve year old brother, hitched a ride on de-

8. James, Last Clear Chance—A Transitional Doctrine (1938) 47 Yale L.J. 704; MacIntyre, Rationale of Last Clear Chance (1940) 53 Harv.L.Rev. 1225.

9. Prosser, The Law of Torts (4th ed. 1971) p. 428 ("[E]xcept in a few cases where a part of the plaintiff's damages have occurred before the 'Last Clear Chance,' it merely transfers from the plaintiff to the defendant an entire loss due to the fault of both").

10. Fleming v. Ayoub, 206 F.Supp. 860 (D.C.D.C.1962), aff'd 315 F.2d 47 (4th Cir.) ("The authorities clearly demonstrate that the purpose of the doctrine of the Last Clear Chance is to avoid the defense of contributory negligence. It has no other function."); Thomas v. Bruton, 270 F. Supp. 33 (D.C.S.C.1967), aff'd 390 F. 2d 658 (4th Cir.) ("It is an exception or a qualification or modification to the doctrine of contributory negligence which presupposes some negligence on the part of the defendant").

11. Lund v. Pacific Elec. Ry. Co., 25 Cal.2d 287, 153 P.2d 705 (1944); Campion v. Eakle, 79 Colo. 320, 246 P. 280, 47 A.L.R. 289 (1926); Vignone v. Pierce & Norton Co., 130 Conn. 309, 33 A.2d 427 (1943); Theurer v. Holland Furnace Co., 124 F.2d 494 (10th Cir. 1941); Gibbs v. Norfolk Southern Ry. Co., 358 F.Supp. 239 (D.C.N.C.1972), aff'd 474 F.2d 1341 (4th Cir.); Stephens v. Balkamp, Inc., 70 F.R.D. 49 (D.C.Tenn.1975); Benson v. United States, 235 F.Supp. 495 (D. C.Alaska 1964); Haydel v. American Emp. Ins. Co., 339 F.2d 201 (5th Cir. 1964).

12. Prosser, The Law of Torts (4th ed. 1971) pp. 428–429 ("It is quite literally true that there are as many variant forms and applications of this doctrine as there are jurisdictions which apply it").

13. 301 N.Y. 176, 93 N.E.2d 625 (1950); 26 N.Y.L.Rev. 224, 36 Cornell L.Q. 394, 1 Buffalo L.Rev. 56.

fendant's truck. The boys crouched on a step fastened to the right front fender, out of the driver's sight. As the truck turned onto a bumpy road, decedent was bounced from his perch, but clung to a handhold with his feet dragging. Finally, he lost his grip and fell under the rear wheel. After the fall the driver continued on for two hundred feet. Decedent's brother testified that when decedent slipped, he, the brother, began banging on the cab window and screamed, "Stop!" The defendant's driver testified that he saw a little hand bang and "so I figured something is in danger, must be, to be there . . . I stopped right then." A judgment dismissing the complaint was reversed and a new trial granted. The court held that it was for the jury to determine if the driver had in fact become actually aware of the danger, and whether he then ignored the warning in an unreasonable manner when he still had a last clear chance to avoid the accident.[14] The California District Court [15] reversed a trial court for failure to give a last clear chance instruction, when a bus pulled away from the intoxicated plaintiff, who was leaning on the vehicle, allowing him to fall.

(2) *Inattentive Plaintiff.* A variant of the Discovered Peril situation is where the facts show that although the danger has actually been discovered by the defendant, the plaintiff is physically able to escape, but inattentive and unaware of this peril. The weight of authority supports the application of last clear chance to this category even though the plaintiff was "guilty of continuing and concurring negligence in the sense of his continued obliviousness of his own danger which it was his duty to discover and realize." [16] Many courts ap-

14. New York has long applied this view of Last Clear Chance. In Clarke v. City of New York, 50 N.Y. S.2d 333 (1944), aff'd 269 App.Div. 821, 56 N.Y.S.2d 413, app. denied 269 App.Div. 928, 57 N.Y.S.2d 843, a verdict for plaintiff was set aside because the "credible evidence indisputably indicates that the motorman did not have knowledge of the deceased's peril in time to avert the accident."

See also Sawyer v. United States, 297 F.Supp. 324 (D.C.N.Y.1969), aff'd 436 F.2d 640 (2d Cir.); Wright v. Standard Oil Co., Inc., 470 F.2d 1280 (5th Cir. 1972), cert. denied, 412 U.S. 938, 93 S.Ct. 2772, 37 L.Ed.2d 398; Texas & N. O. R. Co. v. Cadoree, 333 F.2d 682 (5th Cir. 1964).

15. Simmer v. City and County of San Francisco, 116 Cal.App.2d 724, 254 P. 2d 185 (1953) ("Thus, the jury could have believed that the operator saw plaintiff, who he believed was drunk, staggering alongside the bus holding on with both hands, and yet started up the bus").

16. Hall v. Monongahela West Pennsylvania Public Serv. Co., 128 W.Va. 547, 37 S.E.2d 471 (1946) (Decedent killed by defendant's automobile at a point on defendant's tracks not a public crossing); McCormick v. Gilbertson, 41 Wash.2d 495, 250 P.2d 546, 11 NACCA L.J. 200 (1952) (Held doctrine applicable even if plaintiff could escape, and his negligence continues up to the time of the accident,

ply the theory that defendant's actual knowledge interrupts the chain of causation and creates a new duty on defendant's part.[17]

(3) *Inability to Escape.* Here we find those situations where the plaintiff is physically unable to escape and the defendant, although not having actually discovered the danger, should have.

In most jurisdictions, the doctrine will operate to establish defendant's liability where by exercise of due care he ought to have been aware of plaintiff's peril.[18] The Restatement of Torts accepts

if defendant actually sees the peril, and has a clear chance to save him).

Cal.—Hardin v. Key System Transit Lines, 134 Cal.App.2d 677, 286 P.2d 373 (1955) (Plaintiff drove toward railraod crossing, oblivious to warning signals; defendant's motorman observed plaintiff's approach, but assumed she would stop in time. When he realized she was not going to stop, he applied the emergency brake, but not in time to prevent collision—instruction proper that if circumstances indicate a reasonable chance that plaintiff is inattentive and will not discover his peril, defendant must make a reasonable effort to avoid injuring him); Wylie v. Vellis, 132 Cal.App.2d 854, 283 P.2d 327 (1955) (Plaintiff's and defendant's automobiles approached intersection at same time and speed; when defendant noticed the dazed look on plaintiff's face, he had 4 seconds of reaction time in which to sound his horn or slow down or swerve—where plaintiff is in a dangerous position because of his inattentiveness and defendant knows of plaintiff's situation and has reason to realize plaintiff's peril in time to avoid the accident by use of care, the doctrine is applicable).

La.—Greyhound Corp. v. Dewey, 240 F.2d 899 (5th Cir. 1957) (Decedent while walking on right shoulder of highway in violation of law, struck by rear-view mirror of bus).

Mont.—Feeley v. Northern Pac. Ry. Co., 230 F.2d 316 (9th Cir. 1956).

N.M.—Merrill v. Stringer, 58 N.M. 372, 271 P.2d 405 (1954) (Plaintiff was struck by automobile while running across the street into the path of the car—Last Clear Chance may apply, irrespective of plaintiff's continuing negligence, if defendant after knowing plaintiff's danger and having reason to suppose that he may not save himself, had a Last Clear Chance to avoid the accident by exercise of ordinary care but failed to do so).

Va.—Greear v. Noland Co., Inc., 197 Va. 233, 89 S.E.2d 49 (1955) (Defendant, as he approached in his truck, saw plaintiff standing on shoulder of the road unaware of its approach, and negligently failed to stop, striking plaintiff—error not to instruct jury on doctrine of Last Clear Chance where plaintiff, though not physically helpless, has negligently placed himself in a position of peril and through inattentiveness is oblivious of his danger, and defendant discovers plaintiff's situation and realizes or should realize his danger in time to avoid striking him by the use of care).

17. Locke v. Puget Sound Int'l R. & Power Co., 100 Wash. 432, 171 P. 242 (1918).

18. Capital Transit Co. v. Garcia, 194 F.2d 162, 10 NACCA L.J. 235 (D.C. Cir. 1952) (Streetcar conductor had duty to notice negligent pedestrian, oblivious to danger); Jones v. Atlanta-Charlotte Air Line Ry. Co., 218 S. C. 537, 63 S.E.2d 476, 26 A.L.R.2d 297 (1951) (Helpless intoxicated man on railroad tracks, railroad negligently failed to keep reasonable lookout.

"But one insensible from voluntary intoxication is after all not immediately substantially different from one unconscious because of innocent accident or illness. In both cases helpless human life is at stake. No doubt this consideration has moved this court and others to consistently hold that intoxication to the extent of helplessness interrupts the negligence of the victim so that subsequent negligence of a defendant brings into play the rule of Last Clear Chance—converts plaintiff's prior negligence into the remote, rather than the proximate, cause of the injury.").

See Annotation, Intoxication of Injured or Killed Persons as Affecting Liability Under Doctrine of Last Clear Chance, 26 A.L.R.2d 308.

Ariz—Hirsh v. Manley, 81 Ariz. 94, 300 P.2d 588 (1956) (Plaintiff and defendant drove their automobiles toward the intersection at right angles; plaintiff saw defendant but failed to apply his brakes in time; defendant, negligently inattentive, failed to see plaintiff and a collision resulted—"this doctrine permits a plaintiff to recover, even though negligent, if he finds himself in a situation where he is unable to avoid the accident, and the defendant knows plaintiff's plight or would have discovered it if he had exercised proper vigilance toward plaintiff, thereafter fails to take the necessary steps to avoid harming the plaintiff").

Colo.—Union Pac. R. Co. v. Ward, 230 F.2d 287 (10th Cir. 1956) (Tractor trailer stalled on railroad track).

Del.—Lord v. Poore, 9 Terry 595, 108 A.2d 366 (1954) (Plaintiff standing to rear of automobile parked without lights and unaware of approach of defendant's vehicle on wrong side of road where defendant could have seen plaintiff).

Fla.—Springer v. Morris, 74 So.2d 781 (Fla.1954) (Plaintiff, while crossing the street at night, was struck by defendant's automobile. Evidence that both parties were inattentive. Held, defendant had the last clear chance to avoid the accident, even though he did not discover the danger to plaintiff, if he should have discovered it in time).

Ia.—Lauman v. Dearmin, 246 Iowa 697, 69 N.W.2d 49 (1953) (Plaintiff's automobile skidded on icy road into path of defendant's car).

Kan.—Becker v. Tasker, 177 Kan. 452, 280 P.2d 581 (1955) (Sufficiency of pleading discussed).

Mont.—Sorrells v. Ryan, 129 Mont. 29, 281 P.2d 1028 (1955) (Plaintiff negligently crossing the street inattentive to traffic struck by defendant's car—applies not only where defendant actually saw plaintiff in a position of peril, but also where in the exercise of reasonable care he could have discovered plaintiff in his perilous position in time to avoid the injury).

N.Y.—Kumkumian v. City of New York, 305 N.Y. 167, 111 N.E.2d 865 (1953) (Where lack of knowledge amounted to "willful indifference").

S.C.—Bruin v. Tribble, 238 F.2d 12 (4th Cir. 1956) (Plaintiff pedestrian failed to look to the right whence defendant's truck came as he crossed the street—plaintiff and defendant apparently failed to see each other until the moment of impact although the truck was well lighted. A negligent plaintiff may recover if the defendant has the Last Clear Chance to avoid the accident by exercise of due care if he realizes or should have realized, that the plaintiff is inattentive or unaware of the danger).

Utah—Beckstrom v. Williams, 3 Utah 2d 210, 282 P.2d 309 (1955) (Plaintiff drove his tractor out of a driveway and stopped it when it was several feet onto the highway when defendant, truck driver, approaching on the highway, failed to stop in time to avoid a collision—error to refuse instruction on last clear chance since the jury could reasonably find that after plaintiff was in the lane of traf-

this view.[19] Nevertheless, some jurisdictions still hold that Last Clear Chance will not operate without actual knowledge on defendant's part.[20]

(4) *Unconscious Last Clear Chance.* Where the plaintiff is physically able to escape but is oblivious to his peril, and defendant has no actual knowledge, the majority rule is that the doctrine does not apply, on the theory that plaintiff's and defendant's negligence were co-extensive and actively continued until the moment of injury.[21]

fic defendant should have both braked and turned out); Fielder v. Service Cab Co., 122 W.Va. 522, 11 S.E.2d 115 (1940) (Boy riding bicycle down steep hill out of control struck by taxicab, held doctrine of last clear chance applied, "[W]here a plaintiff cannot escape from his position of peril, it is immaterial whether the defendant had actual knowledge of plaintiff's position and was under a duty to realize the peril, or by the exercise of reasonable care could have seen and realized plaintiff's peril.").

19. Restatement, Second, Torts §§ 479, 480.

20. Floersch v. Merchants Motor Freight, Inc., 248 F.2d 704 (8th Cir. 1957) (Actual knowledge of plaintiff's presence, but only constructive knowledge of plaintiff's peril, required under Iowa law); Pflugh v. United States, 138 F.Supp. 470 (D.C. Pa.1956) (Defendant must have knowledge both of plaintiff's presence and his peril, under Ohio law).

21. Lee v. Cotten Bros. Co., 1 Wash. App. 202, 460 P.2d 694 (1969) (". . . [I]f you simply have a negligent plaintiff and a defendant who is negligent because he fails to see the negligent plaintiff, one is guilty of no more than the other and the contributory negligence of the plaintiff should not be excused").

Cal.—Brandelius v. City and County of San Francisco, 47 Cal.2d 729, 306 P.2d 432 (1957) (Cable car passenger after alighting killed by another car —new trial granted after plaintiff's verdict because instructions failed to clearly inform jury that "actual knowledge of plaintiff's position of danger is required").

Conn.—Porto v. Consolidated Motor Lines, Inc., 117 Conn. 681, 169 A. 48 (1933).

Ind.—Woodrow v. Woodrow, 131 Ind. App. 523, 172 N.E.2d 883 (1961).

Ky.—Ratliff v. Mayo, 290 S.W.2d 479 (Ky.1956) (Last clear chance doctrine not applicable where there is no evidence that defendant became aware of plaintiff's inattentiveness in sufficient time to avert the accident).

La.—McCallum v. Adkerson, 126 So.2d 835 (La.App.1961).

Mont.—Feely v. Northern Pac. Ry. Co., 230 F.2d 316 (9th Cir. 1956).

Wyo.—Davies v. Dugan, 365 P.2d 198 (Wyo.1961) (Doctrine not available where plaintiff negligently stopped in heavy traffic and defendant, not keeping proper lookout, crashed into him).

Contra:

D.C.—Rankin v. Shayne Bros., Inc., 234 F.2d 35 (D.C.Cir. 1956) ("[N]otwithstanding plaintiff's contributory negligence defendant may be found liable if the jury should find that plaintiff was in a position of peril of which he was oblivious, that defendant was aware, or had he exercised reasonable care would have been aware, of plaintiff's peril and obliviousness thereof, and that thereafter defendant by the exercise of reasonable care could have avoided the accident").

In a liberal extension the Missouri courts have applied last clear chance in this situation as a "humanitarian doctrine." [22] Illustrative is the following fact situation: two automobiles approach each other at the same rate of speed with each driver negligently inattentive and unaware of the imminent collision and probable personal injury to both. Each driver could avoid the collision by timely action, but neither does and both are injured in the ensuing collision. At common law both would be barred as each is guilty of contributory negligence in failing to look out for the other vehicle. However, in Missouri under the true humanitarian case, an injured party, whose peril is caused by his own negligent inattentiveness can recover against another who was also negligently inattentive, and not aware of the injured party's peril.[23] Under this doctrine each party can make a case for recovery.

(5) *Last Clear Chance available to defendant.* Only a few courts have declared that the Last Clear Chance doctrine is a two-edged sword and permitted its use by defendant to establish, as proximate cause, that plaintiff had the last chance to avoid the accident.[24]

22. Banks v. Morris & Co., 302 Mo. 254, 257 S.W. 482 (1924) ("Under this doctrine 'the position of peril' is one of the basic facts of liability, it might be denominated the chief one. It is of no consequence what brings about or continues the situation of peril. It may be through the obliviousness of the one in peril, or through his inability to extricate himself from his environment, or through his efforts to rescue another, or through his sheer hardihood or recklessness. But regardless of what occasions his peril, the law out of its extreme regard for human life makes it the duty of another who sees him in peril to exercise ordinary care to prevent injury or death."); Noland v. Pastor, 191 F.2d 1009 (8th Cir. 1951) (At 1:15 o'clock in the morning, a 63 year old pedestrian left a streetcar at an intersection, looked in both directions, saw no automobile and proceeded without looking again. When he came to the center of the street he was struck by defendant's car. The motorist admitted he saw the plaintiff only when he was so close to him that there was no time to swerve the car or to sound the horn. On appeal for a directed verdict for the defendant, it was held that the cause should be submitted to a jury to decide whether the defendant exercised the highest degree of care under the Missouri "humanitarian doctrine." As the court points out, citing Clifford v. Pitcairn, 345 Mo. 60, 131 S.W.2d 508 (1939), any question of the plaintiff's contributory negligence is irrelevant. This doctrine which has evolved in Missouri, in order to stress the importance of safety, is applicable if the defendant operates a dangerous machine, such as a railroad car or automobile).

23. Becker, The Supreme Court and Missouri Humanitarian Doctrine in the Years 1950–51, 17 Mo.L.Rev. 32, 34.

24. Prosser, The Law of Torts (4th ed. 1971) p. 429 ("A few courts, with something resembling billiard-parlor reverse English, have even purported to recognize a 'last clear chance' doctrine in favor of the defendant, to bar plaintiff's recovery; but since this

Most courts view the doctrine as an exception to the contributory negligence rule, and limit its use to plaintiff for that purpose.[25] The doctrine cannot be invoked as between joint defendants,[26] or by a defendant against a third party.[27]

> comes out at exactly the same place as the defense of contributory negligence without the doctrine at all, and is calculated only to bewilder the jury with incomprehensible instructions, most courts have rejected any such idea").
>
> Doctrine available to defendant: Id.—Durrington v. Crooker, 78 Idaho 539, 307 P.2d 227 (1957) (Defendant motorist on county road entered intersection with 4-lane through highway on which plaintiff motorist was traveling and failed to grant the right-of-way required by statute—whether plaintiff had the last clear chance an issue for jury).
>
> *La.*—Chitwood v. King, 155 So. 466 (La.App.1934) (Defendant backed into highway, forcing plaintiff into ditch. Defendant invoked Last Clear Chance against plaintiff. Verdict for defendant sustained on appeal.); Hanover Fire Ins. Co. v. Sides, 320 F.2d 437 (5th Cir. 1963) (Rear-end auto collision: requested Last Clear Chance instruction which did not make doctrine applicable to both parties properly refused).
>
> *Va.*—Virginia Elec. & Power Co. v. Vellines, 162 Va. 671, 175 S.E. 35 (1934) ("This doctrine is not intended to protect the interest of any special class of litigants. Plaintiffs and defendants each may invoke it. Their rights and obligations are the same."); Friedman v. Morris, 209 F.2d 886 (4th Cir. 1954) (Left-turn auto collision: refusal to grant Last Clear Chance instruction for defendant reversible error).
>
> **25.** Doctrine not available to defendant:
>
> *Ariz.*—Alires v. Southern Pac. Co., 93 Ariz. 97, 378 P.2d 913 (1963) (Railroad-automobile collision: instruction which in effect invoked Last Clear Chance to relieve defendants of their negligence was error).
>
> *Colo.*—DeWeese v. United States, 419 F.Supp. 147 (D.C.Colo.1974) (Air crash: "Of course, Last Clear Chance applies only when there is negligence on plaintiff's part, because it is a humanitarian doctrine to relieve negligent plaintiffs. It is not an escape hatch for a negligent defendant.").
>
> *Conn.*—Corey v. Phillips, 126 Conn. 246, 10 A.2d 370 (1939) (Purpose of doctrine limited to eliminating plaintiff's antecedent negligence as bar to recovery).
>
> *Ky.*—Smith v. Wright, 512 S.W.2d 943 (Ky.1974) ("The Last Clear Chance Doctrine is designed to relieve a plaintiff from the harsh effects of the contributory negligence rule. By definition, the Last Clear Chance Doctrine is applicable only to the negligent plaintiff.").
>
> *N.Y.*—Schlimmeyer v. Yurkiw, 50 A.D. 2d 616, 374 N.Y.S.2d 427 (1975) (Doctrine may not be applied for defendants).
>
> *Or.*—Ballard v. Rickabaugh Orchards, Inc., 259 Or. 200, 485 P.2d 1080 (1971) (Doctrine cannot be invoked by defendant—overruling prior holding).
>
> *S.D.*—Wolff v. Stenger, 59 S.D. 231, 239 S.W. 181 (1931) (Last Clear Chance applies only to overcome plaintiff's
>
> **26.** Greene v. Charlotte Chem. Laboratories, Inc., 254 N.C. 680, 120 S.E.2d 82 (1961) (One defendant may not resist recovery on ground that codefendant had Last Clear Chance); Atlantic Coast Line R. Co. v. Coxwell, 93 Ga.App. 159, 91 S.E.2d 135 (1955) (Doctrine cannot be extended into
>
> **27.** See note 27 on page 488.

§ 12.2 Issues—Knowledge, Opportunity, Antecedent Negligence

In the Discovered Peril of either type (1) or (2) above, defendant's *actual* knowledge is a necessary element. It is generally required that defendant appreciate the danger to plaintiff,[28] whether actually or constructively, and it is sometimes necessary to show defendant's awareness of plaintiff's inability to escape.[29] Circumstantial evidence, such as defendant's act of braking or signalling may suffice to infer defendant's actual knowledge.[30] Once there is actual knowledge of plaintiff's presence, constructive knowledge will ordinarily be sufficient as to the danger and inability of plaintiff to escape.[31] In situation (3) above, where defendant has no actual knowledge, but is charged with the duty of vigilance, the issue is whether plaintiff's peril was reasonably apparent.[32]

But did defendant have actual knowledge particularly when he testifies "no"? This is a jury question to determine if he is telling the truth.

field of joint tortfeasor as test of whether only one of them should be held liable by reason of having discovered the peril).

27. Southard v. Lira, 212 Kan. 763, 512 P.2d 409 (1973) (Doctrine cannot be invoked by defendant driver against another driver not sued by plaintiff. Defenses of proximate cause and concurring negligence are fully available to defendant.); Bond v. Rexroat, 339 F.Supp. 585 (D.C. Mont.1972). (Under Montana law, doctrine not available to defendant in automobile collision case where defendant seeks to join third-party defendant.).

28. Restatement, Second, Torts §§ 479, 480.

See also Casey v. Marshall, 64 Ariz. 232, 168 P.2d 240 (1946), reh. denied 64 Ariz. 260, 169 P.2d 84; Spencer v. Fondry, 122 Vt. 149, 167 A.2d 372 (1960).

29. Mast v. Illinois Central R. Co., 176 F.2d 157 (8th Cir. 1949).

30. Gilette v. City and County of San Francisco, 58 Cal.App.2d 434, 136 P. 2d 611 (1943) (Defendant testified that he was looking ahead, inferred that he must have seen plaintiff); Arnold v. Owens, 78 F.2d 495 (4th Cir. 1935) (Evidence at trial sufficient to support contention that driver must have seen plaintiff).

31. *Cal.*—Brandelius v. City and County of San Francisco, 47 Cal.2d 729, 306 P.2d 432 (1957).

Iowa—Menke v. Peterschmidt, 246 Iowa 722, 69 N.W.2d 65 (1955) ("It is actual knowledge of plaintiff's presence that is required . . . but this knowledge may be inferred from circumstantial evidence, in spite of denial by the defendant . . . . Our cases make it clear there must be actual knowledge of plaintiff's presence . . . it is not necessary to show actual knowledge of the danger, but only that it should have been realized in the exercise of reasonable care).

32. Carter v. Snyder, 329 S.W.2d 382, 81 A.L.R.2d 452 (Ky.1959) (Peril of plaintiff helping defendant bulldozer operator extricate stuck blade was not reasonably obvious).

LAST CLEAR CHANCE § 12.2

The Last Clear Chance doctrine is predicated upon defendant's opportunity to avoid the peril, and thus plaintiff must show that the time interval between plaintiff's discovery, or his constructive discovery, and the injury was sufficient to allow him to act effectively to avert the danger.[33] The last chance must be a clear one, not merely a possibility.[34] It has been declared that "the doctrine implies thought,

---

33. *D.C.*—Dean v. Century Motors, 154 F.2d 201 (D.C.Cir. 1946) ("The doctrine presupposes a perilous situation created or existing through the negligence of both the plaintiff and the defendant but assumes that there was a time after such negligence had occurred when the defendant could, and the plaintiff could not, by use of means available, avoid the accident. It is not applicable if the emergency is so sudden that there is no time to avoid the collision, for the defendant is not required to act instantaneously."); Law v. Virginia Stage Lines, Inc., 444 F.2d 990 (D.C.Cir. 1971) (Bus collision with intoxicated plaintiff. j. n. o. v. for defendant sustained on grounds that emergency gave driver no Last Clear Chance).

Ohio—Lones v. Detroit, T. & I. R. Co., 398 F.2d 914 (6th Cir. 1968), cert. denied 393 U.S. 1063, 89 S.Ct. 714, 21 L.Ed.2d 705 ("Under Ohio law for the doctrine of Last Clear Chance to apply, it must be shown that the defendant became aware of the plaintiff's situation in time to avoid the accident by the exercise of ordinary care").

34. Frost v. Benedict, 331 F.2d 772 (D.C.Cir. 1964) (Automobile collision where plaintiff ran stop sign. Verdict for plaintiff reversed—error to give Last Clear Chance instruction where no clear chance to avoid accident.); Hatcher v. Gwaltney, 258 N.C. 527, 128 S.E.2d 862 (1963) (The doctrine contemplates a "clear" chance, not a "possible" chance to avoid the accident).

Ark.—Roland v. Terryland, Inc., 221 Ark. 837, 256 S.W.2d 315 (1953) (Where only a few seconds interval after discovery of peril).

Fla.—Ippolito v. Brenner, 72 So.2d 802 (Fla.1954).

Idaho—Laidlaw v. Barker, 78 Idaho 67, 297 P.2d 287 (1956) (Defendant driving automobile within lawful limit of 60 miles per hour saw decedent run onto highway oblivious of danger 7/10 of second before accident—doctrine not applicable where sudden emergency); Graham v. Milsap, 77 Idaho 179, 290 P.2d 744 (1955) (Head-on collision between plaintiff's automobile and defendant's truck proceeding at 35 miles per hour where plaintiff turned into defendant's lane less than 25 feet before collision—giving instruction on Last Clear Chance reversible error).

Iowa—Menke v. Peterschmidt, 246 Iowa 722, 69 N.W.2d 65 (1955) (Burden on plaintiff to prove sufficient time to exercise Last Clear Chance—intersectional collision where defendant had less than 2 seconds to act); Levendosky v. Chicago, Milwaukee, St. Paul & Pac. Ry. Co., 223 F.2d 395 (8th Cir. 1955) (Truck ran into backing locomotive at crossing).

Ky.—Ratliff v. Mayo, 290 S.W.2d 479 (Ky.1956); Johnson v. J. E. Morris' Adm'x, 282 S.W.2d 835 (Ky.1955) (Intoxicated man lying on highway where not seen until within 15 to 20 feet).

La.—Carlson v. Fidelity Mut. Ins. Co., 88 So.2d 461 (La.App.1956) (Plaintiff motorist, failing to look to right when entering intersection, collided with defendant's car—Last Clear Chance is not applicable unless defendant's superior knowledge of

§ 12.2 TORT LIABILITY AND DEFENSES Pt. 3

appreciation, mental direction and the lapse of sufficient time to act effectually on the impulse to avoid injury," [35] and defendant will not necessarily be held liable where his emergency action, by virtue of hindsight, does not appear to have been the wisest alternative. In *Landers v. Poole*, where a motorist attempted to stop on a slippery road to avoid hitting plaintiff, rather than driving into a ditch, Last Clear Chance was not available to overcome plaintiff's contributory negligence in being on the wrong side of the road.[36]

In jurisdictions where Last Clear Chance is not available if plaintiff's negligence has continued to the moment of injury, situation (2) above, it will be necessary to show a new act of negligence on defendant's part which supercedes plaintiff's negligence.[37] Where

plaintiff's peril is coupled with ability to avoid the accident).

Md.—Meldrum v. Kellam Distributing Co., 211 Md. 504, 128 A.2d 400 (1957).

Miss.—Illinois Central R. Co. v. Underwood, 235 F.2d 868 (5th Cir. 1956), cert. denied 352 U.S. 1001, 77 S.Ct. 557, 1 L.Ed.2d 546 (Railroad crossing accident).

N.C.—Shinault v. Creed, 244 N.C. 217, 92 S.E.2d 787 (1956).

Ohio—Hirsch v. Dairy Express, Inc., 221 F.2d 350 (6th Cir. 1955) (Pedestrian run over and killed by truck driver while asleep on highway).

S.C.—Farrell v. Weinard, 143 F.Supp. 939 (D.C.S.C.1956), aff'd 241 F.2d 562 (4th Cir.).

Tex.—Welch v. Ada Oil Co., 302 S.W. 2d 175 (Tex.Civ.App.1957), ref'd n. r. e., Thompson v. Creed, 284 S.W.2d 256 (Tex.Civ.App.1955), ref'd n. r. e. (Decedent observed on railroad trestle 400 feet away while train operated at speed of 59 to 75 mph).

Va.—Brown v. Vinson, 198 Va. 495, 95 S.E.2d 138 (1956).

Wash.—Stokes v. Johnstone, 47 Wash. 2d 323, 287 P.2d 472 (1955).

W.Va.—Higgs v. Watkins, 138 W.Va. 844, 78 S.E.2d 230 (1953) (Instruction as to issue should not be given unless there is sufficient evidence tending to show not only time for appreciation of the "dangerous situation" but also

time for "effective effort to relieve it").

35. Landeis v. Poole, 69 Wash.2d 515, 418 P.2d 717 (1966).

36. Id. n. 35 ("Where a defendant is confronted by an emergency created by the negligence of plaintiff, and he does what he can to avoid an injury, he is not liable under the doctrine of Last Clear Chance, even though his course of action is not the wisest choice, and though he is unsuccessful").

37. Benton v. Henry, 241 Md. 32, 215 A.2d 226 (1965) (Child riding on running board of ice cream truck injured when he fell off. Held, no Last Clear Chance when theory of driver's negligence was in failure to determine whether children were on the truck before driving away, and no new act of negligence charged. "To invoke the doctrine, the negligence of the defendant must be sequential to that of the plaintiff and not concurrent."); Perry v. McVey, 345 F.2d 897 (4th Cir. 1965) (Pedestrian struck while crossing highway at night. "Where the negligent conduct of the defendant merely continues unchanged up to the time of the accident, the doctrine of Last Clear Chance is inapplicable . . . After his own primary negligence and the decedent's contributory negligence, the defend-

defendant's negligence was antecedent to plaintiff's contributory negligence, application of the doctrine may similarly be denied, with the unjust result that defendant may be advantaged where his negligence operated over an extended time frame. Driving with defective brakes or at excessive speed or in an intoxicated condition for some time before an accident, for instance, would be insulated from the Last Clear Chance Doctrine by the antecedent negligence rule, on the theory that defendant's prior negligence has prevented any chance of averting the injury.[38] Although this logic is supported by the Restatement[39] and at least one eminent commentator,[40] it is not universally recognized in the courts.[41]

§ 12.3 Relation to other Doctrines

While the Last Clear Chance doctrine is often considered as a specific inquiry into proximate cause,[42] it is as often stated to be a

ant must have had a fresh opportunity to avert the consequences.").

38. Anderson v. Bingham & Garfield R. Co., 117 Utah 197, 214 P.2d 607 (1950) (Error to apply Last Clear Chance against railroad where trains equipped with faulty brakes, in violation of safety statutes, were unable to stop to avoid collision with automobile); Lee v. Cotten Bros., supra, n. 21 (Speeding log truck, swerved to avoid stopped vehicle, lost control and struck and killed decedent. Held, Last Clear Chance inapplicable in that driver did all he could to avoid the accident.).

39. Restatement, Second, Torts §§ 479, 480.

40. Prosser, The Law of Torts (4th ed. 1971) p. 432 ("No reason is evident in such a case for distinguishing between the antecedent negligence of the defendant and that of the plaintiff who has got himself into danger . . .").

41. Fairport, P. & E. R. Co. v. Meredith, 46 Ohio App. 457, 189 N.E. 10 (1933), aff'd 292 U.S. 589, 54 S.Ct. 826, 78 L.Ed. 1446 (1934).

42. See 57 Am.Jur.2d Negligence § 388, p. 800 ("Where the doctrine of Last Clear Chance is not viewed as an exception to the contributory negligence rule, the proper application of the doctrine does not permit an injured person to recover in spite of the negligence on his part, but it does permit a recovery notwithstanding a want of due care on the part of plaintiff where the facts are such that it may be said that the plaintiff's want of due care was not the proximate cause of the injury and that the defendant, in the exercise of due care, might have avoided the injury, and that his failure to exercise such care was the proximate cause of the injury").

Prosser, The Law of Torts (4th ed. 1971) p. 427 ("No very satisfactory reason for the rule ever has been suggested. The first explanation given, and the one which is still most often stated, is that if the defendant has the last clear opportunity to avoid the harm, the plaintiff's negligence is not a 'proximate cause' of the result"); Evansville Container Corp. v. McDonald, 132 F.2d 80 (6th Cir. 1943) ("The last clear chance rule is a phase of the question of proximate cause"); Goldsmith v. Martin Marietta Corp., 211 F.Supp. 91 (D.C.Md. 1962) (Under Pennsylvania law, ". . . the condition created by

rule of exception to the Contributory Negligence doctrine.[43] As such it is sometimes held that, with regard to the category of discovered peril, the doctrine of last clear chance amounts to nothing more than a finding that the defendant has been guilty of *wilful* or *wanton* misconduct.[44] However, such an explanation does not meet the situation where defendant's conduct involves only confusion, mistake or inadvertence. An example is the case of *Smith v. Connecticut Ry. & Lighting Co.*[45] In that case plaintiff cut in front of a streetcar moving so slowly that he had time to cross the tracks without being struck. This was negligence, of course. The conductor, although aware of plaintiff's action, because of his inexperience, became confused and, accelerating, caused the streetcar to strike the plaintiff. Plaintiff recovered. Yet this conduct could hardly be characterized as wanton or wilful.[46]

In jurisdictions that have adopted Comparative Negligence,[47] a plaintiff who can show a Last Clear Chance situation may be protected from a reduction in recovery if the jurisdiction interprets the issue as proximate cause, and finds plaintiff's negligence remote.[48] Most comparative negligence jurisdictions refuse the doctrine entirely, however, on the reasoning that the hardships of the contributory

the original tortfeasor is deemed to be but a circumstance of the accident and not its proximate cause . . ."); Eastern Brick & Tile Co. v. United States, 281 F.Supp. 216 (D.C.S.D.1968) (Doctrine not an exception to contributory negligence rule, but characterizes defendant's negligence "as the sole proximate cause of the injury, and the plaintiff's antecedent negligence as a condition or remote cause"); Swift v. Southern Ry. Co., 307 F.2d 315 (4th Cir. 1962) ("Under [the] doctrine, the antecedent negligence of one killed or injured is not treated as a proximate cause of the injury of the other party had an opportunity to avoid the injury and failed to exercise due care to do so").

43. 57 Am.Jur.2d Negligence § 389, p. 802. ("Some courts have expressly repudiated the proximate cause view of the last clear chance doctrine and regard it as a true exception to, rather than a logical qualification of,

the doctrine of contributory negligence, so that when it operates, it permits a recovery in spite of contributory negligence, or, as has been said, it operates to relieve the plaintiff of the consequences of his contributory negligence").

44. Esrey v. Southern P. Co., 103 Cal. 541, 37 P. 500 (1894); Central of Georgia R. Co. v. Thompson, 25 Ga. App. 715, 104 S.E. 515 (1920); Tempfer v. Joplin & P. R. Co., 89 Kan. 374, 131 P. 592 (1913).

45. 80 Conn. 268, 67 A. 888, 17 L.R.A. (N.S.) 707 (1907).

46. *Accord:* Clark v. Wilmington & W. R. Co., 109 N.C. 430, 14 S.E. 43, 14 L.R.A. 749 (1891).

47. See Chapter 10 Comparative Negligence, supra.

48. St. Louis S. R. Co. v. Simpson, 184 Ark. 633, 43 S.W.2d 251 (1931).

negligence rule are already avoided by adoption of comparative negligence itself.[49]

Many jurisdictions require plaintiff to *plead* Last Clear Chance specifically or by facts alleged, so as to give defendant timely notice.[50] The greater number of jurisdictions allow the doctrine to be raised at trial, under general pleadings of negligence, as argument to proximate causation or defense to contributory negligence.[51]

---

49. Loftin v. Nolan, 86 So.2d 161, 59 A.L.R.2d 1257 (Fla.1956) (Last Clear Chance instruction in comparative negligence jurisdiction is reversible error); Li v. Yellow Cab, 13 Cal.3d 804, 824, 119 Cal.Rptr. 858, 872, 532 P.2d 1226, 1240 (1975) ("[T]he better reasoned position seems to be that when true comparative negligence is adopted, the need for Last Clear Chance as a palliative of the hardships of the 'all-or-nothing' rule disappears and its retention results only a windfall to the plaintiff in direct contravention of the principle of liability in proportion to fault").

Admiralty

The Norman B. Beam, 252 F. 409 (7th Cir. 1918) (Last Clear Chance Doctrine not recognized in admiralty).

50. Barnes v. Wright, 123 Colo. 462, 231 P.2d 794 (1951) ("The underlying theory of the well-settled rule that the doctrine of Last Clear Chance must be affirmatively pleaded, is that it affords timely notice to the opposing Party . . ."); Albrecht v. Rausch Trucking Co., 193 N.W.2d 492 (Iowa 1972).

Factual Allegations

Pfeifer v. Johnson Motor Lines, Inc., 47 Del. (8 Terry) 191, 89 A.2d 154 (1952) (Plaintiff must allege facts which will bring him within the protection of the doctrine); Jackson v. Solomon, 228 S.C. 225, 89 S.E.2d 436 (1955) (Plaintiff seeking use of doctrine must allege facts regarding discovery of peril).

Raising Issue in Supplemental Pleadings

Exum v. Boyles, 272 N.C. 567, 158 S.E. 2d 845 (1968) (Plaintiff's factual allegations sufficient when raised in reply).

51. Meadow Gold Products Co. v. Wright, 278 F.2d 867 (D.C.Cir. 1960) (No error in giving instruction although issue not framed in pleadings); Gulf, M. & O. R. Co. v. Sims, 260 Ala. 258, 69 So.2d 449 (1953) (Pleadings charging general negligence suffice to support recovery after discovered peril).

Federal

Kline v. McCorkle, 330 F.Supp. 1089 (D.C.Va.1971) (Doctrine need not be specifically pleaded under FRCP § 8(a)).

---

§§ 12.4–13.0 are reserved for supplementary material.

CHAPTER 13

ASSUMPTION OF RISK

Table of Sections

Sec.
13.1 Origins.
13.2 Relation to Contributory Negligence.
13.3 Express Agreements.
13.4 Implied Acceptance of Risk.
13.5 Demise of the Defense.

Library References:
C.J.S. Negligence §§ 63(136), 119, 155, 156.
West's Key No. Digests, Negligence ☞66.
Prosser, Law of Torts (4th ed. 1971), pp. 439–457.
Blashfield, Automobile Law & Practice, § 64.1 et seq.

§ 13.1 Origins

The doctrine of Assumption of Risk, however analyzed, is in most of its aspects a defendant's doctrine designed to restrict liability and thus to reduce compensation to accident victims. It is a heritage of the extreme individualism of the early industrial revolution.[1] As stated in *Crichton v. Keir:*[2]

"This is a country of free labour. We have no such thing as travaux forces, still less have we anything approaching slavery.

---

1. "Assumption of risk was developed to insulate the employer as much as possible from bearing the 'human overhead' which is the inevitable part of the cost to someone of the doing of industrial business." Tiller v. Atlantic Coast Line Ry. Co., 318 U.S. 54, 63 S.Ct. 444, 87 L.Ed. 610, 143 A. L.R. 967 (1943), quoting from Tuttle v. Detroit, etc. R. Co., 122 U.S. 189, 196, 7 S.Ct. 1166, 1168, 30 L.Ed. 1114 (1887).

   "It will be apparent at once that the whole spirit of the defense and of the reasoning it employs, bears a strong imprint of *laissez faire* and its concomitant philosophy of individualism which has passed its prime." James, Assumption of Risk (1952) 61 Yale L.J. 141, 153. See James, Contributory Negligence (1953) 62 Yale L.J. 691, 698; Bohlen, Voluntary Assumption of Risk (1910) 20 Harv.L.Rev. 14, 91; Gow, The Defense of Volenti Non Fit Injuria (1949) 61 Jurid.Rev. 37. There is some indication that it was recognized by Aristotle. Child (1906) 18 Jurid.Rev. 73.

2. 1 Sess.Cas. (Scot.) (3rd series) 407, 41011 (1863).

... Now, if a servant, in the face of a manifest danger, chooses to go on with his work, he does so at his own risk, and not at the risk of his master."

But looking at it today, and being economically realistic, is it "free labour" when one has to choose between taking the job with its risks and supporting one's family or refusing it because of its dangers and starving?

§ 13.2 Relation to Contributory Negligence

The defenses of Assumption of Risk and Contributory Negligence are not synonymous, though in certain fact situations these defenses may overlap.[3] In contributory negligence, plaintiff is held to have contributed to the proximate cause of his injury by his own departure from the standard of due care.[4] In assumption of the risk, plaintiff has voluntarily chosen to encounter a known danger, and by this consent has relieved defendant of a duty to him.[5] Plaintiff's course of conduct may have been entirely reasonable.[6] Where the risk was unknown to plaintiff due to his failure to discover it by reasonable care, he is contributorily negligent.[7] Thus, it has been said

---

3. Landrum v. Roddy, 143 Neb. 934, 12 N.W.2d 82 (1943).

   Prosser, The Law of Torts (4th ed. 1971) p. 441.

   Jones v. Wittenberg Univ., 534 F.2d 1203 (6th Cir. 1976) ("Although contributory negligence and assumption of . . . risk may overlap in appropriate cases, they are separate and distinct defenses").

4. See Chapter 11, Contributory Negligence, supra.

   Walsh v. West Coast Coal Mines, Inc., 31 Wash.2d 396, 197 P.2d 233 (1948) ("While the defenses of assumption of risk, volenti non fit injuria, and contributory negligence are so closely allied that it is sometimes difficult to draw the line between them, they are not synonymous but are founded on separate, distinct principles of law. Contributory negligence involves some fault of breach of duty on the part of the injured person, or failure on his part to use the required degree of care for his safety, whereas assumption of risk or volenti non fit injuria may bar recovery even though the injured person may be free from contributory negligence.").

5. Prosser, Law of Torts (4th ed. 1971) p. 440.

6. Marlowe v. City of Los Angeles, 147 Cal.App.2d 680, 305 P.2d 604 (1957); Roberts v. Gray, 119 Vt. 153, 122 A.2d 855 (1956).

   Prosser, Law of Torts (4th ed. 1971) p. 440 (". . . [T]he plaintiff may be acting quite reasonably, and not be at all negligent in taking the chance, because the advantages of his conduct outweigh the risk. His decision may be the right one, and he may even act with unusual caution because he knows the danger he is to meet").

7. Prescott v. Ralph's Grocery, 42 Cal.2d 158, 161, 265 P.2d 904, 905 (1954); Fonseca v. Orange County, 28 Cal.App.3d 361, 368, 104 Cal.Rptr. 566, 570 (1972) ("Assumption of risk involves the negation of defendant's duty; contributory negligence is a

that the essence of contributory negligence is carelessness, while the essence of assumption of risk is venturousness.[8] Contributory negligence is measured by the objective standard of the reasonable man, while assumption of risk involves the subjective standard of plaintiff's knowledge and appreciation of the danger.[9]

Where the risk was unreasonably encountered, the defenses overlap. For example, assume X consents to ride with a drunken driver in an unlighted car at night. In a suit by X against the driver,[10] X may be barred from recovery either because he was guilty of contributory negligence or because of plaintiff's consent to relieve the defendant of an obligation of conduct toward him, and to take his chances of harm from a particular risk. In this situation, either defense, or both, may be raised against plaintiff.[11] In *Grey v. Fibreboard Paper Products Co.*, an "overlap" situation where plaintiff sustained injuries to his hand while repairing a machine, the trial court's error in failing to give an assumption of risk instruction was held insufficient to reverse verdict for plaintiff, on the grounds that the instruction on contributory negligence had rendered the error harmless.[12]

defense to a breach of such duty; assumption of risk may involve perfectly reasonable conduct on plaintiff's part, contributory negligence never does; assumption of risk typically embraces the voluntary or deliberate incurring of known peril; contributory negligence frequently involves the inadvertent failure to notice danger").

See also McGowan v. St. Regis Paper Co., Inc., 419 F.Supp. 742 (D.C.Miss. 1976).

8. Hunn v. Windsor Hotel Co., 119 W. Va. 215, 193 S.E. 57 (1937) ("The essence of contributory negligence is carelessness; of assumption of risk, venturousness").

See also Porter v. Toledo Terminal R. Co., 152 Ohio St. 463, 90 N.E.2d 142, 143 (1950); Hopkins v. C. E. Whalen Co., 456 F.2d 205 (4th Cir. 1972); Hubbard v. United States, 295 F. Supp. 524 (D.C.Va.1969).

9. Restatement, Second, Torts § 496 A, Comment (d) ("A subjective standard is applied to *assumption of risk*, in determining whether the plaintiff knows, understands, and appreciates the risk. (See § 496D.) An *objective standard* is applied to *contributory negligence*, and the plaintiff is required to have the knowledge, understanding, and judgment of the standard reasonable man.").

Vierra v. Fifth Avenue Rental Serv., 60 Cal.2d 266, 32 Cal.Rptr. 193, 383 P.2d 777 (1963); Hodge v. Borden 91 Idaho 125, 417 P.2d 75 (1966).

10. Sutherland v. Davis, 286 Ky. 743, 151 S.W.2d 1021 (1941); Hutzler v. McDonnell 242 Wis. 256, 7 N.W.2d 835 (1943).

11. Demarest v. T. C. Bateson Constr. Co., 370 F.2d 281 (10th Cir. 1966); Krolikowski v. Allstate Ins. Co., 283 F.2d 889 (7th Cir. 1960); Evans v. Johns Hopkins Univ., 224 Md. 234, 167 A.2d 591 (1961); Baltimore County v. State, 232 Md. 350, 193 A.2d 30 (1963).

12. Grey v. Fibreboard Paper Products Co., 65 Cal.2d 240, 53 Cal.Rptr. 545, 418 P.2d 153 (1966) ("While contribu-

§ 13.3 Express Agreements

Although there is no general legal prohibition against express agreements to assume risk,[13] such agreements are looked on with disfavor by the courts.[14] Their language must be clear and unequivocal [15] and will be strictly construed against the party claiming immunity.[16] Agreements to assume risk have been held invalid

tory negligence and assumption of risk are two different legal doctrines, one being based on a failure to exercise due care in the circumstances and the other being based upon voluntary exposure to a known risk, it is nevertheless true that the two doctrines overlap in many situations . . . . The jurors necessarily determined that plaintiff was not negligent in any degree; in other words, that his conduct did not fall 'below the standard to which he should conform for his own protection,' and was not a 'contributing cause co-operating with the negligence of the defendant in bringing about the' harm. Thus, the jurors absolved plaintiff of any misconduct in jeopardizing his well-being, and necessarily determined that he did not unreasonably undertake to encounter a specific known risk, the prerequisite upon which the particular defense of assumption of risk must be based.").

13. Laverty, Inc. v. Mel Jarvis Constr. Co., Inc., 513 F.2d 1307 (8th Cir. 1975); U. S. Fibres, Inc. v. Proctor & Schwartz Inc., 358 F.Supp. 449 (D.C. Mich.1972), aff'd 509 F.2d 1043 (6th Cir.); National Steel Corp. v. L. G. Wasson Coal Mining Corp., 338 F.2d 565 (7th Cir. 1964); Foland v. St. Louis-San Francisco Ry. Co., 208 F. Supp. 295 (D.C.Kan.1962).

14. Union Pac. R. R. Co. v. El Paso Natural Gas Co., 17 Utah 2d 255, 408 P.2d 910 (1965) ("A closely related proposition pertinent here is that the law does not look with favor upon one exacting a covenant to relieve himself of the basic duty which the law imposes on everyone: that of using due care for the safety of himself and others. This would tend to encourage carelessness and would not be salutary either for the person seeking to protect himself or for those whose safety may be hazarded by his conduct. For these reasons such covenants are sometimes declared invalid as being against public policy").

See also Kansas City Power & Light Co. v. United Tel. Co. of Kansas, 458 F. 2d 177 (10th Cir. 1972); Jones v. Walt Disney World Co., 409 F.Supp. 526 (D.C.N.Y.1976).

15. Stromberg's v. Victor Gruen & Associates, 384 F.2d 163 (10th Cir. 1967); Sterner Aero AB v. Page Airmotive, Inc., 499 F.2d 709 (10th Cir. 1974) (". . . [A] necessary requisite to recognition of the negligence disclaimer clause is that such a provision must be clear, explicit and unambiguous in its intention to exculpate a contracting party from the consequences of its own negligence"); Neville Chem. Co. v. Union Carbide Corp., 422 F.2d 1205 (3d Cir. 1970), cert. denied 400 U.S. 826, 91 S.Ct. 51, 27 L.Ed.2d 55 ("[T]he provisions and terms of the contract [must] clearly and unequivocally spell out the intent to grant such immunity and relief from liability"); Morton v. Borough of Ambridge, 375 Pa. 630, 101 A.2d 661 (1954) (Such contracts "must spell out the intention of the parties with the greatest particularity").

16. Keystone Aeronautics Corp. v. R. J. Enstrom Corp., 499 F.2d 146 (3d Cir. 1974) (Four prerequisites which must be met before Pennsylvania law

§ 13.3 TORT LIABILITY AND DEFENSES Pt. 3

on grounds of the disparity in *bargaining power* between the parties;[17] such as between an employer and employee.[18] Similarly, public utilities,[19] common carriers,[20] and telegraph companies [21] have been prevented from contracting away their liability. The rule has been extended, in some situations, to landlords,[22] innkeepers [23] and parking lot proprietors.[24] Contractual assumption of risk will not be

will give effect to an exculpatory claim: (1) such clauses must be strictly construed, (2) with every intendment against the party who seeks immunity from liability, (3) the contract must spell out the intention of the parties with the greatest of particularity and (4) the burden is on the party asserting the immunity).

See also Posttape Associates v. Eastman Kodak Co., 537 F.2d 751 (3d Cir. 1976).

17. Restatement, Second, Torts, § 496B, comment (j): (Such agreements "will not, in general, be enforced where there is such disparity of bargaining power between the parties that the agreement does not represent a free choice on the part of the plaintiff"); Bisso v. Inland Waterways Corp., 349 U.S. 85, 75 S.Ct. 629, 99 L.Ed. 911 (1954) ("The two main reasons for the creation and application of the rule have been (1) to discourage negligence by making wrongdoers pay damages, and (2) to protect those in need of goods or services from being overreached by others who have power to drive hard bargains").

18. Blanton v. Dold, 109 Mo. 64, 18 S. W. 1149 (1892); McCarthy v. National Ass'n for Stock Car Auto Racing, Inc., 90 N.J.Super. 574, 218 A.2d 871 (1966), aff'd 48 N.J. 539, 226 A.2d 713 (Release by racing driver immunizing race promoters from liability void as against public policy, does not bar action for negligence in failing to inspect cars before race); Bard v. Board of Educ., 140 N.Y.S.2d 850 (1955) (Plaintiff, applicant for a teaching job, was required to execute a paper releasing defendant from all liability for accidents as condition precedent to taking examination involving physical activity but plaintiff was injured during the examination —the paper was not sufficient to exempt defendant from liability for its negligence).

19. Collins v. Virginia Power & Elec. Co., 204 N.C. 320, 168 S.E. 500 (1933); Oklahoma Natural Gas Co. v. Appel, 266 P.2d 442 (Okl.1954); Reeder v. Western Gas & Power Co., 42 Wash.2d 542, 256 P.2d 825 (1953).

20. Bisso v. Inland Waterways Corp., 349 U.S. 85, 75 S.Ct. 629, 99 L.Ed. 911 (1954); Boston Metals Co. v. The S/S Winding Gulf, 349 U.S. 122, 75 S.Ct. 649, 99 L.Ed. 933 (1955).

21. Bowman & Bull Co. v. Postal Telegraph-Cable Co., 290 Ill. 155, 124 N.E. 851 (1919), cert. denied 251 U.S. 562, 40 S.Ct. 342, 64 L.Ed. 415; Dickerson v. Western Union Tel. Co., 114 Miss. 115, 74 So. 779 (1917).

See 49 U.S.C.A. §§ 1 et seq. permitting limitation of liability for unrepeated interstate messages.

22. Crowell v. Housing Auth. of City of Dallas, 495 S.W.2d 887 (Tex.1973); Thomas v. Housing Auth. of City of Bremerton, 71 Wash.2d 69, 426 P.2d 836 (1967); Nashua Gummed & Coated Paper Co. v. Noyes Buick Co., 93 N.H. 348, 41 A.2d 920 (1945).

23. Oklahoma City Hotel Co. v. Levine, 189 Okl. 331, 116 P.2d 997 (1941).

24. Agricultural Ins. Co. v. Constantine, 56 N.E.2d 687 (Ohio 1943), aff'd 144 Ohio St. 275, 58 N.E.2d 658; Baione v. Heavey, 103 Pa.Super. 529, 153 A. 181 (1932).

upheld where a safety statute has been violated.[25] An express agreement to assume the risk will not protect from liability for wilful or wanton conduct.[26]

In *Tunkl v. Regents of University of California*,[27] a case involving an exculpatory release required for admission to a hospital, the California Supreme Court enunciated six criteria of exculpatory clauses void as violative of public policy: first, a business generally thought suitable for government regulation; second, a business performing services necessary or of great importance to the public; third, services held out to the general public; fourth, disparity in bargaining power; fifth, no provision to avoid exculpatory contract, even by additional payment; and sixth, person or property of purchaser exposed to risk of seller's negligence. In *Tunkl*, the hospital-patient express agreement was held to fall within the above criteria and was held invalid. In *Henrioulle v. Marin Ventures, Inc.*,[28] the same Court held that exculpatory or disclaimer clauses in residential leases were void on the same grounds.

Exculpatory language contained on a *ticket stub* or elsewhere will not be held to establish an agreement to assume risk if plaintiff

---

25. Finnegan v. Royal Realty Co., 35 Cal.2d 409, 218 P.2d 17 (1950) ("There are certain statutes which clearly are intended to protect the plaintiff against his inability to protect himself. Such are the child labor acts, and various safety statutes for the benefit of employees as to which the courts have recognized, in this respect at least, the economic inequality in bargaining power which had induced the passage of the legislation. Since the fundamental purpose of such statutes would be defeated if the plaintiff were permitted to assume the risk, it is generally held that he cannot do so, either expressly or by implication. The workman has no alternative but the loss of his livelihood, it is his 'poverty and not his will' which consents, and economically he is no more free to leave his employment than a soldier or a sailor."); Bragg v. Mobilhome Co. of Los Angeles, 145 Cal.App.2d 326, 302 P.2d 424 (1956); Farmers Co-op Elevator Ass'n Non-stock of Big Springs v. Strand, 382 F.2d 224 (8th Cir. 1967), cert. denied 389 U.S. 1014, 88 S.Ct. 589, 19 L.Ed.2d 659, reh. denied 390 U.S. 913, 88 S.Ct. 815, 19 L.Ed.2d 887.

26. Friedman v. Lockheed Aircraft Corp., 138 F.Supp. 530 (D.C.N.Y.1956) (Document providing that signer was about to take a flight on his own risk, and released U. S. government from any and all claims related thereto, was not a defense to charge of wilful, wanton or gross negligence); Turek v. Pennsylvania R. Co., 369 Pa. 341, 85 A.2d 845 (1952), cert. denied 343 U.S. 929, 72 S.Ct. 762, 96 L.Ed. 1339; Arrington v. Trammell, 83 Ga. App. 107, 62 S.E.2d 451 (1950).

27. 60 Cal.2d 92, 32 Cal.Rptr. 33, 383 P.2d 441 (1963).

28. 20 Cal.3d 512, 143 Cal.Rptr. 247, 573 P.2d 465 (1978).

reasonably was unaware of it, or its terms were not otherwise "brought home" to him,[29] i. e. fine printing not apparent.

§ 13.4 Implied Acceptance of Risk

In the greater number of cases, the courts must deal with *"implied* assumption of risk." As stated by Prosser: "By entering freely and voluntarily into any relation or situation where the negligence of the defendant is obvious, the plaintiff may be found to accept and consent to it, and to undertake to look out for himself and relieve the defendant of the duty."[30]

As in *express* assumption of risk, it is essential that plaintiff have knowledge and appreciation of the *particular* risk, and that the assumption or acceptance of it be voluntary and free.[31] A showing of

29. Kushner v. McGinnis, 289 Mass. 326, 194 N.E. 106, 97 A.L.R. 578 (1935) ("Conceding in the defendant's favor that he lawfully could have exempted himself from liability for negligence in the operation of the device which he invited plaintiff to use, if he had employed adequate means to bring to her attention the fact that his invitation was a qualified and conditional one (see Blanchette v. Union Street Railway Co. 248 Mass. 407, 413 N.E. 310) we think the judge could find that the means employed were not adequate even if the plaintiff had been able to read. Taking into account the facts that the only warning given was by means of printed matter on the back of a small ticket which was purchased at a booth only four or five steps from the place where it was to be collected and torn up, we think the judge was justified in finding not only that the plaintiff did not know what was printed on the ticket, but also that a person of average intelligence and alertness would be unlikely to observe it. . . .").

See also Maynard v. James, 109 Conn. 365, 146 A. 614 (1929) (Reasonable belief that ticket is only token of identification); Van Noy Interstate Co. v. Tucker, 125 Miss. 260, 87 So. 643 (1921).

Contra: Hackbart v. Cincinnati Bengals, Inc., 435 F.Supp. 352 (D.C.Colo.1977).

30. Prosser, The Law of Torts (4th ed. 1971) pp. 445–46.

31. Indiana Natural Gas & Oil Co. v. O'Brien, 160 Ind. 266, 65 N.E. 918, 920 (1903), reh. denied 160 Ind. 266, 66 N.E. 742 ("Where a person has knowledge of and fully appreciates a danger, and under such circumstances, without any special exigency compelling him, he exposes himself to such danger or peril, his act in the premises may be deemed to have been voluntary. Contributory negligence in such a case cannot properly be said to be an element therein, for certainly the voluntary act of a party in exposing himself to a known and appreciated danger is wholly incompatible with an act of negligence or carelessness, for it must be manifest that carelessness in regard to a matter is not the same as the exercise of a deliberate choice in respect thereto. Freedom of the will, in fact, is the thing emphasized by the principle asserted in the maxim volenti non fit injuria.").

See Edwards v. Kirk, 227 Iowa 684, 288 N.W. 875 (1939) (Comprehensive discussion of the cases).

Ch. 13 **ASSUMPTION OF RISK** **§ 13.4**

actual knowledge, rather than constructive notice, is required,[32] though actual knowledge may be inferred from surrounding circumstances.[33] *Plaintiff* must appreciate the particular danger which causes the injury.[34] In case of a child or incompetent person, the capacity to re-

See also Mason v. Hunter, 534 F.2d 822 (8th Cir. 1976); Borel v. Fibreboard Paper Products Corp., 493 F.2d 1076 (5th Cir. 1974), cert. denied 419 U.S. 869, 95 S.Ct. 127, 42 L.Ed.2d 107; Weakley v. Fishbach & Moore, Inc., 515 F.2d 1260 (5th Cir. 1975); U. S. Steel v. Warner, 378 F.2d 995 (10th Cir. 1967); Rhoads v. Service Machine Co., 329 F.Supp. 367 (D.C.Ark. 1971); Clarke v. Brockway Motor Trucks, 372 F.Supp. 1342 (D.C.Pa. 1974); Hubbard v. United States, 295 F.Supp. 524 (D.C.Va.1969); Snodgrass v. Nelson, 369 F.Supp. 1206 (D.C.S.D. 1974), aff'd 503 F.2d 94 (8th Cir.); Ricketson v. Seaboard Airline R. Co., 403 F.2d 836 (5th Cir. 1968); Eisenhower v. United States, 216 F.Supp. 803 (D.C.N.Y.1963), aff'd 372 F.2d 663 (2d Cir.), cert. denied 377 U.S. 991, 84 S.Ct. 1915, 12 L.Ed.2d 1044.

32. Fisher v. United States Steel Corp., 334 F.2d 904 (5th Cir. 1964); Vierra v. Fifth Ave. Rental Serv., 60 Cal.2d 266, 32 Cal.Rptr. 193, 383 P.2d 777 (1963); Chase v. Shasta Lake Union Sch. Dist., 259 Cal.App.2d 612, 66 Cal.Rptr. 517 (1968); Quinn v. United States, 312 F.Supp. 999 (D.C.Ark. 1970), aff'd 439 F.2d 335 (8th Cir.); Dulin v. Circle F Indus., Inc., 558 F. 2d 456 (8th Cir. 1977).

33. Green v. Parisi, 478 F.2d 313 (3d Cir. 1973) (Error to withhold assumption of risk instruction where evidence had been presented from which jury could infer that decedent had actual knowledge of leaking gas and appreciation of its danger).

Gibson v. Beaver, 245 Md. 418, 226 A. 2d 273 (1967) (Demurrer to complaint sustained where plaintiff suffered heart attack while pulling fuel oil hose from delivery truck to his house. "[Plaintiff] must be taken to have been aware of the danger of slipping on snow and of the burden the snow would add to physical effort taken in it; he must be charged with knowledge of the heaviness of a hose of large diameter in which there was fuel oil and of the possible physical effects on a man of his age of the efforts to lift it or drag it through the snow.").

White v. Mississippi Power & Light Co., 196 So.2d 343 (Miss.1967).

34. Csizmadia v. P. Ballantine & Sons, 287 F.2d 423 (2d Cir. 1961) (Plaintiff slipped lifting beer barrel, recovery upheld despite prior warning: "The Connecticut cases assert that assumption of the risk is an effective defense only if the injured party fully comprehended the nature and extent of the danger. . . . Although he knew the floor was 'slippery', the full extent of the danger may not have been brought home to him.").

Diamond Crystal Salt Co. v. Thielman, 395 F.2d 62 (5th Cir. 1968) (Decedent killed during guided tour of salt mine. Held, prior release no defense where dangerous defect, known to defendant, not obvious to others. "The risk and danger must be seen, understood and appreciated before a risk may be legally assumed. In this case, the danger was not obvious, and if the dangerous condition had in fact been observed it would not have been appreciated by persons of ordinary understanding. No warning was given concerning the existence of the 'fault'.").

Swanson v. United States, 229 F.Supp. 217 (D.C.Cal.1964) (Pilot with 21 years experience was aware of "normal flight test risk," but had no

alize the peril may be the crucial issue.³⁵ Although the plaintiff's subjective knowledge and appreciation of the risk are generally questions of fact for the jury,³⁶ in some situations an objective standard may be applied by the court.³⁷

knowledge of the magnitude of the specific risk, created by defendant, which caused fatal injury).

Des Bouillons v. Burke, 418 F.2d 297 (7th Cir. 1969) (Electrical worker, who appreciated risk of working on staging, did not assume risk of aluminum bolt used in place of steel pin, which sheared and caused his injury).

Northwest Airlines, Inc. v. Glenn L. Martin Co., 224 F.2d 120 (6th Cir. 1955) (Action by airline against aircraft manufacturer based on alleged negligence in the manufacture of the airplane—defense of assumption of risk based on fact plaintiff had engineer, inspectors, and pilots observing operations at defendant's plant—assumption of risk should not have been submitted to the jury since plaintiff did not know or appreciate the danger).

Guerro v. Westgate Lumber Co., 164 Cal.App.2d 612, 331 P.2d 107 (1958) (Plaintiff struck by falling log while loading truck. Held error to instruct on assumption of risk where plaintiff had general knowledge of danger, but no evidence indicated knowledge of log which hit him: "Actual knowledge of the existence of a specific danger is an essential and indispensable element of the defense of assumption of the risk.").

Hook v. Point Montara Fire Protection Dist., 213 Cal.App.2d 96, 28 Cal.Rptr. 560 (1963) (Plaintiff knew of danger of walking into darkened room, but did not know that floor level was nine inches below threshold).

Sparks v. Porcher, 109 Ga.App. 334, 136 S.E.2d 153 (1964) (Knowledge that driver has been drinking is not as matter of law knowledge that he is incapacitated to drive).

Curran v. Green Hills Country Club, 24 Cal.App.3d 501, 101 Cal.Rptr. 158 (1972) (Plaintiff, in his backyard swimming pool, struck by golf ball from neighboring golf course. Held, no assumption of risk because no knowledge of particular golfers nearby at time of accident.).

35. Cowden v. Bear Country, Inc., 382 F.Supp. 1321 (D.C.S.D.1974) (Minor child of three years of age cannot be held to have assumed risk of injury when mountain lion entered open window of camper in which he was riding and attacked him); Greene v. Watts, 210 Cal.App.2d 103, 26 Cal. Rptr. 334 (1962) (Child of three and one-half years of age who played with dog was not capable of assuming risk of dog bite); Mudrich v. Standard Oil Co., 87 Ohio App. 8, 86 N.E.2d 324 (1949), aff'd 153 Ohio St. 31, 90 N.E.2d 859 (Seven-year-old child who jumped into burning puddle of gas to extinguish it was not capable of assuming risk of severe injury); Gold v. Hlivyak, 131 Cal.App. 2d 39, 280 P.2d 71 (1955) (Child playing with dangerous toy); Roberts v. Gray, 119 Vt. 153, 122 A.2d 855 (1956) (Intoxicated plaintiff); Nechodomu v. Lindstrom, 273 Wis. 313, 77 N.W.2d 707 (1956), reh. denied 273 Wis. 313, 78 N.W.2d 417 (9 year old child placed in sand mixing machine —capacity to realize danger an issue for injury); Kuemmel v. Vradenburg, 239 S.W.2d 869 (Tex.Civ.App.1951), refused n. r. e. (Hot-rod race where child injured, negligence of parents in standing behind filmsy fence not imputable to child).

36. Meistrich v. Casino Arena Attractions, 31 N.J. 44, 155 A.2d 90 (1959);

37. See note 37 on page 503.

It is more dangerous to work on a railroad than behind the ribbon counter at Macy's, but that's not the *particular* risk contemplated in this doctrine.

One group of cases in which the doctrine has been invoked involves *spectators* at games. Baseball and hockey are two of the most fertile fields of litigation. It is usually held that the spectator assumes the risk "when seated in the unscreened section of the ball park," as long as the proprietor has screened enough seats to accommodate the number reasonably expected to call for them on an ordinary occasion.[38] One problem upon which the courts divide is wheth-

Douglass v. Douglass, 130 Cal.App.2d 609, 279 P.2d 556, 46 A.L.R.2d 1370 (1955); Turner v. Johnson, 333 S.W.2d 749 (Ky.1960); Quigley v. Roath, 227 Or. 336, 362 P.2d 328 (1961) (Plaintiff's knowledge of driver's sleepiness and intoxication a jury question); Booth v. General Mills, Inc., 243 Iowa 206, 49 N.W.2d 561 (1951). The Constitutions of Arizona and Oklahoma contain provisions that the defense of assumption of risk shall be a question of fact and at all times left to the jury.

See also Herron v. Southern P. Co., 283 U.S. 91, 51 S.Ct. 383, 75 L.Ed. 857 (1931) (Ariz.Const. Art. 18 § 5); Chicago, R. I. & P. R. Co. v. Cole, 251 U.S. 54, 40 S.Ct. 68, 64 L.Ed. 133 (1919) (Okl.Const. Art. 23 § 6).

37. Wesson v. Gillespie, 382 S.W.2d 921 (Tex.1964). (Where plaintiff had crossed threshold 500 times, she was held chargeable with knowledge and appreciation of the danger thereof).

Houston Nat'l Bank v. Adair, 146 Tex. 387, 207 S.W.2d 374 (1948) (Plaintiff, who slipped on stairs, chargeable with knowledge of their condition because it was "open and obvious").

Bockman v. Mitchell Bros. Truck Lines, 213 Or. 88, 320 P.2d 266, 69 A.L.R.2d 152 (1958) (Plaintiff, who warned crane operator of danger of contacting electrical wires, held to have assumed the risk when injured by shock while assisting crane).

Celli v. Sports Car Club of America, Inc., 29 Cal.App.3d 511, 105 Cal.Rptr. 904 (1972) (Court ruled that "pit-passes" containing release were inadmissible against plaintiff, where as matter of law they had not assumed particular risk of racing car spinning out on straightaway endangering spectators).

38. Defense Applied

Quinn v. Recreation Park Ass'n, 3 Cal. 2d 725, 46 P.2d 144 (1935) (14-year-old girl familiar with baseball); Wells v. Minneapolis Baseball and Athletic Ass'n, 122 Minn. 327, 142 N.W. 706 (1913); Blackhall v. Capitol Dist. Baseball Ass'n, 154 Misc. 640, 278 N.Y.S. 649 (1935), aff'd 157 Misc. 801, 285 N.Y.S. 695; Erickson v. Lexington Baseball Club, 233 N.C. 627, 65 S.E.2d 140 (1951) (Spectator who selects seat in unscreened stand, accepts "the common hazards incident to the game"); Kavafian v. Seattle Baseball Club Ass'n, 105 Wash. 215, 181 P. 679 (1919); Morton v. California Sports Car Club, 163 Cal.App.2d 685, 329 P.2d 967 (1958) (Plaintiff observed race protected by 4-foot picket fence. Held, assumed risk of injury from spun-out car: "He ignored this hazard in his desire to observe the races from the best (rather than the safest) location.").

Defense Denied

Shurman v. Fresno Ice Rink, 91 Cal. App.2d 469, 205 P.2d 77 (1949) (No

er the inexperienced spectator also assumes the risk.[39] Also, voluntary participants in lawful games, sports, and even roughhouse, assume the risk of injury at the hands of their fellow participants (and, of course, of "hurting themselves") so long as the game is

assumption of risk at hockey game. "[I]t cannot be held, as a matter of law, that the general public has, at this particular date, become so familiar with the hazards of this sport and of the actual appreciation of the seriousness of the risk as to bring them within the 'common knowledge' rule and under the doctrine of assumption of risk").

Alden v. Norwood Arena, Inc., 332 Mass. 267, 124 N.E.2d 505 (1955) (Plaintiff's decedent attended automobile race—wheel from racing car flew into grandstand, and struck and killed decedent—decedent did not assume this risk).

Klinsky v. Hanson Van Winkle Munning Co., Inc., 38 N.J.Super. 439, 119 A.2d 166 (1955) (Plaintiff, invitee at family outing sponsored by defendant athletic association for employees of defendant company, was struck in face by bat which had slipped from defendant batter's hands and sailed through air 90 feet—plaintiff not barred as a matter of law by defense of assumption of risk. "Plaintiff will be held not to have assumed a risk of danger unless he actually appreciated the danger or unless an ordinarily prudent person in his position and with his experience would have appreciated it. . . . He not only must have knowledge of the physical surroundings which create the danger, but he must comprehend and appreciate the danger.").

Schentzel v. Philadelphia Nat'l League Club, 173 Pa.Super. 179, 96 A.2d 181 (1953) (Plaintiff, while attending her first baseball game, was struck by a foul ball driven into the stands—plaintiff assumed the risk even though she did not have full knowledge and appreciation of the danger).

Hunt v. Portland Baseball Club, 207 Or. 337, 296 P.2d 495 (1956) (Plaintiff, a spectator at a baseball game, was struck by a foul ball—no screening had been provided—plaintiff was intimately familiar with the game and the risks inherent in being a spectator—plaintiff assumed the risk and could not recover).

See Prosser, The Law of Torts (4th ed. 1971) p. 309.

Comment

The Promoters' Liability for Sports Spectator Injuries, 46 Cornell L.Q. 140 (1960); Comment, The Perils of Being a Spectator, 2 Lincoln L.Rev. 75 (1966); Solis, Sports Spectators—The Uncompensated Injury Victims, Ins.L.J. 385 (May, 1968); 24 Cal.L. Rev. 429; 89 A.L.R.2d 1163 [basketball]; 14 A.L.R.3d 1018 [Hockey].

39. Baseball

Anderson v. Kansas City Baseball Club, 231 S.W.2d 170 (Mo.1950), 1951 Wash.L.Q. 435 (Woman hit by ball in unscreened portion of stands assumed the risk although she had no knowledge of the rules or strategy of baseball).

Keys v. Alamo City Baseball Co., 150 S.W.2d 368 (Tex.Civ.App.1941) (Baseball company had no duty to warn patrons to occupy screened portion of stands).

Wrestling

As to a spectator being hit by "thrown wrestler" see Dusckiewicz v. Carter, 115 Vt. 122, 52 A.2d 788 (1947) (Wrestler landed in lap of spectator, causing injuries. Held that issue as to assumption of risk properly placed before jury, because plaintiff did not have actual, or implied "common

played in good faith and without negligence.[40] Yet the risk assumed is always the *"usual"* risk of the activity and not that created by abnormal conduct or condition,[41] or by another's negligence.[42]

knowledge" that wrestlers frequently are thrown from the ring.).

Ice Hockey

Morris v. Cleveland Hockey Club, 157 Ohio St. 225, 105 N.E.2d 419 (1952); Shanney v. Boston Madison Square Garden Corp., 296 Mass. 168, 5 N.E. 2d 1 (1936); Tite v. Omaha Coliseum Co., 144 Neb. 22, 12 N.W.2d 90, 149 A.L.R. 1164 (1943); James v. Rhode Island Auditorium, 60 R.I. 405, 199 A. 293 (1938).

40. Scala v. City of New York, 200 Misc. 475, 102 N.Y.S.2d 790 (1951) (Softball player collided with concrete bench).

Hotels El Rancho v. Pray, 64 Nev. 591, 187 P.2d 568 (1947) (Cross-country horse race, where horse stepped into hole made by a bombing demonstration, held this was an extraordinary hazard, the risk of which was not assumed).

Rogers v. Allis Chalmers Mfg. Co., 153 Ohio St. 513, 92 N.E.2d 677 (1950) (Player struck in eye by sliced golf ball).

Mann v. Nutrilite, Inc., 136 Cal.App.2d 729, 289 P.2d 282 (1955) (Plaintiff, chaperone of girls soft ball team, was injured when struck by ball while assisting girls in pregame warm-up. Held, for defendant, the risk of being struck by batted or thrown balls is one of the natural risks assumed by spectators attending a ball game, and, a fortiori, by participants.).

Hawayek v. Simmons, 91 So.2d 49 (La. App.1956) (Plaintiff fisherman struck in eye by lure of defendant fisherman —found a negligent and unusual hazard and therefore not assumed).

Trauman v. City of New York, 208 Misc. 252, 143 N.Y.S.2d 467 (1955) (Defendant, without warning, teed off, the ball striking plaintiff who was on another fairway—all golf players must accept the risk that bad shots may carry the ball to the right or left of an intended line of play).

Getz v. Freed, 377 Pa. 480, 105 A.2d 102 (1954) (Defendant and plaintiff were members of golf foursome—defendant hit two drives, the first of which went out of bounds, and plaintiff volunteered to look for the first ball but as plaintiff walked toward it, defendant, without warning, hit a third drive which hit plaintiff on the back of the head—trial court correctly refused to charge jury on defense of assumption of risk).

Strand v. Conner, 207 Cal.App.2d 473, 24 Cal.Rptr. 584 (1962) (Plaintiff hit by golf ball "pulled" by defendant. Court's nonsuit based on assumption of risk upheld, on grounds that plaintiff had assumed risk of normal game hazard.).

41. Maytnier v. Rush, 80 Ill.App.2d 336, 225 N.E.2d 83 (1967) (Plaintiff spectator at baseball game did not assume risk of being struck by ball thrown from bullpen).

Ratcliffe v. San Diego Baseball Club, 27 Cal.App.2d 733, 81 P.2d 625 (1938) (Plaintiff spectator at baseball game did not assume risk of being hit by flying bat while walking in passageway).

Klause v. Nebraska State Bd. of Agric., 150 Neb. 466, 35 N.W.2d 104 (1948) (Spectator at wrestling match did not assume risk of being hit by referee thrown from ring).

Kaiser v. State, 55 Misc.2d 576, 285 N. Y.S.2d 874 (1967), rev'd on other grounds 30 A.D.2d 482, 294 N.Y.S.2d 410, appeal dismissed 23 N.Y.2d 866,

---

42. See note 42 on page 506.

§ 13.4   TORT LIABILITY AND DEFENSES   Pt. 3

The classic assumption of risk opinion is that of Justice Cardozo in the 1929 "Flopper" case, *Murphy v. Steeplechase Amusement Co.*[43] Plaintiff, visiting the Coney Island amusement park, stepped onto "the Flopper", an inclined conveyor belt, designed to tumble those who attempted to stand upon it. Plaintiff's tumble resulted in a fractured kneecap, but his recovery was reversed by the New York Court of Appeals on the grounds that he had assumed the obvious risk of a fall: "One who takes part in such a sport accepts the dangers that inhere in it so far as they are obvious and necessary . . . . The plaintiff was not seeking a retreat for meditation. Visitors were tumbling about the belt to the merriment of onlookers when he made his choice to join them. He took the chance of a like fate, with whatever damage to his body might ensue from such a fall. The timorous may stay at home." Justice Cardozo noted, however, that "A different case would be here if the dangers inherent in the sport were obscure or unobserved," and further, that "A different case would be here if the accidents had been so many as to show that the game in its inherent nature was too dangerous to be continued without change."

The modern view, however, is exemplified by the holding of the Vermont Supreme Court in *Sunday v. Stratton Corp.*,[44] wherein plaintiff, a novice skier, was tumbled by a bush hidden in snow upon de-

---

298 N.Y.S.2d 74, 245 N.E.2d 806 (Plaintiffs assumed inherent risks of bobsledding, but not risk of unsafe condition of sled run).

Keaton v. Good, 350 S.W.2d 119 (Mo. App.1961) (Jockey did not assume risk of truck driving into racetrack).

Garafano v. Neshobe Beach Club, Inc., 126 Vt. 566, 238 A.2d 70 (1967) (Plaintiff playing softball did not assume risk of stepping into hole in outfield).

42. Carabba v. Anacortes Sch. Dist. No. 103, 72 Wash.2d 939, 435 P.2d 936 (1967) (Highschool wrestler did not assume risk of negligence of referee).

Harrop v. Beckman, 15 Utah 2d 78, 387 P.2d 554 (1963) (Waterskier did not assume risk of being run over by negligently driven boat).

Hairston v. Studio Amusements, 86 Cal.App.2d 735, 195 P.2d 498 (1948) (Plaintiff rollerskater who fell on rink, lay unattended by guards, and was finally struck by reckless skater skating backwards, did not assume risk).

Edwards v. Hollywood Canteen, 27 Cal.2d 802, 167 P.2d 729 (1946) (Plaintiff hostess did not assume risk of injury caused by reckless dancing partner).

43. 250 N.Y. 479, 166 N.E. 173 (1929).

44. 136 Vt. 293, 390 A.2d 398 (1978). See also Garafano v. Neshoba Beach Club, Inc., 126 Vt. 566, 238 A.2d 70 (1967) (Plaintiff injured by hole in softball field did not assume risk as inherent hazard of sport).

Chase v. Shasta Lake Union Sch. Dist., 259 Cal.App.2d 612, 66 Cal.Rptr. 517 (1968) (Plaintiff injured running into incinerator in softball field did not assume risk as inherent hazard of sport).

fendant's ski trail. His tumble resulted in permanent quadriplegia. The jury award of $1.5 million was sustained despite defendants' argument of assumed risk, the Court holding that, "While skiers fall, as a matter of common knowledge, that does not make every fall a danger inherent in the sport." The Court noted defendants' "concerted efforts" to attract the patronage of inexperienced skiers, and based its holding on defendants' duty to make the premises reasonably safe by removing concealed brush, or to warn of its existence.

Though always a jury question, plaintiff's acceptance of a risk will not ordinarily be deemed "voluntary" in situations where he has no reasonable alternative course of conduct.[45] Thus, where plaintiff was negligently locked into defendant's business premises, he did not assume the risk of injuries sustained while effecting his escape.[46] Similarly, where plaintiff is injured attempting to rescue persons or property endangered by defendant's negligence, plaintiff will not be held to have assumed the risk.[47] Plaintiff is not required to surren-

---

45. Restatement, Second, Torts § 496E, Comment (c):

"A defendant who, by his own wrong, has compelled the plaintiff to choose between two evils cannot be permitted to say that plaintiff is barred from recovery because he has made the choice."

Prosser, The Law of Torts (4th ed. 1971), p. 451.

"Even where the plaintiff does not protest, the risk is not assumed where the conduct of the defendant has left him no reasonable alternative. Where the defendant puts him to a choice of evils, there is a species of duress, which destroys all idea of freedom of election."

Littleton v. Western Union Tel. Co., 442 F.2d 1169 (10th Cir. 1971) (Business invitee knew floor was mopped all around her, and had no reasonable alternative to walking across wet floor to exit. Held, no assumption of risk to slip and fall.).

Bitsos v. Red Owl Stores, Inc., 459 F.2d 656 (8th Cir. 1972) (Even assuming business invitee knew defective condition of stairs, he was not precluded from recovering where he had no reasonable alternative to using stairs).

C.C.A., D.C.—Dougherty v. Chas. H. Tompkins Co., 240 F.2d 34 (D.C.Cir. 1957) (Plaintiff, pedestrian, was injured when he fell on temporary sidewalk which defendant had constructed during construction of building—though plaintiff was aware of slippery condition, he did not assume the risk because, inter alia, the risk was not "voluntarily" assumed because defendant had no right to force plaintiff to "take or leave" the risk in traversing the sidewalk).

Jury Question

Fla.—Byers v. Gunn, 81 So.2d 723 (Fla. 1955) (Plaintiff injured by fall from automobile fender where he was seated after being refused a seat—whether peril voluntarily assumed for jury).

Wash.—Ewer v. Johnson, 44 Wash.2d 746, 270 P.2d 813 (1954) (Plaintiff injured by collision of automobiles in dust cloud where he had gone to assist traffic—issue for jury whether he voluntarily assumed known peril).

46. O'Reilly Motor Co. v. Rich, 3 Ariz.App. 21, 411 P.2d 194 (1966).

47. See Chapter 9 Recue Doctrine, supra.

§ 13.4 TORT LIABILITY AND DEFENSES Pt. 3

der a right or privilege by reason of threat of harm from defendant's negligence.[48]

The defense has been denied where the plaintiff can assume safe conditions, such as when traveling upon a highway in the absence of warnings. Where defendant's duty is statutorily imposed, plaintiff's acceptance of a known risk will not constitute voluntary assumption of the risk.[49] In the California case of *Fonseca v. Orange*,[50] plaintiff

Drummond v. Mid-West Growers Coop. Corp., 91 Nev. 698, 542 P.2d 198 (1975) (". . . [T]he individual is not 'voluntarily' accepting the risk if he is compelled by an emergency situation to endanger himself").

Lives

Aylor v. Intercounty Constr. Corp., 381 F.2d 930 (D.C.Cir. 1967).

Schwab v. Allou Corp., 177 Neb. 342, 128 N.W.2d 835 (1964) (Tenant who left apartment building through front door, although she knew entranceway was icy, did not assume risk where all exits were icy).

Bard v. Board of Educ., 140 N.Y.S.2d 850 (1955) (Plaintiff, applicant for teaching job, batted ball and ran to "first base" as directed as part of her examination but the base slid from her on a slippery gymnasium floor and plaintiff broke her leg—there can be no assumption of risk unless it is voluntary; here plaintiff was forced to proceed as directed in order to take the examination).

48. Restatement, Second, Torts § 496E, Comment (c), (1965).

Kanelos v. Kettler, 406 F.2d 951 (D.C. Cir. 1968) (Plaintiff tenant remained in possession of apartment negligently maintained by landlord).

State of Maryland for Use of Pumphrey v. Manor Real Estate & Trust Co., 176 F.2d 414 (4th Cir. 1949) (Tenants remaining in premises where common cellars were infested with rats did not assume risk of typhus infection. Tenants "were entitled to exercise the right of occupancy conferred by their lease and to demand that the landlord perform the duty of keeping the reserved portion of the premises in safe condition for their use.").

49. Finnegan v. Royal Realty Co., 35 Cal.2d 409, 431, 218 P.2d 17, 30 (1950) ("Where an ordinance is a police regulation, made for the protection of human life . . . the doctrine of assumption of the risk does not apply. Public policy forbids that the duty which the defendant owes to the plaintiffs should be waived by plaintiffs' mere passive quiescence, even though with knowledge of the infraction of the ordinance. . . . Since the fundamental purpose of such statutes would be defeated if the plaintiff were permitted to assume the risk, it is generally held that he cannot do so, either expressly or by implication. The workman has no alternative but the loss of his livelihood, it is his 'poverty and not his will' which consents, and economically he is no more free to leave his employment than a soldier or a sailor.").

Dougherty v. Chas. H. Tompkins Co., 240 F.2d 34 (D.C.Cir. 1957) (Plaintiff, pedestrian, was injured when he fell on temporary sidewalk which defendant had constructed during construction of building—plaintiff was aware of slippery condition, he did not assume the risk because, inter alia, defendant had violated a statutory duty).

Bragg v. Mobilhome Co., 145 Cal.App. 2d 326, 302 P.2d 424 (1956) (Plaintiff

50. See note 50 on page 509.

was an experienced cement worker who recognized the need for scaffolding on his job, yet proceeded to work without it. His recovery for injuries incurred in a fall was not precluded by his knowing acceptance of the risk because the failure to erect scaffolding constituted a violation of state industrial safety orders.[51] In general, however, it has been held that duress imposed by "general circumstances", including "economic duress," will not suffice to defeat the "voluntary" element of the assumption of risk defense.[52]

Where plaintiff proceeds on defendant's assurance of safety, or assurance that dangerous conditions will soon be remedied, there is no voluntary assumption of risk.[53] In a California case, plaintiff roofing contractor fell through tarpaper covered chimney hole cut by defendants in roof of house being constructed by them. Held, assumption of risk is not to be applied in cases of violation of safety statutes).

Hrabak v. Madison Gas & Elec. Co., 240 F.2d 472 (7th Cir. 1957) (Defense of assumption of risk not available to occupant of premises under Wisconsin's safe place statute).

50. 28 Cal.App.3d 361, 104 Cal.Rptr. 566 (1972).

51. See also Mason v. Case, 220 Cal. App.2d 170, 33 Cal.Rptr. 710 (1963).

52. Messick v. General Motors Corp., 460 F.2d 485 (5th Cir. 1972) (Plaintiff injured in car accident caused by defect known to him. Plaintiff's claim that "economic duress" forced him to continue to drive car, when dealer and manufacturer refused to exchange it, held insufficient to defeat defense of volenti.).

Employer/Employee

Demarest v. T. C. Bateson Constr. Co., 370 F.2d 281 (10th Cir. 1966) ("It may be conceded that [plaintiff] was under the necessity of assuming the risk of his employment or quitting. Even so, as we read New Mexico law, it does not recognize economic coercion as having any bearing on the question of voluntariness in a non-master-servant situation. In master-servant cases the general rule in this country seems always to have been that economic coercion does not make a servant's act involuntary.").

McKee v. Patterson, 271 S.W.2d 391 (Tex.1954) (Plaintiff sustained injuries when ladder slipped on slick floor: "So far as we have been able to discover the courts of this state have never held that the necessity of performing his duties and/or earning a livelihood was such economic compulsion or constraint as to render involuntary the workman's choice of accepting or retaining employment in the face of known and appreciated dangers").

2 Harper & James, Torts (1956) § 21.3, p. 1147:

"The plaintiff takes a risk *voluntarily* [within the meaning of the present rule] where the defendant has a right to face him with the dilemma of 'take it or leave it'—in other words, where defendant is under no duty to make the conditions of their association any safer than they appear to be. In such a case it does not matter that plaintiff is coerced to assume the risk by some force not emanating from defendant, such as poverty, dearth of living quarters, or a sense of moral responsibility."

53. Restatement, Second, Torts § 496E, Comment a.

Prosser, The Law of Torts (4th ed., 1971), p. 450.

contracted to fly on a kite towed by an automobile as a stunt for defendant's television show "You Asked For It". Defendant agreed to supply a "top qualified" expert stunt driver. At trial, it was determined that plaintiff's injuries were proximately caused by the negligence of the driver, who was not an experienced stunt driver, but rather had been hired as a studio grippe. On appeal of the $135,000 verdict, plaintiff was held not to have assumed the risk of the particular accident, in that he had been "assured repeatedly as to the competency and care of the driver to be furnished by defendant. That was the one feature of the venture that he could not control. He obviously surrendered his judgment as to selection of a driver to defendant and did so upon the faith of such assurances given him." [54] Where plaintiff relied on defendant's promise to repair, the length of time during which such reliance remains reasonable is a jury question.[55]

Express Assurances

Montellier v. United States, 202 F.Supp. 384 (D.C.N.Y.1962), aff'd 315 F.2d 180 (2d Cir.) (Decedent journalist executed release before boarding Air Force plane. Court found that effect of three briefing sessions conducted by Air Force prior to signing of release was not to apprise decedent of dangers, but rather to instill confidence: "Nothing presented at this session was of a nature which would bring any sense of particular danger to the mind of one of ordinary sensibilities. Rather, the stress on safety and careful planning would assure one going on the mission of the care and precaution exercised in his behalf.").

Oltmans v. Driver, 252 Iowa 1066, 109 N.W.2d 446 (1961) (Plaintiff relied on defendant's assurances that scaffolding was safe. Held, error not to include reliance on assurance instruction with assumption of risk instruction.).

Implicit Assurances

Collins v. Musgrave, 28 Ill.App.3d 307, 328 N.E.2d 649 (1975) (Defendant's replacement of wheel axle assembly constituted implicit assurance to plaintiff that repairs were complete and truck was safe for normal use: "Plaintiffs cannot be held to have assumed the risk of harm in the face of defendant Musgrave's implicit assurance that there was no danger of harm").

Promise To Remedy

Deshazer v. Tompkins, 89 Idaho 347, 404 P.2d 604 (1965) (Plaintiff employee injured by sprinkling system which employer promised to make safe: "When the servant has full knowledge of a special risk under which he is working, he is deemed to have assumed the risk, incidental to the employment, subject however to the exception that when a servant notifies the master of the risk and objects thereto, and is induced to continue the employment by the master's promise to remove the danger within a reasonable time, the servant does not assume the risk during such time").

Unreasonable Reliance

Blume v. Ballis, 207 Minn. 393, 291 N. W. 906 (1940) (Danger of unsupported chimney falling was obvious).

54. Woodall v. Wayne Steffner Productions Inc., 201 Cal.App.2d, 800, 20 Cal.Rptr. 572 (1962).

55. Deshazer v. Tompkins, supra, n. 53 ("There still remains the factual question for determination by the

In states where there is no motor vehicle guest statute restricting the owner's liability to "gross negligence" or "wantonness," the defense of assumption of risk is frequently invoked.[56] Mere knowledge that the driver is under the influence of liquor has been held insufficient to establish the defense—the pertinent question is whether plaintiff knew that the driver's driving ability has been dangerously impaired.[57]

§ 13.5 Demise of the Defense

As stated earlier, the doctrine of assumption of risk developed as a device of the common law courts to insulate the employer from what might prove to be "serious responsibilities."[58]

The law has advanced from this *laissez faire* attitude to one of concern for the welfare of the injured worker and the defense minimized. It is notable that almost all industrial accidents are covered by workers' compensation statutes.[59] In a field not so covered, injuries to

jury, whether the time element was reasonable under the circumstances, i. e., between the time of promise, or renewed promise, and the injury").

Buehner v. Creamery Package Mfg. Co., 124 Iowa 445, 100 N.W. 345 (1904) (Employee injured two days after complaining of unsafe condition—not unreasonable length of time to rely on employer's promise to remedy).

56. Notwithstanding guest act restrictions of liability "wilful," "wanton," or "gross negligence," assumption of risk is frequently invoked as a defense for the delinquent motorist. See Pierce v. Clemens, 113 Ind.App. 65, 46 N.E.2d 836 (1942) (Although the Indiana court had previously called the doctrine "part of the doctrine of contributory negligence," policy considerations undoubtedly led the court to attempt a logical separation, since contributory negligence had been declared no defense under the guest act. "It is different from and should not be confounded with acts and omissions amounting to contributory negligence which is not a defense to an action of this kind, or with acts or omissions amounting to contributory misconduct, either wanton or wilful, which is a defense to an action of this kind.").

Assumption of risk not applicable unless guest has actual knowledge of danger, and voluntarily acquiesces: see Bohnsack v. Driftmier, 243 Iowa 383, 52 N.W.2d 79 (1952).

57. Cousins v. Cooper, 232 Ark. 605, 339 S.W.2d 316 (1960); Cox v. Johnston, 139 Colo. 376, 339 P.2d 989 (1959); Sparks v. Porcher, 109 Ga. App. 334, 136 S.E.2d 153 (1964).

58. Tuttle v. Detroit, G. H. & M. Ry. Co., 122 U.S. 189, 7 S.Ct. 1166, 30 L. Ed. 1114 (1887).

59. See Chapter 39 Worker's Compensation, infra.

Sears, Roebuck & Co. v. Robinson, 154 Tex. 336, 280 S.W.2d 238 (1955) (Plaintiff, employee in defendant's warehouse, noticed oil on floor but failed to report it, then slipped on oil and fell—employee's knowledge of condition no defense under workmen's compensation statute abolishing assumption of risk).

Walls v. McKinney, 139 W.Va. 866, 81 S.E.2d 901 (1954) (Upholds work-

seamen and railroad employees engaged in interstate commerce, the doctrine has been abolished by statute.[60]

Admiralty and railroad worker's laws are *almost* absolute liability with common law damages now.

In spite of these advancements there are still fields in which the common law rule applies. One example is provided by agricultural and domestic labor in some states.[61]

The defense is generally held unavailable to commercial airlines where the negligence is in the operation or servicing of the plane, the passenger only assuming those perils which are commonly foreseen before boarding, such as adverse weather.[62]

The defense of implied assumption of risk has been abolished outright in some states.[63] In California, the adoption of the comparative negligence rule abolished the defense "to the extent that it is a

men's compensation statute, depriving employer of defense of assumption of risk where he does not elect to come under the statute).

60. 45 U.S.C.A. § 54, F.C.A. 45, § 54 (railroad employees); 46 U.S.C.A. § 688, F.C.A. 46, § 688 (Made applicable to seamen).

Tiller v. Atlantic Coast Line R. R. Co., 318 U.S. 54, 63 S.Ct. 444, 87 L.Ed. 610, 143 A.L.R. 967 (1943); Becker v. Waterman S. S. Corp., 179 F.2d 713 (2d Cir. 1950); Carter v. Schooner Pilgrim, Inc., 238 F.2d 702 (1st Cir. 1957) (Assumption of risk defense not available under 46 U.S.C.A. § 688); Reyes v. Vantage S. S. Co., Inc., 558 F.2d 238 (5th Cir. 1977) (Assumption of risk never rises to level of even a partial defense, no matter how glaring the negligence of the seaman); Gindville v. American-Hawaiian S. S. Co., 224 F.2d 746 (3d Cir. 1955) (Plaintiff longshoreman was injured in unloading cargo negligently loaded by defendant—doctrines of contributory negligence and assumption of risk do not apply in maritime injury cases); Mason v. Lynch Bros. Co., 228 F.2d 709 (4th Cir. 1956) (Assumption of risk no defense against seaman under Jones Act).

61. Cruzan v. Grace, 165 Kan. 638, 198 P.2d 154 (1948) (Ranch hand injured by runaway horse).

62. Urban v. Frontier Air Lines, 139 F.Supp 288 (D.C.Wyo.1956). (Stewardess authorized plaintiff airline passenger to leave her seat and go to the lavatory despite the fact that the weather was rough and turbulent—plaintiff fell and broke her ankle when plane hit down draft—a passenger on a commercial airliner no longer voluntarily assumes a risk with respect to the plane itself or to its operation.)

63. *Ky.*—Parker v. Redden, 421 S.W. 2d 586 (Ky.1967).

Mich.—Felgner v. Anderson, 375 Mich. 23, 133 N.W.2d 136 (1965). (Defense retained between employer-employee.)

N.H.—Bolduc v. Crain, 104 N.H. 163, 181 A.2d 641 (1962).

N.J.—McGrath v. American Cyanamid Co., 41 N.J. 272, 196 A.2d 238 (1963).

Or.—Horenbeck v. Western States Fire Apparatus, Inc., 280 Or. 647, 572 P.2d 620 (1977). (Interpreting ORS 18.-475(2).)

form of contributory negligence." [64] Wisconsin has taken a similar approach.[65] Other comparative negligence jurisdictions have retained assumption of risk as a complete bar to recovery.[66] The assumption of risk defense was included in the Restatement of Torts, Second, despite a sharp division among the advisers, many of whom advocated striking the entire chapter [67] on the grounds that the issues are adequately treated by examining the questions of duty and contributory negligence.

The burden of proof of plaintiff's assumption of risk in the traditional pattern is clearly on defendant.[68] Treating the question as one of defendant's duty to plaintiff, however, can effectively shift the burden to plaintiff.[69] Moreover, while assumption of risk is a question of fact, the issue of duty is often a question of law for the court.[70]

Some courts will refuse to instruct the jury on assumption of risk if instructions on contributory negligence are given, and this has been upheld on review.[71] Unavoidable accident is also a defense gen-

---

64. Li v. Yellow Cab, 13 Cal.3d 804, 829, 119 Cal.Rptr. 858, 875, 532 P.2d 1226, 1243 (1975).

65. McConville v. State Farm Mut. Auto. Ins. Co., 15 Wis.2d 374, 113 N.W.2d 14 (1962). (Guest statute: "A guest's assumption of risk, heretofore implied from his willingness to proceed in the face of a known hazard is no longer a defense separate from contributory negligence . . . if a guest's exposure of himself to a particular hazard be unreasonable and a failure to exercise ordinary care for his own safety, such conduct is negligence, and is subject to the comparative negligence statute.")

66. *Ark.*—Bugh v. Webb, 231 Ark. 27, 328 S.W.2d 379, 84 A.L.R.2d 444 (1959).
Ga.—Roberts v. King, 102 Ga.App. 518, 116 S.E.2d 885 (1960).
Miss.—Saxton v. Rose, 201 Miss. 814, 29 So.2d 646 (1947).

67. See Halepeska v. Callihan Interests, Inc., 371 S.W.2d 368, 378, note 3 (Tex.1963), on remand 376 S.W.2d 932.

See also James, Assumption of Risk: Unhappy Reincarnation, 78 Yale L.J. 185 (1968).

68. Green v. Parisi, 478 F.2d 313 (3d Cir. 1973) (Under Pa. law, burden of proving assumption of risk is on defendant); Associated Engineers, Inc. v. Job, 370 F.2d 633, (8th Cir. 1966), cert. denied 389 U.S. 823, 88 S.Ct. 59, 19 L.Ed.2d 77; Troy Cannon Constr. Co. v. Job, 389 U.S. 823, 88 S.Ct. 59, 19 L.Ed.2d 77 (1967) (Under S.D. law, burden of proving assumption of risk defense is on defendant).

69. Hannon v. Hayes-Bickford Lunch System, Inc., 336 Mass. 268, 145 N.E.2d 191 (1957); Morril v. Morril, 104 N.J.L. 557, 142 A. 337 (1928).

70. See Prosser, The Law of Torts (4th ed. 1971) p. 455.

71. Smith v. Ritch, 196 N.C. 72, 144 S.E. 537, 59 A.L.R. 1084 (1928); Grey v. Fibreboard Paper Products Co., 65 Cal.2d 240, 53 Cal.Rptr. 545, 418 P.2d 153 (1966); Dorobek v. Ride-A-While Stables, 262 Cal.App.2d 554, 68 Cal. Rptr. 774 (1968).

erally available to a defendant, even though not pleaded,[72] and instructions may be given upon both unavoidable accident and contribu-

72. Unavoidable Accident Defense Approved

C.C.A., D.C.—Moore v. Capital Transit Co., 226 F.2d 57 (D.C.Cir. 1955), cert. denied 350 U.S. 966, 76 S.Ct. 434, 100 L.Ed. 839 (Collision between streetcar and cab—unanticipated convulsive seizure of motorman).

Cal.—Parker v. Womak, 37 Cal.2d 230 P.2d 823 (1951) (See dissent by Justice Carter—"If an instruction on unavoidable accident does not add anything to instructions covering negligence, proximate cause, and the burden of proving these matters there is no reason to give such an instruction").

Md.—Shirks Motor Express v. Oxenham, 204 Md. 626, 106 A.2d 46 (1954) (Claimed unconsciousness of defendant motor driver for jury).

Okl.—Ries v. Cartwright, 297 P.2d 367 (Okl.1956) (Where motor vehicle driver blinded by light and drove into ditch injuring guest).

Or.—Whelpley v. Frye, 199 Or. 530, 263 P.2d 295 (1953) (Motor vehicle head-on collision where expert testimony that decedent dead before accident).

Tenn.—Hooper v. Starkey, 41 Tenn. App. 633, 297 S.W.2d 948 (1957) (Where pedestrian stepped onto highway into path of automobile).

W.Va.—Keller v. Wonn, 140 W.Va. 860, 87 S.E.2d 453 (1955) (Motor vehicle accident following cerebral hemorrhage although decedent tortfeasor knew he had a bad case of hypertension).

Unavoidable Accident Defense Disapproved

Ariz.—Town & Country Securities Co., Inc. v. Place, 79 Ariz. 122, 285 P.2d 165 (1955) (Where defendant motorist after collision with another automobile claimed that her foot slipped from brake).

Cal.—Jensen v. Minard, 44 Cal.2d 325, 282 P.2d 7 (1955) (Death of child from gunshot—instruction tended to suggest to jury that shooting unavoidable and that extreme caution not necessary in use of firearms).

Colo.—Jacobsen v. McGinness, 135 Colo. 357, 311 P.2d 696 (1957) (Instruction erroneous where no genuine issue as to unavoidable accident as tending, "not only to divert the minds of the jurors from the decisive issues of negligence, but suggested that under the evidence, the parties might be held blameless for reasons other than their freedom from negligence or contributory negligence").

Mich.—McClarren v. Buck, 343 Mich. 300, 72 N.W.2d 31 (1955) (Motor vehicle collision—where one or both of parties were negligent, instruction on unavoidable accident reversible error).

Tex.—Amarillo, City of v. Hill, 278 S.W.2d 332 (Tex.Civ.App.1954) ("Unavoidable accident occurs only when neither party is guilty of negligence").

Va.—Smith v. Tatum, 199 Va. 85, 97 S.E. 820 (1957) (Inappropriate where evidence of negligence or contributory negligence).

Act of God Defense Approved

Ga.—Western & Atlantic R. R. v. Hassler, 92 Ga.App. 278, 88 S.E.2d 559 (1955) (Action for flooding of lands because of insufficient culvert-catastrophic flood).

Ill.—Villegas v. Kercher, 11 Ill.App.2d 282, 137 N.E.2d 92 (1956) (Where automobile of decedent careened off of street and killed child in yard—defense that motorist had died from cerebral hemorrhage before accident for jury); McClean v. Chicago Great Western Ry. Co., 3 Ill.App.2d 235, 121 N.E.2d 337 (1954) (Sudden attack of illness).

tory negligence in the same case. It seems to the author that instructions on contributory negligence, assumption of risk and unavoidable accident, all applied to the same defense and factual situation, and frequently argumentative, are unfair to the plaintiff and unduly persuasive in favor of the defense.[73]

Neb.—Cover v. Platte Valley Public Power & Irrigation Dist., 162 Neb. 146, 75 N.W.2d 661 (1956) (Flooding of land by irrigation district—flood Act of God when not reasonably anticipated).

N.C.—Bennett v. Southern Ry. Co., 245 N.C. 261, 96 S.E.2d 31 (1957), cert. denied 353 U.S. 958, 77 S.Ct. 865, 1 L. Ed.2d 909 (FELA—brakeman struck by lightning).

Act of God Defense Disapproved

Ark.—Manila School Dist. v. Sanders, 226 Ark. 270, 289 S.W.2d 529 (1956) (Negligent roofing of gymnasium resulting in rainstorm damage—Act of God insufficient defense where it concurs with negligence).

Ill.—Blue v. St. Clair Country Club, 7 Ill.2d 359, 131 N.E.2d 31 (1956) (Where sudden wind caused table umbrella to upset table against plaintiff invitee at country club jury verdict upheld for injuries on ground that the wind was foreseeable and not Act of God).

Miss.—Jackson, City of v. Brummett, 224 Miss. 501, 80 So.2d 827 (1955) (Damage to airplane by windstorm where negligence in anchoring plane concurred with wind).

Mo.—Buschelberg v. Chicago, Burlington & Quincy R. Co., 289 S.W.2d 447 (Mo.App.1956) (Flooding of land because of embankment construction—where floods ordinary occurrences).

73. See Parker v. Womack, supra, n. 72.

§§ 13.6–14.0 are reserved for supplementary material.

CHAPTER 14

IMMINENT PERIL—"I CAN'T LET GO!"— THE EMERGENCY RULE

Table of Sections

Sec.
14.1 General Considerations.
14.2 Availability of Defense.

Library References:
  C.J.S. Negligence §§ 136(2), 137(3).
  West's Key No. Digests, Negligence ⚖=83.3, 83.6.

§ 14.1 General Considerations

The author once interviewed a client who told of disembarking from a street car which apparently started up as his alighting foot was still off the ground. The passenger hastily alighted but still held on to the stanchion for support. By the time both feet were on the ground, the car was gathering speed. The prospective plaintiff continued to hold on to the stanchion even though he was now being dragged along the ground. He was severely injured before the street car was brought to a stop by an inattentive motorman.

At first, as I listened to the story, I wondered why the plaintiff did not let go, rather than compound the damage and danger. Then I recalled several instances of similar conduct of my own wherein it had seemed that the most reasonable thing to do under the circumstances was to hold on, both because of the fear of being thrown under a moving vehicle and the assurance of remaining at least partially upright, not falling completely prone.

Cartoons wherein the unwilling and unsuspecting balloon ascensionist holds to the rope of a rapidly-rising balloon and "can't let go," are more fact than comedy, are instinctive, rather than insane, conduct.

In these cases of a person holding, grasping, or supporting himself against an offered railing, a stanchion or a moving vehicle, a jury must appreciate that they judge such conduct not at a time of leisurely and deliberate decision, but at a time of great stress, when instincts may be stronger than intellect. The threat of losing one's balance when a chair leans backwards, the giving away of a support upon which one leans, the rapidly changing position of the human body and the moving vehicle are instances in point. Unless a jury is made to realize that the standard of negligence pertaining to this type of case is that of the "reasonable man" unreasonably frightened, conduct will be penalized as aberrant by comparing it with conduct in the more orderly deliberations of the court room.

Instructions on imminent peril, that a passenger remains such until after he has alighted, and that the defendant carrier must furnish a safe place to alight certainly should be offered. The imminent peril instruction shows, perhaps, the ultimate in adaptability of the "ordinarily prudent person."

George J. Engelman, of New York, told the author of a case in which he represented a seaman who, having gone into the lower hold to take a cargo hook out of a sling, was removing the sling when the runner attached to the hook was raised through the hatchway. The seaman was seen to maintain his grip as he was carried to the top. There he lost it, and fell to the bottom of the hold. And the seaman could not explain why he had not "let go" of the cargo hook.

Defendant contended that the seaman had purposely held on to the hook, taking the dangerous procedure of so riding, rather than climbing up the ladder. But this seaman merely did what was instinctive. "Before he knew it" he was off the ground; then, too frightened to let go in time voluntarily, held on until his hold was involuntarily broken.

Mr. Engleman states that, when he, himself, experimented with the actual hook, his normal reaction, when the hook was jerked, was to "hold on."

As regards "imminent peril," there can be no rule prescribing the right conduct in emergencies. All that is required is that the conduct be consistent with that of a man of ordinary prudence, acting under the same circumstances.[1] As expressed in a comment to Re-

---

1. Sills v. Los Angeles Transit Lines, 40 Cal.2d 630, 255 P.2d 795 (1953) ("A person in imminent peril, where immediate action is necessary to avoid it, is not required to exercise all that presence of mind which is normally exacted of a careful and prudent person under ordinary circumstance, nor to show that his inability to escape from the threatened danger was a physical impossibility"); Kardasinski v. Koford, 88 N.H. 444, 190 A. 702, 111 A.L.R. 1017 (1937) ("An unexpected danger suddenly encountered more or less naturally tends, in effect upon one's mental faculties, to slow as well as to disturb them. . . . Not only may the mind in an emergency fail to do its best work, but the emergency may be such as to give no time for, or to delay, the working."); Bennett v. Robertson, 107 Vt. 202, 177 A. 625, 98 A.L.R. 152 (1935); McGowan v. Tayman, 144 Va. 358, 132 S.E. 316 (1926); Kennedy v. Delaware Leasing

statement, Second, Torts, § 296: "The mere fact that his choice is unfortunate does make it improper even though it is one which the actor should not have made had he had sufficient time to consider all the effects likely to follow his action."[2] The jury is the final arbiter of whether the conduct was reasonable under the circumstances,[3] and care should be taken to educate the jury to the application of this rule in determining whether particular conduct met the standard of due care. Instructions, though generally available,[4] may be unnecessary if the "under the circumstances" argument is effectively advanced, and are usually better to avoid since they often constitute reversible error,[5] and always, at least, provide grounds for appeal.

& Rental Corp., 441 F.2d 562 (6th Cir. 1971) (Test is what reasonably prudent man would have done under the circumstances); Cincotta v. United States, 362 F.Supp. 386 (D.C.Md.1973) (Emergency conduct must be analyzed in light of situation where time for deliberate choice is unavailable).

Restatement, Second, Torts § 296(1): ("In determining whether conduct is negligent toward another, the fact that the actor is confronted with a sudden emergency which requires rapid decision is a factor in determining the reasonable character of his choice of action.")

2. Restatement, Second, Torts § 296, comment b; Prosser, The Law of Torts (4th ed. 1971) p. 169.

See also Wagner v. International Ry. Co., 232 N.Y. 176, 133 N.E. 437 (1921) (Defendant's mistake "would not count against him, if it resulted from the excitement and confusion of the moment."—Cardozo, C.J.); Kane v. Worcester Consol. St. Ry. Co., 182 Mass. 201, 65 N.E. 54 (1902) (In an emergency, a choice may be "mistaken, yet prudent."—Holmes, C. J.); M. P. Howlett, Inc. v. Tug Michael Moran, 425 F.2d 619 (2d Cir. 1970), cert. denied 400 U.S. 833, 91 S.Ct. 67, 27 L.Ed.2d 65 (Negligence does not flow from mere errors of judgment in emergency).

3. North River Ins. Co. v. Davis, 274 F.Supp. 146 (W.D.Va.1963), aff'd 392 F.2d 571 (4th Cir.) (Composite judgment of jury is best means to determine conduct of reasonable man under similar circumstances); Leo v. Dunham, 41 Cal.2d 712, 264 P.2d 1 (1953) (Whether party was in a position of imminent peril a question of fact for jury).

4. E. g., California: BAJI 4.40.

See, Annotation, Imminent Peril Instructions in Motor Vehicle Cases, 80 A.L.R.2d 5.

5. Dooley, Modern Tort Law, (1977) § 3.38 (Emergency doctrine instructions are "the most fertile field of error in negligence litigation); Kuist v. Curran, 116 Cal.App.2d 404, 253 P.2d 681 (1953) (Instruction constituted error; necessity for quick action not emergency).

See also Pullin v. Nabors, 240 Miss. 864, 128 So.2d 117 (1961); Lentz v. Northwestern Nat'l Cas. Co., 11 Wis. 2d 462, 185 N.W.2d 759 (1961).

§ 14.2 Availability of Defense

The rule is equally available to defendant, as a defense to negligence, and to plaintiff, as a defense to contributory negligence.[6] Where the actor created the emergency,[7] however, or his tortious con-

---

6. Smith v. Johe, 154 Cal.App.2d 508, 316 P.2d 688 (1957) (Doctrine of imminent peril is available to plaintiff or defendant, or, in a proper case, to both).

Md.—Brehm v. Lorenz, 206 Md. 500, 112 A.2d 475 (1955) (Negligence of defendant motorist not shown where rear end collision caused by sudden stopping of another vehicle).

Mo.—Jones v. Hughey, 283 S.W.2d 550 (Mo.1955) (Defendant applied brakes when dog suddenly crossed in front of him, causing his car to swerve into plaintiff's lane and collide with plaintiff's car).

Neb.—Kiser v. Christensen, 163 Neb. 155, 78 N.W.2d 823 (1956). (Guest case for injuries sustained when truck collided with train, defendant, under the emergency doctrine, was, as a matter of law, not guilty of gross negligence).

Plaintiff: Kan.—Winfough v. Tri-State Ins. Co., 179 Kan. 525, 297 P.2d 159 (1956) (Plaintiff motorist collided with defendant's parked, unlighted truck shortly after sunset—plaintiff was confronted with a sudden emergency and was not bound by the rule that one operating his vehicle in the nighttime must have it under such control that he can stop it within the range of his lights).

La.—Snodgrass v. Centanni, 229 La. 915, 87 So.2d 127 (1956) (Plaintiff motorist entered unbarricaded city street and in an instant saw a workman waving his arms, glanced up and saw a falling tree, and accelerated his speed, rather than stopping, in an unsuccessful effort to avoid the tree—the emergency doctrine applies).

Mass.—Barton v. New York, New Haven & Hartford R. R. Co., 332 Mass. 345, 125 N.E.2d 124 (1955) (Plaintiff's truck stalled on tracks as train approached—plaintiff became "glued to" his truck and "horrified").

Minn.—Shastid v. Shue, 247 Minn. 314, 77 N.W.2d 273 (1956) (Where operator of tractor-trailer, collided with another disabled tractor-trailer parked on highway and lights appear to indicate an approaching vehicle).

Wash.—Poling v. Charbonneau Packing Corp., 45 Wash.2d 845, 278 P.2d 375 (1954) (Tractor driver was injured when, because of heavy rear load, front of tractor tipped over backward —plaintiff's stepping on the brake pedal instead of the clutch pedal was not contributory negligence as a matter of law).

7. Pierce v. Der Wienerschnitzel Int'l, Inc., 313 F.Supp. 740 (W.D.Mo.1970) (Air crash emergency created by defendant when he cut off fuel to engines—emergency doctrine unavailable); Cataldi v. Sal Finocchiaro Motor Freight, 221 F.Supp. 921 (E.D.Pa. 1963) (Rear end vehicle accident. Under New Jersey law, emergency doctrine not available to plaintiff who created emergency.); Trezza v. Dame, 370 F.2d 1006 (5th Cir. 1967) (Head-on collision. Emergency doctrine unavailable where defendant's conduct proximately causes emergency.).

Cal.—Yates v. Morotti, 120 Cal.App. 710, 8 P.2d 519 (1932) (Doctrine does not apply "to one who has muddled his mind by an excessive use of intoxicating liquor and while in such condition is guilty of wilful, wanton

duct preceded it,[8] the defense is not available. Where the emergency was of the sort that should have been foreseen, such as dangerous road conditions in inclement weather,[9] or a child darting out on a residential street,[10] or cattle breaking loose during a stockyard delivery,[11] the rule may not apply since reasonable conduct would have been to anticipate the situation. Further, where the actor engages in an activity which requires special training or experience because of the likelihood of emergency situations, the emergency rule may be inapplicable to excuse his error of judgment.[12]

or reckless driving of an automobile which results in injury . . .").

Wis.—Metz v. Rath, 275 Wis. 12, 81 N.W.2d 34 (1957) (Action for wrongful death of pedestrian who was struck by automobile while crossing highway—emergency doctrine is inapplicable because the emergency was of the pedestrian's own creation).

8. *Ill.*—Duffy v. Cortesi, 2 Ill.2d 511, 119 N.E.2d 241 (1954) (Motorist who continues to drive into heavily traveled intersection while blinded by sun negligent as a matter of law).

S.D.—Dwyer v. Christensen, 76 S.D. 201, 75 N.W.2d 650 (1956) (Plaintiff was injured when his car left the highway to avoid collision with defendant's automobile which had stalled across the highway—plaintiff had been outdriving his headlights and not entitled to protection of emergency rule).

Vt.—Kremer v. Fortin, 119 Vt. 1, 117 A.2d 245 (1955) (Where motorist failed to hear fire truck siren and stop before entering intersection he cannot invoke sudden emergency rule).

Wis.—Ackley v. Farmers Mut. Auto. Ins. Co., 273 Wis. 422, 78 N.W.2d 744 (1956) (Two cars collided head-on, both having been driven with left wheels over center of highway toward crest of hill over which neither driver could see oncoming automobile —emergency doctrine inapplicable.

"One cannot deliberately proceed to a point of danger, and then act within the protection that a sudden emergency might otherwise give him.").

9. Sowizral v. Hughes, 333 F.2d 829 (3d Cir. 1964).

10. *N.C.*—Brunson v. Gainey, 245 N.C. 152, 95 S.E.2d 514 (1956) (Defendant motorist struck and killed child when he darted out in front of car—defendant cannot invoke emergency rule if he drove at excessive speed in a neighborhood where he knew small children were accustomed to play and thereby permitted the emergency to arise).

See also Skeens v. Gemmell, 353 F.2d 38 (6th Cir. 1965); Conery v. Tackmaier, 34 Wis.2d 511, 149 N.W.2d 575 (1967).

11. *Okl.*—Bocock v. Tulsa Stockyards Co., 309 P.2d 279 (Okl.1957) (While plaintiff was delivering his cattle at defendant's stockyards, a calf escaped and injured plaintiff—instruction on "sudden emergency" was properly refused because plaintiff, with his experience at the stockyard, should reasonably have anticipated such danger).

12. Lachman v. Pennsylvania Greyhound Lines, Inc., 160 F.2d 496 (4th Cir. 1947) (Error to give emergency doctrine instruction in case involving bus accident, without explaining training and skills required of bus drivers).

Restatement, Second, Torts § 296, comment c ("In determining whether the actor is to be excused for an error of judgment in a sudden emergency, importance is to be attached to the fact that many activities require that those engaged in them shall have such natural aptitude or special training as to give them the ability to cope with those dangerous situations which are likely to arise in the course of such activities").

Kachman v. Blosberg, 251 Minn. 224, 87 N.W.2d 687 (1958) (High degree of vigilance required of motor vehicle driver where children known or reasonably expected to be in vicinity).

§§ 14.3–15.0 are reserved for supplementary material.

CHAPTER 15

WANTON OR WILFUL MISCONDUCT

Table of Sections

Sec.
15.1 In General.
15.2 Elements.
15.3 Pleadings.
15.4 Corporate Wilful and Wanton Misconduct.

Library References:
C.J.S. Negligence § 203 et seq.
West's Key No. Digests, Negligence ⇨121.1(11).
Prosser, Law of Torts (4th ed. 1971), pp. 180–187.
Blashfield, Automobile Law and Practice, § 67.1 et seq.

§ 15.1 In General

Contributory negligence generally does not bar recovery where the conduct of defendant may be characterized as "wanton" or "wilful,"[1] nor will assumption of risk.[2] In addition to the foregoing

---

1. See Chapter 11, Contributory Negligence, supra.
Seeger v. Odell, 18 Cal.2d 409, 115 P.2d 977, 136 A.L.R. 1291 (1941) (As a general rule negligence of the plaintiff is no defense to an intentional tort); Hinkle v. Minneapolis A. & C. R. Ry. Co., 162 Minn. 340, 202 N.W. 340 (1925) ("Contributory negligence is not a defense to wanton and wilful negligence, for the very simple reason that the parties are not equally delinquent in the violation of duty. In such case the negligence of the defendant is the proximate cause of plaintiff's injury while his negligence is no more than a remote cause."); Most courts hold that wilful or wanton misconduct by a plaintiff is a defense. Schneider v. Brecht, 6 Cal. App.2d 379, 44 P.2d 662 (1935) "[W]here the negligence of the plaintiff is of such a character that it contributes to, and really becomes a part of, and the inducing cause of the defendant's wilful misconduct, no recovery can be or should be had—"); Gulf M. & O. R. Co. v. Freund, 183 F.2d 1005 (8th Cir. 1950).

2. See Chapter 13, Assumption of Risk, supra.
Teeter v. Pugsley, 319 Mich. 508, 29 N.W.2d 850 (1947) (Pistol fired by resident over heads of children, and hit neighbor in leg, assumption of risk not a sufficient defense).
Assumption of risk has been held a good defense to an act of wanton or wilful misconduct: Freedman v. Hurwitz, 116 Conn. 283, 164 A. 647 (1933) (Riding as guest of sleepy driver); Ridgway v. Yenny, 223 Ind. 16, 57 N.E.2d 581 (1944) (Automobile being driven at excessive speed); Pierce v. Clemens, 113 Ind.App. 65,

advantages there are other reasons which commend to the attorney for the plaintiff, a careful scrutiny of the fact situation to determine if he has a case involving "wanton" or "wilful" misconduct.[3] A judgment based on that conduct cannot be discharged by bankruptcy proceedings,[4] and it is held to justify an award of exemplary damages,[5] plaintiff's contributory negligence being no defense.

46 N.E.2d 836 (1943) (Guest driving automobile for owner, as a passenger, told to open throttle on the dash); Garrity v. Mangan, 232 Iowa 1188, 6 N.W.2d 292 (1942) (Automobile guest riding with a driver known to be intoxicated); Davis v. Hollowell, 326 Mich. 673, 40 N.W.2d 641, 15 A.L.R. 2d 1160 (1950) (Riding with intoxicated driver); Gill v. Arthur, 69 Ohio App. 386, 43 N.E.2d 894 (1941) (Automobile guest riding with driver known to be intoxicated.—the rule is "predicated on the factual situation of the defendant's acts alone creating the danger and causing the accident with the plaintiff's acts being that of exposing himself to such obvious danger with appreciation thereof which results in the injury.").

3. Under the so-called "guest act" of numerous states, a guest passenger in a motor vehicle must bring an action for wanton or wilful misconduct, since by legislative prohibition, negligence is not sufficient.

Although the apparent purpose of such statutes is to discourage litigation of this sort, a review of the numerous cases successfully prosecuted under this supposed handicap will demonstrate that there are often manifest advantages to the plaintiff by this enforced procedure.

In 16 Nevada St.Br.J. 51, 61, Dean Prosser comments correctly that the "guest" statutes were the work of liability insurance companies, and often deny recovery to deserving plaintiffs.

See Appleman, Wilful and Wanton Conduct in Automobile Guest Cases (1937) 13 Ind.L.J. 131; Wilful and Wanton—Those Weasel Words (1944)

92 Univ.Pa.L.Rev. 431; Huff, Basis of Liability in Automobile Cases, 1953 Univ.Ill.Law Forum 39.

White, The Liability of an Automobile Driver to a Non-paying Passenger (1934) 20 Va.L.Rev. 326; Rice, The Automobile Guest and the Rationale of Assumption of Risk, 27 Minn.L. Rev. 329; 15 A.L.R.2d 1181.

4. The Bankruptcy Act does not relieve a debtor from liabilities "for wilful and malicious injuries to the person or property of another." 11 U.S.C.A. § 523.

Harrison v. Donnelly, 153 F.2d 588 (8th Cir. 1946) (Judgment for punitive damages obtained against a bankrupt in an action for personal injuries caused by wanton and reckless conduct in the operation of a truck was not dischargeable in bankruptcy); Saueressig v. Jung, 246 Wis. 82, 16 N.W.2d 417 (1944) (Automobile accident judgment where defendant was found to be wanton, reckless and wilful, not dischargeable by bankruptcy).

See also Fitzgerald v. Herzer, 78 Cal. App.2d 127, 177 P.2d 364 (1947).

5. Keller v. Morehead, 247 S.W.2d 218 (Ky.1952) ("It is the general rule that in order to warrant an instruction on punitive damages the negligence must be of such degree as manifests a wanton disregard of the lives or safety of others, or is wilful or malicious"); Southland Broadcasting Co. v. Tracy, 210 Miss. 836, 50 So.2d 572 (1951) (Punitive damages may be recovered "not only for a wilful and intentional wrong, but for such gross and reckless negligence as is equivalent to such a wrong").

It may support recovery by a trespasser [6] or licensee,[7] where ordinary negligence would preclude a cause of action. Plaintiff's prior release will not shield defendant from liability for wanton misconduct.[8] And, in limitation of the duty concept, wanton or wilful misconduct will support an action for damages where plaintiff has suffered no physical impact but mental disturbance only.[9] In *Anderson v. Knox*,[10] an insurance fraud case, defendant insurers were held to have acted in "reckless disregard of the rights of plaintiff," thereby sustaining that portion of damages awarded for plaintiff's resultant psychic tension and anxiety.[11]

But note: Massachusetts Bonding & Ins. Co. v. United States, 352 U.S. 128, 77 S.Ct. 186, 1 L.Ed.2d 189 (1956) (United States not liable for punitive damages under Tort Claim Act.)

6. Reynolds v. Knowles, 185 Tenn. 337, 206 S.W.2d 375 (1947) (Recovery denied to child trespasser on motor vehicle where wilful or wanton misconduct not established); Palmer v. Gordon, 173 Mass. 410, 53 N.E. 909 (1899) (Defendant threw scalding water on stove to frighten child trespasser, resulting in injury); Bremer v. Lake Erie & W. R. Co., 318 Ill. 11, 148 N.E. 862, 41 A.L.R. 1345 (1925) (Railroad held liable where engineer recklessly ran past signal and injured an undiscovered trespasser); Beauchamp v. New York City Housing Auth., 12 N.Y.2d 400, 240 N.Y.S.2d 15, 190 N.E.2d 412, 99 A.L.R.2d 454 (1963) (Child trespasser injured in defendant's vacant house awaiting demolition. Held: maintaining inherently dangerous article without exercising high degree of care constitutes wilful or wanton misconduct.); Puchta v. Rothman, 99 Cal.App.2d 285, 221 P.2d 744 (1950) (Allegation that owner planted contrivance or trap for trespassers on premises would state facts showing wilful act).

7. Sideman v. Guttman, 38 A.D.2d 420, 330 N.Y.S.2d 263 (1972) ("The duty which the owner of premises owes to a social guest is twofold: (1) he must abstain from inflicting intentional, wanton or wilful injuries; and (2) he must exercise reasonable care to disclose any danger known to him but not likely to be discovered by the guest"); Hilker v. Knox, 18 N.C.App. 628, 197 S.E.2d 618 (1963); Steen v. Grenz, 167 Mont. 279, 538 P.2d 16 (1975).

8. Friedman v. Lockheed Aircraft Corp., 138 F.Supp. 530 (E.D.N.Y.1956) (FTCA action where decedent journalist had executed a release before boarding Air Force aircraft for demonstration flight. Held, release no defense to charge of wilful, wanton, or gross negligence.).

9. See Chapter 33, Recovery for Emotional Disturbances, infra.

Prosser, The Law of Torts (4th ed. 1971) pp. 328–30. Blakeley v. Shortal's Estate, 236 Iowa 787, 20 N.W.2d 28 (1945) (Defendant committed suicide by cutting his throat in plaintiff's kitchen; when she returned, she was confronted by his corpse and a kitchen awash with blood; held: even though impact is required in negligent-fright cases, here defendant's estate was liable for plaintiff's mental distress because of defendant's wanton and reckless misconduct); Price v. Yellow Pine Paper Mill Co., 240 S.W. 588 (Tex.Civ.App. 1922) (Mangled husband brought home in shocking condition and delivered abruptly to pregnant wife).

10. 297 F.2d 702 (9th Cir. 1961), cert. denied 370 U.S. 915, 82 S.Ct. 1555, 8 L.Ed.2d 498.

11. 297 F.2d at 730, 731.

§ 15.2 Elements

Having seen the importance of determining whether plaintiff's action was "wilful or wanton," we may ask, what is the distinction between conduct that is merely negligent and conduct that is "wilful or wanton?" [12] In *Donnelly v. Southern Pac. Co.* [13] the court pointed out that "a negligent person has no desire to cause the harm that results from his carelessness." [14] Negligence is an unintentional tort. The court continues: "A tort having some of the characteristics of both negligence and wilfulness occurs when a person with no intent to cause harm intentionally performs an act so unreasonable and dangerous that he knows, or should know, it is highly probable that harm will result. It involves no intention, as does wilful misconduct, to do harm, and it differs from negligence in that it does involve an intention to perform an act that the actor knows, or should know, will very probably cause harm. This is wanton misconduct." [15]

"Wilful" misconduct is sometimes distinguished from "wanton" or "reckless" misconduct in that "wilfulness" involves a somewhat higher degree of purpose, intent or design—short, however, of intentional infliction of injury.[16] The majority of courts today do not dis-

---

12. "One experienced trial judge has evolved a theory. . . . It may be called the 'Oh, my God' theory of wilful and wanton misconduct. . . . If, while listening to a witness recount the facts of an accident, the judge finds himself gripping the arms of his chair and saying to himself, 'Oh, my God, you didn't', then the conduct is wilful and wanton." 1949 Ins.L.J. 716, 723.

13. 18 Cal.2d 863, 118 P.2d 465 (1941).

14. Ibid. at 869.

15. Universal Concrete Pipe Co. v. Bassett, 130 Ohio St. 567, 200 N.E. 843, 119 A.L.R. 646 (1936) ("Wantonness is a synonym for what is popularly known as 'cussedness' and cussedness is a disposition to perversity"); Higbee Co. v. Jackson, 101 Ohio St. 75, 128 N.E. 61, 14 A.L.R. 131 (1920) ("To constitute 'wanton negligence' it is not necessary that there should be ill-will toward the person injured, but an entire absence of care for the safety of others, which exhibits indifference to consequences, establishes legal wantonness. Such a mental attitude distinguishes wrongs caused by wanton negligence from torts arising from mere negligence"); Baines v. Collins, 310 Mass. 523, 38 N.E.2d 626, 138 A.L.R. 1123 (1942) ("It is not necessary to prove that the defendant deliberately intended to injure the plaintiff. It is enough if it is shown that, indifferent to consequences, the defendant intentionally acted in such a way that the natural and probable consequence of his act was injury to the plaintiff."); Gibbard v. Cursan, 225 Mich. 311, 196 N.W. 398 (1923) ("If one wilfully injures another, or if his conduct in doing the injury is so wanton or reckless that it amounts to the same thing, he is guilty of more than negligence. The act is characterized by wilfulness rather than by inadvertence, it transcends negligence —is different in kind.").

16. Everett v. Receivers of Richmond & D. R. Co., 121 N.C. 519, 27 S.E. 991 (1897) ("To constitute willful injury there must be actual knowledge, or

tinguish between the terms, but look rather to the essential characteristic of the actor's indifference to the probable consequences of a known risk.[17] As Prosser indicates:

> "in practice all such distinctions have consistently been ignored, and the three terms have been treated as meaning the same thing, or at least as coming out at the same legal exit. They have been grouped together as an aggravated form of negligence, differing in quality rather than in degree from ordinary lack of care." [18]

The Restatement of Torts treats conduct of this class under the designation "reckless conduct" differentiated from ordinary negligence by the degree of risk involved.[19]

that which the law deems to be the equivalent of actual knowledge, of the peril to be apprehended, coupled with a design, purpose, and intent to do wrong and inflict injury. A wanton act is one which is performed intentionally with a reckless indifference to injurious consequences probable to result therefrom. Ordinary negligence has as its basis that a person charged with negligent conduct should have known the probable consequences of his act. Wanton and willful negligence rests on the assumption that he knew the probable consequences, but was recklessly, wantonly, or intentionally indifferent to the results.").

17. Saunders v. Shaver, 190 Kan. 699, 378 P.2d 70 (1963) ("A wanton act is something more than ordinary negligence, and yet it is something less than willful injury; to constitute wantonness, the act must indicate a realization of the imminence of danger and a reckless disregard and complete indifference and unconcern for the probable consequences of the wrongful act. It is sufficient if it indicates a reckless diregard for the rights of others with a total indifference to the consequences, although a catastrophe might be the natural result."); Williams v. Carr, 68 Cal.2d 579, 584, 68 Cal.Rptr. 305, 309, 440 P.2d 505, 509 (1968) "[W]illful misconduct implies the intentional doing of something either with knowledge, express or implied, that serious injury is a probable, as distinguished from a possible, result, or the intentional doing of an act with a wanton and reckless disregard of its consequences."

18. Prosser, The Law of Torts, (4th ed. 1971) p. 184.

Montellier v. United States, 202 F.Supp. 384 (E.D.N.Y.1962), aff'd 315 F.2d 180 (2d Cir.) ("Wilful, wanton and reckless conduct is defined by the courts of Massachusetts as a positive act or careless omission in reckless disregard of the rights of others which exposes another to a risk of grave bodily injury. . . . All that must be shown is that the defendant acted indifferently to the consequences in such a way that the natural and probable consequence of his act was injury to plaintiff.") 202 F.Supp. at 400.

19. Restatement, Second, Torts § 500.

Golden v. Sommers, 56 F.R.D. 3 (D.C. Pa.1972), aff'd 481 F.2d 1398 (3d Cir.) ("The three elements necessary to make such a finding are present in this evidence. As the jury was charged, these elements are: (1) that defendant consciously chose a course of action which placed plaintiff in a perilous situation; (2) that this course of action involved a risk of harm substantially greater than that

§ 15.2 WANTON OR WILFUL MISCONDUCT

In *Morgan v. Southern Pac. Transp. Co.*, a California court articulated the following elements of wanton or wilful misconduct:

> "Three essential elements must be present to raise a negligent act to the level of wilful misconduct: (1) actual or constructive knowledge of the peril to be apprehended, (2) actual or constructive knowledge that injury is a probable, as opposed to a possible, result of the danger, and (3) conscious failure to act to avoid the peril." [20]

In *Morgan*, a train, backing up at night along an unguarded divider, in a rural residential neighborhood, struck plaintiff and severed both his legs. The court found that the train crew had constructive knowledge that pedestrians commonly used the divider, had actual knowledge of the potential danger presented by the pedestrian use, had backed the train at an unsafe rate of speed, had taken no precautionary measures when approaching the accident site, and had given no warning after discovering plaintiff's peril. The jury instruction on wilful misconduct, and the jury's award of $175,000 to plaintiff were upheld. (Compare the adequacy of this award with today's which would be circa $1,000,000 plus for a double amputation of either both arms or both legs—with liability).

Where defendant's tortious conduct consists of several acts or omissions, the combination may be found to constitute wanton misconduct, although no individual act or omission alone could be so characterized.[21] Thus, in a jurisdiction where driving while intoxicated does not alone support a charge of wanton misconduct, the combination of intoxicated driving, entering an intersection at 60 mph, running a red light, and disregarding approaching traffic was held to support the charge.[22] Where an experienced bartender served a pa-

---

which is required for a finding of negligence; *and* (c) that defendant either knew that his conduct would expose plaintiff to serious danger or had knowledge of facts which would have disclosed the imminence of danger to a reasonable man.").

20. Morgan v. Southern Pac. Transp. Co., 37 Cal.App.3d 1006, 1012, 112 Cal.Rptr. 695, 698 (1974).

21. Pelletti v. Membrila, 234 Cal.App. 2d 606, 44 Cal.Rptr. 588 (1965) ("When several elements of misconduct, including intoxication, are present, the sum of these elements may add up to wilful misconduct even though no single element alone might suffice"); Turner v. McCready, 190 Or. 28, 54, 222 P.2d 1010, 1021 (1950).

22. Palmer v. Agid, 171 Cal.App.2d 271, 340 P.2d 303 (1959); Pelletti v. Membrila, supra, n. 5 (Intoxicated driver speeding, struck and killed pedestrian in crosswalk and left the scene of the accident).

See also Goncalves v. Los Banos Mining Co., 58 Cal.2d 916, 918, 26 Cal. Rptr. 769, 770, 376 P.2d 833, 834 (1962) (sufficient evidence of willful misconduct where driver apparently ignored stop sign and proceeded into intersection without abating excessive speed); Jones v. Ayers, 212 Cal.

§ 15.2 TORT LIABILITY AND DEFENSES Pt. 3

tron, on his twenty-first birthday, ten straight shots of 151 proof rum, plus a vodka collins, and two beers, all within an hour and a half, wilful misconduct was properly charged in the ensuing wrongful death action based on acute alcohol poisoning.[23]

What constitutes reckless, wilful or wanton behavior is a question of fact for the jury, to be determined in the light of the particular facts and circumstances of the case.[24] Plaintiff is entitled to the wanton or wilful instruction when he has presented evidence reasonably sufficient to support the finding.[25] The trial judge's determination of sufficiency of evidentiary support will ordinarily be reviewed only where there appears to be an abuse of discretion.[26]

§ 15.3 Pleadings

Where plaintiff is uncertain as to whether the evidence will show that the injuries were caused by wanton or wilful misconduct or by

---

App.2d 646, 654, 28 Cal.Rptr. 223, 229 (1963) (High speed, knowledge of stop signs, opportunity to slow vehicle, no apparent attention paid to stop signs and entry into intersection without reduction of speed); Bristow v. Brinson, 212 Cal.App.2d 168, 175, 27 Cal.Rptr. 796, 800 (1963) (Driver familiar with intersection drove past warning sign and through stop sign at 40 miles per hour).

23. Ewing v. Cloverleaf Bowl, 20 Cal. 3d 389, 143 Cal.Rptr. 13, 572 P.2d 1155 (1978) (Bartender knew high potency of liquor served, knew decedent was an inexperienced drinker, knew warnings had no effect on decedent, filled shot glasses beyond usual limit, and continued to serve after decedent was intoxicated. Held, sufficient to raise jury question of wilful misconduct.).

24. Bjornquist v. Boston & A. R. Co., 250 F. 929, 5 A.L.R. 951 (1st Cir. 1918), cert. denied 248 U.S. 573, 39 S.Ct. 11, 63 L.Ed. 427; Meyer v. Blackman, 59 Cal.2d 668, 31 Cal.Rptr. 36, 381 P.2d 916 (1963); Reuther v. Viall, 62 Cal.2d 470, 42 Cal.Rptr. 456,
398 P.2d 792 (1965); Hallman v. Richards, 123 Cal.App.2d 274, 266 P.2d 812 (1954) ("In determining whether the driver of the car is guilty of wilful misconduct, his entire course of conduct, including his speed, is to be considered . . .").

25. Bremer v. Lake Erie & W. R. Co., 318 Ill. 11, 148 N.E. 862, 41 A.L.R. 1345 (1925); Phillips v. G. L. Truman Excavation Co., 55 Cal.2d 801, 13 Cal.Rptr. 401, 362 P.2d 33 (1961).

See also Morgan v. Southern Pac. Transp. Co., supra, n. 20.

26. Mahoney v. Corralejo, 36 Cal.App. 3d 966, 112 Cal.Rptr. 61 (1974) (Plaintiff struck from behind by motorcycle while walking in street at night. Court's refusal to give instructions on wanton misconduct held proper. "Since the trial judge . . . was in the best position to have a 'feel' for the evidence, we at the appellate level must give deference to his determination of the issues of the *reasonableness and evidentiary support* of the plaintiff's theory and only look for an abuse of discretion.").

528

simple negligence, the complaint may be framed to avail plaintiff of either contingency.[27] Except where permitted by statute,[28] a complaint may not allege both simple negligence and wanton misconduct in the same count.[29] Rather the complaint will contain one count for simple negligence and another for wilful misconduct.[30] As to wanton or wilful misconduct it is the general rule that it is necessary to plead so that on the face of the complaint there are facts constituting wanton misconduct.[31] Despite the absence of the word "malice" in the pleading, and the absence of a prayer for punitive damages, exemplary damages may be recovered if from the entire pleading it is clear that defendant's misconduct gives rise to an inference of "wantonness or wilfulness." [32]

The actor's actual state of mind is not controlling.[33] Where the unreasonable risk *should* reasonably be appreciated, constructive knowledge will be attributed to the tortfeasor.[34] Similarly, plaintiff

27. Indeed, it may well be malpractice for an attorney to so frame the complaint if the evidence may go either way.

28. Du Pre v. Southern R. Co., 66 S.C. 124, 44 S.E. 580 (1903).

29. Sharp v. Kurth, 245 S.W. 636 (Mo. App.1922).

30. Horstman v. Krumgold, 55 Cal. App.2d 296, 130 P.2d 721 (1942); Wells v. Wildin, 224 Iowa 913, 277 N.W. 308, 115 A.L.R. 169 (1938); Troxell v. De Shom, 279 S.W. 438, 23 A.L.R.2d 117 (Mo.App.1925); Smith v. Williams, 180 Or. 626, 178 P.2d 710, 173 A.L.R. 1220 (1947); Michels v. Boruta, 122 S.W.2d 216 (Tex.Civ. App.1938).

31. Firsvold v. Leahy, 15 Cal.App.2d 752, 60 P.2d 151 (1936) (Where the complaint alleged the time, the place, the parties involved as guests and driver, the act, the intent, the wilful misconduct, the injuries and the proximate cause, the complaint was sufficient against a special demurrer); Universal Concrete Pipe Co. v. Bassett, 130 Ohio St. 567, 200 N.E. 843, 119 A.L.R. 646 (1936) ("Facts must be pleaded which reveal on their face the element of wantonness, and they must be proved as pleaded").

32. Morgan v. French, 70 Cal.App.2d 785, 161 P.2d 800 (1945); Vaughn v. Jonas, 31 Cal.2d 586, 191 P.2d 432 (1948) ("Malice" may be inferred from pleading of an intentional wrongful act which causes harm).

No specific sum in exemplary damages need be prayed. Powell v. West, 208 Ala. 388, 94 So. 475 (1922); Winn & Lovett Grocery Co. v. Archer, 126 Fla. 308, 171 So. 214 (1936); Dwyer v. Libert, 30 Idaho 576, 167 P. 651 (1917).

33. Pelletti v. Membrila, 234 Cal.App. 2d 606, 44 Cal.Rptr. 588 (1965) ("If conduct is sufficiently lacking in consideration for the rights of others, reckless, heedless to an extreme, and indifferent to the consequences it may impose, then, regardless of the actual state of the mind of the actor and his actual concern for the rights of others, we call it willful misconduct . . . .")

34. Restatement, Second Torts § 500(c): "In order that the actor's conduct may be reckless, it is not necessary that he himself recognize it as being extremely dangerous. His inability to realize the danger may be due to his own reckless temperament or to the abnormally favorable results of previous conduct of the same

need not show that defendant was "consciously unconcerned whether or not plaintiff was injured," [35] nor prove "ill will" on defendant's part.[36] Where "malice" is statutorily required to support an award of exemplary damages, wilful conduct done in "reckless disregard of its possible results" has been held to suffice as an equivalent showing, without need for further proof of the actor's state of mind.[37] Some courts, however, have reasoned that "malice" necessarily involves a subjective element, and requires a showing of conscious disregard of a known serious risk. Thus, in a 1975 products liability case, where plaintiff charged that a contraceptive had proximately caused injuries including thrombophlebitis and multiple pulmonary emboli, the court held that plaintiff was required to allege that the manufacturers had acted in "conscious disregard of safety", as *animus malus* to justify her plea for exemplary damages.[38]

sort. It is enough that he knows or has reason to know of circumstances which would bring home to the realization of the ordinary, reasonable man the highly dangerous character of his conduct."

Williamson v. McKenna, 223 Or. 366, 354 P.2d 56 (1960) (" 'Recklessness' is, therefore, not necessarily a 'state of mind' showing a consciousness of the danger and an election to encounter it; 'recklessness' may be found in circumstances where the defendant did not appreciate the extreme risk but where any reasonable man would appreciate it. In other words, the standard is an objective one as it is in the case of negligence.").

35. Taylor v. Lawrence, 229 Or. 259, 366 P.2d 735 (1961).

36. See 57 Am.Jur.2d Negligence § 101.

Higbee Co. v. Jackson, 101 Ohio St. 75, 128 N.E. 61, 14 A.L.R. 131 (1920) ("The authorities are uniform in holding that, to constitute wilful or wanton negligence, it is not necessary to show ill will toward the person injured, but an entire absence of care for the life, person or property of others which exhibits indifference to consequences makes a case of constructive or legal wilfulness. A complete indifference to consequences distinguishes wrongs caused by wantonness and recklessness from torts arising from negligence.").

37. Toole v. Richardson-Merrell, Inc., 251 Cal.App.2d 689, 60 Cal.Rptr. 398 (1967) ("But malice in fact, sufficient to support an award of punitive damages on the basis of malice as that term is used in Civil Code section 3294, may be established by a showing that the defendant's wrongful conduct was wilful, intentional, and done in reckless disregard of its possible results. Where, as here, there is evidence that the conduct in question is taken recklessly and without regard to its injurious consequences, the jury may find malice in fact.").

See also Templeton Feed & Grain v. Ralston Purina Co., 69 Cal.2d 461, 471, 72 Cal.Rptr. 344, 350, 446 P.2d 152, 158 (1968); Dorsey v. Manlove, 14 Cal. 553, 556 (1860); Sturges v. Charles L. Harney, Inc., 165 Cal.App. 2d 306, 322, 331 P.2d 1072, 1081 (1958); McDonell v. American Trust Co., 130 Cal.App.2d 296, 299, 279 P. 2d 138, 140 (1955).

38. G. D. Searle & Co. v. Superior Court, 49 Cal.App.3d 22, 122 Cal. Rptr. 218 (1975).

§ 15.4 Corporate Wilful and Wanton Misconduct

In *Roginsky v. Richardson-Merrell, Inc.*[39] a products liability case wherein plaintiff alleged reckless conduct on the part of defendant drug manufacturing corporation, a Federal Court of Appeals disallowed the jury's award of $100,000 punitive damages. The court held that, under New York law, punitive damages would be awarded against a corporate defendant only when the management "either authorized, participated in, consented to, or after discovery, ratified" the reckless conduct.[40] The court further held that such conduct must involve a conscious disregard of a substantial and unjustifiable risk, and must be clearly established by a standard of proof close to that required in criminal cases.[41] The drug manufacturer had earlier pleaded *nolo contendere* to related criminal charges of withholding evidence and making false statements to the FDA, and had paid an $80,000 fine.[42] In a companion case against the manufacturer in California, $250,000 in punitive damages were upheld on "ample evidence from which the jury could infer that high level management had knowledge of wrongdoing on the part of department heads and other employees and agents."[43] Nevertheless, the *Roginsky* court,

---

39. 378 F.2d 832 (2d Cir. 1967).

40. 378 F.2d at 842.

41. 378 F.2d at 843.

42. United States v. Richardson-Merrell, Inc., Crim. No. 1211–63 (D-D.C., June 4, 1964).

43. Toole v. Richardson-Merrell, Inc., supra, n. 39, $175,000 compensatory damages, $500,000 punitive damages reduced to $250,000. "Besides the falsification of test data under the direction of Dr. Van Maanen and the withholding from the FDA and the medical profession of vital information concerning blood changes and eye opacities in test animals, there was evidence that, after Dr. Fox reported eye opacities and blindness in her test animals, and after Merck, Sharp & Dohme had made a similar report, appellant continued to represent to the medical profession that MER/29 was a proven drug, remarkably free from side effects, virtually nontoxic, having a specific and completely safe action. In light of appellant's knowledge, the jury could infer that these statements were recklessly made with wanton disregard for the safety of all who might use the drug. Moreover, similar representations continued to be made even after the first report of cataracts in a human had been received and after appellant's later tests confirmed the presence of eye opacities in virtually all test animals. When respectable medical publications began to challenge the toxicity and efficacy of MER/29 appellant's salesmen were instructed to blame side effects on other drugs, or at least to suggest that as a good possibility. Even after a number of cases of cataracts in humans from use of MER/29 had been reported to appellant, and when its own tests had established blindness in its test animals, appellant continued to defend sale of its drug. When in November, 1961, Dr. Nestor of the FDA expressed the opinion that MER/29 should be withdrawn from the market, he was told by Vice President Woodward, in President Getman's presence, that MER/29 '. . . .

conceding that plaintiff had shown "wilfulness" on the part of subordinate officials, found that the record presented "no proof from which a jury could properly conclude that defendant's officers manifested deliberate disregard for human welfare." [44] This disingenuous rationale, which, for practical purposes, would put an end to punitive damages in products liability cases, seems to have been motivated primarily by the court's sympathy to defendant's plight in facing the spectre of multiple punitive damages, and the court's astonishing conclusion that: "A manufacturer distributing a drug to many thousands of users under government regulation scarcely requires this additional measure [punitive damages] for manifesting social disapproval and assuring deterrence." [45] The same court expressed greater rationality in a subsequent oil spill case, where it noted:

> "To hold that punitive damages may not be imposed unless there is participation in the tortfeasing decision by the highest corporate executives is unrealistic given the size of giant corporations like appellant whose operations are so far-flung . . . ."

was the biggest and most important drug in Merrell history . . .' and that the company intended '. . . to defend it at every step . . . .' and would withdraw the drug from the market voluntarily only when it determined that its inherent risk outweighed its efficacy. In December, 1961, the FDA compelled appellant to issue a drastic warning letter notifying the medical profession of known cases of cataract in humans from use of the drug. Appellant nevertheless continued with plans vigorously to promote its sale."

From all of the evidence the jury could find that appellant acted recklessly and in wanton disregard of possible harm to others in marketing, promoting, selling and maintaining MER/29 on the market in view of its knowledge of the toxic effect of the drug. Such a finding would necessarily be a finding of malice in fact, and since the jury was instructed only on malice as a foundation for an award of punitive damages and made such an award in respondent's favor, we must presume they found malice in fact."

The court noted that it respectfully differed from the holding in *Roginsky*. 251 Cal.App.2d at 714–715, 60 Cal. Rptr. at 416–417.

44. 378 F.2d at 850 ("But there was no proof from which a jury could properly conclude that defendant's officers manifested deliberate disregard for human welfare; what it shows as to this, apart from negligence in policing subordinates and a somewhat stiff-necked attitude toward the FDA, is rather that they were so convinced of the value of the drug both to the public welfare and to the company's finances that they maintained a sanguine view longer than prudence warranted").

45. 378 F.2d at 840, 841. See Frumer and Friedman, Products Liability, § 33.01[7] for discussion of the Richardson-Merrell MER/29 cases.

Rheingold, The MER/29 Story—An Instance of Successful Mass Disaster Litigation, 56 Cal.L.Rev. 116 (1968).

It is true that stockholders ultimately bear the cost of liability, but those who have been given authority to avert environmental damage should be given some incentive to do so. 'Smart money' is the traditional way, and the type of modern tort represented here is a fair field for punitive damages . . . ."[46]

46. Doralee Estates, Inc. v. Cities Serv. Oil Co., 569 F.2d 716, 722 (2d Cir. 1977).

§§ 15.5–16.0 are reserved for supplementary material.

CHAPTER 16

PUNITIVE DAMAGES *

Table of Sections

Sec.
16.1 Introduction.
16.2 History.
16.3 Statements of Purpose.
16.4 Arguments Against Punitive Damages.
16.5 Requirements for Punitive Damages.
16.6 Survival of Claim.
16.7 Measurement of Punitive Damages.
16.8 Pleadings.
16.9 Insurance Coverage of Punitive Awards.
16.10 Contract Actions.
16.11 Punitive Damages in Products Liability Cases.
16.12 Punitive Damages in Drunk Driving Cases.
16.13 Conclusion.

Library References:
  C.J.S. Damages §§ 117–126.
  West's Key No. Digests, Damages ⚖︎87–94.
  Prosser, Law of Torts (4th ed. 1971), pp. 9–14.
  Blashfield, Automobile Law & Practice, § 480.16.

§ 16.1 Introduction

Punitive, or exemplary, damages have skyrocketed in recent years.[1] Plaintiffs' lawyers and jurors like them. Yet, for some rea-

---

* This article appears in 49 U.Mo.K.C.L. Rev. 1 (1980).

1. Mann v. Alabama-Kraft, No. 77-71-COL (M.D.Ga. March 15, 1979) ($1,000,000 in punitive damages for wrongful death as a result of a negligent repair by machine's owner; machine put back into use violated written safety regulations); Higbee v. Cole, No. 38088 (Ariz. Yuma County Super. Ct. Apr. 24, 1979) ($10,500 compensatory, $289,500 punitive, for intentional infliction of mental distress, assault and property damage as a result of defendant's belief that plaintiff had "stolen his wife" and planned to take over his business); Daniel v. Magma Copper Co., No. 164920 (Ariz. Pima County Super. Ct. Apr. 19, 1979) ($176,000 compensatory, $500,000 punitive for wrongful termination of plaintiff's employment and the intentional infliction of emotional distress as a result of plaintiff's suggestion that he was going to file a medical malpractice claim against the company hospital for a severe injury to his anal sphincter muscle which resulted in embarrass-

son, trial and appellate judges disfavor and generally tend to discourage them,[2] despite the fact that the law plainly allows them to be awarded.

Any lawyer would be remiss if he failed to consider the availability of punitive damages in any given case. Although most jurisdictions [3] do not require that punitive damages be requested in the prayer of the complaint, nonetheless, it is certain that the sooner the attorney begins looking for evidence of wilful or wanton conduct, the more likely he will be able to prove this activity at trial.

§ 16.2 History

The value inherent in a review of the history of a subject should not be regarded lightly. Perhaps Professor Morris most succinctly

---

ing bowel accidents); Sarchett v. Blue Shield, No. 72–10–0416–77 (Cal. Com.Arb. June 4, 1979) (Fox Arb.) (*$13,000 compensatory, $300,000 punitive* for bad faith failure to pay hospital bill on grounds that hospitalization was not "medically necessary"); Ingram v. Commercial Bankers Life Ins. Co., No. 117117 (Cal. Riverside County Super. Ct. May 23, 1979) (*$128,000 compensatory, $872,001 punitive* for bad faith termination of benefits under a credit disability policy); Grimshaw v. Ford Motor Co. (Cal. San Bernadino County Super. Ct. 1978), appeal docketed, No. 4th Civ. 20095 (Cal.Ct.App. 4th Dist. Apr. 26, 1978) (*$125,000,000 punitive* reduced to $6,000,000, including compensatory; Pinto gas tank case); Farish v. MacArthur, No. 76–4516 CA-(L)O1C (Fla. Palm Beach County Cir. Ct. July 12, 1979) (*$50,000 compensatory, $2,000,000 punitive* for tortious interference with attorney-client relationship following defendant insurance company's attempt to settle directly with widow in wrongful death action and to destroy widow-client's confidence in attorney-plaintiff's reputation); Smuckler v. J. M. Fields, Inc., No. 75–24187 (Fla. Dade County Cir.Ct. Sept. 22, 1978) (*$150,000 actual, $350,000 punitive* for wrongful death and survival actions for illegal sale of handgun ammunition and shopping center's failure to provide security which ultimately resulted in decedent's murder; store sold ammunition to youths in violation of federal laws); Gordon v. Grove Mfg. Div. of Walter Kiddle & Co., No. 77–C470 (Ind. Henry County Cir.Ct. Dec. 15, 1978) (*$2,000,000 compensatory, $500,000 punitive* for strict liability action against manufacturer of crane which struck high voltage wire and resulted in amputation of plaintiff's left arm below elbow, two fingers of right hand and portions of both feet at mid-arch; punitives based on evidence manufacturer had failed to investigate safety devices or give warning to workers despite notice of a large number of injuries and deaths).

2. Hatfield v. Max Rouse & Sons N.W., 606 P.2d 944, 955 (Idaho 1980) ("[P]unitive damages 'are not a favorite of the law, and the power to give such damages should be exercised with caution and within the narrowest limits.'") (quoting Williams v. Bone, 74 Idaho 185, 189, 259 P.2d 810, 812 (1953)).

3. Guillen v. Kuykendall, 470 F.2d 745 (5th Cir. 1972); Gibson v. 1013 N. Broad Assoc., 172 N.J.Super. 191, 411 A.2d 711 (1980).

explained the importance of such a study when, in speaking of liability without fault, he noted: "[I]ts age is something of a *prima facie* case for its usefulness."[4] This axiom is equally applicable when one discusses the relative merits and validity of punitive damages.

Early Development

The ancient precursors to the concept of modern punitive damages may be found in the earliest collection of laws known to man. The Code of Hammurabi, dated circa 2000 B.C., provided for multiple recovery of compensatory damages. Section eight thereof, for example, required that if a man were to steal an ox, sheep, ass, pig or goat from a temple or palace, he must pay thirty-fold; were he to steal it from a freeman, then he was to pay ten-fold.[5] The range of recoveries under Babylonian laws of restitution in theft cases ranged from two to thirty times the value of the stolen property.[6]

The harbinger of modern punitive damages further may be traced through the centuries: The Bible contains examples from the Hebrew Code of the Mosaic Law;[7] Roman Law calling for multiple damages commences with the Twelve Tables, dated approximately 450 B.C.,[8] the Hindu Code of Manu with similar reference goes back to 200 B.C.,[9] and other provisions for increased awards are found throughout the ancient Greek codes and writings.[10]

Related to the concept of punitive damages are *qui tam* actions which were common in seventeenth century England.[11] Designed to punish wrongdoers, these statutory actions were pursued by informers who received a portion of the judgment as a reward for their efforts. The balance of the judgment went to the king, the poor or to some public use.[12] Modern versions of *qui tam* statutes are not unknown.[13]

---

4. Morris, Punitive Damages in Tort Cases, 44 Harv.L.Rev. 1173, 1206 (1931).

5. A. Kocourek & J. Wigmore, Sources of Ancient and Primitive Law 391 (1915).

6. Id.

7. If a man shall steal an ox, or sheep, and kill it, or sell it; he shall restore five oxen for an ox, and four sheep for a sheep. . . . If the theft be found in his hand alive, whether it be ox, or ass, or sheep; he shall restore double.
Exodus 22:1, 4.

8. H. Lawson, Negligence in the Civil Law 60 (1950).

9. A. Kocourek & J. Wigmore, supra note 5, at 469.

10. Plato, Protagoras 324b; Plato Laws 9.85b and 9.934a.

11. W. Blackstone, Commentaries *161–62. See Groves v. Morris, 73 N.Y. 478 (1878).

12. Clever crooks of the time simply would have a friend bring a *qui tam* action against them which would

13. See note 13 on page 537.

English Common Law

Punitive damages appeared late in the development of the common law. Early English courts never had to face the prospect of assessing damages; most suits then brought were for the recovery of specific property of which the plaintiff had been deprived. Later, in the thirteenth century, juries, having no prior experience or examples to follow, began to make occasional pecuniary awards which ranged from the ridiculously excessive to the grossly inadequate.[14]

Rather than develop a substantial law of damages, the English courts decided to deal with the problem at its source—the jury. If an erroneous verdict was rendered, a "writ of attaint" could then issue. The punishment for imprudent jurors was severe:

> All of the first jury shall be committed to the King's prison, their possessions seized into the King's hands, their habitations and houses shall be pulled down, their woodland shall be felled, their meadows shall be plowed up and they themselves forever thenceforward be esteemed in the eye of the law infamous.[15]

By the sixteenth century, courts had done away with *attaint* and let jury verdicts stand unless there was contrary precise, calculable information on the amount of damage. Later courts began ordering new trials in cases of inappropriate verdicts because it seemed obvious that some jury controls were needed. From the seminal principle of granting new trials in cases of improper awards was germinated the doctrine of punitive damages.[16]

Punitives appeared discreetly, their importance overshadowed by the legal and moral issues of the cases of which they were a part. Ironically, the first case specifically to award punitive damages is much more celebrated as the basis for the fourth amendment to the

then bar all other recovery suits, including actions by the state. This devious practice was "in some measure prevented by a statute made in the reign of a very sharp-sighted prince in penal laws, 4 Hen. VII, ch. 20, which enacts that no recovery, otherwise than by verdict obtained by collusion in a *[qui tam]* action, shall be a bar to any other action prosecuted in *bona fide*." W. Blackstone, supra note 11, at * 162.

13. See Note, The Federal False Claims Act: The Informer as Plaintiff, 69 Harv.L.Rev. 1106 (1956).

14. T. Plucknett, A Concise History of the Common Law (5th ed. 1956).

15. Id. at 131.

16. All theories regarding the origin of punitive damages agree on one basic precept: Early juries had great difficulty in determining the fair amount of damages. J. Stein, Damages and Recovery in Personal Injury and Death Actions § 183 (1972).

United States Constitution than as a basis for assessing punitive damages.

That case, *Wilkes v. Wood*,[17] arose when Woods and the king's messengers ransacked Wilkes' house with the most general of warrants because of a "libelous" pamphlet which Wilkes had published. The court stated:

> I still continue of the same mind, that a jury have it in their power to give damages for more than the injury received. Damages are designed not only as a satisfaction to the injured person, but likewise as a punishment to the guilty, to deter from any such proceeding for the future, and as a proof of the detestation of the jury to the action itself.[18]

The jury found for the plaintiff and awarded 1000 pounds for the trespass. Thus, in the earliest case expressly using the words "exemplary damages," there is no doubt but that the court intended the damages not only to recompense the plaintiff but also to *punish* the tortfeasor and to deter such future conduct.[19]

Punitive damages have had a checkered history of favor-disfavor in English jurisprudence, just as they have had in American jurisprudence. Criticized and controversial since *Wilkes v. Woods*, punitive damages practically were abolished in England in 1964.[20]

American Common Law

Punitive damages were found in early American cases amid a continual debate over whether their primary function was penal or compensatory. Punitive damages were awarded "for example's sake" in a 1791 case of breach of a promise to marry.[21] A number of other cases awarded punitive damages as compensation for plaintiff's cost of bringing suit.[22]

This is not to assume that these early American cases always spoke of punitive damages with approval. In *Fay v. Parker*, the court spoke of punitive damages as "a monstrous heresy . . .

17. Lofft 1, 98 Eng.Rep. 489 (C.P. 1763).

18. Id. at 18–19, 98 Eng.Rep. 498–99.

19. *Accord,* Huckle v. Money, 2 Wils. K.B. 205, 95 Eng.Rep. 768 (1763) (plaintiff, a printer earning one guinea a week, awarded 300 pounds exemplary damages for having been imprisoned for only six hours and admittedly had been confined "very civilly by treating him with beef-steaks and beer").

20. See Rookes v. Barnard [1964] 1 All E.R. 367.

21. Coryell v. Colbaugh, 1 N.J.L. 90 (1791).

22. E. g., Hanna v. Sweeney, 78 Conn. 492, 62 A. 785 (1906).

an unsightly and an unhealthy excrescence, deforming the symmetry of the body of the law." [23] (The old judicial language was as flamboyant as was the forensic endeavors of counsel, both in opening statements and closing arguments.) And so the debate has continued to modern day: courts favoring, disfavoring; condoning, condemning.

Currently, all but four states permit awards of punitive damages in appropriate situations.[24] And of these four states, all have numerous statutory exceptions to the proscription on this practice.[25]

§ 16.3 Statements of Purpose

Clearly, punitive damages now are permitted almost uniformly. Behind this, though, lies the query: *"Why* are they awarded?" Four different rationales have been advanced in support of punitive damages. Close examination of the cases reveals that these rationales are not used independently, rather they usually are found concurrently, with two or more being given by courts to explain the desirability in allowing these damages.

Revenge

Although the "purist" might revolt upon learning that revenge possibly is one of the guiding forces in the law, the eminent jurist Oliver Wendell Holmes, Jr., in discussing the criminal law, once stated: "If people would gratify the passion of revenge outside of the law, if the law did not help them, the law has no choice but to satisfy the craving itself, and thus avoid the greater evil of private retribution." [26]

Prevention of self-styled revenge was a justification of eighteenth and nineteenth century English courts in awarding exemplary damages. In one case involving a quarrel over who had the right to possession of a turtle, the court held:

> [W]hen a blow is given by one gentleman to another, a challenge and death may ensue, and therefore the jury have done right in giving exemplary damages; the plaintiff has been used unlike a

---

23. 53 N.H. 342, 382 (1873).

24. Louisiana, Massachusetts, Nebraska and Washington.

25. E. g., Jeansonne v. Marath, 61 So. 2d 598 (La.Ct.App.1952) (Louisiana allows multiple damages for personal injury); Mass.Gen.Laws Ann. ch. 130, § 27 (West 1974) (Massachusetts allows treble recovery for discharge of sewage into coastal waters); Neb.Rev.Stat. § 54–1808 (1978) (Nebraska allows double damages for violation of its Livestock Sellers Protective Act); Wash.Rev.Code § 19.86.–090 (1978) (Washington allows treble damage award for violation of the Washington Consumer Protection Act).

26. O. W. Holmes, The Common Law 4 (1881).

gentleman by the defendant in striking him, withholding his property, and insisting upon his privilege, all of them tending to provoke him to seek revenge in another way than by law, and therefore we think the damages are not excessive.[27]

Whether prevention of revenge can be considered a valid modern justification for punitive damages is a philosophical question not within the purview of this article. The fact remains, however, that courts and legal scholars continue to cite it as a possible rationale for the promulgation of punitive damages.[28]

Public Justice

Many of the writings and cases on punitive damages hold that the major reason behind punitive damages is that public justice may be served by awarding such damages to individual plaintiffs.[29] What often occurs is that, although defendant's conduct is reprehensible, plaintiff's resulting injury is relatively minimal. The costs of bringing suit alone would discourage the wrong victim from pursuing any remedy. Thus, the wrongdoer whose conduct does not come within the parameters of a criminal offense escapes all prosecution.

Under this theory, referred to as the "private attorney general" approach, allowance of punitive damages acts to persuade the injured victim to pursue his claim and also acts to entice counsel to accept the case. This, in turn, fulfills a public, or attorney general, function of admonishing the wrongdoer and dissuading him from repeating such or similar antisocial conduct.[30]

Compensation

Compensation to the injured plaintiff often is stated as a reason for awarding punitive damages in some states.[31] Semantic problems

27. Grey v. Grant, 2 Wils.K.B. 251, 95 Eng.Rep. 794, 795 (1764).

28. Roginsky v. Richardson-Merrell, Inc., 378 F.2d 832, 838 (2d Cir. 1967); Note, Exemplary Damages in the Law of Torts, 70 Harv.L.Rev. 517, 521 (1957). See also Long, Punitive Damages: An Unsettled Doctrine, 25 Drake L.Rev. 870, 877 (1976).

29. E. g., H. Oleck, Damages to Persons and Property 541 (1961).

30. The possibility of a punitive damages award sometimes may induce the victim, otherwise unwilling to proceed because of the attendant trouble and expense, to take action against the wrongdoer. Indeed, such self-interest of the plaintiff has been characterized as "[p]erhaps the principal advantage" of sanctioning punitive damages because it "leads to the actual prosecution of the claim for punitive damages, where the same motive would often lead him to refrain from the trouble incident to appearing against the wrongdoer in criminal proceedings." C. McCormick, Damages 276–77 (1935). See also Walker v. Sheldon, 10 N.Y. 2d 401, 179 N.E.2d 497, 223 N.Y.S.2d 488 (1961).

31. Long, supra note 28, contains an excellent discussion of the conflict

with this concept appear to make this practice questionable because most jurisdictions have designed *actual* damages to implement this function. But upon closer examination, it is apparent that courts allow recovery of only those damages not recoverable as compensatory damages. The most common of these is attorney's fees. By so limiting punitive awards, courts avoid any possible conflict with double recovery.[32]

Punishment and Deterrence

The most frequently articulated, and probably most logical, reason for awarding punitive damages is to punish the wrongdoer in order to deter him, and others as well, from again engaging in socially unacceptable conduct.[33] The Restatement Second Torts is in accord with this view.[34]

Concerning this approach, the United States Supreme Court once stated:

> It is a well-established principle of the common law, that . . . a jury may inflict what are called exemplary, punitive, or vindictive damages upon a defendant, having in view the enormity of his offence rather than the measure of compensation to the plaintiff. . . . By the common as well as by statute law, men are often punished for aggravated misconduct or lawless acts, by means of a civil action, and the damages, inflicted by way of penalty or punishment, given to the party injured.[35]

§ 16.4 Arguments Against Punitive Damages

All of the preceding views in favor of awarding exemplary damages properly may be said to be based upon public policy reasons. Yet many judges and commentators continue to disparage such

---

among legal scholars as to states utilizing compensation as a rationale for punitive damages.

32. In Connecticut, exemplary damages are limited in amount to expenses of litigation, less taxable costs. Craney v. Donovan, 92 Conn. 236, 102 A. 640 (1917).

33. This is the view adhered to in California. Section 3294 of West's Ann. California Civil Code states: "[T]he plaintiff, in addition to the actual damages, may recover damages for the sake of example and by way of punishing the defendant." West's Ann. Cal.Civ.Code § 3294 (West 1980).

34. Section 908 states: "Punitive damages are damages, other than compensatory or nominal damages, awarded against a person to punish him for his outrageous conduct and to deter him and others like him from similar conduct in the future." Restatement, Second Torts § 908(1) (1965).

35. Day v. Woodworth, 45 U.S. (13 How.) 534, 536 (1851).

awards and even go so far as to deny them *wholly* in some cases where they unquestionably are valid. What, then, is it about these damages that excites the wrath of these legal scholars?

The best known modern statement against the practice of allowing punitive damages is in *dicta* by the well-known United States District Judge, Henry J. Friendly, in *Roginsky v. Richardson-Merrell, Inc.*[36] That case involved a product liability action which alleged that MER/29, a drug used to lower blood cholesterol levels, caused side-effects such as dermatitis, hair loss and cataracts. Supra, p. ——. Evidence was discovered that the results of tests run by the drug company, indicating that the product caused eye damage in laboratory rats, had been altered by company employees prior to submitting them to the Federal Drug Administration for marketing approval.

Judge Friendly, in discussing the numerous claims against the defendant and the problems which would be created if each plaintiff were to receive a substantial punitive damages award, observed:

> The legal difficulties engendered by claims for punitive damages on the part of hundreds of plaintiffs are staggering. If all recovered punitive damages in the amount here awarded these would run into tens of millions, as contrasted with the maximum criminal penalty . . . . We have the greatest difficulty in perceiving how claims for punitive damages in such a multiplicity of actions throughout the nation can be so administered as to avoid overkill.[37]

Judge Friendly further noted that the cost of companies providing "probably needless insurance" against punitive damages merely is passed on to the consumer and that "many innocent *stockholders* [are] suffering extinction of their investments for a single management sin."[38]

The learned jurist also addressed the argument that these damages fulfilled a public policy need:

> A manufacturer distributing a drug to many thousands of users under government regulation scarcely requires this additional measure [punitive damages] for manifesting social disapproval and assuring deterrence. Criminal penalties and heavy compensatory damages, recoverable under some circumstances even without proof of negligence, should sufficiently meet these objectives.[39]

36. 378 F.2d 832 (2d Cir. 1967).
37. Id. at 839.
38. Id. at 841.
39. Id. at 840–41.

Another strong argument which has been advanced is that punitive damages violate certain constitutional guarantees. Basically, this argument contends that because punitive damages serve to punish, they must be considered penal; fundamental constitutional criminal safeguards therefore must be applied fully.[40]

Punitive damages also are criticized on the ground that the award represents an improper windfall for the plaintiff.[41] These critics assert that if the purpose of exemplary damages is to punish the defendant and not to reward the plaintiff, then the latter truly reaps an unjust and unwarranted reward. Entertained with this argument is the proposal that the government should be the benefactor of the punitive awards.[42] The government then would be in the assumed position to disperse the funds for the general public benefit rather than one person receiving the funds for his own personal use.

Punitive damages in cases of multiple plaintiffs can present a problem when the plaintiff first to trial is awarded huge exemplary damages.

§ 16.5 Requirements for Punitive Damages

State of Mind

Punitive damages are not recoverable unless the defendant has acted with the requisite state of mind. In Missouri, it is held that the defendant must have committed a wrongful act without just cause or excuse.[43] Furthermore, he must know the act was wrong at the time he did it.[44]

Punitive damages are available in California where the defendant has acted with oppression, fraud or malice—whether express or implied.[45] Where the plaintiff proceeds upon a theory of malice, mal-

---

40. See, e. g., Toole v. Richardson-Merrell, Inc., 251 Cal.App.2d 689, 716, 60 Cal.Rptr. 398, 417 (1967).

41. Morris, Punitive Damages in Tort Cases, 44 Harv.L.Rev. 1173, 1206 (1931).

42. Note, Exemplary Damages in the Law of Torts, 70 Harv.L.Rev. 517, 523 (1957).

43. Engman v. Southwestern Bell Tel. Co., 591 S.W.2d 78 (Mo.Ct.App.1979); Murski v. Sportsman Cycles, Inc., 559 S.W.2d 67 (Mo.Ct.App.1977).

44. Price v. Ford Motor Credit Co., 530 S.W.2d 249 (Mo.Ct.App.1975) ("[L]egal malice also can arise from acts done in reckless disregard for another's rights"); Beggs v. Universal C.I.T. Credit Corp., 409 S.W.2d 719 (Mo.1966).

45. Kendall Yacht Corp. v. United Cal. Bank, 50 Cal.App.3d 949, 958, 123 Cal.Rptr. 848, 854 (1975); Cal.Civ. Code § 3294 (West 1980).

ice in fact must be established clearly by the evidence.[46] This may be done by showing that the defendant's wrongful activity was wilful, intentional and done in reckless disregard of the possible results,[47] or that he acted in conscious disregard for the safety of others.[48]

Other jurisdictions permit punitive damages where the defendant has acted in conscious disregard for the rights of others[49] or was *grossly* negligent.[50]

Actual and Nominal Damages

Since punitive damages are merely incidental to a cause of action, they alone never may constitute the basis of the action.[51] Thus, the plaintiff must show that he has been injured or that his rights have been infringed. Missouri allows exemplary damages to lie only where actual or nominal damages have been recovered first.[52] Although some states require actual damages to be proved,[53] most allow punitive damages to be awarded where the damages are merely nominal.[54] California appears to be moving away from strict adherence to the rule that the plaintiff must suffer actual damages before he may recover exemplary damages.[55]

Punitive damages are awarded in the discretion of the jury,[56] not as a matter of right. Generally, punitive damages are not granted by

46. Toole v. Richardson-Merrell, Inc., 251 Cal.App.2d 689, 716, 60 Cal.Rptr. 398, 413 (1967); Roth v. Shell Oil Co., 185 Cal.App.2d 676, 682, 8 Cal. Rptr. 514, 517 (1960).

47. David v. Hearst, 160 Cal. 143, 116 P. 530 (1911).

48. Richards Co. v. Harrison, 262 So. 2d 258 (Fla.Dist.Ct.App.1972); Frizzy Hairstylists, Inc. v. Eagle Star Ins. Co., 89 Misc.2d 822, 392 N.Y.S.2d 554 (1977); Atlas Chem. Indus., Inc. v. Anderson, 524 S.W.2d 681 (Tex.1975).

49. Collens v. New Canaan Water Co., 155 Conn. 477, 234 A.2d 825 (1967).

50. Ryan v. Foster & Marshall, Inc., 556 F.2d 460 (9th Cir. 1977).

51. Gold v. Los Angeles Democratic League, 49 Cal.App.3d 365, 122 Cal. Rptr. 732 (1975).

52. Longmore v. Merwin, 585 S.W.2d 545 (Mo.Ct.App.1979); Schmidt v. Central Hardware Co., 516 S.W.2d 556 (Mo.Ct.App.1974) (Holding that even though punitive damages may be recovered where actual damages are nominal, they are limited by the requirement that they are not to be entirely disproportionate to the actual damages).

53. Stoner v. Houston, 582 S.W.2d 28 (Ark.1979) (Award of $1 held nominal, precluding recovery for punitive damages); Cactus Drilling Co. v. McGinty, 580 S.W.2d 609 (Tex.Civ.App. 1979).

54. Shell Oil Co. v. Parker, 265 Md. 631, 291 A.2d 64 (1972); Beavers v. Lamplighter Realty, Inc., 556 P.2d 1328 (Okla.Ct.App.1976).

55. James v. Public Fin. Corp., 47 Cal. App.3d 995, 121 Cal.Rptr. 670 (1975).

56. Millar v. James, 254 Cal.App.2d 530, 62 Cal.Rptr. 335 (1967). In South Carolina, however, punitive damages *are* a matter of right. Sam-

courts of equity,[57] not because they lack the power, but because they use specific personal orders instead of penal awards as their basic remedial power.[58]

§ 16.6 Survival of Claim

Death of Defendant

Although at least one court has held that a claim for punitive damages survives the death of the tortfeasor,[59] the almost universal rule is that the death of the wrongdoer extinguishes the claim.[60] This view is followed in both Missouri[61] and California.[62] The reason advanced is that courts no longer consider that there is a plausible deterrent effect once the tortfeasor is dead—apparently ignoring the theory that punitive damages also are designed to deter others from similar conduct. In *Evans v. Gibson*,[63] the California Supreme Court touched briefly upon this problem, stating:

> Since the purpose of punitive damages is to punish the wrongdoer for his acts, accompanied by evil motive, and to deter him from the commission of like wrongs in the future, the reason for such damages ceases to exist with his death. It is true that the infliction of punishment serves as a deterrent to the commission of future wrongs by others as well as by the wrongdoer, but punitive damages by way of example to others should be imposed only on actual wrongdoers.[64]

The case also makes an analogy to other situations where only the actual wrongdoer is held liable for punitive damages. One example given is that of the principal not being held liable for punitive damages assessed against the agent unless the principal has ratified the

---

ple v. Gulf Ref. Co., 183 S.C. 399, 191 S.E. 209 (1937). See Bukovac v. Lloyd Ketcham Oldsmobile, Inc., 579 S.W.2d 790 (Mo.Ct.App.1979) (Appellate court affirmed trial court's grant of new trial on ground that jury's failure to award punitive damages went against the weight of evidence).

57. Rivero v. Thomas, 86 Cal.App.2d 225, 194 P.2d 533 (1948).

58. H. Oleck, supra note 29, at § 269.

59. Johnson v. Rinesmith, 238 So.2d 659 (Fla.Dist.Ct.App.1969).

60. Ellis v. Zuck, 546 F.2d 643 (5th Cir. 1977); Paul v. Milburn, 275 F. Supp. 105 (W.D.Tenn.1967); Mervis v. Wolverton, 211 So.2d 847 (Miss. 1968); Hayes v. Gill, 216 Tenn. 39, 390 S.W.2d 213 (1965).

61. State ex rel. Mercantile Nat'l Bank v. Rooney, 402 S.W.2d 354 (Mo.1966).

62. Holm Timber Indus. v. Plywood Corp. of America, 242 Cal.App.2d 492, 51 Cal.Rptr. 597 (1966).

63. 220 Cal. 476, 31 P.2d 389 (1934).

64. Id. at 490, 31 P.2d at 395.

agent's acts.[65] Another example given is that of joint tortfeasors being assessed punitive damages in differing amounts based upon the culpability of each.[66] These two situations hardly can be said to be analogous to the *Evans* case. In *Evans*, the wrongdoer's own coffers would be tapped for his wrongful acts, even though the monies had passed to heirs; the two examples would tap the coffers of innocent persons.

Thus, though the court recognizes that punitives could be utilized to deter the undesirable behavior of others, as well as the orignal tortfeasor, the court apparently feels that it would be undesirable to expand the assessment of punitive damages to the estates of deceased tortfeasors. The author fails to find much judicial logic in a position which would allow punitive damages to be assessed against the tortfeasor if he died the day after a judgment but not if he died the day before the judgment was handed down.

Death of Plaintiff

The maxim that it is cheaper to kill a person than to injure him still rings true in those jurisdictions where punitive damages are not recoverable in a wrongful death action [67] but are recoverable in an action for personal injury.[68] Some states which allow exemplary damages as a means of punishing the defendant have permitted such an award in a wrongful death case in keeping with the intent of the award.[69]

California prohibited punitive damages in a wrongful death case until the United States District Court found such practice a denial of equal protection. That court carefully limited its decision:

> [T]he *sole* purpose of punitive damages under California law is to *deter conduct of the defendant*. This Court does not purport to express an opinion as to those statutes and decisions in states other than California which premise exemplary damages on a theory of compensation only or a mixed theory of compensation and deterrence.[70]

---

65. Id.

66. Id.

67. At the present time, approximately thirty-one states do not allow punitive damages recoveries in wrongful death cases. Comment, 22 Trial Law. Guide 29 (1978).

68. Ray v. City of Detroit, 67 Mich. App. 702, 242 N.W.2d 494 (1976) ("Recovery [of punitive damages] is restricted to the injured party").

69. Leahy v. Morgan, 275 F.Supp. 424 (N.D.Iowa 1967); Atlas Properties, Inc. v. Didich, 226 So.2d 684 (Fla. 1969).

70. In re Paris Air Crash of March 3, 1974, 427 F.Supp. 701 (C.D.Cal.1977), 706, n. 10 rev'd 622 F.2d 1315 (9th Cir. 1980).

§ 16.7 Measurement of Punitive Damages

This case was recently reversed on appeal,[71] so it still stands that California does not allow punitive damages in a wrongful death case.

Juries have wide discretion in determining an award of punitive damages.[72] However, several factors commonly are used by juries in ascertaining proper amounts to assess as punitive damages. Normally, none of these factors considered alone is adequate to assess damages. All of the factors should be considered together.

Relationship to Actual Damages

It often is stated that exemplary damages must bear a reasonable relationship to actual damages.[73] However, there is no fixed ratio by which to determine the proper proportion between the two classes of damages.[74] There is authority that a verdict for punitive damages out of proportion to actual damages must be set aside by the court like any excessive verdict,[75] but it has been stated also that the excessiveness of a punitive damages award cannot be established by reference to the disparate ratio between the punitive award and the compensation award alone.[76] The court summarized the current status of this proposition in California in *Zhadan v. Downtown L. A. Motors:* [77]

> [I]t is apparent that plaintiff made a showing of substantial damage from which the jury could quite properly have awarded in excess of $4,000. Thus, the $175,000 punitive damage award is roughly 40 times the compensatory damage. Though there are cases, relied upon by defendants, holding such a ratio too high . . . , other cases (most of them more recently decided) cited by plaintiff have approved awards in which the ratio of punitive to compensatory damages was much higher than 40 to 1. As our

71. Id. 622 F.2d 1315 (9th Cir. 1980).
72. Richardson v. Employers Liab. Assur. Corp., 25 Cal.App.3d 232, 102 Cal.Rptr. 547 (1972); Price v. Ford Motor Credit Co., 530 S.W.2d 249 (Mo.Ct.App.1975).
73. Zhadan v. Downtown L.A. Motors, 66 Cal.App.3d 481, 136 Cal.Rptr. 132 (1976), aff'd on appeal from remand, 100 Cal.App.3d 821, 161 Cal.Rptr. 225 (1979); Beggs v. Universal C.I.T. Credit Corp., 409 S.W.2d 719 (Mo. 1966); Parker v. McGinnes, 594 S.W.2d 550 (Tex.Civ.App.1980).
74. Finney v. Lockhart, 35 Cal.2d 161, 217 P.2d 19 (1950); State ex rel. St. Joseph Belt Ry. v. Shain, 341 Mo. 733, 108 S.W.2d 351 (1937); Kraus v. Alamo Nat'l Bank, 586 S.W.2d 202, 207–08 (Tex.Civ.App.1979, writ granted) ("[N]o set rule or ratio can be laid down, and such amount must depend upon the facts in the particular case").
75. Wilkinson v. Boor Singh, 93 Cal. App. 337, 269 P. 705 (1928).
76. Zhadan v. Downtown L.A. Motors, 66 Cal.App.3d 481, 136 Cal.Rptr. 132 (1976), aff'd on appeal from remand, 100 Cal.App.3d 821, 161 Cal.Rptr. 225 (1979).
77. Id.

§ **16.7**   TORT LIABILITY AND DEFENSES   Pt. 3

Supreme Court stated . . . "[T]here is no fixed ratio by which to determine the proper proportion between the two classes of damages." In *Finney,* an award of $2,000 exemplary damages in a case in which nominal damages of $1 were awarded was affirmed.[78]

Relationship to Nature of Defendant's Conduct

The outrageous nature of the defendant's conduct has long been held to be one of the factors for a jury to consider in assessing the amount of punitive damages. This refers not only to the type of conduct in which the defendant engaged but also to the degree of offensiveness with which the defendant pursued the conduct.[79] The Supreme Court of California stated it well when it said: "[C]learly, different acts may be of varying degrees of reprehensibility, and the more reprehensible the act, the greater the appropriate punishment, assuming all other factors are equal."[80]

Relationship to Defendant's Wealth

Most jurisdictions which state that the objective of punitive damages is to punish the defendant allow into evidence at trial proof of the defendant's wealth.[81] Obviously, the wealthier the defendant, the larger the award of exemplary damages must be to accomplish this stated purpose. Proof of wealth not only is admissible at trial, but, accordingly, it is a proper subject for discovery.[82] It also is proper to show the defendant's wealth at the time of trial instead of at the time of the injury.[83] Wealth may be determined by reference to the defendant's net worth, his after-tax income or both.[84]

To illustrate this concept, the California Supreme Court has upheld an award of $740,000 in punitive damages which represented less than one-tenth of one percent of the defendant's gross assets and

---

78. Id. at 498, 136 Cal.Rptr. at 141–42 (citations omitted).

79. Cantrell v. Amarillo Hardware Co., 226 Kan. 681, 602 P.2d 1326 (1979); Beggs v. Universal C.I.T. Credit Corp., 409 S.W.2d 719 (Mo.1966); Parker v. McGinnes, 594 S.W.2d 550 (Tex.Civ.App.1980).

80. Neal v. Farmers Ins. Exch., 21 Cal.3d 910, 928, 582 P.2d 980, 990, 148 Cal.Rptr. 389, 399 (1978) (citations omitted).

81. Brown v. Payne, 264 S.W.2d 341 (Mo.1954); Reid v. Kelly, 262 S.E.2d 24 (S.C.1980).

82. Doak v. Superior Ct., 257 Cal. App.2d 825, 65 Cal.Rptr. 193 (1968) (dictum).

83. Marriott v. Williams, 152 Cal. 705, 93 P. 875 (1908).

84. Little v. Stuyvesant Life Ins. Co., 67 Cal.App.3d 451, 136 Cal.Rptr. 653 (1977); Wetherbee v. United Ins. Co. of America, 18 Cal.App.3d 266, 95 Cal.Rptr. 678 (1971).

less than a week's worth of its net income according to 1974 figures.[85] That same court overturned an award of $5 million where the award was "more than 40 times larger than the not-insubstantial assessment of $123,600 in compensatory damages against [the defendant,] Mutual."[86] In the words of the court:

> [T]he punitive damage figure represented two and one-half months of Mutual's entire net income in 1973, and more than seven months of such income in 1974. Viewing the record as a whole and in the light most favorable to the judgments, we conclude that in these circumstances the punitive damage award against Mutual must be deemed the result of passion and prejudice on the part of the jurors and excessive as a matter of law.[87]

Some jurisdictions do not allow evidence of defendant's wealth at trial but allow for a bifurcated trial. After the initial trial, if the jury finds the defendant liable for punitive damages, the court then allows into evidence proof of the defendant's wealth.[88]

Great difficulty is encountered in admitting proof of wealth where *several defendants* are named and the jury is required to return one punitive award verdict against all of the defendants. A single verdict based on the wealth of one defendant would appear to be unjust to other defendants. Conversely, an amount based on the wealth of the poorest defendant would fail to punish the wealthier defendants. To avoid this problem, courts have held that it was improper in a tort action against several defendants for the plaintiff to introduce evidence of the wealth of one of the defendants as a basis for awarding punitive damages against other defendants.[89] Other jurisdictions deal with the problem by allowing juries to assess punitive damages separately among joint tortfeasors based upon evidence as to the varying degress of culpability and wealth.[90]

---

85. Neal v. Farmers Ins. Exch., 21 Cal.3d 910, 582 P.2d 980, 148 Cal. Rptr. 389 (1978).

86. Egan v. Mutual of Omaha Ins. Co., 24 Cal.3d 809, 824, 598 P.2d 452, 460, 157 Cal.Rptr. 482, 490 (1979), appeal dismissed 100 S.Ct. 1271 (1980).

87. Id.

88. Rupert v. Sellers, 48 A.D.2d 265, 368 N.Y.S.2d 904 (1975). See Note, Punitive Damages: An Exception to the Right of Privacy? Coy v. Superior Court, 5 Pepperdine L.Rev. 145 (1977) (Discusses arguments for non-admissibility of evidence of defendant's wealth).

89. Washington Gaslight Co. v. Lansden, 172 U.S. 534 (1899).

90. Huckeby v. Spangler, 563 S.W.2d 555 (Tenn.1978).

§ 16.8 Pleadings

In California, the fact that the exemplary damages are not mentioned expressly in the prayer of a complaint does not preclude allowing such damages upon a contested trial.[91] Decisions as to the sufficiency of various pleadings for punitive damages appear to be disharmonious or, at best, confusing.[92] Conclusionary characterization of defendant's conduct as intentional, wilful and fraudulent is a patently insufficient statement of "oppression, fraud, or malice, express or implied," within the meaning of Civil Code section 3294.[93] Malice properly is pleaded by alleging the wrongful motive, intent or purpose.[94] A general allegation of the wrongful intent is sufficient.[95]

In some jurisdictions where an "intentional" act pleaded and proved voids the insurance policy, knowledgeable trial lawyers suggest that "wantonness" instead of "wilfulness" be pleaded. This may save the policy, but the state's statutes must be examined to determine if "wantonness" is grievous enough conduct to justify punitive damages. Generally it is. The policy of defendant, too, should be examined.

In products liability cases, conclusionary allegations of wrongful, knowing and wilful conduct are insufficient to plead malice as a ground for exemplary awards.[96] Rather, to establish malice in these cases, allegations must show either an intent to injure consumers or that a defendant acted in conscious disregard for the safety of the consumer.[97]

§ 16.9 Insurance Coverage of Punitive Awards

There is a split of authority nationwide as to whether insurance validly may cover liability for punitive damages. Prior to 1962, only

---

91. Forte v. Nolfi, 25 Cal.App.3d 656, 102 Cal.Rptr. 455 (1972); Vaughn v. Jonas, 31 Cal.2d 586, 191 P. 432 (1948).

92. See G. D. Searle & Co. v. Superior Ct., 49 Cal.App.3d 22, 122 Cal.Rptr. 218 (1975), where the court traces three different lines of cases utilizing different requirements for malice.

93. West's Ann.Cal.Civ.Code § 3294.

94. Brousseau v. Jarrett, 73 Cal.App.3d 864, 141 Cal.Rptr. 200 (1977).

95. Unruh v. Truck Ins. Exch., 7 Cal.3d 616, 498 P.2d 1063, 102 Cal.Rptr. 815 (1972).

96. Cyrus v. Haveson, 65 Cal.App.3d 306, 135 Cal.Rptr. 246 (1976). Defendant's appeal of the punitive damages award was upheld based upon plaintiff's failure to allege facts showing wrongful motive or intent and failure to plead that defendant acted intentionally, as opposed to negligently or mistakenly.

97. G. D. Searle & Co. v. Superior Ct., 49 Cal.App.3d 22, 122 Cal.Rptr. 218 (1975).

Colorado[98] and Connecticut[99] had held that an insurance company could *not* be held liable for punitive damages assessed against its insured. In 1962, the Fifth Circuit Court of Appeals held in *Northwestern National Casualty Co. v. McNulty*[1] that Florida public policy would not permit a liability insurer to pay its insured's punitive assessments. Subsequently, approximately ten more states have held that insurance companies may not be held liable for their insured's punitive award liabilities.[2]

States which allow punitive damages to be covered by insurance contracts have used several lines of reasoning. One method courts use to find liability is simply to interpret the insurance contract between the company and the insured to include coverage for punitive damages.[3] Another method courts use to allow coverage is to state that the public policy favoring the enforcement of contracts outweighs the public policy reasons for assessing punitive damages.[4]

The California Court of Appeals recently addressed, for the first time, the question of whether insurance contracts covered punitive damages. In *City Products Corp. v. Globe Indemnity Co.*,[5] the court held:

> [T]he policy of this state with respect to punitive damages would be frustrated by permitting the party against whom they are awarded to pass on the liability to an insurance carrier. The objective is to impose such damages in an amount which will appropriately punish the defendant in view of "the actual damages sustained," "the magnitude and flagrancy of the offense, the importance of the policy violated, and the wealth of the defendant."
> . . . Consideration of the wealth of the defendant would of course be pointless if such damages could be covered by insurance. The onus of the award would depend entirely upon the

---

98. Universal Indem. Ins. Co. v. Tenery, 96 Colo. 10, 39 P.2d 776 (1934).

99. Tedesco v. Maryland Cas. Co., 127 Conn. 533, 18 A.2d 357 (1941). This case involved a statute awarding double damages. In Connecticut, traditional punitive damages are considered to be compensatory. See note 34 supra.

1. 307 F.2d 432 (5th Cir. 1962).

2. See generally Note, Punitive Damages and Liability Insurance: Theory, Reality and Practicality, 9 Cum.L. Rev. 487 (1978).

3. See General Cas. Co. of America v. Woodby, 238 F.2d 452 (6th Cir. 1956); Concord Gen. Mut. Ins. Co. v. Hills, 345 F.Supp. 1090 (S.D.Me.1972); Abbie Uriguen Olds. Buick, Inc. v. United States Fire Ins. Co., 95 Idaho 501, 511 P.2d 783 (1973).

4. See Lazenby v. Universal Underwriters Ins. Co., 214 Tenn. 639, 383 S.W. 2d 1 (1964).

5. 88 Cal.App.3d 31, 151 Cal.Rptr. 494 (1979).

amount of insurance coverage and not upon the legally relevant factors. We conclude, therefore, that the public policy of this state prohibits insurance covering the punitive damages levied against plaintiff.[6]

The court observed that the states which allow punitive damages to be covered by insurance were those states that allow punitive damages based on gross negligence or reckless or wanton conduct.[7] The court quoted *Harrell v. Travelers Indemnity Co.* to the effect that

> "[p]rotection would not be available to a professional person or wage earner or to a housewife or retired person, who might well be ruined financially by a judgment for punitive damages as a result of conduct of no more flagrancy than an act of 'gross negligence,' a momentary 'reckless' act, or conduct 'contrary to societal interests.'"[8]

§ 16.10 Contract Actions

It is almost black letter law that punitive damages are not available in *contract* actions.[9] Like most black letter law, this rule is replete with exceptions. One of the earliest exceptions was for breach of a promise to marry.[10] Another early exception was the concept that suppliers of public services might be held liable for punitive damages for failure to discharge their obligations to the public. The logic for imposing this duty upon the providers was that persons engaged in these positions often enjoyed a monopoly position within the community.[11] Thus, actions against defendants such as common carriers[12] and public utilities[13] were allowed to sound in tort as well as contract, even though actually based upon a contractual relationship.

---

6. Id. at 41, 151 Cal.Rptr. at 500–01 (citation omitted).

7. Id.

8. Id. (quoting Harrell v. Travelers Indem. Co., 279 Or. 199, 567 P.2d 1013, 1021 (1977)). Accord, Levit, Punitive Damages: Recent Developments, 659 Ins.L.J. 719, 723 (1977). A national insurance company now has introduced an insurance policy available for insurers offering protection against punitive damages in suits by policyholders. A policy of this type presumably would be appropriate only in those jurisdictions which allow punitive damages to be paid by insurance companies.

9. 5 A. Corbin, Contracts § 1077 (1963).

10. McQuillen v. Evans, 353 Ill. 239, 187 N.E. 320 (1933); Drobnich v. Bach, 159 Minn. 258, 198 N.W. 669 (1924).

11. Wyman, The Law of the Public Callings as a Solution of the Trust Problem, 17 Harv.L.Rev. 156, 217 (1904).

12. Burrus v. Nevada-Cal.-Ore. Ry., 38 Nev. 156, 145 P. 926 (1915); Hutchinson v. Southern Ry., 140 N.C. 123, 52 S.E. 263 (1905).

13. See note 13 on page 553.

Where the contract "sets up" the tort, punitives are allowed. For example, when the telegraph company contracts to relay the message and grossly distorts it, punitives may be awarded. Thus, where "father dead" was sent instead of "father better," punitives were granted.[14] Two jurisdictions, Texas [15] and South Carolina,[16] early in their common law allowed the recovery of punitive damages in contract actions.

Insurance Contracts

Recently, California and other jurisdictions have favored allowing recovery of punitive damages from an insurance company where the company's conduct has been far short of admirable. Insurance companies decry the trend, and statements such as the following may be found: "No company wants to be taken advantage of, but the environment seems to have been created in California via the punitive damage decisions for venting of the frustrated big-business, consumerism feelings of juries on Life and Health insurers." [17]

The fact remains, however, that the standard for allowing punitive damages is high. Plaintiff must prove that the defendant acted with the "intent to vex, injure, or annoy, or with a conscious disregard of the plaintiff's rights." [18] Though it might be argued that causes of action against insurance companies are in contract and therefore are not compatible with allowing punitive damages, California courts and other jurisdictions are willing to grant punitive damages when the breach of the insurance contract is accompanied by an act that is independent and wilfully tortious.[19] The basis of these causes of action may be in fraud, intentional infliction of emotional distress or tortious breach of an implied covenant of good faith and fair dealing.[20] Holdings in California have expanded greatly this latter concept which generally is known as "bad faith."

13. Birmingham Water Works Co. v. Keiley, 2 Ala.App. 629, 56 So. 838 (1911).

14. Peterson v. Western Union Tel. Co., 75 Minn. 368, 77 N.W. 985 (1899). See Wyman, note 110 supra.

15. National Fin. Co. v. Abernathy, 66 S.W.2d 358 (Tex.Civ.App.1933); Morgan v. Steinberg, 23 S.W.2d 527 (Tex.Civ.App.1929); Ball v. Britton, 58 Tex. 57 (1882).

16. Welborn v. Dixon, 70 S.C. 108, 49 S.E. 232 (1904).

17. Rubin & Scheil, Punitive Damage Awards: The Insurance Industry Is Placed on Notice, 45 Ins. Counsel J. 350, 354 (1978).

18. Silberg v. California Life Ins. Co., 111 Cal.3d 452, 462, 521 P.2d 1103, 1110, 113 Cal.Rptr. 711, 718 (1974).

19. Crisci v. Security Ins. Co., 66 Cal. 2d 425, 432–34, 426 P.2d 173, 178–79, 58 Cal.Rptr. 13, 18–19 (1967). See generally J.C. McCarthy, Punitive Damages in Bad Faith Cases (2d ed. 1978).

20. Gruenberg v. Aetna Ins. Co., 9 Cal.3d 566, 573, 510 P.2d 1032, 1036, 108 Cal.Rptr. 480, 484 (1973); Comunale v. Traders & Gen. Ins. Co., 50

§ 16.10   TORT LIABILITY AND DEFENSES   Pt. 3

"Bad faith" cases may arise when the insured or his beneficiary makes a direct claim against the company and the company unreasonably refuses to make the payments.[21] "Bad faith" claims also may arise when the insurer fails to accept an offer to settle against its insured within policy limits.[22] The insured in this case is held to be unduly exposed to liability at trial for amounts above the policy limits.

Gruenberg v. Aetna Insurance Co.[23] held that plaintiff's breach of a contractual duty would not excuse a defendant insurance company from its duty, implied by law, of good faith and fair dealing. That is, the insurer's duty was held to be unconditional and independent of the performance of the plaintiff's contractual obligation.[24]

Egan v. Mutual of Omaha Insurance Co.[25] held that an insurance company was liable for breach of the covenant of good faith and fair dealing when the company failed to investigate properly a claim by an insured. The court upheld the right of the plaintiff to be awarded punitive damages in such a case, but it reversed this particular award as being based on passion and prejudice.[26]

§ 16.11 Punitive Damages in Products Liability Cases

A corporation or other manufacturer which makes a defective product and markets it with full knowledge of the serious risk of injury it poses to the consuming public in its intended use may be held liable for punitive damages. One of the most important cases in this field, if only to show the extent of the award the jury may give, is *Grimshaw v. Ford Motor Co.*[27] Plaintiff therein had been burned se-

---

Cal.2d 654, 658, 328 P.2d 198, 200 (1958); Fletcher v. Western Nat'l Life Ins. Co., 10 Cal.App.3d 376, 401, 89 Cal.Rptr. 78, 93 (1970) (this implied covenant inherent in not only insurance contracts, but in every contract).

21. Silberg v. California Life Ins. Co., 11 Cal.3d 452, 521 P.2d 1103, 113 Cal.Rptr. 711 (1974); Fletcher v. Western Nat'l Life Ins. Co., 10 Cal. App.3d 376, 89 Cal.Rptr. 78 (1970). See Mo.Rev.Stat. § 375.420 (1978).

22. Crisci v. Security Ins. Co., 66 Cal. 2d 425, 432–34, 426 P.2d 173, 178–79, 58 Cal.Rptr. 13, 18–19 (1967); Cain v. State Farm Mut. Auto. Ins. Co., 47 Cal.App.3d 783, 121 Cal.Rptr. 200 (1975).

23. 9 Cal.3d 566, 510 P.2d 1032, 108 Cal.Rptr. 480 (1973).

24. Id. at 578, 510 P.2d at 1040, 108 Cal.Rptr. at 488.

25. 24 Cal.3d 809, 817, 598 P.2d 452, 455–56, 157 Cal.Rptr. 482, 485 (1979).

26. Id. at 820, 598 P.2d at 458, 157 Cal.Rptr. at 487.

27. (Cal. San Bernadino County Dist. Ct.1978), appeal docketed, No. 4th Civ. 20095 (Cal.Ct.App., 4th Cir., Apr. 26, 1978).

For complete report of this case, see Chapter 43, Products Liability, infra.

verely when the gas tank of the Ford Pinto in which he was riding exploded when the car was rear-ended by another vehicle. Testimony adduced at trial showed that Ford knew about the dangerous condition posed by its placement of the gas tank without any safeguards but marketed the Pintos as originally designed, even though a safety device to prevent this type of occurrence could have been installed in each car at minimal cost. The jury awarded plaintiff $127.8 million, $125 million of which was in punitive damages. The trial court judge reduced the entire award to $3.5 million. The case currently is on appeal.

Missouri, in 1978, joined that group of jurisdictions [28] which allows punitive damages in products liability cases. In *Rinker v. Ford Motor Co.*,[29] the Missouri Court of Appeals affirmed a jury verdict of $100,000 actual and $460,000 punitive damages against Ford for knowingly failing to alleviate a problem in its carburetor mechanism. Addressing itself to appellant Ford's contention that punitive damages were "inappropriate" in products liability cases, the court stated:

> [G]iven the purpose of punitive damages to punish a defendant for an aggravated act of misconduct and to deter similar conduct in the future by the defendant and others, there is no fundamental reason for excluding products liability cases from the cases in which punitive damages may be recovered. One writer suggests that punitive damages are particularly appropriate in such cases.[30]

Section 120 of the United States Department of Commerce's Model Uniform Liability Act would allow plaintiff to recover punitive damages where he shows by clear and convincing evidence that "the harm suffered was the result of the product seller's reckless disregard for the safety of product users . . . ." However, that same section would leave it to the *court* to determine the *amount* of punitive damages to be awarded once the jury has found sufficient culpable conduct to hold defendant liable therefor.[31]

---

28. Gillham v. Admiral Corp., 523 F.2d 102 (6th Cir. 1975), cert. denied, 424 U.S. 913 (1976); Vollert v. Summa Corp., 389 F.Supp. 1348 (D.Hawaii 1975); Drake v. Wham-O Mfg. Corp., 373 F.Supp. 608 (E.D.Wis.1974); Toole v. Richardson-Merrell, Inc., 251 Cal.App.2d 689, 60 Cal.Rptr. 398 (1967); E. R. Squibb & Sons, Inc. v. Stickney, 274 So.2d 898 (Fla.Dist.Ct.App.1973), cert. denied, 416 U.S. 961 (1974); Moore v. Jewel Tea Co., 116 Ill.App.2d 109, 253 N.E.2d 636 (1969).

29. 567 S.W.2d 655 (Mo.Ct.App.1978).

30. Id. at 668.

31. 44 Fed.Reg. 62,748 (1979). Factors which the court is to consider in making the award are the likelihood that serious harm would arise and the seller's awareness thereof; the profitability of the seller's misconduct; whether the seller made any attempt to conceal the danger once discovered; and the financial condition of the product seller.

§ 16.11   TORT LIABILITY AND DEFENSES   Pt. 3

Liability-Producing Conduct

Professor D. G. Owen, in a well-reasoned article [32] advocating the allowance of punitive awards in products liability cases, identified five types of conduct that should be construed as creating the type of aggravated conduct upon which punitive damages should be based. The categories described include:

1. Fraudulent-type misconduct,[33]
2. Knowing violations of safety standards,[34]
3. Inadequate testing or quality control,[35]
4. Failure to warn of known dangers,[36]
5. Post-marketing failure to remedy known dangers.[37]

Company Liability for Employee's Act

A second problem arising in products liability cases [38] is whether a company may be held liable in punitive damages for conduct attributable to an employee of the company. It was on this basis that the

32. Owen, Punitive Damages in Products Liability Litigation, 74 Mich.L.Rev. 1258 (1976).

33. Most notable of cases fitting into this category would be the MER/29 drug cases, discussed at notes 36–37 supra and accompanying text. See Roginsky v. Richardson-Merrell, Inc., 378 F.2d 832 (2d Cir. 1967); Toole v. Richardson-Merrell, Inc., 251 Cal.App.2d 689, 60 Cal.Rptr. 398 (1967).

34. Companies frequently argue that safety standards are more stringent than is required for the public's safety. See Barth v. B. F. Goodrich Tire Co., 265 Cal.App.2d 228, 71 Cal.Rptr. 306 (1968).

35. A notable example is the Dalkon Shield intrauterine contraceptive device which caused many injuries and deaths. The device was tested clinically for an average insertion time of only 5.5 months before marketing. Owen, supra note 31, at 1341 n. 121. See In re A. H. Robins Co. "Dalkon Shield" IUD Prod. Liab. Litigation, 406 F.Supp. 540 (J.P.M.D.L.1975); Tinnerholm v. Parke, Davis & Co., 285 F.Supp. 432, 446 (S.D.N.Y.1968) (Manufacturers failed to test vaccine adequately).

36. Wright v. Carter Prod., Inc., 244 F.2d 53 (2d Cir. 1957) (Deodorant manufacturer failed to warn consumers of potential danger); Hill v. Hursky Briquetting, Inc., 54 Mich.App. 17, 220 N.W.2d 137, aff'd, 393 Mich. 136, 223 N.W.2d 290 (1974) (Warning on charcoal briquettes inadequate as to danger of indoor use).

37. See Gillham v. Admiral Corp., 523 F.2d 102 (6th Cir. 1975), cert. denied, 424 U.S. 913 (1976) (Television manufacturer failed to warn or repair customers' television sets even though manufacturer knew of danger of fire); Basko v. Sterling Drug, Inc., 416 F.2d 417 (2d Cir. 1969) (Manufacturer of drug which caused blindness failed to notify doctors until three years after discovery).

38. The following discussion would be applicable to all cases where the plaintiff is seeking to hold a corporation liable for the acts of one or more of the company's employees.

court denied punitive damages against Richardson-Merrell in the MER/29 case discussed above.[39]

Law varies among the jurisdictions as to when the employer may be held liable for punitive damages for its employee's conduct. Some jurisdictions take the view that punitive damages may be recovered on a respondeat superior basis. This means that an employer is liable for punitive damages based on conduct of its employees that occurs during the course and scope of the employee's job—assuming that the conduct will justify punitive damages.[40] This obviously is the most lenient standard for imposing liability for punitive damages on employers. Florida is an example of this type of jurisdiction.[41] Other jurisdictions hold that an employer is not liable for punitive damages unless he has created liability by implicating himself through an intentional act. This may be accomplished by *authorizing* the act before its performance, by *ratifying* the act after its performance or by negligently hiring an unfit person for the act.[42]

The divergent methods used in applying these rules may be shown by examining the two main MER/29 cases, *Roginsky v. Richardson-Merrell, Inc.*[43] and *Toole v. Richardson-Merrell, Inc.*[44]

Roginsky was decided by a federal court applying New York law, and it stated:

> The parties are in substantial agreement on one point—that New York does not impose punitive damages on a corporation unless, . . . "the officers or directors, that is, the management" of the company or the relevant division "either autho-

---

39. See notes 36–39 supra and accompanying text.

40. H. Oleck, Damages to Persons and Property § 274 (1961).

41. Kreindler, Punitive Damages in Aviation Cases, Trial, Aug. 1978, at 28, 30 ("Florida is one such state, and that is why claims for punitive damages are quite common there").

42. See generally Note, Liability of Employers for Punitive Damages Resulting from Acts of Employees, 54 Chi-Kent L.Rev. 829 (1978). The Restatement, Second, Torts § 909 (1965), lists four conditions, one of which must be met in order to find a corporation employer liable in punitive damages for the tortious acts of an employee:

    1. The principal authorized the doing, and the manner of the acts, or

    2. The agent was unfit and the principal was reckless in employing him, or

    3. The agent was employed in a managerial capacity and was acting in the scope of his employment, or

    4. The principal or managerial agent of the principal ratified or approved the act.

43. 378 F.2d 832 (2d Cir. 1967).

44. 251 Cal.App.2d 689, 60 Cal.Rptr. 398 (1967).

rized, participated in, consented to or, after discovery, ratified the conduct" giving rise to such damages.⁴⁵

Toole, a California case based upon the same fact situation as *Roginsky,* illustrates California's application of the law when it states:

> A corporation may be held liable for punitive damages for the acts of its agents and employees when the act is done in ill will, or is motivated by actual malice, or done under circumstances amounting to fraud or oppression, providing that the act is done with the knowledge or under the direction of corporate officials having power to bind the corporation. . . .
>
> Appellant argues that none of the wrongdoing upon which respondent relies to show fraud was known to any officer or principal having power to bind the corporation; that all of the alleged wrongful acts were done by agents and employees below the level of responsible management and hence, . . . the corporation cannot be held liable for punitive damages. This argument cannot succeed here because its validity depends upon facts favorable to its application, and facts in our record do not support it. There was ample evidence from which the jury could infer that high level management had knowledge of wrongdoing on the part of department heads and other employees and agents.⁴⁶

Multiple Awards of Punitive Damages

Another important problem with products liability awards involving punitive damages is the question of multiple recoveries. In products liability, this question frequently is discussed in connection with aviation cases.⁴⁷ The reason for this is obvious in that one aviation disaster has the potential to kill a large number of people and thus produce a large number of lawsuits. This problem is not, of

---

45. 378 F.2d at 842 (citation omitted).

Because defendant asserts, and plaintiff does not dispute, that for purposes of applying this rule to the case at bar "management" includes only the presidents and vice-presidents of Richardson-Merrell and its Wm. S. Merrell Division, we need not decide whether, under New York law, the acts of inferior supervisory employees would otherwise be deemed the acts of the corporation for purposes of assessing punitive damages.

Id. at 842 n. 17.

46. Toole v. Richardson-Merrell, Inc., 251 Cal.App.2d 689, 716, 60 Cal.Rptr. 398, 414 (1967) (cases omitted).

47. Donnelly, The Importance of the Exemplary Award Issues in Aviation Litigation, 42 J. Air L. & Com. 825 (1976); See Kreindler, Punitive Damages in Aviation Litigation—An Essay, 8 Cum.L.Rev. 607 (1978).

course, unique to the aviation industry. The problem of multiple awards was discussed thoroughly by Judge Friendly in *Roginsky*.[48]

The question usually discussed is whether each successive plaintiff is entitled to an award of punitive damages against the same defendant for the same incident without regard to the punitive awards assessed in prior litigation on the same matter. Some authorities suggest that only one award of punitives should be assessed against the defendant and that then this award should be divided among the plaintiffs.[49]

The Wisconsin Court of Appeals, in a recent decision holding that a plaintiff in a strict products liability action could recover punitive damages, disposed of the multiple awards argument by reasoning that judicial review of the amount of punitive damages awards would prevent overkill by taking into account these awards in other cases.[50]

§ 16.12 Punitive Damages in Drunk Driving Cases

If a person consumes a fair amount of alcohol, becomes intoxicated, and while driving home causes an injury to another by reason of his diminished ability to operate his car, should a claim for punitive damages lie?

If punitive damages are intended to deter the defendant and others like him from engaging in socially unacceptable conduct, punitive damages should be awarded. A number of older decisions considering this issue held that one who became intoxicated with full knowledge that he intended to drive immediately afterwards, was at most grossly negligent. Since his activity lacked the requisite "malice," a claim for punitive damages was not permitted.[51]

Today, most courts permit the plaintiff to include in his complaint a claim for punitive damages in such a situation.[52] In *Taylor*

---

48. See § 16.4 supra.

49. Kreindler, supra note 147, at 615, states that the author attempted to bring the cases resulting from the crash of a DC-10 outside Paris in 1974 as a class action in an effort to avoid the very problem of multiple recoveries of punitive damages. The district court granted the class action, but the court of appeals reversed. See In re Paris Air Crash of March 3, 1974, 427 F.Supp. 701 (C.D. Cal.1977).

50. Wangen v. Ford Motor Co., No. 77–893 (Wis.Ct.App., May 31, 1979). This decision was not published and may be found in the Table of Unpublished Opinions, 284 N.W.2d 120.

51. Gombos v. Ashe, 158 Cal.App.2d 517, 322 P.2d 933 (1958); Gesslein v. Britton, 175 Kan. 661, 266 P.2d 263 (1954) Baker v. Marcus, 201 Va. 905, 114 S.E.2d 617 (1960).

52. Holmes v. Hollingsworth, 234 Ark. 347, 352 S.W.2d 96 (1961); Infeld v. Sullivan, 151 Conn. 506, 199 A.2d 693 (1964); Ingram v. Pettit, 340 So.2d 922 (Fla.1976); Svejcara v. Whitman, 82 N.M. 739, 487 P.2d 167 (1971);

v. Superior Court,[53] the California Supreme Court overruled its holding in *Gombos v. Ashe*,[54] decided some twenty years earlier. The court ventured a little further than most and held that punitive damages were available in *every* case where the driver became intoxicated and knew he would be driving afterwards. The court ruled:

> One who wilfully consumes alcoholic beverages to the point of intoxication, knowing that he thereafter must operate a motor vehicle, thereby combining sharply impaired physical and mental faculties with a vehicle capable of great force and speed, reasonably may be held to exhibit a conscious disregard of the safety of others. The effect may be lethal whether or not the driver had a prior history of drunk driving incidents.[55]

In *Taylor*, the California court emphasized the deterrent effect punitive damages would have in such an instance.[56] This reasoning is directly in accord with that of the Supreme Court of Oregon, which in *Harrell v. Ames* [57] stated:

> Indeed, the fact of common knowledge that the drinking driver is the cause of so many of the more serious automobile accidents is strong evidence in itself to support the need for all possible means of deterring persons from driving automobiles after drinking, including exposure to awards of punitive damages in the event of accidents.[58]

§ 16.13 Conclusion

Punitive damages, or their equivalent, serve and have served for many centuries a valid purpose. Despite their checkered history, such damages have survived to the present day. Perhaps, now, more than ever, punitive damages' stated purpose of punishment and deterrence has an important role to play in society. Civilization is so complex, industries so large, commodities so varied and complicated, and governments so encumbered, that checkmates are needed, wherever

---

Colligan v. Fera, 76 Misc.2d 22, 349 N.Y.S.2d 306 (1973); Payne v. Daley, 51 Ohio Misc. 65, 367 N.E.2d 75 (1977); Harrell v. Ames, 265 Or. 183, 508 P.2d 211 (1973); Focht v. Rabada, 217 Pa.Super.Ct. 35, 268 A.2d 157 (1970).

53. 24 Cal.3d 890, 598 P.2d 854, 157 Cal.Rptr. 693 (1979).

54. 158 Cal.App.2d 517, 322 P.2d 933 (1958).

55. 24 Cal.3d 890, 897, 598 P.2d 854, 857, 157 Cal.Rptr. 693, 697 (1979).

56. "The allowance of punitive damages in such cases may well be appropriate because of another reason, namely, to deter similar future conduct, the 'incalculable cost' of which is well documented." Id.

57. 265 Or. 183, 508 P.2d 211 (1973).

58. 508 P.2d at 214–15.

possible, to assure that a conscience is formed where there is no patent responsibility. Furthermore, trial judges exercise more supervisory restraint than previously. The author, for one, does not care if that conscience is forced on industry and people. Granted, gentle compliance is more preferable than the steel hammer, but this article is replete with examples where gentility was unheard. Therefore, let those who castigate punitive damages look beyond them and castigate instead the people and industries who make punitive damages necessary. Look to the source instead of the prevention. Indeed, punitive damages are the only civil judicial steel hammer we have. Punitives are distinguished historically and modernly authorized. Their excision by philosophically bent trial judges is only another step in the growing curtailment of the modern knowledgeable trial juror's rights.

§§ 16.14–17.0 are reserved for supplementary material.

CHAPTER 17

CONTRIBUTION BETWEEN JOINT TORTFEASORS

Table of Sections

Sec.
17.1 Common Law Rule.
17.2 Criticism—Statutory and Judicial Revision.
17.3 Requirement of Common Liability.
17.4 Apportionment—Pro Rata—Comparative Fault.
17.5 Release.

Library References:
C.J.S. Contribution § 11.
West's Key No. Digests, Contribution ⚖️5.

§ 17.1 Common Law Rule

Suppose a plaintiff, suing X and Y corporations jointly, recovers a judgment of $100,000, both defendants being held liable and both being solvent. Generally, plaintiff's counsel, perhaps with a great deal of pleasure, will arbitrarily collect the entire award from one of the corporations, the other being entirely excused. Can the one that paid enforce contribution from the one that did not? At a very early date, the courts at *common law* formulated the rule concerning contribution. There could be none between joint tortfeasors.

The rule stems from the English case of *Merryweather v. Nixan*.[1] Although the case is often cited in support of the broad proposition of no contribution, the actual ruling of the case limited the denial of contribution as between wilful or intentional wrongdoers.[2] After a period of adherence to the true holding,[3] no

---

1. (1799) 8 Durnf. & E. 186 (K.B.), 8 Term.Rep. 186, 101 Eng.Rep. 1337.

2. The rule of "no contribution" was originally based on the public policy that the affairs of wrongdoers should not be the subject of adjustment in the courts. Demonstrative of this is the Highwayman's case, Ex. 1725, 9 L.Q.Rev. 197 (1893) in which one highwayman brought his partner in crime into court for an accounting of their plunder. The court dealt rather summarily with the case. The plaintiff's attorneys were fined and one was transported, and both plaintiff and defendant were hanged.

3. Hunt v. Lane, 9 Ind. 248 (1857); Atkins v. Johnson, 43 Vt. 78, 5 Am.Rep. 260 (1870).

contribution in cases of wilful misconduct, there was a reversion to the position that there *can* be no contribution without distinguishing between those who are intentional wrongdoers and those whose negligent conduct or mistake resulted in a tort.

§ 17.2 Criticism—Statutory and Judicial Revision

The doctrine denying contribution among joint tortfeasors has been criticized on a wide variety of grounds, including running "counter to tort policy goals of deterrence, equitable loss sharing by all the wrongdoers, effective loss distribution over a large segment of society, and rapid compensation of plaintiff." [4] The Merryweather rule has been abrogated in England by statute, viz., "The Law Reform Act." [5] The Uniform Contribution Among Joint Tortfeasors Act, adopted by the Commission of Uniform State Laws in 1939 and revised in 1955, provided a model for state statutes allowing contribution.[6] Some contribution statutes follow the Uniform Act in

---

4. Werner, Contribution and Indemnity, 57 Cal.L.Rev. 490, 516.

5. 25 and 26 Geo. V. c. 30, § 6 (1935).

6. 12 Uniform Laws Annotated (U.L.A.).

Table of Jurisdictions Wherein Act Has Been Adopted

Jurisdiction	Laws	Effective Date	Statutory Citation
Alaska	1970, c. 80	4-20-1970	AS §§ 09.16.010 to 09.16.060.
Arkansas	1941, Act 315	3-26-1941 *	Ark.Stats. §§ 34-1001 to 34-1009.
Colorado	1977, c. 195	7-1-1977	C.R.S. '73, 13-50.5-101 to 13-50.5-106.
Delaware	1949, c. 151	5-27-1949 *	10 Del.C. §§ 6301 to 6308.
Florida	1975, c. 75-108	6-12-1975	West's F.S.A. § 768.31.
Hawaii	1941, Act 24	4-14-1941 *	HRS §§ 663-11 to 663-17.
Maryland	1941, c. 344	6-1-1941	Code 1957, art. 50, §§ 16 to 24.
Massachusetts	1962, c. 730	1-1-1963	M.G.L.A., c. 231B §§ 1 to 4.
Mississippi	1952, c. 259	4-15-1952	Code 1972, § 85-5-5.
Nevada	1973, c. 693	7-1-1973	N.R.S. 17.225 to 17.305.
New Jersey	1952, c. 335	5-22-1952	N.J.S.A. 2A:53A-1 to 2A:53A-5.
New Mexico	1947, c. 121	3-19-1947 *	NMSA 1978, §§ 41-3-1 to 41-3-8.
North Carolina	1967, c. 847	1-1-1968	G.S. §§ 1B-1 to 1B-6.
North Dakota	1957, c. 223	3-11-1957 *	NDCC 32-38-01 to 32-38-04.
Ohio	1976, H.B. 531	10-1-1976	R.C. §§ 2307.31, 2307.32.
Pennsylvania	1951, p. 1130	7-19-1951 *	42 Pa.C.S.A. §§ 8321 to 8327.
Rhode Island	1940, c. 940	7-1-1940	Gen.Laws 1956, §§ 10-6-1 to 10-6-11.
South Dakota	1945, c. 167	2-24-1945 *	SDCL §§ 15-8-11 to 15-8-22.
Tennessee	1968, c. 575	4-3-1968	T.C.A. §§ 29-11-101 to 29-11-106.
Wyoming	1977, c. 188	1-1-1978	W.S.1977, §§ 1-1-110 to 1-1-113.

* Date of approval.

§ 17.2   TORT LIABILITY AND DEFENSES

allowing recovery generally against others "liable in tort." [7] Other statutes limit recovery to joint judgment defendants.[8] Some statutes simply declare the right of contribution, leaving its development to the courts.[9] In Federal court actions, contribution is a substantive matter, governed by local law.[10]

Although the Restatement of Restitution adheres to the common law rule denying contribution,[11] in a few jurisdictions contribution among joint tortfeasors has been introduced by the courts as a matter of equity, without the benefit of legislation.[12] The right of contribution from the United States by way of impleader under the FTCA was declared in 1951 in *United States v. Yellow Cab Co.*[13]

§ 17.3   Requirement of Common Liability

The right of contribution exists only where there is "common liability" to the injured party.[14] The distinction between joint tortfeasors and concurrent and successive tortfeasors [15] generally will not

---

7. 12 U.L.A. § 1, Alaska, Arkansas, Hawaii, Maryland, Massachusetts, New Jersey, New Mexico, North Dakota, Oregon, Pennsylvania, Rhode Island, South Dakota.

8. California, Delaware, Michigan, Mississippi, Missouri, Nebraska, New York, North Carolina, Oklahoma, Texas, West Virginia. See, e. g., California's statute, West's Ann.C.C.P. § 875(a): "Where a money judgment has been rendered jointly against two or more defendants in a tort action there shall be a right of contribution among them as hereinafter provided."

9. Georgia, Kentucky, Louisiana, New Jersey, Virginia, Wisconsin.

10. Diversity: Blunt v. Brown, 225 F.Supp. 326, 60 A.L.R.2d 1370 (D.C.Iowa 1963); F.T.C.A.: Certain Underwriters At Lloyd's v. United States, 511 F.2d 159, 161 (5th Cir. 1975); United States Lines, Inc. v. United States, 470 F.2d 487, 490 (5th Cir. 1972).

11. Restatement of Restitution § 102.

12. District of Columbia: Georges Radio v. Capital Transit Co., 126 F.2d 219 (D.C.Cir. 1942).

See Best v. Yerkes, 247 Iowa 800, 77 N.W.2d 23, 60 A.L.R.2d 1354 (1956); Quatray v. Wicker, 178 La. 289, 151 So. 208 (1933); Hobbs v. Hurley, 117 Me. 449, 104 A. 815 (1918); Ankeny v. Moffet, 37 Minn. 109, 33 N.W. 320 (1887); Goldman v. Mitchell-Fletcher Co., 292 Pa. 354, 141 A. 231 (1928); Davis v. Broad St. Garage, 191 Tenn. 320, 232 S.W.2d 355 (1950); Ellis v. Chicago & North Western Ry. Co., 167 Wis. 392, 167 N.W. 1048 (1918).

See also Prosser, Law of Torts (4th ed. 1971), pp. 305–310.

13. 340 U.S. 543, 71 S.Ct. 399, 95 L.Ed. 523 (1951).

14. Blunt v. Brown, supra, n. 10.

Allied Mut. Cas. Co. v. Long, 252 Iowa 829, 107 N.W.2d 682, 684 (1961). "The sole basis for contribution among joint tortfeasors is a common liability. . . . It is a fundamental principle of the right and without it the right does not exist."

Certain Underwriters at Lloyd's v. United States, supra, n. 10.

15. "Joint tortfeasors" can be narrowly defined as those who cause harm by acts done *in concert*. Where independent but simultaneous acts

bar an action for contribution where defendants are liable for the same injury,[16] even though the liability of each defendant is based on different grounds.[17] Thus, the subrogees of a defendant whose intoxicated driving has proximately caused plaintiff's injuries, will have a right of contribution from the tavern owner, whose liability to plaintiff arises under a Dramshop statute.[18]

Where, however, a workman's compensation act regulates the obligations of an employer to an injured employee, generally there is held to be no common liability between the employer and a third person tortfeasor, and therefore no right of contribution against the employer.[19]

cause injury, the actors are "concurrent tortfeasors". Where their independent acts are successive in time, they are "successive tortfeasors." 19 Cal.L.Rev. 630; 25 Cal.L.Rev. 413; 68 Harv.L.Rev. 697; Witkin, Torts §§ 30, 34.

16. Cokas v. Perkins, 252 F.Supp. 563 (D.D.C.1966) (Medical malpractice. Held right of contribution exists between physicians rendering successive treatment.); Trieschman v. Eaton, 224 Md. 111, 166 A.2d 892 (1961) (Original tortfeasor and physician and hospital rendering subsequent negligent treatment are joint tortfeasors under Contribution Act).

See Prosser, Law of Torts (4th ed. 1971), pp. 305–310.

17. Chicago, Rock Island & Pac. R. R. Co. v. Chicago & North Western Ry. Co., 280 F.2d 110, 114 (8th Cir. 1960) (Supplier of railroad car liable for implied warranty, employer of injured party liable for failure to inspect); Zontelli Bros. v. Northern Pac. Ry. Co., 263 F.2d 194, 199 (8th Cir. 1959) (F.E.L.A. and Minnesota Wrongful Death Act); Farmers Ins. Exchange v. Village of Hewitt, 274 Minn. 246, 143 N.W.2d 230 (1966) (Dramshop and intoxicated driver); Thorson v. City of Minot, 153 N.W.2d 764 (N.D.1967) (Negligence and nuisance); Duckworth v. Ford Motor Co., 320 F.2d 130, 97 A.L.R.2d 806 (3d Cir. 1963) (Manufacturer of defective steering assembly entitled to contribution from dealer negligent in servicing same part).

18. Federated Mut. Implement & Hardware Ins. Co. v. Dunkelberger, 172 N.W.2d 137 (Iowa 1969) (Dramshop and intoxicated driver).

19. Guillard v. Niagara Machine & Tool Works, 488 F.2d 20, 22 (8th Cir. 1973) (Action by manufacturer of power press for contribution from employer of injured worker. Held, where employer liable through workman's compensation act, no common liability with third person tortfeasor).

Employers Mut. Liab. Ins. Co. v. Griffin Constr. Co., 280 S.W.2d 179, 53 A.L. R.2d 967 (Ky.1955) (Workman's compensation act extinguished employer's liability to employee, therefore no basis for common liability with third person tortfeasor).

American Dist. Tel. Co. v. Kittleson, 179 F.2d 946 (8th Cir. 1950) (Employer's liability under workman's compensation act was contractual, therefore no common liability with third person liable in tort).

Criswell v. Seaman Body Corp., 233 Wis. 606, 290 N.W. 177 (1940) (Liability under workman's compensation act is in lieu of tort liability, therefore no liability in common with third party tortfeasor).

Contra: Justice v. United States, 208 F.Supp. 724 (D.C.Pa.1962) (Employer

§ 17.3   TORT LIABILITY AND DEFENSES   Pt. 3

If the act by its terms provides an exclusive remedy, the employer is insulated, even where his concurrent negligence is established.[20]

Where one party has a defense or immunity to the original action, common liability is not established, and the right of contribution is precluded.[21] Where a party is only vicariously liable, the liability has been considered as primary and secondary, rather than joint and several, thereby barring contribution.[22] Thus, a master liable for the

liable to third person tortfeasor for contribution in amount of unpaid balance due employer under workman's compensation act).

F.E.L.A.: Ryan Stevedoring Co. v. Pan-Atlantic S. S. Corp., 350 U.S. 124, 76 S.Ct. 232, 100 L.Ed. 133 (1956) (Exclusivity provision bars contribution recovery against U. S. unless liability established by contract); United Airlines, Inc. v. Weiner, 335 F.2d 379 (9th Cir. 1964), cert. dism'd 379 U.S. 951, 85 S.Ct. 452, 13 L.Ed.2d 549.

20.   Guillard, supra, n. 19.

Myers v. J. A. McCarthy, 428 F.Supp. 656 (E.D.Pa.1977) (Despite showing of negligence, employer's liability not in tort, therefore no contribution); Christie v. Powder Power Tool Corp., 124 F.Supp. 693 (D.D.C.1954) (FELA establishes exclusive liability, thus U. S. not subject to contribution).

21.   Contributory Negligence

Fort Worth & Denver Ry. Co. v. Threadgill, 228 F.2d 307 (5th Cir. 1955) (Employer, liable under FELA despite employee's contributory negligence, has no right of contribution from a third party defendant for whom the contributory negligence is a complete defense).

Annotation: 6 A.L.R.3d 1307; 19 A.L. R.3d 928.

Guest Statute Immunity

Troutman v. Modlin, 353 F.2d 382 (8th Cir. 1965) (Third person defendant had no right of contribution from host driver who had guest statute defense against injured party); Shonka v. Campbell, 260 Iowa 1178, 152 N. W.2d 242, 26 A.L.R.3d 1274 (1967) (Guest statute precludes common liability between host driver and third person defendant).

Annotation: 26 A.L.R.3d 1283.

Family Immunity

Blunt v. Brown, 225 F.Supp. 326 (D.C. Iowa 1963) (No contribution from husband of injured party); Zaccari v. United States, 130 F.Supp. 50 (D.C. Md.1955) (U. S. cannot recover contribution from father of infant plaintiff).

Contra:

Puller v. Puller, 380 Pa. 219, 110 A.2d 175 (1955) (Third party defendant has right of contribution from joint tortfeasor despite family immunity doctrine); Zarrella v. Miller, 100 R.I. 545, 217 A.2d 673 (1966) (Contribution held to be an equitable duty to share liability, rather than a recovery for tort, therefore interfamilial immunity no bar); Smith v. Southern Farm Bureau Cas. Ins. Co., 247 La. 695, 174 So.2d 122 (1965) (Interspousal immunity a procedural doctrine limited to suit between spouses and does not preclude contribution).

Government Immunity

Hill v. United States, 453 F.2d 839 (6th Cir. 1972) (Plaintiff injured when ROTC cannon fired at state university football game. U. S. action for contribution barred by state's immunity from plaintiff's tort action); Starr v. United States, 393 F.Supp. 1359 (N.D.Tex.1975) (U. S. suit for contribution barred by Texas municipal immunity law).

22.   George v. Brehm, 246 F.Supp. 242 (W.D.Pa.1965) (Sidewalk slip and fall

566

tort of his servant may be able to recover through indemnity,[23] but has no action in contribution.[24]

The true Merryweather rule denying contribution to intentional tortfeasors has been preserved in most jurisdictions [25] and is incorporated into the Uniform Act.[26] In cases of wanton or reckless misconduct, there is less uniformity on the question of contribution.[27]

§ 17.4 Apportionment—Pro Rata—Comparative Fault

Although contribution is a doctrine founded in equity, contribution statutes frequently provide for its operation by the inflexible and mechanistic rule of pro rata, or per capita, sharing of damages without regard to respective fault.[28] While equitable considerations in contribution have been statutorily provided in some jurisdictions,[29] the modern trend to equitable contribution generally has been a creation of the courts.[30]

---

action brought against borough and abutting property owner. Held, not basis for contribution).

23. See Chapter 36, Persons in Control, infra.

24. Melichar v. Frank, 78 S.D. 58, 98 N.W.2d 345 (1959).

But see Smith v. Raparot, 101 R.I. 565, 225 A.2d 666 (1967) (Act providing for contribution where tortfeasors are jointly *or* severally liable held to apply to master-servant relationship).

25. Turner v. Kirkwood, 49 F.2d 590 (10th Cir. 1931), cert. denied 284 U.S. 635, 52 S.Ct. 18, 76 L.Ed. 540; Best v. Yerkes, 247 Iowa 800, 77 N.W.2d 23 (1956); Bartnick v. Dunkin, 1 Cal. App.3d 38, 81 Cal.Rptr. 428 (1969).

26. 12 U.L.A. § 1(c). (Listed as optional).

See also West's Ann.California CCP § 875(d).

27. Cage v. New York Central R. R. Co., 276 F.Supp. 778 (W.D.Pa.1967), aff'd 386 F.2d 998 (3d Cir.) (Contribution denied to wantonly negligent railroad against administrator of estate of negligent deceased, under Penna. Law); Southern Ry. Co. v. Foote Mineral Co., 384 F.2d 224 (6th Cir. 1967) (No recovery of contribution where party seeking it is guilty of gross negligence); McCabe v. Century Theatres, Inc., 18 N.Y.2d 648, 273 N.Y.S.2d 74, 219 N.E.2d 426 (1967).

28. 12 U.L.A. § 2(a).

California: West's Ann. CCP § 876(a).

Based on the Merryweather rationale—"The unwillingness of the law as a matter of policy to make relative value judgments of degrees of culpability among wrongdoers." Dole v. Dow Chem. Co., infra.

Early Settlers Ins. Co. v. Schweid, 221 A.2d 920 (D.C.App.1966); Russell v. United States, 113 F.Supp. 353 (M.D. Pa.1953).

29. Arkansas Stat.Ann. § 32–1002(4) (1962); Hawaii Rev.Laws § 246–11 (1955); South Dakota Code § 33.-04A03(4) (Supp.1960).

30. Where liability is vicarious or constructive, it is generally equitably treated as a unified share with the primary liability, for pro rata purposes.

In the Wisconsin case of *Bielski v. Schulze*, the court reasoned that the state's adoption of a comparative negligence statute favored a rule of proportionate contribution among joint tortfeasors.[31] In 1974, contribution on a comparative negligence basis was announced as the Federal rule of contribution by the 7th Circuit.[32] The rule was held applicable to admiralty cases by the United States Supreme Court in *United States v. Reliable Transfer Co.*[33] In the landmark case of *Dole v. Dow Chem. Co.*,[34] the New York Court of Appeals utilized an "equitable indemnity" approach to overcome the state's pro rata contribution statute. Even without the theoretical support of a comparative negligence statute, the New York court found that the equitable basis of indemnity required a rule of "apportionment of responsibility in negligence" on the basis of comparative fault.[35] Combining both the *Bielski* and *Dole* rationales, the California Supreme Court in *American Motorcycle Ass'n v. Superior Court*[36] found that California's adoption of the comparative negligence doctrine[37] mandated "the more refined stage of permitting the jury to apportion liability in accordance with the tortfeasors' comparative fault," as a rule of "equitable indemnity" not precluded by California's rule of pro rata contribution.[38]

General and Sub-contractor

Larsen v. Minneapolis Gas Co., 282 Minn. 135, 163 N.W.2d 755 (1968).

Master/Servant

Standard Oil Co. of Kentucky v. Illinois Central R. R. Co., 421 F.2d 201 (5th Cir. 1968).

In nuisance cases, courts have apportioned damages according to defendant's contributions to the injury. Connor v. Grosso, 41 Cal.2d 229, 259 P.2d 435 (1953).

31. Bielski v. Schulze, 16 Wis.2d 1, 114 N.W.2d 105 (1962).

32. Kohr v. Allegheny Airlines, Inc., 504 F.2d 400 (7th Cir. 1974), cert. denied 421 U.S. 978, 95 S.Ct. 1980, 44 L.Ed.2d 470, on remand 420 F.Supp. 1339 (S.D.Ind.) (Aviation collision in Federal jurisdiction by diversity and FTCA claim).

33. United States v. Reliable Transfer Co., 421 U.S. 397, 405–411, 95 S.Ct. 1708, 1712–1716, 44 L.Ed.2d 251, 258–262 (1975).

34. Dole v. Dow Chem. Co., 30 N.Y.2d 143, 331 N.Y.S.2d 382, 282 N.E.2d 288, 53 A.L.R.3d 360 (1972).

35. 30 N.Y.2d 143, 149, 331 N.Y.S.2d 382, 387, 282 N.E.2d 288, 292.

36. American Motorcycle Ass'n v. Superior Court, 20 Cal.3d 578, 146 Cal. Rptr. 182, 578 P.2d 899 (1978).

37. Li v. Yellow Cab Co., 13 Cal.3d 804, 119 Cal.Rptr. 858, 532 P.2d 1226, 78 A.L.R.3d 393 (1975).

38. The court reasoned that the contribution statute's provision for administration "in accordance with the principles of equity, principles which the Legislature obviously intended the judiciary to elaborate, "refutes the argument that the Legislature intended to curtail judicial discretion in apportioning damages among multiple tortfeasors." 20 Cal.3d 578, 603, 146 Cal.Rptr. 182, 198, 578 P.2d 899, 915.

§ 17.5 Release

The common law rule that a plaintiff's release of one joint tortfeasor releases all is based on the theory that a cause of action is indivisible in the eyes of the law, and that there can be but one compensation for the joint wrong.[39] This rule, based on a confusion between release and satisfaction,[40] has been rejected in many jurisdictions in favor of looking for full compensation in fact,[41] or intent of the parties to the release.[42]

Where the rule still stands, it is circumvented in practice by the *"covenant not to sue"*, which is theoretically not a release and therefore does not discharge the non-agreeing tortfeasors.[43] The possibility of double recovery is precluded by requiring a pro tanto deduction in the amount received by plaintiff from any eventual recovery.[44]

Several jurisdictions, in the interest of disposition of litigation by settlement, have abrogated the common law rule by statute.[45]

---

39. Bee v. Cooper, 217 Cal. 96, 17 P.2d 740 (1932); Wagner v. Chicago & A. R. Co., 265 Ill. 245, 106 N.E. 809 (1914), aff'd 239 U.S. 452, 36 S.Ct. 135, 60 L.Ed. 379.

40. Prosser, Law of Torts (4th ed. 1971) p. 301.

41. **Full Compensation Releases All**

See Shortt v. Hudson Supply & Equipment Co., 191 Va. 306, 60 S.E.2d 900 (1950); Daily v. Somberg, 28 N.J. 372, 146 A.2d 676, 69 A.L.R.2d 1024 (1958).

42. Zenith Radio Corp. v. Hazeltine Research Inc., 401 U.S. 321, 91 S.Ct. 795, 28 L.Ed.2d 77 (1971), reh. denied 401 U.S. 1015, 91 S.Ct. 1247, 28 L. Ed.2d 552; Adams v. Dion, 109 Ariz. 308, 509 P.2d 201 (1973).
See Restatement, Second, Torts § 885.

43. Johnson v. Harnisch, 259 Iowa 1090, 147 N.W.2d 11 (1966); Pellett v. Sonotone Corp., 26 Cal.2d 705, 160 P.2d 783, 160 A.L.R. 863 (1945).

Covenant Not to Execute on Judgment

See Rager v. Superior Coach Sales & Serv., 110 Ariz. 188, 516 P.2d 324 (1973).

44. Bolton v. Ziegler, 111 F.Supp. 516 (D.C.Iowa 1953).

But see Giem v. Williams, 215 Ark. 705, 222 S.W.2d 800 (1949) (Where release agreement admitted before jury, presumption that award includes deduction).

45. E. g. California, West's Ann. CCP § 877: "Where a release, dismissal with or without prejudice, or a covenant not to sue or not to enforce judgment is given in good faith before verdict or judgment to one or more of a number of tortfeasors claimed to be liable for the same tort—

(a) It shall not discharge any other such tortfeasor from liability unless its terms so provide, but it shall reduce the claims against the others in the amount of the consideration paid for it whichever is the greater; and

(b) It shall discharge the tortfeasor to whom it is given from all liability for any contributions to any other tortfeasors."

Where the released defendant remains liable for contribution to the other defendants, the inducement to settle is impaired by lack of finality. Thus, many statutes provide the agreeing defendant with immunity from contribution. Devices other than formal release have been utilized for the same purpose, such as an agreement to limit one co-tortfeasor's liability in relation to the recovery against the others,[46] or a "loan receipt" from plaintiff to an agreeing defendant to be repaid out of the recovery against the others.[47] The inherent danger of collusion in any such arrangement has led one jurisdiction to hold all such agreements invalid as against public policy.[48] In other jurisdictions, the agreement is required to be disclosed,[49] and may be examined for determination of "good faith."[50] While "good faith" has been recognized to be an inherently nebulous concept,[51] the essential test will be a question of fact as to whether the agreement is "aimed to injure the interests of an absent tortfeasor."[52] Some jurisdictions provide that the agreement may be introduced into evidence, subject to the discretion of the court.[53]

46. Termed "Mary Carter agreements" in Maule Indus., Inc. v. Rountree, 264 So.2d 445 (Fla.App.1972), remanded on other grounds 284 So.2d 389 (Fla.), deriving from the case of Booth v. Mary Carter Paint Co., 202 So.2d 8 (Fla.App.1967). The Florida Supreme Court in Ward v. Ochoa, 284 So.2d 385 (Fla.1973), refined the term to apply only to *secret* liability limitation agreements. See also Daniel v. Penrod Drilling Co., D.C.La., 393 F.Supp. 1056; and, Annotation, 65 A.L.R.3d 602.

47. **Validity Upheld**
Reese v. Chicago, B & Q R. Co., 55 Ill. 2d 356, 303 N.E.2d 382, 62 A.L.R.3d 1101 (1973); Northern Indiana Public Serv. Co. v. Otis, 145 Ind.App. 159, 250 N.E.2d 378 (1969).
But see Biven v. Charlie's Hobby Shop, 500 S.W.2d 597 (Ky.1973) (Loan receipt arrangement held to constitute a release, denied effect as an enforceable loan); Bolton v. Ziegler, 111 F.Supp. 516 (D.C.Iowa 1953) (Loan receipt not between insurer and own insured held to constitute a covenant not to sue).

48. Lum v. Stinnet, 87 Nev. 402, 488 P.2d 347 (1971).

49. River Garden Farms, Inc. v. Superior Court, 26 Cal.App.3d 986, 103 Cal.Rptr. 498 (1972); Lareau v. Southern Pac. Co., 44 Cal.App.3d 783, 118 Cal.Rptr. 837 (1975).

50. Id.

51. River Garden Farms, supra, 26 Cal.App.3d at 997, 103 Cal.Rptr. at 506.

52. 26 Cal.App.3d at 996, 103 Cal.Rptr. at 505.

53. California: West's Ann. CCP § 877.-5(a)(2) provides an exception to admission where the court finds "that such disclosure will create substantial danger of undue prejudice, of confusing the issues, or of misleading the jury."

§§ 17.6–18.0 are reserved for supplementary material.

CHAPTER 18

RELEASES

Table of Sections

Sec.
18.1   In General.
18.2   Mutual Mistake.
18.3   Unilateral Mistake of Fact.
18.4   Ignorance of Releasor.
18.5   Mistake of Law.
18.6   Innocent Misrepresentation.
18.7   Fraud.
18.8   Burden of Proof.
18.9   Restoration of Consideration Upon Repudiation of Release.
18.10 What Law Applies.
18.11 Effect of Release—Joint Tortfeasors.
18.12 Distinguished from Covenant Not to Sue.

Library References:

C.J.S. Release § 1 et seq.
West's Key No. Digests, Release ⚖1 et seq.
Blashfield, Automobile Law and Practice, § 251.15 et seq.

§ 18.1 In General

Suppose plaintiff himself has "released" or "settled" his case for an amount the lawyer he subsequently consults advises is inadequate. Is he without relief? The answer has been firmly established as a solid "no" in many cases.

Whatever practical criticisms, charges of wrong doing or ethical errancy may be placed at the portals of plaintiff's personal injury counsel, in the region of releases blooms the full flower of defendant's derelictions.

A mendacious few insurance companies apparently have as their sole purpose in settlement, the bargain purchase of the case as cheaply as possible. They show no regard for public policy or welfare, social consequences, or appreciation that the premium money is not theirs, but funds of the assured held *in trust* to pay an *adequate settlement* in the contingency of catastrophe.[1]

---

1. There are two aspects motivating insurance: the assured wants protection for himself, and protection for the person he injures. In obtaining releases, too many insurance companies disregard this second motive.

§ 18.1   TORT LIABILITY AND DEFENSES   Pt. 3

I have read adjuster's handbooks proffering practices making Fagin's curriculum, in comparison, seem as noble as the ten commandments. I have heard some adjusters, not so instructed but being motivated by a desire to "please the home office," or because it is an "accepted custom of their trade," brag of their method of "ether settlements":[2] their blandishments to the children of the injured father, the gaining of the confidence of other members of the family, the disparagement of the legal profession ("Don't get a lawyer; he'll take all your money."), the courts ("Don't go to court; it will take five years to get a nickel."), the paternalistic approach ("We'll pay all your doctor and hospital bills."), and the persuasive showing of "ready cash."

It is the author's practice in these cases to telephone the principal, and the insurance company's manager, stating the facts and demanding relief. If such is not forthcoming, I ignore the release, make no repayment, and file suit. In an aggravated case, however, counsel, after exhausting his informal remedy with the defendant's insurance company, should proceed to the insurance commissioner of his particular state, or even to the district attorney if the particular statute permits. If the erring lawyer should be brought before his bar association grievance committee, so, too, should the deceitful adjuster.

Generally, the validity of a release is to be determined in accordance with the rules governing the validity of contracts.[3]

§ 18.2   Mutual Mistake

A release may be set aside for a mutual mistake of fact.[4] The mistake must relate to a past or present material fact at the time the release is executed.[5] A mistake of opinion concerning future condi-

2. Now disapproved by statute in a number of states. An ideal enactment would make any release or settlement, contract employment or retainer, void if executed within two weeks after discharge from the hospital. See Mitschelen v. State Farm Mut. Auto. Ins. Co., 89 N.M. 586, 555 P.2d 707 (1976); Peterson v. Panovitz, 62 N.D. 328, 243 N.W. 798 (1932).

3. Brackeen v. Milner, 88 Ill.App.2d 50, 232 N.E.2d 241, 246 (1967); Swan v. Great Northern R. Co., 40 N.D. 258, 168 N.W. 657 (1918).

4. Meyer v. Murray, 70 Ill.App.3d 106, 26 Ill.Dec. 48, 52, 387 N.E.2d 878, 882 (1979); Mangini v. McClurg, 24 N.Y. 2d 556, 301 N.Y.S.2d 508, 513 (1969); Reynolds v. Merrill, 23 Utah 2d 155, 460 P.2d 323 (1969). Some jurisdictions, however, adhere to the rule that a mistake is *not* a ground for setting aside a release. See, e. g., Benton v. Smith, 389 S.W.2d 392 (Mo.App.1965) (Requiring a show of fraud or overreaching in order to invalidate release).

5. Quartermen v. City of Jacksonville, 347 So.2d 1036, 1038 (Fla.App.1977) ("To avoid a general release, a party must show that there was a mistake as to a past or present material fact

tions as a result of present factors is *not* a basis for invalidating a release.⁶

In order to avoid a release, the mistake must be mutual, material to the transaction, and affect its substance.⁷ Although a few decisions have set aside a release where there is a *known injury*, but the consequences therefrom are unknown and unexpected,⁸ the clear majority is contra. The majority rule is that in order to set aside a release in a personal injury claim, there must be in existence *unknown injuries* which were not within the parties' contemplation in reaching a settlement.⁹

Relief may be granted notwithstanding the fact that the release is broad enough in its terms to cover all injuries resulting from the particular incident. Where the release is executed without any intention to release liability for unknown injuries, the release will not act as a bar to an action for such unknown injuries.¹⁰ However, it has been held that where there is a *conscious intent* to discharge liability for *all* consequences of an accident, the release will be upheld.¹¹ In this context, the courts are fond of reminding plaintiff that the freedom to contract includes the freedom to make a bad bargain.¹²

at the time of the execution of the release).

6. Davis v. Flatiron Materials Co., 182 Colo. 65, 511 P.2d 28 (1973) (Upholding release as mistake was not in relation to plaintiff's present condition, but instead to her future course of recovery); Wheeler v. White Rock Bottling Co. of Oregon, 229 Or. 360, 366 P.2d 527 (1961) (Ordinarily mistaken opinions or bad guesses do not constitute the type of material mistake which will avoid a release); Bauer v. Griffin, 104 N.J.Super. 530, 250 A.2d 603, 610 (1969), aff'd 108 N.J.Super. 414, 261 A.2d 667.

7. Meyer v. Murray, 70 Ill.App.3d 106, 26 Ill.Dec. 48, 52, 387 N.E.2d 878, 882 (1979).

8. Illinois courts do not distinguish between: (1) separate and distinct injuries which were not known or considered at the time the settlement was approved, and (2) known injuries resulting in unknown and unexpected consequences. See Scherer v. Ravenswood Hosp. Medical Center, 21 Ill.App.3d 637, 639, 316 N.E.2d 98, 101 (1974). See also, Meyer v. Murray, 70 Ill.App.3d 106, 26 Ill.Dec. 48, 52, 387 N.E.2d 878, 882 (1979).

9. Hughes v. State Farm Mut. Auto. Ins. Co., 294 So.2d 398, 399 (Fla.App. 1974).

10. Grebe v. McDaniel, 265 Cal.App.2d 901, 71 Cal.Rptr. 662 (1968); Ranta v. Rake, 91 Idaho 376, 421 P.2d 747 (1967) (Court holding that plaintiff did not intend release for an injury, the existence of which was completely unknown at the time of the injury); Kropp v. Diamond K Markets, Inc., 207 Misc. 1030, 141 N.Y.S.2d 542, 543 (1955) (Fracture of left femoral neck incorrectly diagnosed as traumatic arthritis).

11. Mangini v. McClurg, 24 N.Y.2d 556, 301 N.Y.S.2d 508, 514 (1969) (If there was a conscious and deliberate intention to discharge liability from the accident, the release will be sustained and bar any future claims of previously unknown injuries).

12. Sanger v. Yellow Cab Co., Inc., 486 S.W.2d 477, 482 (Mo.1972).

§ 18.3 Unilateral Mistake of Fact

The general rule is that a unilateral or self-induced mistake on the part of the releasor is *not* an adequate basis for invalidating the release.[13] It is considered a unilateral mistake where the defendant accepts plaintiff's own diagnosis and opinion, which subsequently proves inaccurate. In such a case, the release may not be avoided by plaintiff.[14]

The result is contra where the opposite situation presents itself. If the *releasee's* physician makes a mistake upon which the releasor acts, the release may be set aside.[15] And when the mistake exists on the side of the releasor, relief may be granted where there has been inequitable conduct on the side of the releasee.[16] Relief will be granted where the releasee knows of the releasor's mistake.[17]

§ 18.4 Ignorance of Releasor

Generally, a releasor who has no disability preventing him from reading the release is bound thereby, even if he in fact did not read the release.[18] In such a case, he cannot avoid the release by claiming

---

13. Scherer v. Ravenswood Hosp. Medical Center, 70 Ill.App.3d 939, 27 Ill.Dec. 219, 222, 388 N.E.2d 1268, 1271 (1979) (A unilateral or self-induced mistake is insufficient to void a release); Sosa v. Velvet Dairy Stores, Inc., 407 S.W.2d 615 (Mo. App.1966).

14. Kiest v. Schrawder, 56 Ill.App.3d 732, 14 Ill.Dec. 431, 372 N.E.2d 442 (1979). In that case, plaintiff told defendant that her doctor had diagnosed whiplash. After she signed the release, it was discovered that her injuries were much more serious than initially believed. The release was enforced, the court stating that this was a unilateral mistake of plaintiff which had been constructively adopted by defendant. See also, Beaver v. Estate of Harris, 67 Wash.2d 621, 409 P.2d 143 (1965).

15. Thomas v. Hollowell, 20 Ill.App.2d 288, 155 N.E.2d 827, 828 (1959).

16. Baker v. Chicago, Fire & Burglary Detection, Inc., 489 F.2d 953, 955–56 (7th Cir. 1973); Hutcheson v. Frito-Lay, Inc., 315 F.2d 818, 823 (8th Cir. 1963) (The mistake of one party, accompanied by fraud or misrepresentation by the other party, may be sufficient to avoid a release); Coester v. H. H. B. Co., 447 F.Supp. 372, 378 (D.C.S.D.1978); Robles v. Trinidad Corp., 270 F.Supp. 570, 572 (S.D.N.Y. 1966).

17. Limestone Realty Co. v. Town & Country Fine Furniture & Carpeting, Inc., 256 A.2d 676 (Del.Ch.1969); Smiles v. Young, 271 So.2d 798 (Fla. App.1973); Century Plastic Corp. v. Tupper Corp., 333 Mass. 531, 131 N.E.2d 740 (1956).

Equity will step in to prevent a party from taking an unconscionable advantage of another's mistake for the purpose of enriching himself at the other's expense. Spaulding v. Zimmerman, 263 Minn. 346, 116 N.W.2d 704, 710 (1962).

18. Lee v. Allied Sports Associates, Inc., 349 Mass. 544, 209 N.E.2d 329 (1965) (Failure of plaintiff to read the release before signing does not affect its validity).

he was ignorant of its contents.[19] It has even been held that an illiterate is under the obligation to have it read to him by someone whose interests are not antagonistic to his own.[20]

The general rule, however, is inapplicable where there is evidence of misconduct on the part of the releasee.[21] The courts will not enforce a release executed under those circumstances. The same is true when the releasee hires an interpreter to read the release to the releasor, and the interpreter makes a mistake in the interpreting thereof.[22]

Courts refuse to uphold releases where the releasor could not read the instrument he was signing, and the releasor reasonably believed he was signing a different paper, such as a receipt.[23] In one case,[24] the injured plaintiff was allowed to set aside a release which she had signed, thinking it was a thank-you note for a gift received for the tortfeasor. Her inability to read without her glasses, which had been broken in the collision, and her reliance on statements by insurance company adjuster (who incidentally had not identified himself as such) that the paper had nothing to do with the case, convinced the court her inability to read the instrument was not a bar.

---

19. Gingell v. Backus, 246 Md. 83, 227 A.2d 349 (1967) (Plaintiff cannot invoke his own heedlessness to impeach his solemn release, and then call that heedlessness someone else's fraud. If he did not know what he was signing, it was his plain duty to inquire.); Slade v. Phelps, 446 S.W.2d 931 (Tex.Civ.App.1969) (Nobody prevented plaintiff from reading the release; it was her own choice to sign without reading it).

20. Serdenes v. Aetna Life Ins. Co., 21 Md.App. 453, 319 A.2d 858, 863 (1974); Merit Music Serv., Inc. v. Sonneborn, 245 Md. 213, 225 A.2d 470 (1967).

21. DuBois v. Sparrow, 92 Cal.App.3d 290, 154 Cal.Rptr. 717 (1979); Conley v. Fuhrman, 355 S.W.2d 861 (Mo. 1962) (The question is not whether plaintiff was negligent, but whether through defendant's fraudulent representations she was led to sign without further investigation an instrument she did not intend to execute).

22. Southern Pac. Co. v. Gastelum, 36 Ariz. 106, 283 P. 719 (1929); Burik v. Dundee Woolen Co., 66 N.J.L. 420, 49 A. 442 (1901).

23. Dice v. Akron C & Y Ry. Co., 342 U.S. 359, 72 S.Ct. 312, 96 L.Ed. 398 (1951) (U.S. Supreme Court holding that under federal law, a release is void even if employee failed to read it before signing, if the release was induced by fraud); Bergeron v. Port Allan Mortuary, Inc., 178 So.2d 442, 448 (La.App.1965), writ refused 248 La. 441, 179 So.2d 430 ("Releasor" thought she was signing papers necessary for the arrangement of decedent husband's funeral); Whitehead v. Montgomery Ward & Co., Inc., 194 Or. 106, 239 P.2d 226 (1959) (Injured employee relied on statements made that document was not a release, and did not have his glasses at the time of signing).

24. Wise v. Prescott, 244 La. 157, 151 So.2d 356 (1963).

A valid release cannot be obtained from a person mentally incompetent.[25]

§ 18.5 Mistake of Law

For a mutual mistake of law, a release may in some, but not all jurisdictions, be set aside.[26] For a *unilateral* mistake of law, the general rule regarding mistakes applies—there can be no relief from the release unless there has been some inequitable conduct on the part of the releasee.[27]

§ 18.6 Innocent Misrepresentation

A misrepresentation of a material fact to the releasor by the releasee, even though made in good faith and without any intent to deceive, is usually sufficient to avoid a release.[28] This is especially true when the misrepresentation is negligent.[29]

§ 18.7 Fraud

A release may be avoided for fraud or fraudulent representations made by the releasee or his agent and relief upon by the releasor to his injury.[30] The law of fraud, as generally applied to written instruments, controls when the question concerns fraudulently in-

---

25. Gillenwater v. Johnson, 226 Ark. 400, 290 S.W.2d 1 (1956) (Aged and illiterate man under influence of codeine tablets); Bowman v. Illinois Central R. Co., 11 Ill.2d 186, 142 N.E.2d 104 (1957), cert. denied 355 U.S. 837, 78 S.Ct. 63, 2 L.Ed.2d 49.

26. Pennsylvania Mut. Life Ins. Co. v. Forcier, 24 F.Supp. 851 (D.C.Mo. 1937); Smyth v. Kaspar American State Bank, 6 Ill.App.2d 64, 127 N.E. 2d 149 (1955), aff'd 9 Ill.2d 27, 136 N.E.2d 796; Reggio v. Warren, 207 Mass. 525, 93 N.E. 805 (1911).

27. Gelfand v. Tanner Motor Tours, Ltd., 450 F.2d 786 (2d Cir. 1971); Jordan v. Guerra, 23 Cal.2d 469, 144 P. 2d 349 (1943).

28. Doyle v. Teasdale, 263 Wis. 328, 57 N.W.2d 381 (1953). A misrepresentation by the physician employed by the releasee as to the releasor's injuries or physical condition, made in good faith and with no intention to deceive and relied on by the releasor, will be sufficient to avoid a release. See also, Whitehead v. Montgomery Ward & Co., 194 Or. 106, 239 P.2d 226 (1959); Wood v. Dunlop, 8 Wash.App. 957, 510 P.2d 260 (1973), aff'd in part, rev'd in part on other grounds, 83 Wash.2d 719, 521 P.2d 1177.

29. Scarborough v. Atlantic Coast Line Ry. Co., 178 F.2d 253 (4th Cir. 1949), cert. denied 339 U.S. 919, 70 S.Ct. 621, 94 L.Ed. 1343; Fravel v. Pennsylvania Ry. Co., 104 F.Supp. 84 (D. C.Md.1952).

30. Reese v. Cradit, 12 Ariz.App. 233, 469 P.2d 467 (1970); Carruth v. Fritch, 36 Cal.2d 426, 224 P.2d 702 (1950); King v. Motor Mart Garage Co., 336 Mass. 422, 146 N.E.2d 365 (1957).

duced releases and, therefore, the usual elements of fraud must be shown.[31]

Fraud may be evidenced by inadequacy of consideration.[32] After knowledge of the fraud, the innocent party must guard against acts of affirmance.[33]

Where the evidence warrants, questions of fraud and misrepresentation in obtaining a release are for the jury.[34]

§ 18.8 Burden of Proof

A release is usually raised by the defendant as an affirmative defense, and it is up to the defense to prove it by a preponderance of the evidence.[35] With the exception of a seaman's release,[36] once the defendant has met his burden of proof concerning the validity of the release, it is up to the plaintiff to establish those facts which would render the release void.[37]

---

31. Martin v. Po-Jo, Inc., 104 Ill.App. 2d 462, 244 N.E.2d 851 (1969).

32. Wojcik v. Pollock, 97 N.J.Super. 319, 235 A.2d 58, 61 (1967) (One of the proper factors in order to prove fraud is the inadequacy of consideration).

33. Swartz v. Topping, 191 Neb. 41, 213 N.W.2d 718 (1974) (Party estopped to claim release not binding); Davis v. Hargett, 244 N.C. 157, 92 S.E.2d 782 (1956) (Injured person cannot affirm voidable release against one joint tortfeasor and recover the additional damages for which he may be entitled from another); Mitzel v. Schatz, 175 N.W.2d 659 (N.D.1970) (Voidable release may be ratified or confirmed by statements or acts of the releasor).

34. Dice v. Akron, C&Y Ry. Co., 342 U.S. 359, 72 S.Ct. 312, 96 L.Ed. 398 (1951); Allen v. Overturf, 234 Ark. 612, 353 S.W.2d 343 (1962); DuBois v. Sparrow, 92 Cal.App.3d 290, 154 Cal.Rptr. 717 (1979); Bowman v. Illinois Central R. Co., 11 Ill.2d 186, 142 N.E.2d 104 (1957), cert. denied 355 U.S. 837, 78 S.Ct. 63, 2 L.Ed.2d 49; Stewart v. Eldred, 349 Mich. 28, 84 N.W.2d 496 (1957); Bryant v. Greene, 164 Neb. 15, 81 N.W.2d 580 (1957).

35. Eulo v. Deval Aerodynamics, Inc., 430 F.2d 325 (1970), cert. denied 401 U.S. 974, 91 S.Ct. 1191, 28 L.Ed.2d 323 (1971); Brubaker v. United States, 342 F.2d 655 (7th Cir. 1965); Insurance Co. of North America v. Knight, 8 Ill.App.3d 871, 291 N.E.2d 40 (1972), appeal dism'd 414 U.S. 804, 94 S.Ct. 165, 38 L.Ed.2d 40; Tabor v. Lederer, 205 Kan. 746, 472 P.2d 209 (1970); Belli v. Forsyth, 301 Mass. 203, 16 N.E.2d 656 (1938); Romero v. King, 368 Mich. 45, 117 N.W.2d 119 (1962); Tesauro v. Thomas H. Tesauro Lumber Corp., 35 A.D.2d 607, 313 N.Y.S.2d 443 (1970).

36. Cates v. United States, 451 F.2d 411 (5th Cir. 1971); Wooten v. Skibs A/S Samuel Bakke, 431 F.2d 821 (4th Cir. 1969); Comeaux v. Two-R Drilling Co., 236 F.Supp. 735 (E.D.La. 1964).

37. Martin v. Po-Jo, Inc., 104 Ill.App. 2d 462, 244 N.E.2d 851 (1969); Child v. Lincoln Enterprises, Inc., 51 Ill. App.2d 76, 200 N.E.2d 751 (1964);

§ 18.9 Restoration of Consideration Upon Repudiation of Release

There is a split in authority on the question of whether the releasor must restore the consideration for the release before repudiating it.[38] It is clear, though, that where a release of a claim has been obtained through fraud, the majority rule has no requirement to return any consideration received.[39] Admiralty and FELA cases do not require a return.[40]

§ 18.10 What Law Applies

Generally, the law applied to contract law is in force in determining the validity of a release.[41] However, in cases of admiralty[42] or under the FELA,[43] federal law applies. The Federal Tort Claims Act has been construed as permitting suit against the United States although the employee tortfeasor has been released.[44]

At common law, and in the absence of a statute providing otherwise, it is a general proposition that a valid release of one joint tortfeasor releases and discharges *all* of the tortfeasors.[45] The unitary

---

Dixson v. Carter, 138 So.2d 227 (La. App.1962); Jenkins v. Simmons, 472 S.W.2d 417 (Mo.1971); Sexton v. Lilley, 4 N.C.App. 606, 167 S.E.2d 467 (1969); Barnes v. Barnes, 207 Va. 114, 148 S.E.2d 789 (1966).

38. Ted Price Constr. Co. v. Cascade Natural Gas Co., 307 F.2d 741, 743 (9th Cir. 1962) (No tender-back required); Rachesky v. Finklea, 329 F.2d 606 (4th Cir. 1964) (Tender-back required); Chapman v. Ross, 47 Mich.App. 201, 209 N.W.2d 288 (1973) (Tender-back required); Newton v. St. Louis-San Francisco Ry. Co., 405 S.W.2d 489 (Mo.App.1966) (Tender-back required).

39. Reliable Furniture Co. v. Fidelity and Guar. Ins. Underwriters, Inc., 16 Utah 2d 211, 398 P.2d 685 (1965). *Contra,* Hinds v. Plantation Pipe Line Co., 455 F.2d 902 (5th Cir. 1972).

40. Hogue v. Southern R. R. Co., 390 U.S. 516, 88 S.Ct. 1150, 20 L.Ed.2d 73 (1968), conformed to 117 Ga.App. 874, 162 S.E.2d 471; Mohr v. Pennsylvania R. R. Co., 409 F.2d 73 (3d Cir. 1969); Marshall v. New York Central R. R. Co., 218 F.2d 900 (7th Cir. 1955); Apitsch v. Patapsco & Back Rivers R. R. Co., 385 F.Supp. 495 (D.C.Md.1974).

41. Brackeen v. Milner, 88 Ill.App.2d 50, 232 N.E.2d 241 (1967); Swan v. Great Northern R. Co., 40 N.D. 258, 168 N.W. 657 (1918).

42. Garrett v. Moore-McCormack Co., 317 U.S. 239, 63 S.Ct. 246, 87 L.Ed. 239 (1942).

43. Callen v. Pennsylvania Ry. Co., 332 U.S. 625, 68 S.Ct. 296, 92 L.Ed. 242 (1948); Marshall v. New York Central R. Co., 218 F.2d 900 (7th Cir. 1955).

44. Friday v. United States, 239 F.2d 701 (9th Cir. 1957); United States v. First Sec. Bank, 208 F.2d 424 (10th Cir. 1953).

45. Transpac Constr. Co. v. Clark & Groff Engineers, Inc., 466 F.2d 823 (9th Cir. 1972); Whitt v. Hutchison, 43 Ohio St.2d 53, 330 N.E.2d 678 (1975); Hemphill v. Strain, 341 So.2d 1186 (La.App.1976), application denied 343 So.2d 1072 (La.); Weather-

conception of joint tortfeasors at common law, coupled with the equitable principal that an injured person should not be compensated twice for the same injury, is the source of the rule.[46]

In an attempt to avoid this harsh rule, an express reservation of the right to sue other joint tortfeasors is often included in the release.[47] There is a conflict of authority as to the effectiveness of such reservations, some jurisdictions recognizing them, while others do not.[48] In those jurisdictions which do not recognize express reservation, it is on the ground that a release operates to extinguish a claim, and any reservation would be repugnant thereto.[49]

Although initially the rule was that a release of one joint tortfeasor was a release of all applied only where the wrongdoers acted in concert,[50] many jurisdictions apply the same rule where independent tortfeasors are involved, especially where the injuries are inseparable.[51] Where the torts are wholly separate and distinct, the release of one tortfeasor should not be construed as releasing the other.[52]

The release of a tortfeasor has been held also to release a physician or surgeon for medical malpractice in the treatment and aggravation of the original injuries,[53] unless the patient has suffered a new and disconnected injury.[54] Release of an employer under worker's compensation has been held not to release a third party

ford v. Ryder Truck Rental & Leasing, Inc., 344 So.2d 937 (Fla.App. 1977).

46. Dougherty v. California Kettleman Oil Royalties, 13 Cal.2d 174, 88 P.2d 690 (1939).

47. Zenith Radio Corp. v. Hazeltine Research, Inc., 401 U.S. 321, 91 S.Ct. 795, 28 L.Ed.2d 77 (1971), reh. denied 401 U.S. 1015, 91 S.Ct. 1247, 28 L. Ed.2d 552; Sade v. Hemstrom, 205 Kan. 514, 471 P.2d 340 (1970); McMillen v. Klingersmith, 467 S.W.2d 193 (Tex.1971) ("The rule is a simple one. Unless a party is named in a release, he is not released.").

48. Parker v. Baltimore Paint & Chem. Corp., 273 F.Supp. 651 (D.C.Colo. 1967); Atlantic Coast Line R. Co. v. Boone, 85 So.2d 834 (Fla.1956).

49. Simpson v. Plyler, 258 N.C. 390, 128 S.E.2d 843 (1963); Carey v. Bilby, 129 F. 203 (8th Cir. 1904).

50. Union of Russian Societies of St. Michael & St. George v. Koss, 348 Pa. 574, 36 A.2d 433 (1944); Shortt v. Hudson Supply & Equipment Co., 191 Va. 306, 60 S.E.2d 900 (1950).

51. Bittner v. Little, 270 F.2d 286 (3d Cir. 1959); Anderson v. Martzke, 131 Ill.App.2d 61, 266 N.E.2d 137 (1970).

52. Litts v. Pierce County, 5 Wash. App. 531, 488 P.2d 785 (1971).

53. Knight v. Strong, 101 Ohio App. 347, 140 N.E.2d 9 (1955).
Contra, McMillen v. Klingensmith, 467 S.W.2d 193 (Tex.1971).

54. Dickow v. Cookingham, 123 Cal. App.2d 81, 266 P.2d 63 (1954); Frost v. Des Moines Still College of Osteopathy and Surgery, 248 Iowa 294, 79 N.W.2d 306 (1957).

§ **18.11** Effect of Release—Joint Tortfeasors

When a plaintiff releases one joint tortfeasor, does this release any and all remaining tortfeasors? Under strict common law doctrine, the release of one automatically released all joint tortfeasors. The release was thought to be a "satisfaction in law," even though the given compensation was inadequate and the parties had no intention to release the other wrongdoers.[57] One English court justified the rule on the ground that the cause of action was "one and indivisible," and once one was released, all other liable persons were consequently released also.[58]

This rule received enormous and well-founded criticism. Dean Wigmore referred to it as a "surviving relic of the Cokian period of metaphysics."[59] Many courts[60] have voiced similar opposition to a

---

55. Lamoreux v. San Diego & Arizona Eastern Ry. Co., 48 Cal.2d 617, 311 P.2d 1 (1957) (Release of employer under workmen's compensation does not release third party tortfeasor, even if acting in concert).

56. Giem v. Williams, 215 Ark. 705, 222 S.W.2d 800 (1949); Raughley v. Delaware Coach Co., 47 Del. (8 Terry) 343, 91 A.2d 245 (1952); Maryland Lumber Co. v. White, 205 Md. 180, 107 A.2d 73 (1954); Daugherty v. Hershberger, 386 Pa. 367, 126 A. 2d 730 (1956).

57. Cocke v. Jennor, Hob 66, 80 Eng. Rep. 214 (K.B.1614).

58. Duck v. Mayen, [1892] 2 Q.B. 511 (C.A.).

59. Wigmore, Diversities De La Ley, 17 Ill.L.Rev. 563 (1923)
"Our obnoxious old friend, that constant companion of personal injury cases, viz., the rule that a release to one of several joint-tortfeasors is a discharge to all, is receiving numerous hard knocks lately. He is already aged and infirm, being quite anachronistic; and it looks as though he would soon have to retire from active meddling in the affairs of men. The legislatures have begun to deliver blows at him . . . and these legislative remedial statutes sometimes become fashionable and spread rapidly.

. . .

"Considering that personal injury cases have occupied our courts in large degree for sixty years past, and that in that field his offensiveness was most obvious and constant. It is singular that so long a time has elapsed before the movement to blackball this obnoxious old party has developed. Various technicalities have been covertly employed to show our unfriendly sentiments towards him; e. g., the distinction between an out-and-out release and a covenant not to sue

. . .

"In recent years a few courts have further helped by at least giving to well-informed counsel the opportunity to evade the old gentleman, i. e., they refuse to recognize his authority where the release explicitly reserves all right to pursue other tortfeasors

. . .

60. See note 60 on page 581.

rule which so often produces manifestly unfair results. One court noted [61] that the rule is a "trap for the unwary, it stifles the desire of the victim to compromise, and it leads to results not intended by the parties."

In response to the widespread opposition to this rule, the Restatement (Second) of Torts was changed to read: "A valid release of one tortfeasor from liability for a harm . . . does not discharge others liable for the same harm, unless it is agreed that it will discharge them." [62] Most states [63] now follow this rule, and consider the intent of the parties and whether the compensation received for the release was adequate for all of plaintiff's injuries.

§ 18.12 Distinguished from Covenant Not to Sue

At common law, and even today to a fair extent, the viability of plaintiff's claim after he settled with one joint tortfeasor hinged on the distinction between whether he had executed a release, or merely had covenanted not to sue. Unlike a release which operates to extinguish a cause of action, a covenant not to sue operates only against the covenantee.[64] Thus, in the case of joint tortfeasors, a valid covenant not to sue one tortfeasor does not preclude an action against the others.[65] If suit is brought in a jurisdiction following strict common

". . . Nothing but false logic prevents a complete repudiation of this principle. Some courts have indeed not deemed it necessary to wait for the legislature, and have repudiated the hoary fallacy on common law grounds . . . ." Id. at 563–64. (Citations omitted.)

60. Adams v. Dion, 109 Ariz. 308, 509 P.2d 201 (1973); Breen v. Peck, 28 N.J. 351, 146 A.2d 665 (1958) ("The rule was evolved when metaphysics rather than justice was the dominant factor and obviously tends to defeat the fair expectations and intentions of the parties to the release . . .").

61. Kussler v. Burlington Northern, Inc., — Mont. —, 606 P.2d 520, 524 (1980).

62. Restatement, Second, Torts § 885.

63. Wiederhold v. Elgin, J. & E. Ry. Co., 368 F.Supp. 1054 (N.D.Ind.1974)

("Whether the release of one joint tortfeasor operates as a release of all joint tortfeasors depends on whether the injured party has received full satisfaction and whether the parties intended that the release be in full satisfaction of the injured party's claim, thus releasing all tortfeasors from liability"); Adams v. Dion, 109 Ariz. 308, 509 P.2d 201 (1973); Kussler v. Burlington Northern, Inc., — Mont. —, 606 P.2d 520 (1980).

64. Farmers Elevator Co. of Sterling v. Morgan, 172 Colo. 545, 474 P.2d 617 (1970); Pennsylvania Threshermen & Farmers Mut. Cas. Ins. Co. v. Hill, 113 Ga.App. 283, 148 S.E.2d 83 (1966); Memphis State Ry. Co. v. Williams, 47 Tenn.App. 399, 338 S.W.2d 639 (1960).

65. Adler v. Segal, 108 So.2d 773 (Fla.App.1959); Holcomb v. Flavin, 34 Ill.2d 558, 216 N.E.2d 811 (1966); Friedman v. Martini Tile & Terrazzo Co.,

law principles, counsel wishing to settle with one joint tortfeasor only should insist upon a covenant not to sue, the wording of which has been linguistically approved by the appellate courts of the forum state.

Courts have recognized that the distinction between releases and covenants not to sue is an artificial one which looks to form rather than substance, and which tends to trap the unwary.[66] They have relaxed the rules concerning releases, as we have seen, so that much of the distinction has disappeared.[67]

298 S.W.2d 221 (Tex.Civ.App.1957); Lee v. Junkans, 18 Wis.2d 56, 117 N.W.2d 614 (1962).

66. Breen v. Peck, 28 N.J. 351, 146 A.2d 665, 669 (1958).

67. Even where the distinction between releases and covenants not to sue are important, courts often will declare that an agreement is the latter to avoid an unjust result. See, e. g., Mitchell v. Weiger, 56 Ill.App.3d 236, 13 Ill.Dec. 796, 371 N.E.2d 888 (1977) wherein the court held that an agreement was a covenant not sue, even though it was entitled "Release."

§§ 18.13–19.0 are reserved for supplementary material.

PART IV

DEFENSES—SPECIFIC ACTIONS

CHAPTER 19

FEDERAL TORT CLAIMS ACT

Table of Sections

Sec.
19.1 In General.
19.2 Construction of F.T.C.A.
19.3 Limitations.
19.4 Subrogation.
19.5 Armed Forces Personnel.
19.6 Impleader.
19.7 Exclusions.
19.8 Strict Liability.
19.9 Compromise.
19.10 Attorney's Fees.
19.11 Damages.
19.12 Discovery.
19.13 Election of Remedy.
19.14 Within Scope of Office or Employment.

Library References:

C.J.S. United States §§ 117, 118.
West's Key No. Digests, United States ⟜78.
Wright & Miller, Federal Practice and Procedure, § 3656 et seq.
West's Federal Practice Manual, § 1991 et seq.

§ 19.1 In General

The Federal Tort Claims Act,[1] (F.T.C.A.), put into effect the concept of federal governmental liability for torts committed by the

---

1. Statutes relating to tort claims against the United States are as follows:

   Exclusive jurisdiction of district courts, 28 U.S.C.A. § 1346(b).

   Tort claims procedure, 28 U.S.C.A. §§ 2671–2680.

   Death on the High Seas, 46 U.S.C.A. § 761.

   The Amtrak Act or Rail Passenger Service Act of 1970, 45 U.S.C.A. § 547(a).

   The Military Claims Act, 10 U.S.C.A. § 2733.

government's employees during the course and scope of the employees' duties. The need for such a law was recognized years before its passage. Abraham Lincoln said: "It is as much the duty of government to render proper justice against itself, in favor of its citizens, as to administer the same between private individuals."

The F.T.C.A. permits suit against the United States for money damages for injury or loss of property, or personal injury or death caused by *negligence* or wrongful acts or omissions of any employees of the federal government while acting within the scope of his employment. The government may be held liable to a claimant only if a private person would be liable to the claimant in accordance with the law of the place where the act or omission occurred.

Venue is proper either in the district court where the plaintiff resides or the omission complained of occurred.[2] Change of venue for matter of convenience may be granted.[3] Trial is by the court without a jury,[4] and the Federal Rules of Civil Procedure are utilized.

Foreign Claims Act, 10 U.S.C.A. § 2734.

Claims resulting from use of Government property, 10 U.S.C.A. § 2737.

Military Personnel and Civilian Employees' Claims Act of 1964, 31 U.S.C.A. §§ 240–243.

Claims under reciprocal international agreements, 10 U.S.C.A. § 2734b.

The National Guard Claims Act, 32 U.S.C.A. § 715.

The United States Employees' Compensation Act, 5 U.S.C.A. § 8116 (c).

Federal Drivers Act, 28 U.S.C.A. § 2679(b–e).

Medical Care Recovery Act, 42 U.S.C.A. §§ 2651–2653.

Federal Claims Collection Act of 1966, 31 U.S.C.A. §§ 951–953.

Time for commencing tort action against the United States, 28 U.S.C.A. § 2401(b).

Venue, 28 U.S.C.A. § 1402.

No jury trial, 28 U.S.C.A. § 2402.

Appeal to Court of Appeals, 28 U.S.C.A. § 1291.

Appeal to Court of Claims, 28 U.S.C.A. § 1504.

The procedure in district court is governed by the Federal Rules of Civil Procedure.

For additional discussion of the Federal Tort Claims Act, reference should be made to West's Federal Practice Manual, § 1991 et seq., and Wright and Miller, Federal Practice and Procedure § 3656 et seq.

2. 28 U.S.C.A. § 1402(b).

Confusion as to whether this is a venue or jurisdiction statute abounds as a result of the use of the word jurisdiction in the Code. Cases consistently treat the statute as establishing venue requirements. See Nowotny v. Turner, 203 F.Supp. 802 (D.C.N.C. 1962); Buchheit v. United Airlines, Inc., 202 F.Supp. 811 (S.D.N.Y.1962); Shaw v. United States, 422 F.Supp. 339 (S.D.N.Y.1976) (Discusses similar confusion under 28 U.S.C.A. § 1402(a) (1) which is a statute covering tax claims).

3. 28 U.S.C.A. § 1404(a). See also Kephart v. United States, 242 F.Supp. 469 (D.C.Pa.1965).

4. 28 U.S.C.A. § 2402.

If a state defendant is also sued, trial by jury may be had as to him at the same time the Federal Judge sits without a jury.[5] The government may assert any set-off or counterclaim it may have against the plaintiff.[6] The remedy provided by the Act is exclusive, precluding suit against any federal agency as to claims within the purview of the Act.[7] Not all sovereign immunity is absolved by the Act, as there are 13 classes of claims specifically excluded under the Act.[8]

Federal agencies are authorized to make administrative settlements of claims under $2,500.[9] All suits coming within the Act are defended by the Attorney General.[10]

§ 19.2 Construction of F.T.C.A.

Some district courts originally construed the F.T.C.A. strictly as a waiver of an immunity.[11] However, in *United States v. Aetna Cas. and Sur. Co.*,[12] Chief Justice Vinson, writing for a plurality of the Supreme Court, expressly rejected a strict construction of the F.T.C.A. Justice Vinson quoted Justice Cardozo, saying, "The exemption of the sovereign from suit involves hardship enough where consent has been withheld. We are not to add to its rigor by refinement of construction where consent has been announced." [13]

The Court was even more explicit in *United States v. Yellow Cab*,[14] where the Court said, "We recognize the Federal Tort Claims Act waives the government's immunity in sweeping language. Moreover, the Court has stated that the exceptions to the waiver are to be narrowly construed." [15]

5. Moloney v. United States, 354 F.Supp. 480 (S.D.N.Y.1972).

6. 28 U.S.C.A. § 1346(c).

7. 28 U.S.C.A. § 2679(b).

8. 28 U.S.C.A. §§ 2680(a)–(n).

9. 28 U.S.C.A. § 2672.

10. 28 U.S.C.A. § 2679(c).

11. Spelar v. United States, 75 F.Supp. 967 (D.C.N.Y.1948), rev'd 171 F.2d 208 (2d Cir.), rev'd 338 U.S. 217, 70 S.Ct. 10, 94 L.Ed. 3; Grace to Use of Grangers Mut. Ins. Co. v. United States, 76 F.Supp. 174 (D.C.Md.1948).

12. 338 U.S. 366, 70 S.Ct. 207, 94 L.Ed. 171 (1949).

13. Anderson v. John L. Hayes Constr. Co., 243 N.Y. 140, 147, 153 N.E. 28, 29–30 (1926), motion to amend remittititur denied 243 N.Y. 593, 154 N.E. 619.

14. 340 U.S. 543, 547, 71 S.Ct. 399, 402, 95 L.Ed. 523 (1951).

15. Dalehite v. United States, 346 U.S. 15, 73 S.Ct. 956, 97 L.Ed. 1427 (1953), reh. denied 346 U.S. 841, 880, 74 S.Ct. 13, 117, 98 L.Ed. 362, 386, reh. denied, 347 U.S. 924, 74 S.Ct. 511, 98 L.Ed. 1078; First Nat'l Bank in Albuquerque v. United States, 552 F.2d 370 (10th Cir. 1977), cert. denied 434 U.S. 835, 98 S.Ct. 122, 54 L.Ed.2d 96.

§ 19.3 Limitations

Under the Act, a tort claim against the United States will be barred unless presented to the appropriate federal agency within two years after the accrual of the claim or unless an action is commenced within six months after receipt by the claimant of the final denial of the claim.[16] Unlike a statute of limitations, this time limitation is jurisdictional and nonwaivable, and may even be raised by a Court on its own action.[17] A claimant may elect to treat a claim as having been denied six months after its filing.[18]

There is a conflict of authority as to whether federal or state law is controlling as to when the statutory limitation period starts to run. The First Circuit Court of Appeals follows state law,[19] while the majority of circuits follow federal law.[20]

For the purposes of this section, a "Federal Agency" is defined to include the executive departments, the military departments, independent establishments of the United States, and corporations primarily acting as instrumentalities or agencies of the United States, but does not include any contractor with the United States.[21]

Among others, the following have been held to be an agency of the United States: Federal Deposit Insurance Corporation;[22] St.

---

16. 28 U.S.C.A. § 2401(b). Anderson v. John L. Hayes Constr. Co., 243 N.Y. 140, 153 N.E. 28 (1926), motion to amend remittitur denied 243 N.Y. 593, 154 N.E. 619. "Claim" within the meaning of the statute requires notice to the proper Federal Agency of the incident, accompanied by a demand for money damages in a sum certain. Under 28 U.S.C.A. § 2675(b) the filing of an action following the denial of a claim cannot be instituted for an amount in excess of the claim submitted to the agency, except where the increased amount is based upon newly discovered evidence. See Molinar v. United States, 515 F.2d 246 (5th Cir. 1975); Caton v. United States, 495 F.2d 635 (9th Cir. 1974); Bialowas v. United States, 443 F.2d 1047 (3d Cir. 1971).

Minority does not toll the statute of limitations as a legal disability under 28 U.S.C.A. § 2401(a); Simon v. United States, 244 F.2d 703 (5th Cir. 1957); Corcoran v. Allied Supermarkets, Inc., 498 F.2d 527 (8th Cir. 1974).

17. Kielwien v. United States, 540 F.2d 676 (4th Cir. 1976), cert. denied 429 U.S. 979, 97 S.Ct. 491, 50 L.Ed.2d 588; Lien v. Beehner, 453 F.Supp. 604 (N.D.N.Y.1978).

18. 28 U.S.C.A. § 2675.

19. Hau v. United States, 575 F.2d 1000 (1st Cir. 1978).

20. Toal v. United States, 438 F.2d 222 (2d Cir. 1971); Portis v. United States, 483 F.2d 670 (4th Cir. 1973); Tyminski v. United States, 481 F.2d 257 (3d Cir. 1973).

21. 28 U.S.C.A. § 2671.

22. Safeway Portland Employees' Fed. Credit Union v. Federal Deposit Ins. Corp., 506 F.2d 1213 (9th Cir. 1974); Federal Deposit Ins. Corp. v. Citizens Bank and Trust Co., 592 F.2d 364 (7th Cir. 1979), cert. denied 444 U.S. 829, 100 S.Ct. 56, 62 L.Ed.2d 37.

Lawrence Seaway Development Corporation;[23] a civilian swimming pool constructed, maintained and operated by the Government.[24]

The following have been held not to be an agency of the United States: Civil Air Patrol;[25] a community action agency funded by federal grants;[26] a club located on military reservation with primary membership consisting of military personnel, but actually a self-supporting private association;[27] a superintendent of Public Works of the municipality of St. Thomas and St. John of the Virgin Islands, notwithstanding that his salary was paid from federal funds appropriated by Congress;[28] a railroad seized by the Government pursuant to an executive order to prevent a strike.[29]

§ 19.4 Subrogation

The F.T.C.A. specifically allows recovery against the United States if a private person would be liable to the claimant in accordance with the law of the place where the act or omission occurred. Confusion as to whether the word "claimant" allowed a cause of action for a subrogee was dispelled by the Supreme Court in *United States v. Aetna Cas. and Sur. Co.*[30] In that case, Chief Justice Vinson held that an insurance company has a "claim" within the meaning of the Act by virtue of subrogation when an insured, able to bring an action, has been paid by the insurance company.[31]

§ 19.5 Armed Forces Personnel

In *Brooks v. United States*,[32] the Supreme Court held that the plaintiff, a serviceman on leave from duty, could recover against the

---

23. Breitbeck v. United States, 500 F. 2d 556 (Ct.Cl.1974).

24. Brewer v. United States, 108 F. Supp. 889 (D.C.Ga.1952).

25. Kiker v. Estep, 444 F.Supp. 563 (D.C.Ga.1978).

26. United States v. Orleans, 425 U.S. 807, 96 S.Ct. 1971, 48 L.Ed.2d 390 (1976).

27. Scott v. United States, 337 F.2d 471 (5th Cir. 1964), cert. denied 380 U.S. 933, 85 S.Ct. 939, 13 L.Ed.2d 821.

28. Harris v. Boreham, 233 F.2d 110 (3d Cir. 1956).

29. Clark v. United States, 218 F.2d 446 (9th Cir. 1954).

30. 338 U.S. 366, 70 S.Ct. 207, 94 L.Ed. 171 (1949); Edwards, Inc. v. Arlen Realty and Development Corp., 446 F.Supp. 505 (D.C.S.C.1978).

31. It was also held that the Anti-assignment Act, 31 U.S.C.A. § 203, did not apply to an assignment by operation of law.

United States v. South Carolina State Highway Dept., 171 F.2d 893 (4th Cir. 1948) (Foreign insurers can be subrogees within this interpretation of the Act).

32. 337 U.S. 49, 69 S.Ct. 918, 93 L.Ed. 1200 (1949).

United States under the Act for injuries the serviceman received from a civilian employee of the army. In 1950, in *Feres v. United States*,[33] the Court carefully distinguished the *Brooks* case by saying that servicemen could not recover under the F.T.C.A. for "injuries incident to the service". *Feres* involved a death to a serviceman caused by negligence which resulted in a barracks fire. Two companion cases involved death to a serviceman caused by negligence of a service doctor (Griggs) and injury to a serviceman which resulted from negligence of a service doctor in leaving a towel in the stomach of a plaintiff (Jefferson). The rationale for these decisions is found in the specific exclusion of the F.T.C.A. to persons engaged in "combatant activities of the military or naval forces",[34] or while serving in "a foreign country".[35]

Since *Brooks* and *Feres* were decided, opinions based upon the doctrines expressed in the two cases have been conflicting and are best approached on a case-by-case basis.[36]

A serviceman is not precluded, because of his service status, from recovering under the F.T.C.A. for injuries to his wife or children.[37] Also, discharged service personnel negligently treated at a Veterans Administration Hospital may state a cause of action un-

33. 340 U.S. 135, 71 S.Ct. 153, 95 L.Ed. 152 (1950); Stencel Aero Engineering Corp. v. United States, 431 U.S. 666, 97 S.Ct. 2054, 52 L.Ed.2d 665 (1977), reh. denied 434 U.S. 882, 98 S.Ct. 250, 54 L.Ed.2d 168.

34. 28 U.S.C.A. § 2680(j).

35. 28 U.S.C.A. § 2680(k).

36. Mills v. Tucker, 499 F.2d 866 (9th Cir. 1974) (Widow of navy petty officer killed in automobile accident could recover under Act when husband killed while on furlough and returning from secondary civilian employment to his quarters owned by the Navy); Hand v. United States, 260 F.Supp. 38 (D.C.Ga.1966) (Soldier on pass was injured when auto in which he was riding was struck by an Army vehicle). But see cases where relief denied military personnel, Coyne v. United States, 411 F.2d 987 (5th Cir. 1969) (Relief denied in medical malpractice case where treatment by military medical personnel was solely because victim was a serviceman); Herreman v. United States, 476 F.2d 234 (7th Cir. 1973) (Widow of national guard officer denied relief on grounds that husband was subject to military courtesies and discipline while returning from a personal fishing trip on a military plane, space available basis, in uniform as a nonpaying passenger); James v. United States, 358 F.Supp. 1381 (D.C.R.I.1973), vacated and remanded 502 F.2d 1159 (1st Cir.) (Decedent, while on leave, was arrested for causing public disturbance on a military reservation and was fatally beaten by a security guard while under orders to be taken to a dispensary for sobriety test).

37. Costley v. United States, 181 F.2d 723 (5th Cir. 1950); Hall v. United States, 314 F.Supp. 1135 (N.D.Cal. 1970).

der the F.T.C.A.[38] Actions under the Military Claims Act [39] remain the exclusive remedy for servicemen injured incident to the service.

In such cases, however, counsel should determine whether there is any third party liability, such as product manufacturer or someone other than the government or its agent.

§ 19.6 Impleader

In *United States v. Yellow Cab Co.*,[40] the Supreme Court held that a claim for contribution against the United States as a joint tortfeasor comes within the terms of the F.T.C.A. Further, the Court held that the United States had also consented to the impleader provisions of Federal Rule 14(a) and therefore could be impleaded as a third party defendant and forced to answer the claim of a joint tortfeaser for contribution.[41]

The decision in *Yellow Cab* was limited by the Court's decision in *Stencel Aero Engineering Corp. v. United States*.[42] In *Stencel*, the Court held that the rationale of *Feres v. United States* [43] applied to impleader actions.

Stencel involved an action brought against the manufacturer of an ejection system by a National Guard officer who was permanently disabled when the ejection system of his aircraft malfunctioned during a mid-air emergency. The manufacturer cross-claimed against the United States, alleging that any malfunction in the ejection system was caused by faulty Government specifications. The Court applied the rationale of *Feres v. United States*, holding that suits involving active military personnel were barred under the F.T.C.A.[44]

---

38. United States v. Gray, 199 F.2d 239 (10th Cir. 1952); Schwartz v. United States, 230 F.Supp. 536 (E.D. Pa.1964).

But see O'Neil v. United States, 202 F. 2d 366, 367 (D.C.Cir. 1953) where court applied the *Feres* doctrine and denied cause of action to World War I veteran who was negligently treated by a Veteran's Administration hospital in 1949. The Court stated, "Appellant's service led him to get treatment for his allergy in a government hospital and the treatment he got there caused his disability. Accordingly, it may be said that his disability did, though his allergy did not, 'arise out of activity incident to service.'"

39. 31 U.S.C.A. § 240 et seq.; Barr v. Brezina Constr. Co., 464 F.2d 1141 (10th Cir. 1972), cert. denied 409 U.S. 1125, 93 S.Ct. 937, 35 L.Ed.2d 256.

40. 340 U.S. 543, 71 S.Ct. 399, 95 L.Ed. 523 (1951).

41. Fed.R.Civ.P. 14(a).

42. 431 U.S. 666, 97 S.Ct. 2054, 52 L. Ed.2d 665 (1977), reh. denied 434 U.S. 882, 98 S.Ct. 250, 54 L.Ed.2d 168.

43. 340 U.S. 135, 71 S.Ct. 153, 95 L.Ed. 152 (1950).

44. See § 19.5, "Armed Forces Personnel," supra.

Applicable state law determines whether impleader and contribution is allowable in any given fact situation.[45]

§ 19.7 Exclusions

The F.T.C.A. does not completely abrogate the doctrine of sovereign immunity in that the Act contains a list of 13 specific exclusions from liability.[46] Exclusions to the Act are to be narrowly construed.[47] Among the more important of these exclusions are:

> (A) Claims based upon "the exercise or performance or the failure to exercise or perform, a *discretionary* function or duty on the part of a federal agency or an employee of the government, whether or not the discretion involved be abused." [48]

Discretionary exclusion has been litigated in many cases, and opinions vary considerably as to the scope of the exclusion. One factor frequently discussed by the Courts is the distinction between operational versus policy-making levels of government.[49] The Supreme Court first discussed this in *Dalehite v. United States*,[50] stating that "the immunized discretion includes determinations made by executives or administrators in establishing plans, specifications or schedules of operations. Where there is room for policy judgment and decision, there is discretion." A clear example of this is found in *Seaboard Coast Line Railroad Co. v. United States*,[51] where the Court stated, "Once the government decided to build a drainage ditch, it was no longer exercising a discretionary policy-making function, and

---

45. United States v. Yellow Cab Co., 340 U.S. 543, 547, 71 S.Ct. 399, 402, 95 L.Ed. 523 (1951); Kennedy v. Pennsylvania R. R. Co., 282 F.2d 705 (3d Cir. 1960).

46. 28 U.S.C.A. § 2680(a)–(n).

47. See West's Federal Practice Manual §§ 2006, 2007.

48. Dalehite v. United States, 346 U.S. 15, 73 S.Ct. 956, 97 L.Ed. 1427 (1953), reh. denied 346 U.S. 841, 880, 74 S. Ct. 13, 117, 98 L.Ed. 362, 386, reh. denied 347 U.S. 924, 74 S.Ct. 511, 98 L. Ed. 1078.

49. *Id.* But see Rayonier, Inc. v. United States, 352 U.S. 315, 77 S.Ct. 374, 1 L.Ed. 354 (1957); Indian Towing Co. v. United States, 350 U.S. 61, 76 S.Ct. 122, 100 L.Ed. 48 (1955). (Both cases suggest a more restrictive view than Dalehite.)

Downs v. United States, 522 F.2d 990, 997 (6th Cir. 1975), suggests that the test is not the status of the official involved as either within the planning level or operational level, but "whether the judgments of a Government employee are of 'the nature and quality' which Congress intended to put beyond judicial review."

50. 346 U.S. 15, 73 S.Ct. 956, 97 L.Ed. 1427 (1953), reh. denied 346 U.S. 841, 880, 74 S.Ct. 13, 117, 98 L.Ed. 362, 386, reh. denied 347 U.S. 924, 74 S. Ct. 511, 98 L.Ed. 1078.

51. Seaboard Coast Line R. R. Co. v. United States, 473 F.2d 714, 716 (5th Cir. 1973).

it was required to perform the operational function of building the drainage ditch in a non-negligent manner."

Early cases suggested that another factor for the courts to consider in determining exclusion from liability under the discretionary exception was that the exclusion was limited to activities which were governmental rather than proprietary in nature. This concept was put aside in *Indian Towing Co. v. United States*,[52] when the Court said, "[The government] would push the courts into the 'non-governmental'—'governmental' quagmire that has long plagued the law of municipal corporations . . . . The decisions in each of the States are disharmonious and disclose the inevitable chaos when courts try to apply a rule of law that is inherently unsound."

(B) Claims arising out of the *combatant activities* of the military or naval forces, or the Coast Guard, during time of war. "During time of war" has been interpreted to mean during actual hostilities.[53] In the same case, "combatant activities" were defined to "include not only physical violence, but activities both necessary to and in direct connection with actual hostilities."[54] *Kuhne v. United States*[55] involved a wrongful death action where decedent died of a blood disease in 1965. Decedent had been employed during World War II as a civilian engineer in a place where radioactive materials were made. The government argued that the engineer's blood disease arose out of combatant activities. The Court dismissed the argument by stating that plaintiff's decedent was not a soldier and his claim was in no way connected with the military or naval forces. The courts have held that claims arising out of the Vietnamese conflict were properly excluded by the combatant activities exception, even though technically a formal declaration of war was never made.[56]

(C) Claims arising in any *foreign country* are consistently denied recovery under the act. Courts have used the rationale that Congress, in specifically excluding claims arising in a foreign country, refused to subject the United States to liabilities depending on the laws of a foreign power.[57]

---

52. Indian Towing Co. v. United States, 350 U.S. 61, 65, 76 S.Ct. 122, 126, 100 L.Ed. 48, 51 (1955).

53. Johnson v. United States, 170 F.2d 767 (9th Cir. 1948).

54. Id. at 770. The Court held that returning ammunition "to a place of safe keeping after all of the fighting is over cannot logically be catalogued as a 'combat activity.'"

55. 267 F.Supp. 649 (D.C.Tenn.1967).

56. Morrison v. United States, 316 F. Supp. 78 (D.C.Ga.1970); Rotko v. Abrams, 338 F.Supp. 46 (D.C.Conn. 1971), aff'd 455 F.2d 992 (2d Cir.).

57. United States v. Spelar, 338 U.S. 217, 70 S.Ct. 10, 94 L.Ed. 3 (1949) (Newfoundland Airbase leased to United States by Great Britain for 99 years was considered a foreign coun-

(D) Another exclusion from liability is any claim based on specifically enumerated *intentional* torts committed by the government's employees.[58]

Other exceptions to tort liability include such matters as claims arising from faulty transmission of postal matters, assessment or collection of taxes, admiralty, imposition of a quarantine by the United States, the Tennessee Valley Authority, the Panama Canal Company, and operations of the federal treasury.

§ 19.8 Strict Liability

Dalehite v. United States [59] held that the F.T.C.A. did not authorize suit against the federal government based on strict liability for ultra-hazardous activity or ownership of an "inherently dangerous commodity." In that case, plaintiff's decedent was killed in an explosion of fertilizer base which had been produced by the United States government. The explosion resulted when two freighters collided in

---

try under Act); Cobb v. United States, 191 F.2d 604 (9th Cir. 1951), cert. denied 342 U.S. 913, 72 S.Ct. 360, 96 L.Ed. 683 (United States de facto sovereignty over Okinawa held not to preclude Okinawa from being considered a foreign country); Maffei v. Nieves-Reta, 412 F.Supp. 43 (D.C. Cal.1976), aff'd 549 F.2d 807 (9th Cir.) (To extent plaintiff relied on transactions which occurred in Mexico where defendant applied and received a border pass, action was foreclosed by subsection (k) even though fatal auto crash took place in California); Leaf v. United States, 588 F.2d 733 (9th Cir. 1978) (Cause of action not precluded by fact damage to plane occurred in Mexico where negligent acts of Government occurred in California).

58. 28 U.S.C.A. § 2680(h) includes assault, battery, false imprisonment, false arrest, malicious prosecution, abuse of process, libel, slander, misrepresentation, deceit, interference with contract rights.

1974 amendment excludes application of this exclusion to acts or omissions of federal investigative or law enforcement officers.

Authority holds that exception does not apply to battery action where government's negligence was in allowing one federal prisoner to assault another and no assault was committed by a federal employee. United States v. Muniz, 374 U.S. 150, 83 S.Ct. 1850, 10 L.Ed.2d 805 (1963); Jones v. United States, 534 F.2d 53 (5th Cir. 1976), cert. denied 429 U.S. 978, 97 S.Ct. 487, 50 L.Ed.2d 586.

Actions for invasion of privacy are not barred by intentional tort exception because not specifically enumerated in Code. Cruikshank v. United States, 431 F.Supp. 1355 (D.C.Hawaii 1977); Black v. Sheraton Corp. of America, 564 F.2d 531 (D.C.Cir. 1977).

Misrepresentation exclusion applies to negligent as well as intentional misrepresentation. Hall v. United States, 274 F.2d 69 (10th Cir. 1959); Scanwell Laboratories, Inc. v. Thomas, 521 F.2d 941 (D.C.Cir. 1975), cert. denied 425 U.S. 910, 96 S.Ct. 1507, 47 L.Ed.2d 761.

59. 346 U.S. 15, 73 S.Ct. 956, 97 L.Ed. 1427 (1953) reh. denied 346 U.S. 841, 880, 74 S.Ct. 13, 117, 98 L.Ed. 362, 386, reh. denied 347 U.S. 924, 74 S.Ct. 511, 98 L.Ed. 1078.

a Texas port. Many people were killed or injured, and property damage was extensive. Plaintiff argued that the word "wrongful" in the act meant more than negligence. The court, tracing the legislative history, held that the word was merely intended to include trespasses which might not be considered strictly negligent and denied plaintiff's cause of action. The court refined its decision in *Laird v. Nelms* [60] and eliminated the confusion caused by its discussion in *Dalehite* of trespass by declaring that *Dalehite* had not created strict governmental liability based on a theory of trespass which would be within the Act's waiver of immunity. The plaintiff in *Laird* was attempting to recover damages caused by sonic booms from military planes. The Court stated unequivocally that "the F.T.C.A. did not authorize suits against the Government in claims based on strict liability for ultrahazardous activity." [61]

In situations where strict liability actions might be considered because negligence cannot be proved, plaintiff's recourse is to *petition Congress* for relief. This was the method of relief ultimately afforded the victims in the Texas catastrophe discussed in the *Dalehite* case.

§ 19.9 Compromise

The Attorney General or his designee may arbitrate, compromise, or settle any claim after commencement of a tort action under the act.[62] All F.T.C.A. cases go to vigorous settlement conference before trial.

As a practical matter, I have found United States attorneys and assistants particularly unwilling to initiate or negotiate adequate settlements. I try all of my F.T.C.A. cases.

§ 19.10 Attorney's Fees

As modified in 1966, the Federal Tort Claims Act allows attorneys fees up to 25 percent of any judgement pursuant to Section 1346(b) or any settlement pursuant to Section 2677 of Title 28. The amendment also allows for criminal penalties against any attorney who attempts to receive any amount in fees above the statutory limit.[63]

---

60. 406 U.S. 797, 32 L.Ed.2d 499, 92 S.Ct. 1899 (1972), reh. denied 409 U.S. 902, 93 S.Ct. 95, 34 L.Ed.2d 165.

61. Id. at 803, 92 S.Ct. at 1902.

62. 28 U.S.C.A. § 2677.
See United States v. Reilly, 385 F.2d 225 (10th Cir. 1976) holding that the government can receive contribution from a joint tortfeasor only if the release entered into between claimant and the government specifically names the joint tortfeasor. This is based on the fact that the joint tortfeasor might not be relieved of liability if not specifically mentioned.

63. 28 U.S.C.A. § 2678.
For discussion of awarding of attorney's fees in class action claims un-

§ 19.11 Damages

The United States is liable under the Act to the same extent as a private individual under like circumstances but cannot be held liable for prejudgment interest or for *punitive* damages.[64] The measure of damages is based on state law, but if the applicable state law provides for punitive damages, then by statute, the United States is liable only for actual or compensatory damages.[65]

Awards under the F.T.C.A., because based upon applicable state law, are extremely varied and hard to compare. "In assessing the amount of damages in a wrongful death case, each case must stand on its own facts (cites omitted). Courts nonetheless seek to maintain some degree of uniformity in cases involving similar losses."[66] The awards by U. S. District Judges sitting without juries is generally substantial against their employer.

§ 19.12 Discovery

In one case, plaintiff served Interrogatories on defendant (United States) requesting a copy of an investigatory report of an airplane accident. The government refused, claiming the report was confidential and there was no cause for reviewing its contents. The Court said that it would examine the document in camera for confidential material and still the government refused to produce the report. The Court held that the facts in controversy were established in the plaintiff's favor and the defendant could not introduce contrary evidence.[67] On Appeal,[68] the decision was affirmed, the Appellate Court holding that under the F.T.C.A., the defendant, United States, is on the same level as a private party. If there is good cause shown by plaintiff, the

---

der the F.T.C.A., see Pollard v. United States, 69 F.R.D. 646 (D.C.Ala.1976) where Court held that quality of the attorney's work and amount of award were to be considered in determining the amount of fees allowed.

64. 28 U.S.C.A. § 2674.

65. 28 U.S.C.A. § 2674.

See Felder v. United States, 543 F.2d 657, 669 (9th Cir. 1976) stating, "Although the Act does not define punitive damages, they may be thought of generally as damages intended to punish and deter. However, we are not bound to a narrow definition.

Since the interpretation and application of the Act is a matter of federal law, we look to the purpose of the Act for a definition of punitive. Likewise, in deciding if a state statute is punitive, we look not to its language nor to the state court's characterization of it. Rather, we look to its effect. (cites omitted)."

66. Felder v. United States, 543 F.2d 657, 674 (9th Cir. 1976).

67. Fed.R.Civ.P. 37(b)(2)(i).

68. United States v. Reynolds, 345 U.S. 1, 73 S.Ct. 528, 97 L.Ed. 727 (1953).

United States cannot rely on a claim that the records are privileged. However, the United States Supreme Court held that the documents were privileged, and under the circumstances the trial court could not inspect the documents, and further that the offer of the government to produce the surviving crew members was sufficient.

§ 19.13 Election of Remedy

The amount of recovery under the F.T.C.A. is not to be diminished by any benefits which the Claimant may have received in the way of payments from third parties.[69] This principle, known at common law as the *Collateral Source Rule,* has several exceptions where the payments originate from general federal government funds. Thus, amounts may be deducted from the award if received by the plaintiff from military benefits,[70] Veteran's Administration,[71] Social Security,[72] and Federal Workmens' Compensation.[73]

Where collateral federal funds have been supplied from special government funds, the government may not deduct the payments from the award. Examples are found where a National Service Life Insurance Policy is involved,[74] social security from the Federal Old Age and Survivors' Insurance Trust Fund,[75] retirement benefits from the Civil Service Retirement Act,[76] and money received from a public welfare fund.[77]

---

69. See Annotation 12 A.L.R.3d 1245.

70. Brooks v. United States, 337 U.S. 49, 69 S.Ct. 918, 93 L.Ed. 1200 (1949); Hale v. United States, 416 F.2d 355 (6th Cir. 1969).

71. Kubrick v. United States, 581 F.2d 1092 (3d Cir. 1978), rev'd on other grounds 444 U.S. 111, 100 S.Ct. 352, 62 L.Ed.2d 259; Mosley v. United States, 538 F.2d 555 (4th Cir. 1976); Contra, United States v. Gray, 199 F.2d 239 (10th Cir. 1952). (Gray distinguished in Felley v. United States, 337 F.2d 924 (3d Cir. 1964).

72. Cooper v. United States, 313 F.Supp. 1207 (D.C.Neb.1970); Gowdy v. United States, 271 F.Supp. 733 (W.D. Mich.1967), rev'd on other grounds 412 F.2d 525 (6th Cir.), cert. denied 396 U.S. 960, 90 S.Ct. 437, 24 L.Ed.2d 425, reh. denied 396 U.S. 1063, 90 S.Ct. 750, 24 L.Ed.2d 756.

See Steckler v. United States, 549 F.2d 1372 (10th Cir. 1977). (Holding social security collateral as to proportion of amounts contributed by worker and employers; Contra, United States v. Grajeda, 587 F.2d 1017 (9th Cir. 1978). (Stating the government's payments into Social Security Fund are so minimal and difficult to trace that such payments should not be deducted.

73. Martin v. United States, 566 F.2d 895 (4th Cir. 1977).

74. Brooks v. United States, 337 U.S. 49, 69 S.Ct. 918, 93 L.Ed. 1200 (1949).

75. United States v. Harue Hayashi, 282 F.2d 599 (9th Cir. 1960).

76. United States v. Price, 288 F.2d 448 (4th Cir. 1961).

77. Wham v. United States, 180 F.2d 38 (D.C.Cir. 1950).

The Federal Court applies the applicable state law as to the determination of allowable deductions under the Act.[78]

Federal employees injured or killed during the course of their employment must first seek and be denied relief by the Secretary of Labor, acting in his capacity as administrator of the Federal Employees Compensation Act,[79] before proceeding under the F.T.C.A.[80] Similarly, the Supreme Court has uniformly held that a maritime action may be maintained against the United States only under the Suits in Admiralty Act.[81]

§ 19.14 Within Scope of Office or Employment

The Act defines an "employee of the government" to include officers or employees of any federal agency, members of the military or naval forces of the United States, and persons acting in behalf of a federal agency in an official capacity, temporarily or permanently in the service of the United States, whether with or without compensation.[82] Peace Corps volunteers are expressly stated by statute to be employees of the Federal Government for purposes of the Act.[83]

The Act has been held not to include members of the federal judicial branch [84] or members of the National Guard who are not on active federal service.[85]

The application of local laws of respondeat superior determine whether an employee is acting within the scope of his employment under the Act.[86]

---

78. United States v. Price, 288 F.2d 448, 450 (4th Cir. 1961).

79. 5 U.S.C.A. § 8101 et seq.

80. Bailey v. United States, Through Dept. of Army, 451 F.2d 963 (5th Cir. 1971); Concordia v. United States Postal Serv., 581 F.2d 439 (5th Cir. 1978), reh. denied 585 F.2d 731. This applies to claims arising subsequent to 1949.

81. 46 U.S.C.A. § 741 et seq. Brady v. Roosevelt S. S. Co., 317 U.S. 575, 63 S.Ct. 425, 87 L.Ed. 471 (1943), reh. denied 318 U.S. 799, 63 S.Ct. 659, 87 L.Ed. 1163; T. J. Falgout Boats, Inc. v. United States, 508 F.2d 855 (9th Cir. 1974), cert. denied 421 U.S. 1000, 95 S.Ct. 2398, 44 L.Ed.2d 667 (1975).

82. 28 U.S.C.A. § 2671.

83. 22 U.S.C.A. § 2504(h).

84. Foster v. Bork, 425 F.Supp. 1318 (D.D.C.1977).

See United States v. LePatourel, 571 F. 2d 405 (8th Cir. 1978) (Holding that government liable when federal judge was performing an official but not judicial function).

85. Maryland For Use of Levin v. United States, 381 U.S. 41, 85 S.Ct. 1293, 14 L.Ed.2d 205 (1965), vacated on reh. on other grounds, 382 U.S. 159, 86 S.Ct. 305, 15 L.Ed.2d 227 (Members of the National Guard are employees of state and not federal government).

86. Williams v. United States, 350 U.S. 857, 76 S.Ct. 100, 100 L.Ed. 761 (1955).

If a member of the Armed Forces is negligent, the F.T.C.A. defines when he is acting within the scope of his employment to be when he is ". . . acting in the line of duty".[87] Courts have consistently applied the principles of respondeat superior to the military cases and look to local law to determine whether the serviceman was acting in the line of duty.[88] The Courts have held that when a soldier is on leave and injures another, the United States is not liable.[89] Generally, when the tortfeasor acts out of "line of duty" for the United States,[90] or when he is doing something contrary to regulations,[91] or when he has deviated from his instructions, the sovereign is not liable.

87. 28 U.S.C.A. § 2671.

88. McCall v. United States, 338 F.2d 589 (9th Cir. 1964), cert. denied, 380 U.S. 974, 85 S.Ct. 1334, 14 L.Ed.2d 269; Davies v. United States, 542 F.2d 1361 (9th Cir. 1976).

89. King v. United States, 178 F.2d 320 (5th Cir. 1950), cert. denied 339 U.S. 964, 70 S.Ct. 998, 94 L.Ed. 1373 (Student aviator took plane when drunk); Mason and Dixon Lines v. Shore, 409 F.Supp. 1127 (E.D.Tenn. 1975) (Airman failed to notify superiors of termination of leave status).

90. Murphey v. United States, 179 F.2d 743 (9th Cir. 1950) (Soldiers joyriding in truck); Whittle v. United States, 328 F.Supp. 136 (M.D.Ala. 1971) (Army pilot, without authority, took aboard civilians for plane ride).

91. Christian v. United States, 184 F.2d 523 (6th Cir. 1950) (Soldier, after driving truck for transportation of other soldiers, became intoxicated and killed deputy sheriff during argument).

§§ 19.15–20.0 are reserved for supplementary material.

CHAPTER 20

SUING THE INSURER

Table of Sections

Sec.
20.1 The Problem.
20.2 Standards for Recovery.
20.3 Duty to Initiate Settlement.
20.4 Duty to Defend.
20.5 Extent of Liability.
20.6 Punitive Damages.
20.7 Who May Sue.
20.8 Duty of Insurance Agent to Insured.

Library References:
Blashfield, Automobile Law and Practice, § 351.1 et seq.

§ 20.1 The Problem

Although most insurance policies give the insurance company an exclusive right to settle or compromise a claim, the company has no absolute duty to accept settlement offers within the policy limits.[1] An inevitable conflict of interest arises when an insured is sued for an amount beyond the policy limits and the plaintiff offers to settle at or below those limits. In these cases the insured should have his own personal lawyer.[2]

1. Kricar, Inc. v. General Acc. Fire & Life Assur. Corp., 542 F.2d 1135 (9th Cir. 1976); La Rocca v. State Farm Mut. Auto. Ins. Co., 329 F.Supp. 163 (W.D.Pa.1971), aff'd 474 F.2d 1338 (3d Cir.); Olson v. Union Fire Ins. Co., 174 Neb. 375, 118 N.W.2d 318 (1962).

2. When the author has reason to believe defendant's lawyer (usually actually representing the insurance company) has not communicated his offer of settlement at or under policy limits to the assured, the following procedure has been successfully followed: after selection of the jury, in open court, for the record, or in chambers, conference is requested of defendant's counsel, defendant personally, the judge, and reporter. There, for the record, in the absence of the jury, the offer of settlement is formally made.

If defendant's counsel has not communicated this offer to his personal client, some enthusiastic conferring usually ensues. This procedure also makes a record of the actual dollar and cent settlement offer as a benefit to the personal defendant in the case of suit over after judgment, as herein discussed. Some counsel send the offer by registered mail to defense counsel, with copy to the insurance company, and another copy to the defendant personally.

The insurer may believe that it can defeat liability at trial and want to decline the settlement offer, but by going to trial it is gambling with the insured's money. If the plaintiff wins a verdict which exceeds the policy limit, the insured is personally liable for the excess. The insurer is, of course, liable only for the amount of the policy, and so has lost only the cost of the trial. The question is, then, whether the insurer must compensate the insured for the damage caused by its failure to settle?

§ 20.2 Standards for Recovery

Earlier cases, relying on the lack of any duty to settle on the part of the insurer, granted the insurer complete discretion in accepting or rejecting settlement.[3] The insurer had a right to go to trial even if the claim could be settled for a relatively small amount.[4]

Fortunately, modern courts do not allow insurance companies to treat their insured's interests with such disdain. All jurisdictions now require the insurer to take the interests of the insured into account in weighing a settlement offer.[5] The courts disagree, however, on the standard to be applied in determining when an insurer can reject a settlement offer with impunity.

Two basic standards are applied in these cases.[6] The majority view is that the insurer is under a duty to exercise *good faith* in evaluating all settlement offers.[7] In order to recover in these jurisdictions, the insured must show that the refusal to settle was arbitrary

---

If counsel for defendant has reason to suspect that an attorney for a plaintiff has failed to inform his client of a reasonable offer in settlement, such attorney may, often with profit, follow the same procedure.

3. Auerbach v. Maryland Cas. Co., 236 N.Y. 247, 140 N.E. 577 (1923); C. Schmidt & Sons Brewing Co. v. Travelers Ins. Co., 244 Pa. 286, 90 A. 653 (1914); Rumford Falls Paper Co. v. Fidelity & Cas. Co., 92 Me. 574, 43 A. 503 (1899).

4. Mears Mining Co. v. Maryland Cas. Co., 162 Mo.App. 178, 144 S.W. 883 (1912).

5. See Martin v. Travelers Indem. Co., 450 F.2d 542 (5th Cir. 1971). See generally 14 Couch on Insurance 2d § 51.2.

6. Mississippi, apparently alone, still uses an outmoded third standard, refusing to hold an insurer liable "unless its refusal to settle was so arbitrary and unreasonable as to constitute fraud." Martin v. Travelers Indem. Co., 450 F.2d 542, 551 (5th Cir. 1971).

7. E. g., Gibbs v. State Farm Mut. Ins. Co., 544 F.2d 423 (9th Cir. 1976); Ward v. State Farm Mut. Auto. Ins. Co., 539 F.2d 1044 (5th Cir. 1976); Yeomans v. Allstate Ins. Co., 130 N. J.Super. 48, 324 A.2d 906 (1974); Knobloch v. Royal Globe Ins. Co., 38 N.Y.2d 471, 381 N.Y.S.2d 433, 344 N. E.2d 364 (1976); Ammerman v. Farmers Ins. Exchange, 19 Utah 2d 261, 430 P.2d 576 (1967), appeal after remand 22 Utah 2d 187, 450 P.2d 460.

or in bad faith. Since bad faith is a state of mind, it is difficult to define [8] and may offer hazards in the proof. Each case must be decided on its own facts,[9] but certain elements are generally considered. Among these are basic honesty in dealing with the insured,[10] weighing insured's interests equally with its own,[11] belief in nonliability or smaller jury verdict,[12] informing insured of offer,[13] completeness of investigation [14] and probability of recovery in excess of limits.[15]

Simpson v. Motorists Ins. Co. [16] showed an unfortunate example of bad faith. The insurer knew that insured had been negligent and had caused damage well beyond the policy limit, but never informed him of the limits or of his possible participation in the settlement. The company had gotten information from insured while he was drugged, and had withheld vital information from him. Such actions were deemed sufficiently disreputable to constitute bad faith, even though the rule was a strict one requiring "a dishonest purpose or conscious wrongdoing." [17]

A minority of jurisdictions impose liability on the insurer for negligent, rather than bad faith, failure to settle.[18] Although the insurer need not ignore its own interests,[19] it must conduct itself as

8. See Terrell v. Western Cas. & Sur. Co., 427 S.W.2d 825 (Ky.App.1968).

9. Jessen v. O'Daniel, 210 F.Supp. 317 (D.Mont.1962), aff'd 329 F.2d 60 (9th Cir.).

10. Landie v. Century Indem. Co., 390 S.W.2d 558 (Mo.App.1965).

11. Sobus v. Lumbermans Mut. Cas. Co., 393 F.Supp. 661 (D.Md.1975).

12. Capitol Indem. Corp. v. St. Paul Fire & Marine Ins. Co., 357 F.Supp. 399 (W.D.Wis.1972); Jessen v. O'Daniel, 210 F.Supp. 317 (D.Mont. 1962).

13. Id.

14. Riske v. Truck Ins. Exchange, 490 F.2d 1079 (8th Cir. 1974), appeal after remand 541 F.2d 768; State Farm Mut. Auto. Ins. Co. v. Marcum, 420 S.W.2d 113 (Ky.1967); see also Young v. American Cas. Co., 416 F.2d 906 (2d Cir. 1969), cert. dism'd 396 U.S. 997, 90 S.Ct. 580, 24 L.Ed.2d 490; Ward v. State Farm Mut. Auto. Ins. Co., 539 F.2d 1044 (5th Cir. 1976).

15. Fulton v. Woodford, 26 Ariz.App. 17, 545 P.2d 979 (1976).

16. 494 F.2d 850 (1974), cert. denied 419 U.S. 901, 95 S.Ct. 184, 42 L.Ed.2d 147.

17. Id. at 853. For a simpler case, see Riske v. Truck Ins. Exchange, 490 F. 2d 1079 (8th Cir. 1974), appeal after remand 541 F.2d 768 (Bad faith for the failure to advise of settlement or depose claimant's doctor, among other faults).

18. Anderson v. St. Paul Mercury Indem. Co., 340 F.2d 406 (7th Cir. 1965); Knudsen v. Hartford Acc. & Indem. Co., 26 Conn.Sup. 325, 222 A. 2d 811 (1966); Aetna Cas. & Sur. Co. v. Kornbluth, 28 Colo.App. 194, 471 P.2d 609 (1970); Dumas v. State Farm Mut. Auto. Ins. Co., 111 N.H. 43, 274 A.2d 781 (1971).

19. Fidelity & Cas. Co. v. Robb, 267 F.2d 473 (5th Cir. 1959).

would a prudent insurer without policy limits in evaluating the settlement offer.[20] In other words, it must pretend that it alone is responsible for the entire claim,[21] and it will be held liable if the "most reasonable manner of disposing of the claim is a settlement." [22]

Although this would seem to be a much easier standard to meet, in practice there is often little distinction between the two rules.[23] Where the duty of the insurer is to act as if the entire risk of loss was its own, "[m]ost authorities agree there is little difference between the concepts of 'good faith' and 'due care.' " [24]

In any case where the verdict exceeds the policy, any settlement demands by plaintiff should at least be considered.

§ 20.3 Duty to Initiate Settlement

The cases discussed above all involved concrete settlement offers by the claimant which the insurer unwisely rejected. Despite some cases to the contrary,[25] many courts now find a failure to explore settlement opportunities may be bad faith even in the absence of a firm offer.[26] The insurer should initiate settlement if, assuming it alone was liable, it would do so.[27] The court in *Rova Farms Resort, Inc. v. Investors Ins. Co. of America*,[28] extends this duty so that an insurer must show, not only that a settlement within policy limits was impossible, but also that the insured was unwilling to contribute the difference between the limit and the offer.[29]

---

20. Crisci v. Security Ins. Co., 66 Cal. 2d 425, 58 Cal.Rptr. 13, 426 P.2d 173 (1967). See also n. 29 infra.

21. Johansen v. California State Auto Ass'n Inter-Insurance Bureau, 15 Cal. 3d 9, 123 Cal.Rptr. 288, 538 P.2d 744 (1975).

22. Id.

23. See Lienemann v. State Farm Mut. Auto. Fire & Cas. Co., 540 F.2d 333 (8th Cir. 1976).

24. Eastham v. Oregon Auto. Ins. Co., 273 Or. 600, 542 P.2d 895 (1975).

25. E. g., La Rocca v. State Farm Mut. Auto. Ins. Co., 329 F.Supp. 163 (W. D.Pa.1971), aff'd 474 F.2d 1338 (3d Cir.); Fulton v. Woodford, 26 Ariz. App. 17, 545 P.2d 979 (1976); Merritt v. Reserve Ins. Co., 34 Cal.App.3d 858, 110 Cal.Rptr. 511 (1973); Cotton States Mut. Ins. Co. v. Fields, 106 Ga.App. 740, 128 S.E.2d 358 (1962).

26. Farmers Ins. Exchange v. Schropp, 222 Kan. 612, 567 P.2d 1359 (1977); Western World Ins. Co. v. Allstate Ins. Co., 150 N.J.Super. 481, 376 A.2d 177 (1977); State Auto Ins. Co. v. Rowland, 221 Tenn. 421, 427 S.W.2d 30 (1968); Alt v. American Family Mut. Ins. Co., 71 Wis.2d 340, 237 N. W.2d 706 (1976).

27. Farmers Ins. Exchange v. Schropp, 222 Kan. 612, 567 P.2d 1359 (1977).

28. 65 N.J. 474, 323 A.2d 495 (1974).

29. 323 A.2d at 507. This case and Crisci v. Security Ins. Co., 66 Cal.2d 425, 430–31, 58 Cal.Rptr. 13, 16, 17, 426 P.2d 173, 176–177 (1967), come closest to imposing an absolute duty

§ 20.4 Duty to Defend

Most insurance policies impose on the insurer a duty to defend the insured in any cause of action covered by the insurance policy. Although the insurance company may have a good faith doubt that its policy covers the incident, a mistaken failure to defend will render it liable for damages, even where the claim is frivolous.[30] As stated in *Dillon v. Hartford Acc. & Indem. Co.:*[31]

> The duty to defend is not without limitation; it extends only to the defense of those actions of the nature and kind covered by the policy. [Cite omitted]. If the insurer, after taking into consideration facts gathered from its own investigation or information supplied by the insured, determines that there is no potential liability under the policy, it may refuse to defend the lawsuit; "[t]his it does at its own risk, and if it later develops liability or potential liability existed under the policy, the company will be held accountable to its insured, or to one who obtained judgment against its insured in the action it refused to defend." [Cite omitted].

§ 20.5 Extent of Liability

In most cases the insured simply wants to be indemnified for the amount that he has paid above the policy limit, and this is the usual measure of damages.[32] The only other expense involved in most cases is attorney's fees; courts have gone both ways in discussing such legal consequences.[33]

Where the insurer's actions have been particularly egregious, however, there may be further liability. The leading California case of *Crisci v. Security Ins. Co.*[34] noted that *mental suffering* might well to settle within the policy limits on the insurer.

See also Schwartz, Statutory Strict Liability for an Insurer's Failure to Settle: A Balanced Plan for an Unsolved Problem, 1975 Duke L.J. 901.

30. Western Cas. & Sur. Co. v. Herman, 405 F.2d 121 (8th Cir. 1968); Comunale v. Traders & General Ins. Co., 50 Cal.2d 654, 328 P.2d 198 (1958).

31. 38 Cal.App.3d 335, 339–40, 113 Cal.Rptr. 396, 398–99 (1974).

32. Young v. American Cas. Co., 416 F.2d 906 (2d Cir. 1969), cert. dism'd 396 U.S. 997, 90 S.Ct. 580, 24 L.Ed.2d 490; National Indem. Co. v. Donald, 229 So.2d 900 (Fla.App.1969).

33. Canadian Universal Ins. Co. v. Employers Surplus Lines Ins. Co., 325 So.2d 29 (Fla.App.1976) (Legal expenses and costs included); Liberty Mut. Ins. Co. v. Davis, 412 F.2d 475 (5th Cir. 1969) (Attorney's fees under statute); Twentieth Century-Fox Film Corp. v. Harbor Ins. Co., 85 Cal.App.3d 105, 149 Cal.Rptr. 313 (1978) (No attorney's fees).

34. 66 Cal.2d 425, 58 Cal.Rptr. 13, 426 P.2d 173 (1967).

accompany the loss of property caused by an adverse judgment, and said "in this connection mental suffering includes nervousness, grief, anxiety, worry, shock, humiliation and indignity as well as physical pain." [35] The court there upheld a $25,000 award for mental suffering.

Although courts now allow such recoveries for the tortious breach of duty of good faith,[36] they require, as in other emotional distress cases, a very strong showing of causation. Liability may be denied where the insured suffered emotionally but did not actually lose any money.[37] Some jurisdictions still require physical injury unless malice can be shown.[38] In *Butchikas v. Travelers Indemnity Co.*,[39] a recovery for mental anguish was equated with punitive damages and denied because the insurer had not actively injured the insured, but had simply ignored the insured throughout the proceedings.

§ 20.6 Punitive Damages

If the insurer has acted maliciously or with very bad faith it may be liable for punitive damages, which "serve the predominant function of deterrence and punishment." [40] Punitives may be granted for concealing settlement offers and misrepresenting the gravity of the claim,[41] or for refusing to settle or take responsibility for damages when liability is both clear and large.[42] They will be denied if the insurer's eventual payment negates bad faith,[43] or where it simply ignores the insured rather than actively misrepresenting the situation to the insured.[44]

Punitive damages may also be available when an insurer maliciously refused to pay a valid claim to its insured. In *Neal v. Farm-*

---

35. 66 Cal.2d at 433, 58 Cal.Rptr. at 18, 426 P.2d at 178.

36. See Austero v. National Cas. Co., 62 Cal.App.3d 511, 133 Cal.Rptr. 107 (1976); Merlo v. Standard Life & Acc. Ins. Co., 59 Cal.App.3d 5, 130 Cal. Rptr. 416 (1976).

37. Kunkel v. United Sec. Ins. Co., 84 S.D. 116, 168 N.W.2d 723 (1969).

38. Butchikas v. Travelers Indem. Co., 343 So.2d 816 (Fla.1976).

39. Id.

40. Campbell v. Government Employees Ins. Co., 306 So.2d 525 (Fla. 1974). For a complete discussion of punitive damages, see Chapter 16, supra.

41. Id.

42. Cain v. State Farm Mut. Automobile Ins. Co., 47 Cal.App.3d 783, 121 Cal.Rptr. 200 (1975) ($115,000 in punitives upheld).

43. Kricar, Inc. v. General Acc., Fire & Life Assur. Corp., 542 F.2d 1135 (9th Cir. 1976).

44. Butchikas v. Travelers Indem. Co., 343 So.2d 816 (Fla.1976).

ers Ins. Exchange,[45] the defendant had failed to pay a $15,000 uninsured motorist claim filed by its insured, apparently hoping that the strained financial situation of the plaintiff would force a more favorable settlement. The California Supreme Court upheld an award of $10,000 in compensatory damages, and $740,000 in punitives.

Thomas T. Anderson, Esquire,[46] handled a case in which exemplary damages of $8,250,000 were assessed against insurance companies. The conduct of the insurance companies was not what counsel would normally expect to find. The case, however, serves as a fine example of conduct of an insurance company that more than justifies extensive punitive damage award.

The punitive damage case arose out of an automobile accident that occurred when plaintiff was in the process of making a left turn from a northbound lane at the same time that a vehicle owned by Desert Ginning Company was passing the plaintiff from the rear. The basic issue insofar as liability was concerned was whether or not the plaintiff signaled for a left turn. Desert Ginning maintained that the plaintiff did not signal. Plaintiff maintained that he did signal.

Plaintiff was rendered a paraplegic as a result of the accident.

Desert Ginning Company was insured by Reliance Insurance Company. Reliance Insurance hired General Adjustment Bureau for the purpose of investigating the case. General Adjustment in turn hired an employee of Stephen Blewett & Associates to perform accident reconstruction work.

The employee of Blewett examined the plaintiff's car which was located on the premises of the plaintiff's parents. In the process of conducting this examination, the employee removed the left rear taillight bulb for the alleged purpose of testing to see if the bulb was capable of being operated at the time of the accident.

Meanwhile, the plaintiff was visited in the hospital by an adjuster from General Adjustment Bureau. The plaintiff testified that the adjuster represented to plaintiff he was an adjuster with Allstate Insurance Company who insured the plaintiff. The adjuster testified that he fully informed the plaintiff that he was investigating the case on behalf of the insurer of Desert Ginning.

A statement was given and signed by the plaintiff in the hospital. The statement as written was true, with the exception that one essential fact was omitted. This fact was that there was a car behind the plaintiff's vehicle and in front of the Desert Ginning Com-

---

45. 21 Cal.3d 910, 148 Cal.Rptr. 389, 582 P.2d 980 (1978).

46. Thomas T. Anderson, Esq., 45–926 Oasis Street, Indio, California.

pany's car. Plaintiff's counsel argued that defendants were attempting to eliminate the presence of an essential witness.

The instant case for emotional distress with a prayer for punitive damages was filed following the settlement of the original action for personal injuries. The plaintiff also prayed to recover the difference between the true value of the case and the amount that was actually received in settlement.

The trial judge precluded any testimony concerning such compensatory damages and confined all testimony to the value of the parts that were taken. Thus, the only compensatory damages that the jury was allowed to award was the value of the left turn bulb which was $5.93.

The defendants contended that when the part was originally taken, the employee had the permission of the plaintiff's mother. Defendants further contended that the entire circumstances surrounding the taking of the parts was a set-up by plaintiff's attorney in order to obtain punitive damages.

The jury returned a general verdict against Reliance Insurance Company of $50 compensatory damages and $8,000,000 punitive damages. General Adjustment Bureau was found liable for $50 in compensatory damages and $250,000 in punitive damages. Stephen Blewett and Associates was found liable for no punitive damages, but had to pay the $5.93 for the missing lightbulb.

§ 20.7 Who May Sue

Most bad faith suits against insurance companies are brought by the insured to recover for the excess payment that he has made. In some cases, however, the injured claimant may want to bring suit against the insurer because he can recover little or nothing from the insured. Until recently, it was usually assumed that, in the absence of statutory or contractual provisions, the claimant had no privity of contract with the insurer and so had no standing to sue the recalcitrant insurance company.[47] In some of these cases it has been argued that the claimant had not been injured by the failure to settle.[48]

---

47. Rowe v. United States Fidelity & Guar. Co., 421 F.2d 937 (4th Cir. 1970); Yelm v. Country Mut. Ins. Co., 123 Ill.App.2d 401, 259 N.E.2d 83 (1970); Steen v. Aetna Cas. & Sur. Co., 157 Colo. 99, 401 P.2d 254 (1965); Murphy v. Allstate Ins. Co., 17 Cal.3d 937, 132 Cal.Rptr. 424, 553 P.2d 584 (1976).

48. Nichols v. United States Fidelity Guar. Co., 318 F.Supp. 334 (N.D. Miss.1970); Pringle v. Robertson. 258 Or. 389, 465 P.2d 223 (1970), adhered to 258 Or. 389, 483 P.2d 814; Browdy v. State-Wide Ins. Co., 56 Misc.2d 610, 289 N.Y.S.2d 711 (1968).

Certain states now allow the claimant to sue the insurer in a direct action under a variety of theories. California recently allowed a direct action against an insurer who violated statutes forbidding unfair practices. The court distinguished previous cases which found no contractual duty toward the claimant, ruling that the statutory violation was a tortious act running directly to the victim, who could recover for all damages.[49] Florida has granted claimants a direct cause of action, even in the absence of a statute, based upon a claim of fraud or bad faith of the insurer in the conduct or handling of the suit.[50]

Excess liability insurers may also have a cause of action against a primary insurer who fails to exercise good faith in settling a claim.[51] These suits are allowed under a variety of theories, including equitable subrogation[52] and assignment.[53]

The assignment theory has been much discussed in regards to both excess liability insurers and claimants. Some courts which will not otherwise allow a claimant to sue will permit suit following a valid assignment by the insured.[54] Although a few jurisdictions preclude assignments by viewing such suits as unassignable tort actions,[55] most allow the assignments either by treating the action as sounding in contract,[56] or by making certain tort actions assignable.[57]

49. Royal Globe Ins. Co. v. Superior Court, 23 Cal.3d 880, 153 Cal.Rptr. 842, 592 P.2d 329 (1979). Connecticut has a statute explicitly permitting direct actions; see Bourget v. Government Employees Ins. Co., 287 F.Supp. 108 (D.Conn.1968).

50. Boston Old Colony Ins. Co. v. Gutierrez, 360 So.2d 464, 467 (Fla.App. 1978), relying on Thompson v. Commercial Union Ins. Co. of New York, 250 So.2d 259 (Fla.1971).

51. Peters v. Travelers Ins. Co., 375 F.Supp. 1347 (C.D.Cal.1974); Allstate Ins. Co. v. Reserve Ins. Co., 116 N.H. 806, 373 A.2d 339 (1976); St. Paul Fire & Marine Ins. Co. v. United States Fidelity & Guar. Co., 43 N.Y.2d 977, 404 N.Y.S.2d 552, 375 N.E.2d 733 (1978).

52. Peters v. Travelers Ins. Co., 375 F.Supp. 1347 (C.D.Cal.1974).

53. Allstate Ins. Co. v. Reserve Ins. Co., 116 N.H. 806, 373 A.2d 339.

54. Lisiewski v. Countrywide Ins. Co., 75 Mich.App. 631, 255 N.W.2d 714 (1977); Smith v. Transit Cas. Co., 281 F.Supp. 661 (E.D.Tex.1968), aff'd 410 F.2d 210 (5th Cir.); Nichols v. U. S. Fidelity & Guar. Co., 37 Wis.2d 238, 155 N.W.2d 104 (1968).

55. E. g., Dillingham v. Tri-State Ins. Co., 214 Tenn. 592, 381 S.W.2d 914 (1964).

56. Terrell v. Western Cas. & Sur. Co., 427 S.W.2d 825 (Ky.App.1968); Gray v. Nationwide Mut. Ins. Co., 422 Pa. 500, 223 A.2d 8 (1966).

57. Comunale v. Traders & General Ins. Co., 50 Cal.2d 654, 328 P.2d 198 (1958); Harvin v. U. S. Fidelity & Guar. Co., 428 S.W.2d 213 (Ky.App. 1968); Allstate Ins. Co. v. Reserve Ins. Co., 116 N.H. 806, 373 A.2d 339 (1976); Smith v. Transit Cas. Co., 281 F.Supp. 661 (E.D.Tex.1968), aff'd 410 F.2d 210 (5th Cir.).

An important question which can arise in any suit against the insurer is whether the insured must pay the excess judgment before a suit can be maintained. Although recovery has sometimes been denied where the insured has not yet paid,[58] most jurisdictions no longer require payment as a prerequisite to a suit for the excess judgment.[59]

The question arises, may plaintiff's attorney ethically represent the defendant in his suit over against the insurance company after excess judgment has been paid by the defendant personally? Of course if he has not impersonally and unequivocally memorialized his own settlement offer as suggested herein,[60] his personal testimony may be required in the second suit. In this latter contingency, he should not accept the at once embarrassingly inconsistent employment of both witnesses and counsel.

§ 20.8 Duty of Insurance Agent to Insured

An insurance agent or broker who, for compensation, undertakes to obtain insurance for a client is under a duty to exercise due care in the procuring of that insurance.[61] Failure to exercise due care would constitute negligence or breach of contract and the agent or broker would be liable for all damages resulting therefrom.

Richard B. Davis, Jr.[62], Esquire presented a recent Florida case,[63] in which plaintiff pleaded that defendant insurance agent had breached a third party beneficiary contract and was also liable for negligent failure to insure.

The case arose out of an incident in which a child was struck by a taxi cab in Lake City, Florida. Plaintiff sued the cab driver and cab company, as owner of the vehicle and recovered the policy limits of $15,000. The $15,000 was that limit required by Florida state law, but the cab had failed to comply with a Lake City ordinance requiring minimum limits of $125,000/$150,000.

58. State Auto. Mut. Ins. Co. v. York, 104 F.2d 730 (4th Cir. 1939), cert. denied 308 U.S. 591, 60 S.Ct. 120, 84 L. Ed. 495.

59. Farmers Ins. Exchange v. Schropp, 222 Kan. 612, 567 P.2d 1359 (1977); Wolfberg v. Prudence Mut. Cas. Co., 98 Ill.App.2d 190, 240 N.E.2d 176 (1968); Lange v. Fidelity & Cas. Co. of New York, 290 Minn. 61, 185 N. W.2d 881 (1971); Hernandez v. Great American Ins. Co. of New York, 464 S.W.2d 91 (Tex.1971).

60. See note 2 supra.

61. Insurance Management of Washington, Inc. v. Eno & Howard Plumbing Corp., 348 A.2d 310 (D.C.App. 1975).

62. Richard B. Davis, Esquire, P.O. Drawer 1360, N.E. Central, Jasper, Florida.

63. Lane v. Wheeler, Circuit Court of the Third Judicial District, Columbia County, Florida, Docket No. 77-596-CA.

The case withstood all of the Motions to Dismiss, but at the conclusion of the trial the court indicated that it would direct a verdict in favor of the defendants on the basis that plaintiff failed adequately to show negligence on the part of the defendant. Before the court could announce the directed verdict, plaintiff entered a voluntary non-suit, preserving plaintiff's right to try the case on a later date.

Concurrently with this action, plaintiff gave notice to the City of Lake City, Florida, that plaintiff was pursuing a claim against the City for its failure to perform a ministerial function; to wit, insure that the taxi cab applicants had adequate insurance. The city officer in charge of checking that the application was complete failed to notice that the company did not have adequate insurance.

Coincidentally, in examination of the insurance agent as an adverse witness, the insurance agent admitted that he had only advised the owners of the taxi cab company of the premium for a much higher rate than the $25,000 required by City ordinance. The company was only advised of the premium for either $50,000 or $100,000. The agent admitted that the company should have been told what the rate was for the $25,000 premium. A complaint has now been filed against both Lake City and the insurance agent on a theory of mixed liability as well as counts alleging separate liability for each of them.

§§ 20.9–21.0 are reserved for supplementary material.

CHAPTER 21

ACTIO PERSONALIS MORITUR CUM PERSONA

Table of Sections

Sec.
21.1 General Consideration.
21.2 Survival Statutes.
21.3 Distinction from Wrongful Death Statutes.
21.4 Punitive Damages.
21.5 Injury to the Person.

Library References:
C.J.S. Death § 39.
West's Key No. Digests, Death ⚖︎28.

§ 21.1 General Consideration

The maxim, actio personalis moritur cum persona—a personal injury action abates on the death of either plaintiff or defendant—though shrouded in the mist of post-classical origin,[1] has demonstrated a most distressing zest for life and ability to fend off the demand for uniform and sensible reform voiced by the commentators and judges.[2]

1. Van Beeck v. Sabine Towing Co., 300 U.S. 342, 57 S.Ct. 452, 81 L.Ed. 685 (1937) (Opinion of Judge Cardozo: "The rule is often viewed as derivative of the formula 'actio personalis moritur cum persona,' a maxim which is 'one of some antiquity,' though its origin is obscure and post-classical. Even in classical times, however, the Roman law enforced the principle that 'no action of an essentially penal character could be commenced after the death of the person responsible for the injury.' Vengeance, though permissible during life, was not to 'reach beyond the grave.' There was also an accepted doctrine that no money value could be put on the life of a free man. The post-classical maxim, taken up by Coke and his successors, gave a new currency to these teachings of the Digest, and, it seems, a new extension. But the denial of a cause of action for wrongs producing death has been ascribed to other sources also. The explanation has been found at times in the common law notion that trespass as a civil wrong is drowned in a felony. As to the adequacy of this explanation grave doubt has been expressed. None the less, the rule as to felony merger seems to have coalesced, even if in a confused way, with the rule as to abatement, and the effect of the two in combination was to fasten upon the law a doctrine which it took a series of statutes to dislodge.").

See Malone, The Genesis of Wrongful Death, 17 Stan.L.Rev. 1043 (1965).

See also Prosser, Law of Torts (4th Ed. 1971) pp. 898–914.

2. Hyatt v. Adams, 16 Mich. 180 (1867) ("The rule rests more on artificial distinction than any real princi-

§ 21.1 SPECIFIC ACTIONS

Although the injustice of such a rule, characterized by Pollock as "one of the least rational parts of our law," [3] was readily apparent and though many exceptions were added by the judiciary,[4] it was not until 1934 [5] that the right of action for personal injuries was allowed to survive the death of either party in England.[6]

In America, the development of this troublesome maxim paralleled that of the English courts with the reception of the common law as it existed prior to 1833.[7] Following the common law, it became established that, in absence of statute, actions for injuries to the person abate on the death of the person injured, and do not survive to the personal representative.[8] The same result, abatement of the cause of action, was reached where the action was nominally one in contract though in reality for the recovery for personal injuries.[9]

§ 21.2 Survival Statutes

Today, most of the states have adopted survival legislation of one form or another,[10] generally in recognition that, with the substitution

ple, and savors more of the logic of the schoolman than on common sense"); Harris v. Nashville Trust Co., 128 Tenn. 573, 162 S.W. 584 (1914) ("The maxim, 'Actio personalis moritur cum persona,' is by no means a favorite with the courts. It has no champion at this date, nor has any judge or law writer risen to defend it for 200 years past.").

See Winfield, Death As Affecting Liability In Tort, (1929) 29 Col.L.Rev. 239 (Excellent historical treatment).

Rodgers v. Ferguson, 89 N.M. 688, 556 P.2d 844 (1976), cert. denied 90 N.M. 7, 558 P.2d 619.

3. Pollock, The Law of Torts (12 Ed.) p. 60.

4. See Kirk v. Commissioner of Internal Revenue, 179 F.2d 619 (1st Cir. 1950) ("In short, we think the general rule today with respect to the survival of tort actions decedent estates is that actions essentially for penalties do not survive for the reason that a decedent is beyond punishment, but that actions to recompense or compensate a plaintiff for a harm inflicted upon him by a decedent do survive, for an estate can, and we think should, compensate for injury to the same extent as the decedent had he lived").

5. Law Reform Act, 1934.

6. "[T]he damages being payable to or exigible from his estate."

7. Sullivan v. Associated Bill Posters and Distributors, 6 F.2d 1000 (2d Cir. 1925).

8. Ormsby v. Chase, 290 U.S. 387, 54 S.Ct. 211, 78 L.Ed. 378 (1933); Yount v. National Bank of Jackson, 327 Mich. 342, 42 N.W.2d 110 (1950).

9. Singley v. Bigelow, 108 Cal.App. 436, 291 P. 899 (1930); State ex rel. H. E. Wolfe Constr. Co. v. Parks, 129 Fla. 50, 175 So. 786 (1937); Bernstein v. Queens County Jockey Club, 225 N.Y.S. 449 (1927).

10. See Speiser, Recovery for Wrongful Death, (2d ed. 1975) § 14.4 and Appendix A, for compilation of state survival statutes.

of compensation for vengeance as the basis of recovery in civil actions, the *actio personalis* rule is without plausible ground.[11] State survival statutes are generally controlling in Federal actions,[12] including those brought under the FTCA [13] or the Civil Rights statutes,[14] although the FELA and the Jones Act contain their own survival provisions.[15]

State survival statutes vary widely in their wording and in their judicial construction. Most statutes provide that a cause of action will survive the death either of the injured party or of the tortfeasor.[16] Some statutes expressly limit the types of tort actions which will survive,[17] with the tendency to exclude injuries to intangible personal interests, such as defamation. Some statutes limit the damages recoverable, precluding, for instance, recovery for pain and suffering.[18] Many statutes do not distinguish between actions for fatal and non-fatal injuries.[19] Some statutes have been construed to

Evans, A Comparative Study of the Statutory Survival of Tort Claims For and Against Executors and Administrators, 29 Michigan L.Rev. 969.

11. Pollock, The Law of Torts (12th ed.) p. 62.

See also Grant v. McAuliffe, 41 Cal.2d 859, 264 P.2d 944 (1953).

12. Baltimore & Ohio R. Co. v. Joy, 173 U.S. 226, 19 S.Ct. 387, 43 L.Ed. 677 (1899); Patton v. Brady, 184 U.S. 608, 22 S.Ct. 493, 46 L.Ed. 713 (1900).

13. Fed. Rules of Civil Procedure, Rule 17(b). See Mazeau v. United States, 280 F.Supp. 879 (D.N.H.1968).

14. Pritchard v. Smith, 289 F.2d 153 (8th Cir. 1961) (Action survives death of defendant); Brazier v. Cherry, 293 F.2d 401 (5th Cir. 1961), cert. denied 368 U.S. 921, 82 S.Ct. 243, 7 L.Ed.2d 136 (Action survives death of injured person).

15. *FELA:* 46 U.S.C.A. § 59.

Metcalfe v. Atchison, T. & S. F. Ry. Co., 491 F.2d 892 (10th Cir. 1974); Connors v. Gallick, 339 F.2d 381 (6th Cir. 1964).

Jones Act

See 46 U.S.C.A. § 688; Civil v. Waterman S. S. Corp., 217 F.2d 94 (2d Cir. 1954); Wilkes v. Mississippi River Sand and Gravel Co., 202 F.2d 383 (6th Cir. 1953), cert. denied 346 U.S. 817, 74 S.Ct. 29, 98 L.Ed. 344.

16. E.g., West's Ann.California Probate Code § 573: "[N]o cause of action shall be lost by reason of the death of any person but may be maintained by or against his executor or administrator."

17. E.g., West's Florida Statutes Ann. § 45.11: "All actions for personal injuries shall die with the person, to wit: Assault and battery, slander, false imprisonment, and malicious prosecution; all other actions shall and may be maintained in the name of the representatives of the deceased."

18. Arizona, California, Colorado, District of Columbia, Indiana, Rhode Island.

19. Alaska, Arizona, California, Colorado, District of Columbia, Georgia, Hawaii, Illinois, Kansas, Kentucky, Maryland, Massachusetts, Mississippi, Montana, Nebraska, New Jersey, New York, Ohio, Oklahoma, Rhode Island, South Carolina, South Dakota, Texas, Wisconsin.

disallow survival in cases of instantaneous death,[20] others are expressly limited to non-fatal injuries.[21]

Survival statutes often have been strictly construed as intended to derogate as little as possible from the common law rule,[22] but now more frequently the legislative purpose is interpreted more favorably for the beneficiaries.[23]

Notwithstanding the generally accepted common law rule that personal injury claims are not assignable,[24] some courts have logically upheld the right of assignment where the action survives by reason of statute.[25] Although death claims under enabling statutes are usually non-assignable,[26] some statutes have been construed broadly enough to permit such transfer.[27]

20. *Ark.*—Missouri P. R. Co. v. Creekmore, 193 Ark. 722, 102 S.W.2d 553 (1937).

S.C.—Bowers v. Charleston & W. C. Ry. Co., 210 S.C. 367, 42 S.E.2d 705 (1947).

21. Alabama, Indiana, Missouri, Nevada.

22. See, e. g., McDowell v. Henderson Mining Co., 276 Ala. 202, 160 So.2d 486 (1963). (Statutes which help "causes of action to survive are in derogation of common law and should be strictly construed."); Norman v. Murphy, 124 Cal.App.2d 95, 268 P.2d 178 (1954). ("Even if the courts of this state should now hold that an unborn viable child is 'a person' within the meaning of our law, it could not be held to be 'a minor person'" for the purposes of the wrongful death act.); Danis v. New York Central R. Co., 160 Ohio St. 474, 117 N.E.2d 39, 43 A.L.R.2d 1286 (1954). (Where sole statutory beneficiary died pending an action for wrongful death the right of action is extinguished).

23. See, e. g., Pritchard v. Smith, 289 F.2d 153 (8th Cir. 1961). (Trend toward liberal construction.); Reinhardt v. New Haven, 23 Conn.Sup. 321, 182 A.2d 925 (1961). (Survival is rule.); McDaniel v. Bullard, 34 Ill.2d 487, 216 N.E.2d 140 (1966). (Statute includes terms nonexistent at time of enactment.); Massachusetts Banking & Ins. Co. v. United States, 352 U.S. 128, 77 S.Ct. 189, 1 L.Ed.2d 189 (1956) (FTCA amendment applying compensatory damages in states having punitive damage death acts as Massachusetts, construed to also eliminate the ceiling of $20,000 in the state act.); Van Beeck v. Sabine Towing Co., 300 U.S. 342, 57 S.Ct. 482, 81 L.Ed. 685 (1937). (Commentary by Justice Cardozo); Tauch v. Ferguson-Steere Motor Co., 62 N.M. 429, 312 P.2d 83 (1957). (Statute construed to include unmarried adults who had no dependents since punishment for tort intended as well as compensation.)

24. See, e. g., Berlinski v. Ovellette, 164 Conn. 482, 325 A.2d 239 (1973). (Assignment of personal injury action against public policy in absence of statute.); In re Schmelzer, 350 F. Supp. 429 (S.D.Ohio 1972), aff'd 480 F.2d 1074.

25. See, e. g., Davenport v. State Farm Mut. Auto. Ins. Co., 81 Nev. 361, 404 P.2d 10 (1965); Harvey v. Cleman, 65 Wash.2d 853, 400 P.2d 87 (1965).

26. See, e. g., Liberty Mut. Ins. Co. v. Lockwood, Greene Engineers, Inc., 273 Ala. 403, 140 So.2d 821 (1962); Forsthove v. Hardware Dealers Mut. Fire Ins. Co., 416 S.W.2d 208 (Mo. App.1967).

27. Baker & Conrad, Inc. v. Chicago Heights Constr. Co., 364 Ill. 386, 4

§ 21.3 Distinction from Wrongful Death Statutes

Although a survival statute is conceptually distinct from a wrongful death act, the distinction is not always observed in legislative drafting. A survival statute permits recovery by decedent's representatives, on behalf of his estate, of damages decedent could have recovered in his own action had he lived. A wrongful death act creates a new cause of action, whereby decedent's survivors may recover the damages they have sustained by reason of the death.

Nevertheless, some states have provided for wrongful death recovery by way of "enlarged" survival statutes.[28] Where a survival statute provides for recovery of damages for pain and suffering incidental to death, it is often necessary to show that the suffering was consciously experienced.[29] This may be evidenced by decedent's behavior,[30] or inferred from the nature of the injury.[31]

I once proved just that, consciousness, by a nurses' testimony that her patient licked an ice cream cone. Philosophically, was that consciousness? The jury said it was.

The extent of pain and suffering is always a jury question. In a 1969 Louisiana case, an award of $10,000 damages for pain and suffering was upheld in a case where it was established that decedent died 1.76 seconds after the injury.[32]

Juries will award high damages for an injured person's momentary contemplation of that long journey into forever's eternity.

§ 21.4 Punitive Damages

The right to punitive damages generally dies with the tortfeasor, on the theory that the purpose of such damages is to punish the wrongdoer.[33] Recovery of punitive damages by the representatives

---

N.E.2d 953 (1936). (Where recognized by workmen's compensation statute); Shreveport, City of v. Southwestern Gas & Elec. Co., 140 La. 1078, 74 So. 555 (1917).

28. See Chapter 22, "Wrongful Death."

29. Carr v. Arthur D. Little, Inc., 348 Mass. 469, 204 N.E.2d 466 (1965) (Where evidence of conscious suffering only speculative, no basis for recovery of damages).

30. Giles v. Chicago G. W. Ry. Co., 72 F.Supp. 493 (D.C.Minn.1947), appeal dism'd 163 F.2d 631 (8th Cir.) (FELA —railroad employee burned by live steam was conscious and active from time of injury to admission to hospital); Johnson v. State Fire & Cas. Co., 303 So.2d 779 (La.App.1974) (Struggles of drowning man sufficient to justify award of $2,500 for pain and suffering).

31. United States Steel Corp. v. Lamp, 436 F.2d 1256 (6th Cir. 1970). (Evidence giving rise to inference that decedents died by drowning while aware of their fate sufficient to justify award for pain and suffering).

32. Wiggins v. Lane & Co., 298 F.Supp. 194 (D.C.La.1969).

33. Evans v. Gibson, 220 Cal. 476, 31 P.2d 389 (1934) ("Since the purpose

of a decedent plaintiff, however, is generally allowed, absent statutory provision to the contrary.[34] Thus, the award of punitive damages to plaintiff's estate has been upheld in a medical malpractice action,[35] in an action against a labor union for loss of membership,[36] and in a tenant's action for treble damages against his landlord.[37] Some jurisdictions hold to the contrary and deny punitive damages to plaintiff's estate. On this basis, where a physician died during a slander action, punitive damages were denied to his estate, although they were awarded to the joint plaintiff hospital.[38]

§ 21.5 Injury to the Person

At common law, survival was limited to actions involving injury to property as distinguished from injury to the person.[39] The underlying rationale was the reason for redressing "purely personal" wrongs ceases to exist when the person injured cannot benefit by the recovery, whereas since the property or estate of the injured person passes to his representatives, the cause can serve its purpose as well after his death as before.[40] The legacy of this common law rule has persisted, despite the growth and application of survival statutes, in that causes of action deemed "personal" are frequently held to be out-

of punitive damages is to punish the wrongdoer for his acts, accompanied by evil motive, and to deter him from the commission of like wrongs in the future, the reason for such damages ceases to exist with his death. It is true that the infliction of punishment serves as a deterrent to the commission of future wrongs by others, as well as by the wrongdoer, but punitive damages by way of example to others should be imposed only on actual wrongdoers.") 220 Cal. at 490. See also Holm Timber Indus. v. Plywood Corp. of America, 242 Cal.App. 2d 492, 51 Cal.Rptr. 597 (1966).

But see Atlas Properties, Inc. v. Didich, 213 So.2d 278 (Fla.App.1968), writ disch'd 226 So.2d 684 (Punitive action surviving death of either party).

34. Worrie v. Boze, 198 Va. 891, 96 S. E.2d 799 (1957) (Where right to action survives, right to punitive damages based on it also survives, absent statutory provision to the contrary); State ex rel. Smith v. Greene, 494 S. W.2d 55 (Mo.1973) (Action for destruction of deceased's personal property, right to punitive damages survives where cause of action survives).

35. Dunwoody v. Trapnell, 47 Cal. App.3d 367, 120 Cal.Rptr. 859 (1975).

36. Layne v. International Broth. of Elec. Workers, 418 F.Supp. 964 (D.S. C.1976).

37. Staub v. Triangle Oil Co., 349 A.2d 209 (Del.1975).

38. Wolf v. Gold, 41 Misc.2d 548, 246 N.Y.S.2d 458 (1962), aff'd 18 A.D.2d 987, 238 N.Y.S.2d 473 (Doctor's estate awarded $25,000 general damages, no punitive damages. Joint plaintiff hospital awarded $15,000 general damages, $20,000 punitive damages.).

39. Prosser, The Law of Torts (4th ed. 1971) p. 899.

40. Barnes Coal Corp. v. Retail Coal Merchants Ass'n, 128 F.2d 645 (4th Cir. 1942) (Action to recover triple damages under Sherman Anti-Trust Act survives under Virginia law).

side the statute's scope. Slander and libel actions are expressly excluded under several statutes.[41]

I sought in vain for a U. S. jurisdiction in which to sue for the late Errol Flynn's estate, he having been defamed in a book after his death. Our last chance seems Connecticut. (*Emmanuel v. Bovino*, 26 Conn.Sup. 356, 223 A.2d 541 (1966)).

An individual's constitutional rights against unlawful search and seizure have been held to be "personal", and thus abated with the individual's death.[42] In *Maritote v. Desilu Productions, Inc.*, it was held that Al Capone's right to privacy was personal and had died with him, and thus could not be asserted by his widow and son against the producers of a fictionalized television broadcast which falsely attributes more than one hundred acts of violence to him.[43] The modern, liberal approach to survival, however, was expressed by a Connecticut court, where a claim for damages for alienation of affection was held to survive under a general survival statute on the presumption that "every cause or right of action survives until the contrary is made to appear by way of exception to the rule." [44]

---

41. *Alaska*—CCP § 09.55.570.

Arizona—CCP § 14–477.

Colorado—CRS § 153–1–9.

Delaware—10 Del.C. § 3701.

Florida—West's Ann.Fla.Stats. § 45.11.

Hawaii—Stats. § 663–6.

Illinois—Ill.Rev.Stats. § 339.

Kansas—KSA § 60–1802.

Kentucky—KRS § 411.140.

Nebraska—NRS § 25–1402.

North Dakota—Cent.Code § 28–01–26.1.

Oklahoma—Okla.Stats. 12 § 1052.

Pennsylvania—20 PS § 320.601.

42. Ravellette v. Smith, 300 F.2d 854 (7th Cir. 1962) (Blood sample taken from deceased, held no survival of cause for damages: "The law, frequently expressed, is that the rights guaranteed by the search and seizure provisions of state and federal Constitutions are personal rights. . . . Decedent's right, being personal, could not survive his death and cannot validly be urged by plaintiff. The same reasoning applies to the asserted invasion of decedent's privacy.").

43. Maritote v. Desilu Productions, Inc., 230 F.Supp. 721 (D.C.Ill.1964), aff'd 345 F.2d 418 (7th Cir.), cert. denied 382 U.S. 883, 86 S.Ct. 176, 15 L. Ed.2d 124.

See Chapter 30, Defamation, and Chapter 31, Right of Privacy, infra.

44. Emmanuel v. Bovino (1966) 26 Conn.Sup. 356, 223 A.2d 541.

§§ 21.6–22.0 are reserved for supplementary material.

CHAPTER 22

WRONGFUL DEATH

Table of Sections

Sec.
22.1 At Common Law.
22.2 Statutes.
22.3 Application—Proximate Cause, Defenses, Conflicts.
22.4 Beneficiaries—Damages.

Library References:
C.J.S. Death §§ 13, 27.
West's Key No. Digests, Death ⚖7 et seq.
Prosser, Law of Torts (4th ed. 197) pp. 901–914.
Blashfield, Automobile Law and Practice, § 456.2.

§ 22.1 At Common Law

As might have been anticipated, the same obscure reasoning that prevented survival of the personal injury cause of action at common law also prevented any new action arising in decedent's representatives or estate based on the death itself.[1] In an 1808 case, *Baker v. Bolton*,[2] it was stated that the death of a human being could not be complained of as an injury,[3] thus making it more profitable for the defendant to do a thorough job and kill the plaintiff than merely to injure him.

The origins of the common law rule seem to trace from the royal preemption of homicide prosecution. Although in early Anglo-Saxon times, any homicide, whether intentional or involuntary, was a private wrong to the surviving relatives which might be redressed by payment of punitive damages (or other form of retribution), by the 13th century homicide had become an offense to the state, on the the-

---

1. Indeed, such a right may at one time have been allowed a third person, still alive. In 1369, in a case where a writ of trespass was brought by the plaintiff for the ravishment of his wife, and her goods, one defense was that the wife was divorced. The Chief Justice of King's Bench said, "Tho his wife was dead, yet he shall have action of ravishment, so here, tho there is a divorce between them." See 7 Harv.L.Rev. 170 (1893), 29 Col.L. Rev. 239 (1929).

2. 170 Eng.Rep. 1033.

3. Steamer Harrisburg v. Rickards, 119 U.S. 199, 7 S.Ct. 140, 30 L.Ed. 358 (1886); The Mobile Life Ins. Co. v. Brame, 95 U.S. (5 Otto) 754, 24 L.Ed. 580 (1878); Major v. Burlington, C. R. & N. Ry. Co., 115 Iowa 309, 88 N. W. 815 (1902); Perham v. Portland Gen. Elec. Co., 33 Or. 451, 53 P. 14 (1898).

ory that the king had lost a subject. Since the wrongdoer's penalty frequently included complete forfeiture of his property to the crown, the state sanctions acted to exclude any private recovery by the survivors.[4]

Although there is evidence that some early American colonial courts allowed recovery of damages for wrongful death,[5] the common law rule expressed in *Baker* was quickly established in American courts.[6] It was not until 1846 that Lord Campbell's Act, allowing recovery to the heirs and representatives of a person killed by the wrongful act of another, was passed in England as a corrective measure.[7] Acts similar or identical to Campbell's Act have been adopted in the United States,[8] and nearly all wrongful death recovery is pursuant to these statutes.

4. See Hay, "Death as a Civil Cause of Action in Massachusetts", 7 Harv.L. Rev. 170 (1893); Malone, "Genesis of Wrongful Death", 17 Stanford L.Rev. 1043 (1965); Smedley, "Wrongful Death—Bases of the Common Law Rules", 13 Vand.L.Rev. 609 (1960).

See also Moragne v. States Marine Lines, Inc., 398 U.S. 375, 90 S.Ct. 1772, 26 L.Ed.2d 339 (1970), on remand 446 F.2d 906 (5th Cir.); Goheen v. General Motors Corp., 263 Or. 145, 502 P.2d 223 (1972).

Speiser, Recovery for Wrongful Death 2d, (1975) §§ 1:1, 1:2.

5. See Speiser § 1:3.

Foster's Case, 1674, 1 Court of Assistants 54: "In the case of Jno. Ffoster accidently dischardging gun(s) at foules on the neck thereby wounding Samuel Ffacks son so as he died the Court sentent him to pay the father of the boy tenn pounds and to pay tenn more as a like fine to the Countrey, wch was declared and on his humble petition the Court saw cause to remit five pounds of the Country's fine."

Ford's Case, 1675, 1 Court of Assistants 60: "James Fford being bound over to this Court to Ansr for his driving a cart over Abigaile King that the Child died. After the Court had duely considered the case sentenced him to pay the fine of five pounds to the Country and five pounds money to its fathr Samuel King."

6. See Cary v. Berkshire R. Co., 55 Mass. (1 Cush.) 475 (1848); Green v. Hudson R. Co. 28 Barb. 9, 16 How.Pr. 230 (N.Y.1858), aff'd 41 N.Y. (2 Keyes.) 294; Aetna Life Ins. Co. v. Moses, 287 U.S. 530, 53 S.Ct. 231, 77 L.Ed. 477, 88 A.L.R. 647 (1933); Chrisafogeorgis v. Brandenberg, 55 Ill.2d 368, 304 N.E.2d 88 (1973); Incollingo v. Ewing, 444 Pa. 263, 282 A.2d 206 (1971), rearg. 444 Pa. 299, 282 A.2d 225.

Speiser, §§ 1:3, 1:4.

7. 9 and 10 Vict.Ch. 93.

8. Van Beeck v. Sabine Towing Co., 300 U.S. 342, 57 S.Ct. 452, 81 L.Ed. 685 (1937) ("The adoption of Lord Campbell's Act in 1846 (9 and 10 Vict. chap. 93), giving an action to the executor for the use of wife, husband, parent or child, marks the dawn of a new era. In this country, statutes substantially the same in tenor followed in quick succession in one state after another, until today there is not a state of the Union in which a remedy is Lacking").

For compendium of U.S. state wrongful death statutes as well as foreign statutes, see Speiser, Appendix A & B.

§ 22.1 SPECIFIC ACTIONS Pt. 4

The United States Supreme Court in its historic 1970 decision *Moragne v. States Marine Lines, Inc.*,[9] overruled the *Baker* rule and held that a non-statutory action would lie for wrongful death under general maritime law. Noting that the *Baker* rule lacked foundation in reason or precedent,[10] and had been rejected as social policy by the widespread enactment of statutory remedies, the Court established the existence of the common law right to sue for wrongful death, without limitation to the maritime field.[11]

The *Moragne* holding was adopted by the Massachusetts Court in *Gaudette v. Webb*,[12] wherein it was held that, in Massachusetts, a common law wrongful death remedy existed[13] which would co-exist with the state's statutory remedy. A subsequent attempt to utilize the common law remedy to circumvent the statutory limitation on damages, however, was disallowed, on the holding that the statutes still applied to provide the measure and limits of liability.[14]

§ 22.2 Statutes

Acts similar or identical to Campbell's Act have been adopted in the United States [15] and they fall into two categories: (1) Death Acts or those which follow the English act as their guide and create a new cause of action for the death in favor of the decedent's personal representative for the benefit of certain designated persons; (2) Survival Acts or those whose theory is that decedent had a right of action vested at the time of the wrong and then enlarging it to include the damage resulting from the death.[16] The question of who is the prop-

9. 398 U.S. 375, 90 S.Ct. 1772, 26 L. Ed.2d 339 (1970).

10. Id. at 381–392, 90 S.Ct. 1772, 1777–1783, 26 L.Ed.2d 339, 346–52.

11. Gaudette v. Webb, 362 Mass. 60, 284 N.E.2d 222, 61 A.L.R.3d 893 (1972) ("The [*Moragne*] court's decision was founded in large part upon the general prevalence of non-maritime wrongful death statutes, and it is thus applicable with equal force to non-maritime actions for wrongful death").

12. Id.

13. ("Upon consideration of the *Moragne* decision and the sound reasoning upon which it is based, we are convinced that the law in this Commonwealth has also evolved to the point where it may now be held that the right to recovery for wrongful death is of common law origin, and we so hold").

14. Meagher v. Electrolux Corp., 388 F.Supp. 1009 (D.C.Mass.1975).

See also Prunty v. Schwantes, 40 Wis. 2d 418, 162 N.W.2d 34 (1968).

15. See Prosser, Law of Torts (4th ed. 1971), pp. 901–914.

See also n. 8, supra.

16. A comparison of the theories of the two forms will readily suggest that under the survival act, if death is instantaneous, there can be no right of action as decedent suffered no appreciable damage giving rise to a right.

er plaintiff depends for its answer on the particular statute involved. Under the survival acts this usually means the executor or administrator. Other statutes allow a direct right of action by the beneficiary.[17]

Where a jurisdiction has both a wrongful death and a survival act, ordinarily they may be prosecuted concurrently,[18] although some jurisdictions require plaintiff to elect between the two remedies.[19] Where the actions may be brought concurrently, some jurisdictions deny recovery for decedent's future earnings in the survival action,[20] so as to prevent the possibility of double recovery.[21]

Great Northern Ry. Co. v. Capital Trust Co., Adm'r, 242 U.S. 144, 37 S.Ct. 41, 61 L.Ed. 208 (1916); Dillon v. Great Northern Ry. Co., 38 Mont. 485, 100 P. 960 (1909); Slater v. State, 192 Misc. 826, 82 N.Y.S.2d 313 (1948); Hansen v. Hayes, 175 Or. 358, 154 P. 2d 202 (1944); Belding v. Black Hills, Ft. P. R. Co., 3 S.D. 369, 53 N.W. 750 (1892); Carolina C. & O. Ry. v. Shewalter, 128 Tenn. 363, 161 S.W. 1136 (1913).

Schumacher, Rights of Action Under Death and Survival Statutes (1924) 23 Mich.L.Rev. 114.

17. Stewart v. L. & N. R. Co., 83 Ala. 493, 4 So. 373 (1888); Western Union Tel. Co. v. McGill, 57 F. 699, 21 L.R.A. 818 (10th Cir. 1893); Cibulla v. Pennsylvania-Reading Seashore Lines, 25 N.J.Misc. 98, 50 A.2d 461 (1946); Belding v. Black Hills, Ft. P. R. Co., 3 S.D. 369, 53 N.W. 750 (1892); Herro v. Steidl, 255 Wis. 65, 37 N.W.2d 874 (1949).

Right of creditors to share in recovery; Kennedy v. Davis, 171 Ala. 609, 55 So. 104 (1911); Broadnax v. Broadnax, 160 N.C. 432, 76 S.E. 216 (1912); Ghilain v. Couture, 84 N.H. 48, 146 A. 395 (1929).

Death of beneficiary after death of decedent: Thomas, Adm'r v. Maysville Gas Co., 112 Ky. 569, 66 S.W. 398 (1902); Union Steamboat Co. v. Chaffin's Adm'rs, 204 F. 412 (7th Cir. 1913).

18. *Cal.*—Pacific Employers Ins. Co. v. Hartford Steam Boiler Inspection & Ins. Co., 143 Cal.App.2d 747, 299 P.2d 928 (1956). (Not a survival of the decedent's cause of action for injury but as another and independent action, founded upon an event (death) subsequent to the injury, and prosecuted by another plaintiff for the violation of a right appertaining to him and to the decedent.)

N.Y.—Cramer v. Nuccitelli, 151 N.Y.S. 2d 544 (1956). (Cause of action for injuries conferred on fireman by statute survives the subsequent death of the injured fireman and may be prosecuted by his executor or administrator, but action for his death is specifically conferred upon his family or relatives.)

Pa.—Schwab v. P. J. Oesterling & Son, Inc., 386 Pa. 388, 126 A.2d 418 (1956). (Rights under Wrongful Death Act and Survival Act separate action but may be incorporated in same action.)

19. Chesapeake & Ohio R. Co. v. Banks' Adm'r, 142 Ky. 746, 135 S.W. 285 (1911); Cottengim's Adm'r v. Adams' Adm'r, 255 S.W.2d 637, 36 A.L. R.2d 1142 (Ky.1953).

20. *Fla.*—Hooper Constr. Co. v. Drake, 73 So.2d 279 (Fla.1954).

Hawaii—Greene v. Texeira, 54 Hawaii 231, 505 P.2d 1169, 76 A.L.R.3d 111 (1973).

Kan.—Flowers v. Marshall, 208 Kan. 900, 494 P.2d 1184 (1972).

21. See note 21 on page 620.

§ 22.2 SPECIFIC ACTIONS

Where the death occurs under circumstances covered by a Workmen's Compensation Act, wrongful death or survival actions are ordinarily preempted by the "exclusive remedy" provisions of the Compensation Act,[22] unless the death is caused by a third party.[23]

There is a division of opinion as to general construction of wrongful death statutes.[24] Some hold that they should be liberally construed to effect their remedial purpose.[25] Other jurisdictions hold that the statutes are to be strictly construed since they are in derogation of the common law.[26] Still other jurisdictions construe strictly as to determining who are the beneficiaries, and then liberally as to applying the statute in their favor.[27]

§ 22.3 Application—Proximate Cause, Defenses, Conflicts

Most wrongful death statutes, following Lord Campbell's Act, require that defendant's wrongful act be such that, but for his death,

---

Mass.—O'Leary v. United States Lines Co., 111 F.Supp. 745 (D.C.Mass.1953).

Ohio—Allen v. Burdette, 139 Ohio St. 208, 39 N.E.2d 153 (1942).

Wis.—Prunty v. Schwantes, 40 Wis.2d 418, 162 N.W.2d 34 (1968).

21. See, generally, Prosser, Law of Torts (4th ed. 1971), pp. 901–914.

22. Page, "The Exclusivity of the Workmen's Compensation Remedy", 4 Boston College Indus. & Comm.L. Rev. 555 (1963). See also Prosser, Law of Torts (4th ed. 1971), pp. 901 et seq.

McLain v. Llewellyn Iron Works, 56 Cal.App. 60, 204 P. 869 (1921); Mariscal v. American Smelting & Refining Co., 113 Ariz. 148, 548 P.2d 412 (1976).

23. McCord, "The Third Person in the Compensation Picture: A Study of the Liabilities and Rights of Non-Employers", 37 Tex.L.Rev. 389 (1959).

See also Sanders v. Shockley, 468 F.2d 88 (5th Cir. 1972); Mullarkey v. Florida Feed Mills, Inc., 268 So.2d 363 (Fla.1972), appeal dism'd 411 U.S. 944, 93 S.Ct. 1923, 36 L.Ed.2d 406.

24. See Prosser, Law of Torts (4th ed.), pp. 901 et seq.

See also Speiser, § 1:12.

25. *Cal.*—Bond v. United R. Co., 159 Cal. 270, 113 P. 366 (1911).

Fla.—Stokes v. Liberty Mut. Ins. Co., 213 So.2d 695 (Fla.1968).

Mich.—Hunter v. Dampsk A/S Flint, 279 F.Supp. 701 (D.C.Mich.1967).

S.D.—Halvorsen v. Dunlap, 495 F.2d 817 (8th Cir. 1974).

Wash.—Gray v. Goodson, 378 P.2d 413, 61 Wash.2d 319 (1963).

26. *Ark.*—McGinty v. Ballentine Produce, Inc., 241 Ark. 533, 408 S.W.2d 891 (1966).

Del.—Saunders v. Hill, 57 Del. 519, 202 A.2d 807 (1964).

Ill.—Baird v. Chicago, B. & Q. R. Co., 11 Ill.App.3d 264, 296 N.E.2d 365 (1973), appeal after remand 32 Ill.App.3d 1, 334 N.E.2d 920, aff'd 63 Ill.2d 463, 349 N.E.2d 413.

Miss.—Edwards v. Sears, Roebuck & Co., 512 F.2d 276 (5th Cir. 1975).

N.J.—State ex rel. Gosnell v. Gosnell, 106 N.J.Super. 279, 255 A.2d 769 (1969).

27. *Mo.*—Almcrantz v. Carney, 490 S.W.2d 59 (Mo.1973).

Wash.—Whittlesey v. Seattle, 94 Wash. 645, 163 P. 193 (1917).

decedent could have sued on it for damages.[28] In the wrongful death action, it is essential to show that the wrongful act was the proximate cause of the death.[29] Where decedent was suffering a terminal illness, the fact that defendant's wrongful act merely "accelerated" or "precipitated" the death does not protect defendant from liability.[30]

28. Michigan C. R. Co. v. Vreeland, 227 U.S. 59, 33 S.Ct. 192, 57 L.Ed. 417 (1913).
Ala.—Denny v. Seaboard Lacquer, Inc., 487 F.2d 485 (4th Cir. 1973) (applying Alabama Law.)
Del.—Reynolds v. Willis, 58 Del. 368, 209 A.2d 760 (1965).
Fla.—Latimer v. Sears, Roebuck & Co., 285 F.2d 152, 86 A.L.R.2d 307 (5th Cir. 1960).
Mich.—Maiuri v. Sinacola Constr. Co., 382 Mich. 391, 170 N.W.2d 27 (1969).

29. Ark.—Superior Forwarding Co. v. Garner, 236 Ark. 340, 366 S.W.2d 290 (1963).
D.C.—Elliott v. Michael James, Inc., 507 F.2d 1179 (D.C.Cir. 1974), appeal after remand 559 F.2d 759. (Employer's violation of building code requiring unlocked egress was proximate cause of employee's death, where knifed by another employee.)
Fla.—Jolly v. Insurance Co. of North America, 331 So.2d 368 (Fla.App. 1976). (Facts did not show proximate cause where decedent collapsed watching her house burn while firemen could do nothing due to inadequate water supply.)
Ill.—Glenview Park Dist. v. Melhus, 540 F.2d 1321 (7th Cir. 1976), cert. denied 429 U.S. 1094, 97 S.Ct. 1109, 51 L. Ed.2d 541. (Error to rule that there was no negligence on part of defendant park district causing decedent's death where decedent drowned on canoe trip operated by defendant.)
Ind.—Childs v. Rayburn, 169 Ind.App. 147, 346 N.E.2d 655 (1976). (Employer negligent where boy working in open field struck by lightning.)

Mich.—Farwell v. Keaton, 396 Mich. 281, 240 N.W.2d 217 (1976). (Companion's desertion of injured friend after attempting to help was a breach of duty to use reasonable care in performing rescue and constituted proximate cause of death.)
Miss.—Carlson v. Pascagoula, 227 So.2d 279 (Miss.1969). (Drowning on public recreation premises.)
N.Y.—Salsedo v. Palmer, 278 F. 92, 23 A.L.R. 1262 (2d Cir. 1921).
Tex.—Hall v. Atchison, T. & S. F. Ry. Co., 504 F.2d 380 (5th Cir. 1974). (Defendant railroad's negligent blockage of crossing could constitute proximate cause of death through delay in decedent's reaching hospital.)

30. Ark.—Follett v. Jones, 252 Ark. 950, 481 S.W.2d 713 (1972) (Jury question of proximate cause where decedent with lung cancer was injured in car accident shortly before death).
Cal.—Hastie v. Handeland, 274 Cal. App.2d 599, 79 Cal.Rptr. 268 (1969) (Death resulted from infection contracted in operation for back condition aggravated by accident).
Ga.—National Dairy Products Corp. v. Durham, 115 Ga.App. 420, 154 S.E.2d 752 (1967) (Accident precipitated spread of pre-existing testical cancer).
La.—Austin v. Otis Elevator Co., 336 So.2d 914 (La.App.1976) (Accident precipitated death from pre-existing aneurysm, diabetes and hypertension).
Vt.—Harrington v. Shareff, 305 F.2d 333 (2d Cir. 1962) (Automobile accident precipitated spread of preexistent cancer).

Where the injury inflicted creates a subsequent disease or condition, or merely combines with a subsequent disease to cause death, proximate cause is established if absent the injury death would not have ensued.[31]

Defendants may be held liable for decedent's wrongful death through his suicide, where defendants' duty to protect against such risk is established. Proximate cause under these circumstances often may be established in cases involving hospitals and sanitoriums, where the duty to use a reasonable degree of care in supervision is breached.[32] In a Georgia case, a cause of action was held stated against a hotel for a guest's suicide,[33] where the circumstances supported a contention of foreseeability. A cause of action has been held stated for wrongful death where defendant's intentional infliction of emotional distress has resulted in decedent's suicide.[34] Some jurisdictions will impose liability for suicide resulting from defend-

---

31. *Cal.*—Marks v. Reissinger, 35 Cal. App. 44, 169 P. 243 (1917) (Injury produced cerebral meningitis which combined with subsequent pneumonia to cause death); Francis v. Sauve, 222 Cal.App.2d 102, 34 Cal.Rptr. 754 (1963) (Whiplash induced brain hemorrhage causing death).

Mo.—Tharp v. Oberhellmann, 527 S.W. 2d 376 (Mo.App.1975) (Proximate cause not established where not shown that chest injury resulted in heart disease).

Minn.—Mattfeld v. Nester, 226 Minn. 106, 32 N.W.2d 291, 3 A.L.R.2d 909 (1948) (Proximate cause established where decedent died of pneumonia 9 months after accident).

32. *Cal.*—Wood v. Samaritan Inst., 26 Cal.2d 847, 161 P.2d 556 (1945).

Mo.—Stallman v. Robinson, 364 Mo. 275, 260 S.W.2d 743 (1953) (Proximate cause depends on reasonable foreseeability of risk, where patient hanged self in hospital).

N.Y.—Fatuck v. Hillside Hosp., 45 A.D. 2d 708, 356 N.Y.S.2d 105 (1974), aff'd 36 N.Y.2d 736, 368 N.Y.S.2d 161, 328 N.E.2d 791 (Proximate cause established where hospital failed to employ due care to prevent mental patient from escaping shortly before committing suicide).

Tenn.—Rural Educ. Ass'n v. Anderson, 37 Tenn.App. 209, 261 S.W.2d 151 (1953) (Proximate cause a question for jury where hospital knew mental patient needed safeguards before committing suicide).

Tex.—Harris Hosp. v. Pope, 520 S.W.2d 813 (Tex.Civ.App.1975) (Hospital liable for patient's suicide if risk reasonably foreseen).

See also Annotation, 58 A.L.R.3d 828 (Druggist's liability for suicide committed with drugs supplied by him); 79 A.L.R.3d 1210 (Liability of prison for suicide by inmate).

33. Sneider v. Hyatt Corp., 390 F. Supp. 976 (D.C.Ga.1975).

34. Tate v. Canonica, 180 Cal.App.2d 898, 5 Cal.Rptr. 28 (1960) (Held that where defendant's act was intentional, he may be liable if his act was a substantial factor inducing decedent's suicide; but when defendant's act was only negligent, he is liable only when decedent was under an irresistible impulse to commit suicide); Cauverien v. De Metz, 20 Misc.2d 144, 188 N.Y.S.2d 627 (1959) (Liability restricted to defendant's intentional act and decedent's irresistible impulse).

ant's *negligent* infliction of emotional distress, where decedent acted on an irresistible impulse,[35] although others hold to the contrary.[36]

Though some statutes limit or exclude the defense of decedent's contributing negligence,[37] the ordinary rule is that the defense may be raised against the beneficiaries' wrongful death action,[38] on the theory that the beneficiaries are maintaining a cause of action that decedent would have had, had he lived.[39] In most jurisdictions, plain-

---

35. Ga.—Appling v. Jones, 115 Ga. App. 301, 154 S.E.2d 406 (1967).

Ill.—Stasiof v. Chicago Hoist & Body Co., 50 Ill.App.2d 115, 200 N.E.2d 88 (1964).

N.Y.—Fuller v. Preis, 35 N.Y.2d 425, 363 N.Y.S.2d 568, 322 N.E.2d 263 (1974).

Tex.—Exxon Corp. v. Brecheen, 526 S. W.2d 519 (Tex.1975).

Wash.—Orcutt v. Spokane County, 58 Wash.2d 846, 364 P.2d 1102 (1961).

36. U.S.—Scheffer v. Railroad Co., 105 U.S. 249, 26 L.Ed. 1070 (1882).

Ariz.—Tucson Rapid Transit Co. v. Tocci, 3 Ariz.App. 330, 414 P.2d 179 (1966).

Okl.—Runyan v. Reid, 510 P.2d 943, 58 A.L.R.3d 814 (Okl.1973).

Wis.—Bogust v. Iverson, 10 Wis.2d 129, 102 N.W.2d 228 (1960).

37. E. g. Ark.—Ark.Stats. §§ 73–916; 81–1202.

D.C.—D.C.Code § 44–402.

Or.—O.R.S. § 654.335.

S.D.—1939 S.D.Code § 52.0945.

Va.—Va.Code § 8–642.

Wis.—WSA § 895.045.

38. Senior v. Ward, 1 El. & El. 385, 120 Eng. Reprint 954 (1859) (Lord Campbell, J.)

See Restatement, Second, Torts § 494.

U.S.—Martin v. United States, 546 F.2d 1355 (9th Cir. 1976), cert. denied 432 U.S. 906, 97 S.Ct. 2950, 53 L.Ed.2d 1078. (F.T.C.A. death claim for camper killed by bear in national park barred by decedent's negligence in disregarding ranger's advice and camping in unauthorized area.); McGarry v. United States, 549 F.2d 587 (9th Cir. 1976), cert. denied 434 U.S. 922, 98 S.Ct. 398, 54 L.Ed.2d 279.

Ariz.—Quintero v. Continental Rent-A-Car System, Inc., 105 Ariz. 135, 460 P.2d 189 (1969). (Decedent's contributory negligence a defense to action against car rental agency.)

Cal.—Buckley v. Chadwick, 45 Cal.2d 183, 288 P.2d 12 (1955), reh. denied 45 Cal.2d 183, 289 P.2d 242.

Idaho—Kirk v. United States, 161 F. Supp. 722 (D.C.Idaho 1958), aff'd 270 F.2d 110 (9th Cir.).

Mo.—Davis v. Quality Oil Co., 353 S. W.2d 670 (Mo.1962).

Md.—Jennings v. United States, 374 F. 2d 983 (4th Cir. 1973).

N.Y.—Haber v. Nassau County, 418 F. Supp. 1120 (D.C.N.Y.1976), aff'd in part, rev'd in part 557 F.2d 322 (2d Cir.).

N.C.—Bowen v. Constructors Equipment Rental Co., 283 N.C. 395, 196 S.E.2d 789 (1973).

Ohio—Corrigan v. E. W. Bohren Transport Co., 408 F.2d 301 (6th Cir. 1968), cert. denied 393 U.S. 1088, 89 S.Ct. 880, 21 L.Ed.2d 782.

39. See, supra, n. 28.

Neb.—Heinis v. Lawrence, 160 Neb. 652, 71 N.W.2d 127, 52 A.L.R.2d 1428 (1955).

W.Va.—Barr v. Curry, 137 W.Va. 364, 71 S.E.2d 313 (1952).

tiffs enjoy the presumption that decedent was exercising due care at the time of his death.[40] Where the negligence or wrongful act of a *beneficiary* was a contributing cause to the death, the general rule is that the beneficiary's recovery is barred under a wrongful death statutory action,[41] but is *not* necessarily barred where the action is based on a survival statute.[42] The courts are divided on whether a release or covenant not to sue executed by decedent prior to his death will work to defeat the wrongful death action of the beneficiaries.[43]

40. Speiser, § 12:9.
Cal.—Wilkinson v. Southern Pac. Co., 224 Cal.App.2d 478, 36 Cal.Rptr. 689 (1964).
Conn.—Gulia v. Ortowski, 156 Conn. 40, 238 A.2d 396 (1968).
Ill.—Hardware State Bank v. Cotner, 55 Ill.2d 240, 302 N.E.2d 257 (1973).
Md.—Wood v. Abell, 268 Md. 214, 300 A.2d 665 (1973).
Mass.—Montellier v. United States, 202 F.Supp. 384 (E.D.N.Y.1962), aff'd 315 F.2d 180 (2d Cir.). (Applying Mass. law.)
Mich.—Hill v. Harbor Steel & Supply Corp., 374 Mich. 194, 132 N.W.2d 54 (1965).
N.Y.—Brady v. New York, 39 A.D.2d 600, 332 N.Y.S.2d 319 (1972).

41. *Cal.*—Cardenas v. Turlock Irrigation Dist., 267 Cal.App.2d 352, 73 Cal. Rptr. 69 (1968). (Parent's failure to supervise child.)
Kan.—Schmidt v. Martin, 212 Kan. 373, 510 P.2d 1244 (1973).
La.—Hartman v. Allstate Ins. Co., 284 So.2d 559 (La.1973).
Minn.—Minners v. State Farm Mut. Auto. Ins. Co., 284 Minn. 343, 170 N. W.2d 223 (1969).
S.C.—Hall v. United States, 381 F.Supp. 224 (D.C.S.C.1974).
Tex.—Mitchell v. Akers, 401 S.W.2d 907, 20 A.L.R.3d 1385 (Tex.Civ.App. 1966), refused n. r. e.

Negligence of one Parent Bars Recovery by Either for Death of Child
Fla.—Martinez v. Rodriguez, 215 So.2d 305 (Fla.1968).

Ky.—Wheat's Adm'r v. Gray, 309 Ky. 593, 218 S.W.2d 400, 7 A.L.R.2d 1336 (1949).
Tenn.—Nichols v. Nashville Housing Auth., 187 Tenn. 683, 216 S.W.2d 694 (1949).
Contra: See Speiser, § 5:9.

42. *Ark.*—Stockton v. Baker, 213 Ark. 918, 213 S.W.2d 896 (1948).
Iowa—Kuehn v. Jenkins, 251 Iowa 718, 100 N.W.2d 610 (1960).
N.H.—Lundberg v. Hagen, 114 N.H. 110, 316 A.2d 177 (1974).
N.Y.—Guilmetti v. Ritayik, 39 A.D.2d 339, 334 N.Y.S.2d 223 (1972).
Pa.—Frankel v. Burke's Excavatory, Inc., 223 F.Supp. 945 (D.C.Pa.1963).
See, Restatement, Second, Torts § 493, Comment (a).

43. **Decedent's Release Defeats Beneficiaries' Action**
F.E.L.A.—Walrod v. Southern Pac. Co., 447 F.2d 930 (9th Cir. 1971).
Ariz.—Hutton v. Davis, 26 Ariz.App. 215, 547 P.2d 486 (1976).
Idaho—Northern Pac. R. Co. v. Adams, 192 U.S. 440, 24 S.Ct. 408, 48 L.Ed. 513 (1904) (applying Idaho law.)
N.J.—Libera v. Whittaker, Clark & Daniels, Inc., 20 N.J.Super. 292, 89 A.2d 734 (1952).
Okl.—Haws v. Luethje, 503 P.2d 871 (Okl.1972).

Decedent's Release Does Not Release Beneficiaries' Action
Cal.—Earley v. Pacific Elec. R. Co., 176 Cal. 79, 167 P. 513 (1917). Montellier v. United States, 202 F.Supp. 384 (E.

It is usually held that the statute of limitations runs against the death action only after death, regardless of the circumstance that any action by decedent would have been barred while he was living.[44] There are a few courts that hold contrary to the above position, letting the statute run from the time of the original injury.[45] Consequently, the action could be barred prior to the time of its accrual. Under Federal legislation, such as the Jones Act, the federal period rather than the period applied by a state forum applies.[46] Where an action against a municipality is brought, and there is a conflict between a special time prescribed for bringing actions against a city

D.N.Y.1962), aff'd 315 F.2d 180 (2d Cir.).

Pa.—Brown v. Moore, 247 F.2d 711, 69 A.L.R.2d 228 (3d Cir. 1957), cert. denied 355 U.S. 882, 78 S.Ct. 148, 2 L. Ed.2d 112.

S.D.—Rowe v. Richards, 35 S.D. 201, 151 N.W. 1001 (1915).

44. *U.S.*—Varveris v. United States Lines Co., 141 F.Supp. 874 (S.D.N.Y. 1956) (Employee filed timely suit under Jones Act and died while suit was pending after which administratrix moved to be substituted as party plaintiff, amending the complaint to include a death claim, within one year of plaintiff's death but more than three years (the statutory period) after the injury—since the employee's right of action had not been barred at the time of his death, neither was the death claim.).

Fla.—Griffin v. Workman, 73 So.2d 844 (Fla.1954) (Father of decedent brought wrongful death action but was not appointed administrator until after the running of the statute of limitations—held, (1) letters of administration relate back to the time of death, (2) action filed by plaintiff prior to his appointment as administrator is validated upon his qualification, (3) the mere substitution of parties plaintiff, without substantial change from the claims of the original petition, does not constitute setting forth a new cause of action.).

Ga.—Porter v. Lassiter, 91 Ga.App. 712, 87 S.E.2d 100 (1955) (Action for death of child *en ventre sa mere* arose on death of child and not time of injury to mother).

Ill.—Petsel v. Chicago, B. & Q. R. Co., 202 F.2d 817 (8th Cir. 1953) (Illinois law).

Tenn.—Gogan v. Jones, 197 Tenn. 436, 273 S.W.2d 700 (1954) (Change of parties plaintiff from administrative to individual capacity after limitations had run deemed to relate back since cause not changed).

45. Flynn v. New York N. H. & H. R. Co., 283 U.S. 53, 51 S.Ct. 357, 75 L.Ed. 837, 72 A.L.R. 1311 (1931); Kelliher v. New York Central & H. R. R. Co., 212 N.Y. 207, 105 N.E. 824, L.R. A.1915E 1178 (1914); Piukkula v. Pillsbury Astoria Flouring Mills Co., 150 Or. 304, 42 P.2d 921, 44 P.2d 162 (1935); Howard v. Bell Tel. Co. of Pennsylvania, 306 Pa. 518, 160 A. 613 (1932); Street v. Consumers Mining Corp., 185 Va. 561, 39 S.E.2d 271, 167 A.L.R. 886 (1946).

46. *U.S.*—Cox v. Roth, 348 U.S. 207, 75 S.Ct. 242, 99 L.Ed. 260 (1955). (Seaman was killed on the high seas —the 3 year statute of limitations of the Jones Act cannot be diminished by any state statute—here Florida's statute governed the distribution of decedent's estates, with which plaintiff failed to comply.).

and the longer general limitations period for wrongful death, ordinarily the longer period is accepted.[47]

Where the action is brought in some jurisdiction other than the place of the tort, important conflict of laws question as to parties and limitations as well as substantive rights invariably arise.[48] Most jurisdictions have abandoned the inflexible rule of "lex loci delicti"—law of the place of the wrong—in favor of the more reasonable "governmental interests" approach.[49] In *Reich v. Purcell*,[50] where Ohio plaintiffs had been killed in an auto accident with California defendants in Missouri, the California Supreme Court reasoned that application of the Missouri limitation on death damages would have little or no effect on regulating conduct within Missouri, but would defeat Ohio's interest in affording full recovery to injured parties. The Court therefore discarded the lex loci rule and applied Ohio law, to allow damages in excess of the Missouri limitation. The Court noted that the California defendants could not "reasonably complain when compensatory damages are assessed in accordance with the law of [their] domicile and plaintiffs receive no more than they would have had they been injured at home."[51] The Constitutional objection, that refusal to apply lex loci constitutes a denial of full faith and credit, was overruled in *Pearson v. Northeast Airlines, Inc.*,[52] where the Second Circuit upheld application of New York's unrestricted death recovery rule over the Massachusetts $15,000 limitation, in a case involving an

47. *Fla.*—Parker v. City of Jacksonville, 82 So.2d 131 (Fla.1955).

Minn.—Senecal v. City of West St. Paul, 111 Minn. 253, 126 N.W. 826 (1910).

48. See Speiser, Chapter 13, pp. 339–406; 2 Am.Jur.2d Death §§ 277 et seq.

U.S.—Romero v. International Terminal Operating Co., 358 U.S. 354, 79 S.Ct. 468, 3 L.Ed.2d 368 (1959), reh. denied 359 U.S. 962, 79 S.Ct. 795, 3 L.Ed.2d 769. (Admiralty).

49. *Cal.*—Reich v. Purcell, 67 Cal.2d 551, 63 Cal.Rptr. 31, 432 P.2d 727 (1967). (Overruling lex loci delicti rules.); Hurtado v. Superior Court, 11 Cal.3d 574, 114 Cal.Rptr. 106, 522 P.2d 666 (1974).

Ill.—Ingersoll v. Klein, 46 Ill.2d 42, 262 N.E.2d 593 (1970).

Maine—Beaulieu v. Beaulieu, 265 A.2d 610 (Me.1970).

Mass.—In re Air Crash Disaster at Boston, 399 F.Supp. 1106 (D.C.Mass. 1975).

Minn.—Balts v. Balts, 273 Minn. 419, 142 N.W.2d 66 (1966).

Mich.—Branyan v. Alpena Flying Serv., Inc., 65 Mich.App. 1, 236 N.W.2d 739 (1975).

N.Y.—Kilberg v. Northeast Airlines, Inc., 9 N.Y.2d 34, 211 N.Y.S.2d 133, 172 N.E.2d 526 (1961).

Pa.—Griffith v. United Airlines, Inc., 416 Pa. 1, 203 A.2d 796 (1964).

50. 67 Cal.2d 551, 63 Cal.Rptr. 31, 432 P.2d 727 (1967).

51. 67 Cal.2d 551, 556, 63 Cal.Rptr. 31, 34, 432 P.2d 727, 730 (1967).

52. 309 F.2d 553, 92 A.L.R.2d 1162 (2d Cir. 1962), cert. denied 372 U.S. 912, 83 S.Ct. 726, 9 L.Ed.2d 720.

airplane crash in Massachusetts which resulted in the death of a New York resident who had boarded the flight in New York. As to conflicts of statutes of limitations, most jurisdictions will apply their own, unless the foreign death statute sued under contains its own limitation which the forum views as a condition on the "right" to utilize the statute.[53] Where the limitation is viewed as qualifying the "remedy" only, the forum will generally apply its own rule.[54] In Federal diversity actions, statutes of limitation are construed as "substantive" rather than "procedural", and thus the forum's rules, including choice-of-law rules, will be applied.[55]

§ 22.4 Beneficiaries—Damages

Wrongful death statutes modeled on Lord Campbell's Act specifically designate those who are entitled to recovery. Some statutes designate "preferred classes" of beneficiaries, so that recovery is reserved exclusively for the first preferred class, if such beneficiaries exist, and if not, the right passes to the next class.[56] Some statutes provide for recovery according to the state laws of intestacy.[57]

All jurisdictions designate the spouse [58] and children [59] of decedent as beneficiaries, whether directly or indirectly. Decisions in some states grant a right of recovery to a "putative spouse",[60] but the "common law" spouse is not so favored.[61] In *Levy v. Louisiana*,[62] the

---

53. *Ala.*—Battles v. Pierson Chevrolet, Inc., 290 Ala. 98, 274 So.2d 281 (1973).
Del.—Pack v. Beech Aircraft Corp., 50 Del. 413, 132 A.2d 54, 67 A.L.R.2d 207 (1957).
Mo.—Toomes v. Continental Oil Co., 402 S.W.2d 321 (Mo.1966).

54. *Cal.*—Klingebiel v. Lockheed Aircraft Corp., 494 F.2d 345 (9th Cir. 1974); Wohlgemuth v. Meyer, 139 Cal.App.2d 326, 293 P.2d 816 (1956).
N.Y.—Caffaro v. Trayna, 35 N.Y.2d 245, 360 N.Y.S.2d 847, 319 N.E.2d 174 (1974).
N.C.—Brown v. Lumbermens Mut. Cas. Co., 285 N.C. 313, 204 S.E.2d 829 (1974).

55. O'Keefe v. Boeing Co., 335 F.Supp. 1104 (D.C.N.Y.1971).
Schenk v. Piper Aircraft Corp., 377 F. Supp. 477 (D.C.Pa.1974), aff'd 521 F.2d 1399 (3d Cir.).

56. See Speiser, § 10:01.
Downs v. United States, 522 F.2d 990 (6th Cir. 1975). (Reviewing Florida's preferred class system.)

57. E. g.: *Iowa*—Ia.Code § 633.537.
W.Va.—W.Va.Code § 5475[6].

58. Speiser, § 10:2.

59. Speiser, § 10:3.

60. *Cal.*—In re Paris Air Crash, 420 F.Supp. 880 (D.C.Cal.1976).
La.—King v. Cancienne, 316 So.2d 366 (La.1975).

61. *Cal.*—In re Paris Air Crash, supra, n. 60.
Pa.—Headen v. Pope & Talbot, Inc., 252 F.2d 739 (3d Cir. 1958).

62. 391 U.S. 68, 88 S.Ct. 1509, 20 L. Ed.2d 436 (1968), reh. denied 393 U.S. 898, 89 S.Ct. 65, 21 L.Ed.2d 185, on remand 253 La. 73, 216 So.2d 818.

United States Supreme Court ruled that illegitimate children may not be denied the right to sue for the wrongful death of their parent.[63] A companion case upheld the right of a mother to recover for the wrongful death of an illegitimate child.[64]

Damages under the wrongful death statutes are generally measured by the pecuniary loss to the beneficiaries,[65] and include the value of services and financial support which the survivor would have received from the decedent.[66] Some state and federal courts additionally allow recovery for "loss of inheritance",[67] on the theory that the beneficiary ultimately would have received some portion of accumulated earnings beyond decedent's direct life-time contributions. Non-pecuniary damages, such as mental anguish and loss of society and consortium, though traditionally disallowed,[68] are recoverable today in many jurisdictions.[69]

63. *Cal.*—Arizmendi v. System Leasing Corp., 15 Cal.App.3d 790, 93 Cal.Rptr. 411 (1971).

Fla.—Brown v. Bray, 300 So.2d 668 (Fla.1974).

N.J.—Schmoll v. Creecy, 54 N.J. 194, 254 A.2d 525, 38 A.L.R.3d 605 (1969).

Mich.—Cannon v. Transamerican Freight Lines, 37 Mich.App. 313, 194 N.W.2d 736 (1971).

Nev.—Weaks v. Mounter, 88 Nev. 118, 493 P.2d 1307 (1972).

N.Y.—In re Estate of Flores, 78 Misc.2d 481, 357 N.Y.S.2d 825 (1974).

64. Glona v. American Guar. & Liab. Ins. Co., 391 U.S. 73, 88 S.Ct. 1515, 20 L.Ed.2d 441 (1968), reh. denied 393 U.S. 898, 89 S.Ct. 66, 21 L.Ed.2d 185.

65. Although Lord Campbell's original Act provided for "such damages as [the jury] may think proportioned to the injury."

See Speiser § 3:1.

Recovery limited to pecuniary loss to survivors: Arizona, Illinois, Maine, Michigan, Minnesota, New Jersey, New Mexico, New York, Ohio, South Dakota, Vermont, Virginia, West Virginia.

66. Sea-Land Services, Inc. v. Gaudet, 414 U.S. 573, 94 S.Ct. 806, 39 L.Ed.2d 9 (1974), reh. denied 415 U.S. 986, 94 S.Ct. 1582, 39 L.Ed.2d 883.

Mass.—Alden v. Norwood Arena, Inc., 332 Mass. 267, 124 N.E.2d 505 (1955). (Loss of wife's services constitutes pecuniary loss.)

Ark.—Vines v. Arkansas Power & Light Co., 232 Ark. 173, 337 S.W.2d 722 (1960).

Colo.—Metcalfe v. Atchison, T. & S. F. R. Co., 491 F.2d 892 (10th Cir. 1974).

D.H.S.A.—Higginbotham v. Mobil Oil Corp., 360 F.Supp. 1140 (D.C.La. 1973), aff'd in part, rev'd in part 545 F.2d 422 (5th Cir.), cert. denied 434 U.S. 830, 98 S.Ct. 110, 54 L.Ed.2d 89 (Death on High Seas Act.)

67. O'Toole v. United States, 242 F.2d 308 (3d Cir. 1957) (F.T.C.A. case); Martin v. Atlantic Coast Line R. Co., 268 F.2d 397, 91 A.L.R.2d 472 (5th Cir. 1959) (F.E.L.A. case).

See Speiser, §§ 3:39 et seq.

68. American R. Co. v. Didricksen, 227 U.S. 145, 33 S.Ct. 224, 57 L.Ed. 456 (1913).

Cal.—Zeller v. Reid, 38 Cal.App.2d 622, 101 P.2d 730 (1940).

See Speiser & Malawer, "An American Tragedy: Damages for mental anguish of bereaved relatives in wrong-

69. See note 69 on page 629.

In actions brought under the survival-type statutes, damages are measured generally by the loss to decedent's estate.[70] This is variously computed as: (1) probable future earnings minus expenses;[71] (2) probable future accumulations;[72] or (3) probable future gross earnings[73]—in each case, reduced to present value. Under many "enlarged" or "hybrid" survival-wrongful death statutes, recovery may be had for decedent's conscious pain and suffering prior to death;[74] but of course may be barred where the death was instantaneous.[75]

---

ful death actions", 51 Tulane L.Rev. 1 (1976).

69. Mental Anguish

Arizona, Arkansas, Florida, Georgia, Kansas, Louisiana, Maryland, Puerto Rico, South Carolina, Virginia, West Virginia.

General rule against allowing recovery for mental anguish in wrongful death: Speiser, §§ 3:52, 3:55.

Loss of Society

Arizona, California, Florida, Hawaii, Idaho, Kansas, Louisiana, Michigan, Mississippi, Nevada, Puerto Rico, South Carolina, Texas, Utah, Virginia, Washington, West Virginia, Wisconsin, Wyoming.

Sea-Land Services v. Gaudet, supra, n. 66:

> "Recovery for loss of support has been universally recognized, and includes all the financial contributions that the decedent would have made to his dependents had he lived. Similarly, the overwhelming majority of state wrongful-death acts and courts interpreting the Death on the High Seas Act have permitted recovery for the monetary value of services the decedent provided and would have continued to provide but for his wrongful death. Such services include, for example, the nurture, training, education, and guidance that a child would have received had not the parent been wrongfully killed. Services the decedent performed at home or for his spouse are also compensable.

> Compensation for loss of society, however, presents a closer question. The term "society" embraces a broad range of mutual benefits each family member receives from the others' continued existence, including love, affection, care, attention, companionship, comfort, and protection. Unquestionably, the deprivation of these benefits by wrongful death is a grave loss to the decedent's dependents."

See Speiser § 3:48.

70. Speiser, § 3:2.

Conn.—McKirdy v. Cascio, 142 Conn. 80, 111 A.2d 555 (1955).

Iowa—Tedrow v. Fort Des Moines Community Services, Inc., 254 Iowa 193, 117 N.W.2d 62 (1962).

71. Feldman v. Allegheny Airlines, Inc., 382 F.Supp. 1271 (D.C.Conn. 1974), aff'd in part, rev'd in part 524 F.2d 384 (2d Cir.).

Scriven v. McDonald, 264 N.C. 727, 142 S.E.2d 585 (1965).

72. Jones v. Goodman, 114 F.Supp. 110 (D.C.Kan.1953).

Brophy v. Iowa-Illinois Gas & Elec. Co., 254 Iowa 895, 119 N.W.2d 865 (1963).

Goheen v. General Motors Corp., 263 Or. 145, 502 P.2d 223 (1972).

73. Georgia Code §§ 105–1308.

74. *Fla.*—Martin v. United Sec. Services, Inc., 314 So.2d 765 (Fla.1975).

---

75. See note 75 on page 630.

§ 22.4   SPECIFIC ACTIONS   Pt. 4

Many death acts provide for punitive damages.[76] Other statutes have been construed to allow punitives,[77] while many have been construed to exclude them.[78] Thus in many jurisdictions punitive damages may be levied against a tortfeasor for his wilful and wanton infliction of *injury*, but none if he succeeds in killing his victim.

Although the "collateral source rule"—mitigating damages to the extent they have been otherwise compensated [79]—generally applies to wrongful death actions,[80] in practice courts are reluctant to reduce awards on this ground.[81] Insurance proceeds to the beneficiaries or the estate are uniformly held irrelevant to determination of wrongful death damages,[82] as are social security [83] or pension benefits,[84] or ben-

Iowa—Fitzgerald v. Hale, 247 Iowa 1194, 78 N.W.2d 509 (1956).

La.—McFarland v. Illinois Central R. Co., 241 La. 15, 127 So.2d 183, 87 A. L.R.2d 246 (1961).

Tenn.—Knight v. Nurseryman Supply, Inc., 248 F.Supp. 925 (D.C.Tenn.1965).

75. In re Dearborn Marine Serv., Inc., 499 F.2d 263 (5th Cir. 1974), reh. denied 512 F.2d 1061; Feldman v. Allegheny Airlines, Inc., 382 F.Supp. 1271 (D.C.Conn.1974), aff'd in part, rev'd in part 524 F.2d 384 (2d Cir.); Cincotta v. United States, 362 F.Supp. 386 (D.C.Md.1973).

76. Colorado, Kentucky, Massachusetts, Montana, New Mexico, Nevada, North Carolina, South Carolina, Texas.

See Speiser, § 3:4.

77. See McClelland and Truett, "Survival of punitive damages in wrongful death cases," 8 U.S.F.L.Rev. 585 (1974).

Comment, "Punitive Damages in Wrongful Death", 29 Clev.St.L.Rev. 301 (1971).

La Bella v. Southwestern Bell Tel. Co., 224 Mo.App. 708, 24 S.W.2d 1072 (1930); Moffa v. Perkins Trucking Co., 200 F.Supp. 183 (D.C.Conn. 1961); Kindellan v. Arwood Material Co., 338 F.Supp. 1210 (D.C.Tenn. 1972).

78. *Cal.*—Pease v. Beech Aircraft Corp., 38 Cal.App.3d 450, 113 Cal. Rptr. 416 (1974).

Del.—Reynolds v. Willis, 58 Del. 368, 209 A.2d 760 (1965).

Ill.—Mattyasovszky v. West Towns Bus Co., 21 Ill.App.3d 46, 313 N.E.2d 496 (1974), aff'd 61 Ill.2d 31, 330 N.E.2d 509.

N.Y.—Barrett v. State, 85 Misc.2d 456, 378 N.Y.S.2d 946 (1976).

F.E.L.A.—Kozar v. Chesapeake & O. Ry. Co., 449 F.2d 1238 (6th Cir. 1971).

79. See Am.Jur.2d Damages § 206.

80. See Speiser § 6:7.

81. *Cal.*—Stathos v. Lemich, 213 Cal. App.2d 52, 28 Cal.Rptr. 462 (1963). (Damages for future support not to be reduced by amounts from other sources).

Conn.—Perry v. Allegheny Airlines, Inc., 489 F.2d 1349 (2d Cir. 1974). (Proceeds from life insurance properly excluded from evidence).

82. Bangor & A. R. Co. v. Jones, 36 F. 2d 886 (1st Cir. 1929).

Ky.—Taylor v. Jennison, 335 S.W.2d 902 (Ky.1960).

La.—Trahan v. Gulf Crews, Inc., 246 So.2d 280 (La.App.1971), rev'd on

83. See note 83 on page 631.

84. See note 84 on page 631.

630

efits to be derived from the remarriage of decedent's spouse.⁸⁵ On the latter point, counsel for plaintiff is advised to obtain a pre-trial order forbidding defense reference to spouse's remarriage.⁸⁶

Although many wrongful death statutes originally contained damage limitation provisions,⁸⁷ today no state limits the damages recoverable for pecuniary loss from wrongful death.⁸⁸ Although the limitations had withstood attacks on their constitutionality,⁸⁹ they

other grounds 260 La. 29, 255 So.2d 63 (Jones Act).

N.Y.—Healy v. Rennert, 9 N.Y.2d 202, 213 N.Y.S.2d 44, 173 N.E.2d 777 (1961).

Va.—Walthew v. Davis, 201 Va. 557, 111 S.E.2d 784 (1960).

83. United States v. Harue Hayashi, 282 F.2d 599, 84 A.L.R.2d 754 (9th Cir. 1960).

84. Hughes v. Clinchfield R. Co., 289 F.Supp. 374 (D.C.Tenn.1968) (F.E.L. A.); Phelan v. Motor Vehicle Acc. Indemnification Corp., 52 Misc.2d 341, 275 N.Y.S.2d 873 (1966), aff'd 31 A. D.2d 758, 298 N.Y.S.2d 669.

85. See Speiser, § 6:12

Brady v. Finklea, 400 F.2d 352 (5th Cir. 1968).

Cal.—Barth v. B. F. Goodrich Tire Co., 265 Cal.App.2d 228, 71 Cal.Rptr. 306 (1968).

Ga.—Wright v. Dilbeck, 122 Ga.App. 214, 176 S.E.2d 715 (1970).

Ill.—Hardware State Bank v. Cotner, 55 Ill.2d 240, 302 N.E.2d 257 (1973).

La.—McFarland v. Illinois Central R. Co., 241 La. 15, 127 So.2d 183, 87 A. L.R.2d 246 (1961).

Mich.—Bunda v. Hardwick, 376 Mich. 640, 138 N.W.2d 305 (1965).

N.Y.—Luddy v. State, 30 A.D.2d 993, 294 N.Y.S.2d 87 (1968), aff'd 25 N.Y. 2d 773, 303 N.Y.S.2d 522, 250 N.E.2d 581.

S.C.—Smith v. Wells, 258 S.C. 316, 188 S.E.2d 470 (1972).

Tenn.—Phelps v. Magnavox Co. of Tennessee, 497 S.W.2d 898 (Tenn.App. 1972).

Wash.—Stuart v. Consolidated Foods Corp., 6 Wash.App. 841, 496 P.2d 527 (1972).

Contra:

Fla.—West's Ann.Fla.Stats. § 768, 18(6) (c).

Wis.—Jensen v. Heritage Mut. Ins. Co., 23 Wis.2d 344, 127 N.W.2d 228 (1964).

See Note, Damages for Wrongful Death and the Possibility of Remarriage, 32 U.Pitts.L.Rev. 119 (1970).

Note, Remarriage and Wrongful Death, 50 Marquette L.Rev. 653 (1967).

86. See 1959 Belli Seminar, Trial & Tort Trends 265, 266.

Speiser, Exclusion of Evidence of Remarriage of Plaintiff-Widow on Wrongful Death Cases, 1956 Belli Seminar, Trial & Tort Trends 233–238.

87. Speiser, §§ 7:1, 7:2.

88. Speiser, § 7:2 (Supp.1978).

See Note, "Wrongful Death Recovery Limitations—R.I.P.", 17 De Paul L. Rev. 385 (1968).

"Wrongful Death Limitations in Oregon —A Rational Result or a Historical Mistake", 1 Willamette L.Rev. 616, 624.

89. Ill.—Butler v. Chicago Transit Auth., 38 Ill.2d 361, 231 N.E.2d 429 (1967).

Mo.—Glick v. Ballentine Produce, Inc., 396 S.W.2d 607 (Mo.1965), appeal dism'd 385 U.S. 5, 87 S.Ct. 44, 17 L. Ed.2d 5.

N.H.—Gibbs v. Prior, 107 N.H. 218, 220 A.2d 151 (1966).

have succumbed generally to legislative recognition of the right of the innocent victim of tortious conduct to full compensatory recovery.[90] The United States is still a party, however, to the Montreal Agreement of May, 1966, limiting recovery for wrongful death in the course of international air travel to $75,000.[91]

90. See, citations in n. 88, supra.

Kilberg v. Northeast Airlines, Inc., 9 N.Y.2d 34, 211 N.Y.S.2d 133, 172 N.E.2d 526 (1961).

91. See Speiser, § 7:5.

The United States and other countries have signed the "Guatemala Protocol" of March, 1971, to amend the Warsaw Convention, limiting liability for injuries and death in international air travel to $100,000.

See Tompkins, The Warsaw Convention and the Proposed Revisions of 1971, 6 The Forum 151 (1971).

§§ 22.5–23.0 are reserved for supplementary material.

CHAPTER 23

WRONGFUL BIRTH AND WRONGFUL LIFE

Table of Sections

Sec.
23.1 In General.
23.2 Common Law View—No Damages Suffered.
23.3 Wrongful Birth—Origin of Action—Normal Children.
23.4 —— Defective Children.
23.5 —— What Injuries Are Compensable.
23.6 "Wrongful Life"—In General.
23.7 —— Traditional Damages Incapable of Measurement.
23.8 —— Child's Suit Against Laboratory for Negligent Testing.
23.9 —— Birth Under Adverse Circumstances.
23.10 Injuries Resulting from Pre-conception Negligence.

§ 23.1 In General

Advancements in the science of genetics and embryology,[1] the development of new techniques of birth control and sterilization, and social policy changes sanctioning abortion,[2] have combined to foster

1. See Lintgen, "Impact of Medical Knowledge on Law Relating to Prenatal Injuries," U.Pa.L.Rev. 553 (1962); Shaw, "Genetically Defective Children: Legal Considerations," Am. J.L. & Med. 3:333–40 (1977).

2. Note, "Wrongful Birth in the Abortion Context—Critique of existing case law and proposal for future actions." Denver L.J. 53:501–20 (1976); Foley, "Abortion: An inspection of legalizing its destruction," U.Cin. L.Rev. 46:725–821 (1977); Benda, "Impact of Constitutional Law on the Protection of Unborn Human Life: some comparable remarks," Human Rights 6:223–43 (1977); Lenhard, "Abortion and Prenatal Injury: A Legal and Philosophical Analysis"; Pilpel, "Voluntary Sterilization: A Human Right", 7 Col. Human Rights L.Rev. 105 (1975); Dourlen-Rollier, "Legal Problems Related to Abortion and Menstrual Regulation," 7 Col. Human Rights L.Rev. 120 (1975); Quay, "Justifiable Abortion—Medical and Legal Foundations," 49 Geo.L.J. 395 (1961); Niswander, "Medical Abortion Practices in the United States," 17 W.Res.L.Rev. 403 (1965).

Betancourt v. Gaylor, 136 N.J.Super. 69, 344 A.2d 336 (1975) (Citing legal recognition of a woman's right to control her own bodily functions in Roe v. Wade, 410 U.S. 113, 93 S.Ct. 705, 35 L.Ed.2d 147 (1973), reh. denied 410 U.S. 959, 93 S.Ct. 1409, 35 L.Ed.2d 694); Custudio v. Bauer, 251 Cal. App.2d 303, 59 Cal.Rptr. 463, 27 A.L. R.3d 884 (1967) (Sterilization not contrary to public policy, noting that Griswold v. Connecticut, 381 U.S. 479, 85 S.Ct. 1678, 14 L.Ed.2d 510 (1965) gives constitutional protection to dissemination of birth-control in-

§ 23.1   SPECIFIC ACTIONS   Pt. 4

the development of a new concept in tort liability, "wrongful birth" and "wrongful life." [3]

Negligence in sterilization and abortion procedures,[4] or in genetic and obstetric counselling [5] or in drug manufacture and retailing,[6] has predicated tort claims against physicians, hospitals, drug manufacturers and retailers, not only by parents, but also by or on behalf of the "negligently conceived and born" children. Damages have been claimed, and awarded, for the birth of normal, healthy children, as well as for children suffering congenital defects. "Wrongful life" suits have even been brought by illegitimate children against their parents for damages suffered in being born out of wedlock.

§ 23.2   Common Law View—No Damages Suffered

The first courts to consider the question of "wrongful birth" held that, as a matter of law, no cause of action for damages could be stated by parents for the birth of a child, on the theory that any birth was a blessing and a benefit to the parents.[7] A Pennsylvania

formation); Troppi v. Scarf, 31 Mich.App. 240, 187 N.W.2d 511 (1971) (Noting state statutes designed to foster birth-control); Christensen v. Thornby, 192 Minn. 123, 255 N.W. 620 (1934) (Vasectomy to protect wife from dangerous pregnancy not against public policy); Ziemba v. Sternberg, 45 A.D.2d 230, 357 N.Y.S. 2d 265 (1974) (Noting statutory changes authorizing abortion).

3. See Comment, Wrongful Birth, the Emerging Status of a New Tort, 8 St. Mary's L.J. 140 (1976); Note, "Liability for wrongfully causing one to be born: development of a tort for 'wrongful life'", U.W.L.A. L.Rev. 10:53–66 (1978); Tedesclin, "Tort Liability for "Wrongful Life'", 7 J. Family L. 465 (1967). Note: " 'Wrongful Life'—A New Tort?", 17 Hastings L.J. 400 (1965–66).

4. See Note, "Sterilization and Family Planning: The Physicians Liability," 56 Ga.L.J. 976 (1967–68) Comment, "Pregnancy After Sterilization: Causes of Action for Parent and Child", 12 J. Family L. 635 (1972–73). Note, "The Birth of a Child Following an Ineffective Sterilization Operation as Legal Damage," 7 Utah L.Rev. 808 (1964–65). Note, "Remedy for the Reluctant Parent: Physicians' Liability for the Post-Sterilization Conception and Birth of Unplanned Children," 27 U.Fla.L.Rev. 158 (1974–75).

5. Holt v. Nelson, 11 Wash.App. 230, 523 P.2d 211 (1974) (Child born a spastic quadriplegic; doctor negligently failed to inform plaintiffs that cesarean section could have been performed at earlier date).

See also NacRauf, Birth Control and Malpractice, 10 Trial L.Q. 86 (1974).

6. Note, "Unwanted Pregnancy and the Pill—The Question of Liability of the Manufacturer," 41 Cin.L.Rev. 335 (1972). Comment, "Strict Liability: A 'Lady in Waiting' for Wrongful Birth Cases," 11 Calif. Western L. Rev. 136 (1974). "Liability for Failure of Birth Control Methods," Col. L.Rev. 76:1187–204 (1976).

7. Christensen v. Thorny, 192 Minn. 123, 255 N.W. 620 (1934) (Plaintiff underwent vasectomy to protect wife from dangerous second pregnancy: "The purpose of the operation was to save the wife from the hazards to her

court, in *Shaheen v. Knight*,⁸ stated: "We are of the opinion that to allow damages for the normal birth of a normal child is foreign to the universal public sentiment of the people . . . . To allow damages in a suit such as this would mean that the physician would have to pay for the fun, joy and affection which the plaintiff . . . will have in the rearing and educating of this child. . . . In our opinion to allow such damages would be against public policy." The *Shaheen* "overriding benefits" rationale was echoed in a 1975 Delaware case, *Coleman v. Garrison*,⁹ where the court held that "the value of a human life outweighs any 'damage' which might be said to follow from the fact of birth, and recovery on any such thesis would violate both our public policy and the law governing proveable damages." ¹⁰ The Wisconsin Supreme Court, in 1974, rejected a wrongful birth cause of action on the grounds that holding a doctor liable for the expenses of rearing a normal child would create an unreasonable burden, "wholly out of proportion to the culpability involved" in failing to timely diagnose pregnancy.¹¹

life which were incident to childbirth. It was not the alleged purpose to save the expense incident and pregnancy and delivery. The wife has survived. Instead of losing his wife, the plaintiff has been blessed with the fatherhood of another child. The expenses alleged are incident to the bearing of a child, and their avoidance is remote from the avowed purpose of the operation.").

8. 11 Pa.D. & C.2d 41, 6 Lycoming County 19 (1957).

9. 349 A.2d 8 (Del.1975).

10. See also Terrell v. Garcia, 496 S. W.2d 124 (Tex.Civ.App.1973), refused n. r. e., cert. denied 415 U.S. 927, 94 S.Ct. 1434, 39 L.Ed.2d 484 ("Who can place a price tag on a child's or the parental pride in a child's achievement? Even if we consider only the economic point of view, a child is some security for the parents' old age. Rather than attempt to value these intangible benefits, our courts have simply determined that public sentiment recognizes that these benefits to parents outweigh their economic loss in rearing and educating a healthy, normal child.").

11. Rieck v. Medical Protective Co., 64 Wis.2d 514, 219 N.W.2d 242 (1974). "To permit the parents to keep their child and shift the entire cost of its upbringing to a physician who failed to determine or inform them of the fact of pregnancy would be to create a new category of surrogate parent. Every child's smile, every bond of love and affection, every reason for parent pride in a child's achievements, every contribution by the child to the welfare and well-being of the family and parents, is to remain with the mother and father. For the most part, these are intangible benefits, but they are nonetheless real. On the other hand, every financial cost or detriment—what the complaint terms "hard money damages" —including the cost of food, clothing and education, would be shifted to the physician who allegedly failed to timely diagnose the fact of pregnancy. We hold that such result would be wholly out of proportion to the culpability involved, and that the allowance of recovery would place too unreasonable a burden upon physician under the facts and circumstances here alleged.

§ 23.3 Wrongful Birth—Origin of Action—Normal Children

The 1967 California case of *Custudio v. Bauer* [12] rejected the *Shaheen* reasoning and upheld the complaint of a husband and wife against three physicians for unsuccessful tubal ligation surgery which resulted in the birth of the couple's tenth child. The Court held that damages could lie "to replenish the family exchequer so that the new arrival will not deprive the other members of the family of what was planned as their just share of the family income." In the same year, a Federal Court in West Virginia upheld the complaint of another victim of unsuccessful tubal ligation for damages of the medical expenses of the birth and the wife's anguish and physical suffering during pregnancy.[13]

James Hullverson, Esquire,[14] relates a similar situation which created a case [15] of first impression in Missouri. Plaintiff was a 23-year-old woman who had just delivered her third illegitimate child. Following this, the woman elected to have bilateral tubal ligation. This was attempted, and tissue samples were sent to the pathology lab at the hospital where the tubal ligation was undertaken.

The pathology report indicated that specimen A was fallopian tube tissue, and that specimen B was normal tissue and not fallopian tube tissue. The attending surgeon failed to wait the results of the pathology report, failed to read the report which was thereafter lodged in the hospital record, and failed to read the report which the hospital indicated was subsequently mailed to him. The treating doctor who referred plaintiff to the surgeon was also to have received a mailed copy of the path report, according to the hospital.

Since nothing was done, it was shortly thereafter that the woman became pregnant again, ultimately delivering twins. The mother thus had five illegitimate children, had always been on ADC, and the father of the children was in the penitentiary at the time of trial.

The jury returned a verdict of $110,000 to compensate plaintiff for past and future pain and suffering of her body and mind, medical expenses incident to the pregnancy and a subsequent repeat tubal ligation, and the cost of raising the twins, set-off by any benefits conferred on plaintiff by reason of the births.

---

12. 251 Cal.App.2d 303, 59 Cal.Rptr. 463 (1967).

13. Bishop v. Byrne, 265 F.Supp. 460 (D.C.W.Va.1967).

14. James E. Hullverson, Esquire, Eleventh Floor, 722 Chestnut Street, St. Louis, Mo.

15. Davis v. Taylor, Missouri, St. Louis Circuit Court, No. 782–254, April 18, 1979.

In *Troppi v. Scarf*,[16] where a pharmacist had negligently supplied plaintiff's wife with tranquilizers rather than the prescribed birth control pills, the court rejected the *Shaheen* "overriding benefit" theory and applied instead the mitigation rule of the Restatement, Torts, Section 920 [17] allowing the jury to deduct the value of any benefits conferred on the parents by virtue of the birth of a child, from the gross damages awardable.[18] The Court rejected the argument that plaintiff was required to mitigate damages by aborting the child [19] or placing the child for adoption.[20]

The *Troppi* approach has been followed in the majority of subsequent cases upholding a cause of action for the birth of a healthy child

---

16. 31 Mich.App. 240, 187 N.W.2d 511 (1971).

17. § 290 reads: "Where defendant's tortious conduct has caused harm to the plaintiff or to his property and in so doing has conferred upon the plaintiff a special benefit to the interest which was harmed, the value of the benefit conferred is considered in mitigation of damages, where this is equitable".

18. Note, "Damages—The Not So Blessed 'Blessed Event'," 46 N.Car.L. Rev. 948 (1968); Comment, "Busting the Blessed Balloon: Liability for the Birth of an Unplanned Child," 39 Albany L.Rev. 221 (1974–75).

19. "Many women confronted with an unwanted pregnancy will abort the fetus, legally or illegally. Some will bear the child and place him for adoption. Many will bear the child, keep and rear him. The defendant does not have the right to insist that the victim of his negligence have the emotional and mental makeup of a woman who is willing to abort or place a child for adoption." 187 N.W.2d 511, 520.

20. See also Stills v. Gratton, 55 Cal. App.3d 698, 127 Cal.Rptr. 652 (1976) ("No court can say as a matter of law that every mother, wed or unwed, is required to abort or place her child for adoption"); Rivera v. State, 94 Misc.2d 157, 404 N.Y.S.2d 950 (1978) ("We are of the opinion that a rule of law which required claimant to have an abortion would constitute an invasion of privacy of the grossest and most pernicious kind. The decision to have an abortion or not is for the individual to make, based on whatever religious, philosophical or moral principles the individual may adhere to, or upon consideration of the medical risks involved. Just as the law may not impose the philosophy of one group upon the public at large, neither may it permit the public to invade the province of the individual in an area as private as sovereignty over one's own body. We find that claimant had no obligation to mitigate damages by undergoing an abortion."); Ziemba v. Sternberg, 45 A.D.2d 230, 357 N.Y.S.2d 265 (1974) ("The right to have an abortion may not be automatically converted to an obligation to have one"); Martineau v. Nelson, 311 Minn. 92, 247 N.W.2d 409 (1976) ("Moreover, plaintiffs were likewise not negligent in failing to have an abortion or give up their child for adoption. The policy of the law would be thwarted if plaintiffs were forced to make such moral and ethical choices regarding themselves and their child under a cloud of contributory fault.").

as a result of unsuccessful vasectomy,[21] tubal ligation,[22] abortion,[23] or failure to timely diagnose birth defects [24] or pregnancy [25] so as to pre-

21. Hackworth v. Hart, 474 S.W.2d 377 (Ky.1971) (Defendants assured plaintiffs that vasectomy operation was "100 percent sure to produce infertility," gave only one post-operation semen test. Statute of limitations began to run when pregnancy was or should have been discovered.); Sherlock v. Stillwater Clinic, 260 N.W.2d 169 (Minn.1977) ($19,500 jury verdict reversed and remanded for failure to instruct jury to deduct value of benefits. Question of negligence in vasectomy post-operative care for jury.); Cox v. Stretton, 77 Misc.2d 155, 352 N.Y.S.2d 834 (1974) (Complaint of negligence and breach of contract for unsuccessful vasectomy states cause of action on behalf of plaintiff parents).

22. Anonymous v. Hosp., 33 Conn.Sup. 126, 366 A.2d 204 (1976) (Complaint for malpractice in negligent tubal ligation states cause of action for damages of medical expenses, pain and suffering, mental distress, and cost of rearing child, to be mitigated by value of joy, satisfaction, and companionship); Jackson v. Anderson, 230 So.2d 503 (Fla.App.1970); Betancourt v. Gaylor, 136 N.J.Super. 69, 344 A.2d 336 (1975) (Damages for costs, emotional upset, and physical inconvenience of rearing child may be recovered in suit based on birth of healthy child after unsuccessful tubal ligation: "In light of the law's recent recognition of a woman's right to control her own bodily functions, as evidenced by the United States Supreme Court decision in Roe v. Wade, 410 U.S. 113 . . . the trier of fact should be permitted to evaluate whatever damages plaintiffs are entitled to"); Bowman v. Davis, 48 Ohio St.2d 41, 356 N.E.2d 496 (1976) (Cause of action states for negligence in unsuccessful tubal ligation. Verdict of $450,000 for wife for pain and suffering, change in family status, and cost of rearing twins, one retarded, and $12,500 to husband for loss of consortium, affirmed: "The choice not to procreate, as part of one's right to privacy, has become (subject to certain limitations) a constitutional guarantee. . . . For this court to endorse a policy that makes physicians liable for the foreseeable consequences of all negligently performed operations *except* those involving sterilization would constitute an impermissible infringement of a fundamental right."); Vaughn v. Shelton, 514 S.W.2d 870 (Tenn.App. 1974) (Directed verdict for defendants reversed: ("It does not require expert medical evidence to prove that if both of the fallopian tubes are severed and closed, the patient would thereby be rendered immune from pregnancy.") But see Coleman v. Garrison, 327 A.2d 757 (Del.Super. 1974), aff'd 349 A.2d 8 (Del.) ("[S]ince ensuing pregnancy does not necessarily indicate improper performance of the operation, *res ipsa loquitur* is not applicable.").

23. Stills v. Gratton, 55 Cal.App.3d 698, 127 Cal.Rptr. 652 (1976) (Nonsuit against plaintiff mother improper where damages claimed for birth of healthy child after unsuccessful abortion. Plaintiff "should be permitted to recover all the damages to which she is entitled under ordinary tort principles.").

24. Gildiner v. Thomas Jefferson Univ. Hosp., 451 F.Supp. 692 (D.C.Pa.1978) (Physician incorrectly advised that results of amniocentesis tests indicated that child would be born free of Tay-Sachs disease. Held, cause of action stated for medical expenses and emotional suffering.).

25. Ziemba v. Sternberg, 45 A.D.2d 230, 357 N.Y.S.2d 265 (1974) (Cause of action for failing to diagnose preg-

clude the option of abortion. Recoverable damages have included costs of the pregnancy and delivery,[26] costs of medical complications,[27] the mother's pain and suffering,[28] mental anguish,[29] loss of consortium of both husband and wife,[30] husband's loss of wife's services,[31] and the cost of rearing the child to majority,[32] sub-

nancy "within reasonable time of commencement of pregnancy" not barred by plaintiff's failure to undergo abortion later: "The right to have an abortion may not be automatically converted to an obligation to have one. The decision whether or not to undertake that medical procedure must rest on a number of factors, including the stage to which pregnancy has progressed, the health and condition of the woman at that time and the professional judgment and counsel received."); Chapman v. Schultz, 47 A.D.2d 806, 367 N.Y.S.2d 1018 (1975); Debora S. v. Sapega, 56 A.D. 2d 841, 392 N.Y.S.2d 79 (1977) (Negligent failure to diagnose pregnancy of plaintiff 15 year old rape victim, precluding abortion in early stages of pregnancy, states cause of action for malpractice).

26. Bishop v. Byrne, 265 F.Supp. 460 (D.C.W.Va.1967) (Husband's claim for $684 medical expenses allowed as appendage to wife's action for mental and physical suffering in jurisdictional amount).

See also Coleman v. Garrison, 327 A.2d 757 (Del.Super.1974), aff'd 349 A.2d 8 (Del.).

27. Sherlock v. Stillwater Clinic, supra, n. 21.

Bishop v. Byrne, supra, n. 26.
Custudio v. Bauer, supra, n. 12.

28. *Cal.*—Custudio v. Bauer, supra, n. 12.
Del.—Coleman v. Garrison, supra, n. 26.
Mich.—Troppi v. Scarf, supra, n. 16.
Minn.—Sherlock v. Stillwater Clinic, supra, n. 21.
N.Y.—Ziemba v. Sternberg, supra, n. 25.
Ohio—Bowman v. Davis, supra n. 22.

W.Va.—Bishop v. Byrne, supra, n. 26.

29. *Conn.*—Anonymous v. Hosp., supra, n. 22.
Del.—Coleman v. Garrison, supra, n. 26.
N.J.—Betancourt v. Gaylor, supra, n. 22.
N.Y.—Ziemba v. Sternberg, supra, n. 25.

30. *Del.*—Coleman v. Garrison, supra, n. 26.

Ohio—Bowman v. Davis, supra, n. 22.
N.Y.—Ziemba v. Sternberg, supra, n. 25.

31. *Del.*—Coleman v. Garrison, supra, n. 26.

N.Y.—Ziemba v. Sternberg, supra, n. 25.

32. *Cal.*—Pearson v. Pharmacy, (Los Angeles Sup.Ct., Nov. 1971) (Pharmacy supplied sleeping pills instead of contraceptives. Jury verdict of $42,000 for costs of rearing child to majority.) (Reported in ATLA Newsletter, Vol. 15, No. 4, p. 166, May, 1972.); Baig v. Glendale Hosp. (Sup. Ct., Los Angeles, Cal., No. C 123998, July 18, 1978) Reported in 22 ATLA L.Rep. 40 ($100,000 jury verdict for parents of unplanned child after unsuccessful tubal ligation, of which $75,000 represented costs of rearing and educating).

Conn.—Anonymous v. Hosp., supra, n. 22.
Mich.—Troppi v. Scarf, supra, n. 16.
Minn.—Sherlock v. Stillwater Clinic, supra, n. 21.
N.J.—Betancourt v. Gaylor, supra, n. 22.
N.Y.—Cox v. Stretton, supra, n. 21; Ziemba v. Sternberg, supra, n. 25.
Ohio—Bowman v. Davis, supra, n. 22.

ject to the Restatement Section 920 "benefit" deduction. Some courts have approved damages for "change in family status," [33] in recognition that the mother's care will be spread over a greater number. An action on behalf of the siblings for diminution of parental affection, however, has been disallowed.[34] Several decisions have simply permitted "damages according to normal tort principles." [35] Courts adhering to the "overriding benefits" rule may allow damages for expenses and injuries related to the pregnancy and delivery, and refuse damages for rearing or other prospective expenses.[36]

§ 23.4 Wrongful Birth—Defective Children

Wrongful birth cases involving deformed children have addressed similar issues. In *Gleitman v. Cosgrove*,[37] parents brought an action against their doctors for failure to advise of the congenital consequences of rubella (German measles), which the mother had contracted during pregnancy,[38] thereby precluding abortion. The Court held that "the sanctity of the single human life" [39] prevented

33. *Cal.*—Custudio v. Bauer, supra, n. 12 ("Where the mother survives without casualty there is still some loss. She must spread her society, comfort, care, protection and support over a larger group. If this change in family status can be measured economically it should be as compensable as the former loss.").

Ohio—Bowman v. Davis, supra, n. 22 ("[T]he value of Mrs. Bowman's society, comfort, care and protection (including consortium) lost to 'other members of the family' ").

34. Cox v. Stretton, supra, n. 21.

35. *Cal.*—Stills v. Gratton, supra, n. 23.
Mich.—Troppi v. Scarf, supra, n. 16.
N.J.—Betancourt v. Gaylor, supra, n. 22.
N.Y.—Ziemba v. Sternberg, supra, n. 25.
W.Va.—Bishop v. Byrne, supra, n. 26.
See, generally Barrett, "Damages for Wrongful Birth," 21 Cleveland St.L. Rev. 34 (1972).

36. Coleman v. Garrison, supra, n. 26.

See also Bushman v. Burns Clinic Medical Center, 83 Mich.App. 453, 268 N. W.2d 683 (1978).

37. 49 N.J. 22, 227 A.2d 689 (1967).

38. See Roy and Deutsch, "The Congenital Rubella Syndrome—Ocular Pathogenesis and Related Embryology." 62 Am.J.Opthal. 236 (1966). Sheridan, "Final Report of a Prospective Study of Children Whose Mothers Had Rubella in Early Pregnancy," 1964, Brit.Med.J. 536.

39. "It is basic to the human condition to seek life and hold on to it however heavily burdened. If Jeffrey could have been asked as to whether his life should be snuffed out before his full term of gestation could run its course, our felt intuition of human nature tells us he would almost surely choose life with defects as against no life at all. 'For the living there is hope, but for the dead there is none.' Theocritus. See Ryan (M.D.), 'Humane Abortion Laws and the Health Needs of Society,' 17 West.Res.L. Rev. 424, 428–430 (1965).

the allowing of tort damages for the denial of the opportunity to take an embryonic life: "Though we sympathize with the unfortunate situation in which these parents find themselves, we firmly believe the right of the child to live is greater than and precludes their right not to endure emotional and financial injury." A 1970 New York case involving an identical fact situation dismissed the parents' claim as one which should await legislative action, noting that compensatory damages for the mental anguish suffered would be virtually impossible to evaluate in view of the benefits conferred by parenthood.[40]

The Ohio case of *Bowman v. Davis*[41] involved an unsuccessful tubal ligation which resulted in the birth of twins, one normal and one defective. The Supreme Court of Ohio upheld the jury award of $450,000 to the parents for the foreseeable consequences including the costs of raising the child, as well as $12,500 to the husband for loss of consortium and expenses, despite the "consent form" signed by plaintiffs, on the grounds that plaintiffs had never released the hospital or physicians from liability for negligence. A 1975 Texas case[42] involv-

"The right to life is inalienable in our society. A court cannot say what defects should prevent an embryo from being allowed life such that denial of the opportunity to terminate the existence of a defective child in embryo can support a cause for action. Examples of famous persons who have had great achievement despite physical defects come readily to mind, and many of us can think of examples close to home. A child need not be perfect to have a worthwhile life.

"We are not faced here with the necessity of balancing the mother's life against that of her child. The sanctity of the single human life is the decisive factor in this suit in tort. Eugenic considerations are not controlling. We are not talking here about the breeding of prize cattle. It may have been easier for the mother and less expensive for the father to have terminated the life of their child while he was an embryo, but these alleged detriments cannot stand against the preciousness of the single human life to support a remedy in tort. See Jonathan Swift, 'A Modest Proposal' in Gulliver's Travels and Other Writings, 488–496 (Modern Library ed. 1958)." 227 A.2d at 693.

40. Stewart v. Long Island College Hosp., 35 A.D.2d 531, 313 N.Y.S.2d 502 (1979) appeal dism'd 27 N.Y.2d 804, 315 N.Y.S.2d 863, 264 N.E.2d 354, aff'd 30 N.Y.2d 695, 332 N.Y.S.2d 640, 283 N.E.2d 616.

41. 48 Ohio St.2d 41, 356 N.E.2d 496 (1976).

42. Jacobs v. Theimer, 519 S.W.2d 846 (Tex.1975):

"Insofar as the parents sue for damages for all expenses incurred and to be incurred in raising the child and for their own mental or emotional anguish, the objection is more understandable. The objection is to an award based on the quality of life and as to the pluses and minuses of parental mind and emotion.

"The economic burden related solely to the physical defects of the child is a different matter which is free from the above objection. These expenses lie within the methods of proof by which the courts are accustomed to determine awards in personal injury cases. No public policy argument should be interposed to that recovery."

ing rubella held that a cause of action existed for the medical expenses of required treatment of the congenital defects, but that an award for emotional damages would necessarily involve impermissible speculation. In the same year the Wisconsin Supreme Court came to the same conclusion in a rubella case.[43] The New York cases have similarly established the rule that damages for emotional injuries are not recoverable in such cases.[44] Thus although damages for parents' emotional distress are allowed for wrongful birth of a healthy child, they have yet to be awarded for the wrongful birth of a congenitally defective child.[45]

---

43. Dumer v. St. Michael's Hosp., 69 Wis.2d 766, 233 N.W.2d 372 (1975) ("If they obtain a favorable finding as to all of these facts they then are entitled to the damages they have sustained because of the deformity and defects of the child. Their damages must be limited to those expenses which they have reasonably and necessarily suffered, and will to a reasonable medical certainty suffer in the future by reason of the additional medical, hospital and supportive expense occasioned by the deformities of the child as contrasted to a normal, healthy child.").

44. Howard v. Lecher, 53 A.D.2d 420, 386 N.Y.S.2d 460 (1976), aff'd 42 N.Y.2d 109, 397 N.Y.S.2d 363, 366 N.E.2d 64 (1977) (Physicians failed to advise parent of likelihood of child's congenital affliction with Tay-sachs disease, from which child eventually died); Park v. Chessin, 60 A.D.2d 80, 400 N.Y.S.2d 110 (1977), modif. 46 N.Y.2d 401, 413 N.Y.S.2d 895, 386 N.E.2d 807 (Failure to advise of likelihood of infant suffering congenital kidney disease: "The injuries that flow therefrom include the economic injuries represented by proveable medical and support expenses during the lifetime of the child . . . . Specifically excluded from recovery under the parents' cause of action, however, are damages flowing from emotional distress, or mental anguish, to the mother, owing to the inability to calculate, and the absence of duty . . . ."); Becker v. Schwartz, 60 A.D.2d 857, 400 N.Y.S.2d 119 (1977), modif. 46 N.Y.2d 401, 413 N.Y.S.2d 895, 386 N.E.2d 807 (Failure to advise of availability of amniocentesis test to determine existence of congenital defects—cause of action for psychiatric injuries or emotional distress dismissed).

But see Karlsons v. Guerinot, 57 A.D.2d 73, 394 N.Y.S.2d 933 (1977) (Complaint for damages for mental anguish from birth of mongoloid child states cause of action).

45. On the apparent rationale that, in the defective child cases, the parents desired to conceive and bear children, and thus the wrongful birth is attended by complex measurement of damages; whereas in the cases of wrongful birth of a healthy child, the parents wished to be free of any birth at all, and the damages (supposedly) are therefore more amenable to computation.

See Betancourt v. Gaylor, 136 N.J.Super. 69, 344 A.2d 336 (1975).

§ 23.5 Wrongful Birth—What Injuries Are Compensable

The disparity among jurisdictions as to just what damages may be recovered by the parents is evidenced in two 1979 cases,—*Berman v. Allan*,[46] decided by the Supreme Court of New Jersey, and *Speck v. Finegold*,[47] decided in the Superior Court of Pennsylvania.

In the *Berman* case, plaintiff mother was not informed that because of her age, there was a high risk that the child would be born afflicted with Down's syndrome (mongolism), nor was she informed of the availability of amniocentesis, which could have been used to study the genetic structure of fetal cells. Plaintiffs alleged that had they known these facts, and that the child would have been born mongoloid, they would have had the fetus aborted. Plaintiffs sought damages for medical expenses and the costs of raising the child, and also damages for their mental and emotional anguish.

The New Jersey Court denied the claim for medical expenses and costs of raising the child. The reason given in support of this was that it would be wholly disproportionate to allow plaintiffs to retain the benefits inhering in the birth of the child, "while saddling defendants with the enormous expenses upon her rearing".[48]

As to the parents' claim for emotional damages, this was allowed by the court. The court noted that the law had evolved to the point that mental and emotional distress is recognized as being just as "real" as physical pain, and its valuation is no more difficult. The court felt that the monetary equivalent of the distress of giving birth to a child afflicted with Down's syndrome is an appropriate measure of the harm suffered by the parents, deriving from the mother's loss of her right to abort the fetus.[49]

In the *Speck* case, plaintiff father suffered from neurofibromatosis, a crippling disease of the fibrous structures of the nerves. After his first two children were born afflicted with this disease, plaintiff decided to undergo a vasectomy. Following the operation, plaintiff was assured he was sterile.

However, a few months later, plaintiff's wife became pregnant, whereupon they consulted another physician to perform an abortion. The physician did perform the abortion procedure, and informed plaintiffs the operation was a success. Sometime after the operation, however, plaintiff's wife felt that the pregnancy was continuing. The doctor persistently assured her the fetus had been aborted.

---

46. 80 N.J. 421, 404 A.2d 8 (1979).

47. 268 Pa.Super. 342, 408 A.2d 496 (1979).

48. 404 A.2d at 14.

49. 404 A.2d at 15.

However, a few months later plaintiff's wife gave birth to a premature child, afflicted with the crippling disease.

The Pennsylvania court denied the claim of the parents for emotional disturbance and mental stress on the ground that it was not "possible to distinguish the mental and emotional travail which plaintiffs claim here from the pain and suffering of parents who raise a retarded child or whose infant is born blind or mongoloid or falls heir to one of the countless natural diseases or being healthy becomes permanently injured, disfigured or handicapped by reason of accident." [50]

The Pennsylvania court, however, did uphold plaintiff's claim for pecuniary losses which would be incurred in caring for the medical needs of the child and for the costs of raising the child.[51]

§ 23.6 "Wrongful Life"—In General

Where the action is brought on behalf of a child who has been conceived due to the negligence of others, or who is born with severe defects which could have been discovered while the child was *in utero*, giving the parents the option of aborting the fetus, courts are nearly unanimous in denying the child's action for "wrongful life." [52] The two most often stated reasons in support of this denial is that the damages are incalculable of determination (i. e., what is the difference between being born in a severely deformed state, and that of not being born at all), and that the law does not recognize an actionable claim for relief, as life is more precious than non-life.[53] To be is more

---

50. 408 A.2d at 509.

51. 408 A.2d at 508–09. See also Becker v. Schwartz, 46 N.Y.2d 401, 413 N.Y.S.2d 895, 386 N.E.2d 807 (1978) ("Unlike the causes of action brought on behalf of their infants for wrongful life, plaintiffs' causes of action, also founded essentially upon a theory of negligence or medical malpractice, do allege ascertainable damages: the pecuniary expense which they have borne, and must continue to bear, for the care and treatment of their infants").

52. *Ala.*—Elliot v. Brown, 361 So.2d 546 (Ala.1978).

Cal.—Stills v. Gratton, supra, n. 23.

N.J.—Gletiman v. Cosgrove, supra, n. 37.

N.Y.—Stewart v. Long Island College Hosp., supra, n. 40.

Pa.—Gildiner v. Thomas Jefferson Univ. Hosp. 451 F.Supp. 692 (D.C.Pa.1978).

Tex.—Smith v. United States, 392 F. Supp. 654 (D.C.Ohio 1975). (Applying Texas law.)

Wis.—Dumer v. St. Michaels Hosp., supra, n. 43.

53. Berman v. Allan, 80 N.J. 421, 404 A.2d 8 (1979) ("In the case of a claim predicated upon wrongful life, such a computation would require the trier of fact to measure the difference in value between life in an impaired condition and the 'utter void of non-existence' . . . As Chief Justice Weintraub noted, man, 'who knows nothing of death or nothingness', simply cannot affix a price tag to non-life." A few paragraphs later, the court stated: "One of the most deeply held beliefs of our society is that life—whether experienced with or without a major physical handicap—

desirous than not to be at all, although the state of being is not what one would have chosen had he a choice.

§ 23.7 "Wrongful Life"—Traditional Damages Incapable of Measurement

In the *Gleitman* case,[54] one count of the complaint was brought on behalf of the congenitally defective child, claiming, ultimately, that the conduct of defendants prevented his mother from obtaining an abortion, which would have terminated his existence, that he never should have been born at all, and that his very life is "wrongful." In rejecting the child's cause of action the court reasoned: "Damages are measured by comparing the condition plaintiff would have been in, had the defendants not been negligent, with plaintiff's impaired condition as a result of the negligence. The infant plaintiff would have us measure the difference between his life with defects against the utter void of nonexistence, but it is impossible to make such a determination. This Court cannot weigh the value of life with impairments against the nonexistence of life itself. By asserting that he should not have been born, the infant plaintiff makes it logically im-

is more precious than non-life . . . . [Nowhere] is there to be found an indication that the lives of persons suffering from physical handicaps are to be less cherished than those of non-handicapped human beings."); Speck v. Finegold, 268 Pa. Super. 342, 408 A.2d 496 (1979) ("First, there is no precedent in appellate judicial pronouncements that holds a child has a fundamental right to be born as a whole, functional human being. Whether it is better to have never been born at all rather than to have been born with serious mental defects is a mystery more properly left to the philosophers and theologians, a mystery which would lead us into the field of metaphysics, beyond the realm of our understanding or ability to solve. The law cannot assert a knowledge which can resolve this inscrutable and enigmatic issue. Second, it is not a matter of taking into consideration the various and convoluted degrees of the imperfection of life. It is rather the improbability of placing the child in a position she would have occupied if the defendants had not been negligent when to do so would make her nonexistent. The remedy afforded an injured party in negligence is intended to place the injured party in a position he would have occupied but for the negligence of the defendant. Thus, a cause of action brought on behalf of an infant seeking recovery for a 'wrongful life' on grounds she should not have been born demands a calculation of damages dependent on a comparison between Hobson's choice of life in an impaired state and nonexistence. This the law is incapable of doing."). The *Berman* court added the following words: "No man is perfect. Each of us suffers from some ailments or defects, whether major or minor, which make impossible participation in all the activities the world has to offer. But our lives are not thereby rendered less precious than those of others whose defects are less pervasive or less severe." 404 A.2d at 13.

54. Gleitman v. Cosgrove, 49 N.J. 22, 227 A.2d 689 (1967).

§ 23.7   SPECIFIC ACTIONS   Pt. 4

possible for a court to measure his alleged damages because of the impossibility of making the comparison required by compensatory damages." [55]

A 1976 New York case [56] involved a claim of medical malpractice in genetic counseling prior to infant plaintiff's conception, including failure to inform plaintiff's parents of the risk of their child being born with congenital defects, their affirmative advice to the contrary, and their failure to perform necessary tests. One count of the action brought on behalf of the infant plaintiff, who had survived for two and one-half years before succumbing to a hereditary congenital kidney disease, claimed damages for pain and suffering resulting from her wrongful life, that is, in violation of her right not to be conceived and therefore not to be born.

The New York Appellate Division court, noting that the public policy permitting abortions gives *parents* the right not to have a child, held that such right extended "to instances in which it can be determined with reasonable medical certainty that the child would be born deformed." [57] That court concluded that the breach of this right may also be considered tortious to the fundamental right of a child to be born as a "whole, functional human being."

On appeal to the Court of Appeals, the New York high court reversed. The court ruled that the law is not equipped to calculate damages by comparing life in an impaired state to nonexistence, commenting that "whether it is better never to have been born at all than to have been born with even gross deficiencies is a mystery more properly to be left to the philosophers and theologians." [58]

§ 23.8   "Wrongful Life"—Child's Suit Against Laboratory for Negligent Testing

In June of 1980, a California Court of Appeals made a landmark ruling in this area in *Curlender v. Bio-Science Laboratories*,[59] wherein it was recognized that a child born with severe genetic defects may

---

55. 227 A.2d at 692.

See "On Tort Liability for 'Wrongful Life.'". 1 Israel L.Rev. 513, 529 (1966) ("[N]o comparison is possible since were it not for the act of birth the infant would not exist. By his cause of action, the plaintiff cuts from under himself the ground upon which he needs to rely in order to prove his damage.").

56. Park v. Chessin, 60 A.D.2d 80, 400 N.Y.S.2d 110 (1977), modif. sub nom.

Becker v. Schwartz, 46 N.Y.2d 401, 413 N.Y.S.2d 895, 386 N.E.2d 807.

57. 400 N.Y.S.2d at 114.

58. Becker v. Schwartz, 46 N.Y.2d 401, 43 N.Y.S.2d 895, 386 N.E.2d 807 (1978).

59. 106 Cal.App.3d 811, 165 Cal.Rptr. 477 (1980).

bring suit against a laboratory which negligently performed diagnostic tests of its parents.

In the *Curlender* case, plaintiff's parents engaged the professional services of defendant laboratories to administer certain tests which were designed to reveal whether either of the parents were carriers of genes which could lead to a child born afflicted with Tay-Sachs disease. The laboratories erroneously and negligently reported that neither parent was a carrier. The child was later born with the disease, resulting in its suffering from "mental retardation, susceptibility to other diseases, convulsions, sluggishness, apathy, failure to fix objects with her eyes, inability to take an interest in her surroundings, loss of motor reactions, inability to sit up or hold her head up, loss of weight, muscle atrophy, blindness, pseudobulbar palsy, inability to feed orally, decerebrate rigidity and gross physical deformity." The child had a life expectancy of four years.

The California court engaged in an exhaustive study of the major cases which had previously considered the propriety of bringing such wrongful life suit, and despite the obvious lack of precedence, ultimately held that such an action may lie in proper situations. Much reliance for the decision was placed upon *Rowland v. Christian*,[60] the seminal case which abolished class distinctions when one was injured on another's property.[61]

As to whether the breach of the duty owed the child was the approximate cause of an injury *cognizable at law*, the court stated: "The circumstance that the birth and injury have come hand in hand has caused other courts to deal with the problem by barring recovery. The reality of the 'wrongful-life' concept is that such a plaintiff both exists and suffers, due to the negligence of others. It is neither necessary nor just to retreat into meditation on the mysteries of life. We need not be concerned with the fact that had defendants not been negligent, the plaintiff might not have come into existence at all. The certainty of genetic impairment is no longer a mystery. In addition, a reverent appreciation of life compels recognition that plaintiff, however impaired she may be, has come into existence as a living person with certain rights."[62]

Plaintiff sought damages based upon an actuarial life expectancy of more than 70 years—the age she could have expected had she been born without the disease. The court, however, rejected this measure. The amount of damages which could be recovered by a child suing for

60. 69 Cal.2d 108, 70 Cal.Rptr. 97, 443 P.2d 561 (1968).

61. See Chapter 38, "Owners and Possessors of Land," infra.

62. 106 Cal.App.3d at 829, 165 Cal. Rptr. at 488.

"wrongful life" was limited to the pain and suffering the child would endure over its *limited* life span, along with any special pecuniary loss resulting from the impaired condition.

The California Appellate Court properly rejected the age-old argument that damages could not be ascertained; that it is difficult to compute the difference between being born with defects, and not being born at all. A child born afflicted with Tay-Sachs or other genetic diseases, which could be detected if proper diagnostic tests had been performed, has indeed suffered a severe and tragic injury. As such, the policy of the law should be one of compensation to the victim, not one of shielding the wrongdoer on the basis of some tenuous argument.

§ 23.9 "Wrongful Life"—Birth Under Adverse Circumstances

Another line of "wrongful life" cases involves an action by the child against the parent or third party for proximately causing conception and birth under adverse circumstances. In *Williams v. State of New York*,[63] an infant who was born out of wedlock to a mentally deficient mother as a result of a sexual assault while the mother was confined in a mental institution, claimed damages against the state for deprivation of "normal childhood and home life," deprivation of "proper parental care, support, and rearing," and causing her to bear "the stigma of illegitimacy."

In denying her cause of action, the Court pointed out: "If the pleaded facts are true that State was grievously neglectful as to the mother, and as a result the child may have to bear unfair burdens as have many other sons and daughters of shame and sorrow. But the law knows no cure or compensation for it, and the policy and social reasons against providing such compensation are at least as strong as those which might be thought to favor it. Being born under one set of circumstance rather than another or to one pair of parents rather than another is not a suable wrong that is cognizable in court."

In *Zepeda v. Zepeda*,[64] an illegitimate son sued his father for damages to his person, property, and reputation in causing him to be born an adulterine bastard, deprived of the right to be a legitimate child, to have a normal home, to inherit from a legal father and paternal ancestors, and forced to be stigmatized as a bastard. The court, noting that the claim was apparently unprecedented in any common law jurisdiction or civil law country, held that recognition of such a cause of action should be reserved for the legislature in view of its

---

63. 18 N.Y.2d 481, 276 N.Y.S.2d 885, 223 N.E.2d 343 (1966).

64. 41 Ill.App.2d 240, 190 N.E.2d 849 (1963), cert. denied 379 U.S. 945, 85 S.Ct. 444, 13 L.Ed.2d 545.

"vast" legal implications and "staggering" social impact: "Encouragement would extend to all others born into the world under conditions they might regard as adverse. One might seek damages for being born of a certain color, another because of race; one for being born with a hereditary disease, another for inheriting unfortunate family characteristics; one for being born into a large destitute family, another because a parent has an unsavory reputation." [65] Similar judicial restraint has been exercised by other jurisdictions which have addressed the same questions.[66]

§ 23.10 Injuries Resulting from Pre-conception Negligence

A recent line of cases has addressed the logical extension of the cause of action for "pre-viable" injuries—that is, the right to recover for injuries from tortious acts committed *before conception*.[67] The right was first recognized in 1973, in *Jorgensen v. Meade Johnson Laboratories, Inc.*,[68] where an action was brought on behalf of twin girls, one deceased, who had been born afflicted with Down's syndrome (Mongolism).[69]

The complaint alleged that the condition resulted from chromosome alterations within the mother caused by defendant's birth control pills, which the mother had used prior to plaintiff's conception. Damages were claimed for personal injuries including retardation, deformity, and pain and suffering. The Tenth Circuit Court of Appeals, noting that the pleadings alleged that a "deformity was created within the viable fetus of the minor plaintiffs," [70] held that a cause of action was stated. The Court reasoned:

---

65. 190 N.E.2d at 858.

66. Slaweck v. Stroh, 62 Wis.2d 295, 215 N.W.2d 9 (1974).

See Comment, "Illegitimate Child May Not Recover from Father for Lack of Normal Home or Inferior Social Status," 77 Harv.L.Rev. 1349 (1964); Comment, "Does the Bastard have a Legitimate Complaint?" 22 U. Miami L.Rev. 884 (1967–68); Comment, "Illegitimate Child Denied Recovery Against Father for 'Wrongful Life'", 49 Iowa L.Rev. 1005 (1963–64).

67. Note, "Preconception Injuries: Visible extension of pre-natal injury law or inconceivable tort?" 12 Val.U. L.Rev. 143 (1977). Note, "Preconception torts: Foreseeing the unconceived," U.Colo.L.Rev. 48:621–39 (1977); Preconceptional Tort Liability, 27 De-Paul L.Rev. 891 (1978).

68. 483 F.2d 237 (10th Cir. 1973).

69. See Benda, Down's Syndrome; Mongolism and Its Management (Rev.Ed.1969); Lilienfeld, Epidemiology of Mongolism (1969); "Maternal Health and Mongolism" Lancet, 1972, 312–315.

See also, Sinkler v. Kneale, 401 Pa. 267, 164 A.2d 93, 96 (1960) (Treating the cause of a Mongoloid condition as a factual one requiring medical proof).

70. 483 F.2d at 239 ("Specifically, the aforesaid birth control pills altered the chromosome structure within the

§ 23.10   SPECIFIC ACTIONS   Pt. 4

If the view prevailed that tortious conduct occurring prior to conception is not actionable on behalf of an infant ultimately injured by the injury from a defective food product, manufactured before his conception, would be without remedy. Such reasoning runs counter to the various principles of recovery which Oklahoma recognizes for those ultimately suffering injuries proximately caused by a defective product or instrumentality manufactured and placed on the market by the defendant.[71]

Robert C. Strodel, Esquire,[72] relates *Renslow v. Mennonite Hosp.*,[73] an Illinois Supreme Court case he tried involving recovery for prenatal injuries. In October of 1965, eight years before infant plaintiff was born, the mother, at the time a 13-year-old school girl, was negligently transfused by defendant hospital on two occasions with 500 cubic centimeters of Rh-positive blood. The mother's Rh-negative blood was incompatible with, and was sensitized by, the Rh-positive blood.

She had no knowledge of any adverse reaction from the transfusions, nor was she aware that she had been improperly transfused or that her blood had been sensitized. In December, 1973 her condition was first discovered when a routine blood screening was ordered by her physician in the course of prenatal care. Although the defendants discovered they had administered the incompatible blood, they at no time notified the girl or her family to this effect.

The resulting sensitization of the mother's blood caused prenatal damage to the infant's hemolitic processes, which put her (the infant's) life in jeopardy and necessitated her induced premature birth. Plaintiff was born jaundiced, and suffering from hyperbilirubinemia (an excess of bilirubin, a bile pigment). Plaintiff required an im-

body of the plaintiff's wife, Alta J. Jorgensen, and as a result thereof, a Mongoloid deformity was created within the viable fetus of the minor plaintiffs during the period of development prior to birth.
"The plaintiff further alleges and states that as a direct and proximate result of the negligence and breach of warranty on the part of the defendant, the viable fetus of the minor plaintiffs were exposed to the altered chromosome structure within the mother's body thereby inducing the condition of mongolism . . .") (quoting from plaintiff's claim).

71. 483 F.2d at 240.
See also Zepeda v. Zepeda, 41 Ill.App. 2d 240, 190 N.E.2d 849 (1963), cert. denied 379 U.S. 945, 85 S.Ct. 444, 13 L.Ed.2d 545.

72. Robert C. Strodel, Esquire, Strodel & Kingery Assoc., First National Bank Building, Peoria, Illinois 61602.

73. 67 Ill.2d 348, 10 Ill.Dec. 484, 367 N.E.2d 1250 (1977). This case is also the subject of an annotation at 91 A. L.R.3d 316.

mediate, complete exchange transfusion of the blood, followed shortly thereafter by another identical transfusion.

The court first rejected the requirement that a fetus must be "viable" at the time the injury is sustained. Viability, the court stated, "is a relative matter, depending on the health of mother and child and many other matters in addition to the stage of development." Further, the court noted that many meritorious claims for injuries to a previable fetus were being unduly cut off, and thus erased by viability factor.

In extending the right to sue, the court stated:

> The cases allowing relief to an infant for injuries incurred in its previable state make it clear that a defendant may be held liable to a person whose existence was not apparent at the time of his act. We therefore find it illogical to bar relief for an act done prior to conception where the defendant would be liable for this same conduct had the child, unbeknownst to him, been conceived prior to his act. We believe that there is a *right to be born free from prenatal injuries foreseeably caused by a breach of duty to the child's mother.* [Emphasis added.] [74]

The *Renslow* case was ultimately settled four days before the case was scheduled to go to trial on the merits.

In *Bergstreser v. Mitchell*,[75] two physicians had negligently performed a Caesarean section on the plaintiff's mother a few years prior to plaintiff's birth. Plaintiff claimed that defendant's misconduct caused his mother to suffer an occult rupture of the uterus. This resulted in the necessity of a premature emergency Caesarean delivery, during the course of which plaintiff suffered an oxygen deficiency resulting in, among other injuries, brain damage.

Since a Missouri State Court had never ruled on the issue, the United States Court of Appeals for the Eighth Circuit scrutinized other decisions to determine how the Supreme Court of Missouri would most likely decide the issue. The decision the court reached was:

> We think that the Missouri Supreme Court would permit an infant, born alive, to bring action for injuries resulting from

---

74. 367 N.E.2d at 1255. See also Peek v. Lockwood, (Colo. Boulder City Dist.Ct., No. 76–1074–1, May 26, 1978, reported in 21 ATLA L.Rep. 471) ($575,000 jury verdict for infant who suffered erythroblastosis fetalis and stroke resulting in hemiplegia and mild retardation, because of negligently-caused Rh sensitization of mother. Additional $27,000 awarded to mother, $26,608 given for medical expenses, and $8,000 loss of consortium to father awarded.).

75. 577 F.2d 22 (8th Cir. 1978).

negligent acts occurring prior to conception. [Plaintiff] having been born alive, has, therefore, stated a cause of action under the law of Missouri.[76]

These cases are significant as they create a cause of action in favor of a fetus which suffers injury due to someone's malfeasance prior to the time it was conceived. The focus of these courts has rightly been upon foreseeability: If it is foreseeable that defendant's misconduct could cause injury to a fetus, that person should be liable for all consequences he has directly caused. The shadow of old Mrs. Palsgraf should not prevent protection for *all*, including the unconceived child where injuries to it are reasonably foreseeable.

76. Id. at 26.

§§ 23.11–24.0 are reserved for supplementary material.

CHAPTER 24

PRENATAL INJURIES

Table of Sections

Sec.
24.1 Development of the Cause of Action.
24.2 Viability.
24.3 Wrongful Death Resulting from Prenatal Injuries.
24.4 Damages.
24.5 Effect of Statutes of Limitation.

Library References:
C.J.S. Infants §§ 218, 219.
West's Key No. Digests, Infants ⚖︎72(2).
Prosser, Law of Torts (4th ed. 1971) pp. 335–338.

§ 24.1 Development of the Cause of Action

As early as 1893, the Supreme Court of the United States allowed recovery for the reduction in value of cows resulting from the calving caused by a collision of railroad cars in which they rode.[1] Yet 46 years later, in 1939, an Illinois court denied recovery where defendant doctor had negligently diagnosed the mother's pregnant condition as a tumor of the womb. He administered a series of x-ray treatments resulting in the destruction of the infant's brain cells and causing the infant to be a permanent cripple until the time it died at the physical age of 13, and the mental age of 2.[2]

The judicial reluctance in considering pre-natal injuries of human infants and calves with the same dignity is traced to *Dietrich v. Northampton*.[3] Therein, the court, per Justice Holmes, disallowed

---

1. New York, Lake Erie & Western R. R. Co. v. Estill, 147 U.S. 591, 13 S.Ct. 444, 37 L.Ed. 292 (1893).

2. Smith v. Luckhardt, 299 Ill.App. 100, 19 N.E.2d 446 (1939); Stemmer v. Kline, 128 N.J.L. 455, 26 A.2d 489 (1942).

3. Dietrich v. Inhabitants of Northampton, 138 Mass. 14, 52 Am.Rep. 242 (1884) (Mother of deceased child fell because of a defect in highway of town, and suffered miscarriage. Child lived 10 or 15 minutes, and brought an action by administrator. No liability since "the unborn child was a part of the mother at the time of the injury, any damage to it which was not too remote to recover for at all was recoverable by her."); See Cavanaugh v. First Nat'l Stores, 329 Mass. 179, 107 N.E.2d 307 (1952) (6 year old child alleged that his blindness was caused by prenatal injuries to his mother from eating an un-

the medical verity, "that the infant lives with its mother",[4] and is not "part of the mother."[5] The *Dietrich* case was followed in 1890 by *Walker v. Great Northern*.[6] In that case the court refused to allow a suit to be brought on behalf of a child born deformed as the result of railroad accident. Two of the justices enunciated the contract of carriage theory whereby defendant owed the unborn infant no duty of care, the other justices placing the decision on the ground that plaintiff infant was not in being at the time of the wrong. However in 1900,[7] Justice Boggs in a dissenting opinion, urged that a child viable, but in utero, if injured by tort, should, when born, be allowed to sue. Although the majority opinion conformed to the rationale of the *Dietrich* case, this most able dissent led to a tort trend allowing recovery for prenatal injuries.[8]

In *Bonbrest v. Kotz*,[9] a medical malpractice action, the District Court for the District of Columbia became the first American court to hold that injuries to a viable unborn child were compensable in a tort action brought after the child's birth. This holding initiated "the most spectacular abrupt reversal of a well settled rule in the whole history of the law of torts,"[10] culminating in 1972 when Ala-

wholesome turkey. Petition held demurrable. "We are not prepared to overrule our earlier decisions, which began nearly seventy years ago.";

4. See 31 Baylor L.Rev. 131 (1979); 12 Creighton L.Rev. 402 (1978); 45 Tenn. L.Rev. 545 (1978); 21 Vill.L.Rev. 994 (1976); 46 U.Cin.L.Rev. 266 (1977).

5. Dietrich v. Inhabitants of Northampton, 138 Mass. 14, 52 Am.Rep. 242 (1884); 1 Bl.Comm. 129.

6. See Nugent v. Brooklyn Heights R. R. Co., 154 App.Div. 667, 139 N.Y.S. 367 (1913), dism'd 209 N.Y. 515, 102 N.E. 1107 (Careful analysis of Walker v. Great Northern Ry. Co. case); 28 L.R. (Ir) Q.B. and Ex.Div. 69 (1890).

7. Allaire v. St. Luke's Hosp., 184 Ill. 359, 56 N.E. 638, 48 L.R.A. 225, 75 Am.St.Rep. 176 (1900) ("The law should, it seems to me, be, that whenever a child in utero is so far advanced in a prenatal age as that, should parturition by natural or artificial means occur at such age, such child could and would live severable from the mother and grow into the ordinary activities of life, and is afterwards born and becomes a living human being, such child has a right of action for any injuries wantonly or negligently inflicted upon his or her person at such age of viability, though then in the womb of the mother.").

8. Prosser, The Law of Torts (4th ed. 1971) p. 336.

9. 65 F.Supp. 138 (D.D.C.1946) ("Why is the infant a part of the mother under the law of negligence, and a separate entity in that of property and crime? Why a human being under the civil law and a non-entity under the human law? It has, if viable, its own bodily form and members, manifests all the anatomical characteristics of individuals, possesses its own circulatory, vascular, and excretory systems and is capable now of being ushered into the viable world.").

10. Prosser, The Law of Torts (4th ed. 1971) p. 336.

§ 24.2 Viability

The *Bonbrest* decision, and much of its progeny, supported the *Dietrich* rationale of the inseparability of a fetus and mother—and the consequent lack of a being *in esse*—to the extent that their holdings were factually limited to prenatal injuries inflicted upon a "viable" fetus, that is, one "potentially able to live outside the mother's womb, albeit with artificial aid." [12] The viability concept had been introduced in Bogg's *Allaire* dissent to attack the *Dietrich* rationale of absence of legal existence,[13] and subsequently was successfully relied upon to avoid *Dietrich's* harsh results.[14] Yet, as theory, the concept merely shifted the critical stage of "being" from birth to the more nebulous point of "viability" *in utero*. On practical grounds it

---

11. Huskey v. Smith, 289 Ala. 52, 265 So.2d 596 (1972).

12. Roe v. Wade, 410 U.S. 113, 160, 93 S.Ct. 705, 730, 35 L.Ed.2d 147 (1973), reh. denied 410 U.S. 959, 93 S.Ct. 1409, 35 L.Ed.2d 694. In testing a Texas abortion statute, in Roe, the court found that a state's important and legitimate interest in protecting the potentiality of human life became "compelling", with respect to a fetus, at the point of "viability." 410 U.S. at 163, 93 S.Ct. at 732, 35 L.Ed. 182–3.

13. Allaire v. St. Luke's Hosp., 184 Ill. 359, 56 N.E. 638, 48 L.R.A. 225, 75 Am.St.Rep. 176 (1900):

> A foetus in the womb of the mother may well be regarded as but a part of the bowels of the mother during a portion of the period of gestation; but if, while in the womb, it reaches that prenatal age of viability when the destruction of the life of the mother does not necessarily end its existence also, and when, if separated prematurely, and by artificial means, from the mother, it would be so far a matured human being as that it would live and grow, mentally and physically, as other children generally, it is but to deny a palpable fact to argue there is but one life, and that the life of the mother. Medical science and skill and experience have demonstrated that at a period of gestation in advance of the period of parturition the foetus is capable of independent and separate life, and that, though within the body of the mother, it is not merely a part of her body, for her body may die in all of its parts and the child remain alive, and capable of maintaining life, when separated from the dead body of the mother. If at that period a child so advanced is injured in its limbs or members, and is born into the living world suffering from the effects of the injury, is it not sacrificing truth to a mere theoretical abstraction to say the injury was not to the child, but wholly to the mother? 56 N.E. at 641. (Boggs, J., dissenting).

14. *Bonbrest*, 65 F.Supp. 138 (D.C. 1946); Williams v. Marion Rapid Transit, Inc., 152 Ohio St. 114, 87 N.E.2d 334 (1949); Keyes v. Constr. Serv., Inc., 340 Mass. 633, 165 N.E.2d 912 (1960).

has been justified by the supposed difficulties of proof for injuries sustained in the earliest periods of fetal development.[15]

Aside from the impossibility of determining with precision the point at which a fetus becomes "viable",[16] the viability concept suffers from a patent lack of logical relevance to the right of recovery.[17] Medical science demonstrates that many of the most severe prenatal injuries can be sustained only in the earliest "pre-viable" stages.[18]

---

15. See Note: Prenatal Injuries—Viability & Live Birth, 21 Okla.L.Rev. 114 (1968); Gordon, The Unborn Plaintiff, 63 Mich.L.Rev. 579 (1965).

Woods v. Lancet, 303 N.Y. 349, 102 N.E.2d 691 (1961).

16. Smith v. Brennan, 31 N.J. 353, 157 A.2d 497 (1960) ("In the first place, age is not the sole measure of viability and there is no real way of determining in a borderline case whether or not a fetus was viable at the time of injury, unless it was immediately born. Therefore the viability rule is impossible of practical application.")

But see Roe v. Wade, 410 U.S. 113, 93 S.Ct. 705, 35 L.Ed.2d 147 (1973), reh. denied 410 U.S. 959, 93 S.Ct. 1409, 35 L.Ed.2d 694 and Planned Parenthood of Central Missouri v. Danforth, 428 U.S. 52, 96 S.Ct. 2831, 49 L.Ed.2d 788 (1976), wherein the U.S. Supreme Court recognizes the point of "viability" as the point when the state has a "compelling interest" in protecting life so as to regulate abortion. "[I]t is not the proper function of the legislature or the courts to place viability, which is essentially a medical concept, at a specific time in the gestation period. The time when viability is achieved may vary with each pregnancy, and the determination of whether a particular fetus is viable is and must be a matter for the judgment of the responsible attending physician."

17. Sylvia v. Gobeille, 101 R.I. 76, 220 A.2d 222, 224 (1966) ("[W]e are unable logically to conclude that a claim for an injury inflicted prior to viability is any less meritorious than one sustained after"); Smith v. Brennan, 31 N.J. 353, 157 A.2d 497 (1960). ("The most important consideration, however, is that the viability distinction has no relevance to the injustice of denying recovery for harm which can be proved to have resulted from the wrongful act of another. Whether viable or not at the time of injury, the child sustains the same harm after birth, and therefore should be given the same opportunity for redress.") Prosser, The Law of Torts (4th ed. 1971) p. 337: "Certainly the infant may be no less injured; and all logic is in favor of ignoring the state at which it occurs."

18. Trauma to the Unborn Child, 5 Trauma, No. 1, June, 1963, p. 42:

"In the remainder of the first trimester maternal disease exerts its most damaging effects. There is a precise sequence in the development of the various organs in the fetus at this time. If damage occurs, then the organ or organs developing at that particular time may be damaged or completely arrested."

Lintgen, Impact of Medical Knowledge on Law Relating to Prenatal Injuries. Note U.Pa.L.Rev. 553, 562–64 (1962).

Thalidomide
See Gordon, The Unborn Plaintiff, 63 Mich.L.Rev. 579, 619–21 (1965); Mellin & Katzenstein, The Saga of Thalidomide (pts. 1–2), 267 A.M.A.J. 1184, 1187–90, 1238 (1962); Taussig, A Study of the German Outbreak of Phocomelia: The Thalidomide Syndrome, 267 A.M.A.J. 1106 (1962);

Adequate proof, as in other cases requiring medical evidence, is plaintiff's burden, and its theoretical difficulty is no bar to plaintiff's action.[19]

Accordingly, the viability rule has never been utilized to bar an action for injuries,[20] and has been expressly rejected by many jurisdictions.[21] The prevailing view, in reversal of *Dietrich*, is to allow recovery for prenatal injuries incurred at any stage from the moment of conception.[22]

Trueta, Care of Thalidomide Babies, 1962–63, The Lancet 1162; Bennett, Liability of the Manufacturers of Thalidomide to the Affected Children, 39 Aust.L.J. 256 (1965).

Rubella (German Measles)

Sylvia v. Gobeille, 101 R.I. 76, 220 A.2d 222 (1966) (Medical malpractice for failure to prescribe gamma globulin to mother exposed to rubella while fetus previable); Dillon v. SS Kresge Co., 35 Mich.App. 603, 192 N.W.2d 661 (1971).

19. Woods v. Lancet, 303 N.Y. 349, 102 N.E.2d 691 (1951) ("[I]t is an inadmissible concept that uncertainty of proof can ever destroy a legal right. The questions of causation, reasonable certainty, etc., which will arise in these cases are no different, in kind, from the ones which have arisen in thousands of other negligence cases decided in this state, in the past.") 102 N.E.2d at 695.

See also ATLA L.J. 36, p. 75–84 for the interesting problem regarding proof of pre-natal injuries, presented by the "DES" cases, where manufacturers and distributors of an anti-abortion drug were sued by daughters of mothers who took the drug while pregnant, on the theory that it resulted in vaginal and cervical cancer in the maturing daughters. Although plaintiffs were unable to specifically identify the particular manufacturers linked to the individual injuries, the California Supreme Court upheld a complaint against *all* manufacturers of the drug on the theory of "enterprise liability," shifting the burden to the defendants to prove that they did not manufacture the particular drug. Sindell v. Abbott Laboratories, 26 Cal.3d 588, 163 Cal.Rptr. 132, 607 P. 2d 924 (1980).

20. Dooley, Modern Tort Law (1977) § 14.03.

21. See ATLA L.J. Vol. 36 (1974) p. 246–247. Note, Viability is Not a Prerequisite in Action for Injuries Sustained to Fetus, 10 Tulsa L.Rev. 153 (1974).

See also, Bennett v. Hymers, 101 N.H. 483, 147 A.2d 108 (1958); Wolfe v. Isbell, 291 Ala. 327, 280 So.2d 758 (1973).

22. Day v. Nationwide Mut. Ins. Co., 328 So.2d 560 (Fla.App.1976) ("We hold that a child born alive, having suffered prenatal injuries at any time after conception, has a cause of action against the alleged tortfeasor. If the child is born alive, there is a relation-back to the time of injury in order for the infant person to maintain its cause of action."); Labree v. Major, 111 R.I. 657, 306 A.2d 808 (1973); Delgado v. Yandell, 468 S.W. 2d 475 (Tex.Civ.App.1971), refused n. r. e. 471 S.W.2d 569 (Tex.). ("A cause of action does exist for prenatal injuries sustained at any prenatal stage provided the child is born alive and survives".).

§ 24.3 Wrongful Death Resulting from Prenatal Injuries

Where prenatal injuries result in death subsequent to live birth, the wrongful death action is generally allowed, pursuant to the reasoning allowing recovery for non fatal injuries.[23] But where the infant dies unborn, the courts have been slower to allow recovery,[24] with the unjust result that it may be more profitable for defendant to kill a fetus than to injure it.[25] Generally the question will turn on whether the fetus can be considered a "person" within the meaning of the particular state's wrongful death statute. Thus, in the leading California case, *Justus v. Atchison*,[26] recovery was denied where a fetus died in an allegedly negligent delivery, on the grounds that the state's wrongful death statute lacked specific language to include an unborn fetus within its purview.[27]

While presently some 12 states follow this "live birth" rule,[28] the more rational doctrine allowing wrongful death recovery in stillbirth

---

23. Torigian v. Watertown News Co., 352 Mass. 446, 225 N.E.2d 926 (1967) (Defendant's auto struck that of mother, at the time 3½ months pregnant; 40 days later, she delivered a child that lived for 2½ hours).

24. Kilmer v. Hicks, 22 Ariz.App. 552, 529 P.2d 706 (1974); McKillip v. Zimmerman, 191 N.W.2d 706 (Iowa, 1971); State ex rel. Hardin v. Sanders, 538 S.W.2d 336 (Mo.1976).

25. See Prosser, The Law of Torts (4th ed. 1971) p. 902.

Eich v. Town of Gulf Shores, 293 Ala. 95, 300 So.2d 354 (1974) ("To deny recovery where the injury is so severe as to cause the death of a fetus subsequently stillborn, and to allow recovery where injury occurs during pregnancy and death results therefrom after a live birth, would only serve the tortfeasor by rewarding him for his severity in inflicting the injury. It would be bizarre, indeed, to hold that the greater the harm inflicted the better the opportunity for exoneration of the defendant. Logic, fairness and justice compel our recognition of an action, as here, for prenatal injuries causing death before a live birth.") 300 So.2d at 355; Todd v. Sandidge Constr. Co., 341 F. 2d 75 (4th Cir. 1964) ("[I]f the trauma is severe enough to kill the child, then there could be no recovery; but if less serious, allowing the child to survive, there might be recovery. Again, if the fatality was immediate, the suit could not prevail, but if the death was protracted by a few hours, even minutes, beyond birth, the claim could succeed. Practically, it would mean that the greater the harm the better the chance of immunity.") 341 F.2d at 77.

26. 19 Cal.3d 564, 139 Cal.Rptr. 97, 565 P.2d 122 (1977).

27. The court noted that California child support law (Penal Code § 270) had been amended specifically to include "a child conceived but not yet born," and the state's murder statute had been amended to include the unlawful and malicious killing of a fetus.

28. Kilmer v. Hicks, 22 Ariz. App. 552, 529 P.2d 706 (1974); Tyrrell v. City & County of San Francisco, 69 Cal. App.3d 876, 138 Cal.Rptr. 504 (1977); Drabbels v. Skelly Oil Co., 155 Neb. 17, 50 N.W.2d 229 (1951); Graf v. Taggert, 43 N.J. 303, 204 A.2d 140 (1964); Endresz v. Friedberg, 24 N.Y.2d 478, 301 N.Y.S.2d 65, 248 N.E.2d

cases is now followed in many jurisdictions.[29] The majority of these jurisdictions, however, have predicated recovery on the same "viability" requirement which has generally been rejected in cases of non-fatal injury.[30] Thus in Michigan, where a wrongful death action had earlier been granted for an eight-month-old viable fetus,[31] recovery was denied on behalf of a three-month-old infant *en ventre sa mere*, who was miscarried as a result of an automobile accident.[32] The Michigan court relied in part on the U.S. Supreme Court's "viability" ruling in *Roe v. Wade*,[33] that a three-month-old fetus may be aborted free from state interference:

> If the mother can intentionally terminate the pregnancy at three months, without regard to the rights of the fetus, it becomes increasingly difficult to justify holding a third person liable to the fetus for unknowingly and unintentionally, but negligently, causing the pregnancy to end at that same state. There would be an inherent conflict in giving the mother the right to terminate the pregnancy yet holding that an action may be brought on behalf of the same fetus under the wrongful death act.[34]

Whether misplaced reliance on *Roe*, which was addressed to balancing the state's interest in regulating abortion with the right of privacy, will continue to deter the trend to abandon the viability requirement, remains to be seen. As pointed out in the *Toth* dissent: "Certainly a tortfeasor cannot invoke the mother's privacy rights to defend his wrongdoing." [35] The logic which denies the viability re-

901 (1969); Yow v. Nance, 29 N.C. App. 419, 224 S.E.2d 292 (1976), cert. denied 290 N.C. 312, 225 S.E.2d 833; Lawrence v. Craven Tire Co., 210 Va. 138, 169 S.E.2d 440 (1969).

29. Eich v. Town of Gulf Shores, 293 Ala. 95, 300 So.2d 354 (1974); Worgan v. Greggo & Ferrara, Inc., 50 Del. 258, 128 A.2d 557 (1956); Chrisafogeorgis v. Brandenberg, 55 Ill.2d 368, 304 N.E.2d 88 (1973); State v. Sherman, 234 Md. 179, 198 A.2d 71 (1964); Mone v. Greyhound Lines, Inc., 368 Mass. 354, 331 N.E.2d 916 (1975); O'Neill v. Morse, 385 Mich. 130, 188 N.W.2d 785 (1971); Rainey v. Horn, 221 Miss. 269, 72 So.2d 434 (1954); Evans v. Olson, 550 P.2d 924 (Okl.1976); Libbee v. Permanente Clinic, 268 Or. 258, 518 P.2d 636 (1974), reh. denied 268 Or. 258, 520 P.2d 361, appeal after remand 269 Or. 543, 525 P.2d 1296; Kwaterski v. State Farm Mut. Auto. Ins. Co., 34 Wis.2d 14, 148 N.W.2d 107 (1967).

30. Note, Damages for Wrongful Death of a Fetus—Proof of Fetal Viability, 51 Chicago—Kent L.Rev. 227 (1974).

31. O'Neill v. Morse, 385 Mich. 130, 188 N.W.2d 785 (1971).

32. Toth v. Goree, 65 Mich.App. 296, 237 N.W.2d 297 (1975).

33. 410 U.S. 113, 93 S.Ct. 705, 35 L. Ed.2d 147, reh. denied 410 U.S. 959, 93 S.Ct. 1409, 35 L.Ed.2d 694.

34. 237 N.W.2d at 301.

35. 237 N.W.2d at 305 (Maher, J., dissenting).

§ 24.4 Damages

Damages for prenatal injuries may compensate the infant's impaired capacity for physical and mental development, deprivation of normal life expectancy, as well as costs of anticipated future medical care.[36] A California medical malpractice settlement in 1978 provided a lump sum of $750,000 and lifetime annual payments of $36,000 growing at a compounded rate of four percent annually, to a child who lost use of her arms and legs through alleged negligence in delivery. The agreement, which guaranteed the child or her estate a minimum of $1.2 million, ultimately could exceed $14 million in payments if plaintiff lives a normal lifespan of 70 years.[37]

Because of the length of life expectancy, medicals and severity of damages, awards in this field are among the highest. Structured settlements are particularly available.

Elements of damages for wrongful death from prenatal injuries may include loss of companionship and affection,[38] sorrow and mental distress,[39] as well as compensation for loss of future earnings.[40] Failure to furnish direct evidence of the infant's potential earning capacity will not bar recovery.[41]

A mother's personal injury action for physical and mental sufferings occasioned by a miscarriage may be maintained along with an action on behalf of the infant.[42] Damages for the death of the child, however, generally will not be recoverable in the mother's action.[43]

---

36. Sox v. United States, 187 F.Supp. 465 (D.C.S.C.1960) (Damages of $260,000 for prenatal injuries resulting in plaintiff's inability to see, talk, think for herself, use her limbs, or control her muscles).

37. Alameda County Superior Court approved settlement (Coble v. Kaiser Foundation), reported in San Francisco Chronicle July 20, 1978.

38. Todd v. Sandidge Constr. Co., 341 F.2d 75 (4th Cir. 1964).

39. Cox v. Cooper, 510 S.W.2d 530 (Ky.1974) ($50,000 damages to mother included shock and grief).

40. Gullborg v. Rizzo, 331 F.2d 557 (3d Cir. 1964); Cox v. Cooper, 510 S.W.2d 530 (Ky.1974) ($40,000 for infant's loss of earning power).

41. Louisville v. Stuckenborg, 438 S.W.2d 94 (Ky.1968) ($25,000 awarded for death of infant four days after birth resulting from prenatal injuries. "It is impossible to furnish any direct evidence of the earning capacity of a four-day-old child born prematurely. To require such a showing is to deny recovery entirely.").

42. Cox v. Cooper, 510 S.W.2d 530 (Ky.1974).

43. Stafford v. Roadway Transit Co., 70 F.Supp. 555 (D.C.Pa.1947) aff'd 165

David H. White, Esquire,[44] reports a case he tried with *Stephen M. Ohano* in which they received a settlement of *$175,000* for the death of an unborn fetus and its mother. Counsel represented the family of a young woman who was eight and one-half months pregnant at the time of a *head-on collision* between a vehicle in which she was a passenger and another vehicle which was passing a vehicle headed in the opposite direction. The woman was wearing a seatbelt with shoulder harness at the time of the accident, and the force of the impact ripped the placenta from the womb resulting in a condition known as *abruptia placenta,* as a result of which the fetus was diagnosed to have died some two hours prior to its delivery by ceasarean section. The expectant mother also subsequently died as a result of complications of the *abruptia placenta.*

Defense counsel filed a Motion for Summary Judgment asserting that no cause of action existed for the death of an unborn fetus, and asserting that a live birth must first occur before recovery could be had for prenatal injuries, including death. The Motion Judge denied the Motion on the grounds that recovery should not be denied simply because the injury was so grievous as to have caused death before birth, particularly when the fetus was viable at the time of the accident.

§ 24.5 Effect of Statutes of Limitation

Although most statutes of limitation provide for tolling during plaintiff's minority,[45] some states, including California, have enacted special statutes for pre-natal injury actions. The California statute provides a six year limitation period, running from the date of birth, where injuries were sustained prior to or in the course of birth.[46] This statute may be tolled by the common law delayed discovery rule, where circumstances warrant.[47] When presented with a pre-natal injury case, plaintiff's lawyer is advised vigilantly to examine his jurisdiction's statutes. Misplaced reliance that limitations will be tolled during plaintiff's entire minority can spell disaster in a pre-natal case.

F.2d 920 (3d Cir.); Occhipinti v. Rheem Mfg. Co., 252 Miss. 172, 172 So.2d 186 (1965).

44. Okano, Noguchi and Wong, 10th Floor American Savings Tower, Financial Plaza of the Pacific, 915 Fort Street, Honolulu, Hawaii.

45. Chapter 3, Have I a Case?, supra.

46. West's Ann.Cal.Civ.Code § 29.

47. Segura v. Brundage, 91 Cal.App.3d 19, 153 Cal.Rptr. 777 (1979).

§§ 24.6–25.0 are reserved for supplementary material.

CHAPTER 25

LOSS OF CONSORTIUM

Table of Sections

Sec.
25.1 In General.
25.2 "Consortium" Defined.
25.3 Development of Right.
25.4 Rationales Given for Extending Right to Wife.
25.5 Procedural Aspects—Derivative v. Non-derivative.
25.6 Requirement of Marriage.
25.7 Parents' Action for Loss of Filial Consortium.
25.8 Child's Action for Loss of Parental Consortium.
25.9 Why Action Is Denied.
25.10 Recovery When Parent "Severely Injured".

Library References:
C.J.S. Husband and Wife § 400 et seq.
West's Key No. Digests, Husband and Wife ⇔209 et seq.
Prosser, Law of Torts (4th ed. 1971) pp. 888–897.
Blashfield, Automobile Law & Practice, § 481.8.

§ 25.1 In General

When a husband and father or a wife and mother is injured by another's negligent or intentional misconduct, counsel should be careful not to overlook a possible claim for loss of consortium on behalf of the noninjured spouse or children. In our office, we have determined that loss of consortium has evolved so greatly in the past 25 years that it must be regarded as a substantial right,[1] not just an academic addendum to plaintiff's complaint. It is now our practice to advise our clients of the possible claim, and include it whenever possible. Indeed, it may well be considered malpractice for a plaintiff's lawyer not to inform and advise his injured client and his family of this claim.

1. M. M. Belli & A. P. Wilkinson, Loss of Consortium: Academic Addendum or Substantial Right?, 16 Trial 20 (Feb. 1980).

§ 25.2 "Consortium" Defined

The dictionary defines consortium as "conjugal fellowship."[2] However, this definition tends to make the word even more abstract. Consortium is now defined as being much more than mere sexual relations. Encompassed are such elements as love, companionship, affection, society, solace, conjugal life, comfort and more.[3]

Loss of consortium recently has been recognized as being a form of mental suffering,[4] akin to that accompanying the loss of a limb. What consortium is *not* is loss of financial support, or nursing services for the care of the injured spouse. These elements may be fully recovered by the injured spouse. Such damages must also be excluded to prevent defendant from being subjected to a double recovery.

---

2. Black's Law Dictionary (5th) p. 280.

3. City of Fairbanks v. Smith, 525 P.2d 1095 (Alaska 1974) ("Society, companionship and sexual relationship"); Rodriguez v. Bethlehem Steel Corp., 12 Cal.3d 382, 115 Cal.Rptr. 765, 525 P.2d 669 (1974) ("The concept of consortium includes not only loss of support or services, it also embraces such elements as love, companionship, affection, society, sexual relations, solace and more"); Gates v. Foley, 247 So.2d 40 (Fla.1971) ("Consortium means much more than mere sexual relation and consists, also, of that affection, solace, comfort, companionship, conjugal life, fellowship, society and assistance so necessary to a successful marriage"); Rindlisbaker v. Wilson, 95 Idaho 752, 519 P.2d 421 (1974); Deems v. Western Maryland Ry. Co., 247 Md. 95, 231 A.2d 514 (1967) ("Loss of society, affection, assistance and conjugal fellowship"); Diaz v. Eli Lilly & Co., 364 Mass. 153, 302 N.E.2d 555 (1973); Montgomery v. Stephan, 359 Mich. 33, 101 N.W.2d 227 (1960) ("[T]he pleader at the common law (following his practice in deeds, wills, contracts, and what-not) alleged the loss of love, companionship, affection, society, comfort, sexual relations, services, solace, and on and on until his dictionary ran dry. It does, indeed, (since it is fellowship between man and wife), embrace all of these things, and more."); Tribble v. Gregory, 288 So.2d 13 (Miss.1974) ("Society, companionship, love, affection, aid, services, support, sexual relations and . . . comfort"); Millington v. Southeastern Elevator Co., Inc., 22 N.Y.2d 498, 293 N.Y.S.2d 305, 239 N.E.2d 897 (1968) ("Love, companionship, affection, society, sexual relations, solace and more"); General Elec. Co. v. Bush, 88 Nev. 360, 498 P.2d 366 (1972); Clouston v. Remlinger Oldsmobile Cadillac, Inc., 22 Ohio St.2d 65, 258 N.E.2d 230 (1970) ("Society, services, sexual relations and conjugal affection which includes companionship, comfort, love and solace"); Moran v. Quality Aluminum Casting Co., 34 Wis.2d 542, 150 N.W.2d 137 (1967) ("The concept of consortium, however, embraces love, companionship, affection, society, sexual relations, services, solace and more").

4. Rodriguez v. Bethlehem Steel Corp., 12 Cal.3d 382, 115 Cal.Rptr. 765, 525 P.2d 669 (1974) ("Although loss of consortium may have physical consequences, it is principally a form of mental suffering").

§ 25.2   SPECIFIC ACTIONS   Pt. 4

A cautionary instruction from the trial judge should remove this possibility.[5]

§ 25.3   Development of Right
Originally Only Husband Had Right to Sue

At common law, a husband could sue for loss of services, comfort and sexual relations when a third party negligently injured his wife, but she had no right to sue for similar elements when her husband was injured.[6] In effect, she was required to exchange a "heart for a husk,"[7] and to go "from loving wife to lonely nurse."[8] This harsh rule evolved during the times when a woman was regarded as part chattel and part servant.[9] Upon marriage, the personality of the

---

5. If consortium did embrace such economic factors, then defendants' fears of double recovery would be justified. Any threat of double recovery can be eliminated by a jury verdict containing a proper definition of consortium, and a caution concerning economic aspects.

6. Prosser on Torts 889 (4th Ed. 1971); Tyler v. Brown-Service Funeral Homes Co., 250 Ala. 295, 34 So.2d 203 (1948); Giggey v. Gallagher Transp. Co., 101 Colo. 258, 72 P.2d 1100 (1937); Sobolewski v. German, 32 Del. 540, 127 A. 49 (1924); Ripley v. Ewell, 61 So.2d 420 (Fla.1952); McDade v. West, 80 Ga.App. 481, 56 S.E.2d 299 (1949); Brown v. Kistleman, 177 Ind. 692, 98 N.E. 631 (1912); Cravens v. Louisville & N.R. Co., 195 Ky. 257, 242 S.W. 628 (1922); Harker v. Bushouse, 254 Mich. 187, 236 N.W. 222 (1931); Eschenback v. Benjamin, 195 Minn. 378, 263 N.W. 154 (1935); Hinnant v. Tide Water Power Co., 189 N.C. 120, 126 S.E. 307 (1925); Howard v. Verdigris Val. Elec. Co-op., 201 Okl. 504, 207 P.2d 784 (1949); Sheard v. Oregon Elec. Ry. Co., 137 Or. 341, 2 P.2d 916 (1931).

7. Montgomery v. Stephan, 359 Mich. 33, 101 N.W.2d 227 (1960).

8. Ekalo v. Constructive Serv. Co. of America, 46 N.J. 82, 215 A.2d 1 (1965).

9. Sovereign v. Sovereign, 354 Mich. 65, 92 N.W.2d 585 (1958) ("The picture we receive, sketchy as it is, of late 16th and early 17th century women is, by today's standards, a depressing one. She was regarded as a creature (the choice of words is not our own) of limited intellectual attainments or possibilities. Education was largely denied her. There were few schools for even the girls of the wealthier families and the training given in those was limited to that of 'polishing nature, music and the arts.' There was almost no opportunity for the rigorous intellectual discipline given to young men. They were married young, pawns in their father's hands for the attainment of title or prestige. They could not possibly hope to reach, in fact, they were not 'meant' to reach, intellectual equality with their husbands. Their existence, socially and economically, pivoted around that of a dominant husband, authoritarian and paternalistic."); Hoekstra v. Helgeland, 78 S.D. 82, 98 N.W.2d 669 (1959) ("By primitive law, the only member of the family deemed to be harmed by an injustifiable disturbance of family relations was the family head. . . . Under this primitive and Blackstone's common law the wife was regarded as a chattel, or a servant, who owed her service to her master, her husband, and she could not sue for any

wife merged with that of her husband. A husband and wife then were regarded as one person, that person being solely the husband.[10]

Extension of Right to Wife—Present Status

This rule became so archaic that the mouths of the courts became powdered with dust upon each subsequent application thereof.[11] It was not until 1950, in the famous District Court case of *Hitaffer v. Argonne Company*[12] that a wife was given this right. The passage of the Married Woman's Act and other laws changed the status of a married woman from a mere servant to a partner having equal rights in the marriage relation. As such, she was entitled to equal protection of the law.[13] The *Hitaffer* decision was based upon modern truth, not ancient dogma.

injuries sustained by her, as an individual, except by an action in the joint names of the husband and wife, the recovery obtained being vested in the husband, who could discharge the cause of action without her consent, or prevent her suing by refusing to join as a plaintiff.").

10. Clouston v. Remlinger Oldsmobile Cadillac, Inc., 22 Ohio St.2d 65, 258 N.E.2d 230 (1970) ("The reason that, at common law, the husband could pursue such an action but the wife could not is that the common law regarded husband and wife as one person, that person being the husband"); Moran v. Quality Aluminum Casting Co., 34 Wis.2d 542, 150 N.W.2d 137 (1967):

"[U]pon marriage, husband and wife became one, and he was that one. The personal property, money and chattels of the wife became those of her husband. She could neither contract nor bring an action of any kind, for she was a legal nonentity. Blackstone declared:

" 'By marriage, the husband and wife are one person in law: that is, the very being or legal existence of the woman is suspended during the marriage, or at least is incorporated and consolidated into that of the husband. . . . Upon this principle, of a union of person in husband and wife, depend almost all the legal rights, duties, and disabilities, that either of them acquire by the marriage.' "

11. Montgomery v. Stephan, 359 Mich. 33, 101 N.W.2d 227 (1960) ("These precedents are venerable. Their chains may be moss-encrusted and rusty but only a few courts have held that they no longer control or confine. Thus again we reach the conflict that divides us, for the law as Dean Pound put it, must be stable, and yet it cannot stand still. Were we to rule upon precedent along, were stability the only reason for our being, we would have no trouble with this case. We would simply tell the woman to begone, and to take her shattered husband with her, that we need no longer be affronted by a sight to repulsive. In so doing we would have vast support from the dusty books. But dust of the decision would remain in our mouths through the years ahead, a reproach to law and conscience alike. Our oath is to do justice, not to perpetuate error.").

12. 183 F.2d 811 (D.C.Cir. 1950) cert. denied 340 U.S. 852, 71 S.Ct. 80, 95 L.Ed. 624.

13. 183 F.2d at 816:
There can be no doubt that the expressed view of this court is that

Other courts did not move nearly as swiftly in providing the same relief to a wife. Many courts did not recognize the wife's right until the 1970's.[14] California, long regarded as one of the most progressive courts in the nation, did not bestow this right upon the wife until 1974.[15] Four states only recognized this right in the years 1978 to 1980,[16] which seems rather remarkable, in light of the strong movement in the 70's for women's rights. It was not until June 3, 1980 that the Supreme Court of North Carolina recognized a consortium action in favor of either spouse![17]

Most states now recognize the wife's right by judicial decree or legislation.[18] Only a few states remain [19] which do not afford the wife this right, but do give it to the husband. Several other states [20] still refuse to recognize this action in favor of either spouse.

In 1974, the United States Supreme Court ruled [21] that the widow of a longshoreman mortally injured aboard a vessel in state terri-

---

the husband and the wife have equal rights in the marriage relation which will receive equal protection of the law. That these rights existed prior to the passage of the Married Women's Act cannot be doubted. The Act simply removed the wife's disability to invoke the law's protection.

14. Schreiner v. Fruit, 519 P.2d 462 (Alaska 1974); City of Glendale v. Bradshaw, 108 Ariz. 582, 503 P.2d 803 (1972), appeal after remand 114 Ariz. 236, 560 P.2d 420; Gates v. Foley, 247 So.2d 40 (Fla.1971); Kotsiris v. Ling, 451 S.W.2d 411 (Ky.1970); Diaz v. Eli Lilly & Co., 364 Mass. 153, 302 N.E.2d 555 (1973); General Elec. Co. v. Bush, 88 Nev. 360, 498 P.2d 366 (1972); Clouston v. Remlinger Oldsmobile Cadillac, Inc., 22 Ohio St.2d 65, 258 N.E.2d 230 (1970); Hopkins v. Blanco, 224 Pa.Super. 116, 302 A.2d 855 (1973), aff'd 457 Pa. 90, 320 A.2d 139.

15. Rodriguez v. Bethlehem Steel Corp., 12 Cal.3d 382, 115 Cal.Rptr. 765, 525 P.2d 669 (1974).

16. Hopson v. St. Mary's Hosp., 176 Conn. 485, 408 A.2d 260 (1979); Albertson v. Travis, 2 Kan.App.2d 153, 576 P.2d 1090 (1978); Whittlesey v. Miller, 572 S.W.2d 665 (Tex.1978).

17. Nicholson v. Hugh Chatham Memorial Hosp. Inc., 300 N.C. 295, 266 S.E.2d 818 (1980).

18. Other states which have provided such a right to the wife includes: Colorado, see Crouch v. West, 29 Colo.App. 72, 477 P.2d 805 (1970); Mississippi, Tribble v. Gregory, 288 So.2d 13 (Miss.1974); New Hampshire, Bromfield v. Seybolt Motors, Inc., 109 N.H. 501, 256 A.2d 151 (1969); Oregon, Smith v. Smith, 205 Or. 286, 287 P.2d 572 (1955); and Tennessee, Burroughs v. H. E. Jordan, 224 Tenn. 418, 456 S.W.2d 652 (1970).

19. New Mexico: Roseberry v. Starkovich, 73 N.M. 211, 387 P.2d 321 (1963); Washington: Ash v. S. S. Mullen, Inc., 43 Wash.2d 345, 261 P. 2d 118 (1953); Wyoming: Bates v. Donnafield, 481 P.2d 347 (Wyo.1971).

20. Carey v. Foster, 221 F.Supp. 185 (E.D.Va.1963), aff'd 345 F.2d 772 (4th Cir.); McFarland v. Cathy, 349 So.2d 486 (La.App.1977); Nicholson v. Hugh Chatham Memorial Hosp., Inc., 43 N.C.App. 615, 259 S.E.2d 586 (1979); Ellis v. Hathaway, 27 Utah2d 143, 493 P.2d 985 (1972).

21. Sea-Land Services, Inc. v. Guadet, 414 U.S. 573, 94 S.Ct. 806, 39 L.Ed.2d

torial waters could recover for the loss of her deceased husband's "society." The Supreme Court, in May, 1980, held [22] that general maritime law gives the wife a cause of action for loss of consortium when her husband is injured.

§ 25.4 Rationales Given for Extending Right to Wife

The courts' approaches to extending this action to the wife were numerous. Some found it was a denial of equal protection.[23] Others found the old argument that the wife's damages were too speculative [24] were spurious. The loss to the wife was not less substantial nor distinguishable from the loss to the husband, and juries had been computing his loss with no difficulty.[25] Other courts could

9 (1974), reh. denied 415 U.S. 986, 94 S.Ct. 1582, 39 L.Ed.2d 883.

22. American Export Lines, Inc. v. Alvez, 446 U.S. 274, 100 S.Ct. 1673, 64 L.Ed.2d 284 (1980).

23. See e. g., Hitaffer v. Argonne Co., 183 F.2d 811 (D.C.Cir. 1950) cert. denied 340 U.S. 852, 71 S.Ct. 80, 95 L. Ed. 624; Gates v. Foley, 247 So.2d 40 (Fla.1971) ("The intangible segments of the elements comprising a cause of action for loss of consortium are equally previous to both husband and wife. The classification by sex formerly made by this Court discriminates unreasonably and arbitrarily against women and must be abolished."); Moran v. Quality Aluminum Casting Co., 34 Wis.2d 542, 150 N.W. 2d 137 (1967). See also, Owen v. Illinois Baking Corp., 260 F.Supp. 820 (D.C.Mich.1966) ("[T]o grant a husband the right to sue on this right while denying the wife access to the courts in the assertion of this same right is too clearly a violation of Fourteenth Amendment equal protection guarantees to require citation of authority").

24. In Deshotel v. Atchison, Topeka and Santa Fe Ry. Co., 50 Cal.2d 664, 328 P.2d 449 (1958), the Supreme Court of California had stated, "This case was later overruled by Rodriguez v. Bethlehem Steel Corp., 12 Cal. 3d 382, 115 Cal.Rptr. 765, 525 P.2d 669 (1974). Concerning the argument that the damage to the wife was speculative and incapable of determination, the court in Millington v. Southeastern Elevator Co., 22 N.Y.2d 498, 293 N.Y.S.2d 305, 239 N.E.2d 897 (1968) stated: It is also contended that the 'sentimental' damages such as the diminution of the value of her husband's society and affection and the deprivation of sexual relations and the attendant loss of child-bearing opportunity are too personal, intangible, and conjectural to be measured in pecuniary terms by a jury. This argument had no merit. The logic of it would also hold a jury incompetent to award damages for pain and suffering."

See also, Benjamin v. Cleburne Truck & Body Sales, Inc., 424 F.Supp. 1294 (D.C.V.I.1976).

25. In Gist v. French, 136 Cal.App.2d 247, 288 P.2d 1003 (1955), the court held: "A husband is entitled to reasonable compensation for the loss of 'the services, consortium, companionship, and society of his wife.' . . . Like actions for pain and suffering, no definite rule can be prescribed for the measurement of the loss of his wife's society. The value of such loss must be determined by the triers of fact in the exercise of a sound discretion in the light of their own ex-

not understand why the wife could bring a suit for a third party's intentional interference, but not for negligence. How, they queried, did the loss to the wife become any more severe as the result of an intentional act? Was it not true that the loss to the wife was no different whether the tortfeasor was negligent or acting with malice? [26]

Earlier decisions had contended that by allowing a wife to recover for *loss of consortium*, this would be subjecting a defendant to double liability.[27] Modern courts recognized that this threat may be avoided by the court in carefully cautioning the jury that the wife's loss of support is fully compensated by any award to the husband.[28] Collateral estoppel [29] may be applied to ensure the wife is not award-

perience, observation and reflection. No valid arguments exist that the loss to the wife, when her husband has been injured cannot be similarly computed."

26. See, e. g., Diaz v. Eli Lilly & Co., 364 Mass. 153, 302 N.E.2d 555 (1973) (There is an incongruity in allowing either spouse a consortium right for an intentional invasion but denying the right when the conjugal relationship suffers as much or more disturbance and injury through third-party negligence).

27. Deshotel v. Atchison, Topeka & Santa Fe Ry. Co., 50 Cal.2d 664, 328 P.2d 449 (1958) ("A judgment obtained by a husband after he is injured by a third person might include compensation for any impairment of his ability to participate in a normal married life, and, if his wife is allowed redress for loss of consortium in a separate action, there would be danger of double recovery"); Giggey v. Gallagher Transp. Co., 101 Colo. 258, 72 P.2d 1100 (1973) ("The wrongful acts or negligence of which complaint is made in this case were committed against the husband and not directly against plaintiff. His recovery from the defendants, as hereinbefore recited, precludes a double recovery for the same injury or wrong."); Thornton v. First Nat'l Stores, Inc., 340 Mass. 222, 163 N.E. 2d 264 (1960) ("There cannot be a double recovery"); Nickel v. Hardware Mut. Cas. Co., 269 Wis. 647, 70 N.W.2d 205 (1955) "[T]o permit it would result in double recovery to the husband and wife for the same injury").

28. Gates v. Foley, 247 So.2d 40 (Fla. 1971) ("In such actions by the wife, the trial court should carefully caution the jury that any loss to the wife of her husband's material support is fully compensated by any award to him for impairment of his lost earning and that the wife is entitled to recovery only for loss of consortium . . ."); Lombardo v. D. F. Frangioso & Co., Inc., 359 Mass. 529, 269 N.E.2d 836 (1971) "(It has been contended that loss of consortium includes within its scope loss of support and that, since this is an element of damages implicitly contained in the husband's recovery for diminished earning capacity, allowance to the wife for loss of consortium might result in double recovery. . . . A proper charge by the trial judge could eliminate this problem.").

29. Sea-Land Services, Inc. v. Gaudet, 414 U.S. 573, 94 S.Ct. 806, 39 L.Ed.2d 9 (1974) ("Any potential for such double liability can be eliminated by the application of familiar principles of collateral estoppel to preclude a decedent's dependents from attempting to relitigate the issue of the support due from decedent's future

ed damages previously awarded the husband. Loss of support and fees for nursing services should be excluded, as those should have been separately recovered by the injured spouse.[30] As long as the jury understands that the wife's recoveries are for those damages suffered by her, to wit loss of consortium, there is no possibility of a double recovery.

Another classic argument utilized by the courts in denying the wife her just recovery was that no other court gave her this right. Stare decisis precluded the court from opening its eyes. But the older decisions failed to realize that the strong points of common law are its flexibility and capacity for growth and application. Unless the courts remain alert to their obligation and opportunity to change the common law when reason and equity demand, the courts will perpetuate antiquity alone and error, rather than doing justice and modernity.[31]

§ 25.5 Procedural Aspects—Derivative v. Non-derivative

Although most states now recognize the right of consortium in favor of either spouse, there is considerable disparity in its procedural treatment. In many states, it is deemed to be a derivative action: one that arises from the principle tort and is inseparable therefrom.[32]

wages"); Fitzgerald v. Meissner & Hicks, Inc., 38 Wis.2d 571, 157 N.W.2d 595 (1968).

30. Rindlisbaker v. Wilson, 95 Idaho 752, 519 P.2d 421 (1974); Kotsiris v. Ling, 451 S.W.2d 411 (Ky.1970) ("First, the cause does not include any right of recovery for loss of financial support by the husband. That is because the source of the wife's right to support is the husband's earning capacity, for impairment of which he is entitled to recover. Second, the cause does not include any right of recovery for nursing services rendered or to be rendered to the husband by the wife. The reason for this is that according to the general rule (which we hereby adopt) the husband is entitled to recover from the tortfeasor for the value of nursing services even though the services are rendered or to be rendered by the wife."); Hockstra v. Helgeland, 78 S.D. 82, 98 N.W.2d 669 (1959) ("The wife does not lose the right to, and cannot recover for, the support of her husband"); Whittlesey v. Miller, 572 S.W.2d 665 (Tex.1978) ("[T]here is no duplication of recovery. Each spouse recovers for losses peculiar to the injury sustained by each of them.").

31. See Stare Decisis and the Lawyer's Duty, Chapter 3, Have I a Case?, supra.

32. Benjamin v. Cleburne Truck & Body Sales, Inc., 424 F.Supp 1294 (D.C.V.I.1976) ("The right of action is a derivative right and accordingly may accrue only to the extent that the other spouse has a cause of action against the same defendant"); Nelson v. Busby, 246 Ark. 247, 437 S.W.2d 799 (1969) ("[T]he husband's right to special damages for his loss of consortium and his wife's medical expenses was derivative. It is only logical that since his cause of action

The remaining states recognize the right as being non-derivative, a separate and independent action.[33]

Where the right is derivative, it must be joined with the injured spouse's action and is bound by the disposition of the original claim.[34] If the injured spouse settles, loses, or is otherwise barred from pursuing the original claim, the loss of consortium action is similarly barred.[35] The right, when classified derivative, is subject to any de-

is derivative, [plaintiff] can have no better standing in court than is vested in his wife."); Gates v. Foley, 247 So.2d 40 (Fla.1971); Swanson v. Ball, 67 S.D. 161, 290 N.W. 482 (1940); White v. Lunder, 66 Wis.2d 563, 225 N.W.2d 442 (1975) (Holding that although the right is not derivative in the usual sense, it is subject to the defense of the injured spouse's contributory negligence).

33. Macon v. Seaward Constr. Co., Inc., 555 F.2d 1 (1st Cir. 1977); Lantis v. Condon, 95 Cal.App.3d 152, 157, 157 Cal.Rptr. 22, 24 (1979) (Although the wife's cause of action "arises" from the bodily injury to her husband, the injury suffered is personal to the wife. Loss of her husband's consortium impairs a wife's interest which are wholly separate and distinct from that of her husband: "[T]he wife's loss is just as real as it is distinct. She can no longer enjoy her legally sanctioned and morally proper privilege of copulation or procreation, and is otherwise deprived of her full enjoyment of her marital state. These are her rights, not his." Thus, the injury incurred can neither be said to have been "parasitic" upon the husband's cause of action nor can it be properly characterized as an injury to the marital unit as a whole.); La Bonte v. National Gypsum Co., 110 N.H. 314, 269 A.2d 634 (1974) ("[T]he right of action for loss of impairment of consortium granted to the wife (as well as to the husband) is a separate and distinct right from that of her husband to recover for her separate and distinct loss of consortium which results to her from the negligent injury to her husband.").

34. Bitsos v. Red Owl Stores, Inc., 350 F.Supp. 850 (D.C.S.D.1972) ("The wife's cause of action being born of the husband's actionable loss is controlled by its fate. The wife's cause of action must rise or fall upon the success or failure of her husband's cause of action.); "Deems v. Western Maryland Ry. Co., 247 Md. 95, 231 A.2d 514 (1967) (Requiring that the separate actions of the husband for his physical injuries and that of the wife for loss of consortium must be joined for trial); Ekalo v. Constructive Service Corp. of America, 46 N.J. 82, 215 A.2d 1 (1965); Moran v. Quality Aluminum Casting Co., 34 Wis.2d 542, 150 N.W.2d 137 (1967) ("[A] wife may maintain an action for loss of consortium of her husband against a negligent tortfeasor provided, and on condition, that her cause of action is combined with that of her husband for his personal injuries.").

35. Hopson v. St. Mary's Hosp., 176 Conn. 485, 408 A.2d 260 (1979) ("[B]ecause a consortium action is derivative of the injured spouse's cause of action, the consortium claim would be barred when the suit brought by the injured spouse has been terminated by settlement or by an adverse judgment on the merits."); Kolar v. Chicago, 12 Ill.App.3d 887, 299 N.E.2d 479 (1973) (When claim for substantive injury is barred by statute of limitations, suit for loss of consortium is also barred); Thill v. Modern Erecting Co., 284 Minn. 508, 170 N. W.2d 865 (1969) (Holding that the wife may recover for loss of consortium only if her injured husband recovers from the same defendant);

fenses which could be asserted against the injured spouse.[36] Thus, if the injured spouse was negligent in a contributory negligence state, this would act to bar both the original claim and the loss of consortium action.[37] If one happens to be in a comparative negligence state which recognizes the loss of consortium action as derivative, then the award in the consortium action must be reduced by 25 percent if the spouse is 25 percent negligent.

A defendant who has received a favorable judgment may assert res judicata to bar the consortium claim.[38] In the opposite situation, where there has been a finding of negligence against defendant, res judicata acts to bar its contention of non-liability in the consortium action.[39]

If the state in which one files suit treats the action for loss of consortium as non-derivative, it is not affected by the outcome of the injured spouse's claim,[40] nor is it subject to any defense which conceivably could be asserted against the injured spouse. Res judicata is often held [41] not to apply to bar the consortium claim. Although it is preferred that the consortium count be joined with the original tort claim, it is not mandatory when the right is non-derivative.[42]

Millington v. Southeastern Elevator Co., 22 N.Y.2d 498, 293 N.Y.S.2d 305, 239 N.E.2d 897 (1968) ("Where . . . the husband's cause of action has been terminated either by judgment, settlement or otherwise, that should operate to bar the wife's cause of action for consortium").

36. Nelson v. Busby, 246 Ark. 247, 437 S.W.2d 799 (1969); White v. Lunder, 66 Wis.2d 563, 225 N.W.2d 442 (1975).

37. Gates v. Foley, 247 So.2d 40 (Fla. 1971) (Holding that in order for spouse to recover for loss of consortium, injured spouse must have been free of any contributory negligence); White v. Lunder, 66 Wis.2d 563, 225 N.W.2d 442 (1975).

38. Jess v. Great Northern Ry. Co., 401 F.2d 535 (9th Cir. 1968); Stickney v. E. R. Squibb & Sons, Inc., 377 F.Supp. 785 (M.D.Fla.1974); Chandler v. Gately, 119 Ga.App. 513, 167 S.E.2d 697 (1969); Laws v. Fisher, 513 P.2d 876 (Okl.1973); Brown v. University Nursing Home, Inc., 496 S.W.2d 503 (Tenn.App.1973).

39. Bitsos v. Red Owl Stores, Inc., 350 F.Supp. 850 (D.C.S.D.1972); Davis v. Asbell, 328 So.2d 204 (Fla.App.1976); Snodgrass v. General Tele. Co., 275 Or. 79, 549 P.2d 1120 (1976).

40. Macon v. Seaward Constr. Co., Inc., 55 F.2d 1 (1st Cir. 1977); Lantis v. Condon, 95 Cal.App.3d 152, 157 Cal.Rptr. 22 (1979); Kotsiris v. Ling, 451 S.W.2d 411 (Ky.1970).

41. Jones v. Beasley, 476 F.Supp. 116 (M.D.Ga.1979); Wolff v. Du Puis, 233 Or. 317, 378 P2d 707 (1963), overruled on other grounds, Bahler v. Fletcher, 257 Or. 1, 474 P.2d 329 (1970); Palmer v. Clarksdale Hosp., 213 Miss. 611, 57 So.2d 476 (1952).

42. Rodriguez v. Bethlehem Steel Corp., 12 Cal.3d 382, 115 Cal.Rptr. 765, 525 P.2d 669 (1974); Kotsiris v. Ling, 451 S.W.2d 411 (Ky.1970); Shepherd v. Consumers Co-op. Ass'n, 384 S.W.2d 635 (Mo.1964); Fitzgerald v. Meissner & Hicks, Inc., 38 Wis.2d 571, 157 N.W.2d 595 (1968).

§ 25.6 Requirement of Marriage

For a spouse to bring an action for loss of consortium when his or her mate is injured, there is the almost universal requirement that the couple is married at the time of the injury-producing accident.[43] It is said that the right of consortium grows out of the marriage relationship, and in the absence of a lawful husband-wife relationship, there can be no recovery.[44]

When a couple is engaged at the time of the accident, most courts still deny recovery,[45] even if the couple marries within a month.[46] Only one court is known to the author wherein such recovery was permitted. In *Sutherland v. Auch Inter-Borough Transit Co.*,[47] a Federal District Court construing Pennsylvania law, ruled that the Supreme Court of Pennsylvania would make some modification of the rule to permit recovery when the couple were engaged at the time of the accident, and married less than a month afterwards. However, Pennsylvania decisions both before[48] and after[49] have denied such claims.

The author is of the belief that the arbitrary requirement of marriage should be abolished. A couple engaged at the time of the accident and who marry shortly thereafter may suffer more injury to consortium than does a couple married at the time of the accident who divorce shortly thereafter. Furthermore, many couples today are opting for alternative relationships, and do not find it necessary to go through the "mere formality" of marriage. Nonetheless, the injuries they suffer when their loved one is injured is no less severe than the loss suffered by a husband or wife when the other is injured.

---

43. Wagner v. International Harvester Co., 455 F.Supp. 168 (D.Minn.1978); Tribble v. Gregory, 288 So.2d 13 (Miss.1974).

44. Domany v. Otis Elevator Co., 369 F.2d 604 (6th Cir. 1966), cert. denied 387 U.S. 942, 87 S.Ct. 2073, 18 L.Ed. 2d 1327.

45. Rademacher v. Torbensen, 257 App.Div. 91, 13 N.Y.S.2d 124 (1939).

46. Tong v. Jocson, 76 Cal.App.3d 603, 142 Cal.Rptr. 726 (1977) (Couple engaged and living together at time of injury married three weeks later. Court denied recovery, noting that liability must terminate somewhere to prevent an "indefinite extension of liability for loss of consortium to all foreseeable relationships."); Sawyer v. Bailey, 413 A.2d 165 (Me.1980) ("[T]he law is concerned with the protection of the 'relational' interests of married persons and recognizes as an actionable tort any interference, intentional or negligent, with the *continuation* of the relation of husband and wife, such as the right to damages for the loss of consortium of either one of the spouses").

47. 366 F.Supp. 127 (E.D.Pa.1973).

48. Sartori v. Gradison Auto Bus Co., Inc., 42 Pa.D. & C.2d 781, 47 Wash. Co. 246 (1967).

49. Rockwell v. Liston, 71 Pa.D. & C. 2d 756 (1975).

A federal district court has recently made a landmark decision which permits recovery for loss of consortium even though the couple is not married at the time of the injury. Attorney *Gerald M. Eisenstat* [50] of Vineland, New Jersey, reports *Bullock v. United States* [51] in which he is participating as trial counsel.

Plaintiffs therein were married for 26 years. On April 26, 1974, they separated, and a formal Judgment of Divorce was entered on February 17, 1977. On May 21 of that same year, plaintiff's ex-husband was injured in a scuba diving accident. The affidavit alleged that prior to the date of the accident, the couple had agreed to a reconciliation, were planning to resume living together, and ultimately to remarry.

The accident rendered the ex-husband incapable of engaging in sexual relations. Plaintiffs considered entering into a marriage ceremony, but were advised that since it was impossible for them to consummate the marital act, the ceremony would be of no consequence. (The court pointed out that they were incorrectly advised on this, as New Jersey law did not require consummation. However, this was of no effect to the suit, since plaintiffs had sincerely believed the advice they were given.) In September of 1977, plaintiffs resumed living together, and from that date on, held themselves out as husband and wife.

After analyzing decisions by New Jersey courts which recognized a non-marital, co-habitating relationship as a lawful one, the federal court judge stated that it was obvious that a member of a co-habitating couple could suffer identical damage to that suffered by a spouse when his or her mate was injured.

The court continued: "The strong New Jersey policy of compensating those whose injuries are proximately caused by the tortious conduct of others would seem to outweigh the policy favoring marriage. The fact that a cohabitant suffers as much as a spouse would prevent the courts from remaining neutral towards the relationship. . . . Recognizing an action for loss of consortium in circumstances like those at bar only means that tortfeasors will compensate more fully for the actual damage caused. It does not mean that the marital relationship is devalued. While many considerations lead to marriage, I doubt many decide to marry because they want to have a cause of action for loss of consortium. Deciding against a cause of action for cohabitants, therefore, is unlikely to encourage

---

50. Gerald M. Eisenstat, Esquire, Shapiro, Eisenstat, Capizola, O'Neill & Gabage, A Professional Corporation, 1179 East Landis Avenue, P. O. Box O, Vineland, New Jersey.

51. Bulloch v. United States, 487 F. Supp. 1078 (D.C.N.J.1980).

people to wed. Realistically, both married couples and cohabitants dread the possibility of injury to their mate and suffer when that injury occurs. It is the suffering of the mate of the physically injured plaintiff that the tort compensates."

The author agrees that recovery should be allowed even when couples are not married. This is not to infer that a loss of consortium should be awarded regardless of the couple's relationship. Guidlines should, of course, be formulated so that compensation is awarded only when a *bona fide* relationship exists to prevent spurious claims.

§ 25.7   Parents' Action for Loss of Filial Consortium

When a child has been injured, courts have split on the question of whether its parents may bring a claim for loss of filial consortium. At common law, a parent could recover for the loss of services resulting from the injury to the child. This recovery is rooted in older times when the pecuniary contribution of the child to the family was considerably greater than it is today.[52] Many of the jurisdictions which statutorily or otherwise provide for recovery of the lost services do not recognize a claim for loss of filial consortium.[53] The deni-

---

52. Katz, Schroeder & Sidman, "Emancipating Our Children—Coming of Legal Age in America," 7 Family Law Q. 211 (1973) ("In colonial America children occupied the lowest rungs of the social ladder. Various enactments of the Massachusetts Bay Colony suggest that children and servants were treated similarly before the law and were subject to the harshest punishments for relatively trivial offenses. Apprenticeship 'was often merely a specialized form of servitude.' Children owed the strictest obedience toward parents and were expected to assume completely subservient positions within the family unit. Since child labor was crucial to the economic system, the parential right to a minor child's services and wages was also a practical necessity.").

53. Smith v. Richardson, 277 Ala. 389, 171 So.2d 96 (1965) ("[S]ervices means the labor and assistance of a child rendered for the father, and imply a loss measured by pecuniary standards of value. . . . The loss of the society of a child as distinguished from the loss of its services, cannot form the element of recoverable damages."); Baxter v. Superior Court, 19 Cal.3d 461, 138 Cal. Rptr. 315, 563 P.2d 871 (1977) ("In California, however, the parent's cause of action has not expanded beyond the ancient right to recover for loss of earnings and services of economic value. . . . [In view of] the intangible nature of the injury and the danger of multiplication of claims and liability, we decline to enlarge the parent's cause of action to permit recovery for the loss of affection and society."); Deems v. Western Maryland Ry. Co., 247 Md. 95, 231 A.2d 514 (1967); Butler v. Chrestman, 264 So.2d 812 (Miss.1972) ("Loss of the society and companionship of a child [is not] an element in fixing the damages recoverable by a parent for injuries to a sibling"); Brennan v. Biber, 93 N.J.Super. 351,

al of this claim is usually based on the argument that loss of comfort, sustenance and filial support are too remote.[54]

A growing number of courts now permit a count for loss of filial consortium to be included in the complaint.[55] It has been recognized that the society and companionship between parents and their children "are closer to our present day family ideal than the right of the parents to the 'earning capacity during minority,' which once seemed so important when the common law was established." [56]

The restrictive common law pecuniary loss test has been rejected by many states via the modification of their wrongful death statutes.[57] Using these statutes as support, there seems to be no valid reason why loss of filial consortium should not be recoverable, except for arbitrary decisions of judges acting without regard for the values of present-day society. When a child is so severely injured that a nor-

---

225 A.2d 742 (1966), aff'd 99 N.J.Super 247, 239 A.2d 261 ("Parent may not recover damages for loss of society and companionship of an injured child").

54. Michigan Sanitarium & Benevolent Ass'n v. Neal, 194 N.C. 401, 139 S.E. 841 (1927).

55. Drayton v. Jiffee Chem. Corp., 395 F.Supp. 1081 (N.D.Ohio 1975), motion denied 413 F.Supp. 834 (Award of $100,000 for loss of daughter's services and society upheld); Miller v. Subia, 514 P.2d 79 (Colo.App.1973); Yordon v. Savage, 279 So.2d 844 (Fla.1973) (Parent has cause of action for loss of child's companionship, society and services); Hayward v. Yost, 72 Idaho 415, 242 P.2d 971 (1952) (Damages include loss of protection, comfort, society and companionship); Stephens v. Weigel, 336 Ill.App. 36, 82 N.E.2d 697 (1948).

56. Shockley v. Prier, 66 Wis.2d 394, 225 N.W.2d 495 (1975) ("We conclude that the law should recognize the right of parents to recover for loss of aid, comfort, society and companionship of a child during minority when such loss is caused by the negligence of another.").

57. D'Ambra v. United States, 481 F. 2d 14 (1st Cir. 1973), cert. denied 414 U.S. 1075, 94 S.Ct. 592, 38 L.Ed.2d 482 (FTCA case—"An equally but more limited element of compensation for the loss of a minor child, capable of responsible judicial application, seems to us to lie in the loss of society and companionship of the child"); Wardlow v. City of Keokuk, 190 N.W.2d 439 (Iowa 1971), appeal after remand 206 N.W.2d 700 (Iowa); Fussner v. Andert, 261 Minn. 347, 113 N.W.2d 355 (1961) ("We agree with the plaintiff that the strict pecuniary-loss measure of damages, which limits recovery to the parent for the loss of earnings, contributions, and services in terms of dollars which the survivor might have expected to receive during the lifetime of the child, is unduly restrictive and its meaning should be expanded to conform to present-day needs and experience."); Lockhart v. Besel, 71 Wash.2d 112, 426 P.2d 605 (1967) ("We hold that the measure of damages . . . should be extended to include the loss of companionship of a minor child during his minority without giving any consideration for grief, mental anguish or suffering of the parents by reason of such child's wrongful death.").

mal parent-child relationship cannot be enjoyed, courts should provide a remedy against the tortfeasor.[58]

§ 25.8 Child's Action for Loss of Parental Consortium

If a third party negligently injures a parent, all[59] but two[60] states which have considered the question have denied the child's claim for loss of parental consortium.

§ 25.9 Why Action Is Denied

One of the strongest arguments advanced in favor of denying a child's claim is that money is no substitute for a parent,[61] and the

58. Shockley v. Prier, 66 Wis.2d 394, 225 N.W.2d 495 (1975) ("In the case at bar one needs little imagination to see the shattering effect that [the child's] blindness will have on the relationship between him and his parents. The loss of the enjoyment of those experiences normally shared by parents and children need no enumeration here.").

59. The following cases, representing 15 states and the District of Columbia, deny recovery: Early v. United States, 474 F.2d 756 (9th Cir. 1973) (Alaska law); Pleasant v. Washington Sand & Gravel Co., 262 F.2d 471 (D.C. Cir. 1958); Meredith v. Scruggs, 244 F.2d 604 (9th Cir. 1957), rev'g per curiam, 134 F.Supp. 868 (D. Hawaii 1955); Turner v. Atlantic Coast Line R. R. Co., 159 F.Supp. 590 (N.D.Ga. 1958); Hill v. Sibley Memorial Hosp., 108 F.Supp. 739 (D.D.C.1952); Jeune v. Del E. Webb Constr. Co., 77 Ariz. 226, 269 P.2d 723 (1954), overruled on other grounds, Glendale v. Bradshaw, 108 Ariz. 582, 503 P.2d 803 (1972), appeal after remand 114 Ariz. 236, 560 P.2d 430; Borer v. American Airlines, Inc., 19 Cal.3d 441, 138 Cal. Rptr. 302, 563 P.2d 858 (1977); Clark v. Suncoast Hosp. Inc., 338 So.2d 1117 (Fla.App.1976); Halberg v. Young, 41 Hawaii 634 (1957); Hankins v. Derby, 211 N.W.2d 581 (Iowa 1973); Hoffman v. Dautel, 189 Kan. 165, 368 P.2d 57 (1962); Eschenback v. Benjamin, 195 Minn. 378, 263 N.W. 154 (1935), overruled on other grounds, Beaudette v. Frana, 285 Minn. 366, 173 N.W.2d 416 (1969); Stout v. Kansas City Terminal Ry. Co., 172 Mo.App. 113, 157 S.W. 1019 (1913) (dicta), overruled on other grounds, Novak v. Kansas City Transit, Inc., 365 S.W.2d 539 (Mo.1963); General Elec. Co. v. Bush, 88 Nev. 360, 498 P.2d 366 (1972); Russell v. Salem Transp. Co., Inc., 61 N.J. 502, 295 A.2d 862 (1972); Cox v. Streton, 77 Misc.2d 155, 352 N.Y.S.2d 834 (Sup.Ct.1974); Duhan v. Milanowski, 75 Misc.2d 1078, 348 N.Y.S.2d 696 (Sup.Ct.1973); Gibson v. Johnston, 144 N.E.2d 310 (Ohio App.1956), appeal dism'd, 166 Ohio St. 288, 141 N. E.2d 767; Roth v. Bell, 24 Wash. App. 92, 600 P.2d 602 (1979).

60. Ferritter v. Daniel O'Connell's Sons, Inc., — Mass. —, 413 N.E.2d 690 (1980), reported in 23 ATLA Law Reporter 388 (Nov. 1980); Berger v. Weber, 82 Mich.App. 199, 267 N.W.2d 124 (1978).

61. Millington v. Southeastern Elevator Co., 22 N.Y.2d 498, 293 N.Y.S.2d 305, 239 N.E.2d 897 (1968). ("Money is a poor substitute for the loss of an only child or the pain resulting from serious injuries. Likewise, it cannot truly compensate a wife for the destruction of her marriage, but it is the only known means to compensate

only result of an award for loss of parental consortium will be that, upon reaching adulthood, the children will become "unusually wealthy men and women." [62] (This reasoning would void all tort law!) Money is no support for a lost limb, yet it is the only way the law knows of making an injured plaintiff "whole".

The argument that money is no substitute for a parent is spurious. Many courts award a child whose parent has been killed damages for loss of consortium. The Supreme Court of California justified this anomaly on the basis that "the historical purpose of the wrongful death statute fulfills a deeply felt social belief that a tortfeasor who negligently kills someone should not escape liability completely." [63] In the case of a parent who is "merely" disabled, the tortfeasor, according to the court, cannot escape with impunity, being subject to an action by the injured parent.

Another reason often advanced when the child's claim is rejected is that the damages to the child are highly speculative and incapable of measurement.[64] However, courts have no difficulty measuring these damages when there has been intentional interference with the parent-child relationship.[65]

Some courts also place misguided reliance on the fact that as between a husband and wife, consortium includes an element of sexual relations.[66] Since there is no such element inherent in the parent-

for the loss suffered and to symbolize society's recognition that a culpable wrong—even if unintentional—has been done.").

62. In Borer v. American Airlines, Inc., 19 Cal.3d 441, 138 Cal.Rptr. 302, 563 P.2d 858 (1977), Acting Chief Justice Mathew O. Tobriner wrote:
Loss of consortium is an intangible, nonpecuniary loss; monetary compensation will not enable plaintiffs to regain the companionship and guidance of a mother; it will simply establish a fund so that upon reaching adulthood, when plaintiffs will be less in need of maternal guidance, they will be unusually wealthy men and women. To say that plaintiffs have been "compensated" for their loss is superficial; in reality they have suffered a loss for which they can never be compensated; they have obtained, instead, a future benefit essentially unrelated to that loss.

63. Borer v. American Airlines, Inc., 19 Cal.3d 441, 138 Cal.Rptr. 302, 563 P.2d 858 (1977).

64. Id. at 448, 138 Cal.Rptr. 307, 563 P.2d at 863 ("A second reason for rejecting a cause of action for loss of parental consortium is that, because of its intangible character, damages for such a loss are very difficult to measure. Plaintiffs here have prayed for $100,000 each; yet by what standard could we determine that an award of $10,000 was inadequate, or one of $500,000 excessive?").

65. Id. at 451 n. 3, 138 Cal.Rptr. at 309 n. 3, 563 P.2d at 865 n. 3.

66. In Borer v. American Airlines, Inc., 19 Cal.3d at 448, 138 Cal.Rptr. at 307, 563 P.2d at 863 (1977), Justice Tobriner pointed out that "the spousal action for loss of consortium rests in large part on the impairment or destruction of the sexual life of the

child relationship, courts deny the child any recovery. Yet if a husband and wife had a non-existent sex life, it does not seem probable that the courts would deny them relief for loss of consortium.

In addition to the above arguments, courts emphasize the possible multiplicity of suits. Whereas recognizing a right to sue for loss of consortium in favor of a spouse creates only one lawsuit, an injured father having many children would generate that many more claims, each entitled to separate appraisal and award.[67]

Finally, in a typical opinion the court will point out that few other courts allow such recovery. Therefore, since other courts will not wade into new waters, it too will refuse to take the judicial plunge. This specious argument is best answered by Justice Stanley Mosk's stirring dissent stating that "[W]hen that crowd is marching in the wrong direction, we have not heretofore hesitated to break ranks and strike out on our own."[68]

The true reason the courts do not recognize this claim is a purely arbitrary policy determination[69] that liability is not endless, and must terminate somewhere. The author contends that this approach is erroneous. The test which should be applied is that of forseeability: if it is forseeable that children would suffer this harm, then public policy and the most elementary principles of tort law require that they are justly compensated for their injuries.

§ 25.10   Recovery When Parent "Severely Injured"

In 1978, a Michigan appellate court became the first court to recognize this cause of action on behalf of an injured child. In *Berger v. Weber*,[70] the mother of a mentally retarded daughter was "severely" injured due to the negligence of a third party. The court allowed the child's claim for loss of consortium, correctly pointing out that it is of no consequence to the child whether the parent has been killed or so severely injured as to be unable to perform the parental function. In those cases the nisi prius (trial) judge must carefully ex-

couple. . . . No similar element of damage appears in a child's suit for loss of consortium."

67. Russell v. Salem Transp. Co., Inc., 61 N.J. 502, 295 A.2d 862, 864 (1972).

68. Borer v. American Airlines, Inc., 19 Cal.3d 441, 138 Cal.Rptr. 302, 563 P.2d 858 (1977) (Mosk, J., dissenting).

69. Suter v. Leonard, 45 Cal.App.3d 744, 120 Cal.Rptr. 110 (1975) ("[N]ot every loss can be made compensable in money damages, and legal causation must terminate somewhere. In delineating the extent of a tortfeasor's responsibility for damages under the general rule of tort liability . . . , the courts must locate the line between liability and nonliability at some point, a decision which is essentially political."); Roth v. Bell, 24 Wash.App. 92, 600 P.2d 602 (1979).

70. 82 Mich.App. 199, 267 N.W.2d 124 (1978).

amine the state law for compensable elements in wrongful death and see that there is no overlapping or double recovery if consortium loss is allowed, that the latter awards for loss of different elements.

This view is in accord with that of Dean Prosser, who stated:[71] "It is not easy to understand and appreciate this reluctance to compensate this child who has been deprived of the care, companionship and education of his mother, or for that matter, his father, through the defendant's negligence. This is surely a genuine injury and a serious one, which has received a great deal more sympathy from legal writers than from the judges."

On September 9, 1980, the Supreme Judicial Court of Massachusetts became the first court of last resort[72] to recognize a child's claim for loss of consortium when its parent is injured. The court therein agreed with the Michigan Court of Appeals approach in *Berger v. Weber*,[73] and declared that the rationale advanced for denying recovery to the child was unsound.

If the true spirit of the law, and not antiquated principles, is followed, courts should have no problem affording a child whose parent is severely injured his just remedy and due compensation. However, several courts decided after *Berger v. Weber* still deny the child any such right, despite the fact they acknowledge that a child realizes a real and significant loss when a parent is injured by a third party.[74]

---

71. Prosser on Torts 896–897 (4th Ed. 1971) (footnotes omitted).

   Prosser goes on to state:
   . . . There is of course the problem of preventing double compensation . . ., since the child will to some extent benefit by any sum recovered by the injured parent; but it is quite evident that this will not and cannot recompense him for all that he has lost. The obstacles in the way of satisfactory limitation of recovery are no greater than in the case of the wife [suing for loss of consortium]. As has been said even by one court which considered itself forced to deny recovery, it is difficult "on the basis of natural justice to reach the conclusion that this type of action will not lie." It is particularly difficult when recovery is permitted to the wife, but denied to the child.

72. Ferriter v. Daniel O'Connell's Sons, Inc., —— Mass. ——, 413 N.E.2d 690 (1980).

73. 82 Mich.App. 199, 267 N.W.2d 124 (1978).

74. Bradford v. Union Elec. Co., 598 S.W.2d 149, 150 (Mo.App.1979). See also Hoesing v. Sears, Roebuck & Co., 484 F.Supp. 478 (D.C.Neb.1980); Morgel v. Winger, 290 N.W.2d 266 (N.D. 1980).

§§ 25.11–26.0 are reserved for supplementary material.

CHAPTER 26

TORT LIABILITY AND THE FAMILIAL RELATIONSHIP

Table of Sections

Sec.
26.1 In General.
26.2 Husband—Wife Immunities.
26.3 Parent—Child Immunities.
26.4 Family Law—Vicarious Liability.

---

§ 26.1   In General

The structure of the family in America has changed greatly since the first edition of *Modern Trials*. The last twenty-five years has seen not only a decline in the American birth rate but also a large increase in the incidence of divorce. Reflecting this great change within the family structure has been the court's handling of inter-familial immunity and liability.

Whereas the original *Modern Trials* could say, "The majority rule has continually recognized the common law disability of husband and wife to maintain personal tort actions against each other," [1] that rule can no longer be stated to be a majority viewpoint.

§ 26.2   Husband—Wife Immunities

At common law, any tort action between spouses was confronted with the dogma of merged legal identity, and as a result the rule arose that neither spouse could be civilly liable to the other for an act which would have been a tort in absence of the marriage relation.[2]

---

1. Belli, 1 Modern Trials 479 (1954).

2. Rupert v. Stienne, 90 Nev. 397, 528 P.2d 1013, 1015 (1974), "At common law, a husband and wife were regarded as one because a metaphysical merger had taken place, and the legal existence of the wife had merged with that of the husband. Under this concept, either spouse was precluded from maintaining an action against the other for wrongful conduct whether intentional or negligent." 1 Blackstone Commentaries 442; Prosser, The Law of Torts, § 122 (4th ed. 1971). This artificial concept cannot be seriously defended today and is not compatible with our current conditions.

Note, 6 U. of Rich.L.Rev. 379 (1972).

The apparent basis of this was "a mixture of the Bible and medieval metaphysics, the position of the father of the family in Roman law, the natural-law concept of the family as an informal unit of government with the physically stronger person at the head, or the property law of feudalism." [3]

An improvement in this scheme resulted in the 18th century when the courts of equity gave the wife a separate equitable estate.[4] The whole premise of legal entity of spouses belonged to a social order no longer consonant with the actuality of living in the 19th century and, as a result, statutes known as the Married Women's Acts, or Emancipation Acts were passed to secure to a married woman a separate legal estate.[5] Courts have generally agreed that under these acts the wife or husband may recover for torts committed by the other against a property interest.[6]

In 1910, the United States Supreme Court held in interpreting a District of Columbia statute [7] that a wife could not recover for injuries received from an assault and battery by her husband. Initially, a majority of states, following the common law and this case, held similarly.

By 1978, however, the Supreme Court of New Jersey was able to say:

> What unfolds from a canvass of the doctrine of interspousal immunity across the country is that its application is far from consistent or uniform; its efficacy as a legal principle has divided jurisdictions; and its utility as a social tool or instrument of justice has confounded courts, legislators and commentators. It is clear, nonetheless, that despite its survival in varying forms, interspousal immunity is no longer the doctrinal monolith it was in olden times. . . . Upon close analysis one finds that cur-

---

3. Prosser, The Law of Torts (4th ed. 1971) p. 860.

4. Snell, Principles of Equity 364 (19th ed. 1925); Dicey, Law and Public Opinion in England, 13 Oh.L.J. 90 (1914).

5. McCurdy, Torts in Domestic Relation in Selected Essays on Family Law, 96 (1950); 3 Verier, American Family Laws (1935), S.S. 167, 179, 180 (Statutes collected).

6. Kennedy v. Camp, 14 N.J. 390, 102 A.2d 595 (1954) (Contract); Eshom v. Eshom, 18 Ariz. 170, 157 P. 974 (1916); Notes v. Snyder, 55 App.D.C. 233, 4 F.2d 426 (Replevin) (1925); Goodwin v. Goodwin, 172 Misc. 118, 13 N.Y.S.2d 894 (1939) (Ejectment to recover possession of her separate estate).

7. Thompson v. Thompson, 218 U.S. 611, 31 S.Ct. 111, 54 L.Ed. 1180 (1910).

§ 26.2   SPECIFIC ACTIONS   Pt. 4

rently only a handful of courts unqualifiedly retain the doctrine in its pristine formulation.[8]

Various states now find exceptions to the traditional law where the marriage has been terminated by death or divorce,[9] where the immunity has been asserted in negligent handling of vehicle cases [10] and

---

8. Merenoff v. Merenoff, 76 N.J. 535, 388 A.2d 951, 955 (1978) citing Paiewonsky v. Paiewonsky, 446 F.2d 178 (3d Cir. 1971), cert. denied 405 U.S. 919, 92 S.Ct. 944, 30 L.Ed.2d 788 (1972) (Applying Virgin Islands law); see also Monk v. Ramsey, 223 Tenn. 247, 443 S.W.2d 653 (1969); Donsbach v. Offield, 488 S.W.2d 494 (Tex. Civ.App.1972); *Accord*, Steffa v. Stanley 39 Ill.App.3d 915, 350 N.E.2d 886 (1976).

The doctrine of interspousal tort immunity has been perpetuated on the notion that it fosters domestic tranquility and prevents fraud and collusion, and it has been frequently argued that fraudulent and collusive suits would flow from abandonment of the rule. There is a possibility of fraud or collusion in every negligence action where the tort-feasor is insured. Where the adversaries are husband and wife, not only are the parties in close personal relationship, but any recovery will inure to the benefit of the entire family, and the failure to recover will affect the entire family adversely.

However, to deny one spouse the opportunity to recover for the tortious conduct of the other because of the possibility of fraud and collusion, belies the centuries old trust in our jury system. An interspousal tort claim should not be saddled with the presumption of fraud ab initio. Courtney v. Courtney, 184 Okl. 395, 87 P. 2d 660 (1938); Rupert v. Stienne, 90 Nev. 397, 528 P.2d 1013 (1974) ("Our adversary system will ferret out the nonmeritorious claims and dispatch those who would practice fraud upon the courts.").

9. See, e. g., Jones v. Pledger, 363 F.2d 986 (D.C.Cir.1966) (Applying District of Columbia law); Apitz v. Dames, 205 Or. 242, 287 P.2d 585 (1955).

The author fails to see how any state could consider the husband-wife immunity applicable where there is no longer a marriage.

10. See e. g., Rupert v. Stienne, 90 Nev. 397, 528 P.2d 1013 (1974); Richard v. Richard, 131 Vt. 98, 300 A.2d 637 (1973); Surratt v. Thompson, 212 Va. 191, 183 S.E.2d 200 (1971).

With the advent of liability insurance in automobile cases there seems no reason to continue the doctrine of immunity in those states still retaining it. The modern lawsuit is against the insurance company, not the spouse. The family carries insurance to protect against all accidents, not the select ones. The dead hand of the past rules historically rather than practically, economically or socially when suit between spouses is disallowed, particularly in the automobile cases. To disfavor suit in such cases may encourage rather than abate domestic disturbances. In the other actions, such as assault, the criminal law punishes but is not compensatory.

For a kindred problem in many community property states, permitting one spouse to recover would enable the other to benefit by his wrong. In those states perhaps the filing of suit could statutorily be made to assign or release the proceeds of the cause of action solely to the innocent spouse. See Rogers v. Yellowstone Park Co., 97 Idaho 14, 539 P.2d 566 (1974).

where the action can be brought against a third party.[11] Other exceptions are recovery for antenuptial torts [12] and intentional torts.[13] Apparently only 16 states still apply the immunity without serious reservations.[14]

§ 26.3 Parent—Child Immunities [15]

No common law doctrine of parent-child immunity existed in English law. The immunity was purely a creation of American common law and originated with the 1891 Mississippi case of *Hewlett v. George*.[16] That case held that a minor child could not maintain a tort action against the parent for wrongful confinement in an insane asylum. Though offering no precedents for the doctrine, the court stated:

> So long as the parent is under obligation to care for, guide, and control, and the child is under reciprocal obligation to aid and comfort and obey, no such action as this can be maintained. The peace of society, and of the families composing society, and a sound public policy, designed to subserve the repose of families and the best interests of society, forbid to the minor child, a right to appear in court in the assertion of a claim to civil redress for personal injuries suffered at the hands of the parent. The state, through its criminal laws, will give the minor child protection from parental violence and wrong-doing, and this is all the child can be heard to demand.

---

11. See, e. g., Fields v. Synthetic Ropes, Inc., 215 A.2d 427 (Del.1965), on remand 219 A.2d 374 (Wife's suit against husband's employer for injuries negligently inflicted by husband in course of his employment sustainable).

12. See, e. g., O'Grady v. Potts, 193 Kan. 644, 396 P.2d 285 (1964); Chen v. Liao, 420 F.Supp. 472 (D.C.Del. 1976) (Construing Delaware Law); Moulton v. Moulton, 309 A. 2d 224 (Me. 1973); Pearce v. Boberg, 89 Nev. 266, 510 P.2d 1358 (1973).

13. See, e. g., Flores v. Flores, 84 N.M. 601, 506 P.2d 345 (App.1973), cert. denied 84 N.M. 592, 506 P.2d 336.

14. MacDonald v. MacDonald, 412 A. 2d 71, 73 n. 3 (Me.1980).

15. The doctrine of "parental immunity" is reciprocal in that in the overwhelming majority of jurisdictions actions by parents against their unemancipated children are barred as well as actions by unemancipated children against their parents. Rupert v. Stienne, 90 Nev. 397, 528 P.2d 1013, 1017 n. 4 (1974); Wright v. Farmers' Reliance Ins. Co., 314 So.2d 641 (Fla.App.1975).

16. 68 Miss. 703, 9 So. 885, 887 (1891).

§ 26.3   SPECIFIC ACTIONS   Pt. 4

Exactly why jurisdictions followed the Mississippi case remains a mystery to legal scholars,[17] but two cases [18] decided shortly after *Hewlett* firmly entrenched the doctrine into American jurisprudence. *Roller v. Roller* refused recovery to a 15-year-old daughter whose father had been criminally convicted of her rape; [19] *McKelvey v. McKelvey* denied a child the right to sue her father and stepmother for cruel and inhuman treatment.

The first major attack on the blind acceptance of the immunity doctrine appears to be the strong dissent of Chief Justice Clark in *Small v. Morrison*.[20] Clark stated:

> In the progress of the ages we have admitted the right to be heard in the courts of women, of men of all races and complexions, and of convicts. The defendant insurance company asks that we shall now turn back the clock of the ages and the onward sweep of universal justice by decreeing that it shall be exempted from the payment of the damages sustained by this little girl because in this equitable proceeding to subrogate her to the rights accruing to her father for damages sustained, it is necessary to make the father a party, and therefore she cannot be heard.

The rationale of that dissent was picked up by the Supreme Court of New Hampshire in 1930 and the first modification to the immunity was formed.[21] This modification allowed an action against the defendant father by the injured child where a master-servant relationship existed between the two.

Many jurisdictions have now abrogated [22] or modified the immunity doctrine. One modification allows recovery in cases where

---

17. Prosser, The Law of Torts (2nd ed. 1951) p. 865.

18. McKelvey v. McKelvey, 111 Tenn. 388, 77 S.W. 664 (1903); Roller v. Roller, 37 Wash. 242, 79 P. 788 (1905).

19. In defense of its decision the court in the Roller case had this to say: "The rule of law prohibiting suits between parent and child is based upon the interest that society has in preserving harmony in domestic relations, an interest which has been manifested since the earliest organization of civilized government, an interest inspired by the universally recognized fact that the maintenance of harmonious and proper family relations is conducive to good citizenship, and, therefore works to the welfare of the state—".

What interest society has in "preserving harmony in domestic relations" when a father has raped his daughter remains elusive to this author.

20. 185 N.C. 577, 118 S.E. 12, 22 (1923).

21. See, e. g., Dunlap v. Dunlap, 84 N. H. 352, 150 A. 905 (1930).

In Accord, Worrell v. Worrell, 174 Va. 11, 4 S.E.2d 343 (1939); Black v. Solmitz, 409 A.2d 634 (Me.1979).

22. See, e. g., Hebel v. Hebel, 435 P.2d 8 (Alaska, 1967); Balts v. Balts, 273 Minn. 419, 142 N.W.2d 66 (1966);

negligent operation of a motor vehicle by a parent causes injury to a minor child.[23] This modification makes particular sense when viewed in light of the fact that most families carry automobile accident insurance. The father would rather see his child compensated than a stranger.

Another exception recognized in some jurisdictions is the duty to supervise.[24] It has also been held that family immunity does not protect a murdering husband in the case of a suit brought by the stepdaughter for the pecuniary loss resulting from the mother's murder.[25]

An outstanding personal injury decision [26] the court allowed an illegitimate to recover for serious shock without physical impact, where her father, with a shotgun, blew her mother's brains on the kitchen table, splattering the girl with blood.

The court refuses to protect the father from suits by his children when his acts show an abandonment of his parental relation. This, even for the most historically minded, should satisfy.

Parenthetically, where the child has been emancipated, an action against a parent-tortfeasor is allowed.[27]

An action for alienation of affection is denied a minor child against a third party interloper by the great majority of jurisdictions.[28]

Briere v. Briere, 107 N.H. 432, 224 A. 2d 588 (1966); Gelbman v. Gelbman, 23 N.Y.2d 434, 297 N.Y.S.2d 529, 245 N.E.2d 192 (1969); Goller v. White, 20 Wis.2d 402, 122 N.W.2d 193 (1963).

23. Smith v. Kauffman, 212 Va. 181, 183 S.E.2d 190 (1971); France v. A. P.A. Transport Corp., 56 N.J. 500, 267 A.2d 490 (1970); Wood v. Wood, 135 Vt. 119, 370 A.2d 191 (1977); Rigdon v. Rigdon, 465 S.W.2d 921 (Ky.1971); Sanford v. Sanford, 15 Md.App. 390, 290 A.2d 812 (1972).

24. See e. g., Petersen v. City and County of Honolulu, 51 Hawaii 484, 462 P.2d 1007 (1970); Cole v. Sears Roebuck & Co., 47 Wis.2d 629, 177 N.W.2d 866 (1970); Howes v. Hansen, 56 Wis.2d 247, 201 N.W.2d 825 (1972); *Contra* Holodook v. Spencer, 36 N.Y.2d 35, 364 N.Y.S.2d 859, 324 N.E.2d 338 (1974).

25. Welch v. Davis, 410 Ill. 130, 101 N.E.2d 547 (1951); Deposit Guar.

Bank and Trust Co. v. Nelson, 212 Miss. 335, 54 So.2d 476 (1951).

26. Mahnke v. Moore, 197 Md. 61, 77 A.2d 923 (1951).

27. Gillikin v. Burbage, 263 N.C. 317, 139 S.E.2d 753 (1965); Lancaster v. Lancaster, 213 Miss. 536, 57 So.2d 302 (1952) (20 year old emancipated child may sue his father for negligence.)

28. Hunt v. Chang, 60 Hawaii 608, 594 P.2d 118 (1979); Miller v. Kretschmer, 374 Mich. 459, 461, 132 N.W.2d 141, 143 (1965); Roth v. Parsons, 16 N.C.App. 646, 647, 192 S.E.2d 659 (1973), cert. denied 282 N.C. 582, 193 S.E.2d 745; Kane v. Quigley, 1 Ohio St. 1, 3, 203 N.E.2d 338, 340 (1964); Nash v. Baker, 522 P.2d 1335, 1339–40 (Okl.App.1974); Wallace v. Wallace, 155 W.Va. 569, 579, 184 S.E. 2d 327, 332–33 (1971).

§ 26.4 Family Law—Vicarious Liability

At common law a husband was liable for all the torts of his wife which were committed before or during the marriage. This rule applied though the tort occurred without the knowledge, consent, or presence of the husband, or in fact even though the spouses resided apart from one another.[29] That the husband must have been joined with his wife at common law and that he had control over her money and property, and indeed her very conduct, supported the common law rule. Though her negligence was vicariously that of her spouse, the wife at common law was also independently liable for her own torts except when she committed them in the presence of her husband, at which time the law presumed she acted under his direction.[30]

The Married Women's acts, which gave the wife the capacity to be sued alone and which gave her control over her property, abrogated the common law rule and today the mere existence of the marriage relation does not result in the imputation of the wife's negligence to her husband.[31] As there was no imputation to the wife of the husband's negligence at common law the general rule today does not provide for any intermarital vicarious liability for negligence unless there was some joint enterprise or agency relationship apart from the marriage.[32]

In the absence of statute to the contrary, American jurisdictions which have not adopted comparative negligence are unanimous in holding that the contributory negligence of one spouse bars recovery of collateral damages suffered by the other spouse.[33] The same rule is applicable as between child and parent.[34] This rule is vigorously

---

29. Best v. Samuel Fox & Co., 2 K.B. 639, 2 All.Eng. 798 (1951).

30. See, Hill v. Sibley Memorial Hosp., 108 F.Supp. 739 (D.D.C.1952) (Loss of consortium of mother by child denied).

31. Prosser, The Law of Torts (4th ed. 1971) p. 870.

32. Id. at 871–72.

33. Pioneer Constr. Co. v. Bergeron, 170 Colo. 474, 462 P.2d 589 (1969); Resmondo v. International Builders of Florida, Inc., 265 So.2d 72 (Fla.App. 1972); Deskins v. Woodward, 483 P.2d 1134 (Okl.1971).

34. McNally v. Addis, 65 Misc.2d 204, 317 N.Y.S.2d 157 (1970). In action by son for injuries sustained and by his father for medical expenses and loss of services when son fell from rotting bridge, father's derivative claim was not barred by son's contributory negligence, but was reduced pro rata in light of son's comparative culpability pursuant to comparative negligence statute. Meyer v. State, 92 Misc.2d 996, 403 N.Y.S.2d 420 (1978).

Contributory negligence by child, which was not the sole proximate cause of child's injury, did not bar parental claim for medical expenses, loss of services, companionship and society resulting from injury. Handeland v. Brown, 216 N.W.2d 574 (Iowa, 1974).

attacked by scholars [35] but in that small minority of jurisdictions that has not adopted comparative negligence there is little inclination shown to abandon the contributory negligence bar.

A parent may be liable for the acts of a child who is known to be vicious or destructive.[36]

35. Harper and James, Law of Torts § 8.9 (1956); Prosser, The Law of Torts (3d ed. 1964) pp. 892–893.

36. Ellis v. D'Angelo, 116 Cal.App.2d 310, 253 P.2d 675 (1953); Parsons v. Smithey, 109 Ariz. 49, 504 P.2d 1272 (1973).

§§ 26.5–27.0 are reserved for supplementary material.

CHAPTER 27

CHARITABLE AND SOVEREIGN IMMUNITIES

Table of Sections

Sec.
27.1 Immunity of Charities.
27.2 Immunity of National and State Governments.
27.3 Immunity of Municipalities.
27.4 Immunity of Public Officers.
27.5 Actions under 42 U.S.C.A. § 1983.

Library References:

C.J.S. Municipal Corporations § 745 et seq.
West's Key No. Digests, Municipal Corporations ⚖︎723 et seq.
Prosser, Law of Torts (4th ed. 1971) pp. 970 et seq.

§ 27.1 Immunity of Charities

In the last few decades, an almost complete abrogation of tort immunity for charitable organizations has occurred.[1] The reasons for this were well expressed in the case of *Garlington v. Kingsley*;[2] wherein the court stated:

> There is no foundation in civil law for the doctrine of charitable immunity . . . . The doctrine is not accepted in any foreign jurisdiction, civilian or common law, and though once perhaps a majority view in the common law states of the United States, it is now a fast waning and dwindling minority theory. It had an inauspicious and a not too reputable beginning in the United States in a case arising in Massachusetts in 1876, *McDonald v. Massachusetts Gen. Hosp.*, 120 Mass. 432, 10 years after the repudiation of the doctrine in England.[3] Although the doctrine has been embodied into law for periods of time in many states, voluminous opinions in the various jurisdictions have vainly attempted to find a logical rationale for it.[4]

---

1. Rosenthal v. Warren, 374 F.Supp. 522 (S.D.N.Y.1974); Colby v. Carney Hosp., 356 Mass. 527, 254 N.E.2d 407 (1969); Garlington v. Kingsley, 289 So.2d 88 La.1974); Prosser, Handbook of the Laws of Torts, § 127 (4th Ed. 1971).

2. 289 So.2d 88 (La.1974).

3. Heriot's Hosp. v. Ross, 12 Clark and Fin. 507, 8 E.R. 1508 (1846) (cite added).

4. 289 So.2d at 90.

The most frequently espoused "logical rationale" for the doctrine of charitable immunity was the trust fund theory.[5] This theory held that a tort recovery from a charitable institution wrongfully diverted trust funds from the purposes for which the trust was created. If this was permitted, the courts reasoned, the inclination of people to give to charities would be stifled. Another theory courts used to uphold charitable immunity was that liability of charities would wrongfully extend the doctrine of respondeat superior to embrace corporations engaged in businesses not operated for profit.[6] The final rationale courts utilized was to state that by accepting the treatment received, the patient assumed the risk of negligence, and impliedly agreed to waive liability for torts committed.[7] All of these theories are now generally rejected.

§ 27.2 Immunity of National and State Governments

The doctrine that the sovereign is not answerable in damages for the wrongs committed by its officers and employees originated in the feudal conception of the King as the Vicar of God on earth. This rather awesome idea, combined with the great prerogative powers which the King developed, legally placed the King in an "untouchable position." By the end of the 18th Century Blackstone was able to say, ". . . no suit or action can be brought against the King, even in civil matters . . . ."[8]

---

5. The author agrees with Laski, Liability Charitable Corporations in Tort, 31 Harv.L.Rev. 479, 482 (1918): "A negligently administered charity may aim at inducting us all into the Kingdom of Heaven, but it is socially essential to make it adequately careful of the methods employed."

6. Watkins v. Southcrest Baptist Church, 399 S.W.2d 530 (Tex.1966). Perhaps the rule resulted because "in olden days, they were operated by pious monks or nuns whose sole reward for being Good Samaritans was in the hereafter . . . ." Parker, 9 NACCA Law Journal, 191. "The hospital of today has grown into an enormous business. They own and hold large assets, much of it tax-free by statute, and employing many persons. The state has become paternal to an astonishing degree, as evidenced by numerous statutes found in our code . . . . Also, we take judicial notice of the extensive use of the many types of hospital insurance, as well as liability insurance by the institutions. Thus, it is evident that times have changed and are now changing in the business, social, economic and legal world. The basis for, and the need of, such encouragement is no longer existent." Haynes v. Presbyterian Hosp. Ass'n, 241 Iowa 1269, 45 N.W.2d 151 (1950).

    It is even less necessary now, and almost all states have followed the *Haynes* rationale in denying any charitable immunity.

7. Forrest v. Red Cross Hosp., Inc., 265 S.W.2d 80 (Ky.1954).

8. "Thus his (the King) is of right and not wrong, and since he is the author of right, the occasion of wrongs

The non-responsibility of the federal [9] and state governments in the United States, for torts, is based squarely upon this development in the English law.[10] Justice Holmes modernized the reasoning of the doctrine in *Kawananokoa v. Polyblank* [11] by attributing the immunity not to "obsolete theory, but on the logical and practical ground that there can be no legal right as against the authority that makes the law on which the right depends." It is a rule of social policy, which protects the state from burdensome interference with the performance of its governmental functions and preserves its control over state funds, property and instrumentalities.[12]

If there is no immunity provision in the state constitution, there can be statutory consent to suit given by the legislature which waives the sovereign immunity. However, the state's immunity from suit is absolute and unqualified unless the state does consent to suit [13] and the state may qualify its consent.[14]

Though the modern trend is definitely for states to shed immunity and allow recovery for injuries they cause to their citizens and those of other states,[15] cases and state laws still support state governmental immunity in many situations.[16] However, many states now

ought not to arise . . . ." 2 Bracton, DeLegibus et Consuetudinibus (Woodbine's Ed. 1922); earlier feudal theory, however, didn't deify the King, and his immunity from suit was based on the old principle that no feudal lord could be sued in his own courts. Pollock and Maitland, 1 History of English Law 518 (2nd Ed. 1923); Blackstone, 1 Commentaries 242 (9th Ed. 1783). Also see Russell v. Men of Devon, 2 Dunn and East 667, 100 E.R. 359 (1788) (early English decision denying recovery against county—no funds allocated, and prospect of too many suits).

9. In 1946, the federal government passed the Federal Tort Claims Act permitting certain actions against the United States. See infra, Chapter 19.

10. Constitution of the United States, 11th Amendment; Borchard, Government Liability in Tort, 34 Yale L.J. 1 (1924).

11. 205 U.S. 349, 353, 27 S.Ct. 526, 527, 51 L.Ed. 834, 836 (1907).

12. Glassman v. Glassman, 309 N.Y. 436, 131 N.E.2d 721. See also Fitts v. McGhee, 172 U.S. 516, 195 S.Ct. 269, 43 L.Ed. 535.

13. Nevada v. Hall, 440 U.S. 410, 99 S.Ct. 1182, 59 L.Ed.2d 416:
"The immunity of a truly independent sovereign from suit in its own courts has been enjoyed as a matter of absolute right for centuries. Only the sovereign's own consent could qualify the absolute character of that immunity."
440 U.S. at 414.

14. Stanley v. City and County of San Francisco, 48 Cal.App.3d 575, 121 Cal.Rptr. 842 (1975).

15. See cases in Evans v. Board of County Comm'rs, 174 Colo. 97, 482 P.2d 968 (1971) (Colorado Supreme Court prospectively overruling doctrine).

16. See Thomas v. State Highway Dept., 398 Mich. 1, 247 N.W.2d 530, 531, n. 1 (1976). The California Law

have Tort Claims Acts which allow the state to be sued in specified instances.[17]

A state's immunity from suit is limited by provisions of the United States Constitution [18] and even without its consent, it may be sued in the federal system by the federal government or by a federal instrumentality.[19]

§ 27.3 Immunity of Municipalities

The state, as the creator of municipal corporations, may impose liability which would otherwise not exist upon those municipalities.[20] Generally, whether or not a municipal corporation is liable to, or immune from suit, for injuries caused by its officers and agents depends on the nature of the activity engaged in when the accident occurred. Municipalities perform some activities which are considered governmental, public, or political and in such capacity are clothed with the sovereign immunity of the state for which they so act.[21]

Revision Commission, after thorough and thoughtful examination of the governmental immunity problem, concluded that the doctrine did have validity in some instances: "Government cannot merely be made liable as private persons are, for public entities are fundamentally different from private persons. Private persons do not make laws. Private persons do not issue and revoke licenses to engage in various professions and occupations. Private persons do not quarantine sick persons and do not commit mentally disturbed persons to involuntary confinement. Private persons do not prosecute and incarcerate violators of the law or administer prison systems. Only public entities are required to build and maintain thousands of miles of streets, sidewalks and highways. Unlike many private persons, a public entity often cannot reduce its risk of potential liability by refusing to engage in a particular activity, for government must continue to govern and is required to furnish services that cannot be adequately provided by any other agency. Moreover, in our system of government, decision-making has been allocated among three branches of government—legislative, executive and judicial—and in many cases decisions made by the legislative and executive branches should not be subject to review in tort suits for damages, for this would take the ultimate decision-making authority away from those who are responsible politically for making the decisions." 4 Cal. Law Revision Comm.Report, Recommendations and Studies, 810 (1963).

17. For an example of one such Tort Claims Act, see West's Ann.Cal.Gov't Code §§ 810–996.

18. Commonwealth, Dept. of Public Welfare v. Ludlow Clinical Laboratories, 22 Pa.Cmwlth. 614, 350 A.2d 208 (1976), aff'd 473 Pa. 299, 374 A.2d 526.

19. Department of Employment v. United States, 385 U.S. 355, 87 S.Ct. 464, 17 L.Ed. 414 (1966); Matter of Estate of Novotny, 446 F.Supp. 1027 (S.D.N.Y.1978).

20. West's Ann.Cal.Gov't Code § 815 et seq.

21. See Nanna v. Village of McArthur, 44 Ohio App.2d 22, 335 N.E.2d 712, 73 O.O.2d 14 (1974):

"[M]unicipalities are liable for negligence with respect to the exercise

When the municipality functions in a corporate, private, or proprietary manner it has been held since about 1842 that it is liable in tort to those damaged in the course of such activity.[22] Classifying various municipal functions into these categories has led to much difficulty and conflict in authority. Therefore many jurisdictions have now rejected this "rigid dichotomy of the past,"[23] and have abolished much of municipal immunity.[24] Where the distinction between governmental and proprietary functions is maintained, the test is normally whether the particular action involved is for the general benefit of all, or whether it is merely to benefit the municipality involved.[25] Attorneys are cautioned that classifications are made on a case-by-case basis so that generalizations have very little value.[26]

of powers and functions proprietary in character and not liable in the exercise of powers and functions governmental in character. . . . The rationale behind distinguishing between governmental and proprietary functions in determining liability is that in performing the former a city acts as the agent of the state in the exercise of sovereign powers. The state cannot be sued without its consent and, therefore, the municipality cannot be sued. Proprietary functions are acts performed in the pursuit of private or corporate duties for the particular benefit of the corporation and its inhabitants. While performing these functions, municipalities do not act as agents of the state in the exercise of its sovereign powers and the corporation is liable for its negligent acts."

335 N.E.2d at 715.

22. Bailey v. City of New York, 3 (Hill) N.Y. 531, 38 Am.Dec. 669 (1842), aff'd 2 Denio 433.

If the tort violates any constitutional rights, the municipality may now be held liable under 42 U.S.C.A. § 1983. See Monell v. New York City Dept. of Social Servs., 436 U.S. 658, 98 S.Ct. 2018, 56 L.Ed.2d 611 (1978), discussed in § 27.5 infra.

23. Thomas v. State Highway Dept., 398 Mich. 1, 247 N.W.2d 530, 537 n. 7 (1976); Lykins v. Peoples Community Hosp., 355 F.Supp. 52, 54 (E.D.Mich. 1973) ("This court is of the opinion that to . . . define 'government function' to include the operation of a public hospital might raise a constitutional problem. There appears no rational basis to distinguish liability for services delivered by a public hospital and liability for the same services when provided by a private or charitable hospital.").

24. University of Alaska v. National Aircraft Leasing, Inc., 536 P.2d 121 (Alaska 1975); Stone v. Arizona Highway Comm'n, 93 Ariz. 384, 381 P.2d 107 (1963); Muskopf v. Corning Hosp. Dist., 55 Cal.2d 211, 11 Cal. Rptr. 89, 359 P.2d 457 (1961); Molitor v. Kaneland Community Unit Dist., 18 Ill.2d 11, 163 N.E.2d 89, cert. denied 362 U.S. 968, 80 S.Ct. 955, 4 L. Ed.2d 900.

25. Thomas v. State Highway Dept., 398 Mich. 1, 247 N.W.2d 530 (1976).

26. See Indian Towing Co. v. United States, 350 U.S. 61, 76 S.Ct. 122, 100 L.Ed. 48 (1955) in which the Supreme Court successfully avoided the " 'non-governmental' — 'governmental' quagmire that has long plagued the law of municipal corporations. A comparative study of the cases . . . will disclose an irreconcilable conflict. More than that, the

Attorney *Louis Drazin* [27] reports an interesting case [28] wherein sovereign immunity was held not to be a bar to plaintiff's recovery. A young man, while riding a motorcycle, ran a red light and the police gave chase in an unmarked police car. Plaintiff was injured when his motorcycle collided with a second police vehicle. This case was novel in that generally there is no liability where a police officer takes up chase, provided that the vehicle is a marked vehicle. In this case, plaintiff alleged that he was unaware that he was being chased by a police vehicle. Trial resulted in a verdict in favor of the plaintiff on a comparative basis, 75 per cent for the plaintiff.

Some states have modified the governmental proprietary doctrine and determine municipal liability based upon the doctrine of respondeat superior.[29] Another factor extending liability is the accepted view that municipalities are liable if they have created nuisances notwithstanding that the activity involved is considered to be governmental.[30] "Claims" must be filed against the municipality in a period far shorter than the general statute of limitations. There are provisions in some cities to file a "late claim." If no claim is filed at all, no suit can be brought later.

For discussion of actions against municipalities under 42 U.S. C.A. § 1983, see § 27.5, infra.

decisions in each of the States are disharmonious and disclose the inevitable chaos when courts try to apply a rule of law that is inherently unsound. The fact of the matter is that the theory whereby municipalities are made amenable to liability is an endeavor, however awkward and contradictory, to escape from the basic historical doctrine of sovereign immunity."

350 U.S. at 65.

27. Louis M. Drazin, Drazin & Warshaw, 25 Reckless Place, Red Bank, New Jersey.

28. Dorr v. Township of Woodbridge, N.J.Super.Ct.

29. City of Tampa v. Davis, 226 So.2d 450 (Fla.App.1969); Gordon v. City of West Palm Beach, 321 So.2d 78 (Fla. App.1975) writ discharged 349 So.2d 160 (Fla.) (held that municipal activities which fell into proprietary function category created tort liability similar to a private corporation but governmental function activities created municipal tort liability on the basis of respondeat superior as long as contract took place in a direct transaction or confrontation or there was privity between the complainant and the municipality's agent).

30. See Buckeye Union Fire Ins. Co. v. State, 383 Mich. 630, 178 N.W.2d 476 (1970), appeal after remand 38 Mich. App. 155, 195 N.W.2d 915.

§ 27.4 Immunity of Public Officers [31]

Though the 11th Amendment to the United States Constitution bars suits against any party if any judgment leveled would be paid from a public treasury, the amendment does not bar suit against governmental officials as individuals.[32] However, immunity for certain government positions is recognized as follows:

Legislative Officers. It is generally held that legislative officers are not civilly liable for their legislative acts on the ground that they are called upon to exercise judgment and discretion as to the needs and welfare of the public, and that their duties are owed to the public at large and not to individuals.[33]

Judicial officers have always been accorded complete immunity for their judicial actions even when their motives are improper. This rule protects the independence of the judiciary by removing fear of future damage suits which could operate as an influence on the judgments of the court.[34] Judicial officers in some foreign countries are liable in malpractice suits.

Prosecutors. In a majority of states, prosecutors engaged in the performance of their prosecutorial, as opposed to administrative or investigative duties, are afforded absolute immunity.[35] Thus, prose-

---

31. Very often the tortfeasor will be an individual public officer. Consideration should immediately be given to filing a claim, if necessary, under applicable state or local statutes, so that a subsequent tort suit may be brought. Failure to file a timely claim will result in dismissal of the suit in many jurisdictions. Investigation should also be made of the surety or bond of the public officer required under the law. Occasionally the suit may be directed against the surety company directly. The problem of respondeat superior may likewise be presented, and available to a claimant.

32. See Scheuer v. Rhodes, 416 U.S. 232, 237–38, 94 S.Ct. 1683, 1687, 40 L.Ed.2d 90 (1974).

33. U.S.Const. Art. I, § 6, cl. 1; Gravel v. United States, 408 U.S. 606, 92 S. Ct. 2614, 33 L.Ed.2d 583 (1972); Kilbourne v. Thompson, 103 U.S. 168, 26 L.Ed. 377 (1880).

34. Bradley v. Fisher, 80 U.S. (13 Wall.) 335, 20 L.Ed. 646 (1872); Piersen v. Ray, 386 U.S. 547, 87 S.Ct. 1213, 18 L.Ed.2d 288 (1967) (court held *Bradley* immunity doctrine applied in suits brought under section 1 of the Civil Rights Act of 1871 revised 42 U.S.C.A. § 1983; Stump v. Sparkman, 435 U.S. 349, 98 S.Ct. 1099, 55 L.Ed.2d 331 (1978), reh. denied 436 U.S. 951, 98 S.Ct. 2862, 56 L.Ed.2d 795, on remand 601 F.2d 261 (7th Cir.) (reaffirmation of *Bradley* holding that a judge is absolutely immune from liability if the acts complained of are judicial and not taken without jurisdiction); Farish v. Smoot, 58 So.2d 534 (Fla.1952) (action of false imprisonment may be maintained against a municipal court judge, who ordered the rearrest of the plaintiff, who was free on writ of habeas corpus).

35. Imbler v. Pachtman, 424 U.S. 409, 421–422, 96 S.Ct. 984, 990–991, 47 L. Ed.2d 128 (1976); Apton v. Wilson,

cutors are provided protection in such matters as arrest proceedings, filing of criminal complaints and the searching of criminal suspects.[36]

Government Officials—High Executives.[37] High level executive officers have traditionally been protected with absolute immunity,[38] and the majority of states continue to follow this rule.[39] The federal courts allow complete immunity except in cases stating a claim for relief on federal constitutional grounds.[40]

Government Officials—Low Level Executives. There is no absolute immunity for acts committed by administrative officers of a lower rank. Such officers may be held liable for acts done which cause injury to private citizens.[41] There has been a rather crude attempt to classify the activities of these officers into "quasi-judicial", "discretionary" and "ministerial". The first two, by analogy to judicial or executive function, are considered protected activity.[42] On this basis, the attempted removal of a city manager,[43] the denial of a permit,[44] or the parole of a dangerous prisoner,[45] though performed negligently, did not result in liability of the state official. But when the act was merely ministerial, such as the driving of a vehicle,[46] the decision to warn of a psychotic's violent propensities,[47] or the care of prisoners,[48] the officer is fully liable in tort for his negligence. The distinction is hardly considered satisfactory since it is only one of de-

506 F.2d 83, 93 (D.C.Cir. 1974); **Briggs v. Goodwin,** 569 F.2d 10 (D.C.Cir. 1977).

36. Burkhart v. Saxbe, 397 F.Supp. 499 (E.D.Pa.1975).

37. Includes the President of the United States, Governors and Federal Cabinet Officers.

38. Prosser, Handbook of the Law of Torts § 131, at 975–87 (4th ed. 1971); see Barr v. Matteo, 360 U.S. 564, 79 S.Ct. 1335, 3 L.Ed.2d 1434, reh. denied 361 U.S. 155, 80 S.Ct. 41, 4 L.Ed.2d 93 (1959).

39. See, e. g., Stiebitz v. Mahoney, 144 Conn. 443, 134 A.2d 71 (1975); Vickers v. Motle, 109 Ga.App. 615, 137 S.E.2d 77 (1964).

40. Butz v. Economou, 438 U.S. 478, 98 S.Ct. 2894, 57 L.Ed.2d 895, on remand 466 F.Supp. 1351 (D.C.N.Y.) (1978).

41. Prosser, Handbook of the Law of Torts, p. 987 (4th ed. 1971).

42. Id.

43. Gildea v. Ellershaw, 363 Mass. 800, 298 N.E.2d 847 (1972).

44. Movable Homes, Inc. v. North Tonawanda, 56 A.D.2d 718, 392 N.Y.S.2d 772 (1977).

45. Grimm v. Board of Pardons & Paroles, 115 Ariz. 260, 564 P.2d 1227 (1977).

46. Davis v. Little, 362 So.2d 642 (Miss.1978).

47. Tarasoff v. Regents of Univ. of California, 17 Cal.3d 425, 131 Cal.Rptr. 14, 551 P.2d 334 (1976).

48. Clark v. Kelly, 101 W.Va. 650, 133 S.E. 365 (1926).

§ 27.4   SPECIFIC ACTIONS   Pt. 4

gree and an element of discretion is present in the most mechanical of activities.

In addition, it is often said that all governmental officials are liable for injuries caused when they act out of their jurisdiction.[49] Some courts have distinguished acts without the jurisdiction of the officer from those merely in excess thereof, assessing liability only for the former.[50] This distinction has become clouded and its usefulness has been seriously questioned.

§ 27.5   Actions under 42 U.S.C.A. § 1983

Section 1983 of the Civil Rights Act of 1871 [51] provides a remedy to anyone whose federal rights are infringed upon under color of state law.[52] Today, this statute is the basis upon which most civil rights actions are filed against states whether the protection needed is from executive, legislative or judicial officers.[53] Actions brought under section 1983 are a major vehicle for development and enforcement of constitutional rights.

The immunities from prosecution generally afforded to various governmental bodies and officers, discussed in the previous sections, may not fully apply to actions brought under section 1983.

Prior to 1978, municipalities or other governmental agencies could not be sued for damages under this section because it was held that such entities were not "persons" as that term is used in the statute.[54] In June 1978, the United States Supreme Court reversed this circumstance in the case of *Monell v. Department of Social Ser-*

---

49. Prosser, Handbook of the Law of Torts 991 (4th Ed.1971).

50. Id.

51. Act of April 20, 1871, ch. 22, § 1, 17 Stat. 13. 42 U.S.C.A. § 1983 states: "Every person who, under color of any statute, ordinance, regulation, custom, or usage, of any State or Territory, subjects, or causes to be subjected, any citizen of the United States or other person within the jurisdiction thereof to the deprivation of any rights, privileges, or immunities secured by the Constitution and laws, shall be liable to the party injured in an action at law, suit in equity, or other proper proceeding for redress."

52. Section 1343(3) empowers federal courts to hear section 1983 cases.

53. Mitchum v. Foster, 407 U.S. 225, 242, 92 S.Ct. 2151, 2161, 2162, 32 L.Ed.2d 705 (1972). Suits alleging constitutional violations by federal agents are filed with allegations of violations of civil rights. Bivens v. Six Unknown Named Agents of the Federal Bureau of Narcotics, 403 U.S. 388, 91 S.Ct. 1991, 29 L.Ed.2d 619, on remand 456 F.2d 1339 (D.N.Y.) (1971); Butz v. Economou, 438 U.S. 478, 98 S.Ct. 2894, 57 L.Ed.2d 895, on remand 466 F.Supp. 1351 (D.C.N.Y.) (1978).

For compilation of decisions, see 42 U.S.C.A. § 1983.

54. Monroe v. Pape, 365 U.S. 167, 81 S.Ct. 473, 5 L.Ed.2d 492 (1961).

vices.⁵⁵ *Monell* involved a class action by the female employees of the Department of Social Services and Board of Education of the City of New York, alleging deprivation of their constitutional rights by an official policy of the City, which compelled pregnant employees to take unpaid leaves of absence before such leaves were required for medical reasons. The suit sought injunctive relief and back pay for periods of unlawful forced leave.⁵⁶

The Supreme Court concluded, after analyzing the legislative history of the Civil Rights Act of 1871, that the term "persons," as that term is used in Section 1983 of the Act, includes municipalities and other local governmental units.⁵⁷ Thus, under the Court's holding, local governments, like any other Section 1983 "person", may be sued for constitutional deprivations which result from official governmental policy or governmental custom (even where such custom has not received formal approval through the bodies' official decision-making channels.) ⁵⁸

Having established that actions could be brought against local governments under Section 1983, the question remained as to whether the sovereign immunity of municipal governments would repel such an action. The court did not discuss this immunity issue in *Monell*, beyond stating that a "municipal body sued under Section 1983 cannot be entitled to an absolute immunity, lest our decision that such bodies are subject to suit under Section 1983 'be drained of meaning' ".⁵⁹ Thus, the degree of immunity available to local governments against a Section 1983 suit is unclear at this time. It is clear, however, that it is not absolute.

55. 436 U.S. 658, 98 S.Ct. 2018, 56 L.Ed.2d 611 (1978).

56. 436 U.S. at 661, 98 S.Ct. at 2020, 56 L.Ed.2d 611.

57. 436 U.S. at 690, 98 S.Ct. at 2035, 56 L.Ed.2d 611.

58. See generally Schnapper, Civil Rights Litigation after Monell, 75 Colum.L.Rev. 213 (1979).

59. 436 U.S. 658 at 701, 98 S.Ct. 2018 at 2041, 56 L.Ed.2d 611.

See also Parratt v. Taylor, 451 U.S. 527, 101 S.Ct. 1908, 68 L.Ed.2d 420 (1981) wherein the Supreme Court considered whether negligent acts were sufficient to invoke the application of § 1983. The Court stated that nothing in the language of § 1983 or its legislative history limits the statute solely to intentional deprivations of constitutional rights. The Court explained that in any § 1983 action, the initial inquiry must focus on whether the two essential elements to a § 1983 action are present: (1) whether the conduct complained of was committed by a person acting under color of state law; and (2) whether this conduct deprived a person of the rights, privileges, or immunities secured by the Constitution or laws of the United States.

Public officials are also considered persons under Section 1983, and under certain circumstances, actions may be brought against them.[60]

The court has indicated that some governmental officials, such as legislators, judges and prosecutors have absolute immunity against Section 1983 actions.[61] Other local governmental officials are protected to a lesser extent, on a sliding scale. The case of *Scheuer v. Rhodes*[62] sets out the basic test for determining the scope of immunity granted to a governmental official. That case involved a Section 1983 action against the Governor of Ohio, alleging that his willful or reckless deployment of the Ohio National Guard led to the deaths of several students at Kent State University. The Supreme Court held absolute immunity was unavailable, and found that "in varying scope, a qualified immunity is available to officers of the executive branch" under Section 1983.

> [T]he variation [is] dependent upon the scope of discretion and responsibilities of the office and all the circumstances as they reasonably appeared at the time of the action on which the liability is sought to be based. It is the existence of reasonable ground for the belief formed at the time and in light of all the circumstances. Coupled with good-faith belief, that affords a basis for qualified immunity of executive officers for acts performed in the course of official conduct."[63] Therefore, though "a declaration of emergency by the chief executive of the state is entitled to great weight . . . it is not conclusive."[64] Officials with less discretionary power are granted a correspondingly lower degree of immunity.

Although a local government can be sued in a Section 1983 action, a state government, as an entity, cannot be so sued. In the case *Quern v. Jordan*,[65] the Court held that the term "person", as that term is used in Section 1983, does not include a state. Thus a state has absolute immunity against a Section 1983 claim.

---

60. See Leite v. Providence, 463 F. Supp. 585, 590 (D.R.I.1978), in which the court held that supervisory officials could be held liable under Section 1983 if they were directly involved in the governmental action which led to the bringing of the action.

61. See Tenney v. Brandhove, 341 U.S. 367, 71 S.Ct. 783, 95 L.Ed. 1019 (1951), reh. denied 342 U.S. 843, 72 S.Ct. 20, 96 L.Ed. 637; Stump v. Sparkman, 435 U.S. 349, 98 S.Ct. 1099, 55 L.Ed.2d 331 (1978); Imbler v. Pachtman, 424 U.S. 409, 96 S.Ct. 984, 47 L.Ed.2d 128 (1976).

62. 416 U.S. 232, 94 S.Ct. 1683, 40 L.Ed.2d 90 (1974).

63. 416 U.S. 232 at 247, 94 S.Ct. 1683 at 1691, 40 L.Ed.2d 90.

64. Id. at 250.

65. 440 U.S. 332, 99 S.Ct. 1139, 59 L.Ed.2d 358 (1979).

Even before *Monell* held that a municipality was a "person" under § 1983, attorney *Thomas Bellmann* [66] handled a case which was able to survive all motions to dismiss in a 1983 action against a municipality. Plaintiff alleged direct negligence of the Chief of Police and the Board of Police Commissioners in failing to supervise a subordinate known to have a propensity for violence.

In that case,[67] plaintiff had been drinking at a bachelor party with four friends when they decided to go to Kansas City's "hooker district" and "find a woman" for the husband-to-be. While circling the area, plaintiff exited his vehicle and conversed for twenty to thirty minutes at curbside with two plain clothes officers in an unmarked car. Beer and whiskey were exchanged and the officers succeeded in convincing plaintiff to solicit a prostitute for their benefit by denying they were cops and saying that they wanted a good time. The prostitutes informed plaintiff the men were "pigs." Plaintiff informed the officers of this and walked toward his pickup and four buddies parked fifteen feet to the rear of the police car.

Defendant officer exited his auto with "intent to arrest plaintiff for hindering and interfering with a police officer," as his "stake-out" had been fouled up.

Upon approaching plaintiff, he grabbed plaintiff by the arm, spun him around and struck plaintiff with his service revolver, which then "accidently" discharged into plaintiff's throat, breaking his jaw bone and incurring $6,000.00 in special damages.

The Officer claimed self-defense, but no object of any sort was recovered at the scene. Defendant Officer never revealed his I.D., but dragged plaintiff to his unmarked car, emptied the beer cans on the street and sped off. Plaintiff's friends gave chase, rammed the car, assaulted defendant, rescued plaintiff and were then escorted to the hospital where all were charged with assault on a police officer.

After trial by jury, all were acquitted, and a civil rights action was instituted by plaintiff.

Suit was filed based upon 42 U.S.C.A. § 1983, assault, battery and respondent superior, and extensive discovery was had. Plaintiff learned of a prior incidence of violence by defendant through interrogatory and then amended his petition alleging the negligence of the Chief of Police in failure to train and supervise, when he knew or should have known of defendant's propensity to engage in violence.

66. Thomas R. Bellman, Esquire, Bellman, Speck and Handley, Kansas City, Missouri.

67. Litteken v. Liebsch, et al., U.S. District Court, W.D.Mo., No. 76CV504–W–3, Sept. 22, 1977.

The Kansas City Police Department had no insurance bond or other written or oral indemnity agreement protecting the individual officer. When the Chief of Police and the individual Board of Police Commissioners (a statutory body) realized their exposure would exist until at least the close of plaintiff's case, and a possible verdict against each personally, the City made "voluntary" payment of $25,000.00, the largest sum paid by suit or settlement of a brutality claim in Kansas City.

It was also known that the Police Department had settled previous suits, and therefore, was asked by interrogatory the names and details, including all dollar amounts of any suits or settlements for five years prior to plaintiff's incident. The obvious relevancy objection was overruled and defendants were compelled to reveal all to the plaintiff (under protective order) on the theory that by a history of prior acts, defendants had waived immunity and waived their claim of non-indemnity. This proved to be a powerful tool in settlement negotiations, as were the multiple defendants' inconsistent interrogatory answers. Also, a ballistics expert retained by plaintiff, was prepared to testify that defendant's service revolver could not "accidentally" discharge by subjecting it to a sharp blow, such as striking plaintiff in the face.

According to the attorney in the case, the pleadings file, by the time of settlement, approached 400 pages, including seven motions for sanctions based upon refusal to comply with discovery.

§§ 27.6–28.0 are reserved for supplementary material.

CHAPTER 28

UNINSURED MOTORIST COVERAGE

Table of Sections

Sec.
28.1 Introduction.
28.2 "Unsatisfied Judgment" Statutes.
28.3 Financial Responsibility Statutes.
28.4 Uninsured Motorist Statutes.
28.5 Arbitration.
28.6 No-Fault Insurance.

Library References:

C.J.S. Insurance §§ 762 et seq., 1317, 897, 1126, 1247.
West's Key No. Digests, Insurance ⇐467.51, 467.52, 531.3, 574(5.2), 612(4).
Blashfield, Automobile Law & Practice § 274.1 et seq.

§ 28.1 Introduction

In these inflationary times many people simply feel they cannot afford automobile insurance, and the uninsured motorist is now as likely to be the little old lady from Pasadena as the reckless teen-age menace from down the street. Whichever, formerly any hapless motorist who was involved in an accident with the uninsured motorist probably discovered the tragedy and financial devastation such an accident could bring. With the modern concepts of uninsured motorist coverage, unsatisfied judgment laws, and no-fault insurance, the days are past in which an accident with an uninsured motorist almost automatically meant financial devastation for the innocent party.

§ 28.2 "Unsatisfied Judgment" Statutes

"Unsatisfied Judgment" laws are considered the precursor of uninsured motorist laws. The unsatisfied judgment laws created a state fund from which an innocent, injured motorist who unluckily could not collect for his injuries due to the injurer's insolvency or lack of insurance, could receive aid. North Dakota adopted the first such act in 1947. Many states subsequently followed suit.[1] Such

---

1. N. Dak. NDCC § 39–1703; N.J. N.J.S.A., § 39:6–70 (1955); Md.Ann. Code 1957, Motor Vehicles, Art. 66½, § 150; N.Y. Insurance Laws, Art. 17–A, § 600 et seq. (1969); Mich. M.C. L.A., § 9.2803.

funds were generally found to be insufficient to meet many injured motorists' needs.

The unsatisfied judgment acts vary considerably from state to state. In general, all statutes provide that the claimant must show that another driver was at fault for the accident and that the claimant will receive no compensation for his injuries unless the State fund so provides.

The statutes normally provide a stated maximum recovery and the funds are usually available only to State residents for in-state accidents.

The two major problems found with such legislation are that even the maximum amounts fail to provide adequate coverage in woeful cases and State territorial limits often preclude recovery from the funds. A prudent motorist is well advised to purchase uninsured motorist coverage, if available, even though he is a resident of an "Unsatisfied Judgment" state.[2]

§ 28.3   Financial Responsibility Statutes

States attempted to cope with the uninsured motorist by "financial responsibility" laws. Massachusetts did so in 1925, as did New York in 1956 and North Carolina in 1957. Most states now have similar laws. These laws simply mean that all motorists driving in the state are required to carry insurance. As with all laws, people sometimes do not comply. For the motorist struck by an insolvent non-complier, the law does virtually no good.

Enforcement of the act is normally sought to be accomplished by suspension of driving privileges for a period of time if a driver fails to provide financial responsibility. In *Bell v. Burson*,[3] the United States Supreme Court held unconstitutional the Georgia financial responsibility act which authorized the revocation of the license of any driver involved in an accident, regardless of fault, if that driver could not show proof of financial responsibility. The Court held that the state must provide a forum for the determination of the question whether there is a reasonable possibility of a judgment being rendered against the uninsured motorist as a result of the accident.[4]

---

2. P. Pretzel, Uninsured Motorist 165 (1972).

3. 402 U.S. 535, 91 S.Ct. 1586, 29 L. Ed.2d 90 (1971), conformed to 124 Ga.App. 220, 183 S.E.2d 416.

4. 402 U.S. at 540.

§ 28.4 Uninsured Motorist Statutes

The first uninsured motorist coverage was offered in New York in 1955. This basic coverage, although later refined, met with rapid and widespread acceptance.[5] Today, all states but two [6] require by statute that uninsured motorist coverage be available to all drivers.

Uninsured motorist coverage is a relatively inexpensive adjunct to the basic automobile liability insurance policy. Essentially, under the coverage, the insurance company agrees to provide coverage to the company's own insured for damages received as a result of an accident with an uninsured or hit-and-run driver. In effect, uninsured motorist coverage constitutes insurance against a tortfeasor's lack of insurance.[7]

The legislation adopted by the majority of states follows a standard short form model which *requires* the insurer to include or offer such coverage under provisions approved by the state insurance commissioner.[8] However, commissioner approval generally will not validate policy provisions which do not conform with the intent of the statutes [9] and a policy which fails to conform with the statute will be deemed to do so.[10]

Uninsured motorist coverage is mandatory in some states;[11] other states allow the insured the option of rejecting the coverage.[12]

It is imperative to remember that uninsured motorist coverage operates only when the injured party is not responsible for the accident. Moreover, an attempted recovery by the injured party is subject to all applicable legal defenses. For example, in many states a parent cannot recover in tort for injuries received from the parent's own minor child: This legality would also preclude the parent from recovering under his uninsured motorist coverage policy if the parent's injuries were received from his minor child-tortfeasor.[13]

---

5. Pretzel, supra n.2, at 5 (1972).

6. Maryland and New Jersey; see n.1 as to Unsatisfied Judgment Statutes. Twenty-Five Years of Uninsured Motorist Coverage: A Silver Anniversary Cloud with a Silver Lining, Indiana Law Review. Vol. 14, 1981, No. 2.

7. See also Appleman, Insurance Law & Practice, § 5066 et seq.

8. Id.

9. McNutt v. State Farm Mut. Auto. Ins. Co., 369 F.Supp. 381 (W.D.Ky. 1973) aff'd 494 F.2d 1282 (6th Cir.); Simpson v. State Farm Mut. Auto. Ins. Co., 318 F.Supp. 1152 (S.D.Ind. 1970); but see Smith v. Allstate Ins. Co., 224 Tenn. 423, 456 S.W.2d 654 (1970).

10. Hendricks v. Meritplan Ins. Co., 205 Cal.App.2d 133, 22 Cal.Rptr. 682 (1962).

11. Arizona, Connecticut, Illinois, Maine, Massachusetts, Missouri, New Hampshire, North Dakota, Oregon, South Carolina, South Dakota, Vermont, Virginia, West Virginia and Wisconsin.

12. See e. g., V.A.T.S. Tex.Ins. Code, Art. 506–1.

13. Markham v. State Farm Mut. Auto. Ins. Co., 464 F.2d 703 (10th Cir. 1972).

All uninsured motorist statutes require an insurer to offer uninsured motorist coverage with bodily injury limits at least equal to those required by the state financial responsibility act.[14] The total payments to all insureds will not exceed the total maximum recovery for each accident as set forth in the policy.[15] Payment of the maximum recovery amount to one or more claimants to the exclusion of other claimants is allowed unless the insurance company does so in bad faith.[16] If multiple claimants are joined in a single action, the court will generally prorate the amount among the claimants.[17]

Where multiple claimants might quickly deplete the maximum recovery amount, good legal technique for claimant's attorney would be to file his proceeding as quickly as possible or to press for a speedy settlement so as to secure full payment of the client's claim while sufficient funds remain.[18]

A good tactic for the insurance carrier's attorney might be to file an action seeking the court's advice as to proper payment. This will ordinarily preclude a subsequent finding of bad faith.[19]

Standard uninsured motorist policies contain provisions for reductions and exclusions from liability. Among the standard provisions are the tortfeasor recovery credit clauses which permit the insurer to offset sums recovered from a tortfeasor,[20] or sums the insurer was required to pay under the medical payments coverage of the same policy.[21]

Also included in standard uninsured motorist policies is a clause prohibiting subrogation by a workers' compensation carrier.[22] This

14. Schermer, supra n.7, at § 20.01.

15. Pulley v. Allstate Ins. Co., 242 F. Supp. 330 (E.D.Va.1965); Drewry v. State Farm Mut. Auto. Ins. Co., 204 Va. 231, 129 S.E.2d 681 (1963).

16. Liguori v. Allstate Ins. Co., 76 N. J.Super. 204, 184 A.2d 12 (1962); Clarke v. Brown, 101 N.J.Super. 404, 244 A.2d 514 (1968); David v. Bauman, 24 Misc.2d 67, 196 N.Y.S.2d 746 (1960); Duprey v. Security Mut. Cas. Co., 22 A.D.2d 544, 256 N.Y.S.2d 987 (1965).

17. Garner v. O'Connor, 282 So.2d 807 (La.App.1973); Wasserman v. Glen Falls Ins. Co., 19 A.D.2d 552, 240 N. Y.S.2d 917 (1963).

18. Pretzel, supra n.2, at § 19.7.

19. Id.

20. Moreau v. State Farm Mut. Auto. Ins. Co., 298 So.2d 907 (La.App.1974); Chaest v. Union Mut. Ins. Co., 313 A.2d 407 (N.H.1973); Schermer, supra n.7, at § 25.01.

21. Monaco v. United States Fidelity and Guar. Co., 275 Or. 183, 550 P.2d 422 (1976); Woolston v. State Farm Mut. Ins. Co., 306 F.Supp. 738 (W.D. Ark.1969); Northwestern Mut. Ins. Co. v. Rhodes, 238 Cal.App.2d 64, 47 Cal.Rptr. 467 (1965); Fisher v. State Farm Mut. Auto. Ins. Co., 243 Cal. App.2d 749, 52 Cal.Rptr. 721 (1966).

22. Horne v. Superior Life Ins. Co., 203 Va. 282, 123 S.E.2d 401 (1962); State Farm Mut. Auto. Ins. Co., v. Board of Regents, 226 Ga. 310, 174 S.E.2d 920 (Ga.1970); Reliance Ins. Co. v. Robertson, 7 Mass.App. 735, 390 N.E.2d 739 (1979); Hartford Acc.

exclusion is necessary because workers' compensation carriers normally have a right to subrogation for funds received from the tortfeasor. Because uninsured motorists funds are a substitute for funds which should be received from the tortfeasor, workers' compensation insurers could logically extend the argument that the workers' compensation insurers are entitled to the uninsured motorist proceeds. The standard policy clause excludes this possibility and has uniformly been upheld by the courts. In other words, "the (uninsured motorist) carrier is not the alter ego of the tortfeasor, and the provision appropriately reflects this (footnote omitted)." [23]

Attorney *Robert S. Felker* [24] handled a case [25] in which the Washington courts started a "snowballing" effect by requiring insurance carriers to provide uninsured motorist coverage on the basis of public policy and the spirit of the coverage rather than the technical terminology used in the individual policies.

This particular case involved a vehicle of a hit-and-run driver and Attorney Felker's client. Technically, the driver did not hit-and-run. Instead, another car swerved to avoid colliding with the vehicle of the hit-and-run driver. The other car collided with Attorney Felker's clients who were defendants in the instant case.

The defendants sought to bring their uninsured motorist carriers into arbitration in an attempt to receive payments for damage caused by the second driver's attempt to avoid the hit-and-run driver. The carrier filed the instant action with the court for declaratory relief as to the carrier's liability where the insurance policy specifically defined a hit-and-run accident as one "arising out of *physical contact* (emphasis added)." Obviously no physical contact occurred in the instant case.

The court, however, quoted an earlier case saying:

> The statute (RCW 48.22.030) requiring that uninsured motorist coverage shall be provided . . . is but one of many regulatory measures designed to protect the public from the ravages of the negligent and reckless driver. It was enacted to expand insurance protection for the public in using the public streets, highways and walkways and at the same time cut down the incidence and consequences of risk from the careless and insolvent drivers. The statute is both a public safety and a financial security measure . . . .

and Indem. Co. v. Cummings, 66 Ill. App.2d 704, 23 Ill.Dec. 483, 384 N.E. 2d 119 (1978).

23. Schermer, supra n.7, at § 25.03.

24. Robert S. Felker, Esq., Felker & Lazares, Attorneys at Law, Suite 1700, One Washington Plaza, Tacoma, Wash.

25. Hartford Acc. and Indem. Co. v. Novak, 83 Wash.2d 576, 520 P.2d 1368 (1974).

The position taken by courts of this State, and by courts of other States, makes it clear that *restriction* upon the coverage provided by uninsured motorists provisions of automobile insurance policies is against public policy and is void . . . .

We believe it is apparent that the legislature, by its enactment of RCW 48.22.030, intended to afford protection to an insured for injuries or damages proximately caused by a hit-and-run vehicle, irrespective of its actual physical contact with the vehicle of the insured . . . .[26]

§ 28.5 Arbitration

The position between the uninsured motorist carrier and the insured is a curious lot. The carrier is the agent of the insured, yet the interests of the two are often separate.

To handle this situation, uninsured motorist policies typically call for the settling of disputes through arbitration.[27] However, in several states the arbitration provision of the standard policy has been declared unenforceable.[28]

If the arbitration provision of the policy is unenforceable, then the standard consent-to-sue provision is also unenforceable.[29]

§ 28.6 No-Fault Insurance

Library References:
> C.J.S. Motor Vehicles §§ 273.1–273.3.
> West's Key No. Digests, Automobiles ⚖=251.11–251.19.
> Blashfield, Automobile Law & Practice, Ch. 275.
> Appleman, Insurance Law & Practice, § 5151 et seq.

It is imperative that the basic difference between no-fault insurance and uninsured motorist coverage be understood. Uninsured motorist coverage is payable by the insurer only if the person for whose benefit the policy is held is not at fault for the accident in which that person's injuries occur. The tortfeasor-driver must be uninsured or

---

26. Id. at 1371.

27. Schermer, supra n.7 at § 26.01.

28. Logan v. Aetna Cas. and Sur. Co., 309 F.Supp. 402 (S.D.Miss.1970); MFA Mut. Ins. Co. v. Bradshaw, 245 Ark. 95, 431 S.W.2d 252 (1968).

29. Schermer, supra n.7, at § 26.04: "An insured contemplating a third-party action against the tortfeasor should, if possible, attempt to obtain the written consent of the insurer to the institution of the action. Under an early form of exclusion, prosecution of an action to judgment against a tortfeasor without the written consent of the insurer defeated coverage under the policy.

"The coverage loss characteristics of the exclusion were eliminated under a 1963 policy revision. Under the new type of exclusion, the insured agrees that his failure to obtain written consent to sue will deprive him of the right to insist upon the conclusive nature of the judgment as against the insurer. For a discussion of the forfeiture type of clause see Courson v. Maryland Cas. Co. 475 F.2d 1030 (8th Cir. 1973)."

improvident before an innocent, injured person may collect on his own uninsured motorist provision.

No-fault insurance is aptly named. A policy holder may be faulty of negligence but is still entitled to recover under a no-fault policy. This is the basic difference between no-fault and uninsured motorist insurance.

The suggestion of no-fault automobile insurance was made as early as 1932, when Columbia University released the first study on no-fault insurance.[30] The concept reached maturity in 1965, when Professors Richard Keeton and Jeffrey O'Connell published their now-famous book on the subject, Basic Protection for the Traffic Victim.[31]

In that book, the authors recommend compulsory first-party automobile owner coverage of a maximum basic protection benefit of $5,000 in general damages and $10,000 in special damages. In other words, an injured party would have the right to sue a tortfeasor at common law only if the basic protection losses exceeded those quoted. Needless to say, the furor generated by this original work has yet to die down, although the no-fault plan has undergone many modifications.

In 1971, Massachusetts became the first state to adopt no-fault legislation.[32] By 1979, 24 states had adopted some form of compulsory no-fault automobile insurance.[33] Federal legislation which would mandate basic standards for state no-fault benefit plans is continually contemplated by Congress.[34]

The individual state plans vary greatly, and each state's statute would have to be checked before action based upon no-fault would be appropriate. In general, all acts furnish indemnification for loss of insured's income or wages, value of personal services which the injured would have provided for his or her family, and the cost of medical, hospital, or funeral services. Some statutes also cover automobile and property damage loss.[35]

---

30. Smith, Lilly & Dowling, Compensation for Automobile Accidents: A Symposium, 32 Col.L.Rev. 758 (1932).

31. Keeton & O'Connell, Basic Protection for the Traffic Victim (1965).

32. Mass. M.G.L.A. c. 670 §§ 1–5 (1970); M.G.L.A. c. 744 § 3 (1970).

33. Arkansas, Colorado, Connecticut, Delaware, Florida, Georgia, Hawaii, Kansas, Kentucky, Maryland, Massachusetts, Michigan, Minnesota, Nevada, New Jersey, New York, North Dakota, Oregon, Pennsylvania, South Carolina, South Dakota, Texas, Utah, Virginia.

34. See e. g. S. 1381 (1978); H. R. 6601 (1978).

35. Schermer, supra, n.7, at § 2.01.

Attorney *C. Robert Beltz* [36] reports a case [37] he handled in which the Michigan Court of Appeals unanimously reversed a Circuit Court ruling that held that a $20 per day assessment under a no-fault policy for expenses reasonably incurred for a minor child as a result of the death of that child's mother, was not payable after remarriage of the child's father.

MCL 500.3108 provides for:

> Personal protection insurance benefits payable for a survivor's loss * * * not exceeding $20.00 a day reasonably incurred by these dependents during their dependency and after the date on which the deceased died in obtaining ordinary and necessary services in lieu of those that the deceased would have performed for their benefit if he had not suffered the injury causing death . . . .

The Trial Court in the case reasoned that the payment of $20.00 a day for replacement services to the two year old daughter of the deceased was not part of the consideration for a marriage contract between the natural father and his new wife. The court reasoned that once the marriage occurred a family unit was re-established and there were no replacement services "ordinary and necessary."

The Honorable D. J. Brennan, Presiding Judge of the Court of Appeals, in a case of first impression under the Michigan No-Fault Act, held that:

> The insurer should not reap a windfall because ordinary and necessary services rendered to replace those which would have been performed are performed by a wife, instead of a housekeeper or a nursemaid . . . .

> Plaintiff's new wife does not legally replace his daughter's dead mother. The stepmother is not liable for all the duties or entitled to all of the rights of a parent . . . . Nor does a stepmother enjoy any favorable presumption for purposes of child custody under the Child Custody Act.

> Plaintiff's remarriage, while re-establishing the family unit, in no way affected [the child's] need for ordinary and necessary services that her dead mother once provided. The Trial Court improperly concluded that plaintiff's remarriage terminated his daughter's eligibility to receive survivor's loss benefits, Section 3108, of the No-Fault Act."

---

36. C. Robert Beltz, Esquire, Hicks, Beltz, Behm & Nickola, Sixth Floor-Genesee Bank Building, Flint, Michigan.

37. Youmans v. Citizen Insurance Company of America, Circuit Court for the County of Genesee, Michigan, Docket No. 76 41076 NM, February 17, 1978.

The case was reversed and remanded for entry of a judgment, 12 percent interest per annum and the payment of actual attorney fees.

Another variation in no-fault statutes among different jurisdictions is the treatment of releases. Just as the common law concerning releases varies from jurisdiction to jurisdiction, so does the statutory no-fault law.

Typical of many states is the South Carolina Automobile Reform Act of 1974. The Act specifically states that no *general release* may be procured by an insurer based upon payment of no-fault benefits in the absence of a full written disclosure to the insured of all rights accruing to him.

Joel D. Bailey, Esquire, of South Carolina,[38] was plaintiff's attorney in a case[39] concerning this provision. The plaintiff was a passenger in an automobile which had overturned when it was being driven at a high rate of speed. The driver was the plaintiff's brother.

Plaintiff sustained a fractured femur in the accident and, thereafter, approximately $2,500 in medical expenses were paid by Allstate Insurance Company, the liability insurer for the defendant/brother. Of this $2,500, $1,000 had been paid under no-fault insurance coverage.

Allstate procured a general release from the plaintiff, the consideration for which was the $2,500 in medical payments. Both the plaintiff and the insurance carrier assumed that the plaintiff had experienced a normal recovery, and that the only additional medical treatment needed would be a minor operative procedure to remove the pin from the plaintiff's leg. For this reason, the release contained a provision for payment of $1,000 for additional medical expenses. Allstate failed to make a full written disclosure to the plaintiff of all rights accruing to plaintiff, as South Carolina's statute required.

When the pin was subsequently removed from plaintiff's leg, it developed that there was a non-union of the fractured femur and that additional surgery would be required.

Allstate then refused to pay any future medical expenses and asserted the validity of the release. The plaintiff brought suit against his brother and Allstate pleaded the release as an affirmative defense. The release was held invalid as a matter of law in that (a) it was

---

38. Joel D. Bailey, Esquire, Moss, Carter, Branton and Bailey, 1501 North Street, Beaufort, South Carolina.

39. Trent v. Trent, Beaufort County Court of Common Pleas, Docket No. 78–CP–7–580.

based upon a mutual mistake of fact, and (b) the insurer had failed to provide full written disclosure in contravention of the South Carolina statute.

The jury returned a verdict of $30,000 and the case was subsequently settled on appeal.

§§ 28.7–29.0 are reserved for supplementary material.

CHAPTER 29

THE DRAMSHOP RULE

Table of Sections

Sec.
29.1 Development of Common Law Liability.
29.2 Proof in a Dramshop Case.
29.3 Dramshop Acts—Construction and Elements.
29.4 Who May Be Liable.
29.5 Extraterritoriality—Exclusiveness of Remedy.

Library References:

C.J.S. Intoxicating Liquors §§ 428, 430, 449.
West's Key No. Digests, Intoxicating Liquors ⚖=282 et seq.
Blashfield, Automobile Law & Practice 54.3.

§ 29.1 Development of Common Law Liability

Today, most states have statutes (called "Dramshop" or "Civil Damages" Acts) giving a right of action against the supplier of intoxicating beverages [1]. At common law, however, no remedy was afforded for the damage or injury caused by intoxication other than the direct right against the intoxicant in rem.[2]

As stated in the early Illinois case of *Cruse v. Aden*,[3]

"It was not a tort at common law to either sell or give intoxicating liquor to a 'strong and able-bodied man,' and it can be said safely that it is not anywhere laid down in the books that such act was ever held at common law to be culpable negligence that would impose legal liability for damages upon the vendor or donor of such liquor."

The injudicious mixture of liquor and gasoline, however, and its all-too-frequently appalling consequences, has put great pressure on this common law rule. As expressed in an able dissent to an Idaho decision withholding the rule:

---

1. See § 29.3, infra.

2. Megge v. United States, 344 F.2d 31 (6th Cir. 1965), cert. denied 382 U.S. 831, 86 S.Ct. 69, 15 L.Ed.2d 74; Meade v. Freeman, 93 Idaho 389, 462 P.2d 54 (1969); Parsons v. Jow, 480 P.2d 396 (Wyo.1971); Garcia v. Hargrove, 46 Wis.2d 724, 176 N.W.2d 566 (1970).

3. 127 Ill. 231, 20 N.E. 73, 3 LRA 327; see Am.Cas.1917B 533 (1889).

"When most people walked and few had horses or carriages, or even in the days when the horse and buggy was a customary mode of travel, it may have been that the common law rule of non-liability arising from the sale of liquor to an intoxicated person was satisfactory. But the situation then and the problem in today's society of the imbiber going upon the public highways and operating a machine that requires quick response of mind and muscle and capable of producing mass death and destruction are vastly different."[4]

The modern trend is to treat intoxicating liquor as a volatile substance in the same category with firearms or explosives, and require, especially of the commercial dealer, a duty to spare the public a deadly danger in those circumstances where the likelihood of injury is reasonably apparent.[5]

Despite the common law rule, several jurisdictions have found liability for negligence where the act of furnishing the intoxicant is in violation of statute or regulation, such as against serving minors or intoxicated persons. In *Rappaport v. Nichols*,[6] the New Jersey Supreme Court held that a cause of action in negligence was stated against a tavern owner who had illegally served drinks to a minor, in a wrongful death suit brought by the survivors of the victim of a car accident caused by the minor's drunk driving.[7] The Court dismissed the question of proximate cause on the grounds of foreseeable risk,[8] and held that the victim, as a member of the general public, was within the class intended to be protected by the statute forbidding sale of liquor to minors.[9] In *Davis v. Shiappacose*,[10] the Florida

---

4. Meade v. Freeman, supra n.2.

5. See: Cahn, New Common Law Dramshop Rule, 9 Cleve. Marsh.L. Rev. 302 (1960); Note, 18 West.Res. L.Rev. 251 (1966); Dramshop Liability: A Judicial Response, 57 Cal.L. Rev. 995 (1969); Note, Vendor's Liability for Damages by Intoxicated Persons, 74 W.Va.L.Rev. 408 (1972).

6. 31 N.J. 188, 156 A.2d 1 (1959).

7. "If the patron is a minor or is intoxicated when served, the tavern-keeper's sale to him is unlawful; and if the circumstances are such that the tavern-keeper knows or should know that the patron is a minor or is intoxicated, his service to him may also constitute common law negligence." 31 N.J. at 202, 156 A.2d at 9.

8. "And a jury could also reasonably find that Nichols' negligent operation of his motor vehicle after leaving defendant's tavern was a normal incident of the risk they created, or an event which they could reasonably have foreseen, and that consequently there was no effective breach in the chain of causation." 31 N.J. at 204, 156 A.2d at 9.

9. "It seems clear to us that these broadly expressed restrictions were not narrowly intended to benefit the minors and intoxicated persons alone but were wisely intended for the protection of members of the general public as well." 31 N.J. at 202, 156 A.2d at 8.

10. 155 So.2d 365 (Fla.1963).

Supreme Court held that a cause of action was stated on behalf of the deceased minor himself, holding that violation of the statute constituted negligence per se. Illegal sale of liquor to an intoxicated person has similarly been held to constitute negligence in California [11] and other jurisdictions.[12] In a Minnesota case,[13] where 3.2 "near beer" was illegally sold to a minor, the vendor was held liable to a third party injured by the intoxicated minor. Although 3.2 beer was not an intoxicating beverage for purposes of the Minnesota dramshop act, liability was nevertheless predicated on common law negligence, and the sale

---

11. Vesely v. Sager, 5 Cal.3d 153, 95 Cal.Rptr. 623, 486 P.2d 151 (1971) ("Insofar as proximate cause is concerned, we find no basis for a distinction founded solely on the fact that the consumption of an alcoholic beverage is a voluntary act of the consumer and is a link in the chain of causation from the furnishing of the beverage to the injury resulting from intoxication. * * * If such furnishing is a proximate cause, it is so because the consumption, resulting intoxication, and injury-producing conduct are foreseeable intervening causes, or at least the injury-producing conduct is one of the hazards which makes such furnishing negligent." 5 Cal.3d at 164, 95 Cal.Rptr. at 631, 486 P.2d at 159).

12. Waynick v. Chicago's Last Dept. Store, 269 F.2d 322 (7th Cir. 1969), cert. denied 362 U.S. 902, 80 S.Ct. 611, 4 L.Ed.2d 554 ("The Illinois act making unlawful the sale of alcoholic liquor to any intoxicated person is for the protection of any member of the public who might be injured or damaged as a result of the drunkenness to which the particular sale of alcoholic liquor contributes").

Adamian v. Three Sons, Inc., 353 Mass. 498, 233 N.E.2d 18 (1968) ("Henceforth in this Commonwealth waste of human life due to drunken driving on the highways will not be left outside the scope of the foreseeable risk created by the sale of liquor to an already intoxicated individual").

Mason v. Roberts, 35 Ohio App.2d 29, 300 N.E.2d 211 (1971), aff'd 33 Ohio St.2d 29, 294 N.E.2d 884. (Wrongful death action by administrator of decedent beaten to death by intoxicated man whom defendant seller knew was violent when intoxicated. Ohio statute prohibits sale to intoxicated person or "blacklisted" habitual drunk:

("No Ohio case holds that this statute offers immunity to one who knowingly and intentionally sells intoxicants to a person known to him to be physically dangerous to others when such person is drunk. Such conduct is an intentional invasion of the legally protected interest of the public to be free from the intentional loosing upon the community of physical violence. Such conduct is not the mere want of ordinary care or negligence, but is an intentional violation of a substantial socially important legally protected interest at common law.")

Jardine v. Upper Darby Lodge No. 1973, Inc., 413 Pa. 626, 198 A.2d 550 (1964) ("An intoxicated person behind the wheel of an automobile can be as dangerous as an insane person with a firearm. He is as much a hazard to the safety of the community as a stick of dynamite that must be defused in order to be rendered harmless. To serve an intoxicated person more liquor is to light the fuse").

13. Trail v. Christian, 298 Minn. 101, 213 N.W.2d 618 (1973).

in violation of the statute against sale to minors was held to constitute negligence per se.

Where the relevant statute is not restricted to commercial liquor vendors but applies generally to "persons" who "furnish" intoxicants to minors or intoxicates persons, common law liability has been imposed on "social hosts." In *Brockett v. Kitchen Boyd Motor Co.*,[14] a California appellate court overruled the demurrer of a defendant employer who had supplied his minor employee with "copious amounts" of alcoholic beverage at the office Christmas party, with knowledge that the minor would subsequently be driving on the public highway. The California Supreme Court, in *Coulter v. Superior Court*,[15] extended the rule to social hosts serving intoxicated guests, stating, "We think it evident that the service of alcoholic beverages to an obviously intoxicated person by one who knows that such intoxicated person intends to drive a motor vehicle creates a reasonably foreseeable risk of injury to those on the highway. . . . Simply put, one who serves alcoholic beverages under such circumstances fails to exercise reasonable care."[16] Shortly after this decision, the California Legislature amended its applicable code to negate this ruling, and to reinstitute the rule that the proximate cause of any resulting injuries was the consumption of the beverage, not the serving thereof.[17]

14. 24 Cal.App.3d 87, 100 Cal.Rptr. 752 (1972). ("Clearly the impeccable logic of *Vesely* impels the conclusion that any person, whether he is in the business of dispensing alcoholic beverages or not, who disregards the legislative mandate breaches a duty to anyone who is injured as a result of the minor's intoxication and for whose benefit the statute was enacted. If one willfully disobeys the law and knowingly furnishes liquor to a minor with knowledge that the minor is going to drive a vehicle on the public highways, as alleged in this case, he must face the consequences.")

15. 21 Cal.3d 144, 145 Cal.Rptr. 534, 577 P.2d 669 (1978).

16. 21 Cal.3d 152–3, 145 Cal.Rptr. at 539, 577 P.2d at 674. See Lewis v. Wolf, 122 Ariz. 567, 596 P.2d 705 (1979) ("[W]e are not considering here the liability of a social host. Even if we were, what is wrong with making a person who furnishes intoxicants to one who is already visibly and obviously intoxicated liable if the latter gets into the driver's seat of an automobile and kills or maims another? If his act is a proximate cause of the injury, how can he say that he should not be liable? It is a wrong for which a responsible judicial system should provide a remedy").

17. West's Ann.Cal.Bus. & Prof. Code § 25602:

(b) No person who sells, furnishes, gives or causes to be sold, furnished or given away, any alcoholic beverage . . . shall be civilly liable to any injured person or the estate of such person for injuries inflicted on that person as a result of intoxication by the consumer of such alcoholic beverage.

(c) The Legislature hereby declares that this section shall be interpreted so that the holding in such cases as Vesely v. Sager, Bernard v. Harrah's Club and Coulter

Other jurisdictions have applied reasoning similar to the court in *Coulter*, and have imposed liability on the part of college fraternities,[18] a wedding party host,[19] and even a woman who was aware that her 20-year-old brother was taking beer and whiskey from her refrigerator and failed to stop him, even though she had not affirmatively furnished him with liquor.[20] A New Jersey court recently held that a homeowner may be liable for permitting consumption of alcohol by minors on its premises, even though the homeowner did not sell, serve, furnish or observe the drinking.[21]

In an interesting Michigan case,[22] a bar had served drinks to an elderly alcoholic despite prior promises to his family not to do so, and the alcoholic shortly thereafter fell off a bridge to his death. Over defendants' demurrer, the appeals court upheld the wrongful death action based on common law negligence, holding that the charge of selling alcohol to a known compulsive alcoholic, contrary to an agreement not to serve him, stated a cause of action for gross negligence and willful and wanton misconduct.[23]

v. Superior Court be abrogated in favor of prior judicial interpretation finding the consumption of alcoholic beverages rather than the serving of alcoholic beverages as the proximate cause of injuries inflicted upon another by an intoxicated person. [Citations omitted.]

18. Wiener v. Gamma Phi Chapter of Alpha Tan Omega Fraternity, 258 Or. 632, 485 P.2d 18 (1971):
("Ordinarily, a host who makes available intoxicating liquors to an adult guest is not liable for injuries to third persons resulting from the guest's intoxication. There might be circumstances in which the host would have a duty to deny his guest further access to alcohol. This would be the case where the host 'has reason to know that he is dealing with persons whose characteristics make it especially likely that they will do unreasonable things.' Such persons could include those already severely intoxicated, or those whose behavior the host knows to be unusually affected by alcohol. Also included might be young people, if their ages were such that they could be expected, by virtue of their youth alone or in connection with other circumstances, to behave in a dangerous fashion under the influence of alcohol.")

Giardina v. Solomon, 360 F.Supp. 262 (D.C.Pa.1973) (Cause of action stated against fraternity which illegally furnished liquor to minor by plaintiff injured by assault to intoxicated minor).

19. Thaut v. Finley, 50 Mich.App. 611, 213 N.W.2d 820 (1974) (Liquor served to minor in violation of statute).

20. Brattain v. Herron, 159 Ind.App. 663, 309 N.E.2d 150 (1974). Contra: See Hopper v. F. W. Corrdori Roofing Co., 305 A.2d 309 (Del.1973) (Where 18-year-old employee became intoxicated at employer's Christmas party, mere availability of intoxicants did not constitute "giving" in violation of statute).

21. Demes v. Kuligoski, (N.J.App. Docket # A 2886–77, May 10, 1979), cert. denied 81 N.J. 293, 405 A.2d 837 (1979).

22. Grasser v. Fleming, 74 Mich.App. 338, 253 N.W.2d 757 (1977).

23. The Grasser court referred to the earlier cases of Swanson v. Bull, 67

§ 29.1 SPECIFIC ACTIONS Pt. 4

In a Kentucky case,[24] common law liability was based on an intentional wrong where the vendor sold decedent a quart of whiskey knowing that he intended to drink it all on a bet. The Court held that decedent's contributory negligence was no defense to the vendor's intentional wrong.

§ 29.2 Proof in a Dramshop Case

It is, of course, necessary to prove that plaintiff purchased the alcohol from a specific dealer, bar, grocery store, or other defendant. When the latter denies furnishing the plaintiff with the beverage, counsel must perform an imaginative pretrial investigation to identify the particular defendant. Attorney *William M. Shernoff* of Claremont, California,[25] did such an investigation, which combined with appropriate liability theories, resulted in a structured settlement worth as much as $4,681,000 in *Chase v. Chizar.*

Plaintiff therein was rendered a quadriplegic when the car in which he was riding overturned, throwing him from the vehicle. At the time of the accident, plaintiff was eighteen years old; the driver was seventeen.

Prior to the accident the boys had bought two six-packs of malt liquor from a nearby convenience store. They had consumed the alcohol before getting into the car, and plaintiff alleged that the driver's intoxication caused the accident. The driver was a minor, so plaintiff sued both franchisor and franchisee under a dramshop theory for compensatory and punitive damages.

Defendants denied selling alcohol to plaintiff, the driver, or any other minors. They claimed that plaintiff had been contributorily negligent in the purchase and consumption of the beer, and also planned to assert the seatbelt defense.

Defendant franchisor also hoped to avoid any punitive liability (which, as shown below, was likely to be huge) by arguing that it was not responsible for the conduct of its franchisee. Plaintiff planned to counter this argument with two theories of liability: (1) the franchisor exercised control over the franchisee, which was a mere managerial agent; and (2) the franchisor, as co-liquor licensee with franchisee, had a nondelegable duty to prevent the latter from selling alcohol to minors or committing other illegal acts.

S.D. 161, 290 N.W. 482 (1940), and Pratt v. Duly, 55 Ariz. 535, 104 P.2d 147, 130 A.L.R. 341 (1940), wherein wrongful death actions were sustained on the analogy of sale of intoxicating liquor to the sale of a habit-forming drug.

24. Nally v. Blandford, 291 S.W.2d 832 (Ky.1956).

25. William M. Shernoff, Esquire, 600 South Indian Hill Blvd., Claremont, California.

While plaintiff's liability theories were persuasive, they would not have compelled settlement unless defendants anticipated rather large punitive damages. To convince defendants of the potential enormity of the punitives, Attorney Shernoff found seventeen minors willing to sign affidavits stating that they had purchased alcohol from defendants' store on numerous occasions. These minors ranged in age from fourteen to twenty; of these, one had purchased alcohol there on 25 occasions, another on 50 separate instances. A fourteen-year-old stated that he could only purchase liquor after 10:00 p.m. Finally, there was evidence that these minors were charged $0.50 extra per six-pack because they were under age.

Energetic investigation thus provided Attorney Shernoff with compelling evidence that defendant franchisee was not only selling alcohol to minors but also reaping extra profits from his lawlessness. Plaintiff's liability theories tied defendant franchisor to these disreputable acts, opening them to the dangers of a substantial punitive judgment. A structured settlement was negotiated which gave plaintiff $545,000 immediately and installment payments of $22,000 each year, compounded annually at five per cent interest, to continue for the rest of plaintiff's life.

§ 29.3 Dramshop Acts—Construction and Elements

To fill the gap left by the early common law, various state legislatures have enacted statutes giving a right of action against the supplier of intoxicating beverages—the so-called "Dramshop" or "Civil Damages" Acts.

Early cases indicated that the Dramshop Acts were to be considered statutes of a highly penal character and, therefore, should receive a strict construction.[26] This view continues to prevail in many courts.[27] Noting, however, that the acts are primarily for the wel-

---

26. Cruse v. Aden, 127 Ill. 231, 20 N.E. 73, 3 L.R.A. 327. See Am.Cas.1917B 533 (1889).

27. **Strict Statutory Construction.** Noonan v. Galick, 19 Conn.Sup. 308, 112 A.2d 892 (1955) (Statute providing recovery by person injured by purchaser not extended to cover injuries to intoxicated person); Robertson v. White, 11 Ill.App.2d 177, 136 N.E.2d 550 (1956) (Where 4 year old child killed by reason of defendant's dram shop action not maintainable for loss of support where child had no income); Strand v. Village of Watson, 245 Minn. 414, 72 N.W.2d 609 (1955) (Statute prohibiting sale to any person obviously intoxicated requires instructions defining necessary proof); Beck v. Groe, 245 Minn. 28, 70 N.W.2d 886, 52 A.L.R.2d 875 (1955) (Sale of 3.2 beer designated by legislature as non-intoxicating no basis for action under act penalizing furishing "intoxicating liquors"); Christoff v. Gradsky, 140 N.E.2d 586 (Com. Pl.1956) (Statute prohibiting sale to person after order of department of liquor control required such order as basis for any liability).

fare and benefit of the public and are designed to provide a means of indemnification to persons injured by the intoxication of others, a liberal construction is often urged.[28] Indeed, the Illinois Dramshop Act declares specifically that its terms are to receive such a liberal construction.[29]

The Dramshop Acts of various states differ in their language and application, and to undertake a detailed treatment of them is beyond the scope of this section. However, generally, to impose liability under these acts the following conditions must be met: (1) Defendant or his agent must sell or furnish the liquor causing the intoxication upon which the action is predicated. (2) Plaintiff must show that the gift or sale was a cause of the intoxication of the person to whom the liquor was furnished, although, generally, it need not be shown it was the sole, or even most material cause thereof. (3) Death or injury resulting from the intoxication. (4) Damage or loss to the plaintiff as a result thereof.

Some jurisdictions hold that privity between the vendor and the intoxicated person need not be shown where the vendor has knowledge or reason to know that the intoxicant would be consumed by a third party.[30] Such knowledge may be based on the third party's

---

See 52 A.L.R.2d 890 (What constitutes "intoxicating liquor" within civil damage act).

28. Arington v. Phelps, 79 F.Supp. 295 (D.C.Ill.1948).

Wendelin v. Russell, 259 Iowa 1152, 147 N.W.2d 188 (1966) ("In addition it is evident the subject act should be construed liberally to aid in suppressing the mischief and advance the remedial objective which prompted its enactment. . . . Section 123.95, as finally adopted, was disguised to place a hand of restraint upon those licensed or permitted by law to sell or supply intoxicants to others and protect the public, but above all to provide an avenue of relief to those offended who had no recourse or right of action under the common law").

See also Federated Mutual Implement & Hardware Ins. Co. v. Dunkelberger, 172 N.W.2d 137 (Iowa 1969); Bankord v. DeRoch, 423 F.Supp. 602 (D.C.Iowa 1976); Village of Brooten v. Cudahy Packing Co. 291 F.2d 284 (8th Cir. 1961) ("The review of the case law leads us to conclude that the Supreme Court of Minnesota has adopted a generally broad and liberal attitude toward the state's Civil Damage Act").

29. Ill.Rev.Stat.1949, ch. 43, § 94: "This act shall be liberally construed, to the end that the health, safety and welfare of the people of the State of Illinois shall be protected, and temperance in the consumption of alcoholic liquors shall be fostered and promoted by sound and careful control and regulation of the manufacture, sale and distribution of alcoholic liquors."

30. See Annotation: 64 A.L.R.3d 922, Civil Damage Act: Liability of one who furnishes liquor to another for consumption by third parties for injury caused by consumers.

presence at the sale,³¹ or by the excessive quantity of liquor sold.³² Although the rule that the furnishing of intoxicants constitutes only a remote cause to injuries resulting from the intoxication—the rationale of the common law rule against recovery—is no longer accepted as a bar to recovery in most jurisdictions,³³ nonetheless, where the statute establishes liability for injuries inflicted "in consequence of the intoxication" (as opposed to "by an intoxicated person"), plaintiff must show the intoxication to have been the proximate cause of the injuries.³⁴ Sufficient causation has been found in cases of automobile accidents,³⁵ falls,³⁶ exposure,³⁷ and violence.³⁸ Injuries sus-

31. Bell v. Poindexter, 336 Ill.App. 541, 84 N.E.2d 646 (1949) (Liquor purchased when driver present); Anderson v. Dale, 90 Ill.App.2d 332, 232 N.E.2d 767 (1967) (No recovery where vendor had no reason to know).

32. Peterson v. Jack Donelson Sales Co., 4 Ill.App.3d 792, 281 N.E.2d 753, 64 A.L.R.3d 916 (1972) (Bringing beer dispensing truck to picnic site equivalent to bringing dramshop premises, knowledge that beer intended for general consumption inferred).

33. Deeds v. United States, 306 F. Supp. 348 (D.C.Mont.1969): ("The increasing frequency of serious accidents caused by drivers who are intoxicated is a fact which must be well known to those who sell and dispense liquor. This lends support to those cases which have found the automobile accident to be 'the reasonably foreseeable' result of furnishing liquor to the intoxicated driver, at least where the person furnishing the liquor knew that the intoxicated person would be driving on a public highway.")

See also: Village of Brooten v. Cudahy Packing Co., supra, n.28.

34. O'Rorke v. John Day, Oregon Lodge No. 1824 of Benevolent & Protective Order of Elks, 270 Or. 533, 528 P.2d 1030 (1974) ("There must be proof of the causal relationship between defendants' conduct and plaintiff's injuries in order to establish defendants' liability." Question wheth-

er defendants' sale to deceased was proximate cause of his death was properly a jury question).

See also Watson v. Ristow, 42 Mich. App. 318, 201 N.W.2d 289 (1972); Trail v. Village of Elk River, 286 Minn. 380, 175 N.W.2d 916 (1970); Bryant v. Athans, 362 Mich. 17, 106 N.W.2d 389 (1960).

35. Fletcher v. Flynn, 368 Mich. 328, 118 N.W.2d 229 (1962) (Sufficient causation where decedent consumed more than half a fifth of liquor and two beers and later walked directly into path of automobile); Bejnarowicz v. Bakos, 332 Ill.App. 151, 74 N. E.2d 614 (1947) (Decedent drove on wrong side of street into streetcar).

No Proximate Causation. Watson v. Fischbach, 6 Ill.App.3d 166, 284 N.E.2d 720 (1972), rev'd on other grounds 54 Ill.2d 498, 301 N.E.2d 303 (No recovery where no competent evidence of intoxication, and jury could have found that decedent's car left road for other reasons).

36. Grasser v. Fleming, supra, n.22 (Decedent fell off bridge while intoxicated); Jones v. Keilbach, 309 Ill. App. 233, 32 N.E.2d 985 (1941) (Decedent found dead in excavation two or three hours after leaving tavern in intoxicated condition).

37. Curran v. Percival, 21 Neb. 434, 32 N.W. 213 (1887) (It was natural and probable result that customer who

38. See note 38 on page 720.

§ 29.3   SPECIFIC ACTIONS   Pt. 4

tained from a third party in a fight initiated by the intoxicated person may be considered the proximate consequences of the intoxication.[39] Dramshop liability has been upheld where the decedent has committed suicide.[40]

A related proximate cause issue is the need to show that the liquor furnished at least contributed to the intoxication which caused the damage,[41] although unless expressly required by the statute, it need not be its sole cause.[42] The various stations of an inebriant's

became drunk at saloon should become stupefied and unable to reach home, and freeze to death); Rafferty v. Buckman, 46 Iowa 195 (1877) (Decedent found dead in the street morning after obtaining intoxicant from defendant's store); Schwehr v. Badalamenti, 14 Ill.App.2d 128, 143 N.E.2d 558 (1957) ("If the drunk is frozen to death, or falls into a fire, or is drowned in a freshet, the intervening agency of frost, fire, or freshet does not eliminate intoxication as the proximate cause . . . . To hold the contrary would defeat the purpose of the statute").

38. McIntire v. Morris, 199 Ill.App. 20 (1916) (Deceased while intoxicated fired six shots at city marshall and was killed by the latter in self defense); Cook v. Kirgan, 332 Ill.App. 294, 75 N.E.2d 120 (1947) (Deceased provoked fight while intoxicated and was shot to death).

39. Kiriluk v. Cohn, 16 Ill.App.2d 385, 148 N.E.2d 607 (1958) (Where intoxicated husband chased wife threatening to kill her, and she shot and killed him in self defense, liability of tavern was established, where wife's prior requests to tavern not to sell liquor to decedent supported an inference that tavern could foresee consequent harm of further sales).

40. Garrigan v. Kennedy, 19 S.D. 11, 101 N.W. 1081 (1904).

41. Pose v. Roosevelt Hotel Co., 208 N.W.2d 19 (Iowa 1973) (Where decedent had drunk at bar till midnight and left his motel the next morning after sleeping one hour and taking a diet pill, tavern was not liable for his death in auto accident 20 minutes after leaving motel. Court held that plaintiff must show a causal connection between decedent's intoxication at the time of the accident and the furnishing of liquor by the defendant); Hartwig v. Loyal Order of Moose, 253 Minn. 347, 91 N.W.2d 794, 75 A.L.R.2d 459 (1958) (Court held that recovery for death of decedent must be based on proof that defendants unlawfully furnished liquor which caused intoxication and that intoxication was proximate cause of injuries); Danhof v. Osborne, 11 Ill. 2d 77, 142 N.E.2d 20, 65 A.L.R.2d 917 (1957); 45 Am.Jur.2d Intoxicating Liquors § 582.

42. Hahn v. Ortonville, 238 Minn. 428, 57 N.W.2d 254 (1953) (Sufficient causation if liquor furnished is a cooperating, concurring, or contributing factor to the intoxication).

See also Weiner v. Trasatti, 19 Ill.App. 3d 240, 311 N.E.2d 313 (1974); Pesola v. Pawlowski, 45 Mich.App. 516, 206 N.W.2d 780 (1973); Harris v. Hurlburt, 83 Misc.2d 626, 373 N.Y.S.2d 480 (1975).

Contra

Caruso v. Kazense, 20 Ill.App.3d 695, 313 N.E.2d 689 (1974) (Revised Illinois statute supposes liability only upon person who "caused" intoxication rather than on any person who contributed thereto).

O'Rorke v. John Day, Oregon, Lodge # 1824 of Benev. & Protective Order of Elks, supra, n. 34 (Liability for dece-

pilgrimage may be joined as defendants,[43] and it is not necessary to show where the last libation was obtained.[44]

Where the statute is held to impose a rule of strict liability, plaintiff's burden is of course greatly reduced. A line of Connecticut cases, for example, holds that it is not necessary to prove that the sale produced the intoxication which caused the injury.[45]

§ 29.4 Who May Be Liable

The question of who may be held liable depends, of course, upon the construction given the provisions of the particular liquor act.[46] The United States Supreme Court has stated that, "A state statute giving a wife a right of action against any person who injures her means of support by selling intoxicating liquor to her husband, does not violate the due process clause of the Fourteenth Amendment by providing further that the judgment for damages so recovered shall be a lien upon the premises where the liquor was sold, as against an owner who leased, or knowingly permitted the use of, such premises for the sale of intoxicating liquor."[47]

If the act does not specifically list who may be entitled to recovery, then generally an action may be maintained by "any person

dent's death required causal connection between furnishing liquor and death, and could not be based merely on showing contribution to intoxication).

43. Roose v. Perkins, 9 Neb. 304, 2 N. W. 715 (1879) (Statute created liability to all who contributed to intoxication by furnishing liquor); Duncan v. Beres, 15 Mich.App. 318, 166 N.W.2d 678 (1968) (Defendant may implead and seek contribution from any other tavern owner who contributed to the intoxication); Dunkelberger v. Hopkins, 51 Ill.App.2d 205, 200 N.E.2d 905 (1964) (Prima facie case established where shown that liquor served by various taverns contributed to intoxication of person who injured plaintiff); Skaja v. Andrews Hotel Co., 281 Minn. 417, 161 N.W.2d 657 (1968) (Two vendors of liquor to minor may be joined as defendants, but settlement with one by covenant not to sue did not bar recovery against the other against whom action still pending).

44. Wanna v. Miller, 136 N.W.2d 563 (N.D.1965) (Dramshop act does not require that plaintiff prove intoxicated person received his last drink at defendant's place of business).

45. Pierce v. Albanese, 144 Conn. 241, 129 A.2d 606 (1957), appeal dism'd 355 U.S. 15, 78 S.Ct. 36, 2 L.Ed.2d 21 (Not necessary to show that the sale produced the intoxication which caused the injury).

See also Lavieri v. Ulysses, 149 Conn. 396, 180 A.2d 632, 98 A.L.R.2d 1096 (1962); Roberts v. Casey, 4 Conn.Cir. 89, 225 A.2d 836 (1966).

46. Hahn v. City of Ortonville, 238 Minn. 428, 57 N.W.2d 254 (1953) (Minn. Civil Damage Act applies to municipal corporations operating liquor stores); Gibbons v. Cannaven, 393 Ill. 376, 66 N.E.2d 370, 169 A.L.R. 1190 (1946) (Liability of lessor of saloon property).

47. Eiger v. Garrity, 246 U.S. 97, 38 S.Ct. 298, 62 L.Ed. 596 (1918).

injured."[48] However, courts generally feel that no person should profit by his own wrongdoing, and recovery is barred if the person damaged has, himself, contributed in causing the intoxication.[49] For example, a wife has no action against the purveyor of intoxicants for injuries inflicted by her inebriated spouse if she has directly contributed to his state.[50] However, the wife will not defeat her right of action if she secures the liquor under compulsion,[51] or if she merely accompanied her husband even if she drank moderately.[52] The rule against recovery has been characterized as one of complicity, not of contributory negligence,[53] and generally plaintiff's role must be more affirmative than that of drinking companion for the defense to bar recovery.[54] In a New York case,[55] plaintiff had passed out from intoxication while drinking with her companion, who, after several

48. Cope v. Gepford, 326 Ill.App. 171, 61 N.E.2d 394 (1945).

49. Cookinham v. Sullivan, 23 Conn. Sup. 193, 179 A.2d 840 (1962); Sapp v. Johnson, 15 Ill.App.3d 119, 303 N. E.2d 429 (1973) (Plaintiff accompanied driver to bar, drinking with him); Berge v. Harris, 170 N.W.2d 621 (Iowa 1969) (Active drinking companion cannot recover); Turk v. Long Branch Saloon Inc., 280 Minn. 438, 159 N.W.2d 903 (1968); Martinson v. Monticello Municipal Liquors, 297 Minn. 48, 209 N.W.2d 902 (1973) (One who alternated with driver in buying drinks could not recover for injuries sustained in accident).

50. Engleken v. Hilger, 43 Iowa 563 (1876) (Wife voluntarily contributed to intoxication of husband).

51. Masted v. Swedish Brethern, 83 Minn. 40, 85 N.W. 913, 53 L.R.A. 803 (1901).

52. Todd v. Bigelow, 51 Mich.App. 346, 214 N.W.2d 733 (1974) (Merely accompanying and drinking with an intoxicated person does not, as a matter of law, bar recovery).
Hempstead v. Minneapolis Sheraton Corp., 283 Minn. 1, 166 N.W.2d 95 (1969) (Companion of intoxicated driver who did not purchase, procure, or participate in obtaining liquor not barred from recovery).

53. Osinger v. Christian, 43 Ill.App.2d 480, 193 N.E.2d 872 (1963):
("The defense of complicity and the defense of contributory negligence are both children of the doctrine that one cannot profit from his own wrong or neglect. Although the line which divides them may on occasion be thin, the history of the dramshop act justifies the acceptance of complicity and the rejection of contributory negligence as a defense. The common law gave no right of action either on the theory that the sale of liquor was a direct wrong or on the ground that it was negligence, which under any circumstance might impose liability on the seller for damages resulting from intoxication.")

54. Martinson v. Monticello Municipal Liquors, 297 Minn. 48, 209 N.W.2d 902 (1973) (Mere passive participation does not constitute complicity in drinking companion's intoxication); Chapman v. Powers, 30 Ill.App.3d 44, 331 N.E.2d 593 (1975) (Plaintiff who purchased drink for assailant not barred from recovery from tavern for later shooting).

55. Mitchell v. Shoals, Inc., 19 N.Y.2d 338, 280 N.Y.S.2d 113, 227 N.E.2d 21 (1967).

more bourbons, placed her in the front seat of his car and drove off. He subsequently crashed into a building. He was killed and she was seriously injured. Her recovery against the tavern was not barred, the Court finding that:

> ". . . she had not, in any sense, caused or procured his intoxication. She had neither purchased the drinks nor encouraged him to take more than he could weather. The plaintiff had simply had a few drinks and passed out before her escort's inebriacy became really serious. This did not amount to a guilty participation in his intoxication. To deny her a remedy because her own alcoholic capacity was limited would impair, if not go a long way toward defeating, the purpose of the statute."

Contributory negligence is not a permissible defense when the liability is created by statute and not in negligence.[56] This rule has been utilized in a federal case in New Jersey [57] to establish the liability of a tavernkeeper to an intoxicated patron himself for injuries sustained in a car accident. The Court noted: "The theory is that the prohibition in the statute represents a device to protect an incompetent against the consequences of his own incompetency."

In the California case of *Ewing v. Cloverleaf Bowl*,[58] where defendant died of acute alcohol poisoning after celebrating his twenty-first birthday with ten one-ounce shots of 150-proof rum and two beer chasers, decedent's contributory negligence was considered no bar to recovery in view of the willful misconduct of the experienced bartender who furnished, literally, "the poison". Holding that decedent, without appreciation of the danger of alcohol poisoning, had not assumed the risk despite his intention to get drunk, the Court held that a common law cause of action on behalf of the surviving widow and children had been stated.[59]

Since dramshop liability often is imposed statutorily, the terms of a liability insurance policy may not cover the wrongdoer.[60] It has

---

56. Zucker v. Vogt, 329 F.2d 426 (2d Cir. 1964).

See also Williams v. Klemesrud, 197 N. W.2d 614, 64 A.L.R.3d 843 (Iowa 1972); Abram v. Bourrie, 8 Mich.App. 184, 154 N.W.2d 20 (1967).

57. Galvin v. Jennings, 289 F.2d 15 (3d Cir. 1961).

58. 20 Cal.3d 389, 143 Cal.Rptr. 13, 572 P.2d 1155 (1978).

59. See supra, Ch. 15, Wanton or Willful Misconduct.

60. London & Lancashire Indem. Co. v. Duryea, 143 Conn. 53, 119 A.2d 325 (1955) (Policy insuring liquor owner for bodily injury or death "caused by" sale of intoxicating liquor does not cover liability under statute not requiring causal connection between sale and injury).

been held that the insurer of an intoxicated motorist may not recover from the dramshop any sums the insurer has paid in settlement of accident claims,[61] although other courts have held that an insurer may qualify as plaintiff under the category of "the person injured."[62]

§ 29.5 Extraterritoriality—Exclusiveness of Remedy

One field all too often overlooked by the practicing attorney is that of conflict of laws. In the case of *Eldridge v. Don Beachcomber, Inc.*,[63] an attempt to give the Illinois Dramshop Act extraterritorial effect was rejected. In that case defendant sold liquor to A in Illinois. A then drove with plaintiff into Indiana where he crashed his car into another vehicle, injuring plaintiff. The Illinois court phrased the question before it in this manner: Does the Dramshop Act give rise to a cause of action where the intoxication occurs in Illinois and the resulting accident occurs in another state? In answering the question in the negative, the court stated that intoxication alone does not give rise to an action under the statute, but must be coupled with an act which causes injury. Plaintiff suffered no injury in Illinois. The injury occurred in Indiana. The court concluded that if the legislature had intended the Act to have extraterritorial effect, it would have so provided.[64]

In *Waynick v. Chicago's Last Dept. Store*,[65] the sale took place in Illinois and the injury in Michigan. The Federal Appeals Court, on diversity jurisdiction, held that neither state's dramshop act could be applied but that recovery could nevertheless be sought on common law negligence principles.[66] Other jurisdictions, including

---

61. Empire Fire & Marine Ins. Co. v. Williams, 265 Minn. 333, 121 N.W.2d 580 (1963).

62. See Village of Brooten v. Cudahy Packing Co., 291 F.2d 284 (8th Cir. 1961).

63. 342 Ill.App. 151, 95 N.E.2d 512, 22 A.L.R.2d 1123 (1950).

64. See: Graham v. General United States Grant Post No. 2665, V.F.W., 43 Ill.2d 1, 248 N.E.2d 657 (1969). (Illinois statute has no extraterritorial effect: "A relevant fact is that the legislature has not seen fit to amend the Dramshop Act so as to give it extraterritorial applicability since the *Eldridge* case was decided in 1950. . . . In the last analysis, the question of whether the Dramshop Act should be given extraterritorial effect is a question of policy that is peculiarly within the province of the legislature.")

65. 269 F.2d 322 (7th Cir. 1959), cert. denied 362 U.S. 903, 80 S.Ct. 611, 4 L.Ed.2d 554.

66. "In applying the common law to the situation presented in this case, we must consider the law of tort liability, even though the chain of events, which started when the defendant tavern keepers unlawfully sold intoxicating liquor to two drunken men, crossed state boundary lines, and culminated in the tragic collision in Michigan. We hold that, under the facts appearing in the complaint, the tavern keepers are liable in tort for the damages and injuries sus-

Connecticut,[67] Minnesota,[68] and North Dakota[69] have ruled that their dramshop acts have extraterritorial effect under circumstances similar to those in *Eldridge*. In a California case, *Bernhard v. Harrah's Club* (1976),[70] the court took notice that the Nevada club which furnished the liquor advertised extensively and solicited business in California, knowing that California residents would be using the public highways in going to and coming from the club. Although Nevada imposed no civil liability for sale of liquor to an intoxicated person,[71] the California court held that the Nevada defendant's active solicitation in California had subjected defendant to liability under California's common law dramshop doctrine.[72]

Many jurisdictions declare that the rights created under a Dramshop Act are exclusive[73] and that such rights and remedies cannot be enlarged except by legislative enactment.[74] Where, however, the com-

tained by plaintiffs, as a proximate result of the unlawful acts of the farmer." 269 F.2d at 326.

67. Zucker v. Vogt, 200 F.Supp. 340 (D.C.Conn.1961) (Connecticut tavern keeper may be sued under Connecticut Dramshop Act although injuries occurred in New York); Osborn v. Borchetta, 20 Conn.Sup. 163, 129 A. 2d 238 (1956) (New York Dramshop Act gave rise to cause of action in Connecticut where sale of liquor and intoxication took place in New York and accident occurred in Connecticut).

68. Schmidt v. Driscoll Hotel, Inc., 49 Minn. 376, 82 N.W.2d 365 (1957) (Where all parties were Minn. residents and wrongful acts took place in Minnesota, plaintiff's right to recover under Minnesota Dramshop Act established although injury occurred outside state).

69. Trapp v. 4–10 Investment Corp., 424 F.2d 1261 (8th Cir. 1970).

70. 16 Cal.3d 313, 128 Cal.Rptr. 215, 546 P.2d 719 (1976).

71. Hamm v. Carson City Nuggett, Inc., 85 Nev. 99, 450 P.2d 358 (1969).

72. "Defendant by the course of its chosen commercial practice has put itself at the heart of California's regulatory interest, namely to prevent tavern keepers from selling alcoholic beverages to obviously intoxicated persons who are likely to act in California in the intoxicated state. It seems clear that California cannot reasonably effectuate its policy if it does not extend its regulation to include out-of-state tavern keepers such as defendant who regularly and purposely sell intoxicating beverages to California residents in places and under conditions in which it is reasonably certain these residents will return to California and act therein while still in an intoxicated state. California's interest would be very significantly impaired if its policy were not applied to defendant." 16 Cal.3d at 322–323.

73. Thompson v. Capasso, 21 Ill.App. 2d 1, 157 N.E.2d 75, 79 A.L.R.2d 1354 (1959) ("The liability imposed and the nature of the damages recoverable are of statutory origin and are expressly and exclusively defined in the Dramshop Act . . . .").

74. Robinson v. Bognanno, 213 N.W.2d 530 (Iowa 1973) (Patron cannot recover against tavern for injuries resulting from his intoxication. "In adopting the statutory right of recovery against dramshop operators the

mon law right is recognized, the Dramshop Act has been considered not to exclude the common law action [75] which may be pleaded independently. Similarly, an independent action may be brought, under appropriate facts, against a tavern keeper for common law negligence in failing to maintain a suitable place of business and safe conditions for his business invitees.[76]

legislature expressly and carefully limited the class of persons to whom that right was given. It would not be a proper judicial function to amend the legislation by interpretation so as to enlarge the class").

75. Waynick v. Chicago's Last Dept. Store, Inc. supra, n. 53.

76. Manual v. Weitzman, 386 Mich. 157, 191 N.W.2d 474 (1971) (Held that prior decisions "are in error insofar as they purport to hold that the liability provisions of the dramshop act not only preempt any common law action for negligent sale, but also preempt a common law action for 'negligence in failing to maintain a suitable place and safe conditions for business invitees' ").

§§ 29.6–30.0 are reserved for supplementary material.

CHAPTER 30

DEFAMATION

Table of Sections

Sec.
30.1 In General.
30.2 Defamation Defined—Who Can Sue.
30.3 Libel and Slander Distinguished.
30.4 Libel and Slander—When Actionable.
30.5 Interpretation of Dafamatory Meaning.
30.6 Requirement of Publication.
30.7 Truth—A Complete Defense.
30.8 Absolute Privilege.
30.9 Qualified Privilege.
30.10 Constitutional Privilege—Public Officials and Public Figures.
30.11 Burden of Proof—Court and Jury.
30.12 Measure of Damages.

Library References:
C.J.S. Libel and Slander § 1 et seq.
West's Key No. Digests, Libel and Slander ⚖1 et seq.
Prosser, Law of Torts (4th ed.) pp. 737 et seq.

§ 30.1 In General

The field of defamation law, arena of litigious conflict in defense of plaintiff's intangible yet priceless interest in his "good name", abounds in idiosyncracy and anomaly. As the late Dean Prosser commented:

> "It must be confessed at the beginning that there's a great deal of law of defamation which makes no sense. . . . [I]t is a curious compound of a strict liability imposed upon innocent defendants, as rigid and extreme as anything found in the law, with a blind and almost perverse refusal to compensate the plaintiff for real and very serious harm." [1]

The shifting sands of defamation law are blown by the crosscurrents of conflicting social policy goals, upholding both the individual's interest in his personal reputation [2] and society's interest in free expression regarding matters of public concern.[3] The recent

---

1. Prosser, The Law of Torts (4th ed. 1971) p. 737.

2. Rosenblatt v. Baer, 383 U.S. 75, 86 S.Ct. 669, 15 L.Ed.2d 597 (1966).

3. See: Pound, Equitable Relief Against Defamation and Injuries to Personality, 1916, 29 Harv.L.Rev. 640; Shientag, From Seditious Libel to

evolution of defamation in American jurisprudence from common law to constitutional law [4] reflects the same dynamics evident in 700 years of English concern with *scandalous magnatum* (slander of great men)[5]—which ranged from periods of benign neglect of the slander statutes by the common law courts [6] to spirited prosecution of "seditious libel" by the notorious Star Chamber.[7]

Although many elements of modern defamation law trace from Roman and Anglo-Saxon precedents,[8] the term *"diffamatus"* was an expression of the medieval Church courts, signifying one whose reputation was so bad as to itself serve as an accusation.[9] If the *diffamatus* was subsequently acquitted in a trial before the ecclesiastical court, then those who had disseminated the unfounded calumny were guilty of a crime and subject to excommunication.[10]

Civil prosecution of defamation historically was pursued in the King's courts and in the local courts either as "public libel" (against a magistrate, etc.), which was a disturbance to the State, or as "pri-

Freedom of the Press, 1942, 11 Brook L.R. 125; Leflar, Legal Liability for the Exercise of Free Speech, 1956, 10 Ark.L.R. 155; Leflar, the Free-ness of Free Speech, 1962, 15 Vand.L.Rev. 1073; Pedrick, Freedom of Free Press and the Law of Libel, 1964, 49 Corn. L.Q. 581; Beaney, Libel and the First Amendment—A New Constitutional Privilege, 1965, 51 Va.L.R. 1; Anderson, Libel and Press Self-Censorship, 1975, 53 Texas L.R. 422; Robertson, Defamation and the First Amendment, 1976, 54 Texas L.R. 199; Anderson, The Issue is Control of Press Power, 1976, 54 Texas L.R. 271.

4. See infra, § 30.10.

5. Beginning with a statute of 1275, providing that one who publishes false news or scandal tending to produce discord between the King and his people or the magnates shall be kept in prison until he produces in court the origination of the tale. (Westminster I, 1275, c. 34). Plucknett, A Concise History of the Common Law (5th ed., 1956), pp. 485–6.

6. Plucknett, p. 487, n. 2: "The common law courts, . . . were at pains to avoid using the statutes, and so created the impression that seditious words were a common-law misdemeanour." See: Veeder, History and Theory of the Law of Defamation (1903) 3 Col.L.R. 546; Donnelly, History of Defamation (1949) Wis.L.R. 99; Lovell, The Reception of Defamation by the Common Law (1962) 15 Vand.L.R. 1051.

7. See Prosser, Law of Torts, p. 738; Plucknett, pp. 487–498.

8. See Veeder; Donnelly; supra, n. 6. Plucknett, p. 487: "Roman law had distinguished between the defamation which could be remedied by a civil action, and the *libellus famosus* which it visited with extraordinary punishment."

9. Plucknett, p. 484.

10. Gibon, Codex Juris Ecclesiastic (ed. 1761): "Furthermore, we excommunicate all those who for lucre, hate, favour, or any other cause maliciously impute a crime whereby anyone is defamed among good and grave persons in such wise that he has been put to his purgation at least, or otherwise aggrieved." Plucknett, p. 484.

vate libel" (against a private individual). The latter frequently served as an incitement to duelling and thus constituted a breach of the peace.[11] For these purposes, the ancient Roman principle of truth as a complete defense [12] was irrelevant, hence the maxim: "The greater the truth, the greater the libel."

Today, modern methods of communication, a wider dissemination of printed material, and the all-pervasive influence of the electronic media [13] have increased the importance of the tort of defamation. Concurrently, new problems requiring solutions have likewise been created. And as the number of cases reported continues to increase, more and more attention is given the subject by leading authors. Related to, or more aptly, in, the field of defamation are the cases of right of privacy, and infringements on personal liberties, such as false imprisonment, abuse of process, etc.

The inclusion of this section is principally to invite the attention of the personal injury lawyer to monetary awards which, at first impression, might seem completely out of proportion to the "injury",[14] but which by any standard are a far cry from the ancient Anglo-Saxon remedy whereby the defendant was required to hold his nose and call himself a liar.[15] Equally important, however, is the caveat that modern libel litigation is time consuming and expensive [16] and always an uncertain endeavor.[17]

11. See Prosser, p. 796–7; Plucknett, p. 490.

12. See infra, § 30.7.

13. See: Leflar, Radio and T. V. Defamation: Fault or Strict Liability? (1954) 15 Ohio St.L.J. 252; Korbel, Defamation by Broadcast: The Need for Federal Control (1963) 49 A.B.A.J. 771; Annotation, Defamation by Radio and Television (1973) 50 A.L.R.3d 1311.

14. E. g., Rosenbloom v. Metromedia, Inc., 403 U.S. 29, 91 S.Ct. 1811, 29 L.Ed.2d 296 (1971) (Plaintiff awarded $25,000 general damages and $725,000 punitive damages, reduced by remitter to $250,000. Reversal upheld on appeal to U. S. Supreme Court).

15. Pollock & Maitland, History of English Law, ii, 537.

16. See Alioto v. Cowles Communications, Inc., 430 F.Supp. 1363 (N.D.D.C.Cal.1977) (Defendant's affidavit indicates that it had spent over $600,000 in fees and costs, in an unsuccessful motion to dismiss before the fourth trial of the suit. Plaintiff was eventually awarded $350,000).

17. See Rosenbloom v. Metromedia, Inc., 403 U.S. 29, 91 S.Ct. 1811, 29 L.Ed.2d 296 (1971); Phoenix Newspapers, Inc. v. Church, 24 Ariz.App. 287, 537 P.2d 1345 (1975), cert. denied 425 U.S. 908, 96 S.Ct. 1502, 47 L.Ed.2d 759, reh. denied 425 U.S. 985, 96 S.Ct. 1293, 48 L.Ed.2d 811. (Defendants appealed a $50,000 judgment. Award of $485,000 on retrial affirmed on appeal).

§ 30.2 Defamation Defined—Who Can Sue

Defamation is an invasion of the interest in reputation,

"which tends to injure 'reputation' in the popular sense; to diminish the esteem, respect, goodwill, or confidence in which the plaintiff is held, or to excite adverse, derogatory or unpleasant feelings or opinions about him." [18]

The term includes both libel and slander. There must be an unprivileged publication of false and defamatory matter which is either actionable without showing of special harm, or is the legal cause of special harm, before liability will result.[19]

The defamatory communication may consist of false statements of fact [20] or statements of opinion.[21] Statements of opinion may be of two kinds, those based upon facts known or assumed,[22] or those based upon undisclosed facts.[23] The latter are general statements, without reference to any particular act of the plaintiff, which imply the commission of an unidentified specific offense.[24] It is not essential that the communication actually adversely affect the personal or financial reputation of the one defamed. For example, the imputation of certain physical or mental attributes, such as disease or insanity, is defamatory because it tends to deter third persons from associating or dealing with him.[25] It need not tend to prejudice him in the eyes of everyone in the community, and not even necessarily in the majority, but a respectable minority will do.[26]

Any living natural person, unincorporated association,[27] partnership,[28] or corporation [29] may maintain a civil action for defa-

---

18. Prosser, Law of Torts, p. 739.

19. See: infra, § 30.12; Restatement, Second, Torts, Second, §§ 558, 559.

20. Restatement, Second, Torts § 565.

21. But see Gertz v. Welch, 418 U.S. 323, 339–40, 94 S.Ct. 2997, 3006, 3007, 41 L.Ed.2d 789 (1979).

22. Restatement, Second, Torts, § 566.

23. Id., § 566.

24. Id., § 566, Comment b.

25. Id., § 559, Comment c.

26. Id., § 559, Comment e.

27. Kirkman v. Westchester Newspapers, Inc., 287 N.Y. 373, 39 N.E.2d 919 (1942). Labor union's right to recover for statements regarding labor relations or disputes.

See also Daniels v. Sanitarium Ass'n, 59 Cal.2d 602, 30 Cal.Rptr. 828, 381 P.2d 652 (1963) (Labor Union).

28. Both the partnership and individual members may be defamed: see Vogel v. Bushnell, 203 Mo.App. 623, 221 S.W. 819 (1920).

29. Restatement, Second, Torts § 561. A corporation or partnership's cause of action requires a defamation which tends to injure its business reputation.

Western Broadcast Co. v. Times-Mirror Co., 14 Cal.App.2d 120, 57 P.2d 977 (1936) (The defamation "must have a

mation. There is no action for defamation of one who is dead,[30] in any of the American Jurisdictions. Thus, the author was extended to file suit for the children of his late good friend Errol Flynn. Such suit was filed in California on the basis that the California Criminal Code provides that defamation of deceased is a crime and a statutory admonition criminally should be extended by the courts over onto the civil side. (Case pending.) See Satterlee v. Orange Glenn School Dist., 29 Cal.2d 581, 177 P.2d 279 (1947).

Whether or not the cause of action abates upon death of the plaintiff, after institution of the suit but before trial, depends on the statutes of the forum.[31]

A corporation has a business reputation and may be defamed in this respect.[32] However, it will not have a cause of action for communications defamatory of its officers, agents, or stockholders, unless they also reflect discredit upon the way the corporation conducts its business.[33] Also, an individual will have no right of recovery for a libel published of a corporation, even though he alleges he is president, treasurer, and general manager.[34] A corporation, or other principal,

tendency to directly affect the credit or property of the corporation or occasion it pecuniary injury. The mere fact that a publication is unpleasant or hostile does not make it defamatory"); Golden Palace, Inc. v. National Broadcasting Co., Inc., 386 F.Supp. 107 (D.D.C.1974) aff'd 530 F.2d 1094 (D.C.Cir.) (Corporation has no personal reputation and may be defamed only regarding its financial soundness or business ethics).

See 69 Harv.L.R. 892.

A nonprofit corporation may be defamed by something which injures its estimation by the public. Restatement, Second, Torts § 561. See also Restatement, Second, Torts § 560.

30. Wright v. R.K.O. Radio Pictures, 55 F.Supp 639 (D.C.Mass.1944); Renfro Drug Co. v. Lawson, 138 Tex. 434, 160 S.W.2d 246, 146 A.L.R. 732 (1942). Yet it may be a crime, depending on the jurisdiction. E. g., West's Ann.Cal.Penal Code §§ 248, 249.

31. Thompson v. Curtis Pub. Co., 193 F.2d 953 (3rd Cir. 1952).

See also Trans World Accounts, Inc. v. Associated Press, 425 F.Supp. 814 (D.C.Cal.1977). Report of press release of FTC complaint against collection company failed to indicate plaintiff corporation was not charged with all the practices mentioned in the report.

32. See supra, n. 29.

33. Brayton v. Crowell-Collier Pub. Co., 205 F.2d 644 (2d Cir. 1953); Neiman-Marcus Co. v. Lait, 107 F.Supp. 96 (D.C.N.Y.1952).

See Note, 51 Mich.L.R. 611.

34. Gilbert Shoe Co. v. Rumpf Pub. Co., 112 F.Supp. 228 (D.C.Mass.1953). McBride v. Crowell-Collier Pub. Co., 196 F.2d 187, 189 (5th Cir. 1952); Dossett v. New York Mining & Mfg. Co., 451 S.W.2d 843 (Ky.1970); American Life Ins. Co. v. Shell, 265 Ala. 306, 90 So.2d 719 (1956) (Libel).

§ 30.2 SPECIFIC ACTIONS Pt. 4

however, may be liable for defamation published by an agent acting within the scope of his authority.[35]

An individual may have an action for defamation arising from disparaging words about a group with which he is associated.[36] But as the group referred to becomes larger, the damage to the individual becomes more highly conjectural, and the chance of recovery less.[37] The plaintiff need not be named specifically, but he must show, by extrinsic circumstances, that he was the one intended.[38] The requirement that the defamatory statements must be "of and concerning the plaintiff" puts the burden on him to show that persons hearing or reading such communication could understand it to refer to him.[39]

Where defendant's statement accused the entire University of Oklahoma football team of taking drugs, an action was upheld on be-

---

35. Johnson v. Life Ins. Co., 227 S.C. 351, 88 S.E.2d 260, 55 A.L.R.2d 813 (1955) (Slander by insurer's agent that insured had shot his leg off for purpose of collecting insurance—authority of agent for jury).

36. See: Prosser, Law of Torts, pp. 749, 750; Miller, Defamation—A Survey of Recent Decisions (1953) 4 Syracuse L.R. 221, 231; Tannenhaus, Group Libel 35 Corn.L.Q. 261, 264, cit-state statutes; Glick, Group Libel and Criminal Libel (1952) 1 Buffalo L.Rev. 258; see Beauharnais v. Illinois, 343 U.S. 250, 72 S.Ct. 725, 96 L.Ed. 919 (1952) (Involving criminal libel and upholding Illinois statute which may strengthen civil group libel actions); also see (1953) 41 Cal. L.Rev. 290; (1953) 41 Ky.L.J. 436; (1952) 61 Yale L.J. 252.

For actions by a group defamed, see Reisman, Democracy and Defamation; Control of Group Libel (1942) 42 Col.L.Rev. 719; (1947) 47 Col.L.Rev. 595 for discussion of statutory action on this subject.

See also Fenstermaker v. Tribune Pub. Co., 13 Utah 532, 45 P. 1097 (1886) (Recovery allowed "the Fenstermaker family"); Tobin v. Alfred M. Best Co., 120 App.Div. 387, 105 N.Y.S. 294 (1907) ("The members of a named partnership"); Bornmann v. Star Co., 174 N.Y. 212, 66 N.E. 723 (1903) ("The staff of twelve young doctors at a particular hospital");

Recovery denied, Louisville Times v. Stivers, 252 Ky. 943, 68 S.W.2d 411 (1934) (Recovery denied, "the Stivers clan"); Comes v. Cruce, 85 Ark. 29, 107 S.W. 185 (1908) ("The wine joint owners"); McGee v. Collins, 156 La. 291, 100 So. 430 (1924) ("Insurance agents"); Noral v. Hearst Publications, Inc., 40 Cal.App.2d 348, 104 P.2d 860 (1940) ("The officials of a named labor union"); Sumner v. Buel, 12 Johns 475 (N.Y.1815) ("The officers of a military regiment"); Smallwood v. York, 163 Ky. 139, 173 S.W. 380 (1915) ("Member of a jury"). Lewis, the Individual's Right to Recover for a Defamation Leveled at the Group (1963) 17 U. Miami L.R. 519.

37. Fowler v. Curtis Pub. Co., 78 F. Supp. 303 (D.C.D.C.1948) aff'd 182 F. 2d 377 (D.C.Cir.).

See also: (1949) 2 Okl.L.Rev. 377–8; (1951) 24 S.Cal.L.Rev. 213–16.

38. Neiman-Marcus Co. v. Lait, 13 F. R.D. 311 (S.D.N.Y.1952).

39. Marr v. Putman, 196 Or. 1, 246 P. 2d 509 (1952); Gross v. Cantor, 270 N.Y. 93, 200 N.E. 592 (1936);

See also (1953) 41 Cal.L.Rev. 144–8; (1953) 28 N.Y.U.L.Rev. 220–3; (1936) 22 Iowa L.Rev. 159; (1936) 10 Tex.L. Rev. 135.

half of the "sixty or seventy" members of the team.[40] Where defendant alleged that "most" of a department store's sales staff were "fairies", a cause of action was upheld for the store's twenty-five salesmen.[41] But the related allegation, that the store's salesgirls were "call girls", was held insufficient to base a cause of action on behalf of the store's 382 salesgirls, there being "no language referring to some ascertained or ascertainable person." [42]

§ 30.3 Libel and Slander Distinguished

There are two forms of defamation, libel and slander, which generally are distinguishable, but there are areas where exact classification is uncertain and in dispute.[43]

In its simplest form, libel consists of printed words or matter, while slander refers to spoken words.[44] More broadly, libel consists of a fixed representation to the eye, including pictures, cartoons, and effigies, while slander consists of more transitory forms of expression, including oral statements and gestures.[45]

The invention and wide use of radio and television have created new problems of distinction.[46] The premeditated character of the publication, and the persistence of the defamatory conduct are to be considered in determining whether it is libel rather than slander.[47] Broadcast defamation read from a prepared script thus may be treated as libel,[48] but as slander if shown to be extemporaneous.[49] The is-

40. Fawcett Publications, Inc. v. Morris, 377 P.2d 42 (Okl.1962), appeal dism'd cert. denied 376 U.S. 513, 84 S.Ct. 964, 11 L.Ed.2d 968, reh. denied 377 U.S. 925, 84 S.Ct. 1218, 12 L.Ed. 2d 217.

41. Neiman-Marcus v. Lait, 13 F.R.D. 311 at 313 ("Then you learn that the nucleus of the Dallas fairy colony is composed of many Neiman dress and millinery designers, imported from New York and Paris, who sent for their boy friends when the men's store was expanded. Now most of the sales staff are fairies, too").

42. Id. at 316. ("The salesgirls are good, too pretty, and much cheaper —twenty bucks on the average. They're more fun, too, not as snooty as the models." 13 F.R.D. at 313).

43. Miller, supra n. 36, at 222.

44. Restatement, Second Torts, § 568.

45. Prosser, pp. 75 et seq., Witkin, Summary of California Law, (8th ed. 1974), Vol. 4, Torts, p. 2543.

46. See supra, n. 13.

47. Restatement, Second, Torts § 568, Comment f.

48. Hartman v. Winchell, 296 N.Y. 296, 73 N.E.2d 30 (1947); Christy v. Stauffer Publications, Inc., 437 S.W. 2d 814 (Tex. 1969); Landau v. Columbia Broadcasting System, 205 Misc. 357, 128 N.Y.S.2d 254 (1954) aff'd 1 A.D.2d 660, 147 N.Y.S.2d 687.

49. Arno v. Stewart, 245 Cal.App.2d 955, 54 Cal.Rptr. 392 (1966); Remington v. Bentley, 88 F.Supp. 166 (D.C. N.Y.1949).

sue is in many jurisdictions governed by statute—the majority, thanks to broadcast industry lobbying, holding for slander.[50] Defamation by motion pictures, including talking pictures, generally is agreed to be libel.[51]

Oral statements intended to be reduced to writing, such as an interview given to a reporter [52] or even dictation to defendant's secretary or stenographer [53] are generally considered to constitute libel.

§ 30.4 Libel and Slander—When Actionable

The majority rule in the United States and England is that any libel is actionable, without the necessity of proving that special damage was suffered by plaintiff as a result of its publication.[54] Damage is conclusively assumed from the publication of the libel itself.[55] When this is the case, it is said to be *actionable per se* and requires that the defamer justify his publication.[56] Although special harm and loss of reputation are not essential to recovery, if alleged and proven, the jury may take them into account in awarding damages.[57] However, in many jurisdictions, a distinction is made between words libelous *"per se"* (that is, actionable on their face, without extrinsic proof of their defamatory meaning), and those which are said to be libelous *"per quod"* (that is, extrinsic evidence is necessary to establish their defamatory meaning). In case of the latter, allegation and proof of special damages are necessary.[58]

But see: Shor v. Billingsley, 4 Misc.2d 857, 158 N.Y.S.2d 476 (1957), aff'd 4 A.D.2d 1017, 169 N.Y.S.2d 416, appeal denied 5 A.D.2d 768, 170 N.Y.S.2d 976 (Defamatory broadcast or telecast will be treated as libel, although not read from prepared script).

50. Prosser, Law of Torts, p. 754.

51. Youssoupov v. M. G. M. Pictures, 78 S.J. 617, 50 T.L.R. 581, C.O. (1934); 32 Mich.L.Rev. 1013; Newel, Slander and Libel, p. 19 (1924, 4th ed.); Prosser, p. 796.

52. Valentine v. Gonzales, 190 App. Div. 490, 179 N.Y.S. 711 (1920).

53. Nelson v. Whitten, 272 F. 135 (2d Cir. 1921); Hanrahan v. Kelly, 269 Md. 21, 305 A.2d 151, 62 A.L.R.3d 1187 (1973).

54. Restatement, Second, Torts § 569; Prosser, pp. 762–763; Prosser, Interstate Publication (1953) 51 Mich.L.R. 959, 980.

55. Id.

56. Restatement, Second, Torts § 569, Comment b.

57. Id., § 569, Comment c.

58. Whitby v. Associates Discount Corp., 59 Ill.App.2d 337, 207 N.E.2d 482 (1965).

See: West's Ann.Cal. Civil Code, § 45a: "A libel which is defamatory of the plaintiff without the necessity of explanatory matter, such as an inducement, innuendo or other extrinsic fact, is said to be a *libel on its face*. Defamatory language not libelous on its face *is not actionable* unless the plaintiff alleges and proves that he has suffered *special damage* as a proximate result thereof."

Slander is *actionable per se*, and no special harm or loss of reputation need be established, if the slander is within one of the following categories: imputation of a crime,[59] loathsome disease,[60] conduct incompatible with proper exercise of a business, trade, profession, or office,[61] or unchastity of a woman (usually by statute).[62] The actionability of a charge of being a communist has varied with the temper of the times.[63]

If other slanderous statements, not *actionable per se*, are the basis of the action, special harm must be alleged and proved before liability attaches.[64] Damages for loss of general reputation may be included in the award.[65]

The special harm must be of a material and, generally, pecuniary nature.[66] It must be a result of the action of someone other than the

59. Tracing from the original concept of *diffamatus*. See text accompanying footnotes 9 and 10, supra.

60. Hamilton v. Nance, 159 N.C. 56, 74 S.E. 627 (1912). Limited, in practice, to venereal disease and leprosy. (Prosser, pp. 756–757). Accusations of tuberculosis (Kassowitz v. Sentinel Co., 226 Wis. 468, 277 N.W. 177 (1938)) or other communicable diseases (Lowe v. DeHoog, 193 S.W. 969 (Mo.App.1917)) have been held not actionable.

61. Prosser, Law of Torts, pp. 757–759.

62. Restatement, Second, Torts § 574. Note: The California statute includes a charge of unchastity against a man or woman, or a charge of impotence. West's Ann.Cal.Civ.Code § 46.

63. Utah State Farm Bureau Federation v. National Farmers Union Serv. Corp., 198 F.2d 20 (10th Cir. 1952).

See also: (1950) 34 Marquette L.Rev. 31; (1953) 33 B.U.L.Rev. 256; (1953) 15 Ga.B.J. 357; (1953) 27 St. John's L.Rev. 624; (1953) 51 Mich.L.Rev. 946; (1953) 5 Ala.L.Rev. 338; Booker, The Accusation of Communism as Slander Per Se, 1954, 4 Duke Bar J.I.; Faulk v. Aware, Inc., 35 Misc.2d 302, 315, 317, 231 N.Y.S.2d 270, 284–286 (1962), rev'd conditionally 19 A.D.2d 464, 244 N.Y.S.2d 259, motion denied 14 N.Y.2d 719, 250 N.Y.S.2d 64, 199 N.E.2d 163, aff'd 14 N.Y.2d 899, 252 N.Y.S.2d 95, 200 N.E.2d 778; (Accusation of communism, causing plaintiff to be blacklisted. $1,000,000 compensatory damages, and $1,250,000 punitive damages upheld); Cahill v. Hawaiian Paradise Park Corp., 56 Hawaii 522, 543 P.2d 1356 (1975) (Radio broadcast charging plaintiff with being communist actionable per se); Karry v. International Tel. & Tel. Corp., 444 F.Supp. 193 (D.C.N.Y.1978) (Appellation of "communist" not slanderous per se, in "today's more relaxed atmosphere," in regard to freelance journalist).

64. Restatement, Second, Torts § 570 et seq.

65. Craney v. Donovan, 92 Conn. 236, 102 A. 640 (1917).

See also Restatement, Second, Torts § 575; Prosser, Law of Torts, p. 761.

66. Arturie v. Tiebie, 73 N.J.Super. 217, 179 A.2d 539 (1962) (Cost of wardrobe alterations following slander insufficient damages); Restatement, Second, Torts, § 575, Comment b; McCormick, Damages, § 114.

The rule apparently derives from medieval jurisdictional requirements whereby defamation was venued strictly in Church courts unless "tem-

§ 30.4 SPECIFIC ACTIONS Pt. 4

defamer, done as a reaction to the slanderous statements.[67] Rules of legal causation must be met. The resulting damage must have been reasonably foreseeable by the defamer as a normal consequence of the publication, unless the defamer intended to bring about such harm.[68] Loss of reputation or social position is not sufficient, unless reflected in terms of material harm.[69] Plaintiff must plead specific facts which comprise the damage for which the plaintiff seeks compensation.[70]

§ 30.5 Interpretation of Defamatory Meaning

The defendant's understanding of the meaning of the words or his intention as to whom they apply is immaterial, if the recipient reasonably, under the circumstances, gave the words a different meaning or understood them to refer to the plaintiff.[71] The recipient must think that the communication referred to the plaintiff.[72] It is not necessary that every recipient believe that the reference was made to the plaintiff. If anyone reasonably did, it is enough.[73] The

poral" damages could be proved allowing hearing in the common law courts. See: Lovell, The Reception of Defamation by the Common Law, (1962) 15 Vand.L.R. 1051; Prosser, p. 738.

67. Arturie v. Tiebie, 73 N.J.Super 217, 179 A.2d 539 (1962). Restatement, Second, Torts § 575, Comment b.

68. Restatement, Second, Torts § 622A, Comment c.

69. Restatement, Second, Torts § 575, Comment b; Clark, Survey of American Law, § 79.

70. Prosser, Law of Torts, p. 760.

(1953) 6 Okl.L.Rev. 397. For discussion see McCormick, Damages, § 115 (1935). See also Pollard v. Lyon, 91 U.S. 225, 23 L.Ed. 308 (1875); Ellsworth v. Martindale-Hubbell Law Directory, Inc., 66 N.D. 578, 268 N.W. 400, 406, 407 (1936); Denny v. N. W. Credit Ass'n, 55 Wash. 331, 104 P. 769, 25 L.R.A.,N.S. (1909).

71. See McAndrew v. Scranton Republican Pub. Co., 364 Pa. 504, 72 A.2d 180 (1950) (Imputation of "communism"); Ward v. League for Justice, 57 O.L.A. 197, 93 N.E.2d 723 (1950); Dilling v. Illinois Pub. Co., 340 Ill. App. 303, 91 N.E.2d 635 (1950) ("Subversive"); also see (1951) 5 Ark.L. Rev. 106; (1950) 11 Oh.St.L.J. 577–83; 1953 Wash.U.L.Q. 331 (Label of "communist-dominated" held libelous per se). Reaction of "right-thinking persons" as test of defamation discussed: see Sydney v. MacFadden Newspaper Pub. Corp., 242 N.Y. 208, 210, 151 N.E. 209 (1926); Katapodis v. Brooklyn Spectator, Inc., 287 N.Y. 17, 31, 38 N.E.2d 112, 113 (1941); also (1951) 11 La.L.Rev. 327–346.

72. See Miller, n. 36 supra, p. 230, n. 62, "The question is not who is aimed at but who is hit."

73. Restatement, Second, Torts § 564; Prosser, Torts, p. 789; See also: Archibald v. Belleville News Democrat, 51 Ill.App.2d 38, 203 N.E.2d 281 (1964).

defamer takes the risk that the name or description used may be ambiguous and, therefore, misapplied.[74]

In *Montandon v. Triangle Publications*,[75] plaintiff, a San Francisco social figure and author, was scheduled to appear on a television show to promote her book. The producer of the show, unbeknownst to plaintiff, arranged to have an anonymous prostitute appear on the same program. Defendant's *T.V. Guide* announced the show as follows: "'From Party Girl to Call Girl.' Scheduled Guest: T.V. Personality Pat Montandon and author of 'How to Be a Party Girl.'" Plaintiff's witnesses, including a professor of English, a newspaper editor, and two television producers, testified that the average reader would conclude that plaintiff "had progressed from being a party girl to being a call girl." The jury's verdict for $150,000 compensatory damages was affirmed.

Extrinsic evidence is admissible to show that, under all of the circumstances known to the recipient, the damaging material could or could not reasonably be interpreted to refer to the plaintiff.[76] The fact that very few out of a large number of recipients understood the communication as plaintiff contends, is relevant on the issue of the reasonableness of his interpretation.[77]

When the defamatory meaning of the communication, or its applicability to the plaintiff, depends upon extrinsic circumstances, the plaintiff must allege and prove these facts.[78] By the "colloquium," he shows that the communication referred to him; the "innuendo," explains its meaning as being defamatory, and the "inducement" shows facts not apparent upon the fact of the publication which gave rise to its defamatory meaning.[79]

---

74. But see: Restatment, Second, Torts § 580B.

Jacobs v. Transcontinental and Western Air, Inc., 358 Mo. 674, 216 S.W.2d 523, 6 A.L.R.2d 1002 (1948).

75. 45 Cal.App.3d 938, 120 Cal.Rptr. 186 (1975), cert. denied 423 U.S. 893, 96 S.Ct. 193, 46 L.Ed.2d 126.

76. Restatement, Second, Torts § 563, Comment e.

Neal v. Huntington Pub. Co., —— W.Va. ——, 223 S.E.2d 792 (1976) (Identity of defamed person ascertainable by way of extrinsic evidence); Layman v. Reader's Digest Ass'n, 412 P.2d 192 (Okl.1966).

77. Restatement, Second, Torts § 564, comment b. Neal v. Huntington Pub. Co., —— W.Va. ——, 223 S.E.2d 792 (1976).

78. See: Restatement, Second Torts § 563, comment f; Newell, Slander and Libel, pp. 734, 735; Prosser, p. 746; See also Rovira v. Boget, 240 N.Y. 314, 148 N.E. 534 (1925) (Use of the French word "cocotte" which has two meanings, "prostitute" or "poached egg", requires that the jury must determine whether defamatory meaning was the one conveyed).

79. Prosser, pp. 748–751; Restatement, Second, Torts § 563, Comment f; Newell, supra, pp. 583, 588; Neal v.

§ 30.5   SPECIFIC ACTIONS   Pt. 4

Defamation may occur in motion pictures or plays, although the author, producer, or playwright did not believe or have reason to believe that what is said or shown would be interpreted as referring to the plaintiff.[80] It is sufficient if it is shown that the recipient reasonably believed the reference was to the plaintiff.[81] Liability may attach although the defendant has no reason to know that his description fitted an actual living person.[82]

§ 30.6   Requirement of Publication

Publication of defamatory matter consists of its intentional or negligent communication to a third person.[83] Without publication, there can be no liability. Words communicated only to the one defamed will not give rise to an action for defamation, because the interest protected is one's reputation, that is, the estimation in which one is held by others.[84] Communication to one third person is a sufficient publication.[85] One is liable for defamatory statements which

---

Huntington Pub. Co., — W.Va. —, 223 S.E.2d 792.

80. Restatement, Second, Torts § 564, Comments b and f; Wheeler v. Dell Pub. Co., 300 F.2d 372, 376 (7th Cir. 1962).

81. Miller, supra, n. 36, p. 230; Davis v. R.K.O. Radio Pictures, Inc., 191 F. 2d 901 (8th Cir. 1951).

82. One of England's largest defamation awards (amounting to about $126,000) arose from the motion picture, "Rasputin, the Mad Monk," which was based upon historical facts, but advertised as a fictitious play. The plaintiff recovered on her claim that her friends reasonably understood that she was the one portrayed as being ravished.

See: Youssopoff v. Metro-Goldwyn-Mayer Pictures (1934) 50 T.L.R. 581; Hulton & Co. v. Jones (1909) 2 K.B. 44, aff'd (1910) A.C. 20; Prosser, p. 772; Holdsworth, A Chapter of Accidents in the Law of Libel (1941) 57 L.Q.Rev. 74.

But see Wheeler v. Dell Pub. Co., 300 F.2d 372 (7th Cir. 1962) (Where description did not match plaintiff she could not recover, though she was wife of murder victim portrayed in "Anatomy of a Murder").

83. Restatement, Second, Torts, § 577; Prosser, p. 766; Spring, Rights and Risks, chapter IX (1952); Newell, Slander and Libel, § 175 (4th ed. 1924); Miller, supra, n. 36, pp. 227, 228; Prosser, Interstate Publication (1953) 51 Mich.L.Rev. 959, 961.

See also Pinckney v. District of Columbia, 439 F.Supp. 519 (D.C.D.C.1977); Fulton v. Atlantic Coast Line R. Co., 220 S.C. 287, 67 S.E.2d 425 (1952) (Communications between employees of same company).

84. Elliott v. McDonough, 344 Ill.App. 211, 100 N.E.2d 803 (1951); Pinckney v. District of Columbia, 439 F.Supp. 519 (D.C.D.C.1977); Farr v. Bramblett, 132 Cal.App.2d 36, 281 P.2d 372 (1955).

See also Restatement, Second, Torts § 577, Comment b.

85. Cunningham v. Simpson, 1 Cal.3d 301, 81 Cal.Rptr. 855, 461 P.2d 39 (1969) (Bank officer told car seller in presence of buyer, "you've got a hot title").

Restatement, Second, Torts § 577, Comment g. (Delivery of message to tel-

he directs his servant or agent to publish.[86] Many forms of publication, however, may be protected by *privilege*.[87]

The negligent communication of defamatory matter will constitute sufficient publication.[88] But, an accidental communication to a third party will not.[89] The distinction is that, in the former, the communication is made by an act which a reasonable man should realize is likely to communicate the defamatory matter to a third person, while an accidental communication is done by an act which is not intended to, and does not, create an unreasonable risk that such publication will be made.[90]

A person who repeats or otherwise republishes defamatory matter is liable to the same extent as though he had originally published it.[91] Each time the libelous article is brought to the attention of a third person, a new publication has occurred.[92] Each publication is a

egraph company for transmission constitutes publication to employee).

86. Restatement, Second Torts § 577, Comment f.

87. See: infra, §§ 30.8, 30.9.

88. Davis v. Askin's Retail Stores, 211 N.C. 551, 191 S.E. 33 (1937) (Noted in 1938), 22 Minn.L.Rev. 571; See: Restatement, Second, Torts § 577, Comment k.

89. See: Restatement, Second, Torts § 577, Comment o. There is authority for holding an author or publisher to "strict liability" for defamatory articles. See Miller, n. 36, § 288; Prosser, p. 772.

90. Freeman v. Busch Jewelry Co., 98 F.Supp. 963 (D.C.Ga.1951) (Postcard to plaintiff, read by his wife, held publication); Western Union Tel. Co. v. Lesesne, 182 F.2d 135 (4th Cir. 1950) (Sealed telegram to plaintiff, read by his wife, held no publication); Lane v. Schilling, 130 Or. 119, 279 P. 267 (1930) (Letter to plaintiff, known by defendant to be blind, held publication).

Prosser, p. 774:

"There is no liability for publication which the defendant did not intend and could not reasonably anticipate . . . ."

91. Olinger v. American Sav. & Loan Ass'n, 409 F.2d 142 (D.C.Cir. 1969); Theiss v. Scherer, 396 F.2d 646, 36 A.L.R.3d 1321 (6th Cir. 1968); Luster v. Retail Credit Co., 575 F.2d 609 (8th Cir. 1978).

See: Restatement, Second, Torts §§ 576, 578.

And note that the original defamer may be liable for any repetition by a third party, if the republication was foreseeable.

92. For an interesting case see: Hellar v. Bianco, 111 Cal.App.2d 424, 244 P.2d 757, 28 A.L.R.2d 1451 (1952), where the California District Court had occasion to consider a defamation which in method of publication is at least as old as the walls of Pompeii. A defamatory statement concerning plaintiff's chastity was placed on the wall of a Men's Room by an unknown person. Plaintiff complained that the bartender in charge of the tavern failed to comply with a telephoned demand by plaintiff's husband to remove the language "within 30 minutes." A judgment for nonsuit by the trial court was reversed. The holding: persons who invite the pub-

separate tort, and gives rise to a new cause of action.[93] A newspaper editor cannot escape liability for a defamatory publication by naming the author and stating where it was first published.[94] In fact, the publisher may be liable, although the author is protected in his original publication by a privilege.[95] On the other hand, a republication of a libel may be privileged, even though the original publication was not.[96]

To protect the courts and individuals from multiplicity of suits, where there has been a wide distribution of a communication in one state, what is known as the *single publication* rule has been evolved, and has been accepted in many states. This rule, in effect, provides that only one cause of action will arise, and that it arises when the finished product is released for sale. The extent of the publication goes to the measure of the damages only.[97] This rule also is used to determine when the statute of limitations shall commence to run against a publication.[98]

The fact that some states have adopted such rules by statute, while others have not either by statute or decision, has caused conflict of laws problems when the publication is in more than one state, and the decisions have not been uniform.[99]

lic to their premises are responsible for the publication of a libel by knowingly permitting defamatory matter to remain on their walls after a reasonable opportunity to remove the same. See also: Wittenberg, Dangerous Words, (Columbia University Press 1947).

93. Graff v. Arlington Seating Co., 343 Ill.App. 266, 98 N.E.2d 552 (1952).

See also: Restatement, Second, Torts § 578, Comment b.

94. Restatement, Second, Torts § 578; Ashley, Essentials of Libel, p. 31 (1948).

95. Restatement, Second, Torts § 578.

96. Id.

97. Barres v. Holt, Rinehart & Winston, 131 N.J.Super. 371, 330 A.2d 38 (1974); Wheeler v. Dell Pub. Co., 300 F.2d 372 (7th Cir. 1962). Kilian v. Stackpole Sons, Inc., 98 F.Supp. 500 (D.C.Pa.1951), noted in 47 N.W. L.Rev. 252 (1952); Winrod v. Time, Inc., 334 Ill.App. 59, 78 N.E.2d 708 (1948).

Single Publication Rule is also applied to books: see Gregoire v. G. P. Putnam's Sons, 298 N.Y. 119, 81 N.E.2d 45 (1948); (1949) 9 La.L.Rev. 558; (1949) 23 St. John's L.Rev. 363; (1949) 6 Wash. & Lee.L.Rev. 128. Also see: Prosser, Law of Torts (4th Ed. 1971) p. 769; Mattox v. New Syndicate Co., Inc., 176 F.2d 897 (2d Cir. 1949); (1953) 51 Mich.L.Rev. 959; Leflar, The Signal Publication Rule (1953) 25 Rocky Mt. L.Rev. 263; (1949) 62 Harv.L.Rev. 1041; 44 Cal. L.R. 146; 69 Harv.L.R. 950.

98. See: Hartman v. Time, Inc., 166 F.2d 127, 1 A.L.R.2d 370 (3d Cir. 1947), cert. denied 334 U.S. 838, 68 S.Ct. 1495, 92 L.Ed. 1763.

Belli v. Roberts Bros. Furs, 240 Cal. App.2d 284, 49 Cal.Rptr. 625 (1966). (California adoption of rule substitutes "issue" for "edition".)

99. Mattox v. News Syndicate Co., Inc., 176 F.2d 897, 12 A.L.R.2d 988

One who disseminates (that is, circulates by selling, renting, giving, etc.) matter defamatory of another, originally published by a third person, is liable as though it were an original publication by him, unless he had no reason to know of its defamatory character.[1] There is a trend to relieve radio broadcasters from strict liability, both in regard to ad lib departures from prior approved scripts, and where one not associated with the station manages to broadcast defamatory matter over the station's facilities.[2]

§ 30.7 Truth—A Complete Defense

The truth of a defamatory statement of fact is a complete defense to an action for defamation.[3] The only exceptions to this rule

(2d Cir. 1949), cert. denied 338 U.S. 858, 70 S.Ct. 100, 94 L.Ed. 525; Curtis Pub. Co. v. Birdsong, 360 F.2d 344 (5th Cir. 1966); Buckley v. New York Post Corp., 373 F.2d 175 (2d Cir. 1967).

See also Thomas, Multi-state Libel and Conflict of Laws, Substantive Law Applied to Multi-state Libel Cases (1953) 14 Oh.St.L.J. 96; Conflict of Laws Problems in Multi-state Defamation (1953) 4 Syracuse L.Rev. 310 (Discussion of radio and television publications); 2 Socolow, Law of Radio Broadcasting, p. 872. See Restatement, Conflict of Laws 2d, § 379e. (Plaintiff has one cause of action for all damages in state with most significant relationship with the parties and the communication, usually plaintiff's domicile.)

1. Hartmann v. American News Co., (7th Cir. 1948), 171 F.2d 581, cert. denied 337 U.S. 907, 69 S.Ct. 1049, 93 L.Ed. 1719. See also Restatement, Second, Torts § 581; Prosser. pp. 768–769.

2. Adams v. Frontier Broadcasting Co., 555 P.2d 556 (Wyo.1976) (failure to use electronic delay system not reckless); Josephson v. Knickerbocker Broadcasting Co., 179 Misc. 787, 38 N.Y.S.2d 985 (1942).

See also: Moser and Lavine, Radio and The Law, § 61 (1947); 2 Socolow, Law of Radio Broadcasting, § 471, W.

R. Hirsch (1950) Wash.Univ.L.Q. 95; Snyder, Liability of Station Owners for Defamatory Statements Made by Political Candidates (1953) 39 Va.L. Rev. 303. For cases on liability of advertisers, see 2 Socolow, supra, § 481.

Radio broadcasting company which leased its facilities is not liable for defamatory statement during lessee's broadcast by one in station's employ, if it could not have prevented publication by exercise of reasonable care: see Kelly v. Hoffman, 137 N.J.L. 695, 61 A.2d 143, 5 A.L.R.2d 951 (1948).

3. Curtis Pub. Co. v. Butts, 388 U.S. 130, 87 S.Ct. 1975, 18 L.Ed.2d 1094 (1975), reh. denied 389 U.S. 889, 88 S.Ct. 11, 19 L.Ed.2d 197; Cox Broadcasting Corp. v. Cohn, 420 U.S. 469, 95 S.Ct. 1029, 43 L.Ed.2d 328 (1975), on remand 234 Ga. 67, 214 S.E.2d 530; Garrison v. State of Louisiana, 379 U.S. 64, 85 S.Ct. 209, 13 L.Ed.2d 125 (1964); Hotchner v. Castillo-Puche, 551 F.2d 910, (2d Cir. 1977), cert. denied 434 U.S. 834, 98 S.Ct. 120, 54 L.Ed.2d 95; Maheu v. Hughes Tool Co., 569 F.2d 459 (9th Cir. 1977) (Defendant need not prove literal truth if imputation was substantially true as to justify gist or sting of the remark).

See also Restatement, Second, Torts § 581A; Prosser, p. 796; Harnett & Thornton, Truth Hurts, a Critique of

are created by statutes in some states, declaring that truth is a defense unless the publisher's motives are malicious.[4] In other states, his motives must be good, and the publication must be for justifiable ends or in the public interest, if truth is to be relied upon as a defense.[5]

The defendant must plead and has the burden of proving the truth of the defamatory statement.[6] It is not necessary to prove the literal truth of the precise statement made, but only that the charge is true in substance.[7] A mistaken belief in the truth of the publication, although honest and reasonable, is not sufficient, unless the occasion of the publication is privileged. On the other hand, if the statement is in fact true, the publisher's mistaken belief that it is false will not make it actionable.[8] In proving the truth of a charge of a criminal offense, a preponderance of evidence is satisfactory, and it need not be proved beyond a reasonable doubt, as would the criminal offense.[9]

The recent Supreme Court holdings affording constitutional protections to defamation of public officials and public figures [10] have reversed the traditional burden and require plaintiff to prove that the published material was false.[11]

a Defense of Defamation (1949) 35 Va.L.Rev. 425.

4. Perry v. Hearst Corp., 334 F.2d 800 (1st Cir. 1964) (Truth not a defense where publication made with actual malice.) But see: Chagnon v. Union-Leader Corp., 103 N.H. 426, 174 A.2d 825 (1961).

See: Angoff, Handbook of Libel (1946); Franklin, the Origins and Constitutionality of Limitations on Truth as a Defense in Tort Law (1964) 16 Stan. L.R. 789.

5. Restatement, Second, Torts § 581A, Comment a; Prosser, p. 797.

6. Lipman v. Brisbane Elementary Sch. Dist., 55 Cal.2d 224, 11 Cal.Rptr. 97, 359 P.2d 465 (1961).

See also Restatement, Second, Torts §§ 581A, 613. See, infra, n. 11.

7. Restatement, Second, Torts § 581A. Maheu v. Hughes Tool Co., 569 F.2d 459 (9th Cir. 1977); Piracci v. Hearst Corp., 263 F.Supp. 511 (D.C.Md.1966) aff'd 371 F.2d 1016 (4th Cir.).

But see: McNair v. Hearst Corp., 494 F.2d 1309 (9th Cir. 1974) (False impression created by headline and leading paragraph of newspaper story libelous even though majority of article contained true story).

8. Restatement, Second, Torts § 581A, Comment h.

9. Restatement, Second, Torts § 581A, Comment f.

10. See: infra, § 30.10.

11. New York Times Co. v. Sullivan, 376 U.S. 254, 271, 84 S.Ct. 710, 11 L. Ed.2d 686 (1964), motion denied 376 U.S. 967, 84 S.Ct. 1130, 12 L.Ed.2d 83; Goldwater v. Ginzburg, 414 F.2d 324 (2d Cir. 1969), cert. denied 396 U.S. 1049, 90 S.Ct. 701, 24 L.Ed.2d 695, reh. denied 397 U.S. 978, 90 S. Ct. 1085, 25 L.Ed.2d 274.

But see: Restatement, Second, Torts § 581A, Comment b; § 613, Caveat and Comment j.

§ 30.8 Absolute Privilege

Absolute privilege is of two types—the privilege which arises from consent of the person defamed, and that which, irrespective of such person's consent, is conferred by the law because of the character of the occasion on which the defamatory material is published.

Consent by the one defamed is a complete defense.[12] The consent must be such that is legally effective, and does not include an assent obtained by fraud, duress, or from one lacking capacity to give consent. The type of consent given, with the circumstances under which it is given, determines the extent of the privilege. It may be limited to a particular person or to a particular time or a particular purpose.[13] Submission to investigation or acceptance of voluntary membership in an association with rules providing for investigation, may carry with it consent to publications of honest findings.[14] The privileges arising from the character of the occasion are based upon the belief that the ends to be gained by permitting such statements to be published without liability, outweigh the harm which may result to others' reputations.[15]

It is recognized that certain officials and others charged with the performance of important public functions, must be as free as possible from fear that their actions may have an adverse effect upon their own personal interests. This absolute immunity is thus a means of removing any inhibitions which might deprive the public of the best service of its officers and agencies. The privilege protects them not only from liability but also from any danger of an unsuccessful civil action. It is a protection against harassment because, were it merely protection from liability, a conditional privilege would suffice to protect all but those public officials who act in bad faith. The propriety of their conduct cannot be questioned in an action for defamation.[16] Even where the defamation is motivated by actual malice there is no liability—and malice is not a proper subject of inquiry in such a case.[17]

---

12. Royer v. Steinberg, 90 Cal.App.3d 490, 153 Cal.Rptr. 499 (1979) (Consent confers absolute privilege).

13. Restatement, Second, Torts § 583, Comment d.

14. Id.

15. Royer v. Steinberg, 90 Cal.App.3d 490, 153 Cal.Rptr. 499 (1979) (Primary purpose for consent doctrine to prevent plaintiff from inviting publication & then bringing suit).

16. See Schlinkert v. Henderson, 331 Mich. 284, 49 N.W.2d 180 (1952); Sanborn v. Chronicle Pub. Co., 18 Cal.3d 406, 134 Cal.Rptr. 402, 556 P.2d 764 (1976).

    See also Restatement, Second, Torts, §§ 585–591; 69 Harv.L.R. 918.

17. Gosewisch v. Doran, 161 Cal. 511, 119 P. 656 (1911); Royer v. Steinberg, 90 Cal.App.3d 490, 153 Cal.Rptr. 499 (1979).

§ 30.8   SPECIFIC ACTIONS

A judge or other officer performing a judicial function,[18] or a person participating in a judicial proceeding as a lawyer,[19] witness,[20] juror,[21] or grand juror [22] is absolutely privileged to publish false and defamatory matter in the performance of such function, if the publication has some relation to the subject matter of the proceeding.[23] The relevancy test demands "some reference" to the proceeding, but dispenses with the requirement of relevancy, materiality, or pertinency in their technical sense.[24]

A member of the Congress of the United States or of the legislature of any state or territory thereof, is absolutely privileged to publish false and defamatory matter of another in the performance of his legislative function. Members of Congress are granted this privilege by the Federal Constitution, which provides that "for any Speech or Debate in either House, they shall not be questioned in any other Place."[25] A witness in a legislative proceeding is privileged in his testimony just as a witness in a judicial proceeding.[26]

18. Lowenschuss v. West Pub. Co., 542 F.2d 180 (3d Cir. 1976); Owen v. Kronheim, 304 F.2d 957 (D.C.Cir. 1962).

19. Read v. Baker, 430 F.Supp. 472 (D.Del.1977).

20. Lofland v. Meyers, 442 F.Supp. 955 (D.C.N.Y.1977); Dickinson v. French, 416 F.Supp. 429 (D.C.Ala.1976); Gilpin v. Tack, 256 F.Supp. 562 (D.C. Ark.1966).

21. Rainier's Dairies v. Raritan Val. Farms, 19 N.J. 552, 117 A.2d 889 (1955).

22. United States v. Briggs, 514 F.2d 794 (5th Cir. 1975). See also Restatement, Second, Torts § 589.

23. A witness is not required to determine the relevancy of a question put to him in a judicial proceeding. Johnson v. Diver, 201 Ark. 175, 143 S.W.2d 1112 (1940); Greenberg v. Ackerman, 41 N.J.Super. 146, 124 A. 2d 313 (1956).

24. Thornton v. Rhoden, 245 Cal.App. 2d 80, 53 Cal.Rptr. 706 (1966); Smith v. Hatch, 271 Cal.App.2d 39, 76 Cal. Rptr. 350 (1969). (Attorney's letters to client and court related to pending litigation absolutely privileged).

See Restatement, Second, Torts § 586, Comment c.

25. See: U.S.C.A.Const. Art. 1, § 6. The provision confers absolute immunity for any words uttered in debate on the floor of Congress.

See generally Hutchinson v. Proxmire, 443 U.S. 111, 99 S.Ct. 2675, 61 L.Ed. 2d 111 (1979); Saroyan v. Burkett, 57 Cal.2d 706, 21 Cal.Rptr. 557, 371 P.2d 293 (1962). (State Superintendent of Banks).

See also Yankwich, Immunity of Congressional Speech—Its Origin, Meaning, Scope (1951) 99 U. of Pa.L.Rev. 960; Simmons, Freedom of Speech in Congress: The History of a Constitutional Cause (1952) 38 ABA Journal 649; (1952) 5 Ala.L.Rev. 150; (1952) 38 Iowa L.Rev. 186; (1953) 51 Mich. L.Rev. 457; (1953) 37 Minn.L.Rev. 141; (1952) 28 N.D.L.Rev. 142; (1953) 20 U.Chi.L.Rev. 677; also note in 97 U.Pa.L.Rev. 877; Restatement, Torts, § 591.

26. Restatement, Second, Torts § 590A.

The President of the United States, and the Governor of any state or territory thereof, cabinet officers of the United States, and the corresponding officers of any state or territory thereof, are absolutely privileged regarding publications made in the exercise of an executive function, if the matter has some relation to the discharge of official duty.[27] The federal rule extends the privilege to subordinate officers and agencies,[28] and even to agencies or individuals required to report to the government in the normal course of their business.[29]

Communications between husband and wife are absolutely privileged because of the very confidential character of the relationship.[30]

§ 30.9 Qualified Privilege

Privileges also may be of another type, known as conditional or qualified privileges. The immunity granted by these privileges is not absolute but is conditioned upon publication in a reasonable manner and for a proper purpose.[31] They afford protection based upon a public policy which recognizes that it is essential that true information shall be given, whenever it is reasonably necessary for the protection of one's own interests, the interests of third persons, or certain interests of the public. That result is accomplished by providing protection against liability for misinformation given in an honest and reasonable effort to protect or advance the interest in question. One who publishes matter on a conditionally privileged occasion, provided he does not abuse such privilege, is not liable even though it be defamatory and false.[32]

---

27. Barr v. Matteo, 360 U.S. 564, 79 S.Ct. 1335, 3 L.Ed.2d 1434, reh. denied 361 U.S. 855, 80 S.Ct. 41, 4 L.Ed.2d 93. But see Butz v. Economou, 438 U.S. 478, 98 S.Ct. 2894, 57 L.Ed.2d 895 (1928), on remand 466 F.Supp. 1351 (S.D.N.Y.); Barr v. Matteo, 360 U.S. 564, 79 S.Ct. 1335, 3 L.Ed.2d 1434, reh. denied 361 U.S. 855, 80 S.Ct. 41, 4 L.Ed.2d 93.

28. Ingram v. United States, 360 U.S. 672, 79 S.Ct. 1314, 3 L.Ed.2d 1503 (1959), reh. denied 361 U.S. 856, 80 S.Ct. 42, 4 L.Ed.2d 96. (Acting Director of Office of Rent Stabilization); Chavez v. Kelly, 364 F.2d 113 (10th Cir. 1966) (Narcotics officer); Taylor v. Glotfelty, 201 F.2d 51 (6th Cir. 1952) (Government psychiatrist).

29. Becker v. Philco Corp., 372 F.2d 771 (4th Cir. 1964), cert. denied 389 U.S. 979, 88 S.Ct. 408, 19 L.Ed.2d 473 (Employer making report required by defense contract absolutely privileged).

30. Restatement, Second, Torts § 592; Prosser, Law of Torts (4th Ed. 1971) p. 785.

31. Zarate v. Cortinas, 553 S.W.2d 652 (Tex.Civ.App.1977). See also Prosser, pp. 785–796.

32. See: Sheehan v. Tobin, 326 Mass. 185, 93 N.E.2d 524 (1951); Zarate v. Cortinas, 553 S.W.2d 652 (Tex.Civ.App.1977). See also Restatement, Second, Torts § 593.

If the interest to be protected is that of the publisher, his defamatory publication is privileged conditionally if the interest is legitimate and the publisher believes or has reason to believe that the publication is necessary to protect that interest.[33] The privilege has been recognized where the publisher speaks in defense of his own reputation in response to defamation directed against him.[34]

A publication made to protect the interest of others than the publisher may be privileged conditionally if the publisher, under the circumstances, believes or has reason to believe that the interest is important and that the publication to the recipient is required by a legal or "moral" duty, or by generally accepted standards of decent conduct.[35] In the latter instance, the fact that the information is requested tends to indicate that the matter is important to the recipient, and that its publication is reasonable and justified.[36]

An occasion is privileged conditionally when the publisher and the recipient have a common interest in a particular subject matter,

---

33. Faber v. Byrle, 171 Kan. 38, 229 P.2d 718, 25 A.L.R.2d 1379 (1951); Emde v. San Joaquin County Central Labor Council, 23 Cal.2d 146, 154, 143 P.2d 20, 25, 150 A.L.R. 916 (1943); Stewart v. Nationwide Check Corp., 279 N.C. 278, 182 S.E.2d 410 (1971); Southwest Drug Stores, Inc. v. Garner, 195 So.2d 837 (Miss.1967); Meekins v. Mensou, 1 All Eng. 899 (1962).

See also: Restatement, Second, Torts § 594; Prosser, pp. 786–789.

34. Haycox v. Dunn, 200 Va. 212, 104 S.E.2d 800 (1958); Shenkman v. O'Malley, 2 A.D.2d 567, 157 N.Y.S.2d 290 (1956).

See also Prosser, Law of Torts (4th ed.) p. 786.

35. Stewart v. Nationwide Check Corp., 279 N.C. 278, 182 S.E.2d 410 (1971); Stephenson v. Marshall, 104 F.Supp. 26 (D.Alaska 1952), noted in (1953) 7 Ark.L.Rev. 150; Campbell v. Willmark Serv. System, 123 F.2d 204, 206 (3rd Cir. 1941).

Also see: Restatement, Second, Torts § 595 (1); Harper, Privileged Defamation, (1936) 22 Va.L.Rev. 642; Evans, Legal Immunity for Defamation (1940) 24 Minn.L.Rev. 607.

See: Faber v. Byrle, 171 Kan. 38, 229 P.2d 718, 25 A.L.R.2d 1379 (1951) (Alleged slanderous communications made to an official investigator in the sheriff's office, and to a half-brother of the plaintiff were conditionally privileged if not made with malice).

36. Restatement, Second, Torts § 595(2), Comment j.

Credit agencies come within this rule, if their investigation is made carefully and honestly and published upon a legitimate request.

See Restatement, Second, Torts § 595, Comment h; Prosser, p. 790.

See also Levy v. American Mut. Liab. Ins. Co., 196 A.2d 475 (D.C.App.1964); Watwood v. Stone's Mercantile Agency, Inc., 194 F.2d 160, 30 A.L.R.2d 772, 781 (D.C.Cir. 1952), cert. denied 344 U.S. 821, 73 S.Ct. 18, 97 L.Ed. 639, reh. denied 345 U.S. 960, 73 S.Ct. 935, 97 L.Ed. 1380.

and the communication is of facts reasonably calculated to protect or further that interest.[37]

The family relationship also gives rise to a conditionally privileged occasion. One may publish material which, if true, would be of service in protecting the well-being of his family. This includes communications other than between husband and wife, which are absolutely privileged. That the information communicated may have been requested is material in establishing the privileged nature of the publication, although a request is not essential to its establishment.[38]

A conditionally privileged occasion can arise from a correct or reasonable belief that a sufficiently important public interest is affected by and requires the publication of defamatory matters to a public officer or private citizen who is authorized or privileged to act.[39]

Conditional or qualified privileges must be exercised in a reasonable manner and for a proper purpose.[40] The occasion is abused and the protection lost if the publisher does not believe or have reason to believe that the publication is true,[41] or that its publication to the re-

37. See: Soley v. Ampudia, 183 F.2d 277, 19 A.L.R.2d 689 (5th Cir. 1950); Stewart v. Nationwide Check Corp., 279 N.C. 278, 182 S.E.2d 410 (1971); Sheehan v. Tobin, 326 Mass. 185, 93 N.E.2d 524 (1950); Jones v. Hansen, 220 La. 673, 57 So.2d 224 (1952); Ward v. Painters Local Union No. 300, 41 Wash.2d 859, 865, 252 P.2d 253, 256–257 (1953).

See also discharge from employment: privileged nature of communication to other employees' union of reason for plaintiff's discharge. 60 A.L.R.3d 1080; Jackson, Libel Actions Arising from Labor Disputes, 1953 Wis.L.Rev. 537–50; Restatement, Second, Torts § 596; Prosser, pp. 789–791; Miller, Defamation: A Survey of Recent Decisions, 4 Syracuse L.Rev. 221, 240 (1953);

38. Restatement, Second, Torts § 597.

See also Manning v. McAllister, 454 S. W.2d 597 (Mo.App.1970); Zarate v. Cortinas, 553 S.W.2d 652 (Tex.Civ. App.1977).

39. See: City of Mullens v. Davidson, 133 W.Va. 557, 57 S.E.2d 1, 13 A.L. R.2d 887 (1949), annotation 13 A.L.R. 2d 897; Morgan v. Bulletin Co., 369 Pa. 349, 85 A.2d 869 (1952).

Statements to F.B.I. concerning government employee as privileged communications, see: Foltz v. Moore-McCormack Lines, Inc., 189 F.2d 537 (2d Cir. 1951), cert. denied 342 U.S. 871, 72 S.Ct. 106, 96 L.Ed. 655, noted in 51 Col.L.Rev. 244–7.

40. Southwest Drug Stores, Inc. v. Garner, 195 So.2d 837 (Miss.1967) (Privilege lost because defendant broadcast suspicions negligently); Whitcomb v. Hearst Corp., 329 Mass. 193, 107 N.E.2d 295 (1952).

Also see: Restatement, Second, Torts § 599; Prosser, p. 792.

41. Fulton v. Atlantic Coast R. Co., 220 S.C. 287, 67 S.E.2d 425 (1951); Boulet v. Beals, 158 Me. 53, 177 A.2d 665 (1962).

Also see: Restatement, Second, Torts § 600.

Rumors may be published, as such, when necessary, in view of the cir-

cipient is reasonably necessary to accomplish the purpose for which the occasion is privileged,[42] or if it is published for a purpose beyond that for which the privilege is granted.[43] The propriety of the publisher's purpose, or his ill-will or malice, should be considered in the light of his belief or reasonable belief that the publication furthers an interest which should be protected.[44]

§ 30.10 Constitutional Privilege—Public Officials and Public Figures

In 1964, the United States Supreme Court extended constitutional protection to defamation of public officials in the historic decision of *New York Times Co. v. Sullivan*,[45] cited by Dean Prosser as "unquestionably the greatest victory won by the defendants in the modern history of the law of torts."[46] In the interests of "a profound national commitment to the principle that debate on public issues should be uninhibited, robust and wide-open, and that it may well include vehement, caustic, and sometimes unpleasantly sharp attacks on government and public officials,"[47] the Supreme Court held that the First and Fourteenth Amendments prohibit recovery of damages for libel of a public official relating to his official conduct, unless it is shown that the statement was made with actual "malice".[48] The Court further held that the reckless disregard must be shown with "convincing

cumstances, with less risk of abuse of privilege: see Restatement, Second, Torts § 602.

42. Hughes v. Washington Daily News Co., 193 F.2d 922 (D.C.Cir. 1952); Newell, Slander and Libel, p. 418 (4th ed. 1924).

See also Restatement, Second, Torts § 605.

43. Emo v. Milbank Mut. Ins. Co., 183 N.W.2d 508 (N.D.1971); Robinson v. Home Fire and Marine Ins. Co., 242 Iowa 1120, 49 N.W.2d 521 (1951); Mullen v. Lewiston Evening Journal, 147 Me. 286, 86 A.2d 164 (1952); Loeb v. Geronemus, 66 So.2d 241 (Fla.1953); Ward v. Painters Local Union No. 300, 41 Wash.2d 859, 866, 252 P.2d 253 (1953); Veazy v. Blair 86 Ga.App. 72, 72 S.E.2d 481 (1953),

citing statute; Restatement, Second, Torts § 603.

44. See Faber v. Byrle, 171 Kan. 38, 229 P.2d 718, 25 A.L.R.2d 1379 (1951) (Circumstances may repel influence of malice).

See also Prosser, Law of Torts (4th ed. 1971) p. 850.

45. 376 U.S. 254, 84 S.Ct. 710, 11 L. Ed.2d 686 (1964), motion denied 376 U.S. 967, 84 S.Ct. 1130, 12 L.Ed.2d 83.

46. Prosser, Law of Torts (4th ed. 1971) p. 819.

47. 376 U.S. at 270, 84 S.Ct. at 720, 11 L.Ed.2d at 701.

48. 376 U.S. at 279–280, 84 S.Ct. at 725–726, 11 L.Ed.2d at 706.

clarity",[49] and that a jury's finding of reckless disregard would be subject to *de novo* appellate review.[50]

Subsequent decisions have extended the constitutional privilege to defamation of "public figures",[51] and even private persons in reports on matters "of public or general interest".[52] The latter holding was repudiated in *Gertz v. Robert Welch, Inc.*,[53] wherein the Court decided that the states may define standards of liability for defamation of private individuals, short of strict liability. Recovery of presumed or punitive damages, however, remains restricted to cases where "actual malice" is shown.[54] Nevertheless, in practice, the standards for determining who is a "public figure" as opposed to a private individual have evaded definition, and still appear to be resolved on a case-by-case basis. In *Gertz*, a civil liberties lawyer of national prominence, who was author of several books and articles and the frequent subject of newspaper articles, was held not be be a public figure. In *Time, Inc. v. Firestone*,[55] a Palm Beach socialite who employed a newspaper clipping service and held press conferences during her divorce trial was held not to be a public figure.

The standards for finding "actual malice" under the New York Times rule have been amplified, but not clarified, by subsequent decisions. One case defined it as making the statement with "a high degree of awareness" of its probable falsity.[56] Another found "actual malice" where defendant entertained "serious doubts as to the truth" of the matter stated.[57] Although the Court has held that reckless conduct is *not* measured "by whether a reasonably prudent man . . . would have investigated before publishing,"[58] other decisions have held that a failure to investigate thoroughly and verify the facts could support a finding of reckless disregard, where there is no

49. 376 U.S. at 285–286, 84 S.Ct. at 728–729, 11 L.Ed.2d at 710.

50. 376 U.S. at 285, 84 S.Ct. at 728, 11 L.Ed.2d at 709.

51. Curtis Pub. Co. v. Butts, 388 U.S. 130, 154–155, 87 S.Ct. 1975, 1991, 18 L.Ed.2d 1094 (1967), conformed to 418 S.W.2d 379, reh. denied 389 U.S. 889, 88 S.Ct. 11, 19 L.Ed.2d 197, error ref'd, cert. denied 391 S.Ct. 966, 83 S.Ct. 2036, 20 L.Ed.2d 880 (Mr. Justice Harlan, plurality opinion).

52. Rosenbloom v. Metromedia, Inc., 403 U.S. 29, 91 S.Ct. 1811, 29 L.Ed.2d 296 (1971) (Mr. Justice Brennan, plurality opinion).

53. 418 U.S. 323, 94 S.Ct. 2997, 41 L.Ed.2d 789 (1974).

54. 418 U.S. 323 at 345, 94 S.Ct. 2997 at 3009, 41 L.Ed.2d 789.

55. 424 U.S. 448, 96 S.Ct. 958, 47 L.Ed.2d 154 (1976).

56. Garrison v. State of Louisiana, 379 U.S. 64, 74, 85 S.Ct. 209, 215–216, 13 L.Ed.2d 125 (1974).

57. St. Amant v. Thompson, 390 U.S. 727, 731, 88 S.Ct. 1323, 1325, 20 L.Ed.2d 262 (1968).

58. 390 U.S. 727 at 731, 88 S.Ct. 1323 at 1325, 20 L.Ed.2d 262.

need for expeditious publishing, and where the danger of substantial damage to plaintiff's reputation is apparent from the nature of the statement.[59]

With regard to defamation of private individuals, the states have significant variation in standards imposed. Many require a showing of "actual malice" in cases of "public interest",[60] while others require only a showing of negligence.[61] One state requires "gross negligence".[62] Where negligence is the test, either the "reasonable person" standard [63] or a "professional negligence" standard is imposed. The latter requires an inquiry as to the conduct of "the reasonably careful publisher or broadcaster in the community or similar communities."[64]

One significant effect on libel litigation of the *New York Times* decision is the shift of focus from the publisher's attitude towards the person defamed to the publisher's attitude towards the defamatory statement. The defendant's "state of mind" is thus of critical importance in establishing liability.

---

59. Curtis Pub. Co. v. Butts, 388 U.S. 130, 87 S.Ct. 1975, 18 L.Ed.2d 1094 (1967); Goldwater v. Ginzburg, 414 F.2d 324 (2d Cir. 1969), cert. denied 396 U.S. 1049, 90 S.Ct. 701, 24 L.Ed. 2d 695, reh. denied 397 U.S. 978, 90 S.Ct. 1085, 25 L.Ed.2d 274; Carson v. Allied News Co., 529 F.2d 206 (7th Cir. 1976); Fopay v. Noveroske, 31 Ill.App.3d 182, 332 N.E.2d 79 (1975).

See also Vandenburg v. Newsweek, Inc., 507 F.2d 1024 (5th Cir. 1975) ("[W]hen the story is not 'hot news' . . . the investigation must be more thorough, and 'actual malice may be inferred when the investigation . . . was grossly inadequate in the circumstances' ").

60. West v. Northern Pub. Co., 487 P. 2d 1304 (1971); Belli v. Curtis Pub. Co., 25 Cal.App.3d 384, 102 Cal.Rptr. 122 (1972).

Time, Inc. v. Firestone, 424 U.S. 448, 96 S.Ct. 958, 47 L.Ed.2d 154, on remand 332 So.2d 68 (Fla.); State v. Snyder, 277 So.2d 660 (La.1973), writ denied 294 So.2d 543, rev'd 304 So.2d 334; Standke v. B. E. Darby & Sons, Inc., 291 Minn. 468, 193 N.W.2d 139 (1971), cert. dism'd 406 U.S. 902, 92 S.Ct. 1608, 31 L.Ed.2d 813; Matus v. Triangle Publications, Inc., 445 Pa. 384, 286 A.2d 357 (1971), cert. denied 408 U.S. 930, 92 S.Ct. 2494, 33 L.Ed. 2d 343; Sanders v. Harris, 213 Va. 369, 192 S.E.2d 754 (1972); Chase v. Daily Record, Inc., 83 Wash.2d 37, 515 P.2d 154 (1973).

61. Cahill v. Hawaiian Paradise Park Corp., 56 Hawaii 522, 543 P.2d 1356 (1975); Jacron Sales Co. v. Sindorf, 276 Md. 580, 350 A.2d 688 (1976); Martin v. Griffin Television Inc., 549 P.2d 85 (Okl.1976); Foster v. Laredo Newspapers, Inc., 541 S.W.2d 809 (Tex. 1976).

62. Chapadeau v. Utica Observer-Dispatch, Inc., 38 N.Y.2d 196, 379 N.Y. S.2d 61, 341 N.E.2d 569 (1975) ("Gross irresponsibility").

63. E. g. Troman v. Wood, 62 Ill.2d 184, 340 N.E.2d 292 (1975).

64. Gobin v. Globe Pub. Co., 216 Kan. 223, 531 P.2d 76 (1975).

The Supreme Court's recent decision in *Herbert v. Lando* [65] has significantly expanded the methods of proving malice. Questions as to a journalist's subjective conclusions regarding the veracity of his sources and the truth of the published statement, as well as questions as to the editorial procedures followed in verification and editing are now constitutionally permissible.

§ 30.11 Burden of Proof—Court and Jury

In an action for defamation, the plaintiff has the burden of proving, when the issue is properly raised, the defamatory character of the communication, its publication by the defendant, its application to the plaintiff, the recipient's understanding of its defamatory meaning and application to the plaintiff, the special harm resulting to the plaintiff from its publication, and the abuse of a conditionally privileged occasion.[66]

The defendant has the burden of proving, when the issue is properly raised, the truth of the defamatory communication, the privileged character of the occasion on which it was published, and the character of the subject matter of the defamatory comment as of public concern.[67]

The court determines whether a communication is capable of a defamatory meaning, and the jury determines whether such communication was so understood by its recipient.[68] The court also deter-

---

65. 441 U.S. 153, 99 S.Ct. 1635, 60 L. Ed.2d 115 (1979).

66. Hahn v. Kotten, 43 Ohio St.2d 237, 331 N.E.2d 713, 720 O.O.2d 134 (1975); Capps v. Watts, 271 S.C. 276, 246 S.E.2d 606 (1978); Werner v. Southern California Associated Newspapers, 35 Cal.2d 121, 216 P.2d 825, 13 A.L.R.2d 252 (1950); Van Gundy v. Wilson, 84 Ga.App. 429, 66 S.E.2d 93 (1952), 14 Ga.B.J. 358–61 (Admissibility of evidence of malice without pleading same to defeat a privilege, to enhance damages, and to rebut evidence given in mitigation); Hellar v. Bianco, 111 Cal.App.2d 424, 244 P.2d 757, 28 A.L.R.2d 1451 (1952) (Burden on plaintiff of introducing evidence that defendant adopted defamatory matter or republished it).

See also Restatement, Second, Torts § 613(1).

67. See Morgan v. Bulletin Co., 369 Pa. 349, 85 A.2d 869 (1952) (privilege); Sanders v. W. T. Grant Co., 55 So.2d 89 (La.App.1951) (Defense of privilege in slander action must be pleaded).

68. Belli v. Orlando Daily Newspapers, Inc., 389 F.2d 579 (5th Cir. 1967), cert. denied 393 U.S. 825, 89 S.Ct. 88, 21 L.Ed.2d 96.

In Yorty v. Chandler, 13 Cal.App.3d 467, 91 Cal.Rptr. 709 (1970), plaintiff mayor of Los Angeles had held a press conference in which he had expressed interest in the cabinet post of Secretary of Defense. Defendant newspaper published a cartoon showing the mayor at his desk telephone, with white-coated medical orderlies standing beside him, one holding a straightjacket and the other beckoning with his finger. The caption was,

mines whether a crime or disease imputed by spoken language is of such a character as to make the slander actionable *per se*.

Subject to the control of the court whenever the issue arises, the jury determines whether spoken language imputes to another conduct or attributes of character which are incompatible with the proper conduct of his business, trade, or profession.[69]

The court determines what items of harm suffered by plaintiff as a result of the publication of the defamatory matter may be considered by the jury in assessing damages. The jury determines the amount of the damages to be awarded for each item.[70]

The jury determines whether the defamatory matter was published of and concerning the plaintiff, and whether it was true or false.[71]

The Court determines whether an expression of opinion is capable of constituting a defamatory allegation of facts.[72]

Whether criticism was expression of opinion upon known facts or upon true or privileged statement of fact, or whether it carried with it a false implication of defamatory facts, and whether it represented the honest opinion of its author, and whether it was expressed for a proper purpose, is a jury question.[73]

The Court determines whether or not the occasion upon which defendant published the defamatory matter was privileged.[74]

"I've got to go now . . . I've been appointed Secretary of Defense and the Secret Service men are here!" Plaintiff alleged that the cartoon was intended to convey the meaning that he suffered from the delusion that he had been appointed to the post, and that he was therefore insane. Held, judgment for defendants on demurrer affirmed:

"It is simply impossible to believe that a viewer of the cartoon would not have understood exactly what was meant: it was Mayor Yorty's public aspiration for appointment as Secretary of Defense which was being ridiculed. No reader could have thought that either the cartoonist or the editor of the Los Angeles Times was charging Mayor Yorty with mental derangement or mental incompetency. On the contrary, even the most careless reader must have perceived that the cartoon was no more than rhetorical hyperbole, a vigorous expression of opinion by those who considered Mayor Yorty's aspiration for high national office preposterous. To penalize defendants for publishing this political cartoon would subvert the most fundamental meaning of a free press, protected by the First and Fourteenth Amendments."

69. Restatement, Second, Torts § 615.
70. Restatement, Second, Torts § 616.
71. Restatement, Second, Torts § 617.
72. Restatement, Second, Torts § 566, Comment c.
73. Restatement, Second, Torts § 617.
74. Nuyen v. Slater, 372 Mich. 654, 127 N.W.2d 369 (1964); Sheehan v. Tobin, 326 Mass. 185, 93 N.E.2d 524 (1950).

See also Restatement, Second, Torts § 619.

Finally, it is up to the jury to determine whether defendant abused a conditionally privileged occasion.[75]

§ 30.12 Measure of Damages

Although the law used to award at least nominal damages to one who had proved his case for libel or slander per se,[76] *Gertz v. Welch*[77] explicitly held that states "may not permit recovery of presumed or punitive damages, at least when liability is not based on a showing of knowledge of falsity or reckless disregard for the truth."[78] Although compensation is thus limited to "actual injury," the Court does not restrict compensation to "out-of-pocket loss. Indeed, the more customary types of actual harm inflicted by defamatory falsehood include impairment of reputation and standing in the community, personal humiliation, and mental anguish and suffering. [T]here need be no evidence which assigns an actual dollar value to the injury."[79]

In most cases, therefore, there is still no need to prove special, pecuniary losses in establishing damages.[80] The state can still protect such intangible interests as reputation and a freedom from humiliation. Emotional distress is often a likely element of damages, as long as the distress can be traced to the defamation.[81]

In strict slander cases, special damages must still be shown, though these are often difficult to prove.[82] If a valid claim is stated, punitive damages are often the most significant element of damages.[83]

---

75. Robinson v. Home Fire & Marine Ins. Co., 242 Iowa 1120, 49 N.W.2d 521 (1951).

See also Restatement, Second, Torts § 619.

76. Cook v. East Shore Newspapers, Inc., 327 Ill.App. 559, 64 N.E.2d 751 (1945); Kehoe v. New York Tribune, Inc., 229 App.Div. 220, 241 N.Y.S. 676 (1930).

77. 418 U.S. 323, 94 S.Ct. 2997, 41 L. Ed.2d 789 (1974).

78. Id. at 349.

79. Id. at 350.

80. See Rowe v. Metz, 195 Colo. 424, 579 P.2d 83 (1978) (Holding that *Gertz* allows damages to be presumed against nonmedia defendants).

81. Browning v. Birmingham News, 348 So.2d 455 (Ala.1977); Mattox v. News Syndicate Co. Inc., 176 F.2d 897 (2d Cir. 1949), cert. denied 338 U.S. 858, 70 S.Ct. 100, 94 L.Ed. 525.

82. Arturie v. Tiebie, 73 N.J.Super. 217, 179 A.2d 539 (1962) (Plaintiff tried to prove damages by showing cost of altering wardrobe due to loss of weight following defamation).

See Developments in the Law—Defamation, 69 Harv.L.Rev. 875 (1965).

83. International Broth. of Elec. Workers v. Mayo, 281 Md. 475, 379 A.2d 1223 (1977) ($5,000 punitive not excessive despite compensatory award of only $1); General Motors Corp. v. Piskor, 27 Md.App. 95, 340 A.2d 767 (1975) aff'd in part rev'd in part 277 Md. 165, 252 A.2d 810, appeal after

Although plaintiffs have had difficulty in surmounting the *Gertz* requirement of malice for punitive damages, the recent *Herbert v. Lando* [84] decision should ease this burden significantly.

Various factors may be proved by the plainitff in aggravation of damages, and by the defendant in mitigation of those damages. Among these are the character of the plaintiff and his general standing or reputation in the community;[85] the character of the publication and the probable effect of the language used;[86] the area of dissemination and the extent, duration and circulation of the publication;[87] the retraction or apology, if any, and its timeliness and adequacy.[88]

A retraction ordinarily is not a complete defense to defamation. Evidence of retraction may be admissible to show that plaintiff's general reputation has not been damaged as much as he asserts, to negative malice as a basis of punitive damages, or to show good motive in establishing that a privileged occasion has not been abused.[89] An unsuccessful plea of truth may be considered as a matter likely to aggravate the harm which plaintiff's reputation has sustained.[90]

remand 281 Md. 627, 381 A.2d 16. ($1500 compensatory, $25,000 punitive damages); Reynolds v. Pegler, 223 F.2d 429 (2d Cir. 1954), cert. denied 350 U.S. 846, 76 S.Ct. 80, 100 L. Ed. 754 ($1 compensatory, $175,000 punitive); Davis v. Schuchat, 510 F. 2d 731 (D.C.Cir. 1975).

84. 441 U.S. 153, 99 S.Ct. 1635, 60 L. Ed.2d 115 (1979).

85. Towle v. St. Albans Pub. Co., 122 Vt. 134, 165 A.2d 363 (1960).

86. Mattox v. News Syndicate Co. Inc., 176 F.2d 897 (2d Cir. 1949), cert. denied 338 U.S. 858, 70 S.Ct. 100, 94 L.Ed. 525.

87. Utah State Farm Bureau Federation v. National Farmers Union Serv. Corp., 198 F.2d 20 (10th Cir. 1952).

88. Morgan v. Dun & Bradstreet, Inc., 421 F.2d 1241 (5th Cir. 1970).

89. Id.; See Turner v. Hearst, 115 Cal. 394, 47 P. 129 (1896); See also 1A Hanson, Libel & Related Torts (1969) ch. 15.

90. Arnold v. Quillian, 262 So.2d 414 (Miss.1972).

§§ 30.13–31.0 are reserved for supplementary material.

†

MODERN TRIALS

Second Edition

1984 Pocket Parts

By

MELVIN M. BELLI, SR.

of the
San Francisco and Los Angeles Bars

Assisted by
ALLEN P. WILKINSON
of the
California Bar

Volume 1

Sections 1.1 to 30

Insert this Pocket Part in back of Volume

ST. PAUL, MINN.
WEST PUBLISHING CO.
1984

1 Belli Modern Trials—1
1984 P.P.

COPYRIGHT © 1984
By
WEST PUBLISHING CO.

PREFACE

These 1984 pocket parts to *Modern Trials* bring this new Second Edition up-to-date as regards important court decisions and new trial techniques.

Our law is "up to date"! I sincerely and honestly feel that in the United States this is the Golden Age of the trial part of modern common law, both civil and criminal. I am specifically confining this observation to the United States, however, because in Canada the Golden Age of tort law has recently but definitely passed! Trial by jury there is on its way out. Verdicts and judgments are inadequate, and the most of us, particularly including those of the least of us, are not given the adequacy of protection that the common law seemed for a while—at least in England and Canada—to warrant.

From a monetary standpoint, the common law tort plaintiff in the United States has achieved the adequate award and the adequate remedy. More and more and varied plaintiffs are achieving more and more adequate awards. This however is not the case in England and Canada where means are found deliberately, practically, and materially to reduce compensation.

Only one thing can be said for the commonwealth jurisdictions and that is that justice is speedier. However, while it is certainly speedier, it is also "littler." One may get an award much sooner in commonwealth jurisdictions than in the United States, but it's not an "adequate" award at all.

Though we've approached and may have reached the Golden Age of the common law in the United States, particularly in tort law, our particular problem is the delay in getting to trial; the delay in getting any action. It seems to be more than the problem of legislative or case law which prevents us from getting our case to trial for our clients. It seems it's more the action or lack of action of the trial lawyer. If the judges countenance delay, the trial lawyer shouldn't. I'm not so sure where the fault really lies; with the trial judge or the trial lawyer or, for that matter, with the appellate judges. But, something must be done and done soon or the whole house of adequate awards will come tumbling down if it can't be achieved timely.

But, when I say that we've reached the Golden Age of our common tort law, I see ominous legislative clouds on the legal horizon, both federal and state. The present Washington administration is no friend of the civil plaintiff, unless perhaps he's a big corporation. There is

PREFACE

brutal federal legislation being offered to make all consumer and warranty cases federal. With but a slight change in the membership of the United States Supreme Court, an artificial device will be achieved to make interstate jurisdiction a federal question.

However, we must consider how the federal courts will handle this additional litigation in the warranty and consumer cases if their jurisdiction is expanded. These federal courts are already so overburdened with cases that Justice Burger on the other hand wants to limit their activities. Will the answer be some ancillary federal courts or arbitrations, or just what does the present Washington administration have in mind?

And then there is the new "medical malpractice crisis." When every insurance company seeks to raise its premiums, they initiate a new "medical malpractice crisis." Indeed there is now a bill in the Congress that all health providers throughout the United States will come under federal jurisdiction if they receive any federal monies, and their responsibility will be drastically limited monetarily, to even the most deserving plaintiff.

These pocket parts bring us up to our modernity of the Golden Age in plaintiff tort law. They also bring us up to our ultimate protection of the individual defendant in criminal law. But when reading these supplements one must be on the lookout for the complete reversal of the trend of our modern tort law to protect the individual, both in the national and local legislatures. Within a very few years, and a very few changes of legislation, our present whole good system, nationally and federally, can be reversed. Hark to what was done in Canada and England and the commonwealth jurisdictions, which never did achieve the protective benevolence to the civil plaintiff and criminal defendant that we have just achieved in the United States.

So when reading these pocket parts, rejoice in what we trial lawyers, criminal and civil, have done to make of our system the most protective of the individual criminally and the most adequate of the civil plaintiff man has ever achieved.

But, we can't be complacent, we don't want to have to say by the time of the next pocket parts to our new Modern Trials, "we achieved our greatness in 1984—then we achieved a more expedient but less adequate system."

MELVIN M. BELLI

San Francisco and Los Angeles
May, 1984

SUMMARY OF CONTENTS
(Including New or Retitled Sections)

Volume 1

PART I. INTRODUCTION

Chapter		Page
1.	Setting the Stage	1
2.	Investigation and Discovery	4
3.	Have I a Case?	5

PART II. BURDEN OF PROOF

5.	Quantum of Proof: Inferences, Presumptions, Possibilities and Probabilities	8

PART III. TORT LIABILITY AND DEFENSES—GENERALLY

6.	Strict Liability	9
7.	Res Ipsa Loquitur	10
8.	Violation of Statute	11
10.	Comparative Negligence	12
11.	Contributory Negligence	14
12.	Last Clear Chance	16
13.	Assumption of Risk	17
14.	Imminent Peril—"I Can't Let Go!"—The Emergency Rule	18
16.	Punitive Damages	19
18.	Releases	21

PART IV. TORT LIABILITY AND DEFENSES— SPECIFIC ACTIONS

19.	Federal Tort Claims Act	25
20.	Suing the Insurer	28
22.	Wrongful Death	29
	§ 22.5 Effect of Spouse's Remarriage	30
23.	Wrongful Birth and Wrongful Life	31
	§ 23.11 Statutes of Limitations	33
24.	Prenatal Injuries	35
25.	Loss of Consortium	36
26.	Tort Liability and the Familial Relationship	38
27.	Charitable and Sovereign Immunities	39
	§ 27.6 Government Liability for Negligent Design and Maintenance	41

SUMMARY OF CONTENTS

Chapter		Page
28.	Uninsured Motorist Coverage	48
29.	The Dramshop Rule	49
30.	Defamation	52
	§ 30.13 Libel of Trade School	55
	§ 30.14 Fair Comment Privilege	55

Volume 2

PART IV. TORT LIABILITY AND DEFENSES—SPECIFIC ACTIONS—Continued

31.	Right of Privacy	1
32.	Nuisance	4
33.	Recovery for Emotional Disturbances	6
35.	Animal Law	11
	§ 35.6 Guard Dog Attack	12
36.	Persons in Control	15
37.	Landlord's Liability	18
	§ 37.4A Store Parking Lot—Assault	26
38.	Owners and Possessors of Land	36

B. SWIMMING POOL LIABILITY

	§ 38.13 Drownings in Storm Sewer	45
39.	Workers' Compensation	48
	§ 39.22 Suits Against Employer's Insurance Carrier	49
	§ 39.23 Construction Injuries—Roof Collapse	50
	§ 39.24 Loading Dock Injury	54
40.	Aircraft Accident Litigation	59

SUBCHAPTER 1. GENERAL CONCEPTS

B. INVESTIGATION AND DISCOVERY

§ 40.19	Investigation and Reconstruction	59

C. POSSIBLE DEFENDANTS AND THEORIES

§ 40.27A	Failure to Install Fire Detector or Extinguisher	69
§ 40.27B	Crashworthiness—Defective Seats/Restraints	74
§ 40.34	Defendants on the Ground	81

D. DEMONSTRATIVE EVIDENCE IN AVIATION CASES

§ 40.46	Military Aircrashes	81
41.	Railroad Law	86

SUMMARY OF CONTENTS

A. FEDERAL EMPLOYERS' LIABILITY ACT (FELA)

		Page
§ 41.30	Train—Train Collision—Avoiding FELA	88

B. PREPARATION OF RAILROAD CROSSING CASES

§ 41.51 Railroad Crossing—Excessive Speed 92

Chapter
42. Maritime Tort Law 97

L. PLEASURE BOAT LITIGATION

§ 42.101 In General 103
§ 42.102 Defective Cleat 104
§ 42.103 Collisions 112
43. Products Liability 117

I. PERSONS LIABLE

§ 43.86A Used Products: Dealers and Rebuilders 119

U. SPECIFIC PRODUCTS

§ 43.187 Tampons—Toxic Shock Syndrome (TSS) 126
44. Medical Malpractice 132
   § 44.34 Hospitals—Negligence in Permitting Surgeon to Operate 137
   § 44.35 Chiropractic Malpractice—Failure to Diagnose Cancer 141
   § 44.36 Neck Surgery Malpractice 144
   § 44.37 Ambulance Liability—Failure to Transport 144
   § 44.38 Drug Liability—Experimentation/Radioactive Drugs 150
   § 44.39 —— Xylocaine Hydrochloride 155

Volume 3

PART IV. TORT LIABILITY AND DEFENSES—SPECIFIC ACTIONS—Continued

45. Admission of Liability by Words, Acts and Conduct 1
46. Safety History: Prior Accidents and Subsequent Repairs 3

PART V. TESTS AND MEDICAL EXAMINATIONS

47. Tests—Lie Detector, Intoxication, Blood 4
48. The Medical Examination 7

PART VII. SETTLEMENT OF THE CASE

50. The Settlement 8

SUMMARY OF CONTENTS

PART VIII. TRIAL TECHNIQUES

Chapter		Page
51.	The Jury	9

D. JURY INFORMATION

§ 51.30   Use of Community Surveys and Jury Profiles 9

K. PSYCHOLOGICAL FACTORS IN TRIAL

	§ 51.110	Introduction	15
	§ 51.111	The Cognitive or Information-Processing Issues	16
	§ 51.112	Emotional and Attitudinal Issues	23
	§ 51.113	Summary	28
52.	The Opening Statement		30
	§ 52.10	Opening Statements in Falling Tree/Government Liability Case	30
53.	Demonstrative Evidence in Civil Cases		45
54.	Demonstrative Evidence in Divorce Cases		46
55.	Trial by Blackboard, Placards and Charts		47

Volume 4

PART VIII. TRIAL TECHNIQUES—Continued

56.	Experiments	1
57.	Models	3
58.	Photographs and Movies	12
59.	Videotape Depositions: A New Frontier of Advocacy	16
60.	Exhibition of Person	17
61.	Medical Demonstrative Evidence	19
62.	Expert Testimony	20
63.	Examining Witnesses	21
	§ 63.36 Examination of Document Examiner	21

Volume 5

PART VIII. TRIAL TECHNIQUES—Continued

64.	General Damages: Pain and Suffering	1
65.	Closing Argument to Jury in Civil Cases	3
	§ 65.33 Misconduct in Argument—Mention of Insurance —Settlement Offers	3
	§ 65.36 Argument in Wrongful Death of Minor	3

SUMMARY OF CONTENTS

PART XII. TAX CONSIDERATIONS

Chapter		Page
72.	Tax Aspects of Litigation Settlements	10

App.		
C.	Table of Persons	11

Index 13

*

MODERN TRIALS

Second Edition

*

PART I

INTRODUCTION

CHAPTER 1

SETTING THE STAGE

C. ATTORNEY'S FEES, LIENS AND EXPENSES

§ 1.23 Amount of Fees; Fee Schedules

26. Heller v. Frankston, ___ Pa.Cmwlth. ___, 464 A.2d 581 (1983) (Provision of Health Care Services Management Act regulating fees which may be received by plaintiff's attorney upon settlement of medical malpractice actions held violative of constitutional principle of separation of powers.)

§ 1.25 Recovery of Fee by Discharged Attorney

Page 30

... write the former client and the carriers of the amount claimed as fees and costs.[47.5]

46. Harris Trust & Savings Bank v. Chicago College Osteopathic Medicine, 116 Ill. App.3d 906, 72 Ill.Dec. 448, 452 N.E.2d 701 (1983) (Attorney, discharged by clients with medical malpractice action when attorney was disbarred, and who accepted $150,000 payment from clients' new counsel in complete discharge and release for any claims for attorney fees, was not entitled to additional fees when action was settled for $2 million.)

Booker v. Midpac Lumber Co., Ltd., ___ Hawaii ___, 649 P.2d 376 (1982). ("Where the efforts of an attorney who was employed under a contingent fee contract would have a tendency to advance the client's claim or to enhance the possibility of a favorable result, we would also conclude the contract and the reasonably estimated value of the case should be considered in fixing a reasonable attorney's fee. For 'the real value of the service' encompasses 'the benefits resulting to the client.'")

47.5 Adan v. Abbott, 114 Misc.2d 735, 452 N.Y.S.2d 476 (Sup.Ct.1982). ("Under New York Law, there are two kinds of attorney's liens, (1) the general possessory retaining lien established by common law allowing an attorney to keep a client's papers or assets until his legal fee is paid; and (2) the charging or special lien statutorily established against monies recovered for a client by the attorney's efforts in litigation ....")

E. TRAUMATIC NEUROSES AND HYSTERICAL PARALYSES

§ 1.43 Examples of Traumatic Neuroses

Los Angeles attorney *Edward Barker* gained a $1,300,000 award on behalf of a forty-four year old Spanish-American man who suffered back injury and traumatic neurosis after attempting to lift by hand a 100 pound locomotive cylinder head, a task performed by machine on most locomotives.[67.5] Due to his back injury, the plaintiff was unable to work for approximately nine months. During the period he was unable to work and provide for his family and out of fear that he would never be able to return to work, the plaintiff, who by his heritage was very "macho" oriented, went into a very depressed state that ultimately evolved into a psychosis. The plaintiff, who was employed by the Southern Pacific Railroad as a $12,000 a year machinist at the time of the accident, began hearing voices and feared that railroad officials were plotting to kill him. The plaintiff's condition worsened, even though he was receiving psychiatric treatment. Suit was filed under the Federal Employers' Liability Act. Mr. Barker's approach at trial was to base the suit primarily on the psychological damage suffered by the plaintiff. Mr. Barker spent much time at trial establishing the physical injury to the back, but used it not as an injury in itself, but as that which caused the ensuing psychological damage. One of the high points of the trial came during Mr. Barker's cross-examination of a psychiatrist who testified for the defense. That psychiatrist testified that the psychosis was "involutional depression," and was not precipitated by outside causes, but rather was due to hormones, or "male menopause." Mr. Barker had found a textbook written by that psychiatrist, and in the text what he had written on involutional depression disputed his courtroom testimony. The psychiatrist was asked to read aloud the passage from the book. The jury awarded a gross sum of $1,625,585, but this figure was reduced as the plaintiff was found 20% negligent. This resulted in a net award of approximately $1,300,000, the largest award to date for traumatic neurosis. Figure 1.43–1.

[67.5] Chavez v. Southern Pacific Railroad, filed in Los Angeles County (California) Superior Court, # C–134630.

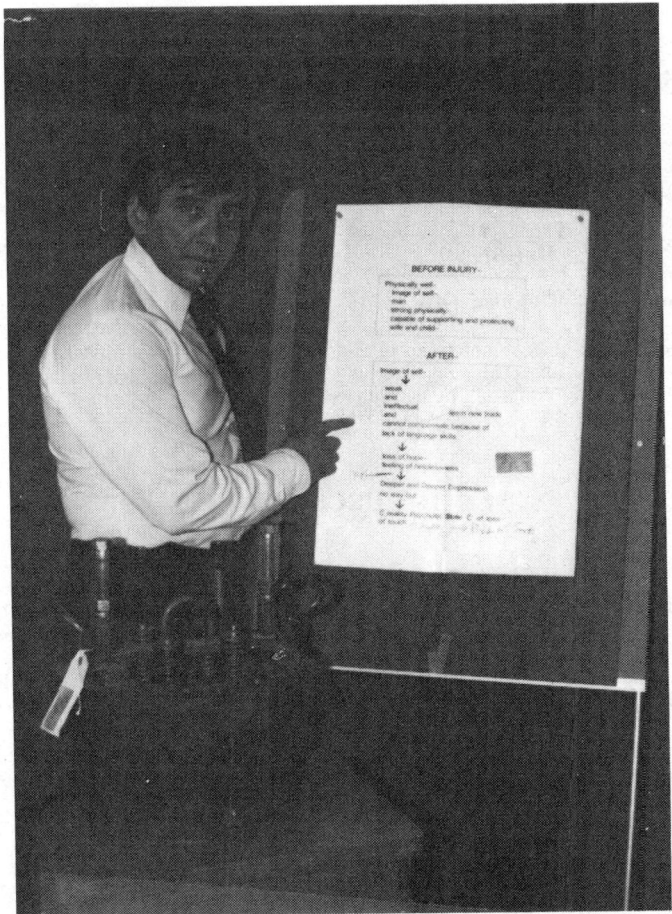

Figure 1.43–1. Edward Barker, Esq., Los Angeles, with chart and 100-pound locomotive cylinder head used to gain net award of $1,300,000, largest award to date for traumatic neurosis.

CHAPTER 2

INVESTIGATION AND DISCOVERY

C. OFFICE FORMS AND RECORDS

§ 2.25 Police Reports [8.5]

8.5 Competency of Police Officer As Witness

A police officer is not competent to testify as to the cause of an accident where his opinion is based on accounts of the accident given by eyewitnesses, but officer himself did not see the accident, and opinion was not based upon facts determined after careful analysis of the physical evidence at the scene of the accident. Lesher v. Henning, 302 Pa.Super. 508, 449 A.2d 32 (1982).

I. DISCOVERY

§ 2.81 In General

57. Summit Chase Condominium Association, Inc. v. Protean Investors, Inc., 421 So.2d 562 (Fla.App.1982). ("The openness of modern discovery is recognized to the point where the discovery process is for the most part self-executing. The superintendence of trial judges should be resorted to only with respect to whether information should be disgorged and the sequence or timing of its proliferation. It is inherent in the present rules of discovery that lawyers, out of respect for the adversary system, should make good faith efforts to comply with one another's reasonable discovery requests without constant recourse to the trial courts. This is especially so when counsel know full well that compliance with discovery is inevitable if sanctions are to be avoided.")

§ 2.84 Lawyer-Client Privilege

83. Goldberg v. Ross, 421 So.2d 669 (Fla. App.1982). ("Documents which are not privileged in the hands of the client cannot be shielded by transferring them to the attorney.")

Page 135

1. State ex rel. Jay Bee Stores, Inc. v. Edwards, 636 S.W.2d 61 (Mo.1982). (Individual's Fifth Amendment privilege against self-incrimination does not attach to records of corporations.)

§ 2.85 Attorney's Work Product

28. Stein v. Trump Village Section No. 4, Inc., 118 Misc.2d 344, 460 N.Y.S.2d 475 (Sup.Ct.1983). ("[R]eports taken by or for carriers or by attorneys of their client's employees ... are protected from disclosure. Reports made by the defendant's employees of an accident, even after the spectre of litigation has arisen, are reports taken in the regular operation of business and will be available for discovery. This is so whether or not that report is to be used solely for defense litigation ....")

CHAPTER 3

HAVE I A CASE?

C. *STARE DECISIS* AND THE LAWYER'S DUTY

§ 3.12 The Doctrine of *Stare Decisis*

43. Goetzman v. Wichern, 327 N.W.2d 742 (Iowa 1982). (In abrogating the doctrine of contributory negligence and replacing it with comparative negligence, the court stated: "Moreover, stare decisis does not preclude the change. That principle does not require blind imitation of the past or adherence to a rule merely because 'it was laid down in the time of Henry IV.' ... We must reform common law doctrines that are unsound and unsuited to present conditions.")

D. THE CRIPPLED CASE

§ 3.22 Intoxication

57. Note, A Common Law Cause of Action for the Injured Inebriate?, 31 Drake L.Rev. 435 (1982).

§ 3.23 Aggravation of Pre-existing Condition

83. Abernathy v. Superior Hardwoods, Inc., 704 F.2d 963 (7th Cir.1983). ("Although [plaintiff] is entitled to a substantial award for the six months of pain and restricted movement that followed the accident, there is little evidence of pain or other disutility since then other than what can be inferred from his wife's testimony. Of course his back may get worse; and not only is a spinal fusion a dangerous procedure, because there is a significant possibility of its causing paralysis, but it often is unsuccessful in relieving pain. On the other hand, the evidence is uncontested that [plaintiff] was suffering from disc disease ("slipped disc") before the accident; his vertebrae were already beginning to disintegrate and press on the nerves. To someone already suffering from disc disease a back injury is a terrible thing; and the fact that a tort victim, because of a preexisting weakness, suffers a worse injury than a normal person would suffer is not in itself a ground for reducing his damage award. ... But it is different when the weakness makes it likely that the injury complained of would have occurred anyway, so that the accident merely accelerated it .... A man who has disc disease yet does heavy work—[plaintiff] at the time of the accident—is quite likely in time to experience symptoms similar to those [plaintiff] experienced prematurely because of the accident. It is unreasonable to ascribe to the accident 100 percent of the back pain that he is expected to suffer over his lifetime.")

E. STATUTES OF LIMITATION

§ 3.31 In General

92. Nelson v. James, 435 So.2d 1189 (Miss.1983) (When last day of six-year statute of limitations for filing personal injury action falls on a Sunday, action filed on following Monday is timely.)

§ 3.39 Computation of Period—Accrual; Estoppel; Tolling

60. Continuous Representation

Where an attorney commits an act of malpractice but continues to represent the client, the statute is tolled during the period of continued representation. Glamm v. Allen, 57 N.Y.2d 87, 453 N.Y.S.2d 674, 439 N.E.2d 390 (1982). (A client is not "expected to jeopardize his pending case or his relationship with the attorney handling that case during the period that the attorney continues to represent the person. Since it is impossible to envision a situation where commencing a malpractice suit would not affect the professional relationship, the rule of continuous representation tolls the running of the Statute of Limitations on the malpractice claim until the ongoing representation is completed.")

62. Asbestos

Redeker v. Johns-Manville Products Corp., 571 F.Supp. 1160 (W.D.Pa.1983) (Wrongful death actions brought within two years of decedents' deaths from exposure to asbestos dust and fibers maintainable under Pennsylvania Wrongful Death and Survival Acts, where decedents had not known cause of their disease during their lifetimes.)

Matthews v. Celotex Corp., 569 F.Supp. 1539 (D.C.N.D.1983) (North Dakota's six year statute of limitations applicable to personal injury action involving asbestos victim, although barring personal representative's survival claim, did not apply to heirs' separate cause of action for wrongful death.)

Pierce v. Johns-Manville Sales Corp., 296 Md. 656, 464 A.2d 1020 (1983) (Widow's survival and wrongful death action not barred by three year statute of limitations, even though husband's exposure to asbestos had resulted in manifestation of asbestosis prior to three-year limitation. Court held that survival and wrongful death causes of action accrued only at time when husband was diagnosed as having asbestos-related lung cancer.)

Neubauer v. Owens-Corning Fiberglass Corp., 686 F.2d 570 (7th Cir.1982), on remand 26 B.R. 644, certiorari denied ___ U.S. ___, 103 S.Ct. 1233, 75 L.Ed.2d 467 (1983), on remand 576 F.Supp. 197 (E.D.Wis.) (In asbestos case, court held that "the 'injury' that starts clock running is not the defendant's allegedly wrongful act of exposing the plaintiffs to asbestos, but instead the onset of harm to each plaintiff sufficient that 'he can come into court, plead and prove certain facts and secure the relief requested.'" However, applying Wisconsin law, the court ruled that the statute begins to run when the injury was diagnosable without regard for any noticeable impairment to the plaintiff. Additionally, court stated that "it is irrelevant whether the evidence of injury leads the plaintiff to realize that the disease was caused by exposure to asbestos.")

McDaniel v. Johns-Manville Sales Corp., 542 F.Supp. 716 (N.D.Ill.1982). (Statute of limitations begins to run when plaintiff is aware of injury and wrongful causation; plaintiff need not know the identity of defendant.)

Nolan v. Johns-Manville Asbestos, 85 Ill.2d 161, 52 Ill.Dec. 1, 421 N.E.2d 864 (1981). ("We hold, therefore, that when a party knows or reasonably should know both that an injury has occurred and that it was wrongfully caused, the statute begins to run and the party is under an obligation to inquire further to determine whether an actionable wrong was committed. In that way, an injured person is not held to a standard of knowing the inherently unknowable ... yet once it reasonably appears that an injury was wrongfully caused, the party may not slumber on his rights.")

Staiano v. Johns Manville Corp., 304 Pa. Super. 280, 450 A.2d 681 (1982). (Holding that once plaintiff has salient facts concerning the occurrence of his injury and who or what caused it, he has the ability to investigate and pursue his claim. It is not necessary that plaintiff know the proper parties to sue and the identities of other potential defendants. Statute of limitations began running when plaintiff knew he had asbestosis, which was caused by the inhalation of asbestos dust emanating from asbestos products on work site. "We find no reason to postpone the commencement of the statute until a plaintiff has in addition discovered who manufactured the products that he knows have injured him.")

64. Date of Injury Not Included

Goldberg v. Charter Medical Corp., ___ Nev. ___, 651 P.2d 94 (1982). (Date of decedent's wrongful death is not included in computing limitations period.)

Olson v. Campbell County Memorial Hospital, 652 P.2d 1365 (Wyo.1982). (Plaintiff filed suit for alleged medical malpractice on November 12, 1981. The alleged malpractice occurred on November 12, 1979. Defendant argued that suit was filed one day late. Court held that rule stating that day of act, event or default from which the designated period of time begins to run shall not be included was applicable, and suit was timely filed.)

Defamation Actions

Chacharis v. Fadell, ___ Ind.App. ___, 438 N.E.2d 1032 (1982). (In defamation action, statute of limitations begins to run when allegedly defamatory matter is published, not when there is a determination that the matter is not privileged.)

70. Herdman v. Smith, 707 F.2d 839 (5th Cir.1983) (Statute of limitations is tolled when defendant actively conceals his identity.); Hershley v. Brown, 655 S.W.2d 671 (Mo.App.1983) (Statute of limitations tolled where physician allegedly concealed fact that he had implanted tubal ring instrument in patient's body without her consent.)

McDaniel v. LaSalle Ambulance Service, Inc., 108 Ill.App.3d 1042, 64 Ill.Dec. 606, 440 N.E.2d 158 (1982). (Plaintiff sustained fractures of both legs in automobile accident on November 6, 1975. On December 24, 1975, while being transported by defendant ambulance service, her leg struck the pavement. Plaintiff's attorney wrote a letter to her physician asking whether plaintiff's drop foot condition, discovered after that incident, might have been caused by the allegedly negligent transportation. Physician replied that plaintiff did not evidence drop foot condition prior to December incident. Suit was filed against ambulance company on December 10, 1976, but in January, 1980, (during) a discovery deposition, the physician testified that the drop foot condition had existed for more than one month prior to the incident. Plaintiff then filed suit for malpractice against physician, and physician defended on ground that statute of limitations barred action. Court held that action of physician did not constitute fraudulent concealment which operated to toll statute: "A cause of action accrues when the plaintiff knows or reasonably should know of an injury and also knows or reasonably should know that the injury was caused by the wrongful acts of another. A complaint for fraudulent concealment must aver facts which establish affirmative acts or representations on the defendant's part, which are calculated to and in fact do prevent the discovery of the cause of action. A mere misrepresentation of a fact does not constitute fraudulent concealment in absence of a showing that it tended to conceal the cause of action. A contention that defendant concealed the identity of a wrongdoer rather than the cause of action does not constitute fraudulent concealment ....") (Citations omitted.)

73. Coons v. American Honda Motor Co., 94 N.J. 307, 463 A.2d 921 (1983) (Statute which tolled running of statute of limitations in actions against foreign corporations which were not represented in state unconstitutionally burdened interstate commerce by requiring foreign corporation engaged exclusively in interstate commerce to obtain certificate to do business in order to gain advantage of statute of limitations.)

83. Rittenhouse v. Erhart, 126 Mich. App. 674, 337 N.W.2d 326 (1983) (Statute of limitations tolled due to plaintiff's mental impairment.).

See Libertelli v. Hoffman-La Roche, Inc., 565 F.Supp. 234 (S.D.N.Y.1983) (If insane plaintiff at any time during three-year period of statute of limitations experienced lucid interval during which she regained her ability to protect her rights, toll was lost.)

Duwe v. Rodgers, ___ Ind.App. ___, 438 N.E.2d 759 (1982). (A distracted person is one "who by reason of his or her mental state is incapable of managing or procuring the management of his or her ordinary affairs." Persons under such disability may bring suit in Indiana within two years after disability removed.)

85. Turner v. Evans, 251 Ga. 486, 306 S.E.2d 921 (1983), certified question conformed to 721 F.2d 341 (11th Cir.) (Statute of limitations is tolled as to causes of action arising while person is imprisoned, despite fact that prisoners may sue or be sued.)

PART II

BURDEN OF PROOF

CHAPTER 5

QUANTUM OF PROOF: INFERENCES, PRESUMPTIONS, POSSIBILITIES AND PROBABILITIES

§ 5.6 Different Standards in Different Proceedings

54. Insurance Co. of State of Pennsylvania v. Estate of Guzman, 421 So.2d 597 (Fla.App.1982). ("Guided by the foregoing principles, we reach the following conclusions. First, the burden of proof in the strict sense always remains on the party initially having it. Second, presumptions affecting the burden of proof declare or implement some strong social policy of the state, like the validity of a marriage, or the legitimacy of a child. Third, presumptions affecting the burden of producing evidence facilitate the determination of the issues. These presumptions negate the necessity of proof in the absence of contradictory evidence.") (Footnotes omitted.)

PART III
TORT LIABILITY AND DEFENSES—GENERALLY

CHAPTER 6
STRICT LIABILITY

§ 6.4 Dangerous Activities

35. Fire

Koos v. Roth, 293 Or. 670, 652 P.2d 1255 (1982). (Plaintiff's property sustained damage when field fire on defendant's property spread to plaintiff's field. Court held that the use of fire is the "aboriginal dangerous activity," and despite legislation dealing with field burning, held that defendant was strictly liable for trespass to plaintiff's property, and therefore liable for the damages done.)

CHAPTER 7

RES IPSA LOQUITUR

§ 7.2 Elements or Conditions

6. Jones v. Tarrant Utility Co., 638 S.W.2d 862 (Tex.1982). (Plaintiff's skating rink sustained damage due to continuous overflowing of defendant's water storage tanks. Supreme Court of Texas ruled it was error for trial court to refuse to apply doctrine of res ipsa, stating: "Water repeatedly overflowing from a water tank, like oil spilling out of an oil pipeline, is the type of accident that normally would not occur absent negligence.")

CHAPTER 8

VIOLATION OF STATUTE

§ 8.3 Criminal Statutes

28. Boyer v. Tenn Tom Constructors, 702 F.2d 609 (5th Cir. 1983). (Under Mississippi law, violation of a regulatory or penal statute constitutes negligence per se and will support a cause of action in tort where the plaintiff is within the class protected by the statute, and the harm sustained is the type sought to be prevented by the statute.)

§ 8.4 Municipal Ordinances and Administrative Regulations

33. Zimmerman v. Moore, ___ Ind.App. ___, 441 N.E.2d 690 (1982). (Violation of administrative regulation is only evidence of negligence in Indiana, and is not treated as negligence per se as is violation of a statute or ordinance.)

CHAPTER 10

COMPARATIVE NEGLIGENCE

§ 10.1 In General

2. Harrison v. Montgomery County Board of Education, 295 Md. 442, 456 A.2d 894 (1983). (Court of Appeals of Maryland refused to judicially abrogate doctrine of contributory negligence in favor of comparative negligence, stating that such decision "involves fundamental and basic public policy considerations properly addressed by the legislature.")

§ 10.2 Forms of Comparative Negligence

42. Goetzman v. Wichern, 327 N.W.2d 742 (Iowa 1982). (Supreme Court of Iowa adopted pure form of comparative negligence: "We are convinced that comparative negligence is a fairer system. It diminishes but does not defeat the right to recover damages caused by another party's fault. We are also convinced that the pure form of comparative negligence should be adopted in Iowa. It gives full rather than partial effect to the principle of comparative fault by reducing a person's recovery based on another party's fault by the percentage of the person's own fault in the occurrence.")

49. Dixon v. Stewart, 658 P.2d 591 (Utah 1982). (Supreme Court of Utah ruled that trial court must inform the jury of the effect of apportioning to the plaintiff 50% or more of the negligence it finds in a comparative negligence case, if the effect of such instruction will not be to confuse or mislead the jury. Utah law precludes a plaintiff from recovering unless the defendant's negligence is greater than plaintiff's.)

Adkins v. Whitten, ___ W.Va. ___, 297 S.E.2d 881 (1982). (West Virginia high court rejects "blindfold rule," and holds that it is proper for trial judge to instruct the jury of the effect of finding some percentage of negligence against the plaintiff. Court states that to withhold such fact from the jury could conceivably mislead them into believing that so long as plaintiff is not 100% at fault he would recover some damages.)

§ 10.3 Proximate Cause—Last Clear Chance—Assumption of Risk

64. Wilson v. Chesapeake & Ohio Railway Co., 118 Mich.App. 123, 324 N.W.2d 552 (1982).

68. Anderson v. Ceccardi, 6 Ohio St.3d 110, 451 N.E.2d 780 (1983) (Merger of defense of assumption of risk and contributory negligence under comparative negligence statute does not merge categories of assumption of risk known as "express assumption of risk" and "primary assumption of risk."); Fish v. Gosnell, ___ Pa.Super. ___, 463 A.2d 1042 (1983) (Comparative negligence statute did not wholly abolish assumption of risk defense, nor did it extend application of assumption of risk defense in cases that have been traditionally evaluated primarily according to contributory negligence principles. Court stated that all voluntary risk-taking that can be described by the ambiguous phrase "assuming risk" does not constitute the defense. Rather, the plaintiff must fully understand the specific risk, voluntarily choose to encounter it, and manifest a willingness to accept it.)

69. Wendland v. Ridgefield Construction Services, 190 Conn. 791, 462 A.2d 1043 (1983) (Although Connecticut comparative negligence statute abolished the harsh common law rule that the doctrines of contributory negligence, assumption of risk, and last clear chance operated as complete bar to recovery, factors relevant to assumption of risk may be considered by trier of fact in regard to determining the relative negligence of each party.)

Simmons v. Frazier, 277 Ark. 452, 642 S.W.2d 314 (1982). (Under Arkansas comparative negligence rules, assumption of risk is not a complete bar but simply a matter to be considered in deciding fault.)

§ 10.4 Multiple Defendants

71. Hurley v. Public Service Co. of New Hampshire, ___ N.H. ___, 465 A.2d 1217 (1983) (Trial court did not abuse its discretion in giving jury special verdict form which provided, in part, that it was jury's obligation to determine damages if percent of negligence attributed to defendants was 50 percent or more "either separately or added together.")

80. Mountain Mobile Mix, Inc. v. Gifford, 660 P.2d 883 (Colo.1983). ("[I]n cases where there are multiple defendants who proximately cause the injury, the degree of fault of each defendant will be combined and compared with the degree of fault of the plaintiff. If the plaintiff is less than 50% at fault, each defendant will be jointly and severally liable for the plaintiff's damages even if the degree of fault of a particular defendant is less than that of the plaintiff.")

CHAPTER 11

CONTRIBUTORY NEGLIGENCE

§ 11.2 Criticism and Defense of the Doctrine

8. Harrison v. Montgomery County Board of Education, 295 Md. 442, 456 A.2d 894 (1983). (High court of Maryland refused to abrogate doctrine of contributory negligence, leaving it to Legislature: "[W]e are unable to say that the circumstances of modern life have so changed as to render contributory negligence a vestige of the past, no longer suitable to the needs of the people of Maryland.")

§ 11.3 Standard of Conduct—Imputed Negligence

22. Davis v. Waterman, 420 So.2d 1063 (Miss.1982). (13-year-old riding motorbike killed in accident with automobile driven by defendant. Rebuttable presumption existed that child under 14 years of age incapable of contributory negligence. However, court held that since child was operating a self-propelled vehicle on a highway, the child must be held to the same standard of care as an adult).

Sharpe by Sharpe v. Quality Education, Inc., 59 N.C.App. 304, 296 S.E.2d 661 (1982). (Rebuttable presumption exists that nine-year-old child is incapable of contributory negligence.)

24. Choice of Paths

Wakenight v. State, 212 Neb. 798, 326 N.W.2d 52 (1982). (Plaintiff was picked up by police for illegal hitchhiking, and was transported off of the Interstate. Plaintiff was struck by a car while walking over a bridge which was unlighted. Court held that although state was negligent in failing to maintain high tower lights, plaintiff was also negligent in failing to walk on correct side of highway and in failing to keep proper lookout. Plaintiff's negligence found more than slight when compared with any negligence of defendant).

McDevitt v. Terminal Warehouse Co., 304 Pa.Super. 438, 450 A.2d 991 (1982). (In the absence of a "compelling reason," one who follows an unfamiliar course in the dark or steps into darkened and unfamiliar space, relying upon his sense of touch instead of obtaining and using adequate lighting facilities, is guilty of contributory negligence as a matter of law.)

27. Buchanan v. Tangipahoa Parish Police Jury, 426 So.2d 720 (La.App.1983). ("Contributory negligence is an affirmative defense to a negligence tort action ... and the party relying upon it has the burden of proving it. Contributory negligence is conduct on the part of a plaintiff which falls below the standard to which he should conform for his own protection. The standard of conduct to which a plaintiff must conform for his own protection is that of a reasonable man under like circumstances. Failure to take every precaution against every foreseeable risk or to use extraordinary skill, caution, and foresight does not constitute negligence or contributory negligence. The alleged victim is required only to use reasonable precautions, and his conduct in this regard is not negligent if, by a commonsense test, it is in accord with that of reasonably prudent persons faced with similar conditions and circumstances.")

28. Rhyner v. Madden, 188 N.J.Super. 544, 457 A.2d 1243 (1983). (Passengers who were injured when intoxicated driver's vehicle struck oncoming traffic not contributorily negligent for riding with intoxicated driver, if tavernkeepers served them alcoholic beverages while they were visibly intoxicated.)

§ 11.4 Avoidable Consequences Rule

52. Watson v. Storie, 60 N.C.App. 736, 300 S.E.2d 55 (1983). (The failure of an injured person to seek prompt medical attention is not contributory negligence, as it is not a cause of the accident that produced the injuries.)

CHAPTER 12

LAST CLEAR CHANCE

§ 12.1 General Considerations

18. Ireland v. Leach Pontiac-GMC, Inc., 420 So.2d 18 (Ala.1982). ("To predicate liability on subsequent negligence it must be shown that the plaintiff was in peril and that the defendant had actual knowledge of plaintiff's peril and negligently failed to prevent the accident when he had the means available to do so.")

Woodard v. Mays, 416 So.2d 1305 (La. App.1982), writ denied 421 So.2d 906. ("In order to use this doctrine [of last clear chance] the party relying upon it [the plaintiff] must prove three elements. First, the plaintiff must have been in a position of peril of which he was unaware or from which he was unable to extricate himself. Second, the defendant must have actually discovered the plaintiff's peril or could have, by the exercise of ordinary and reasonable care, discovered the plaintiff's peril. Third, at that time, the defendant must have been able, with the exercise of reasonable and ordinary care, to have avoided the accident."

Meyers v. City of Louisiana, 637 S.W.2d 219 (Mo.App.1982). ("In order to establish a submissible case under the humanitarian doctrine, a party must establish that: 1) plaintiff was in a position of immediate danger; 2) defendant knew or should have known of plaintiff's position or peril; 3) defendant, after receiving such notice, had the present ability to have averted the impending injury without harming himself or others; 4) defendant failed to exercise the requisite care to avert injury; and 5) damage to plaintiff resulted.")

§ 12.2 Issues—Knowledge, Opportunity, Antecedent Negligence

37. Maricle v. Spiegel, 213 Neb. 223, 329 N.W.2d 80 (1983). (Doctrine of last clear chance did not apply where driver's negligence was active and continued as contributing factor up to time of injuries sustained by other driver.)

Brown v. George, 278 S.C. 183, 294 S.E.2d 35 (1982). (The doctrine of last clear chance "applies only where the antecedent negligence of the plaintiff has become remote in the chain of causation and a mere condition of his injury .... It does not apply where the plaintiff's act combines and concurs with the defendant's act as a proximate cause of the injury .... When the emergency arises so suddenly that the defendant has no time to avert the accident, the last clear chance doctrine does not apply.")

§ 12.3 Relation to Other Doctrines

48. Wilson v. Chesapeake & Ohio Railway Co., 118 Mich.App. 123, 324 N.W.2d 552 (1982). (Doctrine of last clear chance remains viable under doctrine of comparative negligence.)

CHAPTER 13

ASSUMPTION OF RISK

§ 13.3 Express Argeements

Page 500

... "brought home" to him,[29] i.e. fine printing not apparent.

Express assumption of risk has also been applied to cases where a person voluntarily participates in a contact sport.[29.10]

29.10 Kuehner v. Green, 436 So.2d 78 (Fla.1983) (plaintiff injured in karate sparring match during manuever in form of a leg sweep could not recover, as he subjectively recognized the danger of "leg sweeps" and voluntarily proceeded to spar in the face of such danger.)

CHAPTER 14

IMMINENT PERIL—"I CAN'T LET GO!"—THE EMERGENCY RULE

§ 14.1 General Considerations

1. Taylor v. Todd, ___ Ind.App. ___, 439 N.E.2d 190 (1982). (In order to invoke the sudden emergency doctrine, party must prove (1) that the appearance of danger or peril was so imminent that he had no time for deliberation; (2) that the situation relied upon to excuse any failure to exercise legal care was not created by the party's own negligence; and (3) that his conduct under the circumstances was such as the law requires of an ordinarily prudent man under like or similar circumstances.)

§ 14.2 Availability of Defense

6. State Farm Mutual Automobile Insurance Co. v. Hoerner, 426 So.2d 205 (La.App 1982), writ denied 433 So.2d 154 (1983). (Doctrine of sudden emergency does not excuse motorist's improper vigilance, following too close, failure to see an emergency situation in sufficient time to avert a collision, or creation of the emergency by his own negligence.)

CHAPTER 16

PUNITIVE DAMAGES

§ 16.3 Statements of Purpose

33. Matter of GAC Corp., 681 F.2d 1295 (11th Cir. 1982). (Punitive damages not appropriate in bankruptcy court, since it would not be the wrongdoer who would be punished, but rather innocent third parties, that is, other creditors. "[F]uture wrongful conduct will not be deterred when the punitive damages are paid from the wrongdoer's estate rather than from his own pocket.")

§ 16.6 Survival of Claim

60. Thorpe v. Wilson, 58 N.C.App. 292, 293 S.E.2d 675 (1982). ("The general rule in this and other jurisdictions is that there can be no recovery for punitive damages against the personal representative of the deceased wrongdoer, however aggravated the circumstances may be .... The sole purpose of the allowance of punitive damages is to punish the wrongdoer. The death of the wrongdoer precludes his being punished by the assessment of punitive damages.")

§ 16.7 Measurement of Punitive Damages

76. Snodgrass v. Headco Industries, Inc., 640 S.W.2d 147 (Mo.App.1982). (In defamation action, jury awarded $75,000 punitive damages with $1.00 nominal award, and $100,000 punitive damages with $5,000 award for actual damages. Court held that based upon record and degree of malice present, jury did not abuse its discretion in making these awards.)

Wells v. Smith, ___ W.Va. ___, 297 S.E.2d 872 (1982). (In action arising out of theft of jewelry and coins, actual damages were awarded against all but one co-defendants. However, against that defendant the jury did make an award of $10,000 in punitive damages. Court ruled that where a claim for actual damages is sufficiently pleaded and proved, the failure of the jury to allow compensatory damages does not require an award of exemplary or punitive damages to be set aside.)

81. Nienstadt v. Wetzel, 133 Ariz. 348, 651 P.2d 876 (App.1982). ("In Arizona, there is no compensatory-punitive damage ratio limit. Whether punitive damages are excessive is based solely on the circumstances of each case and one of the factors that the jury may consider in assessing the degree of punishment is the wealth of the defendant.")

Vossler v. Richards Manufacturing Co., Inc., 143 Cal.App.3d 952, 192 Cal.Rptr. 219 (1983). (To recover an award of punitive damages, plaintiff is not obligated to introduce evidence of defendant's financial condition. Rather, it is incumbent upon defendant manufacturer, if it deemed itself unable to pay punitive damages, to introduce evidence of its wealth. "Net, not gross, figures are the best yardstick to be used in determining punitive damages." Ratio of 20 to 1 between punitive damages ($500,000) and compensatory damages ($25,000) not disproportionate in light of defendant's conduct.)

§ 16.9 Insurance Coverage of Punitive Awards

3. Skyline Harvestore Systems, Inc. v. Centennial Insurance Co., 331 N.W.2d 106 (Iowa 1983). (Insurance policy stating that insurance company would pay "all sums that the insured shall become legally obligated to pay as damages because of A. bodily injury or B. property damage" obligated insurance company to pay award of

punitive damages. Public policy argument of insurance company fell to insured's argument that freedom to contract for insurance coverage was stronger consideration.)

§ 16.10 Contract Actions

20. R & H Trucking, Inc. v. Occidental Fire & Casualty Co. of North Carolina, 2 Ohio App.3d 269, 441 N.E.2d 816 (1981). (Punitive damages not recoverable in an action for breach of contract, even though it is alleged that the breach was unlawful, wilful, wanton, and malicious.)

§ 16.11 Punitive Damages in Products Liability Cases

28. Thiry v. Armstrong World Industries, 661 P.2d 515 (Okl.1983). (Supreme Court of Oklahoma ruled that punitive damages may be recovered in an action for strict products liability. "We hold that a plaintiff may allege and prove exemplary and punitive damages as an element of damage in an alleged manufacturers' product liability case. In doing so we compliment the 'shield' of compensation provided by strict liability doctrine with a 'sword' of punitive damages. But appropriate control must be exercised to prevent the awarding of *excessive* judgments. Since the primary purpose of punitive damages is to punish the defendant and deter similar wrongdoing in the future, the 'sword' must be used to deter the wrongdoer, not kill him.")

In Gold v. Johns-Manville Sales Corp., 553 F.Supp. 482 (D.C.N.J.1982) and Wolf by Wolf v. Procter & Gamble Co., 555 F.Supp. 613 (D.C.N.J.1982), it was ruled that the Supreme Court of New Jersey most likely would not permit recovery for punitive damages in an action based on strict products liability. However, both courts agreed that where plaintiffs alleged theories of negligent and intentional misconduct, the court could not strike their claims for punitive damages.).

32. Ghiardi & Kircher, Punitive Damage Recovery in Products Liability Cases, 65 Marquette L.Rev. 1 (1981); Owen, Problems in Assessing Punitive Damages Against Manufacturers of Defective Products, 49 Univ. of Chicago L.Rev. 1 (1982).

CHAPTER 18

RELEASES

§ 18.1 In General

Page 572

An agreement not to sue a store, county, and police department in return for the dismissal of criminal charges of theft and disorderly conduct has been upheld against the person seeking to avoid that agreement.[3.5] A release executed by a race driver whereby he agrees not to hold the race track liable may bar a suit by such driver against the track and its employees for ordinary negligence.[3.10] However, the agreement may not bar an action based on gross negligence, nor should it bar other claims, such as a spouse's action for loss of consortium.[3.15]

3. Anderson v. Anderson, 90 A.D.2d 763, 455 N.Y.S.2d 304 (1982). (Relief from a stipulation of settlement may be granted only upon a showing of good cause, as where it resulted from collusion, mistake, accident, or similar cause. Unsupported assertions of coercion cannot form the basis for vacating a stipulation of settlement.)

Yoon Pil Kim v. Shull, 90 A.D.2d 482, 454 N.Y.S.2d 480 (1982). (Written settlement statement was definite and complete on face, constituting a valid and binding contract; if plaintiffs desired the attack the validity of settlement on basis of mutual mistake, plenary suit in equity must be brought.)

Community Development Construction Corp. v. Fleetwood Construction Co., Inc., 640 S.W.2d 331 (Tex.App.1982), error refused n.r.e. (Release properly identified and introduced into evidence, valid on its face, is a bar to suit, where release had never been set aside and no pleadings at trial requested that it be set aside.)

3.5 Brothers v. Rosauer's Supermarkets, Inc., 545 F.Supp. 1041 (D.C.Mont. 1982).

3.10 Lee v. Beauchene, 337 N.W.2d 827 (S.D.1983) (Release signed by stock car driver discharging track operators and owners from liability due to strict liability and ordinary negligence barred driver's suit against track operator and owner when stock car struck hole in track and flipped.).

But see Ferrell v. Southern Nevada Off-Road Enthusiasts, Limited, 147 Cal.App.3d 309, 195 Cal.Rptr. 90 (1983) (Adhesive release agreement prepared by racetrack operator, and given to dune buggy driver on "take it or leave it" basis was not sufficiently clear to release operator from liability for driver's injuries proximately caused by operator's negligence. Word "release" only appeared in document's title, and only exculpatory language appeared in convoluted 147-word sentence.)

Grbac v. Reading Fair Co., 688 F.2d 215 (3d Cir. 1982). ("Release and Waiver of Liability and Indemnity Agreement" executed by race driver before taking part in stockcar race in which he was killed operated to bar driver's widow from bringing suit against racetrack.)

3.15 Gillespie v. Papale, 541 F.Supp. 1042 (D.C.Mass.1982). (Plaintiff rendered quadriplegic in accident while he was driving a race car on defendant's track. Although plaintiff's claims arising from ordinary negligence were barred, court held he could pursue his claims for gross negligence, and release did not bar his wife's claim for loss of consortium.)

§ 18.2 Mutual Mistake

The intention of the parties to make a contract for the specific terms agreed to is essential to a valid release. If there is no "meeting of the minds" the release will not stand.[12.5]

§ 18.2 TORT LIABILITY AND DEFENSES Pt. 3

4. Frahm v. Carlson, 214 Neb. 532, 334 N.W.2d 795 (1983) (Release set aside on grounds of mutual mistake, where both parties believed known, trivial injuries were only injuries sustained, and were ignorant of other and more serious injuries.)

12.5 DeKalb County Hospital Authority v. Davis, 250 Ga. 46, 295 S.E.2d 840 (1982). (Plaintiff was injured in an automobile accident, then suffered further injuries due to alleged negligence of hospital. Plaintiff signed a release with the driver who caused the accident, the release stating that plaintiff released "all other persons . . . of any and all claims . . . arising from, and by reason of any and all known and unknown, foreseen and unforeseen bodily and personal injuries . . . and the consequences thereof." Court held that release did not absolve hospital of liability unless parties intended to release hospital of liability.)

Noroski v. Fallet, 2 Ohio St.3d 77, 442 N.E.2d 1302 (1982). (During telephone call between insurance adjuster and plaintiff, call being recorded with plaintiff's consent, plaintiff replied in the affirmative to adjuster's question whether he agreed that certain amount was "full and complete settlement for your bodily injuries as well as the property damage resulting" from accident. Supreme Court of Ohio holds that plaintiff was not barred from seeking recovery for injuries discovered subsequent to conversation, as he did not intend nor believe conversation would prohibit him from recovering for future discovered injuries. Since there was no meeting of the minds, the release, like any other contract, was invalid.)

§ 18.3 Unilateral Mistake of Fact

13. Indiana Bell Telephone Co., Inc. v. Mygrant, ___ Ind.App. ___, 441 N.E.2d 48_ (1982). (Plaintiff was injured in an automobile accident allegedly caused by defendant's employee. Plaintiff was apparently uninjured, and executed a release relinquishing all claims for $600 for the loss of the car. Approximately three months afterward, plaintiff learned he had in fact sustained injury. After defendant refused his new claim, plaintiff filed suit. Appellate court holds that plaintiff was bound by release, despite his knowledge that he had unknown injuries at the time release was executed. "(I)gnorance of the extent of the releasor's injuries may be said to never constitute a mistake on the part of the releasee which is relevant and material to the terms of the contract.")

§ 18.4 Ignorance of Releasor

Page 574

However, the release must be legible.[18.10]

18.10 Wells v. Peery, 656 S.W.2d 275 (Mo.App.1983) (Illegible rubber stamp release on back of check did not preclude subsequent suit.)

23. Lewis v. Wall, 640 S.W.2d 540 (Mo. App.1982). (Plaintiff injured in rear-end accident caused by defendant. Plaintiff could not read or write, and had not finished first grade. Insurance adjuster had her sign release for $251.05, allegedly explaining that it only covered the damage to her automobile when in fact it served as a general release. Trial court set aside release on grounds it was obtained through fraud: "(Plaintiff's) testimony . . . provided all of the elements of actionable fraud including her right to rely on the adjuster's misrepresentations since the adjuster, as the trial court concluded, obtained the confidence of (plaintiff) by artifice, and anesthetized her sense of caution, thereby overcoming her subjective belief as to whether she should make an independent investigation of the facts.")

§ 18.5 Mistake of Law

26. Wilson v. New York City Transit Authority, 454 N.Y.S.2d 962 (N.Y.Civil Ct. 1982). (Written agreement between parties is binding, and plaintiff cannot use a subse-

quent change in law to set aside a written agreement evidenced by an executed release.)

§ 18.11 Effect of Release—Joint Tortfeasors

Page 581

... release was adequate for all of plaintiff's injuries.[63.5]

The remaining tortfeasors may plead the release as a bar to the amount paid by the released tortfeasor, or may place it in evidence showing payment for the injury up to the amount shown in the release.[63.10] A party which is only vicariously liable for the injuries may seek indemnification from the active tortfeasor, even though the active tortfeasor has obtained a release from the plaintiff.[63.15]

63. Collins v. United States, 708 F.2d 499 (10th Cir. 1983) (Factual issue existed as to whether parties intended release, which only specifically named private hospital, to also release United States from liability based upon alleged negligence of public hospital and staff.); Marchman & Sons, Inc. v. Nelson, 251 Ga. 475, 306 S.E.2d 290 (1983) (Release in full settlement of damages in favor of one joint tortfeasor releases all joint tortfeasors.); Porter v. Ford Motor Co., 96 Ill.2d 190, 70 Ill.Dec. 480, 449 N.E.2d 827 (1983) (Unconditional release of tortfeasor, his insurer, and any person, firm or corporation liable in his stead, from all damages arising out of fatal automobile accident barred subsequent breach of warranty action against automobile manufacturer arising out of same accident.); Gagnon v. Lakes Region General Hospital, ___ N.H. ___, 465 A.2d 1221 (1983) (General release executed by victim in favor of automobile driver did not preclude victim's action against physicians and hospital for negligent treatment of injury.)

63.5 Opposite conclusions have been reached where the release purported to release "all other persons" from liability. *Compare* Beck v. Cianchetti, 1 Ohio St.3d 231, 439 N.E.2d 417 (1982). (Release did not bar plaintiff from suing others even though agreement purported to release "all other persons," as statutory phrase required a release to expressly designate by name or otherwise specifically identify any tortfeasor to be discharged.); *with* White v. General Motors Corp., 541 F.Supp. 190 (D.C.Md.1982). (Agreement signed releasing driver of vehicle which allegedly caused plaintiff's injuries barred suit against automobile manufacturer, where agreement released "any and all other persons, associations and corporations, whether herein named or referred to or not ....")

63.10 Bucyrus-Erie Co. v. Von Haden, 416 So.2d 699 (Ala.1982).

63.15 Rebhan Leasing Corp. v. Trias, 419 So.2d 352 (Fla.App.1982), petition for review denied 427 So.2d 738 (1983). (Original plaintiff injured when tire blew on van in which she was riding. She settled with active tortfeasor, then obtained judgment against other defendants based on its vicarious liability pursuant to Florida's dangerous instrumentality doctrine. Other defendants then brought suit against active tortfeasor for indemnification. "The law is well-settled that one who is only vicariously liable is entitled to indemnification from the active tortfeasors. The fact that the active tortfeasors settled with the plaintiff does not release them from the claim for indemnification by the party held vicariously liable.") (Citations omitted.)

§ 18.12 Distinguished From Covenant Not to Sue

66. Number One Beverage, Inc. v. Miller Brewing Co., ___ Ind.App. ___, 437 N.E.2d 508 (1982). (Intention of parties determines whether an agreement is a release or a covenant not to sue. Here, court found that mutual covenant not-to-sue agreement signed by plaintiff and one defendant did

not constitute a "release" of that defendant, thereby releasing other defendant, as there was no language in instrument showing an intention to "release" one party and reserve claim against the other.)

PART IV

TORT LIABILITY AND DEFENSES—SPECIFIC ACTIONS

CHAPTER 19

FEDERAL TORT CLAIMS ACT

§ 19.3 Limitations

16. Lotrionte v. United States, 560 F.Supp. 41 (D.C.N.Y.1983). (Action for wrongful death of veteran who died in Veterans Administration hospital barred where plaintiff failed to present written claim to V.A. hospital within two years after claim accrued.)

Jackson v. United States, 558 F.Supp. 14 (D.C.D.C.1983). (Widow of federal inmate was barred from bringing suit where she failed to file administrative claim; widow could not rely on the inmate's parents having filed administrative claim.)

Gonzales v. United States Postal Service, 543 F.Supp. 838 (N.D.Calif.1982). (Plaintiff's suit under F.T.C.A. barred where at time of filing administrative claim, she indicated the amount of damages was unknown at the time, and did not submit additional information or update her claim, once the amount of damages was ascertained, within the two-year statutory limit.)

Elements of Administrative Claim

Rogers v. United States, 568 F.Supp. 894 (E.D.N.Y.1983) (District court was divested of jurisdiction where administrative notice of claim failed to contain demand for sum certain in damages or any basis for assessing value of claim within reasonable degree.); accord, Robinson v. United States, 563 F.Supp. 312 (W.D.Pa.1983).

Avery v. United States, 680 F.2d 608 (9th Cir. 1982). (Ninth Circuit Court of Appeals rules that "minimal notice" is all that is required, and that administrative claim requirement is satisfied when the agency is provided with notice of the manner and general circumstances of the injury, and a sum certain representing damages. "Section 2675(A) was not intended to allow an agency to insist on proof of a claim to its satisfaction before the claimant becomes entitled to a day in court. To so hold would permit federal defendants to be judge in their own cause by the initial determination of a claim's sufficiency")

Van Lieu v. United States, 542 F.Supp. 862 (N.D.N.Y.1982). (Filing of administrative claim is not required where plaintiff has no way of knowing that defendant was a government employee, and government fails to communicate the government-employee status of such person. Plaintiff had brought suit against the individual defendant in state court. The government did not petition for removal of the case to federal court until the limitations period for filing an administrative claim had expired. Court held government was estopped from attempting to dismiss the action based on the plaintiff's failure to comply with the administrative claim requirement.)

§ 19.5 Armed Forces Personnel

36. Gaspard v. United States, 713 F.2d 1097 (5th Cir. 1983) (Feres doctrine barred suit by former members of armed services who alleged physical injuries resulting from radiation exposure which occurred when they took part in atmospheric weapons tests on active duty.); Hopkins v. United States, 567 F.Supp. 491 (E.D.N.Y.1983) (Parents could not bring F.T.C.A. action for death of their son who committed suicide while in

§ 19.5 SPECIFIC ACTIONS

Army; complaint alleged that son was negligently treated and released from hospital following diagnosis of paranoid schizophrenia. Fact that army authorized serviceman to return home pending final disposition of his medical status did not overcome government's immunity.)

Cusanelli v. Klaver, 698 F.2d 82 (2d Cir. 1983). (Active duty Coast Guardsman injured during attempt to float grounded vessel while on return voyage to home port could not bring negligence suit against United States.); Williamson v. Sartain, 555 F.Supp. 487 (D.C.Mont.1983). (Heirs could not bring suit against the United States under F.T.C.A. for death of volunteer member of Civil Air Patrol while engaged in U.S. Air Force authorized mission.)

Bloss v. United States, 545 F.Supp. 102 (N.D.N.Y.1982). (National guardsman who was not an employee of the United States could not bring suit under F.T.C.A. for injuries occasioned when military jeep he was driving overturned.)

Wilful Misconduct

Laswell v. Brown, 683 F.2d 261 (8th Cir. 1981), certiorari denied ___ U.S. ___, 103 S.Ct. 1205, 75 L.Ed.2d 446 (1983). (Suit brought by heirs of decedent who, while member of the U.S. Army stationed in the South Pacific in 1947–48, was exposed to three atomic tests in the Eniwetok Atolls in the Marshall Islands. Court dismissed the complaint on the grounds *Feres* was not restricted to cases of simple negligence, but also applied where the allegations constituted a more willful act.)

Off-Duty Servicemen

Johnson v. United States, 704 F.2d 1431 (9th Cir. 1983). (*Feres* doctrine did not apply to serviceman who was injured following after hours party at NCO club. Serviceman had been off duty for the day, and was working at private job as a bartender at the club.)

37. Hinkie v. United States, 715 F.2d 96 (3d Cir. 1983) (Feres doctrine barred suits by serviceman's widow and children that miscarriages and birth defects were caused by serviceman's exposure to radiation during active duty.); Mondelli v. United States, 711 F.2d 567 (3d Cir. 1983) (Feres doctrine barred suit by cancer victim under F.T.C.A. for injuries caused her by exposure of her father to radiation while on active duty in United States Army.)

§ 19.7 Exclusions

Page 592

... the Panama Canal Company, and operations of the federal treasury.[58.5]

48. George v. United States, 703 F.2d 90 (4th Cir. 1983). (Discretionary function exception barred suit alleging that Federal Aviation Administration's failure to prohibit use in aircraft of fuel pickup composed of coterminous dissimilar metals caused air crash.)

Amato v. United States, 549 F.Supp. 863 (D.C.N.J.1982). (Plaintiff, engaged in armed robbery of bank when he was shot by F.B.I. agents, brought suit under F.T.C.A., alleging in part that F.B.I. should have arrested him earlier, before attempt was made to hold up bank, as they had knowledge of robbery plan. Court held that planning decisions involved came under the discretionary exception, as they involved issues of law enforcement policy. Court also held that no duty exists which runs to the criminal in such a situation.)

58. Wine v. United States, 705 F.2d 366 (10th Cir. 1983). (Plaintiff who was sexually assaulted and shot by off-duty air force sergeant could not bring suit under F.T.C.A., such actions being barred by exception covering assault and battery.)

58.5 Misrepresentation

In Sheridan v. United States, 542 F.Supp. 1243 (E.D.N.Y.1982). (Parents of serviceman who died in Vietnam brought suit alleging that defendant United States negligently failed to timely and correctly inform them that their son's death resulted from his prescribed use of the sulfa drug Dapsone. The court ruled that plaintiffs' complaint alleged an action for negligent misrepresentation, and as such was barred by 28 U.S.C.A § 2680(h).)

§ 19.14 Within Scope of Office or Employment

86. Bates v. United States, 701 F.2d 737 (8th Cir. 1983). (United States not liable for acts of military policemen who stopped automobile, killed male occupants, assaulted, raped, and shot the women in the vehicle, as the acts did not arise out of and in the scope of the military policemen's assignment to the Game Warden section.)

Robbins v. United States, 722 F.2d 387 (8th Cir. 1983). (Where government reserved right to control air force major's movement in driving his car between air force bases, major was acting within scope of his employment at time he allegedly negligently caused automobile collision.)

CHAPTER 20

SUING THE INSURER

§ 20.2 Standards for Recovery

20. James v. Aetna Life & Casualty Co., 109 Wis.2d 363, 326 N.W.2d 114 (App.1982). ("To establish the tort of bad faith an objective standard must be met. This standard is met by showing the absence of a reasonable basis for denying the claim, i.e., would a reasonable insurer under the circumstances have denied or delayed payment of the claim under the facts and circumstances.") (Footnote omitted.)

§ 20.6 Punitive Damages

45. Timmons v. Royal Globe Insurance Co., 653 P.2d 907 (Okl.1982). (Action by insured against insurance company for breach of duty to deal fairly and in good faith in dispute arising from airplane crash, wherein insured was piloting the craft. Jury award of approximately $9,000 actual damages, $25,000 in damages for mental pain and suffering, and $3,000,000 in punitive damages affirmed against insurance company, on condition that plaintiff accept remittitur of $1,500,000 of the punitives award.)

CHAPTER 22

WRONGFUL DEATH

Table of New or Retitled Sections

Sec.
22.5 Effect of Spouse's Remarriage.

---

§ 22.3 Application—Proximate Cause, Defenses, Conflicts

The plaintiff in a wrongful death proceeding is not held to as high degree of proof as a plaintiff in a personal injury action. Additionally, a wrongful death plaintiff is entitled to every favorable inference which can reasonably be drawn from the evidence in determining whether a prima facie case has been made.[55.5]

28. Grbac v. Reading Fair Co., 688 F.2d 215 (3d Cir. 1982). (Wrongful death action is purely derivative. If statute of limitations in the personal injury action had run prior to decedent's death, there could be no recovery under wrongful death act.)

39. Gramlich v. Travelers Insurance Co., 640 S.W.2d 180 (Mo.App.1982) ("[S]tatutory beneficiary may not recover in those cases where a deceased never had a cause of action against the defendant or where there was a substantial defense which could be invoked, such as contributory negligence.")

55.5 Locker v. Ford Motor Co., 91 A.D.2d 510, 456 N.Y.S.2d 379 (1982).

§ 22.4 Beneficiaries—Damages

Page 628

... illegitimate child.[64]

It is not necessary for all beneficiaries to join in the wrongful death action. For example, in one case, the two children were entitled to full value for the decedent's life, notwithstanding the fact that the surviving spouse was not a plaintiff in the suit.[64.5]

64. Edenfield v. Jackson, 251 Ga. 491, 306 S.E.2d 911 (1983) (Supreme Court of Georgia interprets wrongful death statute as including both legitimate and illegitimate children, and as so interpreted, statute does not unconstitutionally discriminate against illegitimate children solely on the basis of their illegitimacy.)

64.5 Adams v. Wright, 162 Ga.App. 550, 293 S.E.2d 446 (1982). (Court rejecting defendant's argument that the children were entitled to sue only for two-thirds, with the absent husband-father being entitled to the remaining one-third.)

65. Bellamy v. Sadler, 640 S.W.2d 20 (Tenn.App.1982). ("In an action for damages due to wrongful death the pecuniary value of the decedent's life is to be determined by evidence of the decedent's expectancy of life, his age, condition of health and strength, capacity, if any, for labor and earning money through skill in any art, trade, profession, occupation or business and his personal habits as to sobriety and industry.")

66. Barnhill v. Public Service Co. of Colorado, 649 P.2d 716 (Colo.App.1982). ("(T)he loss compensated is what the surviv-

ing spouse would have reasonably expected to receive from the decedent had the decedent spouse survived, not the surviving spouse's financial situation after the decedent's death."); Wallace v. Couch, 642 S.W.2d 141 (Tenn.1982) (Probable living expenses should be deducted in determining the amount of damages based upon life expectancy and earning capacity in wrongful death actions.)

As to the damages recoverable by parents of a deceased child, see Dolata v. Ohio Edison Co., 2 Ohio App.3d 293, 441 N.E.2d 837 (1981). (Child killed in electrical accident. Jury awarded $52,600. Appellate court held this amount excessive, and reduced figure to $20,000. Court ruled it was erroneous for trial court to allow evidence as to child's probable future income, as there was no showing of a reasonable expectation that the present beneficiaries of the child's services (his parents) would continue to benefit from such services after the child's emancipation.)

68. Washam v. Hughes, 638 S.W.2d 646 (Tex.App.1982), error refused n.r.e. ("a surviving parent in a wrongful death suit has no recovery for damages for mental anguish, grief, bereavement, or loss of companionship occasioned him by the death of his child.")

69. Elliot v. Willis, 92 Ill.2d 530, 65 Ill. Dec. 852, 442 N.E.2d 163 (1982), on remand 113 Ill.App.3d 848, 69 Ill.Dec. 627, 447 N.E.2d 1062 (1983). ("The purpose of the Wrongful Death Act is to compensate the surviving spouse and next of kin for the pecuniary losses sustained due to the decedent's death. It is intended to provide the surviving spouse the benefits that would have been received from the continued life of the decedent. The jury should have been instructed that the value of the decedent's companionship and conjugal relations could be considered in computing the damages to be recovered." (Citations omitted.) Later, "One consideration in assessing the pecuniary value of the decedent's worth is the widow's loss of consortium.")

71. Wallace v. Couch, 642 S.W.2d 141 (Tenn.1982).

§ 22.5 Effect of Spouse's Remarriage

As it may take as many as five years for a case to come to trial, it is not infrequent that the survivor of the deceased spouse has remarried by such time. The question that arises then is whether the jury should be informed of this fact. The majority of decisions which have considered this issue have held that such information is inadmissible, as "(e)vidence of the surviving spouse's remarriage is irrelevant in that the damages in this type of action are calculated at the time of death, and remarriage is highly speculative as proof in mitigation of damages." [92] Other courts, however, have held that there is no error in admitting evidence that the plaintiff has remarried, as "to withhold the fact of remarriage of a surviving spouse in a wrongful death case would be inconsistent with the integrity which the judicial process should maintain." [93]

92. Swartwood v. Burlington Northern, Inc., 669 P.2d 1051 (Colo.App.1983); Wooten v. Amspacher, 279 S.C. 325, 307 S.E.2d 232 (1983) (Evidence that wife separated from husband and remarried following his death inadmissible in wrongful death action against physician.)
Barnhill v. Public Service Co. of Colorado, 649 P.2d 716, 719 (Colo.App.1982). *Accord*, Harbenski v. Upper Peninsula Power Co., 118 Mich.App. 440, 325 N.W.2d 785 (1982); Kimery v. Public Service Co., 562 P.2d 858 (Okl.1977). See Annotation, 88 A.L.R.3d 926.

93. Peters v. Henshaw, 640 S.W.2d 197 (Mo.App.1982).

CHAPTER 23

WRONGFUL BIRTH AND WRONGFUL LIFE

Table of New or Retitled Sections

Sec.
23.11 Statutes of Limitations.

§ 23.3 Wrongful Birth—Origin of Action—Normal Children

21. University of Arizona v. Superior Court, 136 Ariz. 579, 667 P.2d 1294 (1983) (Arizona Supreme Court ruled that in wrongful pregnancy action arising from negligent sterilization procedure, damages can be recovered for the cost of rearing and educating a normal healthy child. However, the trier of fact must also consider any offsetting pecuniary and non-pecuniary benefits which the parents will receive from the parental relationship with the child. Court held that trier of fact may consider parents reason for submitting to sterilization procedures. Court gives the following example: "[W]here the parent sought sterilization in order to avoid the danger of genetic defect, the jury could easily find that the uneventful birth of a healthy, non-defective child was a blessing rather than 'damage' ".)

34. Miller v. Duhart, 637 S.W.2d 183 (Mo.App.1982) (Brothers and sisters of baby born healthy and normal following allegedly negligent sterilization procedure could not recover damages for baby's wrongful birth. Siblings had alleged that baby's birth resulted in the loss of their mother's society, comfort, care, protection and financial support. "[N]o basis in law exists for an action by siblings for the birth of an additional child to their family. ... Although children may expect their mother's society, comfort, care, protection and financial support, they have no vested right to a particular share of it." Later: "It would be ludicrous to find that the defendants owed a duty to the appellant children to prevent the birth of their brother ... or that the breach of that duty resulted in the loss of their share of their mother's society, comfort, care, protection and financial support. No duty owed them has been breached. No fundamental right has been violated. There is no correlation between the alleged negligence or wrongful act of the defendant and the damages sought by [the baby's] siblings."); Holt, Wrongful Pregnancy, 33 South Carolina L.Rev. 759 (1982).

36. Beardsley v. Wierdsma, 650 P.2d 288 (Wyo.1982). (Authorizing parents' suit for wrongful birth of normal and healthy children born following unsuccessful tubal ligations, but restricting recovery to certain damages only. Court rules that once fault and causation are proved, parents may recover "expenses and damages for 1) recovery of any medical expenses associated with the unsuccessful ligation, such as surgical expense, hospital expense, physicians' fees, and expense of medication, 2) medical and hospital expenses for the birth of the unplanned child, 3) wages necessarily lost by the woman because of pregnancy and childbirth or because of an abortion, 4) pain and suffering of the mother in connection with pregnancy, and 5) cost of abortion, together with pain and suffering of the women who elected to have their pregnancies terminated.

"We reject any claim for damages of expenses after the birth of the child. We believe that these latter expenses and damages are too speculative; that the injury is too remote from the negligence; that the injury is out of proportion to the culpability of the tortfeasors; and that the allowance of recovery would place too unreasonable a burden on appellees, since it would likely open the way for fraudulent claims, and since it would enter a field that has no sensible or just stopping point.")

See also Cockrum v. Baumgartner, 95 Ill.2d 193, 69 Ill.Dec. 168, 447 N.E.2d 385 (1983), certiorari denied ___ U.S. ___, 104 S.Ct. 149, 78 L.Ed.2d 139. (Parents of chil-

§ 23.4 Wrongful Birth—Defective Children

Page 642

The Supreme Court of Washington recently ruled that parents of a defective child had a right to sue for the infant's wrongful death, where the parents were not notified of the potential birth defects associated with the use of Dilantin by the mother during pregnancy. Damages recoverable included "the medical, hospital and medication expenses attributable to the child's birth and to its defective condition, and in addition damages for the parents' emotional injury caused by the birth of the defective child." These damages were to be offset by emotional benefits attributable to the birth of the child.[45.5]

45. The Supreme Courts of Virginia and Washington both recently permitted parents of children born afflicted with Tay Sachs disease and mentally retarded, respectively, to recover for emotional distress in addition to other damages. Naccash v. Burger, 223 Va. 406, 290 S.E.2d 825 (1982). (Parents of child born afflicted with Tay Sachs disease could bring cause of action for wrongful birth against doctor and others for negligence in labelling father's blood sample. Parents were entitled to recover damages which were the reasonable and proximate consequences of the breach of the duty owed them, which included damages for expenses incurred in the care and treatment of their afflicted child, but did not include the cost connected with the child's funeral and grave markers since the disease which caused the child's death was not caused by the defendant's negligence, by by hereditary factors. Parents also entitled to recover damages for emotional distress suffered following birth of their fatally defective child.

Harbeson v. Parke-Davis, Inc., 98 Wn.2d 460, 656 P.2d 483 (1983). (Parents of child born mentally retarded due to mother's taking Dilantin on doctor's orders without being informed of risks, have cause of action for wrongful birth. As for damages, the court stated: "[W]e hold that recovery may include the medical, hospital, and medication expenses attributable to the child's birth and to its defective condition, and in addition damages for the parents' emotional injury caused by the birth of the defective child. In considering damages for emotional injury, the jury should be entitled to consider the countervailing emotional benefits attributable to the birth of the child.")

45.5 Harbeson v. Parke-Davis, Inc., 98 Wn.2d 460, 656 P.2d 483 (1983).

§ 23.6 "Wrongful life"—In General

Page 645

The Supreme Court of Washington recently recognized the right of a defectively born child to sue for wrongful life, stating: "It would be illogical and anomalous to permit only parents, and not the child, to recover for the cost of the child's own medical care."[53.5]

52. Nelson v. Krusen, 635 S.W.2d 582 (Tex.App.1982), error granted (1983), judgment affirmed ___ S.W.2d ___. (Holding that while Texas Supreme Court has authorized suit by parents of defectively born child to recover the expenses reasonably

necessary for the care and treatment of their child's physical impairment, a child does not have a right to bring its own action to recover expenses incident to the care and treatment of its physical impairment.)

Healthy Children

Foy v. Greenblott, 141 Cal.App.3d 1, 190 Cal.Rptr. 84 (1983). (Child could not pursue action for wrongful life where he did not allege that he was born "impaired." Child was born to a mentally incompetent mother.)

Miller v. Duhart, 637 S.W.2d 183 (Mo. App.1982). (Baby born due to defendant's alleged negligence in performing sterilization procedure could not bring action for wrongful life, as it was born healthy and normal, and not defective. "[A child] has no fundamental right not to be born, nor does he have a right to be born into a family where he was planned or wanted."); *Accord*, Beardsley v. Wierdsma, 650 P.2d 288 (Wyo.1982).

53.5 Harbeson v. Parke-Davis, Inc., 98 Wn.2d 460, 656 P.2d 483 (1983).

§ 23.8 "Wrongful life"—Child's Suit Against Laboratory for Negligent Testing

59. The California Supreme Court modified the holding in Curlender v. Bio-Science Laboratories to restrict compensable damages to extraordinary special damages. Turpin v. Sortini, 31 Cal.3d 220, 182 Cal. Rptr. 337, 643 P.2d 954 (1982). (In a wrongful birth action, child born in a defective condition may not recover general damages, special damages for the extraordinary expenses necessary to treat the defective condition are compensable.)

Harbeson v. Parke-Davis, Inc., 98 Wn.2d 460, 656 P.2d 483 (1983). (Child born mentally retarded has right to bring cause of action for wrongful life against negligent doctor. Although child may not recover general damages, child permitted to recover special damages for the extraordinary expenses for medical care and special training incurred as a result of its condition.) *Contra*, Strohmaier v. Associates in Obstetrics & Gynecology, 122 Mich.App. 116, 332 N.W.2d 432 (1982) (Child born defectively when defendant failed to advise its mother that she had contracted rubella during first trimester of pregnancy could not bring an action for wrongful life, disapproving of Turpin v. Sortini, 31 Cal.3d 220, 182 Cal. Rptr. 337, 643 P.2d 954 (1982)).

Law Reviews

Rogers, Wrongful Life and Wrongful Birth: Medical Malpractice in Genetic Counseling and Prenatal Testing, 33 South Carolina L.Rev. 713 (1982); Note, a Cause of Action for "Wrongful Life" in California: Breech Birth or Abortion?, 12 Golden Gate Univ.L.Rev. 423 (1982); Comment, On Determining Liability for "Wrongful Life": Curlender v. Bio-Science Laboratories—A Step in the Right Direction?, 17 New England L.Rev. 213 (1981).

§ 23.11 Statutes of Limitations

Wrongful birth and wrongful life cases present special considerations of the statute of limitations.[77] Many times, the injury does not manifest itself until several years after the negligent act or omission. For example, if a negligent sterilization procedure is performed, but a child is not conceived until a few years later, does the statute begin running at the time of the child's birth or conception, or at the time of the negligent act or omission? The cases which have answered this question seem to agree that the statute begins running on the date of the negligent act or omission, rather than upon the child's birth. Additionally, if the particular state has enacted a special medical malpractice statute of limitations, its provisions will govern the action.

77. See Brubaker v. Cavanaugh, 542 F.Supp. 944 (D.C.Kan.1982). (Provisions of Kansas medical malpractice act relating to statute of limitations operated to bar father and husband's claims for wrongful death and wrongful birth, and child's cause of action for wrongful life. Defendant doctor allegedly negligently failed to diagnose plaintiff's wife's father as having a hereditary disease from which he died. Plaintiff also alleged that the defendant negligently failed to diagnose and treat his wife for the same disease, and failed to inform her that her father had died of the same disease. Plaintiff's son was diagnosed as having the disease. Plaintiff's wife's father died in 1959. Plaintiff's wife died in 1981, but her last treatment by defendant occurred in 1968. Plaintiff's son was born in 1971, and was diagnosed as having the disease in 1980. The Kansas statute provided that an action against a health care provider arising out of the rendering of or failure to render professional services must be brought within two years. The statute also provided that if the fact of injury was not reasonably ascertainable until some time after the initial act, then the period of limitation did not commence until the fact of injury became reasonably ascertainable, but in no event could the action be commenced more than four years beyond the time of the negligent act or omission. Since the last time plaintiff's wife was treated by the defendant, her cause of action would have had to have been filed no later than 1972. As for the child's claim, the statute provided that no action on behalf of a person under a legal disability could be brought more than eight years beyond the time of the act giving rise to the cause of action. Accordingly, the court held that the child's suit should have been commenced no later than 1976, some four years before the instant action was brought. Under the court's reasoning, if the child had not been born until 1977, his cause of action would have been time barred, notwithstanding the fact that it would have been medically and scientifically impossible to determine any injury, since the child would not have existed before the statute of limitations expired. Such a result is illogical and unjust.)

Miller v. Duhart, 637 S.W.2d 183 (Mo. App.1982). (Several months short of four years after having undergone a bilateral tubal ligation, plaintiff gave birth to a healthy baby, her fifth child. The court held that in actions for wrongful birth, the medical malpractice statute of limitations applied, not the general tort statute, and therefore the claim was time barred.)

Nelson v. Krusen, 635 S.W.2d 582 (Tex. App.1982), error granted (1983), judgment affirmed ___ S.W.2d ___. (Misdiagnosis of neuromuscular disease in fetus).

CHAPTER 24

PRENATAL INJURIES

§ 24.3 Wrongful Death Resulting from Prenatal Injuries

29. O'Grady v. Brown, 654 S.W.2d 904 (Mo.1983) (Action permitted for wrongful death of viable fetus.)

CHAPTER 25

LOSS OF CONSORTIUM

§ 25.3 Development of Right

20. Mouton v. Armco, Inc., 417 So.2d 889 (La.App.1982), writ denied 421 So.2d 903.

22. The spouse of an injured railroad employee may not sue for loss of consortium under the Federal Employers Liability Act. Kelsaw v. Union Pacific Railroad Co., 686 F.2d 819 (9th Cir. 1982), certiorari denied ___ U.S. ___, 103 S.Ct. 1197, 75 L.Ed.2d 440 (1983).

§ 25.5 Procedural Aspects—Derivative v. Non-derivative

Page 671

... However, an independent consortium claim may be brought when the injured spouse dies during the pendency of the action, or chooses not to, bring any action against the tortfeasor.[39.5]

34. Not all states require that the loss of consortium be joined with the injured spouse's main cause of action, even if consortium is considered derivative. Allstate Insurance Co. v. Collier, 428 So.2d 379 (Fla App.1983). (Loss of consortium, though derivative, may be maintained as separate cause of action.); Board of Commissioners of Cass County v. Nevitt, ___ Ind.App. ___, 448 N.E.2d 333 (1983). (Even though it is a derivative action, husband's inability to recover for his injuries does not preclude his wife's claim for loss of consortium.)

35. White Construction Co. v. Dupont, 430 So.2d 915 (Fla.App.1983). ("An action for loss of consortium is, of course, a derivative action and the jury must first find that the husband has sustained compensable injuries at the hands of another before the wife's action may be considered.")

36. Triloi v. Town of Sudbury, 15 Mass. App.Ct. 394, 446 N.E.2d 92 (1983). (Statute giving cause of action to plaintiff against municipality for defects in a public way was limited in application to injured plaintiff; neither wife nor minor child could recover for loss of consortium.)

39.5 Yamamoto v. Premier Insurance Co., ___ Hawaii App. ___, 668 P.2d 42 (1983).

§ 25.6 Requirement of Marriage

A California appellate court recently ruled that marriage is not required to recover for loss of consortium, and that such an action can be brought by a cohabitant upon proof of a "stable and significant" relationship. *Butcher v. Superior Court* [51.5] involved a man and woman who had been living together for 11½ years prior to the injury-causing accident. The couple maintained joint savings and checking accounts, had two children, referred to each other as husband and wife. The wife testified that she believed they had a valid common law marriage. The court held that in today's society, it was reasonably foreseeable that an injured person may be cohabiting without marriage, as the incidence of such relationships in the United States had increased by 800 percent between 1960 and 1970.

In addition to being foreseeable, the court stated that the harm to the "de facto spouse, like the injury to a legally married spouse, is real, direct, and foreseeable. We believe that, in the conditions of modern society, the possibility that an adult may be cohabiting with another is neither unexpected nor remote; in short, it is reasonably foreseeable." The standard imposed by the court to permit recovery where the couple are not legally married is based upon whether the relationship is "both stable and significant." Factors to be used in making this determination are the duration of the relationship; whether the couple have a mutual contract; the degree of economic cooperation and entanglement; exclusivity of sexual relations; and whether there is a "family" relationship with children.

45. Weaver v. G.D. Searle & Co., 558 F.Supp. 720 (1983). (In a case involving a woman who underwent a hysterectomy necessitated by infection allegedly caused by an IUD, her husband could not recover for loss of consortium where, although they were living together at the time of the accident, they were not married until after it occurred. Court concluded that a valid marriage at the time of injury is a necessary and indispensable element of loss of consortium in Alabama.

Lieding v. Commercial Diving Center, 143 Cal.App.3d 72, 191 Cal.Rptr. 559 (1982). (No cause of action exists where couple engaged to marry before accident, and does in fact marry after accident.)

51.5 139 Cal.App.3d 58, 188 Cal.Rptr. 503 (1983).

§ 25.7 Parents' Action for Loss of Filial Consortium

54. Wilson v. Galt, 100 N.M. 227, 668 P.2d 1104 (App.1983), certiorari quashed 100 N.M. 192, 668 P.2d 308 (Parent has no cause of action for loss of filial consortium).

§ 25.8 Child's Action for Loss of Parental Consortium

59. Audubon-Exira v. Illinois Central Gulf Railroad Co., 335 N.W.2d 148 (Iowa 1983) (Child has no cause of action for loss of parental consortium independent of statute providing for recovery of the value of services and support; however, such damages are not limited to the period of minority.)

Norwest v. Presbyterian Intercommunity Hospital, 293 Or. 543, 652 P.2d 318 (1982). (No cause of action for child for loss of parental consortium where one causes nonfatal injuries to a parent, thereby depriving the child of that parent's society and companionship.)

60. Glicklich v. Spievack, 16 Mass. App.Ct. 488, 452 N.E.2d 287 (1983), review denied ___ Mass. ___, 454 N.E.2d 1276 (Child may maintain action for loss of parental society even though injured parent is not principal wage earner; child need only be living in injured parent's household, and be dependent upon parent for management of child's needs and for emotional guidance and support.)

CHAPTER 26

TORT LIABILITY AND THE FAMILIAL RELATIONSHIP

§ 26.2 Husband-Wife Immunities

8. Davis v. Davis, 657 S.W.2d 753 (Tenn. 1983) (Interspousal tort immunity completely abolished.); Boblitz v. Boblitz, 296 Md. 242, 462 A.2d 506 (1983) (Interspousal tort immunity abrogated as to cases sounding in negligence; thorough discussion and comprehensive citations.)

9. Stone v. Valley Forge Insurance Co., 436 So.2d 1069 (Fla.App.1983); Luna v. Clayton, 655 S.W.2d 893 (Tenn.1983) (Both cases holding that a wrongful death action may be maintained against a spouse when the action is predicated upon an intentional tort to the other spouse during the marriage, which results in the termination of the marriage by death.)

14. Williams v. Williams, 108 Ill.App.3d 936, 64 Ill.Dec. 390, 439 N.E.2d 1055 (1982), judgment modified 98 Ill.2d 128, 74 Ill.Dec. 495, 455 N.E.2d 1388. (Wife injured in automobile accident brought negligence suit against husband. Court held that under the Rights of Married Women Act (Ill.Rev.Stat. 1979, ch. 40, ¶ 1001 et seq.) no personal injury action could be maintained between spouses for torts committed during marriage. "Various reasons sound from different quarters for discarding the notion of interspousal immunity. The common law notion of the marital unity of husband and wife is a concept at odds with our present statutory view of marriage, which, judicially interpreted, incorporates a partnership theory of marriage. On the other hand, a persuasive argument can be advanced that the concept of interspousal immunity prevents collusive litigation between spouses to bilk insurance companies. The debate continues. In our statute, it is not our job to evaluate the merits or shortcomings of these competing arguments. The fact remains that interspousal immunity is a constitutional enactment of our State's public policy.") (Citations omitted).

§ 26.3 Parent-Child Immunities

27. Buffalo v. Buffalo, ___ Ind.App. ___, 441 N.E.2d 711 (1982). (Doctrine of parent-child immunity does not preclude a suit for negligent injury by an *unemancipated* minor against a non-custodial parent where the marriage of the child's parents was dissolved prior to the child's injury. Child was injured while visiting father pursuant to reasonable visitation rights, when father's dog attacked and bit child.)

§ 26.4 Family Law—Vicarious Liability

36. Family purpose doctrine. Beardon v. Derry, 645 S.W.2d 356 (Ky.App.1983). (Father not liable for injuries caused by minor son's operation of automobile even though title to vehicle was in father's name, where minor's mother was owner of vehicle and had been owner since their divorce.

Paprocki v. Stopak, 213 Neb. 523, 330 N.W.2d 475 (1983). (While the negligence of the driver of a family-purpose vehicle is ordinarily imputed to the parent owner in actions by a third party, the negligence of the family-purpose driver is not ordinarily imputed to the family-purpose owner in an action by the owner against a third party for the owner's own injuries or property damage.)

CHAPTER 27

CHARITABLE AND SOVEREIGN IMMUNITIES

Table of New or Retitled Sections

Sec.
27.6 Government Liability for Negligent Highway Design and Maintenance.

§ 27.2 Immunity of National and State Governments

13. Hall v. Roberts, 548 F.Supp. 498 (W.D.Va.1982). (Under Virginia law, a hospital which is an organ of the State is immune, under the doctrine of sovereign immunity, from actions sounding in tort.)

15. Pruett v. City of Rosedale, 421 So.2d 1046 (Miss.1982). (Supreme Court of Mississippi abolished doctrine of sovereign immunity, except as to legislative, judicial and executive acts by individuals acting in their official capacity, or to similar situations of individuals acting in similar capacities in local governments, either county or municipal. "The immunity we abolish in this opinion is the immunity of the 'sovereign,' which broadly speaking is the state, the county, the municipality or any other local subdivision of the sovereign.")

Haverlack v. Portage Homes, Inc., 2 Ohio St.3d 26, 442 N.E.2d 749 (1982). (Supreme Court of Ohio abolishes doctrine of sovereign immunity: "Because Ohio's sovereign immunity for municipalities was judicially created, it can be judicially abolished. When we considered sovereign immunity last year, we noted that only six other states adhered to the traditional common law immunity doctrines. Stare decisis alone is not a sufficient reason to retain the doctrine which serves no purpose and produces such harsh results. Therefore, we join with the other states in abrogating the doctrine.") (Citations omitted.) See also Enghauser Manufacturing Co. v. Eriksson Engineering, 6 Ohio St.3d 31, 451 N.E.2d 228 (1983).

16. Bartley v. Special School District of St. Louis Co., 649 S.W.2d 864 (Mo.1983). (Maintenance of liability insurance by school did not waive its sovereign immunity from suit for damages resulting from its alleged negligence in permitting student of violent propensities to ride school bus.)

King v. Williams, 5 Ohio St.3d 137, 449 N.E.2d 452 (1983). (Neither driver of city-owned ambulance nor city itself was liable to plaintiff for injuries sustained in automobile accident with ambulance while on emergency run.)

(Neither driver of city-owned ambulance nor city itself was liable to plaintiff for injuries sustained in automobile accident with ambulance while on emergency run.)

18. Laird v. Chrysler Corp., ___ R.I. ___, 460 A.2d 425 (1983). (Rhode Island statute waiving sovereign immunity from tort actions in state courts also waives that state's Eleventh Amendment immunity from suit in federal court.)

§ 27.3 Immunity of Municipalities

21. **Public Hospital**

Salcedo v. Diaz, 647 S.W.2d 51 (Tex.App. 1983), writ granted 650 S.W.2d 67, judgment reversed in part 659 S.W.2d 30. (Whether emergency room physician of government hospital was performing a quasi-judicial function or only a ministerial function was a question to be decided based upon the proof in the case in medical malpractice action.)

Police Protection

Failure to Respond—DeLong v. Erie County, 89 A.D.2d 376, 455 N.Y.S.2d 887 (1982), dismissal denied 58 N.Y.2d 860, 460 N.Y.S.2d 526, 447 N.E.2d 74 (1983), order affirmed 60 N.Y.2d 296, 469 N.Y.S.2d 611, 457 N.E.2d 717. (Plaintiff's decedent dialed the emergency telephone number 911 to inform police that a burglar was trying to break into her house. She asked the police to come right away to "319 Victoria." The complaint writer erroneously wrote the address down as "219 Victoria," and further erroneously noted it as being Victoria Avenue in the city of Buffalo, instead of Victoria Boulevard in the Village of Kenmore. Police officers dispatched to 219 Victoria Avenue in Buffalo found there was no such address, and were subsequently called off. Approximately eight minutes later, the decedent ran naked into the street, screaming, and collapsed. She had sustained numerous knife wounds, including one that had severed the jugular vein and carotid artery on the left. She died several minutes later. A medical examiner's report stated that the wounds were inflicted about four minutes after the woman had dialed the emergency number. The police station in the Village of Kenmore was approximately 1375 feet from the woman's house, and police could have been to her door within one minute of being notified of the call. Additionally, the officer would have used his siren during the approach to scare the burglar away. The court held that the county had assumed an obligation to the decedent by "holding out of the 911 number as one to be called by someone in need of assistance, [decedent's] placing of the call in reliance on that holding out, and her further reliance on the response to her plea for immediate help: 'Okay, right away.' This is not a mere failure to furnish police protection owed to the public generally but a case where the municipality has assumed a duty to a particular person which it must perform 'in a nonnegligent manner, [although without the] voluntary assumption of that duty, none would have otherwise existed' ...".)

Jails—Norton v. Brazos County, 640 S.W.2d 690 (Tex.App.1982). (Prisoner assigned to kitchen brought suit after he injured his hand in a bacon slicing machine. Suit alleged failure of defendant county to secure the machine properly, to provide a safety guard, and to maintain the machine. Suit was brought under the Texas Tort Claims Act. Defendant argued that it was immune under the Act since the claim was based on the method of providing police protection. The court rejected this argument, and held that the operation of a jail kitchen was only incidental to and not an integral part of police protection and criminal rehabilitation.)

Intentional Acts–Graves v. Wayne Co., 124 Mich.App. 36, 333 N.W.2d 740 (1983). (Plaintiff who alleged that off-duty deputy sheriff intentionally shot him in back during fight stated cause of action. While "the management, operation, and control of a police department is a governmental function," the "commission of an intentional tort is not in the exercise or discharge of a governmental function.")

Fire Protection

Lewis v. Mendocino Fire Protection District, 142 Cal.App.3d 345, 190 Cal.Rptr. 883 (1983). (Plaintiff could bring suit against fire protection district for injuries suffered due to firemen's negligence in attempting to rescue him when he was trapped beneath a tree which had fallen on his tent. Statute providing immunity to fire protection district was not applicable, as the injuries occurred during a nonfire-fighting incident.)

22. Driving Automobile

Kruger v. Wilson, 325 N.W.2d 851 (S.D. 1982). (Suit against state employee for injuries suffered from employee's negligence in operating automobile not barred by sovereign immunity, as the driving of an automobile is a ministerial function.)

Supplying Water

Ovist v. City of Hancock, 123 Mich.App. 276, 333 N.W.2d 250 (1983). (Maintenance of a public water line by city is a proprietary function, and city is not entitled to immunity from tort liability for injuries occurring in connection with the line.)

Byrd v. Brown, 641 S.W.2d 163 (Mo.App. 1982). (Plaintiff's store burned down when city employee attempted to thaw a frozen water pipe with a butane torch. Court rules that city was liable as any other private supplier of water for profit, as it was acting in a proprietary function.)

Failure to Warn

Miller v. Grants Pass Irrigation District, 62 Or.App. 747, 663 P.2d 30 (1983), on reconsideration 64 Or.App. 40, 667 P.2d 4, review allowed ___ Or. ___, 671 P.2d 1176. (Boat passengers who were injured when the boat on which they were riding was swept over dam brought action against irrigation district and state for maintenance of a nuisance based on negligent or reckless conduct. Court ruled that whether the decision to warn people using the river of the dam's presence was a decision which might or might not have been made in the exercise of governmental discretion, depending on the manner in which the particular decision was made. Further evidence was required. "The decision whether to warn people using the river of the dam's presence is not one that falls automatically within the discretionary exception based on the nature of the function. It is not self-evident that the decision requires the kind of policy choices the governmental immunity is designed to protect.")

City of St. Petersburg v. Collom, 419 So.2d 1082 (Fla.1982). ("[W]hen a governmental entity creates a known dangerous condition, which is not readily apparent to persons who could be injured by the condition, a duty at the operational-level arises to warn the public of, or protect the public from, the known danger. The failure to fulfill this operational-level duty is, therefore, a basis for an action against the governmental entity.")

§ 27.6 Government Liability for Negligent Highway Design and Maintenance

John J. McCarty, Esq., of Raynes, McCarty, Binder, Ross & Mundy, Philadelphia, Pennsylvania reports the case of *Terwilliger v. State of New York*,[68] a highway design and maintenance case tried to a judge of the New York Court of Claims, in which a verdict of $1,895,159.96 was rendered for the injured client. Also representing the plaintiff were *Roger N. Huggins*, Esq., of the same firm and *Donald J. Kemple*, Esq., of Hancock, Estabrook, Ryan, Shove & Hust, Syracuse, New York.

The accident occurred on September 7, 1978, while the plaintiff, a twenty-six-year-old employee of Tent Rental Company, was riding as a passenger in his employer's pick-up truck. The truck was heading south on a two-lane state road near Binghamton, New York. As the road crossed a New York county line, its character changed substantially. North of the county line, the road was a modern, well-constructed route with gentle curves and paved eight-foot shoulders. South of the county line, however, the shoulders became gravel and narrowed suddenly, the width being only two feet seven inches.

The truck driver's attention was diverted momentarily, resulting in the truck leaving the road on a curve and going into a drainage ditch that paralleled the highway. The truck struck a cement culvert headwall in the ditch located only four feet from the road's edge, and overturned, causing serious personal injuries to the plaintiff. At trial, both the driver and plaintiff's highway expert testified that the truck could have been brought to a safe stop but for the presence of the culvert. Other evidence showed that as originally constructed, the culvert headwall was six feet from the edge of the road. However, the road had been widened by two feet on each side, but neither the ditch nor the headwall was moved. The two-foot wide addition to each lane was not "deep base" construction and, as a result, a "crack and failure zone" developed where the original road edge was joined by the addition. This tended to destroy the superelevation of the curve.

Plaintiff proved at trial that in the three years prior to this incident, five other vehicles had left the roadway in this vicinity and hit the same culvert headwall, causing one fatality. It was demonstrated that the culvert served no useful purpose and that, in spite of the risks, the State of New York had a policy of not removing off-road hazards because their removal was not cost effective. The Court found that the culvert presented an extremely hazardous condition, and should have been removed.

Mr. McCarty and his associates maximized the use of demonstrative evidence to prove both liability and damages in the case. Numerous photographs and charts were used to show the sudden and dramatic change in the character of the road and shoulder. Ground level photographs were initially obtained through the State of New York pursuant to a program under which all state highways in New York were photographed and compiled. Due to the purpose for which they were taken, the photographs contained a great deal of self-authenticating information, including location and date of taking. Figures 27.6–1 and 27.6–2 are two of the photographs used to illustrate graphically the dramatic changes encountered by a driver as he crossed the county line. The pictures illustrate the sudden narrowing of the shoulder, the proximity of the ditch and culvert headwall to the road edge, and the presence of the "crack and failure" zone.

Aerial photographs were also employed to give an overview of the scene and show the relative location of the culvert to the road's edge. Figure 27.6–3 is a view looking north. The county line sign is visible in the right hand lane about ⅓ up from the bottom. Figure 27.6–4 shows the vicinity of the county line and the quick change in the shoulders of the road. To identify the culvert headwall, a white sheet was placed over it so it would show up clearly on the aerial photograph. A bright yellow blanket was also used to call attention to the width of the shoulder at the point of the culvert headwall.

Also instrumental to the liability portion of the case was a scaled engineering diagram containing specific and exact measurements of the accident scene, illustrating dimensions, shoulder composition, and the "crack and failure" zone which resulted from the widening procedure.

As the case was filed against the State of New York in its Court of Claims, discovery was significantly restricted. Specifically, plaintiff's attorneys did not have available the discovery tools of Interrogatories and Requests for Admissions. They were permitted to take depositions and present Requests for Production of Documents, but this could be done only upon order of the court.

These discovery limitations led to a unique aspect of the case involving the securing of documents under both Federal and State Freedom of Information Acts. Pursuant to the terms of the Acts, plaintiff's attorneys were able to obtain copies of reports on highway safety made by the State of New York pursuant to the Federal Highway Safety Acts of

1973. Under the terms of this statute, individual states were required to implement programs for the detection of hazardous highway locations and corrective measures for identified hazards. States were also required to submit annual reports to the Federal Highway Administration, which included information on these programs. States were required to include in this information a proposed schedule for the elimination of roadside obstacles and the method employed in establishing project priorities.

Figure 27.6-1. Photograph obtained from State of New York taken pursuant to highway program used to show difference in quality of road.

Figure 27.6-2. Closer view showing drainage ditch and culvert headwall.

Figure 27.6–3. Aerial view looking north shows better condition of road north of county line.

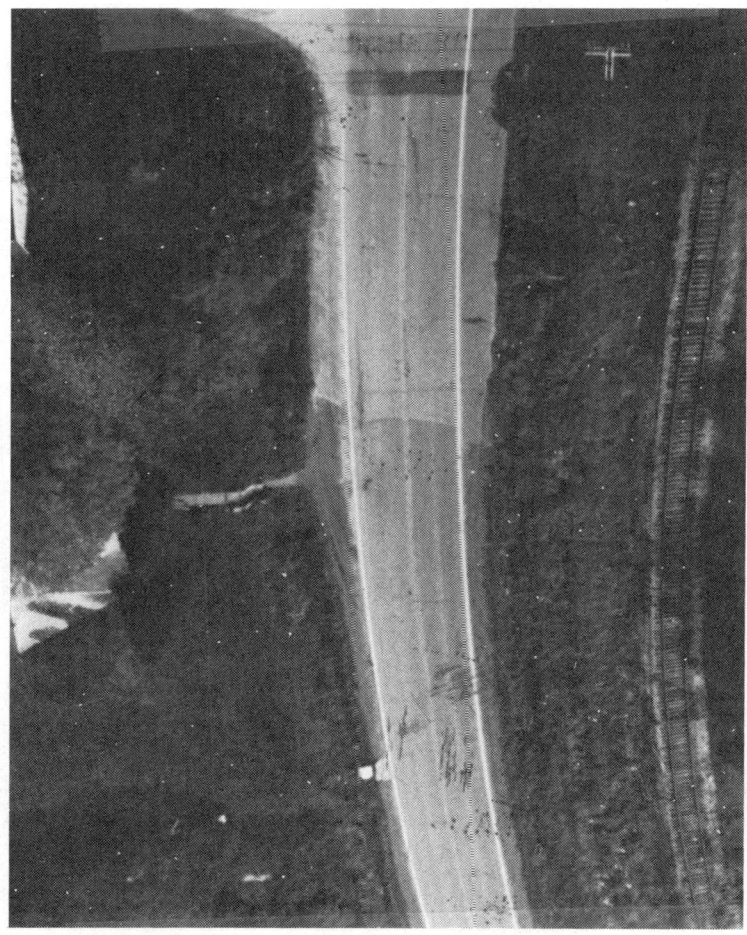

Figure 27.6–4. Differences in road and width of shoulder north and south of county line (approximately center of picture) are clearly evident. White sheet was placed over culvert headwall and yellow blanket on shoulder to demonstrate how close headwall was to edge of road.

With this knowledge and the Freedom of Information Acts, plaintiff's counsel were able to obtain the annual reports prepared by the State of New York. These revealed that the area in question had indeed appeared as a hazardous area prior to this accident, yet nothing had been done to eliminate the hazard because of its low priority. It was discovered that the State of New York had established its priority system through the use of a cost-benefit analysis, in which the cost of eliminating the hazard was measured against the benefits to be derived from its elimination in terms of claims avoided. In other words, the State of New York had a policy of permitting known hazards to exist if the State felt that it would be cheaper to contest or pay claims for injuries. This policy was brought out at trial.

In an attempt to limit the State's responsibility, the plaintiff's non-use of a seatbelt was raised as an affirmative defense. This was rejected by the trial court, as the State failed to prove initially that a seatbelt was available to plaintiff. Additionally, the State failed to establish that the injuries sustained were causally related to the non-use of the seatbelt.

Plaintiff's injuries included paraplegia from a fractured thoracic vertebrae, multiple facial fractures, ruptured spleen, and loss of sexual function as well as bowel and bladder control. The extent of the medical injuries was presented in part by videotape, and the plaintiff conducted physical demonstrations in court to show the extent of his limitations. The Court awarded medical expenses of $70,159.96, loss of earning capacity in the amount of $325,000.00, and $1,500,000.00 for pain, suffering and permanency, for a total award of $1,895,159.96.

68. Terwilliger v. State of New York, filed in the New York Court of Claims, No. 63050, verdict rendered by the Honorable James C. O'Shea on March 30, 1982.

CHAPTER 28

UNINSURED MOTORIST COVERAGE

§ 28.4 Uninsured Motorist Statutes

19. Insurance carrier providing uninsured motorist coverage may intervene as of right as party defendant in tort action between its insured and an uninsured motorist tortfeasor. Lima v. Chambers, 657 P.2d 279 (Utah 1982).

§ 28.6 No-Fault Insurance

33. Crawford v. Allstate Insurance Co., 305 Pa.Super. 167, 451 A.2d 474 (1982). (Plaintiff injured while walking on railroad tracks by pick-up truck adapted to operate on tracks as well as on highways. Supreme Court of Pennsylvania ruled that plaintiff was entitled to benefits under no-fault insurance coverage dealing with the "maintenance or use of a motor vehicle.")

CHAPTER 29

THE DRAMSHOP RULE

§ 29.1 Development of Common Law Liability

Page 712

... such as serving minors [5.5] or intoxicated persons.[5.10] ...

[5.5] Michnik-Zilberman v. Gordon's Liquor, Inc., 390 Mass. 6, 453 N.E.2d 430 (1983) (Sale of alcoholic beverages to minor is evidence of negligence, even though minor is not intoxicated at time of transaction.); Porter v. Ortiz, 100 N.M. 58, 665 P.2d 1149 (App.1983), certiorari quashed 100 N.M. 53, 665 P.2d 809 (Tavern keeper may be held liable for knowingly selling alcohol to minors, where such sale proximately causes accident in which minors are killed or injured); McClellan v. Tottenhoff, 666 P.2d 408 (Wyo.1983) (Allegations that, while in automobile, 17-year-old purchased alcoholic beverages at liquor store drive-in window, and seller made no effort to check his identification, stated cause of action against seller for damages sustained when minor was involved in automobile accident which resulted in death of third party.)

[5.10] Brannigan v. Raybuck, 136 Ariz. 513, 667 P.2d 213 (1983); Ontiveros v. Borak, 136 Ariz. 500, 667 P.2d 200 (1983) (Supreme Court of Arizona abolished common law doctrine of tavern owner non-liability. In *Brannigan*, the court stated: "We hold, therefore, that the common law doctrine of tavern owner nonliability is abolished in Arizona. Tavern owners and other licensed sellers in Arizona will be under a duty of care and may be held liable when they sell liquor to an intoxicated patron or customer under circumstances where the licensee or his employees know or should know that such conduct creates an unreasonable risk of harm to others who may be injured either on or off the premises. If the duty of care is breached, the seller will be liable for the damage caused by his negligence.") (Footnote omitted.); Hutchens v. Hankins, 63 N.C.App. 1, 303 S.E.2d 584 (1983), review denied 309 N.C. 191, 305 S.E.2d 734.

17. See Burke v. Superior Court, 129 Cal.App.3d 570, 181 Cal.Rptr. 149 (1982). (Although the California Legislature enacted a law reverting to the rule that the furnishing of liquor is not a basis for civil liability, that statute does not apply where a bartender or liquor store owner sells liquor to an obviously intoxicated *minor*, who injures a third person in an automobile accident.)

§ 29.2 Proof in a Dramshop Case

Richard D. Stanzione, Esq., Stanzione & Stanzione, Toms River, New Jersey, relates the case of *Dalton v. DeBenedictis et al.*,[25.5] wherein his exhaustive investigative efforts were instrumental in achieving a settlement with a present value of $235,000.00 for the wrongful death of a man allegedly served alcoholic beverages although he was intoxicated.

Suit was filed on behalf of the deceased's widow and three unemancipated children against DeBenedictis/dba Fox Chase Inn and 1000 Madison Avenue/dba Holiday Inn of Lakewood, accusing the taverns of serving alcohol to the deceased when in fact he was intoxicated. The theory of liability was that the taverns knew or should have known by his physical actions that the deceased was intoxicated while in the taverns, and by serving him alcohol, the taverns were negligent as well as in violation of the New Jersey Administrative Code, which prohibits one who holds a liquor license from serving an intoxicated person.

§ 29.2   SPECIFIC ACTIONS   Pt. 4

Mr. Stanzione, assisted by a private investigator, did the investigation personally and was able to locate witnesses to place the deceased in both establishments. The pattern of the deceased's actions that night was that he was sober at approximately 8:00 p.m. Mr. Stanzione was able to place the deceased in the Holiday Inn at about 10:00 p.m., having one or two drinks. This was done through a waitress who saw him there, although she did not make any observations of physical signs of intoxication.

Other witnesses placed the deceased in the Fox Chase Inn at 11:00 p.m., where he showed physical signs of slurred speech, stumbling while walking, and general dishevelment in his appearance. The deceased had four drinks at the Fox Chase Inn before leaving. At 12:30 a.m., the deceased was involved in a single-car accident. His car ran off the road into a tree, causing his death.

The autopsy revealed a blood alcohol content of .171 percent. By having an expert witness extrapolate backwards from the blood alcohol reading at the time of death, Mr. Stanzione was able to get expert testimony and reports that the deceased had shown obvious signs of intoxication in both taverns as a result of the alcoholic beverages. Mr. Stanzione thereupon argued that by being continually served the alcoholic drinks, he was rendered incapable of operating a motor vehicle.

The deceased was a self-employed insurance salesman who had recently started working for an insurance brokerage firm, and showed annual earnings from the last year of approximately $15,000.00. Prior to that time he had been an account executive for a firm in New York where he had been making more than $30,000.00 per year. The current earning made it difficult to establish a high economic loss.

A settlement with a present value of $235,000.00 was reached, with the terms as follows: $65,000.00 was paid to plaintiff immediately upon settlement; $20,000.00 cash was to be paid within two years; and an annuity was purchased which would provide the widow with annual payments of $15,000.00 for life, with a guaranteed payment of twenty years.

25.5 Dalton v. DeBenedictis/dba Fox Chase Inn et al., filed in Ocean County (New Jersey) Superior Court, Law Division, No. L–11617–80.

§ 29.3 Dramshop Acts—Construction and Elements

27. Morella v. Brown, 425 So.2d 123 (Fla.App.1983), petition for review denied 434 So.2d 886. (Vendor of intoxicants is not liable to third persons injured by intoxicated minor's operation of motor vehicle, even though vendor sold liquor to minor in violation of law.)

28. Tomlinson v. McCutcheon, 554 F.Supp. 186 (N.D.Ohio 1982). (Ohio dram shop statute forbidding sales of beer or intoxicating liquor to intoxicated person, imposes liability on tavern owner for injuries suffered by third person, if the injuries

were the proximate result of the serving of the alcohol.)

Carver v. Schafer, 647 S.W.2d 570 (Mo. App.1983). (Tavern owner owes duty of ordinary care to avoid supplying patron with intoxicating liquor once it becomes apparent that patron is intoxicated.)

Lopez v. Maez, 98 N.M. 625, 651 P.2d 1269 (1982). ("In light of the use of automobiles and the increasing frequency of accidents involving drunk drivers, ... the consequences of serving liquor to an intoxicated person whom the server knows or could have known is driving a car, is reasonably foreseeable.")

29. But see Wienke v. Champaign County Grain Association, 113 Ill.App.3d 1005, 69 Ill.Dec. 701, 447 N.E.2d 1388 (1983). (No cause of action at common law for damages received by one injured by an intoxicated driver against persons who, knowing the driver to be intoxicated and likely to drive recklessly, either furnish the driver with intoxicants or aid him in getting to his automobile, or both.)

§ 29.4 Who May Be Liable

46. Social Hosts

Kohler v. Wray, 114 Misc.2d 856, 452 N.Y.S.2d 831 (Sup.Ct.1982). (Dram Shop Act does not apply to social host in a noncommercial setting. Homeowners did not go outside protection of "social host" exception of Dram Shop Act when they asked guests to "chip in" for beer.)

Congini by Congini v. Portersville Valve Co., ___ Pa.Super. ___, 470 A.2d 515 (1983). (Social host held liable for injuries to minor to whom he furnished alcohol. Minor's contributory negligence could be asserted as defense. No liability for returning automobile keys to minor, as host had no right of control over car.)

48. Lucido v. Apollo Lanes & Bar, Inc., 123 Mich.App. 267, 333 N.W.2d 246 (1983). (Intoxicated person, even minor, has no cause of action against bar owner for injuries sustained due to unlawful sale of intoxicants, as he is not an "innocent person" entitled to recover under Dramshop Act.)

49. Rhyner v. Madden, 188 N.J.Super. 544, 457 A.2d 1243 (1983). (Passengers could not be held contributorily negligent for riding with intoxicated driver if tavern keepers served them alcoholic beverages while they were visibly intoxicated.)

Tome v. Berea Pewter Mug, Inc., 4 Ohio App.3d 98, 446 N.E.2d 848 (1982). (Under-aged patron and his passenger brought suit against tavern for injuries suffered in one car accident, after under-aged patron was allegedly furnished alcohol resulting in his intoxication. Court holds that tavern can assert the patron's contributory negligence in driving while intoxicated as a defense in a negligence action, as well as the passenger's contributory negligence in riding with him. However, contributory negligence may not be asserted where willful and wanton misconduct is alleged, but affirmative defense of assumption of risk can be raised.)

53. Morris v. Farley Enterprises, Inc., 661 P.2d 167 (Alaska 1983). (Liquor store held liable for wrongful deaths of two minors arising from unlawful sale of alcohol to one of the minors. Court rules that the complicity of a minor who is a party to an illegal liquor transaction should not preclude his action against the liquor seller, as the policy underlying statute forbidding sale of liquor to minors was in part to protect minors from the effects of alcohol. Court also holds that doctrine of negligence per se applies to violation of law, and the wrongful conduct of one minor furnishing alcohol to another minor who was driving was not a superseding cause as a matter of law.)

56. Buckley v. Estate of Pirolo, 190 N.J. Super. 491, 464 A.2d 1136 (A.D.1983) (Passengers' contributory negligence in going for joyride with obviously intoxicated aircraft pilot precluded recovery under dram shop rule against tavern which allegedly sold intoxicants to pilot of aircraft which crashed, causing passengers' deaths.)

60. Cussans v. Harris, 118 Mich.App. 567, 325 N.W.2d 793 (1982). (Statute requires that intoxicated driver who allegedly caused injuries be named a defendant and retained in the action until the litigation is concluded by trial or settlement. Purpose is to prevent collusion and perjury, by eliminating the "common" practice whereby intoxicated driver enters into settlement with injured plaintiff for a "token sum," and thereafter energetically assists plaintiff in prosecution against tavern owner.)

CHAPTER 30

DEFAMATION

Table of New or Retitled Sections

Sec.
30.13 Libel of Trade School.
30.14 Fair Comment Privilege.

---

§ 30.2 Defamation Defined—Who Can Sue

34. Caruso v. Local Union No. 690, etc., 33 Wn.App. 201, 653 P.2d 638 (1982), reversed on other grounds 100 Wn.2d 343, 670 P.2d 240. (Sole proprietor has right to sue for defamation, where his business is defamed, even though he is not specifically mentioned.)

§ 30.4 Libel and Slander—When Actionable

56. Beneficial Management Corp. of America v. Evans, 421 So.2d 92 (Ala.1982). (Alabama applies to nonmedia defamation defendants the *Gertz* rules which abolish the notion of "presumed damages" and limit compensation in defamation cases which are actionable per se to recover for actual injuries only.)

§ 30.5 Interpretation of Defamatory Meaning

79. Utecht v. Shopko Department Store, 324 N.W.2d 652 (Minn.1982). (After plaintiff's wife lost their checkbook and several credit cards, she called defendant store and so informed it to prevent unauthorized use of cards. Defendant posted sign on cash register stating—"Shopper's Charge—Robert Utecht—Do Not Accept." Trial court granted defendant's motion for summary judgment. Minnesota Supreme Court reverses, finding that notice was reasonably capable of defamatory meaning. "Loss or theft are possible explanations but poor credit is an at least equally likely alternative. The innuendo that one is a deadbeat is clearly defamatory and a jury should determine whether that meaning was the one actually conveyed.")

§ 30.6 Requirement of Publication

84. Fausett v. American Resources Management Corp., 542 F.Supp. 1234 (D.C.Utah 1982). (No publication of allegedly defamatory matter impugning reputation of corporation, where matter is conveyed only to corporation's chief principals. "In essence the management is the corporation for purposes of communication .... The law is clear that there is no publication when the communication is made to the person defamed.")

§ 30.8 Absolute Privilege

20. Meyer v. Hubbell, 117 Mich.App. 699, 324 N.W.2d 139 (1982). ("It is well settled in Michigan that statements made by witnesses in the course of judicial proceedings are absolutely privileged provided they were relevant, material or pertinent to

the issue being tried. This privilege gives witnesses relative freedom to express themselves without fear of retaliation.") (Citations omitted).

27. Moorhead v. Millin, 542 F.Supp. 614 (D.C. Virgin Islands 1982). (Defendant, in his capacity as Lieutenant Governor of Virgin Islands, wrote letter to West Indies Transport Company critical of plaintiff's act in his capacity as Director of Divisions of Utilities and Sanitation of Virgin Islands Department of Public Works. Defendant newspaper accurately reported various quotations from the letter. Court found that defendant Lieutenant Governor was a "superior executive officer of a state" and wrote the letter in the performance of his official duties. As a result, he was entitled to claim executive privilege, which privilege was absolute and barred the present action.)

§ 30.9 Qualified Privilege

Page 745

... whenever it is reasonably necessary for the protection of one's own interests, the interests of third persons, or certain interests of the public.[31.5] ...

31. Hayes v. Irwin, 541 F.Supp. 397 (N.D.Ga.1982). ("(A) publication 'may not be used as a cloak for venting private malice.' This is precisely what (defendant) did. There was a complete absence of good faith; the interest that was to be upheld was not to promote competition but rather to disparage (plaintiff's) integrity and business acumen.")

31.5 Gaines v. CUNA Mutual Insurance Society, 681 F.2d 982 (5th Cir. 1982). (Of the qualified privilege where a business or personal interest is concerned, the court stated: "The protection is based on a public policy that recognizes the need for the free communication of information to protect business and personal interests. To encourage open communication, it is necessary to afford protection from liability for misinformation given in an appropriate effort to protect or advance the interests involved.")

37. Roland v. D'Arazien, 685 F.2d 653 (D.C.Cir.1982). (No abuse of qualified privilege where legislative assistant of Congressman informed him that new intern that had been hired as summer intern had sexually assaulted legislative assistant's wife some years earlier, and that he was unable physically and mentally to work in same office with intern.)

40. Shallenberger v. Scoggins-Tomlinson, Inc., ___ Ind.App. ___, 439 N.E.2d 699 (1982). (Qualified privilege is lost where the defamation goes beyond the group interest, or is made to persons who have no reason to receive the information, or if it is motivated by express or actual malice.)

Snodgrass v. Headco Industries, Inc., 640 S.W.2d 147 (Mo.App.1982). (Plaintiff quit company after he discovered that a newly hired employee was being paid a considerably higher wage than himself and many other salespersons. Little more than one month later, plaintiff began dating the new receptionist at his old employer. The receptionist was told by her superiors that the plaintiff "had raped their other receptionist" who worked before her; "was involved in a murder"; "had mental problems"; "had stole from the company"; and other falsities. After plaintiff applied for a loan, the loan officer called his former employer for information, and was informed that the plaintiff had been fired for "falsifying information to his boss" and had been "caught taking company property." Additionally, a service letter contained alleged falsities.

Defendant alleged the defense of qualified privilege. The court observed that the existence of a qualified privilege does not preclude a party from establishing that a defendant acted outside the scope of such privilege. "Once the qualified privilege is injected into the proceedings, the burden is on the plaintiff to overcome the defense. This may be done, and the plaintiff may recover, if he shows that the statement was made with *malice* by producing substantial evidence that defendant made the statements knowing they were false or without knowledge of whether they were true or false in reckless disregard for the plaintiff's rights."

§ 30.9 SPECIFIC ACTIONS Pt. 4

Jury awarded the plaintiff $1.00 nominal for the statements to the receptionist (Plaintiff convinced the receptionist that the accusations were untrue, and they later married, and $75,000 punitives; and $5,000 actual damages for the refusal of the loan, and $100,000 punitives; and $1.00 actual and $10,000 punitives for violation of Missouri's service letter statutes. Appellate court affirmed, except reduced $5,000 loan damage to $1.00.)

§ 30.10 Constitutional Privilege—Public Officials and Public Figures

Page 749

... and still appear to be resolved on a case-by-case basis.[54.5] ...

54.5 Clark v. American Broadcasting Companies, Inc., 684 F.2d 1208 (6th Cir. 1982), certiorari denied ___ U.S. ___, 103 S.Ct. 1433, 75 L.Ed.2d 792 (1983). (Defamation suit wherein plaintiff alleged that television program falsely depicted her as prostitute. Defendant argued that its report on the effects of sex-related businesses in a community were a matter of public interest, and plaintiff, although otherwise not known or famous, was a limited public figure. Court rejects this argument: "The nature and extent of an individual's participation (in a public controversy) is determined by considering three factors: first, the extent to which participation in the controversy is voluntary; second, the extent to which there is access to channels of effective communication in order to counteract false statements; and third, the prominence of the role played in the public controversy .... Applying these three factors, we conclude that Plaintiff is not a limited public figure.")

Diversified Management Inc. v. Denver Post, Inc., 653 P.2d 1103 (Colo.1982). (One is not a public figure simply because the press is attracted to him. "We are reluctant to make too easy a finding that one is a public figure .... Just as too easy a finding of liability on the part of a newspaper has a chilling effect on its expression, too easy a finding that someone has become a public figure by virtue of responding to unfavorable publicity can have a chilling effect on the expression of a private figure. A private figure subjected to unfavorable publicity should not forfeit protection from defamation as a price of his response.")

Romero v. Abbeville Broadcasting Service, 420 So.2d 1247 (La.App.1982). (Plaintiff falsely accused during radio interview of having been arrested by the FBI for alleged vote buying. Plaintiff was a deputy sheriff and had run for public office on three prior occasions. Court held that plaintiff had "voluntarily injected himself into the public controversy of a hotly contested election, and he assumed a special prominence in the resolution of this public issue." Court concluded that plaintiff was a public officer/public figure, and was required to prove actual malice or reckless disregard of truth.)

Marchiondo v. Brown, 98 N.M. 394, 649 P.2d 462 (1982), certiorari quashed 98 N.M. 336, 648 P.2d 794. (Lawyers, even well known, generally are not public figures unless they voluntarily inject themselves or are drawn into a particular public controversy and thereby become public figures for a limited range of issues.)

§ 30.11 Burden of Proof—Court and Jury

67. Dunlap v. Philadelphia Newspapers, Inc., 301 Pa.Super. 475, 448 A.2d 6 (1982) (*Plaintiff* has burden of proving falsity of alleged defamatory statement. This case breaks from the traditional holding that the law presumes in the first instance that all defamation is false, and the defendant has the burden of pleading and proving truth.)

72. Marchiondo v. Brown, 98 N.M. 394, 649 P.2d 462 (1982), certiorari quashed 98 N.M. 336, 648 P.2d 794. (Where alleged defamatory remark could be found as either fact or opinion, courts can not say as matter of law that statements were not understood as fact; it is for jury to determine whether statements were fact or opinion.)

§ 30.13 Libel of Trade School

Keith S. Erbstein, Esq., of Beasley, Hewson, Casey, Colleran, Erbstein & Thistle, Philadelphia, Pennsylvania, reports *Walder v. Lobel*, Court of Common Pleas, Philadelphia County Trial Division, August Term, 1973, # 5394, an interesting action for libel and slander concerning two competing technical trade schools. Mr. Erbstein's client is the owner of a private trade school that provides instruction in dental technology and allied health areas. The defendant is the owner of another private trade school that provides instruction in the same area.

In 1972, the defendant entered upon a course of conduct that was designed to adversely affect the standing and reputation of the plaintiff. This conduct consisted of the circulation of a series of phony letters aimed at discrediting the plaintiff and causing plaintiff's school to lose its accreditation. These letters were ostensibly written by students of defendant's school, wherein they complained of the recruitment practices of plaintiff's school. If these letters had been true, the plaintiff would have been guilty of a serious breach of ethics in attempting to steal students from defendant's school. In reality, however, these letters had not been written by students, but were in fact the product of the defendant himself.

The testimony indicated that not only did the defendant write these letters, but that he also requested members of his staff to edit the letters in question. In addition to these letters, another letter reported that graduates of the plaintiff's school were so poorly educated that upon graduation it was impossible for them to find employment. In January of 1973, a letter to that effect was sent to the Veteran's Administration. Although this letter was purported to have been written by a former student of the plaintiff's school, the student testified at trial that the letter was a phony. Had the allegations in that letter been true, the plaintiff school would have been in jeopardy of losing governmental approval for the education of veterans and other students. As a result of the circulation of these false letters, the plaintiff school was subject to investigation and peer review.

The jury found in plaintiff's favor in the sum of $950,000, $500,000 of which represents punitive damages, the remainder compensatory damages.

§ 30.14 Fair Comment Privilege

91. Goodrich v. Waterbury Republican-American, Inc., 188 Conn. 107, 448 A.2d 1317 (1982). ("(A)n opinion is privileged as fair comment 'only when the facts on which it is based are truly *stated* or *privileged* or otherwise *known* either because the facts are of common knowledge or because, though perhaps unknown to a particular recipient of the communication, they are readily accessible to him.' ... If the facts that are criticized or commented upon are *not* stated or known, however, then fair comment is no defense. The reason for this distinction is as follows: an opinion must be based upon facts; if the facts are neither known nor stated, then a defamatory opinion implies that there are undisclosed defamatory facts which justify the opinion. ... The damage of such an implication is that the person defamed becomes the victim of the prejudiced and distorted judgment of not only the defamer, but also of everyone who hears and believes the opinion without knowing that it is based on incorrect and untrue facts .... Our review of the case law ... leads us to conclude that expressions of 'pure' opinion (those based upon known or disclosed facts) are guaranteed virtually complete constitutional protection. Expressions of 'mixed' opinion, however, are privileged only where made (1) by members of the press or news media; (2) about matters of public interest or concern; and (3) without knowingly or recklessly distorting the facts upon which they are based.") (Footnotes omitted.)

92. Gaeta v. New York News, Inc., 115 Misc.2d 483, 454 N.Y.S.2d 179 (Sup.Ct.1982), order affirmed 95 A.D.2d 315, 466 N.Y.S.2d 321 (1983). (Higher standard of care required for investigative reporting than for general reporting. "A higher degree of care is justified by the longer period of time the investigative reporter, has to check inconsistencies, seek out corroboration and verify information than is given to a news reporter. In addition, the publisher of an article based on an investigation has the opportunity not available for a news story to examine the research upon which the article is based and ask pertinent questions. In the context of this case, a violation of 'the standards of information gathering ordinarily followed by responsible parties' ... shows a reckless disregard for the truth. Accordingly, plaintiff's claim for punitive damages may stand.")

93. Havalunch, Inc. v. Mazza, ___ W.Va. ___, 294 S.E.2d 70 (1982). (Defendant, a university student who was a paid reporter for the university-sponsored student newspaper, was assigned to write a tongue-in-cheek, humorous piece on local restaurants. In plaintiff's restaurant, defendant received a mediocore sandwich and observed a roach. Of the restaurant she wrote: "HAVA-LUNCH—Bring a can of Raid if you plan to eat here. And paint your neck red; looks like a truck stop. You'll regret everything you eat here, especially the BLT's ...." Plaintiff appealed from jury award of $00.00 general and $15,000 punitives. West Virginia high court reverses, ruling that article was reporter's opinion, and humorous characterization protected by "fair comment.")

†